KT-464-044

Spain

Damien Simonis, Sarah Andrews, Anthony Ham, Susan Forsyth, John Noble, Miles Roddis, Daniel Schlechter

Contents

Asturias p502
Cantabria p488
Galicia p530
Basque Country p440
Andorra p384
Catalonia p326
Castilla y León p170
Aragón p403
Barcelona p263
Comunidad de Madrid p159
Madrid p102
Extremadura p798
Castilla-La Mancha p234
Valencia p571
Balearic Islands p614
Murcia p660
Andalucía p671

Destination Spain

Tapas, the charge of the bull, endless beaches and guaranteed sunshine. Say Spain and these are among the first images that occur to many, but they are also only the beginning…

Spain is a country with four official languages, a rich palette of local cuisines, powerful mountain ranges and desert plains. It is a haven of high art and home to some of the most extraordinary Islamic architecture in the world. Indeed, it's astonishing just how many Spains there are. The cool, green northern regions from Cantabria to Galicia are a world away from hot, dry Andalucía, home of flamenco and bullfighting. Fertile Catalonia, with its separate language and independent spirit, seems a different nation from the Castilian heartland. The crowded tapas bars of sophisticated San Sebastián have little in common with the lazy, limpid waters of Menorca. Grand Gothic and Romanesque monasteries and soaring craggy castles litter the inland expanses. Chichi ski slopes and wilderness walking trails stretch across the Pyrenees and lesser known, if equally majestic, ranges like the Sierra Nevada, Picos de Europa and Sierra de Gredos.

The cities are as diverse as the landscapes. The madness of Madrid's nightlife is as exhilarating as the strange beauty of Barcelona's Gaudí monuments is breathtaking. Home of some of the world's greatest artists (El Greco, Velázquez, Goya, Dalí, Picasso…), Spain is unafraid to match its weighty heritage with daring innovation, exemplified by the Museo Guggenheim in Bilbao or Valencia's ultramodern City of Arts & Sciences.

One thing that never changes is the Spaniards' legendary lust for a fiesta. From traditional sherry bars in Córdoba to the macro-discos of Ibiza, fun is calibrated to all paces and ages. Come and join in!

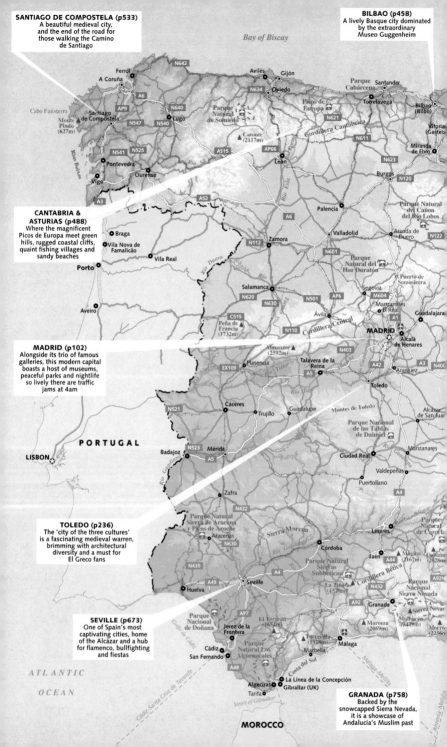

SANTIAGO DE COMPOSTELA (p533)
A beautiful medieval city, and the end of the road for those walking the Camino de Santiago

BILBAO (p458)
A lively Basque city dominated by the extraordinary Museo Guggenheim

Bay of Biscay

CANTABRIA & ASTURIAS (p488)
Where the magnificent Picos de Europa meet green hills, rugged coastal cliffs, quaint fishing villages and sandy beaches

MADRID (p102)
Alongside its trio of famous galleries, this modern capital boasts a host of museums, peaceful parks and nightlife so lively there are traffic jams at 4am

TOLEDO (p236)
The 'city of the three cultures' is a fascinating medieval warren, brimming with architectural diversity and a must for El Greco fans

SEVILLE (p673)
One of Spain's most captivating cities, home of the Alcázar and a hub for flamenco, bullfighting and fiestas

GRANADA (p758)
Backed by the snowcapped Sierra Nevada, it is a showcase of Andalucía's Muslim past

PORTUGAL

LISBON

Porto

ATLANTIC OCEAN

MOROCCO

THE PYRENEES (p350)
Skiers and trekkers flock to this all-season paradise of dramatic mountains, valleys and enchanting medieval villages

BARCELONA (p263)
A stylish, dynamic city with plenty to see and do – Gaudí monuments, the Barri Gòtic and September fiesta fun

BALEARIC ISLANDS (p614)
There's never a dull moment on these four islands – white-sand beaches, walking trails, endless sunshine and wild nights

VALENCIA (p574)
This busy Mediterranean metropolis offers beaches and the extraordinary Ciudad de las Artes y las Ciencias, and will host the 2007 America's Cup

ELEVATION

	3300m
	3000m
	2700m
	2400m
	2100m
	1800m
	1500m
	1200m
	900m
	600m
	300m
	Sea Level

0 ——— 100 km
0 ——— 50 miles

Spain originally built its tourist reputation on the sea-and-sun formula. Small wonder, given the endless variety of coastal delights. The translucent waters of **Menorca** (p649) compete with the picturesque cliff-and-beach Costa Brava combinations, including **Tossa de Mar** (p330). Get off the beaten track and enjoy cooler Atlantic rollers at laid-back fishing villages such as **Zahara de los Atunes** (p722). The north coast is the country's most dramatic. Look over the ocean from the sheer cliff walls of Galicia's **Cabo Ortegal** (p548) and explore the deep bays of the **Rías Altas** (p546). Further east, the pretty beaches around **Llanes** (p513) in Asturias have the mighty Picos de Europa mountains as a backdrop. Surfers head for the Basque Country's breaks, especially **Mundaka** (p457) and **Zarautz** (p456).

Dive into the turquoise waters of Cala Macarella (p659), in the Balearic Islands

DALLAS STRIBLEY

JESSE MECHLING

Discover a desert idyll near El Cabo de Gata village (p793) in Almería

Try kitesurfing at Playa de los Lances (p724), Tarifa

MARTIN FOJ

MARTIN LLADÓ

Soak in the sunshine in Cadaqués' picturesque harbour (p343)

Explore the pretty coast of Lastres
(p512), Asturias

STEPHEN SAKS

Prepare to be charmed by Tamariu
(p335), a beautiful Costa Brava resort

STEPHEN SAKS

Early in the year, the party town of Sitges lets its hair down for **Carnaval** (p321). Seville's **Semana Santa parades** (p689) are surely the single greatest demonstration of centuries-old Catholic emotion and drama in the country. But they are also an occasion for much merriment and drinking. Equally colourful but a little more sober are the parades in Toledo for **Corpus Christi** (p244), the city's most important religious festival. In Buñol, west of Valencia, tonnes of tomatoes are launched in all directions during **La Tomatina** (p588), a festival that attracts up to 30,000 visitors.

Don a colourful costume for Barcelona's religiously inspired Festes de la Mercè (p300)

GUY MOBERLY

NEIL SETCHFIELD

Take in a Semana Santa procession at Málaga (p737)

Hot foot it to Pamplona's Fiesta de San Fermín (p471) and the famous running of the bulls

CHRISTIAN ASLUND

Meet the colourful characters at Granada's Feria de Corpus Christi (p768)

BETHUNE CARMICHAEL

Spain has more World Heritage sites (38 in 2004) than any other country. They range from architectural wonders and awe-inspiring countryside to the extraordinary landscape of **Las Médulas** (p217), the weird formations created by ancient Roman gold mines. In the damp, green hills of the **Vall de Boí** (p365), pious Catalans raised a series of graceful Romanesque churches in the 12th century. A city that was long under Muslim rule is **Toledo** (p236), a labyrinthine medieval city. Of Spain's national parks, Andalucía's **Parque Nacional de Doñana** (p700) is one of the most outstanding.

Witness a feat of Roman engineering: Segovia's mortarless Acueducto (p191)

Get into Gaudí at Barcelona's Palau Güell (p284), with its fantastically shaped chimney pots

DAMIEN SIM

Fall under the spell of the Alhambra's Jardines del Partal (p764), Granada

WAYNE WALTON

Be dazzled by Burgos' Catedral
(p218), a French Gothic masterpiece

BETHUNE CARMICHAEL

Marvel at the splendour that is Córdoba's
ornate Mezquita (p751)

Gaze down on Toledo's World Heritage–listed old city from the imposing
10th-century Alcázar (p241)

KRZYSZTOF DYDYNSKI

You'll know you're in Spain when you encounter the touchstones of its gastronomic heritage, such as saffron-scented **rice dishes** (p584). *Azafrán* (saffron), is the world's most-expensive spice and Spain is the West's largest producer. Spanish cured ham, **jamón serrano** (p94), is a worthy counterpart to its Italian sister, prosciutto. Spain is the world's largest producer of olive oil, though top-of-the-line oil is rare. Called *arbequina*, it's grown almost exclusively in Lleida province. Spanish food is said to be 'thick with garlic and religion'. You'll know when it's garlic, but watch out for dishes such as **tarta de Santiago** (St James' cake; p539). However, only in Spain will you find a cheese so aptly named as *tetilla* (literally, nipple). Yes, it's shaped like a woman's breast. Spain's best-known cheese, *manchego*, comes (like Don Quixote) from La Mancha, as its name implies.

OLIVER STREWE

Try *arroz a la paella* (aka paella), perhaps Spain's best-known dish, at its birthplace, the village of El Palmar (p588)

Give in to temptation and go on a tapas taste fest in Barcelona (p304)

PASCALE BERO

Sample Spain's national treasures: *salchichón* (similar to salami) and *chorizo* (spicy pork sausage; p94)

CHRISTOPHER WOOD

Getting Started

Spain is like a drug – the more you get, the more you want. Vibrant cities (from bustling Barcelona in the northeast to sensual Seville in the southwest), the miraculous secrets of still unspoilt coastal coves, untamed mountain ranges – the menu seems endless. Country castles, hideaway gourmet restaurants, let-your-hair-down festivals, ancient sites and modern art…it's enough to make you wish you were already there!

WHEN TO GO

Depending on what you're after, Spain is a year-round destination. The ideal months to visit are May, June and September (plus April and October in the south). At these times you can rely on good to excellent weather, yet avoid the sometimes extreme heat – and the main crush of Spanish and foreign tourists – of July and August, when temperatures can climb to 45°C in inland Andalucía, and Madrid is unbearable and almost deserted.

See Climate Charts (p832) for more information.

There's decent weather in some parts of Spain virtually year-round. Winter (December to February) along the south and southeast Mediterranean coasts is mild, while in the height of summer (June to August) you can retreat to the northwest, to beaches or high mountains anywhere to escape excessive heat. You can be sitting outside enjoying a beer in a T-shirt in Granada in February, or rugged up against the cold while tramping the Picos de Europa mountains in July.

COSTS & MONEY

Spain is, as locals will quickly tell you, not as cheap as it once was. What you spend on accommodation (probably your single greatest expense) will depend on various factors, such as location (Madrid is pricier than Albacete), season (August along the coast is packed and expensive), the degree of comfort you require and a little dumb luck. At the budget end you'll pay €11 to €22 for a bed in a youth hostel (depending on the hostel, season and your age).

The cheapest bearable *pensión* (small private hotel)/*hostal* (budget hotel) is unlikely to cost less than €15/25, but reckon on more in the cities and resorts. Depending on where you are, you can stumble across good rooms with attached bathroom from as little as €30/50 (up to €50/70 in the more popular locations).

Eating out is still more variable. A *menú del día* (daily set menu) can cost as little as €6 to €12. Bank on spending a minimum of €20 on a full dinner (including house wine).

Most sights are fairly cheap. Keep an eye out for free days (especially on Sunday and set days for EU citizens).

DON'T LEAVE HOME WITHOUT...

- Valid travel insurance (p839)
- Your ID card and passport or visa if required (p845)
- Driving licence and car documents if driving, along with appropriate car insurance (p858)
- A concealed moneybelt or shoulder wallet to help save you from being a petty-theft victim (p834)

TOP TENS
FESTIVALS & EVENTS

Inspired in part by a deeply religious past, Spaniards have stuck to centuries-old traditions to this day. Just about every town and village has at least one annual fiesta. Here are some of our favourites, but there are many more around which you can plan your travels (see p837).

- Carnaval (Sitges, Catalonia), February (p321)
- Semana Santa (Seville), Easter (p690)
- Fiestas de San Isidro (Madrid), May (p138)
- Romería del Rocío (El Rocío, Andalucía), July (p701)
- La Tomatina (Buñol, Valencia), August (p588)

- Las Fallas (Valencia), March (p582)
- Moros y Cristianos (Alcoy, Alicante), April (p610)
- Corpus Cristi (Toledo), May to June (p244)
- Fiesta de San Fermín (Pamplona, Navarra), May to June (p471)
- Festes de la Mercè (Barcelona), September (p300)

SPANISH CINEMA

Spanish cinema has had an uneven run. A handful of classics slipped through the general drivel produced during the Franco era, but since the great dictator's demise Spaniards have been nothing if not cheekily adventurous with celluloid. See p56 for reviews.

- *Todo Sobre Mi Madre* (Pedro Almodóvar, 1999)
- *Amantes* (Vicente Aranda, 1991)
- *La Mala Educación* (Pedro Almodóvar, 2004)
- *My Life Without Me* (Isabel Coixet, 2003)
- *Jamón, Jamón* (José Juan Bigas Luna, 1992)

- *Belle Epoque* (Fernando Trueba, 1992)
- *¡Bienvenido, Mr Marshall!* (Luis García Berlanga, 1952)
- *Flamenco* (Carlos Saura, 1995)
- *Un Chien Andalou* (Luis Buñuel, 1929)
- *Mar Adentro* (Alejandro Amenábar, 2004)

READS

Spanish literature has known periods of greatness and bad patches. Writers past and present have enriched the world's libraries with a host of all-time classics, and the following is barely a wink at the possibilities. See p54 for reviews.

- *La Familia de Pascual Duarte* (The Family of Pascual Duarte; Camilo José Cela, 1942)
- *Fortunata y Jacinta* (Benito Pérez Galdós, 1887)
- *La Ciudad de los Prodigios* (The City of Marvels; Eduardo Mendoza, 1986)
- *El Ingenioso Hidalgo Don Quijote de la Mancha* (Don Quixote; Miguel de Cervantes Saavedra, 1605)
- *Homage to Catalonia* (George Orwell, 1938)
- *Galíndez* (Manuel Vázquez Montalbán, 1990)
- *Invierno en Lisboa* (Winter in Lisbon; Antonio Muñoz Molina, 1987)
- *París No Se Acaba Nunca* (Paris Never Ends; Enrique Vila-Matas, 2003)
- *El Arpista Ciego* (The Blind Harpist; Terenci Moix, 2002)
- *El Capitán Alatriste* (Captain Alatriste; Arturo Pérez-Reverte, 1996)

Public transport is reasonably priced, although high-speed trains are pricey. Internal air transport is generally also steep. See the Transport chapter (p849) for more information.

A backpacker sticking to youth hostels, lunch-time snacks and travelling slowly could scrape by on €40 to €50 a day. A more comfortable mid-range budget, including a sandwich for lunch, a modest evening meal, a couple of sights and travel will come to anything from €100 to €150 a day.

TRAVEL LITERATURE

Much ink has been spilled on the subject of Spain by its observers, both foreign and local. For books on Spanish history, art and architecture, see the appropriate chapters.

Written in 1845, Richard Ford's classic *A Handbook for Travellers* in Spain not only tells us how things once were in places we see now, but also has us chortling as its irascible English author is by turns witty, informative and downright rude.

Between Hopes and Memories: A Spanish Journey by Michael Jacobs is an amusing and personal reflection on contemporary Spain.

Jimmy Burns' book *A Literary Companion – Spain* is an entertaining tour of the country as seen through the eyes of a phalanx of writers and other notables down through the years.

Our Lady of the Sewers by Paul Richardson is a highly mirthful story, if at times a trifle hard to believe, in which the author goes in search of the strange but true.

Robert Hughes' book *Barcelona* is the Australian art critic's account of the Catalan capital, told with mordant wit and a keen eye. It remains the most incisive portrait in English of the city's past and its art.

Madrid by Elizabeth Nash is an informative, entertaining and joyfully written account of various aspects of the city's past and present – the perfect introduction to the city.

INTERNET RESOURCES

Ciudad Hoy (www.ciudadhoy.com) One of the better listings sites (in Spanish) for many Spanish cities. Search for the city of your choice and you'll reach a comprehensive site with broad listings, general news, links to the *White Pages* and *Yellow Pages* websites and more.

Lonely Planet (www.lonelyplanet.com) Can get you started with summaries on Spain, links to Spain-related sites and travellers trading information on the Thorn Tree.

Renfe (www.renfe.es) Timetables, tickets and special offers on Spain's national rail network.

Turespaña (www.tourspain.es) This is the Spanish tourist office's official site, with lots of general information about the country and some useful links.

HOW MUCH?

El País newspaper
€1

Admission to dance clubs
€10-20

Cocktail
€6-8

Seat at a Real Madrid or FC Barcelona match
from €30

City metro ride
€1.10

LONELY PLANET INDEX

Litre of petrol
€0.82-0.98

Litre of bottled water
€0.35

Caña (small glass) of Mahou beer
€1

Souvenir T-shirt
€10-24

A tapa
€1-3

Itineraries
CLASSIC ROUTES

HEADING SOUTH
One Month / Santander to Cádiz

It's a bright spring morning as you drive off the Plymouth ferry in **Santander** (p490), Cantabria's elegant coastal capital. After a little exploration, head east along the coast to the Basque Country and **Bilbao** (p458), with its extraordinary Guggenheim museum. From here the rest of Spain beckons. The road south runs through green, rolling country to the Basque capital **Vitoria** (p467), where you veer southwest to **Burgos** (p217), with its magnificent cathedral. Cross the Río Duero and Sierra de Guadarrama mountains and descend on the capital, mighty **Madrid** (p102). Lap up the hedonism and great museums, then go on to **Toledo** (p236), a medieval jewel hugged by the Río Tajo. From here the road sweeps through La Mancha's plains and olive groves to **Ciudad Real** (p249). Make a left for the striking medieval village of **Almagro** (p250), then take the A4 for **Jaén** (p780) and its gorgeous cathedral. Nearby are the Islamic glories of **Granada** (p758) and **Córdoba** (p750), with its grand **Mezquita** (p751) and animated sherry bars. Rich in monumental splendour, **Seville** (p673), colourful capital of the south, awaits. After passing through the country's sherry and equestrian capital, **Jerez de la Frontera** (p713), the peninsular journey ends in the ancient port of **Cádiz** (p705).

Taking Madrid as a midway point, this 1368km route slices through Spain, from the verdant north and modern art of the Guggenheim in Bilbao to the fiery southern cities of Andalucía, land of flamenco and fine Islamic monuments. On the way, soak up the art and atmosphere of the capital, and stop in the Castilian strongholds of Burgos and Toledo.

ANDALUCIAN ADVENTURE   Three Weeks / Málaga to El Cabo de Gata

Capture the colour, excitement and variety of Spain's southernmost region by combining a visit to its three World Heritage cities – **Seville** (p673), **Córdoba** (p750) and **Granada** (p758) – with an exploration of some of its most beautiful countryside and a relaxing beach spell to finish your trip. If flying in or out of **Málaga** (p733), don't miss its great new **Museo Picasso** (p733).

Andalucía was the heartland of medieval Islamic Spain and each of the World Heritage cities is home to one of Spain's three great Islamic monuments: Seville's **Alcázar** (p683), Córdoba's **Mezquita** (p751) and Granada's **Alhambra** (p759). They also have an array of other treasures, from Seville's great **cathedral** (p682) and baroque churches to Córdoba's **Alcázar de los Reyes Cristianos** (p754) and Granada's historic **Capilla Real** (p765) and old Muslim quarter, the **Albayzín** (p766). Modern Andalucian culture and entertainment, too, are at their strongest in the university cities of Seville and Granada, both hubs of the flamenco scene and both serving up the most delectable tapas in the region.

For a change of key, venture outside the cities to the great Roman site of **Itálica** (p697) near Seville, the caliphs' palace **Medina Azahara** (p757) near Córdoba, or the otherworldly valleys of **Las Alpujarras** (p776) south of Granada. Granada and Las Alpujarras provide easy access to the mainland's highest mountains, the **Sierra Nevada** (p773), great for walking in summer and skiing in winter. Finally, wind down on the beautiful sandy coves of **El Cabo de Gata** (p793), Andalucía's southeastern tip.

The ideal months to visit the inland cities and Las Alpujarras are April to June, September and October. This is when the cities hold their major festivals – book accommodation in advance if you're heading there for one.

The route from Málaga to El Cabo de Gata is 750km. Add another 245km if you need to return to Málaga at the end. Three weeks allows just enough time to savour the places you visit; four weeks would permit you to linger where you like best and follow up your own discoveries.

GREEN SPAIN
One Month / San Sebastián to Santiago de Compostela

Spain's well-drenched northern coast forms a green band from the Basque Country to Galicia, backed up by the Cordillera Cantábrica. Either of the Basque Country's major cities, **San Sebastián** (p445), with its crescent bay and tapas bars, or **Bilbao** (p458), with its renowned Guggenheim museum, would make a fine introduction to the journey. Heading westward, hug the coasts of Cantabria and Asturias, making forays to inland valleys and mountains. Following Cantabria's eastern coast, bask in the quaintness of **Castro Urdiales** (p497), surf at **Oriñón** (p497) and cruise the bars of festive **Santander** (p490). Continuing westward, explore **Santillana del Mar** (p498) and its medieval core, admire **Comillas'** (p500) modernist architecture and catch some waves at sprawling **Playa de Merón** (p501). The eastern Asturias coast is best travelled by train, stopping off at the fishing ports of **Llanes** (p513) and **Ribadesella** (p512). **Arriondas** (p521), the next stop, is one gateway to the majestic **Picos de Europa** (p517). Straddling Cantabria and Asturias, the peaks offer unlimited hiking. Next, head for **Oviedo** (p503), Asturias' capital, with its pre-Romanesque architecture, and **Gijón** (p508), a substantial port where cider flows copiously. West of Gijón, secluded beaches await between the picturesque harbours of **Cudillero** (p514) and **Luarca** (p515). One approach to Galicia is to follow its *rías* (estuaries), a route that covers dynamic cities, like **A Coruña** (p542) and **Vigo** (p559), and low-key resorts, islands and protected areas. Between the Rías Altas (north) and Rías Baixas (west) are the untamed beaches of **Costa da Morte** (p550). **Santiago de Compostela** (p533), a pilgrimage destination for centuries, makes a suitable endpoint for a Green Spain trek. Those with more time could make the final approach on foot via the well-trodden **Camino de Santiago** (p83).

The sea sets the agenda for the Iberian Peninsula's emerald fringe. The great sweep of coastline crosses some 600km from the French to the Portuguese borders, with hundreds of beaches en route. Cosmopolitan Bilbao and some of Europe's tallest peaks present bracing alternatives. All roads lead to Santiago de Compostela in Galicia, Spain's culturally distinct northwest extremity.

ROADS LESS TRAVELLED

THE BASQUE COUNTRY, NAVARRA & LA RIOJA   Two to Three Weeks

The Basque Country is an increasingly popular destination for visitors to Spain, but you can still get off the beaten track, especially if you have your own vehicle. Starting out in **San Sebastián** (p445), well fed from the country's finest tapas, get away from the crowds by following the coast past quiet fishing villages, wonderful beaches and cliffs plunging down to the Bay of Biscay. Among the many picturesque villages worth visiting are **Getaria** (p456), **Mutriku** (p457) and **Lekeitio** (p457), but stunning **Elantxobe** (p457) is the pick of the bunch. From here, head into the rural Basque heartland, passing by **Guernica** (p465) for a moving lesson on Basque history, before seeking out engaging **Oñati** (p456) and **Arantzazu** (p456), where a striking *santuario* (shrine) highlights the prolific output of modern Basque artists. Leave behind the churches and head for the vineyards of La Rioja, where you couldn't find a more enchanting base than **Laguardia** (p485), which surveys Spain's finest wine country from its hilltop perch. For the chance to enjoy your tipple with new-found friends, pause for at least a night in the rarely visited town of **Logroño** (p482), with its great bars and friendly, feel-good ambience. Continue east into Navarra, resting en route in the charming, quiet town of **Olite** (p478), with its castle and state-of-the-art wine museum, adding a brief side trip to time-worn **Ujué** (p478). This small village's hilltop location is merely a foretaste of what's to come in the Navarran Pyrenees, with the precipitous **Foz de Arbayún** (p481), the bucolic splendour of the **Valle del Salazar** (p481), stunning vistas of the **Valle del Roncal** (p481), and beautiful country roads that fan out from the lovely, cobblestone village of **Ochagavía** (p480) – the sort of place you'll want to linger in as long as you can.

This journey (approximately 550km) takes you along the forbidding cliffs of the Bay of Biscay, through the rolling hills of the Basque interior and the sophisticated wine-tasting pleasures of La Rioja before climbing into the Navarran Pyrenees. With your own vehicle, you could accomplish all of this in 10 days but two to three weeks will allow a more leisurely pace.

EXTREME WEST

For many travellers, the plateresque joys of the university town of **Salamanca** (p179), in western Castilla y León, are well known, but relatively few venture south into what was long one of the poorest regions of Spain. A back highway leads into the hill territory of the Peña de Francia, whose main village is pretty **La Alberca** (p188). You would never guess that, until recent decades, misery ruled in this quiet rural retreat. The road continues to climb and then suddenly drops through woods into the region of Extremadura, passing into the once equally poor Las Hurdes region to reach **Plasencia** (p807) to the southeast. Jammed with noble buildings, churches and convents, it was for centuries the principal city of the region, and makes a good base for excursions up the region's northeast valleys and to the **Monasterio de Yuste** (p801). From Plasencia, a circuit takes you first to the charming hill town of **Guadalupe** (p817), lorded over by the monastery complex dedicated to Our Lady of Guadalupe. Country roads then lead westward to the medieval town of **Trujillo** (p814), a fascinating warren of cobbled lanes, churches and the newer Renaissance era additions that were the fruit of American gold. A short drive further west lies the compact, ochre-coloured medieval jewel of **Cáceres** (p809), a town with a lively student nightlife scene, too. To the south stand some of Spain's most impressive Roman ruins in **Mérida** (p819). Further south again across the dry plains lies the white town of **Zafra** (p825). Rather than continue straight into Andalucía, make a westward detour to the hilly town of **Jerez de los Caballeros** (p826) before finally heading southwest for magical **Seville** (p673).

This 810km route opens up the largely unexpected treasures of Extremadura, wedged between two much better-known cities: the Castilian university town of Salamanca in the north and the sparkling sultry mistress of the south, Seville. Along the way you'll discover the Roman wonders of Mérida, fine medieval cities, and the enchanting towns of La Alberca, Guadalupe and Zafra.

TAILORED TRIPS

THE MONSTER TAPEO

While there may be no tradition of the pub crawl in Spain, there is the *tapeo*, the tapas crawl, from *tasca* to *tasca* down the street or around the neighbourhood. But let's go on one through the great *tapeo* heart of Spain. Start in **Madrid** (p142). Cava Baja is upscale, and has a few establishments offering *cecina de caballo* (yes, horsemeat ham). Next day board the AVE train bound for **Seville** (p673), the premier *tasca* town of Spain. Calle del Betis in particular has many *tascas*. Look for one with barrels for tables. In the wee hours find a cluster on Calle de los Alemanes across from the cathedral. Now head for **Jerez de la Frontera** (p713). This is chichi Spain, so bring your gold card. The best *tascas* are on the side streets, away from fancy folk. While you're there, take a tour of a sherry bodega. Now eat your way to **Cádiz** (p705). It's a beautiful, tiny city, perfect for the *tapeo* because of its size. And it's likely to have more *tascas* per capita than any burg in Iberia. Now repeat, in reverse. *¡Salud!*

KIDS' SPAIN

Spain's standard diet of beaches, fiestas, castles and double-decker city tours will keep under 14s content most of the time. There are also many special local attractions. Barcelona has a great aquarium and other amusements at **Port Vell** (p286). Around Catalonia, kids will enjoy Figueres' weird **Teatre-Museu Dalí** (p346), the strange rock pillars and breathtaking cable car of **Montserrat** (p323), and Spain's biggest amusement/adventure park, **Universal Mediterránea** (Port Aventura; p381).

Down the Mediterranean coast, stimulate those little brain cells at Valencia's marvellous **Ciudad de las Artes y las Ciencias** (p577), before you set the adrenaline pumping at Benidorm's **Terra Mítica**, **Aqualandia** and **Mundomar** (p602).

Entering Andalucía, stop for a Wild West shootout at **Mini Hollywood** (p793). Estepona's wildlife park **Selwo Aventura** (p743) stands out among the Costa del Sol's many kid-friendly attractions. In **Gibraltar** (p728) youngsters love the cable car, the apes, the dolphin-spotting boat trips and the tunnels in the upper rock. Next stop: **Jerez de la Frontera** (p713) for its zoo and the prancing horses of the Real Escuela Andaluza del Arte Ecuestre. **Isla Mágica** (p687), in Seville, thrills the white-knuckle brigade.

Up in Madrid head for the **Faunia** (p136) and the **Casa de Campo** (p130), with its big amusement park, then check out **Warner Brothers Movie World** (p164).

GOTHIC SPAIN

Across Spain, the majesty of Gothic construction can be admired. Start in **Barcelona** (p263), which boasts one of the most extensive Gothic city cores in Europe. Its splendours include the Església de Santa Maria del Mar, the Drassanes (medieval shipyards) and Saló del Tinell. From the Catalan capital you can make a grand sweep west to admire some of the country's landmark Gothic monuments. **Burgos** (p218) is home to a soaring Gothic cathedral much influenced by the French style and, further west still, **León** (p210) is home to another of the country's grandest Gothic cathedrals. To the south, the triangle of Castilian cities **Salamanca** (p180), **Segovia** (p192) and **Ávila** (p173) all contain fine Gothic cathedrals. Ávila's was the earliest one raised in the country. They weren't just building cathedrals in those days. The Castilian countryside in particular is littered with castles of all shapes and sizes. Some, like the all-brick castle of **Coca** (p195), are all the more extraordinary for their mix of Gothic and Mudéjar styles. That mix continues in many monuments in medieval **Toledo** (p236), south of Madrid, where yet another Gothic pearl stands in the form of the cathedral at the heart of the city.

MEDITERRANEAN COAST

Let's assume you fly into **Alicante** (p603) and out from Valencia – something local car-hire companies (see p587 & p607) will let you do for only a small, if any, supplement.

Resist, momentarily, the temptation to head for the beach and, from Alicante's airport, head southwest to **Elche** (p611), northeast to **Novelda** (p609), then sweep down the motorway (A7) and head north for a night or two of highlife or lowlife in **Benidorm** (p600).

Work your way up the coast, calling in briefly on **Altea** (p600), for its old town, and **Calpe** (p599), perhaps building in a walk up its Peñon to stretch the legs, then allow yourself a night or two in **Xàbia** (p598) or **Denia** (p597), both popular summer resorts. Hit the A7 again and head for **Valencia city** (p574), Spain's third largest, which merits as much time as your schedule will allow – and then some.

To sample more of the Comunidad Valenciana's discreet inland charms, take the A7 again and leave the coast near Castellón for a typical village of the interior, **Vilafamés** (p591), squatting on a hilltop and with a great modern-art museum. Head for **Sant Mateu** (p595), pausing to sip a coffee in its bijou main square, then stay overnight in **Morella** (p594). The run down to **Vinaròs** (p593) and the coast is fun for its own sake, and a short curl southwards brings you to **Peñíscola** (p592), with a fine castle and old city clustered on the promontory. In high summer, beat a retreat from Peñíscola's crowds and spend a night or two in **Benicàssim** (p591), popular and still very Spanish before returning to Valencia city.

The Authors

DAMIEN SIMONIS
Coordinating Author & Barcelona, Catalonia, Balearic Islands & Extremadura

The spark was lit more years ago than Damien cares to remember on a short trip over the Pyrenees to Barcelona during a summer jaunt in southern France. Damien hadn't given a great deal of thought to Spain in those days, but there was something about the place – the way the people moved, talked and seemed to enjoy themselves. All those little bars and eateries, the colourful markets... It would take some years, but Damien finally came back, living in medieval Toledo, frenetic Madrid and, finally, settling on Barcelona as the perfect Mediterranean base of operations.

Damien's Favourite Trip

With two weeks to spare in wintry London, I like to hop on a flight down to **Málaga** (p733). After some fortifying seafood in the old town, it's in the hire car and off to **Granada** (p758), with its Alhambra and Albaicín quarter. While there, some skiing in the **Sierra Nevada** (p773) is in order. Who knows, if I get an exceptionally warm day I might brave a dip in the Med around **Salobreña** (p779). Then it's time to make tracks with an excursion through the villages of **Las Alpujarras** (p776). A trip north to **Jaén** (p780) for some monumental sightseeing is the prelude to the next main stop in **Córdoba** (p750). From there I wind back down to Málaga via spectacular **Ronda** (p744).

SARAH ANDREWS
Madrid & Comunidad de Madrid

On her very first trip to Spain nearly a decade ago, Sarah toted Lonely Planet's guide to the country, dutifully following its advice but little suspecting that years later she'd be living in Spain and writing part of the book herself. But life is funny that way, and Sarah, who's originally from North Carolina, has been living in and writing about Spain since 2000. When she's not journeying around for LP, Sarah writes travel articles and the occasional guidebook from her home base near Barcelona. Sarah was the lucky one who got to spend her days gawking at the masterpieces of the Prado Museum and her nights living it up on Europe's biggest nightlife scene. She's not one to pick favourites, but the things that stood out the most for her were the 'Big Three' museums, which must have the world's highest masterpiece-to-square-foot ratio, and the summer *terrazas*, the open-air bars that pop up all over the city, making every square and wide sidewalk a party waiting to happen. Sarah also co-wrote LP's *Madrid*.

SUSAN FORSYTH
Andalucía

Susan, originally from Melbourne, Australia, has spent the last decade based in southern Spain, and travelling, researching and writing in Spain, Mexico and Central America, mostly sharing assignments with her husband, travel writer and ace editor John Noble. The hispanification of her life continues apace with her two children, now fluent Spanish speakers and totally immersed in the life of a whitewashed Andalucian hill village. Spanish culture, lifestyle and language continue to fascinate and challenge her: she marvels at Spain's architectural and artistic heritage, loves its varied landscapes and finds many similarities with Australia, including the ocean beaches and arid interior.

ANTHONY HAM
Castilla y León, Castilla La Mancha & Basque Country, Navarra & La Rioja

On his first night in Spain in 2001, Anthony fell irretrievably in love with Madrid. Less than a year later, and despite not speaking a word of Spanish or knowing a single person in the city, Anthony left Australia to start a new life in Spain. The Spanish capital is now his home, a city that inspires him daily with its openness, energy and very Spanish love for the good life. He is also now married to Marina, a *madrileña*, and speaks Spanish, although not as well as he'd like. When he's not writing for Lonely Planet, Anthony is a freelance writer and photographer who travels regularly throughout Africa, the Middle East and Europe.

JOHN NOBLE
Andalucía, History & Environment

In the mid-1990s John, originally from England's Ribble Valley, and his wife, Susan Forsyth, decided to try life in an Andalucian mountain village and they are still there, along with their children Isabella and Jack. A writer specialising in Spain and Latin America, John has travelled throughout Spain and loves its fascinatingly historic cities, wild, empty back country, isolated villages and castles, rugged coasts, and its music, art, tapas, wine and football. He has written large parts of every edition of this guide, and is coordinating author of Lonely Planet's *Andalucía* and a co-author of *Walking in Spain*.

MILES RODDIS
Andorra, Valencia & Murcia

Over a decade ago Miles and his wife, Ingrid, bought a tatty old flat in the Barrio del Carmen, Valencia's oldest and most vibrant quarter. Now renovated, this shoebox-sized apartment is their principal home, the place to which they retreat to recover, unwind and write up.

Miles has written or contributed to over 25 Lonely Planet titles, including *Valencia & the Costa Blanca*, *Walking in Spain* and the *Canary Islands*.

DANIEL C SCHECTER   Aragón, Galicia, Cantabria & Asturias

Born in Brooklyn, Daniel C Schechter refused to heed his father's sage advice, 'When you leave New York you're going nowhere.' In *el mundo hispano*, where he's lived a third of his life, he found an alternate universe that has suited him well. His earliest experience with Latin ways was in *la tierra madre*, teaching English on both sides of the Iberian Peninsula. In Mexico City he has been an editor at *The News*, an English-language daily, and *Business Mexico* magazine. Lonely Planet has taken him deeper into the Spanish-speaking world: he's worked on *Central America* and *Mexico*, and now returns to the source.

CONTRIBUTING AUTHORS

Nancy Frey wrote Outdoor Spain. As a kid, Nancy never guessed that she would live abroad (ie, outside of California). Originally, she went to Spain following the Virgin Mary, but then she discovered the apostle Santiago and became a true convert (not to Catholicism but to Spain). As it turned out, her doctoral dissertation in cultural anthropology from the Univeristy of California-Berkeley focused on the Camino de Santiago pilgrimage rather than Marian devotion. Six years of research and writing culminated in *Pilgrim Stories: On and Off the Road to Santiago*. Nancy now lives on the Galician coast with José. Together they run On Foot In Spain, a walking-tour company. They also run after their two adorable kids, Jacobo and Mariña. When not working, you can find them kayaking in the Ría de Arousa, snorkelling and fishing around Corrubedo, or swimming in the crystalline waters of the Río Lor.

Richard Sterling wrote the Food & Drink chapter. Richard first travelled to Spain as a university student to study Spanish and history. Once there, however, he became besotted with Spanish cuisine and went home with more cookbooks than history texts. He has since studied Spanish cooking in Madrid and San Sebastián, and in countless *tapeos* throughout the land. He is the principal author of Lonely Planet's *World Food* series.

Snapshot

The bomb blasts that ripped apart a series of commuter trains in rush-hour Madrid on 11 March 2004 not only took 192 lives. Attributed to radical Muslims connected with Al-Qaeda, they also underlined and perhaps accelerated a process of political upheaval already underway in Spain.

Three days after the massacre, the Partido Socialista Obrero Español (PSOE; Spanish Socialist Workers Party) surprised everyone by sweeping the right-wing Partido Popular (PP) from power at the general elections. The polls had given Socialist José Luis Rodríguez Zapatero (ZP to his supporters) little chance of toppling the PP, due to the PP's (supposed) spotless record on the economy, the fight against the Basque-nationalist terrorist group Euskadi Ta Askatasuna (ETA; Basques and Freedom) and in the defence of the national interests abroad under Prime Minister José María Aznar. Many attributed the surprise victory to Aznar's attempts to focus blame for the bomb blasts on ETA, and so avoid a potential backlash from an electorate that saw in the Islamic assault the result of Aznar's unpopular support of the USA in Iraq.

Disquiet in Spain had been building in any case and Aznar's detractors saw the PP's 'achievements' in less than glowing terms. The consistently higher growth rate of the Spanish economy (on average around 2.5% a year, versus virtual stagnation in European Union partner states such as France and Germany) was due, they said, mostly to the construction industry and speculation. Improved unemployment figures (still high by EU standards) disguised the fact that more than 30% of employees were on temporary or part-time contracts (as opposed to 6% in the UK).

True, the PP's campaign against ETA, with terrorist cells dismantled and the parliamentary political wing, Batasuna, banned, seemed to be having an effect. Still, the single biggest blow to ETA in decades would come in October 2004 under Zapatero's government, with multiple raids in southern France in which big arms caches were impounded and the group's leader, Mikel Albizu, was arrested. But this very intransigence was part of a wider policy of suffocating the aspirations of the Basque Country, Catalonia and other regions for greater autonomy. The PP used its absolute majority to silence opposition to its centralist politics at home and its policy of unswerving support for the USA, which included (in spite of nationwide demonstrations) sending troops to Iraq.

A growing sense of tension during 2003, especially in Catalonia and the Basque Country, set the scene for March 2004. In December 2003 a Socialist-led left-wing coalition, including the hitherto marginal independence-minded Esquerra Republicana de Catalunya (ERC; Republican Left of Catalonia), had taken power in Catalonia. ERC went on to take eight seats in the national parliament (up from one), making the party indispensable to the new Socialist government in Madrid.

Zapatero set the cat among the pigeons from the beginning, deciding within two weeks of acceding to power that he would honour his campaign pledge to withdraw Spanish troops from Iraq.

Uncompromising on that subject, Zapatero promised open government and dialogue on other fronts. As promised, he appointed women to half his government's ministerial posts, declared a willingness to discuss greater devolution to the regions, and dropped objections to a project

FAST FACTS

Population: 42.7 million

Area: 505,000 sq km

GDP: €730 billion

GDP per head: €17,096

GDP growth: 2.3%

Inflation: 2.6%

Unemployment rate: 11.3%

Average life expectancy: 79 years

Highest point in peninsular Spain: Mulhacén at 3487m

Number of *corridas* (bullfights) around the country in 2003: 987

to give the EU a constitution that Aznar had torpedoed in 2003; in June 2004 EU chiefs finally approved the historic charter.

Pope John Paul II observed in mid-2004 that it was good for Spain to have a young prime minister, but the Vatican has minced no words in its criticism of Zapatero's plans to make abortion and divorce easier, remove religion as a compulsory subject from school curricula, and permit gay and lesbian marriages. The local church was indeed apoplectic when a bill aimed at permitting gay marriages and the right of gay couples to adopt children won initial parliamentary approval just over six months after Zapatero took office. His project for tough new laws to protect female victims of domestic violence, however, has approval from women's groups across the country. He has also wasted no time in freezing a controversial PP plan to transfer vast amounts of water from the Río Ebro to thirsty Valencia and Murcia. Those PP-run regions are not amused; however, Catalonia, ecologists and the very EU considered the Herculean scheme unworkable. Instead, the Socialists suggest the building of desalinisation plants and technical improvements in irrigation.

Zapatero confronts multiple problems. Waves of illegal *clandestinos* (immigrants) continue to disembark on Spain's southern shores; international companies are closing factories and moving to cheaper locations in Eastern Europe and Asia; and the entry of 10 new member states to the EU in May 2004 means that Spain will lose much of its EU funding in coming years.

History

The ancestors of today's Spaniards included Stone-Age hunters from Africa; Greeks, Romans, Visigoths and other European peoples; Berber tribes from Morocco; and Phoenicians, Jews and Arabs from the Middle East. The ancestors of a good half of the people living in the Americas today – and others dotted across the rest of the globe – were Spaniards. The key to this great ebb and flow of peoples, cultures and empires is Spain's location: on both the Mediterranean Sea and the Atlantic Ocean; in Europe yet just a stone's throw from Africa – a pivotal position that has entangled Spain in the affairs of half the world and half the world in Spain's.

IN THE BEGINNING

For a colourful survey of the whole saga of Spanish history, read *The Story of Spain* by Mark Williams.

Caves throughout the country tell us plenty about Spain's earliest inhabitants. The most impressive, with the sophisticated paintings of bison, stag, boar and horses, are at Altamira near Santander, and date from around 12,000 BC. Altamira was part of the Magdalenian hunting culture of southern France and northern Spain, a Palaeolithic (Old Stone Age) culture that lasted from around 20,000 BC to the end of the last Ice Age in about 8000 BC.

However the story goes back much further. The oldest pieces of human bone in Europe have been found in Spain. Human bone fragments found in 1994 in the Sierra de Atapuerca near Burgos are about 780,000 years old and probably come from ancestors of the later Neanderthals. Another piece of bone found in 1976 near Orce, in Granada province, is reckoned to be from the skull of an infant ancestor of *Homo sapiens* eaten by a giant hyena over a million years ago. These finds suggest that the earliest humans in Europe arrived in Spain from Africa.

From the later Neanderthal era, about 30,000 BC, comes 'Gibraltar woman', a skull that was found in 1848. Current thinking is that the Neanderthals were displaced during the last Ice Age by waves of migrants of African origin. The Cueva de Nerja in Andalucía is one of many sites of these Cro-Magnons, the first modern humans, who hunted mammoth, bison and reindeer. After the Ice Age new peoples, probably from North Africa, arrived, and their rock-shelter paintings of hunting and dancing survive in eastern Spain.

The Neolithic (New Stone Age) reached eastern Spain from Mesopotamia and Egypt around 6000 BC, bringing many innovations, such as the plough, crops, livestock, pottery, textiles and permanent villages. Between 3000 and 2000 BC the first metalworking culture began at Los Millares, near Almería, where people began to smelt and shape local copper deposits. The same era saw the building of megalithic tombs (dolmens), constructed of large rocks, around the perimeter of the Iberian Peninsula. The best examples are to be found at Antequera in Andalucía.

In Spain the Bronze Age began at El Argar in Almería province, where, around 1900 BC, people learned how to alloy copper with tin.

TIMELINE

c12,000 BC	c800–600 BC
Stone Age hunters at Altamira paint some of Europe's most sophisticated cave art	The fabled Tartessos culture, influenced by Phoenician and Greek traders, flourishes in western Andalucía

PHOENICIANS & GREEKS

By about 1000 BC a flourishing culture had arisen in western Andalucía. The development of this and other societies in the south and east was influenced by Phoenician and, later, Greek traders, who exchanged oils, textiles, jewels and ivory for local metals. The Phoenicians, a Semitic people from present-day Lebanon, set up permanent trading colonies including Cádiz (which they called Gadir), Huelva (Onuba), Málaga (Malaca) and Almuñécar (Ex or Sex). Greek settlements, which began around 600 BC, tended to be further north on the Mediterranean coast. The main one was Emporion (Empúries) in Catalonia.

These incomers brought the potter's wheel, writing, coinage, the olive tree, the grapevine, the donkey and the hen. Around 700 BC iron replaced bronze as the most important metal in the lower Guadalquivir valley of western Andalucía. This Phoenician-influenced culture was very likely the fabled Tartessos, which later Greek, Roman and biblical writers mythologised as a place of unimaginable wealth. No-one knows whether Tartessos was a city or a state. Some argue it was a trading settlement on the site of modern Huelva; some believe it may lie beneath the marshes near the mouth of the Río Guadalquivir.

IBERIANS & CELTS

Iberians is the general name given to the inhabitants of most of the Iberian Peninsula during the millennium or so before the Romans arrived in 218 BC. The Iberians mixed with other newcomers even before the Romans. From around 1000 to 500 BC, Celts (originally from Central Europe) and other tribes crossed the Pyrenees and settled in northern Spain. In contrast to the dark-featured Iberians, the Celts were fair, drank beer and ate lard. Celts and Iberians who merged on the *meseta* (the high tableland of central Spain) became the Celtiberians. Celts and Celtiberians typically lived in sizable hill-fort towns called *castros*. The Celts introduced iron technology to the north about the same time as the Phoenicians brought it to the south.

Spanish History Index (http://vlib.iue.it/hist -spain/Index.html) provides countless Internet leads for those who want to dig deeper.

CARTHAGINIANS

From about the 6th century BC the Phoenicians and Greeks were pushed out of the western Mediterranean by Carthage, a former Phoenician colony in modern Tunisia. There was a flourishing Carthaginian colony on Ibiza.

The Carthaginians came into conflict with the next rising Mediterranean power – Rome. After losing to Rome in the First Punic War (264–241 BC), fought for control of Sicily, Carthage responded by invading the Iberian Peninsula under generals Hamilcar Barca, Hasdrubal and Hannibal. The first landing was in 237 BC.

The Second Punic War (218–201 BC) saw Hannibal march his elephants over the Alps towards Rome but also brought Roman legions to Spain. Hannibal was eventually forced to retreat, finally being routed in North Africa in 202 BC.

ROMANS

Though the Romans held sway on the Iberian Peninsula for 600 years, it took them 200 years to subdue the fiercest of local tribes.

218–201 BC	AD 410
Rome defeats Carthage in the Second Punic War and begins a 600-year occupation of the Iberian Peninsula	Suevi and Vandals, Germanic peoples from the north, overrun the Iberian Peninsula

The Basques in the north, though defeated, were never Romanised in the same way as the rest of Hispania (as the Romans called the peninsula). Legendary stands against the Romans included the eight-year revolt led by the shepherd-turned-guerrilla Virathius in the west and the centre from around 150 BC, and the siege of Numancia near Soria in 133 BC. Rome had to bring in its most illustrious generals to deal with these insubordinations.

By AD 50 most of the peninsula, particularly the south, had adopted the Roman way of life. This was the Pax Romana, a long, prosperous period of stability. Hispania became urbanised and highly organised. In the 1st century BC the Romans organised the peninsula into three provinces: Baetica (most of Andalucía plus southern Extremadura and southwestern Castilla-La Mancha), with its capital at Corduba; Lusitania (Portugal and northern Extremadura), with its capital at Augusta Emerita (Mérida), the greatest Roman city on the peninsula; and Tarraconensis (the rest), with its capital at Tarraco (Tarragona).

Rome gave the peninsula a road system, aqueducts, theatres, temples, amphitheatres, circuses, baths and the basis of its legal system and languages. The Roman era also brought many Jews, who settled throughout the Mediterranean part of the Roman Empire, and Christianity, which probably came with soldiers from North Africa and merchants in the 3rd century AD. Hispania gave Rome gold, silver, grain, wine, soldiers, emperors (Trajan, Hadrian, Theodosius) and the literature of Seneca, Martial, Quintilian and Lucan. Another notable export was *garum*, a spicy sauce derived from fish and used as a seasoning. The finest of Spain's Roman ruins are at Empúries, Itálica, Mérida, Tarragona and Segovia.

The Pax Romana started to crack when two Germanic tribes, the Franks and the Alemanni, swept across the Pyrenees in the late 3rd century AD, causing devastation. When the Huns arrived in Eastern Europe from Asia a century later, the Germanic peoples they displaced moved westwards. Among these were the Suevi and Vandals, who overran the Iberian Peninsula around AD 410.

VISIGOTHS

Another Germanic people, the Visigoths, sacked Rome itself in AD 410. Within a few years, however, the Visigoths had become Roman allies, being granted lands in southern Gaul (France) and fighting on the emperor's behalf against barbarian invaders on the Iberian Peninsula. When the Visigoths were pushed out of Gaul in the 6th century by another Germanic people, the Franks, they settled on the Iberian Peninsula, making Toledo their capital.

The rule of the roughly 200,000 long-haired Visigoths, who had a penchant for gaudy jewellery, over the several million more-sophisticated Hispano-Romans was precarious and undermined by strife among their own nobility. The Hispano-Roman nobles still ran the fiscal system and their bishops were the senior figures in urban centres. The ties between the Visigoth monarchy and the Hispano-Romans were strengthened in AD 587 when King Reccared converted to orthodox Christianity from the Visigoths' Aryan version, which denied that Christ was identical to God. Culturally, the Visigoths tended to ape Roman ways. Today a few

For an example of Visigothic artisanship, check out the garnet- and gem-inlaid crown of King Recceswinth in Madrid's Museo Arqueológico Nacional (p128).

Visigothic conquest of the Iberian Peninsula begins

Muslims invade the peninsula from North Africa, overrunning it within a few years

Visigothic churches can be seen in northern Spain. One, at Baños de Cerrato near Palencia, dates from 661 and is probably the oldest church in the country.

THE MUSLIM CONQUEST

By 700, with famine and disease in Toledo, strife among the aristocracy and chaos throughout the peninsula, the Visigothic kingdom was falling apart. This paved the way for the Muslim invasion of 711, which set Spain's destiny quite apart from that of the rest of Europe.

Following the death of the prophet Mohammed in 632, Arabs spread through the Middle East and North Africa, carrying Islam with them. If you believe the myth, they were ushered onto the Iberian Peninsula by the sexual exploits of the last Visigoth king, Roderic. Later chronicles relate how Roderic seduced young Florinda, the daughter of Julian, the Visigothic governor of Ceuta in North Africa, and how Julian sought revenge by approaching the Muslims with a plan to invade Spain.

In 711 Tariq ibn Ziyad, the Muslim governor of Tangier, landed at Gibraltar with around 10,000 men, mostly Berbers (indigenous North Africans). Roderic's army was decimated, probably near the Río Guadalete or Río Barbate in Cádiz province, Andalucía, and he is thought to have drowned while fleeing the scene. Visigothic survivors fled north.

Within a few years the Muslims had conquered the whole Iberian Peninsula, except small areas in the Asturian mountains in the north. The Muslims pushed on over the Pyrenees, but were driven back by the Franks.

MUSLIM SPAIN

The Muslims (sometimes referred to as Moors) were the dominant force on the peninsula for nearly four centuries, a potent force for 170 years after that, and a lesser one for a further 250 years. Between wars and rebellions, Al-Andalus, the name given to Muslim territory on the peninsula, developed the most highly cultured society of medieval Europe.

Al-Andalus' frontiers were constantly shifting as the Christians strove to regain territory in the stuttering 800-year Reconquista (Reconquest). Up to the mid-11th century the frontier lay across the north of the peninsula, roughly from just south of Barcelona to northern Portugal, with a protrusion up to the central Pyrenees. Al-Andalus also suffered internal conflicts and, at times, Muslims and Christians even struck up alliances with each other in the course of quarrels with their own co-religionists.

Muslim political power and cultural developments centred initially on Córdoba (756–1031), then Seville (Sevilla; c 1040–1248) and lastly Granada (1248–1492). These cities boasted beautiful palaces, mosques and gardens, universities, public baths and bustling markets (*zocos*). The Muslims developed the Hispano-Roman agricultural base by improving irrigation and introducing new fruits and crops (oranges, lemons, peaches, sugar cane, rice and more).

Though military campaigns against the northern Christians could be extremely bloodthirsty affairs, Al-Andalus' rulers allowed freedom of worship to Jews and Christians (*mozárabes* or Mozarabs) under their rule. Jews mostly flourished, but Christians had to pay a special tax, so most either converted to Islam (coming to be known as *muladíes* or

Richard Fletcher's *Moorish Spain* is an excellent short history of Al-Andalus (the Muslim areas of the peninsula).

756–1031	1085
Córdoba dominates Al-Andalus (the Muslim areas of the peninsula) and becomes the finest city in Western Europe	Castile, a northern Christian kingdom, captures Toledo

Muwallads) or left for the Christian north. It was through Al-Andalus that much of the learning of ancient Greece – picked up by the Arabs in the eastern Mediterranean – was transmitted to Christian Europe.

The Muslim settlers themselves were not a homogeneous group. Beneath the Arab ruling class was a larger group of Berbers, and tension between these two groups broke into Berber rebellion numerous times.

Before long, Muslim and local blood merged. There was even frequent aristocratic intermarriage with the northern Christians.

The Cordoban Emirate & Caliphate

Initially Al-Andalus was part of the Caliphate of Damascus, which ruled the Muslim world. In 750 the Omayyad caliphal dynasty was overthrown by a rival clan, the Abbasids, who shifted the caliphate to Baghdad. However an Omayyad survivor, Abd ar-Rahman I, managed to establish himself in Córdoba in 756 as the independent emir of Al-Andalus. He began constructing Córdoba's *mezquita* (mosque), one of the world's greatest Muslim monuments. Most of Al-Andalus was more or less unified under Cordoban rule for some fairly long periods. In 929 Abd ar-Rahman III bestowed on himself the title caliph, launching the Caliphate of Córdoba (929–1031), during which Al-Andalus reached its peak of power and lustre.

At this time Córdoba was the biggest and most dazzling city in Western Europe. Astronomy, medicine, mathematics and botany flourished and one of the great Muslim libraries was established in the city. Abd ar-Rahman III's court was frequented by Jewish, Arab and Christian scholars.

Later on in the 10th century the fearsome Cordoban general Al-Mansour (or Almanzor) terrorised the Christian north with 50-odd forays in 20 years. He destroyed the cathedral at Santiago de Compostela in northwestern Spain in 997 and forced Christian slaves to carry its doors and bells to Córdoba, where they were incorporated into the great mosque. After his death, however, the caliphate collapsed into a devastating civil war, finally breaking up in 1031 into dozens of *taifas* (small kingdoms), with Seville, Granada, Toledo and Zaragoza among the most powerful.

Almoravids & Almohads

Political unity was restored to Al-Andalus by the Almoravid invasion of 1091. The Almoravids, a strict Muslim sect of Saharan nomads who had conquered North Africa, were initially invited to the Iberian Peninsula to help the Seville *taifa* against the growing Christian threat from the north. Seventy years later a second Berber sect, the Almohads, invaded the peninsula after overthrowing the Almoravids in Morocco. Both sects soundly defeated the Christian armies they encountered.

Under the Almoravids and the Almohads, religious intolerance sent Christian refugees fleeing north. But in time both mellowed in their adopted territory and Almohad rule saw a cultural revival in Seville. The Cordoban philosopher Averroës (1126–98) greatly influenced medieval Christian thought with his commentaries on Aristotle, trying to reconcile science with religion.

1091	1147
The Almoravids invade, helping to unify Muslim Spain	The Almohads defeat the Almoravids in Morocco and invade Muslim Spain

The Nasrid Emirate of Granada

Almohad power eventually disintegrated in the face of internal disputes and Christian advances. After Seville fell to the Christians in 1248, Muslim territory on the Iberian Peninsula was reduced to the Emirate of Granada, comprising about half of modern Andalucía and ruled from the lavish Alhambra palace by the Nasrid dynasty. Granada saw Muslim Spain's final cultural flowering, especially in the 14th century under Yusuf I and Mohammed V, both of whom contributed to the splendours of the Alhambra.

THE RECONQUISTA

The Christian reconquest of the Iberian Peninsula began in about 722 at Covadonga, Asturias, and ended with the fall of Granada in 1492. It was a stuttering affair, conducted by a tangled sequence of emerging, merging and demerging Christian states that were as often at war with each other as with the Muslims. However the Muslims were gradually pushed south, as the northern kingdoms of Asturias, León, Navarra, Castile and Aragón developed.

Following his 1959 success in *Ben-Hur*, Charlton Heston turned to the Spanish Reconquista for his follow-up Hollywood epic, *El Cid* (1961).

An essential ingredient in the Reconquista was the cult of Santiago (St James), one of the 12 apostles. In 813, the saint's supposed tomb was discovered in Galicia. The town of Santiago de Compostela grew up on the spot, to become the third-most popular medieval Christian pilgrimage goal after Rome and Jerusalem. Christian generals experienced visions of Santiago before forays against the Muslims, and Santiago became the inspiration and special protector of soldiers in the Reconquista, earning the sobriquet Matamoros (Moor-slayer). Today he is the patron saint of Spain.

The Rise of Castile

Covadonga lies in the Picos de Europa mountains, where Visigothic nobles took refuge after the Muslim conquest. Christian versions of the battle tell of a small band of fighters under their leader, Pelayo, defeating an enormous force of Muslims; Muslim accounts make it a rather less important skirmish. Whatever the facts of Covadonga, by 757 Christians occupied nearly a quarter of the Iberian Peninsula.

The Asturian kingdom eventually moved its capital to León, which spearheaded the Reconquista until the Christians were set on the defensive by Al-Mansour in the 10th century. Castile, originally a small principality in the east of the kingdom of León, developed into the dominant Reconquista force as hardy adventurers set up towns in the no-man's-land of the Duero basin, spurred on by land grants and other rights and privileges *(fueros)*. It was the capture of Toledo in 1085, by Alfonso VI of Castile, that led the Seville Muslims to call in the Almoravids.

Alfonso I of Aragón, on the southern flank of the Pyrenees, led the counterattack against the Almoravids, taking Zaragoza in 1118. After his death Aragón was united through royal marriage with Catalonia, creating a formidable new Christian power block (known as the Kingdom of Aragón). Portugal emerged as an independent Christian kingdom in the 12th century.

Castile suffered a terrible defeat by the Almohads at Alarcos, south of Toledo, in 1195, but in 1212 the combined Christian armies of Castile,

1248	1469
Seville falls to Fernando III of Castile; the Nasrid Emirate of Granada becomes the last surviving Muslim state on the peninsula	Isabel, heir to Castile, marries Fernando, heir to Aragón, uniting the peninsula's two most powerful Christian states

For details on how Granada became one of Europe's richest cities in the 13th century, see p758.

Aragón and Navarra routed a large Almohad force at Las Navas de Tolosa in Andalucía. This was the beginning of the end for Al-Andalus: León took the key towns of Extremadura in 1229 and 1230; Aragón took Valencia in the 1230s; Fernando III 'El Santo' (Ferdinand the Saint) of Castile took Córdoba in 1236 and Seville in 1248; and Portugal expelled the Muslims in 1249. The sole surviving Muslim state on the peninsula was now the Emirate of Granada.

The Lull

Fernando III's son, Alfonso X El Sabio (the Learned; r 1252–84), proclaimed Castilian the official language of his realm. At Toledo he gathered around him scholars regardless of their religion, particularly Jews who knew Arabic and Latin. Alfonso was, however, plagued by uprisings and plots, even from within his own family. The Castilian nobility repeatedly challenged the crown until the 15th century. This was also an era of growing intolerance towards the Jews and Genoese, who came to dominate Castilian commerce and finance, while the Castilians themselves were preoccupied with their low-effort, high-profit wool production. In the 1390s anti-Jewish feeling culminated in pogroms around the peninsula.

Castile and Aragón laboured under ineffectual monarchs from the late 14th century until the time of Isabel and Fernando (Isabella and Ferdinand), whose marriage in 1469 would merge the two kingdoms. Isabel succeeded to the Castilian throne in 1474 and Fernando to Aragón's in 1479. The joint rule of the Catholic Monarchs (Reyes Católicos), as they are known, dates from 1479. The pious Isabel and the Machiavellian Fernando became an unbeatable team.

The Fall of Granada

After Emir Abu al-Hasan of Granada refused, in 1476, to pay any more tribute to Castile, Isabel and Fernando launched the final crusade of the Reconquista in 1482, with an army largely funded by Jewish loans and the Catholic Church.

By now the rulers of Granada were riven by internal feuds. Matters degenerated into a confused civil war, of which the Christians took full advantage. Fernando and Isabel entered Granada, after a long siege, on 2 January 1492, to kick off what turned out to be the most momentous year in Spanish history.

The surrender terms were fairly generous to Boabdil, the last emir, who got the Alpujarras valleys south of Granada and 30,000 gold coins. The remaining Muslims were promised respect for their religion, culture and property, but this didn't last long.

THE CATHOLIC MONARCHS
The Inquisition

The Catholic Monarchs founded the Spanish Inquisition to root out those who didn't practise Christianity as the Catholic Church wished them to. The Inquisition was responsible for perhaps 12,000 deaths over 300 years, 2000 of them in the 1480s. It focused initially on *conversos* (Jews who had converted to Christianity), accusing many of continuing to practise Judaism in secret.

1478	1492 (January)
Isabel and Fernando, the Catholic Monarchs (Reyes Católicos), set up the Spanish Inquisition	Isabel and Fernando capture Granada

In April 1492, under the influence of Grand Inquisitor Tomás de Torquemada, Isabel and Fernando ordered the expulsion from their territories of all Jews who refused Christian baptism. Up to 100,000 Jews converted, but some 200,000 – the first Sephardic Jews – left for other Mediterranean destinations. The bankrupt monarchy seized all unsold Jewish property. A talented middle class was decimated.

Persecution of the Muslims

Cardinal Cisneros, Isabel's confessor and overseer of the Inquisition, tried to eradicate Muslim culture too. In the former Granada emirate he carried out forced mass baptisms, burnt Islamic books and banned the Arabic language. This, combined with seizures of Muslim land, sparked a revolt in Andalucía in 1500. Afterwards, Muslims were ordered to convert to Christianity or leave. Most (around 300,000) underwent baptism and stayed. They came to be known as *moriscos* (converted Muslims), but their conversion was barely skin-deep and they never assimilated. The *moriscos* were finally expelled between 1609 and 1614.

Gérard Depardieu starred in *1492: Conquest of Paradise*, a powerful 1992 version of the Columbus story.

Columbus

In April 1492 the Catholic Monarchs granted Christopher Columbus (Cristóbal Colón to Spaniards) funds for his long-desired voyage across the Atlantic in search of a new trade route to the Orient.

On 3 August 1492 Columbus set off from the port of Palos de la Frontera (in southwestern Andalucía) with three small ships and 120 men. They stopped at the Canary Islands, then sailed west for 31 days, sighting no land; the rebellious crew gave Columbus two more days. However he landed on the island of Guanahaní (Bahamas), which he named San Salvador, went on to find Cuba and Hispaniola, and returned to a hero's reception from the Catholic Monarchs in Barcelona, eight months after his departure.

Columbus made three more voyages, founding Santo Domingo on Hispaniola, finding Jamaica, Trinidad and other Caribbean islands, and reaching the mouth of the Orinoco and the coast of Central America. But he died poor in Valladolid in 1506.

DID YOU KNOW?

Columbus believed until his death that he had reached Asia.

After Isabel

Fernando and Isabel entangled Spain in European affairs by marrying each of their four children into the royal families of Portugal, Burgundy and England. (The liaison with England went wrong when the youngest child, Catalina, or Catherine of Aragón, was cast aside by Henry VIII.) The early death of two children left the third, Princess Juana, heir to the Castilian throne, when Isabel died in 1504. Juana's husband, Felipe El Hermoso (Philip the Handsome), was heir to the Low Countries and to the lands of the powerful Habsburg family in Central Europe. However, Juana, dubbed Juana la Loca (Joanna the Mad), proved unfit to rule and, when Felipe died soon after Isabel, Fernando took over as regent of Castile until his own death in 1516. His annexation of Navarra in 1512 brought all of Spain under one rule for the first time since Visigothic days.

1492 (April)	1492 (October)
Isabel and Fernando expel Jews who refuse Christian baptism	Christopher Columbus, funded by Isabel and Fernando, lands in the Bahamas

THE HABSBURGS
Carlos I

In 1517, 17-year-old Carlos I (Charles I), son of Juana la Loca and Felipe El Hermoso, came from Flanders to take up his Spanish inheritance. In 1519 Carlos also succeeded to the Habsburg lands in Austria and was elected Holy Roman Emperor (in which capacity he was called Charles V). Carlos now ruled all of Spain, the Low Countries, Austria, several Italian states and parts of France and Germany – more of Europe than anyone since the 9th century – plus the Spanish colonies in the Caribbean and Panama. To these he would add more of Central Europe and further big slices of the Americas.

Carlos spent only 16 years of his 40-year reign in Spain. At first the Spaniards did not care for a king who spoke no Castilian, nor for his appropriating their wealth. Castilian cities revolted in 1520–21 (the Guerra de las Comunidades, or War of the Communities) but were crushed. Eventually the Spanish came around to him, at least for his strong stance against emerging Protestantism and his learning of Castilian. Carlos spent the bulk of the monarchy's new American wealth on an endless series of European conflicts and, war-weary, he abdicated shortly before his death in 1556, dividing his many territories between his son Felipe and his brother Fernando. Felipe got the lion's share, including Spain, the Low Countries and the American possessions.

Carlos I's reign saw ruthless but brilliant Spanish conquistadors conquer vast tracts of the American mainland. Between 1519 and 1521 Hernán Cortés conquered the fearsome Aztec empire with a small band of adventurers. Between 1531 and 1533 Francisco Pizarro did the same to the Inca empire. With their odd mix of brutality, bravery, gold lust and piety, these men were the natural successors to the crusading knights of the Reconquista. The new colonies sent huge cargoes of silver, gold and other riches back to Spain, where the crown was entitled to one-fifth of the bullion (the *quinto real*, or royal fifth). Seville enjoyed a monopoly on this trade and grew into one of Europe's richest cities.

Felipe II

Carlos I's son Felipe II (Philip II; r 1556–98) presided over the zenith of Spanish power. His reign is a study in contradictions. He enlarged the overseas empire – by 1600 Spain controlled Florida, all the biggest Caribbean islands, nearly all of present-day Mexico and Central America, and a large strip of South America – but lost Holland to a long drawn-out rebellion. He received greater flows of silver than ever from the Americas, but went bankrupt. His navy defeated the Ottoman Turks at Lepanto in 1571 but the Spanish Armada of 1588 was routed by England. He was a fanatical Catholic, who spurred the Inquisition to new persecutions, yet readily allied Spain with Protestant England, against Catholic France, when it suited Spain.

When Felipe claimed Portugal on its king's death in 1580, he not only united the Iberian Peninsula but also Europe's two great overseas empires. However the Castilian gentry's disdain for commerce and industry allowed foreign merchants to dominate trade. Money that didn't find its way into foreign pockets, or wasn't owed for European wars, went

1517–56	1556–98
Reign of Carlos I, Spain's first Habsburg monarch	Reign of Felipe II, the zenith of Spanish power

towards building churches, palaces and monasteries. Spain, it was said, had discovered the magic formula for turning silver into stone.

Decline of the Habsburgs

Seventeenth-century Spain was like a gigantic artisans' workshop, in which architecture, sculpture, painting and metalwork consumed around 5% of the nation's income. The gentry and the church, which was entitled to one-tenth of all production, led a quite comfortable existence; however, for most Spaniards life was decidedly underprivileged. The age was immortalised on canvas by artists such as Velázquez, El Greco, Zurbarán and Murillo, and in words by Miguel de Cervantes, the mystics Santa Teresa of Ávila and San Juan de la Cruz (St John of the Cross) and the prolific playwright Lope de Vega.

Under a trio of ineffectual kings, Spain saw its chickens come home to roost during this period. Felipe III (Philip III; r 1598–1621) left government to the self-seeking Duke of Lerma. Felipe IV (Philip IV; r 1621–65) concentrated on a long line of mistresses and handed over affairs of state to Count-Duke Olivares, who tried bravely but retired a broken man in 1643. Spain lost Portugal and faced revolts in Sicily, Naples and Catalonia. Silver shipments from the Americas shrank disastrously. Carlos II (Charles II; r 1665–1700) failed to produce children, a situation that led to the War of the Spanish Succession.

Check out Velázquez's world-famous portrait of Felipe IV's family, *Las Meninas* (sans mistresses), in the Prado (p122).

THE FIRST BOURBONS
Felipe V

Carlos II bequeathed his throne to his young relative Felipe V (Philip V; r 1701–46), who also happened to be second in line to the French throne. The Austrian emperor Leopold, however, wanted to see his son Charles, a nephew of Carlos II, on the Spanish throne. The resulting War of the Spanish Succession (1702–13) was a contest for the balance of power in Europe. Spain lost its last possessions in the Low Countries to Austria, and Gibraltar and Menorca to Britain, while Felipe V renounced his right to the French throne but held on to Spain. He was the first of the Bourbon dynasty, still in place today.

This was Europe's age of the Enlightenment, but Spain's powerful church and Inquisition were at odds with the rationalism that trickled in from France. Two-thirds of the land was in the hands of the nobility and church and was underproductive, and large numbers of males, from nobles to vagrants, were unwilling to work.

Fernando VI & Carlos III

Under the reign of Fernando VI (Ferdinand VI; r 1746–59) the economy took an upturn largely as the result of a revitalised Catalonia and the Basque shipbuilding industry. Agricultural Castile and Andalucía were left behind, however, as they were unable to increase yields due to a lack of land reforms.

Enlightened despot Carlos III (Charles III; r 1759–88) expelled the backward-looking Jesuits, transformed Madrid, established a new road system out to the provinces and tried to improve agriculture. However, food shortages fuelled unrest among the masses.

1609–14	1701
The *moriscos* (converted Muslims) are finally expelled from Spain	Felipe V, first of the Bourbon dynasty, takes the throne

THE PENINSULAR WAR

Carlos IV (Charles IV; r 1788–1808) was dominated by his Italian wife, Maria Luisa of Parma; she hooked up with a handsome royal guard called Manuel Godoy, who became chief minister. This unholy trinity was ill-suited to coping with the crisis presented by the French Revolution of 1789.

When Louis XVI of France (Carlos IV's cousin) was guillotined in 1793, Spain declared war on France. Two years later, with France's Reign of Terror spent, Godoy made peace, pledging military support for France against Britain. In 1805 a combined Spanish-French navy was beaten by the British fleet, under Nelson, off the Cabo de Trafalgar (south of Cádiz). This put an end to Spanish sea power.

In 1807 Napoleon Bonaparte and Godoy agreed to divide Britain's ally Portugal between them. French forces poured into Spain, supposedly on the way to northern Portugal. By 1808 this had become a French occupation of Spain. Napoleon forced Carlos to abdicate in favour of Napoleon's brother Joseph Bonaparte (José I).

In Madrid crowds revolted, and across the country, Spaniards took up arms guerrilla-style, reinforced by British and Portuguese forces led by the Duke of Wellington. The French, hopelessly stretched by Napoleon's Russian campaign, were finally expelled after their defeat at Vitoria in 1813.

THE 19TH CENTURY

During the Peninsular War, a national Cortes (parliament), meeting at Cádiz in 1812, drew up a new liberal constitution, which incorporated many of the principles of the American and French prototypes. This set off a contest lasting most of the 19th century between the church, monarchy and other conservatives who liked the status quo, and liberals who wanted vaguely democratic reforms.

Fernando VII (Ferdinand VII; r 1814–33) revoked the Cádiz constitution, persecuted liberal opponents and re-established the Inquisition. Corrupt government drastically cut his popularity before his death. Meanwhile the American colonies took advantage of Spain's problems to strike out on their own. By 1824 only Cuba, Guam, the Philippines and Puerto Rico remained Spanish.

DID YOU KNOW?

Spain lost the last of its once vast overseas possessions – Cuba, Puerto Rico, the Philippines and Guam – in the humiliating Spanish-American War of 1898.

First Carlist War

Fernando's dithering over his successor resulted in the First Carlist War (1833–39), between supporters of his brother Don Carlos and those loyal to his infant daughter Isabel. Don Carlos was supported by the church, other conservatives and regional rebels in the Basque Country, Navarra, Catalonia and Aragón – together known as the Carlists. The Isabel faction had the support of liberals and the army.

During the war violent anticlericalism emerged. Religious orders were closed and, in the Disentailment of 1836, church property and lands were seized and auctioned off by the government. As usual, only the wealthy benefited. The army emerged victorious.

Isabel II

In 1843 Isabel, now all of 13, declared herself Queen Isabel II (Isabella II; r 1843–68). One achievement of sorts during her inept reign was the creation of a rural police force, the Guardia Civil (Civil Guard), which mainly protected the wealthy in the bandit-ridden countryside. There was an upturn in the economy, with progress in business, banking, mining and railways, plus some reforms in education, but the benefits accrued to few. Eventually radical liberals, and discontented soldiers led by General Juan Prim, overthrew Isabel in the Septembrina Revolution of 1868.

First Republic

Spain still wanted a monarch and in 1870 a liberal-minded Italian prince, Amadeo of Savoy, accepted the job. The aristocracy, which opposed Amadeo, split into two camps: one favouring Isabel II's teenage son Alfonso; the other backing Don Carlos' grandson Carlos. Thus began the three-way Second Carlist War (1872–76).

Amadeo quickly abandoned Spain and the liberal-dominated Cortes proclaimed Spain a federal republic of 17 states. However, this First Republic, unable to control the regions, lasted only 11 months. In the end the army, no longer liberal, put Alfonso on the throne as Alfonso XII (r 1874–85), in a coalition with the church and landowners. The 1876 constitution, recognising both monarchy and parliament, produced a sequence of orderly changes of government *(turnos)* between supposed conservatives and liberals. Little actually separated them in policy, and electoral rigging was the norm.

EARLY 20TH CENTURY

Alfonso XIII (r 1902–30) had his friends among the military, wealthy landowners and the rich, powerful church, and was in the habit of meddling in politics. There were 33 different governments during his reign.

At the other end of the social scale, a powder keg was forming. Industry had brought both prosperity and squalid slums to Barcelona, Madrid and some Basque cities, by attracting much large-scale migration from the country. In the countryside, the old problems of underproduction and oligarchic land ownership persisted. Many Spaniards emigrated to Latin America. The working class gravitated towards Marxism and anarchism.

'There were 33 different governments during Alfonso XIII's reign.'

Social Unrest

The anarchist ideas of the Russian Mikhail Bakunin had reached Spain in the 1860s and gained support rapidly. Bakunin advocated a free society in which people would voluntarily cooperate with each other – a state of affairs to be prepared for by strikes, sabotage and revolts. Anarchism appealed to the peasants of Andalucía, Aragón, Catalonia and the northwest, and to workers living in slums in Barcelona and other cities. In the 1890s and the 1900s anarchists bombed Barcelona's Liceu opera house, assassinated two prime ministers and killed 24 people with a bomb at Alfonso XIII's wedding in 1906. In 1910, the anarchist unions were organised into the powerful Confederación Nacional del Trabajo (CNT; National Confederation of Work).

Socialism grew more slowly than anarchism because of its strategy of steady change through parliamentary processes. The Unión General de Trabajadores (UGT; General Union of Workers), established in 1888, was moderate and disciplined. Its appeal was greatest in Madrid and Bilbao,

1805	1808–13
Spanish-French fleet defeated by Britain at Trafalgar, ending Spanish sea power	French occupation forces driven out in Spanish War of Independence (Peninsular War)

where people were fearful of Catalan separatism. Spanish socialists rejected Soviet-style communism.

Parallel with the rise of the left was the growth of Basque and Catalan separatism. In Catalonia, this was led by big business interests. Basque nationalism emerged in the 1890s among Basques who considered the many Castilians who had flocked to work in Basque industries to be a threat to Basque identity.

In 1909 a contingent of Spanish troops was wiped out by Berbers in Spanish Morocco. The government then called up Catalan reserves to go to Morocco. This sparked off the so-called Semana Trágica (Tragic Week) in Barcelona, which began with a general strike and turned into a frenzy of violence. The government responded by executing many workers.

Spain stayed neutral during WWI and enjoyed an economic boom. But anarchist and socialist numbers grew, inspired by the Russian Revolution, and political violence and general mayhem continued, especially in lawless Barcelona.

PRIMO DE RIVERA

In 1921, 10,000 Spanish soldiers were killed by a small force of Berbers at Anual in Morocco. The finger of blame pointed directly at King Alfonso, who had intervened to select the Spanish commander for the Moroccan campaign. Just as a report on the event was to be submitted to parliament in 1923, however, General Miguel Primo de Rivera, an eccentric Andalucian aristocrat, led an army rising in support of the king that launched his own mild, six-year dictatorship.

Primo was a centralist who censored the press and upset intellectuals but gained the cooperation of the socialist UGT. Anarchists went underground. Primo founded industries, improved roads, made the trains run on time and built dams and power plants. However, eventually, with an economic downturn following the Wall St crash and discontent in the army, Alfonso took the chance to return and dismiss him.

SECOND REPUBLIC

Alfonso had brought the monarchy into too much disrepute to last long himself. When a new republican movement scored sweeping victories in municipal elections in 1931, the king went into exile in Italy. The tumultuous Second Republic that followed – called La Niña Bonita (The Pretty Child) by its supporters – polarised Spain and ended in civil war.

The Left in Charge

Elections in 1931 brought in a government composed of socialists, republicans and so-called radicals (who were actually centrists). The Cortes contained few workers and no-one from the anarchist CNT, which continued with strikes and violence to bring on the revolution.

A new constitution in December 1931 gave women the vote, ended Catholicism's status as the official religion, disbanded the Jesuits, stopped government payment of priests' salaries, legalised divorce, banned priests from teaching and gave autonomy-minded Catalonia its own parliament. It also promised land redistribution, which pleased the Andalucian landless, but failed to deliver much.

1813–24	1860s
Most of Spain's American colonies win independence	Anarchist ideas reach Spain and soon gain a wide following

The Right in Charge

Anarchist disruption, an economic slump, the alienation of big business, the votes of newly enfranchised women, and disunity on the left all helped the right to win the 1933 election. The new Catholic party, Confederación Española de Derechas Autónomas (CEDA; Spanish Confederation of Autonomous Rights), won the most seats. Other new forces on the right included the fascist Falange, led by José Antonio Primo de Rivera, son of the 1920s dictator. The Falange practised blatant street violence.

By 1934 violence was spiralling out of control. The socialist UGT called for a general strike, Catalonia's president declared his region independent (albeit within a putative federal Spanish republic) and workers' committees took over the northern mining region of Asturias, after attacking police and army posts. A violent campaign against the Asturian workers by the Spanish Foreign Legion (set up to fight Moroccan tribes in the 1920s), led by generals Francisco Franco and José Millán Astray, firmly divided the country into left and right.

Army Uprising

In the February 1936 elections the Popular Front, a left-wing coalition with communists at the fore, narrowly defeated the right-wing National Front. Violence continued on both sides. Extremist groups grew (the anarchist CNT now had over a million members) and peasants were on the verge of revolution. However, when the revolt came on 17 July 1936, it was from the other end of the political spectrum. On that day the Spanish army garrison in Melilla, in North Africa, rose up against the left-wing government, followed by some garrisons the next day on the mainland. The leaders of the plot were five generals, among them Franco, who on 19 July flew from the Canary Islands to Morocco to take charge of his legionnaires. The civil war had begun.

Homage to Catalonia recounts George Orwell's personal involvement in the civil war, moving from euphoria to despair.

SPANISH CIVIL WAR

The Spanish Civil War split communities, families and friends. Both sides committed atrocious massacres and reprisals, and employed death squads to eliminate members of opposing organisations. The rebels, who called themselves Nationalists because they thought they were fighting for Spain, shot or hanged tens of thousands of supporters of the republic. Republicans did likewise to Franco sympathisers, including some 7000 priests, monks and nuns. Political affiliation often provided a convenient cover for settling old scores. In the whole war an estimated 350,000 Spaniards died.

Ernest Hemingway's terse and magnificent novel For Whom the Bell Tolls is full of the emotions unleashed in the civil war.

Many of the military and Guardia Civil went over to the Nationalists, whose campaign quickly took on overtones of a crusade against the enemies of God. In Republican areas, anarchists, communists or socialists ended up running many towns and cities. Social revolution followed.

Nationalist Advance

The basic battle lines were drawn within a week of the rebellion in Morocco. Most cities with military garrisons fell immediately into Nationalist hands – this meant everywhere north of Madrid except Catalonia, eastern Aragón, the Basque coast, Cantabria and Asturias, plus western Andalucía and Granada. Franco's force of legionnaires and Moroccan mercenaries was

1873	1909
First Republic, a federal union of 17 states, collapses in chaos, and the monarchy is restored	The Semana Trágica (Tragic Week) in Barcelona: a general strike turns into a frenzy of violence

Hugh Thomas' *The Spanish Civil War* is the classic account of the war: long and dense, yet readable and humane.

airlifted from Morocco to Seville by German warplanes in August. Essential to the success of the revolt, they moved northwards through Extremadura towards Madrid, wiping out fierce resistance in some cities. At Salamanca in October, Franco pulled all the Nationalists into line behind him.

Madrid, reinforced by the first battalions of the International Brigades (armed foreign idealists and adventurers organised by the communists), repulsed Franco's first assault in November then endured, under communist inspiration, over two years' siege.

Foreign Intervention

The International Brigades never numbered more than 20,000 and couldn't turn the tide against the better armed and better organised Nationalist forces.

Nazi Germany and Fascist Italy supported the Nationalists with planes, weapons and men (75,000 from Italy, 17,000 from Germany), turning the war into a rehearsal for WWII. The Republicans had some Soviet support, in the form of planes, tanks, artillery and advisers, but the rest of the international community refused to get involved (although 25,000 or so French fought on the Republican side).

Republican Quarrels

The politics and social movements of pre-civil-war Spain are fascinatingly unravelled in Gerald Brenan's *The Spanish Labyrinth*.

With Madrid besieged, the Republican government moved to Valencia in late 1936 to continue trying to preside over a diversity of political persuasions on its side, from anarchists and communists to moderate democrats and regional secessionists. Barcelona was run for nearly a year by anarchists and a Trotskyite militia called the Partido Obrero de Unificación Marxista (POUM; Workers' Marxist Unification Party).

In April 1937 German planes bombed the Basque town of Gernika (Guernica), causing terrible casualties; this became the subject of Picasso's famous pacifist painting. All of the north coast fell in the summer, giving the Nationalists control of Basque industry. Republican counter-attacks near Madrid and in Aragón failed.

British director Ken Loach's *Tierra y Libertad* (Land and Freedom), made in 1995, is one of the most convincing treatments of the civil war on film.

Meanwhile divisions among the Republicans erupted into fierce street fighting in Barcelona in May 1937, with the Soviet-influenced communists completely crushing the anarchists and Trotskyites. The Republican government moved to Barcelona in autumn 1937.

Nationalist Victory

In early 1938 Franco repulsed a Republican offensive at Teruel in Aragón, then swept eastwards with 100,000 troops, 1000 planes and 150 tanks, isolating Barcelona from Valencia. In July the Republicans launched a last offensive as the Nationalists moved through the Ebro valley. The bloody encounter, won by the Nationalists, resulted in 20,000 dead.

The USSR withdrew from the war in September 1938 and in January 1939 the Nationalists took Barcelona unopposed. The Republican government and hundreds of thousands of supporters fled to France.

The Republicans still held Valencia and Madrid, and had 500,000 people under arms, but in the end the Republican army simply evaporated. The Nationalists entered Madrid on 28 March 1939 and Franco declared the war over on 1 April.

1923–30	1931–36
Mild dictatorship of General Miguel Primo de Rivera	Second Republic: King Alfonso XIII goes into exile, Spanish society polarises, political violence spirals

FRANCO'S SPAIN

The Nationalist victors were merciless. Instead of reconciliation, more blood-letting ensued. An estimated 100,000 people were killed or died in prison after the war. The hundreds of thousands imprisoned included many intellectuals and teachers; others fled abroad, depriving Spain of a generation of scientists, artists, writers, educators and more.

Franco ruled absolutely. The Cortes was merely a rubber stamp for such decrees as Franco chose to submit to it. Regional autonomy aspirations were not tolerated. Franco kept hold of power by never allowing any single powerful group – the church, the Movimiento Nacional (the only legal political party), the army, monarchists or bankers – to dominate. The army provided many ministers and enjoyed a most generous budget. Catholic orthodoxy was fully restored, with secondary schools entrusted to the Jesuits, divorce illegal and church weddings compulsory. Franco won some working-class support with carrots such as job security and paid holidays, but there was no right to strike.

WWII

A few months after the civil war ended, WWII began. Franco promised Hitler an alliance but never committed himself to a date. In 1944 Spanish leftists launched a failed attack on Franco's Spain from France; small leftist guerrilla units continued a hopeless struggle in the north, Extremadura and Andalucía until the 1950s.

After WWII Spain was excluded from the UN and NATO, and suffered a UN-sponsored trade boycott that helped turn the late 1940s into Spain's *años de hambre* (years of hunger). But with the onset of the Cold War, the US sought to establish four bases in Spain. Franco agreed, in return for large sums of aid, and in 1955 Spain was admitted to the UN.

Economic Miracle

The Stabilisation Plan of 1959, with its devaluation of the peseta and other deflationary measures, brought an economic upswing. The plan was engineered by a new breed of technocrats linked to the Catholic group Opus Dei. Spanish industry boomed. Thousands of young Spaniards went abroad to study and returned with a new attitude of teamwork. Modern machinery, techniques and marketing were introduced; transport was modernised; and new dams provided irrigation and hydropower.

The recovery was funded in part by US aid, and remittances from more than a million Spaniards working abroad, but above all by tourism, which developed initially along Andalucía's Costa del Sol and Catalonia's Costa Brava. By 1965, the number of tourists arriving in Spain had jumped to 14 million a year.

A huge population shift from impoverished rural regions to the cities and tourist resorts took place. Many Andalucians went to Barcelona. In the cities, elegant suburbs developed, as did shantytowns and, later, high-rise housing for the workers.

The Final Decade

The year 1964 saw Franco celebrating 25 years of peace, order and material progress. However the jails were still full of political prisoners and

1936–39	1939–75
Spanish Civil War: Nationalist rebels led by General Francisco Franco defeat Republican forces; about 350,000 Spaniards are killed	Franco dictatorship

large garrisons were maintained outside every major city. Over the next decade, labour strife grew and there were rumblings of discontent in the universities and even the army and church.

Regional problems resurfaced too. The Basque-nationalist terrorist group Euskadi Ta Askatasuna (ETA; Basques and Freedom), founded in 1959, gave cause for the declaration of six states of emergency between 1962 and 1975; heavy-handed police tactics won ETA support from Basque moderates.

Franco chose as his successor Prince Juan Carlos, the Spanish-educated grandson of Alfonso XIII. In 1969 Juan Carlos swore loyalty to Franco and the Movimiento Nacional.

Cautious reforms by Franco's last prime minister, Carlos Arias Navarro, provoked violent opposition from right-wing extremists. Spain seemed to be descending into chaos when Franco died on 20 November 1975.

TRANSITION TO DEMOCRACY

Juan Carlos I, aged 37, took the throne two days later. The new king's links with Franco inspired little confidence in a Spain now clamouring for democracy. However, Juan Carlos earned much of the credit for the successful transition to democracy that followed. He sacked prime minister Arias Navarro in July 1976, replacing him with Adolfo Suárez, a 43-year-old former Franco apparatchik with film-star looks. To general surprise, Suárez got the Francoist-filled Cortes to approve a new, two-chamber parliamentary system. Then in early 1977 political parties, trade unions and strikes were all legalised and the Movimiento Nacional was abolished.

New Constitution

Suárez's centrist UCD party won nearly half the seats in the new Cortes in 1977. The left-of-centre Partido Socialista Obrero Español (PSOE; Spanish Socialist Worker Party), led by a charismatic young lawyer from Seville, Felipe González, came second.

In 1978 the Cortes passed a new constitution that made Spain a parliamentary monarchy with no official religion. The constitution provided for a large measure of devolution from the central government to Spain's regions, in response to the local-autonomy fever that gripped Spain after the stiflingly centralist Franco era. By 1983 this resulted in the country being divided into 17 'autonomous communities' with their own regional governments controlling a range of policy areas.

For more information on Madrid's underground scene, which eventually emerged as the *movida*, see Moving with the Movida on p152.

Social Liberation

Personal and social life enjoyed a rapid liberation after Franco. Contraceptives, homosexuality and divorce were legalised and during this era the *movida* (the late-night bar and disco scene that enables people anywhere in Spain to party till dawn or after) emerged. However, Prime Minister Suárez faced mounting resistance from within his own party to further reforms, and in 1981 he resigned.

THE PSOE YEARS

In 1982 Spain made a final break with the past by voting the PSOE into power with a sizable majority. Felipe González was to be prime minister for 14 years.

1975	1976–81
Franco dies and is succeeded by King Juan Carlos I	Prime minister Adolfo Suárez engineers a return to democracy

The PSOE's young, educated leadership came from the generation that had opened the cracks in the Franco regime in the late 1960s and early '70s. The PSOE persuaded the unions to accept wage restraint and job losses in order to streamline industry. Unemployment rose from 16% to 22% by 1986. But that same year Spain joined the European Community (now the EU), bringing on an economic boom that lasted until 1991. The middle class grew ever bigger and Spain's traditionally stay-at-home women streamed into higher education and jobs.

The PSOE put a national health system in place by the early 1990s and made improvements in state education, raising the university population to well over a million.

In October 2003, Esperanza Aguirre was elected as president of the Comunidad de Madrid, making history as Spain's first-ever regional woman president.

Slump & Scandal

Around halfway through the late 1980s boom, the good life began to turn sour. People observed that many of the glamorous new rich were making their money by property or share speculation, or plain corruption. In 1992 – exactly five centuries after the pivotal year of its history – Spain celebrated its return to the modern world in style, staging the Barcelona Olympics and the Expo 92 world fair in Seville. However, the economy was now in a slump (unemployment reached 22.5% the following year) and the PSOE was increasingly mired in scandals. González's longtime deputy, Alfonso Guerra, resigned in 1991 over an affair involving his wheeler-dealer brother's use of a government office.

The slump bottomed out in 1993, but the scandals multiplied. The González-appointed head of the Guardia Civil from 1986 to 1993, Luis Roldán, suddenly vanished in 1994 after being charged with embezzlement and bribery. He was arrested the following year in Bangkok and in 1998 was jailed in Spain for 28 years.

Most damaging of all was the affair of the Grupos Antiterroristas de Liberación (GAL), death squads that had murdered 28 suspected ETA terrorists (several of whom were innocent) in France in the mid-1980s. A constant stream of GAL allegations contributed to the PSOE's electoral defeat in 1996. In 1998 a dozen senior police and PSOE men were jailed in connection with the affair.

PARTIDO POPULAR (PP) RULE

The 1996 general election was won by the centre-right Partido Popular (PP; People's Party), led by José María Aznar, a former tax inspector from Castilla y León. Aznar promised to make politics dull, and he did, but he presided over eight years of solid economic progress.

The PP cut public investment, sold off state enterprises and liberalised various sectors, such as telecommunications. In 1997 employers and unions signed a deal reforming Spain's employment system: severance pay was reduced but it became easier for companies to hire the young, middle-aged and long-term unemployed. By 2000, Spain had the fastest-growing economy in the EU. Unemployment fell from 23% in 1996 to 15% in 2000 – still the highest in the EU – but the statistics concealed the fact that many officially jobless people were benefiting from a big black economy.

The 2000 election was a triumph for Aznar and his party. The PP gained the first-ever absolute parliamentary majority for a centre-right

1982–96	1986
Spain is governed by the centre-left Partido Socialista Obrero Español (PSOE) led by Felipe González	Spain joins the EC (now the EU)

party in democratic Spain. The PSOE, under a new leader, Joaquín Almunia, had made an unpopular electoral alliance with the communist-led Izquierda Unida (IU; United Left). Almunia was soon replaced by José Luis Rodríguez Zapatero, an amiable, sincere young lawyer from Castilla y León. Zapatero immediately swept most previous PSOE high-ups, including Felipe González, out of the party hierarchy.

Aznar's second term proceeded in a similar vein to the first, with continued economic progress (unemployment was down to 11% by 2004) and no seriously damaging scandals, though the government's dozy response to the *Prestige* disaster of 2002, when oil from a broken tanker smothered 600km of northwestern Spanish coast in black sludge, earned it a lot of opprobrium. Aznar adopted a hard line against the Basque terrorist organisation, ETA, banning its political wing, Batasuna, in 2002, and refusing to talk to ETA unless it renounced violence. ETA, which wants an independent, sovereign state covering the Spanish and French Basque Country and Navarra, has murdered about 800 people in its 4½ decades of existence. Several high-profile ETA arrests in 2002 and 2003 seemed to vindicate Aznar's stance, but ETA is unlikely to fade away because even though few support its methods, many in the Basque Country share its goal.

For further information about ETA, see ETA & Basque Nationalism on p443.

Aznar lined up firmly behind US and British international policy after 11 September 2001 attacks on the USA. However, his strong support for the US-led invasion of Iraq in 2003 was unpopular at home, as was his decision to send 1300 Spanish troops to Iraq after the war. Nevertheless, Aznar had seemingly steered the PP firmly into pole position in Spanish politics. He stuck to his own decision not to stand for a third term of office in 2004, but as that year's election approached, his successor as PP leader, Mariano Rajoy, seemed sure to win.

The major social change of the Aznar years was a tripling of the number of foreigners in the population: see p52 for more on this important development.

MADRID BOMBINGS & RETURN OF THE PSOE

Early on the morning of Thursday 11 March 2004, three days before the general election, bombs exploded on four crowded commuter trains in and near Madrid, killing 192 people and injuring over 1800. Many millions of Spaniards poured on to the streets in demonstrations of peace and solidarity the following day. Accompanying the overwhelming feelings of national shock and grief was the question, 'Who did it?' The government pointed a very firm finger at ETA, which had been foiled in at least two attempts to carry out devastating bombings in the preceding months. The evidence this time, however, pointed at least equally strongly to Islamic extremists. Police investigating the bombings were certain by the following day that ETA was not the culprit. The government, however, continued to maintain that ETA was the prime suspect until Saturday 13 March, when police in Madrid arrested three Moroccans and two Indians, with suspected links to Al-Qaeda, in connection with an unexploded bomb found on one of the trains.

The following day the PSOE, which had lagged a distant second in the opinion polls before 11 March, won the election. This shock result was widely attributed to the PP's unpopular policy on Iraq, which most

1996–2004	2002
The centre-right Partido Popular (PP), led by José María Aznar, presides over eight years of steady economic progress	Aznar bans Batasuna (ETA's political wing)

Spaniards believed was the reason the terrorists attacked Spain, and to the PP's apparent attempts to mislead the public by blaming the bombings on ETA.

On 30 March the government named an organisation called the Moroccan Islamic Combatant Group, thought to have connections with Al-Qaeda, as the main focus of investigations. Of 16 people charged in connection with the bombings by the end of April 2004, 14 were Moroccan.

Within two weeks of taking office in April, the new PSOE government led by José Luis Rodríguez Zapatero honoured its campaign pledge to pull Spanish troops out of Iraq.

After 11 September 2001, the Spanish government arrested members of an alleged Spanish Al-Qaeda cell, some of whom are still in custody.

192 killed in Madrid train bombings by Islamic terrorists

PSOE, led by José Luis Rodríguez Zapatero, wins surprise election victory

The Culture

THE NATIONAL PSYCHE

More than five centuries of national unity have done little to erode the regional ticks that distinguish one group of Spaniards from another. Even so, they cannot escape the occasional national generalisation. A visitor to Franco's Spain in the 1960s might have found them uniformly dour and frumpy. Not any more.

Spaniards, from San Sebastián to Seville, share a zest for the fest. The country's calendar creaks beneath the weight of an unending parade of feast days and celebrations that, whether of religious or pagan origin, share the common aim of providing an excuse for much drinking, eating and merrymaking. Not that many of them need an excuse. Urban Spain in particular attaches great importance to what the Irish would call *craic*. From the international rave clubs of Ibiza to the rivers of revellers in the narrow Siete Calles of Bilbao, a live-for-the-moment attitude prevails.

Not that Spaniards are layabouts. Perhaps simply a precariousness about daily life down the centuries in this long-troubled country has engendered the need for momentary escape. A trip around the country reveals a broad spectrum of regional traits. While the people of deep Spain, the two Castiles, tend to be taciturn and dry, their neighbours to the south in Andalucía are the height of instant affability. Your average Andalucian loves a chat over a sherry in a flighty, extrovert and often fickle fashion. In the northeast, the Catalans are famed for their unerring sense of business and a rather Protestant style of work ethic. Further west, the proud Basques can at first hand seem unapproachable but quickly prove effusively hospitable once the ice is broken.

Madrid comes closest to providing a picture of the amalgam. For centuries a magnet for Spaniards from all corners of the country, its people have that air of the capital, burning candles at both ends by working and partying hard, and keeping a curious eye open for newcomers. After all, many of them are from elsewhere, or the sons and daughters of immigrants.

LIFESTYLE

Since Spain passed its new constitution in 1978, the life of its people has changed in leaps and bounds. At the time, 40% of Spanish homes had neither bath nor shower and a quarter of the population above 16 was illiterate. Only a fifth of families could afford to go away on holidays. Now most families have all the standard white goods, a car and take annual holidays at home and abroad.

The rapid rise in living standards has been accompanied by deep social change. Spanish women are having fewer children than they were a couple of generations ago (see Population on p49), divorce is on the rise as are single parent families. De facto couples are gradually acquiring much the same rights as their married counterparts and the new Socialist government is considering legalising homosexual marriage. A landmark decision in the region of Navarra in 2004 allowed a lesbian couple custody of two girls born to one of the couple. All this was utterly unthinkable in the grey days of Franco, when the Church ruled supreme over Spanish mores.

Some things don't change so rapidly. Children still tend to stay in the parental home for longer than their counterparts in northern Europe. It is not uncommon for them to still be living with their parents into their 30s. The reasons given range from unemployment (almost 20% of

A Parrot in the Pepper Tree, by Chris Stewart, in the by now well-worn genre of the funny-thing-happened-to-me-when-I-bought-a-house-in-the-sunny-south books, is the relatively amusing second tome to come from the drummer-cum-sheep-shearer in the Alpujarras.

university graduates take four years or more to find work) to low salaries combined with the high cost of rent.

Machismo is very much alive, and in many families the man of the house still tends to be the king of the castle. The ugly side of this phenomenon are the shocking cases of domestic violence that come to light with greater frequency as the years go by. In 2003, 70 women were murdered by their husband, boyfriend or ex, which is 34% more than in the previous year. In all likelihood the level of violence is not increasing but simply attracting greater attention.

Sometimes economic difficulties are behind the troubled family waters. While the statistics show the gap in per capita earnings between Spain and the European Union closing (to about 80% of the EU average), several deep problems remain. Unemployment remains among the highest in Europe. Wages still trail behind those of most Western European countries. The average gross salary does not exceed €18,000 a year. A senior project manager might earn €40,000 before tax.

John Hooper's *The New Spaniards* gives a crisp and diverse insight in many aspects of modern Spanish society. It is a breezy, well documented account of everything from sex bars to the economy.

POPULATION

With 42.7 million people, Spain is one of the least densely populated of Western European countries – about 84 people per square km. According to surveys in 1999, they happen to be among the shortest and slimmest people in Europe too. In 1594 about 8.2 million lived in Spain. In recent years the population would have fallen had it not been for the massive arrival of immigrants. In early 2004 it was estimated that more than 2.7 million people in Spain were immigrants, more than four times the figure in 1998. Spain has long been at the bottom of the birth-rate list, with Italy, at 1.24 children per fertile woman; in recent years immigrants have been helping out, pushing the rate up to about 1.7.

Spaniards like to live together in cities, towns or villages (pueblos), a habit that probably goes back to past needs for defence. Only in the Basque lands (and to some extent Galicia) do you see countryside dotted with single farmsteads and small fields. As a result, the centre of cities like Madrid and Barcelona have among the highest population concentration in the world, while the countryside is bereft of people. Regional differences persist today. The peoples with the strongest identities – the Catalans, Basques and, to a lesser extent, the Galicians – are on the fringes of the Spanish heartland of Castile and have their own languages and minority independence movements.

Some consider Spain's *gitanós* (Roma people, formerly known as Gypsies) to be its only true long-standing ethnic minority, as interbreeding has made the rest of the population more homogeneous than many regional nationalists would like to admit. Generally reckoned to be the originators – as well as the best performers – of flamenco, the *gitanós* are thought to have originated in India and reached Spain in the 15th century. As elsewhere, they have suffered discrimination. There are about 600,000 *gitanós* in Spain, more than half of them in Andalucía.

SPORT
Football

Fútbol (soccer) seems to be many a Spaniard's prime preoccupation. Around 300,000 fans attend the games in the Primera División (First Division) of the Liga (league) every weekend from September to May, with millions more following the games on TV. Spaniards take their favoured teams' fortunes seriously, although there is little hooliganism of the kind that so blights matches in the UK.

Almost any game in the Primera División is worth attending for the Spanish crowd experience. Those involving eternal rivals Real Madrid and Barcelona have an extra passion to them. These two have large followings and something approaching a monopoly on the silverware: between them they have carried off the league title 45 times. Real Madrid, thanks largely to Franco's support in the 1950s, has won Europe's major club competition, the European Cup (now the Champions League), a record nine times. Real's and Barcelona's players and coaches are celebrities (at least when they are winning) – and their clubs have high expectations: when Real won their seventh European Cup in 1998 they promptly sacked coach Jupp Heynckes because they had only finished fourth in the league. Both teams had a rather frustrating time of it in the 2003–04 season, coming close in various competitions but unable to take victor's laurels in any.

Real Madrid is at home in the **Estadio Santiago Bernabéu** (☎ 91 398 43 00, 902 324324; www.realmadrid.com; Avenida de Concha Espina 1), near metro Santiago Bernabéu, and FC Barcelona at **Camp Nou** (tickets ☎ 902 189900; www.fcbarcelona .com; Avinguda Aristides Maillol s/n), near metro Collblanc.

For the latest information on the next bullfight near you, biographies of *toreros* and more, check out www.portaltaurino.com.

Other leading clubs include Valencia (which snatched the Liga for the second time in three years in the 2003–04 season after Real Madrid had led through almost the entire season and collapsed in the final rounds), Athletic Bilbao, Deportivo La Coruña, Real Betis (of Seville), Málaga and Real Sociedad of San Sebastián. The promotion and relegation system (the three sides at the bottom of the First Division at the end of the season drop down) allows lesser teams their occasional hour of glory among the big boys.

League games are mostly played on Saturday and Sunday, and you can pay at the gate (from about €15 for lesser games, at least €30 for Real Madrid or FC Barcelona matches) for all but the biggest matches, for which tickets have to be bought in advance. Games in the Copa del Rey (Spain's equivalent of the FA Cup) and matches in European competitions are held midweek at night.

Bullfighting

It is difficult to classify this very Spanish activity. Bullfighting occurs in Portugal, southern France and parts of Latin America, but Spain is its true home.

The most important fight season, the *crème de la crème* if you will, takes place in Madrid for a month from mid-May as part of that city's celebrations of its patron saint, San Isidro.

A Spanish animal-rights and anti-bullfighting organisation is the Asociación para la Defensa de los Derechos del Animal (ADDA; www.addaong .org).

To aficionados the fight is an art form and to its protagonists a way of life. To its detractors it is little more than ghoulish torture and slaughter. For others it is a show. If we call it here a spectator sport, it is more than anything for lack of another obvious 'category'.

In early 2004 the Barcelona city council whipped up a storm by declaring itself, after a vote on nonparty lines, an antibullfighting city. The decision in itself has no legal validity and a regional Catalan law on the protection of animals allows bullfights, where there are permanent rings and a tradition. While it is true that the spectacle is no longer as popular in Barcelona as it once was, it is hard to imagine towns or cities in the heartland of central Spain following Barcelona's example. Some regions (like the Balearic Islands) have never shown much interest in the activity while others, such as Andalucía, can hardly be imagined without it.

Bullfighting of one sort or another has a long history. In Roman times tests of human bravery against wild animals included bullfighting.

La lidia, as the art of bullfighting is known, took off in Spain in the mid-18th century. By the mid-19th century breeders were creating the first reliable breeds of *toro bravo* (fighting bull), and a bullfighting school had been launched in Seville.

The bullfighting season begins in the first week of February with the fiestas of Valdemorillo and Ajalvir, near Madrid, to mark the feast day of San Blas.

All over the country, but especially in the two Castiles and Andalucía, *corridas* (bullfights) and the running of the bulls through town (*encierros*), as in Pamplona, are part of town festivals. As a rule they take place on weekends from about 6pm. On the card are six bulls, and hence fights, faced by three teams (*cuadrillas*) of *toreros* (bullfighters).

The matador is the star of the team. It is above all his fancy footwork, skill and bravery before the bull that has the crowd in raptures or in rage, depending on his (or very occasionally her) performance.

A complex series of events takes place in each clash, which can last about 20 minutes. *Peons* dart about with grand capes in front of the bull, horseback picadors (*picadores*) drive lances into the bull's withers and *banderilleros* charge headlong at the bull in an attempt to stab *banderillas* into his neck.

Finally, the matador kills the bull, unless the bull has managed to put him out of action, as sometimes happens.

La lidia is about many things – death, bravery, performance. No doubt the fight is bloody and cruel, but aficionados say the bull is better off dying at the hands of a matador than in the *matadero* (abattoir). To witness it is not necessarily to approve of it, but might give an insight into the tradition and thinking behind *la lidia*.

Other anti-bullfighting organisations are the World Society for the Protection of Animals (WSPA; www.wspa.org.uk) and People for the Ethical Treatment of Animals (PETA; www.peta.org).

Basketball

Basketball (*baloncesto*) is a popular spectator sport, with 18 clubs contesting the Liga Asociación de Clubes de Baloncesto (ACB) national league from late September to late June. Leading teams include Barcelona and Real Madrid (attached to the football clubs), Tau Vitoria, Unicaja of Málaga, Pamesa of Valencia, Caja San Fernando of Seville and Estudiantes of Madrid. For details on upcoming matches around the country, check out the league website www.acb.com.

For Hemingway's exhaustive study of a subject he loved dearly, the bullfight, reach for *Death in the Afternoon*.

Motor Racing

Every year around April or May the dashing knights in shining motorised armour come to the Montmeló track, about a 30-minute drive north of Barcelona, to burn rubber. For more information, see Sport in the Barcelona chapter (p314).

Spain is motorcycle mad. It stages a Grand Prix tournament in the world 500cc championship (as well as in the 250cc and 125cc categories) in May each year at the Jerez de la Frontera track **Circuito Permanente de Velocidad** (☎ 956 15 11 00; www.circuitodejerez.com; Carretera de Arcos, Km 10) in Andalucía. A second Grand Prix round is usually held at the Montmeló circuit a month later.

Cycling

Spain's version of the Tour de France cycling race is the three-week Vuelta a España (www.lavuelta.com), usually in September. The course changes each year.

Tennis

Tennis players such as Carlos Moyá, Juan Carlos Ferrero and Alex Corretja in the men's game, and Arantxa Sánchez Vicario and Conchita Martínez among the women, have inspired the rapidly growing popularity of their sport. Spain's strength in men's tennis finally won it the Davis Cup for the first time in 2000, with the final played in Barcelona. And Madrid's Virginia Ruano Pascual, with teammate Argentinian Paola Suarez, won three Grand Slam doubles events in 2004, winning the Australian, French and US Open titles and scoring three consecutive US Open doubles championships.

Golf

Golf is another sport where Spaniards are increasingly prominent and that's ever more popular in Spain. These days it's not just Severiano Ballesteros and José-María Olazábal figuring on the leader boards of major international tournaments but also Miguel-Ángel Jiménez and Sergio García.

MULTICULTURALISM

Long an exporter of its people (the 'Moroccans of the 1950s' in the words of writer Rosa Montero, one of the country's best-known journalists and novelists), Spaniards have, since the mid-1990s, been rudely confronted by a new reality: multiculturalism. The massive influx of immigrants, who now make up more than 6% of the population (see Population on p49), is rapidly changing the once seemingly homogeneous make-up of the country.

Jason Webster sets off to explore the Muslim roots of Spain in a contemporary journey with a Moroccan immigrant across the south of the country in *Andalus*.

More than half a million Muslims live in this once ultra-Catholic country. More than one million nationals from Spain's former South American colonies have come to claim their birthright in the *madre patria* (mother country). Many South Americans, once legally resident, can request Spanish nationality after just two years' residency, unlike other migrants, who must wait 10 years. More than half a million of the foreigners come from EU countries and a similar number come from Africa (mostly Morocco).

The streets of Spain's big cities have taken on new hues. While the Madrid of the 1980s still had a largely uniform feel, the city today hums to the sounds of many languages, whose speakers have brought new tastes to the dining table. Shawarma stands and Peruvian restaurants abound. Argentines staff call centres and Filipinos wait in certain restaurants. Hordes of retired and wealthy EU citizens are catered for by conationals on the holiday *costas* (coasts). Around 13% of the population of the Balearic Islands, and just over 10% of Madrid are foreigners.

Economists underline that immigration is vital to the country's economic future but the seemingly uncontrolled entry of foreigners has become a major political football.

The image of illegal immigrants crossing the Straits of Gibraltar and the Atlantic (to the Canary Islands) from Morocco in barely seaworthy boats is a daily reminder of the litany of suffering. About half the foreigners living in Spain are illegal *clandestinos* (immigrants). Inevitably driven by poverty and frequently unable to obtain work papers, some turn to crime. Cultural clashes and perhaps too much press don't help. Towns like Premià de Mar (Catalonia) hit the headlines as citizens' groups protest against the opening of mosques in their neighbourhoods. Incidents such as the publication of an alleged defence of domestic violence by an imam in Fuengirola (Andalucía), and his subsequent trial, highlight cultural differences. The refusal of some Muslim families to send their elder daughters to school has also led to controversy.

Spain's multicultural experiment has just begun, although the country had some practice in the 1950s and 1960s with massive internal migration from impoverished regions such as Andalucía and Extremadura to the economic and industrial centres of Madrid, Barcelona and the Basque Country. Cosmopolitan urbanite Spaniards, fascinated by the melting pots of New York, London and Paris, rub their hands, perhaps a little ingenuously, in glee at this 'coming of age'. Others, fearful of being engulfed, recoil in horror. One study predicts that migrants will make up more than a quarter of the population by 2015.

MEDIA

In the charged run-up to the 2004 general elections, Spain's main public-television station, TVE-1, came under heavy criticism at home and in the European Parliament for its lack of impartiality. The ruling right-wing Partido Popular (PP) monopolised airtime, leaving opposition parties largely sidelined.

Happily, the wider media is more fractured. The PP had frequent run-ins with the country's most prestigious newspaper, El País, and not the least of them was unleashed over attempts by the PP to push its line that the bomb attacks in Madrid (see p46) were the work of the Basque-nationalist terror group Euskadi Ta Askatasuna (ETA; Basques and Freedom), rather than Islamic radicals. Indeed, the paper published a special last-minute edition on the day of the blasts attributing them to ETA. Both the paper and Cadena SER, the leading private radio station, subsequently gave space to the radical-Islamic line of investigation, in the tense days between the attacks and the elections. Both were accused by the PP of a malicious misrepresentation of the 'facts', even as it became clear that the PP had been, at best, economical with the truth.

Overall, most media observers in Spain lament the poor quality of much TV news reporting and its frequent partiality. In print, things are considerably healthier. Much as in the UK, the main newspapers each have their own pronounced political leaning. If El País is centre-left, ABC is unashamedly right wing. El Mundo lies much further to the left and loves a scandal. Some regional titles also have axes to grind. A good example is a Catalan-language daily published in Barcelona, Avui, which pushes an openly Catalan-nationalist line.

Probably the sharpest political punditry comes from the biting satirical puppet show, Las Noticias del Guiñol, on Canal+ nightly from Monday to Saturday. Not everyone can be bothered with politics, however. The country's most read newspaper (2.5 million readers) is Marca, dedicated entirely to sport.

RELIGION

Cardenal Antonio María Rouco, head of the Catholic Church in Spain, is unhappy. Although he affirms that at least 80% of the population of this arch-Catholic country retains the faith, he confronts a situation not dissimilar to that in the rest of Western Europe – the ebbing of the faithful from the Church.

A 2004 study showed that 12% of people between 13 and 24 regularly attends Mass. Just 1600 young men are preparing for a religious career in the country's seminaries. Proposals by the new Socialist government elected in 2004 to make access to abortion easier, permit homosexual marriage, allow experimentation with human embryos, consider backing euthanasia and drop the previous government's secondary-school reforms (which included compulsory religious education) have met with vigorous criticism from the country's bishops.

Indeed the church, whose headquarters is in the small conservative town of Toledo (p236), the 'Rome of Spain', is showing signs of becoming increasingly tetchy. In a terse pastoral letter on the family issued in early 2004, Spain's bishops declared that the national problem of domestic violence was a result of the sexual revolution of the 1960s. They went on to call on Catholic lawyers and judges to abstain from divorce cases. The

DID YOU KNOW?

The word Internet was finally accepted as a Spanish word by the Real Academia Española in late 2003.

'problems of divorce' were to have been part of the compulsory religious education programme aborted by the Socialist government.

Spain's most significant religious communities after the Catholics are Protestants (around 800,000) and Muslims (around 500,000). Although religious freedom is guaranteed under the constitution of 1978, leaders of the minority faiths claim frequently that they are victims of discrimination. This is particularly evident in the area of finances. The Catholic Church receives state funds and enjoys certain fiscal benefits that are forbidden other faiths.

ARTS
Literature

It is difficult to talk of a 'Spanish' literature much earlier than the 13th century, if one means literature in Castilian. Before this, troubadours working in Vulgar Latin, Arabic and other tongues were doing the rounds of southern Europe, and the great writers and thinkers in a Spain largely dominated by Muslims produced their treatises more often than not in Arabic or Hebrew.

Alfonso X, king of Castile and León (1252–84) and known as El Sabio (the Learned), did much to encourage the use of Castilian as a language of learning and literature, and wrote about diverse subjects.

Of all the works produced in Spanish in the Middle Ages, the *Poema de Mio Cid*, which has survived in a version penned in 1307 (although first written in 1140), is surely the best known. The epic tale of El Cid Campeador, or Rodrigo Díaz, whose exploits culminated in mastery over Valencia, doesn't let the facts get in way of a good story of derring-do.

Perhaps the greatest of all the Spanish poets was Luis de Góngora (1561–1627). Unconcerned by theories, morals or high-minded sentiments, he manipulated words with a majesty that has largely defied attempts at critical 'explanation'; his verses are above all intended as a source of sensuous pleasure. With Góngora we are in the greatest period of Spanish letters – El Siglo de Oro (the Golden Century), which stretched roughly from the middle of the 16th century to the middle of the 17th.

The advent of the *comedia* in the early 17th century in Madrid produced some of the country's greatest playwrights. Lope de Vega (1562–1635), also an outstanding lyric poet, was perhaps the most prolific: more than 300 of the 800 plays and poems attributed to him remain. He explored the falseness of court life and roamed political subjects with his imaginary historical plays. Less playful is the work of Tirso de Molina (1581–1648), in whose *El Burlador de Sevilla* we meet the immortal character of Don Juan, a likable seducer who meets an unhappy end.

With a life that was something of a jumbled obstacle course of trials, tribulations and peregrinations, Miguel de Cervantes Saavedra (1547–1616) had little success with his forays into theatre and verse. But today he is commonly thought of as the father of the novel. *El Ingenioso Hidalgo Don Quijote de la Mancha* started life as a short story, designed to make a quick peseta, but Cervantes found he had turned it into an epic tale by the time it appeared in 1605. The ruined *ancien régime* knight and his equally impoverished companion, Sancho Panza, embark on a trail through the foibles of his era – a journey whose timelessness and universality marked out the work for greatness.

It was some centuries before Cervantes had a worthy successor. Benito Pérez Galdós (1843–1920) is the closest Spain has come to producing a Dickens or a Balzac. His novels and short stories range from social critique to the simple depiction of society through the lives of its many

Siglo de Oro writer Francisco de Quevedo (1580–1645), a great frequenter of Madrid's taverns, wrote some of the 17th-century's most biting and entertaining prose.

players. His more mature works, such as *Fortunata y Jacinta*, display a bent towards naturalism.

Miguel de Unamuno (1864–1936) was one of the leading figures of the so-called Generation of 98, a group of writers and artists working around and after 1898 (a bad year for Spain with the loss of its last colonies and an economic crisis at home). Unamuno's work is difficult, but among his most enjoyable prose is the *Tres Novelas Ejemplares*, which is imbued, like most of his novels and theatre, with a disquieting existentialism.

A little later came the brief flourishing of Andalucía's Federico García Lorca (1898–1936), whose verse and theatre leaned towards surrealism, leavened by a unique musicality and visual sensibility. His many offerings include the powerful play *Bodas de Sangre* (Blood Wedding). His career was cut short by Nationalist executioners in the early stages of the civil war.

One of the few writers of quality who managed to work through the years of the Franco dictatorship was the Nobel prize–winning Galician novelist Camilo José Cela (1916–2002). His most important novel, *La Familia de Pascual Duarte*, appeared in 1942 and marked a rebirth of the Spanish realist novel. It is said to be the most widely read and translated Spanish novel after Don Quijote.

A member of the Generation of 27 along with Dali and Luis Bunuel, Lorca was seen as a dangerous intellectual by Franco's nationalists. He was shot in August 1936, his books prohibited and his name forbidden.

CONTEMPORARY WRITING

The death of Franco in 1975 signalled the end of the constraints placed on Spanish writers. Many of those who became able to work in complete freedom had already been active in exile during the Franco years and some chose to remain outside Spain. Juan Goytisolo (1931–) started off in the neorealist camp but his more recent works, such as *Señas de Identidad* and *Juan sin Tierra*, are decidedly more experimental. Much of his work revolves around sexuality, as he equates sexual freedom (he is bisexual) with political freedom. In *Juan sin Tierra* he sets homosexuality and heterosexuality in conflict with one another.

Goytisolo's pal, Jaime Gil de Biedma (1929–90), was one of the 20th century's most influential poets in Catalonia and indeed across Spain.

Andalucian Antonio Muñoz Molina (1956–) is an author of note. His *El Invierno en Lisboa* (Winter in Lisbon) is a touching novel and won him considerable acclaim when it first appeared in 1987. Madrid features regularly as the stage for his stories, such as *Los Misterios de Madrid* (Mysteries of Madrid) and *El Dueño del Secreto* (The Master of the Secret). He shifts the geographical focus in his latest work, *Ventanas de Manhattan* (Windows of Manhattan).

Murcia's Arturo Pérez-Reverte (1951–), long-time war correspondent and general man's man, has become one of the most internationally read Spanish novelists. In *El Capitán Alatriste* we are taken into the decadent hurly-burly of 18th-century Madrid. The captain in question has become the protagonist of several other novels too.

Enrique Vila-Matas (1948–) has won fans way beyond his native Barcelona and his novels have been translated into a dozen languages. In *Paris No Se Acaba Nunca* (2003), whose title could be translated as Paris Never Ends, Vila-Matas returns to the 1970s, when he rented a garret in Paris from Marguerite Duras and penned his first novel. It is a curious mix of fiction and autobiography from a writer whose trademark has always been a blurring of lines and genre.

Eduardo Mendoza's (1943–) *La Ciudad de los Prodigios* (The City of Marvels) is an absorbing and at times bizarre novel set in Barcelona in the period between the Universal Exhibition of 1888 and the World Exhibition in 1929.

Manuel Vázquez Montalbán (1939–2003) was one of Barcelona's most prolific writers, best known for his Pepe Carvalho detective novel series and a range of other thrillers. *Galíndez* is about the capture, torture and death of a Basque activist in the Dominican Republic in the 1950s. It was made into a moderately interesting film, *El Misterio Galíndez*, starring Harvey Keitel in 2002.

The writing of Barcelona's Terenci Moix (1942–2003) explores Spanish society and often involves a lot of navel-gazing self-discovery. One of his last novels, *El Arpista Ciego*, is a fantastical journey into the time of the pharaohs.

Cinema & TV

Mention cinema and Spain in the same breath nowadays and just about everyone will say: Pedro Almodóvar (1949–). There is little doubt that the Castilian director with the wild shock of hair, and whose very personal, camp cinema was born in the heady days of the Madrid *movida* (the late-night bar and disco scene) in the years after Franco's death, is inimitable.

His latest, *La Mala Educación* (2004), has many of the typical traits of his film-making: Madrid as protagonist in some fashion, a primary-coloured camp humour combined with a deeply noir story. And there's always an unexpected twist – an unlikely web of relationships. Young Mexican actor Gael García Bernal takes on a tough role as a transvestite who has been sexually abused in school as a child, only he isn't who he appears to be…

The Good, the Bad and the Ugly, a great spaghetti Western by Italian director Sergio Leone was largely shot in the Tabernas desert in southeast Andalucía.

In terms of strangeness, a direct line could perhaps be drawn between Almodóvar and one of the earliest great names in Spanish film, Luis Buñuel (1900–83). This disrespectful icon started off with the disturbing surrealist short *Un Chien Andalou* (1929), which was made with Salvador Dalí ('nuff said). Much of his later film-making was done in exile in Mexico.

A classic to slip through the net of Franco's censorship was Luis García Berlanga's (1921–) *¡Bienvenido, Mr Marshall!* (1952). This is a satire of the folkloric genre beloved of the regime, and at the same time a critique of the deal done with the USA to provide Marshall Plan aid in return for military bases. About the only tangible result for the villagers in the film is a rain of dust as Marshall's VIP cavalcade charges through.

Carlos Saura (1932–) has been incredibly prolific, with more than 35 films to his name, ranging from the dance spectacular *Flamenco* (1995) to the civil war tragicomedy *¡Ay, Carmela!* (1990).

In 1973, Víctor Erice's (1940–) *El Espíritu de la Colmena* (The Spirit of the Beehive) hit the screen; it is a quiet and beautifully crafted picture in which one of the cinema's outcast figures, Frankenstein's monster, becomes real for a beekeeper's little daughter.

Since Franco's demise, Spanish cinema has been busy if uneven. Home-grown films account for less than 20% of box-office earnings, and a lack of public funding (and modest fiscal incentives to invest) plagues the industry. Increasingly the solution for bigger budget productions is coming from international financing and alliances, especially with other European and Latin American countries. When the Socialists came to power in 2004, the film industry became hopeful for a favourable change in funding policy.

In 2000 Almodóvar became one of the few Spaniards to take an Oscar, in this case for possibly his best movie, *Todo Sobre Mi Madre* (All About My Mother; 1999). Another quirky director who had foreign audiences a-giggle was José Juan Bigas Luna (1946–) with the hilarious *Jamón, Jamón* (Ham, Ham), a story of crossed love and murder, in 1992.

Vicente Aranda (1926–) has been less prolific than Almodóvar, but found acclaim with *Amantes* (1991), set in 1950s Madrid and based on the real story of a doomed love triangle. In his Oscar-winning *Belle Epoque*, Fernando Trueba (1955–), examines the melancholy underside to bliss through the story of four sisters' pursuit of a young chap in pre–civil war Spain.

Alejandro Amenábar (1972–) had a hit in 2004 with *Mar Adentro* (Out to Sea), a touching if difficult film on the true story of a man's 30-year struggle to win the right to end his own paralysed life. The lead, Javier Bardem, took the best actor award at the Venice film festival that same year. Barcelona's Isabel Coixet (1960–) went down the English-language route with *My Life Without Me* (2003), about a woman who knows she is going to die and tries to make some order of what remains of her life.

For a while the entire country seemed to be glued to the *caja tonta* ('silly box') absorbed by the antics of *Gran Hermano* (Big Brother) and *Operación Triunfo*, which propels singing unknowns to intergalactic fame. The good news in 2004 is that finally people seem to be tiring of reality TV and going back to sitcoms and soaps, a far superior form of pop culture when you look at it. The musical comedy *Paco y Veva* is top of the charts and in early 2004 *Manolito Gafotas*, extracted from a popular local cartoon character, was also pipping *Gran Hermano*, which has lost half its audience since it first aired in 2000. Manolito, with his outsized glasses, is the most popular kids cartoon character in Spain. He has twice been converted into a movie subject and now there's a TV series that follows this feisty kid's antics in the Madrid suburb of Carabanchel.

DID YOU KNOW?

The WWII blockbuster movies *The Battle of the Bulge* and *Patton* were both shot on location in Spain in the 1960s with Spanish army material, including 75 tanks and 500 infantrymen.

Music

Spain pulsates with music. The country's rock, pop and electronic scene, while not wildly successful beyond Spanish shores, is nonetheless busy and vibrant – and a good deal more so than in many other European countries.

Folk music peculiar to different regions of Spain is also blossoming, and flamenco (see p62), the music most readily associated with Spain by outsiders, may be enjoying its real golden age right now.

POP & ROCK

Every summer throws up one ultra-danceable catchy hit that takes the country by storm. Some of these spread beyond Iberian shores. Remember *Aserejé* by Las Ketchup (2002)?

Among more lasting artists, the undoubted King Midas of Spanish pop, writer of countless hit ballads for himself and others, is Alejandro Sanz, born in Madrid in 1968. Sanz's songs have a wistful lyricality that fails to touch few hearts. Recently he's developed a slightly harder-edged 'urban' image.

Another of the most talented songwriter-performers is Kiko Veneno, from Andalucía, who has been around since the 1970s mixing rock, blues, African and flamenco rhythms with lyrics that range from humorous, simpatico snatches of everyday life to Lorca poems, turning out several hit albums. Another Andalucian evergreen is the iconoclastic Joaquín Sabina, a prolific producer of rock-folk with a protest theme for more than two decades. 'I'll always be against those in power,' he has proclaimed.

Enrique Bunbury, from Zaragoza, made his name as the vocalist of 1990s rock group Héroes del Silencio, and has since broadened his brush as a solo artist mixing glam with Latin American influences. Juan Perro is another singer who found Latin rhythms inspirational after departing from the group he made his name with (in this case popsters Radio Futura).

The flagship pop-rock band is Madrid foursome Dover, led by the sisters Cristina and Amparo Llanos. They're powerful live performers who range from grunge to power pop to punk to garage rock. The indie scene is headed by bands such as Barcelona's psychedelic rockers Sidonie, Madrid '80s-throwbacks Ellos, and Granada's Los Planetas.

In electronic realms, José de Padilla, with his *Café del Mar* compilations, is one of the few Spanish DJs to have exploited Ibiza's status as a world dance-music capital. The duo Najwajean (Najwa Nimri and Carlos Jean) rank as Spain's first trip-hoppers, while Wagon Cookin, two brothers from Navarra (Javier and Luis Garrayalde) are both DJs and instrumentalists, cooking up jazz, soul, club music and Caribbean rhythms into an always intelligent and interesting mix. Also listen out for Fundación Eivissa, whose *Supernatural* won the best electronic track award in Spain's 2004 national music awards.

La Mala Rodríguez, from Seville, and Júnior Míguez stand out in rap and hip-hop.

In purely monetary terms, Julio Iglesias must be Spain's most successful performer ever. Long a resident of the USA, he has for many years had millions swooning with his crooning in Spanish and various other languages. Mind you, in recent years he has been increasingly upstaged by his equally smooth son Enrique, who now sells more records.

It's not too hard to catch a gig by good Spanish or international artists when you're in Spain. The tour circuit, especially from early summer to autumn, is extremely busy. See Indy Rock (www.indyrock.es) for dates and venues of all the main upcoming gigs and festivals. Tourist offices can also tell you what's coming up locally.

FOLK

Although the odd group playing traditional folk music can be found in several regions, Spain's best and most prolific source of folk is Galicia. The region's rich heritage is closely related to that of its Celtic cousins in Brittany and Ireland and has nothing in common with other Spanish music such as flamenco. Emblematic of the music is the *gaita*, Galicia's version of the bagpipes. Top bagpipers are popular heroes in Galicia, and some of the younger generation have greatly broadened the music's appeal by blending it with other genres. One highly versatile performer – not just of the *gaita* but of other wind instruments too – is Carlos Núñez. He presents a slick show involving violins, percussion, guitar and lute, and often invites a wide range of guest artists. Other exciting Galician pipers are Susana Seivane, Xosé Manuel Budiño, and Mercedes Peón whose music is perhaps best characterised as neo-pop-folk.

'Top bag-pipers are popular heroes in Galicia'

Among slightly more traditional performers, Galicia's most successful Celtic group is the highly polished Milladoiro. Other groups to seek out are Berrogüetto, Luar Na Lubre and Fía Na Roca. Uxía is a gutsy female solo vocalist.

The Celtic tradition is also alive in Asturias and even Cantabria. The most commercially successful folk here is that of bagpipe-rocker José Ángel Hevia from Asturias, whose album *Tierra de Nadie* sold over a million copies.

CLASSICAL

While the larger Spanish cities have active classical music scenes, and most of the year it's not hard to find a concert to attend, the music you will hear in the concert halls will not often have been written by Spanish composers. Outsiders have made at least as much serious music as Spaniards themselves from the country's vibrant rhythms. Who has not heard of *Carmen*, an opera whose leading lady epitomises all the fire, guile and flashing beauty conjured up by the typical image of Andalucian women? Its composer, Frenchman Georges Bizet (1838–75), had been mesmerised by the melodies of southern Spain in much the same way as Claude Debussy (1862–1918), whose penchant for the peninsula found expression in *Iberia*. Another Frenchman, Maurice Ravel (1875–1937), whipped up his *Bolero* almost as an aside in 1927. Russians, too, have been swept away by the Hispanic. Mikhail Glinka (1804–57) arrived in Granada in 1845, fell under the spell of *gitanó* song and guitar, and returned home to inspire a new movement in Russian folk music. Nicolai Rimsky-Korsakov (1844–1908) popped into Cádiz for three days' shore leave from the Russian navy, resulting in his delightful *Capriccio Espagnol* (Spanish Caprice) of 1887.

Spain itself was more or less bereft of composers until the likes of Cádiz-born Manuel de Falla (1876–1946) and Enrique Granados (1867–1916) arrived on the scene early in the 20th century. Granados and Isaac Albéniz (1860–1909) became great pianists and interpreters of their own compositions, such as the latter's *Iberia* cycle. The blind Joaquín Rodrigo (1901–99) was one of Spain's leading 20th century composers. Rodrigo's celebrated *Concierto de Aranjuez* for guitar also yielded what for some is the greatest jazz rendering of any classical music work – Miles Davis' 1959 version on his *Sketches of Spain* album.

Andrés Segovia (1893–1987), from Linares in Andalucía and steeped in flamenco, probably did more than any other musician to establish the guitar as a serious classical instrument, taking this formerly humble instrument to dizzying heights of virtuosity and transcribing 150 works for other instruments into pieces for guitar.

In opera, Spain has given the world both Plácido Domingo (1934–) and José Carreras (1946–). With Italian tenor Luciano Pavarotti (1935–), they form the big three of modern male opera singers. Catalonia's Montserrat Caballé (1933–) is one of the world's outstanding sopranos.

Painting

Humans have been creating images in Spain for as long as 14,000 years, as the cave paintings in Altamira attest. Later, the Celtiberian tribes were producing some fine ceramics and statuary, perhaps influenced by the presence of Greeks, Carthaginians and ultimately Romans.

See p499 in the Cantabria & Asturias chapter for more information on Altamira's world-famous cave paintings.

The history of painting in Spain is a chequered one. Long, less exciting periods have been interrupted by moments and individuals of unparalleled greatness.

Mostly anonymous, the painters and decorators of Romanesque churches across the north of the country left behind extraordinary testaments to the religious faith of the early Middle Ages. Some remain *in situ* but the single best concentration of 12th-century Romanesque frescoes can be seen in Barcelona's Museu Nacional d'Art de Catalunya (p295).

Artists began to drop the modesty in the 14th century as Gothic painting, more lifelike and complex than the seemingly naive, didactic Romanesque, took hold. Names such as Catalans Ferrer Bassá (c 1290–c 1348), and Bernat Martorell (c 1400–1452), a master of chiaroscuro, Jaume Huguet (1415–92), and Córdoban Bartolomé Bermejo (c 1405–1495) are thus known to us, and their works identifiable, unlike those of their Romanesque predecessors.

One of the most important artists at work in Spain, in the latter half of the 16th century, was an 'adopted' Spaniard. Domenikos Theotokopoulos (1541–1614), known as El Greco (the Greek), was schooled in his native Crete and Italy, but spent his productive working life in Toledo. His slender, exalted figures can be seen in various locations in that city, as well as in Madrid's Museo del Prado (p121).

THE GOLDEN CENTURY

As the 16th century gave way to the 17th, a remarkably fecund era opened. A plethora of masters, in the service of the Church and state, seemed to appear out of nowhere.

In Italy, José (Jusepe) de Ribera (1591–1652) came under the influence of Caravaggio. Many of his works found their way back to Spain and are now scattered about numerous art galleries, including the solid selection in the Museo del Prado (p121).

A precocious talent, at the age of 24 Velázquez painted a portrait of Felipe IV which so pleased the king that he was appointed court painter and was the only artist allowed to paint the king's portrait.

The star of the period was the genius court painter from Seville, Diego Rodríguez de Silva Velázquez (1599–1660), who stands in a class of his own. With him any trace of the idealised stiffness that characterised a by-now spiritless mannerism fell by the wayside. Realism became the key, and the majesty of his royal subjects springs from his capacity to capture the essence of the person, king or *infanta*, and the detail of their finery. His masterpieces include *Las Meninas* and *La Rendición de Breda* (The Surrender of Breda), both in the Museo del Prado.

A less-exalted contemporary, and close friend of Velázquez, Francisco de Zurbarán (1598–1664) moved to Seville as an official painter. Probably of Basque origin but born in Extremadura, he is best remembered for the startling clarity and light in his portraits of monks. He travelled a great deal and, in Guadalupe, a series of eight portraits can still be seen hanging where Zurbarán left them, in the Hieronymite monastery. Zurbarán fell on hard times in the 1640s and was compelled by the plague to flee Seville. He died in poverty in Madrid.

Zurbarán has come to be seen as one of the masters of the Spanish canvas, but in his lifetime it was a younger and less-inspired colleague who won all the prizes. Bartolomé Esteban Murillo (1618–82) took the safe road and turned out stock religious pieces and images of beggar boys, and the like, with technical polish but little verve. Again, you can see many of his works in the Museo del Prado.

Another solid artist of the period was Alonso Cano (1601–67), who spent his working life in Granada. Also a gifted sculptor and architect, he is sometimes referred to as the Michelangelo of Spain. Not a great deal of his work remains, and his stormy life didn't help matters. He might well have joined the Velázquez gravy train in Madrid, had he not been accused of his second wife's murder and been obliged to leave.

GOYA & THE 19TH CENTURY

Francisco José de Goya y Lucientes (1746–1828), a provincial hick from Fuendetodos (p414) in Aragón, went to Madrid to work as a cartoonist in the Real Fábrica de Tapices (p121) in Madrid. Here began the long and varied career of Spain's only truly great artist of the 18th (and, indeed, even the 19th) century. By 1799 he was Carlos IV's court painter.

Several distinct series and individual paintings mark the progress of his life and work. In the last years of the century he painted such enigmatic masterpieces as *La Maja Vestida* and *La Maja Desnuda*, identical portraits but for the lack of clothes in the latter. At about the same time he did the frescoes in Madrid's Ermita de San Antonio de la Florida (p129) and *Los Caprichos*, a biting series of 80 etchings lambasting the follies of court life and ignorant clergy.

The arrival of the French and war in 1808 profoundly affected his work. Unforgiving portrayals of the brutality of war are *El Dos de Mayo* and, more dramatically, *El Tres de Mayo*. The latter depicts the execution of Madrid rebels by French troops and both hang in the Museo del Prado (p121).

It is difficult to do justice to Goya's role in the evolution of European painting. An obvious precursor to many subsequent strands of modern art, he was an island of grandeur in a sea of mediocrity in Spain. He also marked a transition from art in the service of the state or Church to art as a pure expression of its creator's feeling and whim. His commissions for royalty and nobility allowed him the financial freedom he needed to do his own thing.

Long after Goya's death the Valencian Joaquín Sorolla (1863–1923) set off on his own path, ignoring the fashionable French impressionists and preferring the blinding light of the Valencian coast to the muted tones favoured in Paris. He is known for his cheerful, large-format images of beach life and much of his work can be admired in Madrid's Museo Sorolla (p129).

THE SHOCK OF THE NEW

It came out of nowhere. Like a thunderclap in an otherwise anything but sensational artistic scene came the genius of the mischievous Malagueño, Pablo Ruiz Picasso (1881–1973). A child when he moved with his family to Barcelona, Picasso was formed in an atmosphere laden with the avant-garde freedom of Modernisme (see the Architecture chapter, p66).

He must have been one of the most restless artists of all time. His work underwent repeated revolutions as he passed from one creative phase to another. From his gloomy Blue Period, through the brighter Pink Period and on to Cubism – in which he was accompanied by Madrid's Juan Gris (1887–1927) – Picasso was nothing if not a surprise package.

By the mid-1920s he was dabbling with surrealism. His best-known work is *Guernica*, a complex canvas portraying the horror of war and inspired by the German aerial bombing of the Basque town, Guernica, in 1937. Picasso's output during and after WWII remained prolific and indeed he was cranking out paintings, sculptures, ceramics and etchings until the day he died. A good selection of his early work can be seen in Barcelona's Museu Picasso (p285). Other works are scattered about different galleries, notably Madrid's Centro de Arte Reina Sofía (p123).

Separated from Picasso by barely a generation, two other artists reinforced the Catalan contingent in the vanguard of first-class Spanish contributions to this century's art: Dalí and Miró. Although he started off dabbling in cubism, Salvador Dalí (1904–89) became more readily identified with the surrealists. This complex character's 'handpainted dream photographs', as he called them, are virtuoso executions brimming with fine detail and nightmare images dragged up from a feverish and Freud-fed imagination. Preoccupied with Picasso's fame, Dalí built himself a reputation as an outrageous showman and shameless self-promoter. The single best display of his work can be seen at the Teatre-Museu Dalí in Figueres (p346).

Slower to find his feet, Barcelona-born Joan Miró (1893–1983) developed a joyous and almost childlike style that earned him the epithet 'the most surrealist of us all' from André Breton. His later period is his best known, characterised by the simple use of bright colours and forms in combinations of symbols that represented women, birds (the link between earth and the heavens), stars (the unattainable heavenly world, source of imagination) and a sort of net, which entraps all these levels of the cosmos. Galleries of his work adorn Barcelona (p296) and Palma de Mallorca (p623).

Inspired by memory, fantasy and the irrational, Miró created works with a humorous, whimsical quality. Apart from paintings he made ceramics, bronze sculptures and murals, including two ceramic murals for Paris' Unesco building.

THE CONTEMPORARY SCENE

The two main artistic movements of the 1950s, El Paso and the Catalan Dau el Set, launched names such Antonio Saura (1930–98), Manuel Millares (1926–72) and Barcelona's tireless Antoni Tàpies (1923–). To experience the latter's work, head for Fundació Antoni Tàpies in Barcelona (p289). The art of Madrid's Eduardo Arroyo (1937–) is steeped in the radical spirit that kept him in exile from Spain for 15 years from 1962. His paintings, brimming with ironic socio-political comment, tend, in part, to pop art.

The death of Franco acted as a catalyst for the Spanish art movement. New talent popped up, and galleries enthusiastically took on anything new, revolutionary, contrary, or cheeky. The 1970s and '80s were a time of almost childish self-indulgence. Things have since calmed down but there is still much activity.

Seville's Luis Gordillo (1934–) started his artistic career with surrealism, from where he branched out into pop art and photography. His later work in particular features the serialisation of different versions of the same image.

Mallorcan Miquel Barceló (1957–) is one of the country's big success stories. His work is heavily expressionist, although it touches classic themes from self-portraiture to architectural images.

Throughout 2002 and 2003, the Basque Country farewelled several important artistic sons in quick succession. Eduardo Chillida (1924–2002) and Jorge Oteiza (1908–2003) were two of Spain's leading modern sculptors, while Eduardo Úrculo (1938–2003) had a light pop-art brush that has had less public attention than it merits.

Joan Hernández Pijuan (1931–) is one of the most important abstract painters to come out of Barcelona in the latter decades of the 20th century. His work is often referred to as informalist and it concentrates on natural shapes and figures, often with neutral colours on different surfaces.

Barcelona's Susana Solano (1946–) is a painter and above all sculptor, considered to be one of the most important at work in Spain today.

For a peek at what is happening in contemporary art, both Spanish and foreign, it is worth making a date with Madrid's annual Arco exhibition, usually held in February (see p137 for more information).

Flamenco

Federico García Lorca's dramatic play, *Bodas de Sangre*, was brought to the screen in a modern remake by Carlos Saura with dancers of the calibre of the late Antonio Gades in this flamenco film of 1981.

The passionate and uniquely Spanish constellation of singing, dancing and instrumental arts known as flamenco first took recognisable form in the late 18th and early 19th centuries among *gitanós* in the lower Guadalquivir valley of Andalucía (still flamenco's heartland). The first flamenco was *cante jondo* (deep song), an anguished instrument of expression for a group on the margins of society. *Jondura* (depth) is still the essence of flamenco. Flamenco performers who successfully communicate their passion will have you unwittingly on the edge of your seat, oblivious to all else. The ability to evoke this kind of response is known as *duende* (spirit).

A flamenco singer is known as a *cantaor* (male) or *cantaora* (female); a dancer is a *bailaor/a*. Most of the songs and dances are performed to a blood-rush of guitar from the *tocaor/a*. Percussion is provided by tapping feet, clapping hands and sometimes castanets. Flamenco *coplas* (songs) come in many different types, from the anguished *soleá* or the intensely despairing *siguiriya* to the livelier *alegría* or the upbeat *bulería*. The traditional flamenco costume – shawl, fan and long, frilly *bata de cola* dress, and for men flat Cordoban hats and tight black trousers – dates from Andalucian fashions of the 19th century.

FLAMENCO TODAY

Never before has flamenco been so popular or so innovative. While long-established singers such as Enrique Morente, Carmen Linares, Chano Lobato and Juan Peña 'El Lebrijano' remain at the top of the profession, new generations continue to broaden flamenco's audience. Perhaps the most popular and universally acclaimed singer of all at present is José Mercé, from Jerez. El Barrio from Cádiz, with his 21st-century urban flamenco, Estrella Morente from Granada (Enrique's daughter) and Miguel Poveda, a non-*gitanó* from Barcelona, are young singers steadily carving out niches in the first rank of performers.

Dance, always the readiest of flamenco arts to cross boundaries, has reached its most adventurous horizons in the person of Joaquin Cortés, born in Córdoba in 1969. Cortés fuses flamenco with contemporary dance, ballet and jazz, to music at rock-concert amplification. The most exciting younger dance talent is Farruquito, born into a famous flamenco family in Seville in 1983 (he made his Broadway debut at the age of five). Other stars to look out for – you may find them dancing solo or with their own companies – include Sara Baras, Antonio Canales, Manuela Carrasco and the innovative Israel Galván, who has turned Kafka's *Metamorphosis* and the music of The Doors into flamenco – not to some purists' liking.

Guitarists to keep an ear open for include José Mercé's accompanist Vicente Amigo, Tomatito from Almería, Cádiz's Manolo Sanlúcar, and Juan and Pepe Habichuela from Granada's voluminous Montoya family of flamenco artists.

In his first book, *Duende*, Jason Webster immersed his body and soul for two years in Spain's passionate and dangerous flamenco world in search of the true flamenco spirit.

FLAMENCO FUSION

Given a cue, perhaps, by Paco de Lucía (see p64), 1970s musicians began mixing flamenco with jazz, rock, blues, rap and other genres. This *nuevo* (new) flamenco greatly broadened flamenco's appeal. The seminal recording was a 1977 flamenco-folk-rock album, *Veneno* (Poison), by the group of the same name centred on Kiko Veneno (see p57) and Raimundo Amador, both from Seville. Amador then formed the group Pata Negra, which produced four fine flamenco-jazz-blues albums, before going solo. His 2003 album *Isla Menor* adds rap, reggae and paso doble to the fusion.

Ketama, originally from Granada, mixes flamenco with African, Cuban, Brazilian and other rhythms. Radio Tarifa emerged in 1993 with a mesmerising mix of flamenco, North African and medieval sounds. Cádiz's Niña Pastori arrived in the late 1990s singing jazz- and Latin-influenced flamenco. The most recent big crossover triumph has been the collaboration between flamenco singer Diego El Cigala and the octogenarian Cuban pianist Bebo Valdés: their 2003 album *Lágrimas Negras* (Black Tears) was a huge success.

10 GREAT FLAMENCO & FUSION ALBUMS

- *Paco de Lucía Antología* – Paco de Lucía (1995)
- *Una Leyenda Flamenca* – El Camarón de la Isla (1993)
- *Cañailla* – Niña Pastori (2000)
- *La Fuente del Deseo* – El Barrio (2000)
- *Lágrimas Negras* – Bebo Valdés & Diego El Cigala (2003)
- *Del Amanecer* – José Mercé (1999)
- *Noche de Flamenco y Blues* – Raimundo Amador, BB King et al (1998)
- *Blues de la Frontera* – Pata Negra (1986)
- *Carmen Linares en Antología* – Carmen Linares (1996)
- *Rumba Argelina* – Radio Tarifa (1993)

FLAMENCO LEGENDS

The great singers of the 19th century were Silverio Franconetti, from Seville, and Antonio Chacón, from Jerez de la Frontera. The early 20th century threw up Seville's La Niña de los Peines, the first great *cantaora*, and Manuel Torre, from Jerez, whose singing, legend has it, could drive people to rip their shirts open and upturn tables.

La Macarrona and Pastora Imperio, the first great *bailaoras*, took flamenco to Paris and South America. Their successors La Argentina and La Argentinita formed dance troupes and turned flamenco dance into a theatrical show. The dynamic dancing and wild lifestyle of Carmen Amaya (1913–63), from Barcelona, made her the *gitana* dance legend of all time. Her long-time partner Sabicas was the father of the modern solo flamenco guitar, inventing a host of now-indispensable techniques.

Singers Antonio Mairena and Manolo Caracol carried the flamenco torch through the mid-20th century, when it seemed that the debased flamenco of the *tablaos* – touristy shows emphasising the sexy and the jolly – was in danger of taking over. *Flamenco puro* got a new lease of life in the 1970s through singers such as Terremoto, La Paquera, Enrique Morente and above all, El Camarón de la Isla from San Fernando near Cádiz. Camarón's incredible vocal and emotional range and his wayward lifestyle made him a legend well before his tragically early death in 1992. As his great guitar accompanist Paco de Lucía observed, 'Camarón's cracked voice could evoke, on its own, the desperation of a people'.

De Lucía himself, born in Algeciras in 1947, is the flamenco artist known most widely outside Spain, and with good reason. So gifted as a boy that by the time he was 14 his teachers had nothing left to teach him, de Lucía has since transformed the guitar, formerly the junior partner of the flamenco trinity, into an instrument of solo expression with new techniques, scales, melodies and harmonies that have gone far beyond traditional limits. He can sound like two or three people playing together. De Lucía said that his 2004 world tour would be his last tour – hopefully he'll reconsider.

SEEING FLAMENCO

Read more about flamenco and hear, see and buy flamenco recordings and videos at www .flamenco-world.com. Also check the Centro Andaluz de Flamenco (caf .cica.es) and Deflamenco .com (www.deflamenco .com). All three are great resources, with calendars of upcoming concerts and performances.

Flamenco is easiest to catch in Andalucía, Madrid and Barcelona. In the south, many towns' summer *ferias* (fairs) and fiestas include flamenco performances, and some places stage special night-long flamenco festivals. Longer festivals include the two-week Festival de Jerez in Jerez de la Frontera (p715) in late February/early March every year; the Festival de Cante de las Minas, in La Unión, Murcia (Map p662), over several days in mid-August; and the month-long Bienal de Flamenco (p695), held in Seville in September of even-numbered years with the participation of just about every big star of the flamenco world. Otherwise, look out for intermittent big-name performances in theatres, occasional seasons of concerts, and regular flamenco nights at bars and clubs in some cities – often just for the price of your drinks. Flamenco fans also band together in clubs called *peñas*, which stage live performance nights; most will admit interested visitors and the atmosphere here will be authentic and at times very intimate.

Tablaos are regular shows put on for largely undiscriminating tourist audiences, usually with high prices. These are what tourist offices are likely to steer you towards unless otherwise asked.

Theatre & Dance

Thanks mainly to a big development programme by the Partido Socialista Obrero Español (PSOE; Spanish Socialist Worker Party) governments of the 1980s and '90s, most Spanish cities now boast at least one theatre worthy of the name, and drama is an increasingly vibrant field. Larger cities like Madrid, Barcelona and Seville have plenty of smaller locales staging avant-garde and experimental productions as well as larger venues for more orthodox shows. Straight theatre, though, is unlikely to appeal if your understanding of Spanish – or, in Barcelona, Catalan – is less than fluent.

Dance too thrives and not just in the context of flamenco (p62). Again, the bigger cities are the epicentres. Barcelona is the capital of modern dance, with several shows to choose from almost any week, though the Madrid-based Compañía Nacional de Danza is also one of Europe's most exciting contemporary ensembles. The Ballet Nacional de España, founded in 1978, mixes classical ballet with Spanish dance.

Here and there you'll find the occasional regional folk dance, such as Catalunya's *sardana* round-dance, or the Málaga area's *verdiales* (flag dances), which are done to exhilarating fiddle-and-percussion music.

Under the artistic direction of Nacho Duato since 1990, the Compañía Nacional de Danza has performed to critical acclaim around the world and won many awards.

Architecture

As you look up in awe at the arches of the great Roman aqueduct in Segovia you can almost see centurions marching beneath it. Soothed by the gentle bubbling of its cool fountains, the mesmerising beauty of the Alhambra induces a dream sense of a mythical Arab world long past. Wandering along the echoing corridors of the Romanesque cloisters of the Monasterio de Santo Domingo de Silos on a grey winter's day, the Middle Ages seem to have returned with all their mystical fervour. Towering, at times half-ruined, castles dot the countryside from Catalonia to Castile. To gaze up, eyes turned to God, at the great Gothic cathedrals of Burgos and Toledo, you can only feel the awe inspired when they were first raised. And who cannot be carried away by the whimsy of Gaudí's Modernista fantasy in Barcelona's La Sagrada Família and Casa Batlló? Spain's architecture presents one of the broadest and richest testimonies in Europe to thousands of years of building ingenuity.

ANCIENT SPAIN

The tribes that first inhabited the Iberian Peninsula, collectively known as Celtiberians, left behind a wealth of evidence of their existence. The most common living arrangement, called the *castro,* was a hamlet surrounded by stone walls and made up of circular stone houses. Several have been partly preserved in locations mostly across northern Spain. Among the better known ones are those at A Guarda (La Guardia; p563), on Galicia's southern coast, and near Coaña (p516) in Asturias.

The Greeks and Carthaginians rarely made it far into the Spanish interior. Greek remains at Empúries (p341) in Catalonia are the most impressive reminder of their Iberian presence.

The Romans left behind more clues. Among the more spectacular sites are the aqueduct in Segovia (p191), the bridge at Alcántara (p813) and the stout walls of Lugo (p568).

Vestiges of some Roman towns can also still be seen. Among the more important are the ancient town of Augusta Emerita (p819) in Mérida, ancient Tarraco, now known as Tarragona (p376), the amphitheatre and other ruins at Itálica (p697) near Seville, and Sagunto (p588) in Valencia. Modest remains have been imaginatively converted into underground museums in Barcelona (p283) and Zaragoza (p408).

EARLY CHRISTIANITY

Filling the vacuum left by the departing Romans, the Visigoths employed a more humble but remarkably attractive style, which survives in a handful of small churches. The 7th-century Ermita de Santa María de Lara (p223), at Quintanilla de las Viñas in Burgos province, is one of the best. Fragments of this unique style can be seen in several cities across Spain, including Toledo.

Guía de Arquitectura España 1920–2000 presents almost 800 seminal buildings raised around the country in this modern era in a handy single volume.

Reputedly the oldest church in Spain is the 7th-century Basílica de San Juan (p207) in Baños de Cerrato, while the cathedral in nearby Palencia (p205) has Visigothic origins in the crypt. The horseshoe arch, later perfected by the Arabs, is characteristic of the Visigothic aesthetic.

When Spain was swamped by the Muslim invasion of 711 AD, only the unruly northern strip of the country in what is today Asturias held out. During the 9th century a unique building style emerged in this green corner of Spain cut off from the rest of Christian Europe. Out of the 30-odd examples of pre-Romanesque architecture scattered about the Asturian countryside, the little Palacio de Santa María del Naranco (p505) and Iglesia de San Miguel de Lillo (p505), both in Oviedo, are the finest. The complete vaulting of the nave, the semicircular arches in the windows and porches, and the angular simplicity of these buildings offer a foretaste of the Romanesque style.

THE MARK OF ISLAM

Córdoba was the centre of Muslim political power and culture for its first 300 years in Spain, but they remained for almost another 800 years in their longest-lasting enclave, Granada.

The Syrian Omayyad dynasty that set up shop in Spain brought with it architects imbued with ideas and experience won from Damascus. This was soon put to use in the construction of the Mezquita (mosque) in Córdoba (p751), the style of which was echoed across Muslim Spain. Horseshoe-shaped and lobed arches, the use of exquisite tiles in the decoration (mostly calligraphy and floral motifs), complex stucco, peaceful inner courtyards and stalactite ceiling adornments are all features reminiscent of Damascus.

Remnants of this Muslim legacy abound across Spain, although many grand examples have been lost. The most striking piece of Islamic architecture in northern Spain is the palace of the Aljafería (p409) in Zaragoza.

In the 12th century the armies of Morocco's Almohad dynasty stormed across the by now hopelessly divided lands of Muslim Spain. To them we owe some of the marvels of Seville, in particular the square-based minaret known as Giralda (p682), even more beautiful than the minaret of the Koutoubia mosque in Marrakesh.

Muslim art reached new heights of elegance with the construction of the Alhambra (p759) in Granada. Built from the 13th to the 15th centuries, it is symptomatic of the direction taken by Islamic art at the time. Eschewing innovation, the Alhambra expresses a desire to refine already well-tried forms (geometric patterns, use of calligraphy in decoration, stalactite décor). It is one of the Muslim world's most beautiful creations.

MOZARABIC & MUDÉJAR

Already in the 10th century, Mozarabs – Christians practising in Muslim territory – began to adopt elements of classic Islamic construction and export them to Christian-held territory. Although Mozarabic artisans contributed to many buildings, there are few 'purely' Mozarabic structures. Among the outstanding examples are the Iglesia de San Miguel de Escalada (p214), east of León, the Ermita de San Baudelio (p228), beyond Berlanga de Duero in Soria province, and the Iglesia de Santa María de Lebeña (p527) on the east side of the Picos de Europa.

More important was the influence of the Mudéjars, Muslims who remained behind in the lands of the Reconquista. Their skills were found to be priceless (but cheap) and their influence is evident throughout Spain.

One unmistakable Mudéjar feature is the preponderance of brick: castles, churches and mansions all over the country were built of this material. Another telltale feature is in the ceilings. Extravagantly decorated timber creations, often ornately carved, are a mark of the Mudéjar hand. Several different types get constant mention. The term *armadura* refers to any of these wooden ceilings, especially when they have the appearance of being an inverted boat. *Artesonado* ceilings are characterised by interlaced beams leaving regular spaces (triangular, square or polygonal) for the insertion of decorative *artesas*. The term *techumbre* (which can simply mean 'roof')

The Alhambra comes alive in the entertaining and learned study, *Alhambra* (Michael Jacobs); it's beautifully illustrated with photographs of one of Andalucía's most emblematic buildings.

applies more specifically to the most common of *armaduras*, where the skeleton of the ceiling (looked at from the end) looks like a series of 'A's.

In the Convento de Santa Clara (Las Claras; p183) in Salamanca, ramps have been installed, allowing close inspection of the original ceiling.

FROM ROMANESQUE TO GOTHIC

As the Muslim tide was turned back and the Reconquista gathered momentum, the first great medieval European movement in design began to take hold in Spain, spreading from Italy and France. From about the 11th century churches, monasteries, bridges, pilgrims' hospices and other buildings in the Romanesque style mushroomed in the north.

The first wave came in Catalonia, where Lombard artisans influenced by Byzantine building techniques soon covered the countryside with simple churches – the church of Sant Climent de Taüll (p365) and others scattered around nearby are emblematic.

An exhaustive website covering monasteries old and new in Spain, www .catolicos.com/mona steriosespana.htm (in Spanish) has links that will lead you to many sites of great architectural interest around the country.

Romanesque is identified by a few basic characteristics. The exteriors of most edifices bear little decoration and tend to be simple, angular structures. In the case of churches in particular, the concession to curves comes with the semicylindrical apse – or, in many cases, triple apse. The single most striking decorative element is the semicircular arch or arches that grace doorways, windows, cloisters and naves. The humble church of the **Monasterio de Sigena** (☎ 974 57 81 58; Villanueva de Sigena; admission free; ☼ 11.30am-1.30pm & 3.30-4.30pm Fri & Sat, 1-2pm & 4.30-6.30pm Sun), 93km east of Zaragoza, has a doorway boasting 14 such arches, one encased in the other.

The Camino de Santiago is studded with Romanesque beauties. These include (travelling from east to west) the Monasterio de Santo Domingo de Silos (p223), the smaller cloister (Las Claustrillas) in the Monasterio de las Huelgas (p220) in Burgos and the restored Iglesia de San Martín (p207) in Frómista.

During the 12th century modifications in the Romanesque recipe became apparent. The pointed arch and ribbed vault of various kinds are clear precursors to the Gothic revolution to come.

The Monasterio de la Oliva (p479) in Navarra was among the first to incorporate such features, and other buildings followed. Cathedrals in Ávila (p173), Sigüenza (p260), Tarragona (p378) and Tudela (p479) all display at least some transitional elements.

A peculiar side development affected southwest Castile. The cathedrals in Salamanca (p180), Zamora (p203) and Toro (p202) all boast Byzantine lines, particularly in the cupola.

Everyone in northern Europe marvelled at the towering new cathedrals built from the 12th century, made possible by the use of flying buttresses and other technical innovations. The idea caught on later in Spain, but three of the most important Gothic cathedrals in the country, in Burgos (p218), León (p210) and Toledo (p241), were built in the 13th century.

The first two owe much to French models, but the Spaniards soon introduced other elements. The huge decorative altarpieces towering over the high altar were one such innovation. And, although not an exclusively Spanish touch, the placing of the choir stalls in the centre of the nave became the rule rather than the exception in Spanish Gothic style.

The main structural novelty in Spanish Gothic was star-vaulting, a method of weight distribution in the roof in which ribbed vaults project outwards from a series of centre points.

Monuments often belong to several styles. Many great buildings begun at the height of Romanesque glory were only completed long after Gothic had gained the upper hand. And although, for instance, the cathedral in

Burgos was one of the first to go up, its magnificent spires were a result of German-inspired late-Gothic imagination. In many cases, these Gothic or Romanesque-Gothic buildings received a Plateresque or baroque over-lay at a later date.

Mudéjar influences still made themselves felt, particularly in the use of brick rather than stone. Toledo and the region of Aragón, particularly Zaragoza, Teruel, Tarazona and Calatayud, have many buildings of a Gothic-Mudéjar combination.

The so-called Isabelline style was a late addition to the cocktail. Taking some cues from the more curvaceous traits of Islamic design, it was in some ways an indirect precursor to Plateresque. Its ultimate expression would be Toledo's San Juan de los Reyes (p243), originally destined to be the final resting place of the Catholic Monarchs. Designed by French-born Juan Güas (1453–96), it is a medley of earlier Gothic and Mudéjar elements, with a final decorative Isabelline flourish.

The 16th century saw a revival of pure Gothic, perhaps best exempli-fied in the new cathedral in Salamanca (p180), although the Segovia cathedral (p192) was about the last, and possibly most pure, Gothic house of worship to be constructed in Spain.

Not only religious buildings flourished. Most of the innumerable castles scattered across the country went up in Gothic times. Many never saw action and were not intended to – a couple of the more extraordinary sam-ples of Mudéjar castle-building from this era are the Castillo de la Mota (p200) in Medina del Campo and the sumptuous castle at Coca (p195).

THE RENAISSANCE

The Renaissance in Spain can be roughly divided into three distinct styles. First was the Italian-influenced special flavour of Plateresque. To visit Salamanca is to receive a concentrated dose of the most splendid work in the genre. The University façade (p182), especially, is a virtuoso piece, featuring busts, medallions and swathes of complex floral design. Not far behind in intensity comes the façade of the Convento de San Esteban (p183). Little of the work can be convincingly traced to any one hand, and it appears that the principal exponent of Plateresque, Alonso de Co-varrubias (1488–1570), was busier in his home city of Toledo (the Alcázar, p241, and the Capilla de los Nuevos Reyes in the cathedral, p241).

Next was the more purist Renaissance style that prevailed in Andalucía, and had its maximum expression in the Palacio de Carlos V (p764) in Granada's Alhambra. Diego de Siloé (1495–1563) and his followers are regarded as masters. Siloé made his mark with Granada's cathedral (p765); others followed him with such masterpieces as the Jaén cathedral (p780).

Juan de Herrera (1530–97) is the last and perhaps greatest figure of the Spanish Renaissance, but his work bears almost no resemblance to any-thing else of the period. His austere masterpiece is the palace-monastery complex of San Lorenzo de El Escorial (p161).

Spanish Splendour: Palaces, Castles & Country Homes (Roberto Schezen, photographer) is a sumptuous photographic presentation of some of the most spectacular noble buildings in Spain.

BAROQUE BAUBLES

The heady frills and spills of the baroque aesthetic can be seen all over Spain, but usually in the form of additions rather than complete build-ings. Cádiz's cathedral (p707) is an exception (although some neoclassical work was added). Three loose phases can be identified, starting with a sober baroque still heavily influenced by Herrera, followed by a period of greater architectural exuberance (some would say, a sickening amount) and finally running into a mixture of baroque with the beginnings of neoclassicism.

Gaudí: The Man & His Work (Joan Masso Bergos) is a beautifully illustrated study of the man and his architecture, based on the writings of one of his confidants.

The leading exponents of this often overblown approach to building and decoration were the Churriguera brothers. Alberto (1676–1750) designed Salamanca's Plaza Mayor (p180), but he and brother José (1665–1735) are best known for their extraordinary *retablos,* huge, carved wooden altar backdrops. Their memorable works feature twisting gilded columns, burdened with all manner of angels and saints.

Baroque reached new heights of opulence with the Sagrario in Granada's Monasterio de La Cartuja (p767) and the Transparente in Toledo's cathedral (p242). Seville is jammed with gems. But baroque appears elsewhere, too: the façade superimposed over the Romanesque original in the cathedral of Santiago de Compostela (p535) and the cathedral in Murcia (p663) are notable.

MODERNISME MADNESS

Catalonia, at the end of the 19th century, was the powerhouse of the country. And over its capital was unleashed one of the most imaginative periods in Spanish architecture by a group of architects who came to be known as the Modernistas. Leading the way was Antoni Gaudí (1852–1926), who sprinkled the city with jewels of his singular imagination. They range from his immense, and still unfinished, Sagrada Família church (p289) to the simply weird Casa Batlló (p288) and only slightly more sober La Pedrera (p289).

DID YOU KNOW?

When Antoni Gaudí was struck down by a tram in Barcelona's Gran Via de les Corts Catalanes on 7 June 1926, no-one recognised him as the genius architect but assumed the white-bearded man was a vagrant.

Hot on Gaudí's heels were two other Catalan architects, Lluís Domènech i Montaner (1850–1923) and Josep Puig i Cadafalch (1867–1957). Domènech i Montaner's works include the Palau de la Música Catalana (p285), while Puig i Cadafalch built such townhouses as Casa Amatller (p289).

Modernisme did not appear in isolation in Barcelona. To the British and French the style was called Art Nouveau, to the Italians it was *lo stile Liberty* (Liberty Style), while the Germans called it Jugendstil (Youth Style) and the Austrians Sezession (Secession). Elsewhere in Spain, it made little impact.

BUILDING INTO THE FUTURE

If Barcelona is the seat of Modernisme, Madrid is the capital of Spanish Art Deco. In the 1920s the newly created Gran Vía provided a perfect opportunity for new building, and a number of Art Deco caprices raised in that era still line the boulevard today. Overwhelming (and of questionable taste) is the Palacio de Comunicaciones (or post office to some; p125) on Plaza de la Cibeles.

For a good introduction to the Modernista genius Antoni Gaudí and his works, have a look at www.gaudiallgaudi .com, with links to photographic sections on a range of his works, as well as that of other Modernista architects, designers and artists.

Ambitious building and urban redevelopment programmes continue to change the main cityscapes. In Barcelona, for instance, the 1992 Olympics provided an enormous impulse for new construction and urban renewal. The Macba art museum (p284) shines white and boldly bright in the once slummy El Raval district. And Jean Nouvel is building a spangly cucumber-shaped lone skyscraper, the Torre Agbar, just off Plaça de les Glòries Catalanes.

Further south, Valencia has chimed in with its futuristic Ciudad de las Artes y las Ciencias (City of Arts and Sciences; p577) complex. But the single most eye-catching modern addition to the Spanish cityscape is Frank Gehry's Museo Guggenheim (p460) in Bilbao, which looms like a shiny fantasy vessel in the heart of town.

Environment

THE LAND

The Iberian Peninsula (Spain and Portugal), having previously wobbled around off the western end of Europe for millions of years, settled into its present position about 70 million years ago. Its collision at that time with the European and African landmasses caused the peninsula's main mountain chains to rise up. The resulting rugged topography not only separated Spain's destiny from the rest of Europe's for long periods in historical times, but also encouraged the rise of separate small states in the medieval period.

The Meseta

At the heart of Spain and occupying 40% of the country is the *meseta*, a sparsely populated tableland (apart from a few cities, such as Madrid) that's much given to grain growing. Contrary to what Professor Henry Higgins taught Eliza Dolittle, the *meseta* is not where most of Spain's rain falls. In fact it has a continental climate: scorching in summer, cold in winter, and dry. Nor is it really a plain: much of it is rolling hills and it's split in two by the Cordillera Central mountain chain. Three of Spain's five major rivers, the Duero, Tajo and Guadiana, flow west across the *meseta* into Portugal and, ultimately, into the Atlantic Ocean. Like many other Spanish rivers, these three are dammed here and there into long, snaking reservoirs to provide much of the country's water and electricity.

The Mountains

On all sides, except the west (where it slopes gradually down across Portugal), the *meseta* is bounded by mountain chains.

Across the north, close to the Bay of Biscay (Mar Cantábrico), is the damp Cordillera Cantábrica, which rises above 2500m in the spectacular Picos de Europa. The Sistema Ibérico runs down from La Rioja in the central north to southern Aragón, peaking at 2316m in the Sierra de Moncayo, and varying from plateaus and high moorland to deep gorges and strangely eroded rock formations, such as the Serranía de Cuenca. The southern boundary of the *meseta* is the low, wooded Sierra Morena, running across northern Andalucía.

Spain's highest mountains lie on or towards its extremities. The Pyrenees stretch 400km along the French border, with numerous 3000m peaks in Catalonia and Aragón, the highest being Pico de Aneto (3408m). Across Andalucía stretches the Cordillera Bética, a rumpled mass of ranges that includes mainland Spain's highest peak, Mulhacén (3479m), in the Sierra Nevada southeast of Granada.

The Lowlands

Around and between all the mountains are five main lower-lying areas.

The basin of the Río Ebro, Spain's most voluminous river, stretches from the central north to the Mediterranean coast, yielding a variety of crops, though parts of central Aragón are near-desert.

North of the lower Ebro stretches fertile Catalonia, composed mainly of ranges of low hills. Further south, the coastal areas of Valencia and Murcia are dry plains transformed by irrigation into green market gardens and orchards.

AUTONOMOUS COMMUNITIES & PROVINCES

The basin of Spain's fifth major river, the Guadalquivir, stretches across central Andalucía, a fertile zone with a wide range of crops. The summer here sees high temperatures, with a daily average high of 36°C in Seville in July and August.

In northwest Spain is the region of Galicia, hilly, rainy and green, with mixed farming.

The Coasts

Spain's coast is as varied as its interior. The Mediterranean coast alternates between rocky coves and inlets (as on Catalonia's Costa Brava, the Balearic Islands and Andalucía's Cabo de Gata), and flatter, straighter stretches with some long beaches, such as the Costa Daurada, Costa Blanca and Costa del Sol. Sea temperatures along the Mediterranean average 19°C or 20°C in June or October, and a reasonably comfortable 22°C to 25°C between July and September – slightly more in the Balearic Islands and around Alicante.

The Atlantic coast has colder seas and whiter, sandier beaches. The Costa de la Luz, from Tarifa and the Strait of Gibraltar to the Portuguese

Where are Spain's cleanest beaches? Visit the website of the Foundation for Environmental Education (www.fee-international.org), which annually awards blue flags to beaches that meet international standards of hygiene, facilities and environmental management.

border, has many long sandy beaches backed by dunes. In the northwest, Galicia is deeply indented by long estuaries called *rías*, with plenty of sandy beaches. It also has Spain's most awesome cliffs, at Cabo Ortegal and the Serra da Capelada. Along the Bay of Biscay, the Cordillera Cantábrica comes almost down to the coast, and the beaches are mostly coves and small bays, though still sandy.

WILDLIFE

Spain's animal life is among Europe's most varied thanks to its wild terrain, which has allowed the survival of several species that have died out elsewhere. It's possible to see plenty of exciting wildlife if you know where to look. But sadly, some species are now in perilously small numbers. The variety of Spain's plant life is astonishing, as the spectacular wildflower displays on roadsides and pastures in spring and early summer testify.

Animals

There are about 80 *osos pardos* (brown bears) in the Cordillera Cantábrica, and a tiny handful, effectively extinct, in the Pyrenees. Although hunting or killing Spain's bears has been banned since 1973, their numbers have failed to increase since the mid-1980s, despite expensive conservation programmes. In 1900 Spain had about 1000 brown bears; as with many other species, hunting and poison have been the main reasons for their decline.

The *lobo* (wolf), by contrast, is on the increase. From a population of about 500 in 1970, Spain now has around 2000. Their heartland is the mountains of Galicia and northwestern Castilla y León (Zamora is the province with most wolves). Though heavily protected, wolves are still regarded as an enemy by many country people.

The outlook is much brighter for the *cabra montés* (ibex), a stocky mountain goat whose males have distinctive, long horns. Almost hunted to extinction by 1900, the ibex was protected by royal decree a few years later (though still subject to controlled hunting today). There may now be 20,000 in the country, chiefly in the Sierra de Gredos and the mountains of Andalucía.

The beautiful *lince ibérico* (Iberian or pardel lynx), unique to the Iberian Peninsula, is in grave danger of becoming the first extinct feline since the sabre-toothed tiger. Its numbers have dropped to probably less than 400 in Spain (some observers say only 150), and possibly none at all in Portugal, due to hunting and a decline in the number of rabbits, its staple food. The only known breeding populations are in the eastern Sierra Morena and the Doñana national and natural parks in western Andalucía. After years of dithering, expensive save-the-lynx programmes are now underway. A key to its prospects is an in-captivity breeding centre at Doñana.

Other interesting and less uncommon beasts – all fairly widely distributed, though you'd still need to go looking for them – include the *jabalí* (wild boar), the *ciervo, corzo* and *gamo* (red, roe and fallow deer), the *gineta* (genet), a nocturnal catlike creature with a white and black coat, and the *ardilla* (red squirrel). Varieties of the chamois *(rebeco, sarrio, isard* or *gamuza),* a small antelope, live mainly above the tree line in the Pyrenees and the Cordillera Cantábrica. Southwestern Spain is home to the Egyptian *meloncillo* (mongoose). Twenty-seven marine mammal species live off Spain's shores. Dolphin- and whale-spotting boat trips are a popular attraction at Gibraltar and nearby Tarifa.

Birds

Around 25 species of birds of prey, including the *águila real* (golden eagle), *buitre leonado* (griffon vulture) and *alimoche* (Egyptian vulture),

Wildlife Travelling Companion Spain by John Measures (1992) and *Wild Spain* by Frederic V Grunfeld (1999) are useful practical guides to Spain's wilderness and wildlife areas, both with illustrations of animals and plants.

DID YOU KNOW?

The Gibraltar 'apes' – actually Barbary macaques – are the only wild monkeys in Europe.

Practical bird-watching guides include John R Butler's *Birdwatching on Spain's Southern Coast,* Ernest Garcia and Andrew Paterson's *Where to Watch Birds in Southern & Western Spain* and Michael Rebane's *Where to Watch Birds in North and East Spain.*

DID YOU KNOW?

The lammergeier's Spanish name, *quebrantahuesos* (bone breaker), describes its habit of smashing bones by dropping them on to rocks, so that it can get at the marrow.

breed in Spain. Extremadura's Parque Natural Monfragüe is the single most spectacular place to observe birds of prey. You'll often see them circling or hovering in mountain areas or on the *meseta*.

The *quebrantahuesos* (lammergeier or bearded vulture), with its majestic 2m-plus wingspan, is still a threatened species but is recovering slowly in the Pyrenees, where there are about 55 breeding pairs.

Spain's few hundred pairs of *buitre negro* (black vulture), Europe's biggest bird of prey, probably make up the world's largest population. Its strongholds include Monfragüe and the Sierra Pelada in western Andalucía.

Another emblematic bird is the *águila imperial ibérica* (Spanish imperial eagle), of which only around 130 pairs remain, in such places as Doñana and Monfragüe.

One spectacular bird that you are, happily, almost certain to see if you're in western Andalucía, Extremadura or either of the Castillas in spring or summer, is the white stork. Actually black and white, this creature makes its large, ungainly nests on electricity pylons, trees, towers – in fact, any vertical protuberance it can find, even right in the middle of towns – and your attention will be drawn by the loud clacking of chicks' beaks from these lofty perches. Thousands of white storks migrate north from Africa across the Strait of Gibraltar in January and February – as do much smaller numbers of Europe's only other stork, the *cigüeña negra* (black stork), which is down to about 200 pairs in Spain.

Spain's extensive wetlands make it a haven for water birds. The most important of the wetlands is the Parque Nacional de Doñana and surrounding areas in the Guadalquivir delta in Andalucía. Hundreds of thousands of birds winter here, and many more call in during spring and autumn migrations. Other important coastal wetlands include the Albufera de Valencia and the Ebro delta. Inland, thousands of *patos* (ducks) and *grullas* (cranes) winter at Laguna de Gallocanta in Aragón, Spain's biggest natural lake. Laguna de Fuente de Piedra near Antequera in Andalucía is Europe's main breeding site for the greater *flamenco* (flamingo), with as many as 20,000 pairs rearing chicks in spring and summer.

Plants

Mainland Spain and the Balearic Islands contain around 8000 of Europe's 9000 plant species, and 2000 of them are unique to the Iberian Peninsula (and North Africa). This abundance is largely due to the fact that the last ice age did not cover the entire peninsula, enabling plants killed off further north to survive in Spain.

Mountain areas claim much of the variety. The Pyrenees have about 150 unique species and the much smaller Sierra Nevada in Andalucía has about 60 species. When the snows melt, zones above the tree line bloom with small rock-clinging plants and gentians, orchids, crocuses, narcissi and sundews. A particularly good orchid area is the alpine meadows of the Picos de Europa, with 40 species.

The silver fir and the Scots pine, with its flaking red bark, are common on the cooler northern mountains, while the black pine, with horizontally spreading branches clustering near the top, and the maritime pine, with its rounded top, flourish on mountains further south. The rare but beautiful Spanish fir is confined to the Sierra de Grazalema and a few other small areas in western Andalucía. The lovely umbrella pine, with its large spreading top and edible kernel, grows near coasts.

The natural vegetation of many lower slopes in the east and south is Mediterranean woodland, with trees such as the wild olive, carob, holm oak and cork oak that are adapted to a warm, fairly dry climate. The holm and cork oaks are smaller and have pricklier leaves than the tall oaks of more temperate regions. They're also very useful: large expanses of oak woodland in the west and south have been converted over the centuries into woodland pastures known as *dehesas*, where the cork oak's thick outer bark is stripped every ninth summer for cork, while the holm oak can be pruned about every four years and the offcuts used for charcoal. Meanwhile, livestock can graze the pastures, and in autumn pigs are turned out to gobble up the acorns, a diet considered to produce the tastiest ham of all.

The best guide to Spain's flowers and shrubs is *Flowers of South-West Europe* by Oleg Polunin and BE Smythies. In the south, Betty Molesworth Allen's *A Selection of Wildflowers of Southern Spain* is handy.

NATIONAL & NATURAL PARKS

Much of Spain's most spectacular and ecologically important country – about 40,000 sq km, 8% of the entire country, if you include national hunting reserves – is under some kind of official protection. Nearly all these areas are at least partly open to visitors, but degrees of conservation and access vary. For example, *parques naturales* (natural parks), the most widespread category of protected area, may include villages with hotels and camping grounds, or may limit access to a few walking trails with the nearest accommodation 10km away. Fortunately, the most interesting parks and reserves usually have visitor centres.

The *parques nacionales* (national parks) are areas of exceptional importance for their fauna, flora, geomorphology or landscape, and are the country's most strictly controlled protected areas. They are declared such by the national parliament. So far Spain has 13 national parks – eight on the mainland, four on the Canary Islands and one in the Balearic Islands. The hundreds of other protected areas, declared and administered by Spain's 17 regional governments, fall into at least 16 classifications and range in size from 100-sq-m rocks off the Balearics to Andalucía's 2140-sq-km Parque Natural de Cazorla.

For official information on national parks, visit the website of the Ministerio de Medio Ambiente, Spain's environment ministry (www.mma .es) – in Spanish, but the diagrams, maps, lists and pictures are informative to everyone.

ENVIRONMENTAL ISSUES

Human hands have been wreaking radical change in Spain's environment for over two millennia. It was the Romans who began to cut country's woodlands – for timber, fuel and weapons – which until then covered half the *meseta*. Deforestation since then, along with overtilling and overgrazing (especially by huge sheep herds), has brought substantial topsoil erosion; most of the fertile Doñana wetlands and the 300-sq-km delta of the Río Ebro have been formed by eroded deposits. Urban and industrial growth, and in the 20th century the construction of hundreds of dams for hydroelectricity and irrigation, has caused further change. And over the centuries many animal species were drastically depleted by hunting.

But there's still lots of wilderness. By European standards Spain is sparsely populated, and most of its people live in towns and cities, which reduces their impact on the countryside.

Conservation

Environmental awareness took a huge leap forward in the post-Franco 1980s. The Partido Socialista Obrero Español (PSOE) government spurred a range of actions by regional governments, which now have responsibility for most environmental matters. In 1981 Spain had just 35 environmentally protected areas, covering 2200 sq km. Now there are over 400, covering some 40,000 sq km. But different regions give varied priority to conservation: Andalucía has over 80 protected areas, while neighbouring Extremadura has just three. Nor are protected areas always well protected, often because their ecosystems extend beyond their

SPAIN'S HIGHLIGHT PARKS

park	features	activities	best time to visit	page
Parc Nacional d'Aigüestortes i Estany de Sant Maurici	beautiful Pyrenees lake region	walking, wildlife-spotting	Jun–Sep	p363
Parques Nacional de Doñana	bird & mammal haven in Guadalquivir delta	4WD tours, wildlife-watching, walking, horse riding	year-round	p700
Parque Nacional de Ordesa y Monte Perdido	spectacular section of the Pyrenees, with chamois, raptors and highly varied vegetation	walking, rock climbing	Mid-Jun–Jul, Mid-Aug–Sep	p424
Parque Nacional de los Picos de Europa	beautiful mountain refuge for chamois and a few wolves and bears	walking, rock climbing, caving	May-Jul, Sep	p517
Parques Nacional & Natural Sierra Nevada	mainland Spain's highest mountain range, with many ibex and 60 endemic plants	walking, rock climbing, mountain biking, horse riding, skiing	depends on activity	p773
Parque Natural de Cazorla	abundant wildlife, 2300 plant species, beautiful mountain scenery	walking, driving, 4WD tours, wildlife-watching, mountain biking	Apr-Oct	p786
Áreas Naturales Serra de Tramuntana	spectacular mountain range on Mallorca	walks, bird-watching	Late Feb–early Oct	p626
Parque Natural Monfragüe	spectacular birds of prey	bird-watching	Mar-Oct	p808
Parque Natural Sierra de Grazalema	lovely, green, mountainous area with rich bird life	walking, rock climbing, bird-watching, caving, canyoning, paragliding	Oct-Jun	p718
Parc Natural del Cadí-Moixeró	steep pre-Pyrenees range	rock climbing, walking	Jun-Sep	p359
Parc Natural de la Zona Volcànica de la Garrotxa	beautiful wooded region with 30 volcanic cones	walking	Apr-Oct	p351
Parque Natural Sierra de Gredos	beautiful mountain region, home to Spain's biggest ibex population	walking, rock climbing, mountain biking	May, Jun, Sep	p178
Parque Natural de Somiedo	dramatic section of Cordillera Cantábrica	walking	Jul-Sep	p517
Parque Natural de Cabo de Gata-Níjar	sandy beaches, volcanic cliffs, flamingo colony, semidesert vegetation	swimming, bird-watching, walking, horse riding, diving, snorkelling	year-round	p793

own boundaries. Most notoriously, in 1998 the vital Doñana wetlands in Andalucía were damaged by a major spill of acids and heavy metals 50km away into a river that feeds them.

Of Spain's approximately 630 vertebrate species, 41 are considered in danger of extinction and a further 119 are vulnerable. In the plant realm, of the 8000 species on the mainland and Balearic Islands, some 80 are in danger of extinction and about 580 are vulnerable. Plants are threatened by such factors as ploughing and grazing, as well as by tourism and collection.

Water

Potentially Spain's worst environmental problem is drought. It struck in the 1950s and '60s, and again in the first half of the 1990s, despite a gigantic investment in reservoirs (which number around 1300 and cover a higher proportion of Spain than of any other country in the world) and projects such as the Tajo-Segura water-diversion system, which can transfer 600 million cubic metres of water a year from the Tajo basin in central Spain to the heavily irrigated Valencia and Murcia regions on the Mediterranean coast. Although Spain's many dams and reservoirs provide irrigation and hydroelectricity (reducing the need for nuclear or dirtier forms of power) and conserve water, they inevitably destroy habitats.

Water is money in Spain and people are generally not keen to see it transferred out of their regions. The country's 'dry' regions are Andalucía, Castilla-La Mancha, Extremadura, Valencia, Murcia and parts of the Ebro basin in Aragón. Intensive agriculture and the spread of towns and cities (including tourist resorts) have lowered water tables in some areas. Growing vegetables under huge areas of plastic in the southeast, especially Almería province, with intense fertiliser and pesticide use and water pumped up from deep underground, is drying up some of the underground aquifers it depends upon.

In 2000 the Partido Popular (PP) government announced its Plan Hidrológico Nacional (National Water Plan), the key element of which was to double (to 1 billion cu metres a year) the amount of water diverted from the Río Ebro, flowing across the north of the country, to develop agriculture in Mediterranean coastal regions. Inhabitants of the Ebro region poured onto the streets in protest and environmentalists had objections, too. When the PP was defeated in the 2004 elections, the incoming PSOE government immediately cancelled the planned Ebro transfer.

Other Problems

Seaside tourism development, often slackly controlled, and the growth of coastal urban areas in general, have undoubtedly degraded many coastal environments and added to the pollution of the seas, although sewage-treatment facilities are being steadily improved. Spain gets creditable numbers of EU 'blue flags' for its beaches, indicating that they meet certain minimal standards of hygiene, facilities and environmental management.

Industrial pollution is probably at its worst around Bilbao in the Basque Country and the small, chemical-producing town of Avilés in Asturias.

Arguably the worst environmental disaster to strike Spain happened in November 2002, when the ageing oil tanker *Prestige* sank off Galicia, spilling over 14,000 tonnes of oil into the sea. Some 600km of beautiful coastline in Galicia and the neighbouring Asturias and Cantabria were smothered in black sludge, causing incalculable damage to the important local fishing and seafood industries.

For more information on this massive ecological disaster, see the boxed text The Big Spill on p551.

Spain Outdoors

Spain is a land of a thousand remarkable faces and getting outdoors is a great way to experience a few of them. For some this means flopping on the beach or sipping sherry while watching prancing Andalucian thoroughbreds. But if you want the thrill of a lifetime zipping down a gorge, walking peacefully in some of Europe's finest wilderness, or paddling through ocean caves in turquoise water, then you'll also find your niche.

Spain offers a wide breadth of year-round land and water activities suitable for families, novices and seasoned travellers alike. If you're already in Spain, it's easy to hook up with an organised tour or strike out on your own. Countless tour operators (within Spain and abroad) offer day and multi-day packages for every activity imaginable. In general the Mediterranean coast has more readily available, English-friendly outfits and services than the north, but don't let this put you off – many outstanding opportunities await you there too.

DID YOU KNOW?
With an average altitude of 660m, Spain is the second-highest country in Europe after Switzerland.

WALKING

Feel like bagging Spain's highest mainland peak, Mulhacén (3479m; p773) above Granada; following in the footsteps of Carlos V in Extremadura (p803); walking along Galicia's deserted Costa da Morte (Death Coast; p550); or sauntering through alpine meadows in the Pyrenees (p350)? Spain offers a tremendous range of walking, hiking and climbing opportunities for every taste.

GRs, PRs & Other Paths

Spain has a great network of short and long-distance trails called PRs *(senderos de pequeno recorrido)* and GRs *(senderos de gran recorrido)* respectively: PRs, marked with yellow-and-white slashes, and GRs, marked red-and-white, follow old Roman, royal and pilgrimage roads, cart trails and shepherds' migratory paths, as well as trails developed for their beauty or cultural interest. While these are a great concept, maintenance of the trails is unfortunately sporadic. Local or regional groups also create and maintain their own trails using their own trail marking. Tourist offices may have pamphlets describing nearby walks and trailheads sometimes have informative panels.

When to Go

Spain is blessed with an abundance of ranges, valleys and coastal areas in different climate zones, so it's possible to walk and hike here year-round. If your feet are starting to itch in early spring, head to Andalucía, where conditions are most pleasant from March to June and in September and October, but downright unbearable in midsummer. If you want to walk in summer, do what Spaniards have traditionally done: escape to the north. The Basque Country, Asturias, Cantabria and Galicia are best from June to September. Starting in mid-June, the Pyrenees (p350) are accessible, while July and August are the ideal months for the high Sierra Nevada (p773). August is the busiest month on the trails and if you plan to head to popular national parks and stay in *refugios* (mountain refuges), book ahead.

What to Take

On any hike it's sensible to have proper footwear, sufficient water, a hat and sunscreen, as well as emergency phone numbers.

Prime Spots

Most famous are the Pyrenees, separating Spain from France and containing two outstanding national parks: Aigüestortes i Estany de Sant Maurici (p363) and Ordesa y Monte Perdido (p424). The spectacular GR11 or Senda Pirenáica traverses the Pyrenees by connecting the Atlantic (at Hondarribia in the Basque Country) with the Mediterranean (at Cap de Creus in Catalonia). Walking the whole route to appreciate its beauty is unnecessary, as there are day hikes in the national parks that coincide with the GR11.

Highly scenic and accessible limestone ranges with their distinctive craggy peaks (usually hot climbing destinations, too) include the Picos de Europa (p517), Spain's first national park and straddling Cantabria, Asturias and León provinces; the Basque mountains; Valencia's Els Ports area (p595); and the Sierras de Cazorla (p786) and de Grazalema (p718) in Andalucía.

To walk in mountain villages, the classic spot is Las Alpujarras (p776), near the Parque Nacional Sierra Nevada (p773) in Andalucía. Less well known and more remote are the villages of Galicia's Sierras de Courel and Ancares.

Great coastal walking abounds even along the heavily visited south on Mallorca (p618), the Islas Canarias (Canary Islands) and Cabo de Gata (p793) just east of Almería. The easy walking on Galicia's Islas Cíes (p562), part of Spain's newest national park, makes it ideal for families.

Spain's most famous long walk is the Camino de Santiago (p83).

For more information on parks and protected areas, see p75.

Information

Lonely Planet's *Walking in Spain* covers a wide range of routes across the country and contains plenty of advice on books, equipment, preparation, seasons and accommodation. Cicerone Press publishes region-specific walking (and climbing) guides for Mallorca, the Cordillera Cantábrica, the Vía de la Plata pilgrim's route from Sevilla to Santiago, the Costa Blanca, the Sierra Nevada and the GR11 route across the Spanish Pyrenees. Specialist bookshops in your home country, Barcelona's Altaïr (p277) and Madrid's La Tienda Verde sell maps (the best Spanish ones are Prames and Adrados) and guides. In Spanish, the website www .andarines.com gives route descriptions and useful links for books, sports shops and Spanish mountaineering associations.

> Wild camping is generally not permitted in Spain. The website www .campingsonline.com lets you locate campsites anywhere in the country.

CYCLING

Whether you're looking for a gentle family pedal, challenging single tracks, or tours that will take you two weeks or more, here you'll find everything. Spain is a cycle-friendly country and drivers are accustomed to sharing the roads with platoons of Lycra-clad cyclists. Spain has an excellent network of secondary roads, usually with a comfortable shoulder, ideal for road touring.

When to Go

In terms of when to go, the same information holds true for cycling as it does for walking (see p78).

What to Take

Bike rental along the popular Mediterranean coastal areas, the islands and major cities is relatively easy but is hit-and-miss just about anywhere else. Bring your helmet (helmets are required but enforcement is inconsistent) and bicycle if you're planning to do serious touring. Bicycle shops are common everywhere, making it unnecessary to load yourself down with supplies.

Prime Spots

Every region has both off-road (in Spanish called BTT, from *bici todo terreno;* mountain bike) and touring trails and routes. Mountain bikers can head to just about any sierra and use the extensive *pistas forestales* (forestry tracks). A challenging off-road excursion takes you along the Altiplano across the Sierra Nevada. Classic touring routes include the Camino de Santiago (see p83), the Vía de la Plata and the 600km Camino del Cid, which follows in the footsteps of Spain's epic hero from Burgos to Valencia. Guides in Spanish exist for all of these.

Information

An indispensable website for readers of Spanish is www.amigosdel ciclismo.com, which gives useful information on restrictions, updates on laws, circulation norms, contact information for the hundreds of cycling clubs all over the country, and lists of guidebooks, as well as a lifetime's worth of route descriptions organised region by region. There are more than 200 cycling guidebooks published (the vast majority in Spanish). *España en Bici* by Paco Tortosa and María del Mar Fornés is a good overview guide. *Cycle Touring in Spain: Eight Detailed Routes* by Harry Dowdell is a helpful planning tool, as well as being practical once you're in Spain.

For information on bicycle purchase and transport in Spain, see p857. The Real Federación Española de Ciclismo (www.rfec.com) provides contact information for bicycle clubs.

> www.wild-spain.com is an excellent English-language site with articles on wildlife, outdoor sports and conservation.

SKIING & SNOWBOARDING

For winter powder, Spain's skiers (and the royal family) head to the Pyrenees of Aragón and Catalonia. Outside of the peak periods (which are the beginning of December, 20 December to 6 January, Carnival and Semana Santa – Holy Week), Spain's top resorts are relatively quiet, cheap and warm in comparison to their counterparts in the Alps, making them a good alternative. Resorts now also cater to snowboarders, with shops, schools and the installation of on-slope half-pipes. The season runs from December to April, though January and February are generally the best, most reliable times for snow.

Prime Spots

In Aragón two popular resorts are Formigal (p430) and Candanchú (p430). Just above the town of Jaca, Candanchú has some 42km of runs with 51 pistes (as well as 35km of cross-country track). In Catalonia, Spain's first resort, La Molina (p358), is still going strong and is a good place for families and beginners. Considered to have the Pyrenees' best snow (especially in January), the 73-piste resort of Baqueira-Beret (p368) boasts 24 modern lifts with 104km of downhill runs for all levels (and 25km of cross-country track). The après-ski scene also gets high ratings. Andorra, also in the Pyrenees, has popular, well-known resorts. Pas de la Casa-Grau Roig (p398) is Andorra's biggest, with 100km of runs.

Spain's other major resort is Europe's southernmost: the Sierra Nevada (p773), outside Granada. With completely overhauled facilities for the 1996 World Cup ski championships, the 76km of runs are at their prime in March. Despite their World Cup status, the slopes are particularly suited for families and for novice to intermediate skiers.

Minor ski stations with poorer snow and a shorter season can be found in Madrid (Navacerrada is closest to the city), La Rioja (Valdezcaray has 14 runs) and Galicia (Manzaneda boasts a 230m elevation drop). At 60 kilometres from Madrid, Puerto Navacerrada is the closest ski centre. With its 16 runs, Navacerrada caters to beginners and intermediates. Valdezcaray, located in the Sierra de la Demanda just 45 minutes from Santo Domingo de la Calzada, has 20 runs reaching a maximum altitude of 1530m. Manzaneda, 90km northeast of Ourense, has extensive snow-making machines and its 15 runs along treeless trails range from 1500m to 1800m.

Information
If you don't want to bring your own gear, Spanish resorts have equipment rental, as well as ski schools. Lift tickets range between €26 and €31 for adults, and €18 and €21 for children; equipment rental runs at around €15 a day. If you prefer to organise ahead of time, Spanish travel agencies frequently advertise affordable single- or multi-day packages with lodging included.

WATER SPORTS
Scuba Diving & Snorkelling
With Spain's 4000km of shoreline, abundant marine life, relatively warm Mediterranean water, and varied underwater features including wrecks, sheer walls and long cavern swim-throughs, you'll find great scuba diving (*buceo* in Spanish) and snorkelling opportunities year-round. The numerous Mediterranean dive centres cater heavily to an English-speaking market and offer single- and multi-day trips, equipment rental and certification courses. Their Atlantic counterparts (in San Sebastián, Santander and A Coruña) deal mostly in Spanish, but if that's not an obstacle for you, then the colder waters of the Atlantic will offer a completely different underwater experience.

For a list of hyperbaric chambers and diving-accident facilities in Spain, check www.scuba-doc.com/divsp.htm.

Well-known spots include the Costa Brava's coral reefs around the Illes Medes marine reserve (p340) off L'Estartit (near Girona). The Costa del Sol outfits of Málaga, Nerja and Mijas launch to such places as the La Herradura Wall, the 1937 cargo vessel the Motril Wreck and the Cavern of Cerro Gordo. Spain's Balearic and Canary island chains are also popular dive destinations with excellent services.

Paco Nadal's *Buceo en España* provides information province by province, with descriptions of ocean floors, dive centres and equipment rental. The website www.dogbreathdivers.com/spain.htm has helpful diving information, including dive centres.

Surfing
Vans of European surfers following the best waves along Spain's Atlantic coast are a sure sign that summer has arrived. Prime from September to April, Spain's north shore has consistent, tubing waves (in winter) and innumerable beaches that offer ideal conditions for all levels of surfer. Cold water is the only drawback; a full wetsuit is required in winter, but a shorty is sufficient in summer. Some people complain of localism (territorial locals) at the best spots on good and therefore crowded days. Surf shops abound in the popular surfing areas and usually offer board and wetsuit hire.

Mundaka's legendary left (p457), considered Europe's best, is the Basque Country's mecca. Heading east throughout the Basque Country (and even in downtown San Sebastián at the city beach, Zurriola; p448), Cantabria and Asturias, there are well-charted surf beaches. If you're looking for solitude, along Galicia's Costa da Morte (p550) some isolated beaches remain empty even in summer. In September surfers head to Galicia's Pantín Classic surf competition north of Ferrol (p547). Overall, Mediterranean Spain can't compete with the north, but southwest Spain gets powerful, winter beach breaks, and weekdays off Conil de la Frontera can be sublimely lonely.

José Pellón's *Guía del Surf en España* provides comprehensive recommendations on surf shops, surfing schools, clubs and prime spots. Both www.globalsurfers.com and www.wannasurf.com have Spain pages with A to Z surfing information.

Wanna swim? Check out www.swimmersguide.com to find public pools in Spain. Don't forget your swim cap!

Windsurfing & Kitesurfing

The Straits of Gibraltar (aka the Wind Machine) are responsible for Tarifa's (p724) fame as Spain's year-round wind capital and here, along 10km of white, sandy beaches, windsurfers and kitesurfers find their haven. Renting equipment is easy, and many outfits have schools where you can learn and improve. The less well known Empuriabrava in Catalonia also has great conditions, especially from March to July. If you're looking for waves, try Spain's northwest coast, where the northeast trade winds keep the wind constant all year. Compared to windsurfing, kitesurfing has cheaper equipment, and the jumping is higher and requires less wind. The Spanish website www.windsurfesp.com/sp.asp gives very thorough descriptions of spots, conditions and schools all over Spain.

Kayaking, Canoeing & Rafting

Looking for hot wave trains, curlers and reversals? With 1800 rivers and streams, opportunities abound to take off downstream. Most rivers are dammed for electric power at some point along their flow. Consequently, there are many reservoirs with excellent low-level kayaking and canoeing where you can rent equipment. The downside is that to follow a river's course to the sea means getting out and picking up your boat.

Top white-water rivers include Catalonia's turbulent Noguera Pallaresa (p362), Aragón's Gállego, Cantabria's Carasa and Galicia's Miño. In general, May and June are best for kayaking, rafting, canoeing and hydrospeed (water-tobogganing). For fun and competition, in the first weekend in August the 22km crazy, en masse Descenso Internacional del Sella canoe race (p521) from Arriondas in Asturias to coastal Ribadesella is a blast. Patrick Santal's *White Water Pyrenees* thoroughly covers 85 rivers in France and Spain for kayakers, canoers and rafters.

For more-tranquil sea kayaking around caves and cliffs, the Costa Brava's rugged shore by Cala Montgó, Tamariu (p335) and Cadaqués (p343) is tops. Guided excursions, classes and rental from beaches are easy to locate. Exciting surf kayak spots coincide with the surfing ones: Mundaka (p457), with its own Surf Kayak Club (www.ur2000.com), and Llanes (p513) in Asturias.

DID YOU KNOW?

Spain's biggest river is the Ebro, its longest is the Tajo and the river with the second-highest flow is the Miño.

Sailing

Spain has some 250 harbours for sport sailing and stages many sailing competitions (*regatas*); and many companies specialise in chartering sailboats both with and without a skipper and crew. The **Real Federación Española de Vela** (☎ 91 519 50 08; website www.rfev.es) maintains a calendar of windsurfing and sailing *regatas*, as well as regulations governing sailing in Spanish waters.

Itching to cast your line? Check out www.angling-in-spain.com.

Canyoning & Puenting

Canyoning (*barranquismo*) involves walking, sliding, diving, jumping and swimming down canyons. The sport is rapidly evolving in the

ON LITTLE WHEELS

Most coastal cities have flat, wide seaside promenades (eg Barcelona, San Sebastián and A Coruña) ideal for rollerblading (called *patinaje* in Spanish), except when Spaniards come out in droves for their evening (usually 7.30pm to 9pm) *paseo* (stroll). Skateboard-friendly cities such as Pamplona have skating tracks and skateboard parks.

Pyrenees and new routes are constantly explored. Top centres include Aragón's Parque de la Sierra y Cañones de Guara, famous for its deep throats, powerful torrents and narrow gorges, as well as the Río Verde north of Almuñecar (p779) in southern Spain. May to September are generally the best months.

Another popular activity run by adventure outfits all over Spain is swing jumping or *puenting* (which is the Spanglish way of saying 'jumping from a high bridge'). Unlike bungee jumping, where there's rebound, the idea is to jump out far, snug in two harnesses and two cords, and free fall (reaching up to 170km/h) into a pendulum-like swing action.

HANG-GLIDING & PARAGLIDING

If you want to take to the skies either hang-gliding (in Spanish it's called *ala delta*) or paragliding *(parapente)*, there are a number of specialised clubs and adventure tour companies. The **Real Federación Aeronáutica España** (☎ 91 508 29 50; www.rfae.org) gives information on recognised schools and lists clubs and events.

DID YOU KNOW?

The Costa del Sol is also known as the Costa del Golf. Spain has hundreds of courses, many open 365 days a year, with green fees from €30 to €275.

CAMINO DE SANTIAGO

Pilgrimage is back in style. In an unprecedented revival, unlike anything since the 13th century, people are once again following the medieval Camino de Santiago (Way of St James) pilgrimage across northern Spain. Driving down any road running parallel to the Camino, you'll see pilgrims of all sizes, ages and nationalities, heading ever westward loaded down under weighty backpacks or cycling along trails marked with yellow arrows and scallop shells (Santiago's pre-eminent symbol). Medieval pilgrims came for faith, penance and hope for the future (adventure was also mixed in there). Modern pilgrims do it for the Romanesque and Gothic art, the physical challenge, the gorgeous ever-changing landscapes, to decide what's next in life, take a spiritual or religious journey, enjoy a cheap holiday, or to work out mid-life crises; inevitably, they end up having the adventure of a lifetime.

Before people could take a plane or drive to Santiago, millions of pilgrims simply walked out their doors in Germany, the British Isles, Scandinavia, Poland and France and made a beeline for Compostela along a huge network of trade routes, royal roads and trails that eventually came together in Spain. Although in Spain there are many Caminos to Santiago, by far the most popular is, and was, the Camino Francés (p87), which originated in France, crossed the Pyrenees at Roncesvalles and then headed west for 750km across the mountains, wheat and wine fields and forests of the regions of Navarra, La Rioja, Castilla and Galicia. In between this vast space are Pamplona, Logroño, Burgos and León, as well as an endless string of villages, each with its own pilgrimage vestige. Whether you go by car or under your own power, it's bound to be a highlight of your Spanish holiday.

HISTORY

What originally set Europe's feet moving? Tradition tells us that Pelayo, a 9th-century religious hermit living in the remote areas of northwestern Iberia, followed a mysterious shining star to a Roman mausoleum hidden under briars. Inside were the remains of the apostle James the Greater (in Spanish, Santiago). Confirmed by the local bishop Teodomiro and Asturian king Alfonso the Chaste, the earthshaking discovery spread like wildfire and put the incipient Compostela indelibly on European maps. Today it's hard to imagine the impact of this news, but in that age pilgrimage to holy sites with relics was tantamount to obtaining a ticket to eternal salvation. Relics were sacred commodities: the more important the relic, the more important the shrine that held them. And Santiago's relics were gold: nearly intact and belonging to one of Jesus' apostles, making them Europe's finest. When word got out, the devoted hightailed it to Spain. See the boxed text below to find out how James the Greater's remains got to Iberia in the first place.

Bad for early pilgrims, but very good for monarchs, was the lack of roads, bridges, towns, churches and basic services for people trying to get to Compostela. The road had to be built and settled. Taking advantage of the dearth of able-bodied souls, monarchs offered enormous privileges to settlers, who soon populated town after town. Northern Spain was also plagued by Christian and Moorish skirmishes that made the going hazardous. Monarchs and ecclesiasts were no fools: they quickly put the apostle's image to work and he was reborn as the legendary Santiago Matamoros (Moorslayer), heading up the Christian troops and supposedly helping slaughter Moorish forces mounted on a white charger at key Reconquista battles. Benedictine monks from Cluny in France also recognised the advantage of close ties to the Camino and founded many monasteries and attendant churches along the Camino, helping to spread Romanesque art forms and the order's power. In the 12th century a French cleric compiled the *Liber Sancti Jacobi* (aka the *Book of St James*), a masterwork on the Santiago pilgrimage that includes a guidebook dividing the route from the Pyrenees into 13 stages.

After its 11th- to 13th-century heyday (rivalling even Rome and Jerusalem), the Camino suffered through the Protestant Reformation and nearly died out until its late-20th-century revival. The route's current success has pumped life into some lost little corners of northern Spain.

INFORMATION

The Camino is not the yellow-brick road to Santiago. While it is way-marked with cheerful yellow arrows on everything including telephone

---

DID YOU KNOW?

The Camino is also called the Way of the Stars (Vía Láctea in Spanish) because the heavenly Milky Way appears to parallel the Camino on the ground. Charlemagne, it is said, dreamt that Santiago told him to follow the Milky Way to his tomb, making him the legendary first pilgrim.

PAGAN QUEENS & STONE BOATS

In the year AD 44 pagan Queen Lupa was more than a little suspicious when two Palestinian refugees landed in her territory, near Padrón in western Galicia, with the decomposing and headless body of a Christian martyr, and requested permission to bury him. The apostle James, son of Zebedee and María Salomé, is by tradition thought to have preached in Iberia. Herod Agrippa had him executed on his return to Jerusalem and Santiago's followers whisked the body to Jaffa, from where they let Providence guide their stone boat on a miraculous sea voyage through the Straits of Gibraltar back to Galicia. Promising safe passage and burial, Queen Lupa sent the loyal disciples out to a field to retrieve two oxen to pull the body on a cart. Instead they found two wild bulls eager to gore them. Not to be daunted, the disciples prayed to Santiago, who transformed the bulls' ire into cowed obedience and the two bowed their heads and were peacefully yoked. Impressed by this and other exploits, Queen Lupa converted to Christianity. Santiago remained forgotten until Pelayo saw the star in the woods.

CAMINO DE SANTIAGO

poles, rocks, trees and the ground, the 'trail' itself is a mishmash of forest path, rural lanes, field track running parallel to the highway, paved secondary roads and sidewalks all strung together. Scallop shells, stuck in cement markers or stylised on metal signs, also show the way.

Tourist offices in northern Spain frequently offer local and region-specific information on the Camino. 'Friends of the Camino' associations also provide invaluable information, especially the **Confraternity of St James** (☎ 020 7928 9988; 27 Blackfriars Rd, London, SE1 8NY). Lonely Planet's *Walking in Spain* thoroughly describes a 30-day itinerary for walkers.

The Confraternity of St James website (with great links, online bookstore, and historical and practical information) is the one not to miss: www.csj.org.uk!

Pilgrim's Credential & Compostela Certificate
Modern pilgrims carry a Pilgrim's Credential (Credencial del Peregrino) that they get stamped daily in churches, bars and *albergues* (refuges), to gain access to the network of *albergues* and acquire a certificate of completion, the Compostela. Pilgrims who walk (or ride a horse) the last (not simply any) 100km or cycle the last 200km and claim a religious or spiritual motive for the journey can receive the Compostela from the Santiago cathedral's **Oficina del Peregrino** (☎ 981 56 24 19; Rúa do Vilar 1; www.archicompostela.org; ☼ 9am-9pm). Get the Credential (cost €0.25) in Roncesvalles (there it costs €1), in the *albergues* of major cities, or via a Friends of the Camino association.

Both documents are useful for pilgrims' discounts: ask about applicability at museums along the Camino and discount one-way airfares with Iberia.

Tours
Numerous outfits, both in and outside Spain, organise walking and cycling tours of varying duration. Among the established companies are **Experience Plus** (www.experienceplus.com), which leads both walking and cycling tours from Burgos and León; and **Bravo Bike** (www.bravobike.com), which specialises in cycling. **On Foot In Spain** (www.onfootinspain.com) and **Iberian Adventures** (www.iberianadventures.com) guide walking and self-guided trips. **Saranjan** (www.saranjantours.com) runs upmarket bus tours with some walking involved.

PLANNING
Remember: the Camino changes – sleeping facilities open and close, trails are detoured and prices fluctuate.

CAMINO BOOKS
Outstanding books include David Gitlitz and Linda Davidson's *The Pilgrimage Road to Santiago: The Complete Cultural Handbook*; William Melczer's translation of the 12th-century *Pilgrim's Guide to Santiago de Compostela*; Jack Hitt's quirky, modern, personal account *Off the Road*; and Nancy Frey's contemporary analysis of the pilgrimage's popularity, *Pilgrim Stories: On and Off the Road to Santiago*. The best general guide is Millán Bravo's *A Practical Guide for Pilgrims*.

Where to Start

No official Camino starting point exists. People usually decide where to start depending on the time available and what they want to see. To walk the 'whole' route (meaning from Roncesvalles) allow at least five weeks, to cycle it two weeks and give yourself a week by car. Touring cyclists riding on the roads will inevitably go faster than mountain bikers using the mostly off-road walkers' trail. Having a car gives you flexibility to explore many additional sites associated with the pilgrimage otherwise unfeasible if on foot or bicycle.

When to Go

The Camino can be done any time of the year. From October to May there are few people on the road but in winter there will be snow, rain and bitter winds. In May and June the wildflowers are glorious and the endless fields of cereals turn from green to toasty gold, making the landscapes a huge draw. July and August bring crowds of summer vacationers, as well as scorching heat, especially in the middle section through Castilla y León. September is less crowded and the weather still stable, making it a pleasant month to travel. Santiago's feast day, 25 July, is another popular time to converge on the city. See Santiago de Compostela (p533) for more details.

What to Take

The lighter the load, the easier the walking and cycling. In summer, pilgrims ideally get by with about 8kg to 10kg of clothing (quick-drying trousers, shorts, T-shirts, jumper, socks and footgear), sleeping bag, guidebook and any favourite personal items (camera, sunscreen, toiletries, blister pack). Winter pilgrims will need adequate all-weather gear. For walkers, lightweight, flexible boots with good ankle support are sufficient. Even experienced hikers often get tendonitis (and blisters) from wearing heavy boots on the relatively flat terrain of the *meseta* (the high tableland of central Spain). Cyclists will need panniers and helmet as a minimum. With the yellow arrows and detailed guidebooks, buying maps is unnecessary.

Cyclists seeking practical information and advice will want to check out the website: http://groups.yahoo.com/group/santiago_bicicleta.

Sleeping

Those carrying the Credential can stay in *albergues*. Charging €3 to €6 (in Galicia, only a donation is required in the public *albergues*), most *albergues* have dorm rooms, bathrooms, space to hang laundry and sometimes kitchen facilities. As a rule it's first come, first served. Cyclists may have to wait until 8pm before being admitted to give preference to walkers. Pilgrims with support vehicles are at the bottom of the preference totem pole. In summer the *albergues* quickly fill and people start getting up earlier and earlier to race to the next *albergue* to ensure a bed space instead of enjoying the Camino.

Numerous alternatives, albeit more expensive, exist all along the Camino: *hostales* (budget hotels), hotels, rural guesthouses. Another option is to carry a tent. Campsites intermittently coincide with the Camino (see www.campingsonline.com). For lodging information, see the specific towns in the Basque Country, Navarra & La Rioja (p440), Castilla y León (p170) and Galicia (p530) chapters.

Some 300 *albergues* along all of the Caminos are listed (in Spanish, but it's easy to follow) by route on the website www.caminosantiago.org/cpperegrino/cpalbergues/camino frances.html.

Eating

Restaurants all along the route offer an economical *menú del día* (daily set menu) from €7 to €12, which most often includes three courses, wine or water and bread. Bread, cheese, fruit and cold cuts for picnics are readily available at small markets in the many towns and villages en route.

Getting There & Around

Since the Camino Francés has no fixed starting point, you can join the trail at any point along the way. See the corresponding city in the Basque Country, Navarra & La Rioja (p440), Castilla y León (p170) and Galicia (p530) chapters for transport details.

You can parallel the route by car following the blue and yellow highway signs. Covering the entire route by public transport is difficult unless you're travelling from one major town to the next and skipping the smaller villages. Information boards in the *albergues* usually have updated transport information.

CAMINO FRANCÉS

The highlights of the Camino Francés from Roncesvalles to Santiago de Compostela are detailed here. For more specific information on the major towns in Navarra, La Rioja, Castilla y León and Galicia, please see the corresponding chapters.

Roncesvalles to Pamplona   Map p87

Just north of Roncesvalles, the Camino Francés dramatically enters Spain at the same Pyrenean pass immortalised in the French epic *Song of Roland* and which Napoleon used to launch his 1802 occupation of Spain. Diminutive Roncesvalles, 45km from Pamplona, admirably sets the tone for this extraordinary route. Its 13th-century Gothic church contains the first Santiago statue dressed as a pilgrim (with scallop shells and staff) and a finely sculpted 13th-century Virgin (and child) encased in silver. At the daily mass, the church's canons bless pilgrims using a prayer dating from the 12th century.

Beautiful beech forests surround Roncesvalles and are the Camino's first and last. The trail progressively descends through rural pastures, dense mixed forests and picturesque villages, whose three-storey white houses with brightly coloured shutters and steep peaked rooves (for the winter snows), line the undulating road.

Long before people were running with the bulls down the streets of Pamplona in a frenzy of San Fermín madness, pilgrims overnighted here. In the 11th century Pamplona became an official stop along the way,

DID YOU KNOW?

Yellow arrows, the unofficial Camino blaze, were invented by the indomitable priest from O Cebreiro (Galicia), Elías Valiña Sampedro, back in the 1980s. He and his nephews went out with cans of yellow paint (because yellow is easy to see) and marked the historical ways.

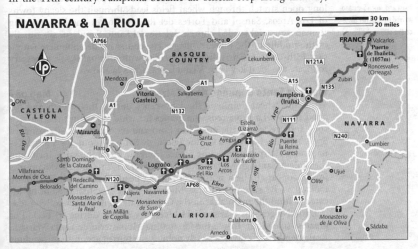

cementing its prosperity. Be sure not to be put off by the cathedral's bland neoclassical façade: just inside are the pure, soaring lines of the 14th-century Gothic interior. The 15th-century alabaster tombs of Carlos III el Noble and his wife, Leonor, are particularly fine.

Pamplona to Estella   Map p87
Heading west out of Pamplona, the Sierra del Perdón, with its long line of electricity-producing windmills, rises ahead of you. From the pass over the sierra, you can see down the long valley that leads to Puente la Reina, where the Camino Aragonés, coming from the east, joins up with the Camino Francés. Also in the valley (a patchwork quilt of wheat, white asparagus, grapes and the first olive trees) is one of the Camino's emblematic spots: Eunate, a remarkable 12th-century, octagonal chapel sitting in the middle of a wheat field.

Puente la Reina's main draw is its striking 11th-century bridge. Notice its diamond-shaped piers and hollows in the arches that help reduce water resistance when the Río Arga rises during floods.

The Romanesque portals of Puente la Reina's Iglesia de Santiago, Cirauqui's Iglesia de San Román and Estella's Iglesia de San Pedro de la Rúa, with Mudéjar-influenced Romanesque lobed arches carved with complicated knots, are the only ones along the Camino. The area's microclimate makes the flowers (especially the roses and geraniums) the envy of any gardener.

The first monumental Romanesque architecture along the route finally makes an appearance in Estella: the outstanding portal of the Iglesia de San Miguel, the cloister of the Iglesia de San Pedro de la Rúa and the Palacio de los Reyes de Navarra. On the Palacio, look for the vices of sloth (a donkey playing a harp while a dog listens), lust (snakes sucking on the breasts of a woman) and avarice (naked people with money bags around their necks) high up on the street corner capital.

Estella to Viana   Map p87

Just outside of Estella, at the Bodega de Irache, the winery owners tempt virtuous pilgrims with a free wine and water fountain. If you're tempted to take the wine away, it's sold cheap in an adjacent vending machine! Evergreen oaks and wine groves fill the undulating landscapes until a very long open stretch through wheat fields leads through the sleepy towns of Los Arcos, Sansol and Torres del Río. In Torres another stunning Romanesque eight-sided church, Iglesia del Santo Sepulcro, sits quietly in the middle of the hillside village. To see the inside, complete with a rare 13th-century Christ figure (crucified with four nails), it's necessary to locate the local key lady. Viana is Navarra's last town.

Viana to Santo Domingo de la Calzada   Map p87
Wine and wheat dominate the landscapes during this stretch and for good reason: La Rioja reds, the grapes for which grow in the iron-rich soils and are fed by the great Río Ebro and its tributaries, are some of Spain's finest. Logroño's Gothic Iglesia de Santiago contains a large Renaissance altarpiece depicting scenes from the life of the saint, including the violent Santiago Matamoros. The façade's 17th-century Matamoros image appears to be a musketeer cutting heads that are Mt Rushmore lookalikes. Be sure not to miss Michelangelo's crucifixion painting located behind the main altar in the Catedral de Santa María la Redonda.

Little Nájera was Navarra's 11th-century capital during its period of greatest splendour. Inside the fascinating Monasterio de Santa María la Real, members of Navarra's early nobility are buried around a miraculous

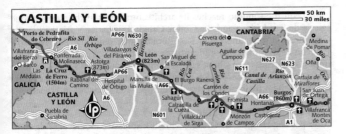

cave where a statue of the Virgin was discovered by the king while out hunting. The 15th-century walnut choir stalls are arguably the finest along the Camino. At the time of writing, the monastery was scheduled for restoration in 2005.

From Nájera the Camino heads to one of the road's wackiest places, Santo Domingo de la Calzada. Named for its energetic, 11th-century founder Santo Domingo (who cleared forest, built roadways, a bridge, a pilgrim's hospice and a church), the cathedral has long been the major attraction (see the boxed text, p486).

Santo Domingo to Burgos   Map p89

After entering Castilla y León province, the Camino passes through the densely forested Montes de Oca, once a thieves' haven, to the isolated monastery at San Juan de Ortega, whose do-gooder founder was Santo Domingo's disciple. On the vernal and autumnal equinoxes, the Miracle of the Light draws thousands to the church to see a shaft of light hit a Romanesque capital depicting the Annunciation. In the hills after San Juan, the Camino runs by Atapuerca, Europe's most productive palaeontological site, loaded with human fossil remains dating back 1.3 million years.

To visit Atapuerca, check the website www.atapuerca.net.

Burgos overwhelms with its art and architectural riches. Not to be missed is the 13th-century Gothic cathedral, with its three eight-pointed-star vaults magnificently illuminating the main aisle and two chapels.

Burgos to León   Map p89

The *meseta* begins after Burgos and continues in endless rolls of waving wheat for the next 200km across Burgos, Palencia and (most of) León provinces. People usually either love or hate this section of open, exposed territory where the largely adobe villages are few and far between. Villages are set low in long valleys (intermittently bisected by small, poplar-lined rivers), which rise up to the high, barren plains. Despite its apparent monotony, the stretch is filled with important testaments to the Camino's historical importance.

The crumbling ruins of Castrojeríz's castle rise majestically from the valley floor and the town's four large churches attest to more prosperous times. In Frómista, find one of the jewels of early Spanish Romanesque architecture, the Iglesia de San Martín, with 315 corbels and fine interior capitals. Between Carrión de los Condes and Calzadilla de la Cueza, the Camino coincides with a long stretch of Roman road. By the 11th century Sahagún was a powerful and wealthy Benedictine centre (now most traces are gone). The brick, Mudéjar-influenced (look for the horseshoe arches and clever way the bricks are placed in geometric patterns) Romanesque churches merit a visit. Before reaching León, the Camino runs through a long series of villages that run together along paved, busy roads.

In León the Camino reaches its architectural apex at the Romanesque Iglesia de San Isidoro and the Gothic Catedral de Santa María La Blanca. Considered the Sistine Chapel of Romanesque painting, San Isidoro's Panteón Real contains magnificently preserved frescoes depicting the most important scenes from Christ's life. The sublime cathedral's nearly 2000 sq metres of stained-glass windows, dating from the 13th to the 19th centuries, make them the best collection in Europe after Chartres in France.

León to Villafranca del Bierzo
Map p89

After passing Hospital de Órbigo, with its impressive medieval bridge and famed for its association with the outlandish chivalry of a 15th-century knight, Don Suero de Quiñones, the Camino finally returns to the mountains. Gateway to the mountain villages collectively known as the Maragatería, Astorga has good Roman ruins and Gaudí's fantastical neo-Gothic Palacio Episcopal (inside you'll find an excellent Camino museum).

From Astorga the Camino progressively ascends through small villages (now back to wood and stone houses) nearly abandoned before the pilgrimage's revitalisation in the early 1990s, including Rabanal del Camino (a favourite stopover that even has a tiny Benedictine monastery founded in 2001). The high point (in more ways than one) is La Cruz de Ferro (1504m); the tiny iron cross is lodged in a long wooden pole set into an ancient pile of rocks. Pilgrims bring stones to this pile (sometimes from home and sometimes picked up a few yards away) and in the last several years have also left behind all manner of personal items on and around the pole: photos, bandanas, a braid of hair, cigarette lighter, messages etc.

The trail makes a long, steep descent to the large, fertile valley, surrounded by mountains, known as the El Bierzo. The Camino cuts straight across the fairly industrialised valley through the large city of Ponferrada, most famous for its impressive castle (the Templars only occupied it for about 20 years) and then various towns before reaching its western edge at Villafranca del Bierzo. At Villafranca's Romanesque Iglesia de Santiago, pilgrims too ill to go further could receive pardon at the Puerta del Perdón (the church's north door), just as if they had reached Santiago.

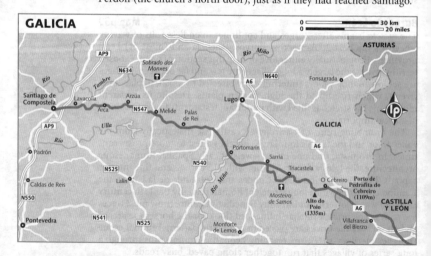

SLEEPING ON THE HOME STRETCH

To do the last 100km walking village to village, Sarria is the most convenient starting point. The towns listed here go from stage to stage and at each end point various sleeping options exist. The lodgings listed here are mid-range, centrally located (except the hotel in Sarria, which is by the train station) and have en-suite facilities. Taxi services, posted in *albergues* and hotels, can ferry luggage if you'd rather not carry it yourself. Once you've reached Santiago, accommodation options are plentiful.

Sarria Hotel Roma (☎ 982 53 22 11; Calvo Sotelo 2; s/d €32/45)
Portomarín Pensión Arenas (☎ 982 54 53 86; Plaza Condes Fenosa; s/d €25/35)
Palas de Rei Hostal Vilariño (☎ 982 38 01 52; Avenida Compostela 16; s/d €24/36)
Arzúa Hostal Teodora (☎ 981 50 00 83; Avenida Lugo 38; s/d €24/36)
Arca Hotel O Pino (☎ 981 51 10 35; Rúa de Arca 5; s/d €27/40)
Santiago See Santiago de Compostela on p538

Villafranca del Bierzo to Samos   Map p90

After gently ascending the long Valcarce river valley to Herrerías, the Camino abruptly rises up the imposing hillside to the pass at O Cebreiro, famous not only for attracting terrible weather, but as one of the earliest pilgrim way stations (a monastery was founded here in 836!) and the legendary locale of the Holy Grail, culminating in a 14th-century miracle in which the host and wine literally turned into the flesh and blood of Christ. Nine *pallozas* (circular, thatched-roof dwellings used since pre-Roman times) and adjacent stone houses (nearly every second one is a bar or hostel) make up this singular village.

In Galicia everything changes: it's permanently green and hilly, there are countless villages and hamlets, the grand monuments disappear and are replaced by small country churches, the houses are all stone, the roofs are slate and the rural people speak the local language, Galego. The first section through Lugo province is particularly beautiful, with old-growth oak and chestnut stands lining the way. Peeking in barn doors you'll see cobwebbed remnants of the area's strong ties to the land and late move towards mechanisation, such as wooden ploughs and carts. Don't be surprised to see wizened old men and women (the latter dressed in black) carrying huge scythes to the field or trundling high wheelbarrow loads of hay, greens or potatoes.

In Triacastela the Camino diverges, with both paths reuniting in Sarria. Going by way of Samos permits you to see the grand Benedictine monastery, Mosteiro de Samos, founded in the 6th century; it has two lovely cloisters (one with odd, busty mermaids and the other filled with roses), an imposing 18th-century church and four walls of murals detailing the life of St Benedict painted in the 1950s after the monastery burnt down.

Destroyed by fire in the 12th and 16th centuries and in 1951, the Mosteiro de Samos has been just as often rebuilt. A visit to the exquisite cloister gardens is a must.

Samos to Melide   Map p90

Built on a hill topped by a crumbling castle, Sarria is the usual launching point for people wanting to undertake the last 100km. The Camino winds through village after hamlet after village (such as Barbadelo, with a well-preserved Romanesque church) and steeply descends to Portomarín, set on a hill above the Río Miño. In the 1960s the old town was flooded to make way for a hydroelectric plant further downriver and the most important buildings, such as the fortress-like Romanesque Iglesia de San Juan, were moved stone by stone to the new town centre. Despite being the next town, Palas de Rei has little to attract attention. From Palas to

Melide there are lovely rural lanes, and the villages of Leboreiro and Furelos are particularly well preserved.

Melide offers not only Galicia's oldest *cruceiro* (standing crucifix) along the main drag but also a good ethnographic museum in the town's small historical quarter. The museum covers the area's prehistory (pre-Roman and Roman) as well as local trades practised for centuries and lost in the last 50 years, such as shoemaking, blacksmithing and carpentry.

A short detour from Melide is the Cistercian monastery of Sobrado dos Monxes, featuring an ornate Galician baroque façade. Though it fell into disrepair in the 19th century, the monastery has since been restored.

Melide to Santiago de Compostela   Map p90

The Camino rolls through numerous hamlets bridged by eucalyptus forest to finally reach Arzúa (the cow's-milk cheese and honey are great) and then Arca, a common last-night stopover. Lavacolla, where pilgrims used to cleanse themselves before heading into town, sits at the base of the last great hill, the climax of which is the Monte do Gozo (meaning Mount Joy), crowned by a huge sculpture in honour of the Pope's 1989 visit to Compostela. Pilgrims once used to see the cathedral's towers from here but now the moving view is obscured by eucalyptus trees! The last six kilometres into town are paved and poorly marked.

From the Rúa de San Pedro it's downhill to the old medieval gateway of Porta do Camiño. Head up the pedestrian street and then down past the cathedral's northern façade and through the tunnel under the Archbishop's Palace to the magnificent cathedral square, the Praza do Obradoiro. The most important pilgrims' rituals revolve around the 12th-century Pórtico da Gloria at the cathedral's western end and behind the main altar, where pilgrims climb stairs to hug a Romanesque Santiago statue and then descend to the crypt below to pay respect to the relics. A fitting end to the pilgrimage is witnessing the cathedral's big finale staged before mass ends: the swinging of the mighty Botafumeiro incense burner. It's truly a spectacle not to be missed.

OTHER CAMINOS DE SANTIAGO

The other Caminos de Santiago have yellow arrows (more sporadic), *albergues* (fewer) and important pilgrimage monuments, but lack the marvellous infrastructure and crowds of the Camino Francés.

Pilgrims coming via Toulouse in southern France would cross the Pyrenees at the Somport pass (1632m) and take the Camino Aragonés through Jaca and Sangüesa to join the main route at Puente la Reina.

Those who crossed into Iberia at Irún or sailed down to ports such as Santander, San Vicente de la Barquera and Avilés, connected up with the Caminos del Norte, following the Basque, Cantabrian and Asturian coasts, and turned inland at any number of spots to join up with the Camino Francés. The oldest known pilgrimage route to Santiago connected the Asturian city of Oviedo with Compostela.

The Vía de la Plata brought pilgrims north from southern Spain via Seville, Zafra, Mérida, Cáceres, Salamanca and Zamora along a Roman

---

THE BOTAFUMEIRO

Santiago's singular censer, the Botafumeiro (meaning loosely 'smoke spitter'), dates from the 13th century, weighs 53kg, reaches a speed of 68km/h, misses hitting the north and south transept vaults by only 51cm while reaching an angle of 82°, swings a minimum of 25 days per year, fell in 1499 and 1622 (to the horror of those below) and is a perfect, gigantic pendulum conceived of three centuries before pendulum physics was worked out. To see it best, be sure to stand in the north or south transept.

trade route. This trail either heads north to Astorga and the main route or enters Galicia via the Puebla de Sanabria towards Ourense.

The Camino Portugués also had inland and coastal versions and crossed into Galicia at Verín or Tui. Fourteenth-century British pilgrims popularised the Camino Inglés by sailing to the Galician ports of A Coruña and Ferrol then proceeding south on foot via Pontedeume and Betanzos to Sigüeiro and finally Compostela.

From Santiago pilgrims continued trekking to the end of the known world, Fisterra. They still do today, but most take the bus. Off the end of Fisterra's lighthouse, pilgrims burn stinking bits of clothes while watching the sun set into the endless blue horizon.

The Confraternity of St James (www.csj.org .ukpublishes excellent guides to all of the alternative *caminos*.

Food & Drink

Gypsies! Bullfights! Prancing stallions! Hot-blooded romance and deadly duels! These are all images of Spain, but so are paella, rough red wine and sublime sherry, roasted suckling pig and little tit-bits known as tapas. And let's not forget saffron-scented stews, sauces made from almonds, recipes that go back to ancient days and leading-edge cooks in the Basque Country. In Spain you will find a cuisine that vividly reflects its culture and its long and varied history. At its table you will dine with the memories of Romans, Moors and Aztecs, Basque fishermen, La Manchan peasants, Spanish grandees and French tourists. You'll encounter a confusion of styles and an unerring kitchen philosophy, sensuality balanced by moderation, culinary routine punctuated by indulgence.

DID YOU KNOW?

Spaniards spend more money per capita on food than any other Europeans.

Spanish cooking is straightforward: 'it should taste of what it is' goes the mantra. Except for garlic, herbs and spices are used sparingly. The cook will seldom alter, mash, puree or mould a food beyond recognition, for it must also look of what it is. To these ends simplicity is prized and simplicity can be a very difficult thing to achieve. It takes close attention and kitchen alchemy to draw out a delicate flavour by means of fire and oil and little else. A dish of Spain is generous: you will never have to lift up a sprig of parsley to find your portion of meat. And Spanish cookery is unpretentious; your food will not be tarted up and made to look cute. So tuck in, and *buen provecho*!

STAPLES & SPECIALITIES

Take a seat at any table in Spain. Almost without exception you will face what we call the Holy Trinity of Spanish cuisine: bread, olive oil and wine. This triumvirate is the cornerstone of Spain's culinary history. The legacy of Rome is both gastronomic and religious; it was Rome that gave Spain the Trinity of Father, Son and Holy Ghost; the Trinity of Wheat, Olive and the Vine. Other essentials of the Spanish table include cured ham from the high plateau, known as *jamón serrano*. Every *tasca* (tapas bar) has it. *Jamón ibérico* is the Cadillac of ham in Spain, being made from the hindquarters of wild pigs that have fed exclusively on acorns. Highly seasoned *chorizo* (pork sausage) is also made from acorn-fed pigs. The Spanish will cure almost any kind of meat, including cows and horses; it's then called *cecina*. The recipe for all of these treats comes from a noble Roman, Cato the Elder, in his tome *De Re Rustica*. Spanish cured meats are a bit like Italian prosciutto, but are deep red rather than blushing pink, offer more to the teeth, have a richer aroma and last longer in the mouth. They also go well with a dry martini!

DID YOU KNOW?

Spain is the world's largest producer of olive oil.

When it comes to fin fish the Spanish favourites are *bonito* (tuna), *bacalao* (dried and salted cod), *sardinas* (sardines) and *anchoas* (anchovies). Shellfish is also a favourite – if it has a house on its back the Spanish love it. No Spaniard is more than a few hours from the sea, and so seafood is never more than a few hours from any Spaniard. And the distribution of seafood in Spain is admirable. With all roads converging on Madrid, much of the sea's harvest arrives there daily, thus this landlocked city is called 'the best seaport in Spain'.

The fish with which the Spaniards have the closest relationship, historically, indeed almost spiritually, is *bacalao*. For many centuries roving Spanish fishermen have harvested the codfish from the grand banks of Newfoundland and Norway, salting it and bringing it home looking more like a rock than food. After soaking it several times in water it is rehydrated and relieved of its salt content, enriching the flavour and improving the texture. Originally it was considered food for the poor and some called it 'vigil day beef' for its use during fasts. Now it's rather pricy stuff. The best place to enjoy it is in the Basque Country, where they absolutely revere it. Try sweet red peppers stuffed with *bacalao*.

Tapas are the quintessential *culinario* that you will simply not find outside Spain. For these are not things to eat, but a uniquely Spanish way of eating things. Anything can be a tapa: a handful of olives, a slice of ham and cheese on bread, a bit of *tortilla española* (potato and onion omelette). Anything. Tapas are always taken at a bar with a glass of wine or beer, and almost always while standing at the bar. The tapa is a way of drinking without getting drunk; a way of socialising; a way of enjoying a little moment in life, with hopefully many more to follow. Tapas are as integral to Spanish life as garlic and religion. If you don't go out on a *tapeo* (tapas-bar crawl), then you will not have experienced Spain.

The Spanish begin their day simply: coffee and a cigarette and perhaps a piece of toast with jam. Lunch is the big and leisurely meal of the day, it's taken around 2pm and will easily last two hours, usually starting with soup or salad. In the north it might begin with *fabada*, a pork and bean stew, in the south with a dish of sweet *almejas* (raw clams). Main courses might be paella in Valencia, fried sardines with potatoes in Basque Country, but in Andalucía people will make a meal of nothing but tapas. Dinner starts late, between 9pm and 10pm; dishes are the same as the lunch menu, but usually lighter. The Spanish are not much given to snacking throughout the day, but they do like a piece of fruit or sweets – they'll dose their coffee with enough sugar to make it into a dessert.

DID YOU KNOW?

Many Spaniards' days begin with a glass of sherry. We call it the 'morning tipple'.

DRINKS
Wine

For as often as the Spanish drink wine you'd think them a nation of drunkards, but the opposite is the truth. The Spanish are a people of

---

TRAVEL YOUR TASTEBUDS

Culinary exotica is not something Spain is well known for. By and large it's a meat and potatoes culture, it just happens to be a superior meat and potatoes culture. There are some things you will find daily in Spain that are not at your local supermarket or café. *Turrón* is a uniquely Spanish kind of nougat, whose recipe goes back to the 14th century and incorporates honey, almonds and sugar. While it is said to have originated in the Jewish quarter of Jijona, it is a traditional Christmas treat. You'll find it at sweet shops everywhere. You may be familiar with *gazpacho*, but if you've encountered it outside Spain you probably haven't had the genuine article. This cold tomato soup is actually based on dry bread crumbs that are flavoured with tomato. It's the old Spanish peasant's way of making use of leftovers. The best place to get the real thing is in someone's home or perhaps a budget restaurant.

We Dare You

When you go to the market, whether to a traditional farmers' market or a modern *supermercado*, be prepared. A lot of dead animals are going to be looking you square in the eye and saying 'take me home for supper'. Their entrails will be hung from hooks, their organs piled high, their brains arranged in geometric patterns and their little disembodied feet resting daintily on their neighbours. So why don't you order a *cabeza de ternero* (calf's head) – boiled, skinned and split down the middle, exposing both hemispheres of the brain? Are you a right-brain person, or a left-brain person?

moderation and regular habits. Sometimes they'll mix wine with water, especially when giving it to drinkers of a youngish age. Eighteen is the legal age, but generally Spaniards are ready to drink wine when they start to ask for it. They grow up with responsible attitudes towards drink, and they keep that attitude for life. So don't look for a piss-up or a Bacchanalian revel. Here wine is a food, not a drug.

Perhaps your first encounter with a Spanish wine import was with Freixenet Cava (sparkling wine) in its trademark black bottle. Or it might have been a burlap-wrapped bottle of a rich-red Rioja. Maybe you came of age sipping sherry. You'll find the wines in Spain to be 'user friendly', easy to understand both on the label and in the bottle. Like their solid food, the Spaniards' liquid nourishment is straightforward and unpretentious. They do not like fussy wine any more than fussy food. They like it to taste good, smell good and feel good going down.

Perhaps the most common premium red table wine you'll encounter will be from Rioja, in the north. The principal grape of Rioja is the Tempranillo, widely believed to be a mutant form of the Pinot Noir. Its wine is smooth and fruity, seldom as dry as its supposed French counterpart. Look for the DO (*Denominación de Origen*: Denomination of Origin) Rioja on the label and you'll find a good wine. One of Spain's most charming white wines is Albariño, from Galicia. It's usually made crisp, dry and refreshing. It isn't sparkling, but it often has a slight 'schpritz', just a suggestion of very tiny bubbles. This is a rare Spanish wine as it's designated by grape rather than region. Sherry, the unique wine of Andalucía, is Spain's national dram. It's in every bar, *tasca* and restaurant in the land. Dry sherry, called *fino*, begins as a fairly ordinary white wine of the Palomino grape, but it's 'fortified' with grape brandy. This stops fermentation and gives the wine taste and smell constituents that enable it to age into something sublime. It's taken as an *aperitivo* or as a table wine with seafood. Amontillado and Oloroso are sweeter sherries, good for after dinner. Manzanilla is grown only in Sanlúcar de Barrameda near the coast and develops a slightly salty taste that is very appetising. When ordering it be sure to say '*vino de Manzanilla*', since *manzanilla* alone means chamomile tea.

Then there is that famous Spanish wine drink, sangria. Don't expect much from it and remember that it was developed as a way to make use of bad wine. It's usually a red wine mixed with citrus juice and zest, a bit of cinnamon, and diabetes-inducing amounts of sugar. It is sold to tourists.

Other Drinks

It will come as a surprise to many that beer outsells wine in Spain. This makes good sense though. The weather is often beastly hot and the food is salty. In Madrid there is a craze for microbrew, and you can find a

A Traveler's Wine Guide to Spain, written by Desmond Begg (1998), is a very authoritative and well-illustrated guide through the wine country of Spain.

CREATING CAVA

There are many criteria to be met for a sparkling wine to be called cava, but the most important is that it be made by the method known as *méthode champenoise*. In this process, the original for Champagne, a still wine is fermented in vats per the usual custom. It is then bottled, but before corking a dosage of yeast is added. The yeast feeds on the residual sugars, causing a secondary fermentation. The products of fermentation are alcohol and carbon dioxide, hence the bubbly. The discovery of this process is credited, at least in France, to Dom Pérignon. Upon tasting it for the first time he is said to have called out to his brethren, 'Come quickly! I am drinking stars!' In Spain these stars are produced almost exclusively in Catalonia.

string of microbreweries alongside Plaza de Santa Ana. In bars and *tascas* almost all the beer is on tap. So waltz in and order *una caña,* for a small beer, or *una jarra* for a greater thirst. Common brands are Cruzcampo, Mahou and San Miguel, which is the strongest at 5.4%. Similar to beer, *sidra* (cider) is the speciality of Galicia and Asturias; you can enjoy it fresh in a *sidrería* (cider bar). Elsewhere *sidra* is found in bottles and cans. *Aguardiente* is the term for strong spirits, the most famous being Ponche Caballero. Order this in a restaurant and the waiter is likely to set the bottle before you and charge you by the centimetre.

You can get any of these drinks in almost any bar, *tasca* or restaurant and there are some dedicated sherry bars in Andalucía, and some cava bars in Catalonia. Most *sidrerías* will serve beer and wine, but the selections might be few.

The favourite soft drink in Spain is *agua* (water). There are over 100 brands of bottled water, but in Spain even the tap water is good. *Horchata* is a sweet, milky drink made from tiger nuts and sugar, and is enjoyed mainly in Catalonia. Tea and coffee are unremarkable in Spain, but the hot chocolate is thick, rich and delicious.

CELEBRATIONS

In addition to the feasts of the calendar, there are many other reasons and excuses for Spaniards to have a fiesta – birthdays, anniversaries, first communions, graduations, weddings. Nowadays, sometimes, a divorce is ample reason to pour the wine, say grace and tuck in. More often than not they are family affairs and often have religious overtones. Even the Running of the Bulls is preceded by fervent prayer.

Spanish fiestas will almost always be accompanied by music. It might be a lone guitarist struggling to be heard, it might be a brass band or a rock band. Groups of women will spontaneously break into song, clapping out Gypsy rhythms. On occasion they will be answered by a chorus of the menfolk singing ballads, or songs with suggestive lyrics. The Spanish love food; music is the food of love and they love love too.

The most important week of the year culminates in Easter, and there are special dishes associated with Holy Week. In some communities there is a Good Friday procession in which heavy floats are borne by penitents. In order to keep up their strength, they breakfast on *bacalao a la vizcaína* (dried and salted cod with chillies and capsicum).

As this is the biggest and most important holiday on the Spanish calendar, there will always be food shared as families and friends come together. Dishes that appear during this time include *monas de pascua* (figures made of chocolate), *torta pascualina* (spinach and egg pie) and *torrija* (French toast). A popular Easter dish in Mallorca is *flan de pascuas* (Easter cheese flan), and *cordero pascual* (spring lamb) is common fare everywhere. In rural areas the village priest pays a visit to all his parishioners and blesses their houses. With some blessed salt and holy water he'll ensure your house has a clean bill of spiritual health for the coming year. An honorarium is expected in the form of a couple of eggs or a small cheese, placed in the basket he carries for this purpose.

WHERE TO EAT & DRINK

If the restaurant is full of Spanish diners the food is authentic (although paella can be dodgy unless you're in Valencia), and that can be said of most restaurants. The great exception is in the coastal resorts where the British, Americans and Germans tend to loiter. There you can have authentic fish and chips, hamburgers and knackwurst.

A Taste of Spain, written by Xavier Domingo (1992), is a gorgeous coffee-table book by one of Spain's most admired men of letters.

The *horno asador* is a restaurant with a wood-burning roasting oven. Baby lambs or kids, suckling pigs and sometimes a fowl of some kind are placed in *cazuelas* (earthenware cooking dishes) and slid into the *horno*. In summer, if the *asador* has no air-conditioning, dining can be uncomfortable, but in the bitter Spanish winter there is no better place to be. The air is thick with convivial conversation, the aromas are maddeningly delicious. This is the oldest type of restaurant in Spain and to dine in one is almost to slip from this century into one past. *Hornos asadores* are very popular with tourists and locals alike, so during the high season be sure to make a reservation. Dinner can run anywhere from €8 to €25, even more if you drink a fine wine.

DID YOU KNOW?

The oldest restaurant in the world is Sobrino de Botín (p143) in Madrid, established in 1725.

You will find pavement restaurants called *terrazas* in every city. To find one, walk down the street and you will eventually encounter several. There will be awnings and umbrellas to sit under to fend off the sun, and in some places, trees. Reservations are generally not taken, but if there is a crowd a waiting list will be started. A proper sit-down *restaurante* in Spain is like any other in the Western world. The customs and protocols are pretty much the same – there are no real pitfalls. One style point is that they tend to be small and intimate. Reservations are accepted, and advised or even required in high season.

Then there is the *tasca,* probably the single most common type of restaurant in Spain. They can be large, grand or the bar of a proper sit-down restaurant, though they are often small and sometimes even grotty. They can have marble floors or floors covered with sawdust, spit, cigarette butts and substances you'd rather not contemplate. You gingerly shoulder your way in through the bustle and hubbub, surrendering yourself to the aromas of garlic, vinegar, boiled shrimp, ham, cheese and saffron, all floating upon the air from a bar groaning with bowls and platters heaped high with tapas. Stand at the bar and enjoy your food and drink. In some *tascas*, tapas are served on toothpicks, which the barman will count to add up your tariff. Let's see, three toothpicks and a *vino de la casa* or *una caña* of draft beer should cost you about €4 – plenty left in your pocket for the next *tasca*.

For the most authoritative and comprehensive periodical on Spanish gastronomy, check www .spaingourmetour.com.

Stand-up fare in the morning is most commonly *churros con chocolate.* Ropes of deep-fried sugar-coated dough (call it a doughnut if you must) and a thick and rich chocolate brew fuels many Spaniards on the way to work or school. Get this treat at the local *chocolateria.*

VEGETARIANS & VEGANS

Vegetarians and vegans will survive. You may get tired of living on salad and bread and the odd vegetarian paella, but you'll get by. You'll probably become a familiar face at the local *frutería* (fruit shop), whose owner will be glad to see you. At the *tasca* you will usually find more veggie foods than at a proper sit-down restaurant. Many tapas consist of vegetables or fruits. *Garbanzos con espinacas* (chickpeas and spinach) is a favourite, as are salads of beetroot and onion, and numerous potato dishes, such as *patatas bravas* (potatoes in a spicy tomato sauce). Dishes of pulses, such

TIP OFF

Tipping is not really the custom among Spaniards. There is always a service charge in restaurants. If you pay by credit card there isn't even a space on your charge form for a tip. Our advice? Leave your small change. It accumulates in your purse or pocket very quickly. And while on the subject of money, restaurants usually accept credit cards. *Tascas,* as a rule, do not. Even the grand and expensive ones normally deal only *en efectivo* (in cash).

as *lentejas* (lentils) are here and there, and cheese is plentiful. Artichokes are popular and olives are always good. Be aware that most Spaniards don't comprehend vegetarianism, so if you're vegan it's wise to ask if dishes contain eggs or dairy. Be aware too that cooked vegetable dishes often contain ham, so speak up. In Madrid there are a few vegetarian restaurants on Calle de Ventura de la Vega, but your best bet is Barcelona, where there are some 50 vegetarian restaurants.

To the Heart of Spain, written by Ann & Larry Walker (1997), is an insightful cookbook, wine book and account of their travels through Iberia.

WHINING & DINING

Children's menus are rare. However, Spanish fare is not very spicy and kids tend to like it. Toddlers are usually fed straight from their parents' plate and if highchairs or risers aren't available staff will improvise. When kids get hungry between meals it's easy to zip into the nearest *tasca* and get them a little snack. There are also sweet shops every few blocks. See p831 for further information on travelling with children.

HABITS & CUSTOMS

Spanish table manners and settings are studies in simplicity. Unless you find yourself in a very smart restaurant you will keep the same knife and fork throughout the meal. You might also have a spoon, and that will be that for your implements of destruction. There will be one wine glass and one water glass, unless you also order cava. In this instance you may be given a flute or a tulip for the bubbly. Your water glass will be larger than your wine glass; the message of this should be clear. The only bit of arcana to remember at the Spanish table is that you should always keep your hands in view, never let them be hidden in the folds of napery or under the table. The reason for this is not known, but speculation suggests that it goes back to days of blood feuds and hidden daggers…

The Spanish seem to think that tobacco belongs to one of the basic food groups – there are no nonsmoking sections in restaurants. So in a *terraza*, take a table upwind; in a café sit as close as possible to the door; and inside a proper sit-down restaurant select a table near the air-conditioner if there is one, or a table off to the side, and put on your stiff upper lip.

COOKING COURSES

There are many great cooking courses throughout Spain. The following run courses for the inspired:

For a fair collection of recipes and some very good links, go to www .xmission.com/~dderhak /recipes.html.

Catacurian (☎ 1 800 601 5008 or 941 723 7588; www.catacurian.com; El Masroig, Tarragona, Catalonia; 3 days from €1000) Head down to the rural wine region of Priorat for three- to 10-day wine and cooking classes. Catalan chef Alicia Juanpere and her American partner Jonathan Perret lead tours around the area and teach the classes, which are offered in English.

L'Atelier (☎ 958 85 75 01; www.ivu.org/atelier; Calle Alberca 21, Mecina, Granada; 1 day €40) Award-winning vegetarian chef Jean-Claude Juston (formerly of Neal's Yard Bakery, the LSE vegetarian restaurant and other celebrated veggie eateries in London) runs vegetarian cookery courses the first week of every month at his welcoming little guesthouse in a centuries-old village house in the magical Alpujarras valleys of Andalucía.

For online shopping www.tienda.com can deliver Spain to your table. It has good recipes, too.

Seu-Xerea (☎ 96 392 40 00; Calle Conde Almodóvar 4, Valencia; 1 day €80) Under the direction of two of Valencia's premier chefs, Seu-Xerea does one-day modular courses in Mediterranean cooking. Visit Valencia's wondrous central market, then get your hands floury as the group prepares, cooks, then consumes the dishes of the day, accompanied by the best of local wines.

EAT YOUR WORDS

Want to know *pil pil* from *pimiento*? *Salsa* from *sandía*? Get behind the cuisine scene by getting to know the language. For pronunciation guidelines see p867 and for a complete rundown on useful phrases check out Lonely Planet's *Spanish Phrasebook*.

Useful Phrases

Table for..., please.	*Una mesa para..., por favor.*
Can I see the menu, please?	*¿Puedo ver el menú, por favor?*
Can I see the wine list, please?	*¿La lista de vinos, por favor?*
Can you recommend a good local wine?	*¿Me recomienda un buen vino del país?*
Can I have a beer, please?	*Una cerveza, por favor.*
Good health/Cheers!	*¡Salud!*
Do you have children's meals?	*¿Comidas para niños?*
Can I have the bill, please?	*La cuenta, por favor.*
I'm vegetarian.	*Soy vegetariano*
I don't eat red meat.	*No como carne roja.*

Menu Decoder

albóndiga – meatballs
champiñones al ajillo – mushrooms fried in garlic
ensaladilla mixta – mixed salad
fideuá – paella made with noodles instead of rice
frito variado – mixture of deep-fried seafood
gambas a la plancha – grilled prawns
menú del día – daily set menu
paella – rice dish which has many regional variations
patatas a lo pobre – poor man's potatoes (potato dish with peppers and garlic)
pipirrana – capsicum, onion, tomato and marinated fish salad
pulpo a la gallego – spicy boiled octopus

Food Glossary

a la parrilla	grilled	*cochinillo*	suckling pig
aceitunas	olives	*codorniz*	quail
adobo	marinade	*coliflor*	cauliflower
aguacate	avocado	*conejo*	rabbit
ajo	garlic	*confitura*	jam
arroz	rice	*cordero*	lamb
asado	roasted	*empanadillas*	small pie, either savoury or
bacalao	dried and salted cod		sweet
berenjena	aubergine, eggplant	*ensalada*	salad
bistec	steak	*escabeche*	pickle, marinade
bocadillo	bread roll with filling	*estofado*	stew
boquerones	anchovies marinated in	*frito*	fried
	wine vinegar	*galleta*	biscuit
butifarra	sausage	*granada*	pomegranate
cabrito	kid, baby goat	*helado*	ice cream
calamares	squid rings	*langosta*	lobster
caldo	broth, stock	*langostino*	king prawn
callos	tripe	*leche*	milk
camarón	small prawn, shrimp	*lechuga*	lettuce
camarónes fritos	deep-fried prawns	*lomo*	loin (pork unless specified
caracol	snail		otherwise)
cebolla	onion	*maíz*	corn
cerdo	pork	*mantequilla*	butter
chorizo	cooked spicy red sausage	*manzana*	apple
chuleta	chop, cutlet	*mejillones*	mussels
churro	long, deep-fried doughnut	*merluza*	hake

miel	honey	*raciónes*	large tapas serving
morcilla	black pudding	*relleno*	stuffing
naranja	orange	*riñón*	kidney
ostra	oyster	*salsa*	sauce
pan	bread	*sandía*	watermelon
pastel	cake	*sesos*	brains
pato	duck	*seta*	wild mushroom
pescaíto frito	fried fish	*solomillo*	sirloin (usually of pork)
pil pil	garlic sauce spiked with chilli	*sopa*	soup
		tarta	cake
pimentón	paprika	*ternasco*	lamb ribs
pimiento	pepper, capsicum	*ternera*	veal
plátano	banana	*tortilla española*	potato and onion omelette
platija	flounder, plaice		
plato combinado	combination plate	*trucha*	trout
queso	cheese	*zarzuela*	fish stew

MADRID

Madrid

CONTENTS

Madrileños have a saying about their city: 'She may not be beautiful, but she sure is a looker!' It's true that this accidental capital doesn't have the effortless glamour of Paris or the stateliness of London, but Madrid has a style and attitude that sets it in a class of its own. Where else will you find dinners that begin at midnight, traffic jams in the wee hours of the morning, and workdays that start at 10am?

Madrileños are nicknamed *gatos* (cats) for their incurable night prowling, and if you stay here long enough, your own feline traits will likely come to light. With endless options for night-time entertainment, you'll find plenty of excuses to stay out late. But the *madrileños* similarity with cats ends with their nocturnal habits; the people here are by and large a friendly, easy-going bunch and known for being open with outsiders. That may be because most of them are outsiders themselves. Traditionally, Madrid has been a city of immigrants, bringing together workers, government officials, students and fun-seekers from all over Spain and beyond.

Madrid became Spain's capital in 1561 because of its geographical location rather than for any merit of its own. But it took this dusty little town centuries to come into its own as a major European city. Today, it boasts one of the world's best cultural scenes, with a triangle of top museums (the Prado, Reina Sofía and Thyssen-Bornemisza) that can stand up against collections anywhere on the globe. Beyond the museums, the lifeblood of the city flows through its streets and squares, which are every bit as important to Madrid culture. To really know Madrid, lose yourself in the tangled streets of the historic city, or in the whirring activity of Chueca and Huertas. It won't take you long to agree that, beautiful or not, Madrid sure is a looker.

HIGHLIGHTS

- See Velázquez's masterpiece *Las Meninas* at the world-famous **Museo del Prado** (p122)
- Join the fashionable *madrileños* strolling through **El Retiro park** (p125)
- Stay out till the wee hours, then feast on hot chocolate and *churros* (long, deep-fried doughnuts) at **Chocolatería San Ginés** (p147)
- Sit back with a *caña* (small beer) on the **Plaza de Santa Ana** (p147)
- Fight your way through the crowds at **El Rastro flea market** (p126)
- Take in a flamenco show at **Casa Patas** (p151)
- Explore the treasures of the **Palacio Real** (p119)
- Bar- or café-hop in lively **Chueca** (p148)
- Hit the streets around **Calle de Serrano** (p154) for window shopping guaranteed to make your wallet ache
- Check out the **live jazz** (p151) at joints such as Café Central, Populart or Calle 54

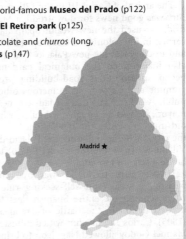

Madrid ★

| AREA: 505,000 SQ KM | POP: 3.09 MILLION | AVE SUMMER TEMP: HIGH 32°C, LOW 16°C |

HISTORY

Madrid was little more than a dusty stop along the road, when Felipe II declared it the seat of the Spanish empire in 1561. Though as early as the 10th century there was a Muslim settlement here called Magerit, the town was basically a blank slate for Felipe to create his capital upon. Nearby Toledo, already a rich and powerful city, would have been a more obvious choice for the capital, but as the headquarters of Spain's Church and its power-hungry clergy, it was too confining for Felipe's taste. The eager monarch preferred to start from scratch, forming an administrative centre, from which the spokes of power would reach into the furthest corners of the empire. Later historians would devise a more fitting background for the capital, claiming a Roman settlement on the site and adding in a few details about ruins that were supposedly found here.

In those first years the Buen Retiro Palace (now destroyed) and park were built for the royals' comfort, but little else was added to the city. The rulers and nobles hid away in posh palaces, while workers were left to wallow in a city that was fast earning the reputation as being Europe's filthiest. Madrid's population grew steadily as the city attracted civil servants, craftsmen and the cultured; writers such as Cervantes, Lope de Vega and Calderón all lived and worked here through the 17th century.

The arrival of Carlos III in the 18th century was good news for downtrodden Madrid. He used the new wealth Spain had earned in the colonies to clean up the city and to complete the new Palacio Real. He also inaugurated the botanical gardens, began an ambitious road-building programme and carried out numerous other public works. Known as 'Madrid's best mayor', he was an enlightened ruler, who did much to foster the intellectual life of the city, including building the Palacio de Villanueva (now the Museo del Prado) to house a science museum.

His successor, Carlos IV, was, by comparison, a weak and self-seeking ruler. After sending the entire Spanish fleet to its destruction in the Battle of Trafalgar (1805), Carlos and his dim-witted minister Manuel Godoy allowed Napoleon to bring his troops into Spain on their way to do battle with Portugal. Big mistake. Napoleon didn't think twice about sending in his brother Joseph to occupy Madrid, which the French held until 1813.

After a long, ugly campaign to oust the French, Fernando VII returned to a miserably poor Madrid to claim the crown, marking the restoration of the Bourbon family to the throne. But the country's problems were far from over. The turbulent Carlist wars followed, and political uncertainty persisted well into the 20th century. In 1931 the Second Republic was proclaimed in Madrid. Franco's troops first tried, but failed, to take the city in 1936. The subsequent siege, and the slow, grinding advance of his Nationalist forces, lasted until the civil war ended in 1939.

With Franco in power, a grey era began for the city that had resisted him for nearly three years. His death in 1975 unleashed a flood of pent-up energy, which took its most colourful form in the years of the *movida* – the endless party that swept up the city in a frenzy of creativity and open-minded freedom. Though Madrid has matured into its modern role as a respectable democratic capital, the partying still goes on.

ORIENTATION

In Spain, all roads lead to Madrid and, more specifically, to the Puerta del Sol, kilometre zero, the physical and emotional heart of the city. Radiating out from this harried plaza are arms – Calle Mayor, Calle del Arenal, Calle Preciados, Calle de la Montera and Calle de Alcalá – that stretch into the city.

South of the Puerta del Sol is the oldest part of the city, with Plaza Mayor to the southwest and the busy streets of the Huertas district to the southeast. North of the plaza is a modern shopping district, and beyond that, the east-west thoroughfare Gran Vía and the bohemian *barrio* (district or quarter of a town or city) Chueca. To the east is the stately Palacio Real, while to the west lies the city's lungs, El Retiro park.

The city is surrounded by a series of ring roads making maps of Madrid look something like a bull's-eye. Though often hellishly crowded, these highways are the best (and sometimes only) way to get out of the city and into the *comunidad autónoma* (autonomous community or region) that surrounds it.

(Continued on page 117)

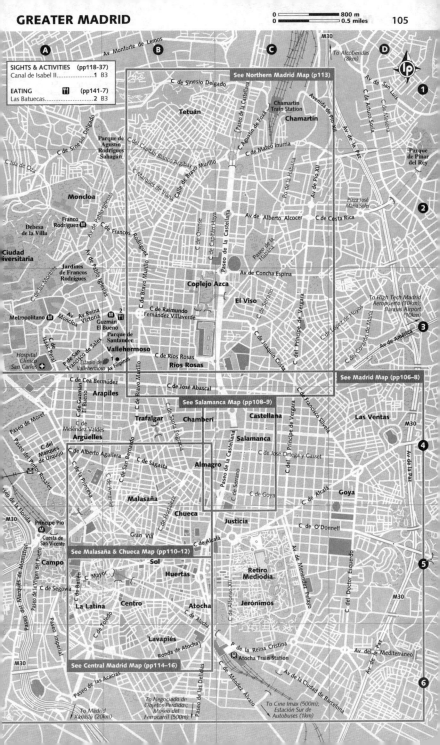

GREATER MADRID

Plaza del Cardenal Cisneros
Hospital Clínico San Carlos
Estudio de Vallehermoso
Vallehermoso
Plaza del Descubridor Diego de Ordás
Ríos Rosas

Av del Arco de la Victoria
Av de los Reyes Católicos
Plaza de Cristo Rey
Av de Filipinas
C de Cea Bermúdez
Jardines Enrique Herreros
Ríos Rosas

Av de Séneca
Av de Isaac Peral
Glorieta de Guzmán El Bueno
Arapiles
Canal
Canal
Glorieta del General Álvarez de Castro
C de José Abascal

Parque del Oeste
C de Fernando El Católico
C de Vallehermoso
C de Bravo Murillo
Glorieta del Pintor Sorolla
Iglesia
Paseo del General Martínez
Chamberí

C Ruperto Chapí
Plaza de la Moncloa
Moncloa
Calle de Meléndez Valdés
Glorieta de Quevedo
C de Eloy Gonzalo
Iglesia
Iglesia

Paseo de Moret
Plaza del Conde del Valle de Suchil
Quevedo
Trafalgar
Plaza de Olavide
Paseo de Eduardo D
Almagro

Argüelles
Argüelles
See Malasaña & Chueca Map (pp110–12)
Bilbao

Paseo del Pintor Rosales
C del Marqués de Urquijo
C de Alberto Aguilera
San Bernardo
Glorieta de Ruiz Jiménez
C de Carranza
Glorieta de Bilbao
Bilbao
Plaza de Alonso Martínez
Alonso Martínez

La Rosaleda
C de la Princesa
C de Santa Cruz de Marcenado
San Bernardo
C de Sagasta
Plaza de Alonso Martínez

Río Manzanares
Paseo del Marqués de Monistrol
Ventura Rodríguez
Plaza de las Comendadoras
Plaza del Dos de Mayo
Tribunal
Jardines Arquitecto Ribera
Plaza de Santa Bárbara

Parque de la Montaña
Plaza del Marqués de Cerralbo
Plaza de Guardias de Corps
Plaza del Conde de Toreno
Plaza de Juan Pujol
Malasaña
Chueca

Jardines de Ferraz
Plaza de Emilio Jiménez Millas
Plaza de España
Noviciado
Plaza de San Ildefonso

Príncipe Pío
Cuesta de San Vicente
Plaza de España
Plaza de Mostenses
Gran Vía
Plaza de Chueca
Recoletos

Casa de Campo
Glorieta San Antonio de la Florida
Príncipe Pío
Cuesta de San Vicente
Jardines de Sabatini
Plaza de la Marina Española
Plaza de Santa María Soledad
Gran Vía
Plaza del Rey

To Parque de Atracciones de la Casa del Campo (3km)
Puente del Rey
Jardines Cabo Noval
Plaza de la Encarnación
Santo Domingo
Plaza de Santo Domingo
Callao
Gran Vía
Gran Vía
Plaza de Callao
Plaza de la Red de San Luis

Campo del Moro
See Central Madrid Map (pp114–16)
Santo Domingo
Plaza de San Martín las Descalzas
Plaza del Carmen
Sevilla
C de Alcalá
Banco de España

To Pool (800m); Tennis Courts (800m); Zoo (4km)
Glorieta de Asorín
Parque de Atenas
Glorieta de Boccherini
C Mayor
Arenal
Sol
Carrera de San Jerónimo
Sevilla

Puente de Segovia
C de Segovia
Jardines de las Vistillas
Plaza de Gabriel Miró
C Mayor
Sol
Sol
Carreras
Plaza de Canalejas
Huertas

Parque de Caramuel
La Latina
C de Segovia
Plaza de Santa Ana
Plaza de Matute
Plaza de Jesús

Río Manzanares
Carrera de San Francisco
Plaza de la Cebada
Plaza del Duque de Alba
Tirso de Molina
C de la Magdalena
Antón Martín
Plaza de Antón Martín
Plaza de San Juan
Plaza de Platería Martínez

Gran Vía de San Francisco
Plaza de San Francisco
La Latina
Plaza de Cascorro
El Rastro
Antón Martín
C de Atocha
Atocha

Ronda de Segovia
Plaza General Vara del Rey
Plaza de Lavapiés
Plaza de Emperador Carlos V

Puente de San Isidro
Paseo Imperial
C de Toledo
Puerta de Toledo
Glorieta de Puerta de Toledo
Plaza Campillo del Mundo Nuevo
Jardín del Rastro
Lavapiés
Ronda de Atocha

Av de Manzanares
Paseo de la Ermita del Santo
Ronda de Segovia
Puerto de los Pontones
Plaza de Francisco Morano
Ronda de Toledo
Glorieta de Embajadores
Ronda de Valencia
Embajadores

Paseo de los Pontones
C del Toledo
Paseo de los Olmos
Paseo de las Acacias
Acacias
C de Embajadores

Jardines de Doña Concha Piquer
Pirámides
Plaza de Ortega y Munilla
Paseo del Doctor Vallejo
Paseo de la Esperanza
Nájera
Palos de la Frontera
C de Tarragona

Paseo de los Melancólicos
To Negociado de Objetos Perdidos (500m); Museo del Ferrocarril (700m)
Paseo de las Delicias

INFORMATION

Andorra Embassy..............................(see 1)
Andorra Tourism Office.........................**1** E3
Anglo-American Medical Unit..................**2** E3
Bookstalls...**3** E5
British Council.....................................**4** D1
Ermita de San Isidro.............................**5** A6
French Embassy...................................**6** E3
Fundación Triángulo.............................**7** C1

SIGHTS & ACTIVITIES　　　(pp118–37)

Antigua Estación de Atocha....................**8** E5
Casón del Buen Retiro............................**9** E4
Cementerio de la Florida......................**10** A3
El Ángel Caído....................................**11** E5
Entry to Campo del Moro......................**12** A4
Ermita de San Antonio de la Florida......**13** A3
Estadio Vicente Calderón.....................**14** A6
Faro de Moncloa.................................**15** A1
Iglesia de San Jerónimo el Real............**16** E4
La Rosaleda (Rose Garden)...................**17** F5
Mausoleum of Alfonso XII.................(see 18)
Monumento a Alfonso XII......................**18** E4
Museo Casa de la Moneda....................**19** G3

Museo de América................................**20** A1
Museo de Artes Decorativos..................**21** E4
Museo de los Carruajes.........................**22** A4
Museo del Ejército...............................**23** E4
Museo del Traje..................................**24** A1
Palacio de Cristal................................**25** F4
Palacio de Exposiciones........................**26** F4
Parque Secreto...................................**27** C2
Plaza de Toros Monumental de las
　Ventas..**28** H2
Polideportivo La Chopera.....................**29** E5
Polideportivo Virgen del Puerto.............**30** A4
Puente de Segovia...............................**31** A4
Puerta de Alcalá.................................**32** E4
Real Academia Española de la Lengua....**33** E4
Real Fábrica de Tapices........................**34** F6
Templo de Debod.................................**35** B3

EATING　　🍴　　(pp141–7)

Balzac...**36** E4
Casa Domingo....................................**37** E3
El Pescador..**38** G2
Goizeko Wellington.............................**39** E3
Mallorca..**40** E3

Sambar Kanda...................................(see 8)

DRINKING　　🍸　　(pp147–9)

Geographic Club.................................**41** F3
Independencia....................................**42** E3

ENTERTAINMENT　　🎭　　(pp150–54)

Galileo Galilei....................................**43** C1
La Cripta Mágica................................**44** D6
La Riviera..**45** A5
Sala Divino..**46** A5

SHOPPING　　🛍　　(pp154–6)

BD Madrid...**47** E3
Farrutx...**48** E3

TRANSPORT　　　(pp157–8)

AutoRes Bus Station............................**49** G6
Bus No 601 (El Pardo)..........................**50** B2
Teleférico..**51** A2

OTHER

Escuela Oficial de Idiomas....................**52** B1
Real Automovil Club de España.............**53** D1

SALAMANCA KEY (p109)

INFORMATION

Alliance Française.................................**1** D2
Canadian Embassy.................................**2** D5
German Embassy...................................**3** B4
Goethe Institut.....................................**4** A4
Institut Français...................................**5** A6
Irish Embassy......................................**6** B2
UK Consulate......................................**7** A5
UK Embassy..**8** A4
US Embassy..**9** C2
Work Center.......................................**10** D5

SIGHTS & ACTIVITIES　　(pp118–37)

Biblioteca Nacional...........................(see 16)
Monumento a
　Colón...**11** B6

Monumento al Descubrimiento.............**12** B5
Museo Arqueológico Nacional..............**13** B6
Museo de Cera....................................**14** A6
Museo de la Escultura
　Abstracta...**15** B2
Museo del Libro..................................**16** B6
Museo Lázaro Galdiano........................**17** C1
Museo Sorolla....................................**18** A1

EATING　　🍴　　(pp141–7)

El Lateral..**19** D4
El Septimo..**20** C2
Estay...**21** D5

DRINKING　　🍸　　(pp147–9)

Terrabacus Vinoteca............................**22** C4

ENTERTAINMENT　　🎭　　(pp150–54)

Centro Cultural de la Villa....................**23** B5

SHOPPING　　🛍　　(pp154–6)

ABC Serrano......................................**24** C3
Alcolea..**25** D6
Amaya Arzuaga..................................**26** C5
Camper...**27** C4
El Corte Inglés...................................**28** C4
Lladró..**29** C4
Loewe..**30** B6
Purificación García.............................**31** B6
Tous & Tous......................................**32** C4

TRANSPORT　　　(pp157–8)

Airport Bus.......................................**33** B5

0   200 m
0   0.1 miles

A   **B**   **C**   **D**

C de García de Paredes

Gregorio Marañón

17

C de López de Hoyos

C del General Oráa

C de Velázquez

Paseo de la Castellana

C de los Hermanos Bécquer

1

Glorieta de Emilio Castelar

eo del General Martínez Campos   18

C de Diego de León

20

Castellana

C de Miguel Ángel

C de Fortuny

9

C de Rafael Calvo

C de Maldonado

2

C de Alfonso X

Rubén Darío

C de Juan Bravo

1

6

C de Juan Bravo

Glorieta de Rubén Darío

Paseo de Eduardo Dato

15

Núñez de Balboa

Rubén Darío

C de Lagasca

Puente de Enrique de la Mata Gorostizaga

C de Jenner

24

C de Serrano

C de Padilla

C de Marqués de Villamejor

C de Claudio Coello

Salamanca

3

C del Marqués de Riscal

C de Fortuny

3

C de José Ortega y Gasset

See Malasaña & Chueca Map (pp110–12)

4

C de Zurbarán

29

C de Monte Esquinza

28

32

Almagro

C del Marqués de Villamagna

C de Don Ramón de la Cruz

C de Zurbano

Almagro

C de Amador de los Ríos

22

19

C de Velázquez

C de Núñez de Balboa

4

C de Fernando el Santo

8

C de Ayala

27

C de Orfila

C de Alcalá Galiano

C de Claudio Coello

e Génova

@ 10

C de la Hermosilla

21

5

C de García Gutiérrez

Torres de Colón

26

Recoletos

Orellana

Colón

P

Plaza de la Villa de Paris

7

Colón

Paseo de la Castellana

C de Marqués Zugena

C de Lagasca

2

Velázquez

5

14

Plaza de Colón

23

33

Serrano

12

Serrano

C de Goya

30

11

Jardines de Descubrimiento

31

16

13

C de Jorge Juan

6

e Bárbara de Bragança

Recoletos

C de Villanueva

C de Jorge Juan

25

P

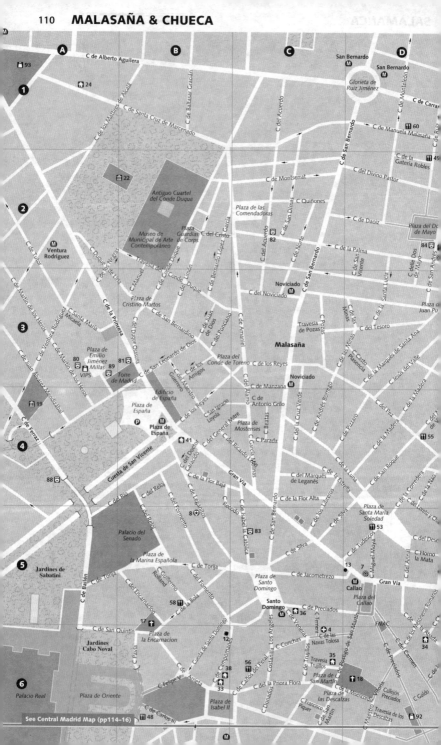

0 — 600 m
0 — 0.4 miles

See Madrid Map (pp106–8)

A   B   C   D

1

2

3

4

5

6

Plaza de Oriente
Statue of Felipe IV
C de Felipe V   Arrieta
Plaza de Isabel II
C de Carlos III
● 40
Ópera
C Francisco Canto Martín
Plaza de las Descalzas
C de la Misericordia
Plaza de Celenque
Travesia de los Descalzas
C de Tetuán
C de Galda

Plaza de la Armería
Jardines de Lepanto
C de Requena
C de Noblejas
Plaza de Ramales
C de Vergara
C de la
Amnistía
C de las Fuentes
C de Escalinata
109
104
C del Arenal
la Pue
del S

38
P
C de la Cruzada
114
96
C del Conde de Lemos
Plaza Herradores
Plaza de San Ginés
61
Sol   70

Plaza de Santiago
C de Santiago
78
Costanilla de Santiago
C Mayor
5
79
@
1

22
C del Biombo
Plaza del Biombo
Juan de Herrera
30
Plaza del Comandante las Morenas
19
Plaza Mayor
46
C del Marqués
Viudo de Pontejos
43
118

6
C Mayor
26
15
C del Duque
113
21
Plaza de San Miguel
77
45
74
9
C de Zaragoza
Plaza de Santa Cruz
117
C de la Bolsa

33
Cuesta de la Vega
32
Plaza de la Villa
18
C del Sacramento
C del Rollo
C de
Antón
Plaza del Conde de Miranda
Plaza del Conde de Barajas
110
80
C del Maestro Villa
C de
Gómez de
C de la Concepción
Plaza de la Provincia
Exteriores
53
27
Plaza Jaci
Benav

Parque del Emir Mohamed I
C de Bailén
Plaza de la Villa
Plaza de la Cruz Verde
Plaza del Alamillo
Condé
Plaza del Cordón
C de Segovia
Plaza de Puerta Cerrada
82
C del Nuncio
Plaza de Segovia Nueva
60
C de la Colegiada
Tirso de Molina

Jardines de las Vistillas
Costanilla de Ramón
103
Plaza de la Morería
Plaza de la Paja
C del Príncipe Anglona
31
93
66
87
59
Instituto de San Isidro
Plaza de Tirso de Molina

Plaza de Gabriel Miró
Plaza de Granado
85
63
92
67
88
81
58
57
Plaza del Humilladero
28
Plaza de la Puerta Cerrada
86
Plaza del Duque de Alba
C del Duque de Alba
C Soler y González

Plaza de San Francisco
16
Carrera de San Francisco
La Latina
Plaza de Oriente
Plaza de San Andrés
Plaza de la Puerta de Moros
76
39
La Latina
C de las Maldonadas
Plaza de Cascorro
El Rastro

Gran Vía de San Francisco
C de Calatrava
C del Ángel
C de Don Pedro
C del Mediodía Grande
C de Sierpe
C de López Silva
C de las Hermanas
C de Abades
C del Oso

Rosario
C de la Ventosa
C de la Paloma
Plaza Genral Vara del Rey
C de santa Ana
115

Ronda de Segovia
Travesía de Gilinch
C de Aguila
C del Carnero
Centro Comercial de la Puerta de Toledo
Callejón Mellizo
C de Carlos Arniches
C de Rodas

P
C de Toledo
C de Capitán San Martínez
35
Mira el Río Baja
C Mira el Sol

Glorieta de Puerta de Toledo
Puerta de Toledo
13
Plaza Campillo del Mundo Nuevo

Puerto de los Pontones
Paseo de los Olmos
C de Toledo
C del Concejal Benito Martín
Jardín del Rastro
Ronda de Toledo

San Isidro de Sevilla Gasómetro

(Continued from page 104)

INFORMATION
Bookshops
Bookstalls (Map pp106-8; Cuesta de Claudio Moyano) On the southern edge of the botanical gardens, a row of 30-odd bookstalls burst with second-hand books, mostly in Spanish.

Casa del Libro (Map pp110-12; ☎ 91 524 19 00; Gran Vía 29) At Spain's answer to Barnes & Nobles, there's a large English- and foreign-language literature section.

Librería Desnivel (Map pp114-16; ☎ 902 248848; Plaza Matute 6) Focused on hiking, travel and outdoor sports.

Petra's International Bookshop (Map pp114-16; ☎ 91 541 72 91; Calle de Campomanes 13) A lively expat community hosts conversation groups at this English-language bookshop.

Cultural Centres
If you're yearning for a whiff of home, consider wandering into one of the foreign cultural centres. They all have libraries and organise film nights and other activities.

British Council (Map pp106-8; ☎ 91 337 35 00; Paseo del General Martínez Campos 31)

Casa de América (Map pp110-12; ☎ 91 595 48 00; Paseo de los Recoletos 2)

Goethe Institut (Map pp108-9; ☎ 91 391 39 44; Calle de Zurbarán 21)

Institut Français (Map pp108-9; ☎ 91 700 48 00; Calle del Marqués de la Ensenada 12)

Istituto Italiano di Cultura (Map pp114-16; ☎ 91 547 86 02; Calle Mayor 86)

Emergency
Ambulance (☎ 061)
Crime Reports (☎ 902 102112)
Cruz Roja (Red Cross; ☎ 91 522 22 22)
Jefatura de Policía (Police Station; Map pp110-12; ☎ 91 541 05 35; Calle de Leganitos 19)
Medical & Fire Emergencies (☎ 112)
Police (☎ 091)

Internet Access
Internet cafés seem to open and close faster than elevator doors, but you're almost guaranteed to find a high-speed connection if you poke around the streets surrounding the Puerta del Sol, Plaza Mayor and intersection of Gran Vía and Calle de Montera.

BBiGG (Map pp110-12; ☎ 91 521 92 07; www.bbigg .com; Calle de Alcalá 21; per hr €2; ☯ 9am-midnight Sun-Thu, 9-2am Fri & Sat) You'll find another branch at Calle Mayor 1 (Map pp114-16; metro Sol).

Ciber Zahara (Map pp110-12; ☎ 91 521 84 24; Gran Vía 31; per 50min €3; ☯ 9-12.30am Sun-Thu, 9-1.30am

> ### MADRID IN TWO DAYS
> Start with breakfast in the Plaza de Santa Ana and then a visit to the Prado Museum. Afterwards, walk around El Retiro, but save energy for the Palacio Real and afternoon shopping and tapas in Chueca. At night, catch a flamenco show.
>
> On day two, sign up for the tourist office's walking tour of historic Madrid, and then visit either the Thyssen-Bornemisza or the Reina Sofía art museum. At night, head to Viva Madrid for drinks in uniquely *madrileño*-style.

Fri-Sat) A coin-operated computer lab sits above this noisy cafeteria.

Enjoy Express (Map pp110-12; ☎ 91 521 79 79; Gran Vía 46; per hr €2; ☯ 8am-midnight)

Nets (Map pp110-12; ☎ 91 522 20 17; Calle de la Palma 24; per hr €1.50; ☯ noon-1am Mon-Sat, noon-midnight Sun) To just skim email, you can log on for up to five minutes for free.

Work Center (Map pp114-16; ☎ 91 360 13 95; www .workcenter.es in Spanish; Calle del Príncipe 1; per hr €2; ☯ 24hr) Find other branches of this photocopy-fax-Net centre at Paseo de la Castellana 149 (Map p113; ☎ 91 121 76 30) and Calle de Velázquez 41 (Map pp108-9; ☎ 91 781 22 56; metro Velázquez.)

Laundry
Lavandería Cervantes (Map pp114-16; ☎ 91 429 92 16; Calle de León 6; ☯ 9am-9pm; per load €2)

Onda Blu (Map pp114-16; ☎ 91 369 50 71; www.onda blu.com in Spanish & Italian; Calle de León 3; per 8kg load €3.50; ☯ 9am-10.30pm)

Left Luggage
Both Chamartín and Atocha train stations have *consignas* (lockers), where you can leave luggage for €3 per day. If you're leaving large boxes or suitcases, the Estación Sur bus station is better; you check your belongings into a large storage room and pay by the day.

Two left-luggage offices operate at the airport, one in the T1 terminal (near the bus stop and taxi stand) and the other in T2 (near the metro entrance).

Lost Property
You can try looking for lost property at the **Negociado de Objetos Perdidos** (☎ 91 588 43 46; Plaza de Legazpi 7; ☯ 9am-2pm). The nearest metro station is Legazpi.

MADRID

If you leave something in a taxi, call ☎ 91 588 43 44. If you lose something on a local train, check at the information desk at Atocha train station.

Medical Services

Anglo-American Medical Unit (Map pp114-16; ☎ 91 435 18 23; Calle Conde de Aranda 1; metro Retiro) For help in English.

Centro de Salud (Map p113; ☎ 91 517 83 03; Calle de Bravo Murillo 317; ◷ 8am-8pm)

Farmacia del Globo (Map pp114-16; ☎ 91 369 20 00; Plaza Antón Martín 46; ◷ 24hr)

Farmacia Mayor (Map pp114-16; ☎ 91 366 46 16; Calle Mayor 13; ◷ 24hr) For help with minor medical problems, ask a pharmacist.

Money

Large banks such as Caja de Madrid usually have the best exchange rates, but check their commissions. Banks usually open 8.30am to 2pm weekdays, and until 1pm Saturday (except during the winter months, when they are only open weekdays). Using your ATM card will give you these same low bank rates, no matter where or what time of day you use it.

If you're desperate, around Puerta del Sol and Plaza Mayor there are plenty of *bureaux de change*, which have the predictable rip-off rates but are often open until midnight.

Post

Post Office (Map pp110-12; ☎ 91 396 24 43; www .correos.es; Plaza Cibeles; ◷ 8.30am-9.30pm Mon-Sat) The main post office is in the gigantic Palacio de Comunicaciones. Other branches are dotted throughout the city.

Tourist Information

The city's general-information telephone line (☎ 010) deals with everything from public transport to shows. You can also try the Comunidad de Madrid's regional information line (☎ 012). Finally, there is a nationwide tourist information line (☎ 902 100007; www.comadrid.es/turismo).

Municipal tourist office (Map pp114-16; ☎ 91 366 54 77; www.munimadrid.es; Plaza Mayor 3; ◷ 10am-8pm Mon-Sat, 10am-3pm Sun)

Regional tourist office (Map pp114-16; ☎ 91 429 49 51, 902 100007; www.madrid.org in Spanish; Calle del Duque de Medinaceli 2; ◷ 9am-7pm Mon-Sat, 9am-3pm Sun) There are also tourist offices at Barajas Airport, Chamartín train station and Atocha train station.

DANGERS & ANNOYANCES

Madrid is not a dangerous city, but you need to be constantly aware of pickpockets, especially in touristy areas such as Plaza Mayor (where thieves are astonishingly brash), Huertas and Chueca. The prostitution (and the slimy clients it attracts) along Calle de la Montera and in the Casa de Campo park means that you need to exercise extra caution in these areas. Females walking alone should try not to linger here, even if you're just looking at a map, as it could give the wrong idea.

Scams

Be on the lookout for classic scams like the old bird-dropping trick: a thief will drop something brown on you then help you clean it off as he helps himself to your wallet. Another common scheme is the group of 'lost' kids, who will crowd around you with a map and sneak away with your stuff as you give directions. Of course, the grab-the-bag-and-run technique is still as popular as ever, as are attempts to reach into your back pocket or to unzip your backpack as you walk.

SIGHTS

No one should leave Madrid without dedicating at least a morning to Spain's temple of art, El Museo del Prado. If you have time and like the idea of seeing priceless masterpieces up close and personal, also be sure to stop by the Centro de Arte Reina Sofía, packed with modern Spanish art, and the Museo Thyssen-Bornemisza, with its fantastic variety of styles and periods.

This triangle of art is one of the city's major attractions, but don't plan to spend your entire trip cooped up in museums. Madrid's charm hides in the maze-like streets of the district of Los Austrias and in the bustle around Plaza Mayor. History comes alive in the Palacio Real and the Convento de las Descalzas Reales, while modern Madrid shows its energy in El Rastro market and the green Parque del Retiro.

Los Austrias & Centro

Madrid's oldest quarter, **Madrid de los Austrias**, is a charming district that's so called because many of its buildings were put up during the reign of the Austrian Habsburgs. The streets wind and twist their way past small squares and stately old palaces where nobles once lived. These days this is a stylish *barrio* that houses many of the city's major sights.

PLAZA MAYOR

Projected in the 17th century by Felipe III (whose statue adorns its centre), the arcaded **Plaza Mayor** (Map pp114–16) was designed by Juan Gómez de Mora and built atop a modest fairground that once sat outside the city walls. Once built, the plaza was the site of bullfights, spectacles, public executions and a fresh market, serving as the centre of city trade and life. The harmonious plaza that today we see lined with touristy bars is the result of three separate fires and subsequent re-buildings through the years, but the greatest aesthetic changes came in the early 1990s, when the historic plaza was renovated and huge, colourful frescoes were added to the façade of the **Casa de la Panadería**.

PALACIO REAL

Spain's lavish **Palacio Real** (Royal Palace; Map pp114-16; ☎ 91 542 00 59; Calle de Bailén s/n; adult/child €9/3.50; ☼ 9.30am-5pm Mon-Sat, 9am-2pm Sun Oct-Mar; 9am-6pm Mon-Sat, 9am-3pm Sun Apr-Sep) is a jewel box of a palace, with priceless tapestries, paintings, frescoes, statues and more crowded into every nook and cranny. Used only occasionally for royal ceremonies (the royal family went to live in the more modest Palacio de la Zarzuela years ago), the palace is an interesting way to learn more about the Bourbon dynasty in Spain.

When the old Alcázar, a patchwork of Austrian improvements atop an Islamic fortress, burned down on this spot on Christmas Day 1734, Felipe V immediately went about planning a splendid palace intended to outshine the royal residences of his European rivals. It was designed by Italian master architect Filippo Juvarra, who unfortunately up and died as soon as the designs were finished. The mammoth project was actually carried out, on a smaller scale than originally planned, by the master's student, Giovanni Battista. The final tally of 2800 rooms was nearly a quarter of the size of the monstrosity originally planned.

Shuffle through the official tour to see 50 of the palace rooms, which hold a good selection of Goyas, 215 absurdly ornate clocks from the Royal Clock Collection and five Stradivarius violins still used for concerts and balls. Most of the tapestries in the palace were made in the Royal Tapestry Factory, and all the chandeliers are original. The **main stairway** is a grand statement of imperial power, leading first to the Halberdiers' rooms and eventually to the **Salón del Trono** (Throne Room). This sumptuous room has crimson-velvet wall coverings complemented by a Tiepolo ceiling. Shortly after, you reach the **Salón de Gasparini**, its exquisite stucco ceiling and walls resplendent with embroidered silks.

Outside the main palace, visit the **Farmacia Real**, at the southern end of the patio known as the **Plaza de Armas** (or Plaza de la Armería). The pharmacy is an endless parade of medicine jars and stills for mixing royal concoctions. Westwards across the plaza is the **Armería Real** (Royal Armoury), a shiny collection of weapons and armour, mostly dating from the 16th and 17th centuries. The full suits of armour, such as those of Felipe III, are among the most striking items on show.

The palace closes on days when official receptions are held.

PLAZA DE ORIENTE

Practically forming the Palacio Real's front lawn is the **Plaza de Oriente**, a luxurious garden lined with statues of monarchs and nobles, many of which had been destined to adorn the roof of the Palacio Real until Carlos III said they were too heavy. This was the site of the old Alcázar until it burned down in 1734; the square was cleared by French occupier Joseph Bonaparte but only laid out in 1844.

On the eastern side of the square is the ill-fated **Teatro Real** (Map pp114-16; ☎ 91 516 06 60; www.teatro-real.com; Plaza de Oriente), the city's opera house. Started in 1818, it was finished in 1850 but has since burned down, been blown up in the civil war, and been shuttered up for decades. After a €100-million renovation in the late 1990s, it's finally ready to claim its role as Madrid's premier stage. **Guided visits** (adult/child €4/2; ☼ every 15min 10.30am-1.30pm Wed-Mon) are available, and no reservations are necessary.

CAMPO DEL MORO & JARDINES DE SABATINI

In proper palace style, lush gardens surround the Palacio Real. To the north are the formal (if slightly neglected) French-style **Jardines de Sabatini** (Map pp110–12). Directly behind the palace are the forest and fountains of the **Campo del Moro**, so named because this

MADRID

is where the Muslim army camped before a 12th-century attack on the Alcázar. Now shady paths, a thatch-roofed pagoda and palace views are the main attractions.

CATEDRAL DE NUESTRA SEÑORA DE LA ALMUDENA

Sitting just beside the Palacio Real, **Catedral de Nuestra Señora de la Almudena** (Map pp114-16; ☎ 91 542 22 00; Calle de Bailén; ☷ 10am-2pm & 5-9pm) is a gleaming white, cavernous temple dedicated to the city's patroness. Its construction began in 1883 but wasn't finished until 1993. Amazingly, this is the first cathedral ever to be built in the capital of Catholic Spain. Until it was finished, the Basílica de San Isidro on Calle de Toledo had functioned as the city's leading church.

The cathedral was originally intended to be a neo-Gothic creation. What we see today is a neoclassical structure with plenty of adornment but little real charm. In May 2004 the heir to the Spanish throne, Felipe de Borbón, was married here to Doña Letizia Ortiz in a splendorous but solemn ceremony.

MURALLA ÁRABE

Behind the cathedral apse, and down Cuesta de la Vega, is a short stretch of the so-called **Arab Wall** (Map pp114-16), the city wall built by Madrid's early medieval Islamic rulers. Some of it dates as far back as the 9th century, when the initial Islamic fort was raised. In summer, there are open-air performances.

PLAZA DE LA VILLA

Though it has served as Spain's capital for nearly half a millennium, Madrid is still officially a *villa* (small town), not a city. So it's in the **Plaza de la Villa** (Map pp114-16), off Calle Mayor, that town business is conducted. On the western side of the square is the 17th-century **Ayuntamiento** (town hall) with its Herrerian slate-tile spires and Habsburg baroque style. On the opposite side of the square is the Gothic-esque **Casa de los Lujanes**, whose brickwork tower is said to have been 'home' to the imprisoned French monarch François I, after his capture in the Battle of Pavia. Perhaps the most interesting building on the square is the Plateresque **Casa de Cisneros**, built in 1537.

MONASTERIO DE LAS DESCALZAS REALES

Built in the 1500s as a gentleman's palace, this rather plain-fronted building is home to the luxurious **Monasterio de las Descalzas Reales** (Convent of the Barefoot Royals; Map pp110-12; ☎ 91 554 88 00; www.patrimonionacional.es; Plaza de las Descalzas; adult/child €5/2.50; ☷ 10.30am-12.45pm & 4-5.45pm Tue-Thu & Sat, 10.30am-12.45pm Fri, 11am-1.45pm Sun, last admission 30min before closing). Founded in 1559 by Juana of Austria, the widowed daughter of the Spanish king Carlos I, the convent was named after the simple sandals these Franciscan nuns wore. The convent quickly became one of Spain's richest religious houses thanks to gifts from Juana's noble friends, many of whom joined the order and adorned the place with their favourite sculptures and paintings. On the obligatory guided tour you'll see a number of tapestries based on works by Rubens, and a wonderful painting entitled *The Voyage of the 11,000 Virgins*. Some 30 nuns still live here.

MONASTERIO DE LA ENCARNACIÓN

Though not as well known as the Monasterio de las Descalzas Reales, this Augustine order is nevertheless an interesting stop. The **Monasterio de la Encarnación** (Monastery of the Incarnation; Map pp110-12; ☎ 91 547 05 10; Plaza de la Encarnación; adult/child €3.60/2, EU citizens free Wed; ☷ 10.30am-12.30pm & 4-5.30pm Wed & Sat, 10am-2pm Sun) was founded by Empress Margarita de Austria, and is still inhabited by nuns of the Augustine order. Inside there is a unique collection of 17th- and 18th-century sculptures and paintings, as well as a handful of silver and gold reliquaries. The most famous of these contains the blood of San Pantaleón, which purportedly liquefies every year on 28 June, drawing throngs of the curious and the faithful.

You can buy a combined ticket (€6) to both the Monasterio de la Encarnación and the Monasterio de las Descalzas Reales.

IGLESIA DE SAN NICOLÁS DE LOS SERVITAS

Considered Madrid's oldest surviving church, **Iglesia de San Nicolás de los Servitas** (Map pp114-16; ☎ 91 559 40 64; Plaza de San Nicolás; ☷ during services) may well have been built on the site of Muslim Magerit's second mosque – if such a mosque existed. Apart from the restored 12th-century Mudéjar bell tower, most of the present church dates to the 15th century.

IGLESIA DE SAN GINÉS

Between Calle Mayor and Calle del Arenal, north of Plaza Mayor, **Iglesia de San Ginés** (Map pp114-16; Calle del Arenal 13; ⏰ during services) is another of Madrid's oldest churches and has been here since at least the 14th century. It houses some fine paintings, including an El Greco, but is only open for services.

Sol, Huertas & Atocha
This lively central quarter is known more for its shops and bars than for its cultural offerings, but there are a few monuments and museums worth seeking out.

PUERTA DEL SOL
Madrid's kilometre zero, this busy **square** is in constant movement, with street vendors flaunting wares, tourists and locals marching past and a major bus stop bringing in passengers from across the city. It comes into its own on New Year's Eve, when all Madrid packs into the square waiting for the clock that gives Spain its official time to strike midnight, as the rest of Spain watches on TV.

The Puerta del Sol (Sun Gate) was once the easternmost gate into the city, but it's now in the dead centre of Madrid. Look out for the statue of a bear nuzzling a *madroño* (strawberry tree); this is the symbol of the city.

BARRIO DE LAS LETRAS
The area around Plaza de Santa Ana is often referred to as the **Barrio de las Letras** (Literature District), because of the writers who lived here during Spain's golden age of the 16th and 17th centuries. Many writers have left their mark in the form of street names and small plaques, so keep your eyes open.

Miguel de Cervantes was originally buried in the baroque **Convento de las Trinitarias** (Map pp114-16; closed to the public) and a commemorative Mass is held for him every year on the anniversary of his death, 23 April. Cervantes' house is long gone, but it once sat at Calle de Cervantes 2. Just down the street is the **Casa de Lope de Vega** (House of Lope de Vega; Map pp114-16; ☎ 91 429 92 16; Calle de Cervantes 11; admission €2, Sat free; ⏰ 9.30am-2pm Tue-Fri, 10am-2pm Sat), which is now a museum about the great writer's life and work. The playwright lived here for 25 years until his death in 1635, and the place is filled with memorabilia related to his life and times.

ANTIGUA ESTACIÓN DE ATOCHA
Walking into the old **Atocha train station** is like walking into a lush greenhouse. The AVE (Tren de Alta Velocidad Española) high-speed train departure lounge is one big botanical garden – a moist green burst of life inside the pretty old station. There is a fine restaurant Sambar Kanda (p143), and plenty of benches for waiting, though thanks to the misty air (the watering system) it can get awfully sweaty in here.

REAL FÁBRICA DE TAPICES
Fancy a wall tapestry or a rug based on some of Goya's sketches? The **Real Fábrica de Tapices** (Royal Tapestry Factory; Map pp106-8; ☎ 91 434 05 51; Calle de Fuenterrabía 2; admission €2; ⏰ 10am-2pm Mon-Fri) can whip one up for you in just a few months for a measly €10,000 or so. Founded in 1720 to provide the royal family and other bigwigs with tapestries befitting their grandeur, this workshop is still producing works today. The Ritz hotel is a regular client, as is the current royal family. Many works are based on cartoons by Goya, who was a long-time employee here creating 63 different drawings to use as models for elaborate tapestries.

Paseo del Prado & El Retiro
Home to Madrid's three top museums, the Prado, Reina Sofía and Thyssen-Bornemisza, the Paseo del Prado has been justly dubbed the 'Paseo del Arte' (Art Boulevard) and is truly one of the world's most thrilling areas for art lovers. At any of these museums you can buy a combined entry ticket (€7.65) that will get you into all three.

MUSEO DEL PRADO
One of the world's top museums, the **Museo del Prado** (Map pp114-16; ☎ 91 330 28 00; http://museo prado.mcu.es; Palacio de Villanueva, Paseo del Prado; adult/student/under 18 €3/1.50/free, admission free Sun; ⏰ 9am-7pm Tue-Sun, last admission 6.30pm) has a privileged collection of Spanish and European art, much of it originally from royal collections. Built towards the end of the 18th century in the Prado (Meadow) de los Jerónimos, the Palacio de Villanueva was originally conceived as a science museum. It later endured a brief spell as cavalry barracks during the Napoleonic occupation, and finally opened as an art gallery in 1819, under Fernando VII.

The Prado has a peerless collection of Spanish art and is best known for its extensive collection of works by three of Spain's greatest artists: Velázquez, Goya and El Greco. You can't help but get a solid lesson in Spanish art history here, but don't overlook the museum's important collections of Flemish and Italian art, both on the ground floor. The extensive collection demands a long visit; to really soak in the art on show you should plan to come more than once, but don't even think about trying to see El Prado in less than three hours.

For the past few years the Prado has been in the midst of a major renovation project that will allow it to stretch its arms a bit further. The museum's main building, the Palacio de Villanueva, has been fixed up, and the secondary building, the Casón del Retiro, is partially closed because of work going on there as well. Eventually the Prado's collection will enjoy a privileged setting, covering the newly updated Palacio de Villanueva, the Casón del Prado and a neighbouring building that currently houses the Museo del Ejército (p126). All that means that visitors will need to spend more time than ever in the museum to hit all the highlights!

Velázquez

The Prado has more than 50 works of Felipe IV's official court painter, Diego Rodríguez de Silva Velázquez (1599–1660). The collection includes his 1656 masterpiece of realism *Las Meninas* (Maids of Honour), originally called *La Familia de Felipe IV*. It depicts Velázquez himself on the left and, in the centre, the Infanta Margarita. There is more to it than that, though: the artist portrays himself painting the king and queen, whose images appear in mirrors behind Velázquez. This painting is so beloved because of the mastery of light, colour, space and depth.

Other Velázquez works to look out for are *Las Hilanderas* (The Spinners, 1650), supposedly inspired by a visit to the Real Fábrica de Tapices, *La Infanta Doña Margarita de Austria* (who stars in *Las Meninas*) and *Baltasar Carlos a Caballo*. *Cristo Crucificado*, which conveys the agony of the Crucifixion with great dignity. *La Rendición de Breda* (The Surrender of Breda) is another classic. You'll find all these works on the 1st floor, in Rooms 12, 14, 15, 15a, 16 and 27.

Goya

The impossibly diverse works of Francisco José de Goya y Lucientes (1746–1828) range from religious paintings and passionate portraits to grotesque war images. Late to reach

the heights of his grandeur, Goya, more than anyone, captured the extremes of hope and misery his country experienced before, during and after the Napoleonic invasion. The horrors of war had a profound effect on Goya's view of the world. *El Dos de Mayo* and, even more dramatically, *El Tres de Mayo* bring to life the 1808 anti-French revolt and subsequent execution of insurgents in Madrid. They're both on the 1st floor.

On the 2nd floor hang probably his best-known and most intriguing oils, *La Maja Vestida* (The Dressed Beauty) and *La Maja Desnuda* (The Nude Beauty). These portraits of an unknown woman, commonly believed to be the Duquesa de Alba (who may have been Goya's lover), are identical save for the lack of clothing in the latter.

The whole southern wing of the 2nd floor is devoted to Goya, and includes many of his preparatory paintings for tapestries, his religious paintings and drawings. On the 1st floor, Rooms 32 and 34 to 39 contain more of his work, including the Pinturas Negras (Black Paintings), so-called because of the dark browns and black that dominate, and the distorted animalistic appearance of their characters. Among the most disturbing of these works is *Saturno Devorando a Su Hijo* (Saturn Devouring His Son).

El Greco

Cretan-born Domenikos Theotokopoulos (1541–1614), known simply as El Greco (the Greek), lived and worked in Toledo, where he spent most of his time painting for the Church. Particularly striking are *La Crucifixión* (The Crucifixion) and *San Andrés y San Francisco* (Saint Andrew and Saint Francis), finished towards the end of the 16th century. The long, slender figures characteristic of this singular Cretan artist, who lived and worked in Toledo, are hard to mistake. His best portrait is *El Caballero de la Mano en el Pecho* (Gentleman with his Hand on his Breast). Most of his works are on the ground floor, in Rooms 60a, 61a and 62a.

Ground Floor

Other than the smattering of works by El Greco, here you'll find an excellent collection of Spanish medieval paintings. To get a solid grip on the roots of Spanish art, pay attention to the Romanesque religious works, such as the Frescoes of Santa Cruz de Maderuelo.

In Rooms 55 to 58 you'll find paintings of the 15th- and 16th-century Flemish school. Search out the work of Hieronymus Bosch (1450–1516), especially *The Garden of Earthly Delights,* a fantastical creation that looks like a 16th-century version of surrealism.

Italian artists such as Sandro Botticelli (1445–1510), Andrea Mantegna (1431–1506), Raphael (1483–1520), Tintoretto (1518–94) and, especially, Titian (1487–1576) are spread over Rooms 49, 56b, 60 to 63b and 75.

First Floor

Works by Velázquez and Goya are the focal point of this floor, but there are more Flemish works here too. *Las Tres Gracias* (Three Graces) by Peter Paul Rubens (1577–1640) is the most sought-after work of the bunch.

In the shadow of these greats comes a small contingent of important 17th- to 19th-century Spanish artists, most of them in Rooms 16 to 23. There are substantial collections of work by Bartolomé Esteban Murillo, José de Ribera (in Rooms 25 to 29 on the 1st floor), Francisco de Zurbarán (Rooms 17A and 18A) and Claudio Coello (plus other Spanish baroque artists in Room 16A).

Second Floor

Though much of this floor was closed at the time of writing, there are fascinating works usually on display here. Much of the floor is devoted to Goya, but you'll also find a small collection of French painting by artists such as Nicolas Poussin (1594–1665), Jean-Antoine Watteau (1684–1721) and Louis Michel Van Loo (1707–71). Once the room is reopened you'll even see a couple of portraits by Gainsborough (1727–88) in Room 83.

Casón del Buen Retiro

A couple of blocks from the main museum, the **Casón del Buen Retiro** (Map pp106–8) is housed in what was the ballroom of the now non-existent Palacio del Buen Retiro. Here you'll find a varied collection of lesser-known works such as portraits by Vicente López (including his imposing portrait of Goya), and several noteworthy paintings such as *The Death of Viriatus* by José de Madrazo, *Las Presidentas* by Eugenio Lucas and *The Countess of Vilches* by Federico de Madrazo. One of Sorolla's first paintings, *They Still Say that Fish is Expensive,* hangs here, as do several landscapes by Carlos Haes.

Guides & Information

With so much to look at, getting a guidebook or joining a guided tour can be a huge help in El Prado. There is little printed information given out free; the hand-out map will guide you to the main schools and the major artists, but it won't tell you anything about the works themselves. Coin-operated machines sell booklets (€1 each) in several languages and the bookshop sells a more complete guide to the highlights for €9. You can also get an audio guide at the entrance for €3.

CENTRO DE ARTE REINA SOFÍA

A fantastic collection of modern, predominately Spanish art, the **Centro de Arte Reina Sofía** (Map pp114-16; ☎ 91 467 50 62; http://museoreina sofia.mcu.es; Calle de Santa Isabel 52; admission €3, 2.30-9pm Sat & Sun free; ☒ 10am-9pm Mon-Sat, 10am-2.30pm Sun) is one of the city's premier showcases of Spanish contemporary culture. Housed in the shell of an 18th-century hospital, the museum is an open, airy place that's perfectly suited to modern art.

To begin the visit of the permanent collection, take the enormous glass elevator (which has awesome views of the plaza below) to the 2nd floor. The first three rooms here provide an introduction to Catalan Modernisme and other turn-of-the-century work. Room 4 is dedicated to Juan Gris' cubism and Room 5 to the bronze sculptures of Pablo Gargallo.

Picasso's famous painting **Guernica**, his protest of the German bombing of the Basque town of Guernica during the Spanish Civil War in 1937, dominates the long hall that is Room 6. It's surrounded by a plethora of preparatory sketches and, usually, a school or tour group. Already associated with the Republicans when the civil war broke out in 1936, Picasso was commissioned by Madrid to do the painting for the Paris Exposition Universelle in 1937. Picasso incorporated features from his other works into this eloquent condemnation of the horrors of war.

The remarkably simple works of Catalan artist Joan Miró take up a parallel corridor (Room 7), and some 20 canvases by Dalí hang in Room 10, including a portrait of the film maker Luis Buñuel (1924), and the surrealist extravaganza *El Gran Masturbador* (The Great Masturbator, 1929). The remaining 1st-floor rooms are given over to a range of international artists who worked from the early 20th century through to the 1940s.

The top-floor collection takes up the baton and marches through the 1980s, with works by Antoni Tàpies, Eduardo Arroyo, Eduardo Chillida and Pablo Palazuelo. A sprinkling of works by non-Spaniards (usually no more than one item apiece) can also be seen, including Francis Bacon and Henry Moore (both Room 24).

MUSEO THYSSEN-BORNEMISZA

Sitting just opposite the Prado, the **Museo Thyssen-Bornemisza** (Map pp114-16; ☎ 91 369 01 51; Paseo del Prado 8; adult/child €4.80/3; ◑ 10am-7pm Tue-Sun) is a themeless collection of priceless works, offering one of the most comprehensive art-history lessons you'll ever have. Starting with medieval religious art, it moves on through Titian, El Greco and Rubens to Cézanne, Monet and Van Gogh, then from Miró, Picasso and Gris to Pollock, Dalí and Lichtenstein.

Formerly the private collection of the German-Hungarian family of magnates, the Thyssen-Bornemiszas, the collection was purchased by Spain in 1993 for a mere US$300 million. Almost 800 works have hung here since 1992, with a further 80 at the Monestir de Pedralbes in Barcelona (p293). An additional collection of more than 300 paintings is on show in a brand-new wing, adjacent to the museum, that opened in June 2004. A further 300 to 400 will go on show soon in a recently acquired adjacent building.

The core is spread out over three floors; you start at the top (2nd) floor, with 13th- and 14th-century religious art, and work your way downstairs to the avant-garde and pop art on the ground floor. You can get a helpful audio guide for €3.

Second Floor

The first three rooms on the 2nd floor are dedicated to medieval art, with a series of remarkable triptychs and paintings (predominantly Italian, German and Flemish) to get the ball rolling. They include work by Duccio di Buoninsegna (1255–1318), who led the Sienese school into a gentle break from Byzantine forms in the late 13th and early 14th centuries.

Room 5 contains, among others, some works by Italy's Piero della Francesca (1410–92) and a *Henry VIII* by Holbein the Younger (1497–1543). Room 6 (the long Galería Villahermosa) includes a sampling of Italian

masters such as Raphael, Lorenzo Lotto (c 1480–1556) and Tintoretto (1518–94).

In Room 7 are some exemplary works by the brothers Gentile (1429–1507) and Giovanni Bellini (1430–1516), who together with their father, Jacopo (1400–70), launched the Venetian Renaissance in painting. Rooms 8, 9 and 10 are given over to German and Dutch 16th-century masters; among them are a few works by Cranach (1472–1553).

Room 11 is dedicated to four pieces by El Greco, and works by Venetian contemporaries Tintoretto, Titian and Jacopo Bassano (1517–92).

Caravaggio and José de Ribera (aka Lo Spagnoletto), who was much influenced by the former, dominate the next room. Look out for the fine views of Venice by Canaletto (1697–1768), accompanied by some of the best works of Francesco Guardi (1712–93), in Rooms 16 and 17.

Rubens leads the way in the last rooms (19 to 21) on this floor, which are devoted to 17th-century Dutch and Flemish masters.

First Floor

The Dutch theme continues on the next floor, with interiors and landscapes. They are followed by Room 27, which is devoted to a still-life series; in Room 28 you'll find a Gainsborough (1727–88), one of the few British works in the collection. Next comes a representative look at North American art of the 19th century, including three pieces by John Singer Sargent (1856–1925).

A series of great impressionist and post-impressionist names get a mention in Rooms 32 and 33, with works by Pissarro, Renoir, Degas, Monet, Manet, Toulouse-Lautrec, Cézanne and Van Gogh. The rest of the floor is dedicated to various movements in expressionist painting. In Room 35 you'll find canvases by Egon Schiele, Henri Matisse and Edvard Munch.

Rooms 36 to 39 feature works by, among others, Ernst Ludwig Kirchner (1880–1938), Wassily Kandinsky (1866–1944) and George Grosz (1893–1959).

Ground Floor

Here you move into the 20th century, from cubism through to pop art. In Room 41, you'll see a nice mix of Picasso, Juan Gris and Georges Braque. There's more Picasso in Room 45, accompanied by works of Marc

Chagall, Max Ernst and Wassily Kandinsky. Miró turns up in Room 46, along with Jackson Pollock (1912–56), Willem de Kooning (1904–97), Mark Rothko (1903–70) and Georgia O'Keefe (1887–1980). Lucian Freud (1922–), Sigmund's Berlin-born grandson, is joined by David Hockney (1937–) and Roy Lichtenstein (1923–97) in Rooms 47 and 48.

PARQUE DEL BUEN RETIRO

A Sunday walk in **El Retiro** (Map pp106-8; 7am-midnight May-Sep, 7am-10pm Oct-Apr) is as much a Madrid tradition as tapas and terrace cafés. Though this was once the privileged strolling zone of royals and their entourages, it's now open to one and all. Street performers, (including a new breed of vendor that provide traveller-friendly back massages for €5) line the boulevards around the small lake, and ice-cream and snack vendors abound. Time it right and in summer you may even catch a puppet show in **Tiritilandia** (Puppet Land).

Walk along **Paseo de las Estatuas**, a path lined with statues originally from the Palacio Real. It ends at the **estanque** (pond), overlooked by a massive stone creation that eerily houses the **mausoleum of Alfonso XII**. There are **row boats** (Map pp106-8; 91 574 40 24; 10am-dusk; boat rental per 45min €4) for hire at the northern end of the pond, though this can be a punishing activity under a blazing summer sun. You can also hop on the optimistically named 'cruise boat' for a short ride that costs €1.10.

The **Palacio de Exposiciones** is the place to go to for art and photo exhibitions, and the **Palacio de Cristal**, a charming metal and glass structure, is also the scene of occasional exhibitions. It was built in 1887 as a winter garden for exotic flowers. You can also search out the **El Ángel Caído** (The Fallen Angel), supposedly the first ever statue dedicated to the devil, and gardens such as **La Rosaleda** (Rose Garden), and the **Chinese Garden** on a tiny island near the Fallen Angel. The southwestern end of the park is a popular cruising zone for young gay men.

REAL JARDÍN BOTÁNICO

With its manicured flowerbeds and neat paths, the **Royal Botanical Garden** (Map pp106-8; 91 420 30 17; Plaza Murillo 2; adult/child €2/0.75; 10am-7pm Oct & Mar, 10am-6pm Nov-Feb, 10am-8pm Apr-Sep, 10am-9pm May-Aug) is a refuge more beautiful than El Retiro, although not nearly

as large. Though it was first created in 1755 on the banks of the Río Manzanares, the garden was moved here in 1781 by Carlos III. These days you can see more than 2000 plants and 1000 trees. There were supposedly once more than 7000 specimens here in the mid-1800s, but most of them were blown away in the cyclone of 1886.

PLAZA DE LA CIBELES

This emblematic landmark is really just the decorative touch in the centre of a busy traffic circle, but since its creation in 1780 by Ventura Rodríguez, **La Cibeles** (Map pp110–12) has been one of Madrid's favourite and most beautiful plazas. It's the place fans flock to when the Real Madrid soccer team wins, and it has been the site of many a protest demonstration.

The statue crowning the plaza tells the story of how the goddess Cybele had lovers Atalanta and Hippomenes, who had recently paired off thanks to the intervention of Aphrodite, converted into lions and shackled to her chariot for having profaned her temple. (They had been put up to this by Aphrodite, who was irritated by the apparent ingratitude of the newlyweds for her good work.)

Even as traffic zooms around the mythic statue, you can't help but gawk at the impossibly elaborate **Palacio de Comunicaciones** – newcomers find it hard to accept that this is only the main post office. Diametrically opposite this is the **Palacio Buenavista**, which now belongs to the army. The buildings are decidedly over the top, but when they're lit up at night the effect is simply magical.

A block behind the plaza to the west on the tiny Plaza del Rey is the **Casa de las Siete Chimeneas** (Map pp110–12), a 16th-century mansion that received its name because of the seven chimneys it still boasts. Nowadays, it is home to the Ministry of Culture.

MUSEO NAVAL

Boat lovers will get a thrill from the **Museo Naval** (Map pp114-16; 91 379 52 99; Paseo del Prado 5; admission free; 10am-2pm Tue-Sun), an interesting look at seafaring through the ages. It is jammed with models, maps, arms and more. The most important exhibit is Juan de la Cosa's parchment map of the known world, put together in 1500. Its accuracy on Europe is quite astounding, and it is supposedly the first map to show the Americas.

MUSEO DE ARTES DECORATIVAS

Give your inner antique dealer a thrill at the **Museo de Artes Decorativas** (Museum of Decorative Arts; Map pp106-8; ☎ 91 532 64 99; Calle de Montalbán 12; 🕙 9.30am-3pm Tue-Sat, 10am-3pm Sun; adult/child €2.40/1.20), a surprisingly interesting museum that gives an inside perspective on high-class life from the 15th to the 19th centuries, with a huge collection of sumptuous period furniture, ceramics and carpets. Spread over five floors, it could keep you occupied for hours but probably only deserves an hour's visit.

MUSEO DEL EJÉRCITO

If you want to see the displays of the Spanish military's weapons, flags and uniforms, you'd better act fast; the contents of the **Museo del Ejército** (Map pp106-8; ☎ 91 522 89 77; Calle de Méndez Núñez 1; admission €1; 🕙 10am-2pm Tue-Sun) are slated to join the collection of Toledo's Alcázar Military Museum (see p241), when it is completed, making room for the Prado to shift some of its collection here.

In 1803 the chief minister, Manuel Godoy, established an army museum in one of the few remaining parts of the one-time Palacio del Buen Retiro. It's housed in what was the Salón de Reinos del Buen Retiro.

A room containing portraits of Franco is devoted to the Nationalist campaign in the civil war, while the Sala Árabe (decorated Alhambra-style) holds various curios, including the sword of Boabdil, the last Muslim ruler of Granada. He signed the instrument of surrender to the Catholic monarchs, marking the end of the Reconquista in 1492.

IGLESIA DE SAN JERÓNIMO EL REAL

The beautiful **Iglesia de San Jerónimo el Real** (Map pp106-8; ☎ 91 420 35 78; Calle de Ruiz de Alarcón 19; 🕙 8am-1.30pm & 5-8.30pm) is essentially a Gothic creation, though it was rebuilt in the 19th century after the Peninsular War, which destroyed the cloister and the monastery that once formed part of the complex. Founded in 1503 by the Catholic Monarchs, Fernando and Isabel, San Jerónimo has always been tightly linked with royals. It was the setting of numerous ceremonies and royal services, including Alfonso XIII's wedding and, more recently, the crowning of Spain's present king, Juan Carlos I. What remained of the cloisters next door has been demolished (despite vociferous local protests) to make way for the Prado extension.

PLAZA DE NEPTUNO

Officially known as **Plaza de Cánovas del Castillo** (Map pp114–16), the traffic circle just south of Cibeles is commanded by an 18th-century sculpture of the sea god Neptune by Juan Pascual de Mena. *Neptune* has attracted some pretty highfalutin neighbours: the plaza is flanked by the Prado, the Museo Thyssen-Bornemisza and the city's classiest hotels, the Ritz and the Westin Palace.

PUERTA DE ALCALÁ

This **gate** (Map pp106–8) was begun under the supervision of Francesco Sabatini at Plaza de la Cibeles to celebrate the arrival of Carlos III in Madrid in 1769. Completed in 1778, it was later moved to its present spot on Plaza de la Independencia.

La Latina & Lavapiés

The working-class districts of La Latina and Lavapiés are right in the city centre, but they feel a world away from the souvenir shops and tour groups. There are few monuments or museums in the area; the real draw is the gritty feel of one of the city's last true *barrios*. Thought to be where the bulk of the city's Jewish population once lived (the existence centuries ago of at least one synagogue in the area is documented), it now hosts an interesting mix of locals from all over Spain, and immigrants from Eastern Europe, North Africa and beyond.

EL RASTRO

This thriving mass of vendors, buyers and pickpockets is as much a part of Madrileño culture as tapas and Plaza Mayor. A classic flea market, **El Rastro** (Map pp114-16; 🕙 Sun morning only) is the place to find everything from faux designer purses and 1960s flamenco cassette tapes to furniture, kitchen appliances and underwear. Locals say the selection is not what it used to be, but there are still treasures to be found if you have the patience to dig through the heaps of second-hand goods.

El Rastro owes its name (the Stain) to the blood that once trickled down these streets from the slaughterhouses, which sat up the hill. It's been an open-air market for half a millennium and is generally considered the largest in Europe.

The madness begins at Plaza de Cascorro, near La Latina metro stop, and worms its way downhill along Calle de la Ribera de Curtidores and the streets branching off it. The shopping starts at 8am and lasts until lunch (2pm or 3pm), but for many *madrileños* the best of El Rastro comes after the stalls have shut down and everyone crowds into nearby bars for an *aperitivo* (appetizer) of vermouth and tapas. Families, friends and die-hard partiers who are still awake from the night before, stroll from bar to bar (especially those along Calle de la Cava Baja), turning the *barrio* into the site of a spontaneous Sunday fiesta. In fine weather, the Plaza de San Andrés attracts a light-hearted Bohemian crowd that fills the area with music and dancing.

VIADUCTO & PUENTE DE SEGOVIA
For a great view of Campo de Moro, take a stroll down Calle de Segovia, where a **viaduct** gives a good vantage point. This was a popular suicide spot until plastic barriers were put up in the late 1990s. Just west of the viaduct is the **Puente de Segovia**, a nine-arched bridge built by Juan de Herrera in 1584. The massive bridge looks almost comical as it spans the wimpy Río Manzanares that trickles underneath it.

LA MORERÍA
The area stretching from Calle de Segovia south to the Basílica de San Francisco el Grande and southeast to the Iglesia de San Andrés was the heart of the *morería* (Moorish quarter). Strain the imagination a little and the maze of winding and hilly lanes even now retains a whiff of the North African medina. This is where the Muslim population of Magerit concentrated, in the wake of the 11th-century Christian takeover of the town.

BASÍLICA DE SAN FRANCISCO EL GRANDE
One of the largest churches in the city, the **Basílica de San Francisco el Grande** (Map pp114-16; ☎ 91 365 38 00; Plaza de San Francisco 1; admission museum €3; ☺ 11am-12.30pm & 4-6.30pm Tue-Fri, 11am-noon Sat) dominates the skyline here, its pretty yellow dome peeking above the rooftops. Completed under the guidance of Francesco Sabatini, the baroque basilica has some outstanding features, including frescoed cupolas and chapel ceilings by Francisco Bayeu. Goya's *The Prediction of San Bernardino of Siena for the King of Aragon* is here too. According to legend, the basilica sits atop the site where St Francis of Assisi built a chapel in 1217.

IGLESIA DE SAN ANDRÉS & AROUND
The stately **Iglesia de San Andrés** (Map pp114-16; Plaza de San Andrés 1; ☺ during services) crowns the plaza of the same name, providing a lovely backdrop for the impromptu parties that fill this plaza on Sunday afternoons after El Rastro flea market. The church was pretty much destroyed during Spain's civil war but has since been rebuilt. It was long the resting place of the remains of Madrid's patron saint, San Isidro Labrador (who supposedly prayed here regularly), until they were moved to the Basílica de San Isidro.

Around the back is the **Capilla del Obispo**, considered the best Renaissance church in Madrid, though it's not strictly of the period. Look out for the mostly Gothic vaulting in the ceilings, the Plateresque tombs and the fine Renaissance reredos (screens).

IGLESIA DE SAN PEDRO EL VIEJO
Built atop the site of the old Mezquita de la Morería (Mosque of the Muslim Quarter), **San Pedro el Viejo** (Map pp114-16; ☎ 91 365 12 84; Calle del Nuncio 14) recalls the mosque's days only in its 14th-century Mudéjar bell tower, which is the most interesting part of the church. Along with the bell tower of the Iglesia de San Nicolás de los Servitas (p120), it's one of the few remnants that remain in Madrid of the masterful Mudéjar builders.

Malasaña & Chueca
Packed with unique shops and lively bars, trendy Chueca and rough-and-ready Malasaña aren't the most obvious districts to head to for museum visits. Nevertheless, you'll find a few places worth a stop.

GRAN VÍA

This grand **boulevard**, which slices across the city centre, is a constantly clogged thoroughfare lined with everything from luxury hotels to sex shops, glitzy theatres to dark pinball parlours, and swanky boutiques to sidewalk hawkers. While it might not be one of Madrid's most charming quarters, it is a vibrant stretch day and night. On Fridays, traffic jams tend to last from evening rush hour right through till dawn.

The street was pushed through here in the early decades of the 20th century, sweeping away entire neighbourhoods. In the following years, many grand buildings were raised along much of its length. Among the more interesting is the **Edificio Metropolis** (Map pp110–12), which was finished in 1910 and marks the beginning of Gran Vía.

MUSEO MUNICIPAL

Offering an interesting but hardly masterful tour through the history of Madrid, the **Museo Municipal** (Map pp110-12; ☎ 91 588 86 72; Calle de Fuencarral 78; admission free; ✆ 9.30am-8pm Tue-Fri, 10am-2pm Sat & Sun) is a worthwhile stop, if you have a strong interest in Madrid's slow transformation into a modern capital city.

The main attraction here is the restored baroque entrance, originally raised in 1721 by Pedro de Ribera. Until its conversion into a museum in 1929, the building had served as a hospice.

On the ground floor, Madrid de los Austrias (Habsburg Madrid) is brought to life, up to a point, through paintings and models. The theme continues on the floor above, where the various rooms take you from Bourbon Madrid through to the final years of the 19th century. Of interest are a couple of Goyas and, possibly more than anything else, a huge model of Madrid done in 1830 by a military engineer called León Gil de Palacios (1778–1849).

SOCIEDAD GENERAL DE AUTORES Y EDITORES

The **Sociedad General de Autores y Editores** (General Society of Authors & Editors; Map pp110-12; ☎ 91 349 95 50; Calle Fernando VI 4; ✆ 1st Mon in Oct), a joyously self-indulgent ode to Modernisme, looks like a huge ice-cream cake half-melted by the summer sun. Built in 1902 by José Grases Riera, the creation is a clear nod to the Catalan architect Antoni Gaudí. There are a few other modestly Modernista buildings in Madrid, but this one takes the cake, as it were, as the most flamboyant.

MUSEO DE CERRALBO

Inside the opulent **Museo de Cerralbo** (Map pp110-12; ☎ 91 547 36 46; Calle de Ventura Rodríguez 17; adult/child €2.40/1.20; ✆ 9.30am-3pm Tue-Sat, 10am-3pm Sun) is an interesting look at the life and times of the 19th-century upper class. Though you could walk past this noble mansion and barely notice it amid the bustle of the tight, narrow streets, inside there's a sensory barrage of classic art and furniture. The upper floor boasts a gala dining hall and a grand ballroom. The mansion is jammed with the fruits of the collector's eclectic meanderings, from religious paintings to Oriental pieces, to clocks and suits of armour. Occasionally there's a gem, such as El Greco's *Éxtasis de San Francisco*.

The 17th Marqués de Cerralbo – politician, poet and archaeologist – was also an inveterate collector. You can see the results of his efforts in what were once his Madrid lodgings.

Salamanca & Las Ventas

You probably won't be impressed with your first view of the modern Plaza de Colón, with the almost surreal Edificio de Colón on its western side. Its physical aspect, although softened by the fountains of the Centro Cultural de la Villa, is certainly nothing to write home about. The statue of Colón (Columbus) seems neglected and the **Monumento al Descubrimiento** (Map pp108–9; Monument to the Discovery – of America, that is), for all its cleverness, does not leave a lasting impression. It was cobbled together in the 1970s.

MUSEO ARQUEOLÓGICO NACIONAL

Madrid's **Museo Arqueológico Nacional** (Map pp108-9; ☎ 91 577 79 12; www.man.es in Spanish; Calle de Serrano 13; admission €3; ✆ 9.30am-8.30pm Tue-Sat, 9.30am-2.30pm Sun) houses a delightfully varied collection spanning everything from prehistory to the Iberian tribes, imperial Rome, Visigothic Spain, the Muslim conquest, and specimens of Romanesque, Gothic and Mudéjar handiwork.

The basement contains displays on prehistoric man, the Neolithic age and on to the Iron Age. Modest collections from ancient Egypt, Etruscan civilisation in Italy, classical

Greece and southern Italy under imperial Rome can also be seen. There are also some Spanish specialities: ancient civilisation in the Balearic and Canary Islands.

The ground floor is the most interesting. Sculpted figures such as the *Dama de Ibiza* and *Dama de Elche* reveal a flourishing artistic tradition among the Iberian tribes, no doubt influenced by contact with Greek, Phoenician and Carthaginian civilisation. The latter bust still attracts controversy over its authenticity a century after it was found.

The arrival of imperial Rome brought predictable changes. Some of the mosaics here are splendid. The display on Visigothic Spain, and especially material from Toledo, marks a clear break, but only previous experience with Muslim Spain (such as the great cities of Andalucía) or other Muslim countries can prepare you for the wonders of Muslim art. The arches, taken from Zaragoza's Aljafería, are the centrepiece.

The influences of pure Islamic precepts persist in the later Mudéjar style of re-Christianised Spain, which contrasts with Romanesque and later Gothic developments, all of which can be appreciated by soaking up the best of this eclectic collection.

Outside, stairs lead down to a partial copy of the prehistoric cave paintings of Altamira (Cantabria), which will be as close to the paintings as many people get.

BIBLIOTECA NACIONAL & MUSEO DEL LIBRO

The **Museo del Libro** (Map pp108-9; ☎ 91 580 77 59; Paseo de los Recoletos 20; admission free; 🕑 10am-9pm Tue-Sat, 10am-2pm Sun) is a worthwhile stop for any bibliophile yearning to see Arabic texts, illuminated manuscripts, centuries-old books of the Torah and more, all made much more interesting if you can understand the video commentaries in Spanish. Some of the library's collections have been imaginatively arranged in displays recounting the history of writing and the storage of knowledge.

One of the most outstanding of the many grand edifices erected in the 19th century on the avenues of Madrid, the **Biblioteca Nacional** was commissioned by Isabel II in 1865 and completed in 1892.

MUSEO SOROLLA

Doubling as an art museum and a period house, the **Museo Sorolla** (Map pp108-9; ☎ 91 310 15 84; Paseo del General Martínez Campos 37; adult/child €2.40/1.20; 🕑 9.30am-3pm Tue-Sat, 10am-3pm Sun) has a fantastic collection of Joaquín Sorolla's paintings, including many sunny Valencian beach scenes, for which he is best known. Housed in the artist's former residence, it's also a showcase for early 20th-century furniture, sculpture and jewellery. It's set amid lovely, cool gardens designed by Sorolla himself.

MUSEO LÁZARO GALDIANO

A surprisingly rich, formerly private collection awaits you in the **Museo Lázaro Galdiano** (Map pp108-9; ☎ 91 561 60 84; Calle de Serrano 122; admission €4; 🕑 10am-4.30pm Wed-Mon). Aside from some fine works by artists such as Van Eyck, Bosch, Zurbarán, Ribera, Goya, Gainsborough and Constable, this is a rather oddball assembly of all sorts of collectables. The ceilings were all painted according to their room's function. The exception is Room 14, where the artist created a collage from some of Goya's more famous works, including *La Maja* and the frescoes of the Ermita de San Antonio de la Florida, in honour of the genius.

MUSEO DE LA ESCULTURA ABSTRACTA

This interesting open-air collection of 17 abstracts (Map pp108–9) includes works by Eduardo Chillida, Joan Miró, Eusebio Sempere and Alberto Sánchez. The sculptures are under the overpass where Paseo de Eduardo Dato crosses Paseo de la Castellana. All but one of the sculptures are on the eastern side of Paseo de la Castellana.

Chamberí & Argüelles

ERMITA DE SAN ANTONIO DE LA FLORIDA

The *panteón* (burial site) of Francisco Goya, the **Ermita de San Antonio de la Florida** (Map pp106-8; ☎ 91 542 07 22; Glorieta de San Antonio de la Florida 5; admission free; 🕑 10am-2pm & 4-8pm Tue-Fri, 10am-2pm Sat & Sun) contains some of the master's most interesting frescoes. Here you'll find two small chapels. In the southern one the ceiling and dome are covered in frescoes (restored in 1993). Those on the dome depict the miracle of St Anthony, who is calling on a young man to rise from the grave and absolve his father, unjustly accused of his murder. Around them swarms a typical Madrid crowd. Usually in this kind of scene the angels and cherubs appear in the cupola, above all the terrestrial activity, but Goya places the human above the divine. The painter is buried in front of the altar. His remains were transferred here in 1919 from France, where he had died in self-imposed exile. The chapel is about a 10-minute walk north from Campo del Moro.

Across the train tracks is the **Cementerio de la Florida** (Calle de Francisco Jacinto), where 43 rebels lie, executed by Napoleon's troops; they were killed on the nearby Montaña del Príncipe Pío in the pre-dawn of 3 May 1808, after the Dos de Mayo rising. The forlorn cemetery, established in 1796, is generally closed.

ANTIGUO CUARTEL DEL CONDE DUQUE & PALACIO DE LIRIA

On the western edge of Malasaña, over Calle de la Princesa, is the grand barracks known as the **Antiguo Cuartel del Conde Duque** (Map pp110-12; Calle Conde Duque 9; ☉ 10am-2pm & 5.30-9pm Tue-Sat, 10.30am-2.30pm Sun, plus during performances). Occasional art exhibitions, concerts and theatre are held here. It's also the site of the **Museo Municipal de Arte Contemporáneo de Madrid** (☎ 91 588 29 28; admission free; ☉ 10am-2pm & 5.30-9pm Tue-Sat, 10.30am-2.30pm Sun Sep-Jun; 10am-2pm & 6-9pm Tue-Sat, 10.30am-2pm Sun Jul & Aug), with contemporary Spanish and international paintings, sculpture, photography and graphic art.

Virtually next door, the 18th-century **Palacio de Liria** (Map pp110-12; ☎ 91 547 53 02; Calle de la Princesa 20; ☉ guided visits Fri 10am, 11am & noon; metro Ventura Rodríguez), rebuilt after fire in 1936 and surrounded by an enviably green oasis, holds an impressive collection of art, period furniture and *objets d'art*. To join a guided visit, send a formal request with your personal details. The waiting list is long and most mortals content themselves with staring through the gates into the grounds.

TEMPLO DE DEBOD

Remarkably, this authentic 4th-century-BC Egyptian temple sits in the heart of Madrid. Looking out of place in the Parque de la Montaña, past the Jardines del Paseo del Pintor Rosales, the **Templo de Debod** (Map pp106-8; ☎ 91 366 74 15; Paseo del Pintor Rosales; admission free; ☉ 9.45am-1.45pm & 4.15-6.15pm Tue-Fri, 10am-2pm Sat & Sun Oct-Mar; 10am-2pm & 6-8pm Tue-Fri Apr-Sep) was saved from the rising waters of Lake Nasser, formed by the Aswan High Dam, and sent block by block to Spain in 1970.

PARQUE DEL OESTE

Spread out between the university and Moncloa metro station, this is a tranquil and, in parts, quite beautiful **park** for a wander or shady laze in the heat of the day. Until recently it would undergo a nocturnal transformation when the city's transsexual-prostitute population and their clients came out to play. For the moment the area seems to have been cleared by the police.

Northern Madrid
MUSEO DE CERA

Most major cities have wax versions of immortal Marilyn Monroe and the Beatles, and Madrid is no different. The **Museo de Cera** (Wax Museum; Map pp108-9; ☎ 91 319 26 49; Paseo de los Recoletos 41; adult/child 4-7 €10/6; ☉ 10am-2.30pm & 4.30-8.30pm Mon-Fri, 10am-8.30pm Sat & Sun) is pricey but fun, if you get a kick out of taking pictures of yourself beside fake famous people. Some 450 characters have been captured here, although some are less convincing than others.

If you need more action, a few other attractions await. Board the Tren del Terror (€3) or the Simulador (€3); the latter shakes you up a bit, as though you were inside a washing machine. Another sideshow is the Multivisión animated 'experience' (€2). You'll probably get the feeling that you've been overcharged at all of the above, but keeping the kiddies entertained for a few hours just might be worth it.

Beyond the Centre
CASA DE CAMPO

A sprawling park that once served as Felipe II's private hunting ground, the huge **Casa de Campo** (Map pp106-8; ☎ 91 479 60 02; ☉ 24hr) is home to the Zoo-Aquarium (p136), an amusement park (p136), tennis court and both indoor and, in season, outdoor swimming pools (p131).

This unkempt semiwilderness, stretching west of the Río Manzanares, was in royal hands until 1931, when the recently proclaimed Republic threw open its 1200 hectares to the people. By day it fills with cyclists and walkers eager for a glimpse of nature near the capital.

To get here take a **cable car** (teleférico; Map pp106-8; ☎ 91 541 74 50; www.teleferico.com in Spanish; round trip adult/child €4.20/3.30; ☉ noon-dusk); it starts at Paseo del Pintor Rosales, on the corner of Calle del Marqués de Urquijo, and ends at a high point in the middle of the park.

At night the park takes on a different feel, becoming the playground of prostitutes, pimps and junkies. It's a place best avoided after sundown.

ESTADIO SANTIAGO BERNABÉU

If you're a fan of Real Madrid, or of football (soccer) in general, a visit to the mythic club's stadium is a must. Visits to the **Estadio Santiago Bernabéu** (Map p113; ☎ 91 398 43 00; Avenida de Concha Espina 1; adult/child €9/7; ☺ 10.30am-6.30pm, closes 2hr before game) include a visit to the stadium itself, the locker rooms, the players' bench and the trophy exposition, where you'll see the seemingly endless line-up of trophies earned by this championship team.

MUSEO DE AMÉRICA & FARO DE MONCLOA

Travel to, and trade with, the newly discovered Americas was a central part of Spain's culture and economy from 1492 until the early 20th century. Ships carried gold one way, and adventurers the other, and the cultural exchange that went on affected both sides in profound ways.

The two levels of the **Museo de América** (Map pp106-8; ☎ 91 543 94 37; Avenida de los Reyes Católicos 6; adult/child €3/1.50; ☺ 9.30am-3pm Tue-Sat, 10am-2.30pm Sun) show off a representative display of ceramics, statuary, jewellery and instruments of hunting, fishing and war, along with some of the paraphernalia of the colonisers. The Colombian gold collection, dating as far back as the 2nd century AD, and a couple of shrunken heads are eye-catching. Temporary exhibitions with Latin American themes are regularly held too.

The odd tower (it's actually a lighthouse) just in front of the Museo de América, the **Faro de Moncloa** (Map pp106-8; ☎ 91 544 81 04; Avenida Arco de la Victoria; adult/child €1/0.50; ☺ 10am-2pm & 5-7pm Tue-Fri, 10am-6pm Sat & Sun 15 Oct-May; 10am-2pm & 5-8pm Tue-Sun May-16 Sep; 10am-2pm & 5-9pm Tue-Sun Jun-15 Sep), is designed not to control air traffic but to transport visitors to panoramic views of Madrid. Zip up the elevator for unparalleled views of the city's rooftops. On stormy or excessively windy days the tower is closed.

MUSEO DE LA CIUDAD

Don't put it on your list of unmissable sights, but if you've fallen in love with Madrid, and want to learn a bit more about her inner workings, you may enjoy the **Museo de la Ciudad** (Map p113; ☎ 91 588 65 99; Calle del Príncipe de Vergara 140; admission free; ☺ 10am-2pm & 4-7pm Tue-Fri, 10am-2pm Sat & Sun Sep-Jun; 10am-2pm & 5.30-8pm Tue-Fri, 10am-2pm Sat & Sun Jul & Aug). The exhibits here are spaced out over three floors and trace the growth and spread of Madrid, with abundant information on municipal services and the like. Some of the most interesting things here are the small-scale models of famous buildings and landmarks in Madrid.

MUSEO CASA DE LA MONEDA & NATIONAL MINT

Coin collectors rejoice: this is the place for you. The **Museo Casa de la Moneda** (Map pp106-8; ☎ 91 566 65 44; Calle del Doctor Esquerdo 36; admission free; ☺ 10am-7.30pm Tue-Fri, 10am-2pm Sat & Sun) is a slightly dingy museum, whose collection includes moulds, etchings and other artefacts covering the history of the coin from ancient Greece to the recently defunct peseta.

ACTIVITIES

If the idea of shuffling down the corridor of one more museum makes you want to scream, then it's time for a change of pace. Madrid has plenty of parks, gyms and swimming pools to keep you active.

Cycling

Madrid is not as bike-friendly as many northern European cities, but a cycle through Casa de Campo or El Parque del Retiro is a fantastic way to spend an afternoon. You can rent bikes at **Bicimania** (Map p113; ☎ 91 533 11 89; Calle de Palencia 20; www.bicimania.com in Spanish; ☺ 10.30am-2pm & 5-8.30pm Mon-Sat). Prices start at €15 per day, but you can also rent by the week (€80) or weekend (€24).

Swimming

In the sticky heat of Madrid's endless summer, there are few things more satisfying than a dip in a cool pool. The huge outdoor pool at **Canal de Isabel II** (Map p105; ☎ 91 533 17 91; www.cyii.es; Avenida Filipinas 54; admission €3.20-3.50; ☺ 11am-8pm Jun-early Sep), in northern Madrid, is the perfect place to cool off on a hot summer's day. Also try the **Casa de Campo** (Map pp106-8; ☎ 91 463 00 50; Avenida Ángel; admission pool €3.80; ☺ 11.30am-9pm May-Sep, 9am-noon & 3-7pm & 9-10pm Oct-Apr), where you'll find a watery oasis in the midst of the sprawling park. The indoor and outdoor swimming pools here are some of Madrid's best.

MADRID

Tennis

If you like rackets, the **Polideportivo Virgen del Puerto** (Map pp106-8; ☎ 91 366 28 40; Paseo de la Virgen del Puerto s/n; court rental from €4.90; ☒ 8.30am-8.30pm) is just the place for you. Run by the municipal government, this modern sports centre, located near the Puente de Segovia, has eight regulation-size tennis courts, eight paddle-ball courts and 12 table-tennis courts.

Skiing

That's right, skiing in Madrid. **Madrid Xanadú** (☎ 902 263026; www.madridxanadu.com; Calle Puerto de Navacerrada, Arroyomolinos; ☒ 10am-2pm Sun-Thu, 10am-4pm Fri & Sat) is the largest covered ski centre in Europe, and you can slide down it's snowy slopes all year long. Within the same complex there's a mammoth mall, a 15-screen movie theatre, a kart track and a kiddie amusement park. To get here, take bus No 529, 531 or 536 from the Méndez Álvaro transportation hub.

Fitness Clubs & Yoga

Public gyms and indoor pools (normally for lap swimming only) are scattered throughout Madrid. They generally charge a modest €3 to €6 per day. A full listing of Madrid's *polideportivos* (sports centres), and the services they offer, is found online at www .imd.es (in Spanish). For swankier sweating options, head to one of Madrid's endless privately owned health centres. You'll pay €9 to €12 for a day's admission, but you'll usually find less-crowded workout rooms.

Polideportivo La Chopera (Map pp106-8; ☎ 91 420 11 54; Parque del Buen Retiro; admission €4.50; ☒ 9am-8pm Mon-Fri) is one of Madrid's oldest and most complete sports centres, boasting a fine new workout centre, several football fields and a tennis court. Sitting in the southwestern corner of El Retiro, it's easily accessible too.

Polideportivo La Latina (Map pp114-16; ☎ 91 365 80 31; Plaza de la Cebada s/n; swimming per adult/child €3.80/2.15; ☒ 8.15am-7pm Mon-Thu, 8.15am-6pm Fri, 10am-8.30pm Sat & Sun) is busy day and night. It's one of the most central municipal gyms (and one of the few that has a pool, though it's for indoor lap swimming only). While it's not all that new or clean, it offers fairly complete weight and workout rooms.

Bring out the mats and get bendy at **City Yoga** (Map p113; ☎ 91 553 47 51; www.city-yoga.com in Spanish; Calle de Artistas 43; 1st class €3; ☒ 10am-10pm Mon-Sat) This yoga centre is one of the most popular in the city, with a variety of classes to suit all styles and abilities.

Hammam Medina Mayrit

A visit to the **Hammam Medina Mayrit** (Map pp114-16; ☎ 91 429 90 20; www.medinamayrit.com; Calle de Atocha 14; ☒ 10am-midnight) might just be the most relaxing cultural experience you've ever had. Imitating a traditional Arab bath, this place is a hybrid – a tea room, restaurant and spa, where you can soak in warm baths and get massages until midnight.

GOING GREEN

When the hustle and bustle of Madrid get to you, take a brief respite in the city's parks and gardens, which dot the capital liberally. The most famous parks, the **Parque del Buen Retiro** (p125), **Casa de Campo** (p130), **Real Jardín Botánico** (p125) and **Campo del Moro** (p119) are listed elsewhere in this chapter, but other lesser-known parks are worth checking out:

- **Parque de la Dehesa de la Villa** (Map p105; metro Francos Rodríguez) A spacious pine forest dotted with sports facilities, this park feels worlds away from Madrid.

- **Parque del Oeste** (p130) Green and perfectly manicured, this immaculate park near the Moncloa metro station, is designed in an English style and includes a pretty rose garden, from which you can take a cable car to the Casa de Campo.

- **Parque de Berlín** (Map p113; Avenida Ramón y Cajal; metro Concha Espina) With a great kids' play area and modern sports facilities, this is a fun park by day. By night the small auditorium is often the stage of concerts.

- **Jardines del Arquitecto Rivera** (Map pp110–12; Calle Barceló & Calle de Fuencarral; metro Tribunal) Next to the Municipal Museum, the highlight of this well-kept garden is a lavish fountain.

WALKING TOURS
Walk 1: Historic Madrid

This route takes you through the oldest quarters of Madrid, meandering among the monuments left by the Habsburg and Bourbon dynasties. If you power-walk it, this route could take you all of two hours. A much better idea is to take things nice and slow, allowing at least a full day to soak up the sights and sounds as you stop in to visit the monuments that most interest you.

The route starts at **Puerta del Sol** (**1**; p121), a busy square at the very centre of Madrid that was once the site of the eastern gate. With your back to the famous clock tower on the southern side of the square, turn left and walk down Calle del Arenal. Take the third street on your left and you'll come to the **Iglesia de San Ginés** (**2**; p120). Built in the 1300s, it's one of Madrid's oldest churches. On the crooked street behind the church hides the Chocolatería San Ginés (p147), famous for the *churros* (long doughnuts) it sells late at night.

From here, continue down Calle de los Bordadores, and you reach Calle Mayor. Directly in front of you is **Plaza Mayor** (**3**; p119),

an orderly arcaded square built in 1619. Designed to hold an open market and occasional special events, such as joustings and public hangings, it can fit more than 100,000 spectators. On a weekend night, it can still feel as if too many people have crowded in to hang out in the bars that line the plaza.

If you like, you can take a detour down Calle de Cuchilleros to stop in at one of the cave-like taverns that serve drinks and tapas in cool and cosy underground rooms. As you enter the plaza from Calle Mayor, Cuchilleros will be just off the far right-hand corner.

Make the loop around Plaza Mayor and exit back onto Calle Mayor. Head southwest down the street, leaving the open Plaza de San Miguel and Mercado de San Miguel (p146) on your left. A block further on you'll come across the elegant **Plaza de la Villa** (**4**; p120), home to Madrid's 17th-century

---

WALKING TOUR

Distance Approximately 5km
Duration Two hours to full day

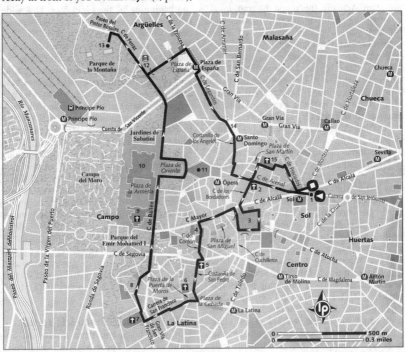

Ayuntamiento), with its pretty slate spire. Designed by Juan Gómez de Mora in 1644, this Madrid-baroque creation was originally intended to be a prison! On the same square stand the 16th-century, Plateresque Casa de Cisneros and the Gothic-Mudéjar Torre de los Lujanes, one of the city's oldest buildings, dating to the Middle Ages.

Take the street down the left side of the Casa de Cisneros, cross the road at the end, go down the stairs and follow the cobbled Calle del Cordón out onto Calle de Segovia. Almost directly in front of you is the Mudéjar tower of the **Iglesia de San Pedro el Viejo** (**5**; p127), a church built on top of the mosque that once stood on this site. This quarter was one of the places Muslim converts congregated in the Middle Ages, though little remains of those days.

Proceeding down Costanilla de San Pedro you reach the **Iglesia de San Andrés** (**6**; p127). The city's patron saint, San Isidro Labrador, was long interred here. The plaza out front is a cheerful, sunny spot with benches and a fountain. Stop by on a Sunday morning and you'll think there's a neighbourhood party going on. Actually, this is just the traditional congregating point for the free spirits and bongo players who aren't ready to go home after their Saturday night out.

From here cross Plaza de la Puerta de Moros (Plaza of the Moorish Door), so called because travellers coming up from North Africa entered the city by this gate. Head southwest to the impressive **Basílica de San Francisco el Grande** (**7**; p127) or go east, past the market along Plaza de la Cebada – once a popular spot for public executions – to arrive at the Sunday flea market of El Rastro.

From Basílica de San Francisco el Grande you can plunge into the small tangle of lanes that forms what was once the *morería*, and emerge onto Calle de Bailén and the wonderful *terrazas* (outdoor cafés) of **Las Vistillas** (**8**), great for drinking in the views. Take a minute to stroll the manicured gardens and, in summer, rest at one of the cafés here.

After a soothing *cerveza* (beer), follow Calle Bailén north to **Catedral de Nuestra Señora de la Almudena** (**9**; p120), built atop part of the old *morería*. Only finished in 1993, the cathedral took over 100 years to build. Next door is the majestic **Palacio Real** (**10**; p119). The palace's Plaza de la Armería opens onto the cathedral, linking the two monuments into

what seems like a single site. Gardens surround the complex on all sides: the Jardines de Sabatini to the north, Campo del Moro to the west, Parque del Emir Mohamed I to the south and Plaza de Oriente, with its statues, fountains and hedge mazes, to the east.

The elegant Plaza de Oriente is one of Madrid's most beautiful squares. It's well worth stopping here for a rest or a drink in the pricey Café de Oriente (p143). Just off the plaza to the east is the **Teatro Real** (**11**; p151), Madrid's opera house.

Continuing on from Plaza de Oriente north along Calle de Bailén, you will come to Plaza de España. The centre of the plaza is a pleasant place for walking, with clipped trees and fountains lining the neat paths. Continue on past the plaza to visit the **Museo de Cerralbo** (**12**; p128) and, further along Calle de Ferraz, the fantastically out-of-place **Templo de Debod** (**13**; p130). If you were to continue north from here, you would pass through the *barrio* of Argüelles, with some pleasant summer *terrazas*, and on towards Madrid's university district.

The eastern flank of Plaza de España marks the beginning of the Gran Vía. This wide boulevard was slammed through the tumbledown slums north of Sol in the 1910s and 1920s, so many buildings of that period line the sidewalks. You could stroll the length of this noisy, humming avenue, an artery simply bursting with shops, hotels, cinemas, bars and just a hint of louche nocturnal activity.

But our route turns here, heading southeast on Calle de Leganitos, which leads directly to **Plaza de Santo Domingo (14)**, a nondescript square surrounded by neighbourhood shops. Cross the plaza and head south on Costanilla de los Angeles, home to several quirky music shops. When the street meets up with Calle del Arenal, take a left here. Take your second left and you'll find yourself at Plaza de San Martín, beside the **Monasterio de las Descalzas Reales** (**15**; p120), whose plain façade hides a wealth of artistic and religious treasures.

Continue past the monastery and you'll reach the bustling shopping avenue of Calle de los Preciados. Take a right, and in just two blocks you'll find yourself back at the Puerta del Sol.

Walk 2: Around El Prado & El Retiro
This walk takes you from Puerta del Sol around the 'Big Three' Museums and along

some of Madrid's most elegant boulevards. If you don't stop, you could walk the entire route in a little over two hours. If you count in breaks at all the sights, the same walk will take days.

Begin at the **Puerta del Sol** (1; p121) and walk southeast down the Carrera de San Jerónimo. You'll soon run into the **Plaza de Canalejas** (2), where four different streets meet. The bustling plaza owes its stately air to the two early-20th-century buildings here: the Casa Meneses (1914) at the corner of Calle del Príncipe, whose round dome can be seen from afar; and the Casa Allende (1916), whose lovely tower is an interesting mesh of Mudéjar and *belle époque* styles.

Head down Calle del Príncipe to reach Calle de las Huertas and the heart of the Barrio de las Letras (Literature District). Turn left onto Huertas, then immediately swing left again, to head up to Calle de Cervantes, where, at No 11, you'll pass the **Casa de Lope de Vega** (3; p121). After passing the house, take your first right onto Calle de San Agustín to reach the 17th-century **Convento de las Trinitarias** (4; p121), where Cervantes lies buried.

Now continue down Calle de las Huertas until it spills into Paseo del Prado. Turn right to reach the **Centro de Arte Reina Sofía** (5; p123) and the **Real Jardín Botánico** (6; p125), or turn left to visit the **Museo del Prado** (7; p121), which will be immediately on your left as you head up the Paseo del Prado.

From here swing into the **Parque del Buen Retiro** (8; p125) or go past the Prado to the third museum in the city's crown, the **Museo Thyssen-Bornemisza** (9; p124). If you choose not to linger here, head north up Paseo del Prado, passing **Plaza de Cibeles** (10; p125), before turning right onto Calle de Alcalá, to reach the emblematic **Puerta de Cibeles** (11).

Turn north up Madrid's best shopping avenue, Calle de Serrano and drool over the offerings in the window displays until you reach the **Museo Arqueológico Nacional** (12; p128) and behind it, the **Biblioteca Nacional** (13;

WALKING TOUR

Distance Approximately 6km
Duration Two hours to full day

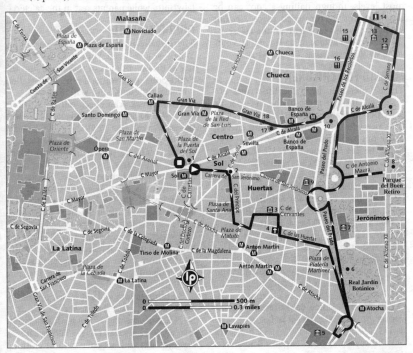

p129). Now on Paseo de los Recoletos, glance to the right at the **Monumento de Colón (14)**, before heading south down the boulevard. Stop for a drink at the emblematic cafés **Pabellón del Espejo (15)**, with its Modernista touches, or **Gran Café de Gijón (16)**, known as the meeting point of Madrid's literary elite.

Now head back towards Plaza de Cibeles and turn right at the ornate **Edificio Metrópolis Building (17)** at the start of **Gran Vía (18**; p128). Get into some heavy-duty window-shopping and people-watching as you make your way down Gran Vía to Calle Preciados, where you go left and stroll back to the Puerta del Sol.

COURSES

Language schools fill the city centre; keep your eye on the 2nd-floor window signs as you stroll along and you're sure to stumble across more than one centre offering classes in Spanish and a variety of other languages. Some of the more reputable courses are offered through the **Escuela Oficial de Idiomas** (Map pp106-8; ☎ 91 553 00 88, 91 554 99 77; Calle de Jesús Maestro). It offers courses in Spanish for foreigners (Español para Extranjeros) at most levels, though nailing a spot can be tough in this overcrowded place. Serious students can also look into taking classes at the **Universidad Autónoma de Madrid** (Map p105; ☎ 91 497 4029; www.uam.es; Ciudad Universitaria).

MADRID FOR CHILDREN

There's plenty to keep the little ones entertained, though most of the kid-specific activities available are fairly pricey. If all they need to do is burn up some energy, check out one of the city parks.

At the **Zoo-Aquarium** (☎ 91 512 37 70; Casa de Campo; adult/child €12.75/10.30; ☉ 10am-7pm) watch dolphins, sharks and fish in the aquarium, or visit the smallish zoo, where elaborate habitats have been created for animals big and small. The nearest metro station is Batán.

Faunia (☎ 91 301 62 10; Avenida de las Comunidades 28; adult/child €17.50/12; ☉ 10am-5.30pm Wed-Sun), a plant-and-animal paradise, is a great place for kids to learn about the natural world. They'll love the accurately recreated 'Amazon Jungle' and 'Polar Eco-System'. The nearest metro station is Valdebernardo.

All aboard! **Museo del Ferrocarril** (Railway Museum; ☎ 902 228822; Paseo de las Delicias 61; adult/child €3.50/2; ☉ 10am-3pm Tue-Sun) is home to old railway cars, train engines and more.

It's definitely guaranteed to fascinate budding engineers. The nearest metro station is Delicias.

Parque de Atracciones de la Casa de Campo (☎ 91 463 29 00; Casa de Campo; admission from €5, plus ride tickets; ☉ noon-7pm Sat & Sun) is a low-key theme park that sits right in the Casa de Campo. Don't expect upside-down roller coasters, but do expect to have a good time. The nearest metro station is Batán.

Cine Imax (☎ 91 467 48 00; Camino de Meneses), in the Parque Enrique Tierno Galván, south of Atocha train station, features a 3D megascreen. Movies such as *Alien Adventure* and *The Human Body* cost €7. The nearest metro stop is Méndez Álvaro.

La Cripta Magica (Map pp106-8; ☎ 91 539 96 96; Calle de Tarragona 15; ☉ 5-7pm Sat & Sun) magic show is great fun for kids and adults; there are also adult-oriented shows some nights.

At the mammoth indoor playground **Parque Secreto** (Map pp106-8; ☎ 91 593 14 80; www .parquesecreto.com in Spanish; Plaza Conde Suchil; admission per 30min from €2.50; ☉ 5-6pm Mon, 5-9pm Tue-Fri, 11.30am-2pm Sat & Sun) kids can romp around in tubs of plastic balls, on slides and in a snaking labyrinth, while parents rest in the cafeteria.

QUIRKY MADRID

There really is a museum for everything. When you've tired your eyes out gawking at the splendours of the Prado and the Reina Sofía, give yourself (and your wallet) a break at these off-the-wall museums.

Phone freaks can check out the displays at the **Museo del Teléfono Antiguo** (Old Telephone Museum; Map pp114-16; ☎ 91 539 17 93; Calle Arganzuela 29; admission free; ☉ 11am-2pm & 5-8pm Mon-Fri), where you'll see phone models from the talking box's early days through to today.

If you truly believe the old adage that cleanliness is next to godliness, you will surely love the **Museo de Sanidad e Higiene Pública** (Public Hygiene & Health Museum; Map p113; ☎ 91 387 78 00; www.isciii.es/museo/museo0.html in Spanish; Calle Sinesio Delgado 6; admission free; ☉ 9am-2pm Mon-Fri), where you'll learn all about Spain's efforts through the ages to prevent diseases and epidemics. Guided tours are available for those who call ahead.

Budding tailors will get a kick out of the **Museo del Traje** (Suit Museum; Map pp106-8; ☎ 91 549 71 50; http://museodeltraje.mcu.es; Avenida Juan de Herrera 2; admission €3; ☉ 9.30am-7pm Tue-Sat, 10am-3pm Sun), with its collection of clothing through the ages. The nearest metro station is Ciudad Universitaria.

TOURS

If you're pushed for time and want to fit a lot of sightseeing into a short visit, guided tours may be the ideal way to see the city.

Madrid Vision

The orange double-decker buses of **Madrid Vision** (☎ 91 779 18 88; adult/aged 7-16/child €10.60/5.30/free; ⏰ 9.30am-midnight Jul-Sep, 10am-9pm Apr-Jun & Oct-Dec, 10am-7pm Jan-Mar) are hard to miss as they go round the busy streets of the city. Hop on one of the three routes to get a great overview of the city; you can hop on or off at any major sight. Route 1 makes a jaunt around 'Historical Madrid', while Route 2 is dedicated to 'Modern Madrid', and Route 3 takes you around 'Monumental Madrid'. Several stops are included on more than one tour.

You can get more information at tourist offices or most travel agencies. You purchase tickets directly on the bus and can start at any stop along the three routes. A couple of private companies offering similar deals seem to come and go, so keep your eyes peeled.

Walking Tours

The tourist office (p118) organises Saturday-morning walks (in English and Spanish) around the centre of old Madrid called **Paseo por el Madrid de los Austrias** (adult/child €3.10/2.50; ⏰ tours at 10am). Meet outside the office half an hour before.

The tourist office also offers **Descubre Madrid** (Map pp114-16; ☎ 91 588 29 06; www.descubre madrid.munimadrid.es; Calle Mayor 69; adult €3.15-6.10, student €2.50-2.55) – dozens of separate itineraries that follow themes ranging from 'Neoclassic Madrid' to 'Madrid's Ceramics' to 'Classic Taverns of Madrid'. Generally three different itineraries are offered daily. You can pick up a booklet with information about times and itineraries at the tourist office or at branches of the bank Caja Madrid.

Cycling Tours

Londoner Mike Chandler has just started up **Madrid Bike Tours** (☎ 680 58 17 82; www.madrid biketours.com; tours incl picnic lunch €55), which offers 10 different guided two-wheel tours in and around Madrid. Make reservations by phone or email, and the tour guide will either pick you up or meet you at a central location.

FESTIVALS & EVENTS

Madrid loves to party, and seemingly any excuse is good for a *fiesta* (festival). For details about national festivals see p837, but here in the city be sure to look out for the following events. There's more information about most of them online at www.munimadrid.es.

Arco (Arte Contemporáneo; mid-February) Spain's premier art festival has gained international renown over its nearly 25 years of existence. Hundreds of galleries from around the world display new work here. Get more details at www.arco.ifema.es.

Gay Pride Parade (March) This wildly colourful spectacle sets out from the Puerta de Alcalá in the early evening, and

---

GAY & LESBIAN MADRID

Chueca is Madrid's gay and lesbian quarter, and while the *barrio* is open to all, there is an abundance of gay-friendly bars, restaurants and shops here. Bookshops such as **A Different Life** (Map pp110-12; ☎ 91 532 96 52; Calle Pelayo 30) not only sell books, but also magazines, videos and apparel, and are more geared towards gays and lesbians. Find a community feel at cafés such as **Mamá Inés** (Map pp110-12; ☎ 91 523 23 33; www.mamaines.com in Spanish; Calle de la Hortaleza 22; ⏰ 10am-2pm Sun-Thu, 10am-3.30am Fri & Sat), where you'll get the inside scoop on where the night's hotspot will be.

Gay bars and nightclubs spill out of Chueca and onto Gran Vía and the streets around it. For a low-key night out, head to the sophisticated **Antik Café** (Map pp110-12; ☎ 620 42 71 68; Calle de la Hortaleza 4 & 6; ⏰ 10am-3am), a bar by night and a tearoom by day that's perfect for a drink and some quiet conversation. Head downstairs to the old cellar, a dungeon-like space tastefully decorated in an Asian style. For something a little more upbeat, the cosy **Why Not?** (Map pp110-12; Calle de San Bartolomé 7; ⏰ 10.30pm-late) has the look and feel of the inside of a train car, and is packed nightly with gays and straights bobbing to pop and Top-40 music.

Two of the best house clubs are **Ohm** (Map pp110-12; ☎ 91 541 35 00; Plaza del Callao 4; ⏰ midnight-6am Fri & Sat), the Saturday-night party at Sala Bash, and **Cool** (Map pp110-12; ☎ 91 542 34 39; Calle Isabel la Católica 6; ⏰ midnight-6am), a sexy place that draws a fashionable crowd.

winds its way around the city in an explosion of music and energy, ending up at the Puerta del Sol later in the night.

Dos de Mayo (2 May) Malasaña hosts its biggest party of the year on this day, which follows the 1 May bank holiday that celebrates workers by giving them all a day off. The Plaza del Dos de Mayo, named in honour of those killed on that day, in 1808, is the scene for a day-long celebration of music and culture.

Fiesta de San Isidro (15 May) Madrid's patron saint is honoured with a week of nonstop processions, parties and bullfights. Free concerts are held throughout the city, and this week marks the start of the city's bullfighting season.

Fiesta de Flamenco Caja Madrid (mid-May) Hosted by the large bank Caja Madrid, this is a week-long celebration of stomping heels and Andalucian *duende* (magic).

Summer Festivals (mid-August to September) Small-time but fun, the neighbourhood summer festivals, such as San Cayetano in Lavapiés, and San Lorenzo and La Paloma in La Latina, are great places to find cheap entertainment.

Fiesta del Partido Comunista Español (PCE; mid-September) The yearly fundraiser of Spain's communist party, this fiesta lasts a weekend and is a mixed bag of regional food pavilions, rock concerts and political soapboxing.

Fiesta de Otoño (mid-October to mid-November) Music, dance and theatre take over Madrid during the fantastically cultural weeks of the Autumn Festival.

SLEEPING

Madrid has an excellent range of hotels, with plenty of decent budget options (doubles up to €50), stylish mid-range choices (doubles €51 to €130) and a handful of luxurious top-end hotels (doubles over €130) that rival those found in any European city. Finding a place to lay your head shouldn't be a problem, but booking ahead is always a good idea, especially in summer or during holidays.

The price of any type of accommodation may vary with the season. Some places have separate price structures for the high season (*temporada alta*), mid-season (*temporada media*) or low season (*temporada baja*); all are usually displayed on a notice in reception or close by. Hoteliers are not bound by these displayed prices. They are free to charge less, which they quite often do, or more, which happens rarely. Not all hoteliers consider the same periods to be high season either.

Accommodation prices in this book are a guide (based on high-season prices). Always check room charges before putting down your bags. Virtually all accommodation prices are subject to IVA, the Spanish version of value-added tax, which is 7%. This is often included in the quoted price at cheaper places, but less often at more expensive ones. To check, ask: *¿Está incluido el IVA?* (Is IVA included?). In some cases you will be charged IVA only if you ask for a receipt.

Los Austrias & Centro

If you like being in the thick of things, this lively quarter is for you. Within walking distance from most major sites and nightlife options, this *barrio* has oodles of budget *hostales* (budget hotels) and some charming mid-range hotels too.

BUDGET

Hostal Orly (Map pp110-12; ☎ 91 531 30 12; 7th fl, Calle de la Montera 47; s/d/tr €29/39/51) In a grand old 19th-century building, this is excellent value (especially spacious corner room No 11). Rooms are cheerful with tall ceilings and wooden floors. Many boast fabulous views.

Hostal Cruz Sol (Map pp114-16; ☎ 91 532 71 97; www.hostalcruzsol.com; 3rd fl, Plaza de Santa Cruz 6; s/d €38/48; ⊠) Set on a small, sunny plaza in the centre, the Cruz Sol is a clean hostel that makes a great base for seeing the sights. The newly renovated rooms have yellow walls and cheerful décor.

Los Amigos Backpackers' Hostel (Map pp110-12; ☎ 91 547 17 07; www.losamigoshostel.com; 4th fl, Calle de Campomanes 6; dm €15; 🖳) Clean, friendly and with English-speaking staff, this is far and away one of the city's best budget options. Cheerful dorm-style rooms have four to 10 bunk beds and free lockers.

United World International Youth Hostel (Map pp110-12; ☎ 91 548 00 48; www.unitedworldinternational.com; Gran Vía 73; dm incl breakfast & linen €15) A great deal, this friendly youth hostel offers kitchen access and intimate-feeling rooms with bunk beds.

MID-RANGE

Hostal Luis XV (Map pp110-12; ☎ 91 522 13 50; www.hrluisxv.net in Spanish; 8th fl, Calle de la Montera 47; s/d/tr €42/55/70; ⊠) All-new everything makes this place feel pricier than it is, as do the balconies outside every exterior room. Rooms are clean and modern, and exterior ones have beautiful views over old Madrid (the sight from triple room, No 820, is better than you'll find at any five-star in the city). At the time of writing, the owners were getting ready to open two other hostels in the same building.

Hostal Acapulco (Map pp110-12; ☎ 91 531 19 45; www.hostalacapulco.com; 4th fl, Calle de la Salud 13;

s/d/tr/q €41/51/69/85; ⊠ ▣) Overlooking a sunny plaza, this immaculate hostal is a great bet thanks to its marble floors, newly renovated bathrooms and gloriously thick double-glazed windows.

Hostal Madrid (Map pp114-16; ☎ 91 522 00 60; www.hostal-madrid.info; 2nd fl, Calle de Esparteros 6; s €50-58, d/tr €70/88; ⊠) Rooms here are simple, with rustic décor and fully equipped bathrooms. The owner also rents apartments starting at €100 per night.

Hotel Plaza Mayor (Map pp114-16; ☎ 91 360 06 06; www.h-plazamayor.com; Calle de Atocha 2; s/d €48/70; ⊠) Sitting just across from Plaza Mayor, here you'll find stylish décor and charming original elements of this 150-year-old building – super value.

Hotel HH Campomanes (Map pp110-12; ☎ 91 548 85 48; www.hhcampomanes.com; Calle de Campomanes 4; s €77-99, d €87-111; ⊠ ▣) For the ultimate in minimalism, head to this swanky boutique hotel with black walls and red lighting in the lobby. Rooms are spacious, with high ceilings and simple furniture.

Hotel Anaco (Map pp110-12; ☎ 91 522 46 04; www.anacohotel.com; Calle de las Tres Cruces 3; s/d/tr €77/97/130; ⊠) The Anaco seems to have it all: a fair price, a central location, attentive service and attractive décor. Recently renovated, rooms are stylish and extremely quiet.

Hotel II Castillas (Map pp110-12; ☎ 91 524 97 50; www.hoteldoscastillas.com; Calle de la Abada 7; s €84-110, d €99-125; ⊠) Open since late 2003, this central hotel has casual, smallish rooms with hardwood floors, and a pretty beige-and-blue colour motif. The spacious bath has some unexpected perks, such as a heated towel rack and a makeup mirror.

Hotel Preciados (Map pp110-12; ☎ 91 454 44 00; www.preciadoshotel.com; Calle de Preciados 37; s €120, d €138-150; ⊠ ▣) Near the Puerta del Sol and the busy commercial district, this stylish

---

TOP FIVE SLEEPS

■ **Catalonia Moratín** (p140) For history.

■ **Hotel HH Campomanes** (above) For being chic.

■ **Hostal Luis XV** (opposite) For value.

■ **Hostal La Macarena** (p140) For charm.

■ **Hostal La Zona** (p141) For gay friendliness.

---

hotel has comfortable rooms with all the amenities (even a free minibar) and a pretty historic façade. It has received rave reviews from readers for having excellent service, and for offering all-round good value for money.

TOP END

Hotel Intur Palacio San Martín (Map pp110-12; ☎ 91 701 50 00; www.intur.com; Plaza San Martín 5; s €109-165, d €109-204; ⊠ ▣) Set on a picturesque plaza, and housed in the former American embassy, this beautiful hotel offers simple luxury in a unique historical setting.

Hotel Senator (Map pp110-12; ☎ 91 531 41 51; www.senatorhoteles.com; Gran Vía 21; s €95-120, d €115-140; ⊠ ▣) One of Madrid's best new hotels is housed in a restored building you can best appreciate from the glass elevator that zips up its airy central patio. Rooms are sophisticated, though not grand, and there's a stylish rooftop pool open in summer.

Sol, Huertas & Atocha   Map pp114-16

The narrow streets and café-filled plazas of this *barrio* are full of people, life and laughter day and night, so if you're after a quiet escape, look elsewhere.

BUDGET

Hostal Internacional La Posada de Huertas (☎ 91 429 35 26; www.posadadehuertas.com; Calle de las Huertas 21; dm from €16) This simple youth hostel offers dorm-style rooms with metal beds and lockers. Though the place is clean, with warm blankets and decent (albeit tiny) bathrooms, it rates a zero on the charm scale.

Hostal Aguilar (☎ 91 429 59 26; www.hostalaguilar.com in Spanish; 2nd fl, Carrera de San Jerónimo 32; s/d/tr €40/47/63; ▣) The décor is tacky but pluses such as double-glazed, noise-blocking windows and a computer offering Internet access for €3 per hour make this a good option.

MID-RANGE

Hotel Mediodia (☎ 91 527 30 60; fax 91 530 70 08; Plaza del Emperador Carlos V 8; s/d/tr €54/64/82; ⊠) Just across from the Atocha train station, this attractive hotel is perfect if you're arriving on a late train.

Hostal Sardinero (☎ 91 429 57 56; 3rd fl, Calle del Prado 16; s/d from €45/60; ⊠) With its cheerful rooms and tall ceilings, this is one of the best hostales in the *barrio*. Fine wooden

MADRID

furniture, newly renovated bathrooms and a clean look make you feel at home.

Hostal Martín (☎ 91 429 95 79; www.hostalmartin .com; Calle de Atocha 43; s €36-58, d €45-70; ✖) This fine hostal is luminous and sparklingly clean, with a look you'd expect to see in a two- or three-star hotel.

TOP END

Catalonia Moratín (☎ 91 369 71 71; www.hoteles -catalonia.es; Calle de Atocha 23; s/d €136/177; ✖ ▯) Housed in a meticulously restored 18th-century palace, this is one of the most charming places to stay in Madrid. Rooms are rustic chic, each with a balcony.

Hotel El Prado (☎ 91 369 02 34; www.pradohotel .com; Calle del Prado 11; s €74-125, d €115-155; ✖) This newly renovated hotel offers style beyond its modest three-star category. Adding to the charm is the wine theme running throughout: rooms are decorated with an attractive grape motif and each room is named for a Spanish wine region.

Paseo del Prado & El Retiro
Map pp114-16

Near the 'Big Three' and the shady Parque del Retiro, this sophisticated district is high on charm but rather low on hotel options.

MID-RANGE

Hotel Mora (☎ 91 420 15 69; Paseo del Prado 32; s/d €57/75; ✖) Near the main museums, this simple hotel offers great value. Rooms are a bit sparse but some overlook the botanical gardens.

TOP END

Hotel Ritz (☎ 91 701 67 67; www.ritzmadrid.com; Plaza de la Lealtad 5; r from €480; ✖ ▯) Spain's most

legendary hotel, the Ritz is the last word in old-world luxury, and has been the hotel of choice for royals and dignitaries since it was built in 1910. If you can't dish out a few hundred euros to stay the night, stop by for a leisurely coffee at the elegant café downstairs.

Westin Palace (☎ 91 360 80 00; www.westin.com; Plaza de las Cortes 7; r from €200; ✖ ▯) A Madrid institution that opened in 1911, the Palace is Spain's second luxury hotel. For a splurge, stop in for one of their elegant theme dinners, such as the monthly 'opera dinner' with live opera, or the Thursday 'jazz and sushi dinners'.

Malasaña & Chueca
Map pp110-12

With its quirky charm and wild nights, this district is a fun place to stay, especially if you're into shopping or nightlife.

BUDGET

Hostal Don Juan (☎ 91 522 77 46; 2nd fl, Plaza de Vazquez de Mella 1; s/d €34/48) This elegant two-story hostal is filled with art (each room has original works) and antique furniture. Rooms are simple but luminous.

Hostal El Catalan (☎ 91 532 30 17; 2nd fl, Calle de Hortaleza 17; s €27-30, d/tr €42/54) El Catalan is one of the best-value places in Chueca, with clean, quiet rooms and especially nice bathrooms.

Hostal Maria Cristina (☎ 91 531 63 00; www .iespana.es/hostalmariacristina; Calle de Fuencarral 20; s/d/ tr €32/44/62) The tidy, quiet Maria Cristina has lots of light and a friendly atmosphere.

MID-RANGE

Hostal San Lorenzo (☎ 91 521 30 57; www.hostal -lorenzo.com; Calle Clavel 8; s €45-50, d €55-65, tr €75-90) The original stone walls of this 19th-century building have been left unexposed, adding

MADRID TRANSPORT MAP

Stations and lines (labelled):

Barajas 8 · Aeropuerto · Parque de Santa María 4 · San Lorenzo · Canillejas 5 · Las Musas 7 · Campo de las Naciones · Torre Arias · San Blas · Suanzes · Simancas · Arganda del Rey 9 · La Poveda · Rivas Vaciamadrid · Rivas Urbanizaciones · Puerta de Arganda · Vicálvaro · Valdebernardo · Mar de Cristal · Canillas · Esperanza · Arturo Soria · Avda. XIII · Parque de las Avenidas · Barrio de la Concepción · Pueblo Nuevo · Ascao · Ciudad Lineal · García Noblejas · Pavones · Artilleria · Cartagena · Concha Espina · Prosperidad · Alfonso XIII · El Carmen · Quintana · Ventas 2 · Manuel Becerra · O'Donnell · Goya · Ibiza · Sainz de Baranda · Estrella · Conde de Casal · Sierra de Guadalupe · Alto del Arenal · Miguel Hernández · Buenos Aires · Portazgo · Nueva Numancia · Puente de Vallecas · Villa de Vallecas · Congosto · Pío XII · Colombia · Cruz del Rayo · Duque de Pastrana · Plaza de Castilla 1 · Fuencarral 10 · Begoña · Chamartín · Ventilla · Valdeacederas · Tetuán · Estrecho · Alvarado · Herrera Oria 9 · Barrio del Pilar · Lacoma · Avda. Ilustración · Peñagrande · Antonio Machado · Valdezarza · Francos Rodríguez · Metropolitano · Cuatro Caminos 2 · Ríos Rosas · Canal · Nuevos Ministerios 8 · Gregorio Marañón · Santiago Bernabéu · Cuzco · República Argentina · Avda. de América 4 6 · Núñez de Balboa · Príncipe de Vergara · Velázquez · Serrano · Retiro · Rubén Darío · Colón · Alonso Martínez · Chueca · Sevilla · Banco de España · Atocha Renfe · Menéndez Pelayo · Pacífico · Méndez Álvaro · Paseo de la Frontera · Bilbao · Iglesia · Alonso Cano · Quevedo · Tribunal · San Bernardo · Noviciado · Gran Vía · Callao · Sol · Tirso de Molina · Antón Martín · Embajadores · Lavapiés · La Latina · Acacias · Pirámides · Marqués de Vadillo · Legazpi 3 · Delicias · Usera · Plaza Elíptica 11 · Abrantes · Oporto · Opañel · Vista Alegre · Carpetana · Puerta del Ángel · Alto de Extremadura · Lucero · Laguna · Empalme · Eugenia de Montijo · Aluche · Carabanchel · San Nicasio · Campamento · Batán · Lago · Casa de Campo · Colonia Jardín · Cuatro Vientos · Joaquín Vilumbrales · Puerta de España · Plaza de España · Opera R · Santo Domingo · Ventura Rodríguez · Guzmán el Bueno · Islas Filipinas · Moncloa 3 · Argüelles 4 · Principe Pío R · Ciudad Universitaria · Filipinas

TFM

zona
- **B1**
- **B2**
- **B3**

leyenda

1. Plaza de Castilla / Congosto
2. Ventas / Cuatros Caminos
3. Legazpi / Moncloa
4. Argüelles / Parque de Santa María
5. Canillejas / Casa de Campo
6. Circular
7. Las Musas / Pitis
8. Nuevos Ministerios / Barajas
9. Herrera Oria / Arganda del Rey
10. Fuencarral / Puerta del Sur
11. Plaza Elíptica / Pan Bendito
   MetroSur
R Opera / Principe Pío

simbología

○ Transbordo entre líneas de Metro
⌒ Transbordo largo entre líneas de Metro
Estación con horario restringido
Estación con acceso para personas con movilidad reducida. Ascensor
Acceso con rampa
◉ Estación de Cercanías Renfe
Estación Renfe
Terminal de autobús interurbano

🅺 Aeropuerto de Madrid • Barajas
🅿 Aparcamiento Libre en estación
🅿 Aparcamiento de Pago en estación
● Oficina de Información al Cliente

B1 B2 B3
Cambio tarifario exclusivamente para abonos mensuales y anuales, y títulos de 10 viajes

Metro ▶

Comunidad de Madrid
CONSEJERÍA DE TRANSPORTES E INFRAESTRUCTURAS

madrid

MetroSur

zona
- **B1**
- **B2**

El Casar · Los Espartales · Juan de la Cueva · El Bercial · Alonso de Mendoza · El Carrascal · Getafe Central · Conservatorio · Arroyo Culebro · Parque de los Estados · Julián Besteiro · Casa del Reloj · Parque Europa · Fuenlabrada Central · San Nicasio · Leganés Central · Hospital Severo Ochoa · Loranca · Manuela Malasaña · Hospital de Fuenlabrada · Parque Oeste · Alcorcón Central · Universidad Rey Juan Carlos · Móstoles Central · Pradillo · Hospital de Móstoles · Parque Laboa · Joaquín Vilumbrales · Puerta del Sur 12 10

Early evening drinks on Plaza de Santa Ana in Madrid's Barrio de las Letras (p121)

Fans at El Rastro flea market
(p126) in central Madrid

Artworks in Madrid's Museo del Prado (p121)

Rowing on the lake in Madrid's Parque del Buen Retiro (p125)

unique character. Renovated in 2003, its rooms are small but modern.

Hostal La Zona (☎ 91 521 99 04; www.hostallazona .com; 1st fl, Calle Valverde 7; d €45-65) Catering to a gay clientele, this place has rooms that are simple but stylish and very well kept. Spacious room No 203 is one of the best.

TOP END

Petit Palace Hotel Ducal (☎ 91 521 10 43; www.ht hoteles.com; Calle de Hortaleza 3; s €115-160, d €120-175; 🖳 🖳) With free computer access and ADSL lines in all rooms, this is the place for those who can't go a day without their high-speed Internet connection. Open since 2003, rooms here are modern and clean-lined, with wooden floors and perks such as a hydromassage shower.

Siete Islas Hotel (☎ 91 523 46 88; www.hotelsiete islas.com; Calle de Valverde 14-16; s €80-120, d €100-145; 🖳) The owners of this hotel are from the Canary Islands, and their heritage shows in every aspect of the place, from the marine-theme lobby to the rooms, which are all named after Canary towns. Rooms are comfortable and stylish, with a generous bathroom each and cool beige-and-navy-blue tones throughout.

Beyond the Centre

If you need to be near the University, the airport or the Chamartín train station, staying in the centre may not be the best option. Try these instead.

BUDGET

Albergue Santa Cruz de Marcenado (Map pp110-12; ☎ 91 547 45 32; Calle de Santa Cruz de Marcenado 28; dm under/over 26 incl carnet & breakfast €7.80/11.25) This HI hostel offers rooms for four, six and eight people and is a good choice if you want to be near the city's university district.

MID-RANGE

La Residencia del Viso (Map p113; ☎ 91 564 03 70; www.residenciadelviso.com; Calle del Nervión 8; s €77-103, d €129; 🖳) A little city oasis, this quiet B&B has rooms that look rather like a favourite aunt's guest room.

Husa Chamartín (Map p113; ☎ 91 334 49 00; www .hotelchamartin.com; Calle Agustín de Foxá s/n; s €60-111, d €60-130; 🖳) A great option if you're arriving late at the Chamartín train station; rooms here have all the comforts.

TOP END

High Tech Madrid Aeropuerto (☎ 91 564 59 06; www .hthoteles.com; Calle Galeón 25; s €100-135, d €120-150; 🖳 🖳 🅿 🖳) Within shouting distance of the airport (they provide free airport transport), the High Tech has stylish rooms, free Internet access and an outdoor pool. The nearest metro station is Aeropuerto.

EATING

Like much of central Spain, Madrid is a meat-lover's paradise, with delicious local specialities, such as *cochinillo asado* (roast suckling pig) and *cocido madrileño* (a hearty local stew made of beans, broth, veggies and various animals' innards). Don't think about what you're eating and it will all taste delicious, honest. Typical tapas include anything from innocuous olives and potato chips to blood sausages and boiled octopus.

Vegetarians can try flavoursome Spanish tortillas, made with potatoes, eggs and plenty of olive oil and salt. Also look out for pasta, salads and *bocadillos vegetales* (vegetable sandwiches), which usually have cheese.

Lunch runs from 1.30pm to 3.30pm, and dinner starts at 9pm and lasts till late. Many *madrileños* head out for a *caña* (small beer) and a tapa or two before meal times.

Eating in Madrid doesn't have to be expensive. To save money head to the impossibly cheap Chinese restaurants, where a full meal costs about €6, or to one of the many kebab cafeterias that dot Chueca, where you'll get a tasty pita sandwich for between €2 and €3. But if you want to dine in style, the city has tempting options ranging from traditional Castilian fare, to the freshest of Galician seafood, to the progressive *cocina de autor* (signature cuisine) of the top chefs.

Budget restaurants charge €8 and under for mains, mid-range restaurants charge €9 to €15 for mains, and anything more expensive than that is top end. Some restaurants with cheap fixed-priced meals *(menúes)* are also classified as budget.

Unless otherwise stated, restaurants listed here are open for both lunch and dinner.

Los Austrias & Centro

In the streets around Plaza Mayor you'll find dozens of character-filled restaurants serving *madrileño* favourites such as *cocido* and roasted meats.

MADRID

BUDGET

La Gloria de Montera (Map pp110-12; ☎ 91 523 44 07; Caballero de Gracia 10; menú €6.60) There's no beating this popular eatery for cheap sit-down fare. With a sleek, minimal décor and a combination of local and international flavours, it's oh-so-stylish, oh-so-cheap and oh-so-good. Lunch is especially crowded; be prepared to wait in line if you arrive after 2pm.

Museo del Jamón (Map p114-16; ☎ 91 531 45 50; www.museodeljamon.com in Spanish; Calle Mayor 7; menúes from €6.90; ☺ 8-1am) The 'Ham Museum' has a very clear focus: Spain's renowned salt-cured *jamón serrano*. You can get it on sandwiches, in tortillas, or sliced to carry home.

The dozens of hams hanging from the ceiling are a great photo op. There are branches of this Spanish chain all over the city.

La Mallorquina (Map pp114-16; ☎ 91 521 12 01; Plaza de la Puerta del Sol 8; pastries around €1.50; ☺ 8am-9pm) Start the day sweet at this bustling pastry shop, where a throng of white-jacketed waiters serve up croissants, truffles and sweets.

MID-RANGE

La Bola (Map pp110-12; ☎ 91 547 69 30; Calle de la Bola 5; mains €13; ☺ closed Aug) A neighbourhood classic, this traditional tavern has been serving up *cocido madrileño* for hungry locals since

---

TOP TAPAS

Madrid's tapas bars are crowded, raucous affairs with impatient crowds and permanently harried waiters. Don't expect service with a smile or extra elbow room, just make your way to the bar and add your shout of an order to the din. You may get a small tapa free with your drink; tapas-bar etiquette mandates that you accept what you're given, even if you don't particularly like it.

Simple tapas start at around €1.50, but the nicer options (such as *manchego* cheese or *jamón serrano* – cured ham) can cost up to €10 or €15 a plate. A full tapas meal can get pricey, so eat slowly and savour every bite!

Expect tapas bars to be open from about 1pm until 4pm for the pre-lunch and lunch crowd, and again from 8pm until midnight or later for the after-work and dinner crowd.

Tapas Tour

In the centre, your nose will tell you when you've reached the garlicky prawns (€4.35) grilling away at **La Casa del Abuelo** (Map pp114-16; ☎ 91 521 23 19; Calle de la Victoria 12). The house wine here is famously cheap. Next head to cafeteria-style **Las Bravas** (Map pp114-16; ☎ 91 532 26 20; Calle Espoz y Mina 13), known for its patented version of the classic Spanish *salsa brava*, a spicy sauce slathered over fried potatoes, Spanish tortillas and even seafood. For the city's best Spanish tortilla, and perfectly golden fried calamari, it's got to be the **Cervecería Alemana** (Map pp114-16; ☎ 91 429 70 33; Plaza de Santa Ana 6; ☺ closed Aug).

La Latina is also home to throngs of tapas bars. This area is especially crowded on Sundays, when everyone heads out for a drink and an appetizer after visiting the nearby Rastro flea market. Here you can try **La Chata** (Map pp114-16; ☎ 91 366 14 58; Calle de la Cava Baja 24), with a great cheese plate (€11) and bullfighter-themed décor. **La Carpanta** (Map pp114-16; ☎ 91 366 57 83; Calle del Almendro 22) is a classic neighbourhood bar with tapas that are so elaborate, they seem like sit-down food.

In Chueca, be sure to try an *empanada* (small meat or tuna pie) at the classic **Angel Sierra** (Map pp110-12; ☎ 91 531 01 26; Calle de Gravina 11), where munchers spill out onto Plaza de Chueca with their tapas and drinks. Nearby, **Stop Madrid** (Map pp110-12; ☎ 91 521 88 87; Calle de Hortaleza 11) is known for is *jamón serrano* and boisterously friendly feel. Gritty **Santander** (Map pp110-12; ☎ 91 522 49 10; Calle de Augusto Figueroa 2; ☺ closed Sun) is one of the most authentic-feeling tapas bars around, with dozens of cheap tapas available, waiters who've been there since before you were born, and a wildly mixed crowd. In nearby Malasaña don't miss **El Pez Gordo** (Map pp110-12; ☎ 91 522 32 08; Calle del Pez 6).

For upscale tapas, head to **El Lateral** (Map pp108-9; ☎ 91 435 06 04; Calle de Velázquez 57), a chic bar in Salamanca, where wearing hair gel seems to be required for entry. Still, it's a popular place to see and be seen. There are two branches: one at Paseo de la Castellana 132 (Map p113) and another at Fuencarral 43 (Map pp110-12).

the 1800s. It offers a unique Madrid flavour you won't find in more modern eateries.

Entre Suspiro y Suspiro (Map pp110-12; ☎ 91 542 06 44; Calle de Caños del Peral 3; mains €15) One of the city's best Mexican restaurants, this stylish place has the look of a Santa Fe café, and serves delicious Mexican dishes that are a world away from the standard tacos and burritos. Try the *mandinga* salad, which comes with prawns, mango and *cilantro* (coriander).

Mi Pueblo (Map pp114-16; ☎ 91 548 20 73; Calle Costanilla de Santiago 2; menú €11.71; ⏳ closed Sun dinner & Mon) For home-style meals such as *la abuela* (grandma) used to make, head to 'My Town', where the fixed-price menu is served day and night, and is a great way to taste regional specialities from all over Spain.

TOP END

Café de Oriente (Map pp110-12 ☎ 91 547 15 64; Plaza de Oriente 2; mains €10-29) The best thing about this sleek and upscale café is the view. It overlooks the Palacio Real and the elegant Plaza de Oriente, providing one of the most privileged eating vistas in Madrid. The elaborate, French-style food is good, if overpriced.

Sobrino de Botín (Map pp114-16; ☎ 91 366 42 17; Calle de los Cuchilleros 17; mains €11-18) This is the oldest restaurant in Madrid and it couldn't be more atmospheric. The delicious speciality is roast suckling pig, which is served whole at your table. If you're lucky, your meal may be accompanied by the music of *tunos*, university students who play traditional music for tips.

Las Cuevas de Luis Candelas (Map pp114-16; ☎ 91 366 54 28; Calle de los Cuchilleros 1; mains €12-22) One of several cave-like restaurants along this street, this hole-in-the-wall is built into the foundation of Plaza Mayor. Serving roasted lamb and suckling pig since 1949, 'The Caves of Luis Candelas' is a *barrio* classic.

Sol, Huertas & Atocha

Full of restaurants ranging from tourist traps to some of Madrid's best dining establishments, this quarter is a good place to find traditional food.

BUDGET

Cuevas El Secreto (Map pp114-16; ☎ 91 531 82 91; Calle de Barcelona 2; ⏳ 6.30pm-2am; mains €4-8) This rustic tavern serves tasty grilled meat and a few basic tapas. Everything is fresh and served with style, but it's refreshingly cheap.

La Finca de Susana (Map pp114-16; ☎ 91 369 35 57; Calle de Arlabán 4; menú €7) Priced right, this trendy spot serves a mix of Spanish and international fare to a professional crowd. Its sister restaurants, La Gloria de Montera (opposite) and Bazaar (p145) have a similar style.

Ducados Café (Map pp114-16; ☎ 91 360 00 89; Calle Plaza de Canalejas 3; mains €4-6, menú €8; ⏳ lunch) By night a popular place for drinks and dancing, by day a great place to grab an informal lunch. The *menú* is good value.

MID-RANGE

La Trucha (Map pp114-16; ☎ 91 429 58 33; Calle Manuel Fernández y González 3; mains €6-12) For fish, traditional dishes and tasty tapas, go for this classic restaurant in the heart of the Huertas. Try the local specialities, such as *rabo de toro* (oxtail) and roast veal. There's also a La Trucha at Calle Núñez de Arce 6 (Map pp114-16).

Edelweiss (Map pp114-16; ☎ 91 532 33 83; Calle de Jovellanos 7; mains €10) This is Madrid's best-loved German restaurant. From the outside it's not much to look at, and the old-fashioned interior hasn't changed in years, but specialities such as *chucrut* (sauerkraut) and German potato salad are excellent. The beer is top-notch too.

Al Natural (Map pp114-16; ☎ 91 369 47 09; Calle de Zorilla 11; mains €9-14; ⏳ closed dinner Sun) You want to eat vegetarian food, not rabbit food? Offering far more than salads and soups, Al Natural has hearty vegetarian dishes such as stuffed eggplant and mushroom stroganoff.

Sambar Kanda (Map pp106-8; ☎ 91 530 97 46; AVE terminal, Antigua Estación de Atocha, Carretera de Carlos V;

TOP FIVE MENÚES

The set menu *(menú)* is like manna from heaven for the hungry traveller. You'll find these three-course godsends all over the city, but some are better than others:

- **Bazaar** (p145) For fresh, fast fusion fare.
- **El Armario** (p145) For variety and fresh market cuisine.
- **Mi Pueblo** (above) For Spanish specialities.
- **La Musa de La Latina** (p145) For creative cuisine.
- **Al Natural** (above) For vegetarian options.

mains €13) A refined restaurant in the midst of the old Atocha station's tropical garden (p121), this is a relaxing place to enjoy elaborate salads and upscale takes on traditional dishes. There is also an informal café where you can get sandwiches.

TOP END

Lhardy (Map pp114–16; ☎ 91 522 22 07; Carrera de San Jerónimo 8; mains €12-20) In business since 1839, this emblematic restaurant is an elegant affair serving traditional Madrileño dishes to a spiffed-up crowd. With a baroque-ish atmosphere and attentive service, Lhardy offers a special dining experience. Order the famous *cocido madrileño* or a delicious game dish.

La Latina & Lavapiés   Map pp114–16

The working-class *barrios* of La Latina and Lavapiés are home to some of Madrid's most traditional restaurants. Calle de la Cava Baja is packed with great eateries, while informal cafés cluster around Plaza de la Paja.

BUDGET

Delic (☎ 91 364 54 50; Costanilla de San Andrés 14; sandwiches €3-5; ⏱ 11am-2am Tue-Sun) This cutesy deli and café serves creative sandwiches and amazing desserts to eat in or take away. There are a few tapas too, and by night it's a low-key spot for drinks and conversation.

Bar Salamanca (☎ 91 366 31 10; Calle de la Cava Baja 31; mains €4-8) Want to eat great Madrileño-style food without blowing your budget? This no-frills bar and restaurant is a great option.

MID-RANGE

Casa Maxi (☎ 91 365 12 49; Calle de la Cava Alta 4; mains €6-12, menú €8; ⏱ closed Mon & Aug) Grungy-looking Casa Maxi proves that even a no-frills joint can dish up delicious food. Known for old-style Madrid dishes, it's not for the weak of stomach. Fancy some *rabo de toro* (oxtail), *revuelto de morcilla* (fried-blood sausage) or *callos a la madrileña* (Madrid-style tripe)?

Julián de Tolosa (☎ 91 365 82 10; Calle de la Cava Baja 18; mains €9-15; ⏱ closed dinner Sun) If you're hungry for some great grilled steaks, this Basque institution will surely satisfy. The house speciality is *chuletón de buey* (steak); the other items on the limited menu are similarly hearty.

TOP END

Casa Lucio (☎ 91 365 32 52; Calle de la Cava Baja 35; mains €9-18) A popular option with politicians

and other *famosos* (celebrities), the traditional Casa Lucio is famous for its *huevos rotos* (fried eggs served runny over potatoes). The place is usually packed, so reservations are necessary, especially for lunch.

Paseo del Prado & El Retiro
MID-RANGE & TOP END

Gran Café de Gijón (Map pp110–12; ☎ 91 521 54 25; Paseo de Recoletos 21; mains €9) This is one of Madrid's best-loved cafés, an elegant old place that has been serving coffee, pastries and simple meals since 1888. It's long been known as a literary hang-out, and writers still meet here to give readings and discuss bookish topics.

Casa Domingo (Map pp106–8; ☎ 91 576 01 37; Calle de Alcalá 99; mains €8-13) A family-owned place that's been here since 1920, Casa Domingo is known for its generous portions of hearty local fare, such as tripe and roast tongue, but have no fear, it also serves up standard dishes such as baked chicken and codfish.

Paradís Madrid (Map pp110–12; ☎ 91 575 45 40; Paseo de Recoletos 2; mains €10-18; ⏱ closed Sat lunch & Sun) For great Catalan food, this is your best bet in central Spain. The terrace is a perfect place to enjoy regional dishes such as grilled *butifarra* (sausage) and codfish in flaky pastry.

Malasaña & Chueca   Map pp110–12

You'll find a little of everything, from homely traditional restaurants to funky fusion food, in this anything-goes neighbourhood. Busy streets such as Calle de Fuencarral and Calle de Hortaleza are lined with cheap eating options like the Middle-Eastern kebab restaurants, which serve tasty pita sandwiches and good vegetarian options. You'll also find a huge selection of newer, trendy restaurants in this area.

BUDGET

Omertá (☎ 91 701 02 42; Calle de Gravina 17; menú €7.50) Bare brick walls and a tall ceiling give Omertá the feel of an old warehouse, though the friendly service and piping-hot square pizza prove its worth as a pizzeria. It gets crowded at lunch, but if you get here by 2pm, you won't have a problem nabbing a table.

El Bierzo (☎ 91 531 91 10; Calle de Barbieri 16; mains €7; ⏱ closed Sun & Aug) With its fantastic midday *menú*, this place has become a favourite with office workers out for a reliably good, quick lunch. Fresh fish, game meat and local veggies usually show up on the ever-changing menu.

Bluefish (☎ 91 448 67 65; Calle de San Andrés 26; mains €5-8, menú €8.50; 🕙 closed Mon) Run by two young expats, this tiny restaurant, off Plaza Dos de Mayo, serves up a delicious array of international dishes. Service (in English, if you like) is always with a smile, and the atmosphere is open and friendly.

Areia (☎ 91 310 03 07; www.areiachillout.com in Spanish; Calle de Hortaleza 92; menú €8) Areia is best known as a bar (p149), but with its chill Arabian vibe, this is a relaxed place for lunch. The *menú* usually offers good vegetarian options.

Chez Pomme (☎ 91 532 16 46; Calle de Pelayo 4; mains €6-8, menú from €9; 🕙 closed Sun & Aug) One of the few vegetarian options in this part of town, this smallish restaurant serves tasty dishes based on fresh vegetables and tofu.

El Buda Feliz (☎ 91 531 95 24; Calle Tudescos 5; mains €5-8) For tasty Chinese food that's cheap but reliable, you can't beat the Happy Buddha, a popular spot for lunch, thanks to its *menú*.

Patatus (☎ 91 532 6129; Calle de Fuencarral 98; shared dishes €9-16) Open late and popular with the under 20s, this tavern is where you go after hours for cheap, filling fare. The speciality is the French-fry tray, which comes with multiple dipping sauces.

Café Comercial (☎ 91 521 65 55; Glorieta de Bilbao 7) With the look of a 1930s salon, this café is a city classic. Join the regulars who stop by for breakfast or a coffee later in the day.

Café de Ruiz (☎ 91 446 12 32; Calle de Ruiz 11) This cosy café looks like it was lifted out of a 1930s movie, with marble tables, velvet-covered seats and a welcoming attitude. Try the awesome desserts (there's little else food-wise) and the tasty speciality coffees.

AUTHOR'S CHOICE

For an eating experience that's fun, filling and fabulously delicious, there's no beating **La Musa de La Latina** (Map pp114-16; ☎ 91 354 02 55; Costanilla de San Andrés 12, Plaza de la Paja; mains €9). Fun and funky, this is a fantastic lunch or dinner spot, with tasty, innovative dishes, such as fried green tomatoes topped with goat's cheese, or foie-and-apple pastry, all served up by one of the hottest wait staffs in town. By night the basement becomes a popular bar.

MID-RANGE

Wokcafé (☎ 91 422 90 69; Calle de los Infantas 44; mains €8-12; 🕙 closed Sun) The Asian-inspired Wokcafé lives by the motto *'sexy y sano'* (sexy and healthy). The romantic atmosphere and light dishes here live up to the claim. The so-called 'woks', bowls of stir-fried rice, veggies, meats or seafood, are the yummy house specialities.

Bazaar (☎ 91 523 39 05; Calle de la Libertad 21; menú €7, mains €7-11) This popular place is priced right and offers creative fusion food that obviously appeals to Madrid's young and trendy, who pack the place for both lunch and dinner. Reservations aren't accepted, so be prepared to wait in line. Your reward is tasty, light fare with an international spin.

El Armario (☎ 91 532 50 12; Calle de San Bartolomé 7; lunch menú €8, dinner €18) Serving seasonal Mediterranean food, this place is great value at lunch, and a reliable choice for a pleasant dinner. The fantastic *menúes* are always surprising and provide a wide variety (six or seven options for each course) of creative market cuisine.

Zara (☎ 91 532 20 74; Calle de las Infantas 5; mains €5-10, menú €12; 🕙 closed Sun & Aug) One of the best Cuban restaurants in Madrid, this homely place has red-chequered tablecloths and homemade dishes such as *arroz a la Cubana* (rice with fried banana, egg and tomato) and *ropa vieja*.

La Musa (☎ 91 448 75 58; Calle de Manuela Malasaña 18; mains €6-12, menú €8-11; tapas €4; 🕙 closed Mon) A trendy place catering to diners who are looking for something a little different, this fabulous restaurant offers unique dishes and a selection of gourmet tapas. The sister branch La Musa de La Latina (see the boxed text Author's Choice opposite) is even better.

Luna Mulata (☎ 91 522 13 26; Calle Reina 4; mains €9-15, menú €8) The stylish Luna Mulata looks like something straight out of Manhattan. With enormous windows and black benches, the restaurant has sleek décor, while the menu is limited but reliable, with lots of lite options.

TOP END

Arce (☎ 91 522 04 40; Calle Augusto Figueroa; mains €9-23; 🕙 closed Sun & Aug) Offering very good value, Arce combines modern style with the most traditional ingredients. The house specialities change with the season, but game dishes are nearly always present in some surprising, delicious form. Chef Iñaki

Camba has made Arce one of Madrid's top new restaurants.

Salamanca & Las Ventas
MID-RANGE
Estay (Map pp108-9; ☎ 91 578 04 70; Calle de la Hermosilla 46; tapas €2-5; ♡ 9am-1am) 'Fine dining in miniature' is this stylish restaurant's claim to fame. In food terms that means tiny tapas-like dishes of yummy things, such as foie gras with raspberry sauce, and zucchini stuffed with shrimp. You'll need to make a reservation, especially at lunch.

El Septimo (Map pp108-9; ☎ 91 562 29 40; Calle de Diego de León 7; mains €13) With its rustic interior and cosy wooden tables, this vegetarian-friendly restaurant is an unusual find in central Madrid. Elaborate salads and delicious concoctions, such as mushrooms with goat's cheese, will keep vegetarians happy, while meat eaters can choose from internationally tweaked options, such as duck *confit* or roasted potatoes with bacon.

TOP END
Balzac (Map pp106-8; ☎ 91 420 06 13; Calle Morato 7; mains €26-30, menú €60) Young and informal, the shaggy-haired, unshaven chef Andrés Madrigal is the last person you'd expect to find behind the sophisticated restaurant Balzac. Madrigal (who also runs Azul Profundo; see opposite) has made this elegant dining spot one of Madrid's best restaurants. Only top ingredients are used for unique dishes such as false couscous and winter gazpacho.

Restaurante El Pescador (Map pp106-8; ☎ 91 402 12 90; Calle de José Ortega y Gasset 75; mains €12-28) High-end but worth a splurge, this is one of the city's best and most emblematic spots for seafood. The smell alone will draw you in and tempt you to try the delicious prawns, oysters and flaky baked fish dishes.

Goizeko Wellington (Map pp106-8; ☎ 91 577 01 38; Calle de la Villanueva 34; mains €15-25; ♡ closed Sun) This Basque restaurant, at the elegant five-star Hotel Wellington, is a romantic spot for an upscale meal. With a superb wine list and heavenly desserts, this place will provide you with a meal to remember.

Northern Madrid
MID-RANGE
Las Batuecas (Map p105; ☎ 91 554 04 52; Av Reina Victoria 17; mains €10) Red-chequered tablecloths and black-and-white photos of old Madrid

---

AUTHOR'S CHOICE
Always creative, always delicious, trendy **Azul Profundo** (Map pp110-12; ☎ 91 532 25 64; Plaza de Chueca; mains €8-12, menú €34; ♡ closed Mon & dinner Sun) is a new restaurant that has skyrocketed to the top of Madrid's most popular eateries list. The menu of tiny tapas-like dishes changes constantly, but expect to be surprised with innovative creations and wonderfully fresh ingredients. Owner Andrés Madrigal is also the chef of the excellent restaurant Balzac (see below).

---

decorate this homely restaurant. The large menu features dozens of local specialities, such as the *tortilla de callos* (tripe omelette); it may not sound appetizing but it ain't famous for nothing.

TOP END
El Bodegón (Map p113; ☎ 91 562 31 37; Calle del Pinar 15; mains €16-27; ♡ closed Sat lunch, Sun & Aug) One of the city's top restaurants, El Bodegón has been serving top-quality Catalan- and Basque-inspired cuisine for years, and its reputation for excellence is as solid as ever. Reservations are usually necessary.

Calle 54 (Map p113; ☎ 91 535 39 02; Paseo de la Habana 3; mains €20) One of the best jazz joints (p151) in Madrid, Calle 54 also has a fantastic restaurant where you can order simple but well-planned dishes, such as hake with vegetables and tuna tar-tar.

Self-Catering
Champion Supermarket (Map pp114-16; ☎ 91 365 55 22; Calle de Toledo 32; ♡ 9am-9.30pm Mon-Sat) Find everything from bananas to baby diapers to bleach at this modern grocery store.

Mercado de San Miguel (Map pp114-16; Plaza de San Miguel; ♡ 8am-2pm & 5-8pm Mon-Fri, 8am-2pm Sat) Madrid's most central fresh market, this is the spot to stock up on ingredients for sandwiches and picnics.

Mercado de La Cebada (Map pp114-16; ☎ 91 365 91 76; Plaza de la Cebada; ♡ 8am-2pm & 5-8pm Mon-Fri) Another easy-to-reach fresh market, this is a great place to take the pulse of 'real' Madrid.

Mallorca (Map pp108-9; ☎ 91 577 18 59; Calle de Serrano 6; ♡ 9.30am-9pm) For fine takeaway food, head to this Madrid institution. Everything here, from gourmet mains to snacks and desserts, is delicious. There are branches throughout the city.

DRINKING

Madrid's bar and café culture is one of its most endearing features, and character-filled bars, pubs and neighbourhood cafés line streets all over the city. If you're after traditional style, with tiled walls and flamenco tunes, head to the *barrio* of Huertas. For gay-friendly drinking holes Chueca is the place. Malasaña caters to a grungy, funky crowd, while La Latina has friendly, no-frills bars that guarantee atmosphere every night of the week. In summer, head to the outdoor cafés in the city's plazas.

Though many bars open in the afternoon for happy hour, most of the places listed here don't get into full swing until after dinner, usually around midnight, but stay open until about 3am. If you want more *marcha* (action) after that, head to a disco (see p152).

Los Austrias & Centro   Map pp114–16

The centre itself is low on really special bars, but head towards Gran Vía for some of Madrid's best dance clubs (see p152) or down near La Latina for a few classic bars.

Café del Nuncio (☎ 91 366 09 06; Calle de Segovia 9) Straggling down a stairway passage to Calle de Segovia, this sprawling café has several cosy levels inside and a fabulous outdoor *terraza*.

Chocolatería San Ginés (☎ 91 365 65 46; Pasadizo San Ginés 5) At least once, you've got to end

the night at this classic café, where the speciality is an eye-opening dose of syrupy hot chocolate and some freshly fried *churros* for dipping. It's open until 7am!

Taberna de Cien Vinos (☎ 91 365 47 04; Calle del Nuncio 17; ✆ closed Mon) This unpretentious wine bar is the perfect place to order by the glass or by the bottle. The classic décor and friendly service have made it one of the best-known wine bars in town.

Sol, Huertas & Atocha   Map pp114–16

This atmospheric *barrio* is a treasure chest of bars and nightspots, and you could stay here night after night and never tire of the offerings. Some of the busiest areas here are Calle de Huertas and the Plaza de Santa Ana.

Cervecería Alemana (☎ 91 429 70 33; Plaza de Santa Ana 6; ✆ closed Aug) Renowned for its cold, frothy beers and delicious tapas, this old-time bar surely hasn't changed much since the time when Hemingway was a regular. The worn wooden benches and bow-tied waiters will take you back to those days.

Los Gabrieles (☎ 91 429 62 61; Calle de Echegaray 17) Smothered in gorgeous tiles, this bar is worth a peek at, even if you don't order a thing. Flamenco music and occasional live music give it a unique Madrileño flavour.

Taberna de Dolores (☎ 91 429 22 43; Plaza de Jesús 4) Old bottles and beer mugs line shelves behind the bar at this Madrid institution, known for its blue-and-white tiled exterior. You can get good house wine and some of Madrid's best beer for €1.50 a pop, though the tapas are pricey.

UNDER THE STARS

From April to October, when the evening temperatures in Madrid are balmy and rain is rare, **summer terrazas** (terraces, or tables set up outdoors) spring up like mushrooms all over town. Though many of the bars listed put up *terrazas*, the most popular places to go for a drink under the stars are along **Paseo de la Castellana** and **Paseo de los Recoletos** (Map pp110–12), where tables run up and down the sidewalks. The drinks are pricey and the crowd a bit pretentious, but the atmosphere is lively and inviting. Even more pleasant are the *terrazas* that set up in Argüelles, especially those on **Paseo del Pintor Rosales** (Map pp106–9). With parkland on one side and considerably less traffic than Paseo de la Castellana, these places also exercise a little more control over their prices. The **Parque de Berlín** (Map p113), way up in Chamartín, is another peaceful spot, and the *terrazas* of **Las Vistillas** (Map pp114–16), just across Calle de Bailén, offer views to the Sierra de Guadarrama.

Yet there's no need to go so far afield to find *terrazas*; Madrid's squares make perfect locations for outdoor drinking. Several of the bars on **Plaza de Santa Ana** (Map pp114–16) operate *terrazas*, as do those at **Plaza del Dos de Mayo** (Map pp110–12) in Malasaña, and **Plaza de la Paja** (Map pp114–16) near the Plaza Mayor.

Matador (☎ 91 531 89 81; Calle Cruz 39) For a more Andalucian atmosphere, come to this utterly unpretentious bar, where soulful flamenco tunes fill the dark corners, and old farm equipment hangs from the walls.

Casa Alberto (☎ 91 429 93 56; www.casaalberto.es; Calle de las Huertas 18) Stop by on Sunday for a traditional pre-lunch aperitif at this classy bar, which has been serving vermouth on tap since 1827. There's also a restaurant at the back, which has a lunch *menú* for €12.50.

Salon del Prado (☎ 91 429 33 61; Calle Prado 4) Curl up with a tea and a book at this elegant café just off Plaza de Santa Ana. The desserts are OK, but the best of Salon del Prado is the ambience.

La Latina & Lavapiés   Map pp114–16

Wander down and around Calle de la Cava Baja for a myriad of options. You'll find everything from Andalucian-styled taverns, where flamenco singers gather, to up-to-the-minute trendy bars drawing Madrid's yuppie scene.

Bonanno (☎ 91 366 68 86; Plaza del Humilladero 4) Due to the *madrileños* genetic aversion to sleep, it can be hard to find a bar with a buzz before midnight. Not so in Bonanno, a stylish cocktail bar that has quickly become wildly popular with young professional *madrileños*. It gets crowded early, so be prepared to snuggle up close to those around you if you want a spot at the bar.

El Viajero (☎ 91 366 90 64; Plaza de la Cebada 11; ⌾ closed Mon) You can get an informal dinner downstairs (tapas €3.50 to €8), but even bet-

ter is the bar upstairs, a dark, low-key place overlooking the plaza and the glorious Iglesia de San Pedro. In summer you can head up another floor to the rooftop terrace, where the view is unbeatable.

Taberna Chica (☎ 91 364 53 48; Costanilla de San Pedro 7) Most of those who come to this narrow little bar are after one thing, the famous Santa Teresa rum that comes served in an extra-large mug. The mood is chilled, and tables at the front and back are perfect for conversation in the early evening – for a rest, if the rum proves too much.

Vinos el Mentidero (☎ 91 354 64 92; Calle del Almendro 22) Get the night started at this fun flamenco bar, where tapas and *copas* (drinks) are served around the bustling upstairs bar. The downstairs area is somewhat more low-key – a place where groups of friends huddle around tall barrels that serve as tables. House wine is just €1.80, and tapas cost from €3 to €8.

Lámiak (☎ 91 365 52 12; Calle de la Cava Baja 42) This place is new but already a hit with the young, arty types of the *barrio*. Here you'll find a good selection of drinks, and a few tapas and canapés to go along with them. If the bar area gets too crowded, you can head downstairs to the dining room for a bite to eat (mains €6 to €12).

Malasaña & Chueca   Map pp110–12

One of Madrid's liveliest nightlife areas, gay-friendly Chueca and let-it-all-hang-loose Malasaña are packed with bars of all styles and attitudes. Head for the streets around

---

A BAR BY ANY OTHER NAME...

So you thought a bar was a bar was a bar? Think again. Sure, a 'bar' describes any place where you can get a beer or a few tapas, but *madrileños* have a complex vocabulary to classify their drinking habits. Here are a few tips on making sense of it all.

- **Bar de Ambiente** A place with a gay *ambiente* (ambience).
- **Bar de Copas** Gets going after dinner (around midnight) and primarily hard drinks are served.
- **Bar Musical** Music, sometimes live, is the defining atmospheric element.
- **Cervecería** Naturally, the focus is on *cerveza* (beer) and there's probably plenty of the foamy stuff on tap.
- **Pub** A pub; nearly always serves Guinness.
- **Terraza** An open-air bar, for warm-weather tippling only.
- **Taberna** Usually a rustic place: expect to see barrels used as tables and lots of tile décor.
- **Vinoteca** A bit more upmarket; wine bars where you can order by the glass.

Plaza de Chueca for a trendy crowd and lots of good-looking boys, or head to Malasaña for a low-key attitude and lots of grunge and rock bars.

Museo Chicote (☎ 91 532 67 37; Gran Vía 12) A city classic, this cocktail bar has a lounge atmosphere late at night and a stream of small-time famous faces all day. For years the place was renowned for its extensive collection of decorative liquor bottles, which is no longer here.

Bar Cock (☎ 91 532 28 26; Calle de la Reina 16) Though it looks drab from the street, the elegant Bar Cock (that's cock as in rooster, and the lower level is full of drawings and paintings of them) is one of Madrid's classic bars and almost always offers a lively atmosphere. It has the look of an old gentleman's club, and is popular with A-listers and a refined older crowd looking for good drinks and funky music.

Café Pepe Botella (☎ 91 522 43 09; Calle de San Andrés 12) The cosy velvet benches and marble-topped tables give this popular place a quirky charm. Old photos line the walls and the atmosphere is bohemian chic.

Quiet Man (☎ 91 523 46 89; Calle de Valverde 44) One of the first bars outside Ireland to serve Guinness beer, the Quiet Man is an institution in Madrid – a dark, spacious bar, where you can play darts, have a seat on the refined velvet benches, or park yourself at the bar.

Areia (☎ 91 310 03 07; www.areiachillout.com in Spanish; Calle de Hortaleza 92) To chill out, there's no place better than this cool café and bar, where an Arabian vibe dominates the décor and chill-out music drifts up to the rafters. By day, you can order a tasty lunch *menú* (see p145).

AUTHOR'S CHOICE

Bow-tied waiters stir classic cocktails at **Del Diego** (Map pp110-12; ☎ 91 523 31 06; Calle de la Reina 12), while a relaxed crowd squashes around the small tables scattered about. Opened by an ex-waiter from Museo del Chicote, this place has become a Madrid classic and is known for its upmarket-yet-welcoming attitude. The wall of old liquor and brandy bottles (a pretty sight in itself) was featured in the Spanish film *Amor, Curiosidad, Prozac & Dudas* (Love, Curiosity, Prozac & Doubts).

AUTHOR'S CHOICE

Smothered with beautiful tiles, **Viva Madrid** (Map pp114-16; ☎ 91 429 36 40; www.barviva madrid.com; Calle de Manuel Fernandez y González 7) is a Madrid landmark. Wildly popular with both tourists and locals, it's a great place to meet people, and since there are several bars spread out over two levels, you're never far from one of their famous *mojitos*.

La Vía Láctea (☎ 91 446 75 81; Calle de Velarde 18) For grouchy, grungy rock and roll, it's got to be La Vía Láctea, a classic bar that earned its fame during the *movida* and hasn't let go since. The tipplers apparently haven't changed their wardrobe since then either: eye shadow for the girls and the boys is definitely the order of the day. Expect to find a mixed, informal crowd and a good drink selection.

La Ida (☎ 91 522 91 07; Calle de Colón 7) Mismatched furniture, arty black-and-white photos, and green walls set the tone at this friendly bar, which draws a surprising number of customers with multiple face-piercings. Hopping most nights of the week, this is a good place to meet up with friends, and it's known for having great *mojitos*.

Finnegan's (☎ 91 310 05 21; Plaza de las Salesas 9) The friendliest pub in town, this laid-back place is full of regulars, who'll make you feel at home.

Salamanca & Las Ventas

Bars in this posh *barrio* tend to draw well-heeled crowds. Get the Salamanca look with preppy clothes for him, and a trendy, ultra-accessorised look for her.

Terrabacus Vinoteca (Map pp108-9; ☎ 91 435 37 18; Calle de Lagasca 74) This stylish wine bar offers more than 60 by-the-glass wines, and has some 300 more labels you can try by the bottle. If a tasting at the bar isn't enough for you, sign up for their club to get wine news and invites to formal tastings.

Geographic Club (Map pp106-8; ☎ 91 578 08 62; Calle de Alcalá 141) With its elaborate stained-glass windows and mountain explorer theme, this is an atmospheric place for a happy-hour drink. Sip at a table on the main floor (like the one built around an old hot-air balloon basket) or head down to the cavern-like pub. There is a restaurant here too.

MADRID

Independencia (Map pp106-8; ☎ 91 7819 540; Calle de Salustiano Olózaga 11) This is one of those places where you can eat breakfast, then stay on for lunch, coffee, tapas, cocktails and dancing. The bar gets lively at around 11pm and dancing comes later.

ENTERTAINMENT

There's something going on in Madrid just about all the time, and to make sure you're not missing out, there are numerous *ocio* (entertainment) publications with what's-on information. The best and best-known guide is *Guía del Ocio*, a Spanish-only weekly magazine that will cost you €1 at a news kiosk. Also keep an eye out for the monthly *Salir*, also €1 and in Spanish. The monthly English-expat publication *In Madrid* is given out free, and has lots of information about what to see and do in town. Find it at some hotels, original-version *(VO)* cinemas and English-language bookshops. The top gay guide is *Shangay*, which also includes listings for Barcelona and other cities.

The local press is always a good bet, with daily listings of films, concerts and special events. On Fridays pick up *Metropoli*, a magazine supplement in *El Mundo*, for additional information on the week's offerings. Specialised publications, such as the free all-flamenco *Alma 100*, available in *tablaos* (tourist-orientated performance venues) and flamenco shops, or the free theatre guide *Teatros*, available from local venues, are helpful too.

Before you get to Madrid, you can check out the scene online. The website for *Guía del Ocio* (www.guiadelocio.com) is a virtual version of the publication, and it has some information in English. Also helpful is the extremely complete guide La Netro (http://madrid.lanetro.com in Spanish). The Madrid page of www.whatsonwhen.com hits the highlights (in English) of sport and cultural activities. It includes information on getting tickets too. The town hall's website (www.munimadrid.es) has practical details for nearly all the city's theatres and stages.

You can buy cinema, theatre, opera or concert tickets *(entradas)* at box offices or at ticket vendors including the following:

Madrid Rock (Map pp110-12; ☎ 91 521 02 39; Gran Vía 25; ⊘ 10.30am-3pm & 4.30-8.30pm Mon-Sat) This music megastore has tickets to most big-name concerts.

Servicaixa (☎ 902 332211; www.servicaixa.com in Spanish) You can also get tickets from Servicaixa ATM machines.

Tel-Entrada (☎ 902 101212, 93 326 29 46 outside Spain; www.entradas.com) Buy the tickets by phone, then pick them up at the box office.

Cinemas

Several movie theatres are huddled around Gran Vía and Calle de Princesa.

La Enana Marrón (Map pp110-12; ☎ 91 308 14 97; Travesía de San Mateo 8) For alternative theatre, there's no beating this great arty, alternative theatre, showing documentaries, animated films, international flicks and oldies.

Cine Doré (Map pp114-16; ☎ 91 549 00 11; Calle de Santa Isabel 3) The National Film Library offers fantastic classic and vanguard films at this cinema. It's always crowded, but what's on offer is great.

Alphaville (Map pp110-12; ☎ 91 559 38 36; Calle de Martín de los Heros 14) Shows quirky, *VO* films from Europe and the USA.

Princesa (Map pp110-12; ☎ 91 541 41 00; Calle Princesa 3) Screens all kinds of *VO* films, from Hollywood blockbusters to arty flicks.

Theatre & Dance

Most Madrid theatre is performed in Spanish, but those who understand the language (or are good at interpreting facial expressions) will find a fairly broad range of plays and musicals on around town. For details pick up a copy of the *Guía del Ocio* at newsstands.

Spain's dynamic Compañía Nacional de Danza, directed by Nacho Duato, performs worldwide and has won accolades for its marvellous technicality and style. The company, which is made up of Spanish and international dancers, performs original and contemporary pieces and is considered a major player on the international dance scene.

Madrid is also home to the Ballet Nacional de España, a classical-dance company that's renowned for its unique mix of ballet and traditional Spanish styles such as flamenco and *zarzuela*. Both companies perform abroad more often than they do at home. When in town, their works are staged in major venues; check local newspapers for details.

Teatro Albéniz (Map pp114-16; ☎ 91 531 83 11; Calle de la Paz 11) Staging both commercial and

---

LA ZARZUELA

What began in the late 17th century as a way to amuse King Philip IV and his court, has become one of Spain's most unique theatre styles. With a light-hearted combination of music and dance, and a focus on everyday people's problems, *zarzuelas* quickly became popular in the capital, and *madrileños'* fondness for the genre has only faded slightly since. Though you may have trouble following the storyline (they are notoriously full of local references and jokes), seeing a *zarzuela* gives an entertaining look into local culture. Catch a show at the Teatro de la Zarzuela (opposite).

---

vanguard drama, this is one of Madrid's better-known theatres. It's also the site of the Fiesta del Flamenco Caja Madrid (p138), held in late winter.

Centro Cultural de la Villa (Map pp108-9; ☎ 91 575 60 80; Plaza de Colón) Located under the waterfall at Plaza de Colón, this cultural centre stages everything from classical-music concerts to comic theatre, opera and quality flamenco performances.

Teatro Español (Map pp114-16; ☎ 91 360 14 80; Calle del Príncipe 25) This is a good choice for mainstream Spanish drama. A theatre has stood on this spot since 1583, when it was known as the Corral del Príncipe. It later became the Teatro del Príncipe, and in 1849 was renamed the Teatro Español.

Live Music

FLAMENCO

Madrid is a good place to see professional interpretations of this Andalucian art. Most shows are set up like a dinner theatre, and while squarely aimed at tourists, the quality is generally top-notch. One of the best of these *tablaos* is **Casa Patas** (Map pp110-12; ☎ 91 369 04 96; www.casapatas.com; Calle Cañizares 10; admission about €30; ☽ noon-5pm & 8pm-3am, shows 10.30pm Mon-Thu, 9pm & midnight Fri & Sat; metro Antón Martín).

Less established (but cheaper) is **Las Tablas** (Map pp114-16; ☎ 91 542 05 20; Plaza de España 9; admission €12-15; ☽ nightly show at 10.30pm).

CLASSICAL MUSIC & OPERA

Auditorio Nacional de Música (Map p113; ☎ 91 337 01 00; www.auditorionacional.mcu.es; Calle del Príncipe de Vergara 146) Resounding to the sounds of

classical music, this modern venue offers a varied calendar of classical music led by conductors from all over the world. In season, there are concerts here almost every day, and you can usually get same-day tickets at the box office.

Teatro de la Zarzuela (Map pp114-16; ☎ 91 524 54 00; Calle de Jovellanos 4) This 1856 theatre is the premier place to see *zarzuela*, a very Spanish mix of theatre, music and dance. The theatre also hosts mainstream shows, as well as a smattering of classical music and opera.

Teatro Real (Map pp114-16; ☎ 91 516 06 06; www .teatro-real.com in Spanish; Plaza de Oriente s/n) After more than €100 million was spent on its rebuilding, the Teatro Real is as technologically advanced as any venue in Europe, and is without a doubt the city's grandest stage. Elaborate operas and occasional ballets are shown in this sumptuous theatre, and tickets are among the priciest in town. To see opera or ballet you'll pay as little as €15 for a spot so far away you will need a telescope, or more than €100. You can buy tickets through the theatre's website or through www.entradas.com. You can also visit the theatre (p119).

JAZZ

Jazz lovers will find several excellent venues in the city. For quality shows that may include anything from blues to fusion flamenco, **Café Central** (Map pp114-16; ☎ 91 369 41 43; www.cafecentralmadrid.com in Spanish; Plaza del Angel 10; admission €10-12) is an excellent option.

More informal is **Café Populart** (Map pp114-16; ☎ 91 429 84 07; www.populart.es in Spanish; Calle de las Huertas 22; admission free), a smoky, usually overcrowded place, where you don't have to pay an entry charge, and can come and go as you please.

AUTHOR'S CHOICE

For great Latin jazz, head out to **Calle 54** (Map p113; ☎ 91 561 28 32; Paseo de la Habana 3), a wildly popular restaurant (p146) and bar that was responsible for putting Madrid on the European jazz circuit. Partly owned by filmmaker Fernando Trueba, whose movie *Calle 54* was its inspiration, it's an upscale place that attracts a mixed audience of musicians, film stars and locals. Live shows start at around 11pm.

ROCK

Performances at these intimate concert venues usually start around 10pm or 11pm, though many open earlier for drinks. Information about the night's concert offerings can be found in publications such as *Guía del Ocio* (p150).

Sala Caracol (Map pp114-16; ☎ 91 527 35 94; Calle Bernardino de Obregón 18) A temple to variety, this popular club hosts a different style of group every night of the week, with shows ranging from hip hop to flamenco.

Galileo Galilei (Map pp106-8; ☎ 91 534 75 57; Calle Galileo 100) A Madrid classic, this club in northern Madrid has been known to stage everything from comedy acts to magic shows, though its strength remains up-and-coming bands.

La Riviera (Map pp106-8; ☎ 91 365 24 15; Paseo Bajo de la Virgen del Puerto) A club and concert venue all in one, La Riviera has a pretty Art Deco interior and hosts open-air concerts in summer.

Honky Tonk (Map pp110-12; ☎ 91 445 68 86; Calle de Covarrubias 24) Despite the name, this casual club is a great place to see local rock and roll, though many acts have a little country thrown in the mix too. A very mixed crowd packs in to this smallish club, so arrive early – the place fills up fast.

Arena (Map pp110-12; ☎ 91 547 57 11; Calle de la Princesa 1) Once a classic rock-and-roll venue, this club has hosted former Guns n' Roses drummer Steve Adler and big-name groups such as Love (led by Arthur Lee). Nowadays you're more likely to find alternative music shows and, later, a club atmosphere.

Nightclubs

There isn't a *barrio* in Madrid that doesn't have a decent club or disco, but the most popular dance spots are along and around Gran Vía, where you'll find mega nightclubs catering to just about every taste and style. For a more intimate experience, head to the small nightclubs of Chueca or Malasaña, especially those along Calle de la Palma, which is lined with quirky nightclubs.

Entry fees vary wildly, but most charge between €8 and €12, though you can get discounts for arriving early, or if you're a girl (sorry guys). Keep your eyes open for discount tickets given out in bars or on the street. At most places, dancing starts at around 1am and lasts until daybreak.

Come Thursday through Saturday for the best atmosphere. The university crowd is generally out in force on Thursday nights, so this is a great time for students to meet other students.

LOS AUSTRIAS & CENTRO

El Sol (Map pp110-12; ☎ 91 532 64 90; Calle de los Jardines 3) Guaranteed for great dancing on weekends, El Sol is a sprawling club that plays a groove-able mixture of house, rock and soul. Open late, it's the perfect place to end the night on a high note.

Palacio Gaviria (Map pp114-16; ☎ 91 526 60 69; Calle del Arenal 9) This palace-turned-club still has some of its original décor, making it temptingly atmospheric but pricier than most nightclubs. Thursday is international student night, when you're guaranteed a thousand-and-one opportunities to meet new people.

Teatro Joy Eslava (Map pp114-16; ☎ 91 366 37 33; www.joy-eslava.com in Spanish; Calle del Arenal 11) Just beside Palacio Gaviria, this old theatre is another sure bet. Popular with locals and visitors.

El Son (Map pp110-12; ☎ 91 532 32 83; Calle de la Victoria 6) The best Latino grooves are found at this friendly club, where you can show off

---

MOVING WITH THE MOVIDA

Anyone who went wild when they first moved out of their parents' house can identify with Madrid's *movida*. After four decades of living under the glaring gaze of an ultra-Catholic, ultra-conservative dictator, *madrileños* took the news of Generalísimo Franco's death in 1975 as an excuse to do everything they hadn't been able to do under his regime, and the party lasted well into the 1980s. A cultural movement that adopted elements of the sexual revolution, free love and other things that had been changing the world while Spain lived under the dark cloth of a dictatorship, the *movida* showed its face in art, music, film and most famously in the city's nightlife. Madrid's reputation as the real 'city that never sleeps' comes in large part from the excesses of the early 1980s. Though things have calmed some since then, Madrid is still a city that loves to show it knows how to party.

your salsa moves to a crowd that's mostly made up of Madrid's large Latin American population. There are live shows Monday to Thursday, and a great atmosphere every night of the week.

SANTA ANA, HUERTAS & ATOCHA

Kapital (Map pp114-16; ☎ 91 420 29 06; Calle de Atocha 125; metro Atocha) If you can't make up your mind about dance styles, this seven-storey mega-club does the trick. Every floor offers a different mood, so you can float between hip-hop, house and latino music without having to leave (or pay a separate cover charge).

Ducados Café (Map pp114-16; ☎ 91 360 00 89; Plaza de Canalejas 3; metro Sevilla) The upstairs bar (p143) is open all day for tapas, lunch or snacks, but at night it becomes a chill bar with DJs downstairs rolling through hip hop, house, funk and soul. Since there's no cover charge, this is a great place to start the night.

LA LATINA & LAVAPIÉS

La Musa de La Latina (Map pp114-16; ☎ 91 354 02 55; Costanilla de San Andres 12; metro La Latina) La Musa has a divided soul. Upstairs is the trendy restaurant (p145) while downstairs a chic bar and club takes over. The old cave-like bodega has been outfitted with blue-toned lights and a fabulous bar area, creating a cool but constantly crowded atmosphere.

Sala Divino (Map pp106-8; ☎ 91 470 24 61; Paseo de la Ermita del Santo 48) Sala Divino hosts the wildly popular super-club of the Madrid scene: a Friday-night party called Deep. A youngish crowd keeps moving until daybreak on weekend nights, moving to the mixes of some of the best local and international DJs.

MALASAÑA & CHUECA

There's more information about Chueca nightclubs in the boxed text Gay & Lesbian Madrid on p137.

Antícafé (Map pp114-16; ☎ 91 599 41 63; Calle de la Unión 2; metro Ópera) The nonstop events going on at this kitschy-cool club put it a step above the rest. New bands play regularly and there are comedy shows, poetry readings and DJs pumping out everything from Latin jazz to Brazilian or soul. In the afternoons, classic films take the stage.

Corto Maltes (Map pp110-12; ☎ 91 531 13 17; Plaza del Dos de Mayo 9; metro Tribunal or Noviciado)

On weekend nights the downstairs dance floor hosts a long, strong dose of house and in summer one of the best terraces in the *barrio* stretches clear across the Plaza Dos de Mayo. Mid-week '80s rock-and-roll tunes are the norm and drinks are served till late.

Café La Palma (Map pp110-12; ☎ 91 522 50 31; Calle de la Palma 62; metro Noviciado) For variety, head to this lively café-club, where live shows featuring hot local bands are held in back, while DJs mix up front. The place is made of several different rooms, one looking like an Arab tea room, pillows on the floor and all. Every night is a little different, so expect to be surprised.

Sport

To get the latest on which team Real Madrid is up against, or which big-name bullfighters will be in the ring this Sunday, check out daily newspapers and team websites. Sports-only dailies, such as the aptly named *Sport*, are wildly popular and will give you the inside scoop on upcoming matches and events – if you read in Spanish that is.

FOOTBALL

Football (soccer) fans will love Madrid. As the home of the Real Madrid – the team FIFA has declared the all-time greatest team in football – and the first-division Atlético de Madrid, Madrid offers a sports line-up few cities can match. The city's pride in its teams turns into football frenzy during games with rivals such as Barça, or big teams from the Champions League; see the frenzy first-hand when Real Madrid fans head to Plaza de la Cibeles (p125) to celebrate the team's victories by cutting off traffic and swarming the statue in the centre of the plaza, sometimes even knocking off bits of it to keep as souvenirs.

Tickets for football matches in Madrid start at around €10 and run up to the rafters for major matches. For some games, tickets can be impossible to get hold of. You can buy tickets directly from the stadiums, either at the box offices or by phone (see individual listings), or from the numerous ticket agents scattered around the city, although the latter tend to be more expensive. One of the best agents is **Localidades Galicia** (Map pp110-12; ☎ 91 531 27 32, 629-218291; Plaza del Carmen 1; ⌚ 9.30am-1pm & 4.30-7pm Tue-Sat).

Holding 80,000 delirious fans, the **Estadio Santiago Bernabéu** (Map p113; ☎ 91 398 43 00, 902 324324; www.realmadrid.com; Calle de Concha Espina 1; ☒ visits 10.30am-6.30pm except day after game), named after the club's longtime president, is a mecca for football fans worldwide. Those who aren't able to come to a game in the mythic stadium can at least stop by for a tour (adult/child €9/7) and a peek at the trophies exhibit (see p131 for more information).

Estadio Vicente Calderón (Map pp106-8; ☎ 91 366 47 07; www.at-madrid.com in Spanish; Calle de la Virgen del Puerto), the home of first-division team Atlético de Madrid, isn't as large as Real Madrid's stadium (Vicente Calderón seats less than 60,000) but what it lacks in size it certainly makes up for in raw energy. A solid group of devoted fans stuck with the club through a few rough years, and now Atlético is back at the top (well, top 10) of division one.

BULLFIGHTING

Bullfighters aren't inducted into the upper echelons until they face off with a bull here in the capital, and the Sunday afternoon fights held here between the Fiesta de San Isidro (p138) in mid-May and the end of October, are some of Spain's best.

The ethical debate about bullfighting is not as loud in Madrid as in other parts of Spain (in Catalonia a law was recently passed forbidding kids under 14 to see the bloody spectacle) but it's not silent. Animal-rights groups argue, not without reason, that the slaughter is cruel, a jabbing, mocking, painful 30 minutes that leaves the bull exhausted and defeated. Yet supporters of this 'art' say that *toros bravos* (wild bulls) live like kings until the day of the slaughter, enjoying freedom that cattle bred for meat only dream about. Both sides have a point, and whether or not you want to see this often-disturbing tradition must be a personal decision.

Tickets are divided into *sol* (sun) and *sombra* (shade) seating, the former being considerably cheaper than the latter. Ticket sales for Sunday *corridas* (bullfights) begin on Friday, and are sold at Las Ventas box office from 10am to 2pm and 5pm to 8pm. A few (very few) ticket agencies sell before then, tacking on an extra 20% for their trouble. You can also get tickets at the authorised sales offices on Calle de la Victoria.

For most bullfights you'll have no problem buying a ticket at the door, but during the Fiesta de San Isidro, or when a popular torero comes to town, book ahead.

The cheapest tickets (€3.60) are for standing-room *sol*, though on a broiling hot summer day it's infinitely more enjoyable to pay the extra €3 for a *sombra* ticket, especially since most of the action is directed at the shady seats. The very best seats – on the front row in the shade – will cost more than €100.

For information on who's in the ring, pay attention to the colourful posters tacked around town. You can also check the daily newspapers or specialist magazines.

Plaza de Toros Monumental de Las Ventas (Map pp106-8; ☎ 91 356 22 00; www.las-ventas.com in Spanish; Calle de Alcalá 237) is the stage for some of Spain's most important confrontations between matadors (bullfighters) and *toros* (bulls). A grand Mudéjar exterior greets you from the street, and inside, the broad sandy ring provides the stage for the fights.

SHOPPING

Madrid is a shopper's city with great options, whether you're searching for the latest designer handbag, the best Spanish wine or traditional Spanish articles, such as fans and shawls. Salamanca is the glitziest shopping district, with designer shops, guaranteed to make you drool, and dozens of art galleries. Off-beat fashion is sold in the shops of Chueca, especially along Calle de Fuencarral; this lively *barrio* is also a magnet for shoe shops – there are a dozen of them along and around Calle Augusto Figueroa. For artisan goods and typically Spanish items, explore the maze of streets in Huerta and Los Austrias.

Bargain hunters flock to the shops during *las rebajas*, the annual winter and summer sales when prices, on just about everything, are slashed. The winter sales begin around 7 January, just after Three Kings' Day, and last well into February. Summer sales begin in early July and last into August.

Among some of the most common buys are leather shoes and handbags; Spanish shoe brands, such as Farrutx, Camper and Jaime Mascaró are popular. Majorica faux pearls and Lladró porcelain are other classic buys. You'll find all these things in shops along Calle de Serrano and Gran Vía.

The *madrileños'* shopping day starts at about 10am, and is almost always broken up by a long lunch between 2pm and 5pm. Shops then reopen after lunch and stay busy until 8pm. Almost all stores are closed on Sundays, and many are only open half the day on Saturday.

Handicrafts

José Ramírez (Map pp114-16; ☎ 91 531 42 29; Calle de la Paz 8) Discover the fine hand-made guitars at this family-run shop near the Plaza Mayor. For the curious, or true aficionados, there's a small museum in back where you can check out old guitars that were made here and elsewhere.

Justo Algaba (Map pp114-16; ☎ 91 523 35 95; Calle de la Paz 4) For an authentic *traje de luz* (bullfighter's suit) stop at this old-fashioned store. You can pick up some pink tights and a cape while you're here, too.

El Flamenco Vive (Map pp114-16; ☎ 91 547 39 17; www.elflamencovive.es; Calle del Conde de Lemos 7) This temple to flamenco has it all, from guitars and songbooks to albums, polkadot dancing costumes, shoes, colourful plastic jewellery and even literature about flamenco.

Gil (Map pp114-16; ☎ 91 521 25 49; Carrera de San Jerónimo 2) Traditional Spanish shawls and veils are the speciality at this old store, where the huge wooden shop counter is a relic of days gone by.

Casa de Diego (Map pp114-16; ☎ 91 522 66 43; www.casadediego.com; Plaza de la Puerta del Sol 12) Since 1858 Casa de Diego has been selling and repairing Spanish fans, shawls, umbrellas and canes. The grumpy old men who serve you seem as if they could have been around for the original shop's opening.

Santarrufina (Map pp114-16; ☎ 91 522 23 83; Calle de la Paz 9) A glittering shop filled with religious items; you'll find everything from simple rosaries imposing statues of saints and even a litter used to carry the Virgin in processions.

Books

For a list of bookshops in Madrid, see Bookshops on p117.

Fashion & Shoes

Mercado de Fuencarral (Map pp110-12; ☎ 91 521 41 52; Calle de Fuencarral 45) Find a little bit of every-

thing at this mall-like centre. It's known for its alternative fashion and is the perfect spot to buy an outfit for a night out.

Loewe (Map pp108-9; ☎ 91 426 35 88; Calle de Serrano 34) Rub shoulders with funkier labels.

Camper (Map pp108-9; ☎ 91 431 43 45; www.camper.es; Calle de Ayala 13) The quirky and cool brand that made bowling shoes chic the world over has several shops in Madrid. The brand is designed in Mallorca and its colourful, fun designs are all about comfort.

Farrutx (Map pp106-8; ☎ 91 577 09 24; Calle de Serrano 7) This chic boutique sells exquisite leather shoes and accessories for men and women. Well made and always fashionable, Mallorca-based Farrutx is arguably Spain's top shoe brand.

Purificación García (Map pp108-9; ☎ 91 576 72 76; Calle de Serrano 92) One of the most successful Spanish designers, 'Puri' offers elegant, mature designs for men and women. With the variety of styles here, you could get an outfit for a wedding or work.

Amaya Arzuaga (Map pp108-9; ☎ 91 426 28 15; Calle de Lagasca 50) Amaya Arzuaga is one of Spain's top designers, with sexy, bold options for women. She loves mixing black with bright colours (think 1980s fuchsia

---

TO MARKET, TO MARKET

Madrid's biggest and best market is the famous El Rastro (p126), which is a thriving mass of vendors, buyers and pickpockets. Though El Rastro takes the prize as Madrid's most colourful market, shoppers will want to check out some of the city's other bargain haunts too.

- **Art Market** (Map pp114-16; Plaza de Conde de Barajas; ☼ 10am-2pm Sun) For local art and prints of the greats.

- **Cuesta de Moyano Bookstalls** (Map pp106-8; Calle Claudio Moyano; ☼ 9am-dusk Mon-Sat, 9am-2pm Sun) Second-hand and new books in many languages.

- **Mercadillo Marqués de Viana** (El Rastrillo; Map p113; Calle del Marqués de Viana; ☼ 9am-2pm Sun) A calmer version of El Rastro.

- **Mercado de Monedas y Sellos** (Map pp106-8; Plaza Mayor; ☼ 9am-2pm Sun) Old coins and stamps.

MADRID

and turquoise) and has earned a reputation as one of the most creative designers in Spain today.

Tous & Tous (Map pp108–9; ☎ 91 578 17 72; www.tous.es; Calle de Don Ramón de la Cruz 5) Designer Rosa Tous has somehow managed to make the teddy bear one of the most popular insignias of *pija* (yuppie) Spain. The ubiquitous teddy covers bags, scarves and jewellery, and though it really is quite cute, the label is finally starting to expand in other, less-cuddly, directions.

Food & Drink

Convento de las Carbonaras (Map pp114-16; Plaza del Conde de Miranda 3) You'll think you've gone to heaven when you taste the pastries these cloistered nuns make with almonds and egg yolks. To the right of the convent's main entrance is a small door with a call button. Ring the for nuns, and you'll be let inside, where you'll walk to a small, dark room (so that the nuns never even see their customers) with a rotating countertop.

Casa Mira (Map pp114-16; ☎ 91 429 88 95; Carrera de San Jerónimo 30) The twirling display of goodies in the window draws lots of oohs and ahs from those passing by, but the real delight is trying the candied fruits, fat pastries and creamy cakes (all made right here) for yourself.

Licorilandia (Map pp114-16; ☎ 91 429 12 57; Calle de León 30) The only shop in Madrid dedicated to selling tiny airline bottles of sherry, brandy and whisky, Licorilandia makes packing souvenirs a cinch.

Cacao Sampaka (Map pp110-12; ☎ 91 319 48 40; Calle de Orellana 4) A paradise for chocoholics, this sprawling shop is dedicated to nothing but rich, dark cocoa. And light sweet cocoa. And cocoa with raspberries. And cocoa with lilacs and roses. And…you get the idea. There's also a bar at the back.

Patrimonio Comunal Olivero (Map pp110-12; ☎ 91 308 05 05; Calle de Mejia Lequerica 1) Olive oil from all over Spain is sold at this simple shop. For a wide sample, try the box of 10 minibottles for just €7.75.

Reserva & Cata (Map pp110-12; ☎ 91 319 04 01; www.reservaycata.com; Calle del Conde de Xiquena 13) With a fantastic selection of Spanish wine, and a knowledgeable staff who can help you pick out a great one, this is a great place to shop for gifts or tasty souvenirs.

Art & Homewares

Lladró (Map pp108-9; ☎ 91 435 51 12; www.lladro.com; Calle de Serrano 68; metro Serrano) The classic porcelain figures of Lladró have changed little since your grandmother started collecting them decades ago. Get a little something as a souvenir or gift, or splurge for something really special – a €30,000 scene of a train station, say?

BD Madrid (Map pp106-8; ☎ 91 435 06 27; bdmadrid@wanadoo.es; Calle de la Villanueva 5) Is it a gallery or is it a shop? A little of both really. In this ultra-fashionable furniture showroom you can spot the latest from Spanish and international designers, along with classics from Spanish greats, such as Oscar Tusquets and Javier Mariscal. Everything you see is available to order.

Alcolea (Map pp108-9; ☎ 91 4352 347; Calle de Velázquez 12) This sprawling gallery specialises in contemporary Spanish art, and it's a great place to hunt for traditional styles, such as landscapes, portraits and paintings, reflecting the Spanish lifestyle.

Shopping Centres

El Corte Ingles (☎ 91 418 88 00) Sells everything from food and furniture to clothes, appliances and toiletries. It's truly one-stop shopping. There's branches all over the city on Calle Princesa, Calle Preciados and Calle Serrano.

ABC Serrano (Map pp108-9; ☎ 91 577 50 31; Calle de Serrano 61) This multilevel shopping mall has shops ranging from trendy Zara to the elegant baby shop, Musgo. Restaurants and cafés are scattered about in case all that shopping wears you out.

GETTING THERE & AWAY
Air
Madrid's **Barajas Airport** (Aeropuerto de Barajas; ☎ 91 305 83 46, 902 353570; www.aena.es) is a busy place, with regular flights arriving from all over the globe. Some 16km northeast of the city, this is central Spain's major hub.

Inside the airport you'll find several banks with ATMs, a post office, tourist information, a hotel booking stand, and general information offices throughout the airport. The airport is well connected to the centre, with regular buses and taxis (about €20) and a metro line that takes you to the centre in minutes (see p158).

The major airlines operate at Barajas:

Air Europa (☎ 902 401501)
Air France (☎ 901 112266)
American Airlines (☎ 902 115570)
British Airways (☎ 902 111333, 91 387 43 03)
Delta Airlines (☎ 91 305 82 75)
Easy Jet (☎ 902 299992)
Iberia (☎ 902 400500)
KLM (☎ 902 222747)
Lufthansa (☎ 902 220103)
Spanair (☎ 902 131415, 91 393 83 19)
US Airways (☎ 91 444 47 00)

Bus
Most out-of-town buses call in at **Estación Sur de Autobuses** (☎ 91 468 42 00; Calle de Méndez Álvaro), the city's principal bus station (the nearest metro station is Méndez Álvaro). Main bus companies here include **Alsa** (☎ 902 422242; www.alsa.es), which runs countless buses to southern Spain, and **AutoRes** (☎ 902 020999; www.auto-res.net), which operates buses to Extremadura, western Castilla y León and Valencia.

Just south of the M30 ring road, the Estación Sur de Autobuses serves most destinations to the south, and many in other parts of the country. Most bus companies have a ticket office here, even if their buses depart from one of the other, smaller stations scattered around the city. From the station you can easily get to central Madrid thanks to the nearby metro stop, Méndez Álvarez.

Car & Motorcycle
If you arrive by car, be prepared to face gridlock traffic. The city is surrounded by three ring roads, the M30, M40 and brand-new M50 (still not 100% completed). You'll probably be herded onto one of these, which in turn give access to the city centre.

RENTAL
The big-name car-rental agencies have offices all over Madrid. Avis, Budget, Hertz, Europcar and Atesa/EuroDollar have booths at the airport. See the Transport chapter (p858) for more information.

Train
Madrid is served by two main train stations. The bigger of the two is Antigua Estación de Atocha, at the southern end of the city centre. Trains from here fan out right across the country. Chamartín train station lies in the north of the city.

The bulk of trains for the rest of Spain depart from Atocha, especially those going south. International services arrive at and leave from Chamartín, as do several services for northern destinations. Be sure to find out which station your train leaves from. Of the two, Atocha is handier for the centre of town.

For bookings, contact **Renfe** (☎ 902 240202; www.renfe.es) at either train station.

GETTING AROUND
Madrid is well served by an excellent and rapidly expanding underground rail system (metro) and an extensive bus service. In addition, you can get from the north to the south of the city quickly by using *cercanías* (local trains) between Chamartín and Atocha train stations. Taxis are also a viable option.

To/From the Airport
The metro (line 8) zips you into the city from the airport's Terminal 2. The 12-minute trip to the Nuevos Ministerios station costs €1.15; from there, you can easily connect to all other stations, though depending on where you're heading, you may have to change lines. This is an easy way to get into town, if you are travelling light. If you're toting a lead-weight suitcase, you may run into trouble, as several metro stops have no escalator or elevator service.

The blue **airport bus** (Map pp108–9; ☎ 91 408 68 10) will take you from Terminals 1, 2 or 3 to Plaza Colón in central Madrid. The trip takes about 30 minutes in normal traffic (but it's best to budget a bit extra) and costs €2.50 per person. If you carry more than two suitcases, you may have to pay a supplement. Buses leave the airport every 15 to 30 minutes between 4.45am and 2am. From Plaza de Colón buses run by between 4.45am and 1.30am.

A taxi to/from the city centre will cost €15 to €18 (if it's more than €20, get suspicious). Taxis wait outside all terminals.

Bus

Buses run by **EMT** (Empresa Municipal de Transportes de Madrid; ☎ 91 406 88 10; www.emtmadrid.es) go along most city routes regularly between about 6.30am and 11.30pm. Between midnight and 6am 20 night-bus routes operate. They run from Puerta del Sol and Plaza de la Cibeles.

Car & Motorcycle

Traffic in Madrid could be worse. But not much worse. The city is in a continual state of gridlock, so driving here is just no fun. Especially avoid peak hour, when the whole city heaves with the masses struggling to and from work. But from about 2pm to 4pm, the streets are relatively quiet. Once in the city, search for a car park. Driving from sight to sight within Madrid is pointless.

Parking is complicated in the centre, as most spaces are reserved for locals with permits. That said, many locals without permits park on the streets, and you could do that too, if you're willing to run the risk of getting a ticket. Lot parking is easier and safer, but of course you'll pay for the privilege. There is a lot beside Plaza Mayor and several others in the centre. All are marked with big blue signs featuring a telltale 'P', and charge upwards of €1 an hour.

Should your car be towed, call the **Grúa Municipal** (City Towing Service; ☎ 91 345 06 66); getting it back costs €8.15 plus a parking fee, and whatever fine you have to pay.

Cercanías

These short-range regional trains go to Madrid suburbs, and nearby towns such as El Escorial, Alcalá de Henares, Aranjuez and other points in the Comunidad de Madrid. They are also handy for making a quick north–south hop between Chamartín and Atocha main-line train stations (with stops at Nuevos Ministerios and in front of the Biblioteca Nacional, on Paseo de los Recoletos, only). Another line links Chamartín, Atocha and Príncipe Pío stations. Single tickets, valid on *cercanías* only, cost €1.15. Since this network is part of the national railways, most international rail passes are also valid.

Metro

Madrid's extensive **metro network** (www.metro madrid.es) can get you to just about any corner of the city with its 11 colour-coded lines. It's quick, clean, relatively safe, and runs from 6am to 2am. You can buy tickets from staffed booths or machines at most stations. Single-ride tickets cost €1.10, while the Metrobus ticket, good for 10 rides on bus or metro, costs €5.20. See the metro map on pp140–1.

Taxi

Madrid's taxis are inexpensive by European standards. They're handy late at night, although in peak hours it's quicker to walk or get the metro. Flag fall is €1.55, after which you are charged by time (about €0.60 per hour), so avoid rush hour. At night and on holidays you'll pay a little more.

Several supplementary charges, usually posted up inside the taxi, apply; these include extra charges for airport runs, taxis hailed at certain taxi ranks, and trips you take on major holidays such as Christmas.

To book a taxi, call ☎ 91 405 55 00, ☎ 91 447 51 80 or ☎ 91 445 90 08.

Comunidad de Madrid

COMUNIDAD DE MADRID

Sitting in the very heart of Spain, the Comunidad de Madrid is a rough triangle surrounding the capital city. Opulent royal palaces, lush gardens and hearty rural restaurants make this a great destination for day trips from the city, though it could also be a base for exploring central Spain.

The fresh mountain air of the sierras to the north and east of the capital has long been a draw for city dwellers looking for the respite of nature. For centuries royals and nobles were the only ones able to escape to the countryside, but now Madrid's sierras are claimed by all, and on weekends it may seem like the entire city has arrived to enjoy them. Hiking, rock climbing and, in winter, skiing are some of the most popular activities. That said, most people come simply to soak up the surroundings over a nice long lunch and a bottle of wine.

Nature is a major attraction here, but there are also cities worth visiting. Too often dismissed as mere suburbs of the capital, cities like Alcalá de Henares (Cervantes' birthplace), Aranjuez (home to one of the Comunidad's finest castles) and Chinchón (famous for its suckling pig) are fascinating places in their own right. All are easily accessible by train or bus from the capital.

HIGHLIGHTS

- Watch a bullfight from a terrace café during Chinchón's **Fiesta Mayor** (p166)
- Stroll the gardens of **Aranjuez** (p164) like the kings of old
- Feast on roast suckling pig at **Mesón Cuevas del Vino** (p166) in Chinchón
- Tour the fairy-tale castle in **Manzanares El Real** (p167)
- Hike the trails in the **Sierra de Guadarrama** (p167)
- Learn all about the life and times of Miguel de Cervantes at his childhood home in **Alcalá de Henares** (p167)
- Visit Franco's spooky **Valle de los Caídos** (p163), the dictator's mausoleum and monument to the fallen soldiers of the Spanish Civil War
- Head to the quiet **Sierra Pobre** (p169), where you'll probably have the trails all to yourself

Map labels: Sierra Pobre, Sierra de Guadarrama, Manzanares El Real, Valle de los Caídos, Alcalá de Henares, Chinchón, Aranjuez

| ■ AREA: 7995 SQ KM | ■ POP: 5 MILLION | ■ AVE SUMMER TEMP: HIGH 30°C, LOW°13 C |

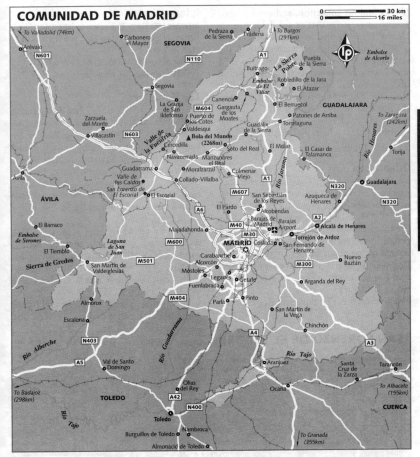

COMUNIDAD DE MADRID

0 — 30 km
0 — 16 miles

SAN LORENZO DE EL ESCORIAL
pop 14,358 / elevation 1032m

The tourist board optimistically calls the palace and monastery complex of San Lorenzo de El Escorial the 'eighth wonder of the world'. While that may be stretching things, this imposing monastic complex is an impressive place. The heart of a quaint resort town, the one-time royal getaway is now a prim little town overflowing with quaint shops, restaurants and hotels, many of them closed in the low season, catering to throngs of weekending *madrileños*. The fresh, cool air here (the climate really is quite good) has been drawing city dwellers since the complex was first ordered to be built by Felipe II in the 16th century.

Kings and princes have a habit of promising extravagant offerings to God, the angels, saints and anyone else who'll listen, in return for help in defeating their foes. Felipe II was no exception before the Battle of St Quentin against the French on St Lawrence's Day, 10 August 1557. Felipe's victory was decisive, and in thanks he ordered the construction of the complex in the saint's name above the hamlet of El Escorial. A huge monastery, royal palace and mausoleum for Felipe's parents, Carlos I and Isabel, were raised under the watchful eye of the architect Juan de Herrera. The austere style reflects Felipe's own severe outlook.

The palace-monastery became an important intellectual centre, with a burgeoning library and art collection, and even a laboratory where scientists could dabble in alchemy. Felipe II died here on 13 September 1598. Various additions were made to the complex in the following centuries. In 1854 the monks belonging to the Hieronymite order, who had occupied the monastery from the beginning, were obliged to leave during one of the 19th-century waves of confiscation of religious property by the Spanish state, to be replaced 30 years later by Augustinians.

Orientation

You can't miss the monastic complex that marks the town's southern border. Running parallel to the monastery's main wall is Calle Floridablanca, where you'll find the tourist office as well as some shops and restaurants. North of here are the narrow streets of the town proper, with Calle del Rey serving as the main thoroughfare and Plaza de la Constitución providing another major landmark.

The monastery's main entrance is on its western façade.

Information

Internet (☎ 918 90 15 33; Plaza de San Lorenzo, Galería Martín; per hour €2; 🕙 11am-10pm Mon-Thu, 11am-11pm Fri-Sun)
Tourist office (☎ 918 90 53 13; Calle de Grimaldi 2; 🕙 10am-6pm Mon-Thu, 10am-7pm Fri-Sun)

The Monastery

The main entrance to the **Real Monasterio de San Lorenzo** (☎ 918 90 59 02; www.patrimonionacional.es; admission €6; 🕙 10am-6pm Apr-Sep, 10am-5pm Oct-Mar, closed Mon) is on the west. Above the gateway a statue of St Lawrence stands watch, holding a symbolic gridiron, the instrument of his martyrdom (he was roasted alive on one). From here you'll first enter the **Patio de los Reyes**, which houses the statues of the six kings of Judah.

Directly ahead lies the sombre **basilica**. As you enter, look up to the unusual flat vaulting below the choir stalls. Once inside the church proper, turn left to view Benvenuto Cellini's white Carrara marble statue of Christ crucified (1576).

Next you'll be led through several rooms containing tapestries and an El Greco, and

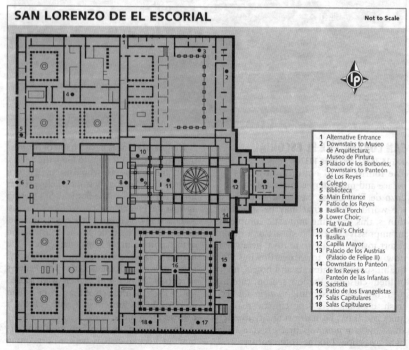

SAN LORENZO DE EL ESCORIAL   Not to Scale

1 Alternative Entrance
2 Downstairs to Museo de Arquitectura; Museo de Pintura
3 Palacio de los Borbones; Downstairs to Panteón de Los Reyes
4 Colegio
5 Biblioteca
6 Main Entrance
7 Patio de los Reyes
8 Basilica Porch
9 Lower Choir; Flat Vault
10 Cellini's Christ
11 Basilica
12 Capilla Mayor
13 Palacio de los Austrias (Palacio de Felipe II)
14 Downstairs to Panteón de los Reyes & Panteón de las Infantas
15 Sacristía
16 Patio de los Evangelistas
17 Salas Capitulares
18 Salas Capitulares

then downstairs to the northeastern corner of the complex. You pass through the **Museo de Arquitectura** and the **Museo de Pintura**. The former covers (in Spanish) the story of how the complex was built, while the latter contains a range of Italian, Spanish and Flemish art from the 16th and 17th centuries.

At this point you are obliged to head upstairs again into a gallery around the eastern protuberance of the complex known as the **Palacio de Felipe II** or **Palacio de los Austrias**. You'll then descend to the 17th-century **Panteón de los Reyes**, where almost all Spain's monarchs since Carlos I lie interred with their spouses. Backtracking a little, you'll find yourself in the **Panteón de los Infantes**. Don Juan de Austria (ie Don John of Austria), victor over the Turks at the Battle of Lepanto, lies in the fifth vault.

Stairs lead up from the Patio de los Evangelistas to the **Salas Capitulares** (chapterhouses) in the southeastern corner of the monastery. These bright, airy rooms, the ceilings of which are richly frescoed, contain a minor treasure chest of works by El Greco, Titian, Tintoretto, José de Ribera and Hieronymus Bosch (El Bosco to Spaniards).

You can wander around the **Huerta de los Frailes**, the orderly gardens just south of the monastery. In the **Jardín del Príncipe**, which leads down to the town of El Escorial (and the train station), is the **Casita del Príncipe**, a little neoclassical caprice built under Carlos III for his heir. The **Casita de Arriba** (Casa del Infant; ☎ 918 90 59 03; admission €3; ☿ daily Jul-Sep, Sat & Sun Oct-May), another 18th-century neoclassical gem, is along the road to Ávila.

Sleeping & Eating
La Cueva (☎ 918 90 15 16; www.mesonlacueva.com; Calle de San Antón 4; mains €9-18; ☿ Tue-Sun) A dark place founded in 1768, this is one of the town's classic eateries. Nibble at the cosy bar downstairs or head up to the more formal dining room, where hearty Castilian dishes await.

Parrilla Príncipe (☎ 918 90 16 11; www.inicia.es /de/parillaprincipe; Calle de la Floridablanca 6; meals €30; ☿ Wed-Mon) A popular but unpretentious place specialising in grilled meats, this is considered by many to be the best dining room in town. It also has a **hotel** (s/d €42-44/53-59) with bare but clean rooms, some with views of the monastery.

Getting There & Away
Every 15 minutes (every 30 minutes on weekends) **Herranz** (☎ 918 96 90 28) sends a bus to El Escorial from the bus depot outside Moncloa metro station, platform 3. The one-hour trip costs €2.85.

San Lorenzo de El Escorial is 59km from Madrid and it takes well under an hour to drive. Take the A6 motorway to the M600 Hwy, then follow the signs to town.

A few dozen **Renfe** (☎ 902 24 02 02; www.renfe .es) C8 *cercanías* (local trains serving large cities) make the one-hour trip daily from Madrid to El Escorial (€2.10).

VALLE DE LOS CAÍDOS
Dictator Francisco Franco's memorial of the 'fallen' to Spain's civil war, this basilica and stone monument are sure to evoke emotional responses from supporters of both sides of the war. The scale is impressive, though the monuments take on a new meaning when one stops to think that everything here was built by Franco's war prisoners.

At the **memorial site** (☎ 918 90 13 98; Ctra 600; admission €5; ☿ 10am-6pm Apr-Oct, 10am-5pm Nov-Mar) you'll find a mammoth stone cross sitting atop a bunker-like basilica dug into the mountainside in the middle of a pristine pine forest. Walking into the basilica, you basically enter into the heart of the mountain. By the altar lies Franco.

The turn-off and ticket booth is 9km north of El Escorial. It's another 6km drive to the shrine. Coming on or around 20 November (the anniversary of the dictator's death) is a curious experience that proves that some Spaniards still revere the man who led their country for three decades.

Near the basilica are walking trails, a picnic area and a small restaurant. You can take a **funicular** (admission €2.50; ☿ 11am-5.30pm Apr-Oct, 11am-4.30pm Nov-Mar) up the mountain to the base of the cross, where if the wind doesn't blow you away, you can enjoy great views of the surrounding sierra.

Getting There & Away
One **Herranz** (☎ 918 96 90 28) bus heads to the monument at 3.15pm Tuesday to Sunday. It returns at 5.30pm. You can catch the bus at El Escorial's Plaza de la Virgen de Gracia. The combined price of the bus and entry ticket to the site is €7.80.

If you're driving, you'll pass the entry to the Valle de los Caídos a few kilometres before you hit El Escorial coming from the A6 Hwy.

SOUTH OF MADRID

Warner Brothers Movie World

An American-style theme park featuring American cartoon characters and American attractions, **Warner Brothers Movie World** (☎ 918 21 12 34; www.warnerbrospark.com; A4 motorway Km22, San Martín de la Vega; adult/child aged 5-11 €32/24; 🕑 10am-8pm Mon-Fri, 10am-10pm Sat summer, winter hrs vary, call ahead) is not the best place to delve into Spanish culture. But it is a whole lotta fun for kids and kids at heart. Rattle around on a mammoth wooden roller coaster, take a splash in the water rides or catch a show at the Looney Tunes theatre.

You enter by Hollywood Boulevard, not unlike LA's Sunset Boulevard, and can then explore four different worlds: Cartoon World, the Old West, DC Super Heroes (featuring Superman, Batman and the finks of Gotham City) and finally the Warner Brothers Studio.

GETTING THERE & AWAY

If you have your own vehicle, take the A4 motorway (aka Carretera de Andalucía) to Km22, where you can exit the highway directly into the park.

You can also catch one of the C3 *cercanías* that leave the Atocha train station regularly headed towards Pinto. In Pinto change trains and get on the C3A line that goes to 'Parque de Ocio'.

Aranjuez

pop 37,670 / elevation 489m

Modern-day visitors to Aranjuez aren't that different from the royals that established this town as a city escape centuries ago. We're still looking for a breath of fresh air, a stroll among the gardens and a chance to soak up the opulent art and architecture of the Palacio Real.

Getting around here is easy; when you come into town, you'll cross the Río Tajo and will immediately enter into a large traffic circle. The *palacio* and its gardens are to your right, while the rest of town spreads out to your left and in front of you. The bus station is right off the central throughway Calle Infantas.

Information

The surprisingly helpful and friendly **Tourist Office** (☎ 918 91 04 27; www.aranjuez.com; Plaza de San Antonio 9; 🕑 10am-6.30pm Nov-Apr, 10am-8.30pm May-Oct) will load you down with information about the town and its attractions.

PALACIO REAL & GARDENS

The **Palacio Real** (☎ 918 91 07 40; admission €3.40, EU citizens free Wed; ☎ 11am-5.30pm Oct-Mar, 11am-7.30pm Apr-Sep) started as one of Felipe II's modest summer palaces, but was converted into this extravaganza by the 18th century. With more than 300 rooms and inspired by Versailles (an ever-popular model with European monarchs), this sprawling box of a palace is filled with a cornucopia of ornamentation. Of all the rulers who spent time here, Carlos III and Isabel II left the greatest mark.

Most of the *palacio* was closed for renovation at the time of writing, but was due to reopen soon. Taking the obligatory guided tour (in Spanish) gives an interesting look at the palace history and the art that fills it. The **Sala de Porcelana** (Porcelain Room) is extravagant, its walls covered in handcrafted porcelain figures (more than vaguely reminiscent of a similar chamber in Madrid's Palacio Real). It took two years to complete the decoration. The **Sala Fumadora** (Smoking Room) is almost as remarkable – a florid imitation of an Alhambra interior, with Arabic inscriptions in stucco and an intricate stalactite ceiling carved in wood.

Afterwards, stroll in the lush **gardens** (admission free; ☎ 8am-6.30pm Oct-Mar, 8am-8.30pm Apr-Sep). They're a mix of local and exotic species that have rubbed along nicely since Spanish botanists and explorers started bringing back seeds from all over the world in the 19th century (an audio guide is available). Within their shady perimeter, which stretches a few kilometres from the palace base, you'll find two other man-made attractions: the **Casa de Marinos**, which contains the **Museo de Falúas** (☎ 918 91 03 05; admission €3; 🕑 10am-5.15pm Oct-Mar, 10am-6.15pm Apr-Sep, reservation required), a museum of royal pleasure boats from days gone by.

JARDÍN DEL PRÍNCIPE

Farther away, towards Chinchón, is the **Casa del Labrador** (☎ 918 91 03 05; admission €3; 🕑 10am-5.15pm Oct-Mar, 10am-6.15pm Apr-Sep, reservation required), a tasteless royal jewellery box crammed to the rafters with gold, silver, silk and some second-rate art. It sits in the Jardín del Príncipe, an extension of the massive Palacio Real gardens.

CHIQUITREN

Offering a fun tour around town and a very practical way to get to the Jardín del Príncipe, the **Chiquitren** (☎ 902 08 80 89; train stop near Palacio Real entrance; adult/child €5/3; ☷ 11am-5.30pm Tue-Sun Oct-Feb, 10am-8pm Tue-Sun Mar-Sep) is a tourist train that loops around Aranjuez. It makes stops at the Casa del Labrador and the Casa de Marinos, allowing you to get off if you choose.

PLAZA DE TOROS

Regardless of your views on the sport (or torture) that is bullfighting, the **museum** (☎ 918 92 16 43; admission €1; ☷ 11am-7.30pm Tue-Sun Apr-Sep, 11am-5.30pm Tue-Sun Oct-Mar) housed in the Plaza de Toros makes for an interesting stop. You'll find displays on the history of bullfighting, the natural attractions of Aranjuez and the entertainments to which the royal court once treated itself.

SLEEPING & EATING

Hostal Castilla (☎ 918 91 26 27; www.hostalesaranjuez .com; Carretera Andalucía 98; s/d €35/45) A short walk from the *palacio* and the town centre, this friendly, charming *hostal* (budget hotel) offers impeccable little rooms with attached bathrooms.

NH Príncipe de la Paz hotel (☎ 918 09 92 22; www.nh-hoteles.com; Calle de San Antonio 22; r €97/126) Sleek, modern design and attentive service make this the best hotel in town.

El Rana Verde (☎ 918 01 15 71; Plaza Santiago Rusiñol; mains €8-18; ☷ 9am-11pm) For scenery, there's no beating this sprawling riverside restaurant near the *palacio*. A classic that's been here for decades, it's famous for its frogs' legs.

Casa José (☎ 918 91 14 88; Calle de Abastos 32; mains €8-16; ☷ 1.30-3.45pm & 9pm-12am Tue-Sat, 1.30-3.45pm Sun) An elegant restaurant, it's widely considered the best in town for meats and local specialities.

GETTING THERE & AWAY

If you're driving from Madrid, take the A4 south to the M305, which leads to the city centre. Aranjuez is about 50km away.

The bus company **AISA** (☎ 902 19 87 88; www .aisa-grupo.com) sends buses to Aranjuez from Madrid's Estación Sur every 15 minutes (€3, 30 minutes).

The easiest way to get here is by train. **Renfe** (☎ 902 24 02 02; www.renfe.es) *cercanías* leave every 15 or 20 minutes from Atocha train station. The 42-minute trip to Aranjuez costs €2.10.

Chinchón

A weekend retreat for city-sick *Madrileños* looking for a slice of country life, Chinchón's main attractions are its unique round plaza (whose *terrazas*, or terraces, make for a heavenly spot for a drink) and the smorgasbord of traditional *mesón*-style (tavern-style) restaurants scattered around town. Otherwise, Chinchón is simply a dusty little town that hasn't significantly changed its style in the past 200 years or so. That, of course, is its charm.

INFORMATION

Police (☎ 629 16 70 70; Plaza Mayor)
Tourist office (☎ 918 93 53 23; www.ciudad -chinchon.com; Plaza Mayor 6; ☷ 10am-8pm Mon-Fri, 11.30am-8pm Sat & Sun May-Jun & Sep-Oct; 10am-9pm Mon-Fri, 11.30am-9pm Sat & Sun Jul-Aug; 10am-7pm Mon-Fri, 11.30am-7pm Sat & Sun Nov-Feb) Small office but very helpful.

TRAILBLAZERS

You don't have to go to the sierras to get in touch with nature. Aranjuez is surrounded by lush natural areas ideal for exploring on foot or bicycle, and the town's recent efforts to repair and promote the trails near town have made it easier than ever to walk here.

The tourist office has maps and trail information for a number of interesting strolls of varying lengths and difficulties (though most are fairly easy, and suitable for walkers of almost all ages and abilities). Several walks begin on the historic paths that run through the Jardín del Príncipe or other palace gardens before branching off into forests or fields.

One of the most popular walks leads you by the 'Mar de Ontígola, a swampy area with unusual vegetation, and along the banks of the Río Tajo, where you can spot a variety of birds and other animals.

SIGHTS

The few historical monuments here won't detain you long, but you can take a look at the 16th-century **Iglesia de la Asunción** (closed for repairs at the time of writing) that rises above the Plaza Mayor. The late-16th-century Renaissance **Castillo de los Condes** sits out of town to the south. The castle was abandoned in the 1700s and was last used as a liquor factory. Both are usually closed to the public, but the local tourist office has recently begun a program allowing sporadic visits. Ask at the tourist office for details.

To get an idea of the traditional lifestyle in the area, head to the **Museo Etnológico La Posada** (☎ 918 94 02 07; Calle Morata 5; adult/child €3/2; ☺ 11am-2pm & 4-8pm Mon-Fri, closed Wed, 11am-8pm Sat & Sun), a well-run museum exhibiting old farm equipment, household items and traditional garb.

FESTIVALS & EVENTS

The **Fiesta Mayor** is held from 12 to 18 August, when the town's main plaza is turned into a bullring that dominates the centre, and morning bullfights are held daily. Cheer from the surrounding balconies over breakfast and coffee.

SLEEPING

Parador Nacional (☎ 918 94 08 36; www.parador.es; Avenida Generalísimo 1; r from €113) The former Convento de Agustinos (Augustine Convent), the Parador Nacional is one of the town's most important historical buildings and can't be beaten for luxury. It's worth stopping by for a meal or coffee (and a peek around) even if you don't plan to stay here.

EATING

Chinchón is loaded with traditional-style restaurants, but for lighter fare there's nothing better than savouring a few tapas and

---

drinks on the sunny Plaza Mayor. There are several restaurants here, all of which serve similar fare.

Mesón Cuevas de la Comendadora (☎ 918 94 09 47; Calle Teniente Ortíz de Zárate; mains €8-16, menu €12; ☺ 1-4.30pm & 8-11pm) For something substantial head to this homely place. Its basement is a maze of old cellars dug into the earth. They're worth seeing even if you decide not to eat here.

Mesón Cuevas del Vino (☎ 918 94 02 06; www.cuevasdelvino.com; Calle Benito Hortelano 13; ☺ 1-4pm & 8-11pm Wed-Mon) The atmospheric Meson 'Caves of Wine' is guaranteed to be an experience you'll write postcards about. From the huge goatskins (used to keep wine) and the barrels covered in famous signatures to the caves underground, it's sure to be memorable.

GETTING THERE & AWAY

The bus company **La Veloz** (☎ 914 09 76 02) has regular (roughly one an hour) services to Chinchón (€3, 50 minutes). The buses leave from a stop on the Plaza Conde de Casal.

Sitting 45km southeast of Madrid, Chinchón is easy to reach by car. Take the A4 motorway and exit onto the M404, which makes its way to Chinchón.

ALCALÁ DE HENARES

With its pretty historical centre, welcoming plazas and legendary university, Alcalá de Henares hides a few treasures behind its façade as a mundane suburb.

Information

Ciber TK (☎ 918 83 40 24; Calle de San Diego de Alcalá 3; ☺ 10am-2pm & 3-9.30pm Mon-Fri, 10am-2pm & 3-9pm Sat, 3-9pm Sun) Get online at this simple Net café.

Tourist office (☎ 918 81 06 34; Plaza de los Santos Niños; ☺ 10am-2pm & 5-7.30pm Jun-15 Sep, 10am-2pm & 4-6.30pm 16 Sep-May) There is also a smaller info kiosk on Plaza de Cervantes.

Sights

The city entered an era of prosperity when Cardinal Cisneros founded a **university** (☎ 918 83 43 84; ☺ 9am-9pm) here in 1486. Now centred on a much-restored Renaissance building, the university was one of the country's principal seats of learning for a long period. You can wander around various faculty buildings, dating mostly from the 17th century, but more interesting is

---

AUTHOR'S CHOICE

Hostal Chinchón (☎ 918 93 53 98; www.hostal chinchon.com; Calle de José Antonio 12; s/d €27/40) If you stay in town, this is an excellent bet. The smallish rooms are clean, but worn around the edges. The best feature of this *hostal* is the surprise rooftop pool, which overlooks Plaza Mayor.

the **guided tour** (6 per day Mon-Fri, 11 per day Sat & Sun), which gives a peek into the Mudéjar **chapel** and the **Paraninfo** auditorium, where the king and queen of Spain give out the prestigious Premio Cervantes literary award every year.

The town is also dear to the hearts of Spaniards as the birthplace of the country's literary figurehead, Miguel de Cervantes Saavedra (see p54). The site believed to be Cervantes' birth place is re-created in the **Museo Casa Natal de Miguel de Cervantes** (☎ 918 89 96 54; Calle de la Imagen 2; admission free; 10am-6pm Tue-Sun Jun-Sep, 10am-1.30pm & 4-6.30pm Tue-Sun Oct-May). It's filled with period furniture and bits and pieces relating to his life.

Sleeping & Eating

Husa El Bedel (☎ 918 89 37 00; www.husa.es; Plaza San Diego 6; s/d €96/108) A sophisticated hotel that offers spacious accommodation and a perfect location.

El Ruedo (☎ 918 80 69 19; Calle de los Libreros 38; 9am-11pm Thu-Tue) Offers light fare, such as salads and *platos combinados* (combined plates). There's a quiet patio for outdoor eating in fine weather.

Hostería del Estudiante (☎ 918 88 03 30; Calle de los Colegios 3; menú €24.50; 1-4pm & 9-11pm) Run by the national Parador hotels, this elegant *hostería* is considered the best restaurant in town. It's very near the main university building.

Getting There & Away

Alcalá de Henares is just 35km east of Madrid, heading towards Zaragoza.

Several buses leave Madrid regularly (every five to 15 minutes) from depots at the Avenida de América and Estación Sur (€1.35, one hour).

If you're driving, you'll find the town just off the A2 Hwy some 40 minutes outside Madrid (depending on traffic).

A constant stream of C1, C2 and C7 Renfe *cercanías* make the trip to Alcalá de Henares (€1.10, 48 minutes) daily.

SIERRA DE GUADARRAMA

To the north of the city lies the Sierra de Guadamarra, a popular hiking and skiing destination. Charming towns such as Manzanares El Real and Cercedilla make great base towns for those wanting to explore the mountains.

Colmenar Viejo

pop 37,240 / elevation 883m

There's little to see in this Madrid satellite. But if you are in Madrid in the first days of February, get up here to witness the colourful **Vaquilla**, a fiesta with pagan origins dating back to the 13th century. A highly ornamental 'heifer' prances about town before being 'slaughtered' by *toreros* (bullfighters) dressed in Andalucian style.

Manzanares El Real

pop 2340 / elevation 908m

This is a sweet little mountain town, but what makes it stand out from others like it is the 15th-century storybook **Castillo de los Mendoza** (☎ 918 53 00 08; admission €1.80; 10am-2pm & 3-6pm Tue-Sun Apr-Sep, 10am-5pm Tue-Sun Oct-Mar). The perfectly preserved (almost too perfectly) castle looks like something out of a Disney cartoon with its evenly spaced turrets and strong round towers. There are great views of the sierra from the top.

Near town, several trails lead into the Parque de la Pedriza, a natural space just outside Manzanares El Real. One trail brings you to freshwater pools. Rock climbers have a wealth of options, with 1500 climbing routes in the park. For advice check out the **Centro de Educación Ambiental de Manzanares el Real** (Environmental Education Centre of Manzanares el Real; ☎ 91 853 9978; Camino de la Pedriza, Manzanares el Real; 9am-6pm).

Bus No 724 runs regularly to Manzanares from Plaza de Castilla in Madrid (€2.55, 40 minutes).

Cercedilla

pop 6297 / elevation 1188m

This mountain town and its surroundings are, are popular with walkers and mountain bikers. Several trails are marked out through the hills, the main one known as the **Cuerda Larga** or **Cuerda Castellana**. This is a forest track that takes in 55 peaks between the Puerto de Somosierra in the north and Puerto de la Cruz Verde in the southwest. It would take days to complete, but there are several options for shorter walks, including day excursions up the Valle de la Fuenfría and a climb up Monte de Siete Picos. Get more information from Lonely Planet's *Walking in Spain*.

Mountain bikers can take their bikes up on the local train to Puerto de los Cotos (a lovely ride in itself), scoot across to the Bola del Mundo (in good winters the top end of Guadarrama's best ski piste) and pedal downhill to Cercedilla.

You can get information at the **Centro de Información Valle de la Fuenfría** (☎ 918 52 22 13; Carretera de las Dehesas Km2), which is a couple of kilometres from Cercedilla train station. Accommodation is scarce in this area.

From Madrid's Chamartín train station, the C2 *cercanías* line goes to Cercedilla (€1.20, 80 minutes, 15 daily).

Skiing

If you're here in winter, you may want to head up to the modest ski resorts in the Guadarrama. The slopes aren't anything to write home about, but hey, it's only 60km from Madrid! Snowless years are common and the available pistes are not extensive, but it's a popular business at the weekend, when the area is best avoided.

The main centre is **Navacerrada** (☎ 915 94 30 34; www.puertonavacerrada.com; admission €17-26), with 13km of mostly easy – and frustratingly short – runs. The **Valdesqui Ski Resort** (☎ 915 70 12 24; Puerto de Cotos; admission €22-30) is another option.

From Madrid's Chamartín train station, you can get to Puerto de Navacerrada on the C8B *cercanías* line (€1.43, two hours with train change in Cercedilla, four daily). Bus No 691 from platform 14 of Madrid's Intercambiador de Autobuses de Moncloa runs here regularly (€2.55, one hour).

Sleeping

Parador Nacional (☎ 920 34 80 48; www.parador.es; Carretera Barraco-Béjar Km42; r from €74.40) Spain's very first *parador*, this elegant stone hotel overlooks the sierra. The refined restaurant serves tasty local dishes.

Arcipreste de Hita (☎ 918 56 01 25; www.hotel arciprestedehita.com; Carretera Nacional 601 Km2, Navacerrada; s/d €120/220) This stone inn is a reliable choice. The outdoor pool is a big plus in summer, and the restaurant is good if not stellar.

Hotel La Barranca (☎ 918 56 00 00; fax 918 56 05 40; Valle del Pinar de La Barranca, Navacerrada; s with breakfast €71-75, d with breakfast €92-98) Tucked into a picturesque valley, the large La Barranca offers all the comforts, including pool and tennis courts. Its restaurant is also recommended.

Eating

La Barranca (☎ 918 56 00 00; fax 918 56 05 40; Valle del Pinar de La Barranca, Navacerrada; mains €8-14) For excellent Castilian fare, head to the homey La Barranca for typical dishes such as roast suckling pig or pigs' trotters.

Sala de Guadarrama (☎ 918 54 21 21; Carretera de los Molinos Km2, Guadarrama; mains €14-24; ◷ 1-4pm & 8.30-11pm, closed 20 Sep-20 Oct) A solid bet, known for its pricey but delicious seafood dishes. This is a popular place, so you'll need to reserve far in advance if you plan to come on a weekend.

NORTH OF MADRID
Palacio Real de El Pardo

Built in the 15th century and remodelled in the 17th, this opulent **palacio** (☎ 913 76 15 00; www.patrimonionacional.es; Calle de Manuel Alonso; admission €3; ◷ 10.30am-5pm Mon-Sat, 9.30am-1.30pm Sun Oct-May; 10.30am-6pm Mon-Sat, 9.30am-1.30pm Sun Jun-Sep) was Franco's favourite residence. It's surrounded by lush gardens, and on Sunday fills with *madrileño* families looking for a bit of fresh air and a hearty lunch. Just outside Madrid, it's the nearest of several regal retreats. Of the art displayed inside, the tapestries stand out, particularly those based on cartoons by Goya.

GETTING THERE & AWAY

If you're driving from Madrid take the M40 Hwy to the C601, which leads to El Pardo. The 13km trip takes just 15 minutes. You can also take bus No 601, which leaves every five to 10 minutes from the bus depot (Map pp106-8) near the Moncloa metro station (€1.05, 25 minutes).

El Molar
pop 4607 / elevation 850m

At first glance El Molar may not seem too exciting. Sitting 33km north of Madrid along the N1 Hwy to Burgos, most of the town is fairly nondescript, with a tiny old centre surrounded by cheap modern housing and scrappy suburban-style spread. But before you head for the door wait, just a moment. To the south is a small rise peppered with *cuevas* (cellars) old and new. Madrileños crowd into them to gorge on grilled meat in the relative cool during the summer months, although they are open year-round. To find them, follow the yellow signs from the town centre to the **Bodegón de**

Olivares. There you will find this *cueva* and all the others huddled together. Plenty of buses zip up from Plaza de Castilla (€2.25, 45 minutes).

Buitrago & Sierra Pobre

Buitrago is the entryway into the Sierra Pobre, a quiet stretch of mountain east of the busier Sierra de Guadarrama. Popular with hikers and others looking for nature without quite so many creature comforts, the sleepy Sierra Pobre has yet to develop the tourism industry of its neighbours. And that's just why we like it.

In Buitrago you can stroll along part of the old **city walls**. You can also take a peek into the 15th-century Mudéjar and Romanesque **Iglesia de Santa María del Castillo** and the small **Picasso Museum** (☎ 918 68 00 56/04; Plaza Picasso; admission free; ☸ 11am-1.30pm & 4-6pm Wed-Mon), which contains a few works that the artist gave to his barber, Eugenio Arias.

Tiny hamlets are scattered throughout the rest of the Sierra Pobre; some, like **Puebla de la Sierra** and **El Atazar**, are pretty to stroll through and are the base for trails that wind into the hills.

SLEEPING & EATING

Posada de los Vientos (☎ 918 69 91 95; Calle Encerradero 2, La Acebeda; r from €60; ☸ weekends & holidays winter only) Housed in a tastefully converted barn, this is a charming small family inn.

El Arco (☎ 918 68 09 11; Calle Arco 6; mains €12-15; ☸ lunch only Fri-Sun 15 Sep-15 Jun) The best restaurant in Buitrago, this is known for its fresh, creative cuisine based on local ingredients and traditional Spanish dishes.

GETTING THERE & AWAY

The Continental Auto Company has a dozen daily buses connecting Madrid's Plaza de la Castilla with Buitrago (€4.19, 1½ hours).

COMUNIDAD DE MADRID

Castilla y León

The vast Castilian heartland, former home to the kingdoms of León and Castilla la Vieja (Old Castilla), is a treasure-trove of cities set in a diverse landscape of sweeping plains and scenic mountain ranges.

Belying Castilla's reputation for conservatism and reserve, Salamanca is a gem of Renaissance sandstone architecture enlivened by a massive student population who know how to party. Enchanting Segovia seems to have also acquired a propensity for lively nights, while its days offer views of an exceptional Roman aqueduct, a fairy-tale castle and restaurants of distinction. And having lost out in its desire to be Spain's capital, Valladolid consoles itself nightly with an energy that's hard to resist. Further north, the attractive towns of León and Burgos boast *catedrals* (cathedrals) that are among Europe's finest. The Catholic monumental legacy survives equally in Ávila, a beautiful town surrounded by stunning defensive walls.

Beyond the cities, this is a region dominated by its terrain. Picturesque mountain ranges shelter villages holding onto traditions and architecture that died out elsewhere long ago. The Sierra de Francia (near Extremadura) and the Sierra de Gredos (bordering Castilla-La Mancha) are magical remnants of a bygone era, with stone-and-timber villages and superb mountain scenery. The villages near Burgos and Soria are similarly pretty, nowhere more so than Covarrubias.

Long, bitter winters have also made their unmistakable mark, most rewardingly on the area's cuisine. Spaniards readily recognise the region as the best for eating roast everything; *cochinillo* (suckling pig) is a particular speciality in Segovia, while *cordero asado* (roast lamb) is the order of the day elsewhere, particularly in Aranda de Duero and Sepúlveda.

Searing summers find some respite in the fact that the riverbank of the Río Duero produces some of the best wines in Spain; particularly noteworthy is the Ribera del Duero.

CASTILLA Y LEÓN

HIGHLIGHTS

- Savour **Salamanca's** (p179) fiery nightlife, lively university scene and Plateresque (early Renaissance) architecture
- Marvel at Segovia's monuments, especially the **Alcázar** (p191) and **aqueduct** (p192)
- Be awestruck in León's **catedral** (p210), a kaleidoscopic vision of glass and stone
- Get off the beaten track to the villages of the **Sierra de Francia** (p188), one of Spain's forgotten corners
- Be uplifted by live Gregorian chanting in the monastery of **Santo Domingo de Silos** (p223)
- Visit the enchanting village of **Covarrubias** (p223) with it's half-timbered houses

León ★
Covarrubias ★
★ Santo Domingo de Silos
Salamanca ★   Segovia ★
Sierra de ★ Francia

■ AREA: 94,224 SQ KM	■ POP: 2,487,646	■ AVE SUMMER TEMP: HIGH 31°C, LOW 14°C

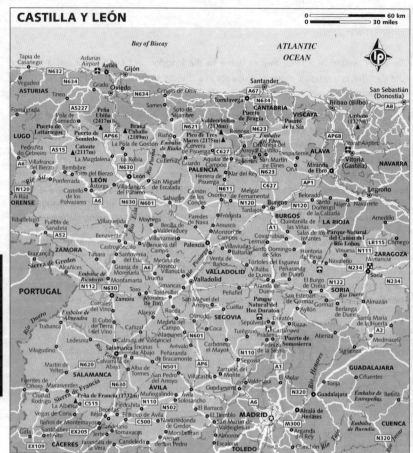

CASTILLA Y LEÓN

CASTILLA Y LEÓN

THE SOUTHWEST

Southwestern Castilla y León is a delight, encompassing beautiful towns such as Salamanca, Ávila and Ciudad Rodrigo, the beautiful mountain scenery of the Sierra de Gredos (ideal for walking) and the timeless villages of the Sierra de Francia.

ÁVILA

pop 51,331 / elevation 1130m

Ávila is like a picture of a bygone age. Encircled by a fairy-tale stone wall with 88 watchtowers, it's easy to imagine Ávila's days on the battleground of medieval kingdoms. This is also a town of enormous spiritual

significance as the home town of Santa Teresa de Ávila, a fact which has bequeathed to the town a rich architectural heritage dating largely from the 16th century.

The Peruvian novelist Mario Vargas Llosa described Ávila as a place 'where the past seems more alive than the present'. It's true that Ávila lacks the lively enchantments of Salamanca or the captivating charm of Toledo and it can get bitterly cold in winter. Nonetheless, it's a wonderful day trip from Madrid, or even better, an overnight stay along one of its quiet medieval streets.

History

According to myth, one of Hercules' sons founded Ávila. The more prosaic truth,

The Hall of Statues inside Madrid's Museo del Prado (p121)

Traditional flamenco dancing in Madrid
(p150)

Catedral de Nuestra Señora de
la Almudena (p120), Madrid

Saaha Sokol Band at Calle 54 jazz club
in northern Madrid (p151))

One of Cuenca's striking *casas colgadas* (hanging houses, p255) at night, Castilla-La Mancha

Segovia's distinctive Alcázar (p192) at sunset, Castilla y León

Detail of the porticoed Plaza Mayor in Almagro (p250), Castilla-La Mancha

Consuegra's classic windmills (p252), Castilla-La Mancha

however, gives the honour to obscure Iberian tribes who were later Romanised and Christianised. For almost 300 years, Ávila changed hands regularly between Muslims and Christians, until the fall of Toledo to Alfonso VI in 1085.

In the following centuries, 'Ávila of the Knights' became an important commercial centre with a well-established noble class. The edict issued in 1492 expelling all Jews from Spain robbed the city of much of its lifeblood. Meanwhile, Fray Tomás de Torquemada, the infamous 15th-century leader of the Spanish Inquisition, ended his days in Ávila.

By the end of the 16th century, the city's heyday was over and it has only recently begun to shake off the deep slumber of neglect that ensued.

Orientation

The old centre fans out to the west from the *catedral* which abuts the eastern wall. The bus and train stations are a five- and 10-minute walk respectively northeast of the catedral. The best accommodation and eating options are all close to the eastern end of the old town.

Information

EMERGENCY
Cruz Roja (☎ 920 22 22 22) For ambulances.
Policía Nacional (☎ 920 25 10 00, emergencies ☎ 091; Paseo San Roque 34)

MEDICAL SERVICES
Hospital Provincial (☎ 920 35 72 00; Calle de Jesús de Gran Poder 42)

MONEY
Banks that will exchange money and have ATMs abound in the eastern end of the old town and in the streets around Plaza de Santa Teresa.

POST
Main post office (correos; ☎ 920 35 31 06; Plaza de la Catedral) Almost opposite the catedral.

TELEPHONE
Telephone office (Plaza de la Catedral; ⊗ 8am-8pm)

TOURIST INFORMATION
Tourist information kiosk (☎ 920 35 71 26; ⊗ 4-7pm Fri, 10am-2pm & 4-7pm Sat, 10am-2pm Sun summer) Outside Puerta de San Vicente, this kiosk – and another

outside the train station (⊗ 9am-2pm & 5-8pm summer) – complements the main tourist office during summer.
Tourist office (☎ 920 21 13 87; turismo@ayuntavila .com; Plaza de la Catedral 4; ⊗ 9am-2pm & 5-8pm)

Catedral

Ávila's 12th-century **catedral** (☎ 920 21 16 41; admission €2.50; ⊗ 10am-7pm Mon-Sat, noon-7pm Sun) is not just a house of worship, but also an ingenious fortress: its stout granite apse forms the central bulwark in the heavily fortified eastern wall of the town. The *catedral* is the earliest Gothic church in Spain, and the grey, sombre façade betrays some unhappy 18th-century meddling in the main portal.

The interior is a different story, with red and white limestone featuring in the columns. To fully appreciate its splendour, you'll need to seek out the inner sanctum, cloisters, sacristy and small museum, which are superb. In the museum, highlights include a painting by El Greco and a splendid silver monstrance by Juan de Arfe. Within the church itself are Renaissance-era carved walnut choir stalls and a dazzling altar painting begun by Pedro de Berruguete, showing the life of Jesus in 24 scenes.

SANTA TERESA DE ÁVILA

Teresa de Cepeda y Ahumada – a Catholic mystic and reformer – was born in Ávila on 28 March 1515, one of 10 children of a merchant family. Raised by Augustinian nuns after her mother's death, she joined the Carmelite Order at age 20. Shortly thereafter, Teresa nearly succumbed to a mysterious illness that paralysed her legs for three years. After her early, undistinguished years as a nun, her visions crystallised her true vocation: she would reform the Carmelites.

With the help of supporters, Teresa founded convents of the Carmelitas Descalzas (Shoeless Carmelites) all over Spain. She also co-opted San Juan de la Cruz (St John of the Cross) to begin a similar reform in the masculine order, a task that earned him several stints of incarceration by mainstream Carmelites. Santa Teresa's writings were first published in 1588 and proved enormously popular, perhaps for their earthy style. She died in 1582 in Alba de Tormes, where she is buried. She was canonised by Pope Gregory XV in 1622.

ÁVILA

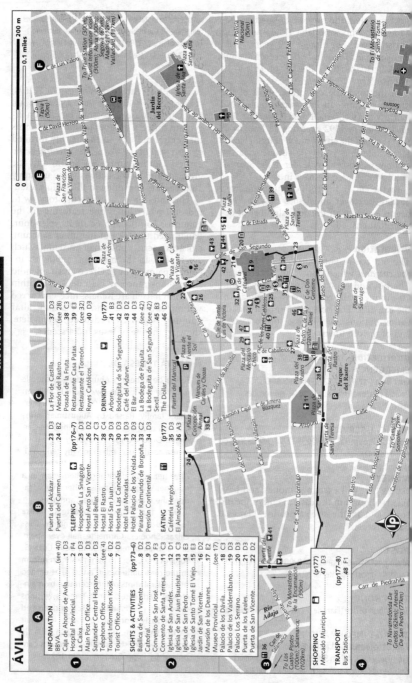

INFORMATION
BBVA...................................(see 40)
Caja de Ahorros de Ávila...............1 D3
Hospital Provincial....................2 F4
La Caixa...............................3 D3
Main Post Office.......................4 D3
Santander Central Hispano..............5 D3
Telephone Office.....................(see 4)
Tourist Information Kiosk..............6 D2
Tourist Office.........................7 D3

SIGHTS & ACTIVITIES   (pp173-6)
Basílica de San Vicente................8 D2
Catedral...............................9 D3
Convento de San José..................10 F3
Convento de Santa Teresa..............11 C3
Iglesia de San Andrés.................12 C1
Iglesia de San Juan Bautista..........13 C3
Iglesia de San Pedro..................14 E3
Iglesia de Santo Tomé El Viejo........15 E3
Jardín de San Vicente.................16 D2
Mansión de los Deanes.................17 E2
Museo Provincial....................(see 17)
Palacio de los Dávila.................18 C3
Palacio Los Valderrábano..............19 D3
Palacio Los Serrano...................20 D3
Puerta de los Leales..................21 D3
Puerta San Vicente....................22 D2

Puerta del Alcázar....................23 D3
Puerta del Carmen.....................24 B2

SLEEPING   (pp176-7)
Hospedería La Sinagoga................25 D3
Hostal Arco San Vicente...............26 D2
Hostal Bellas.........................27 C3
Hostal El Rastro......................28 C4
Hostal San Juan.......................29 D3
Hostería Las Cancelas.................30 D3
Hotel Las Moradas.....................31 D3
Hotel Palacio de los Velada...........32 D3
Parador Raimundo de Borgoña...........33 C2
Pensión Continental...................34 D3

EATING   (p177)
Cafetería Hergós......................35 D3
El Almacén............................36 A3

La Flor de Castilla...................37 D3
Mesón del Rastro.....................(see 28)
Posada de la Fruta....................38 C3
Restaurante Casa Patas................39 E3
Restaurante el Torreón..............(see 32)
Reyes Católicos.......................40 D3

DRINKING   (p177)
Arbore................................41 B3
Bodeguita de San Segundo..............42 D3
Café del Adarve.......................43 D2
El Bar................................44 D3
La Bodega de Paquita................(see 42)
La Bodeguita de San Segundo.........(see 42)
Sextil................................45 B3
The Dollar............................46 D3

SHOPPING   (p177)
Mercado Municipal.....................47 D3

TRANSPORT   (pp177-8)
Bus Station...........................48 F1

You can catch a partial peek of the interior for free, but to see the inner sanctum (and museum) you'll have to produce the €2.50.

Basílica de San Vicente

Outside the great fortified gate of the same name, the subdued elegance of the Romanesque **basilica** (☎ 920 25 52 30; admission €1.40, free Sun; ⏰ 10am-1.30pm) makes it one of the most striking buildings in Ávila. A series of largely Gothic modifications in sober granite contrasts with the warm sandstone of the Romanesque original. Work started in the 11th century, supposedly on the site where three martyrs – Vicente and his sisters – were slaughtered by the Romans in the early 4th century. Their canopied sepulchre is an attractive piece of Romanesque work. The Jardín de San Vicente across the road was once a Roman cemetery.

El Monasterio de Santo Tomás

Commissioned by the Catholic Monarchs, Fernando and Isabel, and completed in 1492, this **complex** (☎ 920 22 04 00; admission €1; ⏰ 10am-1pm & 4-8pm) is an exquisite example of the Isabelline style of architecture. Three interconnected cloisters lead up to the church that contains the alabaster tomb of Don Juan, the monarchs' only son. It's backed by an altarpiece by Pedro de Berruguete depicting scenes from the life of St Thomas Aquinas. The magnificent choir stalls, in Flemish Gothic style, are accessible from the upper level of the third cloister, the Claustro de los Reyes, so called because Fernando and Isabel often attended Mass here. It's thought that the inquisitor Torquemada is buried in the sacristy.

In Santa Teresa's Footsteps

Santa Teresa casts a long shadow over Ávila.

The **Convento de Santa Teresa** (☎ 920 21 10 30; admission free; ⏰ 8.30am-1.30pm & 3.30-8.30pm), built in 1636 over the saint's birthplace, is the epicentre of the cult surrounding Teresa. The room where she was born is now a chapel smothered in gold and lorded over by a baroque altar by Gregorio Fernández and featuring a statue of the saint. An adjoining **room** (admission free; ⏰ 9.30am-1.30pm & 3.30-7pm) is crammed with Teresa relics, including her ring finger (complete with ring), which supposedly spent the Franco years by the Generalísimo's bedside. There's also a small **museum** (admission €2; ⏰ 10am-1.30pm & 3.30-5.30pm) dedicated to the saint, accessible from Calle Aizpuru.

Nearby, the 16th-century **Iglesia de San Juan Bautista** (☎ 920 21 11 27; admission free) contains the baptismal font in which Teresa was baptised. A five-minute walk east of the *catedral* is the unremarkable **Convento de San José** (☎ 920 22 21 27; admission €1; ⏰ 10am-1.30pm & 3-6pm), the first convent Teresa founded in 1562; the saint herself is said to have helped build it.

North of the city walls, the unadorned **Monasterio de la Encarnación** (☎ 920 21 12 12; admission €1.30; ⏰ 9.30am-1.30pm & 3.30-6pm Mon-Fri, 10am-1pm & 4-6pm Sat & Sun) is where Santa Teresa fully took on the monastic life and lived for 27 years, launching her reform movement. A Renaissance complex modified in the 18th century, it contains further mementos of her life as well as a replica of her cell.

City Wall

With its eight monumental gates and 88 towers, Ávila's **muralla** (city wall; adult/concession €3.50/2; ⏰ 11am-6pm Tue-Sun Oct-Apr; 11am-8pm Tue-Sun May-Sep) is one of the world's best-preserved medieval defensive perimeters. Raised to a height of 12m between the 11th and 12th centuries, on the remains of earlier efforts by the Muslims and Romans, the wall has been much restored and modified, with various Gothic and Renaissance touches and some Roman stones re-used in the construction.

The most impressive gates, the Puerta de San Vicente and Puerta del Alcázar, are flanked by towers more than 20m high and stand on either side of the *catedral's* apse.

You can walk atop more than 1km of the 2.5km wall and enjoy the fabulous views. Access is from Puerta del Alcázar, Puerta de los Leales and Puerta del Carmen. The last tickets are sold 45 minutes before closing time.

Churches & Mansions

The Romanesque **Iglesia de Santo Tomé El Viejo** (Plaza de Italia; admission €1.20, free Sat & Sun; ⏰ 10am-2pm & 4.30-7.30pm Tue-Sat, 10am-2pm Sun) dates from the 13th century, and it was from this pulpit that Santa Teresa was castigated most vehemently for her reforms of the Carmelite order. It has been impressively restored to house mostly Roman foundation stones and a splendid floor mosaic. It's an annexe of the **Museo Provincial** (☎ 920 21 10 03; adult/

concession €1.20/0.90, free Sat & Sun; ☉ 10am-2pm & 4-7pm Tue-Sat, 10am-2pm Sun), housed in the adjacent and austere granite 16th-century Mansión de los Deanes. Both can be entered on the same ticket.

Built a little later is the **Iglesia de San Pedro** (Plaza de Santa Teresa; admission free; ☉ 10am-12.30pm & 6.30-8pm). With its light, sandstone exterior, it is a pleasant complement to the granite austerity that reigns inside the city walls. North of the old city, the 12th-century **Iglesia de San Andrés**, a pure example of the Romanesque, is Ávila's oldest church. The interior is closed to the public.

The city also has its fair share of noble mansions, some of which now serve as top-end hotels. The **Palacio de los Velada** and the **Palacio de los Valderrábano**, both on Plaza de la Catedral, fall into this category. The **Palacio de los Dávila** once belonged to one of the city's most illustrious noble families. **Palacio Los Serrano** (☎ 920 21 22 23; Plaza de Italia; admission free; ☉ 7.30-9.30pm Mon-Fri, noon-2pm & 7.30-9.30pm Sat & Sun) is a typically successful Spanish fusion of the old and the new and is used for contemporary art exhibitions.

Los Cuatro Postes

Just northwest of the city on the road to Salamanca, this spot not only affords fine views of Ávila's walls, but also marks the place where Santa Teresa and her brother were caught by their uncle as they tried to run away from home. They were hoping to achieve martyrdom at the hands of the Muslims.

Festivals & Events

Ávila's principal festival, **Fiesta de Santa Teresa**, honours, not surprisingly, Santa Teresa. The city kicks up its heels for 10 days around 15 October, celebrating with processions, concerts and fireworks.

Easter is marked by a stream of solemn marches and other events, beginning on Holy Thursday. The most noteworthy event is the early morning (around 5am) Good Friday procession, which circles the outside of the city wall.

Sleeping

Pensión Continental (☎ 920 21 15 02; fax 920 21 15 63; Plaza de la Catedral 6; s/d with washbasin €15.05/25.85, d with bathroom €33.10) The old-world charm here is most evident in the perilously sloping

staircase, polished floorboards and high ceilings. Some rooms have views of the *catedral*.

Hostal San Juan (☎ 920 25 14 75; Calle de los Comuneros de Castilla 3; www.hostalsanjuanavila.com; s/d from €24/36) A better choice than the Continental, the San Juan is pleasant and friendly, although the rooms lack character.

Hostal Bellas (☎ /fax 920 35 24 49; Calle de Caballeros 19; s/d from €24/33) This tidy, well-run place is friendly (once they warm up). The rooms are good and the bathrooms sparkle.

Hostal El Rastro (☎ 920 21 12 18; fax 920 25 16 26; Plaza del Rastro 4; s/d from €28.50/35) With eight quaint rooms overlooking a quiet square, this is another good choice.

Hostería Las Cancelas (☎ 920 21 22 49; www.las cancelas.com; Calle de la Cruz Vieja 6; s/d €42.50/64.20) Another top choice, the rooms here are spacious and the traditional furniture adds a touch of character.

Hotel Las Moradas (☎ 920 22 24 88; www.hotel asmoradas.com; Calle de Don Gerónimo 3; s/d/tr from €63/79/105) This place offers large, gorgeous rooms, most with kitchenette, and the staff are very helpful.

Hospedería La Sinagoga (☎ 920 35 23 21; lasina goga@airtel.net; Calle de los Reyes Católicos 22; s/d €54/75) Centrally located and quiet, this delightful hotel, built on the site of a synagogue, has bright, good-sized rooms.

Parador Raimundo de Borgoña (☎ 920 21 13 40; avila@parador.es; Marques de Canales y Chozas 2; s/d €77.70/97.10) Occupying a 16th-century palace, the *parador* has all of the essential elements of this chain: elegant public areas, helpful staff and stylish bedrooms.

Hotel Palacio de los Velada (☎ 920 25 51 00; Plaza de la Catedral 10; s/d €108/130) This fancy option boasts great architecture (the colonnaded courtyard is superb) and plush rooms that are a bit overdone. It also offers cheaper weekend deals.

Camping Sonsoles (☎ 920 25 63 36; camping per person/tent/car €4.25/3.75/3.75; ⊙ Jun-Sep) Ávila's nearest camping ground, this place is just 2km south of town on the N403 highway to Toledo.

Eating
RESTAURANTS & CAFES

Ávila is famous for its *chuleton de avileño* (T-bone steak) and *judias del barco de Ávila* (white beans, often with chorizo, in a thick sauce).

Caféteria Hergós (☎ 920 21 33 70; Calle de Don Gerónimo 1; meals from €3.50) This pastry shop and café is the place to tuck into good-value *platos combinados* (combination plate; €6 to €8), burgers (€3) and *bocadillos* (bread rolls with filling; €2.25 to €4).

Restaurante Casa Patas (☎ 920 21 31 94; Calle de San Millán 4; mains €5-15, menú €10) Good *raciónes* (meal-sized tapas) and filling *menú del día* (daily set menu) are the orders of the day at this restaurant. It's very popular with locals.

Posada de la Fruta (☎ 920 22 09 84; Plaza de Pedro Dávila 8; mains €8-15) Two restaurants in one. Simple, informal meals can be had at the café-bar in a light-filled courtyard, while the traditional *comedor* (dining room) serves *menús* and à la carte dishes.

Mesón del Rastro (☎ 920 21 12 18; Plaza del Rastro 4; menú lunch/dinner €13/14.50) This atmospheric mid-range choice is rare in that it serves superb-value *menús* for both lunch and dinner. The dining room, with its dark-wood beams, exudes Castilian charm, and the *cochinillo* is particularly good.

El Almacén (☎ 920 25 44 55; Carretera de Salamanca 6; starters €6-12, mains €12-23) One of Ávila's premier restaurants, you'll pay top dollar here for excellent food (*chuleton de avileño* is €16), wine and views of the city wall.

Other excellent, upmarket options closer to the *catedral*:

Restaurante el Torreón (☎ 920 21 31 71; Calle Tostado; menú €20) Excellent *menú* includes both *chuleton* and *judias*.

Reyes Católicos (☎ 920 25 56 27; Calle de Reyes Católicos; mains €12-15, menú €17.85) A chic and super-modern alternative to Castilian wood-panelled places.

PASTELERÍAS

Ávila's local speciality is the *yema de Ávila*, an ultra-sweet, sticky business made of egg yolk and sugar, allegedly invented by Teresa herself. You'll see it all over town, but one of the best places is **La Flor de Castilla** (☎ 920 25 28 66; Calle de San Gerónimo).

Drinking

Ávila nights aren't particularly lively, but there are a few spots worth seeking out. Most bars in town serve free tapas with drinks.

Café del Adarve (Calle de San Segundo 40; ⊙ 3pm-late) To soak up a youthful vibe, drop in at this hip spot, which has coffee during the day, drinks at night and live music during winter.

El Bar (Calle de San Segundo; ⊙ 11am-3am) Almost next door to Café del Adarve, El Bar is an appealing place with its much-coveted outdoor seats looking out towards the city wall.

Bodeguita de San Segundo (Calle de San Segundo 19; ⊙ 11am-late) Almost opposite El Bar and a real treat, this wine and tapas bar is often standing-room only, and the setting in the 16th-century Casa de la Misericordia is superb. **La Bodega de Paquita** (Calle de San Segundo), next door, is similarly good.

Otherwise, the streets around Plaza del Mercado Chico have bars and tapas.

On Thursday to Saturday you'll find some major *marcha* (action) along Calle de Vallespín and down by the Puerta del Puente. Look out for Sextil and Arbore, which start up at around 11pm. Remember, however, that it's a long uphill walk along cobbled streets at the end of the night, so you might try **The Dollar** (Calle de Plá y Deniel) for an easier walk home.

Shopping

To stock up on supermarket goods, head to the **Mercado Municipal** (Calle de Teresa de Victoría; ⊙ 8am-2pm Mon-Fri).

Getting There & Away
BUS

Buses leave from Ávila's **bus station** (☎ 920 22 01 54; Avenida de Madrid) for Madrid (€6.30, 1½ hours, eight departures daily on weekdays, four daily on weekends), Salamanca (€4.65, 1½ hours, four daily Monday to Saturday, twice on Sundays) and Segovia (€3.75, one hour, six times daily on weekdays, twice daily on weekends). Destinations in the Sierra de Gredos include Navarredonda de Gredos (€3.65, 1¼ hours, two to three times daily) and Arenas de San Pedro (€4.65, 1¼ hours, twice daily).

CAR & MOTORCYCLE

To get to Madrid, head northeast on the N110 and at Villacastín turn onto the NVI or the parallel A6 *autopista* (tollway). From Ávila, the N501 heads north to Salamanca, the N110 east will take you to Segovia, the N110 west to Plasencia and the N403 north to Valladolid. For the Sierra de Gredos, take the N502.

For the Sierra de Gredos, public transport ranges from impractical to nonexistent. Among the car-rental agencies to try are **Atesa** (☎ 920 25 59 02; train station) and **Tapia** (☎ 920 22 22 33; Calle de Segovia 24).

TRAIN

From the **train station** (☎ 920 24 02 02; Paseo de la Estación), more than 30 trains run daily to Madrid (€5.60, 1½ hours) and a handful to Salamanca (€5, 1½ hours). Other Castilian cities with direct service include Burgos, León and Valladolid.

Getting Around

Local bus No 1 runs past the train station to Plaza de la Catedral.

SIERRA DE GREDOS

The picturesque Sierra de Gredos form a formidable barrier between Castilla y León and Castilla-La Mancha. It's a land of precipitous terrain, numerous lakes and granite mountains, including the Pico de Almanzor (2592m), which is surrounded by slightly smaller mountains that together form the Circo de Gredos.

The occasional castle or sanctuary may warrant attention, but the main attraction here is the scenery. Walking ranges from good to excellent, and activities such as mountain biking and rock climbing are popular. Spring and autumn are the best times for outdoor activity; summer can be stifling, while in winter the trails are often covered in snow.

Although there are bus services from Ávila and Madrid, they're sporadic, slow and often limited to weekdays. You might want to consider renting a car to avoid frustration.

There are three main routes through the Sierra. The C502 travels north–south, paralleling an old Roman road (still visible in parts) through a steep valley. Cutting across the northern foothills, the C500 af-

fords scenic views of the mountains while passing through several hamlets. Following the southern flank of the mountain chain, the C501 offers a pretty drive from Arenas de San Pedro towards Candeleda and on into Extremadura's La Vera Valle.

Arenas de San Pedro & Around

Arenas de San Pedro pop 6581 / elevation 620m

Arenas de San Pedro, the southern Sierra's hub, is a popular summer escape for sun-stunned Castilians and *madrileños* (Madrid-dwellers).

The **tourist office** (☎ 920 37 23 68; Plaza de la Nueva España 1; ⏰ 10.30am-1pm & 4.30-7.30pm Tue-Sat, 10am-2pm Sun) in Arenas has walking suggestions, as does the Ávila tourist office (p173).

In the town centre, sights worth at least a quick look include the stout 15th-century **Castillo de la Triste Condesa**, the sober 14th-century Gothic **parish church** and the **Roman bridge**. A 10-minute walk north of here is the neoclassical **Palacio del Infante Don Luis de Borbón**, a gilded cage for Carlos III's imprisoned brother.

Far more attractive, with access to walking trails, are **Guisando**, **El Hornillo** and **El Arenal**, a trio of villages at a distance of 5km, 6km and 9km from Arenas, respectively. All three are served by a daily bus (weekdays only).

One popular walking trail leads from El Arenal to Puerto de la Cabrilla. Gaining some 1000m over a distance of 4.5km, it makes for a rather strenuous workout; it's best to budget about five to seven hours for a return trip.

SLEEPING & EATING

Hostal El Castillo (☎ 920 37 00 91; Carretera de Candeleda 2, Arenas de San Pedro; s/d €23/33) On the main road through Arenas is Hostal El Castillo, with pleasant, clean rooms with heating and TV.

Hostería Los Galayos (☎ 920 37 13 79; losgalayos@lycosmail.com; Plaza de Condestable Dávalos 2, Arenas de San Pedro; s/d €40/48) Adjacent to Hostal El Castillo, this comfortable three-star place is worth the extra euros, with very good rooms and a similarly winning location.

Hostal Isabel (☎ 920 37 51 48; Calle de las Angustias s/n, El Arenal; d with washbasin/bathroom €28/32) In El Arenal, Hostal Isabel is the only game in town, but fortunately it's not a bad choice, offering comfortable rooms.

Hostal El Fogon de Gredos (☎ 920 37 40 18; Calle Linarejo 6; s/d €45/60) This is the most attractive option in Guisando, offering pretty rooms with minibar, heating and satellite TV. You could also try **Hostal Los Galayos** (☎ 920 37 42 42; Paraje de Husero s/n; s/d €25/30), which is simple but adequate. **Camping Los Galayos** (☎ 920 37 40 21; Carretera Linarejos; per person/tent/car €2.70/2.70/2.70) is also in town.

GETTING THERE & AWAY

At least four buses run daily from Arenas de San Pedro to Madrid (€10.35, twice daily except Sunday), and two buses per weekday do the trip to Ávila (€4.65, 1¼ hours).

Northern Flank of the Sierra de Gredos

Veering off the C502 near Puerta de Picos, the C500 connects a series of nondescript, but scenically located, small hamlets. From Hoyos del Espino, a small road, the AV931, leads into the Sierras, ending after 12km at La Plataforma. This is the jumping-off point for one of the most popular and picturesque walks, leading to the **Laguna Grande**, a glassy mountain lake in the shadow of the Pico de Almanzor.

The easy-to-moderate walk along a well-defined 8km trail takes about 2½ hours each way. Next to the lake is a *refugio* (shelter), which is often full, and good camping. From here it's possible to climb to the top of the **Almanzor** (2592m; difficult) in about two hours or to continue for two hours west to the **Circo de Cinco Lagunas** (easy to moderate). From there you could either backtrack or descend via the Garganta del Pinar towards the town of Navalperral de Tormes, a strenuous endeavour that can take as long as five hours.

SLEEPING

Most villages along the C500 route offer accommodation.

Albergue Juvenil (☎ 920348005; albngredos@dvnet .es; Navarredonda de Gredos; dm under/over 26 €7/10; ⏰ 15 Mar-15 Dec; ☒) This place offers spotless rooms, its own Olympic-sized swimming pool and breathtaking mountain views.

Parador de Gredos (☎ 920 34 80 48; gredos@parador .es; s/d from €59.55/74.40, d with terrace €97.80) Not far from Albergue Juvenil and similarly well signposted, this *parador* is supremely comfortable. It has the same views as Albergue Juvenil and a whole lot more charm.

Camping Navagredos (☎ 920 20 74 76; per person/ car/tent €3.01/2.25/2.40) This is a fine camping

ground located on the access road to La Plataforma.

Hoyos del Espino has dozens of places to stay, including many *casas rurales* (rooms in private homes).

Hostal Alfonso (☎ 920 34 90 06; Avenida de la Constitución 6, Hoyos de Espina; s/d €23/43) This is a very good choice, with bathroom, TV and even a hairdryer in each room.

El Milano Real (☎ 920 34 91 08; www.elmilano real.com; Calle de Toleo s/n, Hoyos de Espina; d from €77) This is a gorgeous place to stay with stylish, spacious rooms, wonderful views and a delightfully peaceful setting. The restaurant is also excellent, rounding an excellent package that's worth every euro.

SALAMANCA

pop 157,906

Salamanca is one of Spain's greatest highlights. The uniformity of ancient sandstone architecture is without equal in Spain – in few other places will you witness such virtuosity in Plateresque (early Renaissance) and Renaissance styles – with wonderful Plaza Mayor the undoubted jewel in the city's considerable crown. But this is not a city living in the past. Underneath the sandstone façades with their ochre hints of Latin inscriptions, you'll find an eclectic and vibrant collection of bars, cafés and restaurants invariably filled with Salamanca's enormous student population (Spanish and international). This is Castilla's liveliest, most stunning city and should on no account be missed.

History

In 220 BC, Celtiberian Salamanca was besieged by Hannibal. Later, under Roman rule, it was an important staging post on the Via Lata (Ruta de la Plata, or Silver Route) from the mines in northern Spain to the south. After the Muslim invasion of Spain, it changed hands repeatedly.

Possibly the greatest turning point in the city's history was the founding of the university (initially the Estudio General) in 1218. It became the equal of Oxford and Bologna, and by the end of the 15th century was the focal point of some of the richest artistic activity in the country, in part due to the generous patronage of Queen Isabel of Castile.

The city followed the rest of Castilla into decline in the 17th century, although by the time Spanish literary hero Miguel de Una-muno became rector at the university in 1900, Salamanca had essentially recovered.

Orientation

The old centre, north of the Río Tormes and with the Plaza Mayor at its heart, is compact and easily walked. The train and bus stations are about equidistant from the centre of town, the former to the northeast and the latter to the northwest. Buses connect both to the town centre and taxis are cheap. Most accommodation and eating options, as well as the major monuments, can be found between Plaza Mayor and the river.

Information

EMERGENCY
Cruz Roja (☎ 923 22 22 22) For ambulances.
Policía Nacional (☎ 091; Ronda de Sancti-Spíritus 8)

INTERNET ACCESS
Ciberspace (Plaza Mayor 10; ☽ 10.30am-2am)
Cyber Anuario (Calle de La Latina 8; ☽ 9am-1am Mon-Fri, 10am-1am Sat & Sun) Also offers cheap international phone calls. Internet prices start from as low as €0.75, depending on the time of day.

LAUNDRY
Laundry (Calle de Pasaje Azafranal 18; per wash €3.15; ☽ 9.30am-2pm & 4-8pm Mon-Fri, 10.30am-2pm Sat) Coin operated and offers free soap powder and Internet access (per hour €2).

MEDICAL SERVICES
Hospital Clínico Universitario (☎ 923 29 11 00; Paseo de San Vicente 108)
Hospital Santísima Trinidad (☎ 923 26 93 00; Paseo Carmelitas 74-94)

MONEY
There's no shortage of banks around the centre, particularly along Rúa Mayor.

POST
Main post office (Calle Gran Vía 25)

TOURIST INFORMATION
Municipal tourist office (☎ 923 21 83 42; Plaza Mayor 14; ☽ 9am-2pm & 4.30-6.30pm) Concentrates on the city.
Tourist office (☎ 923 26 85 71; Rúa Mayor s/n; ☽ 9am-2pm & 5-7pm) This helpful office in the Casa de las Conchas covers both the city and the surrounding province.

Plaza Mayor

Built between 1729 and 1755, Salamanca's exceptional grand square is widely considered Spain's most beautiful central plaza, particularly at night when illuminated to magical effect. Designed by Alberto Churriguera, it's a remarkably harmonious and controlled baroque display. The medallions placed around the plaza bear the busts of famous figures, and bullfights were held here well into the 19th century (the last ceremonial occasion took place here in 1992). Its outdoor tables are a place to linger, watch the passing parade and marvel at the beguiling beauty of the architecture. Chances are, you'll find yourself drawn here again and again.

Just off the square, the 12th-century **Iglesia de San Martín** (Plaza del Corrillo) lies wedged among a huddle of houses. It's one of several nice examples of Romanesque religious architecture dotted about the city.

Catedrales

The tower of the late-Gothic **Catedral Nueva** (☎ 923 21 74 76; admission free; ☽ 9am-8pm) lords over the centre of Salamanca, its churrigueresque dome visible from almost every angle. It is, however, the magnificent Renaissance doorways, particularly the **Puerta del Nacimiento** on the western face, that stand out as one of several miracles worked in the city's sandstone façades. Walk around to the **Puerta de Ramos**, facing Plaza Anaya, which is decorated with similar flourish. It also contains an encore to the 'frog spotting' challenge on the university façade (see the boxed text Frog Spotting on p182): look for the little astronaut and ice-cream cone chiselled into the portal by stonemasons in charge of the recent restoration.

Inside, the most notable features include the elaborate choir stalls, main chapel and retrochoir, all courtesy of the prolific José Churriguera.

The Catedral Nueva was raised abutting its largely Romanesque predecessor, which is predictably known as the **Catedral Vieja** (adult/student €3/2.25; ☽ 10am-7.30pm). Begun as early as 1120, this church is something of a hybrid, incorporating some Gothic elements. The unusual ribbed cupola, the Torre del Gallo, reflects a Byzantine influence, while the main altarpiece in the apse of the *capilla mayor* (chapel containing the

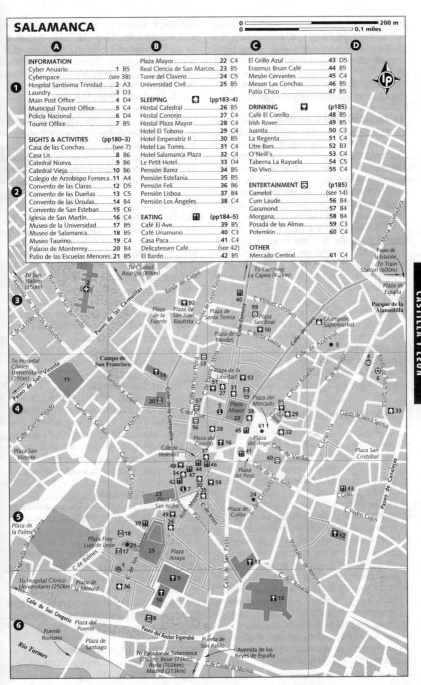

SALAMANCA

| 0 | 200 m |
| 0 | 0.1 miles |

To Ciudad Rodrigo (89km)
To Camping La Capea (4.2km)
To Bus Station (350m)
To Hospital Clínico Universitario (250m)
To Hospital Clínico Universitario (250km)
To Parador de Salamanca (750m); Bejar (73km); Ávila (102km); Madrid (213km)
Paseo de la Estación; To Train Station (600m)

CASTILLA Y LEÓN

high altar) is a sumptuous work depicting scenes from the life of Christ and Mary. It's all topped by a representation of the Final Judgement. The cloister was largely ruined in the 1755 Lisbon earthquake, but in the Capilla de San Bartolomé you can still admire one of Europe's oldest organs.

Universidad Civil & Around

The visual feast of the entrance façade to Salamanca's **university** (Calle de los Libreros; adult/student €4/2, free Mon morning; ☼ 9.30am-1.30pm & 4-7pm Mon-Fri, 9.30am-1pm & 4-6.30pm Sat, 10am-1pm Sun) is simply stunning. Founded initially as the Estudio Generál in 1218, the university came into being in 1254 and reached the peak of its renown in the 15th and 16th centuries. These were heady times for Spain, fully 'reconquered' from the Muslims in 1492 and bent on expansion in the Americas. The façade, more a tapestry in sandstone, bursts with images of mythical heroes, religious scenes and coats of arms. It's dominated in the centre by busts of Fernando and Isabel, but it's the elusive frog that draws the crowds.

Among the small lecture rooms arranged around the courtyard inside the building, the **Aula de Fray Luis de León** was named after the celebrated 16th-century theologian and writer who taught here and whose statue stands in the Patio de las Escuelas Menoras

---

FROG SPOTTING

A compulsory task facing all visitors to Salamanca is to search out the frog sculpted into the façade of the Universidad Civil. Once pointed out, it's easily enough seen, but you can spend considerable time in vain searching otherwise.

Why bother? Well, they say that those who detect it without help can be assured of good luck and even marriage (if you consider that good luck) within a year. Some hopeful students see a guaranteed examinations victory in it. If you believe all this, stop reading now. If you do want help, look at the busts of Fernando and Isabel. From there, turn your gaze to the largest column on the extreme right of the façade. Slightly above the level of the busts is sculpted a series of skulls, atop the leftmost of which sits our little amphibious friend (or what's left of his eroded self).

---

outside. It conserves the original benches and lectern from Fray Luis' day. Arrested by the Inquisition for having translated the Song of Solomon into Spanish, the sardonic theologian returned to his class after five years in jail and resumed lecturing with the words, 'As I was saying yesterday…'.

Upstairs, the university library has fine late-Gothic features and a beautiful *techumbre* (carved wooden ceiling). Some 2800 ancient manuscripts lie in the custody of what is one of the oldest university libraries in Europe. The entry fee to the university includes entry to the Museo de la Universidad (see below).

PATIO DE LAS ESCUELAS MENORES

Head out of the university and walk over to the southwestern corner of the little square, off which opens the cloister of the Escuelas Menores. Among the arches lies the **Museo de la Universidad** (admission free if visiting the university; ☼ 9.30am-1.30pm & 4-7pm Mon-Fri, 9.30am-1pm & 4-6.30pm Sat, 10am-1pm Sun), where you can see an impressive ceiling fresco of the zodiac along with a fairly standard collection of clerical robes and art. Check out the **Sala de Exposiciones**, where you can admire two *techumbres:* one clearly Mudéjar and the other with Italian Renaissance influences.

MUSEO DE SALAMANCA

This modest **gallery** (☎ 923 21 22 35; Patio de las Escuelas Menores 2; adult/concession €1.20/0.60, free Sat & Sun; ☼ 10am-2pm & 4-7pm Tue-Sat, 10am-2pm Sun), in the former residence of Queen Isabel's doctor, is as interesting for its architecture as for the paintings and sculptures within. Notable are the little patio and the *techumbre* in Sala 1.

CASA DE LAS CONCHAS

One of the city's most endearing buildings **Casa de las Conchas** (☼ 923 26 93 17; admission free; ☼ 9am-9pm Mon-Fri, 9am-2pm & 4-7pm Sat, 10am-2pm & 4-7pm Sun) is named after the scallop shells clinging to its façade. Its owner, Dr Rodrigo Maldonado de Talavera, was a doctor at the court of Isabel and a member of the Order of Santiago, whose symbol is the shell. It now houses the public library, entered via a charming bi-level courtyard, and the regional tourist office.

REAL CLERICÍA DE SAN MARCOS

Across the street from the Casa de las Conchas is the Universidad Pontificia, whose main attraction is the colossal baroque church. It's only open in the half-hour before Mass; times are posted by the entrance.

Convento de San Esteban & Around

Standing proudly in the southeastern corner of the old city, the Convento de San Esteban's **church** (☎ 923 21 50 00; admission €1.50; 9.30am-1pm & 4-8pm Wed-Sat, 9.30am-1pm Sun, 4-8pm Mon & Tue) has a façade that is in effect a huge altar in stone, with the stoning of San Esteban (St Stephen) as its central motif. Inside, the centrepiece is a *retablo* (altarpiece), this time an ornate masterpiece by José Churriguera. Through the Gothic–Renaissance **cloister** you can climb upstairs to the church's choir stalls.

CONVENTO DE LAS DUEÑAS

Easily the city's most beautiful cloister is the irregular, pentagonal cloister that graces this **convent** (☎ 923 21 54 42; admission €1.50; 10.30am-12.45pm & 4.30-6.45pm Mon-Sat, 11am-12.45pm & 4.30-6.45pm Sun). This is a convent of Dominican nuns, who still make and sell a range of traditional pastries.

TORRE DEL CLAVERO

Not far away from the Convento de las Dueñas, this defensive **tower** of a 15th-century octagonal fortress is worth seeking out, especially for its unusual square base adorned with smaller cylindrical towers.

CONVENTO DE SANTA CLARA

This **convent** (Convento de las Claras; ☎ 923 26 96 23; adult/child €2/0.50; 9.30am-2pm & 4.20-7.15pm Mon-Fri, 9am-3pm Sat & Sun) started life as a Romanesque building, but it has been rebuilt on several occasions. You can climb up some stairs to inspect at close quarters the 14th- and 15th-century *artesonado* (Mudéjar ceiling), hidden from view for almost three centuries by a lower ceiling. You can only visit this part of the convent with a guide, and you will enjoy your visit more if you understand Spanish.

Colegio del Arzobispo Fonseca & Around

A short stroll west of Plaza Mayor brings you to another series of Salamantine monuments. The **Colegio del Arzobispo Fonseca** (Colegio de los Irlandeses, Irish College; ☎ 923 29 45 70; adult/student €0.60/0.30; 10am-2pm & 4-7pm) was built in the 16th century in a sober Plater-

esque style. Of particular note are the main entrance and harmoniously proportioned courtyard. The college also has an **antique clock collection** (admission €1; 4-6pm Tue-Fri, 11am-2pm Sat & Sun).

CONVENTO DE LAS ÚRSULAS

Nearby, this late-Gothic **nunnery** (☎ 923 21 98 77; admission €2; 11am-1pm & 4.30-6.30pm, closed last Sun each month) was founded by Archbishop Alonso de Fonseca in 1512 and now contains his magnificent marble tomb, sculpted by Diego de Siloé. There's a Spanish twist: the nuns rent out part of the space to a nightclub called Camelot (p185).

PALACIO DE MONTERREY

A 16th-century holiday home of the Duques de Alba, this **palace** is a seminal piece of Spanish Renaissance architecture. The dukes pop in every now and then, and visitors are not permitted inside, but it can be admired from the outside.

Other Museums

Fans of Art Nouveau and Art Deco will probably get a kick out of **Casa Lis** (☎ 923 12 14 25; Calle de Gibraltar 14; adult/student €2.50/1.50; 11am-2pm & 5-9pm Tue-Fri, 11am-9pm Sat & Sun), a gallery devoted to both styles in this Modernista (Catalan Art Nouveau) house.

Salamanca province is bull-breeding territory and is one of the more important sources of *toros bravos* (fighting bulls) for the country. Those interested can learn a more at **Museo Taurino** (☎ 923 21 94 25; admission €3; 11.30am-1.30pm & 6-8pm Tue-Sat, 11.30am-1.30pm Sun), just north of Plaza Mayor.

Sleeping
BUDGET

Pensión Lisboa (☎ 923 21 43 33; Calle de Meléndez 1; s/d with shared bathroom €15/22, d with private bathroom €30) Run by a friendly young owner, this very good choice has comfortable rooms. Some of the singles are on the small side but some have a private terrace, while the rooftop terrace with *catedral* views is a huge bonus.

Pensión Barez (☎ 923 21 74 95; Calle de Meléndez 19; s/d with shared bathroom €12/22) The rooms here are tidy, some come with balcony, and the no-nonsense owner is quite friendly once you get to know her.

Pensión Los Ángeles (☎ 923 21 81 66; Plaza Mayor 10; s/d from €15/26) In a prime location –

smack-bang on Plaza Mayor – and with cheap prices to boot, this place is a winner. Those with balconies overlooking the plaza are for three to five people (up to €75).

Pensión Feli (☎ 923 21 60 10; Calle de los Libreros 58; s/d with shared bathroom €12/24) Pleasant, simple rooms with high ceilings are the order of the day here. At the quieter end of town, it's nonetheless central and the owner is friendly.

Pensión Estefania (☎ 923 21 73 72; Calle de Jesús 3-5; d €23.90) This place is excellent value. Most rooms have their own bathroom, and it's just off Rúa Mayor.

Camping La Capea (☎ 923 25 10 66; per person/tent/car €3.25/3.25/3.25; ⏲ 1 Apr-30 Sep) Of the four camping grounds near Salamanca, this is the closest and cheapest, about 4km out of town on the N630.

MID-RANGE
All rooms in this category have private bathroom or shower, TV, phone and air-con.

Hotel El Toboso (☎ 923 27 14 62; Calle del Clavel 7; s/d €30/45.25, 3/4/5-person self-contained apt €76/84/93) Even if the rooms are ageing at this friendly place, they're super value, especially the enormous apartments.

Hostal Plaza Mayor (☎ 923 26 20 20; Plaza del Corrillo 20; s/d/tr €36/60/90) Just off Plaza Mayor, this hostel is one of the best in this price range, with stylish and clean rooms with satellite TV. Prices drop during low season (October to March).

Hostal Concejo (⏲ 923 21 47 37; Plaza de la Libertad, 1; s/d Sun-Thu €40/50, s/d Fri & Sat €45/58) Also good value is the stylish Concejo, a stone's throw from the Plaza Mayor and located on a pretty square.

Le Petit Hotel (☎ 923 60 07 73; Ronda de Sancti-Spíritus 39; s/d €33/43) Overlooking a peaceful square in a quiet part of town, this place has individually designed rooms that are good

---

AUTHOR'S CHOICE

Hostal Catedral (☎ 923 27 06 14; Rúa Mayor 46; s/d €30/45) Just across from the *catedrals*, this well-run hostel has a few extremely pretty, clean-as-a-whistle, bright bedrooms with shower. All look out onto the street or *catedrals*, which is a real bonus, as is the friendly owner who treats her visitors with discretion, yet also as honoured guests.

---

value. It's a popular place and the motherly owner is a plus.

Hotel Emperatriz II (☎ 923 21 91 56; www.empera trizhotel.com; Rúa Mayor 18; s/d €36/51) Not the most stylish place in town, the rooms are nonetheless very comfortable; those at the front are better (but also noisier). The location is also a winner.

Hotel Salamanca Plaza (☎ 923 27 22 50; http://salamancaplaza.com; Plaza del Mercado 16; s/d from €48/72) Also in the upper mid-range bracket, this pleasant place has very comfortable rooms that come with a bounty of bathroom goodies.

TOP END
Parador de Salamanca (☎ 923 19 20 82; fax 923 19 20 87; Calle Teso de la Feria 2; s/d €95.75/119.70; ⏲) Boasting the city's best vistas and stylish, generously sized rooms with all the amenities you'd expect from a *parador*, this place also gets big bonus points for its swimming pool and tennis courts.

Hotel Las Torres (⏲ 923 212 100; tor@hthoteles.com; Calle de Concejo 4-6) It doesn't get much more central than this. This place is part of the quality High-Tech chain, and was undergoing refurbishment at the time of writing. Expect stylish and super-modern rooms with all the amenities. Doubles with balconies overlooking the Plaza Mayor are expected to cost €120.

Eating
Café Unamuno (Calle Zamora 55; ⏲ from 8am) A good place for breakfast, Café Unamuno serves pastries and good coffee from €1.50.

Café El Ave (☎ 923 26 45 11; Calle de los Libreros 24; menú €10.60) Recently (and pleasantly) renovated, this place serves decent breakfasts, *platos combinados* (€5.95) and lunch-time *menús*.

El Bardo (Calle de la Compañía 8; menú €11) A step up in quality, this high-calibre option bustles with eaters enjoying moreish tapas; its *menú* (with separate choices for carnivores and vegetarians) is pretty good, too.

Mesón Cervantes (☎ 923 21 72 13; Plaza Mayor 15; menú 12) This is another great place, though the tables overlooking the Plaza Mayor are always at a premium. Here you can eat good-quality *raciónes* for €5 to €12 in the atmospheric bar area.

Meson Las Conchas (☎ 923 21 21 67; Rúa Mayor 16; |menú €11) Specialising in *embutidos* (cured meats), this is another reasonably priced choice (*platos combinados* cost €6.60 to €8.20), with good tapas and a lively Spanish ambience.

El Grillo Azul (☎ 923 21 92 33; Calle Grillo 1; mains €6-8, menú €8.40) Vegetarians need look no further than this place, offering quality salads, organic rice and pasta. The *calabacín relleno de soufle a los tres quesos* (zucchini stuffed with three cheeses) is superb.

Casa Paca (☎ 923 21 89 93; Plaza del Peso 10; mains €11-22) Established in 1928 and still going strong, Casa Paca is rumoured to be where royalty dine when in town. Expect to pay at least €35 for a full meal – a bargain.

Along Calle de Meléndez, you'll find a number of excellent places serving tapas and sit-down meals. They include **Erasmus Bruin Café** (☎ 923 26 57 42; Calle de Meléndez 7; menú €10), which specialises in fondue (€9.65); **Patio Chico** (☎ 923 26 86 16; Calle de Meléndez 13; menú €11), a lively place with an extensive and creative menu; and the super-chic **Delicatessen Café** (☎ 923 28 03 09; Calle de Meléndez 25; platos combinados €6-9) which is a very cool place to be seen.

Drinking

Salamanca, with its myriad bars, is the perfect after-dark playground. Nightlife starts very late – even on weeknights – with many bars not filling until midnight or even later and the partying continuing until the wee hours.

If you don't mind forking out €2 for your coffee, it's hard to beat sipping your way through the morning at a café on the magnificent Plaza Mayor.

Taberna La Rayuela (Rúa Mayor 19) This pleasantly low-lit and intimate place is popular early in the evening for 'first drinks'.

Café El Corrillo (Calle de Meléndez 18) Close to Taberna La Rayuela, Café El Corrillo is great for a beer and tapas at any time, and live jazz on Friday and Saturday nights.

Tío Vivo (Calle de Clavel 3; ☽ 3.30pm-late) Here you can sip drinks by flickering candlelight. It's in the must-visit category, if only to peek at the whimsical décor of carousel horses and oddball antiquities.

Juanita (Plaza de San Boal) Hidden behind leadlight windows, Juanita gets the nod as a suave café for early evening drinks.

La Regenta (Espoz y Mina 19-20) This place recreates a pre-industrial coffeehouse ambience complete with heavy curtains and antique furniture.

Delicatessen Café (Calle de Meléndez 25) This super-cool café opened while we were in Salamanca. Expect it to last the distance, although it's more *pijo* (beautiful people) than student hang-out.

Salamanca's two lively Irish pubs, **O'Neill's** (Calle Zamora 14) and the **Irish Rover** (Calle Rúa Antigua), near the Casa de las Conchas, both pull in the thirsty crowds and both serve good, cheap food.

The collection of so-called 'litre bars' on Plaza de San Juan de Bautista are fun nighttime hang-outs, where you can guzzle a 1L *cerveza* (beer) for €2.50 or a *cubalibre* (rum and coke with lemon juice) for €5.10.

Another hive of *marcha* lies just east of the Mercado Central; Calle de San Justo, Calle de Varillas and Calle del Consuelo in particular are brimming with bars.

Entertainment

Many of Salamanca's café-bars morph into dance clubs after midnight, and there's usually no cover charge. The following venues are worth adding to your *discoteca* itinerary.

Posada de las Almas (Plaza de San Boal) Decked out in a curious design mix of looming papier-mâché figures, doll houses and velvet curtains, this place attracts a mixed crowd – gay and straight, Spanish and foreign.

Camelot (Calle de la Compañía) One of our favourites, this lively disco is actually part of the Convento de las Úrsulas. The décor is incongruously industrial.

Cum Laude (Calle del Prior 7) This is a sprawling space that apes the elegance of a *palacio* and plays mostly dance music to a young, fresh crowd.

Garamond (Calle del Prior 24) A few dance steps from Cum Laude, Garamond has rather baronial décor and a great selection of music to which you can dance or swig your *copas* (drinks).

Morgana (cnr Cuesta del Carmen & Calle de Iscar Peira) This club lively combines two floors – one with rave music, the other with Latino – to create one helluva good time, especially around 5am.

Potemkin (Calle del Consuelo) Salamanca's grungy alternative with live music on most nights, Potemkin is a dark cavern on a bar-lined street.

CASTILLA Y LEÓN

Getting There & Away

BUS

The **bus station** (☎ 923 23 67 17; Avenida de Filiberto Villalobos) is northwest of the town centre. Auto Res has 24 daily buses to Madrid (regular/express €10.20/15, 3/2½ hours); six buses also serve Valladolid (€6.55, 1½ hours) and four go to Ávila (€4.80, 1½ hours).

There's at least one bus daily, except Sunday, going to La Alberca (€2.55). Regular buses head to Ciudad Rodrigo (€5, 1½ hours), Segovia (€8.90, three hours) and Zamora (€3.70, one hour), and there are also services to Béjar (€4, one hour), Candelario (€4.75, 1¾ hours) and throughout the province.

CAR & MOTORCYCLE

The N501 leads southeast to Madrid via Ávila, while the N630 heads north to Zamora. Heading for Portugal, take the N620 west via Ciudad Rodrigo; its eastern continuation goes to Valladolid and Burgos. For the Sierra de la Peña de Francia, take the C512 and head southwest.

TRAIN

Five trains depart daily for Madrid's Chamartín station (€14.15 express, 2½ hours) via Ávila (from €5.60, 1¾ hours). There are also frequent services to Valladolid (from €5.60, 2½ hours).

Getting Around

Bus No 4 runs past the bus station and around the old town perimeter to Gran Vía. From the train station, the best bet is bus No 1, which heads into the centre along Calle de Azafranal. Going the other way, it can be picked up at the Mercado Central. You can also call a **taxi** (☎ 923 25 00 00).

AROUND SALAMANCA

Following the Río Tormes northwest, you will reach the small town of **Ledesma**, a grey, partly walled settlement. A medieval bridge still spans the river and there are a few churches of minor interest, including the Gothic Iglesia de Santa María la Mayor on Plaza Mayor. You can also see the remains of the castle of the Duques de Alburquerque. A couple of buses serve the town each day from Salamanca.

The town of **Alba de Tormes** is a mildly interesting and easily accomplished half-day excursion from Salamanca. Apart from the stout and highly visible **Torreón** – the only surviving section of the former castle of the Duques de Alba – people come to visit Santa Teresa, buried in the Convento de las Carmelitas she founded in 1570. There are plenty of buses from Salamanca.

CIUDAD RODRIGO

pop 13,750

About 80km southwest of Salamanca and less than 30km from the Portuguese border, Ciudad Rodrigo is a sleepy but attractive walled town. With its walls, views over the surrounding plains and the attractive, sloping Plaza Mayor, it makes for a pleasant final stop on the way out of Spain.

Information

The town has a **tourist office** (☎ 923 46 05 61; Plaza de las Amayuelas 6; ❤ 9am-2pm & 5-7pm Mon-Fri, 10am-2pm & 5-8pm Sat & Sun) and a **post office** (Calle de Dámaso Ledesma 12).

Sights

The **catedral** (admission €1.50, free Wed afternoon; ❤ 9am-1pm & 4-6pm Mon-Sat, 4-6pm Sun), the construction of which began in 1165, is without doubt the city's outstanding sight. Its Puerta de las Cadenas, with Gothic reliefs of Old Testament figures, is impressive and it opens onto Plaza de San Salvador. More striking, though, is the elegant Pórtico del Perdón. Inside, the *pièce de résistance* is the dizzyingly detailed carved-oak choir stalls.

Pay a visit to the **correos** (post office) to admire the *artesonado*. The first-floor gallery of the **ayuntamiento** (town hall) is a good spot to photograph the Plaza Mayor.

Ciudad Rodrigo is liberally strewn with interesting palaces, mansions and churches. Among the latter is the **Iglesia de San Isidoro**, with 12th-century Romanesque–Mudéjar elements, particularly the apse, as well as later Gothic modifications. The 16th-century **Palacio de los Castro** (Plaza del Conde) boasts one of the town's most engaging Plateresque façades.

You can climb up onto the **city walls** and follow their length of about 2.2km around the town.

Festivals & Events

Carnaval in February is a unique time to be in Ciudad Rodrigo. Apart from the outlandish fancy dress and festivities, you can witness (or join in) a colourful *encierro* (running of the bulls) and *capeas* (amateur bullfights). It's one of the earliest events in the Spanish bullfighting calendar.

Sleeping & Eating

Pensión Madrid (☎ 923 46 24 67; Calle de Madrid 20; s/d with washbasin €9/18, s/d with private bathroom €18/30) Here you'll find basic no-frills rooms in the heart of the old town.

Pensión París (☎ 923 48 23 49; Calle del Toro 10; s/d with shared bathroom 15 Jul-15 Sep €20/40, 16 Sep-14 Jul €16/28) Another no-frills option that is overpriced in summer.

Hotel Conde Rodrigo I (☎ 923 46 14 08; Plaza de San Salvador 9; s/d Apr-Oct €44/50, s/d Nov-Mar

€41/44) Comfortable and central, this is far and away the best mid-range choice.

Parador Enrique II (☎ 923 46 01 50; ciudad rodrigo@parador.es; Plaza del Castillo; s/d €83.80/104.70) In a spruced-up crenellated castle built into the town's western wall, this is an elegant *parador* offering fine views, rooms filled with character and an excellent restaurant to boot.

Arcos (Plaza Mayor; ⏰ 9am-late) A good spot for breakfast and snacks or just a coffee, this is a pleasant vantage point for watching the town's goings-on.

La Rural (Plaza Mayor; ⏰ 8am-midnight Mon-Sat) Across the square from Arcos, La Rural is always busy serving cheap tapas (from €0.50) and *raciónes* (€2.50 to €4).

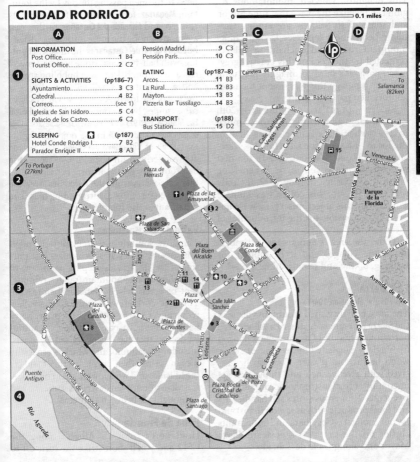

CIUDAD RODRIGO

0 — 200 m
0 — 0.1 miles

CASTILLA Y LEÓN

To Salamanca (82km)

To Portugal (27km)

Parque de la Florida

Río Agueda

Puente Antiguo

Pizzeria Bar Tussilago (Calle Julián Sánchez 7; ☜ Fri-Wed) This place does wonderful things with salads and makes great thin-crusted pizzas, all for under €6.

Mayton (Calle Colada 9; mains €5.50-11, menú €9.20) Offering a formal ambience in an old stony mansion but without the prohibitive price tag, Mayton serves *menús* and mains that are tasty and filling.

Getting There & Away

Up to 11 buses run daily to Salamanca (€4.97, 1½ hours). There are no direct buses from Ciudad Rodrigo into the Sierra de Francia; you need to go via Salamanca.

SIERRA DE FRANCIA

This delightful wooded, mountainous region can feel like the place that time forgot, and some of its villages are among Castilla y León's best-kept secrets. With quiet mountain roads and enchanting villages protected by the cool of this craggy, grey-green oasis, it's hard to imagine that until not very long ago this was one of the most godforsaken parts of Spain.

Ridden with malaria until the early 20th century, the region hadn't improved much in 1932 when Luís Buñuel came to film the locals' 'lifestyle' for *Las Hurdes – Terre Sans Pain* (Land Without Bread), the first part of which was shot here. When King Alfonso XIII visited in June 1922, the only milk available for his coffee was human! Touched by this abject misery, he was supposedly responsible for the introduction of the area's first cows.

Today the area is famous for its timber-and-stone villages and it is popular for walking, biking and trout fishing.

La Alberca

pop 1099 / elevation 1048m

The most heavily visited mountain village in the Sierra de Francia, historic La Alberca is a harmonious huddle of narrow alleys flanked by higgledy-piggledy houses built of stone, wood beams and plaster. Tourism has arrived with a vengeance, and things can get uncomfortably claustrophobic on summer weekends. Numerous stores sell handicrafts and local products such as *jamón* (ham) and *turrón* (nougat). Cosy bars and restaurants cluster on the pretty-as-a-postcard Plaza Mayor and along Calle de Tablado.

Hostal La Alberca (☎ 923 41 51 16; Plaza del Padre Arsenio s/n; s/d with bathroom €24/33) is a charming place in a historical old building with comfortable, renovated rooms. For even more comfort, **Hostal Antiguas Eras La Alberca** (☎ 923 41 51 13; laseras@teleline.es; Calle de Las Eras 29; s/d €50/60) is a very good choice.

Buses travel between La Alberca and Salamanca (€4) twice daily on weekdays and once a day on weekends.

Around La Alberca

If you have a car, the villages surrounding La Alberca are more authentically caught up in the past and are without the crowds. You can even see the village mayor riding through town on a horse and announcing the latest news to the men passing the day by the fountain. **Mogarraz**, to the east and famous for its chorizo, and **Miranda del Castañar**, further east again, are among the more intriguing villages, but **San Martín del Castañar** is the most enchanting, with half-timbered stone houses, flowers cascading from balconies, a bubbling stream and a delightfully small village bullring at the top of the town. All of these villages have *casas rurales,* but a wonderful choice is **Hostal Las Madras** (☎ 923 43 71 15; www.lasmadras.com; Calle de Barrionuevo 27; d €38.60) in the quiet, pretty little village of **Villanueva del Condé**. The rooms are wonderful, with liberal use of wood, the bathrooms are great, the owners friendly and there are views from the balconies over the village square or to the surrounding hills. The restaurant is also top quality.

Valle de las Batuecas

The drive south into Extremadura through this dreamy valley is spectacular. Just outside of La Alberca, a sweeping panorama of cascading lower mountain ranges reminiscent of green velvet opens up before you. The road corkscrews down into the valley, requiring you to negotiate some pretty hairy hairpin curves. It passes through beautiful landscape that has been praised by poets, including Unamuno, and which is especially nice in spring when purple heather blankets the hillsides and wildflowers are in bloom. A Castilian idiom even describes someone lost in thought as 'being in Batuecas'.

Peña de Francia

Head north from La Alberca along the C512 and you'll soon strike the turn-off to the highest peak in the area, the Peña de Francia (1732m), topped by a monastery and reached by a road that turns perilous after rain. From here views extend east to the Sierra de Gredos, south into Extremadura and west to Portugal.

SIERRA DE BÉJAR

The C500 continues west to **El Barco de Ávila**, which has a pretty setting on the Río Tormes and is lorded over by a proud if ruinous castle. After about 30km you'll reach the eye-catching town of **Béjar**, whose partly walled old quarters line up at the western end of a high ridge. Among worthwhile sights is the eye-catching 16th-century Palacio Ducal, just west of Plaza Mayor, now serving as a college. The best place to stay in Béjar is the **Antigua Posada** (☎ 923 41 03 33; Calle Victor Gorzo 1; d €45), close to the centre of town and in a lovely old building.

Candelario

The most scenic village in this region, tiny Candelario is about a 5km detour from Béjar. Rubbing against a steep mountain face, this charming enclave is a popular summer resort and a great base for outdoor activities. It features enchanting mountain architecture of stone and wood houses clustered closely together to protect against the harsh winter climate. A special feature is the little streams that parallel many of the cobbled lanes and the ornate *batipuertas* (wooden half-doors) in front of the regular entrance doors.

If you're counting your euros, **Hostal El Pasaje** (☎ 923 41 32 10; Calle Las Eras; s/d €25/36), not far from Plaza Mayor, offers adequate rooms. For more comfort, try **Hotel La Fuente** (☎ 923 41 31 76; fax 923 41 31 83; Avenida Humilladero s/n; s/d €46/65 Oct-Jun, €52/75 Jul-Sep) or **Hotel Cinco Castaños** (☎ 923 41 32 04; www.candelariohotel.com; Carretera de la Sierra s/n; s/d €50/57 Oct-Jun, €57/63 Jul-Sep), both of which offer high levels of comfort. The latter also has **camping ground** (per person/car/tent €3.40/3.15/3.40). There's another **camping ground** (☎ 923 41 32 04) about 400m from the town.

Meson La Romana (☎ 923 41 32 72; Calle de Núñez Losada; mains from €6; menú €10) does reasonably priced meats cooked on an open wood-fire grill.

Getting There & Away

Béjar and Candelario are served by bus from Salamanca and various other destinations, including Madrid and Plasencia. Drivers could follow the C515 to La Alberca in the Sierra de Francia.

THE CENTRAL PLATEAU

The sweeping rural plains of Castilla y León's central plateau are home to the legendary and magical town of Segovia, the energetic city of Valladolid and smaller towns such as Zamora and Palencia, which are off the tourist trail but well worth a visit. The further north you go, the more spectacular the scenery.

SEGOVIA

pop 53,631 / elevation 1002m

Segovia is a gem. To some, this ridgetop city resembles a warship ploughing through the sea of Castilla, the base of its prow formed by the confluence of the Río Eresma and Río Clamores. The town is loaded with monuments, primary among them the aqueduct, *catedral* and Alcázar. In 1985, Unesco recognised the old city section and aqueduct of Segovia as World Heritage sites. You could see Segovia on a day trip from Madrid, but this is one place which rewards those who linger.

History

The Celtic settlement of Segobriga was occupied by the Romans in 80 BC and rose to some importance in the imperial network. As Christian Spain recovered from the initial shock of the Muslim attack, Segovia became something of a frontline city until the invaders were definitively evicted by 1085. Later a favourite residence of Castile's roaming royalty, the city backed Isabel and saw her proclaimed queen in the Iglesia de San Miguel in 1474.

During the War of the Communities in 1520, the rebellious Comuneros found unequivocal support in Segovia, led by one of its main leaders, Juan Bravo. From then on it was all downhill for the town until the 1960s, when tourism helped begin the process of regeneration.

Orientation

The old town of Segovia is strung out along a ridge, rising in the east and peaking in the fanciful towers of the Alcázar to the west. If

SEGOVIA

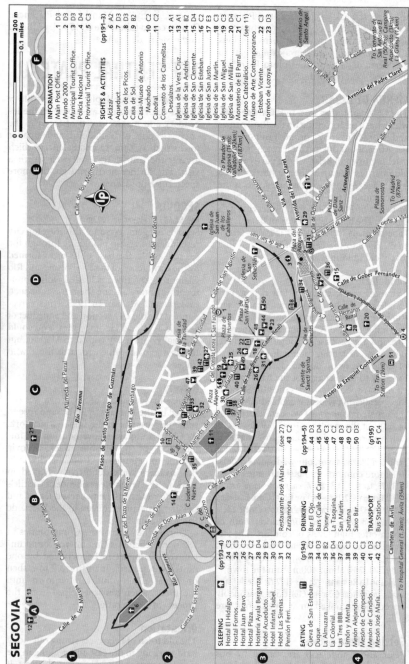

you arrive by train, bus No 2 will take you to Plaza Mayor, site of the *catedral,* tourist office and plenty of hotels, restaurants and bars. From the bus station, it's about a 10-minute walk north. The main road connecting Plaza Mayor and the aqueduct is a pedestrian thoroughfare that changes name several times along the way; locals know it simply as Calle Real.

Information

EMERGENCY
Cruz Roja (☎ 921 44 02 02 or ☎ 061) For ambulances.
Policía Nacional (☎ 091; Cnr Paseo Ezequiel González & Carretera de Ávila)

INTERNET ACCESS
Mundo 2000 (☺ 11am-11pm; per hr €2.40) Opposite the tourist office near the aqueduct.

MEDICAL SERVICES
Hospital General (☎ 921 41 91 00) 1.5km southwest of the aqueduct on the Ávila Hwy.

MONEY
Banks abound along Calle de Juan Bravo, near Plaza Mayor, and on Avenida de Fernández Ladreda near the aqueduct.

POST
Main post office (Plaza de los Huertos 5)

TOURIST INFORMATION
Municipal tourist office (☎ 921 46 29 06; Plaza del Azoguejo 1; ☺ 8am-8pm Mon-Fri, 10am-8pm Sat & Sun) By the aqueduct. This office concentrates on the city itself.
Provincial tourist office (☎ 921 46 03 34; Plaza Mayor 10; ☺ 9am-2pm & 5-7pm Mon-Fri, 10am-2pm & 5-8pm Sat & Sun) Has information about Segovia and the entire region.

Acueducto & Around
Segovia's most recognisable symbol is an extraordinary feat of engineering, made even more remarkable by the fact that it was first raised here by the Romans in the 1st century AD. The 728m granite block bridge you see today is made up of 163 arches and, remarkably, not a drop of mortar was used to hold the whole thing together. The **aqueduct** was part of a complex system of aqueducts and underground canals which once brought water from the mountains 15km away, reaching as far as where the Alcázar now stands. At its highest point in Plaza del Azoguejo, it is 28m high.

THE DEVIL'S WORK
Although no-one really doubts that the Romans built the aqueduct, a local legend asserts that two millennia ago a young girl, tired of carrying water from the well, voiced a willingness to sell her soul to the devil if an easier solution could be found. No sooner said than done. The devil reportedly worked throughout the night, while the girl recanted and prayed to God for forgiveness. Hearing her prayers, God sent the sun into the sky earlier than usual catching the devil unawares, and with only a single stone lacking to complete the structure. The girl's soul was saved, but it seems like she got what she wanted anyway – perhaps God didn't have the heart to tear down the aqueduct.

At this end of town, there are a few churches worth your time. **Iglesia de San Millán**, off Avenida de Fernández Ladreda, is a time-worn example of the Romanesque style typical of Segovia, with porticoes and a Mudéjar bell tower. A couple of other late Romanesque churches around here include the **Iglesia de San Justo** and the **Iglesia de San Clemente**.

To the Catedral
From the Plaza del Azoguejo, beside the aqueduct, Calle Real winds up into the delightful heart of Segovia. About a quarter of the way up to Plaza Mayor, you strike the **Casa de los Picos**, a Renaissance mansion with diamond-shaped façade detail that is home to a school of applied arts and usually hosts free exhibitions.

A little further on you reach **Plaza de San Martín**, one of the most captivating little squares in Segovia. The square is presided over by a statue of Juan Bravo and the 14th-century **Torreón de Lozoya**; the *pièce de résistance* is, however, the Romanesque **Iglesia de San Martín**, with the Segovian touch of Mudéjar tower and arched gallery. The interior boasts a Flemish Gothic chapel.

The shady **Plaza Mayor** is the nerve centre of old Segovia, lined by an eclectic assortment of buildings, arcades and cafés and with an open pavilion in its centre. The **Iglesia de San Miguel**, where Isabel was proclaimed Queen of Castile, recedes humbly into the background before the splendour of the *catedral* across the square.

Catedral

Started in 1525 after its Romanesque predecessor had burned to the ground in the revolt of the Comuneros, the **catedral** (☎ 921 46 22 05; admission free; ☺ 10am-2pm & 4-8pm Tue-Fri Sep-Jul, 10am-8pm Sat & Sun year-round, 10am-8pm daily Aug) is a final, powerful expression of Gothic architecture in Spain that took almost 200 years to complete. The austere three-naved interior is anchored by an imposing choir stall and enlivened by 20-odd chapels. One of these, the Capilla del Cristo del Consuelo, houses a magnificent Romanesque doorway preserved from the original church. The Capilla del Cristo Yacente houses a compelling sculpture of a reclining Christ, while the Capilla de la Piedad contains an important altarpiece by Juan de Juni. The Capilla del Santísimo Sacramento is also beautiful. Don't miss the Gothic cloister or the **Museo Catedralicio** (☎ 921 46 22 05; admission €2; ☺ 9am-5.30pm Mon-Sat, 2.30-5.30pm Sun Sep-Feb, 9.30am-6.30pm Mon-Sat, 1.30-6.30pm Sun Mar-Aug) featuring predominantly religious art.

To the Alcázar

The direct route to the Alcázar from Plaza Mayor is via Calle Marqués del Arco. About halfway along you pass yet another Romanesque church, the **Iglesia de San Andrés**. Before getting this far, you could turn right for the **Casa-Museo de Antonio Machado** (☎ 921 46 03 77; Calle de los Desamparados 5; admission €1.50, free Wed; ☺ 11am-2pm & 4.30-7.30pm Wed-Sun). Machado, one of Spain's pre-eminent 20th-century poets, lived in this house from 1919 to 1932 and it still contains his furnishings and personal effects. A few paces further down the road rises the six-level tower of the 13th-century Romanesque **Iglesia de San Esteban**, which has a baroque interior.

Turning left off Calle Marqués del Arco, via Calle Judería Nueva, will take you down to the **Casa de Sol** (Calle del Socorro 11). This former abattoir usually houses the Museo de Segovia, but at the time of research the museum was still undergoing renovation.

Alcázar

Rapunzel towers, turrets topped with slate witches' hats and a deeeeep moat at its base, are just a few of the more distinctive features of the **Alcázar** (adult/concession €3.50/2.30; ☺ 10am-7pm Mar-Aug, 10am-6pm Sep-Feb). Its fairytale design inspired Walt Disney's vision of Sleeping Beauty's castle in Disneyland – or so Segovia's wily town propagandists would have you believe. Fortified since Roman days, the site takes its name from the Arabic *al-qasr* (castle) and was rebuilt and expanded in the 13th and 14th centuries, but the whole lot burned down in 1862. What you see today is an evocative over-the-top reconstruction of the original.

Highlights include the **Sala de las Piñas**, the ceiling of which drips with a crop of 392 pineapple-shaped 'stalactites', and the **Sala de Reyes** (Kings' Room), featuring a three-dimensional frieze of 52 sculptures of kings who fought during the Reconquista. The views from the Torre de Juan II out across the surrounding hills are exceptional, and put the old town's hill-top location into full context.

Churches & Convents

Another smorgasbord of religious buildings stretches across the luxuriant valley of the Río Eresma to the north of the city, a pleasant place for a wander in the shadow of the walls.

The most interesting of Segovia's churches, and the best preserved of its kind in Europe, is the 12-sided **Iglesia de la Vera Cruz** (admission €1.50; ☺ 10.30am-1.30pm & 3.30-7pm Tue-Sun Mar-Aug; 10.30am-1.30pm & 3.30-6pm Tue-Sun Sep-Feb; closed Nov). Built in the 13th century by the Knights Templar and based on the pattern of the Church of the Holy Sepulchre in Jerusalem, it long housed what is said to be a piece of the Vera Cruz (True Cross), now in the nearby village church of Zamarramala (on view only at Easter). The curious two-storey chamber in the circular nave is where the knights stood vigil over the holy relic. For fantastic views of the town and the Sierra de Guadarrama, walk uphill behind the church for approximately 1km.

Just west of Vera Cruz is the **Convento de los Carmelitas Descalzos**, where San Juan de la Cruz is buried. A bit further east is the **Monasterio de El Parral** (☎ 921 43 12 98; admission by donation; ☺ 10am-12.30pm & 4-6.30pm Mon-Sat, 10-11.30am & 4.30-6.30pm Sun Sep-Jun; 4.30-7.30pm Wed, 10am-2pm & 4.30-7.30pm Thu-Mon Jul & Aug). Ring the bell to see part of the cloister and church, the latter a proud, Flamboyant Gothic structure. The monks chant a Gregorian Mass daily at 1pm (noon on Sunday).

About 1.3km southeast of the aqueduct, just off Avenida de Padre Claret, the **Convento de San Antonio El Real** (adult/child under 12 €2/free; 🕑 10am-2pm & 4-7pm Tue-Sun) is also worth a look. Once the summer residence of Enrique IV, it includes a Gothic–Mudéjar church with a splendid ceiling.

Museo de Arte Contemporaneo Esteban Vicente

In a perfect marriage of space and function, this contemporary **art museum** (☎ 921 46 20 10; www.museoestebanvicente.es; Plazuela de las Bellas Artes s/n; adult/concession €2.40/1.20, free Thu; 🕑 11am-2pm & 4-7pm Tue-Fri, 11am-7pm Sat, 11am-3pm Sun), just north of Plaza de San Martín, occupies a 15th-century palace of Enrique IV, complete with Renaissance chapel and Mudéjar ceiling. A donation of 148 abstract paintings and sculptures by Segovian-born artist Esteban Vicente (1903–2000), a representative of the Abstract Expressionist school, forms the core of the exhibit, which is supplemented by high-calibre temporary shows.

Festivals & Events

Segovians let their hair down for the **Fiestas de San Juan y San Pedro**, celebrated on 24 to 29 June with parades, concerts and bullfights. **Fiesta San Frutos**, on 25 October, celebrates the town's patron saint.

Sleeping

BUDGET

Pensión Ferri (☎ 921 46 09 57; Calle de Escuderos 10; s/d with shared bathroom €14/20) Occupying an old house in a superb location, this is a good budget choice. The rooms are simple but quaint and incorporate some of the building's original wood and brick work.

Hostal Juan Bravo (☎ 921 46 34 13; Calle de Juan Bravo 12; d with shared/private bathroom €31/36) Another excellent choice. Some of the sparkling clean rooms (those at the back) come with stunning views of the Sierra de Guadarrama; the friendly owners round out a great package.

Hostal Plaza (☎ 921 46 03 03; fax 921 46 03 05; Calle del Cronista Lecea 11; s/d with washbasin from €18.65/27.65, s/d with private bathroom from €27.05/30.65) The real drawcard here is the location, a few steps off Plaza Mayor. Ask to see a few rooms as size and comfort levels vary, but most are worth what is asked.

Camping Acueducto (☎ 921 42 50 00; www.camping acueducto.com; Avenida Don Juan de Borbon 49; camping per person/tent/car €4.95/4.95/4.95; Jul-Aug, €4.50/4.50/4.50 Apr-Jun & Sep; 🛇) This camping ground is about 3km southeast of town. From the train station, take bus No 2 to the aqueduct, then No 3 to Carmen/Segovia Nueva.

MID-RANGE

The following rates are for rooms with bathroom, TV and phone.

Hostal Fornos (☎ /fax 921 46 01 98; Calle Infanta Isabel 13; s/d €36.10/48.10) This is surely the best mid-range choice and is deservedly popular. Delightful, spacious rooms have that fresh white-linen-and-wicker-chair look, the owners are welcoming and the location's a winner.

Hotel las Sirenas (☎ 921 46 26 63; hotelsirenas@ terra.es; Calle de Juan Bravo 30; s/d from €45/60) This is also a very popular choice and it's not hard to see why. The rooms are spacious enough and some come with the barest hint of character.

Hotel Infanta Isabel (☎ 921 46 13 00; www .hotelinfantaisabel.com; Plaza Mayor 12; s/d from €50/78) A great place in a great location, this historic hotel has period touches (some are a bit overdone) and the rooms with balconies overlooking the plaza are wonderful.

Hostal El Hidalgo (☎ 921 46 35 29; fax 921 46 35 31; Calle de José Canalejas 3-5; s/d from €33.50/35) Also in the old centre, the rooms here are a minor disappointment given that they're in a lovely 13th-century house, but they're clean and comfortable nonetheless.

Hotel Acueducto (☎ 902 25 05 50; www.hotel acueducto.com; Calle de Padre Claret 10; s/d €52.15/79) If you don't mind being just outside the old town, this place is a very comfortable choice. The rooms are modern and spacious, but what sets it above the others are the views towards the aqueduct from some of the balconies and the rooftop terrace.

TOP END

Hostería Ayala Berganza (☎ 921 46 04 48; ayala berganza@partner-hotels.com; Calle de Carretas 5; d from €110) This charming boutique hotel has supremely elegant, individually designed rooms within a restored 15th-century palace. It's not far from the aqueduct, but it's quiet and it oozes style.

Parador de Segovia (☎ 921 44 37 37; segovia@ parador.es; Carretera de Valladolid; s/d €95.80/119.70) On a hilltop perch about five minutes' drive from the centre, this is one of the more modern *paradors* in Spain. It's certainly deluxe and you'll leave pampered, but it lacks the charm of the old restored *paradors*. The compensation comes in the great views of Segovia.

Eating

Segovians have a culinary love affair with the pig. Just about every restaurant proudly boasts its *horno de asar* (roasts) and they say that 'pork has 40 flavours – all of them good'. The main speciality is *cochinillo asado* (roast suckling pig), but *judiones de la granja* (a lima bean dish with pork chunks) also figures big on menus. The local dessert is a rich, sweet concoction drenched in *ponche*, a popular Spanish spirit, and hence known as *ponche segoviano*.

RESTAURANTS

Although it's no San Sebastián, Segovia has an ample selection of tapas bars.

Mesón José María (☎ 921 46 60 17; Calle del Cronista Lecea 11) This is arguably the best tapas bar in town. It's a widely respected Segovian favourite with a rustic bar, where you can also dine on *cochinillo* (€15) in the formal dining room.

Mesón Alejandro (☎ 921 46 00 09; Plaza Potro 5; menú €11-16) This place is so popular that it's not uncommon to see queues snaking from the front door.

Cueva de San Esteban (☎ 921 46 09 82; Calle de Valdeláguila 15; menú €11) Great atmosphere, tapas and *menú*.

Mesón de Campesino (Calle de Santa Isabel 12; menú €6) This place dishes up the cheapest *menú* in town – it's as simple as that.

Las Tres BBB (☎ 921 46 21 26; Plaza Mayor 13; ☽ 8am-11pm) With initials standing for *bueno, bonito y barato* (good, attractive and cheap), Las Tres BBB serves dishes that meet just those criteria.

Zarzamora (☎ 921 46 12 47; ☽ 5pm-midnight Tue-Sun) Around the corner from Cueva de San Esteban, this is another gem offering healthy pasta and meat dishes, fruit tarts and other home cooking. It's like eating in your own cosy kitchen.

La Almuzara (☎ 921 46 06 22; Calle Marqués del Arco 3; dishes under €8; ☽ closed Sun lunch & Mon) If you're a vegetarian, you don't need to feel like an outcast in this overwhelmingly carnivorous city. La Almuzara features lots of vegetarian dishes, pastas and salads and the ambience is warm and artsy. It even has a nonsmoking section.

Duque (☎ 921 46 24 87; Calle de Cervantes 12; mains €11-19, meals €30; ☽ noon-11.30pm) Segovia's oldest dining establishment (open since 1895) is a local institution and a great place to sample *cochinillo*. It's a class place with an old-world atmosphere and consistently great food and wine. For less formality, try its *cueva* (cave) – which can be entered at Calle de Santa Engracia 10 – in the same building.

Other long-standing Segovian institutions serving traditional roasted cuisine include: **Mesón de Cándido** (☎ 921 42 81 03; Plaza del Azoguejo 5; mains €10-16, meals €30), at the foot of the aqueduct; and **Restaurante José María** (☎ 921 46 60 17; Calle de Cronista Lecea 11; meals from €30). At these last three places, reservations are essential on weekends.

CAFÉS

La Colonial (Avenida de Fernández Ladreda 19; ☽ 8.30am-11pm) Near the aqueduct, La Colonial does a roaring trade in coffees and cakes served at its outdoor tables.

Limón y Menta (☎ 921 44 21 41; Calle Isabel de Católica 2; ☽ 8am-11pm) This is the place to head for a mouthwatering array of biscuits and pastries, including some of the best *ponche segoviano* around.

Entertainment

Locals quite appropriately call Calle de la Infanta Isabel 'Calle de los Bares' (Street of the Bars). This is the destination for serious drinking, cheap eating and merriment all around – **Disney** (Calle de la Infanta Isabel 5), **Santana** (Calle de la Infanta Isabel 18) and **Mesón de Campesino** (Calle de la Infanta Isabel 12) are three of the more popular watering holes.

Bars and discos also cluster at the plaza end of Calle de los Escuderos and along Calle de Carmen near the aqueduct, but they don't launch into action until at least 10pm (Thursday to Saturday only).

In fine weather, Plaza Mayor is the obvious place for hanging out and people-watching, but a quieter alternative is Plaza de San Martín, where Bar El Ojo and San Martín are the gathering spots of choice. Near here is **Saxo Bar** (Seminario 2), which has live music, usually jazz.

La Tasquina (☎ 921 46 19 54; Calle de Valdeláguila 3; ⏲ 9am-late) is a wine bar that can get so busy the crowds spill onto the pavement. You'll get good wines, *cavas* (sparkling wines) and cheeses here.

Getting There & Away

BUS
The bus station is just off Paseo de Ezequiel González, near Avenida de Fernández Ladreda. Buses head to Madrid up to 30 times daily (€5.60, 1½ hours). Regular buses go to Coca (€2.75, one hour), Salamanca (€8.90, three hours), Valladolid (€6.25, 2¾ hours) and Ávila (€3.75, 1 hour), although there are significantly fewer services on weekends.

CAR & MOTORCYCLE
Of the two main roads down to the NVI, which links Madrid and Galicia, the N603 is the prettier. The alternative N110 cuts southwest across to Ávila and northeast to the main Madrid–Burgos highway.

TRAIN
Madrid-bound trains leave at two-hour intervals up to nine times daily (€4.85, 1¾ hours). All other destinations from Segovia are served by bus.

Getting Around
Bus No 2 connects the train station with the aqueduct and Plaza Mayor.

AROUND SEGOVIA
La Granja de San Ildefonso
It's not hard to see why the Bourbon king Felipe V chose this site to create his version of Versailles, the palace of his French grandfather Louis XIV. In 1720 French architects and gardeners, together with some Italian help, began laying out the very elaborate **gardens** (admission €3 during Semana Santa, otherwise free; ⏲ 10am-9pm Jul-Aug, 10am-6pm Sep-Jun) in the western foothills of the Sierra de Guadarrama, 12km east of Segovia. La Granja's centrepiece is the garden's 28 extravagant **fountains**. Some are switched on at 5.30pm on Wednesday, Saturday and Sunday during Semana Santa (Holy Week).

The 300-room **Palacio Real** (☎ 921 47 00 19; www.patrimonionacional.es/granja/granja.htm; adult/concession €5/2.50; ⏲ 10am-6pm Tue-Sun Apr-Sep, 10am-1.30pm & 3-5pm Tue-Sat, 10am-2pm Sun Oct-Mar), once

a favoured summer residence for Spanish royalty and restored after a fire in 1918, is impressive but perhaps the lesser of La Granja's jewels. You can visit about half of the rooms, including its **Museo de Tapices** (Tapestry Museum).

The village that surrounds the palace has several bars, restaurants and hotels encircling Plaza de los Dolores, the central square.

Buses to La Granja depart regularly from Segovia's main bus station (€1, 20 minutes).

Pedraza de la Sierra
The captivating walled village of Pedraza de la Sierra, about 37km northeast of Segovia, is eerily quiet during the week – but its considerable number of restaurants and bars spring to life with the arrival of swarms of weekend visitors. At the far end of town stands the lonely **Castillo de Pedraza** (admission €4; ⏲ 11am-2pm & 5-8pm Wed-Sun Mar-Aug, shorter hrs Sep-Feb), unusual for its intact outer wall. At the opposite end of town, by the only town gate, is the 14th-century **prison** (admission €2.50; ⏲ 11.30am-2pm & 3.30-7pm Sat & Sun). Bus services to Pedraza are sporadic at best.

Turégano
pop 1074
Turégano, about 30km north of Segovia, is dominated by a unique 15th-century castle-church complex built by the then Archbishop of Segovia, Juan Arias Dávila, who decided to make a personal fortress of the town. The castle walls are built around the façade of the Iglesia de San Miguel.

Coca
pop 1960
A typically dusty, inward-looking Castilian village 50km northwest of Segovia, Coca is presided over by a stunning all-brick **castle** (guided tours €2.50; ⏲ tours 10.30am-1pm & 4.30-7pm Mon-Fri, 11am-1pm & 4-7pm Sat & Sun), a virtuoso piece of Gothic–Mudéjar architecture. It was built in 1453 by the powerful Fonseca family and is surrounded by a deep moat. The beautiful exterior was once matched by an equally breathtaking Renaissance interior, which was stripped of its ornamentation in the 19th century. Entry is by guided tour only. Up to five buses run daily between Coca and Segovia (€2.75, one hour).

VALLADOLID

pop 317,592

Once the de facto capital of imperial Spain and a flourishing centre of the Spanish Renaissance, Valladolid is now a modern giant with a lively and down-to-earth character. Although it does have a sprinkling of first-rate monuments, a fine Plaza Mayor and museums, Valladolid lives very much in the present, thanks to its large student population, which nightly fills its many spirited bars; if you can, make it an overnight stop. Valladolid is also considered by many to be the cradle of the purest form of spoken Castellano (Spanish), although Spaniards from Salamanca tend to disagree.

History

Little more than a hamlet in the early Middle Ages, Valladolid had become a major centre of commerce, education and art by the time Fernando of Aragón and Isabel of Castile discreetly contracted matrimony here in 1469. As Spain's greatest-ever ruling duo, they carried Valladolid to the height of its splendour. Its university was one of the most dynamic on the peninsula and Carlos I based the Consejo Real here, thereby making Valladolid the seat of imperial government. In 1420, Isabel's confessor and merciless Inquisitor General Fray Tomás de Torquemada was born here (see the boxed text Torquemada & the Inquisition, below), while in 1506, a sad and unrewarded Christopher Columbus ended his days in the city.

Felipe II was born here in 1527. Thirty-three years later he chose to make Madrid the capital, much to the displeasure of the Vallasoletanas. Today it is a major manufacturing and trade centre and also the administrative capital of the Autonomía de Castilla y León.

TORQUEMADA & THE INQUISITION

There's hardly a more notorious body in the history of the Catholic Church than the Spanish Inquisition, and its most infamous member was undoubtedly the zealot Fray Tomás de Torquemada (1420–98). Dostoevsky immortalised him as the articulate Grand Inquisitor who puts Jesus himself on trial in *Brothers Karamazov*, and Monty Python created a parody of the zealot in the Flying Circus.

Born in Valladolid of well-placed Jewish *conversos* (converts to Christianity), Torquemada was deeply affected by the Spanish cult of *sangre limpia* (pure blood), the racist doctrine that inevitably accompanied the 800-year struggle to rid Spain of non-Christian peoples.

After joining the Dominicans, Fray Tomás was appointed Queen Isabel's personal confessor in 1479. Four years later he was nominated by Pope Sixtus IV to head the Castilian Inquisition, and he took to his duties with relish, rooting out *conversos* and other heretics, including his favourite targets, the *marranos* (Jews who only pretended to convert but continued to practise Judaism in private).

If convicted, the lightest punishment dished out by Torquemada and his cronies was the confiscation of the victim's property, a convenient fund-raiser for the war of Reconquista against the Muslims. The condemned were then paraded through town wearing the *sambenito*, a yellow shirt emblazoned with crosses that was short enough to expose their genitals. They were marched to the doors of the local church, where they were then flogged.

If you were unlucky, you underwent unimaginable tortures before going through an *auto-da-fé*, a public burning at the stake. Those that recanted and kissed the cross were garrotted before the fire was set, while those that recanted only were burnt quickly with dry wood. If you stayed firm and didn't recant, the wood used for the fire was green and slow-burning.

In the 15 years Torquemada was Inquisitor General of the Castilian Inquisition, he ran some 100,000 trials and sent about 2000 people to burn at the stake. On 31 March 1492, Fernando and Isabel, on Torquemada's insistence, issued their Edict of Expulsion, as a result of which all Jews were forced to leave Spain within two months on pain of death.

The following year, Torquemada retired to the monastery of Santo Tomás in Ávila, from where he continued to administer the affairs of the Inquisition. In his final years he became obsessed with the fear that he might be poisoned, and refused to eat anything without having a unicorn's horn nearby as an antidote. He died in his sleep in 1498.

Orientation & Information

The centre of Valladolid lies east of the Río Pisuerga. At its southern edge are the train and bus stations.

You'll find the key facilities, including banks with ATMs, along Calle de Santiago, the main street.

Algún Lugar (Plaza de la Universidad; per hr €2; 🕑 11am-2pm & 5-11pm Mon-Sat)

Bocattanet (Calle María de Molina 16; per hr €2; 🕑 11am-2pm & 5-11pm Mon-Sat)

Hospital de la Cruz Roja Española (☎ 983 22 22 22)

Tourist office (☎ 983 34 40 13; Calle de Santiago 19; 🕑 9am-2pm & 5-8pm)

Main post office (Plaza de la Rinconada) Near Plaza Mayor.

Policía Nacional (☎ 983 36 61 00; Calle de Felipe II 11)

Museo Nacional de Escultura

This **museum** (☎ 983 25 03 75; www.mne.es; Calle de San Gregorio 2; adult/concession €2.40/1.20, free Sun; 🕑 10am-2pm & 4-9pm Tue-Fri, 11am-2pm & 6-9pm Sat, 10am-2pm Sun), Spain's premier showcase of polychrome wood sculpture, is housed in the former Colegio de San Gregorio (1496), a flamboyant example of the Isabelline Gothic style. The dizzying façade is especially intricate and spills over with statues, heraldic symbols and floral motifs. Exhibition rooms line a splendid two-storey galleried courtyard.

Alonso de Berruguete, Juan de Juní and Gregorio Fernández are the star attractions, especially some enormously expressive fragments from Berruguete's main commission, the high altar for Valladolid's Iglesia de San Benito. Other works to look out for are Juní's *El Entierro de Cristo* in Room XV upstairs and *El Belén Napolitano*, a room-sized crèche with hundreds of figurines in Room XXX. Back downstairs is a small wing dedicated to Fernández, whose melodramatic intensity is especially well reflected in his painfully lifelike sculpture of a dead Christ.

Plaza de San Pablo

Virtually next to the Museo Nacional de Escultura, this lovely square is dominated by the **Iglesia de San Pablo**, the main façade of which is an extravagant masterpiece of Isabelline Gothic, with every square inch finely worked, carved and twisted to produce a unique fabric in stone. Also fronting the square is the **Palacio de Pimentel**, where, on 12 July 1527, Felipe II was born. A fantastic tiled mural in the entrance hall shows

scenes from the life of the king. Even more impressive are the dazzling *artesonado* ceilings in the Salón de Plenos and the Sala de Comisiones, but to see these, you must first call ☎ 983 42 71 00.

Catedral & Around

Valladolid's 16th-century *catedral* is not one of Castilla's finest, but it does have a fine altarpiece by Juní and a processional monstrance by Juan de Arfe in the attached **Museo Diocesano y Catedralicio** (☎ 983 30 43 62; Calle de Arribas 1; admission €2.50; 🕑 10am-1.30pm & 4.30-7pm Tue-Fri, 10am-2pm Sat & Sun).

More interesting is the **Iglesia de Santa María la Antigua**, a 14th-century Gothic church with an elegant Romanesque tower. The grand baroque façade to the east of the *catedral* belongs to the main building of the **universidad** and is the work of Narciso Tomé.

Further east is the early Renaissance **Colegio de Santa Cruz** (1487). The main portal is an early Plateresque example; wander inside to see the three-tiered and colonnaded patio and, in the chapel, Fernández' super-realistic *Cristo de la Luz sculpture*.

Casas de Cervantes & Columbus

Cervantes was briefly imprisoned in Valladolid, and his **house** (☎ 983 30 88 10; Calle del Rastro 7; adult/under 18 & senior €2.40/free Mon-Sat, free Sun; 🕑 9.30am-3.30pm Tue-Sat, 10am-3pm Sun) is happily preserved behind a quiet little garden.

The **Casa-Museo de Colón** (☎ 983 29 13 53; Calle de Colón; admission free; 🕑 10am-2pm & 5-7pm Tue-Sat, 10am-2pm Sun) is a replica of the house in which Columbus, that ultimately hapless Genoese explorer, lived and ended his days in 1506. Now an interesting museum, it contains a motley collection of Aztec, Incan and Mayan art, as well as some fine replica antique maps charting his journeys.

Sleeping

Hostal Colón (☎ 983 30 40 44; Acera de Recoletos 12; s/d without shower €18/28.85, s/d with shower €30/35.60) Close to the train station, this place is great budget-value with roomy, clean quarters, lofty ceilings and a friendly owner.

Pensión Argentina (☎ 983 39 00 81; Calle de Macías Picavea 7; s/d with washbasin €17/22) There's nothing pretentious about this place (ie the rooms are very simple), on a lively bar street (ie noisy on weekends), but it's well kept and friendly enough.

CASTILLA Y LEÓN

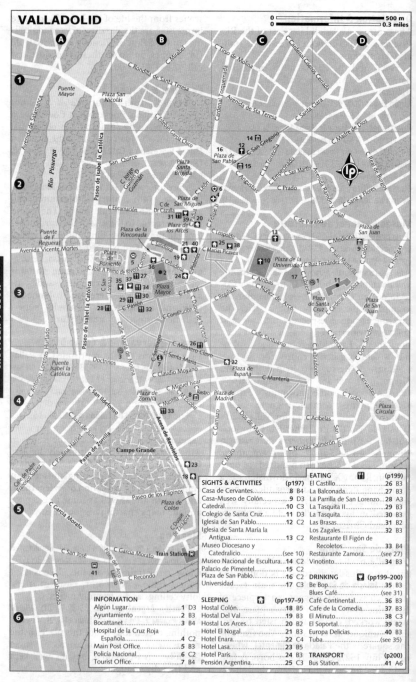

VALLADOLID

0   500 m
0   0.3 miles

Hostal Los Arces (☎ 983 35 38 53; benidiopor@terra.es; Calle de San Antonio de Padua 2; s/d with washbasin €15/27, s/d with bathroom €27/36) This place is outstanding value with pleasant, renovated rooms with TV, most of which overlook a reasonably quiet square. The owner is also friendly in an understated, Castilian kind of way.

Hostal Del Val (☎ 983 37 57 52; benidiopor@terra.es; Plaza del Val 6; s/d with washbasin €15/27, s/d with bathroom €27/36) Run by the same owner as Hostal Los Arces, this place was being renovated when we were there. When finished, it should be a good choice in a central location.

Hotel Enara (☎ 983 30 02 11; Plaza de España 5; s/d from €36/50) This hotel is in that transition stage, where charming and time-worn becomes poorly maintained and run-down. The rooms are OK, but won't be for long.

Hotel París (☎ 983 37 06 25; fax 983 35 83 01; Calle de la Especería 2; s/d €42.30/58) For a step up in quality, Hotel Paris is a fine choice, offering comfortable rooms with all the trimmings and good service.

Hotel El Nogal (☎ 983 29 77 77; hotelelnogal@hot elelnogal.com; Calle Conde Ansúrez 10; s/d €49/76) Even better again, Hotel El Nogal is terrific, a newish 24-room boutique hotel providing modern, stylish accommodation and helpful service.

Hotel Lasa (☎ 983 39 02 55; hotellasa@infonegocio .com; Acera de Recoletos 21; s/d €51.50/70.50 Mon-Thu, s/d €48/55 Fri-Sun) Handy for the train station and geared towards business travellers, Hotel Lasa's warmly decorated rooms have a few luxuries thrown in.

Eating

El Castillo (Calle de Montero Calvo; ☯ from 8am Mon-Sat) This buzzing *churrería* (Spanish-style doughnut shop) is ideal for breakfast. Kickstart your day with good coffee and *tostada* (toasted rolls) or *churros* for €1.20.

La Balconada (Calle de Correos 13) At this goodvalue place, you can nibble at big cheese platters (€11) downstairs, or dine upstairs.

Restaurante Zamora (☎ 983 33 00 71; starters from €5.50, mains €6.50-25.50, menú €25) Just down the road from La Balconada, this is a good place for a splurge, with steak dishes the highlight.

Vinotinto (☎ 983 34 22 91; Calle de Campanas 4; menú €18) In keeping with the hip, buzzy atmosphere of the area, this is a wine-bar-meets-steakhouse sort of place that sizzles nightly with local gossip and spare ribs.

Restaurante El Figón de Recoletos (☎ 983 39 60 43; Acera de Recoletos 3; mains from €12) One of the fanciest and best places in Valladolid to eat classic Castilian fare, this place is renowned for its meat dishes, although they also serve fish. You'll get little change from €35 per person.

Las Brasas (☎ 983 33 31 55; Calle de Dr Cazalla 1; starters €5-11, mains €11.50-25) Fine wines, excellent steaks and an attractive split-level dining area make this a great choice.

La Parrilla de San Lorenzo (☎ 983 33 50 88; Calle de Pedro Niño; mains €11-15; ☯ bar 10.30am-late, restaurant 2-4pm & 9pm-midnight) Both a rustic stand-up bar and a much-lauded restaurant, this place has upmarket cuisine with a relaxed ambience and a menu that looks like a medieval religious document!

Tapas bar–hopping is a favourite pastime in Valladolid – the best areas to explore are the streets just west of Plaza Mayor. Highlights include **La Tasquita** (Calle de Fernandez de la Torre 3), **La Tasquita II** (Calle Caridad) and **Los Zagales** (Calle de la Pasión 13r). The bar-packed Calle de Correos is also worth trying, as are the streets around the university.

Drinking

Central Valladolid brims with welcoming bars and cafés and you'll quickly find a personal favourite.

El Minuto (Calle de Macias Picavea 15; ☯ 9am-late) Near the *catedral,* this popular, smooth café-bar is flanked by several other prospects for late-night drinking.

Café Continental (Plaza Mayor 23; ☯ 8am-3am) This hip spot is the pick of the bars and *terrazas* (terraces) that surround the delightful Plaza Mayor. It features live music upstairs every night, and you could easily spend the best part of a night here without feeling the need to move.

Calle de Paraíso and its surrounding streets (called 'El Portu' by locals) and Plaza de San Miguel draw bar-hoppers like moths to a flame. At the latter, **El Soportal** is a good place to start your night, while the **Blues Cafe** (Calle de Dr Cazalla 1) is similarly good. Not far away, **Europa Delicias** (Calle Conde Ansúrez 18) is one of those places that comes into its own the longer the night goes on.

The Plaza Martí y Monso also has a sprinkling of bars. Cafe de la Comedia is noisy with people and a convivial atmosphere while at Be Bop and Tuba the music all but drowns out conversation. All three are open until late.

Getting There & Away

BUS
Buses travel to Madrid at least hourly between 6.30am and 9.30pm (€10.15, 2¼ hours), while others go hourly to Palencia (€2.70, 45 minutes). Also served several times daily are Tordesillas (€1.85, 30 minutes), Medina del Campo (€2.75, one hour) and Zamora (€5.25, 1½ hours), as well as other Castilian capitals and larger cities throughout Spain.

CAR & MOTORCYCLE
The N620 motorway passes Valladolid en route from Burgos to Tordesillas, where it picks up with the NVI between Madrid and A Coruña in Galicia. The N601 heads northwest to León and south to hit the NVI and A6 west of Segovia.

TRAIN
Valladolid is a major train hub and it's easy to travel to just about anywhere in Spain from here. Up to 20 trains daily go to Madrid (from €12.60, about three hours), around 11 run to León (from €8.05, about two hours) and 14 to Burgos (€7, about 1½ hours). There are also frequent services to Medina del Campo (€2.15, 35 minutes), Palencia (€3.10, 35 minutes) and Salamanca (€11.30, 1¾ hours), one train to Zamora (€6.60, 1½ hours) and three to Bilbao (from €19, about 3½ hours).

Getting Around
Local bus Nos 2 and 10 pass the train and bus stations on their way to Plaza de España, while No 19 terminates in Plaza de Zorrilla.

AROUND VALLADOLID
Medina de Rioseco
pop 4936
Medina de Rioseco, a once-wealthy, 14th-century trading centre, is today a shadow of its former medieval grandeur, but it retains a couple of very worthwhile sights and is ideal for Semana Santa. The **tourist office** (☎ 983 72 50 43; ﹖ 10am-1.30pm & 5-7.30pm Tue-Sat, 10am-1.30pm Sun) is on Plaza Mayor.

The **Iglesia de Santa María de Mediavilla** (admission free) is a grandiose Isabelline Gothic

work with three star-vaulted naves and the famous **Capilla de los Benavente**. Anchored by an eye-popping altarpiece by Juan de Juní, it's referred to as 'the Sistine Chapel of Castile'. Down the hill, the portals of the light-flooded **Iglesia de Santiago** allow for a study in architectural styles: the northern is Gothic, the main one neoclassical and the southern one Plateresque.

The **Museo de Semana Santa** (☎ 983 70 03 27; adult/child under 14 €3/free; ﹖ 11am-2pm & 4-7pm Tue-Sun Sep-May, 11am-2pm & 5-8pm Jun-Aug) has displays of *pasos* (Holy Week figures) and an extensive range of other Easter memorabilia within an old church.

Hostal Duque de Osuna (☎ 983 70 01 79; Avenida de Castilviejo 16; s/d from €18/27), not far from the bus station, is excellent value, especially as the rooms come with private bathroom. You'll be very comfortable here.

Hostal La Muralla (☎ 983 70 05 77; Plaza de Santo Domingo 4; d €18.05) offers huge, bright rooms, small bathrooms, balcony and fan.

Two places for a great feed are **Restaurante La Rúa** (☎ 983 70 07 83; Calle de San Juan 25; menú €7.80) and the slightly more upmarket **Restaurante Pasos** (☎ 983 70 10 02; Calle de Lázaro Alonso 44; menú €11.50).

At last count the town had 66 bars, so you're spoilt for choice.

Each day up to eight buses run to León (€4.95, 1¼ hours) and up to 10 go to Valladolid (€2.45, 30 minutes). The bus station is just off Avenida Juan Carlos I.

Medina del Campo
pop 20,567
A mostly morose stop 45km southwest of Valladolid, Medina del Campo does boast the dignified Mudéjar **Castillo de la Mota** (admission free; ﹖ 11am-2pm & 4-6pm Mon-Sat, 11am-2pm Sun), once a residence of the Catholic Monarchs and subsequently transformed into a state prison.

In town, make for the huge rambling Plaza Mayor de la Hispanidad (Plaza de España). Queen Isabel died in the **Palacio Real**, an unassuming edifice on the western side of the square.

There are loads of eating options around Plaza Mayor. If you're after a spot of bar-hopping, head to Calle de Ángel Molina.

More than 20 trains run daily to Madrid and there are regular services to Ávila, Salamanca and Valladolid.

Tordesillas

pop 7772

Commanding a rise on the northern flank of the Río Duero, this charming little town has a historical significance that belies its size. Originally a Roman town, it later became part of the frontline between the Christians and Muslims, after the latter had been pushed back from the north in the 9th century.

There's a **tourist office** (☎ 983 77 10 67; ☽ 10.30am-1.30pm & 5-7.30pm Tue-Sat, 10am-2pm Sun) in Casas del Tratado, near the Iglesia de San Antolín.

REAL CONVENTO DE SANTA CLARA

Much of the history of Tordesillas has been dominated by this Mudéjar-style **convent** (☎ 983 77 00 71; adult/student & senior incl tour €3.60/2; ☽ 10am-1.30pm & 4-6.30pm Tue-Sat, 10.30am-1.30pm & 3.30-5.30pm Sun Apr-Sep, shorter hrs Oct-Mar), still home to a few Franciscan nuns living in almost total isolation from the outside world. What started in 1363 as a palace for Alfonso XI later became a residence for the mistress of Pedro I. In his testament, Pedro I charged his daughter Beatriz with turning it into a convent. In 1494, the signing of the Treaty of Tordesillas took place here (see the boxed text The Treaty of Tordesillas, below).

It was home to the crazy queen Juana la Loca after her husband, Felipe I, died

---

THE TREATY OF TORDESILLAS

In 1494, only two years after Columbus' 'discovery' of America, Isabel and Fernando, the Catholic Monarchs, sat down with Portugal at the negotiating table in Tordesillas to hammer out a treaty regulating who got what in the New World. The Spanish-born Borgia pope, Alexander VI, had earlier simply pronounced that everything west of the Azores Islands belonged to Spain, something Lisbon considered slightly lopsided. The Tordesillas deal pushed the limiting line 370 leagues (a little less than 1800km) further west, giving Brazil to Portugal. Later on, Spain and Portugal began to recognise that more than one demarcation line for America, or at least the southern half of it, was required, and they thrashed it all out again in the Treaty of Zaragoza in 1529.

---

in 1506; she stayed until her own death in 1555 and in fact was buried here for 19 years before her body was transferred to Granada (as she had wished).

The guided tour takes in some remarkable rooms, including a wonderful Mudéjar patio left over from the palace, and the church, the stunning *techumbre* (roof) of which is a masterpiece of woodwork. The Mudéjar door, Gothic arches and Islamic inscriptions are also superb, as are the **Arab baths** (admission €2.25), which contain some extremely delicate paintings; entry to the baths is by appointment only.

AROUND TOWN

The **Museo de San Antolín** (Calle de Tratado de Tordesillas s/n; admission €2; ☽ 10.30am-1.30pm & 4-7pm Tue-Sun), in a deconsecrated Gothic church, houses a collection of religious art. The heart of town is formed by the pretty, porticoed **Plaza Mayor**, the mustard-yellow paintwork of which contrasts with dark brown woodwork and black grilles.

SLEEPING & EATING

Almost all of Tordesillas' hotels are on or near the highways to Madrid, Valladolid and Salamanca.

Hostal Bastida (☎ 983 77 08 42; Calle Villamarciel 16; s/d €18/35) A good place to start, Hostal Bastida is quiet, clean, and close to the bus station.

Hostal San Antolín (☎ 983 79 67 71; santantolin@telefonica.net; Calle San Antolín 8; s/d €30/60) This is the best place to stay in the old town. The modern rooms have the lot – even piped music. It has a restaurant, too, the Mesón San Antolín, which is a popular spot. It has good *raciónes* downstairs and a fine fancy restaurant upstairs. It's on a street off Plaza Mayor.

Parador (☎ 983 77 00 51; tordesillas@parador.es; Carretera de Salamanca 5; s/d €77.70/97.10) The best choice of all, this *parador* has a rural, patrician air and luxurious rooms with period furnishings.

There are a few pleasant cafés and restaurants on Plaza Mayor, including **Don Pancho** (☎ 983 77 01 74; Plaza Mayor 9).

GETTING THERE & AWAY

The **bus station** (☎ 983 77 00 72) is on Avenida de Valladolid, near Calle de Santa María. Regular buses depart for Madrid (€8.85, 2¼ hours), Salamanca (€4.70, 1¼ hours),

Valladolid (€1.85, 30 minutes) and Zamora (€3.90, one hour).

Toro
pop 8564

Toro lies north of the Río Duero, about equidistant (35km) between Tordesillas and Zamora. Having seen the whole historical parade – Celts, Romans, Visigoths and Muslims to name just a few – Toro reached the height of its glory between the 13th and 16th centuries. Fernando and Isabel cemented their primacy in Christian Spain at the Battle of Toro in 1476. Today the town is at the heart of a much-loved red wine region.

The **tourist office** (☎ 980 69 18 62; Plaza de España; ⏰ 10.30am-1.30pm & 4-7pm Tue-Sun) is in the *ayuntamiento*.

SIGHTS

Toro is studded with Romanesque churches, the most prominent of which is the **Colegiata Santa María La Mayor** (admission free; ⏰ 10am-1pm & 4-7pm). It boasts a fine Romanesque doorway on the northern façade and the even more magnificent Romanesque–Gothic **Pórtico de la Majestad**. Treasures inside include the famous 15th-century painting called Virgen de la Mosca (Virgin of the Fly). See if you can spot the fly on the virgin's robe.

From behind the *catedral* you have a superb view south across the fields to the Romanesque bridge over Río Duero. The nearby 10th-century **Alcázar** conserves its walls and seven towers.

Southwest of town, the **Monasterio Sancti Spiritus** (guided tours €2.40; tours 10.30am, 11.30am, noon, 5.30pm & 7pm Tue-Sun summer, 10.30am, 11.30am, noon, 4.30pm, 5.15pm & 6pm Tue-Sun winter) features a fine Renaissance cloister and the striking alabaster tomb of Beatriz de Portugal, wife of Juan I. It also has a small **museum**.

SLEEPING & EATING

Toro has half a dozen places to stay, accommodating all budgets.

Hostal Doña Elvira (☎ 980 69 00 62; Calle Antonio Miguelez 47; s/d with washbasin €12.65/18.05, d with private bathroom €27.65) One of the cheapest, Hostal Doña Elvira has a few floors of simple, clean rooms, all with TV.

Hotel Maria de Molina (☎ /fax 980 69 14 14; h.molina@helcom.es; Plaza de San Julián 1; s/d from €33.45/46.65) A big step up in comfort, this

place is central and spacious, and the rooms have the occasional nice touch. There's also a decent *menú* for €8.50.

Plaza Mayor and surrounds bustle with plenty of little places to eat.

GETTING THERE & AWAY

Regular buses operate to Valladolid (€2.80, one hour) and Zamora (€1.75, 25 minutes), leaving from near the junction of Avenida de Carlos Pinilla and Calle de la Corredera. There are two direct services to Salamanca (€4.20, 1½ hours) on weekdays.

ZAMORA
pop 65,498

Another strategic fortress town on the northern bank of the Río Duero, Zamora is off the tourist trail – which indeed is part of its charm. It's a subdued place, its religious character reflected in a dozen or so medieval churches to which the town owes its nickname 'Romanesque Museum.'

History

Roman Ocelum Durii was a significant way station along the Ruta de la Plata (Silver Route) from Astorga to southern Spain. The Romans were replaced by the Visigoths, who were in turn overwhelmed by the Muslims, who twice laid waste to Zamora. By the 12th and 13th centuries, when a fever of church-building formed the architectural core of what you see today, Zamora had reached its zenith as a commercial centre.

Orientation

The bus and train stations are a good half-hour walk northeast of the town centre. In the opposite direction, the *catedral* and the heart of the old town are a 15-minute walk southwest from the modern centre. Accommodation is spread out between Plaza Mayor and Calle Alfonso IX, which marks the eastern boundary of the city centre.

Information
Cyber Zamora (☎ 980 67 24 13; Calle de San Juan II 10; ⏰ 10.30am-1am; per hr €2)
Emergency (☎ 091)
Hospital Virgen de la Concha (☎ 980 54 82 00; Avenida Requejo s/n) 1km east of the old town.
Policía Nacional (☎ 980 53 04 62; Calle San Atilano 3)
Post office (Calle de Santa Clara 15)

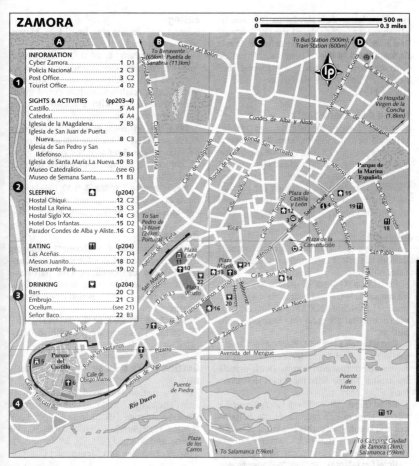

ZAMORA

INFORMATION	
Cyber Zamora	1 D1
Policía Nacional	2 C3
Post Office	3 C2
Tourist Office	4 D2

SIGHTS & ACTIVITIES	(pp203–4)
Castillo	5 A4
Catedral	6 A4
Iglesia de la Magdalena	7 B3
Iglesia de San Juan de Puerta Nueva	8 C3
Iglesia de San Pedro y San Ildefonso	9 B4
Iglesia de Santa María La Nueva	10 B3
Museo Catedralicio	(see 6)
Museo de Semana Santa	11 B3

SLEEPING	(p204)
Hostal Chiqui	12 C2
Hostal La Reina	13 C3
Hostal Siglo XX	14 C3
Hotel Dos Infantas	15 D2
Parador Condes de Alba y Aliste	16 C3

EATING	(p204)
Las Aceñas	17 D4
Meson Juanito	18 D2
Restaurante París	19 D2

DRINKING	(p204)
Bars	20 C3
Embrujo	21 C3
Ocellum	(see 21)
Señor Baco	22 B3

CASTILLA Y LEÓN

Tourist office (☎ 980 53 18 45; Calle de Santa Clara 20; ❨ 9am-2pm & 5-7pm Mon-Fri, 10am-2pm & 5-8pm Sat & Sun)

Catedral & Around

Crowning medieval Zamora's highest point, the largely Romanesque **catedral** (❨ 10am-1pm & 5-8pm Tue-Sun Mar-Sep, 10am-2pm & 4.30-6.30pm Oct-Dec, closed Jan & Feb) features a square tower, a landmark Byzantine-style dome surrounded by little turrets, and notable portals, especially the ornate southern **Puerta del Obispo**. Inside this pleasing 12th-century structure, the early Renaissance **choir stalls** are a masterpiece; carvings depict clerics, animals and even a naughty encounter between a monk and a nun.

Adjacent to the main entrance is the **Museo Catedralicio** (admission €2; ❨ 11am-1pm & 5-8pm Tue-Sun Apr-Sep, 11am-2pm & 4.30-6.30pm Tue-Sun Oct-Mar). Its star attraction is a collection of Flemish tapestries, the oldest of which, depicting the Trojan War, dates from the 15th century.

For a look at what's left of the city wall and its **castillo** (castle), head to the little park just west of the *catedral*.

Churches

Zamora's **churches** (❨ 10am-1pm & 5-8pm Mar-Oct, 10am-1pm & 4-7pm Fri-Sun Nov-Apr) are of Romanesque origin, but all have been subjected to other influences. Among those retaining some of their Romanesque charm are the **Iglesia de San Pedro y San Ildefonso** (with Gothic touches), **Iglesia de la Magdalena** (the southern doorway is considered the city's finest) and **Iglesia de San Juan de Puerta Nueva**. **Iglesia de Santa María La Nueva**, near the Museo de Semana Santa, is actually a medieval replica of a 7th-century church destroyed by fire in 1158.

Museo de Semana Santa

Zamora is famous for its elaborate celebrations of Semana Santa, and this **museum** (adult/child under 12 €2.70/1.20; 10am-2pm & 5-8pm Mon-Sat, 10am-2pm Sun) is a great place to get an overview, particularly of the carved and painted *pasos* (statues depicting the Passion of Christ) that are paraded around town during the colourful processions.

Sleeping

Zamora has a decent spread of accommodation, but prices can almost double during Semana Santa.

Hostal Siglo XX (980 53 29 08; Plaza del Seminario 3; s/d with washbasin €20/30) Located in a secluded nook, Hostal Siglo XX has five bright, simple rooms that are great for those on a tight budget.

Hostal La Reina (980 53 39 39; Calle de la Reina 1; s/d €30/33) A slightly better deal, Hostal La Reina offers spacious rooms (with private bathroom), some with balconies that overlook Plaza Mayor.

Hostal Chiqui (980 53 14 80; Calle de Benavente 2; s/d €25/37) Not quite as good as Hostal la Reina but still comfortable, this is a good place for standard rooms that lack character but are clean, well-located and come with TV.

Hotel Dos Infantas (980 50 98 98; www.hoteldos infantas.com; Calle Cortinas de San Miguel 3; s/d €50/72) This place is superb value: a real touch of class at upper mid-range prices. The large rooms come with minibar, satellite TV and a warm welcome.

Parador Condes de Alba y Aliste (980 51 44 97; Zamora@parador.es; Plaza Viriato 5; s/d €90.65/113.30) Set in a sumptuous 15th-century palace (previous 'guests' included Isabel and Fernando), this is modern luxury with myriad period touches and an impressive attention to detail. A fantastic choice.

Camping Ciudad de Zamora (980 53 72 95; camping per person/tent/car €4.70/5.10/3; Apr-Sep;) This camping ground is on the C605, about 2.5km south of town, and has a swimming pool.

Eating

Several café-restaurants line Plaza Mayor, so take your pick.

Restaurante París (980 51 43 25; Avenida de Portugal 14; menú €12.40) This is one of the town's cheapest high-quality options at which to taste local specialities (such as cured meats and cheeses), and with a friendlier price tag than most.

Las Aceñas (980 53 02 34; Calle de Aceñas de Pinilla s/n; menú €7.60; 1.30-9pm) Just over Puente de Hierro, Las Aceñas has riverside views of Zamora, a filling *menú* and a devoted local following.

Mesón Juanito (980 51 19 59; Calle Diego de Losada 10; menú €6.60) If cheap, simple meals are your thing, this is a good choice.

Drinking

Plaza Mayor and the streets emanating from it are great places for cafés and bars: try Embrujo and Ocellum. One particular street abuzz with evening *marcha* is Calle de los Herreros, which is just one bar after another.

Señor Baco (980 53 04 61; Calle Corral Pintado 5; 9am-late) This is a café-bar with sophisticated surrounds.

Getting There & Away
BUS

The bus station is a good 30-minute walk from the centre. Regular services run to/from Salamanca (€3.70, one hour), León (€6.15, 1½ hours), Valladolid (€5.30, 1½ hours) and Madrid (€16.75, 2¾ hours) via Toro, Tordesillas and Medina del Campo.

TRAIN

The train station is just beyond the bus station. Trains head to Valladolid (€6.65, 1½ hours, one daily), Madrid (€23, 3¾ hours, three daily), Ávila (€17, two hours, three daily) and Ourense (€21.50, two hours, two daily), from where trains branch off to other destinations in Galicia. There are also services to Puebla de Sanabria (from €5.35, 1¼ hours).

AROUND ZAMORA
San Pedro de la Nave

This 7th-century church, about 23km northwest of Zamora, is a rare and outstanding example of Visigothic church architecture, with blended Celtic, Germanic and Byzantine elements. Of special note are the intricately sculpted capitals, a stylistic touch not common until the 12th century. The church was moved a few kilometres to its present site in El Campillo during the construction of the Esla reservoir in 1930. To get there from Zamora, take the N122, then follow the signs to El Campillo after 12km.

North to León

The N630 heads directly north from Zamora to León. There's precious little to hold you up on the way, but just south of the village of Granja de Moreruela, 35km north of Zamora, lie the ramshackle ruins of a 12th-century **monastery** in a perfect state of bucolic abandon; it's signposted 4km down a track west of the highway. A further 30km north, in **Benavente**, a delightful **Parador** (☎ 980 63 03 00; benavente@parador.es; s/d from €77.70/97.10) has been built around the impressive Torre del Caracol, a squat 15th-century castle tower.

To Galicia

An alternative route to Galicia runs northwest from Zamora between the Sierra de la Culebra and Sierra de la Cabrera. Leave the town on the N630 north, then pick up the N631 at the Embalse de Ricobayo, which eventually merges with the N525. Heading west on this road takes you through the **Lago de Sanabria Nature Park**, a popular outdoor recreation area. The heart of the region is the little town of **Puebla de Sanabria**. Its captivating web of medieval alleyways unfolds around the 15th-century castle and trickle down the hill. You can enter the castle at will and wander around the walls.

There are sporadic services to Puebla de Sanabria from Zamora (from €5.35, 1¼ hours).

PALENCIA

pop 81,355

Palencia has a pleasant small-town character, which contrasts with its immense Gothic *catedral*, the sober exterior of which belies the extraordinary riches that await within; it's widely known as 'La Bella Desconocida' (the Unknown Beauty). You'll also find some pretty squares (in particular Plaza Mayor and Plaza de la Immaculada) and a slew of other churches and several museums to make this a worthwhile detour.

History

Known to the Romans as Pallantia and later an important Visigothic centre, Palencia was repeatedly destroyed in the early centuries AD. King Sancho el Mayor de Navarra restored the town in 1035 and Palencia reached its zenith when King Alfonso VIII founded Spain's first university here in 1208. Decline set in rapidly after the 15th century, since which time it has settled comfortably into provinciality.

Orientation

The bus and train stations are both just north of the town centre. From nearby Plaza de León, Calle Mayor forms the main north–south axis, part of it pedestrianised and with columns along one side. Hotels lie just off it, as do most banks, bars and restaurants.

Information

Hospital Géneral (☎ 979 16 70 00; Avenida Ponce de León s/n) West of the city centre.
Post office (Plaza de León)
Telephone office (Avenida Modesto Lafuente 33)
Tourist kiosk (Plaza de San Pablo)
Tourist office (☎ 979 74 00 68; Calle Mayor 105; ☎ 10am-2pm & 4-9pm Mon-Fri, 10am-2pm Sat & Sun) At the southern end of the town centre.

Sights

The **Puerta del Obispo** (Bishop's Door) is the highlight of the façade of the **catedral** (admission free; 🕒 9am-1.30pm & 4-6.30pm Mon-Sat, 9am-1.30pm Sun), which, at 130m long, 56m wide and 30m high, is one of the most massive of the Castilian *catedrals*.

The interior contains a treasure-trove of art. One of the most stunning chapels is the **Capilla El Sagrario**; the ceiling-high altarpiece tells the story of Christ in dozens of exquisitely carved and painted panels. High up on a ledge is the sarcophagus of Queen Doña Urraca. The stone screen behind the choir stalls, or *trascoro*, is a masterpiece of bas-relief attributed to Gil de Siloé and is considered by many to be the most beautiful retrochoir in Spain.

From the retrochoir, a Plateresque stairwell leads down to the crypt, a remnant of the original Visigothic church and a later Romanesque replacement. Near the stairwell is the oak pulpit, with delicate carvings of the Evangelists by Juan de Ortiz allegedly made from a single tree.

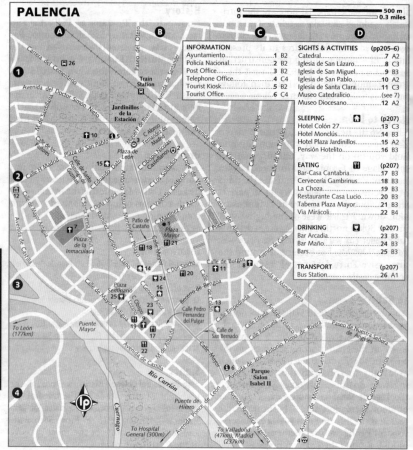

PALENCIA

In the attached **Museo Catedralicio** (guided 45min tours €3; ☒ tours hourly 10am-4pm Mon-Sat, 11am Sun) you'll see some fine Flemish tapestries and a San Sebastián by El Greco. A whimsical highlight is a trick painting by 16th-century German artist Lucas Cranach the Elder. Looking at it straight on, it seems to be a surreal dreamscape that predates Dalí by some 400 years. Only when viewed from the side is the true image revealed – a portrait of Emperor Carlos V. Guided tours are the only way to access the museum and cloister.

Of the numerous other churches around town, it's worth seeking out the **Iglesia de San Pablo** (Plaza de San Pablo), which bears a Renaissance façade and an enormous Plateresque

altarpiece in the main chapel. **Iglesia de San Miguel** (Calle de Mayor Antigua) stands out for its tall Gothic tower; according to the legend, El Cid was betrothed to his Doña Jimena here. If you've got the time, you could also swing by the pretty **Iglesia de San Lázaro** (Calle de Burgos).

Of note too is the **Museo Diocesano** (☎ 979 70 69 13; Calle de Mayor Antigua; admission €3; ☒ 10.30-11.30am Tue-Sat), within the 18th-century Palacio Episcopal, although its opening hours are such that you'll have to be quick. Its 10 rooms exhibit art from the Middle Ages through to the Renaissance; pride of place goes to works by Pedro Berruguete and an altarpiece starring the Virgin (attributed to Diego de Siloé).

Sleeping

Pensión Hotelito (☎ 979 74 69 13; hotelito@yahoo.com; Calle del General Amor 5; s/d with washbasin €16.50/27.80, d with bathroom €32.10) The best of Palencia's budget hotels, this *pensión* is tidy, friendly and quiet, despite being quite central.

Hotel Colón 27 (☎ 979 74 07 00; fax 979 74 07 20; Calle de Colón 27; s/d €29/41) This place is excellent value with bright, spacious and attractive rooms with good bathrooms and TV.

Hotel Monclús (☎ 979 74 43 00; hotelmonclus@turwl .com; Calle de Menéndez Pelayo 3; s/d €33/50) This place is a little old and dark but still reasonable value and generally well kept.

Hotel Plaza Jardinillos (☎ 979 75 00 22; info@ jardinillos.com; Calle de Eduardo Dato 2; s/d €42/51) Another good value mid-range place, this hotel offers tastefully decorated rooms.

Eating & Drinking

Restaurante Casa Lucio (☎ 979 74 81 90; mains €11-16.50; Calle de Don Sancho 2; ☽ 1.30-11.30pm) Great tapas and even better sit-down meals are the orders of the day at this elegant and popular place. The menu is creative and varied; the *foie* (pâté) dishes are particularly good.

La Choza (☎ 979 75 09 12; Calle del Obispo Lozano 6; mains €7.50-16.20) This cosy little restaurant has well-priced, sit-down meals, with a mixture of meat and fish dishes.

Via Mirácoli (☎ 979 75 20 50; Calle de Mayor Antigua 72; menú €11.90) Another small and intimate place, this Italian gem serves home-made pasta and wood-fired pizzas that are very, very good.

Taberna Plaza Mayor (Plaza Mayor 8) This is a popular place and one of a few eateries around the plaza.

Bar Maño (Calle del General Franco 5; ☽ 8am-11pm Mon-Fri, 9am-3am Sat, 10am-11pm Sun) Another good choice, with hip magenta walls.

Bar-Casa Cantabria (Calle de Pedro Fernandez del Pulgar 11) For tapas with a Cantabrian bent, try this tiny, popular place where the *caracoles* (snails) are a treat.

Cervecería Gambrinus (Patio de Castaño) Bar-Casa is also good for tapas, although its sit-down meals are overpriced.

Another convivial spot to hang out is Plaza Seminario; it's ringed by 10 bars, which are open from 7pm to late. In summer, most revellers mill in the open-air plaza. This also happens at **Bar Arcadia** (Plaza San Miguel) where the setting is nicer.

Getting There & Away

BUS

From the **bus station** (☎ 979 74 32 22), there are regular services to Valladolid (€2.70, 45 minutes), Madrid (€12.65, 3¼ hours, seven daily), Aguilar de Campóo (€4.20, 1½ hours, four daily), Frómista (€2.10, 30 minutes, two daily) and Paredes de Nava (€1.25, 25 minutes, five daily).

CAR & MOTORCYCLE

The N620 leads southwest to Valladolid and Salamanca, and northeast to Burgos. The N611 travels north to Santander via Frómista and Aguilar de Campóo, while the N610 heads west to pick up the N601 from Valladolid to León.

TRAIN

Trains are usually a good bet, with regular departures from Palencia's busy little **train station** (☎ 979 74 30 19) throughout the day to Madrid (€15.75, 3¼ hours), Burgos (€3.80, one hour), León (from €7, 1¾ hours) and Valladolid (€2.70, 45 minutes), as well as smaller nearby towns.

AROUND PALENCIA

Baños de Cerrato

A couple of kilometres west of the belching industrial rail junction of Venta de Baños lies Spain's oldest church, the 7th-century **Basílica de San Juan** (☽ 10.30am-1pm Tue-Sun) in Baños de Cerrato. Built by the Visigoths and modified many times since, it has a pleasing simplicity. Get a train from Palencia to Venta de Baños, then walk the 2km or so.

Paredes de Nava

The eminent 16th-century sculptor Alonso de Berruguete was born in Paredes in 1488. Sadly, most of Paredes' churches are in great disrepair, save for the eclectic, 13th-century **Iglesia de Santa Eulalia** (Plaza Mayor; ☽ 10am-2pm & 4-7pm) with its multicoloured steeple. Its museum contains some important artworks, including several pieces by Berruguete and his father, himself a renowned artist.

Several trains travel daily to Palencia (€1.95, 15 minutes), and a couple of buses (€1.25) also ply the route.

Frómista

The main reason for stopping in here is the exceptional Romanesque **Iglesia de San**

Martín (admission free; 10am-2pm & 4.30-8pm Mar-Nov, 10am-2pm & 3.30-6.30pm Dec-Feb), which harks back to 1066. Restored in the early 20th century, the façade of this harmoniously proportioned church is adorned with a veritable menagerie of human and zoomorphic figures, while the capitals inside are also richly decorated.

The best choice for sleeping is undoubtedly **Pensión Marisa** (979 81 00 23; Plaza Obispo Almaraz 2; s/d €15/23), which has spotless, bright rooms as well as some great home cooking. For slightly more comfort, try **Hotel San Martín** (/fax 979 81 00 00; Plaza San Martín 7; s/d €30.05/36.10).

There are two buses daily from Palencia (€2.10, 30 minutes) and another from Burgos. The Palencia–Santander train line also passes through Frómista.

MONTAÑA PALENTINA

The hills straddling the northern fringe of the province of Palencia are collectively known as the Montaña Palentina, an attractive, little-visited foretaste of the Cordillera Cantábrica, which divides Castilla from Spain's northern Atlantic regions.

Aguilar de Campóo

The squat form of Aguilar de Campóo's medieval **castle** stands watch over this quiet town which makes a pleasant base for exploring the region; there are no less than 55 Romanesque churches in the cool, hilly countryside.

The **tourist office** (Plaza de España 30; 10am-1.30pm & 5-7.30pm Tue-Sat, 10am-1.30pm Sun) is on the elongated Plaza de España, capped at its eastern end by the **Colegiata de San Miguel**, a 14th-century Gothic church with a fine Romanesque entrance and a small **museum** (guided tours noon Mon-Sat & 1pm Sun & holidays) of religious art in one of its chapels.

Downhill from the castle is the graceful Romanesque **Ermita de Santa Cecilia**. Just outside town on the highway to Cervera de Pisuerga is the restored **Monasterio de Santa María la Real** of Romanesque origin. Its 13th-century Gothic cloister with delicate capitals is a masterpiece.

The town offers plenty of accommodation and the square is swarming with cafés, bars and a couple of restaurants.

Hostal Siglo XX (979 12 29 00; sigloxxhostal@wanadoo.es; Plaza de España 9; s/d with shared bathroom

Oct-Jun €15/20, Jul-Sep €18/24) is a comfortable, friendly and central place, with a restaurant offering a side-splitting *menú* for €9. Also central and with a touch more character is **Hotel Valentín** (979 12 21 25; Avenida Generalísimo 21; s/d Oct-Jun €33/47, Jul-Sep €42/54).

Regular trains link Aguilar de Campóo with Palencia (€4.70, 1¼ hours), but the station is 4km from town. Buses bound for Burgos, Palencia and Santander depart at least once daily.

Romanesque Circuit

The area around Aguilar is studded with little villages and churches. One scenic circuit for those with their own transport takes you south along the N611 towards Palencia. At **Olleros de Pisuerga** there's a little church carved into rock, while further south, on a back road, the Benedictine **Monasterio de Santa María de Mave** has an interesting 13th-century Romanesque church. The prize in this area lies to the southwest, along the P222: the **Monasterio de San Andrés de Arroyo** (guided tours €1.50; tours hourly 10am-1pm & 4-6pm) is an outstanding Romanesque gem, especially its cloister.

The C627 highway heading to **Cervera de Pisuerga** is lined with still more little churches dating from as far back as the 12th century. Cervera de Pisuerga itself is dominated by an imposing late-Gothic church, the **Iglesia de Santa María del Castillo**.

The N621 north from Cervera is a lovely road into Cantabria and to the southern face of the Picos de Europa.

THE NORTHWEST

Once the centre of Christian Spain, León now stands like a sentinel at the rim of the great Castilian heartland. The last major city on the Camino de Santiago before it climbs west into the sierras that separate Castilla from Galicia, León certainly gets the lion's share of visitors, but the countryside is full of interesting diversions as well. To the west lies Astorga, capital of La Maragatería, where the people are still successfully clinging to century-old traditions. Closer to Galicia is the El Bierzo valley, with the town of Ponferrada as its anchor, and the almost Martian landscape of Las Médulas.

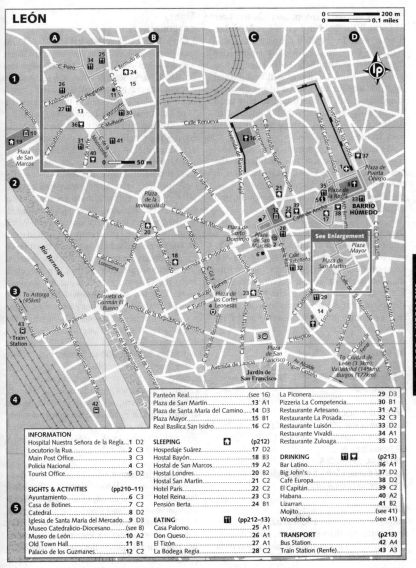

LEÓN

pop 128,565 / elevation 527m

If you arrive in León by bus or train, you may wonder what all the fuss is about. By the time you reach the spectacular *catedral*, chances are León will have begun to cast its spell. Once the flourishing capital of the expanding Christian kingdom of Asturias and León, this cosmopolitan city has some exceptional monuments and, in the Barrio Humedo south of the *catedral*, a picturesque old quarter with enchanting plazas.

History

In AD 70 a Roman legion made camp at a place where later the city of León would

CASTILLA Y LEÓN

rise. The imperial troops were based here to control the gold mines of Las Médulas, further west. In the 10th century, the Asturian king Ordoño II moved his capital here from Oviedo. Although it was later sacked by Al-Mansour, León was still maintained by Alfonso V as the capital of his growing kingdom, a role it continued to play until union with Castilla in 1230. Centuries of decline followed, but mining brought León back to life in the 1800s.

With more in common with its Asturian neighbours across the Cordillera to the north than with its Castilian sister cities to the south and east, León's workers joined their Asturian comrades in the bloody, and ultimately futile, October Revolt of 1934.

Orientation

The train and bus stations lie on the western bank of the Río Bernesga, while the heart of the city is on the eastern side. From the river to the *catedral* it's about 1km, with Plaza de Santo Domingo halfway along. Plenty of banks and hotels are on or off this axis, with many restaurants and bars near the *catedral*.

Information

EMERGENCY
Policía Nacional (☎ 091, 987 20 73 12; Calle de Villa de Benavente 6)

INTERNET ACCESS
Locutorio la Rua (☎ 987 23 01 06; Calle de la Rúa 8; ✆ 9.30am-2.30pm & 4-10.30pm Mon-Fri, 10am-2pm & 5-9.30pm Sat; per hr €2)

MEDICAL SERVICES
Hospital Nuestra Señora de la Regla (☎ 987 23 69 00; Calle del Cardenal Landázuri 2)

MONEY
Banks with ATMs and exchange services are scattered throughout the city centre, with a high concentration along Avenida de Ordoño II.

POST
Main post office (☎ 987 87 60 81; Avenida de la Independencia) Just off Plaza de San Francisco.

TOURIST INFORMATION
Tourist office (☎ 987 23 70 82; ✆ 9am-2pm & 5-7pm Mon-Fri, 10am-2pm & 5-8pm Sat & Sun) Opposite the *catedral*.

Sights

CATEDRAL
León's 13th-century **catedral** (☎ 987 87 57 70; www.catedraldeleon.org; admission free; ✆ 8.30am-1.30pm & 4-7pm Mon-Sat, 8.30am-2.30pm & 5-7pm Sun Oct-May; 8.30am-1.30pm & 4-8pm Mon-Sat, 8.30am-2.30pm & 5-8pm Sun Jun-Sep), with its soaring towers and flying buttresses, is the pinnacle of Castilian houses of worship, not to mention the city's spiritual heart. Whether spot-lit by night or bathed in the glorious northern sunshine, the *catedral*, Spain's premier masterpiece of Gothic fancy, exudes a glorious, almost luminous quality.

Approaching from the west, you'll be captivated by an extraordinary façade with a radiant rose window, three richly sculpted doorways and two muscular towers. After going through the main entrance, lorded over by the scene of the Last Supper, a breathtaking gallery of stained-glass windows awaits. French in inspiration and mostly executed from the 13th to the 16th centuries, the *vidrieras* (stained-glass windows) evoke an atmosphere unlike any other *catedral* in Spain, the kaleidoscope of coloured light offset by the otherwise gloomy interior. There seems to be more glass than brick – 128 windows with a surface of 1800 sq metres in all – but mere numbers cannot convey the ethereal quality of light permeating this *catedral*.

Other treasures include a silver urn on the altar, by Enrique de Arfe, containing the remains of San Froilán, León's patron saint. Also note the magnificent choir stalls and the rich chapels in the ambulatory behind the altar, especially the one containing the tomb of Ordoño II.

The florid **cloister**, with 15th-century frescoes, leads to the **Museo Catedralicio-Diocesano** (admission €3.50, to cloister only €1; ✆ 9.30am-1.30pm & 4-6.30pm Mon-Fri, 9.30am-1.30pm Oct-Jun; 9.30am-1.30pm & 4-7.30pm Mon-Fri, 9.30am-2pm & 4-7pm Sat Jul-Sep). Its high-quality collection encompasses works by Juní and Gaspar Becerra alongside a precious assemblage of early Romanesque carved statues of the Virgin Mary.

The museum and cloister can be visited on a tour (in Spanish), during which the guides open and close each room as they go. The full tour lasts 1¼ hours. You can enter the museum by paying just €2 for a shorter visit under your own steam (but unfortunately you'll only have access to the more boring bits).

CASTILLA Y LEÓN

REAL BASÍLICA DE SAN ISIDORO

A step back further in history, **San Isidoro** is as seminal a work of Romanesque as the *catedral* is a gem of Gothic architecture. Fernando I and Doña Sancha founded the church in 1063 to house the remains not just of the saint, but also of themselves and 21 other early Leónese and Castilian kings and queens. Napoleon's troops sacked San Isidoro in the early 19th century, leaving behind a handful of sarcophagi.

The main basilica is a hotchpotch of styles, but the two main portals on the southern façade are again pure Romanesque. Of particular note is the **Puerta del Perdón** (on the right), which has been attributed to Maestro Mateo, the genius of the *catedral* at Santiago de Compostela.

The church remains open night and day by historical royal edict.

The attached **Panteón Real** (☎ 987 87 61 61; admission €3, Thu afternoon free; 🕑 10am-1.30pm & 4-6.30pm Mon-Sat, 10am-1.30pm Sun Sep-Jun; 9am-8pm Mon-Sat, 9am-2pm Sun Jul & Aug) houses the remaining sarcophagi, which rest with quiet dignity beneath a canopy of some of the finest Romanesque frescoes in all of Spain. Motif after colourful motif drenches the vaults and arches of this extraordinary hall, held aloft by marble columns with intricately carved capitals. Biblical scenes dominate and include the Annunciation, King Herod's slaughter of the innocents, the Last Supper and a striking representation of Christ Pantocrator. The agricultural calendar on one of the arches adds a worldly dimension.

The pantheon once formed the portico of the original church, now a small **museum** where you can admire the shrine of San Isidoro, a mummified finger of the saint and treasures such as an agate chalice and polychrome wood Madonnas. A **library** houses a priceless collection of manuscripts.

HOSTAL DE SAN MARCOS

More than 100m long and blessed with a glorious façade, the **Convent of San Marcos** has more the appearance of a palace than the pilgrim's hospital it was at its founding in 1173. The Plateresque exterior, sectioned off by slender columns and decorated with delicate medallions and friezes, dates to 1513, by which time the edifice had become a monastery of the Knights of Santiago.

Much of the former convent is now a supremely elegant *parador* (p212). As you enter, take a peek into the former chapterhouse, with its splendid *artesonado*, immediately to your right. Continue on, with confidence, to gain free access to the exquisite cloister with ancient tombstones and sculpture. The cloister is technically part of the **Museo de León** (☎ 987 24 50 61; adult/student €1.25/free; Tue-Wed & Fri-Sun, free Thu; 🕑 10am-2pm & 3-7pm Tue-Sat, 10am-2pm Sun), accessible through the church at the eastern end of the structure and given over mostly to archaeology.

Walking Tour

Starting from Plaza de Santo Domingo and heading east towards Plaza de San Marcelo, you'll see the Renaissance-era palace that now houses the **ayuntamiento** (**1**; see map on p212). A few paces further east along the latter plaza stands Antoni Gaudí's contribution to León's skyline, the rather subdued and castle-like neo-Gothic **Casa de Botines** (**2**; 1893). Almost next door, the Renaissance theme continues in the form of the splendid **Palacio de los Guzmanes** (**3**; 1560), where the façade and patio stand out.

From here, the attractive narrow pedestrianised street of Calle de la Rua runs south, leading into the medieval heart of León. After about 400m, turn east in search of the captivating **Plaza de Santa María del Camino** (**4**; also known as Plaza del Grano), which feels like a cobblestone Castilian village square. Apart from its quiet air of provinciality, the outstanding feature is the Romanesque **Iglesia de Santa María del Mercado** (**5**). A short distance up the hill to the northwest, the attractive **Plaza de San Martin** (**6**) comes into its own after dark as the crowds fill the countless bars around the perimeter. Also not far away is the beautiful and time-worn 17th-century **Plaza Mayor** (**7**). Sealed off on three sides by shady porticoes, this sleepy plaza is home to a bustling fruit and vegetable market on Wednesday and Saturday. On the west side of the square is the superb late-17th-century baroque **old town hall**.

If you continue your meanderings to the north, you'll reach the peerless splendour of the **catedral** (**8**; p210). Northwest of here is the equally unmissable **Real Basílica de San Isidoro** (**9**; p211), while veering west for a further 15 minutes takes you to the **Hostal de San Marcos** (**10**; p212).

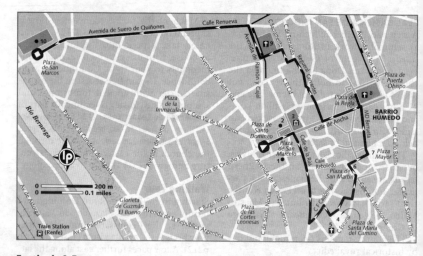

Festivals & Events

León stirs for **Semana Santa** and, more so, from 21 to 30 June for the **Fiestas de San Juan y San Pedro**.

Sleeping

Pensión Berta (☎ 987 25 70 39; Plaza Mayor 8; s/d €15/20) The main drawcards here are the unbeatable views across the plaza and the friendly owners, although the rooms themselves are rickety if clean.

Hospedaje Suárez (☎ 987 25 42 88; Calle de Ancha 7; s/d with shared bathroom €13/20) The businesslike owner does *not* take reservations and *does* close the door at midnight, but she's more friendly than her rules suggest. She also offers fabulously spacious rooms right in the heart of town.

Hostal Bayón (☎ 987 23 14 46; Calle del Alcázar de Toledo 6; s/d with washbasin €15/23) The atmosphere here couldn't be more different than at the Hospedaje Suárez. At Hostal Bayón, the laid-back and friendly young owner watches over cheerful, brightly painted rooms with pine floors.

Hotel Reina (☎ 987 20 52 12; Calle de Puerta de la Reina 2; s/d with washbasin €15/26, d with bathroom €35) On the fringe of the Barrio Húmedo (see p212, the reasonable Hotel Reina has a wide range of rooms, with TV and telephone, in a modern building.

Hostal San Martín (☎ 987 87 51 87; fax 987 87 52 49; Plaza Torres de Omaña; s/d €26/36) This engaging little place is an excellent choice, with light and airy rooms (with balcony) in a

splendid, recently overhauled 18th-century building. The owners are friendly, the location central but quiet and the rooms and private bathrooms immaculate.

Hostal Londres (☎ 987 22 22 74; Avenida de Roma 1; s/d from €25/35) Another good choice, this place has charming rooms and owners. The location in modern León lacks the charm of the Hostal San Martín, but the Barrio Húmedo is just a five-minute walk away. Rooms facing the street are bigger, but noisier too.

Hotel París (☎ 987 23 86 00; www.hotelparisleon .com; Calle de Ancha 18; s/d from €40/55) A good, central three-star place, Hotel París has pleasant, attractively furnished rooms filled with mod cons and painted in soothing amber hues.

Hostal de San Marcos (☎ 987 23 73 00; leon@parador .es; Plaza de San Marcos 7; rooms €124.65-141.05) León's sumptuous *parador* (see p211) is one of the finest hotels in Spain. With palatial rooms fit for royalty and filled with old-world charm in a former convent and pilgrim's hospital, it's a great place for a splurge.

Ciudad de León (☎ 987 68 02 33; camping per person/tent/car €3.25/3.75/3.75; Jun-mid-Sep) The nearest camping ground, about 3km south on the N601 (exit Golpejar).

Eating

Lizarran (Calle de Misericordia 11) Just down the hill from the Plaza de San Martín, Lizarran is part of a nationwide chain serving quality Basque-inspired tapas.

El Tizón (☎ 987 25 60 49; Plaza de San Martín 1; menú from €11) The tapas are good, but the sit-down restaurant, with an abundant set lunch, is even better. House specialities include *embutidos* (cured meats) and the delicious *gambas envueltas con bacon a la crema* (prawns wrapped in bacon with a cream sauce; €10.50). It also has an extensive wine list.

Pizzería La Competencia (☎ 987 84 94 77; Calle Mulhacín) This rustic place is one of the city's best pizzerias and a stalwart among students, especially for its deliciously crispy, generously topped offerings and salads.

Restaurante Luisón (☎ 987 25 40 29; Plaza Puerta Obispo 16; mains €4.85-8.45, menú €6.65) Also great value, this small, exceedingly popular place (book ahead) has great food and reasonable prices and is a good spot to sample the local *botillo berciano*, a succulent pork dish (€9.65), or *cocido leónes* (€8.40).

La Piconera (☎ 987 21 26 07; Plaza de Santa María del Camino 2; meals about €20) Down the hill and on a lovely plaza, La Piconera is worth a visit for its setting alone. It specialises in meat dishes cooked over hot coals but the salads are great too.

Restaurante Zuloaga (☎ 987 23 78 14; Sierra Pambley 3; meals about €25) This fabulous place in the vaults of an early 20th-century palace has a well-stocked cellar and classy menu. The walls feature original mosaics by the artist Ignacio Zuloaga. Try the house speciality: *hojaldre de puerros con salsa de mariscos* (leek filo pastry parcels with a seafood dressing).

Restaurante Artesano (☎ 987 21 53 22; Calle de Juan de Arfe, 2; mains €11.90-16.90, menú €15) Another imaginative choice that is worth the extra euros, this stylish, high-quality restaurant is set in the 17th-century Palacio Jabal Quinto and is a great place to sample the local *embutidos*.

Don Queso (Calle Azabachería 20) Cheese lovers will want to make a stop here. This store stocks every imaginable variety.

Other high-quality choices near the *catedral* include: **La Bodega Regia** (☎ 987 21 31 73; Calle del General Mola 9; menú €15.50), a good spot for outdoor eating in summer; **Restaurante La Posada** (☎ 987 25 82 66; Calle de la Rúa 33; menú €7), which is popular for regional specialities; **Casa Palomo** (☎ 987 25 42 25; Calle de la Escalerilla 8; mains €3.80-13, menú €10), a quality establishment serving up generous fish and meat dishes; and **Restaurante Vivaldi** (☎ 987 26 07 60; Calle Platerías 4; mains €10-18, menú €38), where the menu is stacked with creative *leonese* dishes, including tasty *garbanzos con gambas al ajillo* (a chickpea stew with garlicky prawns; €11).

Drinking

The lifeblood of León's drinking activity flows most thickly through the aptly dubbed Barrio Húmedo (Wet Quarter), a strong concentration of bars and restaurants packed into the crowded tangle of lanes south off Calle de Ancha. Its epicentre is Plaza de San Martín, where popular bars include **Bar Latino** (Plaza de San Martín 10) and **Mojito** (Calle de la Misericordia 3), but you could pretty much take your pick.

A great place day or night for a drink is the hip **El Capitán** (Calle de Ancha 8) with red velvet curtains, candlelight, mirrors and an ambience somewhere between boudoir and retro. Not far away, opposite the *catedral*, **Café Europa** (Plaza de Regla s/n) is also a fun and popular spot for some socialising.

Big John's (Avenida de los Cubos; ⏰ 7pm-2am), behind the *catedral*, is a good hang-out for jazz aficionados. For jazz, you could also try **Habana** (Calle de Juan de Arfe 15). If the '60s and '70s were your era (or you'd like it to have been), head for **Woodstock** (Calle de la Misericordia 9; ⏰ 11pm-5am Thu-Sat), where the young, friendly owners have the whole peace-and-love thing going strong.

Getting There & Away

BUS

ALSA has buses going to Madrid (€18.30, 3½ hours, 12 daily), Burgos (€11.75, 3¾ hours, four daily), Astorga (€2.80, 40 minutes, 16 daily), Ponferrada (€6.95, two hours, 12 daily), Oviedo (€7.10, 1½ hours, nine daily) and Valladolid (€7.50, two hours, eight daily).

CAR & MOTORCYCLE

The N630 heads north to Oviedo, though the A66 *autopista* (tollway) parallel to the west is faster (the two roads merge at Campomanes). The N630 also continues south to Seville via Salamanca. The N120 goes west to Galicia via Astorga, where it merges with the A6. The N601 heads southeast for Valladolid.

TRAIN

Trains travel to Astorga (€2.75, 40 minutes, four daily), Oviedo (€12.55, two hours, seven daily), Valladolid (€8.20, two hours, 10 daily), Burgos (€14.75, two hours, four daily), Madrid (from €19.20, 4¼ hours, seven daily) and Barcelona (from €38, 10 hours, three daily).

EAST OF LEÓN
Iglesia de San Miguel de Escalada
In simplicity often lies a potent beauty: this restored and somewhat out-of-place treasure is a fine demonstration of the thought. Originally built in 930 by refugee monks from Córdoba, the **church** (⊙ 10am-2pm & 4-7pm Tue-Sat, 10am-2pm Sun) displays the horseshoe arch that is typical of Muslim-inspired architecture but rarely seen so far north in Spain. The graceful exterior porch is balanced by the impressive marble columns within.

To get there by private vehicle (the only feasible option), take the N601 southeast of León. After about 14km, take the small LE213 to the east; the church is 16km after the turn-off.

Sahagún
pop 2413 / elevation 807m
An unremarkable place today, Sahagún was once home to one of Spain's more powerful abbeys, in charge of some 90 monasteries. Today the abbey is a crumbling ruin, its more important remnants kept in a small museum run by Benedictine nuns. More often than not the place is closed and there's not a nun to be seen.

Next to the former abbey is the early 12th-century **Iglesia de San Tirso** (⊙ 10.30am-1.30pm & 4-6pm Tue-Sat, 10am-3pm Sun), an important stop on the Camino de Santiago. It's of pure Romanesque design and sports a Mudéjar bell tower laced with rounded arches. The **Iglesia San Lorenzo**, just north of Plaza Mayor, has a similar bell tower but is open only for Sunday Mass.

A good place to stay is the central **Hostal Alfonso VI** (☎ 987 78 11 44; fax 987 78 12 58; Calle Antonio Nicolás 4; s/d Oct-Apr €27/33, May-Sep €33/40).

Trains run regularly throughout the day from León (€3.85, 40 minutes) and Palencia (€3.85, 35 minutes).

WEST OF LEÓN
From León, the Camino de Santiago climbs over the Montes de León and beyond into El Bierzo country, an area that is more reminiscent of Galicia than Castilla. Along the way are Astorga, with a grand *catedral*, Roman remains and a splash of Gaudí, while Ponferrada's castle and the former Roman gold mines of Las Médulas are also pleasing detours.

Astorga
pop 11,901 / elevation 816m
Astorga is a compact, pleasant town. Complete with an attractive *catedral*, a distinctive palace designed by Gaudí, an attractive Plaza Mayor and a smattering of Roman ruins, it also has a surprising sophistication that belies its size. It's all enough to make it a worthwhile day trip from León or overnight staging post for pilgrims along the Camino de Santiago.

HISTORY
The Romans first put Astúrica Augusta on the map, at the head of the Ruta del Oro. The trade in precious metals gave way to pilgrim traffic in the Middle Ages. By the 15th century, Astorga had become wealthy and important, which inspired the construction of the *catedral* and the rebuilding of its 3rd-century walls.

Astorga is the capital of a district known as the Maragatería. Many claim the Maragatos, who, with their mule trains, dedicated themselves almost exclusively to the carrying trade, were descendants of the first Berbers to enter Spain in the Muslim armies of the 8th century. Other theories argue that Celtic and Phoenician tribes were their long-time ancestors, but the mystery of their origin essentially remains unsolved.

ORIENTATION & INFORMATION
Astorga's old centre is small and easily navigated. The *catedral* and Palacio Episcopal huddle together in the northwestern corner of the old town, along with the **tourist office** (☎ 987 61 82 22; turismo@ayuntamientodeastorga.com; ⊙ 10am-2pm & 4-8pm May-Oct; 10.30am-1.30pm & 4-7pm Mon-Fri, 10.30am-1.30pm Sat & Sun Nov-Apr).

CATEDRAL
The most striking element of Astorga's **catedral** (☎ 987 61 58 20; ⊙ 9.30am-noon & 4.30-6pm Oct-Mar, 9am-noon & 5-6.30pm Apr-Sep) is its Plateresque southern façade, made from caramel-coloured sandstone and dripping in sculptural detail. Work began in 1471 on the site of its Romanesque predecessor, and proceeded in stop-start fashion over three centuries, resulting in a mix of styles. The interior is mainly Gothic, with the 16th-century altarpiece by Gaspar Becerra monopolising the visitor's gaze. The attached

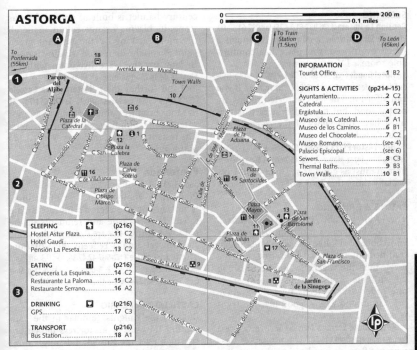

Museo de la Catedral (admission €2.50; ☟ 10am-2pm & 4-8pm Apr-Sep; 11am-2pm & 3.30-6.30pm Oct-Mar) features the usual religious art, documents and artefacts. A combined ticket for €4 is also good for the Museo de los Caminos.

PALACIO EPISCOPAL

Fairy-tale turrets, frilly façades and surprising details – the playful Palacio Episcopal integrates all the stylistic flourishes of its Catalan architect, Antoni Gaudí. Built for the local bishop from the end of the 19th century, it now houses the **Museo de los Caminos** (☎ 987 61 82 22; admission €2.50; ☟ 10am-2pm & 4-8pm Tue-Sat, 10am-2pm Sun Apr-Sep; 11am-2pm & 4-6pm Tue-Sat, 11am-2pm Sun Oct-Mar), with a moderately interesting assemblage of Roman artefacts and coins, medieval sculpture, Gothic tombs and items related to the Camino de Santiago.

MUSEO DEL CHOCOLATE

Chocolate ruled Astorga's local economy in the 18th and 19th centuries, a fact commemorated by this eclectic small private **museum** (☎ 987 61 62 20; Calle de José María Goy 5; admission €1; ☟ 10.30am-2pm & 4.30-8pm Tue-Sat, 11am-

2pm Sun) crammed with quirky old machinery, colourful advertising and fascinating lithographs. It offers a refreshing break from Castile's religious art circuit and, best of all, you get a free chocolate sample at the end.

THE RUTA ROMANA

Housed in the Roman *ergástula* (slave prison), the **Museo Romano** (☎ 987 61 69 37; Plaza de San Bartolomé 2; admission €2.50; ☟ 10am-1.30pm & 4.30-7pm Tue-Sat, 10.30am-1.30pm Sun Jul-Sep; 10.30am-1.30pm & 4-6pm Tue-Sat, 10.30am-1.30pm Sun Oct-Jun) has a modest selection of artefacts, supplemented by an enjoyable big-screen slide show on Roman Astorga. Other Roman ruins can be seen on 1½-hour Spanish-language **guided tours** (tours €1.50; ☟ noon & 5pm Easter-Oct) that leave from the tourist office. Other highlights around town include the **town walls**, **thermal baths** and **sewers**.

FESTIVALS & EVENTS

During the last week of August, Astorga awakes from its customary slumber to celebrate the **Festividad de Santa Marta** with fireworks and bullfights.

SLEEPING

Pensión La Peseta (☎ 987 61 72 75; fax 987 61 53 00; Plaza de San Bartolomé 3; s/d €42/49) Although a touch overpriced, this place has comfortable rooms, TV and phone.

Hotel Gaudí (☎ 987 61 56 54; fax 987 61 50 40; Calle de Eduardo de Castro 6; s/d to €48/60) Stay here if you can afford it. The large carpeted rooms are pretty good, but the real drawcard is that most have fine views of the *catedral* and Gaudí's *palacio*.

Hotel Astur Plaza (☎ 987 61 89 00; asturhplaza@tpi .infomail.es; Plaza Mayor 2; s/d €50/66) The rooms here are just as good as at Hotel Gaudí, especially those that look out over the plaza.

EATING & DRINKING

The local speciality is *cocido maragato*, a stew of chickpeas, various meats, potatoes and cabbage. Unlike elsewhere, Astorgan tradition dictates that you first eat the meat, then the vegetables before finishing up with the broth. Portions are huge, so one order usually feeds two; the average price is around €14. A good place to try it is Pensión La Peseta (above).

Restaurante Serrano (☎ 987 61 78 66; Calle de la Portería 2; menú from €15.50) The upmarket Restaurante Serrano combines a pleasant dining experience with reasonable prices and a creative menu.

Cervecería La Esquina (Plaza Mayor) For tapas, this is probably the best place for local *leonese* specialities and has a pleasant setting.

Restaurante La Paloma (☎ 987 61 68 63; Calle de Pío Gullón 16) The décor here is more basic but the tapas and drinks are good and cheap.

GPS (Calle La Bañeza 9) This café-pub is popular with Astorga's younger set; it has a cosy, living-room ambience and an abundance of framed artwork.

GETTING THERE & AWAY

By far the most convenient way in and out of Astorga is by bus, with regular services to León (€2.80, 40 minutes, 16 daily) and Ponferrada (€4.20, 1¼ hours, 10 daily). If you do arrive by train, the station is a couple of kilometres north of town.

Around Astorga

To give some context to the stories surrounding the Maragatos (see p214), the 6km detour west to **Castrillo de los Polvazares** is definitely worthwhile. This 17th-century hamlet is built of a vivid ferrous stone, its blazing orange colour made all the more striking by the brilliant green paint job on the doors and window frames. In late July the place livens up with the **Fiestas de la Magdalena**. If you'd like to stay, look no further than **Hostería Casa Cascolo** (☎ 987 69 19 84; www.casacoscolo.tk; d/tr €54/74). It has four brightly painted rooms in a renovated stone building with open rafters. The restaurant downstairs serves up *cocido maragato*.

Ponferrada

pop 63,233 / elevation 508m
Ponferrada, about 60km west of Astorga, is not among the region's more enticing towns, but its castle and remnants of the old town centre (the area around the stone clocktower) almost redeem the situation. The **tourist office** (☎ 987 42 42 36; ⊗ 9.30am-3pm Mon-Fri, 10.30am-1.30pm & 4-6pm Sat, 11am-1pm Sun) lies in the shadow of the castle walls.

CASTILLO TEMPLARIO

Built by the Knights Templar in the 13th century, the walls of this fortress-monastery rise high over the Río Sil and simply ooze romance and history. The **castle** (adult/student €2/1; ⊗ 11am-2pm & 5-8.30pm Tue-Sat, 11am-2pm Sun May-Sep; 11am-2pm & 4-7pm Tue-Sat, 11am-2pm Sun Oct-Apr) has a lonely and impregnable air and is a striking and unmistakable landmark in Ponferrada's otherwise bleak urban landscape. To get here, take the old bridge from the town centre over the river and head right for the castle and Plaza de la Virgen de la Encina.

CHURCHES

Among Ponferrada's churches, the Gothic–Renaissance **Basílica de la Virgen de la Encina**, up the hill past the tourist office on the square of the same name, is the most impressive, especially its 17th-century painted wood altarpiece from the school of Gregorio Fernández.

SLEEPING & EATING

Finding accommodation here should not be a problem.

Hostal Roma (☎ 987 41 19 08; Avenida Ferrocarril 16; s/d with washbasin €7.85/15.65) Near the train station. The rock-bottom prices accurately reflect very basic rooms.

Hostal Santa Cruz (☎ /fax 987 42 83 51; hsanta cruz@wanadoo.es; Calle Marcelo Macias 4; s/d €26/33) A largish place with reasonable rates, Hostal Santa Cruz is a good mid-range choice, and the rooms all come with TV and a smile.

Hotel Temple Ponferrada (☎ 987 41 00 58; fax 987 42 35 25; Avenida de Portugal 2; s/d €65/96) This is undoubtedly the most comfortable place to lay your head in town, and the rooms come with all the semi-luxurious 'bells and whistles' and attentive service you'd expect for the price.

For meals, both **Mesón Mosteiro** (☎ 987 42 68 05; Calle del Reloj 10; meals from €4.85) and **Mesón El Quijote** (☎ 987 42 88 90; Calle de Gregoria Campillo 3; menú €5), in the new town, offer cheap set meals.

GETTING THERE & AWAY

The bus station is at the northern end of town (take local bus No 3 to/from the centre). Regular buses run through Ponferrada between Villafranca del Bierzo and León (via Astorga). ALSA runs buses to Madrid (€21.90, five hours, seven daily). Heading west, there are buses to most main Galician cities, including Lugo.

The train station is west of the centre. Nine trains daily run to León (€6.20, two hours) via Astorga (€3.45, one hour), and four go east into Galicia. Madrid (from €24.65, seven hours) is served twice daily.

Las Médulas

The ancient Roman gold mines at Las Médulas, about 20km southwest of Ponferrada, once served as the main source of gold for the entire Roman Empire. The final tally allegedly came to some three million kilograms. An army of slaves honeycombed the area with canals and tunnels (some over 40km long!) through which they pumped water to break up the rock and free it from the precious metal. The result is a singularly unnatural natural phenomenon and one of the more bizarre landscapes you'll see in Spain.

Exploring the area is best done under your own steam. To get to the heart of the former quarries, drive beyond Las Médulas village (4km south of Carucedo and the N536 highway). Several trails weave among chestnut patches and bizarre sunset-coloured formations left behind by the miners.

THE EAST

BURGOS

pop 165,531 / elevation 861m

Burgos is home to one of Spain's greatest Gothic *catedrals*, surrounded by a compact and genuinely beautiful city of pretty promenades and noble buildings. There's even a touch of legend about the place – beneath the majestic spires of the *catedral* lies buried the local and almost mythical El Cid (see the boxed text El Cid: Myth & Man, below).

One point about the climate. Spaniards frequently described the climate of central Spain as having 'nine months of winter and three months of hell.' Nowhere does it apply more than in Burgos.

CASTILLA Y LEÓN

EL CID: MYTH & MAN

In Spanish history, the name of El Cid is often associated with bravery, unswerving loyalty and superhuman strength. It's a romantic, idealised image, based less on historic accounts than on a 12th-century epic poem in which the anonymous author extols the virtues and exploits of this legendary soldier. Reality, though, presents a very different picture.

El Cid (from the Arabic *sidi* for 'chief' or 'lord') was born Rodrígo Diaz in Vivar, a hamlet about 10km north of Burgos, in 1043. After the death of Ferdinand I, he became involved in the power struggle among the king's five heirs, which ended in his banishment from Castilla in 1076. He embarked on a career as a soldier of fortune, offering his services to the ruler and not caring whether they were Christian or Muslim but growing more powerful and wealthy with each exploit.

Eventually though, upon hearing that the Muslims had expelled all the Christians from Valencia, El Cid decided to recapture the city and become its ruler. This he accomplished in 1094 after a devastating siege. After this final adventure, the man also known as *El Campeador* (the Champion) decided it was time to retire. He spent the remainder of his days in Valencia where he died in 1099. His remains were returned to Burgos, where he lies buried along with his wife, Jimena, in the *catedral*.

History

Like so many Castilian towns, Burgos started life as a strategic fortress – in AD 884, most historians believe – facing off both the Muslims and the rival kingdom of Navarra. It was surrounded by several *burgos* (villages), which eventually melded together to form the basis of a new city. Centuries later, Burgos thrived as a way station on the Camino de Santiago pilgrim route and as a trading centre between the interior and the northern ports.

During the civil war, Franco made Burgos his 'capital' and the industrial development he encouraged here in the 1950s and '60s brought a degree of prosperity.

Orientation

The heart of old Burgos, dominated by the *catedral*, is wedged between the Río Arlanzón and the hill to the northwest on which stands the town's old castle. South of the river, in the newer half of town, you'll find the bus and train stations.

Information

EMERGENCY
Policía Nacional (☎ 947 22 04 66 or 091; Avenida de Castilla y León 3)

INTERNET ACCESS
Ciber-Café Cabaret (Calle de la Puebla 21; per 10min to 1hr €0.50/4; ☺ 4pm-2am) A hip place but the charges are rather steep.

MEDICAL SERVICES
Hospital General Yagüe (☎ 947 28 18 00; Avenida del Cid Campeador 96)

MONEY
There are banks all over central Burgos.

POST
Main post office (Plaza del Conde de Castro)

TELEPHONE
Telephone locutorio (Plaza de Alonso Martínez 3; ☺ 10am-2pm & 5-10.30pm) Good international rates.

TOURIST OFFICES
Municipal tourist office (☎ 947 28 88 74, festejos@ aytoburgos.es; ☺ 10am-2pm & 4.30-7.30pm Mon-Sat, 10am-2pm Sun)
Regional tourist office (☎ 947 20 31 25; Plaza Alonso Martínez 7; ☺ 9am-2pm & 5-8pm)

Old Quarter

Burgos' pleasant old quarter is growing old gracefully, stately rather than grand. It can be accessed via two main bridges across the Río Arlanzón. One is the historic **Puente de San Pablo**, beyond which looms a romanticised **statue of El Cid** with his swirling cloak and sword held aloft, looking as if he were about to set off in hot pursuit of some recalcitrant Muslims. About 300m to the west, the **Puente de Santa María** culminates in the magnificent **Arco de Santa María** (☎ 947 28 88 68; admission free; ☺ 11am-2pm & 5-9pm Tue-Sat, 11am-2pm Sun), once part of the 14th-century walls and now home to temporary exhibitions. Between the two bridges is the **Paseo de Espolón**, a lovely tree-lined pedestrian area, ideal for strolling or a picnic. Northwest of the *catedral* is another fine gate, the sturdy **Arco de San Martín**, surrounded by remnants of the original wall.

Catedral

The **catedral** (☺ 8.30am-1pm & 5-8pm) is a Gothic masterpiece that is probably worth the trip here on its own. From humble origins as a modest Romanesque church, work began on a grander scale in 1221. Remarkably, within 40 years most of the French Gothic structure that you see today had been completed. The twin towers, which went up later in the 15th century, each represent 84m of richly decorated fantasy and they're surrounded by a sea of similarly intricate spires. Probably the most impressive of the portals is the **Puerta del Sarmental**, on the southern flank, although the honour could also go to the **Puerta de la Coronería**, on the northern side, which shows Christ surrounded by the Evangelists.

It's possible to enter the *catedral* from Plaza de Santa María for free, but doing so ensures that the most worthwhile sections are off-limits. Nonetheless, you'll still have access to the **Capilla del Santísimo Cristo**, which harbours a much-revered 13th-century crucifix (known as the Cristo de Burgos) made from buffalo hide, and the **Capilla de Santa Tecla** with its extraordinary ceiling.

Inside the **main entrance** (Plaza del Rey Fernando; admission adult/child €3/1), the main altar is a typically overwhelming piece of gold-encrusted extravagance, while directly beneath the star-vaulted central dome lies the **tomb of El Cid**. Another highlight is the **Escalera Dorada** (Gilded Stairway; 1520) on the northern side, the handiwork of Diego de Siloé.

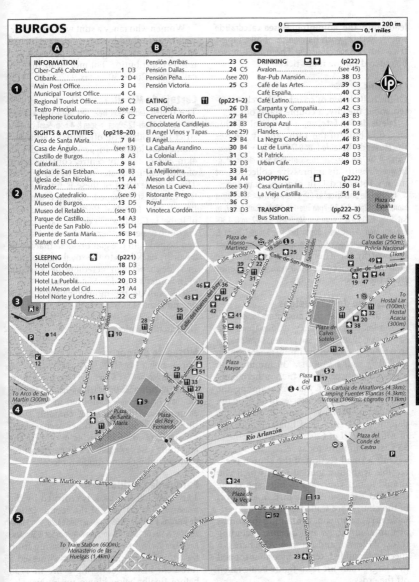

BURGOS

The **Capilla del Condestable**, on the eastern end of the ambulatory behind the main altar, is a remarkable late-15th-century production. Bridging Gothic and Plateresque styles, its highlights include the tombs of the Constable of Castilla and his wife (their statues are carved from Carrara marble), elegant pillars and three altars, all looked upon by unusual star-shaped vaulting in the dome. The sculptures facing the entrance to the *capilla* are astonishing 15th- and 16th-century masterpieces of stone carving, portraying the passion, death, resurrection and ascension of Christ.

Also worth a look is the peaceful **cloister**, with its sculpted medieval tombs, which leads into the adjoining **Museo Catedralicio** (☎ 947 20 47 12), with its wealth of oils, tapestries and ornate chalices. The museum can be entered on the main ticket.

Churches

Of the half-dozen or so other churches dotted about the city, a couple stand out.

Iglesia de San Esteban, a powerful Gothic structure built in the 14th century, houses the **Museo del Retablo** (☎ 947 27 37 52; ☒ 10.30am-2pm & 4.30-7pm Tue-Sat, 10.30am-2pm Sun, closed Mon-Fri winter), with an impressive collection of mainly 16th- and 17th-century altarpieces.

Iglesia de San Nicolás (☒ 9am-2pm & 4.30-8.30pm Mon, 10am-2pm & 4.30-7pm Tue-Fri, 10am-noon & 5-7pm Sat, 9am-1.30pm & 5-6pm Sun May-Sep; 9am-2pm & 4.30-8.30pm Mon, 11.30am-1.30pm Tue-Fri, 11am-1.30pm & 5-7pm Sat, 10am-noon & 5-6pm Sun Oct-May) is most noteworthy for its enormous carved-stone altar by Francisco de Colonia, with scenes from the life of St Nicolas.

Monasterio de las Huelgas

After the *catedral*, this **monastery** (guided tours adult/student €5/4, free Wed; ☒ 10.30am-1pm & 3.30-6pm Tue-Sat, 10.30am-1pm Sun Apr-Sep, slightly shorter hrs Oct-Mar) is second in importance among the city's sights. About a 30-minute walk west of the city centre on the southern bank of Río Arlanzón, it was once among the most prominent monasteries in all of Spain. Founded in 1187 by Eleanor of Aquitaine, daughter of Henry II of England and wife of Alfonso VIII of Castilla, it's still home to 35 Cistercian nuns today.

Only a small section of the church is accessible without a guided tour, which you should join if you want to fully appreciate this place's treasures. The three main naves of the church are walled off and are a veritable royal pantheon, containing the tombs of numerous kings and queens, including those of Eleanor and Alfonso. Also here is a spectacular gilded Renaissance altar topped by a larger-than-life Jesus figure being taken off the cross.

The highlight, though, is the **Museo de Ricas Telas**, reached via a lovely Romanesque cloister known as Las Claustrillas. It contains bejewelled robes and garments once worn by the very royals interred in the aforementioned tombs. These were opened in 1942 and the clothes removed for conservation purposes.

Women who fancy a stint with the Cistercian nuns in the Monasterio de las Huelgas can stay for up to eight days, paying a voluntary contribution. For more information, call ☎ 947 20 16 30 or fax 947 27 36 86.

Cartuja de Miraflores

The **church** (admission free; ☒ 10am-3pm & 4-6pm Mon-Sat, 11.30am-12.30pm, 1-3pm & 4-6pm Sun) of this strict (and otherwise off-limits) Carthusian monastery, located in peaceful woodlands 4km east of the city centre, contains a trio of 15th-century masterworks by Gil de Siloé. The most dazzling of these is undoubtedly the ornate star-shaped alabaster tomb of Juan II and Isabel of Portugal, the parents of Isabel la Católica. Gil de Siloé also carved the tomb of her brother, the Infante Alfonso, and helped with the giant *retablo* that forms a worthy backdrop to the royal mausoleum. In a side chapel is an incredibly lifelike statue of the order's founder, San Bruno.

The walk to the monastery takes about one hour and leads along the Río Arlanzón through the lush Parque de la Quinta, and is particularly pleasant.

Museo de Burgos

This **museum** (☎ 947 26 58 75; adult/student €1.20/free, admission free Sat & Sun; ☒ 10am-2pm & 4-7pm Tue-Sat, 10am-2pm Sun Oct-Jun, 10am-2pm & 5-8pm Tue-Sat, 10am-2pm Sun Jul-Sep), housed in the 16th-century Casa de Miranda, contains some fine Gothic tombs and other archaeological artefacts covering a wide period. In the adjoining **Casa de Ángulo** is a fine-arts collection, including some modern pieces.

Parque de Castillo

This leafy hill-top park is crowned by the massive fortifications of the rebuilt **Castillo de Burgos** (☎ 947 28 88 74; admission €1.20; ☒ 11am-2pm Sat & Sun Oct-Mar; 11am-2pm & 4-7pm Sat & Sun Apr-Jun; 11am-2pm & 5-8pm daily Jul-Sep). Dating from the 9th century, the castle has witnessed a turbulent history, suffering a fire in 1736 before finally being blown up by Napoleon's retreating troops in 1813. Just south of the car park is a **mirador** (lookout) which offers fine views over the town.

Festivals & Events

Burgos' big fiestas take place in the last days of June and the first two weeks of July to celebrate the **Festividad de San Pedro y San Pablo**

(Feast of Saints Peter and Paul). There are bullfights, processions and much merry-making, particularly on the first Sunday of July, the **Día de las Peñas**. A slightly more low-key event is the **Festividad de San Lesmes** (for the city's patron saint) on 30 January.

Sleeping
BUDGET
Pensión Peña (☎ 947 20 63 23; Calle de la Puebla 18; s/d with shared bathroom from €14/22) This impeccable little place has rooms with delightful individual touches, such as hand-painted washbasins.

Pensión Victoria (☎ /fax 947 20 15 42; Calle de San Juan 3; s/d with shared bathroom €17/30) Centrally located and in a crumbling building, this *pensión's* rooms (with washbasin) are basic but spacious and clean, and the management is very friendly. The rooms at the front can be noisy.

Across the river, try either **Pensión Arribas** (☎ 947 26 62 92; Calle de los Defensores de Oviedo 6; s/d with shared bathroom €13/22) or **Pensión Dallas** (☎ 947 20 54 57; Plaza de la Vega 6; s/d €13/25), which has the advantage of being by the river.

Camping Fuentes Blancas (☎ /fax 947 48 60 16; camping per person/tent/car €3.50/3/3.50; ☼ Apr-Sep) The nearest camping ground is about 4km east of the centre on the road to the Cartuja de Miraflores. It's served by hourly bus Nos 26 and 27 from Plaza de España.

MID-RANGE
Hostal Acacia (☎ /fax 947 20 51 34; Calle de Bernabe Perez Ortiz 1; s/d from €25/35) Though some of the rooms here are ageing, most are pleasant and all come with TV, shower and toilet. Run by a quirky but helpful Trotsky-lookalike proprietor, this place is easy to recommend.

Hostal Lar (☎ 947 20 96 55; fax 947 27 82 67; Calle de Cardenal Benlloch 1; s/d €31/50) Not far away, this is another good bet. The rooms are slightly better maintained and quite spacious.

Hotel La Puebla (☎ 947 20 00 11; info@hotellapuebla .com; Calle de la Puebla 20; s/d from €53/69; ☼ ▣) Another great choice, this boutique hotel oozes style, fusing chic minimalism with professional service. The rooms aren't huge, but they are supremely comfortable. Great value.

Hotel Cordón (☎ 947 26 50 00; hotelcordon@cyl .com; Calle de la Puebla 6; s/d €56/75) Now somewhat overshadowed by Hotel La Puebla a few

doors up, Hotel Cordón is still a decent choice with excellent service and attractive (if characterless) rooms filled with all the mod cons.

Hotel Jacobeo (☎ 947 26 01 02; hoteljacobeo@ todoburgos.com; Calle de San Juan 24; s/d €40/50) Stylish and well run, this place is very good value with comfortable rooms and helpful staff.

Hotel Meson del Cid (☎ 947 20 87 15; mesondel cid@mesondelcid.es; Plaza de Santa María 8; s/d/ste €96/ 120/141) In terms of quality (the rooms ooze old-world charm) and location (some rooms face the *catedral*), this is a good, up-market choice. However, for this price you don't expect indifferent service.

Eating
TAPAS
Cervecería Morito (Calle de la Sombrerería; ☼ 1pm-midnight) A classic Spanish tapas bar (noisy, attractive interior and great food), it's always crowded, even on the quietest of Burgos nights. It's deservedly popular for its cheap drinks and budget-friendly *platos combinados*.

La Cabaña Arandino (Calle de la Sombrerería; ☼ 1-11pm) Opposite Cervecería Morito, this place has a more modern feel and doesn't quite match the atmosphere, but it's popular with a young crowd and the tapas are good.

La Mejillonera (Calle de la Paloma 33; ☼ 10am-11pm) A stand-up place which doesn't get as busy as Cervecería Morito, a few doors up, but it's renowned locally for its variety of mussel snacks (€2.10 per plate).

El Angel Vinos y Tapas (Calle de la Paloma 24; ☼ noon-11pm) and **La Colonial** (Calle de Lain Calvo 36; ☼ noon-11.30pm) are other lively places to try for a wide selection of tapas.

CASTILLA Y LEÓN

RESTAURANTS

Royal (Calle del Huerto del Rey 23) If you can withstand the glaringly lit dining area, Royal serves a wide range of *raciones* (€2.40 to €4.80) and *bocadillos* (€1.90 to €2.80) that are consistently tasty.

Ristorante Prego (☎ 947 26 04 47; Calle del Huerto del Rey 4; pasta from €6) Italian food doesn't come any better in Burgos than at the intimate Ristorante Prego, especially the scrummy pizzas (from €12) which are large enough to share between two.

Casa Ojeda (☎ 947 20 90 52; Calle de Vitoria 5) This Burgos classic, all sheathed in dark wood, specialises in plate-bending meat dishes cooked in a clay oven. The upstairs dining room is popular, good, but pricey: *cordero asado* (roast lamb) costs €15.05. You can save money by eating in the equally cosy downstairs bar area where *platos combinados* clock in at around €10.

Other dark-panelled places specialising in a subdued Castilian atmosphere and fine local specialities include: **Meson del Cid** (☎ 947 20 87 15; Plaza de Santa Maria; starters €6-15.60, mains €11.20-19.20) and **Meson La Cueva** (☎ 947 20 86 71; Plaza de Santa Maria; starters €4.50-8, mains €12.50-16). Both offer the local Burgos specialities, *morcilla* (blood sausage) and *cordero asado*.

Burgos also has its fair share of places with a more contemporary flair.

El Angel (☎ 947 20 86 08; Calle de la Paloma 24; starters €7.80-15.50, mains €11.60-17.90) This is an excellent choice for its imaginative menu, patient staff and fusion architecture, which (almost) works aesthetically.

La Fabula (☎ 947 26 30 92; Calle de la Puebla 18; mains from around €12) Another good place for nouveau Castilian cuisine, La Fabula offers slimmed-down rice and fish dishes.

Vinoteca Cordón (☎ 947 27 72 79; Calle de la Puebla 3; menú €14) This place stands out for the impressive wine selection that complements the gourmet food.

Chocolatería Candilejas (Calle de Fernán González 36; desserts start at €2; ⏰ from 6.30pm) A great place for dessert, come here for killer cakes, *churros* (long, deep-fried doughnut) (€2) and *batidos* (milkshakes; €2.30), all home-made.

Drinking
CAFÉS

Café España (Calle de Lain Calvo 12) has been a bastion of the Burgos café scene for over 80 years and one of the better ones with its old-world elegance, while **Café Latino** (Calle de Lain Calvo 16) is also good. Not far away, **Café de las Artes** (Calle de Lain Calvo 31) has a magazine rack, occasional live music and an artsy vibe.

BARS

A great place to get your night started is along Calle de San Juan. **Luz de Luna** (Calle de San Juan; ⏰ 5pm-late Tue-Sun) is always popular. **Europa Azul** (Calle de San Juan 34) doesn't get the crowds until later, but they're pretty cool when they arrive, while **Urban Café** (Calle de San Juan) is seriously funky. Around the corner, **Bar-Pub Mansión** (Calle de la Puebla) is intimate and popular with a student crowd. For a Guinness try **St Patrick** (Calle de San Juan 23).

Alternatively, if you're not keen on walking too far to the next bar, you could spend the whole night on Calle del Huerto del Rey, locally known as Las Llanas. You could start at Flandes, which attracts a student crowd, Avalon or La Negra Candela, before pursuing more energetic *marcha* a few doors up at the noisy music bars of Carpanta y Compañia and El Chupito.

Shopping

Although every tourist-oriented shop in Burgos offers local specialities, the quality varies. Head-and-shoulders above the rest is **La Vieja Castilla** (Calle de la Paloma; ⏰ 10am-2pm & 5-8pm Mon-Fri, 10am-2pm Sat) with a crowded range of wines, cheeses and a host of other delights. A few doors north, **Casa Quinantilla** (Calle de la Paloma; ⏰ 10am-2pm & 5-8pm Mon-Fri, 10am-2pm Sat), is probably the next best bet.

Getting There & Away
BUS

From the **bus station** (Calle de Miranda 4), **Continental-Auto** (☎ 947 26 20 17) runs buses to Madrid (€13.65, 2¾ hours, 10 daily), Vitoria (€6.45, 1½ hours, eight daily), Bilbao (€9.95, two hours, four daily) and San Sebastián (€13, 3½ hours, six daily). **ALSA** (☎ 947 26 63 70) also has buses going to León (€11.75, 3¼ hours, two daily), Pamplona (€12.25, 3½ hours, four daily), Logroño (€5.80, two hours, six daily) and Valladolid (€6.95, two hours, five daily), as well as to most towns in Burgos province.

CAR & MOTORCYCLE

For Madrid, take the N1 directly south. The N234 branches off southeast to Soria and on to Zaragoza and ultimately Barcelona. The N623 leads north to Santander, while the A1 *autopista* goes most of the way to Vitoria and hooks up with the A68 *autopista* to Bilbao.

TRAIN

Burgos is connected with Madrid (€19.90, four hours, seven daily), Bilbao (€13.80, three hours, five daily), León (€14.75, two hours, three daily), Valladolid (€7, 1¼ hours, seven daily) and Salamanca (€17.40, 2½ hours, three daily) among other cities.

AROUND BURGOS

Quintanilla de las Viñas

If you take the Soria road (N234) out of Burgos, a worthwhile stop some 35km out is the 7th-century **Ermita de Santa María de Lara** (admission free). This modest Visigothic hermitage preserves some fine bas-reliefs around its external walls, which are among the better examples of religious art from the 7th century to survive in Spain. To get in, you may have to track down the guardian in the village itself, as the opening hours can be erratic.

Covarrubias

pop 627 / elevation 975m

This pretty hamlet gets somewhat overwhelmed by visitors on weekends, but they come for a good reason. Spread along the banks of the Río Arlanza, the town is made up of a cluster of attractive arcaded half-timbered houses fronting a network of little squares. Highlights include the squat 10th-century **Torreón de Doña Urraca**, towering over the remains of Covarrubias' medieval walls; the late-Gothic **Colegiata de San Cosme y Damián** (☎ 947 40 63 11; admission €2; ⏲ 10.30am-2pm & 4-7pm Wed-Mon), which has attractive cloisters and contains the stone tomb of Fernán González, the 10th-century founder of Castilla; and **Casa Doña Sancha**, the best preserved of the town's 15th-century half-timbered houses.

SLEEPING & EATING

Casa Galín (☎ 947 40 65 52; info@casagalin.com; Plaza de Doña Urraca 4; s/d with shared bathroom €12/21, d with bathroom €30) This place has comfortable rooms with creaky wooden floorboards in an old-fashioned timbered building overlooking the main plaza. It's also home to a popular restaurant with a well-priced *menú* (€7.65).

Los Castros (☎ 947 40 63 68; Calle de los Castros 10; d with breakfast €50) A historic *casa rural*, Los Castros has just five gorgeous doubles filled with all sorts of eclectic furnishings, which somehow reflect this enchanting town.

Two other excellent hotels, both with good restaurants, are **Hotel Arlanza** (☎ 947 40 64 41; www.hotelarlanza.com; Plaza Mayor 11; s/d €35/60) and **Hotel Rey Chindasvinto** (☎ 947 40 65 60; www.hotelchindasvinto.com; Plaza del Rey Chindasvinto 5; s/d from €30/50).

Just east of the town centre, **Camping Covarrubias** (☎ 983 29 58 41; camping per person/tent €3.40/2.70; ⓧ) has two swimming pools and a café. You can also hire mountain bikes here.

Restaurante de Galo (☎ 947 40 63 93; mains about €11, menú €9.60) comes recommended for its robust traditional dishes cooked in a wood-fired oven.

GETTING THERE & AWAY

Two buses travel from Burgos to Covarrubias on weekdays, and one runs on Saturday (€2.40, one hour). The C110 leads west to Lerma and east to hook up with the Burgos–Soria highway (N234).

Santo Domingo de Silos

Monks from this monastery made the pop charts in the mid-1990s in Britain and elsewhere with recordings of Gregorian chants. It appears probable that, as long ago as the 7th century, the Visigoths had a religious centre here. But it was not until the arrival of Santo Domingo (St Dominic) in 1040 that a surer light penetrated the swirling mists of Dark Age ignorance; Santo Domingo began construction of the Benedictine abbey, still inhabited by 27 monks today, after a period of disuse in the wake of the great confiscation of church property in the 19th century.

You can visit the **church** (☎ 947 39 00 68; admission free, guided tours €2.40 Tue-Sun, free Mon; ⏲ 6am-2pm & 4-9.30pm) and the **cloister** and **pharmacy** (⏲ 10am-1pm & 4.30-6pm Tue-Sat, 4.30-6pm Sun & Mon). The jewel is the cloister, a treasure chest of some of the most remarkable and imaginative Romanesque art in all Spain. As you proceed around the courtyard, take a closer look at the sculpted capitals depicting everything from lions to Harpies, intermingled with occasional floral and geometrical motifs betraying the never-distant influence of Islamic art in Spain. More important still are the pieces executed on the corner pillars, representing episodes from the life of Christ.

The galleries are covered by Mudéjar ceilings from the 14th century. In the northeastern corner sits a 13th-century image of the Virgin Mary carved in stone, and nearby is the original burial spot of Santo Domingo.

Although much of the monastery is off-limits to visitors, the compulsory guide will show you inside the 17th-century *botica* (pharmacy), which is now a museum containing a predictable collection of religious artworks, Flemish tapestries and the odd medieval sarcophagus.

You can come to the church to hear the monks **chant** (admission free; ☺ 9am Mon-Sat, noon Sun). Hours may vary slightly throughout the year.

Men can rent a heated **room** (r with meals €24) here, but it's a popular thing to do and you'll need to book well ahead. Call the **Padre Hospedero** (☎ 947 39 00 68) between 11am and 1pm. You can stay for a period of three to 10 days.

Otherwise, there's a handful of lodging options. **Hostal Cruces** (☎ 947 39 00 64; Plaza Mayor 2; s/d €21/36) offers decent rooms and is the cheapest option. **Hotel Arco de San Juan** (☎ 947 39 00 74; fax 947 39 02 00; Pradera de San Juan 1; s/d €35/45) has good rooms with bathroom and phone in the centre of town. For more comfort again, **Hotel Tres Coronas** (☎ 947 39 00 47; fax 947 39 00 65; Plaza Mayor 6; s/d €52/76) has excellent, well-appointed rooms in a historic building; one bonus is the 24-hour room service in case you get peckish at 3am.

Autobuses Arceredillo runs one daily bus from Burgos to Santo Domingo de Silos (€4.55, 1½ hours) from Monday to Saturday.

Desfiladero de Yecla

A couple of kilometres down the back road (BU911) to Caleruega from Santo Domingo, the spectacular Desfiladero de Yecla, a magnificent gorge of limestone cliffs, opens up. It's easily visited thanks to the installation of a walkway. There's a small **information office** (☎ 947 39 01 23; 9am-3pm Mon, Tue & Thu) in the *ayuntamiento* building in Santo Domingo de Silos, where you'll find information on the gorge.

NORTH OF BURGOS

The N623 highway carves a pretty trail from Burgos, particularly between the mountain passes of **Portillo de Fresno** and **Puerto de Car-**

rales. About 15km north of the Portillo de Fresno, a side road takes you through a series of intriguing villages in the **Valle de Sedano**. The town of the same name has a fine 17th-century church, but more interesting is the little Romanesque one above Moradillo de Sedano: the sculpted main doorway is outstanding.

Plenty of villages flank the highway on the way north, but **Orbaneja del Castillo** is the area's best-kept secret. Take the turn-off for Escalada and follow the bumpy road until you reach the waterfall. Park where you can, then climb up beside the waterfall to the village, which is completely hidden from the road. A dramatic backdrop of strange rock walls lends this charming spot a uniquely enchanting air.

SOUTH TO THE RÍO DUERO

As you head south from Burgos to Madrid, you cross some particularly bleak Castilian country. Still, there are some worthwhile places to check out, particularly those towns that spread east and west along Río Duero, the third-longest and second-biggest river in the Iberian Peninsula. Ribera del Duero wines also have a strong reputation for quality.

Lerma

pop 1671 / elevation 827m

An ancient settlement, Lerma hit the big time in the early 17th century when Grand Duke Don Francisco de Rojas y Sandoval, a minister under Felipe II from 1598 to 1618, launched an ambitious project to create another El Escorial. He clearly failed, but the cobbled streets and delightful plazas of the old town retain bags of charm today.

Pass through the **Arco de la Cárcel** (Prison Gate), off the main road to Burgos, climbing up the long Calle del General Mola to the massive Plaza Mayor which is fronted by the oversized **Palacio Ducal**, symbol of the duke's megalomania and notable for its courtyards (closed for restoration at the time of writing) and 210 balconies. To the right of the square is the Dominican nuns' **Convento de San Blas**; the nuns produce some wonderful painted ceramics for sale, ranging from tiles to tea cups. A short distance northwest of Plaza Mayor, at the opposite end from the palace, a pretty passageway and viewpoint opens up over the Río Arlanza. Its arches connect with the 17th-century **Convento de Santa Teresa** (Plaza de Santa Clara), which is also home to the **tourist office** (☎ 947 17 70 02; ⏰ 10am-2pm & 4-7pm Tue-Sat, 11am-2pm Sun). Guided tours (€2.50) of the town and most of its monuments depart from here.

Pensión Martín (☎ 947 17 00 28; Calle Mayor 23; s/d with shared bathroom €10/20) combines a quirky early-19th-century mansion and a secluded garden with basic rooms that are in need of an overhaul.

Hostal Docar (☎ 947 17 10 73; Calle de Santa Teresa de Jesús 18; s/d €28/41) lies outside the old city walls. It's comfortable but the rooms are functional rather than fanciful.

El Zaguan (☎ 947 17 21 65; zaguan.lerma@lycos.es; Calle de Barquillo 6; d/tr €40/53), a charming *casa rural* in the centre of the old town is the most imaginative choice. Set in an 18th-century home with stone walls and beamed ceilings, the rooms are warm and intimate and the owners are friendly.

The traditional **Mesón del Duque** (☎ 947 17 21 22; Calle de Audiencia 2; meals from €35), off Plaza Mayor, is a good place for reliable Castilian cooking and great wines from the region.

Regular buses from Burgos (€2.75, 30 minutes) stop here and some buses coming north from Aranda de Duero or Madrid also pass through.

Aranda de Duero
pop 30,205 / elevation 802m
The big attraction in this crossroads town, apart from its food, is the main portal of the late-Gothic **Iglesia de Santa María**. Its remarkably rich sculptural flourish was executed in the 15th and 16th centuries.

Other than that, people flock here on weekends for lunch (some restaurants don't even bother opening in the evenings) as Aranda de Duero is renowned as a bastion of classic Castilian cooking and is especially famous for its *cordero* (roast lamb).

Few people stay overnight, but if you can't move after the feast, there are plenty of sleeping choices. **Hostal Elvira** (☎ 947 50 08 85; Calle Burgo de Osma 9; s/d €21/30) and **Hotel Julia** (☎ 947 50 12 00; hoteljulia@lycos.es; Calle de San Gregorio 2; s/d €31.20/49.40) are both comfortable options near the centre of town.

But it's most likely the food that drew you here. The most fruitful place to search is on and around Plaza del Arco Isilla; look for the 'Asador' signs.

Probably Aranda's premier *asador* is **Mesón de la Villa** (☎ 947 50 10 25; Calle de la Sal 3; meals around €40, closed Monday) which does succulent lamb and complements it with excellent local wines. Reservations are essential on weekends.

Numerous buses and trains connect Aranda with Madrid and most major cities in Castilla y León.

Peñaranda de Duero
pop 513 / elevation 877m
About 20km east of Aranda on the C111, the village of Peñaranda de Duero exudes considerable charm. Originally a Celtic fortress village, most of its surviving riches are grouped around the attractive Plaza Mayor. The **Palacio Condes de Miranda** is a grand Renaissance palace with a fine Plateresque entrance, double-arched patio and beautiful ceilings in various styles. Free guided tours operate up to eight times Tuesday to Sunday. The 16th-century **Iglesia de Santa Ana** is also impressive in that it integrates columns and busts found at the Roman settlement of Clunia into an otherwise baroque design. For superb views of the village and surrounding country, take a walk up to the medieval **castle** ruins.

There are at least four *casas rurales* in the area for you to choose from should you wish to stay. Most buses between Valladolid (€5.80, 1½ hours) and Soria (€5.65, 1½ hours) pass through town (five daily).

Sepúlveda
pop 1046 / elevation 1313m
With its houses staggered along a ridge carved out by the gorge of the Río Duratón, Sepúlveda is one of many weekend escapes for *madrileños* and this place rivals Aranda de Duero as the destination of choice for *cordero* aficionados. Indeed, the warm ochre tones of Sepúlveda's public buildings, fronting the central Plaza de España, are an enviable setting for a hot Sunday roast.

The *ayuntamiento* backs onto what remains of the old castle, while high above it all the 11th-century **Iglesia del Salvador** rises impassively. It is considered the prototype of this variant of Castilian Romanesque, marked by the single arched portico.

Mirador del Caslilla (☎ 921 54 03 53; Calle del Conde Sepúlveda 26; s/d €40/50) is housed in a traditional building in a delightful cobbled street, just off Plaza de España. The rooms are very comfortable.

CASTILLA Y LEÓN

Hostal Hernanz (☎ 921 54 03 78; www.el-panadero .com; Calle del Conde Sepúlveda 4; s/d €36.05/60) with comfortable, bright and attractive rooms, offers a good range of amenities. Some rooms have views and there's also a decent restaurant.

For the *cordero* feast, you could pretty much take your pick (places serving mediocre *cordero* don't last long here), but **Restaurante Cristóbal** (☎ 921 54 01 00; Calle Conde de Sepúlveda 9; meals €26) and **Restaurante Figón Zute el Mayor** (☎ 921 54 01 65; Calle de Lope Tablada 6; meals €24) are both long-standing favourites with good wine lists. Reservations are highly recommended.

At least two buses link Sepúlveda daily with Madrid, while Segovia is served once daily except Sunday.

Parque Natural del Hoz del Duratón

A sizable chunk of land northwest of Sepúlveda has been constituted as a natural park. The centrepiece is the Hoz del Duratón (Duratón Gorge), in particular where it widens out behind the dam just south of Burgomillodo. A dirt track leads 5km west from the hamlet of Villaseca to the **Ermita de San Frutos**. In ruins now, the hermitage was founded in the 7th century by San Frutos and his siblings, San Valentín and Santa Engracia. They lie buried in a tiny chapel nearby. This is a magical place, overlooking one of the many serpentine bends in the gorge, with squadrons of buzzards and eagles soaring above. Weekends can get claustrophobic as a surprising number of people crowd in. Some people take kayaks up to Burgomillodo to launch themselves down the waters of the canyon.

Castilnovo

Some 12km south of Sepúlveda, this rather cute little **castle** (☎ 921 53 11 33; admission €3; 9am-1pm & 4-6pm Mon-Fri; groups only Sat & Sun) has the air of a private conceit by some moneyed eccentric. Originally built in the 14th century and largely Mudéjar, it has undergone a lot of alterations.

WEST ALONG THE RÍO DUERO
Peñafiel
pop 5257 / elevation 758m

At the heart of the Ribera del Duero wine region, Peñafiel is home to the new state-of-the-art **Museo Provincial del Vino**, cleverly en-

sconced within the walls of the mighty **Castillo de Peñafiel** (admission to museum & castle €5, castle only €2; ⏰ 11.30am-2.30pm & 4.30-8.30pm Tue-Sun Apr-Sep, shorter hrs Oct-Mar). Showcasing the ins and outs of wine – growing, production and history – this exhaustive museum grabs the attention with interactive displays, dioramas, backlit panels and computer terminals. The pleasures of the end product are not neglected: wine tasting costs €7. Not to be missed.

The castle itself is also worth exploring. Riding high above the medieval Castilian stronghold of Peñafiel, it must be about the longest and narrowest castle in Spain. Its crenellated walls and towers stretch over 200m, but little more than 20m across, and were raised and modified over 400 years from the 11th century onward. The sight of it in the distance alone is worth the effort of getting here.

There's a handful of lodging options, including the central **Hostal Linares** (☎ 983 88 09 42; Calle del Mercado Viejo 11; s/d €15.05/27.05), which is pretty good value for rooms with bathroom. For more comfort and euros, **Hotel Ribera del Duero** (☎ 983 88 16 16; www.hotelribera delduero.com; Avenida de Escalona 17; s/d €56.65/67.60) has some attractive touches and character, and some rooms have good views.

Just off the square is the small, pedestrianised town centre, and on Calle Girón de Velasco you'll find several bars and **Restaurante El Bodegón** (☎ 983 88 07 43; Calle Girón de Velasco 16; menú €10.40), where you can dig into a moderately priced meal.

Four or five buses a day run to Valladolid, about 60km west of here.

EAST ALONG THE RÍO DUERO

From Aranda, you can follow the Río Duero east towards Almazán, or take the N122 direct for Soria (p228), Castilla y León's easternmost provincial capital. Both routes are dotted with curious little pueblos and plenty of worthwhile detours. Some of the hamlets you encounter in this area really give the impression that time has stood still for centuries.

San Esteban de Gormaz
pop 2354 / elevation 911m

This dusty little town contains a couple of Romanesque gems hidden away in its centre: the 11th-century **Iglesia de San Miguel** and **Iglesia del Rivero**. Both sport the porticoed side-galleries that characterise the Romanesque style of the Segovia and Burgos areas, and indeed San Miguel is thought by some to have served as a model for other churches.

El Burgo de Osma
pop 3434 / elevation 943m

Some 12km east of San Esteban de Gormaz and veering away from the Duero, this town is a real surprise packet. Once important enough to host its own university, it's now a somewhat run-down little old town, dominated by a quite remarkable *catedral* and infused with an air of decaying elegance.

Begun in the 12th century as an essentially Romanesque building, the **catedral** (☎ 975 36 00 48; admission free; ☼ 10am-1pm & 4-6pm Tue-Sun Oct-Mar; 10am-1pm & 4-7pm Tue-Sun Apr-Sep) was continued in a Gothic vein and finally topped with a weighty baroque tower. It's filled with art treasures, including the 16th-century main **altarpiece** (a collaboration by Juan de Juní and Juan Picardo). Don't miss the so-called **Beato de Osma**, a precious 11th-century *codex* (manuscript) that can be seen in the Capilla Mayor. Also of note is the light-flooded, circular **Capilla de Palafox**, a rare example of the neoclassical style in this region. The **Museo Catedralicio** (guided tours €2.50; ☼ 10am-1pm & 4-7pm Tue-Sat Jun-Oct; 10.30am-1pm & 4.30-6pm Tue-Sun Nov-May) is just off the late-Gothic cloister and contains a worthwhile exhibit of religious artefacts. Entry is by guided tour only.

From Plaza de San Pedro, where the *catedral* stands, Calle Mayor – its portico borne by an uneven phalanx of stone and wooden pillars – leads into **Plaza Mayor**. It is fronted by the 18th-century **ayuntamiento** and the more sumptuous **Hospital de San Agustín** (admission free), now a contemporary art gallery.

Outside the main approach to the town is the 16th-century Renaissance **former university**. If you exit El Burgo from near Plaza de San Pedro, take a left for the village of Osma; high up on a hill you'll see the ruins of the **Castillo de Osma**.

El Burgo is one place where it's definitely worth paying a bit extra for a hotel.

Posada del Canónigo (☎ 975 36 03 62; www .posadadelcanonigo.es; Plaza San Pedro de Osma 19; s/d from €60/70), overlooking the *catedral* in an enchanting 17th-century building, has excellent rooms.

Hotel Il Virrey (☎ 975 34 13 11; www.virreypalafox .com; Calle Mayor 2-4; s/d €52.90/79.35) oozes old

Spanish charm, with its sweeping staircase and heavily gilded furniture. Rates soar on weekends in the last half of January, February and March when people flock here for the ritual slaughter of a pig in the morning, after which diners indulge in all-you-can-eat feasts. At €36 per head it's not bad for one of the more unusual dining experiences. There is even a pig museum…

There are plenty of cafés and tapas bars in town where you can grab a snack, although restaurant choices are rather limited.

Asador El Burgo (☎ 975 34 04 89; Calle Mayor 71; mains from €8, menú especial €23.50) is popular with locals and does the usual meaty Castilian fare with aplomb.

Buses link El Burgo with Soria (€2.95, 50 minutes, six daily) and places as far afield as Valladolid (€13.80, 2¼ hours, three daily). Minor roads lead south to Berlanga de Duero and north to the Cañón del Río Lobos.

Parque Natural del Cañón del Río Lobos

Some 15km north of El Burgo de Osma, this park not only presents some rather bizarre rockscapes and a magnificent deep river canyon, but is also home to vultures and various other birds of prey. Just outside the park is an **information centre** (☎ 975 36 35 64; ☼ mid-Mar–mid-Dec), and about 4km in from the road stands the Romanesque **Ermita de San Bartolomé**. You can walk deeper into the park but free camping is forbidden.

If you decide to stay in the area, the best choice is El Burgo de Osma. **Camping Cañón del Río Lobos** (☎ 975 36 35 65; per person/ tent/car €4.35/4.35/5.55; ☼ Easter-15 Sep; ☒) is near Ucero.

Gormaz
pop 14

Some 14km south of El Burgo, on the Río Duero, is the virtual ghost town of Gormaz. The great **castle** with 21 towers was built by the Muslims in the 10th century and altered in the 13th. Its ruins still convey enormous dignity and the views alone justify the effort of getting here. The nearest place to stay is in nearby Quintanas de Gormaz where **Casa Grande de Gormaz** (☎ 975 34 09 82; Camino de las Fuentes, Quintanas de Gormaz; s/d €55/65) is a delightful, grand old house with 11 imaginatively designed rooms, friendly owners, a sunny terrace and a tennis court. In fact it's the perfect place for curling up with a good book.

For sustenance, you've got a couple of reasonably priced restaurants to choose from.

Berlanga de Duero
pop 888 / elevation 978m

About 15km east of Gormaz, Berlanga is lorded over by a powerful but ruinous castle. Down below, the squat **Colegiata de Santa María del Mercado** is a fine late-Gothic church, with the star-shaped vaulting inside perhaps its most pleasing aspect. It's usually closed (ask in town for María Jesus Moreno, or call ☎ 975 35 30 57, if you want to take a peek inside). The area around the pretty Plaza Mayor, with the occasional Renaissance house, is equally charming. Outside the old town centre, on a desolate open plot, is the **Picota**, to which petty criminals were tied in the good old days.

Hotel Fray Tomás (☎ 975 34 30 33, fax 975 34 31 69; Calle Real 16; s/d €30/48) has comfortable rooms in a modified 14th-century building, while **Posada Los Leones** (☎ 975 34 32 75; Calle de los Leones; s/d €27.05/48.10), a *casa rural* with attached restaurant, has light and breezy rooms with tiled floors and all the charm and family feel you'd expect of a *casa rural*.

Around Berlanga de Duero

About 8km southeast of Berlanga de Duero stands the **Ermita de San Baudelio** (admission €0.75; ☻ 10am-2pm & 4-6.30pm Wed-Sat, 10am-2pm Sun). The simple exterior belies a real gem: a remarkable 11th-century Mozarabic interior. A great pillar in the centre of the only nave opens up at the top like a palm tree to create horseshoe arches. Until recently, the hermitage's walls were decorated with Mozarabic and 12th-century Romanesque frescoes, but these have now been moved to the Prado in Madrid. Opening hours in the afternoon may vary slightly by season. Another 17km south, **Rello** still retains much of its medieval defensive walls.

The Road to Madrid

The N110 winds southwest from San Esteban de Gormaz to join up with the A1 highway between Madrid and Burgos, just short of the Puerto de Somosierra mountain pass. En route, Ayllón and Riaza are particularly worth your time.

AYLLÓN
pop 1254

This village, about 50km southwest of El Burgo de Osma, bathes in the same orange glow that characterises El Burgo's townscape. You enter by a medieval **archway** and are immediately faced on the right by the ornate façade of a late-15th-century noble family's **mansion** in Isabelline style. The uneven, porticoed Plaza Mayor is capped at one end by the Romanesque **Iglesia de San Miguel**, and nearby stands the Renaissance-era **Iglesia de Santa María la Mayor**. Turn right behind this and follow the narrow street for about half a kilometre and you'll come to the extensive remains of another Romanesque **church**, now oddly incorporated into a rambling private residence. **Hostal Vellosillo** (☎ 921 55 30 62; Avenida Conde Vallellano s/n; s/d with washbasin €10.85/18.05, d with private bathroom €30.65) is marginally the better of the two hostales in town.

RIAZA
pop 1988

About 20km south of Ayllón, Riaza's main claim to fame is its charming old circular **Plaza Mayor**. The sandy arena in the centre is still used for bullfights.

Hostal Las Robles (☎ 921 55 00 54; s/d with washbasin €12.05/18.05) is the cheapest place if you want to stay, but **Hotel Plaza** (☎ /fax 921 55 11 28; Plaza Mayor 4; s/d €36/48 Oct-Jun, €50/60 Jul-Sep) offers considerably more charm and comfort, and overlooks the Plaza Mayor.

Restaurante Matimore (Plaza Mayor; meals €7-10) is the place to eat for bull fans. It's a mini-museum of bullfight posters and four rather large stuffed bulls' heads.

SORIA
pop 34,971 / elevation 1055m

Soria, one of Spain's smaller provincial capitals, has a delightful small-town feel, not to mention an appealing old centre and a sprinkling of stunning monuments. Its setting on the Río Duero has also inspired several poets, most notably Antonio Machado. Calm and laid-back by day, Soria has a surprisingly lively nightlife.

History

Possibly populated before Roman times, Soria only appears in the history books with the arrival of the Muslims. Until the crowns

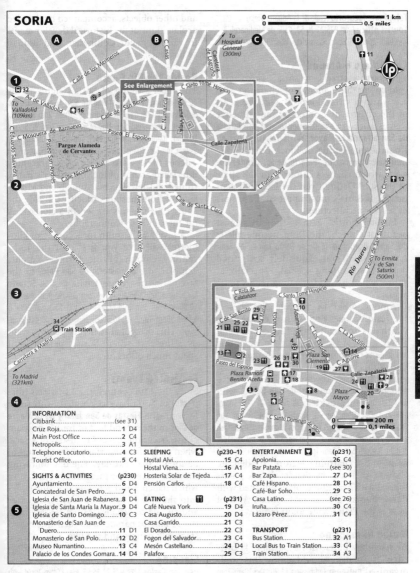

SORIA

0 — 1 km
0 — 0.5 miles

See Enlargement

CASTILLA Y LEÓN

INFORMATION	
Citibank......................................(see 31)	
Cruz Roja...**1** D4	
Main Post Office **2** C4	
Netropolis...**3** A1	
Telephone Locutorio......................**4** C3	
Tourist Office..................................**5** C4	

SIGHTS & ACTIVITIES	(p230)
Ayuntamiento...................................**6** D4
Concatedral de San Pedro...............**7** C1
Iglesia de San Juan de Rabanera......**8** D4
Iglesia de Santa María la Mayor...**9** D4
Iglesia de Santo Domingo.............**10** C3
Monasterio de San Juan de
Duero...**11** D1
Monasterio de San Polo.................**12** D2
Museo Numantino............................**13** C4
Palacio de los Condes Gomara..**14** D4

SLEEPING	(p230–1)
Hostal Alvi.......................................**15** C4
Hostal Viena....................................**16** A1
Hostería Solar de Tejeda................**17** C4
Pensión Carlos.................................**18** C4

EATING	(p231)
Café Nueva York.............................**19** D4
Casa Augusto..................................**20** C4
Casa Garrido...................................**21** C3
El Dorado..**22** C3
Fogon del Salvador.........................**23** C4
Mesón Castellano............................**24** D4
Palafox...**25** C3

ENTERTAINMENT	(p231)
Apolonia..**26** C4
Bar Patata....................................(see 30)
Bar Zapa...**27** D4
Café Hispano...................................**28** D4
Café-Bar Soho.................................**29** C3
Casa Latino...................................(see 26)
Iruña...**30** C4
Lázaro Pérez...................................**31** C4

TRANSPORT	(p231)
Bus Station......................................**32** A1
Local Bus to Train Station...............**33** C4
Train Station...................................**34** A3

of Castile and Aragón were united at the end of the 15th century, Soria was a hive of commercial and political activity, straddling the frontier territory between Old Castilla, Aragón and Navarra. With the decline of the wool trade after the 16th century, however, it lost importance and, along with the expulsion of the Jews, much of its business drive.

Information

Several banks are near the tourist office.

Cruz Roja (☎ 975 22 22 22) For ambulances.

Hospital General (☎ 975 23 43 00; Paseo de Santa Barbara) This is Soria's most central hospital.

Main post office (Paseo del Espolón)

Netropolis (Calle las Navas de Tolosa 17; per hr €4; ☺ 10am-11pm Mon-Sat) For Internet access.

Telephone locutorio (Calle de la Aduana Vieja)
Tourist office (☎ 975 21 20 52; Calle de Medinaceli 2;
🕙 9am-2pm & 5-8pm) Has shorter hours in winter.

Casco Viejo & Around

The narrow streets of Soria's *casco viejo* (old town) have plenty of character and are worth a stroll. Plaza Mayor, the heart of the quarter, is fronted by the attractive Renaissance-era **ayuntamiento** and the **Iglesia de Santa María la Mayor**, with its unadorned Romanesque façade. A block north is the majestic sandstone **Palacio de los Condes Gomara**, which changes colour with the angle of the sun. Dating from the late 16th century, it is Soria's most impressive example of secular architecture.

Further north again is the city's most beautiful church, the Romanesque **Iglesia de Santo Domingo** (Calle de Santo Tomé; 🕙 7am-7pm). Its small but exquisitely sculptured portal is something special, especially at sunset when its reddish stone seems to be aglow.

Among other worthwhile churches is the restored **Iglesia de San Juan de Rabanera**, which was first built in the 12th century and where hints of Gothic and even Byzantine art gleam through the mainly Romanesque hue of this building.

Heading east towards the Río Duero you pass the **Concatedral de San Pedro**, with a 12th-century **cloister** (admission €1; 🕙 10am-1pm & 4.30-5.30pm Tue-Sat, 10am-1pm & 4.30-7pm Sun Feb-Jun; 10am-1.30pm & 4.30-8pm Mon-Sat, 10am-1pm & 4.30-7pm Sun Jul & Aug; 10am-1pm Tue-Fri, 10am-1pm & 4.30-5.30pm Sat, 10am-1pm & 4.30-7pm Sun Sep-Jan) as its most charming feature. Its delicate arches are divided by slender double pillars topped with beautiful capitals adorned with floral, human and animal motifs. Also of note is the Plateresque main façade.

Museo Numantino

Archaeology buffs with a passable knowledge of Spanish should enjoy this well-organised **museum** (admission €1.20; 🕙 10am-2pm & 4-7pm Tue-Sat, 10am-2pm Sun Oct-Jun, 10am-2pm & 5-8pm Tue-Sat, 10am-2pm Sun Jul-Sep), dedicated to finds from ancient sites across the province of Soria (especially Numancia; see p231). The exhibit starts out with bones of mammoths found south of Soria in what might have been a hunting-ground swamp. It continues with ceramics, tools, jewellery and other objects, accompanied by detailed explanations of the historical developments in various major Celtiberian and Roman settlements.

Beside the Río Duero

The most striking of Soria's sights is the 12th-century **Monasterio de San Juan de Duero** (admission €0.75, free Sat & Sun; 🕙 10am-2pm & 5-6pm Tue-Sat, 10am-2pm Sun Nov-Mar, 10am-2pm & 5-7pm Tue-Sat, 10am-2pm Sun Apr, May, Sep & Oct, 10am-2pm & 5-9pm Tue-Sat, 10am-2pm Sun Jun-Aug). What most catches the eye are the exposed, gracefully interlaced arches of the monastery's partly ruined cloister, which artfully blend Mudéjar and Romanesque influences. Inside the church the capitals are worth a closer look for their intense iconography.

A lovely walk south for a couple of kilometres will take you first past the 13th-century church of the former Knights Templar, the **Monasterio de San Polo**, to the fascinating, baroque **Ermita de San Saturio** (admission free; 🕙 10.30am-2pm & 4.30-9pm Tue-Sat, 10.30am-2pm Sun mid-May–mid-Oct; 10.30am-2pm & 4.30-6.30pm Tue-Sat, 10.30am-2pm Sun mid-Oct–mid-May). This octagonal structure perches right over the cave where Soria's patron saint spent much of his life.

Festivals & Events

Since the 13th century, the 12 *barrios* (districts) of Soria have celebrated, with some fervour, the **Fiestas de San Juan y de la Madre de Dios** in the second half of June. The main events occur on Jueves (Thursday) La Saca, when each of the *barrios* presents a bull to be fought the next day. The day following the fight some of the meat is auctioned, after which dancing and general carousing go on into the wee hours of Sunday. Hangovers and all, the *cuadrillas* (teams) representing the 12 *barrios* parade in all their finery and stage folk dances and the like.

Sleeping

Pensión Carlos (☎ 975 21 15 55; Plaza Olivo 2; s/d with washbasin €10/20) This good, family-run cheapie, is well located with simple rooms on the second and third floors of a balconied building.

Hostal Alvi (☎ 975 22 81 12; fax 975 22 81 40; Calle de Alberca 2; s/d €26/46) Spotless and central, this is one of the best-value places, with good rooms complete with TV and phone.

Hostal Viena (☎ /fax 975 22 21 09; Calle de García Solier 5; s/d with washbasin €16/30, d with bathroom €37; 🕱) Despite a depressing façade and 1970s décor in varying shades of brown, this place offers reasonable value and has some reasonably large singles. Rooms have TV, phone and air-con.

Hostería Solar de Tejeda (☎ /fax 975 23 00 54; solardetejeda@wanadoo.es; Calle de Claustrilla 1; s/d €47/52) This charming boutique hotel right in the middle of the pedestrianised zone is the best choice in Soria. Rooms, each individually designed, have whimsical décor, lots of Bohemian touches and beautifully tiled bathrooms.

Eating

Mesón Castellano (☎ 975 21 30 45; Plaza Mayor 2; mains mostly €13-22) With beamed ceilings and dangling flanks of ham, Mesón Castellano is a local institution, with some of the best tapas in town and delicious full meals in its *comedor* (dining room).

Fogon del Salvador (☎ 975 23 01 94; Plaza El Salvador 1; mains from €12.65, menú €15) Soria's other culinary stalwart has a wine list as long as your arm (literally) and a fabulous wood-fired oven churning out succulent meat-based dishes.

Casa Augusto (☎ 975 21 30 41; Plaza Mayor 5; starters €5-7, mains €8-12) This is a classy alternative, with an intimate dining area, very reasonable prices, an extensive wine list and a friendly owner.

Casa Garrido (☎ 975 22 20 68; Calle Vicente Tutor 8; mains €12-16, menú €9.40) This cosy spot is a classic Castilian dark-wood restaurant featuring meaty Castilian cooking.

Palafox (☎ 975 22 00 76; Calle Vicente Tutor 2; menú from €7.65) and **El Dorado** (☎ 975 22 02 72), next door, make substantial *bocadillos*, but also serve sit-down meals and tapas.

Café Nueva York (Plaza San Blas y el Rosel; ☾ 7am-6pm) serves up great breakfasts until midday and is also a good spot to fill up on divine pastries.

Entertainment

Plaza San Clemente is perfect for kicking off the *marcha*. Of the handful or so bars around here, **Iruña** (Plaza San Clemente 2) and **Bar Patata** (Plaza San Clemente 1) have the best range of tapas to go with your drinks. **Lázaro Pérez** (Calle del Collado 52) is also worth a look for the spit-and-sawdust crowd, although it's a bit macho.

Another good spot to start the evening is Plaza Ramon Benito Aceña, where you'll find the hugely popular Apolonia and the very cool Casa Latino.

Down the hill towards the Plaza Mayor, **Bar Zapa** (Calle Zapatería 38) is an exotic spot and **Café Hispano** (Plaza San Gil; ☾ from 3pm) is a comfortable place to hang out, with its low ceilings and wood-panelled walls.

A super-cool alternative is **Café-Bar Soho** (☎ 975 221 911; Calle de Campo 16; ☾ 8am-late), which is good at any time of the day.

For dancing try any of the late-night clubs that line Rota de Calatañazor, just north of the centre.

Getting There & Away

From the **bus station** (☎ 975 22 51 60), a 15-minute walk west of the centre, there are services to Burgos (€8.90, 2¼ hours, three daily), Logroño (€5.62, 1¾ hours, five daily), Madrid (€11.50, 2½ hours, eight hours) and Valladolid (€11.29, three hours, five daily).

Provincial towns such as Medinaceli (€4, 45 minutes, twice daily), Almazán (€1.80, 25 minutes, twice daily) and Peñafiel (€8.33, 2¼ hours, five daily) are served as well.

If you're driving, take the N111 north for Logroño; for Madrid, the same road connects with the N11 south of Soria. The N122 goes west to El Burgo de Osma. Going east, it merges with the A68 to Zaragoza.

Getting Around

Local buses connect the train station with Plaza Ramón Benito Aceña.

AROUND SORIA
Numancia

The low-slung, mainly Roman **ruins** (admission €0.60, free Sat & Sun; ☾ 10am-2pm & 3.30-6pm Tue-Sat, 10am-2pm Sun Nov-Mar; 10am-2pm & 4-7pm Tue-Sat, 10am-2pm Sun Apr, May, Sep & Oct; 10am-2pm & 5-9pm Tue-Sat, 10am-2pm Sun Jun-Aug) left at Numancia, 8km north of Soria, suggest little of the long history of this city, inhabited as early as the Bronze Age. Ironically, given that it has survived longer than many other Roman ruins in the region, Numancia proved one of the most resistant cities to Roman rule. Several attempts by the Romans to take control of it were frustrated until finally Scipio, who had crushed Carthage, managed to starve the city into submission in 134 BC.

Under Roman rule, Numancia was an important stop on the road from Caesaraugusta (Zaragoza) to Asturica (Astorga). Ceramics unearthed here have revealed an advanced artistic tradition among not only the Romanised inhabitants of the city, but also their Celtiberian forebears.

To get there, take the N111 for around 5km north of Soria and then follow the signs to Garray.

Sierra de Urbión

Some of the most surprisingly green and unspoiled country in Castilla y León lies to the northwest of Soria, with the Sierra de Urbión stretching north into La Rioja – a popular weekend destination with the local people. The focal point is the **Laguna Negra**, 18km north of the pretty village of **Vinuesa**. The glacial lake lies still like a mirror at the base of brooding rock walls and partially wooded hills. Although the road is not in great shape, the objective is well worth the battering to your shock absorbers (there are no buses) to get there. It's possible to walk to the Laguna de Urbión in La Rioja or to the summit of the Pico de Urbión, above the village of Duruelo de la Sierra, and then on to a series of other tiny glacial lakes. Vinuesa makes a good base for the area.

Hostal Virginia (☎ 975 37 85 55; www.hotelvirginia rh.com; s/d €42.10/60.10), in the village of Vinuesa, offers bright and pleasant rooms with wrought-iron beds, and some rooms also have nice views.

Casa La Pinariega (☎ 975 37 80 16; Calle de Reina Sofia 4; d €42) is a more homely alternative to the hostal.

Camping El Cobijo (☎ 975 37 83 31; www.camping cobijo.com; camping per person/tent/car €3.90/3.75/3.90; ☒ Easter-Sep) is the nearest camping ground to the Laguna Negra. It's a pleasant place set among ample greenery, 2km northwest of Vinuesa.

Calatañazor

pop 40 / elevation 1071m

This dusty, yet oddly romantic village, about 30km west of Soria, is certainly an original place to stop. As you round a tight bend in the road, the gravestone walls and odd modest turret of this one-time Muslim fort (the name comes from the Arabic Qala'at an-Nassur, literally 'the vulture's

citadel') present a timeless face. Believe it or not, scenes from the movie *Doctor Zhivago* were shot here. Climb the crooked, cobbled lanes through the town gate and step back hundreds of years into a medieval village. Then simply wander through this little maze, which is lined by ochre stone and adobe houses topped with red-tile roofs and conical chimneys typical of the area.

There are two tiny **museums**, a **church** and splendid views from the ruined fortress over a vast field called **Valle de la Sangre** (Valley of Blood). This was the setting of an epic AD 1002 battle that left Muslim ruler Almanzor defeated (he later died in nearby Medinaceli).

If you want to stay, there are three *casas rurales*.

SOUTH OF SORIA
Almazán
pop 5634 / elevation 940m

Three of this small town's massive gates remain to testify to a past more illustrious than the present in this quiet backwater. It frequently changed hands between the Muslims and Christians, and for three short months was chosen by Fernando and Isabel as their residence.

The Romanesque **Iglesia de San Miguel** (Plaza Mayor; admission free; ☒ 10.30am-2pm & 5-7pm Tue-Sun Jul-Oct) sports an unusual octagonal cupola-cum-bell tower that reveals Mudéjar influences. Inside is a bas-relief depicting the killing of Thomas à Beckett at the hands of the British king Henry II. The work was commissioned by Henry's daughter, Eleanor of Aquitaine, the wife of Alfonso VII, as a gesture of penance on behalf of her father.

The most attractive façade of the Gothic–Renaissance **Palacio de los Hurtado de Mendoza** also looks out over Plaza Mayor. Inside is a nice patio and *artesonado*.

Hostal El Arco (☎ 975 31 02 28; Calle de San Andrés 5-7; s with washbasin €15, d with private bathroom €27) Situated by one of the three city gates, El Arco is a reasonable place to rest your head.

Restaurante Puerto Rico (☎ 975 30 00 73; Calle de los Caballeros 10; meals from €5) This is a good, cheap restaurant in the old town.

There are four daily buses to/from Soria (€1.80, 30 minutes) and three trains (€2.15, 35 minutes).

Medinaceli

pop 505 / elevation 1270m

Entering Medinaceli along a slip road just north of the A2 motorway, you'll find the modern equivalent of a one-horse town. The old Medinaceli is further on, draped along a high, windswept ridge 3km to the north. Its most incongruously placed landmark is a 2nd-century AD **triumphal arch**, which is all that remains of the Roman settlement. Little is left to remind you of Medinaceli's Muslim occupiers either: the quiet streets are more redolent of the noble families that lived here after the town fell to the Reconquista in 1124. The most notable religious building is the Gothic **Colegiata de Santa María**. There's also a **tourist office** (☎ 689 734 176; Plaza Mayor 2; 10am-2pm & 4-8pm Wed-Sun).

Hostal Rafa (☎ 975 32 60 32; Avenida de Madrid 30; s/d €24.05/48.10) is probably the pick of the hotels in the town itself.

Regular buses to Soria (€4, one hour) leave from outside the *ayuntamiento* in the new town. Three trains daily pass by en route between Madrid and Zaragoza line. There's no transport between the old and new towns; it's quite a hike.

Santa María de la Huerta

pop 436 / elevation 818m

This dusty, largely insignificant village off the N11 and just short of the Aragonese frontier, contains a gem in the form of a **Cistercian monastery** (☎ 975 32 70 02; admission €2; 10am-1pm & 4-6pm Mon-Sat, 10am-1pm Sun), founded in 1162 and where monks lived until the monastery was expropriated in 1835. The order was allowed to return in 1930 and 25 Cistercians are now in residence. Before entering the monastery, note the church's impressive 12th-century façade with its attractive rose window.

Inside the monastery, you pass through two cloisters, the second of which is by far the more beautiful. Known as the **Claustro de los Caballeros**, it's Spanish Gothic in style, although the medallions on the 2nd floor bearing coats of arms and assorted illustrious busts, such as that of Christopher Columbus, are a successful Plateresque touch. Off this cloister is the *refectorio* (dining hall). Built in the 13th century, it is remarkable, especially for the absence of columns to support the vault.

A couple of buses per day connect the village with Almazán and Soria.

Castilla-La Mancha

CONTENTS

CASTILLA-LA MANCHA

Castilla-La Mancha can be a wonderful surprise for first-time visitors. Not as immediately captivating as some other parts of Spain – La Mancha (the name comes from an Arabic expression meaning 'dry, waterless land') consists of great swathes of Central Spain's harsh, dry *meseta* (plateau), which bakes in summer – Castilla-La Mancha nonetheless conceals a number of real gems.

Toledo, one of Spain's most enchanting and popular towns, is the undoubted highlight, a city where Spain's multicultural, multifaith history shines through in an unrivalled fusion of architectural styles. At times dark and brooding, Toledo is the perfect place to contemplate Spain's unrivalled beauty and the enduring scars of its tumultuous past.

Also bearing considerable medieval charm, Cuenca's stunning old town is seemingly about to spill over into the gorges that surround it, while Sigüenza's quiet, twisting streets climb up a hillside to a forbidding castle. Further south, Almagro is a hidden treasure of white buildings, cobblestone streets and one of Spain's more unusual and attractive main squares.

Castilla-La Mancha is, however, perhaps most famous of all as the home of the potty, errant and idealistic *manchego* knight, Don Quijote, whose legend remains very much alive in the Spanish imagination. The masterpiece of Miguel de Cervantes comes alive throughout the region – the windmills with which Don Quijote and Sancho Panza did battle are everywhere to be seen, most evocatively in Consuegra and Campo de la Criptana.

Even Castilla-La Mancha's bleakest stretches can evoke a grim fascination in those who visit – the empty expanses alone are quite unique in Western Europe. But if you tire of this hot, lonely land, there are quiet mountainous stretches offering respite – not least among them the Sierra de Alcaraz, Montes de Toledo and, best of all, the gorge around Alcalá del Júcar.

HIGHLIGHTS

- Delight in the medieval splendour of the imperial city of **Toledo** (p236)
- Sip a coffee on Almagro's unusual **Plaza Mayor**, and sample some theatre at the unique **Corral de Comedias** (p250)
- Let your imagination roam free and tilt at windmills like Don Quijote on the hill over-looking **Consuegra** (p252)
- Escape the central plains by the river beneath **Alcalá del Júcar's** (p254) cascade of houses
- Be amazed at how the hanging houses of **Cuenca** (p254) stay put

| AREA: 79,461 SQ KM | POP: 1,815,781 | AVE SUMMER TEMP: HIGH 34°C, LOW 16°C |

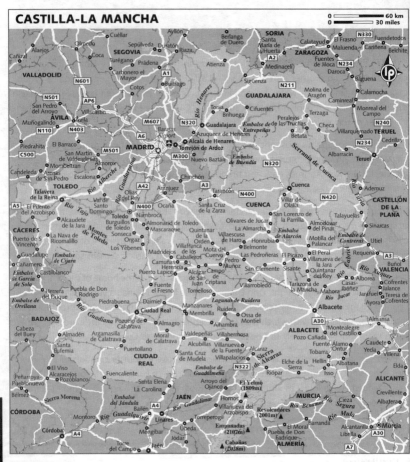

CASTILLA-LA MANCHA

TOLEDO

pop 55,062

Visiting Toledo is a journey to the heart of the polyglot Spain. Still known as La Ciudad Imperial (the Imperial City), Toledo is Iberia's Rome, a remarkable medieval city that bristles with monumental splendour.

Toledo is like the Middle East grafted onto Catholic Spain. The twisting lanes, blind alleys and decorated internal patios hidden by sombre façades are reminiscent of the labyrinthine medinas of Damascus, Cairo or Fés. Yet from its heart rises the Gothic grandeur of the cathedral and the grim composure of Toledo's Alcázar.

Like a creaky old museum, *la ciudad de la tres culturas* (the city of the three cultures) has survived as a unique centre where traces of all of Iberia's conquerors and communities – Romans, Visigoths, Jews, Muslims and Christians – remain strongly in evidence. The artistic legacy is a complex mosaic of European and Middle Eastern values that can be seen elsewhere in Spain, but rarely with the intensity found here.

HISTORY

The Romans were the first to single out this site as a strategic crossroads near the geographical centre of the Iberian Peninsula; ancient Toletum became an important way-station in Roman Hispania. By the 6th century, Roman influence was already a distant memory and the Visigothic king Atanagild moved the site of his capital from Seville to Toletum, which became the Catholic heartland of the Visigothic kingdom. Over time, endless feuds between Visigothic nobles sent the kingdom into decline and its capital became vulnerable, ensuring that soon after the Muslims crossed the Strait of Gibraltar in 711 they conquered Toledo with little difficulty.

Toledo was the main city of central Muslim Spain. After the collapse of the caliphate in Córdoba in 1031 it became the capital of an independent Arab *taifa* (small kingdom). For the following 50 years the city was unrivalled as a centre of learning and arts in Spain, and for a brief period its power ranged across all modern Castilla-La Mancha, to Valencia and to Córdoba itself.

Alfonso VI marched into Toledo in 1085, a significant victory on the long road of the Reconquista. Shortly thereafter, the Vatican recognised Toledo as a seat of the Church in Spain. In the centuries that followed, the city was one of the primary residences of choice for the Castilian monarchy. Their alliance with the Archbishop of Toledo, a vocal proponent of the Reconquista and the monarchs' right-hand man at this time, ensured that Toledo became a place of considerable power. Initially, Toledo's Christians, Jews and Muslims coexisted tolerably well. However, soon after Granada fell to the Reyes Católicos (Catholic Monarchs) in 1492, Spain's Muslims and Jews were compelled to convert to Christianity or flee, a grievous tragedy in this city of many faiths.

In the 16th century, Carlos I considered making Toledo his permanent capital, but his successor, Felipe II, dashed such ideas with his definitive move to Madrid, and Toledo went into decline.

In the early months of the 1936–39 civil war, Nationalist troops (and some civilians) were kept under siege in the Alcázar, but were eventually relieved by a force from the south. However, by diverting his units to Toledo, Franco missed an opportunity to get to Madrid before the arrival of the International Brigades, a miscalculation that many believe prolonged the war.

In 1986 Unesco declared the city a monument of world interest to humanity. In spite of this, people are abandoning the old city for the characterless but comfortable new suburbs sprawled out beneath it, leaving behind only public servants, students, the rent-protected elderly and a medieval city in urgent need of attention.

ORIENTATION

Toledo is built upon a hill around which the Río Tajo (Tagus River) flows on three sides. Modern suburbs spread beyond the river and the walls of the *casco antiguo* (old town). The bus station is northeast of the old town, and the train station is further east across the Tajo. Both are connected by local buses to the centre. Plaza de Zocodover (known as Zoco to the locals) is the main square of the old town.

INFORMATION

Emergency

Cruz Roja (☎ 925 22 22 22) For ambulances.
Policía Nacional (☎ 092; Plaza de la Ropería)

Internet Access

Locutorio Toledo (Plaza de Magdalena 7; per hr €2.50; ⏰ 11am-3pm & 4-11pm Mon-Wed & Fri & Sat, 4-11pm Thu, 11am-3pm Sun)

Money

You're never far from a bank or ATM in central Toledo, especially along Calle de Comercio and Cuesta de Carlos V, both running off Plaza de Zocodover.

Post

Main post office (Calle de la Plata 1)

Tourist Information

Information kiosk (☎ 925 25 40 30; Plaza del Ayuntamiento; ⏰ 10.30am-2.30pm Mon, 10.30am-2.30pm & 4.30-7pm Tue-Sun) This small kiosk is looking for a permanent home but was adjacent to the cathedral at the time of research.
Tourist office (☎ 925 22 08 43, fax 925 25 26 48; Carretera de Madrid; ⏰ 9am-6pm Mon-Fri, 9am-7pm Sat, 9am-3pm Sun) The main tourist office is just outside Puerta Nueva de Bisagra.

SIGHTS

In summer, many of Toledo's attractions open for up to three hours later than the times cited.

Walking Tour

Most of the sights within Toledo's old town can be explored on foot, in a journey

CASTILLA-LA MANCHA

TOLEDO

To Talavera
de la Reina
(80km)

500 m
0.3 miles

INFORMATION	
Ayuntamiento	(see 4)
BBVA	1 E6
Centro de Salud	2 D5
Hospital Provincial	3 F5
Information Kiosk	4 C7
Locutorio Toledo	5 D6
Main Post Office	6 D6
Policía Nacional	7 D6
Santander Central Hispano	(see 1)
Tourist Office	8 C4

SIGHTS & ACTIVITIES	(pp237-44)
Alcázar	9 E6
Cable Ferry	10 E8
Casa-Museo de El Greco	11 B7
Catedral de Toledo	12 D6
Circo Romano Remains	13 B4
Iglesia de San Román	14 C6
Iglesia de Santo Tomé	15 B7
Mezquita de Cristo de la Luz	16 D5
Mezquita de las Tornerías	17 D6
Monasterio de Santo Domingo	
El Antiguo	18 B6
Museo de Arte Contemporáneo	19 B6
Museo de los Concilios y Cultura	
Visigoda	(see 14)
Museo de Santa Cruz	20 E5
Museo Duque de Lerma	(see 26)
Museo Sefardí	21 D3
Plaza de Zocodover	22 D6
Puerta Nueva de Bisagra	23 C4
San Juan de los Reyes	24 A6
Sinagoga de Santa María La Blanca	25 B7
Sinagoga del Tránsito	26 B7
Taller del Moro	27 C7

SLEEPING	(pp244-5)
Circo Romano	28 B4
HI Albergue Juvenil en San Servando	29 D5
Hostal del Cardenal	30 C5
Hostal Nuevo Labrador	31 D6
Hostal Santo Tomé	32 C7
Hotel Carlos V	33 D6
Hotel El Diamantista	34 D8
Hotel Santa Isabel	35 C7
La Posada de Manolo	36 D7
Pensión Castilla	37 D5
Pensión Santa Úrsula	38 D6
Pensión Segovia	39 C7
	40 D5

EATING	(pp245-6)
Aurelio	41 D6
Aurelio	42 D7

Bacus	43 C7
El Trébol	44 E5
Gambrinus	45 C7
Hierbabuena	46 D5
La Abadía	47 D5
La Boveda	48 D6
La Naviera	49 C6
Naca Naca	50 E6
O'Brien's	51 E5
Pastucci	52 D6

DRINKING	(p246)
Bar El Corralito	(see 55)
Bar-Restaurante Ludeña	(see 55)
Camelot	53 D5
Cervecería 1700	54 C6
El Corral de Don Diego	55 C6
El Pellejito	56 C6
El Último	57 D7
Enebro	58 E6
La Tabernita	59 E5
La Venta del Alma	60 A8
Lúpulo	61 C6
Pícaro	62 D6
Sithons	63 D6

ENTERTAINMENT	(p246)
María Cristina Cinema Complex	64 D3
Teatro Rojas	65 D6

SHOPPING	(pp246-7)
Convento Santa Úrsula	66 C7

TRANSPORT	(p247)
Bus Station	67 E3
Taxi Rank	68 E6

Río Tajo

Puente de
Azarquiel

To Train
Station
(130m);
Ocaña;
Orgaz
(34km)

Bda Castilla La Mancha

Calle Río

Calle de los Trinitarios

Plaza
Honda

Calle del Río Llano

Plaza del
Solar

Covachuelas

To
Madrid
(68km)

Calle Honda

Plaza
de Toros

Calle de Madrid

Calle de Cardenal Tavera

Costanilla Santo Lázaro

Iglesia de Santiago
del Arrabal

Puerta de
Alfonso VI

del Arrabal

Av Duque Lerma

Calle de Talavera la Reina

Av de la Reconquista

Plaza
República

Calle de la
Dominicana

Calle de Cuba Chile

Plaza
de Cuba Chile

Avenida de América

Calle de Colombia

Calle de Molinero

Av de Carlos III

Paseo del Circo Romano

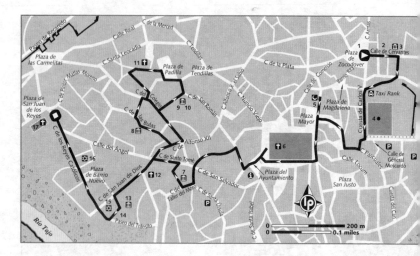

through history that could be completed in three hours or could last all day. Start in the attractive **Plaza de Zocodover** (**1**; below), then pass through the **Arco de la Sangre** (**2**) on the eastern side of the square to the rewarding **Museo de Santa Cruz** (**3**; opposite). Up the hill to the south is Toledo's signature **Alcázar** (**4**; opposite), beyond which there are some fine views over the Río Tajo. Follow the spires down the hill to the west, passing en route the remnants of a mosque, **Mezquita de las Tornerías** (**5**), before reaching the **Catedral de Toledo** (**6**; opposite), the spiritual home of Catholic Spain.

From the nearby Plaza del Ayuntamiento, twist your way west to the 14th-century **Taller del Moro** (**7**; ☎ 925 22 45 00; Calle del Taller del Moro s/n; admission €0.60; ☺ 10am-2pm & 4-6.30pm Tue-Sat, 10am-2pm Sun). It houses a museum with a small collection of Mudéjar decorative items, although it's more interesting for its architecture. Up the hill to the northwest, the **Museo de Arte Contemporáneo** (**8**; ☎ 925 22 78 71; Calle de las Bulas; admission €0.60; ☺ 10am-2pm & 4-6.30pm Tue-Sat, 10am-2pm Sun), housed in the restored 16th-century Mudéjar Casa de las Cadenas, is elevated beyond the mundane by two outstanding works by Joan Miró.

From here, possible detours include heading northeast to the **Iglesia de San Román** (**9**), an impressive hybrid of Mudéjar and Renaissance styles and home to the **Museo de los Concilios y Cultura Visigoda** (**10**; ☎ 925 22 78 72; Calle de San Román; adult/child & senior €0.60/free; ☺ 10am-2pm & 4-6.30pm Tue-Sat, 10am-2pm Sun),

with Visigothic artefacts; or to the **Monasterio de Santo Domingo El Antiguo** (**11**; p243).

Down the hill are a cluster of must-sees for El Greco fans – the wonderful **Iglesia de Santo Tomé** (**12**; p243) and the **Casa-Museo de El Greco** (**13**; p243) – encountered before entering the heart of Toledo's old **Jewish Quarter** (**14**). Here, the **Sinagoga del Tránsito** (**15**; p243) should on no account be missed, while the **Sinagoga de Santa María La Blanca** (**16**; p243) is also worth a look. These synagogues take on special poignancy if you continue along Calle de los Reyes Católicos to the splendid **San Juan de los Reyes** (**17**; p243), which Spain's Catholic rulers hoped would represent the ultimate endpoint of Toledo's history.

Plaza de Zocodover

This picturesque square is most people's introduction to Toledo, and its cafés are lovely places from which to watch the world go by and pass the summer siesta hours.

From 1465 until the 1960s, Zocodover was the scene of El Martes, the city's Tuesday market and successor to the Arab *souq ad-dawab* (livestock market), from which the square derives its unusual name. It was also here that *toledanos* for centuries enjoyed their bullfights or gathered to witness autos-da-fé (public burnings at the stake) carried out by the Inquisition.

Juan de Herrera, who built El Escorial, wanted to convert the square into a grand Castilian *plaza mayor* (main plaza) in the late 16th century, but he was blocked by

Church interests. The result is something of a hotchpotch of architectural styles. The elegant eastern façade is all Juan de Herrera managed to erect along the line of the former Arab city wall, punctuated by the gate now known as the Arco de la Sangre. The southern flank dates from the 17th century, the McDonald's notwithstanding.

Alcázar

Just south off Zocodover, at the highest point in the city, looms Toledo's most recognisable edifice, the Alcázar. Abd ar-Rahman III raised a *al-qasr* (fortress) here in the 10th century and it was altered after the Christians retook the town in the following century. Alonso Covarrubias and Herrera rebuilt it as a royal residence for Carlos I, but the court moved to Madrid and it became a white elephant, eventually winding up as the Academia de la Infantería, one of the most significant army academies in Spain (now located across the Tajo valley to the east).

The Alcázar was largely destroyed during the republican siege of Franco's forces in 1936, but Franco had it rebuilt and turned into a military museum. At the time of research the museum was closed for major renovations, to enable the relocation here of Madrid's Museo del Ejército (Army Museum). It's not expected to reopen until 2006 (at the earliest), although some completed sections may open in the interim.

Prior to the renovation, the exhibits eloquently reflected Spain's ambiguous approach to its past and to Franco himself. Historians eagerly await the reopening to see how this sensitive period of Spanish history will be portrayed.

Museo de Santa Cruz

Just outside what were once the Arab city walls, the **Museo de Santa Cruz** (☎ 925 22 10 36; Calle de Cervantes 3; admission free; ☼ 10am-2pm & 4-6.30pm Mon, 10am-6.30pm Tue-Sat, 10am-2pm Sun) was built in the early 16th century and is a mix of Gothic and Spanish Renaissance styles. The cloisters are superb, as are the upstairs displays of ceramics from across Spain. The ground-level gallery contains a number of El Grecos (look particularly for the *Asunción de la Virgen* and the superbly rendered *La Veronica*); a painting attributed to Goya (*Cristo Crucificado*); the wonderful 15th-

century *Tapestry of the Astrolabes*; and a mixed bag of religious objects.

Catedral de Toledo

Toledo's **catedral** (admission €5.50, free after 4pm; ☼ 10.30am-6.30pm Mon-Sat, 2-6pm Sun) dominates the city skyline, reflecting the city's historical significance as the heart of Catholic Spain.

From the earliest days of the Visigothic occupation of the ancient Roman Toletum, the modern site of the cathedral has been the centre of worship in the city. In 646, Toledo's archbishop was first recognised as the primate of the Catholic Church in Spain. During the three centuries of Muslim rule, the Visigoths' basilica converted into Toledo's central mosque. Alfonso VI promised, in the instruments of surrender signed by Christians and Muslims in 1085, that the mosque would be preserved as a place of worship for Toledo's considerable Muslim population. The promise was broken and the mosque destroyed. The construction of the cathedral began in the 13th century and proceeded slowly over the following centuries.

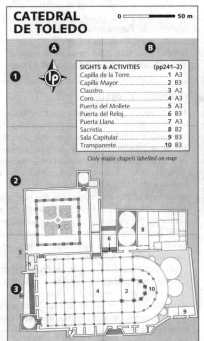

CATEDRAL DE TOLEDO

0 ——— 50 m

SIGHTS & ACTIVITIES	(pp241–2)
Capilla de la Torre	1 A3
Capilla Mayor	2 B3
Claustro	3 A2
Coro	4 A3
Puerta del Mollete	5 A3
Puerta del Reloj	6 B3
Puerta Llana	7 A3
Sacristía	8 B2
Sala Capitular	9 B3
Transparente	10 B3

Only major chapels labelled on map

Essentially a Gothic structure, the cathedral is nevertheless a melting pot of styles, reflecting the mixed history of the city. Mudéjar elements are plain to see in the interior decoration, and the Spanish Renaissance makes itself felt in the many chapels that line the church naves.

The **Puerta Llana** at the side takes you into the cathedral's main nave. The centre is dominated by the **coro** (choir stalls), a feast of sculpture and carved wooden stalls. The lower tier was carved in the 15th century in late Gothic style and depicts the conquest of Granada, while the Renaissance upper level features images of saints and apostles, many by Alonso de Berruguete.

Opposite is the **Capilla Mayor**, too small to accommodate the choir stalls as originally planned, but an extravagant work of art dating back to 1498. This altar serves in part as a mausoleum for Cardinal Mendoza (prelate and adviser to Fernando and Isabel) and several kings. The masterpiece is the *retablo* (altarpiece) in Flemish Gothic style, depicting scenes from the life of Christ and culminating with a *Calvario* and an *Asunción de la Virgen*. The oldest of the cathedral's magnificent stained glass is the rose window above the **Puerta del Reloj**, to your left as you're facing the *capilla* (chapel).

Behind the main altar lies a mesmerising piece of churrigueresque baroque, the **Trans-parente**. A lavish 18th-century embellishment, it also serves to remedy the lack of light in the cathedral.

All the chapels and rooms off the main church body are worth visiting, but the highlights are the **Capilla de la Torre**, in the northwestern corner, and the **sacristía** (sacristy). The latter contains a small gallery packed to the rafters with artwork (many by El Greco), while the former houses what must be one of the most extraordinary monstrances in existence, the **Custodia de Arfe**, by the celebrated 16th-century goldsmith Enrique de Arfe. With 18kg of pure gold and 183kg of silver, this 16th-century conceit bristles with some 260 statuettes. Its big day out is the feast of Corpus Christi (p244), when it is paraded around the streets of Toledo.

The **sala capitular** (chapterhouse) features a remarkable 500-year-old *artesonado* (Mudéjar ceiling) in the so-called Cisneros style and Renaissance murals depicting the life of Christ and the Virgin Mary.

The cathedral's cool and pretty **claustro** (cloister) is entered through the **Puerta del Mollete** facing the square under the Arco del Palacio, which links the cathedral to the Palacio Arzobispal (Archbishop's Palace).

El Greco Trail

The exceptional paintings of El Greco are among the most popular of Toledo's sights

CASTILLA-LA MANCHA

EL GRECO IN TOLEDO

After a long apprenticeship in Crete, where he was born in 1541, Domenikos Theotokopoulos moved to Venice in 1567 to be schooled as a Renaissance artist. He learned to extract the maximum effect from few colours, concentrating the observer's interest in the faces of his portraits and leaving the rest in relative obscurity, a characteristic that remained one of his hallmarks. From 1572 he learned from the mannerists of Rome and the work left behind by Michelangelo.

He came to Toledo in 1577 hoping to get a job decorating El Escorial. Things didn't quite work out, and Felipe II rejected him as a court artist. In Toledo, itself recently knocked back as permanent seat of the royal court, the man who came to be known simply as El Greco felt sufficiently at home to hang around, painting in a style different from anything local artists were producing. He even managed to cultivate a healthy clientele and command good prices. His rather high opinion of himself and his work, however, did not endear him to all and sundry. He had to do without the patronage of the cathedral administrators, the first of many clients to haul him to court for his obscenely high fees.

El Greco liked the high life, and with things going well in the last decade of the 16th century, he took rooms in a mansion on the Paseo del Tránsito, where he often hired musicians to accompany his meals. As Toledo's fortunes declined, so did El Greco's personal finances, and although the works of his final years are among his best, he often found himself unable to pay the rent. He died in 1614, leaving his works scattered about the city, where many have remained to this day.

and they adorn many of the monuments across town. **Iglesia de Santo Tomé** (☎ 925 25 60 98; www.santotome.org; Plaza del Conde; adult/concession €1.50/1.20; ⊙ 10am-6pm) is a must-see, containing as it does El Greco's masterpiece, *El Entierro del Conde de Orgaz* (The Burial of the Count of Orgaz). When the count, a 14th-century benefactor of the church, was buried in 1322, Saints Augustine and Stephen supposedly descended from heaven to attend the funeral. El Greco's work depicts the miracle and features himself, his son and Cervantes among the onlookers.

Similarly rewarding is the **Casa-Museo de El Greco** (☎ 925 22 40 46; Calle de Samuel Leví s/n; admission €2.40; ⊙ 10am-2pm & 4-9pm Tue-Sat, 10am-2pm Sun), although it's unlikely that El Greco actually lived here. Inside you'll find an assortment of his works, including *Vista y Plano de Toledo*, and a small collection of pieces from the 17th-century Toledo, Madrid and Seville schools.

One of the oldest convents in Toledo, the **Monasterio de Santo Domingo El Antiguo** (☎ 925 22 29 30; admission €1.50; ⊙ 11am-1.30pm & 4-7pm Mon-Sat, 4-7pm Sun), dates from the 11th century and includes some of El Greco's early commissions (most are copies). Visible through an iron grating is the crypt and wooden coffin of the painter himself.

Other spots in Toledo where you can see El Greco's works include the **Museo de Santa Cruz** (p241), the *sacristía* of the **Catedral de Toledo** (opposite), and the **Museo Duque de Lerma** (p244).

Jewish Quarter

Near Casa-Museo de El Greco is what was once the *judería* (Jewish quarter). 'Once' because, as a huge plaque in the cathedral proudly proclaims, the bulk of Toledo's Jews, like those elsewhere in Spain, were expelled in 1492. In the centuries prior to this, Toledo's Jews worshipped in 11 synagogues.

Of the two synagogues still standing, the more interesting is **Sinagoga del Tránsito** (☎ 925 22 36 65; Calle de los Reyes Católicos; admission €4.50; ⊙ 10am-2pm & 4-6pm Tue-Sat, 10am-2pm Sun). Built in 1355 by special permission of Pedro I (construction of synagogues was by then prohibited in Christian Spain), its main prayer hall has since been expertly restored. The Mudéjar decoration is particularly striking. From 1492 until 1877 it was variously used as a priory, hermitage

and military barracks. It now houses the **Museo Sefardí** (www.museosefardi.net in Spanish), which gives an insight into the history of Jewish culture in Spain.

A short way north, **Sinagoga de Santa María La Blanca** (☎ 925 22 72 57; Calle de los Reyes Católicos 4; adult/child €1.50/free; ⊙ 10am-5.45pm) is characterised by the horseshoe arches that delineate the five naves – classic Almohade architecture. Originally the upper arches opened onto rooms where women worshipped; the men worshipped down below.

San Juan de los Reyes

A little further north lies one of the city's most worthwhile sights. The Franciscan **monastery and church** (☎ 925 22 38 02; admission €1.50; ⊙ 10am-6pm) is one of the more light-filled churches in Toledo and is notable for its delightful cloisters.

Provocatively built in the heart of the Jewish Quarter, San Juan de los Reyes was founded by Fernando and Isabel to demonstrate the power of the crown over the nobles and the supremacy of the Catholic faith in Spain. The rulers had planned to be buried here, but when they took the greater prize of Granada in 1492 they opted for it purpose-built Capilla Real.

Begun by the Breton architect Juan Güas in 1477, San Juan de los Reyes was finished only in 1606. Throughout the church and two-storey cloister the coat of arms of Fernando and Isabel dominates, and the chains of Christian prisoners liberated in Granada dangle from the walls, most graphically on the northern exterior façade. The prevalent late Flemish Gothic style is enhanced with lavish Isabelline ornament and counterbalanced by unmistakable Mudéjar decoration, especially in the cloister, where typical geometric and vegetal designs stand out.

Muslim Toledo

Though architectural traces of Toledo's medieval Muslim conquerors remain, there's little that's specifically Muslim.

On the northern slopes of town you'll find the **Mezquita de Cristo de la Luz** (admission free; ⊙ closed about 1-4pm), a modest mosque which is nonetheless quite beautiful. Built at the turn of the first millennium, it suffered the usual fate of being converted to a church – as the religious frescoes make clear. The narrow, steep Calle del Cristo de la Luz

CASTILLA-LA MANCHA

continues past the mosque and its charming gardens, and under a gate the Muslims knew as **Bab al-Mardum** (also the original name of the mosque). Entry is possible only when the guardian is around. If you can't see the guardian, try calling at No 11.

Outside the City Walls

Large portions of the old city walls remain intact, and for many people the first sight of old Toledo is the imposing turrets of **Puerta Nueva de Bisagra** (1550), emblazoned with Carlos I's coat of arms, which once greeted visitors coming from Madrid along the Camino Real de Castilla.

Just outside the Puerta Nueva de Bisagra is a shady park that hosts the *mercadillo* (market) every Tuesday. Down the hill to the west is another park, in which you can see the ruins of the former **Circo Romano** (Roman Circus).

Nearby, on the road to Madrid, is the onetime Hospital de Tavera, which now houses the **Museo Duque de Lerma** (☎ 925 22 04 51; Calle de Cardenal Tavera 2; admission €3; ⏲ 10.30am-1.30pm & 3.30-6pm). Built in 1541, it contains an interesting array of art, including some of El Greco's last paintings.

For some of the best views of the city, head over the Puente de Alcántara to the other side of the Río Tajo. Alternatively, you can get the tiny, free **cable ferry** in summer from near Hotel El Diamantista (opposite), and walk up the opposite bank. Scattered about this hinterland are many *cigarrales* (country estates of wealthy *toledanos*).

FESTIVALS & EVENTS

The **Feast of Corpus Christi** falls on the Thursday of the ninth week after Easter and is the most extraordinary event on Toledo's religious calendar – and one of the finest Corpus Christi celebrations in Spain. Several days of festivities reach a crescendo with a solemn procession featuring the massive Custodia de Arfe (see p242).

Easter in Toledo is also marked by several days of solemn processions by masked members of *cofradías* (brotherhoods). In the key days of Holy Week some of these processions take place around midnight.

The **Feast of the Assumption** is on 15 August. On this day of the Sagrario de la Virgen, you can drink of the cathedral's well water, believed by many to have miraculous qualities – the queues for a swig from an earthenware *botijo* (jug) can be equally astonishing.

SLEEPING

Toledo's good range of accommodation is offset by the number of people searching for a bed, especially from Easter to September. Making a reservation is the best bet, especially as wandering up and down the cobblestone lanes with suitcases can be exhausting.

Budget

The following places all have shared bathroom facilities.

HI Albergue Juvenil en San Servando (☎ 925 22 45 54; ralberguesto@jccm.es; r with breakfast under/over 26 €12/15) In a castle just across the Río Tajo, this youth hostel has a better setting than many in Spain and has fine views. A membership card is required.

Pensión Segovia (☎ 925 21 11 24; Calle de Recoletos 2; s/d €15/19) This place has simple rooms with washbasin and has a family atmosphere. The rooms can be very dark, even during the day.

Pensión Castilla (☎ 925 25 63 18; Calle de Recoletos 6; s/d €15/25). Just around the corner from Pensión Segovia, this is a much brighter option although the rooms are similar: tiny spaces with just the bare essentials. The doubles aren't particularly good value.

Pensión Lumbreras (☎ 925 22 15 71; Calle de Juan Labrador 9; s/d €18.70/33.30) This quiet place has clean, unadorned rooms around a tiled courtyard, and good shared bathrooms. One of the singles has cathedral views. The reception is around the corner at Hotel Carlos V.

El Greco (☎ /fax 925 22 00 90; elgreco@retemail.es; camping per person/tent/car €4.50/4.30/4.30, pool adult/child €3.50/2.50; ⚑) Camping is offered 2.5km southwest of town (catch bus No 7), on the road to La Puebla de Montalbán. El Greco has good views of Toledo from the pool.

Circo Romano (☎ 925 22 04 42; Avenida de Carlos III 19; camping per person/tent/car €4.50/4.30/4.30) This camping ground is more conveniently located.

Mid-Range & Top End

All of the following have private bathroom and TV.

Hostal Nuevo Labrador (☎ 925 22 26 20; fax 925 22 93 99; s/d/tr €28/42/55; ⚑) This friendly hotel offers smart-looking but smallish rooms in a good location.

Pensión Santa Úrsula (☎ 925 21 33 25; Calle de Santa Úrsula 14; s/d €29/37.50) Another decent choice, this *pensión* (small, private hotel) has six spacious, comfortable rooms. It is often full, so ring ahead.

Hostal Santo Tomé (☎ 925 22 17 12; www.hostal santotome.com; Calle de Santo Tomé 13; s/d €39/48; 🕮 **P**) A step-up in quality, this friendly place is a great choice, with 10 spacious, spotless rooms that come with satellite TV. The back rooms have leafy views, while the front ones have balconies overlooking the street – both are winners. The location is excellent.

Hotel El Diamantista (☎ 925 25 14 27; fax 925 21 05 86; Plaza de Retama 4; s/d €28.50/44) Way down by the river, this is a good option, but only if you snag a room with a balcony overlooking the Tajo and don't mind a punishing uphill walk into town (or have a car).

La Posada de Manolo (☎ 925 28 22 50; www .laposadademanolo.com; Calle de Sixto Ramón Parro 8; s/d with breakfast from €42/60) You can't get much closer to the cathedral than this thoughtfully designed, well-run hotel, with each floor reflecting one of the 'three cultures' of Toledo. The views of the old town and cathedral from the rooftop terrace are stunning. Highly recommended.

Hostal del Cardenal (☎ 925 22 49 00; www.hostal delcardenal.com; Paseo de Recaredo 24; s €49.80-80.30, d €63.45-102.30) Just down from Puerta Nueva de Bisagra, Hostal del Cardenal is an old mansion loaded with character and set in a beautiful garden. The whole setup is charming, although the rooms are overpriced in high season, which lasts from March to December.

Parador Nacional Conde de Orgaz (☎ 925 22 18 50; s/d €95.80/119.70) High above the southern bank of the Tajo, Toledo's *parador* (luxury state-owned hotel) boasts a classy interior and breathtaking views of the city.

EATING
Restaurants

The cuisine of Toledo is based on simple peasant fare. Partridge, cooked in a variety of fashions, is probably most distinctive of Toledo cuisine. *Carcamusa*, a pork dish, is also typical, as is *cuchifritos*, a potpourri of lamb, tomato and egg cooked in white wine with saffron.

Ñaca Ñaca (Plaza de Zocodover; bocadillos €2-5; 🕑 9am-11pm Mon-Thu, 9-4am Fri, 9am Sat-11pm Sun) What this place lacks in atmosphere it makes up for with good, chunky *bocadillos* (bread rolls with filling) and lengthy opening hours. It's especially good for 3am-bar-hopping hunger when there's nothing else open.

La Boveda (Calle de Tornerías; raciones €2-4.30; 🕑 8am-late) This pleasant no-nonsense bar-café serves tasty snacks and the usual array of drinks; its 1.5L jug of good sangria is an easy €6. It's also a cosy spot for breakfast.

El Trébol (Calle de Santa Fe 1; raciones €4) El Trébol gets a great rap from locals for its consistently good food and relaxed bar atmosphere. Don't leave without trying a *bomba* (crumbed potato stuffed with minced meat).

O'Brien's (Calle de las Armas 12; meals €2.50-6; 🕑 noon-2.30am Sun-Thu, noon-4am Fri & Sat, kitchen closes 9pm) Toledo's Irish bar doesn't serve much that's Spanish, but servings are generous.

Pastucci (☎ 925 25 77 42; Calle de la Sinagoga 10; pizza €6.50-18.50, pasta around €7; 🕑 closed Monday) This excellent Italian place is understandably popular for its 40 varieties of good pizza and filling helpings of pasta.

Bacus (☎ 925 25 01 64; Calle de Travesi Descalzos 1; menú €10; 🕑 9am-11pm Mon-Sat, 9am-5pm Sun) The huge *menú del día* (daily set menu) is the order or the day here and its paella is home-made, unlike those at many other eateries.

Gambrinus (☎ 925 21 44 40; Calle de Santo Tomé; raciones €5-12, mains €7-14, menú €9.50) The outdoor tables here are very popular and it's a good place for a full meal or simply beer and tapas. The *menú* must be eaten inside; the alfresco umbrellas attract pricier meals.

La Abadía (Plaza de San Nicolás 3; menú €10; meals €6-15; 🕑 8am-midnight Sun-Thu, 8-2.30am Fri & Sat) Known more as a bar, La Abadía downstairs restaurant nonetheless serves up excellent typical Toledano dishes. The breakfasts are good and it has a loyal local following.

CASTILLA-LA MANCHA

La Naviera (☎ 925 25 25 32; Calle de la Campana 8; seafood dishes €10-15, menú €15; ⏰ 9am-late Tue-Sun) Diners swoop like seagulls on La Naviera's free tables, ready for the best seafood in Toledo. For an excellent meal, you'll pay at least €20.

Hierbabuena (☎ 925 22 39 24; Calle de Navalpino 45; entrées €9-15, mains €16-21, menú €28.20; ⏰ 1.30-4pm & 9.30pm-midnight Mon-Sat, 1.30-4pm Sun) Hierbabuena is expensive but classy – a considerable step up from the usual traditional fare.

Aurelio (Calle de la Sinagoga 1 & 6 & Plaza del Ayuntamiento 4; mains €13-19; ⏰ 2-4pm & 9.30pm-midnight Mon-Sat, 2-4pm Sun) The three restaurants under this name are among the best of Toledo's expensive restaurants. You'll dine on typical Toledan dishes such as *perdiz estofado* (stewed partridge). You'll eat well for about €30 and it's worth every *céntimo*.

Cafés

The outdoor cafés on Plaza de Zocodover are pleasant for a coffee or drink. La Boveda (p245) also offers alfresco sipping but at slightly cheaper prices. Indoor alternatives include Pícaro (below) and La Abadía (p245).

La Venta del Alma (☎ 925 25 42 45; Carretera de Piedrabuena 35; ⏰ 3.30pm-2am Sun-Thu, 3.30pm-6am Fri & Sat), just outside the city, is a charming old homestead and a very civilised spot to enjoy your brew of choice on the patio. Cross Puente de San Martín and turn left up the hill; it's about 200m up on your left.

For sweeping views and even more expensive drinks, head to the fancy Parador Nacional Conde de Orgaz (p245).

DRINKING & ENTERTAINMENT
Bars & Discotecas

Toledo doesn't have the most dynamic nightlife in Spain, but there are enough bars and discos to keep you cheerful for a couple of days.

Cervecería 1700 (☎ 925 22 25 60; Plaza de las Tendillas 1; ⏰ 10am-11pm Mon-Sat) For a sedate start to your evening, try this relaxed beer bar, with tables spilling out onto the cobblestones, and with decent tapas.

El Pellejito (☎ 925 25 46 16; Calle de las Tendillas 14; ⏰ 9am-late Mon-Sat) Located near Cervecería 1700, and cosier.

Also great in summer are the outdoor tables in the courtyard just off Plaza de Magdalena. Among them are El Corral de Don Diego, Bar-Restaurante Ludeña and Bar el Corralito.

Serving a variety of Spanish and foreign beers are **Lúpulo** (Calle de Aljibillo 4) and, for a cooler crowd, **La Abadía** (see p245). In the streets around La Abadía, particularly Calle de los Alfileritos and Calle de la Sillería, are many of the busier, student-oriented bars; you'll hear them before you see them.

On Calle de Santa Fe there's **El Trébol** (p245) and, at No 10, **La Tabernita**, if you're in the mood for *sidra* (cider) with your tapas. Nearby, on a hidden-away square, is **Enebro** (Plaza de Santiago de los Caballeros), a very popular laid-back spot for all ages. Like the others in the area, you're spared an uphill walk home (or to the next bar) at the end of the night.

Pícaro (☎ 925 22 13 01; Calle de las Cadenas 6; ⏰ 4pm-2.30am Sun-Wed, 4pm-6.30am Thu-Sat) is a popular café-*teatro* (theatre) serving an eclectic range of *copas* (drinks). From Monday to Thursday it's perfect for a quiet beverage, while the weekend gets rowdy, peaking on Friday and Saturday nights when the disco ball starts spinning at 2.30am. Another big drawcard is the live music every Friday night.

Other venues to hunt down for live music are **O'Brien's** (⏰ shows 11pm-late Thu) and **El Último** (☎ 925 21 00 02; Plaza del Colegio de Infantes 4; ⏰ 7.30pm-3am Mon-Sat, shows in winter only) for jazz, blues and soul.

Camelot (Calle del Cristo de la Luz 10), a disco with its name emblazoned above the door in shiny gold, gets the thumbs up from young locals and expats.

For an older crowd, La Venta del Alma (above), mild-mannered during the day, really gets going on Friday and Saturday when people haven't even warmed up by 3am.

Most of the young people finish the night at **Sithons** (Callejón del Lucio; ⏰ late-early), a *discoteca* (disco) for DJs and dancers who just never want to stop.

Theatre & Cinema

The **Teatro Rojas** (☎ 925 22 39 70; Plaza Mayor) often has a rewarding programme of theatre and dance. Tuesday nights are reserved for a 'film club', Toledo's only cinema for films in their original language. Check for weekend kids' matinées.

SHOPPING

For centuries, Toledo was renowned for the excellence of its swords, and you'll see them for sale everywhere you look. Another big seller in Toledo is anything decorated with *damasquinado* (damascene), a fine encrustation of gold or silver in Arab artistic tradition – choose from sword sheaths, plates, lighters etc. Another Arab bequest is the art of ceramics, which the whole region churns out in all imaginable forms.

Toledo is also famed for its *mazapán* (marzipan), which every shop seems to sell regardless of the quality. The Santo Tomé brand is reputable and there are several of its outlets in town, including one on Zocodover. Even the local nuns get in on the marzipan act – two places to try are **Convento Santa Úrsula** (11am-1.30pm & 4-7pm), around the corner from Museo de Taller del Moro, and **Monasterio de Santo Domingo El Antiguo** (11am-1.30pm & 4-7pm), behind the church of the same name (see p243).

GETTING THERE & AWAY

For most major destinations, you'll need to backtrack to Madrid.

Bus

From Toledo's **bus station** (925 22 36 41) buses depart for Madrid every half-hour from about 6am to 10pm daily (8.30am to 11.30pm Sunday and holidays). Direct buses (€4, one hour) run every hour; other services (1½ hours) go via villages along the way. Regular buses go to Alcázar de San Juan (€3.80, 1¼ hours, nine daily), Consuegra (€3.85, one hour) and Talavera de la Reina (€5.20, 1¼ hours), while occasional buses do the run to El Toboso (€6.85, two hours) and Guadalajara (€7, 2¼ hours). There are also services on weekdays and Sunday to Albacete (€11.50, 2¾ hours), Ciudad Real (€6.40, 1½ hours) and Cuenca (€9.10, 2¼ hours).

Car & Motorcycle

The N401 connects Toledo with Madrid. If you want the A4 Autovía de Andalucía, the main motorway running south from Madrid to Córdoba and Seville, take the N400 for Aranjuez. The N403 heads northwest for Ávila and continues as the N501 for Salamanca.

Train

Built in 1920 in neo-Mudéjar style, Toledo's **train station** (925 22 30 99) is a pretty introduction to the city. Trains run every couple

of hours to Madrid's Atocha station (€4.75, one hour), and a new AVE (high-speed) service is due to open in mid-2005.

GETTING AROUND

You won't need wheels to explore the cobblestone laneways of Toledo's old town, but buses do circulate through it and connect with outlying suburbs. Handy buses run between Plaza de Zocodover and the bus station (No 5) and train station (Nos 5 and 6).

A fun way to toot in and around Toledo is aboard the **Zocotren** (adult/child €3.75/2.30; 11am-9pm), a 50-minute nonstop train trip. It departs from Zocodover on the hour from October to March, every half-hour April to September. There are also night rides (after 9pm, depending on demand) throughout the year.

A **remonte peatonal** (escalator; 7am-10pm Mon-Fri, 8am-10pm Sat & Sun), which starts near the Puerta de Alfonso VI and ends near the Monasterio de Santo Domingo El Antiguo, is another way you can minimise the steep uphill climb.

There's a taxi rank just south of Plaza de Zocodover and another at the bus station, or you can call a **taxi** (925 25 50 50).

AROUND TOLEDO

CARRANQUE

Since 1983, archaeologists at **Carranque** (925 59 20 14; admission free; 9am-9pm Tue-Sun 15 Apr-15 Sep; 10am-6pm Tue-Sat 16 Sep-14 Apr) have been excavating what they believe to be the foundations of a late-4th-century Roman basilica, which would make it the oldest in Spain. The skeletal remains of Roman villas and temple-fountains are among the site's other highlights, while the remains of a 12th-century monastery with some valuable mosaics are also undergoing excavation and study. There's a small interpretation centre and museum on the site. Check with the tourist office in Toledo for details. Carranque is just off the N401 highway some 35km north of Toledo.

CASTLES

The area around Toledo is littered with castles in varying states of upkeep. But you'd be hard-pressed to reach most of them without a car.

Some 20km southeast of Toledo along the CM400 is the ruined Arab castle of **Almonacid de Toledo**, which rises up in front of you. Some legends suggest El Cid lived here, but the lonely ruins have long been abandoned. A few kilometres further down the road is a smaller castle in the village of **Mascaraque**. Continue on to Mora then take the CM410 for 10km to the village of **Orgaz**, which has a modest 15th-century **castle** (☿ every 2nd Wed Apr-Nov) in good nick.

Around 30km southwest of Toledo, the hulking, isolated ruin of **Castillo de Montalbán** stands majestically over the Río Torcón valley. This evocative castle is believed to have been erected by 12th-century Knights Templar. Officially, it's open from May to January, but there's little to stop you wandering around at any time. To get there from Toledo, take the CM401 to the CM403 junction and turn right towards La Puebla de Montalbán. Ten kilometres up the road you'll see signs pointing to the castle.

The town of **Escalona**, 52km northwest of Toledo on the N403, boasts a castle ruin of Arab origin, in a pretty location on the banks of the Río Alberche.

THE WEST

TALAVERA DE LA REINA
pop 77,142
Talavera de la Reina, with old city walls and ceramic façades, is worth a stop if you're in the area. Overrun by the Muslim Almoravid dynasty in the 12th century, Talavera was later the birthplace of Fernando de Rojas, whose *Celestina* (published in 1499) is judged by some as Europe's first great novel. In 1809, the town was the scene of a key battle between the Duke of Wellington's forces and the French.

These days, Talavera has settled into comfortable provinciality and has long been famous for its ceramic work, which adorns many buildings around town. The finest example is the façade of the **Teatro Victoria**, just off Plaza del Padre Juan de Mariana.

Within the old city walls is **Museo Ruiz de Luna** (☎ 925 80 01 49; Calle de San Agustín el Viejo s/n; admission €0.60; ☿ 10am-2pm & 4-6.30pm Tue-Sat, 10am-2pm Sun), which houses a good collection of local ceramics, much of which dates from the 16th and 17th centuries. To make

your own purchases, the best places are in the ceramics factories and shops along the road leading north to the A5 motorway. The **tourist office** (☎ 925 82 63 22; Ronda del Cañello s/n; ☿ 10.30am-1.30pm & 4-6pm Mon-Sat, 10.30am-12.30pm Sun) is east of the old city walls.

There's not a huge range of accommodation, but **Hostal Edan** (☎ 925 80 69 89; Paseo de Extremadura 24; s/d with bathroom €15/30) is a popular choice for its simple, clean rooms; reservations are recommended on weekends.

The bus station is in the town centre. Regular buses between Madrid and Badajoz stop here and up to nine per day go to Toledo (€5.20, 1¼ hours). Buses also head to Cáceres, Mérida, Oropesa, Plasencia and Trujillo.

AROUND TALAVERA DE LA REINA
The charming village of **Oropesa**, 34km west of Talavera, makes a far better overnight stop than Talavera. Its hill-top 14th-century **castle** (admission €1.50; ☿ 10am-2pm & 4-7pm Tue-Sun) looks north across the plains to the mighty Sierra de Gredos and also hosts an elegant **parador** (☎ 925 43 00 00; s/d €77.70/97). There's also **La Hostelería** (☎ /fax 925 43 08 75; www.lahosteriadeoropesa.com; Plaza del Palacio 5; s/d with bathroom & breakfast €45/55) just below the castle, which has attractive, light-filled rooms with beamed ceilings.

From Talavera, buses do the trip here three or four times daily. If you're driving, follow the signs to the A5 motorway to Extremadura or Badajoz, and don't be tempted to take the turnoff for Torralba de Oropesa – continue on.

By the Río Tajo just 14km south of Oropesa sits **El Puente del Arzobispo**, another well-known centre for ceramics with showrooms galore. The multiarched bridge after which the town is named – and over which you're most likely to drive on your way out of town – was built in the 14th century.

MONTES DE TOLEDO
Beginning as the low foothills that lie south of Toledo astride the road to Ciudad Real, the Montes de Toledo rise westwards towards Extremadura. Exploring the Montes takes you into the heart of some of the most sparsely populated country of Spain's interior, and a long way off the tourist routes. Long stretches of the region's roads are lined by either patches of terracotta earth dotted

with olive trees or green fields covered in yellow wildflowers during spring. Most towns are served by the occasional bus – usually once daily on weekdays – from Toledo.

If you're travelling by car, the most straightforward route from Toledo is the CM401, which skirts the northern slopes of the Montes. Eleven kilometres short of Navahermosa, a trail leads south to **Embalse del Torcón**, a popular lakeshore picnic spot.

Beyond Navahermosa you have several options for branching south. Some of the more heavily wooded areas offer gorgeous vistas, and apart from the odd tiny pueblo, you'll hardly see a soul. One longish route that gives a taste of the area would see you dropping south off the CM401 at Los Navalmorales. Take the CM4155 towards Los Navalucillos, and keep heading south past seemingly deserted villages until you hit a T-junction after 48km. Turning right (west) you wind 35km to the northern reaches of the huge **Embalse de Cijara**, part of a chain of reservoirs fed by the Río Guadiana and actually part of Extremadura. After the tiny village of Cijara, swing north towards **Puerto Rey**, a mountain pass from where you can branch off west along a back road to the EX102 and the last curvy stretch towards Guadalupe (p817).

THE SOUTH

CIUDAD REAL
pop 64,794

Although once the royal counterpart of Toledo, Ciudad Real is only worth a fleeting visit.

Founded by Castilian King Alfonso X El Sabio (the Wise) in 1255 to check the power of the Knights of Calatrava, based in nearby Almagro, Ciudad Real quickly became an important provincial capital, finally eclipsing Almagro in the 18th century.

Information

The **tourist office** (☎ 926 20 00 37; Calle de Alarcos 21; ⏱ 10am-2pm & 4-7pm Mon-Sat, 10am-2pm Sun) has a reasonable stock of information on the province. The **main post office** (Plaza de la Constitución) is northeast of the tourist office.

Sights & Activities

Coming from the north, you'll enter Ciudad Real by the **Puerta de Toledo** (1328), the

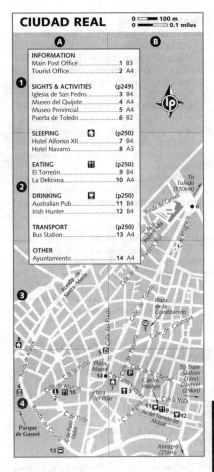

CIUDAD REAL

0 — 100 m
0 — 0.1 miles

INFORMATION	
Main Post Office	1 B3
Tourist Office	2 A4

SIGHTS & ACTIVITIES	(p249)
Iglesia de San Pedro	3 B4
Museo del Quijote	4 A4
Museo Provincial	5 A4
Puerta de Toledo	6 B2

SLEEPING	(p250)
Hotel Alfonso XII	7 B4
Hotel Navarro	8 A3

EATING	(p250)
El Torreón	9 B4
La Deliciosa	10 A4

DRINKING	(p250)
Australian Pub	11 B4
Irish Hunter	12 B4

TRANSPORT	(p250)
Bus Station	13 A4

OTHER	
Ayuntamiento	14 A4

last remaining gate of the original eight, built in Mudéjar style by Alfonso XI.

The **Museo Provincial** (Calle del Prado 4; admission free; ⏱ 10am-2pm & 5-8pm Tue-Sat, 10am-2pm Sun) has exhibits of archaeological finds and an art collection covering the past four centuries. For Quijote fans, the one-of-a-kind **Museo del Quijote** (Ronda de Alarcos 1; admission free; ⏱ 10am-2pm & 6-9pm Mon-Sat, 10am-2pm Sun) has a Cervantes library stocked with hundreds of Don Quijote books, including some in Esperanto and Braille, and others dating back to 1724. You'll have to understand Spanish to get the most out of the inventive audiovisual displays.

Of the swag of churches to be seen, the most striking is the 14th-century Gothic **Iglesia de San Pedro**, the work of Gil de Siloé.

CASTILLA-LA MANCHA

Sleeping & Eating

Hotel Navarro (☎ 926 21 43 77; Avenida de Pío XII 16; s/d with bathroom €28/40) About 1km northwest of the bus station, Hotel Navarro is good value, with large, bright rooms decked out in matching pine furniture.

Hotel Alfonso XII (☎ 926 22 42 81; Calle de Carlos Vázquez 8; d with bathroom Mon-Thu €72, Fri-Sun €58) Not far from Plaza Mayor, this is an up-market place where old façade meets renovated interior with pleasing results. Modern rooms come with all the swish trimmings.

La Deliciosa (Calle de Alarcos 11; ⏰ 8.30am-11pm) Located near the tourist office, this is a handy spot for breakfast, *bocadillos* and good coffee.

The handful of café-bars along Calle de Palma serve some of the best-sized tapas in town. But for most of your dining and drinking pleasures, head for Avenida del Torreón del Alcázar and the parallel Calle de los Hidalgos. The former is lined with eateries such as **El Torreón** (Avenida del Torreón del Alcázar 7), which specialises in game.

Drinking

You'll find bars such as **Australian Pub** (Avenida del Torreón del Alcázar) and **Irish Hunter** (Avenida del Torreón del Alcázar) near El Torreón. On Calle de los Hidalgos you can nibble tapas and sip *cervezas* (beers) in bars, then dance all night at its string of *discotecas*.

Getting There & Away

BUS

The **bus station** (☎ 926 21 13 42) is southwest of the town centre. Up to three daily buses head to Albacete (€12.15, 2¾ hours) and Toledo (€6.40, 1½ hours), and five per day head off to Madrid (€9.85, 2½ hours). Most surrounding towns, including Almagro (€1.50, 30 minutes, up to five daily), can be reached by bus.

TRAIN

You'll find the **train station** (☎ 926 22 02 02) east of the town centre. The bulk of trains linking Madrid with Andalucía call in at Ciudad Real. There are regular departures to Madrid (from €17.10, one hour) and Córdoba (from €21, one hour), while there are less regular departures for Valencia (from €21, five hours, two daily) and southeast to Almagro (€1.50, 30 minutes).

Getting Around

Local bus No 5 swings past both the train and bus stations bound for the town centre; catch it from Plaza del Pilar when you're leaving town.

CIUDAD REAL PROVINCE

Almagro

pop 8397

Almagro is a delight. Though it may not have scored first prize in the struggle for local supremacy with Ciudad Real, it has retained a charm long lost in its competitor. De facto medieval capital of what today is still known as the Campo de Calatrava, Almagro underwent a unique face-lift in the 16th century after the arrival of several German families, including the Fuggers of Augsburg, bankers to Spain's Carlos I. It's largely to them and their successors that Almagro's dark-green porticoed **Plaza Mayor** owes its present distinctive appearance.

INFORMATION

The **tourist office** (☎ 926 86 07 17; Plaza Mayor 1; ⏰ 10am-2pm & 5-8pm Tue-Fri, 10am-2pm & 5-7pm Sat, 11am-2pm Sun), in the *ayuntamiento* (town hall), has information about a number of distinguished buildings around town. It also has a helpful accommodation and restaurant guide.

SIGHTS & ACTIVITIES

Opening onto the plaza is the wonderful **Corral de Comedias** (Plaza Mayor 18; adult/concession €2/1.50; ⏰ 10am-2pm & 5-8pm Tue-Fri, 10am-2pm & 5-7pm Sat, 11am-2pm & 5-7pm Sun), a 17th-century open-air theatre built of wood and surrounded on three sides by enchanting balconies. It's still used for performances, especially during July's **Festival Internacional de Teatro Clásico** (see www.festivaldealmagro.com for dates). This is nicely complemented by the **Museo Nacional de Teatro** (Calle de Gran Maestre 2; adult/concession €2/1.50; ⏰ 10am-2pm & 4-7pm Tue-Fri, 10am-2pm & 4-6pm Sat, 11am-2pm Sun), just across the square, with exhibits on Spanish theatre from the 18th century in rooms around a restored courtyard.

SLEEPING

Almagro has some great accommodation. The following places all come with private bathrooms.

Hospedería Almagro (☎ 926 88 20 87; fax 926 88 21 22; Calle de Ejido de Calatrava s/n; s/d from €19.55/22.55)

Housed in a 15th-century convent within walking distance of Plaza Mayor, this excellent place has modern, spacious rooms and is fabulous value.

La Posada de Almagro (☎ /fax 926 26 12 01; www .laposadadealmagro.com; Calle de Gran Maestre 5; s/d from €36/55) Just around the corner from Plaza Mayor, La Posada is a terrific choice. The rooms have a touch of character and the location is unrivalled. If you're planning to come in July, you'll need to reserve months in advance. The only drawback is that it can be difficult to sleep in some rooms when the restaurant's full.

Parador (☎ 926 86 01 00; almagro@parador.es; Ronda de San Francisco 13; s/d €90.65/113.30) In a spruced-up convent in a quiet but reasonably central corner of town, this *parador* has a luxurious, old-world charm.

EATING

There are several cafés and bars on Plaza Mayor, most with outdoor tables, and they all serve the usual suspects (*raciones, platos* etc) at the usual Plaza Mayor prices.

Bar Las Nieves (☎ 926 86 12 90; Plaza Mayor 52) This is one of the better Plaza Mayor eateries.

El Corregidor (☎ 926 86 06 48; Calle de Jerónimo Ceballos 2; meals around €42; ☺ closed Mon except Jul) Try this place for fine dining. It does high-quality *manchegan* cooking.

Calatrava (Calle de Bolaños 3; menú €9.30) Those on a tight budget should head here. West of the centre, Calatrava doesn't look like much but it serves decent food.

Both La Posada de Almagro and the *parador* have good restaurants.

GETTING THERE & AWAY

Two trains go daily to Madrid (€11.90, 2¾ hours), with up to four to Ciudad Real (€1.95, 15 minutes) and one daily to Valencia (€20.10, five hours); for destinations to the south, you'll need to change in Ciudad Real. Buses also run reasonably often to Ciudad Real (€1.50, 30 minutes), but there are none on Sunday.

Castillo de Calatrava

About 30km south of Almagro, the brooding walls of the castle-and-monastery complex of **Castillo de Calatrava** (Calatrava La Nueva; admission free; ☺ 10am-2pm & 4-7pm Tue-Sun) commands magnificent views across the sierra of the same name. The complex was once

---

THE WINES OF VALDEPEÑAS

Standing at the exact midpoint between Madrid and Córdoba, the large and otherwise uninviting town of Valdepeñas offers weary travellers one (and only one) very good reason to break up the journey. Surrounding the town is what some experts believe to be the largest expanse of vineyards in the world, although true aficionados of the humble grape argue that quantity does not easily translate into quality. There's an element of truth to this view – Valdepeñas has historically been to the mass market what La Rioja is to the quality end of the market (see the boxed text In Search of the Finest Drop p485).

That said, things are changing. You're still more likely to come across Valdepeñas wines in the cheap, cask variety than served in Spain's finest restaurants, but some of the Valdepeñas *bodegas* (cellars) have begun to make inroads into the quality end of the market. Doubtless you'll want to form your own opinion; some of the town's *bodegas* offer wine-tasting. They line the main street into town, but the best are north of town on the road to Madrid.

---

a forward base of the medieval order of knights that long controlled this frontier area of La Mancha during the Reconquista. Even if it's closed, it merits a visit for the site and view alone. From Calzada de Calatrava, it's 7km southwest along the CR504 and is accessible only with your own vehicle.

Parque Nacional de Las Tablas de Daimiel

The reedy lakes of Las Tablas, 11km north of Daimiel, are no great inspiration, but an early morning stroll here in spring or autumn can be profitable for the bird-watcher. The park's **tourist centre** (☺ 8am-dusk) has information, but there's no public transport to the park.

Parque Natural de las Lagunas de Ruidera

A green patch in the middle of parched Castilla-La Mancha is the Parque Natural de las Lagunas de Ruidera, about halfway between Ciudad Real and Albacete on the N430 highway. Surrounding a series of 15 small lakes, with the odd waterfall and diverse bird life, it's a favoured summer retreat for hot and bothered Castilians.

The **tourist office** (🕑 10am-2pm & 4-6pm Wed-Sat, 10am-2pm Sun) is in the nearby town of Ruidera.

Alonso Quijano – Albergue Juvenil (☎ 967 55 80 24; dm under/over 26 €9/11) is a spotless HI youth hostel on Laguna Colgada. Meals are available and a membership card is required.

Camping Los Batanes (☎ 926 69 90 76; camping per person/tent/car €3.30/3.15/3.15, d bungalow €42) is another good option, further along on Laguna Redondilla.

You really need wheels to get into and around the park.

Villanueva de los Infantes
pop 5839

About 30km east of Valdepeñas along the CM415 to Alcaraz lies Villanueva de los Infantes, the fruit of a repopulation campaign in La Mancha as the Muslims fell back into Andalucía after the Battle of Las Navas de Tolosa in 1212. The **Plaza Mayor**, with its deep ochre-coloured buildings and heavy wooden balconies, is one of its most striking features.

On the square stands **Iglesia de San Andrés**, where the 16th-century poet Francisco Gómez Quevedo y Villegas is buried. Like Almagro, Villanueva is studded with the houses of the old nobles and deserves a wander. There's a **tourist office** (☎ 926 36 13 21; 🕑 10am-2pm & 5-8pm Mon-Sat, 10am-2pm Sun) on Plaza Mayor.

Hospedería El Buscón Quevedo (☎ /fax 926 36 17 88; Calle Frailes 1; s/d with bathroom from €40/50 Sun-Thu, €28/45 Fri & Sat), a lovely former convent four streets south of Plaza Mayor, has some good-value rooms. Quevedo spent his last days here, and his room is set up as though he is about to return. Buses head west to Ciudad Real.

SOUTHEAST TO ALBACETE

The sweeping, windswept plains of southeastern Castilla-La Mancha may not offer Spain's prettiest countryside but this is Don Quijote country. Once you get off the highway, it's a land of ancient windmills and quiet villages.

Consuegra

Set in classic La Mancha country, Consuegra has some of the finest *molinos de viento*

(windmills) in the area. Huddled below a hill topped by a 13th-century **castle** (admission €2; 🕑 9.30am-1.30pm & 3.30-5.30pm), Consuegra once belonged to the Knights of Malta; a few rooms in the castle have been done up to give a good indication of how the knights would have lived. A dozen restored windmills flank the castle, which makes for a memorable sight.

The **tourist office** (☎ 925 47 57 31; 🕑 9am-2pm & 4.30-7pm Mon-Fri, from 10.30am Sat & Sun) is in the Bolero mill (they all have names), which is the first you come to as the road winds up from the town.

Of the town's two hotels, **Hotel Las Provincias** (☎ 925 48 03 00; s/d with bathroom €26/46), on the Toledo–Alcázar de San Juan highway, is the better option.

There are regular weekday buses (three on weekends) running between Consuegra and Toledo (€3.85, one hour), and up to three buses daily to Madrid.

Campo de la Criptana & Around

The windmills of Don Quijote fame are the main feature of this quiet, pleasant town all dressed in white. The windmills sit atop the town's summit and their proximity to the surrounding houses marks an interesting contrast with Consuegra. The **tourist office** (☎ 926 56 22 31; 🕑 10am-2pm & 5-8pm Tue-Sat, 10am-2pm Sun) is in the Poyatos mill.

There are a few small *hostales* (cheap hotels) in town, including the simple but adequate **Hostal Ego's** (☎ 926 56 43 04; Calle de García León 51; s/d with bathroom €25/44), which is about a 500m walk from Plaza Mayor.

Campo de la Criptana is served by the odd train and regional bus, but options are greater 8km away in Alcázar de San Juan. About four buses run daily between the two towns, but none on Sunday.

Alcázar

Apart from the 18th-century **Iglesia de Santa María** (it's thought Cervantes was baptised here), there's nothing much to draw you to Alcázar but its transport options.

Hostal Aldonza (☎ 926 54 15 54; Calle de Alvarez Guerra 28; s/d with bathroom €18/30), near the train station, has clean, quaint rooms with TV.

Trains leave from here for destinations throughout the country, including Albacete, Alicante, Barcelona, Ciudad Real, Jaén, Madrid, Málaga, Seville and Valencia. There

IN SEARCH OF DON QUIJOTE

Part of the charm of a visit to Castilla-La Mancha is the chance to track down the real-life locations into which Miguel de Cervantes placed his picaresque hero. The *molinos de vientos* are the most obvious places to start, for it was these 'monstrous giants' that so haunted El Quijote and with which he tried to join battle. Although Consuegra's are the most attractive, those that are mentioned specifically in Cerventes' novel are the windmills of **Campo de la Criptana** (opposite) and **Mota del Cuervo** (below).

But there was more than windmills to Cervantes' epic tale. Don Quijote and his long-suffering sidekick, Sancho Panza, dined in the castle of **Belmonte** (below), and it was in **El Toboso** (below) that the knight discovered the lovely Dulcinea. Other towns that can claim a Don Quijote lineage include **Herencia** (11km northwest of Puerto Lapice off the A4), where the hero killed an innocent monk, and **Quintanar de la Orden** (17km northwest of Mota del Cuervo), where the knight had one of his first encounters.

Before you get too zealous, however, remember that Don Quijote's tales of disaster seem to rub off on those who would seek him. A multimillion dollar film about the mythical knight, supposed to star Johnny Depp and Jean Rochefort, never made it to the screen, and Cervantes himself, some four centuries earlier, was imprisoned, sold into slavery and lost his left hand in battle.

---

are occasional buses that serve Belmonte, Cuenca and Toledo.

El Toboso

Another stop on the Quijote trail is **El Toboso**, a 12km detour off the N420. This pretty town is the literary home of Dulcinea, and in her honour stands the **Casa-Museo de Dulcinea** (admission €0.60; ◷ 10am-2pm & 4-6.30pm Tue-Sat, 10am-2pm Sun). There's a small **tourist office** (◷ 10am-2pm & 4-7pm Tue-Sat, 10am-2pm Sun) in the centre. There are three direct buses every day to Madrid (€6.35, two hours).

There are more pretty windmills at **Mota del Cuervo**, 29km northeast of Campo de la Criptana, at the junction of the N301.

Belmonte

About 25km northeast of Mota del Cuervo, Belmonte has one of the better-preserved Castilian castles. Locals love telling visitors that the village is the birthplace of the well-known poet Fray Luis de León. Set on a low knoll above the pretty village, the 15th-century **castle** (adult/child €2/1; ◷ 10.30am-1pm & 4-6pm Tue-Sun Sep-Mar, 5-7pm Tue-Sun Apr-Aug), with its six round towers, was for a while home to France's Empress Eugénie after her husband Napoleon III lost the French throne in 1871. Also well worth a visit is **Iglesia Colegial de San Bartolomé** (Colegiata), which has an impressive altarpiece.

La Muralla (☎ 967 17 10 45; s/d with bathroom €12/24) is the town's cheapest place to stay and has comfortable rooms, while **Palacio**

Buenavista Hospedería (☎ 967 18 75 80; fax 967 18 75 88; Calle José Antonio González 2; s/d with bathroom & breakfast from €30.90/45), just near Colegiata, is a lovely place, up a notch from La Muralla. Rooms are good value and have balconies; try to get one with a castle view.

By bus from Belmonte, you can get to Alcázar de San Juan and Cuenca.

ALBACETE
pop 149,331

This dull provincial city would never win a beauty contest, but it is a transport hub and a place to pause between Spain's central plains and the Mediterranean *costas* (coast).

If you're passing through, the town's **cathedral** is appealing enough with its four Ionic columns. On a hot summer's afternoon, the leafy **Parque de Abelardo Sánchez** (Calle de Tesifonte Gallego), home of the **Museo Provincial** (admission €1.20; ◷ 10am-2pm & 4.30-7pm Mon-Sat, 10am-2pm Sun), offers some respite. The **tourist office** (☎ 967 58 05 22; Calle del Tinte 2; ◷ 10am-2pm & 4.30-6.30pm Mon-Fri, to 6pm Sat, to 3pm Sun) should be able to muster more enthusiasm for the town than we can.

Hostal Atienza (☎ 967 21 05 95; Calle de Carmen 49; s/d with shared bathroom €16/27, with private bathroom €22/33) About five minutes' walk north of the cathedral, this place has a good selection of large, clean rooms with air-con and TV.

For a whole lot more comfort and charm, the **parador** (☎ 967 24 53 21; s/d with bathroom €70/87.50) is possibly the highlight of the town.

The bus and train stations are next to each other at the northeastern end of town.

Buses serve many major cities around the country. There are up to six buses per day to Cuenca (€8.70, two hours), up to two to Toledo (€11.50, 2¾ hours, none on Saturday) and at least daily weekday services to Almansa, Chinchilla de Monte Aragón and Ruidera. Trains head to Alicante (€11, 1½ hours, up to 11 daily), Ciudad Real (€11.90, 2¾ hours, two daily), Madrid (€15.75, three hours, hourly), Murcia (€20.50, two hours, five daily) and Valencia (€22, 1½ hours, up to 15 daily).

AROUND ALBACETE

Just off the N430 motorway to Valencia, a restored fortress overlooks **Chinchilla de Monte Aragón**, a whitewashed village with a beautiful Plaza Mayor. About 60km further on, a square-turreted castle built by the Muslims stands high above the town of **Almansa**. Both towns are served by bus from Albacete.

Río Júcar

Northeast of Albacete, the deep, tree-filled gorge of the Río Júcar is a wonderful detour. About halfway along the CM3218, the breathtaking town of **Alcalá del Júcar** comes into view as you descend via hairpin turns. Its restored 15th-century **castle**, an unmistakable landmark, towers over the houses that spill down the steep bank of the Júcar gorge. At the foot of the town there are several spots where you can have a drink or long lunch while admiring the views above.

There are a few very well priced hotels, including **Hostal El Júcar** (☎ 967 47 30 55; Calle Batán 1; s/d with bathroom & breakfast €22/42) and **Hostal Rambla** (☎ 967 47 40 64; Paseo Los Robles 2; s/d with bathroom & breakfast €25/37). Both have attached restaurants; the one at Hostal Rambla does great chargrilled meats served at outdoor tables.

For an alternative route back to Albacete, a small back road takes you through the gorge, which has houses cut into the cliff-face. The more picturesque towns are at the western end, where the gorge narrows: **Calzada de Vergara**, **Cubas** and **Alcozarejos**.

Sierra de Alcaraz

Stretching across the southern strip of Albacete province, the cool, green peaks of the Sierra de Alcaraz, laced with small, intensively farmed plots and dotted with villages, offer a great escape from the dusty plains around Albacete.

The prettiest town in the area is **Alcaraz**, with a lovely Plaza Mayor and overlooked by the skeletal remains of castle walls. The most scenic countryside is to be found along the CM412, particularly between **Puerto de las Crucetas** (1300m) and **Elche de la Sierra**, although a detour to **Vianos** is also worthwhile. Apart from in the wooded hills and on some craggy rock formations, donkey-mounted shepherds still watch over their small flocks of sheep in the more remote corners of the sierra.

The largest choice of accommodation is in leafy Riópar where **Hotel Riópar** (☎ /fax 967 43 51 91, Avenida Choperas 2; s/d with bathroom €32.60/65.20) is the most comfortable choice. You could also try **Hostal Los Bronces** (☎ 967 43 50 33; Calle de Haza de San Luis 2; s/d with bathroom €25/40), and **Camping Río Mundo** (person/tent/car €4.10/4/4.10) is 6km east of town. In Elche de la Sierra, **Hotel Moreno** (☎ 967 41 02 62; fax 967 41 04 38; Calle de Bolea 44; s/d with bathroom €30/40) is your best bet.

The odd bus gets to some of these towns, but you'd be better off with a vehicle – and good hiking boots.

THE NORTHEAST

CUENCA

pop 46,668

Cuenca rises up from the parched countryside of Castilla-La Mancha, and is as enchanting a spot as any Tuscan hill-town. Once you escape the nondescript new town, up the hill lies another world: its most emblematic sights are the *casas colgadas*, the hanging houses of Cuenca, which perch above the deep gorges that surround the town.

History

Probably inhabited in Roman times, Cuenca remained obscure until Muslim occupation. Fortified by one Ismail bin Dilnun early in the 11th century, the city became a flourishing textile centre. The Christians took their time conquering the place, and it fell only in 1177 to Alfonso VIII. Like much of Spain's interior, 16th-century Cuenca slipped once again into decline and hardship, something from which it only began to recover during the 20th century.

Orientation

Cuenca is compact and easily negotiable. The old town is home to all the sights and occupies the narrow hill at the northeastern end of town, between the river gorges of the Júcar and Huécar. At the foot of the hill down which the old town tumbles, the new town spreads out to the south. Near Cuenca's southern outskirts (a 10-minute walk from the foot of the hill), the train and bus stations are almost opposite each other, southwest of Calle de Fermín Caballero. The nominal centre of town surrounds Parque de San Julián.

Information

EMERGENCY
Cruz Roja (☎ 969 22 22 00) For ambulances.
Police (☎ 091)

INTERNET ACCESS
Cyber Viajero (Avenida de la República Argentina 3; ☽ 10am-2pm & 5-11pm Mon-Sat; per hr €1.75)

MEDICAL SERVICES
Hospital de la Luz Virgen (☎ 969 17 99 00) Off Avenida de la Cruz Roja.

MONEY
There are banks in the new town, especially around Calle de la Carretería.

POST
Post office (cnr Calle del Parque de San Julián & Calle del Dr Fleming)

TELEPHONE
Telephone office (Paseo de San Antonio 42)

TOURIST INFORMATION
Tourist office (☎ 969 23 21 19; turismo@ayuntocuenca .org; Calle de Alfonso VIII 2; ☽ 9.30am-2pm & 4-6.30pm Mon-Sat, 9.30am-2.30pm Sun)

Catedral

The main façade of Cuenca's **cathedral** (admission free; ☽ 9am-2pm & 4-7pm) is hardly Spain's finest – a pastiche of unfortunate 16th-century Gothic experimentation and 20th-century restoration. Built on the site of a mosque, the relatively unadorned nave dates back to the early 13th century, although other elements, such as the apse, were constructed in the mid-15th century. The cathedral's aesthetics are redeemed somewhat by the cheery, modern stained-glass windows and a small museum, the **Tesoro Catedralicio** (☎ 969 21 20 11; admission €1.50; ☽ 11am-2pm & 4-6pm Tue-Sat, 11am-2pm Sun), which is worth the entry fee.

Casas Colgadas

The most striking element of medieval Cuenca, the **casas colgadas** jut out precariously over the steep defile of the Huécar. First built in the 16th century, the houses with their characteristic layers of wooden balconies seem to emerge from the rock as if an extension of the cliffs. The finest restored examples now house an upmarket restaurant (Mesón Casas Colgadas; p257) and an art museum (Museo de Arte Abstracto Español; below), which make excellent use of what was once an economical adaptation of limited living space. For the best views of the *casas colgadas*, cross the **Puente de San Pablo** footbridge, or walk to the northernmost tip of the old town where a *mirador* (lookout) offers unparalleled views over the town.

Museums

Old Cuenca can feel like a medieval museum, but there are some good museums to provide a focus for your wanderings.

Cuenca is not just a place to enjoy ancient history. The **Museo de Arte Abstracto Español** (☎ 969 21 29 83; museocuenca@expo.march.es; admission €3; ☽ 11am-2pm & 4-6pm Tue-Fri, 11am-2pm & 4-8pm Sat, 11am-2.30pm Sun) is a superb exhibition space, occupying one of the *casas colgadas* and with a fine *artesonado*. Begun as an attempt by Fernando Zobel to unite the works of his fellow artists from the 1950s Generación Abstracta, the museum's constantly evolving displays include works by Chillida, Millares and Sempere. A range of art appreciation courses is also run.

Another innovative museum is the **Museo de Las Ciencias** (Science Museum; admission €1.20; ☽ 10am-2pm & 4-7pm Tue-Sat, 10am-2pm Sun), where displays range from a time machine to the development of the human species and a study of the resources of Castilla-La Mancha. There are plenty of interactive gadgets to keep visitors of all ages happy, as well as a **planetarium** (admission €1.20).

The **Museo de Cuenca** (☎ 969 21 30 69; Calle del Obispo Valero 6; adult/senior & child €1.20/free; ☽ 10am-2pm & 4-7pm Tue-Sat, 11am-2pm Sun) houses a modest archaeological collection from the Cuenca area in which Roman artefacts from classical Hispania are the highlight.

Almost opposite, the **Museo Diocesano** (☎ 969 22 42 10; Calle del Obispo Valero 3; adult/senior & child €1.80/free; ☽ 11am-2pm & 4-7pm Tue-Sat, 11am-2pm Sun) offers the usual collection of

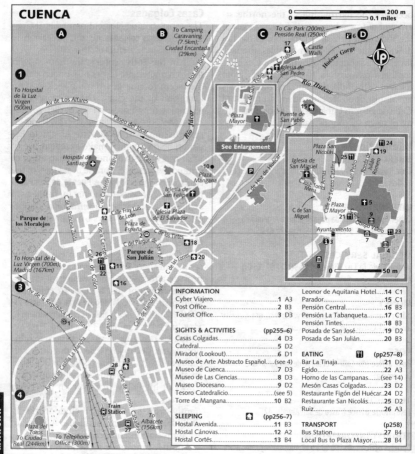

CUENCA

INFORMATION		Leonor de Aquitania Hotel.....**14** C1
Cyber Viajero.....................................**1** A3		Parador......................................**15** C1
Post Office...................................**2** B3		Pensión Central.......................**16** B3
Tourist Office..............................**3** D3		Pensión La Tabanqueta.........**17** C1
		Pensión Tintes..........................**18** B3
SIGHTS & ACTIVITIES	(pp255–6)	Posada de San José..................**19** D2
Casas Colgadas..........................**4** D3		Posada de San Julián...............**20** B3
Catedral.......................................**5** D2		
Mirador (Lookout)....................**6** D1		EATING 🍴 (pp257–8)
Museo de Arte Abstracto Español.....(see 4)		Bar La Tinaja...........................**21** D2
Museo de Cuenca......................**7** D3		Egido...**22** A3
Museo de Las Ciencias.............**8** D3		Horno de las Campanas..........(see 14)
Museo Diocesano.......................**9** D2		Mesón Casas Colgadas............**23** D2
Tesoro Catedralicio..................(see 5)		Restaurante Figón del Huécar..**24** D2
Torre de Mangana....................**10** B2		Restaurante San Nicolás.........**25** D2
		Ruiz..**26** A3
SLEEPING 🏠 (pp256–7)		
Hostal Avenida.........................**11** B3		TRANSPORT (p258)
Hostal Cánovas.........................**12** A2		Bus Station...............................**27** B4
Hostal Cortés............................**13** B4		Local Bus to Plaza Mayor........**28** B4

religious art and artefacts, with a 14th-century Byzantine diptych the jewel in the crown. How such a piece ended up in Cuenca, no-one seems to know.

Torre de Mangana

The elegant Torre de Mangana, halfway down the hill in the old town near Plaza Mangana, is the last remnant of a fortress that was built by Cuenca's Muslim rulers. It is all that remains of Cuenca's days as a Muslim town.

Festivals & Events

Cuenca's **Semana Santa** celebrations are renowned throughout Spain, particularly for the eerie, silent processions through the

streets of the old town. Also gaining international acclaim is the **Semana de Música Religiosa de Cuenca** (www.citelan.es/semana_musica_religiosa_cuenca), the city's celebration of sacred music. Usually held in March or April, it attracts international performers and spectators and is a good time to be in town.

Sleeping

The most imaginative accommodation choices are in the old town, but there are also some reasonable options down the hill. Most places increase their rates during Semana Santa (Holy Week; above) and, sometimes, in summer or on weekends.

If you decide to camp, **Camping Caravaning** (☎ 969 23 16 56; per person/tent/car €3.30/3.30/3.30;

(🗓 1 Mar-31 Oct) is 8km out of town on the road towards the Ciudad Encantada.

OLD TOWN
Many of the hotel rooms in the old town have amazing views, so it's worthwhile seeing if you can get a room with *una vista*.

Pensión Real (☎ 969 22 99 77; Calle de Larga 39; s/d without bathroom €20/25) At the very tip of the old town, this appealing little place offers simple rooms. Those at the front have tantalising (but partially concealed) views down over the town, and it doesn't get any quieter than this.

Pensión La Tabanqueta (☎ 969 21 12 90; Calle de Trabuco 13; s/d without bathroom €15/30) The rooms here are slightly better that at the Real and a bit closer to the centre. Some even have views over the Rio Júcar, which is picturesque if not quite as spectacular as the eastern side of town. There's a popular eatery attached (p258). A decent choice.

Leonor de Aquitania Hotel (☎ 969 23 10 00; www.hotelleonordeaquitania.com; Calle de San Pedro 60; s/d with bathroom & buffet breakfast from €73/99) Housed in an 18th-century house, this is a classy place, although the rooms perhaps lack the character you would expect given the price and location. They are, however, well equipped and well maintained and the bathrooms are very stylish.

Parador (☎ 969 23 23 20; cuenca@parador.es; Calle de Hoz de Huécar; s/d with bathroom €92.90/113.30) If you choose Cuenca's *parador* you're in good company; the prince and princess chose it for the first night of their honeymoon in May 2004. Set in the huge 16th-century Dominican Convento de San Pablo, this place oozes the usual old-world *parador* charm and the views across to the old town are exceptional (rooms with views need to be booked well in advance).

NEW TOWN
Pensión Central (☎ 969 21 15 11; Calle de Alonso Chirino 7; s/d/tr without bathroom €12/20/27) This is one of the better cheapies in the new town, with tidy, bright rooms. Excellent value.

Hostal Cánovas (☎ 969 21 39 73; www.servinet.net/canovas; Calle Fray Luis de León 38; s/d with bathroom Sun-Thu €25/40, d Fri & Sat €45) With spacious rooms featuring polished floorboards, high ceilings and nice furnishings, not to mention young and friendly staff, this place offers outstanding value.

Hostal Avenida (☎ 969 21 43 43; Calle de la Carretería 25; s/d with bathroom Sun-Thu €24/35, Sat & Sun 28/45) This well-run place has friendly staff and offers spacious and comfortable rooms with large bathrooms. Most rooms are *interiores* (rooms without a street view), but many are still quite bright.

Other recommended places:
Pensión Tintes (☎ 969 21 23 98; Calle de los Tintes 7; s/d with bathroom €21/33)
Posada de San Julián (☎ 969 21 17 04; Calle de las Torres 1; d with/without bathroom €34/20)
Hostal Cortés (☎ 969 21 43 43; Calle de Ramón y Cajal 49; s/d with bathroom from €27.50/38.50)

Eating
RESTAURANTS
Mesón Casas Colgadas (☎ 969 22 35 52; Calle de los Canónigos 3; starters €6-12, mains €9-21) Cuenca's pride and joy, this high-quality restaurant fuses an amazing location with great food. For less formality and money (but the same views), enjoy a *ración* (meal-sized tapas) and beer in the downstairs *comedor* (dining room).

Restaurante Figón del Huécar (☎ 969 24 00 62; Ronda Julián Romero 6; mains €16-18, menú €18) Run by the same owners as Mesón Casas Colgadas, this place is also top-notch with fine views.

Horno de las Campanas (🗓 969 23 10 00; Calle de San Pedro 58-60; starters €5.90-10, mains €9-16, menú €13.50) Although it lacks the views, this is another high-standard restaurant with an atmospheric dining room among the stone arches, and prices a touch below the others.

Restaurante San Nicolás (☎ 969 21 22 05; Calle de San Pedro 15; starters €5-12, mains €8-18, menú €18) Another fine establishment for solid Castellano–Manchego food. The *carpaccio de lomo de jabali* (thin cuts of wild boar; €17.75) is particularly good.

CASTILLA-LA MANCHA

There are also several restaurants scattered around Plaza Mayor in the heart of the old town – easily the nicest part of Cuenca to have a meal. Most of them serve pretty good *raciones, bocadillos* etc, so take your pick. Probably the best is the friendly **Bar La Tinaja** (Calle del Obispo Valero 4; raciones €5-12), just off the plaza, which is a little winner. Up the hill, the restaurant at **Pensión La Tabanqueta** (Calle de Trabuco 13; menú €10) is popular and has pleasant views.

CAFÉS

The cafés on Plaza Mayor are perfect for drinking and people-watching. For breakfast or a quick bite in the new town, these two *cafeterías* might do the trick: **Ruiz** (Calle de Carretería 12; ☿ 8.30am-10pm Mon-Sat, closed Sun), where the olive-green seating and wood panelling scream early '70s, and **Egido** (Calle de Carretería 16; ☿ 8.30am-10pm Wed-Mon). Both open from around 8.30am until 10pm.

Entertainment

You can join the under 26s who gather together along Calle de San Miguel (old town) or Plaza de España (new town) for loads of noisy evening *copas*. There's a gaggle of bars in both areas, but many of the locals just bring their own drinks.

If you're looking for a bit more excitement later on in the evening, you'll find some discos along Calle del Doctor Galíndez, near Plaza de España, and a few others across the road from the train station.

Getting There & Away

BUS

Up to nine buses daily serve Madrid (€9, two hours) between 7.30am and 8pm. Other services include Valencia (€10.60, 2½ hours, up to three a day), Albacete (€8.70, two hours, up to three daily) and Alcázar de San Juan (€10, three hours, 3pm weekdays) via Belmonte. There are also two buses to Toledo (€9.10, 2¼ hours) on weekdays and one on Sunday.

CAR & MOTORCYCLE

From Cuenca, the quickest route to Madrid is west along the N400, turning northwest onto the A3 at Tarancón.

TRAIN

Cuenca lies on the train line connecting Madrid and Valencia. Trains to Madrid's Atocha station depart six times on weekdays and four times on weekends (€9.15, 2½ hours). Trains to Valencia leave four times daily (€10, 3¼ hours).

Getting Around

Local bus Nos 1 and 2 for Plaza Mayor leave from just north of the train station. There's free street parking at the top of the old town (follow the signs to *estacionamiento*).

SERRANÍA DE CUENCA

Spreading north and east of Cuenca, the Serranía de Cuenca is a heavily wooded and fertile zone of low mountains and green fields. The Río Júcar and Río Huécar flow through Cuenca from the high hinterland through landscapes which are well worth exploring if you have your own transport.

From Cuenca, take the CM2105 about 30km to the so-called **Ciudad Encantada** (Enchanted City; admission €3; ☿ 10am-sunset). Extremely popular with locals, this series of rocks has been eroded into fantastical shapes by nature. If you let your imagination carry you away, it's possible to see a boat on its keel, a dog and a Roman bridge. The shaded 40-minute circuit around the open-air rock museum is great for breaking up a car journey.

There's an overpriced **hostal** (☎ 969 28 81 94; d with bathroom from €50) opposite the Ciudad Encantada entrance. The rooms are fine for a night and there's an attached restaurant and bar.

You could then head back to the CM2105 and turn right in the direction of Uña and Tragacete. This part of the province is very pretty, dotted with sleepy villages and the clear blue lake of the **Embalse de la Toba**. About 5km on from the eye-catching **Huélamo**, a turn-off to the right (the sign says Teruel) leads 60km across the Montes Universales to the mesmerising medieval town of **Albarracín** (p436) – a perfect place to end a day's drive and stay overnight.

An alternative route to the road east to Teruel, the CM2105 continues north to the **Nacimiento del Río Cuervo** (17km), a couple of small waterfalls where the Río Cuervo rises. From here you could loop around towards **Beteta** (29km) and the gorge of the same name, or cross the provincial frontier into Guadalajara to make for the pleasant if unspectacular **Parque Natural del Alto Tajo**. To the west lies La Alcarria (p259).

AROUND CUENCA
Alarcón
One hundred kilometres or so south of Cuenca is the triangle-based Muslim **castle** at Alarcón, which has been converted into a sumptuous **parador** (☎ 969 33 03 15; s/d with bathroom €116.30/145.40) offering old-world charm and supremely comfortable rooms.

Segóbriga
These **ruins** (☎ 679-090444; adult/student €4/2; 9am-9pm Tue-Sun 15 Apr-15 Sep, 10am-6pm Tue-Sat 16 Sep-14 Apr) may date as far back as the 5th century BC. The best-preserved structures are a **Roman theatre** and **amphitheatre** on the fringes of the ancient city, looking out towards a wooded hillside. Other remains include the outlines of a Visigothic basilica and a section of the aqueduct, which helped keep the city green in what is otherwise a desert. On site is the small **Museo de Segóbriga** and it seems you can explore the ruins at any time.

The site is near Saelices, 2km south of the A3 motorway between Madrid and Albacete. From Cuenca, drive west 55km on the N400, then turn south on the CM202.

GUADALAJARA
pop 69,521
The small provincial capital of Guadalajara is more of historical than aesthetic interest.

Guadalajara (from the Arabic *wad al-hijaara*, or 'stony river') was, in its medieval Muslim heyday, the principal city of a large swathe of northern Spain under the green banner of Islam at a time when Madrid was no more than a military observation point. In 1085 Alfonso VI finally took Guadalajara as the Reconquista moved ponderously south. The city was repeatedly sacked during the War of Spanish Succession, the Napoleonic occupation and the Spanish Civil War.

While little remains of Guadalajara's glory days, the much-restored **Palacio de los Duques del Infantado** (admission €2; 10am-2pm & 4-7pm Tue-Sat, 10am-2pm Sun), where the Mendoza family held court, is worth a visit if you're passing by. Its striking façade is a fine example of Gothic–Mudéjar work, and the heavily ornamental patio is equally entrancing. The town's **tourist office** (☎ 949 21 16 26; Plaza de los Caídos 6; 10am-2pm & 4-7.30pm Mon-Sat, 10am-2pm Sun) is opposite the *palacio*.

Guadalajara is a simple day trip from Madrid, but if you're stuck, both **Pensión**

Venecia (☎ 949 21 13 52; Calle de Dr Benito; s/d with bathroom €14/22), a cheap, no-frills possibility, and the slightly more comfortable **Hostal Infante** (☎ 949 22 35 55; Calle de San Juan de Dios 14; s/d with bathroom €26/38) are worth trying.

The **bus station** (☎ 949 88 70 94; Calle del Dos de Mayo) is a short walk from the *palacio*. Regular buses depart for Madrid (€3.45, 45 minutes) throughout the day between 6.15am and 10pm. Sigüenza (€4.85, 1½ hours) and Pastrana (€2.80, 25 minutes) get two connections daily on weekdays, one on Saturday, but none on Sunday.

From the **train station** (☎ 949 21 28 50), 2km north of town, regular trains head to Madrid (€3.25, 30 minutes) from about 5am to 11.30pm. Regional trains go to Sigüenza (€4.70, one hour), but there's a bit of a lull in the middle of the day.

LA ALCARRIA & AROUND
Mar de Castilla
Southeast of Guadalajara along the N320 (it soon becomes the CM200) is the Mar de Castilla, a collection of lakes formed by dams built in the late 1950s, in an area known as La Alcarria. Hardly spectacular, La Alcarria was nonetheless immortalised in an enchantingly simple account of a walking trip made there in 1946 by the Nobel Prize–winning writer Camilo José Cela, *Viaje a La Alcarria*.

Pastrana
pop 1057
Of the many pueblos Cela called in at during his walking trip, Pastrana is the most enchanting with narrow, cobbled streets and bubbling fountains. Forty-two kilometres south of Guadalajara along the CM200, this tranquil, medieval town hosts in its centre **Plaza de la Hora**, a large square dotted with acacias and fronted by the sturdy **Palacio Ducal**. It is here that the one-eyed princess of Éboli, Ana Mendoza de la Cerda, was confined in 1581 for a love affair with the Spanish King Felipe II's secretary. You can see the caged window of her 'cell', where she died 10 years later, but the palace itself is closed to the public.

Walk from the square along Calle Mayor and you'll soon reach the massive **Iglesia de Nuestra Señora de la Asunción** (Colegiata). Inside, the interesting little **museum** (admission €1.80; 10.30am-1.30pm & 4.30-6.30pm) contains the jewels of the princess, some exquisite 15th-century tapestries and even an El Greco. There's also a helpful **tourist office** (☎ 949 37 06 72; Plaza del Deán 5; ☷ 10am-2pm & 4-7pm Mon-Sat, 10am-2pm Sun).

Hostal Moratín (☎ 949 37 01 16; Calle de Moratín 7; s/d with bathroom from €16.05/28.90), just in from the main highway, is a homely *hostal* with simple, comfortable rooms, a restaurant and a family feel.

Hostería Real de Pastrana (☎ /fax 949 37 10 60; s/d with bathroom from €45/56) is a deluxe place in the Convento del Carmen, 2km from town. The rooms are bright and attractive with a few period touches.

Pastrana is peppered with eateries and bars. Two of the nicest are **Casa de Ruy** (☎ 949 37 00 43; Calle Mayor 1; ☷ noon-4pm & 7pm-midnight Tue-Thu, until 3am Fri-Sun), where you can dine or just sink into one of its sofas and sip the night away, and **Fuente Permanente** (☎ 949 37 01 61; menú €7.20; ☷ Tue-Sun), on the road to Tarancón, which serves roasted meats in a shady courtyard.

Two buses travel to Madrid (€3.75, 1½ hours) via Guadalajara every weekday morning.

Around Pastrana

Some 20km northeast of Pastrana is the area's main reservoir, the white-rimmed **Embalse de Entrepeñas**, where swimming is more an attraction than the views. From there you can push north on the CM204 to **Cifuentes**, with its 14th-century castle.

An alternative route to the lake goes via Guadalajara, from where you could follow the A2 northeast and turn off at **Torija**, which has a rather impressive castle out of proportion to the size of the town. The **museum** (admission free; ☷ 10am-2pm & 4-6pm Tue-Sat, 10am-2pm Sun) within the castle is dedicated to Cela's *Viaje a La Alcarria*. From here, take the CM201 for La Alcarria's second town after Pastrana, **Brihuega**, a leafy village with stretches of its medieval walls intact. The drive east along the Río Tajuña is one of the more pleasant in this part of Castilla-La Mancha. The road forms a T-junction with the CM204, from where you can head north for Sigüenza or south to the Embalse de Entrepeñas.

Yet another option from La Alcarria is to head east from the lake towards **Parque Natural del Alto Tajo**, which offers some pretty scenery. Along with the Serranía de Cuenca (p258) further south and east, the area is very popular with *madrileños* (Madrid residents) on weekends.

SIGÜENZA
pop 4312

Sleepy, medieval and filled with the ghosts of a turbulent past, Sigüenza is a lovely town. Built on a low hill cradled by the Río Henares and a slender tributary, its twisting lanes and well-preserved stone architecture make for a wonderful detour.

History

Originally a Celtiberian settlement, Segontia (as the town was previously named) became an important Roman and, later, Visigothic military outpost. The 8th-century arrival of the Muslims put the town in the frontline provinces facing the Christians. Sigüenza stayed in Muslim hands for considerably longer than towns further southwest, such as Guadalajara and Toledo, resisting until the 1120s. After a period of Aragonese occupation, the town was later ceded to the Castilians, who turned Sigüenza and its hinterland into a vast Church property. The bishops remained complete masters – material and spiritual – of the town and land until the end of the 18th century. Sigüenza's decline was long and painful as the town found itself repeatedly in the way of advancing armies: again a frontline during the War of the Spanish Succession and the civil war, when fighting here was heavy.

Information

The **tourist office** (☎ 949 39 32 51; www.siguenza .com; ☷ 10am-2pm & 4-6pm Mon-Thu, 10am-2pm & 4-8pm Fri, 9.30am-3pm & 4-7pm Sat, 10am-2pm Sun) is in the delightful Ermita del Humilladero; there's another **tourist kiosk** (☎ 949 347 007; Calle de Medina 9) just down the hill from the cathedral.

There are several banks on and near Calle del Cardenal Mendoza, and the **post office** (Calle de la Villa Viciosa) is also central. In an emergency, call ☎ 112 or ☎ 949 39 00 19.

Catedral

Rising up from the heart of the old town is the city's centrepiece, the **catedral** (admission free; ☷ 9.30am-1.30pm & 4.30-7.30pm Tue-Sat, noon-5.30pm Sun). Begun as a Romanesque

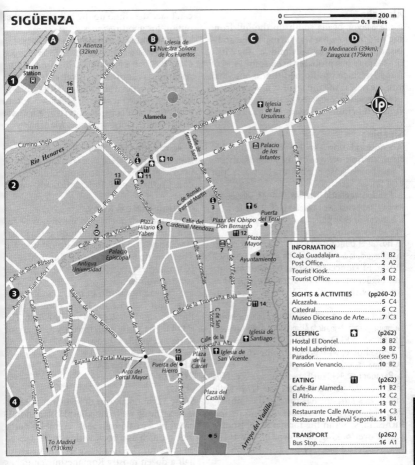

SIGÜENZA

| 0 | 200 m |
| 0 | 0.1 miles |

To Atienza (32km)

Train Station

Iglesia de Nuestra Señora de los Huertos

To Medinaceli (39km); Zaragoza (175km)

Alameda

Paseo de la Alameda

Iglesia de las Ursulinas

Camino Viejo

Río Henares

Calle de San Roque

Palacio de los Infantes

C de Román Pascual Martín

Plaza del Obispo Don Bernardo

Puerta del Torii

Plaza Mayor

Ayuntamiento

Palacio Episcopal

Antigua Universidad

Iglesia de Santiago

Iglesia de San Vicente

Plaza de la Cárcel

Arco del Portal Mayor

Puerta del Hierro

Plaza del Castillo

To Madrid (130km)

Arroyo del Vadillo

INFORMATION	
Caja Guadalajara............................1 B2	
Post Office.......................................2 A2	
Tourist Kiosk..................................3 C2	
Tourist Office.................................4 B2	

SIGHTS & ACTIVITIES	(pp260-2)
Alcazaba..5 C4	
Catedral...6 C2	
Museo Diocesano de Arte................7 C3	

SLEEPING	(p262)
Hostal El Doncel.............................8 B2	
Hotel Laberinto...............................9 B2	
Parador....................................(see 5)	
Pensión Venancio..........................10 B2	

EATING	(p262)
Cafe-Bar Alameda.........................11 B2	
El Atrio..12 B2	
Irene...13 B2	
Restaurante Calle Mayor................14 C3	
Restaurante Medieval Segontia.......15 B4	

| TRANSPORT | (p262) |
| Bus Stop.......................................16 A1 | |

structure in 1130, work continued for four centuries as the church was expanded and adorned. The largely Gothic result is laced with elements of other styles, from Plateresque through Renaissance to Mudéjar. The church was heavily damaged during the civil war.

The dark (and very cold) **nave** (admission free) has some fine stained-glass windows and an impressive 15th-century altarpiece along the south wall. To enter the chapels, sacristy and Gothic cloister, you'll need to join a Spanish-language only **guided tour** (€3; ☒ 11am, noon, 4.30pm & 5.30pm Tue-Sat). The highlights of the tour include the **Capilla Mayor**, home of the reclining marble statue of Don Martín Vázquez de Arce (the statue

is named *El Doncel*) who died fighting the Muslims in the final stages of the Reconquista. Particularly beautiful is the **Sacristía de las Cabezas**, with a ceiling adorned with hundreds of heads sculpted by Covarrubias. The **Capilla del Espíritu Santo** boasts a doorway combining Plateresque, Mudéjar and Gothic styles, and inside is a remarkable dome and an Anunciación by El Greco.

Museo Diocesano de Arte

Across the square from the cathedral, this **museum** (admission €3; ☒ 11am-2pm & 4-7pm Tue-Sun) has an impressive selection of religious art from Sigüenza and the surrounding area, including a series of mainly 15th-century altarpieces.

Alcazaba

Calle Mayor heads south up the hill from the *catedral* to what was formerly the archbishops' castle, originally built by the Muslims. There has probably been some kind of fort here since pre-Roman times, but what you see new is the much-revamped and imposing residence erected by the archbishops. It now functions as a *parador* (p262).

Sleeping

Accommodation can be surprisingly difficult to find on weekends so book ahead. Some hotels close their doors between 2pm and 5pm.

Pensión Venancio (☎ 949 39 03 47; Calle de San Roque 1; s/d with shared bathroom €14/26) Basic with a capital B, this place is only for those who are really counting their euros.

Hostal El Doncel (☎ 949 39 00 01; www.eldoncel .com; Paseo de la Alameda 3; s/d with bathroom €35.25/48) Hostal El Doncel is a great base for exploring Sigüenza, and has attractive, spacious rooms with satellite TV. Highly recommended.

Hotel Laberinto (☎ 949 39 11 65; laberintohotel@ turismosngu.com; Paseo de la Alameda 1; s/d with bathroom from €30/42) If El Doncel is full, this is another decent choice, with good, if somewhat characterless, rooms.

Parador (☎ 949 39 01 00; siguenza@parador.es; Plaza del Castillo, s/n; s/d with bathroom from €77.70/97.10) Sigüenza's *parador* has the usual combination of luxury, attentive service and period furnishings. Set in the former archbishop's palace overlooking the town, its courtyard is a wonderful place to pass the time.

Eating

Irene (Avenida de Pío XII; bocadillos €2-4; ☺ 8am-9pm) This is a good, low-key spot to nip into for breakfast, pastry or a *bocadillo*.

El Atrio (Plaza del Obispo Don Bernado; mains €5-11.20; ☺ 9am-late Tue-Sun) Opposite the *catedral*, this buzzing place is great at any time of the day, with good tapas, *platos combinados* (combination plates) and speedy service.

Cafe-Bar Alameda (☎ 949 39 05 53; Paseo de la Alameda 2; mains €5-9.80; ☺ 10am-midnight) If you

can't face the climb up the hill, this another option for good *raciones*.

Restaurante Medieval Segontia (☎ 949 39 32 33; Calle del Portal Mayor 2; starters €3.80-13.20, mains €11.15-15.60, menú from 11.70) This fine dining restaurant is known for its variety of *menús*. There's a vegetarian *menú* (€19.60), and the great value *menú especial* allows you to enjoy the Castilian speciality, *cordero asado* (roast lamb), along with a La Mancha twist, *migas* (bread crumbs).

Restaurante Calle Mayor (☎ 949 39 17 48; Calle Mayor 21; mains €11.10-14.60, menú €15) Another good, upmarket choice, Restaurante Calle Mayor does Castilian specialities particularly well.

Getting There & Away

Buses are infrequent and mostly serve towns around Sigüenza, including Guadalajara. They stop on Avenida de Alfonso VI. There are up to 10 regional trains to Madrid (Chamartín station; €7.40, 1½ hours). Some continue on to Soria.

Sigüenza lies north of the A2 motorway. The main exits are the C204, coming from the west, and the C114, from the east. The C114 then heads north towards Almazán or Soria in Castilla y León.

AROUND SIGÜENZA
Atienza
pop 397

Some 31km northwest of Sigüenza, Atienza is a charming walled medieval village dominated by a castle ruin that resembles nothing so much as a rock with a turret tacked on one end. This tiny place is crammed with half a dozen mostly Romanesque churches and has two small **museums** (admission €1.50 per museum, or €2 for both; ☺ 10.30am-1.30pm & 4.30-6.30pm) in the Iglesia de San Gil and Iglesia de San Bartolomé.

If you come by bus you'll have to stay. Fortunately, **El Mirador** (☎ 949 39 90 38; d with/ without bathroom €45/26) offers good, if slightly overpriced, rooms and a cosy restaurant.

A couple of buses leave early in the morning, bound for Guadalajara, Madrid and Sigüenza.

Barcelona

BARCELONA

CONTENTS

Some say Barcelona is the most southern city of northern Europe. A short hop from France, it is an industrious, densely packed city that oozes style. In many respects it is a far cry from the fiesta-and-siesta image of more southerly Spanish regions. Probably Spain's most cosmopolitan city, and certainly one of its richest, Barcelona is a hard-working place, yet its people have a strong sybaritic side. Restaurants, bars and clubs are always packed, as is the seaside in summer.

Set on a plain rising gently from the sea to a range of wooded hills, Barcelona enjoys fine vistas, lovely and unusual parks and a fascinating medieval core dotted with pearls of Gothic construction. Beyond this core is perhaps some of the world's most bizarre architecture: surreal spectacles capped by Antoni Gaudí's La Sagrada Família church.

Barcelona has been breaking ground in art, architecture and style for at least a century, from the Modernista architects led by Gaudí to the adventurous redevelopments now being carried out on the city's northeastern waterfront; from Pablo Picasso and Joan Miró, whose spirits haunt the city, to the likes of Antoni Tàpies today. It is the national capital of cooking, with avant-garde chefs whipping up a storm that has even the French trembling with envy.

Barcelona is the capital of Catalonia (Catalunya in Catalan, Cataluña in Castilian), a region with its own language, character and turbulent history – many Catalans think of their home as a separate country. The city itself could keep you occupied for weeks but just outside it there are some fine sandy beaches, the hedonistic seaside town of Sitges and the jagged local mountains of Montserrat.

HIGHLIGHTS

- Marvel at **La Sagrada Família** (p289), Antoni Gaudí's still-unfolding Modernista masterpiece
- Stroll along the **Rambla** (p280), a 24-hour avenue with attitude
- Lose yourself in the hippest part of town for **tippling and snacking** (p309)
- Study the earliest of Pablo's works in the **Museu Picasso** (p285)
- Grab your towel and tastebuds and head for **La Barceloneta** (p287), with a beach to crash on and succulent seafood
- Visit the **Casa Batlló** (p288), Gaudí's kookiest building
- Explore **Montjuïc** (p293), home to botanical gardens, Romanesque art and Miró
- Sip *cava* (Catalan sparkling wine) on the roof of **La Pedrera** (p289)
- Get out of Barcelona and head out for **Sitges** (p321), Spain's most outrageous resort

Barcelona ★

| ▪ METRO AREA: 477 SQ KM | ▪ POP: 1.6 MILLION | ▪ AVE SUMMER TEMP: HIGH 28°C, LOW 20°C |

BARCELONA

HISTORY

Barcelona may have been founded by the Carthaginians in about 230 BC, taking the surname of Hamilcar Barca, Hannibal's father. Roman Barcelona (known as Barcino) covered an area within today's Barri Gòtic and was overshadowed by Tarraco (Tarragona), 90km to the southwest.

In the wake of Muslim occupation, and then Frankish domination, Guifré el Pilós (Wilfrid the Hairy) founded the house of the Counts of Barcelona (Comtes de Barcelona) in 878. Barcelona grew rich on pickings from the collapse of the Muslim caliphate of Córdoba in the 11th century. Under Ramon Berenguer III (1082–1131), Catalonia launched its own fleet and sea trade developed.

In 1137 Ramon Berenguer IV married Petronilla, heiress of Catalonia's western neighbour Aragón, creating a joint state and setting the scene for Catalonia's golden age. Jaume I (1213–76) took the Balearic Islands and Valencia from the Muslims in the 1230s. Jaume I's son Pere II followed with Sicily in 1282. Then followed a spectacular expansion of Catalonia's Mediterranean trade-based empire, albeit hampered at home by divisions in the ruling family, the odd clash with Castile and trouble with the aristocracy in Aragón. Malta (1283), Athens (1310), Corsica (1323), Sardinia (1324) and Naples (1423) fell, for varying periods, under Catalan dominance.

The accession of the Aragonese noble Fernando to the throne in 1479 did not augur well for Barcelona, and his marriage to Queen Isabel of Castile less still. Catalonia effectively became a subordinate part of the Castilian state. In the War of the Spanish Succession (1702–13), Barcelona was abandoned by its European allies and fell to the Bourbon king, Felipe V on 11 September 1714. Felipe abolished the Generalitat (parliament), built a huge fort, the Ciutadella, to watch over Barcelona, and banned the writing and teaching of Catalan.

Modernisme, Anarchy & Civil War

The 19th century brought an economic resurgence. Wine, cotton, cork and iron industries developed, as did urban working-class poverty and unrest. To ease the crush, Barcelona's medieval walls were demolished in 1854 and in 1869 work began on L'Eixample, an extension of the city beyond Plaça de Catalunya. The flourishing bourgeoisie paid for lavish buildings, many of them in the unique Modernista style, whose leading exponent was Antoni Gaudí.

Modernisme was the most visible aspect of the Catalan Renaixença (Renaissance), a movement for the revival of Catalan language and culture in the late 19th century. By the turn of the century, Barcelona was also Spain's hotbed of avant-garde art, with close links to Paris.

In the decades around the turn of the 20th century Barcelona became a vortex of anarchists, Republicans, bourgeois regionalists, gangsters, police terrorists, political gunmen called *pistoleros*, and meddling by Madrid.

Within days of the formation of Spain's Second Republic in 1931, Catalan nationalists, led by Francesc Macià and Lluís Companys, proclaimed Catalonia a republic within an imaginary 'Iberian Federation'. Madrid pressured them into accepting a unitary Spanish state, but Catalonia got a new regional government, with the old title of Generalitat.

For nearly a year after Franco's rising in 1936, Barcelona was run by revolutionary anarchists and the Partido Obrero de Unificación Marxista (POUM; Workers' Marxist Unification Party) Trotskyist militia, with Companys as president only in name. In 1937 the Catalan communist party (PSUC; Partit Socialista Unificat de Catalunya) took control and disarmed the anarchists and POUM. One of those to watch on in distress at this fratricidal conflict was George Orwell, who recorded his war efforts in his classic *Homage to Catalonia*. The city fell to Franco in 1939, and there followed a long period of repression.

From Franco to the Present

The big social change under Franco was the flood of immigrants from poorer parts of Spain, chiefly Andalucía, attracted by economic growth in Catalonia. Some 750,000 people came to Barcelona in the 1950s and '60s, and almost as many to the rest of Catalonia. Many lived in appalling conditions.

Three years after the death of Franco in 1975, a new Spanish constitution created the autonomous community of Catalonia, with Barcelona as its capital, in the context

(Continued on page 276)

BARCELONA

2 km
1 mile

CosmoCaixa..17 B1
Dona i Ocell Sculpture.........................18 C4
Estadi Olímpic.......................................19 D5
Fundació Joan Miró..............................20 D5
Galería Olímpica...................................21 D6
Institut Nacional d'Educació Física de
    Catalunya...22 C5
Jardí Botànic...23 D6
Jardins de Mossèn Costa i Llobera......24 E5
La Font Màgica......................................25 D5
Museu d'Arqueologia de
    Catalunya...26 D5
Museu de Ceràmica...........................(see 32)
Museu de les Arts Decoratives.........(see 32)
Museu del Futbol Club Barcelona........27 A4
Museu Etnològic...................................28 D5
Museu Militar..29 E6
Museu Nacional d'Art de
    Catalunya...30 D5
Museu-Monestir de Pedralbes..............31 A3
Palau Nacional de Montjuïc...............(see 30)
Palau Reial de Pedralbes......................32 A3
Palau Sant Jordi....................................33 D6
Pavelló Mies van der Rohe....................34 D5
Peix Sculpture......................................35 G4
Piscines Bernat Picornell.......................36 D5
Plaça de Braus Monumental.................37 F2
Poble Espanyol.....................................38 C5
Poliesportiu Marítim.............................39 G4
Torre de Collserola...............................40 A1
World Trade Center...............................41 F5

SLEEPING   (pp300–4)
Alberg Mare de Déu de Montserrat......42 C1
Grand Marina Hotel..............................43 F5
Hotel Arts Barcelona.............................44 G3
Hotel Turó de Vilana............................45 B2
Punt d'Informació Juvenil.....................46 D4

EATING   (pp304–9)
Bestial...47 G4
El Peixerot..48 C4
Torre d'Alta Mar.................................(see B3)

DRINKING   (pp309–11)
CDLC..49 G4
Daguiri..50 F4
Mirablau...51 B1

ENTERTAINMENT   (pp311–15)
Bikini..52 C3
Camp Nou...53 B4
Discothèque..54 C3
Icària Yelmo Cineplex..........................55 G3
La Cove del Drac..................................56 C2
L'Auditori...57 F2
Méliès Cinemes.....................................58 D4
Razzmatazz...59 F3
Renoir Les Corts...................................60 B4
Tablao de Carmen..............................(see 38)
Teatre Lliure...61 D5
Teatre Mercat de les Flors.....................62 D5
Teatre Nacional de Catalunya..............63 F2
Terrrazza..(see 54)

SHOPPING   (pp315–16)
Els Encants Vells...................................64 F2
L'Illa del Diagonal................................65 C3

INFORMATION
Andorran Embassy.............................(see 41)
Australian Consulate...............................1 B3
British Council...2 C3
Canadian Consulate................................3 A2
Centre Gestor del Parc de
    Montjuïc...4 D5
Coordinadora Gai-Lesbiana
    Barcelona..5 C5
Dutch Consulate.....................................6 B3
Hospital de la Santa Creu i Sant Pau..7 E1
Hospital Dos de Mayo............................8 E1
Irish Consulate..9 B4
US Consulate..10 A2

SIGHTS & ACTIVITIES   (pp279–300)
Arc de Triomf..11 F3
CaixaForum...12 C5
Casa Museu Gaudí................................13 D1
Castell de Montjuïc...............................14 D6
Cementiri del Sud-Oest.........................15 D6
Club Natació Atlètic-Barcelona.............16 F5

MEDITERRANEAN
SEA

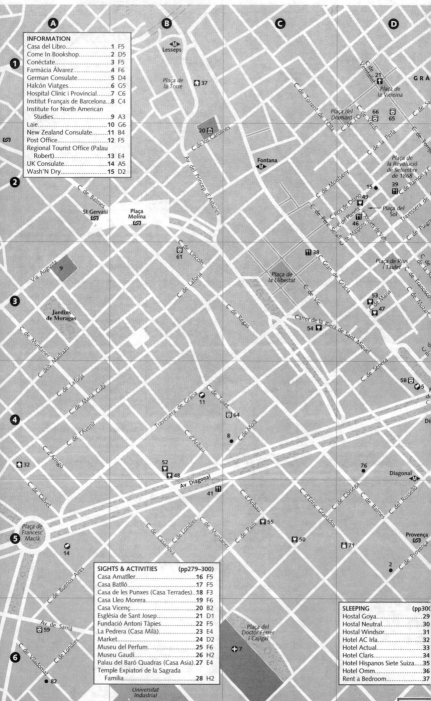

INFORMATION
Casa del Libro	**1** F5
Come In Bookshop	**2** D5
Conéctate	**3** F5
Farmàcia Álvarez	**4** F6
German Consulate	**5** D4
Halcón Viatges	**6** G5
Hospital Clínic i Provincial	**7** C6
Institut Français de Barcelona	**8** C4
Institute for North American Studies	**9** A3
Laie	**10** G6
New Zealand Consulate	**11** B4
Post Office	**12** F5
Regional Tourist Office (Palau Robert)	**13** E4
UK Consulate	**14** A5
Wash'N Dry	**15** D2

SIGHTS & ACTIVITIES (pp279–300)
Casa Amatller	**16** F5
Casa Batlló	**17** F5
Casa de les Punxes (Casa Terrades)	**18** F3
Casa Lleó Morera	**19** F6
Casa Vicenç	**20** B2
Església de Sant Josep	**21** D1
Fundació Antoni Tàpies	**22** F5
La Pedrera (Casa Milà)	**23** E4
Market	**24** D2
Museu del Perfum	**25** F6
Museu Gaudí	**26** H2
Palau del Baró Quadras (Casa Asia)	**27** E4
Temple Expiatori de la Sagrada Família	**28** H2

SLEEPING (pp300
Hostal Goya	**29**
Hostal Neutral	**30**
Hostal Windsor	**31**
Hotel AC Irla	**32**
Hotel Actual	**33**
Hotel Claris	**34**
Hotel Hispanos Siete Suiza	**35**
Hotel Omm	**36**
Rent a Bedroom	**37**

Lesseps

Plaça de la Torre

GRÀ

C de Verdi

Plaça de la Virreina

Plaça del Diamant

C de la Perla

Plaça de los Carolines

Fontana

Plaça de la Revolució de Setembre de 1868

Plaça del Sol

C de Balmes

St Gervasi

Plaça Molina

C de Montseny

C de Puig

Av del Príncep d'Astúries

C de Lincoln

Plaça de la Llibertat

Plaça de Rius i Taulet

C de Francesc

Via Augusta

C de Laforja

C de Regàs

Carrer de la Riera de Sant Miquel

C de Mozart

Jardins de Moragas

C de Muntaner

C dels Madrazo

C de Maria Cubí

C de Senecà

Travessera de Gràcia

C de Tuset

C de Mola

C de l'Avenir

C d'Aribau

C d'Amigó

C de Calvet

Av Diagonal

Diagonal

C d'Aribau

C d'Enric Granados

C de Còrsega

C de Balmes

C del Rosselló

Plaça de Francesc Macià

C de Buenos Aires

C de Casanova

C de Londres

C de París

Provença

Av de Sarrià

C de Viladomat

C de Londres

Plaça del Doctor Ferrer i Cajigal

Universitat Industrial

0 — 400 m
0 — 0.2 miles

...TING (pp304–9)
...afumeiro ... 38 C3
...n Juanito ... 39 D2
...rveseria Catalana ... 40 E5
...s Diagonal ... 41 B5
...Tapa Madre ... 42 F4
...lma ... 43 F5
...liard ... 44 E3
...ostal de Rita ... 45 F5
...Soler ... 46 D2

...NKING (pp309–11)
...1 ... 47 D3
...lin ... 48 B4
...'é del Sol ... 49 D2
... Martini ... 50 C5
...Gens Que J'Aime ... 51 F5
... de Gas ... 52 B4
...ria ... 53 D3
...55 ... 54 C3
...scano Antico ... 55 C5
...us Cave ... 56 E5

...TERTAINMENT (pp311–15)
...enbrut ... 57 E3
...sablanca ... 58 D4
...noteca ... 59 A6
...Boîte ... (see 14)

Michael Collins Pub ... 60 H2
Otto Zutz ... 61 B3
Sala Cibeles ... 62 E3
Salvation ... 63 H6
Sutton Club ... 64 C4
Verdi Park ... 65 D1
Verdi ... 66 D1

SHOPPING (pp315–16)
Antonio Miró ... 67 F6
Bulevard Rosa ... 68 E5
Camper ... 69 E5
Farrutx ... 70 D4
Galeria Victor Saavedra ... 71 D5
J Murrià ... 72 F4
Mango ... 73 E5
Vinçon ... 74 E4
Zara ... 75 G6

TRANSPORT (pp316–20)
Avis ... 76 D4
Barcelona Bus ... 77 H4
Europcar ... 78 H5
Hertz ... 79 H3
Pous Bus for Rupit ... 80 G6
TEISA Buses ... 81 G5
Vanguard ... 82 A6

See Central Barcelona Map (pp270–1)

Ⓐ   Ⓑ   Ⓒ   Ⓓ

1

C. de València

Rambla de Catalunya

Pg. de Gràcia

Gran Via de les Corts Catalanes

C. de Pau Clarís

See L'Eixample & Gràcia Map (pp268–9)

49

Plaça del Doctor Leandri

7

C. d'Enric Granados

40

37 P

C. de Balmes

59

Jardins de la Reina Victoria

Pg. de Gràcia

C. de Calàbria

Ronda de Sant Pere

C. d'Aragó

C. d'Arbau

52

38

56

C. del Consell de Cent

75

C. de Muntaner

Universitat de Barcelona

82

Gran Via de les Corts Catalanes

1

5

8

Catalunya

Estació Catalunya

Plaça de Catalunya

76 65

80

71

70

10

C. de Fontanella

C. d'Estruc

2

74 35

68 44

Plaça de la Universitat

Universitat

Ronda de l'Universitat

C. de Pelai

C. de Bergara

4

72

Església Santa Anna

Plaça de Ramon Amadeu

El Triangle

C. de Pelai

3

C. de la Diputació

C. de Vilamarí

Urgell

12

C. de Casanova

62

43

Plaça Goya

Ronda de Sant Antoni

39

C. de Montalegre

15

22

36

16

57

55

El Raval

Plaça de Castella

Plaça dels Tallers

Plaça dels Àngels

LA RAMBLA

Plaça de la Vila de Madrid

Església de Betlem

Plaça de Vicenç Martorell

Plaça del Bonsuccès

4

69

C. de Sepúlveda

63

Plaça del Pes de la Palla

9

C. de Ferlandina

C. del Tigre

61

C. de Floridablanca

C. de Joaquín Costa

C. del Peu de la Creu

C. del Carme

Mercat de la Boqueria

Jardins Doctor Fleming

Plaça de la Gardunya

C. de la Lluna

C. de Sant Vicenç

C. de la Cera

C. de la Riera Alta

C. de la Riera Baixa

Plaça de Sant Agustí

Església de Sant Agustí

5

C. del Comte d'Urgell

C. del Comte Borrell

Sant Antoni

67

C. de Tamarit

C. de Manso

C. de Sant Antoni Abat

Plaça del Pedró

Ronda de Sant Pau

C. de l'Aurora

C. de Sant Rafael

C. de les Carretes

C. de Sant Ramon

Rambla del Raval

Plaça de Salvador Seguí

Barri Xinès

6

Poble Sec

6

Poble Sec

64

C. de Margarit

Av. del Paral·lel

Plaça de Josep Maria Folch i Torres

45

17

51

53

Paral·lel

Paral·lel (Funicular)

58

Av. del Paral·lel

C. de Sta. Madrona

11

Parc de les Tres Xemeneies

Drassanes

Sant Antoni

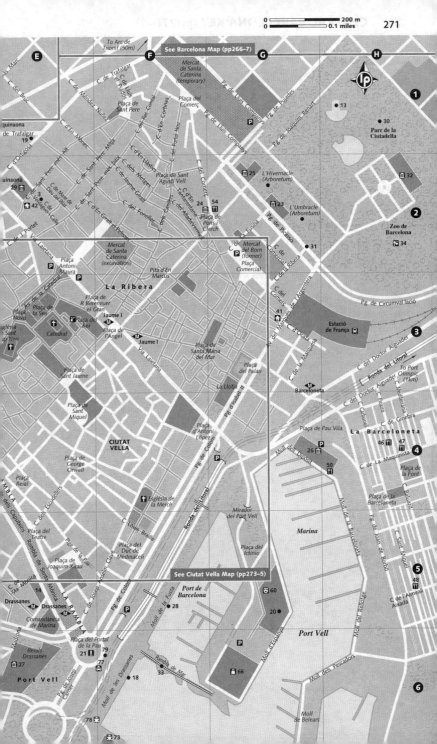

200 m
0.1 miles

To Arc de
Triomf (50m)

See Barcelona Map (pp266–7)

E
F
G
H

Mercat
de Santa
Caterina
(temporary)

Plaça del
Comerç

quinaona
de Trafalgar
19

Plaça de
Sant Pere

Plaça de Sant
Agustí Vell

13

30

Parc de la
Ciutadella

1

quinaona
29

25

L'Hivernacle
(Arboretum)

32

3

42

54

24

Plaça de
Pons i
Clerch

23

L'Umbracle
(Arboretum)

Zoo de
Barcelona

34

2

Mercat
de Santa
Caterina
(excavation)

Mercat
del Born
(former)

Plaça
Comercial

31

Plaça
Antoni
Maura

Pla d'En
Marcús

La Ribera

41

Estació
de França

Plaça de
R Berenguer
el Gran

Plaça de
la Seu

Jaume I

Plaça del
Rei

Catedral

Plaça de
l'Àngel

Jaume I

Plaça de
Santa Maria
del Mar

Pg. de Circumval·lació

3

To Port
Olímpic
(1km)

Plaça de
Sant Jaume

Via Laietana

Plaça
del Palau

Ronda del Litoral

La Llotja

Barceloneta

Plaça de
Sant
Miquel

CIUTAT
VELLA

Plaça
d'Antoni
López

Plaça de Pau Vila

La Barceloneta

46
47
4

Plaça de
George
Orwell

26

50

Plaça de
la Font

Plaça
Reial

Plaça de la
Barceloneta

Església de
la Mercè

Mirador
del Port Vell

Marina

Plaça del
Teatre

Plaça del
Duc de
Medinaceli

Plaça del
Ictinio

5

Plaça de
Joaquim Xirau

See Ciutat Vella Map (pp273–5)

48

14

Drassanes

Drassanes

Port de
Barcelona

60

C de l'Almirall
Aixada

Comandància
de Marina

28

20

Port Vell

Reials
Drassanes

27

Plaça del Portal
de la Pau

21

79

77

18

33

66

Moll dels Pescadors

Port Vell

78

Moll
de Belears

73

6

A

El Triangle

Plaça de Catalunya

B

124

Església Santa Anna

Plaça de Ramon Amadeu

C

C. Comtal

Pg. de Patriarca

C. de Montsió

D

C. de N'Amargós

C. de Ripoll

79

122

100

C. de Petal

1

4

55

C. de Rivadeneyra

C. de Santa Anna

59

C. de Bertrellans

C. de la Canuda

50

Plaça de la Vila de Madrid

C. del Duc de la Victoria

Duran i Bas

49

93

C. dels Sagristans

C. dels Arcs

Plaça Nova

2

RAMBLA de Canaletes

C. dels Tallers

98

Plaça de Vicenç Martorell

C. dels Ramelleres

Plaça del Bonsuccés

71

C. d'En Xuclà

77

67

42

C. d'En Bot

LA RAMBLA

Rambla dels Estudis

C. de la Portaferrissa

C. dels Boters

35

Cape de Sa Lluc

Església de Sant Felip Neri

63

58

Plaça de Sant Felip Neri

C. de la Palla

C. de Sant Sever

C. d'Elisabets

Església de Betlem

8

11

Barri Gòtic

C. de'n Rauric

Baixada de Sta Eulàlia

C. del Pintor Fortuny

C. del Doctor Dou

C. de'n Roca

C. de'n Patritxol

38

16

Plaça del Pi

Plaça de St. Josep Oriol

46

52

C. del Carme

84

69

C. dels Àngels

Rambla de Sant Josep

26

C del Cardenal Cassañas

89

Mercat de la Boqueria

85

6

31

82

C. de les Flors de la Rambla

C. de Beriellam

Jardins Doctor Fleming

Plaça de la Gardunya

18

Plaça de la Boqueria

28

Liceu

2

C. de la Boqueria

C. d'En Quintana

C. d'En Ferran

54

23

119

Plaça de Sant Agustí

65

92

72

C. de l'Hospital

48

Església de Sant Agustí

62

86

C. de la Junta de Comerç

111

C. de les Heures

97

Plaça Reial

116

113

1

9

C. de Sant Rafael

90

C. d'En Robador

70

61

57

60

7

56

C. de la Unió

Rambla dels Caputxins

C. de les Penedides

75

El Raval

Rambla del Raval

Plaça de Salvador Seguí

C. de Sant Pau

96

41

118

5

Plaça Te

Rambla de Santa

C. de Lancaster

110

C. del Marquès de Barberà

C. de St. Ramon

109

115

C. de la Reïeta

C. Nou de la Rambla

C. de la Guàrdia

C. de l'Arc del Teatre

C. del Tist

105

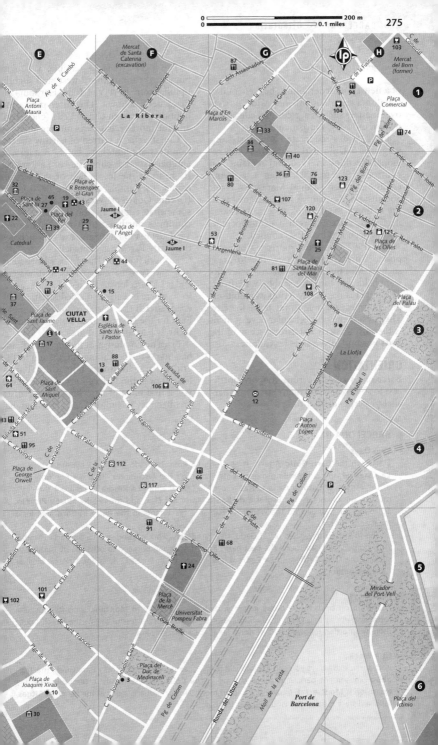

(Continued from page 265)

of a new quasi-federation. The Generalitat, Catalonia's parliament, has wide powers over matters such as agriculture, education, health, industry, tourism and trade.

Jordi Pujol's moderate nationalist Convergència i Unió (CiU) coalition won regional elections in 1980 and remained in control until late 2003, when a left-wing coalition under Pasqual Maragall's Partit Socialista de Catalunya (PSC, aligned with the national PSOE) took power. Barcelona itself has, since the return of democracy, always been run by a PSC council.

The 1992 Olympics spurred a burst of public works, bringing new life to areas such as Montjuïc, where the major events were held, and the once-shabby waterfront. The impetus has barely let up as ambitious programmes continue to revitalise the city. The latest scene of spectacular development is the northeastern waterfront, scene of the 2004 Fòrum Universal de les Cultures.

ORIENTATION

Barcelona's coastline runs roughly northeast to southwest, and many streets are parallel or perpendicular to it.

The focal axis is La Rambla, a 1.25km boulevard running northwest, and slightly uphill, from Port Vell (Old Harbour) to Plaça de Catalunya. The latter marks the boundary between Ciutat Vella (Old City), and the more recent parts further inland.

Ciutat Vella, a warren of narrow streets, centuries-old buildings, hotels, restaurants and bars, spreads either side of La Rambla. Its heart is the lower half of the section east of La Rambla, called the Barri Gòtic (Gothic Quarter). West of La Rambla is somewhat edgier El Raval. Ciutat Vella continues northeast of Barri Gòtic across Via Laietana to La Ribera, east of which lies the pretty Parc de la Ciutadella.

Port Vell (Old Port) has an excellent aquarium and two marinas. At its northeastern end is La Barceloneta, the old sailors' quarter, from where beaches and a pedestrian promenade stretch 1km northeast to Port Olímpic, built for the Olympics and now surrounded by lively bars and restaurants.

Plaça de Catalunya, at the top of La Rambla, marks the beginning of L'Eixample, the grid of straight streets into which Barcelona grew in the 19th century. This is where you'll find most of Barcelona's Modernista architecture, including La Sagrada Família.

BARCELONA IN...

Two Days

Start with the **Barri Gòtic**. After a stroll along **La Rambla**, wade into the labyrinth to admire **La Catedral** and surrounding monuments, including the fascinating Plaça del Rei, now part of the **Museu d'Història de la Ciutat**. Cross Via Laietana into **La Ribera** to confront the city's most beautiful church, the **Església de Santa Maria del Mar**, and the nearby **Museu Picasso**. To round off, plunge into the warren of bars and restaurants in the funky **El Born** area for a meal and cocktails.

The following day, start off at Gaudí's extraordinary work in progress, **La Sagrada Família**. Thus primed, you can spend the best part of the day paying homage to other Gaudí highlights, such as the **Casa Batlló** and **La Pedrera**. For dinner, plunge into El Raval for a classic meal at **Casa Leopoldo**.

Four Days

Following on from the two-day itinerary, dedicate a full day to **Montjuïc**, with its museum, fortress, gardens and Olympic stadium. After so much effort, a restful day at the beach might then be in order, followed by a seafood meal at **La Barceloneta**.

One Week

With three extra days you can explore still further, taking in Gaudí's wacky **Parc Güell**, the **Tibidabo** amusement park, and some walking in the **Collserola** parklands. A tempting one-day excursion is **Montserrat**, Catalonia's 'sacred mountain', or perhaps a day at the beach at **Sitges**, followed by a meal and a wild night at the bars.

Gràcia, beyond the wide Avinguda Diagonal on the northern edge of central L'Eixample, is a net of narrow streets and small squares with a varied population, and can be a lively place to spend a Friday or Saturday night. Just north of Gràcia is Gaudí's Parc Güell.

Two good landmarks are the hills of Montjuïc and Tibidabo. Montjuïc, the lower of the two, begins about 700m southwest of the bottom (southeastern end) of La Rambla. Tibidabo, with its TV tower and enormous Christ statue, is 6km northwest of Plaça de Catalunya. It's the high point of the Collserola range of wooded hills that forms the backdrop to the city.

El Prat airport is just 12km to the southwest of central Barcelona and easily reached by bus and train (see p318).

Maps

Tourist offices hand out free city and transport maps but Lonely Planet's *Barcelona City Map* (1:24,000 with a complete index of streets and sights) is better. Also handy is Michelin's ring-bound *Barcelona*, scaled at 1:12,000. More complete for long-termers is *Guia Barcelona i Poblacions Limítrofes*, published by Oceano.

INFORMATION
Bookshops

Altaïr (Map pp270-2; ☎ 93 342 71 71; Gran Via de les Corts Catalanes 616) Excellent travel bookshop with maps, guides and travel literature.

Antinous (Map pp273-5; ☎ 93 301 90 70; Carrer de Josep Anselm Clavé 6) Good gay bookshop and café.

Casa del Llibre (Map pp268-9; ☎ 93 272 34 80; Passeig de Gràcia 62) Enormous general bookshop.

Come In Bookshop (Map pp268-9; ☎ 93 453 12 04; Carrer de Provença 203) Specialists in English-language teaching books.

Elephant (Map pp270-2; ☎ 93 443 05 94; Carrer de la Creu dels Molers 12) A bright little English-language bookshop.

Laie (Map pp268-9; ☎ 93 518 17 39; Carrer de Pau Claris 85) Attractive bookshop with novels and books on architecture, art and film, in English and French, and a fine café.

Llibreria & Informaciò Cultural de la Generalitat de Catalunya (Map pp273-5; ☎ 93 302 64 62; La Rambla dels Estudis 118) First stop for books on all things Catalan.

Pròleg (Map pp273-5; ☎ 93 319 24 25; Carrer de la Dagueria 13) Well-stocked women's bookshop.

Quera (Map pp273-5; ☎ 93 318 07 43; Carrer de Petritxol 2) Map and guidebook specialists, particularly for hiking.

Cultural Centres

British Council (Map pp266-7; ☎ 93 241 99 77; Carrer d'Amigó 83; FGC Muntaner) Language school, library and occasional cultural events.

Institut Français de Barcelona (Map pp268-9; ☎ 93 209 59 11; Carrer de Moià 8) French-language school that also puts on films, concerts and exhibitions.

Institute for North American Studies (Map pp268-9; ☎ 93 240 51 10; Via Augusta 123) The main centre for learning North American English; also has library services.

Emergency

Tourists who want to report thefts need to go to the **Policía Nacional** (National Police; Map pp270-2; Carrer Nou de la Rambla 80; ☎ 091) or the **Guàrdia Urbana** (Local Police; Map pp273-5; La Rambla 43; ☎ 092).

Ambulance ☎ 061

EU standard emergency number ☎ 112

Fire Brigade (Bombers); ☎ 080 & ☎ 085

Guardia Civil (Military Police); ☎ 062

Institut Català de la Dona (Map pp273-5; ☎ 93 317 92 91; Carrer del Pintor Fortuny 21) For rape counselling.

Mossos d'Esquadra (Catalan State Police); ☎ 088

Internet Access

BBiGG (Map pp270-2; ☎ 93 301 40 20; www.bbigg.com; Carrer Comtal 9; per 24 min €1.30, per hr €2-2.50, membership €6, 30-day unlimited pass €25; ☾ 9am-11pm Mon-Sat, 10am-11pm Sun)

Conéctate (Map pp268-9; ☎ 93 467 04 43; Carrer d'Aragó 283; ☾ 24hr) A similar place providing Net time for as little as €1.20 an hour (it depends on usage at any given time).

Cybermundo (Map pp270-2; ☎ 93 317 71 42; Carrer de Bergara 3; per hr €2.90; ☾ 9am-midnight Mon-Thu, 9-1am Fri, 10-1am Sat, 11am-midnight Sun) Students and Barcelona residents pay less. Become a member (€6) and pay €1.20 an hour (five hours free).

easyInternetcafé (Map pp270-2; ☎ 93 412 13 97; www.easyeverything.com; Ronda de l'Universitat 35; ☾ 8-2am) With 300 terminals and a café, this is an Internet temple. For €1 you get about 30 minutes (depending on demand). Unlimited access costs €5/7/12 per day/week/month. There is another branch at **El Raval** (Map pp273-5; ☎ 93 318 24 35; La Rambla 31; ☾ 8-2.30am).

Laundry

Lavaxpress (Map pp270-2; Carrer de Ferlandina 34; per 8kg wash €3.50, per 30min drying €3.50; ☾ 8am-11pm)

Lavomatic Barri Gòtic (Map pp273-5; ☎ 93 342 51 19; Plaça de Joaquim Xirau 1; per 7kg wash €4, per 5min drying €0.80; ☺ 9am-9pm Mon-Sat); La Ribera (Map pp273-5; ☎ 93 268 47 68; Carrer del Consolat de Mar 43-45)

Wash'N Dry (Map pp268-9; www.washndry.net; Carrer de Torrent 105; per 8kg wash €4.50, per 10min drying €1; ☺ 7am-10pm) There are six other branches around town; wash, dry and fold service for an extra fee.

Left Luggage

At the airport, **left luggage** (consigna; ☺ open 24 hours) is on the ground floor of Terminal B, at the end closest to Terminal C.

Estació Sants, the train station, has **lockers** (small/big per 24hr €3/4.50; ☺ 5.30am-11pm), as does the main bus station, Estació del Nord.

Lost Property

Objectes Perduts (Lost Property; Map pp273-5; ☎ 010; Carrer de la Ciutat 9; ☺ 9am-2pm Mon-Fri)

Taxis Lost Property (☎ 93 223 40 12)

TMB Bus & Metro Lost Property – Centre d'Atenció al Client (☎ 93 318 70 74; Metro Universitat)

Media

El País includes a daily supplement devoted to Catalonia, but the region has a lively home-grown press too. *La Vanguardia* and *El Periódico* are the main local Castilian-language dailies. The latter also publishes an award-winning Catalan version. *Avui* is the more conservative and Catalan-nationalist daily. *El Punt*, a local Catalan daily that first appeared in late 2003, concentrates on news in and around Barcelona.

Medical Services

Hospital Clínic i Provincial (Map pp268-9; ☎ 93 227 54 00; Carrer de Villarroel 170)

Hospital de la Santa Creu i de Sant Pau (Map pp266-7; ☎ 93 291 90 00; Carrer de Sant Antoni Maria Claret 167)

Hospital Dos de Mayo (Map pp266-7; ☎ 93 507 27 00; Carrer del Dos de Maig 301)

Call ☎ 010 to find out where the nearest late-opening duty pharmacy is. There are also several 24-hour pharmacies scattered across town:

Farmàcia Álvarez (Map pp268-9; ☎ 93 302 11 24; Passeig de Gràcia 26)

Farmàcia Clapés (Map pp273-5; ☎ 93 301 28 43; La Rambla de Sant Joseph 98)

Farmàcia Torres (Map pp270-2; ☎ 93 453 92 20; Carrer d'Aribau 62)

Money

Barcelona abounds in banks, many with ATMs, including several around Plaça de Catalunya, on La Rambla and on Plaça de Sant Jaume in Barri Gòtic.

The foreign-exchange offices that you see along La Rambla and elsewhere are open for longer hours than banks but generally offer poorer rates.

American Express (Amex; Map pp273-5; ☎ 93 342 73 11; La Rambla dels Caputxins 74; ☺ 9am-midnight daily Apr-Sep, 9am-9pm Mon-Sat Oct-Mar) This office has a cash machine for Amex cardholders.

Post

The **main post office** (Map pp273-5; Plaça d'Antoni López; ☺ 8.30am-9.30pm Mon-Sat, 9am-2pm Sun) is just opposite the northeastern end of Port Vell. There's a handy **branch** (Map pp273-5; Carrer d'Aragó 282; ☺ 8.30am-8.30pm Mon-Fri, 9.30am-1pm Sat) just off Passeig de Gràcia.

Tourist Information

A couple of general information lines worth bearing in mind are ☎ 010 and ☎ 012. The first is for Barcelona and the latter is for all of Catalonia (run by the Generalitat). You may sometimes strike English-speakers but most operators are Catalan-Castilian bilingual.

Several tourist offices operate in town:

Oficina d'Informació de Turisme de Barcelona (Aeroport del Prat; ☺ 9am-9pm) In the airport's EU arrivals hall, it has information on all of Catalonia. A smaller office at the international arrivals hall opens the same hours.

Oficina d'Informació de Turisme de Barcelona (Map pp266-7; Estació Sants; ☺ 8am-8pm Jun-Sep, 8am-8pm Mon-Fri, 8am-2pm Sat, Sun & holidays Oct-May) Train-station branch with limited city information.

Oficina d'Informació de Turisme de Barcelona (Map pp270-2; ☎ 807 117222, outside Spain 93 368 97 30/1; www.barcelonaturisme.com; Plaça de Catalunya 17-S underground; ☺ 9am-9pm) The main Barcelona tourist information office concentrates on city information and can help book accommodation. Expect to queue.

Oficina d'Informació de Turisme de Barcelona (Map pp273-5; Plaça de Sant Jaume; ☺ 9am-8pm Mon-Fri, 10am-8pm Sat, 10am-2pm Sun & holidays). A branch in the *ajuntament* (town hall).

Palau de la Virreina Arts Information Office (Map pp273-5; ☎ 93 301 77 75; La Rambla de Sant Josep 99; ☺ 10am-8pm Mon-Sat, 11am-3pm Sun) A useful office for events information (and tickets).

Regional tourist office (Map pp268-9; ☎ 93 238 40 00; Passeig de Gràcia 107; ☺ 10am-7pm Mon-Sat,

10am-2pm Sun) Housed in the Palau Robert, it has a host of material on Catalonia, audiovisual stuff, a bookshop and a branch of Turisme Juvenil de Catalunya (for youth travel).

Travel Agencies

Asatej (Map pp273-5; ☎ 93 412 63 38; www.almundo .com in Spanish; La Rambla de Canaletes 140) Can organise anything from car rental to trips outside Spain.

Halcón Viatges (Map pp268-9; ☎ 902 433000; www .halconviajes.com in Spanish; Carrer de Pau Claris 108) Reliable chain of travel agents that sometimes has good deals. This is one of many branches around town.

Viajes Zeppelin (Map pp270-2; ☎ 93 412 00 13; www .viajeszeppelin.com in Spanish; Carrer de Villarroel 49) Small chain that often finds good-value fares.

DANGERS & ANNOYANCES

Every year a contingent of aggrieved readers writes in with tales of woe from Barcelona. Petty crime and theft, with tourists as the prey of choice, is a problem, so you need to take a few common-sense precautions to avoid joining this regrettable list. Nine times out of 10 it is easy enough to avoid.

Thieves and pickpockets operate on airport trains and the metro, especially around stops popular with tourists (such as La Sagrada Família). The Old City (Ciutat Vella), which attracts the greatest concentration of visitors, and usually in their first days in town, is the pickpockets' and bag-snatchers' prime hunting ground. Take special care on and around La Rambla. Prostitutes working the lower (waterfront) end often do a double trade in wallet snatching. Also, stay well clear of the ball-and-three-cups (*trileros*) brigades on La Rambla. This is always a set-up and you will lose your money (and maybe have your pockets emptied as you watch the game).

SIGHTS

Barcelona could be divided up into thematic chunks. In Ciutat Vella (especially the Barri Gòtic and La Ribera) are clustered the bulk of the city's ancient and medieval splendours. Along with El Raval, on the other side of La Rambla, and Port Vell, where old

---

DISCOUNTS & OPENING TIMES

Admission prices to Barcelona's museums and sights vary greatly, but €3 to €8 covers the range of most. Students generally pay a little over half this, as do senior citizens (aged 65 and over) with appropriate ID, and children aged under 12. Several sights have free-entry days, often just once a month. For example the Museu Picasso (p285) is free on the first Sunday of the month and the Museu Nacional d'Art de Catalunya (MNAC; p295) on the first Thursday. Details of free days appear under each entry in the course of the chapter.

Possession of a Bus Turístic ticket (p300) entitles you to discounts to some museums.

The **Ruta del Modernisme** ticket (€3, valid for 30 days) is not as hot as it was, but if you intend to visit the Palau de la Música Catalana, the Fundació Antoni Tàpies and the Museu de Zoologia, the half-price discount is worthwhile. You also get a Modernisme itinerary map and a modest guide booklet. You can pick up the ticket at **Casa de Amatller** (☎ 93 488 01 39; Passeig de Gràcia 41), one of the fine Modernista buildings of the Manzana de la Discordia (p288).

Articket (€15) gives you admission to six important sights: MNAC; Museu d'Art Contemporani de Barcelona (Macba); Fundació Antoni Tàpies; Centre de Cultura Contemporània de Barcelona (CCCB); Fundació Joan Miró; and La Pedrera. You can pick up the ticket through **Tel-Entrada** (☎ 902 101212; www.telentrada.com), at the tourist offices on Plaça de Catalunya, Plaça de Sant Jaume and Sants train station, or at selected branches of the Caixa de Catalunya bank.

If you intend to get around Barcelona fast, and want to visit multiple museums in the blink of an eye, the **Barcelona Card** might come in handy. It costs €17/20/23/25/27 (a little less for children aged four to 12) for one/two/three/four/five days. You get free transport and up to 100% off admission prices to many museums and other sights, as well as minor discounts on purchases at a limited number of shops, restaurants and bars. The card is available at the tourist offices, where you should have a look at the pamphlet first to see whether the discounted sights are what you were hoping to see. You can see details online at www.barcelonaturisme.com.

Museum and art-gallery opening hours vary considerably, but as a rule of thumb you should be OK between 10am and 6pm in most places (many shut for lunch from around 2pm to 4pm, though). Most museums and galleries close all day Monday, and from 2pm Sunday.

Barcelona meets the sea, this is the core of the city's life, by day and by night.

L'Eixample is where the Modernistas went to town. Here the attractions are more spread out. Passeig de Gràcia is a concentrated showcase for some of the most outlandish of their work, but La Sagrada Família, Gaudí's masterpiece, and other outstanding buildings are scattered about.

The beaches and working-class district of La Barceloneta (which is riddled with seafood restaurants) form a separate summery side of the city, just as Montjuïc, with its gardens, museums, art galleries and Olympic Games sites, forms a microcosm on its own.

Gaudí's Parc Güell is just beyond the area of Gràcia, whose narrow lanes and interlocking squares set the scene for much lively nightlife.

Further sights, ranging from FC Barcelona's Camp Nou football stadium to the peaceful haven of the Museu-Monestir de Pedralbes, glitter like distant stars away from the centre.

La Rambla

Head to Spain's most famous street for a first taste of Barcelona's atmosphere. Flanked by narrow traffic lanes, the middle of La Rambla is a broad, pedestrian boulevard, lined with cafés and restaurants, and crowded every day until well beyond midnight with a cross-section of Barcelona's permanent and transient populace.

La Rambla gets its name from a seasonal stream (*raml* in Arabic) that once ran here. It was outside the city walls until the 14th century, and built up with monastic buildings and palaces in the 16th to 18th centuries. Unofficially it's divided into five sections with their own names.

From Plaça de Catalunya, La Rambla de Canaletes is the first stretch of the boulevard and named after an unobtrusive fount, whose drinking water (despite claims that anyone drinking of it will return to Barcelona) nowadays leaves a lot to be desired. A block off to the east along Carrer de la Canuda is Plaça de la Vila de Madrid, with a sunken garden where some Roman tombs lie exposed.

The second stretch, La Rambla dels Estudis, from below Carrer de la Canuda to Carrer de la Portaferrissa, is also called Rambla dels Ocells (Birds) because of its twittering bird market. From Carrer de la Portaferrissa to Plaça Boqueria, what is officially called La Rambla de Sant Josep is lined with flower stalls, which give it the alternative name Rambla de les Flors.

The **Palau de la Virreina** (Map pp273-5; La Rambla de Sant Josep 99) is a grand 18th-century rococo mansion housing an arts-entertainment information and ticket office that's run by the municipality. Next up is the **Mercat de la Boqueria**, one of the best stocked and most colourful of its kind in or beyond Barcelona. Plaça Boqueria, where four side streets meet just north of Liceu metro station, is your chance to walk all over a Miró – the colourful **Mosaïc de Miró** (Map pp273–5) in the pavement, with one tile signed by the artist.

Barcelona seems to take pride in being a pleasure centre and in the **Museu de l'Eròtica** (Map pp273-5; ☎ 93 318 98 65; www.erotica-museum .com; La Rambla de Sant Josep 96; admission €7.50; ☾ 10am-midnight Jun-Sep, 11am-9pm Oct-May), you can observe just how people have been enjoying themselves since ancient times – lots of Kamasutra and 1920s porn flicks.

La Rambla dels Caputxins (also known as Rambla del Centre) runs from Plaça de la Boqueria to Carrer dels Escudellers. On the western side is the Gran Teatre del Liceu.

Further south on the eastern side of Rambla dels Caputxins is the entrance to the palm-shaded Plaça Reial. Below this point La Rambla gets seedier, with a few strip clubs and peep shows. The final stretch, La Rambla de Santa Mònica, widens out to approach the Monument a Colom overlooking Port Vell. La Rambla here is named after the Convento de Santa Mònica that once stood on the western flank of the street and has since been converted into an art gallery and cultural centre, the **Centre d'Art Santa Mònica** (Map pp270-2; ☎ 93 316 28 10; La Rambla de Santa Mònica 7; ☾ 11am-8pm Tue-Sat, 11am-3pm Sun & holidays).

On the east side lurks the **Museu de Cera** (Map pp273-5; ☎ 93 317 26 49; www.museocerabcn .com; Passatge de la Banca 7; adult/child under 12 €6.65/3.75; ☾ 10am-1.30pm & 4-7.30pm Mon-Fri, 11am-2pm & 4.30-8.30pm Sat, Sun & holidays), a wax museum with a hall of horror and everyone from Lady Di to General Franco.

GRAN TEATRE DEL LICEU

Barcelona's grand **opera house** (Map pp273-5; ☎ 93 485 99 14; www.liceubarcelona.com; La Rambla dels Caputxins 51-59; admission €3.50, guided tour adult/ student/child under 10 €5.50/4/free, guided tour incl El

Cercle del Liceu €8.50/7/free; 🕐 guided tours 10am, unguided visits 11.30am, noon & 1pm) was built in 1847, largely destroyed by fire in 1994, and reopened better than ever in 1999.

The Liceu launched such Catalan stars as Josep (aka José) Carreras and Montserrat Caballé, and can seat up to 2300. On the standard visit you are taken to the grand foyer, and then up the marble staircase to the glittering, neo-baroque **Saló dels Miralls** (Hall of Mirrors). You are then led up to the 4th floor to admire the theatre in all its splendour from the high stalls. The longer tour takes in the above and a collection of Modernista art, El Cercle del Liceu.

MONUMENT A COLOM

The bottom end of La Rambla, and the harbour beyond, lie under the supervision of this late-19th-century **monument** (Map pp270-2; ☎ 93 302 52 24; Portal de la Pau; lift adult/child €2/1.30; 🕐 9am-8.30pm Jun-Sep, 10am-6.30pm Oct-May) to the glory of Christopher Columbus. Take the lift to the top for spectacular views over the city.

MUSEU MARÍTIM

West of the Monument a Colom stand the Reials Drassanes (Royal Shipyards), now home to the **Maritime Museum** (Map pp270-2; ☎ 93 342 99 20; www.diba.es/mmaritim; Avinguda de les Drassanes; adult/student & senior €5.40/2.70; 🕐 10am-7pm), a rare work of nonreligious Gothic architecture. The museum, together with its setting, forms a fascinating tribute to the seafaring that shaped much of Barcelona's history and is worth an hour or so of your time.

The shipyards, first built in the 13th century, gained their present form (a series of long bays divided by stone arches) a century later. Extensions in the 17th century made them big enough to accommodate the building of 30 galleys. In their shipbuilding days (up to the 18th century) the sea came right up to them.

Inside is an impressive array of boats, models, maps, paintings and more, with sections devoted to ships' figureheads, Columbus and Magellan, and 16th-century galleys (the full-scale replica of Don Juan of Austria's royal galley from the Battle of Lepanto is the highlight).

Barri Gòtic   Map pp273-5

Barcelona's 'Gothic Quarter', east of La Rambla, is a classic medieval warren of nar-

> ### TOP FIVE WHAT'S FREE?
>
> - **Parc Güell** (p291) Gaudí's weird and wonderful landscaped park.
> - **CaixaForum** (p294) A grand gallery of modern art with constantly changing exhibitions.
> - **Estadi Olímpic** (p295) The site of the 1992 Olympics.
> - **Temple Romà d'Augustí** (p282) The soaring columns left over from a great Roman temple.
> - **Ajuntament** (below) The gorgeous rooms of the city's town hall.

row, winding streets, quaint little *plaças* (plazas), and grand mansions and monuments from the city's golden age. Few of its great buildings date from after the early 15th century. The district is liberally seasoned with a sprinkling of restaurants, cafés and bars, so sight-seeing relief is always close to hand!

Barri Gòtic stretches from La Rambla in the west, to Via Laietana in the east, and roughly from Carrer de la Portaferrissa in the north, to Carrer de la Mercè in the south. Carrer de Ferran and Carrer de Jaume I, cutting across the middle, form a kind of halfway line: these streets and those to their north tend to be peppered with chic little shops, while those to their south become marginally seedier (if in general no less lively).

PLAÇA DE SANT JAUME

This square at the eastern end of Carrer de Ferran has been Barcelona's political hub on and off since the 15th century. Facing each other across it are the Palau de la Generalitat (the seat of Catalonia's government), on the northern side, and the *ajuntament* (town hall) on the southern side. Both have fine Gothic interiors, which the general public can only enter at limited times.

The **Palau de la Generalitat**, founded in the early 15th century, is open only on 23 April, the Dia de Sant Jordi (St George, Catalonia's patron saint), when it's decked out with roses and also very crowded, and 24 September (Festes de la Mercè). At any time, however, you can admire the original Gothic main entrance on Carrer del Bisbe Irurita.

BARCELONA

Outside, the only feature of the **Ajunta-ment** (☎ 93 403 70 00; 🕑 10am-2pm Sat & Sun) that's now worthy of note is the disused Gothic entrance on Carrer de la Ciutat. Inside you can visit, above all, the Saló de Cent, a fine arched hall created in the 14th century (but since remodelled) for the medieval city council, the Consell de Cent. Guided visits start every 30 minutes, and English and French are catered for.

CATEDRAL & AROUND

You can reach Barcelona's **cathedral** (☎ 93 315 15 54; Plaça de la Seu; admission free, special visit €4; 🕑 8am-1.15pm & 5pm-7.30pm, special visit 1.30-5pm), its most magnificent Gothic structure, by following Carrer del Bisbe Irurita northwest from Plaça de Sant Jaume. The narrow old streets around the cathedral are traffic-free, and dotted with occasionally very talented buskers.

The best view of the cathedral is from Plaça de la Seu beneath its main **north-western façade**. Unlike most of the building, which dates from between 1298 and 1460, this façade was not created until the 1870s, although it is closely based on a 1408 design. It is unusual in that it reflects northern-European Gothic styles rather than the sparer, Catalan version.

The interior of the cathedral is a broad, soaring space divided into a central nave and two aisles, by lines of elegant, thin pillars.

In the first chapel, on the right from the northwestern entrance, the main Crucifixion figure above the altar is **Sant Crist de Lepant**, carried on the prow of the Spanish flagship at the battle of Lepanto. Further along this same wall, past the southwestern transept, are the wooden **coffins** of Count Ramon Berenguer I and Almodis, his wife, the founders of the 11th-century Romanesque predecessor to the present cathedral.

Smack bang in the middle of the central nave is the late-14th-century exquisitely sculpted timber **coro** (choir stalls; admission €1.50). The coats of arms belong to members of the Barcelona chapter of the Order of the Golden Fleece.

The **crypt** beneath the main altar contains the tomb of Santa Eulàlia, one of Barcelona's patron saints and a good Christian lass of the 4th century, who is said to have suffered terrible tortures and death at the hands of the pagan Romans.

For a bird's-eye (mind the poop) view of medieval Barcelona, visit the cathedral's **roof** and tower by a lift (admission €2) from the Capella de les Animes del Purgatori, near the northeastern transept.

From the southwestern transept, exit to the lovely **claustre** (cloister), with its trees, fountains and geese (there have been geese here for centuries). One of the cloister chapels commemorates 930 priests, monks and nuns, who were martyred in the civil war.

Along the northern flank of the cloister you can enter the **Sala Capitular** (chapterhouse; admission €1.50). Although bathed in the rich reds of the carpet, and cosseted by fine-timber seating, the few artworks gathered here are of minor interest. Among them is a *Pietat* by Bartolomeo Bermejo.

You can visit the cathedral in one of two ways. In the morning or the afternoon entrance is free and you can opt to visit any combination of the choir stalls, chapter house and roof you choose. If you want to visit all three, it costs less (and is less crowded) to enter for the so-called 'special visit'.

At the northern end of Carrer del Bisbe Irurita, poke your head into the courtyards of the 16th-century **Casa de l'Ardiaca** (Archdeacon's House) and the 13th-century **Palau de Bispat** (Bishop's Palace). On the outside of both buildings, at the very end of Carrer del Bisbe Irurita, you can make out the foundations of the rounded towers that guarded a Roman gate here. The lower part of the Casa de l'Ardiaca's northwestern wall was part of the **Roman walls** (🕑 9am-9pm Mon-Fri, 9am-2pm Sat). Inside the building itself you can see parts of the wall.

The walls ran along present-day Plaça de la Seu into what subsequently became the **Casa de la Pia Almoina**, a medieval centre of charity that now houses the **Museu Diocesà** (Diocesan Museum; ☎ 93 315 22 13; Avinguda de la Catedral 4; admission €3; 🕑 10am-3pm & 4-8pm Tue-Sun), where you can see a sparse collection of medieval religious art, usually supplemented by a temporary exposition.

Just beyond the southeastern end of the cathedral stand four columns of the **Temple Romà d'Augustí** (Roman Temple of Augustus; Carrer de Paradis 10; admission free; 🕑 10am-2pm Mon-Sat).

PLAÇA DEL REI

Just a stone's throw east of the cathedral, Plaça del Rei is the former courtyard of the

Palau Reial Major, the palace of the Counts of Barcelona and monarchs of Aragón.

Most of the tall, centuries-old buildings surrounding Plaça del Rei are now open to visitors as the **Museu d'Història de la Ciutat** (☎ 93 315 11 11; www.museuhistoria.bcn.es; Carrer del Veguer; adult/student incl Museu-Monestir de Pedralbes €4/2.50, admission free 4-8pm 1st Sat of month, temporary exhibitions adult/student €3.50/1.50; ☉ 10am-2pm & 4-8pm Tue-Sat, 10am-3pm Sun Oct-May; 10am-8pm Tue-Sat, 10am-3pm Sun Jun-Sep). This City History Museum is one of Barcelona's most fascinating sights, combining large sections of the palace with a subterranean walk through Roman and Visigothic Barcelona. Set aside a good hour for the visit.

The entrance to the museum is through the **Casa Padellàs**, just south of Plaça del Rei. Casa Padellàs, built for a 16th-century noble family, has a courtyard typical of Barcelona's late-Gothic and baroque mansions, with an external staircase up to the 1st floor. Today the staircase leads to a restored Roman tower and a section of Roman wall. Below ground is a remarkable walk through excavated Roman and Visigothic **ruins** – complete with sections of a Roman street, Roman baths, remains of a Visigothic basilica and a Visigothic baptismal pool. You emerge inside the former palace on the northern side of the Plaça del Rei. To your right is the Saló del Tinell and to the left ahead of you is the Capella Reial de Santa Àgata.

The **Saló del Tinell** was the royal palace's throne hall, a masterpiece of strong, unfussy Catalan Gothic, built in the mid-14th century with wide, rounded arches holding up a wooden roof. The **Capella Reial de Santa Àgata**, whose spindly bell tower rises from the northeastern side of Plaça del Rei, was the palace's chapel and also dates from the 14th century.

Head into Plaça del Rei down the fanshaped stairs and bear right to the entrance to the multitiered **Mirador del Rei Martí** (Lookout Tower of King Martin), built in 1555, from where you can enjoy excellent views over the city.

PALAU DEL LLOCTINENT

The southwest side of Plaça del Rei is taken up by the **Palau del Lloctinent** (Viceroy's Palace), built in the 1550s as the residence of the Spanish viceroy of Catalonia.

MUSEU FREDERIC MARÈS

A short distance north, along Carrer dels Comtes de Barcelona, is the **Museu Frederic Marès** (☎ 93 310 58 00; www.museumares.bcn.es; Plaça de Sant Iu 5-6; admission €3, free Wed afternoon & 1st Sun of month; ☉ 10am-7pm Tue-Sat, 10am-3pm Sun & holidays), in another part of the Palau Reial Major. Marès was a rich 20th-century Catalan sculptor and collector. He specialised in medieval Spanish sculpture, huge quantities of which are displayed on the ground and 1st floors. The top two floors, which are known as the Museu Sentimental, hold a mindboggling array of other Marès knick-knacks, from toy soldiers and cribs to scissors and tarot cards. Take a load off in the pleasant courtyard café.

ROMAN WALLS

From Plaça del Rei it's worth a detour to see the two best surviving stretches of Barcelona's Roman walls. One is on the southwestern side of Plaça de Ramon Berenguer el Gran, with the Capella Reial de Santa Àgata atop them. The other is further south, by the northern end of Carrer del Sotstinent Navarro. They date from the 3rd and 4th centuries, when the Romans rebuilt their walls after the first attacks by Germanic tribes from the north.

PLAÇA DE SANT JOSEP ORIOL & AROUND

This small plaza, not far off La Rambla, is the prettiest in the Barri Gòtic. Its bars and cafés attract buskers and artists, and make it a lively place to hang out at for a while. It's surrounded by quaint streets, many of them dotted with appealing cafés, restaurants and shops. The plaza is dominated by the **Església de Santa Maria del Pi** (☉ 8.30am-1pm & 4.30-9pm Mon-Sat, 9am-2pm & 5-9pm Sun & holidays), a Gothic church built from the 14th to 16th centuries. The beautiful rose window above its entrance on Plaça del Pi is claimed to be the world's biggest. The inside of the church was gutted by fire in 1936, and most of the stained glass is modern.

SINAGOGA MAJOR

The area between Carrer dels Banys Nous, to the east of the church, and Plaça de Sant Jaume is known as the Call, and was Barcelona's **Jewish quarter** – and centre of learning – from at least the 11th century until anti-Semitism saw the Jews expelled from it in 1424. Here the sparse remains of the **Sinagoga Major** (Main Synagogue; ☎ 93 317 07 90; www.calldebarcelona.org; Carrer de Marlet 5; admission free; ⏰ 11am-2.30pm & 4-7.30pm) have been revealed. Remnants of medieval and Roman-era walls remain, suggesting to some (given their orientation towards Jerusalem) that there may even have been a Jewish place of worship on this spot in Roman times.

PLAÇA REIAL & AROUND
Just south of Carrer de Ferran is **Plaça Reial**, an elegant shady square surrounded by eateries, bars, nightspots and budget accommodation. The plaza's 19th-century neoclassical architecture looks as if it would be at home in some Parisian quarter. The lampposts next to the central fountain are Gaudí's first known works.

Until the 1980s the square and surrounding streets had long been a den of poverty, drug abuse and prostitution. A whiff of its dodgy past remains, mainly in the form of a few down-and-outs, and the occasional pickpocket, being all that remain of those grim days. Today locals and tourists fill the square's bars and restaurants with chatter and laughter.

El Raval
West of La Rambla, Ciutat Vella spreads to Ronda de Sant Antoni, Ronda de Sant Pau and Avinguda del Paral.lel, which together trace the line of Barcelona's 14th-century walls. Known as El Raval, the area contains what remains of one of the city's more dispiriting slums, the seedy red-light zone and drug-abusers' haunt of the Barri Xinès, at its southern end. Steps to improve the area are being taken, but you should take care of your pockets around here.

MUSEU D'ART CONTEMPORÀNI & AROUND
The vast, white **Museu d'Art Contemporàni de Barcelona** (Macba; Map pp270-2; ☎ 93 412 08 10; www.macba.es; Plaça dels Àngels 1; admission €7; ⏰ 11am-7.30pm Mon & Wed-Fri, 10am-8pm Sat, 10am-3pm Sun & holidays) opened in 1995 as part of the campaign to give El Raval a lift. Artists frequently on show include Antoni Tàpies, Joan Brossa, Paul Klee, Alexander Calder and Miquel Barceló.

Behind the museum is the **Centre de Cultura Contemporània de Barcelona** (CCCB; Map pp270-2;

☎ 93 306 41 00; Carrer de Montalegre 5; adult/student €4/3; ⏰ 11am-8pm Tue-Sat, 11am-3pm Sun & holidays 21 Jun–21 Sep; 11am-2pm & 4-8pm Tue & Thu-Fri, 11am-8pm Wed & Sat, 11am-7pm Sun & holidays 22 Sep–20 Jun), a complex of auditoriums and exhibition and conference halls created in the early 1990s from an 18th-century hospice. The big courtyard, with a vast glass wall on one side, is spectacular. Exhibitions are held here regularly.

On the south side of the square is the Gothic shell of the 16th-century **Convent dels Àngels** (Map pp270-2; ☎ 93 301 77 75; Plaça dels Àngels), renovated as exhibition space.

Two blocks southeast of Plaça dels Àngels is an architectural masterpiece from another age. Founded in the early 15th century as the city's main hospital, the **Antic Hospital de la Santa Creu** (Map pp273-5; ☎ 93 270 23 00; Carrer de l'Hospital 56; admission free; ⏰ 9am-8pm Mon-Fri, 9am-2pm Sat) today houses the Biblioteca de Catalunya (Catalonia's national library). Take a look inside to admire some fine Catalan-Gothic construction.

The **chapel** (☎ 93 442 71 71; Carrer de l'Hospital 56; ⏰ noon-2pm & 4-8pm Tue-Sat, 11am-2pm Sun) of the former hospital is worth poking your nose into as well. It is often used for temporary exhibitions.

PALAU GÜELL
Gaudí's **Palau Güell** (Map pp273-5; ☎ 93 317 39 74; Carrer Nou de la Rambla 3-5; adult/student €3/1.50; ⏰ 10am-6.15pm Mon-Sat Jun-Sep, 10am-4.15pm Oct-Apr) is one of the few Modernista buildings in Ciutat Vella. Gaudí built it in the late 1880s for his most important patron, the industrialist Eusebi Güell. It lacks some of Gaudí's later playfulness but is still a characteristic riot of styles – Art Nouveau, Gothic, Islamic – and materials. After the civil war it was in police hands and political prisoners were tortured in its basement.

Features to look out for include the carved wooden ceilings and fireplace, the stonework, the use of mirrors, stained glass and wrought iron, and the main hall with its dome reaching right up to the roof. The roof is a weird world of fantastically shaped and polychrome tiled chimneypots. Tours usually start on the hour and take about an hour.

La Ribera
La Ribera is cut off from the Barri Gòtic by noisy Via Laietana, which was driven

through the city in 1907. La Ribera, whose name refers to the waterfront that once lay much further inland, was the pumping commercial heart of medieval Barcelona. Its intriguing, narrow streets house some major sights and a warren of good bars and restaurants, mainly in the hip El Born area.

PALAU DE LA MÚSICA CATALANA

This **Palace of Catalan Music** (Map pp270-2; ☎ 93 295 72 00; www.palaumusica.org; Carrer de Sant Francesc de Paula 2; adult/student/child under 12 by guided tour €7/6/free; ☒ 50min tour every 30min 10am-3.30pm) is one of the city's Modernista high points. It's not exactly a symphony, more a series of crescendos in tile, brick, sculptured stone and stained glass. Built between 1905 and 1908, by Lluís Domènech i Montaner for the Orfeo Català musical society, it was conceived as a temple for the Catalan Renaixença.

You can see some of its splendours – such as the main façade with its mosaics, floral capitals and sculpture cluster representing Catalan popular music – from the outside and glimpse lovely tiled pillars inside the ticket-office entrance on Carrer de Sant Francesc de Paula.

Best of all is the richly colourful auditorium upstairs, with its ceiling of blue-and-gold stained glass and, above a bust of Beethoven, a towering sculpture of Wagner's Valkyries (Wagner was No 1 on the Renaixença charts). To see this, you need to attend a concert or join a guided tour.

MUSEU PICASSO

Barcelona's most visited museum, the **Museu Picasso** (Map pp273-5; ☎ 93 319 63 10; www.museupicasso.bcn.es; Carrer de Montcada 15-23; adult/child/child under 12 €4.80/2.40/free, admission free 1st Sun of month; ☒ 10am-8pm Tue-Sat & holidays, 10am-3pm Sun), occupies five of the many fine medieval stone mansions on narrow Carrer de Montcada (alone worth wandering into to see the courtyards and galleries). The collection concentrates on Picasso's formative years and several highly specific moments in his later life. Allow one to two hours.

The permanent collection is housed in the first three houses, the **Palau Aguilar**, **Palau del Baró de Castellet** and the **Palau Meca**, all dating to the 14th century. The 18th-century **Casa Mauri**, built over medieval remains (even some Roman leftovers have been identified), and the adjacent 14th-century

Palau Finestres accommodate temporary exhibitions.

A visit starts, naturally enough, at the beginning, with sketches, oils and doodling from Picasso's earliest years in Málaga and La Coruña – most of it done between 1893 and 1895. Some of his self-portraits, and the portraits of his father, which date from 1896, are evidence enough of his precocious talent. The enormous *Ciència i Caritat* (Science and Charity) is proof to anyone that, had he wanted, Picasso would have made a fine mainstream artist. His first consciously thematic adventure, the Blue Period is well covered. His nocturnal blue-tinted views of *Terrats de Barcelona* (The Rooftops of Barcelona) and *El Foll* (The Madman) are cold and cheerless, and yet somehow alive.

Among the later works, done in Cannes in 1957, there's a complex technical series *(Las Meninas)*. These consist of studies on Diego Velázquez's masterpiece of the same name (which hangs in the Prado in Madrid). There are additional charges for special exhibitions.

MUSEU TÈXTIL I D'INDUMENTÀRIA

This **museum** (Map pp273-5; ☎ 93 319 76 03; www.museutextil.bcn.es; Carrer de Montcada 12-14; admission €3.50, free 1st Sun of month; ☒ 10am-6pm Tue-Sat, 10am-3pm Sun & holidays) is in the 14th-century Palau dels Marquesos de Llió, across the road from the Museu Picasso. Its 4000 items range from 4th-century Coptic textiles to 20th-century local embroidery. The highlight is the big collection of clothing from the 16th century to the 1930s. The courtyard is graced with an agreeable café.

MUSEU BARBIER-MUELLER D'ART PRECOLOMBÍ

Occupying Palau Nadal, this **museum** (Map pp273-5; ☎ 93 310 45 16; www.barbier-mueller.ch; Carrer de Montcada 12-14; adult/student/child under 16 €3/1.50/free, admission free 1st Sun of month; ☒ 10am-6pm Tue-Sat, 10am-3pm Sun & holidays) holds part of one of the world's most prestigious collections of pre-Colombian art, including gold jewellery, ceramics, statues and textiles. The artefacts from South American 'primitive' cultures come from the collections of the Swiss businessman Josef Mueller (who died in 1977) and his son-in-law Jean-Paul Barbier, who directs the Musée Barbier-Mueller in Geneva.

BARCELONA

CARRER DE MONTCADA

Several other mansions on this once wealthy street of Barcelona merchant barons are now commercial art galleries where you're welcome to browse. The 16th-century **Palau dels Cervelló** (Map pp273-5; Carrer de Montcada 25), for instance, houses the **Galeria Maeght**. The baroque courtyard of the originally medieval **Palau de Dalmases** (Map pp273-5; Carrer de Montcada 20) is one of the finest on the strip. The building is home to a delightfully far-fetched baroque-flavoured wine bar too (p310).

ESGLÉSIA DE SANTA MARIA DEL MAR

Carrer de Montcada opens at its southeastern end into **Passeig del Born**, a plaza where jousting tournaments took place in the Middle Ages, and drinking, eating and carousing take place today. At its southwestern end rises Barcelona's finest Gothic church, the **Església de Santa Maria del Mar** (Map pp273-5; ☎ 93 319 05 16; Plaça de Santa Maria del Mar; admission free; ⏰ 9am-1.30pm & 4.30-8pm). Built in the 14th century, Santa Maria was lacking in superfluous decoration even before anarchists gutted it in 1909 and 1936. This only serves to highlight its fine proportions, purity of line and sense of space.

MUSEU DE LA XOCOLATA

In this **Museum of Chocolate** (Map pp270-2; ☎ 93 268 78 78; www.museuxocolata.com in Spanish; Plaça de Pons i Clerch s/n; admission €3.80, free 1st Mon of month; ⏰ 10am-7pm Mon & Wed-Sat, 10am-3pm Sun & holidays) you can trace the origins of this fundamental foodstuff and admire chocolate models of buildings such as La Pedrera and La Sagrada Família.

Parc de la Ciutadella

East of La Ribera and north of La Barceloneta, **Parc de la Ciutadella** (Map pp270-2; ⏰ 8am-6pm Nov-Feb, 8am-8pm Oct & Mar, 8am-9pm Apr-Sep) makes a fine antidote to the noise and bustle of the city, and is worth a little exploration.

After the War of the Spanish Succession, Felipe V built a huge fort (La Ciutadella) to keep watch over Barcelona. Only in 1869 did the government allow its demolition, after which the site was turned into a park and used to host the Universal Exhibition of 1888.

The single most impressive object in the park is the monumental **Cascada** near the Passeig de les Pujades entrance, created between 1875 and 1881 by Josep Fontsère, with the help of a young Gaudí. It's a dramatic combination of classical statuary, rugged rocks, greenery and thundering water.

Southeast, in the fort's former arsenal, is the regional **Parlament de Catalunya** (Map pp270-2; ☎ 93 304 65 00; admission free, guided group visits by appointment; ⏰ 9am-2pm & 4-8pm Mon-Fri).

The southern end of the park is occupied by the **Zoo de Barcelona** (Map pp270-2; ☎ 93 225 67 80; adult/child €12.90/8.30; ⏰ 10am-7.30pm Apr-Sep, 10am-5pm Oct-Mar), which is destined to be moved to another site, although when remains a mystery. It holds about 7000 living thingies, from gorillas to insects.

Along the Passeig de Picasso side of the park are several buildings constructed for, or just before, the Universal Exhibition. These include two arboretums, the **Museu de Geologia** (Map pp270-2; ☎ 93 319 68 95; Passeig de Picasso; admission with Museu de Zoologia €3; ⏰ 10am-2pm Tue-Wed & Fri-Sun, 10am-6.30pm Thu), for rock- and fossil-lovers, and the **Museu de Zoologia** (Map pp270-2; ☎ 93 319 69 12; Passeig de Picasso; admission with Museu de Geologia €3; ⏰ 10am-2pm Tue-Wed & Fri-Sun, 10am-6.30pm Thu). The contents of this museum (stuffed animals and the kind of displays on the animal kingdom that once formed a part of the young child's school-outings programmes) are less interesting than the building itself, the Castell dels Tres Dragons (Dragons Castle), a whimsical effort by Lluís Domènech i Montaner, who put medieval-castle trimmings on a pioneering steel frame for the Universal Exhibition.

Northwest of the park is the imposing Modernista **Arc de Triomf** (Map pp266-7; Passeig de Lluís Companys), with unusual, Islamic-style brickwork.

Port Vell

Barcelona's old port at the bottom of La Rambla, once such an eyesore that it caused public protests, has been transformed since the 1980s into a people-friendly leisure zone.

For a view of the harbour from the water, you can take a **golondrina** (excursion boat; Map pp270-2; ☎ 93 442 31 06; www.lasgolodrinas.com; Moll de les Drassanes; trips adult/child 11-18/child 4-10 €8.80/6.30/3.85) from in front of the Monument a Colom. The 1½-hour trip takes you out to sea and as far north as the Fòrum 2004 site before returning. The number of departures depends largely on season and demand. As a rule the trips are only done between March and November. Otherwise you can opt for a 35-minute (€3.70/3.70/1.80) or one-hour (€6.25/5.50/1.80) excursion around the port.

Northeast from the quay stretches the palm-lined promenade **Moll de la Fusta**. Usually the **Pailebot de Santa Eulàlia** (Map pp270–2; Moll de la Fusta; adult/child €2.40/1.20, admission free with Museu Marítim ticket; ☺ noon-5pm Tue-Fri, 10am-5pm Sat & Sun), a fully functioning 1918 schooner, restored by the Museu Marítim, is moored here for visits.

At the centre of the redeveloped harbour is the **Moll d'Espanya**, a former wharf linked to Moll de la Fusta by a wave-shaped footbridge, **Rambla de Mar**, which rotates to let boats enter the marina behind it. At the end of Moll d'Espanya is the glossy Maremàgnum shopping and eating complex, but the major attraction is **L'Aquàrium** (Map pp270–2; ☎ 93 221 74 74; www.aquariumbcn.com; Maremàgnum, adult/child €13.50/9.25; ☺ 9.30am-9pm Mon-Fri, 9am-9.30pm Sat & Sun Oct-May; 9.30am-9.30pm daily Jun & Sep; 9am-11pm daily Jul & Aug) behind it – an ultra-modern aquarium said to be Europe's biggest. One of the highlights is the 80m-long shark tunnel. Beyond L'Aquàrium is the big-screen **Imax Port Vell** (Map pp270–2; ☎ 93 225 11 11; www.imaxportvell.com; Maremàgnum; admission €7-10; 8 sessions daily).

The **Teleféric** (Cable Car; Map pp266–7; Passeig Escullera; one way/return €7.50/9; ☺ 10.30am-8pm mid-Jun–mid-Sep, 10.30am-7pm Mar–mid-Jun & mid-Sep–mid-Oct, noon-5.30pm mid-Oct–Feb), strung across the harbour to Montjuïc, provides a seagull's view of the city. You can get tickets at Miramar (Montjuïc) and the Torre de Sant Sebastiá (in La Barceloneta). As well as the metro, you can take bus Nos 17, 39 and 64 to get to the Torre de San Sebastiá.

La Barceloneta & the Coast

It used to be said that Barcelona had 'turned its back on the sea', but the ambitious 1992 Olympics-inspired redevelopment programme returned a long stretch of coast northeast of Port Vell to life. A similar programme in full swing aims to completely turn around the city's extreme northeast coastline too.

La Barceloneta, laid out in the 18th century and subsequently heavily overdeveloped, was long a factory-workers' and fishermen's quarter. It still retains a gritty flavour although the factories are a distant memory. Some of the fishing families remain and the area is laced with seafood restaurants.

In the Palau de Mar (former warehouses) building facing the harbour is the **Museu d'Història de Catalunya** (Map pp270–2; ☎ 93 225 47 00; www.mhcat.net; Plaça de Pau Vila 3; admission €3; ☺ 10am-7pm Tue & Thu-Sat, 10am-8pm Wed, 10am-2.30pm Sun & holidays). The place incorporates lots of audiovisuals and interactive information points in a series of colourful displays, recounting Catalonia's history from the caves to 1980. All sorts of scenes are recreated, from a prehistoric Pyrenean cave dwelling, through to a Roman house to a Spanish Civil War air-raid shelter.

Barcelona's fishing fleet ties up along the Moll del Rellotge, south of the museum. On La Barceloneta's seaward side are the first of Barcelona's **beaches**, which are popular on summer weekends. The pleasant **Passeig Marítim** (Map pp270–2), a 1.25km promenade from La Barceloneta to Port Olímpic, is a haunt for strollers and rollers (this is the best spot in town for Rollerblade enthusiasts).

Port Olímpic (Map pp266–7), a busy marina built for the Olympic sailing events, is surrounded by bars and restaurants. An eye-catcher, on the approach from La Barceloneta, is the giant copper *Peix* (Fish) sculpture by Frank Gehry.

The area behind Port Olímpic, which is dominated by twin-tower blocks (the luxury Hotel Arts Barcelona and Torre Mapfre office block), is the Vila Olímpica. It was the living quarters for the Olympic participants, but has now mostly been sold off as expensive apartments.

More and better beaches stretch northeast along the coast from Port Olímpic. They reach the huge development project known variously as Diagonal Mar and **Fòrum 2004**, after the five-month Fòrum Universal de les Cultures held in 2004. The regeneration project around here, still something of a work in progress, has led to the creation of new marinas, protected beaches, high-rise hotels, apartment blocks and conference centres.

L'Eixample   Map pp268–9

Stretching north, east and west of Plaça de Catalunya, L'Eixample (the Extension) was Barcelona's 19th-century answer to overcrowding in the medieval city.

Work on L'Eixample began in 1869, following a design by the architect Ildefons Cerdà, who specified a grid of wide streets with plazas that were formed by their cut-off corners. Cerdà also planned numerous green spaces but these didn't survive the ensuing scramble for real estate.

L'Eixample has been inhabited from the start by the city's middle classes, many of whom still think it's the best thing about Barcelona. Along its grid of straight streets are the majority of the city's most expensive shops and hotels, plus a range of eateries and several concentrations of bars and clubs. The development of L'Eixample coincided with the city's Modernisme period and so it is home to many Modernista creations. These are the area's main sight-seeing attraction and, apart from La Sagrada Família, are clustered on or near L'Eixample's main avenue, Passeig de Gràcia.

CASA BATLLÓ & THE MANZANA DE LA DISCORDIA

If La Sagrada Família is his master symphony, the **Casa Batlló** (☎ 93 216 03 06; www.casa batllo.es; Passeig de Gràcia 43; admission €10, incl roof €16; ⊗ 9am-2pm Mon-Sat, 9am-8pm Sun) is Gaudí's whimsical waltz. The façade, sprinkled with bits of blue, mauve and green tile, and studded with wave-shaped window frames and balconies, rises to an uneven blue tiled roof

with a solitary tower. The roof represents Sant Jordi (St George) and the dragon, and if you stare long enough at the building, it seems almost to be a living being. The main salon looks on to Passeig de Gràcia. Everything swirls. The ceiling is twisted into a vortex around the sun-like roof lamp. The doors, window and skylights are dreamy waves of wood and coloured glass. The same themes continue in the other rooms and covered terrace. Opened in 2004, the roof, with its twisting chimneys, is equally astonishing, and provides a chance for a close-up look at the St George-and-the-dragon motif that dominates the view from the street. Opened in 2002, Casa Batlló has become one of the city's most popular sights, and will take about an hour to explore.

Casa Batlló is the centrepiece of the so-called **Manzana de la Discordia** (Apple of Discord – in a play on words, *manzana* means both city block and apple) on the western side of Passeig de Gràcia, between Carrer del Consell de Cent and Carrer d'Aragó. According to Greek myth, the original Apple of Discord was tossed onto Mt Olympus by Eris (Discord) with orders that it be given to the most beautiful goddess, sparking jealousies that helped start the Trojan War.

On the same block are two utterly different houses by the other two senior figures of Modernista architecture, Lluís Domènech

---

THE MODERNISTAS

Most visitors to Barcelona will have heard of Antoni Gaudí (gow-*dee*), whose La Sagrada Família church is one of the city's major drawcards. However Gaudí (1852–1926) was just one, albeit the most spectacular, of a generation of inventive architects who left their mark on Barcelona between 1880 and the 1920s. These were the Modernistas.

Modernisme is usually described as a version of Art Nouveau, from which it certainly derived its taste for sinuous, flowing lines. Art Nouveau also inspired Modernisme's adventurous combinations of materials such as tile, glass, brick, and iron and steel (which provide the unseen frames of many buildings). But Barcelona's Modernistas used an astonishing variety of other styles too: Gothic and Islamic, Renaissance and Romanesque, Byzantine and baroque. They were trying to create a specifically Catalan architecture, often looking back to Catalonia's medieval golden age for inspiration.

It's significant that the two other leading Modernista architects, Lluís Domènech i Montaner (1850–1923) and Josep Puig i Cadafalch (1867–1957), were also prominent Catalan nationalists. Gaudí too was a Catalan nationalist, although he turned increasingly to spiritual concerns as he grew older.

L'Eixample, where most of Barcelona's new building was happening at the time, is home to the bulk of the Modernista creations. Others in the city include Gaudí's Palau Güell and Parc Güell (p284); Domènech i Montaner's Palau de la Música Catalana (p285); Castell dels Tres Dragons (p286) and Hotel España restaurant (p302); and Puig i Cadafalch's Els Quatre Gats (p305).

i Montaner's **Casa Lleo Morera** (Map pp268-9; Passeig de Gràcia 35; closed to the public) and **Casa Amatller** (Map pp268-9; ☎ 93 488 01 39; Passeig de Gràcia 41; admission free; 10am-7pm Mon-Sat, 10am-2pm Sun) by Josep Puig i Cadafalch. The former is swathed in Art Nouveau carving on the outside and has a bright, tiled lobby, in which floral motifs predominate. The 1st floor is giddy with swirling sculptures, rich mosaics and whimsical decoration. The latter is altogether different, with Gothic window frames and a stepped gable borrowed (deliberately) from the urban architecture of the Netherlands. The pillared foyer (which you can enter) and the staircase lit by stained glass are like the inside of some romantic castle. All three of the buildings were done by the 'Big Three' of Modernisme from 1898 to 1906.

The **Museu del Perfum** (Map pp268-9; ☎ 93 216 01 46; www.museodelperfume.com; Passeig de Gràcia 39; admission free; 10.30am-1.30pm & 4.30-8pm Mon-Fri, 10.30am-1.30pm Sat), in the Regia store, contains everything from ancient scent receptacles to classic eau de Cologne bottles.

FUNDACIÓ ANTONI TÀPIES

Around the corner from the Manzana de la Discordia, the **Fundació** (☎ 93 487 03 15; www.fundaciotapies.org; Carrer d'Aragó 255; adult/student €4.20/2.10; 10am-8pm Tue-Sun) is both a pioneering Modernista building of the early 1880s, and the major collection of a leading 20th-century Catalan artist. Tàpies does not appeal to everyone. He frequently uses all sorts of 3-D materials – everything from scrap wood to sand and rocks – in his grand canvases that to many will look like meaningless blobs and splotches. Those who do like him may also be a little frustrated here, as frequently only a fairly limited selection of his work is on show. Throughout most of the year much exposition space is devoted to temporary displays of other contemporary artists' work.

LA PEDRERA

Back on Passeig de Gràcia is another Gaudí masterpiece, built between 1905 and 1910 as a combined apartment and office block. Formally called the Casa Milà, after the businessman who commissioned it, it's better known as **La Pedrera** (The Quarry; ☎ 902 400973; www.caixacatalunya.es; Carrer de Provença 261-265; adult/student & senior €7/3.50; 10am-8pm)

because of its uneven grey-stone façade, which ripples around the corner of Carrer de Provença. The wave effect is emphasised by elaborate wrought-iron balconies.

The Fundació Caixa Catalunya has opened the top-floor flat, attic and roof to visitors, organising it as the **Espai Gaudí** (Gaudí Space). The roof is the most extraordinary element, with its giant chimney pots looking like multicoloured medieval knights. One floor below, where you can appreciate Gaudí's gracious parabolic arches, is a modest museum dedicated to his work. You can see models and videos dealing with each of his buildings.

Downstairs on the next floor you can inspect the apartment (El Pis de la Pedrera). It is fascinating to wander around this elegantly furnished home, done up in the style a well-to-do family might have enjoyed in the early 20th century.

From July to September, La Pedrera opens on Friday and Saturday evenings (9pm to midnight). The roof is lit up in an eerie fashion and, while you are taking in the night views of Barcelona, you also get to sip a flute of *cava* (Catalan sparkling wine) and listen to live music in the background (€10).

PALAU DEL BARÓ QUADRAS & CASA DE LES PUNXES

A few blocks north and east of La Pedrera are two of Puig i Cadafalch's major buildings. The nearer is the **Palau del Baró Quadras** (☎ 93 238 73 37; www.casaasia.es; Avinguda Diagonal 373; 10am-8pm Tue-Sat, 10am-2pm Sun), built between 1902 and 1904 with detailed neo-Gothic carvings on the façade and fine stained glass. Since 2003 it has housed the Casa Asia, a cultural centre building on the theme of relations between Spain and the Asia-Pacific region. Visiting the variegated temporary exhibitions allows you to get a peek at the inside of this intriguing building.

Casa Terrades is better known as **Casa de les Punxes** (House of Spikes; Avinguda Diagonal 420) because of its pointed turrets. It's on the other side of Avinguda Diagonal, 1½ blocks east of Palau del Baró Quadras. This apartment block (1903–1905) is more like a fairy-tale castle.

LA SAGRADA FAMÍLIA

If you only have time for one sightseeing outing in Barcelona, this should probably be it. The **Temple Expiatori de la Sagrada Família**

(Expiatory Temple of the Holy Family; ☎ 93 207 30 31; www.sagradafamilia.org; Carrer de Mallorca 401; adult/student €8/5, combined with Casa Museu Gaudí in Parc Güell €9; ⌚ 9am-8pm Apr-Sep, 9am-6pm Oct-Mar) inspires awe with its sheer verticality and, in the true manner of the great medieval cathedrals it emulates, it's still only half-built after more than 100 years. If it's ever finished, the topmost tower will be more than half as high again as those standing today. You could easily spend up to two hours wandering around the site and climbing the towers.

The church, in the east of L'Eixample, was the project to which Antoni Gaudí dedicated the latter part of his life. Building continues today but the completed sections and the museum can be explored at leisure. Guided tours (€3, 50 minutes up to four daily) are offered. You can enter from Carrer de Sardenya and Carrer de la Marina. Audioguides (€3) are available and it costs a further €1.50 per ride on the lifts that take you up inside one of the towers on each side of the church.

The northeast, or **Nativity Façade**, is the building's artistic pinnacle, and was mostly done under Gaudí's personal supervision. You can climb high up inside some of the four towers by a combination of lifts and narrow spiral staircases – a vertiginous experience. The towers are destined to hold tubular bells capable of playing complicated music at great volume. Beneath the towers is a tall, three-part portal on the theme of Christ's birth and childhood. It seems to lean outwards as you stand beneath, looking up. Gaudí used real people and animals as models for many of the sculptures. The three sections of the portal represent, from left to right, Hope, Charity and Faith. Among the forest of sculpture on the Charity portal, you can make out, low down, the manger surrounded by an ox, an ass, the shepherds and kings, with angel musicians above.

The southwest **Passion Façade**, which has the theme of Christ's last days and death, has been constructed since the 1950s with, like the Nativity Façade, four needling towers and a large, sculpture-bedecked portal. The sculptor, Josep Subirachs, has not attempted to imitate Gaudí's work but has produced strong images of his own. The sculptures, on three levels, are in an S-shaped sequence, starting with the Last Supper at bottom left and ending with Christ's burial at top right.

The semicircular **apse** was the first part to be finished (in 1894). The interior of the church remains a building site but the nave has now largely been roofed over, and a forest of extraordinary angled pillars is in place. The image of the tree is in no way fortuitous, for Gaudí's plan envisaged such an effect.

GAUDÍ & LA SAGRADA FAMÍLIA

The idea for La Sagrada Família came from Josep Maria Bocabella, a rich publisher who was worried about the growth of revolutionary ideas in Barcelona, and set up a religious society dedicated to Sant Josep, patron saint of workers and the family. Construction of the society's church (it's not a cathedral) began in 1882 under Francesc de Villar, who planned a relatively conventional neo-Gothic structure. Villar fell out with Bocabella and was replaced, in 1884, by the 31-year-old Antoni Gaudí.

Gaudí stuck to the basic Gothic cross-shaped ground plan, but devised a temple 95m long and 60m wide that was able to seat 13,000 people, it also had a central tower 170m high, and 17 other towers of 100m or more. With his characteristic dislike for straight lines (there are none in nature, he said), Gaudí gave his towers swelling outlines inspired by the weird peaks of Montserrat (p324) outside Barcelona, and encrusted them with a tangle of sculpture that seems to be an outgrowth of the stone.

At Gaudí's death only the crypt, the apse walls, one portal and one tower had been finished. Three more towers were added by 1930 – completing the Nativity Façade – but in 1936 anarchists burned and smashed everything they could in La Sagrada Família, including workshops, models and plans. Work restarted in the 1950s using restored models and photographs of drawings, with only limited guidance on how Gaudí had thought of solving the huge technical problems of the building. Today the southwestern (Passion) façade, with four more towers, is close to completion, the nave has been roofed over and work has begun on the Glory Façade. The way things are going, it might be finished by 2020 – a truly medieval construction timetable.

The **Glory Façade** will, like the others, be crowned by four towers – the total of 12 representing the 12 apostles. Further decoration will make the whole building a microcosmic symbol of the Christian church, with Christ represented by the massive 170m central tower above the transept, and the five remaining planned towers symbolising the Virgin Mary and the four Evangelists.

Open the same times as the church, the **Museu Gaudí**, below ground level, includes interesting material on Gaudí's life and other work, as well as models and photos of La Sagrada Família. You can see a good example of his plumb-line models, which showed him the stresses and strains he could get away with in construction. Gaudí is buried in the simple crypt at the far end.

Gràcia
Map pp268–9

Gràcia lies north of L'Eixample. Once a separate village, then in the 19th century an industrial district famous for its republican and liberal ideas, it became fashionable among radical and bohemian types in the 1960s and '70s. Although now more sedate and gentrified, it retains much of its style of 20 years ago, with a mixed-class population. Gràcia's interest lies in the atmosphere of its narrow streets, small plazas and the multitude of bars and restaurants lining them.

The liveliest plazas are Plaça del Sol, Plaça de Rius i Taulet with its **clock tower**, and Plaça de la Virreina with the 17th-century **Església de Sant Josep**. Three blocks northeast of Plaça de Rius i Taulet there's a big cover ed **market**. West of Gràcia's main street, Carrer Gran de Gràcia, there's an early Gaudí house, the turreted, vaguely Mudéjar **Casa Vicenç** (Carrer de les Carolines 22; no admission).

Parc Güell
Map pp266–7

North of Gràcia, **Parc Güell** (☎ 93 413 24 00; Carrer d'Olot 7; admission free; ⏰ 9am-9pm Jun-Sep, 9am-8pm Apr, May & Oct, 9am-7pm Mar & Nov, 10am-6pm Dec-Feb) is where Gaudí turned his hand to landscape gardening and where the artificial almost seems more natural than the natural.

Parc Güell originated in 1900 when Count Eusebi Güell bought a hillside property (then outside Barcelona) and hired Gaudí to create a miniature garden city of houses for the wealthy. The project was abandoned in 1914, but not before Gaudí had created 3km of roads and walks, steps

and a plaza in his inimitable manner, plus the two Hansel-and-Gretel–style gatehouses on Carrer d'Olot.

Just inside the entrance, visit the park's visitor centre, **Centre d'Interpretació i Acollida** (☎ 93 285 68 99; adult/student/child under 16 €2/1.50/free; ⏰ 11am-3pm), in the Pavelló de Con900sergeria, the one-time porter's home that now hosts a display on Gaudí's building methods.

The steps up from the entrance, guarded by a mosaic dragon-lizard, lead to the **Sala Hipóstila**, a forest of 84 stone columns (some of them leaning), intended as a market. On top of the Sala Hipóstila is a broad open space, the highlight of which is the **Banc de Trencadís**, a tiled bench curving sinuously around its perimeter.

The spired house to the right is the **Casa Museu Gaudí** (☎ 93 219 38 11; admission €4; ⏰ 10am-8pm Apr-Sep, 10am-6pm Oct-Mar), where Gaudí lived for most of his last 20 years (1906–26). It contains furniture by him and other memorabilia.

If you don't want to take the metro, bus No 24 will get you there.

Tibidabo

Tibidabo (512m) is the highest hill in the wooded range that forms the backdrop to Barcelona. It's a good place for some fresh air and fine views. Tibidabo gets its name from the devil, who, trying to tempt Christ, took him to a high place and said, in the Latin version: '*Haec omnia tibi dabo si cadens adoraberis me.*' ('All this I will give you, if you will fall down and worship me.')

TEMPLE DEL SAGRAT COR

The **Church of the Sacred Heart** (Map pp266-7; ☎ 93 417 56 86; Plaça de Tibidabo; admission free; ⏰ 8am-7pm), looming above the top funicular station, is meant to be Barcelona's answer to Paris' Sacré Cœur. It's certainly equally as visible, and even more vilified by aesthetes (perhaps with good reason). It's actually two churches, one on top of the other. The top one is surmounted by a giant Christ and has a lift to the **roof** (tickets €1.50; ⏰ 10am-2pm & 3-7pm).

PARC D'ATRACCIONS

Barcelonins (residents of Barcelona) come to Tibidabo for a bit of an airing at this **funfair** (Map pp266-7; ☎ 93 211 79 42; Plaça de Tibidabo; admission & 6 rides €11, access to all rides €22, child under

1.1m €9; ⊙ noon-10pm or 11pm Aug, otherwise times vary (from noon-5pm to noon-9pm) Sat, Sun & holidays & in summer) Give yourself a bit of a scare in the Hotel Krueger, an *hospedaje* (guesthouse) of horrors inhabited by actors playing out their Dracula, Hannibal Lecter and other fantasies. A curious sideline is the Museu d'Autòmats, which is 35 automated puppets that go back as far as 1880 and are part of the original amusement park. You can still see some of these gizmos go.

COSMOCAIXA

Located in a transformed Modernista building and reopened for business in late 2004, this **science museum** (☎ 93 212 60 50; Carrer de Teodor Roviralta 47-51, Zona Alta; admission free until Jan 2005; ⊙ 10am-8pm Tue-Sun) is four times bigger than the original – a giant interactive paradise with knobs (and buttons and levers and lots more besides).

GETTING THERE & AWAY

First, get an FGC train to Avinguda de Tibidabo (€1.10, 10 minutes) from Catalunya station on Plaça de Catalunya. Outside Avinguda de Tibidabo station, hop on the **Tramvia Blau** (one way/return €2.10/3.10), Barcelona's last-surviving old-style tram, which runs to Plaça del Doctor Andreu. The tram runs daily in summer, on Saturday, Sunday and holidays the rest of the year, they run every 15 or 30 minutes from 9am to 9.30pm April to September (10am to 6pm rest of the year). When the tram isn't operating, a bus serves the route (€1.10, 7.45am to 9pm Monday to Friday, 6pm to 10pm Saturday, Sunday and holidays).

From Plaça del Doctor Andreu, the Tibidabo funicular railway (Map pp266–7) climbs through the woods to Plaça de Tibidabo at the top of the hill (one way/return €2/3), every 15 to 30 minutes (7.15am to 9.45pm April to September, 10.45am to 7.15pm Saturday, Sunday and holidays October to March). If you're feeling active, you can walk up or down through the woods instead. The funicular only operates when the Parc d'Atraccions is open.

The cheaper alternative is bus No T2, the Tibibús, from Plaça de Catalunya to Plaça de Tibidabo (€2.10, buy your ticket on the bus). This runs every 30 minutes from 10.30am on Saturday, Sunday and holidays year-round. From late June to early September it runs

every hour from 10.30am Monday to Friday. The last bus down leaves Tibidabo 30 minutes after the Parc d'Atraccions closes. You can also buy a ticket that includes the bus and entry to the Parc d'Atraccions (€22).

Collserola
PARC DE COLLSEROLA

Stretching over 8000ha, this **park** (☎ 93 280 35 52; Carretera de l'Església 92; Centre d'Interpretació ⊙ 9.30am-3pm) makes an ideal escape hatch from the city, with ample walking and mountain biking possibilities. Aside from the nature, the principal point of interest is the sprawling **Museu-Casa Verdaguer** (☎ 93 204 78 05; Vil.la Joana, Carretera de l'Església 104; admission free; ⊙ 10am-2pm Sat & Sun & holidays), 100 metres from the information centre and a short walk from the train station. In this late-18th-century country house, Catalonia's revered and reverend writer, Jacint Verdaguer, spent his last days before dying on 10 July 1902.

To get there, take the FGC train from Plaça de Catalunya to Baixador de Vallvidrera.

TORRE DE COLLSEROLA

The 288m **Torre de Collserola** (Map pp266-7; ☎ 93 406 93 54; www.torredecollserola.com; adult/child €4.60/3.30; ⊙ 11am-2.30pm & 3.30-7pm Wed-Sun) telecommunications tower was completed by Norman Foster in 1992. An external glass lift takes you up 115m to the visitors' observation area, from where you can see for 70km on a clear day.

To get there, take bus No 211 to the Funicular de Vallvidrera.

Jardins del Laberint d'Horta

Laid out in the twilight years of the 18th century by Antoni Desvalls, Marquès d'Alfarras i de Llupià, this carefully manicured **park** (☎ 93 428 39 34; Carrer dels Germans Desvalls; adult/student with Carnet Jove €1.90/1.25, admission free Wed & Sun; ⊙ 10am-sunset) remained a private family idyll until the 1970s, when it was opened to the public. Many a fine party and theatrical performance was held here over the years, but now it serves as a kind of museum-park. The gardens take their name from a maze in their centre, but other paths take you past a pleasant artificial lake *(estany)*, waterfalls, a neoclassical pavilion and a false cemetery. The latter was inspired by 19th-century romanticism, often characterised by an obsession with a swooning, anaemic (some might say plain silly) vision of death.

The park is about 3km from central Barcelona. To get there, take the metro to Mundet station.

Pedralbes   Map pp266–7

This is a wealthy residential area north of the Zona Universitària.

PALAU REIAL DE PEDRALBES

Across Avinguda Diagonal from the main campus of the Universitat de Barcelona, set in a lush, green park is the 20th century **Palau Reial de Pedralbes** (☎ 93 280 16 21 or ☎ 93 280 50 24; Avinguda Diagonal 686; adult/student incl museums & Museu Tèxtil i d'Indumentària €3.50/2, admission free 1st Sun of month; ☼ 10am-6pm Tue-Sat, 10am-3pm Sun & holidays, park ☼ 10am-6pm), which belonged to the family of Eusebi Güell (Gaudí's patron), until they handed it over to the city in 1926. Then it served as a royal residence – King Alfonso XIII, the president of Catalonia and General Franco, among others, have been its guests.

Today the palace houses two museums. The **Museu de Ceràmica** (www.museuceramica.bcn.es) has a good collection of Spanish ceramics from the 13th to 19th centuries, including work by Picasso and Miró. Across the corridor, the **Museu de les Arts Decoratives** (www.museuartsdecoratives.bcn.es) brings together an eclectic assortment of furnishings, ornaments, and knick-knacks dating as far back as the Romanesque period.

Over by Avinguda de Pedralbes are the Gaudí-designed stables and porter's lodge for the **Finca Güell**, as the Güell estate here was called. They were done in the mid-1880s, when Gaudí was strongly impressed by Islamic architecture. They can't be visited, although there is nothing to stop you admiring Gaudí's wrought-iron dragon gate from the outside.

MUSEU-MONESTIR DE PEDRALBES

This peaceful old **convent** (☎ 93 203 92 82; Baixada del Monestir 9; admission €5.50, monastery only incl Museu d'Història de la Ciutat €4; ☼ 10am-2pm Tue-Sun), now also a museum of monastic life that houses part of the Thyssen-Bornemisza art collection, stands at the top of Avinguda de Pedralbes.

The convent, founded in 1326, still houses a community of nuns who inhabit separate closed quarters. The museum entrance is on Plaça del Monestir, a divinely quiet corner of Barcelona. Once inside, the displays on monastic life are distributed in cells and dependencies distributed around the elegant, three-storey cloister, which was a jewel of Catalan Gothic and built in the early 14th century.

The **Col.lecció Thyssen-Bornemisza** (entry from the ground floor), quartered in the one-time dormitories of the nuns and the Saló Principal, is part of a wide-ranging art collection acquired by Spain in 1993. Most of it went to Madrid's Museo Thyssen-Bornemisza; what's here is mainly religious work by European masters, including Canaletto, Titian, Tintoretto, Rubens, Zurbarán and Velázquez. The collection is due to be transferred to the Museu Nacional d'Art de Catalunya (p295) at Montjuïc by 2005.

To get there, take FGC train to Reina Elisenda or bus Nos 22 (from Plaça de Catalunya), 64 (from Plaça de l'Universitat) or 75 (from Plaça de Kennedy).

Camp Nou

One of Barcelona's most visited museums is the **Museu del Futbol Club Barcelona** (Map pp266-7; ☎ 93 496 36 08; www.fcbarcelona.es; Carrer d'Aristides Maillol; adult/child €5.30/3.70; ☼ 10am-6.30pm Mon-Sat, 10am-2pm Sun & holidays), next to the club's giant Camp Nou stadium. Barça is one of Europe's top football clubs and its museum is a hit with football fans the world over.

Camp Nou, built in 1957, is one of the world's biggest stadiums, holding 100,000 people, and the club has a world-record membership of 112,000. Soccer fans who can't get to a game (see p314) should find the museum worthwhile. The best bits are the photo section, the goal videos, and the views out over the stadium. Among the quirkier paraphernalia are old sports board games, the life-size diorama of old-time dressing rooms, magazines from way back, and the *futbolín* (table-soccer) collection. You can also join a guided museum and stadium **tour** (adult/child €9.50/6.60; ☼ 10am-5.30pm Mon-Sat, 10am-1pm Sun & holidays).

Montjuïc   Map pp266–7

Montjuïc, the hill overlooking the city centre from the southwest, is home to some fine museums and leisure attractions, soothing gardens and the main group of 1992 Olympic sites, along with a handful of theatres and clubs. It's definitely worth a day or two of your time.

The name Montjuïc (Jewish Mountain) indicates there was once a Jewish cemetery, and possibly settlement, here. Montjuïc also has a darker history: its castle was used by the Madrid government as a political prison right up to the Franco era. The first main burst of building on Montjuïc came in the 1920s, when it was chosen as the stage for Barcelona's 1929 World Exhibition. The Estadi Olímpic, the Poble Espanyol and some museums all date from this time. Montjuïc got a face-lift and more new buildings for the 1992 Olympics, and cosmetic surgery on the gardens has continued until today.

Abundant roads and paths, with occasional escalators, plus buses and even a chairlift allow you to visit Montjuïc's sights in any order you choose. You can even hire bicycles for the day. The main attractions – the Poble Espanyol, the Museu Nacional d'Art de Catalunya, CaixaForum, the Pavelló Mies van der Rohe, the Estadi Olímpic, the Fundació Joan Miró and the views from the castle – would make for a very full day's sightseeing.

For information on the park, head for the **Centre Gestor del Parc de Montjuïc** (☎ 93 289 28 30; Passeig de Santa Madrona 28; ✆ 10am-8pm Apr-Sep, 10am-6pm Nov-Mar) in the Font del Gat building, a short walk in off Passeig de Santa Madrona, east of the Museu Etnològic. It also has a pleasant bar-restaurant. Another information office, open the same hours, operates at the castle (see p296).

AROUND PLAÇA D'ESPANYA

The approach to Montjuïc from **Plaça d'Espanya** gives you the full benefit of the landscaping on the hill's northern side and allows Montjuïc to unfold for you from the bottom up. On Plaça d'Espanya's northern side is the dilapidated **Plaça de Braus Les Arenes bullring**, built in 1900. It hasn't seen a bullfight in decades, but the Beatles played here in 1966.

Behind the bullring is **Parc Joan Miró**, created in the 1980s, and worth a quick detour mainly for Miró's giant, highly phallic sculpture *Dona i Ocell* (Woman and Bird) in the northwestern corner.

LA FONT MÀGICA & AROUND

Avinguda de la Reina Maria Cristina, lined with exhibition and congress halls, leads

---

MONTJUÏC CARD

If you're up for a big day on the hill and visiting all of its varied museums and sights, the **Montjuïc Card** (adult/child under 13 €20/10) is a good investment. Valid for a day (it is not issued on Mondays), the card gives entry to all the museums and galleries mentioned below, including temporary exhibitions.

In addition, you can ride the Telefèric de Montjuïc and Tren Turístic for free, as well as pick up one of the hire bicycles available on weekends at various points around the park. For more details, see Getting There & Away on p297.

The card also allows entry to the Olympic-sized **Piscines Bernat Picornell** (p297) and will get you free entry to a theatre performance (if one is on) at either the **Teatre Lliure** (p315) or **Teatre Mercat de les Flors** (p315) at the foot of Montjuïc.

The card is available from the park information office in the Font del Gat building, at bicycle rental points, tourist offices, and by telephone and online with **ServiCaixa** (☎ 902 332211; www.servicaixa.com in Spanish).

---

from Plaça d'Espanya towards Montjuïc. On the hill ahead of you is the Palau Nacional de Montjuïc, and stretching up a series of terraces below it are Montjuïc's fountains, starting with the biggest, **La Font Màgica** (Avinguda de la Reina Maria Cristina; admission free; ✆ every 30min 7-8.30pm Fri & Sat Oct–late Jun, 9.30-11.30pm Thu-Sun late Jun–Sep), which comes alive with a 15-minute lights-water-and-music show on certain evenings.

Just to the west of La Font Màgica is the strange **Pavelló Mies van der Rohe** (☎ 93 423 40 16; www.miesbcn.com; Avinguda del Marquès de Comillas; adult/student/child under 18 €3/1.50/free; ✆ 10am-8pm). Architect Ludwig Mies van der Rohe erected the Pavelló Alemany (German pavilion) for the 1929 World Exhibition. It was a startling modern experiment. What you see now is a 1980s-built replica; the original was taken down after the exhibition.

CaixaForum (☎ 93 476 86 00; www.fundaciolacaixa .es in Spanish; Avinguda del Marquès de Comillas 6-8; admission free; ✆ 10am-8pm Tue-Sun) hosts part of the Caixa bank's extensive collection of modern art from around the globe. It is housed in a former Modernista factory designed by Puig i Cadafalch.

MUSEU NACIONAL D'ART DE CATALUNYA

The **Palau Nacional**, built in the 1920s for displays in the World Exhibition, houses a **museum** (☎ 93 622 03 75; www.mnac.es; Mirador del Palau Nacional; admission €4.80, temporary exhibitions €4.20, free 1st Thu of month; ☺ 10am-7pm Tue-Sat, 10am-2.30pm Sun & holidays) that's considered one of the city's most important. Its Romanesque section consists mainly of 11th- and 12th-century murals, woodcarvings and altar frontals – painted, low-relief wooden panels that were forerunners of the elaborate *retablos* (altarpieces) that adorned later churches. These works, gathered from decaying country churches in northern Catalonia, early in the 20th century, constitute one of Europe's greatest collections of Romanesque art. The museum's other main section is devoted to Gothic art, but is less captivating.

The first thing you see as you enter the Romanesque section is a remake of the apse of the church of Sant Pere de la Seu d'Urgell, dominated by a beautiful fresco from the early 12th century. In Àmbit (Hall) III, the frescoes from the church of Sant Pere d'Àger stand out (item No 31). One of the star attractions is the fresco of Mary and the Christ Child from the apse of the church of Santa Maria de Taüll (No 102 in Àmbit VII).

The extensive Gothic-art section contains works by such Catalan painters as Bernat Martorell and Jaume Huguet. A smaller collection of art from the 16th to 18th centuries is growing and will be complemented (it is planned by early 2005) by a broad collection of 19th and early 20th century Catalan artists (mostly of the Modernista and Noucentista schools) and the transfer of the Thyssen-Bornemisza collection from the Museu-Monestir de Pedralbes (p293).

POBLE ESPANYOL

This so-called **Spanish Village** (☎ 93 508 63 30; www.poble-espanyol.com; Avinguda del Marquès de Comillas; adult/student & senior/child under 12 €7/5/3.90; ☺ 9am-8pm Mon, 9-2am Tue-Thu, 9-4am Fri & Sat, 9am-midnight Sun) is both a cheesy souvenir-hunters' haunt and an intriguing scrapbook of Spanish architecture. Built for the Spanish crafts section of the 1929 exhibition, it's composed of plazas and streets lined with surprisingly good copies of characteristic buildings from across the country's regions.

You enter from Avinguda del Marquès de Comillas, beneath a towered medieval gate from Ávila. Inside, to the right, is an information office with free maps. Straight ahead from the gate is a Plaza Mayor, or town square, surrounded by mainly Castilian and Aragonese buildings. Elsewhere you'll find an Andalucian *barrio* (district), a Basque street, Galician and Catalan quarters, and even – at the eastern end – a Dominican monastery. The buildings house dozens of moderate to expensive restaurants, cafés, bars, craft shops and workshops, and a few souvenir stores.

The **Fundació Fran Daurel** (☎ 93 423 41 72; admission free; ☺ 10am-7pm) is an eclectic collection of 200 works of art including sculptures, prints, ceramics and tapestries by modern artists ranging from Picasso to Miquel Barceló.

MUSEU ETNOLÒGIC & MUSEU D'ARQUEOLOGIA

Down the hill east of the Museu Nacional d'Art, these museums are worth a visit if their subjects interest you, although neither is excitingly presented and most explanatory material is in Catalan.

The **Museu Etnològic** (Ethnology Museum; ☎ 93 424 68 07; Passeig de Santa Madrona; adult/child €3/free, admission free 1st Sun of month; ☺ 10am-2pm Wed & Fri-Sun, 10am-2pm & 3-7pm Tue & Thu) organises temporary exhibitions on a range of cultures from other continents. In 2004 the museum opened what could wind up being a permanent exposition, Ètnic, which presents a broad range of themes on traditional societies from around the world.

The **Museu d'Arqueologia de Catalunya** (Archaeology Museum; ☎ 93 424 65 77; www.mac.es; Passeig de Santa Madrona 39-41; adult/child €2.40/1.70; ☺ 9.30am-7pm Tue-Sat, 10am-2.30pm Sun) covers Catalonia and neighbouring areas in Spain. Items range from copies of pre-Neanderthal skulls to lovely Carthaginian necklaces and jewel-studded Visigothic crosses. There's good material on the Balearic Islands (p614) and Empúries (p341) and Roman finds dug up in Barcelona.

ANELLA OLÍMPICA

The 'Olympic Ring' is the group of sports installations where the main events of the 1992 Olympics were held, on the ridge above the Palau Nacional. Westernmost is the **Institut Nacional d'Educació Física de Catalunya** (INEFC), a kind of sports university, designed by one of the best-known contemporary Catalan architects, Ricardo Bofill. Past a circular arena, the Plaça d'Europa, with the Torre Calatrava telephone tower behind it, is the **Piscines Bernat Picornell** building, where the swimming and diving events were held. For details on swimming here, see p297.

Next comes a pleasant park, the Jardí d'Aclimatació, followed by the **Estadi Olímpic** (Avinguda de l'Estadi; admission free; ✹ 10am-6pm Oct-Apr, 10am-8pm May-Sep), the main stadium of the games; enter at the northern end. If you saw the Olympics on TV, the 65,000-capacity stadium may seem surprisingly small. So may the Olympic flame-holder, rising at the northern end, into which a long-range archer spectacularly deposited a flaming arrow during the opening ceremony. The stadium was opened in 1929, and restored for 1992.

At the southern end of the stadium (enter from the outside) is the **Galería Olímpica** (☎ 93 426 06 60; www.fundaciobarcelonaolimpica.es; Passeig Olímpic s/n; admission €2.50; ✹ 10am-1pm & 4-6pm Mon-Fri), which has an exhibition, including videos, on the 1992 games.

West of the stadium is the **Palau Sant Jordi**, a 17,000-capacity indoor sports, concert and exhibition hall, designed by the Japanese architect Arata Isozaki.

JARDÍ BOTÀNIC
South across the road from the Estadi, this **botanical garden** (☎ 93 426 49 35; www.jardibotanic .bcn.es; Carrer del Doctor Font i Quer; adult/student €4/2; ✹ 10am-8pm Apr-Oct, 10am-5pm Nov-Mar) was created atop what was an old municipal dump. The theme is 'Mediterranean' flora and the collection includes some 2000 species thriving in areas with a climate similar to that of the Med, including the Eastern Mediterranean, Spain (including the Balearic and Canary Islands), North Africa, Australia, California, Chile and South Africa.

CEMENTIRI DEL SUD-OEST
On the hill south of the Anella Olímpica you can see the top of a huge cemetery, the **Cementiri del Sud-Oest** (✹ 8am-5.30pm), which extends right down the southern side of the hill. It was opened in 1883, and is an odd combination of elaborate architect-designed tombs for rich families and small niches for the rest. It contains the graves of numerous Catalan artists and politicians, including Joan Miró, Carmen Amaya (the flamenco star from La Barceloneta) and Lluís Companys

(a nationalist president of Catalonia, who was executed by Franco's henchmen in the nearby Montjuïc castle in 1940).

FUNDACIÓ JOAN MIRÓ
The **Fundació Joan Miró** (☎ 93 443 94 70; www .bcn.fjmiro.es; Plaça Neptu; admission €7.20, temporary exhibitions €3.60; ✹ 10am-7pm Tue-Wed & Fri & Sat, 10am-9.30pm Thu, 10am-2.30pm Sun & holidays) is a must-see gallery dedicated to one of the greatest artists to emerge in Barcelona in the 20th century, Joan Miró.

Miró gave 379 paintings, sculptures and textile works, and almost 5000 drawings, to the collection, but only a selection of these is shown at any one time. The displays tend to concentrate on Miró's more settled last 20 years, but there are some important exceptions. The ground-floor Sala Joan Prats shows the younger Miró moving away, under surrealist influence, from his *relative* realism, then starting to work towards his own recognisable style. This section also includes the *Barcelona* series (1939–44) of tortured lithographs, which was Miró's comment on the civil war.

The Sala Pilar Juncosa, upstairs, also displays works from the 1930s and '40s. Another interesting section is devoted to the 'Miró Papers', which include many preparatory drawings and sketches, some on bits of newspaper or cigarette packets. A Joan Miró is a collection of work by other contemporary artists, donated in tribute to Miró.

Reckon on a couple of hours to take in the permanent and temporary exhibitions.

CASTELL DE MONTJUÏC & AROUND
The southeast of Montjuïc is dominated by the *castell* (castle). It dates in its present form from the late 17th and 18th centuries. For most of its existence it has been used to watch over the city and as a political prison and killing ground. Although the army opened it to the city's populace as a museum in 1960, it was only in June 2004 that the central government, in a moment charged with symbolism, declared that the fort would be fully handed over to the city council for conversion into a European Peace Museum. The castle is surrounded by a network of ditches and walls, and at present houses the **Museu Militar** (☎ 93 329 86 13; admission €2.50; ✹ 9.30am-5pm Tue-Sun Nov–mid-Mar, 9.30am-8pm daily mid-Mar–Oct) with a section

on Catalan military history, a discreetly half-hidden statue of Franco, plus old weapons, uniforms, maps, castle models and so on. Best of all are the excellent views from the castle area of the port and city below.

Towards the foot of this part of Montjuïc, above the thundering traffic of the main road to Tarragona, the **Jardins de Mossèn Costa i Llobera** (Map pp266-7; admission free; ⏱ 10am-sunset) have a good collection of tropical and desert plants – including a veritable forest of cacti. Near the Estació Parc Montjuïc (funicular station) are the ornamental **Jardins de Mossèn Cinto Verdaguer**. From the **Jardins del Mirador**, opposite the Estació Mirador, you have fine views over the port of Barcelona.

GETTING THERE & AWAY

You *could* walk from Ciutat Vella (the foot of La Rambla is 700m from the eastern end of Montjuïc). A series of escalators run up to the Palau Nacional from Avinguda de Rius i Taulet and Passeig de les Cascades. They continue as far as Avinguda de l'Estadi.

Bicycle

On weekends and holidays there's a bike-hire service (€3 per day); you can pick one up at various points. The handiest are at Plaça d'Espanya and the Estació Parc Montjuïc. It's a case of first in, best dressed, as availability is limited.

Bus

Several local buses make their way up here from other parts of town, including Nos 50, 55 and 61. A local bus, the PM (Parc de Montjuïc) line, does a circle trip from Plaça d'Espanya to the Castell de Montjuïc, making 17 stops at points of interest along the way.

Metro & Funicular

Take the metro (lines 2 and 3) to Paral.lel station and jump on the funicular railway (9am to 10pm) from there to Estació Parc Montjuïc. Tickets cost €1.65/2.40 one way/return, but you're better off using one of the public transport multi-ride tickets such as the T-10.

Telefèric (Funicular Aeri)

The quickest way to get to the mountain from the beach is the Telefèric (Funicular Aeri), which runs between Torre de Sant Sebastiá in La Barceloneta (p287) and the Miramar stop on Montjuïc.

Telefèric de Montjuïc

From Estació Parc Montjuïc, this cable car will carry you yet higher, to the Castell de Montjuïc (Castell stop), with an intermediate stop at Mirador (a lookout point). The chair lift operates between 11.15am and 9pm daily, from mid-June to mid-September; 11am to 7.15pm daily from mid-September to early November, and the Easter and Christmas periods; 11am to 7.15pm on Saturday, Sunday and holidays only during the rest of the year. Tickets cost €3.40/4.80 one way/return.

Tren Turístic

This is one of those silly little road trains. It runs every half-hour, 10am to 8pm daily from late June to early September, and on weekends and holidays from late April to late June (subject to change) from Plaça d'Espanya. It stops at all the museums and other points of interest. An all-day ticket costs €3.20/2.50 per adult/child (get on and off as often as you like).

ACTIVITIES
Cycling

For information on bicycle hire, see p319. Cycle lanes have been laid out along many main arteries across the city. Montjuïc (p293), where you can hire bikes for the day, and the Parc de Collserola (p292), are both hilly, but less stressful than the rest of the city, in terms of traffic.

Swimming

Down by La Barceloneta beach, **Club Natació Atlètic-Barcelona** (Map pp266-7; ☎ 93 221 00 10; www.cnab.org; Plaça de Mar s/n; adult/child up to 10 €8/3.50; ⏱ 6.30am-11pm Mon-Fri, 7am-11pm Sat year-round, 8am-5pm Sun & holidays Oct–mid-May, 8am-8pm Sun & holidays mid-May–Sep) has one indoor and two outdoor pools. Of the latter, one is heated for lap swimming in winter. Admission includes use of the gym and private-beach access.

Included in the standard price for access to Barcelona's Olympic pool, **Piscines Bernat Picornell** (Map pp266-7; ☎ 93 423 40 41; www.picornell.com in Spanish; Avinguda de l'Estadi 30-40, Montjuïc; adult over 25/youth 15-25/child & senior €8.10/5.40/4.35, outdoor pool only Jun-Sep adult/child & senior €4.36/3; ⏱ 7am-midnight Mon-Fri, 7am-9pm Sat 7.30am-4pm

Sun, outdoor pool 10am-6pm Mon-Sat 10am-2.30pm Sun Oct-May, 9am-9pm Mon-Sat, 9am-8pm Sun Jun-Sep), is use of the gym, saunas and spa bath.

Water babies will squeal with delight in this thalassotherapeutic sports centre, **Poliesportiu Marítim** (Map pp266-7; ☎ 93 224 04 40; www.claror.org in Spanish; Passeig Marítim 33-35; admission Mon-Fri €12.50, Sat, Sun & holidays €15; ☒ 7am-midnight Mon-Fri, 8am-9pm Sat, 8am-5pm Sun & holidays). Apart from the smallish training pool, the centre is a minor labyrinth of spa pools that are hot, warm and freezing cold, along with thundering waterfalls for massage relief. When you're sufficiently relaxed, you can stumble outside and flop on to the beach.

WALKING TOUR

A great deal of what makes Barcelona fascinating is crowded into a relatively compact space, making an introductory strolling tour a great way to make the city's acquaintance.

WALKING TOUR

Start/Finish Plaça de Catalunya/Palau de la Música Catalana

Distance 3.5km

Duration 1½ hours

There's nothing wrong with following the crowds to start off with, so wander down La Rambla from **Plaça de Catalunya (1)**. Along the way, sniff around the **Mercat de la Boqueria (2**; p309), pop into the **Gran Teatre del Liceu (3**; p280) and visit one of Gaudí's earlier efforts, the **Palau Güell (4**; p284). From here, cross La Rambla and busy **Plaça Reial (5)** and make for **Plaça de Sant Jaume (6**; p281), at the core of the Barri Gòtic and the political heart of the city for two thousand years. You can examine the city's Roman origins in the nearby **Museu d'Història de la Ciutat (7**; p283). From the complex of buildings huddled around the museum and Plaça del Rei, you pass the **Museu Frederic Marès (8**; p283) en route for the main façade of the **Catedral (9**; p282). From there, make the loop down Via Laietana to admire what remains of the **Roman walls (10**; p283), and then branch off down Carrer de l'Argenteria to reach the splendid Gothic **Església de Santa Maria del Mar (11**; p286). Circle around it and up noble Carrer de Montcada, home to several museums in-

cluding the **Museu Picasso (12**; p285). Proceed north past the **Mercat de Santa Caterina (13)**, a huge produce market being rebuilt in daring form, and located on the site of a medieval convent, and then dogleg on to the stunning **Palau de la Música Catalana (14**; p285).

COURSES

Barcelona is bristling with schools offering Spanish- and Catalan-language courses:

Escola Oficial d'Idiomes de Barcelona (Map pp270-2; ☎ 93 324 93 30; www.eoibd.es in Spanish; Avinguda de les Drassanes s/n) Part-time courses (around 10 hours a week) in Spanish and Catalan (around €160 for a semester). Because of the demand for Spanish, there is no guarantee of a place. Generally there is no problem with Catalan.

International House (Map pp270-2; ☎ 93 268 45 11; www.ihes.com/bcn; Carrer de Trafalgar 14) Intensive courses from around €340 for two weeks. They can also organise accommodation.

Universitat de Barcelona (Map pp270-2; for Spanish ☎ 93 403 55 19, for Catalan ☎ 93 403 54 77; www.ub .es/ieh, www.ub.es/slc; Gran Via de les Corts Catalanes 585; ☒ 9am-2pm Mon-Fri) Intensive courses (40 hours' tuition over periods ranging from two weeks to a month; €310) in Spanish year-round. Longer Spanish and Catalan courses also available.

BARCELONA FOR CHILDREN

Barcelona is a relatively child-friendly city. There's plenty to interest kids, from street theatre on La Rambla to the beaches. Transport is good, many attractions are huddled fairly close together and children are generally welcome in restaurants and the like.

An initial stroll along La Rambla is full of potential distractions and wonders, from the bird stands to the living statues and buskers, and the **Wax Museum** (Museu de Cera, p280) further down the boulevard is bound to keep kids engaged.

At the bottom end of La Rambla, more options present themselves: a ride up to the top of the **Monument a Colom** (p281) or **L'Aquàrium** (p287). You might score points with a visit to the nearby 3-D **Imax cinema** (p287) too.

The **Telefèric** (p297) strung across the harbour between La Barceloneta and Montjuïc is an irresistible ride. Or scare the willies out of them with a ride on the Hotel Kruger horror house at Tibidabo's **Parc d'Atraccions** (p291) amusement park!

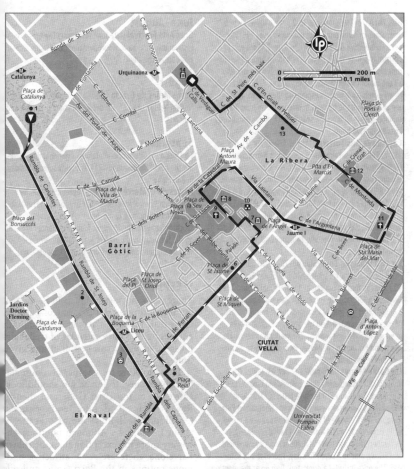

Of the city's many museums, those most likely to capture children's imagination and maintain their attention are the **Museu Marítim** (p281), the **Museu de la Xocolata** (p286) and the interactive **CosmoCaixa** (p292).

In the hot summer months you will doubtless be rewarded by squeals of delight if you take the bairns to one of the city's **swimming pools** (p297) or, better still, the **beach** (p287). In cooler weather, parks can be a good choice. A roam around Montjuïc, including some exploration of its **Castell** (p296), should appeal to young lads. A wander around the maze of the **Jardins del Laberint d'Horta** (p292) could also work. The animal touch usually mollifies truculent toddlers, so why not drop by the **Zoo de Barcelona** (p286)?

Baby-sitting

Most of the mid-range and top-end hotels in Barcelona can organise a baby-sitting service. A company that many hotels use, and which you can also contact directly, is **5 Serveis** (☎ 93 412 56 76, 639-361111; Carrer de Pelai 50). Multilingual baby-sitters (*canguros*) are available.

TOURS

Several tour options present themselves, if you want a hand getting around the sights: **Barri Gòtic Walking Tour** (Map pp270-2; ☎ 807 117222; Plaça de Catalunya 17; adult/child €8/3; English at 10am, Spanish & Catalan at noon, Sat & Sun, also English at 10am Thu & Fri Apr-Sep) The Oficina d'Informació de Turisme de Barcelona organises guided walking tours of the historic heart of the city.

Bus Turístic (TMB; Map pp270-2 ; ☎ 010; www.tmb
.net; adult/children per day of unlimited rides €16/10,
per 2 consecutive days €20/13; ⊕ 9am-7.45pm except
Christmas & New Year's Days) This hop-on hop-off service
runs along two circuit routes (32 stops), linking virtually
all the major tourist sights. Tourist offices, TMB offices and
many hotels have leaflets explaining the system. Tickets
are available on the bus and frequency varies from 10 to 30
minutes, depending on the season. Each of the full circuits
lasts about two hours.

Catalunya Bus Turístic (Map pp270-2; ☎ 93 285
38 32) This new service offers tours from Barcelona,
leaving from Plaça de Catalunya, to the surrounding
region. There are 3 day-tour routes: Girona and Figueres
(€55, 8.30am to 8pm); Colònia Güell, Sant Sadurní d'Anoia
and Sitges (€35, 9am to 5.30pm), and Tarragona via Reus
(€55, 8.30am to 8pm), where Antoni Gaudí was born. The
first two run daily (except Monday) from April to October.
The last one runs on Tuesday, Thursday and Saturday,
April to October.

Picasso Walking Tour (Map pp270-2; ☎ 807 117222;
Plaça de Catalunya 17; adult/child €10/5; ⊕ English at
10.30am, Spanish & Catalan at 11.30am, Sat & Sun) The
Oficina d'Informació de Turisme de Barcelona organises
a guided walking tour of locations, in the historic heart
of the city, connected with the artist, including places
in which he lived and worked. The walk takes about 1½
hours and finishes at the Museu Picasso, entry to which is
included in the price.

Un Cotxe Menys (Map pp273-5; ☎ 93 268 21 05;
www.biketoursbarcelona.com; Carrer de la Espartería 3;
⊕ 10am-2pm Mon-Fri) For bike tours (€22) around
the old city, La Barceloneta, La Sagrada Família and Port
Olímpic. There's no need to book unless you are a group
of 15 or more. Tours take place at 11am daily, March to
December. They also leave at 4.30pm Monday, Wednesday
and Friday, and at 7.30pm Tuesday, Thursday and Saturday. The price includes a drink stop. Turn up at the meeting
spot outside the tourist office on Plaça de Sant Jaume.

FESTIVALS & EVENTS
April
Dia de Sant Jordi (23 April) This is the day of Catalonia's
patron saint (George) and also the Day of the Book: men
give women a rose, women give men a book, publishers
launch new titles; La Rambla and Plaça de Sant Jaume are
filled with book and flower stalls.

June
Dia de Sant Joan (24 June) This is a colourful midsummer celebration with bonfires, even in the squares of
L'Eixample, and fireworks marking the evening preceding
this holiday.
Dia per l'Alliberament Lesbià i Gai (Saturday nearest
28 June) This is the gay and lesbian festival and parade.

June–August
Grec Arts Festival (late June to August) The Grec Arts
Festival involves music, dance and theatre at many loca-
tions across the city.

August
Festa Major de Gràcia (around 15 August) A big local
festival held in Gràcia, with decorated streets, dancing and
concerts.

September
La Diada (11 September) Catalonia's national day, marking the fall of Barcelona in 1714, is a fairly solemn holiday
in Barcelona.
Festes de la Mercè (around 24 September) The city's
biggest party involves around four days of concerts, dancing, *castellers* (human castle-builders), a fireworks display
synchronised with the Montjuïc fountains, dances of giants
on the Saturday, and *correfocs* – a parade of firework-
spitting dragons and devils from all over Catalonia, on
the Sunday.

SLEEPING
There is no shortage of hotels in Barcelona,
but its continuing status as one of Europe's
city-break getaway flavours-of-the-month
and centre of a busy calendar of trade fairs
means that many can be full at any given
time.

Those looking for cheaper accommodation that's close to the action should look,
above all, in the Barri Gòtic and then El
Raval. Some good lower-end *pensiones*
(small private hotels) are also scattered
about L'Eixample. Although boutique hotels are more the exception than the rule in
Barcelona, there are some attractive mid-
range options in the Barri Gòtic, and one
or two in El Raval and La Ribera. A greater
range of mid-range and top-end places are
spread across L'Eixample, most of them in
easy striking distance of the old town.

Camping
A series of vast but well-equipped camping grounds lie virtually side by side to the
southwest of Barcelona on the coastal C31
road towards Castelldefels. All are reachable
by bus No L95 from the corner of Ronda de
la Universitat and Rambla de Catalunya.

A couple of other camping grounds are
located to the north of the city. All are in-
convenient if you want late nights in Barcelona, because the only way back late at
night is by taxi.

BARCELONA TRANSPORT MAP

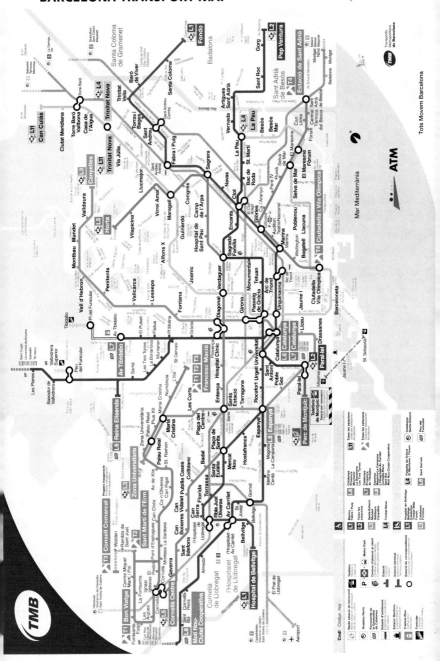

GREG ELMS

Gaudí's La Sagrada Família (p289) at dusk, Barcelona

RICHARD NEBESKY

Picasso's *Guernica* (p123), in the Centro de Arte Reina Sofía, Madrid

VERONICA GARBUTT

Party town Sitges (p321), on the Catalan coast

Nighttime display at La Font Mágica (p294) in Montjuïc, Barcelona

BILL

Filipinas (Map pp266-7; ☎ 93 658 28 95; Carretera C31, Km 186.5, Viladecans; 2-person site €23.20; ⊙ year-round; [P] [R]) Just back from a broad, sandy beach, this three-star camping ground, around 12km southwest of Barcelona, is one of several along this stretch of road. It has shops, restaurants, bars and laundry facilities. It's a quick stroll to the beach.

La Ballena Alegre (Map pp266-7; ☎ 902 500 527; www .ballena-alegre.es; Carretera C31, Km187, Viladecans; sites €32, plus per person €5.35, bungalows from €50; ⊙ Apr-Sep; [P] [□] [R]) Also just back from the beach, and sited amid pine stands, this vast camping ground has full amenities, including shops, laundry facilities, pizzeria, bars and (perhaps unfortunately) a little disco. Prices halve in low season.

Camping Masnou (☎ 93 555 15 03; Camí Fabra 33, El Masnou; 2-person site €20; ⊙ year-round) This is 11km northeast of the city, and only 200m from El Masnou train station (reached by *rodalies* trains from Catalunya station on Plaça de Catalunya). It offers some shade, is near the beach and reasonable value.

La Rambla   Map pp273–5
MID-RANGE
Hotel Continental (☎ 93 301 25 70; www.hotel continental.com; La Rambla 138; s/d €70/90; [R]) Rooms in this classic old Barcelona hotel are a little spartan but have romantic touches such as ceiling fans. The best are easily the doubles, with a balcony looking out over La Rambla (for which you pay €10 extra). You can have breakfast in your room.

Hotel Oriente (☎ 93 302 25 58; www.husa.es; La Rambla 45; s/d €123.05/155.15; [R]) One of Barcelona's oldest hotels is built into the shell of a former convent, among whose most spectacular leftovers is the cloister that is now a skylit restaurant.

Hotel Cuatro Naciones (☎ 93 317 36 24; www .h4n.com; La Rambla 40; s/d €53.50/85.60; [R]) Built in 1849 and a little worse for wear, the Four Nations was once – a long time ago – Barcelona's top hotel. Buffalo Bill preferred it to a wagon when he was in town, back in 1889. It retains a ramshackle charm in its public areas and the rooms are functional.

Barri Gòtic   Map pp273–5
BUDGET
Alberg Hostel Itaca (☎ 93 301 97 51; www.itacahostel .com; Carrer de Ripoll 21; dm €18, d €44) This bright, quiet hostel option near the cathedral has

spacious dorms (for six, eight and 12 people). Breakfast costs €2, and you can make use of the upstairs kitchen.

Hostal Campi (☎ 93 301 35 45; hcampi@terra.es; Carrer de la Canuda 4; s without bathroom €22, d with/ without bathroom €52/44) This is an excellent bottom-end deal. The best rooms are the doubles with own loo and shower. They are extremely roomy and bright.

Hostal Levante (☎ 93 317 95 65; www.hostal levante.com; Baixada de Sant Miquel 2; s without bathroom €33, d with/without bathroom €65/56) Off Plaça de Sant Miquel, this large, bright *hostal* (budget hotel) has rooms of all shapes and sizes. Try for a double with a balcony.

MID-RANGE
Hotel Neri (☎ 93 304 06 55; www.hotelneri.com; Carrer de Sant Sever 5; d €170; [R] [□]) Occupying a beautifully adapted centuries-old building, this stunningly renovated medieval mansion combines history with cutting-edge new – rooms of stone and timber have plasma screen TVs. Sun yourself on the roof deck.

Hotel Nouvel (☎ 93 301 82 74; www.hotelnouvel .com; Carrer de Santa Anna 18-20; s/d €112.80/177.60; [R]) Located near Plaça de Catalunya on one of the Barri Gòtic's more elegant streets, and a few seconds from the shops of Avinguda de Portal de l'Àngel, the hotel has some appealing Modernista touches and lofty ceilings.

Hotel California (☎ 93 317 77 66; www.hotel californiabcn.com; Carrer d'En Rauric 14; s/d €55/85; [R]) This friendly and central hotel, which is popular with gays, has straightforward, but perfectly acceptable, rooms with light, neutral colours, good-size beds and a bustling breakfast room.

Hotel Rialto (☎ 93 318 52 12; www.gargallo-hotels .com; Carrer de Ferran 40-42; s/d €87.10/99.70; [R]) Situated near the passage that was Joan Miró's childhood address, this modest three-star has straightforward rooms, the best of them with little balconies looking onto the street below.

TOP END
Hotel Racó del Pi (☎ 93 342 61 90; www.hotel h10racodelpi.com; Carrer del Pi 7; s/d €177.60/206.50; [R] [□]) Stylishly carved out of a historic Barri Gòtic building, the hotel's 37 rooms have dark-wood beams, parquet floors and prettily tiled attached bathrooms and are fully soundproofed. The location is terrific. Rates can halve in slow periods.

BARCELONA

El Raval

BUDGET

Hostal Gat Raval (Map pp270–2; ☎ 93 481 66 70; www.gataccommodation.com; Carrer de Joaquín Costa 44; s without bathroom €39, d with/without bathroom €71/54.10; ⊠ ⬜) They've opted for a pea-green and lemon-lime colour scheme in this hip young 2nd-floor hostal, on one of the grittier lanes of El Raval. Rooms are pleasant, secure and each behind a green door but only some have private bathroom.

Alberg Center Rambles (Map pp273–5; ☎ 93 412 40 69; www.tujuca.com; Carrer de l'Hospital 63; dm adults/under 26 or ISIC card-holders incl breakfast €21.60/18.10; ⊠ ⬜) This HI hostel is right in the thick of things, just off La Rambla. Beds are in single-sex dorms of four to 10 people. Safes, and kitchen and laundry facilities are available.

MID-RANGE

Hotel Mesón de Castilla (Map pp270–2; ☎ 93 318 21 82; www.husa.es; Carrer de Valldonzella 5; s/d €101.65/130.55; ⓟ ⊠) Some characterful Modernista touches remain on the first floor of this elegant hotel. Heavy wooden furniture, across several timeless sitting rooms, contrasts with playful stained glass and murals, and Gaudíesque window mouldings. Rooms have a classic charm.

Hotel Peninsular (Map pp273–5; ☎ 93 302 31 38; Carrer de Sant Pau 34; s with/without bathroom €50/30, d €70/50; ⊠) This is an oasis on the edge of the slightly louche Barri Xinès. Once part of a convent, it has a plant-draped atrium extending the full height of the hotel. Rooms are simple, clean and (mostly) spacious.

Hotel Aneto (Map pp273–5; ☎ 93 301 99 89; www.hotelaneto.com; Carrer del Carme 38; s/d €60/80; ⊠) This good mid-range hotel, at the lower end of the scale, is nestled in a lively street, in one of the nicer parts of El Raval. The best rooms are the doubles with the shuttered street-side balconies.

Hotel España (Map pp273–5; ☎ 93 318 17 58; Carrer de Sant Pau 9–11; s/d €65/90; ⊠) The hotel is famous for its two marvellous dining rooms designed by the Modernista architect Lluís Domènech i Montaner. One has big sea-life murals by Ramon Casas; the other has floral tiling and a wood-beamed roof. The rooms are a little on the dingy side but have high ceilings and certainly exude the flavour of a past era.

Hotel Principal (Map pp273–5; ☎ 93 318 89 70; www.hotelprincipal.es; Carrer de la Junta del Comerç 8; s/d

€90.95/119.85; ⓟ ⊠ ⬜) The hotel has clean-lined functional rooms, and also some 'superior' options, whose additional features include parquet floors, hairdryers and original art depicting Barcelona. You can sunbathe on the roof.

Hotel San Agustín (Map pp273–5; ☎ 93 318 16 58; www.hotelsa.com; Plaça de Sant Agustí 3; s/d €117.70/160.50; ⊠ ⬜) This one-time 18th-century monastery opened as a hotel in 1840, making it the city's oldest (it's undergone various refits since then!). The location is perfect: a quick stroll off La Rambla, on a curious square. Consider an attic double, with a sloping ceiling and wonderful bird's-eye views.

La Ribera   Map pp270–2

MID-RANGE

Park Hotel (☎ 93 319 60 00; www.parkhotelbarcelona.com; Avinguda del Marquès de l'Argentera 11; s/d €107/155.70; ⓟ ⊠) This 1950s hotel, which oozies details of that period, such as the angular spiral stairway, is a minor Barcelona landmark. Dark wood and fabrics dominate the rooms, some of which have terraces. The Àbac restaurant downstairs (see p307) is also the hotel breakfast room.

Pensió 2000 (☎ 93 310 74 66; www.pensio2000.com; Carrer de Sant Pere més Alt 6; s/d with bathroom €49.50/62; ⬜) Sitting in front of the Modernista chocolate box that is the Palau de la Música Catalana (p285), this cheerful *pensión*, with its seven canary-yellow rooms, is a handily placed option. The best rooms have their own bathroom. You can also take time out on the little terrace.

Port Vell & the Coast   Map pp266–7

TOP END

Hotel Arts Barcelona (☎ 93 221 10 00; www.ritzcarlton.com; Carrer de la Marina 19–21; r €375–460;

P 🔀 🖳 🚇) In one of the two sky-high towers that dominate Port Olímpic, these are Barcelona's most fashionable digs, and frequented by VIPs from all over the planet. The rooms have unbeatable views. Prices vary greatly according to the size and position of the rooms.

Grand Marina Hotel (☎ 93 603 90 00; www .grandmarinahotel.com; Moll de Barcelona s/n; r €235/310, ste €695; **P 🔀 🖳 🚇**) Housed in the World Trade Center, the hotel and its rooms have a maritime flavour, with lots of polished-timber touches. Some of the lateral rooms, the best, offer splendid views of the city, port and open sea.

L'Eixample
BUDGET
Hostal Goya (Map pp268-9; ☎ 93 302 25 65; www .hostalgoya.com; Carrer de Pau Claris 74; s without bathroom €34.25, d with/without bathroom €88.25/72.75; **🔀**) There's no doubt that the address is a chichi one. Half of the rooms are tastefully renovated (stylish parquet floors and light colour scheme) and dearer than those that remain to be overhauled.

Hostal Central (Map pp270-2; ☎ 93 302 24 20; Ronda de l'Universitat 11; s with/without bathroom €33/50, d €60/40) Spread out over several renovated flats, some of the larger rooms have charming enclosed terraces looking onto the admittedly noisy street. Mosaic and parquet floors and some nice decorative touches make it an attractive option.

Hostal Australia (Map pp270-2; ☎ 93 317 41 77; www .residenciaustralia.com; Ronda de l'Universitat 11; s without bathroom €28, d with/without bathroom €58/48; **P**) Up on the 4th floor is this charming, tiny family establishment. Rooms are kept fragrant and prim. With only a handful of rooms, and a faithful clientele, this hostal has the luxury of working almost exclusively with phone bookings.

Hostal Neutral (Map pp268-9; ☎ 93 487 63 90; La Rambla de Catalunya 42; d with/without bathroom €50/44) Although ageing, this is a reliable old-style option, in a privileged and leafy location. It has a couple of little singles without bathrooms but they are generally occupied. The doubles without a loo do have a shower.

MID-RANGE
Hostal Palacios (Map pp270-2; ☎ 93 301 37 92; Rambla de Catalunya 27; s/d €65/100, ste €150; **🔀 🖳**) This classy hostal offers fine, sunny rooms with high ceilings and old-style furnishings. The 'suites', which can be taken as triples, are roomy and worth the extra outlay.

Hostal Windsor (Map pp268-9; ☎ 93 215 11 98; Rambla de Catalunya 84; s/d €48/78) An immaculately maintained, elegant hostal, the Windsor offers a good deal. Try for a room facing the street. Cheaper rooms without a bathroom are also available.

Hotel Hispanos Siete Suiza (Map pp268-9; ☎ 93 208 20 51; www.hispanos7suiza.com; Carrer de Sicilia 255; q €180-210; **P 🔀 🖳**) Near La Sagrada Família, this hotel's apartments have two double rooms and separate bathrooms, a lounge, a fully equipped kitchen and a terrace.

Hotel Onix Rambla (Map pp270-2; ☎ 93 342 79 80; www.hotelsonix.com; Rambla de Catalunya 24; s/d €123/133.75; **P 🔀 🖳 🚇**) Modern rooms are spread through this former urban mansion, just a few steps away from Plaça de Catalunya. They are simple enough but fully equipped, and pluses include a small outdoor pool, a solarium and a handful of exercise machines.

Hotel Actual (Map pp268-9; ☎ 93 552 05 50; www .hotelactual.com; Carrer del Rosselló 238; s/d €138/152; **🔀 🖳**) A minimalist designer hotel that attracts a business clientele, and is handily placed. Its rooms have a sleek, contemporary feel, with cream and dark-oak colours predominating.

Splendid (Map pp270-2; ☎ 93 451 21 42; www .apsishotels.com; Carrer de Muntaner 2; s/d €117.70/142.30; **P 🔀 🖳**) Situated just outside the northern end of El Raval, this three-star is a comfortable, modern option. Rooms are straightforward, have carpet and are dominated by warm browns and yellows.

Hotel AC Irla (Map pp268-9; ☎ 902 292293; www .ac-hotels.com; Carrer de Calvet 32-34; d €182; **🔀 🖳**) This sleek business hotel that's part of a chain, is set just north of L'Eixample and the stylish high-end shopping and business district, around Avinguda Diagonal. Several of the rooms are nonsmoking rooms. Rates drop considerably on weekends. There are no single rooms or rates.

TOP END
Hotel Axel (Map pp270-2; ☎ 93 323 93 93; www .hotelaxel.com; Carrer d'Aribau 33; s/d €133.75/197.95; **🔀 🖳 🚇**) Favoured by a mixed fashion-and-gay set, the sleek-lined corner-block Axel offers modern touches in its designer rooms. Plasma-screen TVs and (in the double

rooms) king-size beds are just some of the pluses. Take a break in the rooftop pool, the Finnish sauna or the Jacuzzi.

Hotel Claris (Map pp268-9; ☎ 93 487 62 62; www.derbyhotels.es; Carrer de Pau Claris 150; d €225-270; ☒ ☒ ☒) The designer upgrade of the 19th-century Palacio Verdura has resulted in one of the city's most stylish hotels. It houses a permanent art collection. Room décor varies greatly: some rooms are strikingly modern, while others cede to more classic tastes in luxury.

Tibidabo & Around
BUDGET
Alberg Mare de Déu de Montserrat (Map pp266-7; ☎ 93 210 51 51; www.tujuca.com; Passeig de la Mare de Déu del Coll 41-51; dm adult/under 26 or ISIC card-holders €21.60/18.10) Four kilometres north of the city, this hostel's main building is a magnificent former mansion with a Mudéjar-style lobby. Most rooms sleep six. Take the metro to Vallcarca station, or bus Nos 25, 28 and N4.

MID-RANGE
Hotel Turó de Vilana (Map pp266-7; ☎ 93 434 03 63; www.turodevilana.com; Carrer de Vilana 7; s/d €139.10/176.55; FGC Les Tres Torres or bus 64; ☒ ☒ ☒) This bright, designer hotel in residential Sarrià has hardwood floors, marble bathrooms and plenty of natural sunlight. For those who like the idea of being able to dip in and out of central Barcelona at will, this is an attractive option. Take the FGC train to Les Torres or bus No 64 (from Plaça de l'Universitat).

TOP END
Gran Hotel La Florida (Map pp266-7; ☎ 93 259 30 00; www.hotellaflorida.com; Carretera de Vallvidrera al Tibidabo

83-93; d from €374.50; ☒ ☒ ☒) Spreading out in all its glory, 500 metres above the city, this luxury hotel has rooms and suites that are all quite different, along with a gourmet restaurant, a jazz bar, disco, outdoor heated pools and a spa. The main drawback is shuttling there and back from the city centre: you must take the funicular or a taxi.

Long-Term Rentals
The **Universitat de Barcelona** (Map pp266-7; ☎ 93 402 11 00; Gran Via de les Corts Catalanes 585), the **British Council** (Map pp266-7; ☎ 93 241 99 77; Carrer d' Amigó 83) and **International House** (Map pp270-2; ☎ 93 268 45 11; Carrer de Trafalgar 14) have noticeboards with ads for flat shares.

Young people and students should also check out options at **Punt d'Informació Juvenil** (Map pp266-7; ☎ 93 483 83 84; Carrer de Calàbria 147; ☒ 9am-2pm & 3-7pm Mon-Fri). Another option for students coming to Barcelona to study is the private **Rent a Bedroom** (Map pp268-9; ☎ 93 217 88 12; www.rentabedroom.com; Avinguda del Príncep d'Astúries 52). They can organise rooms in share houses for between €300 and €690, inclusive of bills.

The free English-language monthly *Barcelona Metropolitan*, found in bars, some hotels and occasionally tourist offices, carries rental classifieds in English, as does another monthly freebie, *Barcelona Connect*. Rooms can come as cheap as €200 per month, but for something halfway decent and central, you're generally looking at around €300. To this, you also need to add your share of bills (gas, electricity, water, phone and *comunidad*-building maintenance charges).

EATING
Barcelona is packed with good places to eat. *Cartas* (menus) may be in Catalan, Spanish, or both; some places also have foreign-language menus. Barcelona has become something of a foodies' paradise on earth in recent years, combining the already rich Catalan cooking traditions with a new wave of cutting-edge chefs at the vanguard of *nueva cocina española*, tipped by some (perhaps a trifle precipitately) to unseat the *nouvelle cuisine* of Spain's northern neighbour. The city has taken on quite a cosmopolitan hue too. Whereas Thai, Japanese and other exotic cuisines were barely represented in the mid-1990s, they are now springing up all over the city.

The main concentration of new and experimental cuisine is in El Born, the trendy, BoHo lower side of La Ribera in the old city. More traditional restaurants, often not too demanding fiscally speaking, are scattered across the Barri Gòtic, and there are some gems in El Raval too. Gràcia is also full of tempting little eateries, among them a legion of Middle Eastern and Greek joints.

Across the broad expanse of L'Eixample, and further outlying districts, you'll find all sorts. The majority of the seriously top-level joints are to be found secreted away in such areas, but there is a range of all sorts. You need to know where you are going, however, as just wandering about aimlessly, and picking whatever takes your fancy, is not as feasible as in the old city.

La Rambla
MID-RANGE
Attic (Map pp273-5; ☎ 93 302 48 66; La Rambla dels Estudis 120; meals €25-30) Attic offers a mix of international dishes, in this superb spot, overlooking the animated activity of La Rambla. Try the *filet de bou* (beef filet).

Barri Gòtic   Map pp273–5
BUDGET
Can Conesa (☎ 93 310 57 95; Carrer de la Llibreteria 1; bocadillos €3-5; ❤ Mon-Sat) They have been doling out delicious *bocadillos* (bread roll with filling), frankfurters and toasted sandwiches here for more than 50 years – *barcelonins* swear by it and queue for it.

Bar Celta (☎ 93 315 00 06; Carrer de la Mercè 16; meals €15-20; ❤ noon-midnight) Specialists in *pulpo* (octopus) and other delights from Galicia in the country's northwest, the waiters waste no time in serving up bottles of crisp white Ribeiro wine to wash down the *raciónes* (large tapas serving).

La Cereria (☎ 93 301 85 10; Baixada de Sant Miquel 3-5; meals €10; ❤ 10.30am-11.30pm) A cross between the café of a century gone by, and a hippy hang-out, this culinary cooperative offers tasty vegetarian cooking, great desserts and low prices. Sip on a chunky fruit shake or pop in for a late breakfast of muesli.

Juicy Jones (☎ 93 302 43 30; Carrer del Cardenal Cassañas 7; menú del día €8.75) In this psychedelic eatery you sit down to a set vegetarian meal, or just sip the wonderful fruit juices.

MID-RANGE
Agut (☎ 93 315 17 09; Carrer d'En Gignàs 16; meals €25-30; ❤ Tue-Sat, lunch only Sun) Contemporary paintings set a contrast with the fine traditional Catalan dishes offered in this timeless restaurant. Start with a platter of cured ham, and proceed with a menu of meat or fish – the *bacallà* (cod) is good.

Pla (☎ 93 412 65 52; Carrer de Bellafila 5; meals €30-35; ❤ dinner) In this modern den of inventive cooking, and music worthy of a club, the chefs present deliciously strange combinations such as *bacallà amb salsa de pomes verdes* (cod in a green apple sauce).

Shunka (☎ 93 412 49 91; Carrer dels Sagristans 5; meals €30; ❤ Tue-Sun) Grab a seat near the open-plan kitchen and you can watch at close quarters exactly what they are doing with your tempura and sashimi. So many Japanese punters can't be wrong.

Els Quatre Gats (☎ 93 302 41 40; Carrer de Montsió 3 bis; meals €30; ❤ 1pm-1am) Once a turn-of-the-

---

COOL CATS OF THE 1900s
Els Quatre Gats was opened in 1897 by four *barcelonins*, who had spent time in Paris' artistic circles: the Modernista artists Ramon Casas and Santiago Rusiñol, and their friends Miquel Utrillo and Pere Romeu, who, among other things, were deeply interested in shadow puppetry. Romeu, the manager, was a colourful character equally devoted to cabaret and cycling.

The name Els Quatre Gats is Catalan for 'the four cats', and alludes both to the café's four founders and to Le Chat Noir, an artistic café in Montmartre, Paris. Idiomatically, it means 'a handful of people, a minority' – no doubt a reference to how its avant-garde clientele saw themselves. Situated in the first Barcelona creation of the Modernista architect Josep Puig i Cadafalch, Els Quatre Gats soon became a meeting, drinking and cavorting place of young artists, writers, actors, musicians and their circles.

The group published its own magazine and staged exhibitions, recitals and, of course, shadow-puppet shows. Picasso's first exhibition was held here in 1900, and included drawings of many of the customers. Els Quatre Gats closed in 1903. Later it was used as an art gallery, before its present incarnation as a restaurant.

20th-century artists' lair (see the boxed text Cool Cats of the 1900s on p305) Els Quatre Gats has been restored to its original appearance. Full of charming tile and timberwork, it also displays reproductions of some of its former customers' portraits, painted by other former customers. Head out past the bar to the grand rear dining area.

Restaurant Pitarra (☎ 93 301 16 47; Carrer d'Avinyó 56; meals €30; ☽ Mon-Sat Sep-Jul) At home in what could be a family home, the chefs here put on fine Catalan fare. It's best in autumn and winter, when escaping from the cold into such a warm retreat and being greeted with venison and other meaty specialities is a treat.

El Raval
BUDGET
Buenas Migas (Map pp273-5; ☎ 93 412 16 86; Plaça del Bonsuccés 6). This charming hole-in-the-wall, in a busy little square just off La Rambla, offers decent focaccia, pizza slices and other snacks.

Bar Pinotxo (Map pp273-5; ☎ 93 317 17 31; Mercat de la Boqueria; meals €15; ☽ 6am-5pm Mon-Sat Sep-Jul) Of the half-dozen or so tapas bars and informal eateries scattered about the market, this one near the Rambla entrance is the most popular.

MID-RANGE
Ra (Map pp273-5; ☎ 93 301 41 63; Plaça de la Gardunya; meals €20; ☽ Mon-Sat) It looks like a beach bar that got lost and ended up in the car park, and offers a vaguely vegetarian menu with a couple of meat options thrown in.

Lupino (Map pp273-5; ☎ 93 412 36 97; Carrer del Carme 33; meals €30; ☽ 1pm-3am) Proceed down the long hall of this 'designer lounge' to eat outside on Plaça de Gardunya. Try the *couscous al xai* (lamb). Hang around in the bar for post-prandial drinks.

Restaurant El Cafetí (Map pp273-5; ☎ 93 329 24 19; Passatge de Bernardí; meals €25; ☽ Tue-Sat, lunch only Sun) This diminutive eatery is filled with antique furniture and proposes traditional local cooking, with one or two unorthodox variations. Paella and other rice dishes dominate. This place is off Carrer de Sant Rafael.

Biblioteca (Map pp273-5; ☎ 93 412 62 21; Carrer de la Junta de Comerç 28, meals €30-35; ☽ Tue-Sat) Exposed-brick and creamy-white décor dominate in the 'Library', where the food represents a broad sweep across Spain, with careful creative touches and a good wine list.

Rita Blue (Map pp273-5; ☎ 93 412 34 38; Plaça de St Agustí 3; meals €20-25; ☽ dinner only Mon-Fri, lunch & dinner Sat & Sun) The funky New York ambience is perfect for hanging at the bar, and then proceeding to dine on a mix of Mediterranean and Mexican fare. They run a little dance space downstairs on Friday and Saturday nights.

TOP END
Ca l'Isidre (Map pp270-2; ☎ 93 441 11 39; Carrer de les Flors 12; meals €45; ☽ Mon-Sat) Ca L'Isidre is one of those old-world gems, where immaculately kept dining areas are dominated by warm timber and tiles. Chefs use only the best of ingredients gathered in the morning at La Boqueria market to produce quality local cuisine.

Casa Leopoldo (Map pp273-5; ☎ 93 441 30 14; Carrer de Sant Rafael 24; meals €50; ☽ Tue-Sat, lunch only Sun) Several rambling dining areas with magnificent tiled walls and exposed timber-beam ceilings, make this a fine option. The seafood menu is extensive and the wine list strong.

La Ribera
BUDGET
Casa Delfín (Map pp273-5; ☎ 93 319 50 88; Passeig del Born 36; menú €8.50; ☽ 6am-7pm Mon-Sat) Under siege from triremes of ultra avant-garde cookeries, the 'Dolphin House' continues to do what it has always done best – a bountiful lunch from an extensive menu of Spanish favourites.

Comme-Bio (La Botiga; Map pp273-5; ☎ 93 319 89 68; Via Laietana 28; lunch buffet €9) This chemical- and additive-free vegetarian restaurant (part of a small chain) and wholefood shop is a vegetarian stalwart. Go for the all-you-can-eat buffet at lunch.

MID-RANGE

Pla de la Garsa (Map pp273-5; ☎ 93 315 23 13; Carrer dels Assaonadors 13; meals €25; ☒ dinner) This 17th-century house is the ideal location for a romantic candle-lit dinner. Timber beams, anarchically scattered tables and soft ambience music combine to make an enchanting setting for traditional and hearty Catalan cooking.

Santa Maria (Map pp270-2; ☎ 93 315 12 27; Carrer de Comerç 17; meals €30-40; ☒ Mon-Sat) It comes as no surprise that this irreverent little gastrodome should be located snugly amid other avant-garde El Born kitchens. Forget your standard tapas. Here your bar snack is as likely to be a serving of Sichuan pepper yucca chips.

Centre Cultural Euskal Etxea (Map pp273-5; ☎ 93 310 21 85; Placeta de Montcada 1; meals €15-20; ☒ Tue-Sat, lunch only Sun) Barcelona is awash with Basque and pseudo-Basque eateries, but this is the real deal. It captures the feel of San Sebastián better than many of its newer competitors. Choose your *pintxos* (snacks), sip *txacoli* wine, and keep the toothpicks so the staff can count them up and work out your bill.

Sikkim (Map pp273-5; ☎ 93 268 43 13; Plaça Comercial 1; meals €30; ☒ 9pm-1am) The tapestries and candle-light give the two separate levels of this dynamic young restaurant a dreamy, exotic air. Cooking is light, and ranges from grapefruit-based salads to filets of Argentinian beef.

Habana Vieja (Map pp273-5; ☎ 93 268 25 04; Carrer dels Banys Vells 2; meals €20) Since the early 1990s this Cuban hideaway has offered old island faves such as the stringy meat – *ropa vieja* ('old clothes') and rice dishes. With its antique light fittings and predilection for timber furnishings, this old Ribera house could easily be an Old Havana eatery.

TOP END

Àbac (Map pp270-2; ☎ 93 319 66 00; Carrer del Rec 79-89; meals €90-100; ☒ Tue-Sat, dinner only Mon Sep-Jul) Minimalist designer décor, dominated by neutral, light furnishings provides the setting for what is considered by some the best avant-garde eatery in town. You never quite know what might emerge from the kitchen, but it does so with a rare aplomb.

La Barceloneta & the Coast
BUDGET

Can Maño (Map pp270-2; ☎ 93 319 30 82; Carrer del Baluard 12; meals €15; ☒ Mon-Sat) You'll need to be

prepared to wait, before being squeezed in at a packed table for a raucous night of *raciones* (posted on a board at the back) over a bottle of *turbio* – a cloudy white plonk. You can breakfast on *gambes* (prawns) too if you want!

MID-RANGE

Bestial (Map pp266-7; ☎ 93 224 04 07; Carrer de Ramon Trías Fargas 2-4; meals €30-35) As your meal of pasta, risotto or huge salad comes to an end the DJ ups the musical ante. Lots of light in a minimalist setting with a palm-fringed, beachside terrace, make the location as attractive as the musical-food offerings.

Merendero de la Mari (Map pp270-2; ☎ 93 221 31 41; Plaça Pau Vila 1; meals €35) This is one of the most consistent of the restaurants lining the waterfront in the shadow of the Palau de Mar. The *fideuá* (paella made with noodles instead of rice; €11) is cooked to just the right point, and they do a range of reasonable paellas for around €16.

Can Ramonet (Map pp270-2; ☎ 93 319 30 64; Carrer de la Maquinista 17; meals €25-30; ☒ Mon-Sat) Perching at one of the little tables, set up across the lane from the restaurant proper, is the perfect way to pass a warm summer evening over an *arròs caldós amb llamàntol* (rice and lobster stew).

Can Ros (Map pp270-2; ☎ 93 221 45 79; Carrer de l'Almirall Aixada 7; meals €25-30; ☒ Thu-Tue) Little has changed over the decades in this seafood fave. In a restaurant where the décor is a reminder of simpler times, a simple rule guides – give the punters succulent fresh fish cooked with a light touch.

AUTHOR'S CHOICE

Hofmann (Map pp273-5; ☎ 93 319 58 89; Carrer de l'Argenteria 74; meals €50-60; ☒ Mon-Fri) Discreetly tucked away, upstairs in the plant-filled annexe to one of the city's renowned cuisine schools, is this refined restaurant. Some of the nation's great chefs learned the trade here, and you will not be disappointed with the present students' efforts. An imaginative and constantly changing menu keeps chefs and diners on their toes. Special care is put into the desserts, and there's a lunch *menú del día* for around €30.

TOP END
Torre d'Alta Mar (Map pp266-7; ☎ 93 221 00 07; Torre de Sant Sebastiá, Passeig de Joan Borbò 88; meals €70-80; ☑ Tue-Sat, lunch only Mon) Head up to the top of the Torre de Sant Sebastiá and take a ringside seat for the best views of the city and reasonable seafood. The setting alone makes this ideal for impressing a date.

L'Eixample
BUDGET
L'Hostal de Rita (Map pp268-9; ☎ 93 487 23 76; Carrer d'Aragó 279; meals €15) Locals love to line up to dine here, if only because the price-quality rapport is excellent. So join the queue to get inside this boisterous restaurant. You have a choice between classic local cooking and some more inventive dishes.

Bar Estudiantil (Map pp270-2; ☎ 93 302 31 25; Gran Via de les Corts Catalanes 592; meals around €10) Has economical *plats combinats* (basically meat-and-three-veg meals), hamburgers and sandwiches. This place is filled with an odd crowd of students, bums and, on early weekend mornings (from 6am), bleary-eyed clubbers.

MID-RANGE
Cerveseria Catalana (Map pp268-9; ☎ 93 216 03 68; Carrer de Mallorca 236; meals €20-25) This 'Catalan brewery' is great for its cornucopia of tapas and *montaditos* (canapés). You can sit at the bar, outside or in the restaurant at the back. The variety of hot tapas, mouthwatering salads and other snacks draws a well dressed crowd.

de Tapa Madre (Map pp268-9; ☎ 93 459 31 34; Carrer de Mallorca 301; meals €30-35; ☑ 8am-midnight Sun-Thu, 8am-3pm & 5pm-1am Fri & Sat) Dine at the bar on tapas, or head upstairs for a table on the open gallery that hangs above the bar. Choose from a range of tapas (€3 to €5.50), or opt for a full meal. The *arròs caldós amb llagostins* (a hearty rice dish with king prawns) is delicious.

Cros Diagonal (Map pp268-9; ☎ 93 414 37 48; Avingudal Diagonal 433; meals €25-30; ☑ 1pm-1.30am) Drop by anytime during opening hours for tapas over a beer, or a full sit-down meal of Spanish fare in this bright restaurant full of Mediterranean colour.

El Rincón Maya (Map pp270-2; ☎ 93 451 39 46; Carrer de València 183; meals €15-20; ☑ Tue-Sun) The setting in this Mexican restaurant is warm and crowded. The nachos, guacamole and

fajitas burst with flavour, and you may have to queue for a spot.

TOP END
Drolma (Map pp268-9; ☎ 93 496 77 10; Passeig de Gràcia 68; meals €100-120; ☑ Mon-Sat, dinner only Aug) In the grand Hotel Majèstic is housed one of the city's top restaurants. Everything oozes luxury. The menu, ranging from Catalan to international, depends largely on produce available in season.

El Peixerot (Map pp266-7; ☎ 93 424 69 69; Carrer de Tarragona 177; meals €40-50; ☑ Mon-Sat, lunch only Sun) With its sea-blue décor and long-standing fame for fresh seafood (sold by weight) and rice dishes, this is a quality stop in the rather unlikely train-station area.

Gràcia
BUDGET
Sol Soler (Map pp268-9; ☎ 93 217 44 40; Plaça del Sol 21-22; meals €15; ☑ dinner) This is a pleasant corner of a busy, bar-lined square. Gather around the marble-top tables for a drink and enticing, inventive snacks, which you choose at the bar.

MID-RANGE
Goliard (Map pp268-9; ☎ 93 207 31 75; Carrer de Progrés 6; meals €25-30; ☑ lunch daily, dinner Sat & Sun) This quiet diner is a haven of exquisite designer cooking at modest prices. Try the *lassanya de pops i patates* (a 'lasagne' in which sliced potatoes take the place of pasta, and slightly spicy, tender octopus is the meat).

Can Juanito (Map pp268-9; ☎ 93 213 30 43; Carrer de Ramon i Cajal 3; meals €25-30; ☑ Tue-Sat, lunch only Sun) At a time when even many Catalan restaurants are tempted to fiddle and experiment, this delightful place comes as a reassuring ambassador of home-cooked Catalan classics such as *botifarra amb mongetes* (pork sausage with fried white beans) and steaming, oven-baked *canelons* (cannelloni).

TOP END

Botafumeiro (Map pp268-9; ☎ 93 218 42 30; Carrer Gran de Gràcia 81; meals €60-70; ☒ 1pm-1am) Limos frequently front this Galician seafood temple. Look up from your plate of *navajas* (a long tubular shellfish) and you might espy anyone from the mayor to Bruce Springsteen. Booking is essential.

Montjuïc & Poble Sec
MID-RANGE

Quimet i Quimet (Map pp270-2; ☎ 93 442 31 42; Carrer del Poeta Cabanyes 25; meals €25; ☒ Tue-Sat, lunch only Sun) Quimet i Quimet is proof that good things come in small packages. Cram into this bottle-lined quad for tapas and fine wine.

Restaurant Elche (Map pp270-2; ☎ 93 441 30 89; Carrer de Vila i Vilà 71; meals €25) With tables spreading over two floors, and old-world style in service and settings, this spot has been doing some of Barcelona's best paella (of various types) and *fideuá* (vaguely similar to paella, but made with vermicelli noodles) since the 1960s.

Self-Catering

Shop in the **Mercat de la Boqueria** (Map pp273-5; La Rambla de Sant Josep; ☒ 8am-8pm Mon-Sat), one of the world's great produce markets, and complement with any other necessities from a local supermarket. Handy ones include **Champion** (Map pp273-5; La Rambla dels Estudis 113; ☒ 9am-10pm Mon-Sat), near the northern end of La Rambla, and **Superservis** (Map pp273-5; Carrer d'Avinyó 13; ☒ 8am-2pm & 4-8pm Mon-Sat), in the heart of Barri Gòtic.

For freshly baked bread, head for a *forn* or *panadería*. For a gourmet touch, the food sections of **El Corte Inglés** department store (p315) have some tempting local and imported goodies.

DRINKING

Barcelona's bars run the gamut from wood-panelled wine cellars to bright waterfront places and trendy designer bars. Most are at their liveliest from about 10pm to 2am or 3am, especially from Thursday to Saturday, as people get into their night-time stride.

The old town is the most fruitful area to search. The single hippest area since the late 1990s has been El Born, in the lower end of La Ribera, but there is a good scattering of bars across the lower half of the Barri Gòtic too, while El Raval has recently begun to be discovered – it is home to some fine old drinking institutions as well as a swelling new wave of funky, inner city locales.

A word of warning on La Rambla: While it can be pleasant enough to tipple here, few locals would even think about it and bar prices tend to be exorbitant – €25 for a carafe of *sangría* is not unheard of.

Elsewhere, the series of squares and some streets of Gràcia are loaded up with bars. In the broad expanse of L'Eixample you need to know where to go. Carrer d'Aribau is the single most fruitful area, along with the area around its continuation northwest of Avinguda Diagonal.

La Rambla   Map pp273–5

Cafè Zurich (☎ 93 317 91 53; Carrer de Pelai 39; coffee & pastry €3-4) This is a prime spot, virtually on Plaça de Catalunya, for coffee, a paper and the passing street theatre at this crucial city crossroads.

Cafè de l'Òpera (☎ 93 317 75 85; La Rambla 74) Opposite the Gran Teatre del Liceu opera house is La Rambla's most interesting café. Founded in 1876, it is pleasant for an early evening tipple or coffee and croissants. Head upstairs for a seat overlooking the boulevard.

Barri Gòtic   Map pp273–5

Barcelona Pipa Club (☎ 93 302 47 32; Plaça Reial 3; ☒ Mon-Sat) This pipe-smokers' club is like someone's flat, with all sorts of interconnecting rooms and knick-knacks – notably the pipes after which the place is named. You buzz at the door and head two floors up. It is for members only until 11pm.

Café Royale (☎ 93 412 14 33; Carrer Nou de Zurbano 3) A high blue-fabric cover covers the wall opposite the bar, so grab a lounge in the spacious hardwood back area.

Dot Light Club (☎ 93 302 70 26; Carrer Nou de Sant Francesc 7) Since the late 1990s this has been one of the hippest hang-outs in this part of town. Each night the DJs change the musical theme, ranging from deep funk to deeper house.

Fantástico (Passatge dels Escudellers 3; ☒ Wed-Sat) This long-time Barri Gòtic dive has gone pop – past and present. The décor is a little

BARCELONA

loud but it's an endearingly unpretentious place for a beer and a bit of a dance.

La Clandestina (☎ 93 319 05 33; Baixada de Viladecols 2bis; ☼ 10am-10pm Sun-Thu, 9am-midnight Sat & Sun) Opt for tea, a beer or a Middle Eastern narghile (the most elaborate way to smoke). You can even get a head massage or eat cake in this chilled tea shop.

El Raval

Bar Marsella (Map pp273-5; Carrer de Sant Pau 65; ☼ Mon-Sat) In business since 1820, the Marsella specialises in *absenta* (absinthe) a beverage that's hard to find, because of its supposed narcotic qualities. Nothing much has changed here since the 19th century.

Casa Almirall (Map pp270-2; Carrer de Joaquim Costa 33) In business since the 1860s, this unchanged corner drinkery is dark and intriguing, with Modernista décor and a mixed clientele.

Kentucky (Map pp273-5; ☎ 93 318 28 78; Carrer de l'Arc del Teatre 11) All sorts of odd bods from the *barri* (district) and beyond squeeze in here late at night. Opening times (which can mean until 5am) depend in part on the presence (or rather absence) of the law in the street.

London Bar (Map pp273-5; ☎ 93 318 52 61; Carrer Nou de la Rambla 34-36; ☼ Tue-Sun) If you still need a drink after 3am this is your best bet. Open since 1909, the bar started as a hangout for circus hands and has some Modernista touches and the occasional music act out back.

Raval Bar (Map pp270-2; ☎ 93 302 41 33; Carrer del Doctor Dou 19) Theatre types and local poseurs sink into lounges and huddle around teensy tables in this long, low and comfortable arty bar.

Zentraus (Map pp273-5; ☎ 93 442 13 23; Rambla del Raval 41; ☼ Tue-Sat) Mellow drum 'n' bass earlier in the week rises to a deep-house crescendo on Saturdays in this deep, dark early-evening dance-and-drink den.

AUTHOR'S CHOICE

Boadas (Map pp273-5; ☎ 93 318 88 26; Carrer dels Tallers 1; ☼ Mon-Sat) Inside the unprepossessing entrance is one of the city's oldest cocktail bars (famed for its daiquiris). The bow-tied waiters have been serving up their poison since 1933, and both Joan Miró and Hemingway tippled here.

La Ribera　　　　　　　Map pp273-5

Flow Fussina Bar (☎ 93 310 06 67; Carrer de Fusina 6) A touched-up old-time bar, with a mirror ball and a little-used pool table, this is a curious spot for a mixed drink, where you may find yourself witness to anything from experimental classical music to amateur theatre.

Gimlet (☎ 93 310 10 27; Carrer del Rec 24) White-jacketed bar staff, with all the appropriate aplomb will whip you up a gimlet, or any other classic cocktail (around €5) your heart desires.

La Fianna (☎ 93 315 18 10; Carrer dels Banys Vells 15) There is something medieval-Oriental about this bar, with its bare stone walls, forged iron candelabras and cushion-covered lounges. They do Sunday brunch (2pm to 7pm) too.

La Vinya Del Senyor (☎ 93 310 33 79; Plaça de Santa Maria del Mar 5; ☼ Tue-Sun) The wine list is as long as *War & Peace,* and the terrace lies in the shadow of Santa Maria del Mar. Or crowd inside the tiny wine bar.

Palau De Dalmases – Espai Barroc (☎ 93 310 06 73; Carrer de Montcada 20; ☼ 8pm-2am Tue-Sat, 6-10pm Sun) This centuries-old mansion has a baroque magnificence that is matched by the Peter Greenaway–style luxury inside. You almost feel you should don a powdered wig to sip on your pricey cocktails.

Port Vell & The Coast　　Map pp266-7

CDLC (☎ 93 224 04 70; Passeig Marítim 32) Seize the night by the scruff at the Carpe Diem Lounge Club, the perfect place for your first drinks lounging back in semi-Oriental surrounds. Ideal for a slow warm-up before heading to the nearby clubs. The nearest metro station is Ciutadella-Villa Olímpica.

Daguiri (☎ 93 221 51 09; Carrer de Grau i Torras 59; h 10am-midnight) Foreigners who have found seaside nirvana in Barcelona, hang out in this chilled bar back from the beach. A curious crowd of crusties and switched-on dudes chats over light meals and a beer. The nearest metro station is Barceloneta.

L'Eixample & Around　　Map pp268-9

Berlin (☎ 93 200 65 42; Carrer de Muntaner 240; ☼ Mon-Sat) This elegant corner chill-out space offers views over the Diagonal, a cluster of tables outside on the first floor, and designer lounges downstairs. Punters tend to be beautiful (or think they are) but there's a relaxed feel about the place and all ages snuggle in well.

Dry Martini (☎ 93 217 50 72; Carrer d'Aribau 162-166) Waiters will serve up the best dry martini in town, or whatever else your heart desires, in this classic cocktail lounge.

Les Gens Que J'aime (☎ 93 215 68 79; Carrer de València 286) This intimate relic of the 1960s offers chilled jazz music in the background, and a cosy scattering of velvet-backed lounges around tiny dark tables.

Michael Collins Pub (☎ 93 459 19 64; Plaça de la Sagrada Família 4) This is one of the city's best-loved (by locals and expats alike) Irish pubs. To be sure of a little Catalan-Irish craic, this barn-sized and storming pub is just the ticket.

Gràcia
Map pp268-9

Maria (Carrer de Maria 5) Even the music hasn't changed since this place got going in the late 1970s. Lovers of rock 'n' roll will enjoy sinking beers here.

Alfa (☎ 93 415 18 24; Carrer Gran de Gràcia 36; ✆ 11pm-4am Thu-Sat) Aficionados of good old-fashioned rock, with a mix of '90s hits, love this unchanging bar-cum-miniature-disco – a Gràcia classic. Take up a stool for a drink and chat, or head for the no-frills dance area just beyond.

Café del Sol (☎ 93 415 56 63; Plaça del Sol 16) This is a lively bar on one of Gràcia's liveliest squares, with a BoHo and grunge set mixing freely over an Estrella or six, inside or at the terrace tables.

Tibidabo & Around

Mirablau (Map pp266-7; ☎ 93 418 58 79; Plaça del Doctor Andreu) Make your way upstairs and gaze out over the entire city from this privileged balcony spot on the way up to Tibidabo. Then wander downstairs after 11pm to join the beautiful people in the squeeze-me small dance space. You can get there by taxi, or an FGC train to Avinguada del Tibidabo.

Montjuïc & Poble Sec

Tinta Roja (Map pp270-2; ☎ 93 443 32 43; Carrer de la Creu dels Molers 17; ✆ Wed-Sun) Sprinkled with an eclectic collection of furnishings, dimly lit in violets, reds and yellows, the 'Red Ink' is an intimate spot for a drink, and the occasional show in the back.

ENTERTAINMENT

To keep up with what's on, pick up a copy of the weekly listings magazine, *Guía del Ocio* (€1) from newsstands. The daily papers also have listings sections and the **Palau de la Virreina** (Map pp273-5; ☎ 93 301 77 75; La Rambla de Sant Josep 99; ✆ 10am-8pm Mon-Sat, 11am-3pm Sun) information office can clue you in to present and forthcoming events.

The easiest way to get hold of *entradas* (tickets) for most venues throughout the city is through the **Caixa de Catalunya's Tel-Entrada service** (☎ 902 101212; www.telentrada.com) or **ServiCaixa** (☎ 902 332211; www.servicaixa.com in Spanish). There's also a *venta de localidades* (ticket office) on the ground floor of **El Corte Inglés** (Map pp270-2; ☎ 902 400222; http://entradas .elcorteingles.es in Spanish; Plaça de Catalunya; ✆ 9am-10pm Mon-Sat) and at other branches around town (you can also buy tickets through El Corte Inglés by phone and online), and at **FNAC** (Map pp273-5; ☎ 93 344 18 00; www.fnac.es; El Triangle, Plaça de Catalunya 4; ✆ 10am-10pm Mon-Sat).

To get half-price on some tickets, you can buy them personally at the Caixa de Catalunya desk in the tourist office, **Oficina d'Informació de Turisme de Barcelona** (Map pp270-2; ☎ 807 117222, outside Spain 93 368 97 30/1; www .barcelonaturisme.com; Plaça de Catalunya 17-S – underground; ✆ 9am-9pm). To qualify you must purchase the tickets in person, no more than three hours before the start of the show you wish to see. The system is known as Tiquet-3. In *Guía del Ocio*, shows for which you can get such tickets are marked with an asterisk.

Cinemas

Foreign films, shown with subtitles and their original soundtrack, rather than dubbed, are marked *VO (versión original)* in movie listings. A ticket usually costs between €5.50 and €5.80 but most cinemas have a weekly *día del espectador* (viewer's day), often Monday or Wednesday, when they charge around €4. The cinemas listed here show *VO* films.

GAY & LESBIAN VENUES

Barcelona has a fairly busy gay scene, much of it concentrated in the 'Gaixample', between Carrer de Muntaner and Carrer de Balmes, around Carrer del Consell de Cent.

Dietrich Gay Teatro Café (Map pp270-2; ☎ 93 451 77 07; Carrer del Consell de Cent 255) It's show time at 1am, with at least one drag-queen gala a night at this cabaret-style locale dedicated to Marlene.

Sm 55 (Map pp268-9; Carrer de la Riera de Sant Miquel 55) With its cosy cabins and dark corners, this gay haunt openly prizes its sex-oriented evenings, with theme nights ranging from bondage and spanking through to pyjama sessions.

Ursus Cave (Map pp268-9; Carrer de Balmes 88; ☽ Mon-Sat) Big burly hairy men with soft centres and frequently leathery gear gather here to admire and fondle one another.

Salvation (Map pp268-9; ☎ 93 318 06 86; Ronda de Sant Pere 19-21; ☽ Fri-Sun) Beautiful boys and fluttering fag hags crowd into this club, where the sexy-boy barmen will warm the hearts of some and the occasional naughty shows will do the rest.

Metro (Map pp270-2; ☎ 93 323 52 27; Carrer de Sepúlveda 185) Metro attracts a casual gay crowd with its two dance floors, three bars and very dark room.

Arena (Map pp270-2; ☎ 93 487 83 42; Carrer de Balmes 32; admission €5-10; ☽ Tue-Sun) Popular with a young, cruisy gay crowd, Arena is one of the top clubs in town for boys seeking boys. Find 'em in the dark room, and keep an eye on Wednesday's drag shows, and handbag nights on Thursday.

Casablanca (Map pp268-9; ☎ 93 218 43 45; Passeig de Gràcia 115) A small cinema handy for central L'Eixample.

Filmoteca (Map pp268-9; ☎ 93 410 75 90; Avinguda de Sarrià 31-33; admission €2.70) Specialises in film seasons that concentrate on particular directors, styles and eras of film.

Icària Yelmo Cineplex (Map pp266-7; ☎ 93 221 75 85; www.yelmocineplex.es in Spanish; Carrer de Salvador Espriu 61) A massive complex where all the cinemas offer undubbed movies.

Méliès Cinemes (Map pp266-7; ☎ 93 451 00 51; Carrer de Villarroel 102) Old classics in the original.

Renoir Floridablanca (Map pp270-2; ☎ 93 426 33 37; www.cinesrenoir.com in Spanish, bookings www.cinentradas.com in Spanish; Carrer de Floridablanca 135) Art-house cinema on the edge of El Raval.

Renoir Les Corts (Map pp266-7; ☎ 93 490 55 10; www.cinesrenoir.com in Spanish, bookings www.cinentradas.com in Spanish; Carrer de Eugeni d'Ors 12) A more distant member of the same art-house chain.

Verdi (Map pp266-7; ☎ 93 238 79 90; Carrer de Verdi 32) One of the most popular art-house cinemas in town, in the heart of Gràcia, and surrounded by bars and eateries.

Verdi Park (Map pp268-9; ☎ 93 238 79 90; Carrer de Torrijos 49) A block away from Verdi, and run by the same people.

Classical Music & Opera

Guía del Ocio has ample listings, but the monthly *Informatiu Musical* leaflet has the best coverage of classical music (as well as

other genres). You can pick it up at tourist offices and the Palau de la Virreina.

Gran Teatre del Liceu (Map pp273-5; ☎ 93 485 99 13; www.liceubarcelona.com; La Rambla dels Caputxins 51-59; box office ☽ 2-8.30pm Mon-Fri & 1hr before show Sat & Sun) Barcelona's grand old opera house, rebuilt after fire in 1999, offers world-class opera, dance and classical-music recitals. Tickets can cost anything from €7.50, for a cheap seat behind a pillar, to €150, for a well-positioned night at the opera.

Palau de la Música Catalana (Map pp270-2; ☎ 93 295 72 00; www.palaumusica.org; Carrer de Sant Francesc de Paula 2) This Modernista delight is the traditional centre for classical and choral music. It has a busy and wide-ranging programme that includes many groups and orchestras from abroad. You could pay from €6, for a cheap seat in a middling concert, to €160 or more for prestigious international performances.

L'Auditori (Map pp266-7; ☎ 93 247 93 00; www.auditori.org; Carrer de Lepant 150; admission €10-43) Barcelona's impressive modern home for serious music lovers, L'Auditori puts on plenty of orchestral, chamber, religious and other music throughout the year.

Clubs

Barcelona clubs are spread a little more thinly than bars across the city. They tend to open from around midnight until 5am or 6am.

Karma (Map pp273-5; ☎ 93 302 56 80; Plaça Reial 10; admission €8; ☽ Tue-Sun) Since the 1980s this basement place has heaved to the sounds of rock, punk and more contemporary hits that lend themselves to joyous leaping about.

La Paloma (Map pp270-2; ☎ 93 301 68 97; Carrer del Tigre 27; admission €8; ✆ Thu-Sat) Draped in voluptuous red, this former theatre and still functioning ballroom metamorphoses into a club later in the night. The Bongo Lounge DJ team reigns on Thursday, and on Friday and Saturday the ballroom theme continues until 3am, so don't come before.

Moog (Map pp273-5; ☎ 93 301 72 82; Carrer de l'Arc del Teatre 3; admission €8) This fun, minuscule club has become a standing favourite with downtown folk. In the main downstairs dance area DJs dish out house, techno and electro, while upstairs you can groove to Latin and pop.

Razzmatazz (Map pp266-7; ☎ 93 320 82 00; Carrer dels Almogàvars 122 & Carrer de Pamplona 88; ✆ Fri & Sat) A half-dozen blocks back from Port Olímpic is this stalwart of Barcelona's club and concert scene. The Loft does house and electronic dance music, while the Pop Bar can be about anything from garage to soul.

Luz De Gas (Map pp268-9; ☎ 93 209 77 11; Carrer de Muntaner 246; admission up to €15) Set in a grand theatre that is frequently the scene of live acts, this club attracts a crowd of well-dressed beautiful people, whose tastes in music vary according to the night: rock on Friday, '60s on Saturday, soul on Thursday.

Sala Cibeles (Map pp268-9; ☎ 93 457 38 77; Carrer de Còrsega 363) Old-time ballroom dancing has gone the way of the dodo at this now-classic nocturnal bop stop. Mond Club is the Friday fixture at this wonderfully time-stuck dance hall.

Sutton Club (Map pp268-9; ☎ 93 414 42 17; Carrer de Tuset 13; admission €12; ✆ Tue-Sat) A classic disco with mainstream sounds, this place inevitably attracts just about everyone pouring in and out of the nearby bars, at some stage in the evening.

Otto Zutz (Map pp268-9; ☎ 93 238 07 22; Carrer de Lincoln 15; admission €15; ✆ Tue-Sat) Beautiful people only need apply for entry into this three-floor dance den. Shake it all up to house downstairs or head upstairs for funk and soul.

Discothèque (Map pp266-7; ☎ 93 423 12 85; Avinguda del Marquès de Comillas; admission €18; ✆ Fri & Sat) Dress to kill (no jackets and ties, and the sexier the better) for this classy club in the heart of the Poble Espanyol. Don't arrive too late or you'll queue for ages. In summer its twin, Terrrazza, takes over.

TOP FIVE CLUBS
▪ **Razzmatazz** (left)
▪ **Discothèque/Terrrazza** (below)
▪ **Sala Cibeles** (below)
▪ **La Paloma** (left)
▪ **Otto Zutz** (below)

Sala Apolo (Map pp270-2; ☎ 93 301 00 90; Carrer Nou de la Rambla 113; admission €6-9; ✆ 12.30am-5am Wed-Sat, 10.30pm-3.30am Sun) In this old theatre the Nitsaclub team provides house, techno and break-beat sounds on weekends. During the week musical themes change regularly and live performances are frequent.

Dance

SARDANA

The best chance you have of seeing people dancing the *sardana* (the Catalan folk dance) is at noon on Sunday in front of the Catedral. Other possibilities are at 6.30pm on Saturday and 7pm on Wednesday. You can also see them during some of the city's festivals. The dancers join hands to form ever-widening circles, placing their bags or coats in the centre. The dance is intricate but hardly flamboyant. The steps and the accompanying brass-and-reed music are at times jolly, at times melancholy, rising to occasional crescendos, then quietening down again.

FLAMENCO

Although quite a few important flamenco artists grew up in the *barris* of Barcelona, opportunities for seeing good performances of this essentially Andalucian dance and music are limited. A few *tablaos* (tourist-oriented locales that stage flamenco performances) are scattered about. If this is the only way you can see it, perhaps it's better than nothing. For more on flamenco see The Culture chapter on p62.

Sala Tarantos (Map pp273-5; ☎ 93 318 30 67; regular flamenco show 616 803497; Plaça Reial 17; admission depends on performance €5-20; ✆ 10pm-5am Mon-Sat) This basement locale is the stage for some of the best of flamenco to pass through Barcelona. You have to keep an eye out for quality acts. Otherwise, a cheesier flamenco show is put on most nights around 10.15pm. The place converts into a club later.

Soniquete (Map pp273-5; Carrer de Milans 5; ⊙ 9pm-3am Thu-Sun) Pop along for the impromptu flamenco sessions in this tile-lined, friendly bar. The music is not always live.

Tablao Cordobés (Map pp273-5; ☎ 93 317 66 53; La Rambla 35; show €28.50, dinner & show €50.50; ⊙ show 10pm) This long-standing *tablao* is typical of the genre. Generally people book for the dinner and show, although you can skip the food and just come along for the performance.

Tablao de Carmen (Map pp266-7; ☎ 93 325 68 95; Carrer dels Arcs 9, Poble Espanyol; show €29, dinner & show €55; ⊙ shows 9.30pm & 11.30pm Tue-Sun) Named after the great Barcelona *bailaora* (flamenco dancer) Carmen Amaya, the set-up here is similar to that at the Tablao Cordobés.

Live Music

There's a good choice most nights of the week. Many venues double as bars and/or clubs. Starting time is rarely before 10pm. Admission charges range from nothing to €20 – the higher prices often include a drink. Note that some of the clubs mentioned including Razzmatazz (p313), Sala Apolo (p313), Sala Cibeles (p313) and La Paloma (p313), occasionally stage concerts too. Keep an eye on listings.

To see big-name acts, either Spanish or from abroad, you will probably pay more. They often perform at venues such as the 17,000-capacity Palau Sant Jordi (Map pp266-7) on Montjuïc or the Teatre Mercat de les Flors (Map pp266-7), at the foot of Montjuïc.

Bikini (Map pp266-7; ☎ 93 322 08 00; Carrer de Déu i Mata 105; admission €10-20; ⊙ midnight-5am Tue-Sat) This multi-hall dance space frequently stages quality acts ranging from funk guitar to rock, mostly on Friday and Saturday nights. Performances generally start around 10pm and the club swings into gear around midnight.

Harlem Jazz Club (Map pp273-5; ☎ 93 310 07 55; Carrer de la Comtessa de Sobradiel 8; admission up to €10; ⊙ 8pm-4am Tue-Thu & Sun, 8pm-5am Fri & Sat) This narrow, smoky old-town dive is one of the best spots in town for jazz. Every now and then they mix it up with a little rock, Latin or blues.

Jamboree (Map pp273-5; ☎ 93 319 17 89; Plaça Reial 17; admission up to €10; ⊙ 10.30pm-5am) Concerts start at 11pm and proceed until about 2am at the latest, at which point punters convert

themselves into clubbers. Some of the great names of jazz and blues have filled the air with their sonorous contributions.

La Boîte (Map pp268-9; ☎ 93 319 17 89; Avinguda Diagonal 477; admission €3-15; ⊙ 11pm-5.30am Tue-Sat) This is one of the classic live-music haunts of Barcelona and offers jazz, R&B, blues and swing, with the occasional jam session several nights a week at midnight. Later on the place morphs into a club.

La Cova del Drac (Map pp266-7; ☎ 93 200 70 32; Carrer de Vallmajor 33; admission €8-10; ⊙ 9pm-3am) Also known as Jazzroom, this is a good, if awkwardly located, spot for jazz sessions most nights of the week. On weekends it can stay open as late as 5am.

Sport
BULLFIGHTING

Barcelona city council has declared itself against bullfighting but some citizens continue to be strongly attached to this controversial activity. Fights are staged on Sunday afternoon in spring and summer at the **Plaça de Braus Monumental** (Map pp266-7; ☎ 93 245 58 02; cnr Gran Via de les Corts Catalanes & Carrer de la Marina; admission €15-75; tickets ⊙ 10.30am-2pm & 6-7pm Wed-Sat, 10am-6pm Sun). The 'fun' starts at around 6pm. Tickets are available at the arena or through ServiCaixa.

FOOTBALL

FC Barcelona (Barça for aficionados) has one of the best stadiums in Europe – the 100,000-capacity **Camp Nou** (Map pp266-7; ☎ 902 189900; tickets ⊙ 9am-1.30pm & 3.30-6pm Mon-Fri) in the west of the city. Tickets for national-league games are available at the stadium and through the ServiCaixa ticketing service. They cost around €30 to €90, depending on the seat and match.

FORMULA ONE

Schumacher and Co come to Barcelona every April to rip around the track at Montmeló, about a 30-minute drive north of the city. A seat for the Grand Prix race at the **Circuit de Catalunya** (☎ 93 571 97 71; www.circuitcat.com) can cost anything from €240 to €375, depending largely on how far in advance you book. Purchase by phone, at the track, or online with ServiCaixa. You can get a regular *rodalies* train to Montmeló (€1.20, 30 minutes) but will need to walk about 3km, or find a local taxi (about €8 to 10) to reach the track.

Theatre

Theatre is almost always performed in Catalan or Spanish (*Guía del Ocio* specifies which). For more information on all that's happening in theatre, head for the information office at Palau de la Virreina (p278), where you'll find leaflets and *Teatre BCN*, the monthly listings guide.

Artenbrut (Map pp268-9; ☎ 93 457 97 05; Carrer del Perill 9-11) One of seven 'alternative' theatres around the city, this spot concentrates on new and rising directors. Performances are usually in Catalan and range from experimental drama to dance.

Teatre Lliure (Map pp266-7; ☎ 93 289 27 70; www.teatrelliure.com; Plaça de Margarida Xirgu s/n, Montjuïc; box office ☺ 5-8pm) Consisting of two separate theatre spaces, the 'Free Theatre' puts on a variety of serious, quality drama, pretty much exclusively in Catalan.

Teatre Mercat de les Flors (Map pp266-7; ☎ 93 426 18 75; Carrer de Lleida 59) At the foot of Montjuïc, this is an important venue for music, dance and drama.

Teatre Nacional de Catalunya (Map pp266-7; ☎ 93 306 57 00; www.tnc.es in Spanish; Plaça de les Arts 1) Ricard Bofill's ultra neoclassical theatre hosts a wide range of performances, principally drama (frequently worthies of the ilk of Ibsen or Catalonia's own Àngel Guimerà) but occasionally also dance and other performances.

Teatre Romea (Map pp273-5; ☎ 93 301 55 04; www.focus.es in Spanish; Carrer de l'Hospital 51; box office ☺ 4.30-8pm Tue-Sun) This theatre is a reference point for quality drama in Barcelona. It puts on a range of interesting plays – usually classics with a contemporary flavour.

SHOPPING

Barcelona is unquestionably a centre of style in Europe, and this is reflected in its unending ranks of fashion and design stores. Maxing out credit cards is a definite risk in this town! Alongside the latest modes, all sorts of curious traditional shops offer everything from coffee and nuts to candles, from sweets made in convents across the country to amusing condoms.

Most of the mainstream fashion and design stores can be found on a shopping 'axis' that looks like the hands of a clock set at a quarter to five. From Plaça de Catalunya it heads along Passeig de Gràcia, turning left into Avinguda Diagonal. From here as far as Plaça de la Reina Maria Cristina (especially the final stretch from Plaça de Francesc Macià) the Diagonal is jammed with places where you can empty your bank account. The T1 Tombbús service (see p319) has been laid on for the ardent shopper.

Fashion does not end in the chic streets of L'Eixample and Avinguda Diagonal. Since the mid-1990s, the El Born area in La Ribera has been humming and, in the wake of bars and restaurants, have come hip little boutiques, especially those purveying young, fun fashion. Custo Barcelona has a branch down here for instance. Another bubbling fashion strip is Barri Gòtic's Carrer d'Avinyó. For second-hand stuff, head for El Raval, especially Carrer de la Riera Baixa.

A growing squadron of antiques stores is scattered about Carrer dels Banys Nous in the Barri Gòtic, in whose labyrinthine lanes you can find all sorts of curious stores. For food, from cheese to nuts, some gems are scattered around El Born.

The single best-known department store is **El Corte Inglés** (Map pp270-2; ☎ 93 306 38 00; Plaça de Catalunya 14; ☺ 9am-10pm Mon-Sat), with several branches around town, including

---

POKING ABOUT THE MARKETS

Large **Els Encants Vells** ('The Old Charms'; Map pp266-7; ☺ 8am-7pm Mon, Wed, Fri & Sat), also known as the Fira de Bellcaire, is the city's principal flea market. There is an awful lot of junk here, but you can turn up interesting items, if you are prepared to hunt around.

The Barri Gòtic is livened up by an **arts and crafts market** (Plaça de Sant Josep Oriol; ☺ 9am-8pm) on Saturday and Sunday, the antiques **Mercat Gòtic** (Plaça Nova; ☺ 9am-10pm) on Thursday, and a **coin- and stamp-collectors' market** (Plaça Reial; ☺ 9am-2pm) on Sunday morning (what a contrast to the previous night's revelry). Just beyond the western edge of El Raval, the punters at the **Mercat de Sant Antoni** (☺ 7am-8.30pm) dedicate Sunday morning to old maps, stamps, books and cards.

Once every fortnight, gourmands can poke about the homemade honey, sweets, cheese and other edible delights at the **Fira Alimentació** (Plaça del Pi) from Friday to Sunday.

---

one at **Plaça de la Reina Maria Cristina** (Map pp266-7; Avinguda Diagonal 617).

Winter sales officially start on or around 10 January and their summer equivalents on or around 5 July.

Art Galleries

Want some contemporary art? You'll also find more small galleries and designer stores on Carrer del Doctor Dou, Carrer d'Elisabets and Carrer dels Àngels (Map pp273–5). The classiest concentration of galleries is on the short stretch of Carrer del Consell de Cent between Rambla de Catalunya and Carrer de Balmes (Map pp270–2). Several others lurk in the nearby streets.

Homewares

Vinçon (Map pp268-9; ☎ 93 215 60 50; Passeig de Gràcia 96; ⏰ 10am-8.30pm Mon-Sat) Vinçon has the slickest designs in furniture and household goods (particularly lighting), local and imported. The building once belonged to the Modernista artist Ramon Casas.

Fashion

Big international names in fashion, especially Italian and French *grifes*, jostle for position along Avinguda Diagonal, between Plaça de Joan Carlos I and Plaça de la Reina Maria Cristina. Passeig de Gràcia is also heavily laden with high fashion stores. Check out what's going on in El Born too.

Custo Barcelona (Map pp273-5; ☎ 93 268 78 93; Plaça de les Olles 7) Custo bewitches young folk the world over with a youthful, psychedelic panoply of women's and men's fashion.

Antonio Miró (Map pp268-9; ☎ 93 487 06 70; Carrer del Consell de Cent 349) Mr Miró is one of Barcelona's *haute couture* kings. He concentrates on light, natural fibres to produce smart, unpretentious men's and women's fashion.

Mango (Map pp268-9; ☎ 93 215 75 30; Passeig de Gràcia 21; ⏰ 10am-8pm Mon-Sat) At home in the basement of a modest Modernista townhouse (and in endless other locations around town), this busy hall of a store shines bright with the local fashion-chain's flagship items – a host of light, fun women's clothing and leather accessories.

Zara (Map pp268-9; ☎ 93 301 74 43; Passeig de Gràcia 16) Started in Galicia, Zara has become one of the great success stories of modern *prêt-à-porter*. Women's fashion is the name of the game and this megastore on Barcelona's

top shopping street is just the most obvious of its outlets around town.

Food & Drink

Casa Gispert (Map pp273-5; ☎ 93 319 75 35; Carrer dels Sombrerers 23) Prize-winning Casa Gispert, has been toasting almonds and selling all manner of dried fruit since 1851. Pots and jars piled high on the shelves contain an unending variety of crunchy titbits.

Tot Formatge (Map pp273-5; ☎ 93 319 53 75; Passeig del Born 13) Little platters are scattered about with samples of some of the tempting array of local and European cheeses on sale here.

J Murrià (Map pp268-9; ☎ 93 215 57 89; Carrer de Roger de Llúria 85) Ramon Casas designed the Modernista shop-front ads for this delicious delicatessen, where the shelves groan under the weight of speciality food from around Catalonia and beyond.

Shoes

Camper (Map pp268-9; ☎ 93 215 63 90; Carrer de València 249) This Mallorcan success story is something of a Clark's of Spain. Their shoes range from the eminently sensible to the stylishly fashionable.

Farrutx (Map pp268-9; ☎ 93 215 06 85; Carrer del Rosselló 218; ⏰ 10am-8.30pm) Farrutx specialises in exclusive footwear for uptown gals.

GETTING THERE & AWAY
Air

Aeroport del Prat (☎ 93 298 38 38) is 12km southwest of the centre at El Prat de Llobregat. Barcelona is a big international and domestic destination, with direct flights from North America as well as many European cities.

Several budget airlines, including Ryanair, use **Girona airport** (☎ 972 18 66 00), 11km south of Girona and about 80km north of Barcelona. Buses connect Barcelona with the airport (see p318).

For information on flights and airfares, see the Transport chapter (p849). See Travel Agencies on p279 for some suggestions on where to pick up air tickets.

Boat
BALEARIC ISLANDS

Regular passenger and vehicular ferries to/from the Balearic Islands, operated by **Trasmediterránea** (☎ 902 454645; www.trasmediterranea.es), dock along both sides of the

Moll de Barcelona wharf in Port Vell (Map pp266–7).

For information on schedules and fares, see p617 in the Balearic Islands chapter.

ITALY

The Grimaldi group's **Grandi Navi Veloci** (in Italy ☎ 010 209 45 91, 902 410200; in Spain ☎ 93 295 70 00; www1.gnv.it) runs a high-speed, roll-on roll-off luxury ferry service from Genoa to Barcelona three times a week. The journey takes 18 hours and costs anything from €62 for an economy class airline-style seat in low season to €184 for a single cabin suite. The boat docks at Moll de San Beltran (Map pp266–7).

Bus

Long distance buses for destinations within Spain leave from the **Estació del Nord** (Map pp266-7; ☎ 902 260606; www.barcelonanord.com; Carrer d'Ali Bei 80). A plethora of companies operates to different parts of the country, although many come under the umbrella of **Alsa-Enatcar** (☎ 902 422242; www.alsa.es). There are frequent services to Madrid, Valencia and Zaragoza (up to 20 a day) and several daily departures to such distant destinations as Burgos, Santiago de Compostela and Seville.

Eurolines (☎ 902 405040, ☎ 93 490 40 00; www.eurolines.es in Spanish), in conjunction with local carriers all over Europe, is the main international carrier. It runs across Europe and to Morocco from the **Estació d'Autobusos de Sants** (Map pp266–7), although many call in at Estació del Nord too.

Within Catalonia, much of the Pyrenees and the entire Costa Brava are served only by buses, as train services are limited to important railheads such as Girona, Figueres, Lleida, Ripoll and Puigcerdà. If there is a train, take it – they're usually more comfortable and convenient. Various bus companies

operate across the region, mostly from Estació del Nord:

Alsina Graells (☎ 93 265 65 92) Runs buses from Barcelona to destinations west and northwest, such as Vielha, La Seu d'Urgell and Lleida.

Barcelona Bus (☎ 902 130014; www.barcelonabus .com in Spanish) Runs buses from the capital to Girona (and airport), Figueres and parts of the Costa Brava.

Hispano-Igualadina (☎ 93 804 44 51) Serves much of central Catalonia.

Sarfa (☎ 902 287000; www.sarfa.com) The main operator on and around the Costa Brava.

Teisa (☎ 972 20 48 68; www.teisa-bus.com in Spanish; Carrer de Pau Claris 117 in Barcelona) Covers a large part of the eastern Catalan Pyrenees from Girona and Figueres.

Departures from Estació del Nord include the following, with journey time and fare (where frequencies vary, the lowest figure is usually for Sunday; fares quoted are the lowest available):

Car & Motorcycle

Autopistas (tollways) head out of Barcelona in most directions, including the C31/C32 to the southern Costa Brava; the C32 to Sitges; the C16 to Manresa (with a turn-off for Montserrat); and the AP7 north to Girona, Figueres and France, and south to Tarragona and Valencia (turn off along the AP2 for Lleida, Zaragoza and Madrid). The toll-free alternatives, such as the A2 north to Girona, Figueres and France, and west to Lleida and beyond, or the A7 to Tarragona, tend to be busy and slow.

RENTAL

Avis, Europcar, Hertz and several other big companies have desks at the airport, Estació Sants train station and Estació del Nord bus terminus:

Avis (Map pp268-9; ☎ 902 135531 or ☎ 93 237 56 80; Carrer de Còrsega 293-295)

Destination	Frequency (per day)	Duration	Cost
Almería	4	11¼–13¼ hr	€52.85
Burgos	3-4	7¾-9 hr	€29.40
Granada	6	12-14¾ hr	€58.15
Madrid	up to 20	7½ hr	€23.55
Seville	1-2	14¼-16½ hr	€76.90
Valencia	up to 16	4-5¾ hr	€21.45
Zaragoza	up to 18	3½ hr	€11.50

Europcar (Map pp268-9; ☎ 902 105030; Gran Via de les Corts Catalanes 680)

Hertz (Map pp268-9; ☎ 902 402405; Carrer d'Aragó 382-384)

National/Atesa (Map pp270-2; ☎ 902 100101 or ☎ 93 323 07 01; Carrer de Muntaner 45)

Pepecar La Rambla (Map pp273-5; ☎ 807 212121; www .pepecar.com; Plaça de Catalunya); Estació Sants Barcelona (Carrer de Béjar 68) This company specialises in cheap rentals of Mercedes Class A cars and Smarts. If you book far enough ahead, it can cost around €12 a day (with a free 100km), plus a credit-card handling fee and a €12 cleaning charge. There's also an outlet at Aeroport del Prat.

Vanguard (Map pp268-9; ☎ 93 439 38 80; Carrer de Viladomat 297)

Train

The main international and domestic station is **Estació Sants** (Map pp266-7; Plaça dels Països Catalans), 2.5km west of La Rambla.

Estació Catalunya (Map pp270-2; Plaça de Catalunya) and **Estació Passeig de Gràcia** (Map pp268-9; cnr Passeig de Gràcia & Carrer d'Aragó), 10 minutes' walk north of Plaça de Catalunya, both have long-distance and regional train services.

INFORMATION

There's a **Renfe information and booking office** (☒ 7am-10pm Mon-Sat, 7am-9pm Sun) in Estació Passeig de Gràcia station. You'll find left-luggage lockers on Via (Platform) 2.

At Estació Sants, the **Informació** (☒ 6.30am-11pm) windows are behind the stairs down to platforms six and seven and give information on all except suburban trains. The station has a **consigna** (left-luggage lockers; small/big locker per 24hr €3/4.50; ☒ 5.30am-11pm), a tourist office, a telephone and fax office, currency-exchange booths (8am to 10pm), and ATMs.

INTERNATIONAL

For details on getting to Barcelona by rail from London, Paris and other cities, see the Transport chapter (p853).

Two daily direct Talgo services connect Montpellier in France with Barcelona (€44 each way in *turista* class, 4¼ hours). A couple of other slower services (with a change of train at Portbou) also make this run. All stop in Perpignan.

From Estació Sants, up to 10 trains daily run to Cerbère (€22, 2½ hours), on the French side of the border, and four to Latour-de-Carol (€7.30, 3½ hours). From these stations you have several onwards

connections to Montpellier and Toulouse, respectively.

DOMESTIC

There are trains to most large Spanish cities, with the usual huge range of train types and fares. All services depart from or pass through Estació Sants.

GETTING AROUND

The metro is the easiest way of getting around and reaches most places you're likely to visit (although not the airport). For some trips you need buses or FGC suburban trains. The **Oficina d'Informació de Turisme de Barcelona** (Map pp270-2; ☎ 807 117222, outside Spain 93 368 97 30/1; www .barcelonaturisme.com; Plaça de Catalunya 17-S – underground; ☒ 9am-9pm) gives out the comprehensive *Guia d'Autobusos Urbans de Barcelona*, which has a metro map and all bus routes.

For public-transport information call ☎ 010.

To/From the Airport

The **A1 Aerobús** (☎ 93 415 60 20; one way €3.45; 30-40 min depending on traffic) service runs from the airport to Plaça de Catalunya via Plaça d'Espanya (Map pp270-2), Gran Via de les Corts Catalanes (Map pp270-2; on corner of Carrer del Comte d'Urgell) and Plaça de l'Universitat (Map pp270-2) every 12 minutes from 6am to midnight Monday to Friday (from 6.30am on weekends and holidays). Departures from Plaça de Catalunya are between 5.30am and 11.30pm Monday to Friday (6am) and go via Estació Sants Barcelona (Map pp266-7) and Plaça de Espanya (Map pp268-9). Buy tickets on the bus. Local bus 105 runs between the airport and Plaça d'Espanya (€1.10) but runs only every half-hour or so. Its night version, the No 106, is even less frequent and serves late incoming flights.

A new metro line (No 9) is being laid between the airport and the future high-speed train (AVE) station in the suburb of Sagrera. In the meantime, you can take Renfe's *rodalies* train. Trains stop at several stations with metro connections, including Estació Sants, Catalunya, Passeig de Gràcia, Arc de Triomf and Clot. A one-way ticket costs €2.25 (unless you have a multi-ride ticket for Barcelona public transport – see p320). Trains run every 30 minutes from 6.13am to 11.15pm daily. It takes 17 minutes to get to

Sants, and 23 minutes to Catalunya. Departures from Sants to the airport are between 5.43am and 10.16pm; from Catalunya they're six minutes earlier.

A taxi to/from the centre, about a half-hour ride depending on traffic, costs between €18 and €20.

Direct **Barcelona Bus** (Map pp268-9; ☎ 902 130014; Passeig de Sant Joan 52) services in Barcelona connect with Girona's airport (70 minutes, one way/return €9/16).

Bicycle

Bike lanes have been laid out along quite a few main roads (such as Gran Via de les Corts Catalanes, Avinguda Diagonal, Carrer d'Aragó, Avinguda de la Meridiana and Carrer de la Marina) and a growing web of secondary streets, so it is quite possible to get around on two ecological wheels.
Biciclot (Map pp266-7; ☎ 93 221 97 78; www.biciclot .net; Passeig Marítim; per hour/day €5/19; ☺ 9am-3pm & 4-7pm Mon-Fri, 9am-3pm & 4-8pm Sat-Sun) A handy seaside location.
Un Cotxe Menys (Map pp273-5; ☎ 93 268 21 05; www.bicicletabarcelona.com; Carrer de la Espartería 3; per hour/half-day/full day/week €5/10/15/48; ☺ 10am-2pm Mon-Fri) Can also organise bike tours around the old city and port on weekends.

Bus

The city transport authority, **TMB** (☎ 010; www .tmb.net), runs buses along most city routes every few minutes from 5am or 6am to 10pm or 11pm. Many routes pass through Plaça de Catalunya and/or Plaça de la Universitat (both on Map pp270-2). After 11pm, a reduced network of yellow *nitbusos* (night buses) runs until 3am or 5am. All *nitbus* routes pass through Plaça de Catalunya and most run about every 30 to 45 minutes.

BUS TURÍSTIC

This TMB-run service covers two circuits (32 stops) linking virtually all the major tourist sights. Tourist offices, TMB offices and many hotels have leaflets explaining the system. Tickets, available on the bus, cost adult/child €16/10 for one day of unlimited rides, or €20/13 for two consecutive days. Buses run from 9am to 7.45pm and the frequency varies from 10 to 30 minutes, depending on the season. It does not operate on Christmas Day or New Year's Day. Each of the full circuits lasts about two hours.

TOMBBÚS

TMB's T1 Tombbús route (€1.25) is designed for shoppers and runs regularly from Plaça de Catalunya up to Avinguda Diagonal, along which it proceeds west to Plaça de Pius XII (Map pp270–2), at which point it turns around. On the way you pass such landmarks as El Corte Inglés (several of them), the Bulevard Rosa arcade (Map pp268–9), off Passeig de Gràcia, and **l'Illa del Diagonal shopping centre** (Map pp266-7; Avinguda Diagonal) with an **FNAC CD-and-book store** (Map pp266-7; Avinguda Diagonal).

Car & Motorcycle

An effective one-way system makes traffic flow fairly smoothly, but you'll often find yourself flowing the way you don't want to go, unless you happen to have an adept navigator and a map that shows one-way streets. Parking is tricky so once you've found a spot leave the car alone and use public transport.

Metro & FGC

The **Transports Metropolitans de Barcelona (TMB) metro** (☎ 010; www.tmb.net) has six lines, which are numbered and colour coded, and is easy to use (see the map on pp300–1). The metro runs from 5am to midnight Sunday to Thursday, and 5am to 2am on Friday, Saturday and days immediately preceding holidays. Line 2 has access for the disabled and a handful of stations on other lines also have lifts (it is hoped all metro stations will have disabled access by 2007).

Suburban trains run by the **Ferrocarrils de la Generalitat de Catalunya** (FGC; ☎ 93 205 15 15; www.fgc.net) include a couple of useful city lines. One heads north from Plaça de Catalunya. A branch of it will get you to Tibidabo, and another within spitting distance of the Monestir de Pedralbes. Some trains along this line continue beyond Barcelona to Sant Cugat, Sabadell and Terrassa.

The other FGC line heads to Manresa from Plaça d'Espanya, and is handy for the trip to Montserrat (p323).

These trains run from about 5am (only one or two services before 6am) to 11pm or midnight (depending on the line) Sunday to Thursday, and 5am to 2am on Friday and Saturday.

A new system of tramways is also being introduced. At the moment they run into the suburbs of greater Barcelona from Plaça

BARCELONA

de Francesc Macià, and are of limited interest to visitors.

Taxi

Taxis charge €1.20 flagfall (€1.35 from 10pm to 6am weekdays and all day Saturday, Sunday and holidays) plus meter charges of €0.71 per kilometre (€0.91). A further €2.10 is added for all trips to/from the airport, and €0.85 for luggage bigger than 55cm x 35cm x 35cm. The trip from Estació Sants to Plaça de Catalunya (about 3km) costs roughly €5. You can call a **taxi** (☎ 93 225 00 00, 93 300 11 00, 93 303 30 33, 93 322 22 22) or flag one down in the streets. General information is available on ☎ 010. The call-out charge is €2.80 (€3.50 at night and weekends). There are several ranks around town, including a handy one on Plaça del Portal de la Pau, at the bottom end of La Rambla.

Fono Taxi (☎ 93 300 11 00) is one of several taxi companies with wheelchair-adapted taxis.

Tickets & Targetas

Single-ride tickets on all standard transport within Zone 1 (which extends beyond the airport), except on Renfe trains, cost €1.10.

Targetas are multiple-trip transport tickets and offer worthwhile savings. They are sold at most city-centre metro stations. The T-10 (€6) gives you 10 rides on the metro, buses, FGC and *rodalies* (Renfe-run local trains). Each ride is valid for 1¼ hours and permits you to make changes between the metro, FGC trains, *rodalies* and buses. On each change you validate the ticket again – if you are within the allotted time, only the one trip will be deducted from your ticket (except for the metro, in which you can only make one continuous trip, with interchanges). The T-DIA (€4.60) gives unlimited travel on all transport for one day.

Two-/three-/four-/five-day tickets for unlimited travel on all transport, except *rodalies*, cost €8.40/11.80/15.20/18.20. These tickets, which can be good value if you move around a lot, can be bought at metro stations, tourist offices and on the Aerobús to the airport.

Trixis

These **three-wheel cycle taxis** (☎ 93 310 13 79; www.trixi.info) operate on the waterfront. They can take two people and cost €1.50 per person per kilometre. Or you can hire them for

a while (€10/18 per half-hour/hour). Children aged three to 12 pay half-price. There's also a set waterfront route from their base, near the Monument a Colom, to the Fòrum 2004 site.

Train

Renfe runs local trains (*rodalies* or *cercanías*) to towns around Barcelona, as well as the airport.

AROUND BARCELONA

Only a short way out of town are several great excursion destinations. On the coast to the southwest, Sitges is a pretty seaside town with thumping nightlife. From the hedonistic to the heavenly, you could head north for Catalonia's sacred mountains, Montserrat, or west to explore the Penedès wine-making region. Closer to home, admire the genius of Gaudí at Colònia Güell.

THE OUTSKIRTS
Colònia Güell

Apart from La Sagrada Família, the last grand project Gaudí turned his hand to was the creation of a Utopian textile-workers' complex, which was known as the **Colònia Güell** (Map below; ☎ 93 630 58 07; Santa Coloma de Cervelló; admission to crypt €4, guided visit to crypt €5, guided visit to crypt & Colònia Güell €8; ☀ 10am-2pm & 3-7pm Mon-Sat, 10am-3pm Sun Apr-Oct; 10am-3pm daily Nov-Mar) outside Barcelona at Santa Coloma de Cervelló.

His main role was to erect the colony's church – workers' housing and the local co-operative were in the hands of other architects. He first thought about it in 1898, but work on the church's crypt started in 1908. It proceeded for eight years, at which point interest in the whole idea fizzled. The crypt today still serves as a working church.

This structure is an important part of Gaudí's oeuvre. The mostly brick-clad columns that support the ribbed vaults in the ceiling are inclined in much the way you might expect trees in a forest to lean at all angles (reminiscent also of Parc Güell, which Gaudí was working on at much the same time). Gaudí had worked out the angles in such a way that their load would be transmitted from the ceiling to the earth, without the help of extra buttressing. Down to the wavy design of the pews, Gaudí's hand is visible.

The Modernista industrial complex, with 23 factory buildings that have stood idle since 1970, is being restored in a project that should be completed in 2005.

To get here, take FGC train No S4, S7 or S8 from Plaça d'Espanya.

SITGES
pop 20,890

Sitges attracts everyone from jet-setters to young travellers, honeymooners to week-ending families, and from Barcelona's night owls to an international gay crowd. The beach is long and sandy, the nightlife thumps until breakfast and there are lots of groovy boutiques, if you need to spruce up your wardrobe. In winter Sitges can be dead, but it wakes up with a vengeance for Carnaval, when the gay crowd puts on an outrageous show.

Information

The main **tourist office** (☎ 93 894 42 51; www .sitges.org; Carrer de Sínia Morera 1; ⏰ 9am-9pm Jul-Sep, 9am-2pm & 4pm-6.30pm Mon-Fri Oct-Jun) can help with information. There is a **branch** (Carrer Fonollar s/n; ⏰ 10am-1.30pm & 5-9pm Jul–mid-Sep; 10.30am-1.45pm Wed-Fri, 11am-2pm & 4-7pm Sat, 11am-2pm Sun mid-Sep–Jun) next door to Palau Maricel.

The **Policía Local** (☎ 93 811 76 25; Plaça d'Ajuntament) is behind the parish church and the **Hospital Sant Joan** (☎ 93 894 00 03; Carrer del Hospital) is in the upper part of town.

Sights & Activities
MUSEUMS

Three **museums** (☎ 93 894 03 64; Carrer de Fonollar; adult/child €3/1.50, combined ticket to all museums €5.40/3; ⏰ 10am-1.30pm & 3pm-6.30pm Tue-Fri, 10am-7pm Sat, 10am-3pm Sun Oct-Jun; 10am-2pm & 5-9pm Tue-Sun Jul-Sep) serve as a timid counterweight to the general hedonism.

The **Museu Cau Ferrat** (Carrer de Fonollar) was built in the 1890s as a house-cum-studio by Santiago Rusiñol, a co-founder of Els Quatre Gats in Barcelona, and the man who attracted the art world to Sitges. In 1894 Rusiñol reawakened the public to the then unfashionable work of El Greco, by parading two of the Cretan's canvases in from Sitges train station to Cau Ferrat. These are on show, along with the remainder of Rusiñol's large art-and-craft collection, which includes paintings by the likes of Picasso, Ramon Casas (another of the 'four cats') and Rusiñol himself.

Next door, the **Museu Maricel del Mar** houses art and handcrafts from the Middle Ages to the 20th century. The museum is part of the Palau Maricel, a stylistic fantasy built around 1910 by Miquel Utrillo (yet another 'cat').

The **Museu Romàntic** (Carrer de Sant Gaudenci 1) recreates the lifestyle of a 19th-century Catalan landowning family, and contains a collection of several hundred antique dolls.

BEACHES

The main beach is divided by a series of breakwaters into sections with different names. A pedestrian promenade runs its whole length. In high summer, especially on the weekend, the end nearest the Esgésia de Sant Bartomeu i Santa Tecla gets jam-packed. Crowds thin out slightly towards the southwest end.

Festivals & Events

Carnaval in Sitges is a week-long riot just made for the extrovert, ambiguous and exhibitionist, capped by an extravagant gay parade that's held on the last night. June sees the **Sitges International Theatre Festival** (www.teatresitges.com), with a strong experimental leaning. Sitges' **festa major** (major festival) in late August features a huge firework show on the 23rd. And early October is the time for Sitges' **International Fantasy Film Festival** (www.cinemasitges.com).

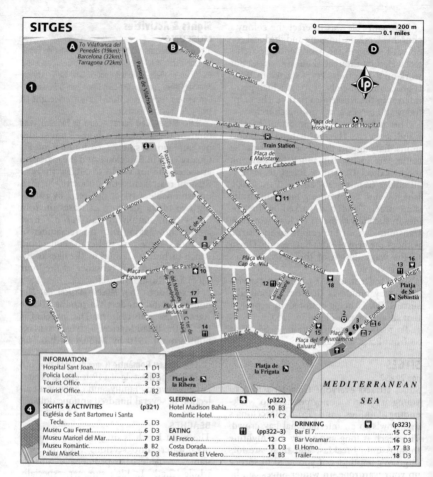

SITGES

INFORMATION
Hospital Sant Joan	1 D1
Policía Local	2 D3
Tourist Office	3 D3
Tourist Office	4 B2

SIGHTS & ACTIVITIES (p321)
Església de Sant Bartomeu i Santa Tecla	5 D3
Museu Cau Ferrat	6 D3
Museu Maricel del Mar	7 D3
Museu Romàntic	8 B2
Palau Maricel	9 D3

SLEEPING (p322)
Hotel Madison Bahía	10 B3
Romàntic Hotel	11 C2

EATING (pp322–3)
Al Fresco	12 C3
Costa Dorada	13 D3
Restaurant El Velero	14 B3

DRINKING (p323)
Bar El 7	15 C3
Bar Voramar	16 D3
El Horno	17 B3
Trailer	18 D3

Sleeping

Sitges has about 45 hotels and hostales, but many close from around October to April, then are full in July and August, when prices are at their highest. If you haven't booked ahead, ask the tourist office to ring around for you, especially if you arrive late in the day.

Hotel Madison Bahía (☎ 93 894 00 12; Carrer de les Parellades 31-33; s/d €60/75; ⊠) This friendly hotel, in the centre of the action, has simple but well-maintained rooms, some with their own balcony. All have satellite TV, and you can relax on the hotel terrace, when fatigue sets in.

Romàntic Hotel (☎ 93 894 83 75; romantic@ hotelromantic.com; Carrer de Sant Isidre 33; s/d €68/101; ⊠)

These three adjoining 19th-century villas are presented in sensuous period style, with a leafy dining courtyard. It's popular with gay visitors, although not exclusively so.

Eating

Restaurante El Velero (☎ 93 894 20 51; Passeig de la Ribera 38; meals €30-35; ⊠ Wed-Sun, dinner only Tue Jun-Sep; Wed-Sat, lunch only Sun & dinner only Tue Oct-May) Hunker down behind the glass fronting, across the road from the beach, to tuck into good seafood at this classic, one of several restaurants offering the fruits of the sea along this strip.

Costa Dorada (☎ 93 894 35 43; Carrer del Port Alegre; meals €30; ⊠ Fri-Tue, lunch only Wed) Old-world service with 1970s atmosphere (lots of tiles and bottles of wine on display) and reliable standards make the 'Gold Coast' a safe bet, especially for seafood, paella and *fideuá*.

Al Fresco (☎ 93 894 06 00; Carrer de Pau Barrabeig 4; meals €25-30; ☯ dinner only Wed-Sun) Hidden along a narrow stairway masquerading as a street, is a charming hideaway with some interesting gastronomic twists. You could indulge in light curries or a *solomillo de canguro* (a prime cut of Australia's bouncing beast).

Drinking & Entertainment

Much of Sitges' nightlife happens on one short pedestrian strip packed with humanity right through the night in summer: Carrer del 1er de Maig, Plaça de la Industria and Carrer del Marqués de Montroig, all in a short line off the seafront. Carrer del 1er de Maig – also known as Calle del Pecado (Sin Street) – vibrates to the volume of 10 or so disco-bars all trying to outdo each other in decibels.

You'll find more of the same, if slightly less intense, around the corner on Carrer de les Parellades, Carrer de Bonaire and Carrer de Sant Pere.

Bar Voramar (Carrer del Port Alegre 55) On Platja de Sant Sebastiá, this is a 1960s throwback with nautical decoration and good music. Check it out for live jazz sessions.

Gay and gay-friendly bars abound. **Bar El 7** (Carrer Nou 7) is popular and occasionally whoops it up with a bit of a show, while **El Horno** (Carrer de Juan Tarrida Ferratges 6) has a dark room to fumble about in. For dancing late into the night, **Trailer** (Carrer d'Àngel Vidal 36; ☯ May-Sep) is a popular gay club, one of two in town. It organises events, such as foam parties, and has a dark room to play in. Opening times out of season vary enormously.

Getting There & Away

From about 6am to 10pm, four *rodalies* per hour run from Estació Sants Barcelona to Sitges (€2.25, 30 minutes). The best road from Barcelona to Sitges is the C32 tollway.

MONTSERRAT

Montserrat (Serrated Mountain), 50km northwest of Barcelona, is a 1236m-high mountain of truly weird rock pillars, shaped by wind, rain and frost from a conglomeration of limestone, pebbles and sand that

once lay under the sea. With the historic Benedictine Monestir de Montserrat, one of Catalonia's most important shrines, cradled at 725m on its side, it makes a great outing from Barcelona. From the mountain, on a clear day, you can see as far as the Pyrenees and even, if you're lucky, Mallorca.

Orientation & Information

The *cremallera* (rack-and-pinion train) and cable car both arrive on the mountainside, just below the monastery. From either of these, the main road curves (past a snack bar, cafeteria, information office and the Espai Audiovisual) round and up to the right, passing the blocks of Cel.les Abat Marcel, to enter Plaça de Santa Maria, at the centre of the monastery complex.

The **information office** (☎ 93 877 77 01; www .abadiamontserrat.net; ☯ 9am-6pm) has information on the complex and walking trails.

Sights & Activities
MONESTIR DE MONTSERRAT

The monastery was founded in 1025 to commemorate a 'vision' of the Virgin on the mountain. Wrecked by Napoleon's troops in 1811, then abandoned as a result of anticlerical legislation in the 1830s, it was rebuilt from 1858. Today a community of about 80 monks lives here. Pilgrims come from far and wide to venerate *La Moreneta* (The Black Virgin), a 12th-century Romanesque wooden sculpture of Mary with the infant Jesus, which has been Catalonia's patron since 1881.

The two-part **Museu de Montserrat** (Plaça de Santa Maria; admission €5.50; ☯ 10am-6pm Mon-Fri, 10am-7pm Sat & Sun) has an excellent collection, ranging from an Egyptian mummy and Gothic altarpieces to art by El Greco, Monet, Degas and Picasso. The **Espai Audiovisual** (admission €2 or free with Museu de Montserrat ticket; ☯ 10am-6pm Mon-Fri, 10am-7pm Sat & Sun) is a walk-through multimedia space (with images and sounds) that illustrates the daily life and activities of the monks and the history and spirituality of the monastery.

From Plaça de Santa Maria you enter the courtyard of the 16th-century **basilica** (☯ 8am-8.15pm Jul-Sep, earlier closing rest of year), the monastery's church. The basilica's façade, with its carvings of Christ and the 12 Apostles, dates from 1900, despite its 16th-century Plateresque style. Opening times, when you can file past the image of the

Black Virgin high above the basilica's main altar, vary according to season. Follow the signs to the **Cambril de la Mare de Déu** (admission free; ☻ 8am-10.30am & 12.15-6.30pm Mon-Sat, 8am-10.30am, 12.15-6.30pm & 7.30-8.15pm Sun & holidays) to the right of the main basilica entrance.

If you're around the basilica at the right time, you'll catch a performance by the **Montserrat Boys' Choir** (Escolania; admission free; ☻ 1pm & 7.10pm Mon-Sat, 1pm Sun Aug-Jun), reckoned to be Europe's oldest music school.

On your way out, have a look in the room, across the courtyard from the basilica entrance, filled with gifts and thank-you messages to the Montserrat Virgin, from people who give her the credit for all manner of happy events. The souvenirs range from plaster casts to wedding dresses.

If you want to see where the holy image of the Virgin was discovered, take the **Santa Cova funicular** (€1.60/2.50 one way/return; ☻ every 20min 10am-1pm & 3.20-7pm) down from the main area.

THE MOUNTAIN

You can explore the mountain above the monastery on a web of paths leading to some of the peaks and to 13 empty and rather dilapidated hermitages. The **Funicular de Sant Joan** (one way/return €3.80/6.10; ☻ every 20min 10am-7pm) will carry you up the first 250m from the monastery. If you prefer to walk, the road past the funicular's bottom station leads to its top station in about one hour (3km).

From the Sant Joan top station, it's a 20-minute stroll (signposted) to the **Sant Joan hermitage**, with fine westward views. More exciting is the one-hour walk northwest, along a path marked with occasional blobs of yellow paint, to Montserrat's highest peak, **Sant Jeroni**, from where there's an awesome sheer drop on the northern side. The walk takes you across the upper part of the mountain, with a close-up experience of some of the weird rock pillars. Many have names: on your way to Sant Jeroni look over to the right for **La Prenyada** (The Pregnant Woman), **La Mòmia** (The Mummy), **L'Elefant** (The Elephant) and **El Cap de Mort** (The Death's Head).

Sleeping & Eating

For accommodation options call ☎ 93 877 77 01.

Cel·les Abat Marcel (☎ 93 877 77 01; 2-/4-person apt €43.60/78; ℗) Here you will find comfort-

able apartments equipped with full bathroom and kitchenette.

Hotel Abat Cisneros (☎ 93 877 77 01; s/d €48.85/85; ℗) The only hotel in the monastery complex has modern, comfortable rooms, some looking on to Plaça de Santa Maria. It has a **restaurant** (meals €25-30), a **cafeteria** (meals €10-15) and a couple of cafés for breakfast.

Getting There & Away

BUS

A daily bus from Barcelona with **Julià Tours** (Map pp270-2; ☎ 93 317 64 54; Ronda de l'Universitat 5) to the monastery (€42.50) leaves at 9.30am (returning at 2.30pm). The price includes travel, all entry prices, use of funiculars at Montserrat and a meal at the cafeteria.

CAR & MOTORCYCLE

The most straightforward route from Barcelona is by Avinguda Diagonal, Via Augusta, the Túnel de Vallvidrera and the C16. Shortly after Terrassa, follow the exit signs to Montserrat, which will put you on the C58 road. Follow it northwest to the C55. Then head 2km south on this road to Monistrol de Montserrat, from where a road snakes 7km up the mountain. You could leave the car at the parking station in Monistrol Vila and take the *cremallera* up to the top.

TRAIN, CREMALLERA & CABLE CAR

FGC (☎ 93 205 15 15) runs trains on its R5 line from Plaça d'Espanya station in Barcelona to Monistrol, up to 18 times daily starting at 8.36am. They connect with the **cremallera** (☎ 902 312020; www.cremallerademont serrat.com; €3.80/6 one way/return), which takes 17 minutes to make the upward journey. One-way/return from Barcelona to Montserrat with the FGC train and *cremallera* costs €7.60/13.60. If you prefer, you could get off the train from Barcelona one stop earlier, at Montserrat Aeri, and get the old cable car up to Montserrat. Prices are the same for the cable car as for the *cremallera*.

Some all-in-one tickets are also available (and cost the same whether you take the cable car or *cremallera*).

TransMontserrat tickets (€20.50) include the train, cable car or *cremallera*, two metro rides, the Espai Audiovisual and unlimited use of the funiculars. For €34.50 you can have all this with the TotMontserrat card, which also includes museum entrance and a modest dinner at the self-service restaurant. Two further ticketing options are available for those who get to the cable car or *cremallera* under their own steam. The Combi 1 ticket (€12.94) includes unlimited use of the funiculars and entrance to the Espai Audiovisual, while the Combi 2 ticket (€26.70) also includes the museum entrance and a meal at the cafeteria.

There are discounts for children, students and senior citizens on all the above fares.

PENEDÈS WINE COUNTRY

Some of Spain's best wines come from this area. Sant Sadurní d'Anoia, a half-hour train ride west of Barcelona, is the capital of *cava*. Vilafranca del Penedès, 12km down the track, is the heart of the Penedès DO (*denominación de origen*) region, which produces noteworthy light whites. Some reasonable reds also come out of the area. Visitors are welcomed on tours of numerous wineries; there'll often be a free glass along the way and plenty more for sale.

Sant Sadurní d'Anoia
pop 10,380

A hundred or so wineries around Sant Sadurní produce 140 million bottles of *cava* a year – something like 85% of the entire national output. *Cava* is made by the same method as French champagne. If you happen to be in town in October, you may catch the **Mostra de Caves i Gastronomia**, a *cava* and food-tasting fest.

Freixenet (☎ 93 891 70 00; www.freixenet.com; Carrer de Joan Sala 2, Sant Sadurní d'Anoia; ☺ 1hr tours at 10am, 11.30am, 3.30pm & 5pm Mon-Thu Jan-Nov, 10am & 11.30am Fri 10am, 11.30am, 3.30pm & 5pm Sat-Thu Dec), the best-known *cava* company, is based right next to the train station.

Codorníu (☎ 93 818 32 32; www.codorniu.es; admission free; ☺ 9am-5pm Mon-Fri, 9am-1pm Sat & Sun) is at Can Codorníu, at the entry to the town by road from Barcelona. Manuel Raventós, head of this firm back in 1872, was the first Spaniard to be successful in producing sparkling wine by the champagne method. The Codorníu headquarters, a Modernista building, is open for visits.

Vilafranca del Penedès
pop 33,020

Vilafranca is larger than Sant Sadurní and more interesting. The **tourist office** (☎ 93

892 03 58; Plaça de la Vila; ☺ 9am-1pm & 4-7pm Tue-Fri, 10am-1pm Sat & 4-7pm Mon) can provide tips on visiting some of the smaller wineries in the area.

SIGHTS

The mainly Gothic **Basílica de Santa Maria** (Plaça de Jaume I) faces the combined **Museu de Vilafranca** and **Museu del Vi** (Wine Museum; ☎ 93 890 05 82; Plaça de Jaume I; adult/child €3/0.90; ☺ 10am-2pm & 4-7pm Tue-Sat, 10am-2pm Sun & holidays) in the old centre of this straggling town. The museum, a fine Gothic building, covers local archaeology, art, geology and bird life, and also has an excellent section on wine. A statue on Plaça de Jaume I pays tribute to Vilafranca's famous *castellers* (Catalan human-castle builders), who do their thing during Vilafranca's lively *festa major* (main annual festival) at the end of August. For more on castellers, see the boxed text Of Giants, Dragons & Human Castles (p379).

Vilafranca's premier winery is **Torres** (☎ 93 817 74 87; www.torres.es; ☺ 9am-5pm Mon-Sat, 9am-1pm Sun & holidays), 3km northwest of the town centre on the BP2121 near Pacs del Penedès. The Torres family revolutionised Spanish wine-making in the 1960s by introducing new temperature-controlled, stainless-steel technology and French grape varieties.

The UK-based **Arblaster & Clarke Wine Tours** (☎ 01730-893344; www.winetours.co.uk) organises occasional tasting tours of the Penedès wine region.

EATING

While there's no need to stay in Vilafranca and little attraction in doing so, eating is another story altogether. **Cal Ton** (☎ 93 890 37 41; Carrer Casal 8; meals €35-40; ☺ Wed-Sat, lunch only Sun & Tue) is one of several enticing options in town. Hidden away down a narrow side street, Cal Ton has a crisp, modern décor and offers inventive Mediterranean cuisine – all washed down with local wines of course!

Getting There & Away

Up to three *rodalies* trains an hour run from Estació Sants Barcelona to Sant Sadurní (€2.25, 40 minutes) and Vilafranca (€2.75, 50 minutes). By car, take the AP7 and follow the exit signs.

BARCELONA

Catalonia

North, south and west of Barcelona spreads a land of such diversity that, although its furthest-flung corner is no more than 200km (seven hours by bus) from Barcelona, you could spend weeks exploring it and still feel you'd barely begun. The Costa Brava, though blighted by dreary pockets of mass tourism, still boasts the wild beauty that first drew visitors here. Just inland are the riverside medieval city of Girona and Figueres, home of the loopy 'theatre-museum' of that city's unique son, Salvador Dalí.

Running across the north, the Pyrenees rise to mighty 3000m peaks from a series of green and often remote valleys, dotted with villages that retain a palpable air of the Middle Ages. These mountains provide some magnificent walking and excellent skiing. Enchanting Romanesque churches are scattered across the mountain valleys of the north.

Excitement runs thinner in the flatter far west and south, but there's enough to keep you happily exploring for days, from the wetlands of the Ebro delta to the historic cities of Tarragona and Lleida. Strike out a little off the well-beaten track and you'll discover grand medieval monasteries, lush vineyards and hilltop villages.

Throughout Catalonia (Catalunya in Catalan, Cataluña in Castilian Spanish) the sense of difference from the rest of Spain is intense, not only in the use of Catalan (though everyone speaks Castilian too) but in the unusual festivals, cuisine and reminders of the region's unique history.

HIGHLIGHTS

- Chill out on the Costa Brava coves and beaches near **Palafrugell** (p333) or **Begur** (p335)
- Discover the magical village of **Cadaqués** (p343), haunted by the memory of Salvador Dalí
- Contemplate the absurd with a visit to the **Teatre-Museu Dalí** (p346) in Figueres
- Conquer the trails of the **Parc Nacional d'Aigüestortes i Estany de Sant Maurici** (p363)
- Take the *cremallera* (rack-and-pinion railway) up to **Vall de Núria** (p356)
- Ski the region's premier slopes at **Baqueira-Beret** (p368)
- Explore the compact medieval city of **Girona** (p336)
- Climb the region's highest mountain, **Pica d'Estats** (p352)
- White-water raft down the Riu Noguera Pallaresa from **Llavorsí** (p362)
- Wander through the monastery complex of the **Reial Monestir de Santa Maria de Poblet** (p371)

| AREA: 32,113 SQ KM | POP: 6,704,145 | AVE SUMMER TEMP: HIGH 30°C, LOW 22°C |

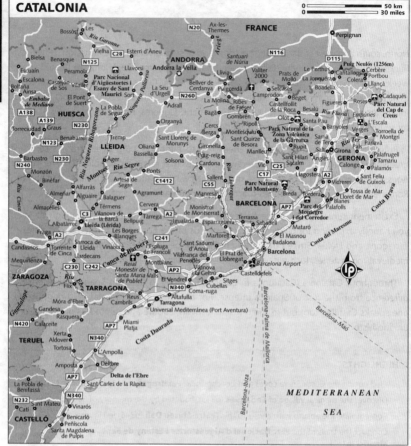

COSTA BRAVA

The Costa Brava (stretching from Blanes, 60km northeast of Barcelona, to the French border) ranks with the Costa Blanca and Costa del Sol as one of Spain's three great holiday *costas* (coasts). But alongside some occasionally awful concrete development, English breakfasts and *konditoreien* (pastry shops), the 'Rugged Coast' offers some spectacular stretches.

Nestling in the hilly back country – green and covered in umbrella pine in the south, barer and browner in the north – are scattered charming stone villages, the towering monastery of St Pere de Rodes and Salvador Dalí's fantasy castle home at Púbol. A little further inland are the bigger towns of Girona (Gerona in Castilian), with a sizable and strikingly well preserved medieval centre, and Figueres (Figueras), famous for its bizarre Teatre-Museu Dalí, the foremost of a series of sites associated with the eccentric surrealist artist Salvador Dalí.

The ruggedness of the Costa Brava continues under the sea and provides some of the best diving in Spain. Diving centres with certified instructors operate at a dozen or more places. The Illes Medes, off L'Estartit, is a group of protected islets with probably the most diverse sea life along the Spanish coast. Other top diving spots include the Illes Formigues (rocky islets off

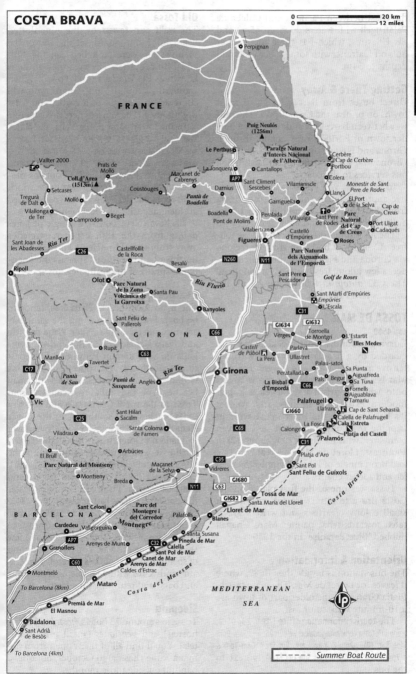

COSTA BRAVA

| 0 | 20 km |
| 0 | 12 miles |

FRANCE

Perpignan

Puig Neulós
(1256m)

Le Perthus

Paratge Natural
d'Interès Nacional
de l'Albera

Cerbère
Cap de Cerbère
Portbou

La Jonquera   Cantallops

Vallíter 2000   Prats de
                        Molló

Coll d'Area   Maçanet de
(1513m) ▲   Cabrenys   Darnius   Sant Climent
                                                        Sescebes   Vilamaniscle   Colera

Setcases   Coustouges   Monestir de Sant
Tregurà   Llançà   Pere de Rodes
de Dalt   Molló   Panta de   Garriguella
                                                    Boadella   El Port   Cap de
Vilallonga   Boadella   Peralada   Sant Pere   de la Selva   Creus
de Ter   Beget   Camprodon   Pont de Molins   de Rodes   Parc   Port Lligat
                                                    Vilabertran   Vilajuïga   Natural   Cadaqués
Sant Joan de   Castelló   del Cap
les Abadesses   Riu Ter   d'Empúries   de Creus
                                                            Figueres   Roses
Ripoll   C26   Castellfollit
                              de la Roca   Parc Natural
                                            Besalú   Riu Fluvià   dels Aiguamolls
                                                    N260   N11   de l'Empordà
Olot   Parc Natural   Golf de Roses
              de la Zona   Santa Pau   Sant Pere
              Volcànica de   Pescador   Sant Martí d'Empúries
              la Garrotxa   Empúries
                                                        Banyoles   L'Escala
Sant Feliu de
Pallerols   GI634   GI632
                          G I R O N A   C66   Verges   Torroella   L'Estartit
Manlleu   Rupit   de Montgrí   Illes Medes
        Tavertet   C63   Castell   Parlavà
                                            Riu Ter   de Púbol   Ullastret   Palau-sator
C17   La Pera   Sa Punta
        Panta   Panta de   Anglès   Peratallada   Begur   Aiguafreda
        de Sau   Susqueda   La Bisbal   Pals   Sa Tuna
Vic   d'Empordà   C66   Fornells
        C25   Palafrugell   Aiguablava
                                        Sant Hilari   Tamariu
Viladrau   Sacalm   GI660   Llafranc
                                                                                            Cap de Sant Sebastià
                        Santa Coloma   Calonge   Calella de Palafrugell
El Brull   de Farners   C65   La Fosca   Cala Estreta
        Parc Natural del Montseny   Platja del Castell
                        Arbúcies   C31   Palamós
        Montseny   Platja d'Aro
                        Maçanet   C35   Sant Pol   Costa Brava
B A R C E L O N A   de la Selva   Vidreres   Sant Feliu de Guíxols
                                            GI680
Sant Celoni   Parc del   N11   C63   Tossà de Mar
                      Montegre i   GI682   Santa Maria del Llorell   Costa Brava
Cardedeu   del Corredor   Palafolls   Lloret de Mar
        Vallgorguina   Montnegre   Blanes
AP7   Arenys de Munt   Santa Susana
Granollers   Pineda de Mar
C60   C32   Calella
Montmeló   Canet de Mar   Sant Pol de Mar
        Arenys de Mar
        Caldes d'Estrac
To Barcelona (8km)   Mataró   Costa del Maresme   MEDITERRANEAN
                                                                        SEA
Premià de Mar
El Masnou
Badalona
Sant Adrià
de Besòs
To Barcelona (4km)

- - - - - - Summer Boat Route

the coast between Palamós and Calella de Palafrugell with waters down to 45m) and Els Ullastres, which has three underwater hills off Llafranc, with some sheer walls and depths to 54m.

Getting There & Away

Direct buses from Barcelona go to most towns on or near the Costa Brava. The railway between Barcelona and the coastal border town of Portbou runs inland, through Girona and Figueres, most of the way. From Girona and Figueres there are fairly good bus services to the coast.

In summer, you could take an alternative approach to the southern Costa Brava from Barcelona by a combination of *rodalies* (local trains) and boat.

The AP7 *autopista* (tollway) and the toll-free A2 highway both run from Barcelona via Girona and Figueres to the French border, a few kilometres north of La Jonquera. The C32 *autopista* follows the A2 up the coast as far as Blanes.

TOSSA DE MAR
pop 4560

Curving around a boat-speckled bay and guarded by a headland crowned with defensive medieval walls and towers, Tossa de Mar is a village of crooked, narrow streets onto which tourism has tacked a larger, modern extension. In July and August it's hard to reach the water's edge without tripping over oily limbs, but it is heaven compared with its bigger neighbour 12km southeast, Lloret de Mar – a real concrete and neon jungle of Piccadilly pubs, *Bierkeller* and soccer chants.

Tossa was one of the first places on the Costa Brava to attract foreign visitors – a small colony of artists and writers gravitated towards what painter Marc Chagall dubbed 'Blue Paradise' in the 1930s.

Orientation & Information

The bus station is beside the GI682, where it leaves for Lloret de Mar. The main beach, Platja Gran, and the older part of town are a 10-minute walk southeast.

The **tourist information office** (☎ 972 34 01 08; www.infotossa.com; Avinguda del Pelegrí 25; ☉ 9am-9pm Mon-Sat, 10am-2pm & 4-8pm Sun Jun-Sep; 10am-1pm & 4-7pm Mon-Sat, 10am-1pm Sun Oct-May) is next to the bus station.

Old Tossa

The **walls** and **towers** on the pine-dotted headland, Mont Guardí, at the end of the main beach, were built between the 12th and 14th centuries. The area they girdle is known as the **Vila Vella** (Old Town). When wandering around Mont Guardí you will come across vestiges of a castle, and a **far** (lighthouse). The sunsets here are superb.

In the lower part of Vila Vella, the **Museu Municipal** (☎ 972 34 07 09; Plaça de Roig i Soler 1; admission €3; ☉ 10am-9pm mid-Jun–mid-Sep, 10am-2pm & 4-6pm Tue-Sun mid-Sep–mid-Jun), set in the 14th- and 15th-century Palau del Batlle, contains mosaics and other finds from a **Roman villa**, which is off Avinguda del Pelegrí, and Tossa-related art including Chagall's *El Violinista*.

Vila Nova (New Town), a tangle of lanes dating from the 18th century, stretches away from the old nucleus. Further north, northwest and northeast spreads the unenticing sprawl of the really new town.

Beaches & Coves

The main town beach, **Platja Gran**, tends to be busy. Further north along the same bay are the quieter and smaller **Platja del Reig** and **Platja Mar Menuda** at the end of Avinguda de Sant Ramon Penyafort. The coast to the northeast and southwest of Tossa is dotted by rocky coves, some with small beaches. You can walk cross-country from Tossa to the small **Cala Llevado** and **Cala d'En Carles** beaches, 3km southwest, or the longer **Platja de Llorell** (3.5km away), or drive down to Platja de Llorell from the GI682. To the northeast, you can walk down from the GI682 to sandy coves such as **Cala Pola** (4km), **Cala Giverola** (5km), **Cala Salions** (8km) and **Platja Vallpregona** (11km). In summer (Easter to September), **glass-bottom boats** (☎ 972 34 22 29; return adult/child aged 3-12/infant €8/5.50/free) run about hourly to some of these northeastern beaches from Platja Gran, calling in at a few sea caves along the way. You have the option of spending the day at Cala Giverola (a pleasant sandy cove with a couple of restaurants and bars) and returning on a later boat.

Sleeping

Tossa has around 75 hotels, *hostales* (budget hostels) and *pensiones* (small private hotels). You'll find all of them open from Semana Santa (Easter) to October, but only a handful outside those months.

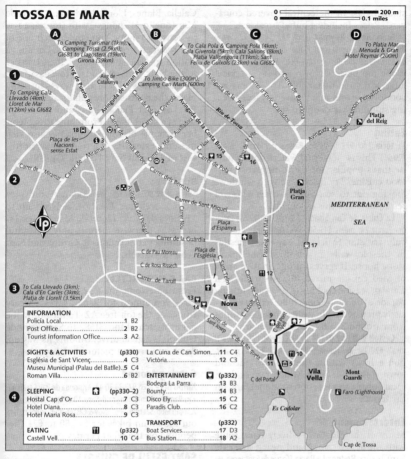

TOSSA DE MAR

Map legend:

INFORMATION
Policía Local.....................................1 B2
Post Office.......................................2 B2
Tourist Information Office..........3 A2

SIGHTS & ACTIVITIES (p330)
Església de Sant Vicenç...............4 C3
Museu Municipal (Palau del Batlle)..5 C4
Roman Villa.....................................6 B2

SLEEPING (pp330–2)
Hostal Cap d'Or..............................7 C3
Hotel Diana......................................8 C3
Hotel Maria Rosa............................9 C3

EATING (p332)
Castell Vell......................................10 C4

La Cuina de Can Simon.............11 C4
Victòria..12 C3

ENTERTAINMENT (p332)
Bodega La Parra.............................13 B3
Bounty..14 B3
Disco Ely..15 C2
Paradís Club...................................16 C2

TRANSPORT (p332)
Boat Services..................................17 D3
Bus Station.....................................18 A2

CAMPING

Five camping grounds are spread out around the town. The nearest is **Camping Can Martí** (☎ 972 34 08 51; Rambla Pau Casals; 2-person tent & car €25.70; ☼ mid-May–late Sep), 1km back from the beach and well equipped. Of the others, **Camping Cala Llevadó** (☎ 972 340314; www.cala llevado.com; Cala Llevadó; 2-person tent & car €32; ☼ May-Sep; ☒) is probably the best. It stretches back from a cove 4km southwest of Tossa in the settlement of Santa Maria de Llorell. This high-quality facility, apart from its shady camping spots and prime location near a pretty beach, offers tennis courts, a pool, a restaurant, shops and bars.

The remaining ones, should you get stuck, are **Camping Tossa**, **Camping Turismar** and **Camping Pola**. The latter is 4km out of town on a cove below the winding road northeast of Tossa.

HOSTALES & HOTELS

Hostal Cap d'Or (☎ 972 34 00 81; Passeig de la Vila Vella 1; s/d with bathroom including breakfast €35/70.50) Rub up against the town's history in this spot right in front of the walls. Rooms are comfortable and the best look out onto the beach.

Hotel Diana (☎ 972 34 18 86; www.diana-hotel.com; Plaça d'Espanya 6; s/d €72.80/115.60, d with sea view €140; ☼ Apr-Nov; ☒) You'll relax simply on entering this small-scale, older hotel fronting Platja Gran. It has a Gaudí-built fireplace in the lounge and oozes Modernista décor and stained glass in the central covered court-yard. Prices include a buffet breakfast.

Gran Hotel Reymar (☎ 972 34 03 12; www
.bestwesternghreymar.com; Platja de Mar Menuda; s/d
up to €142.30/195.80; ☙ May-Oct; Ⓟ ☒ ☒) This
is the top place in town and it's a typical
large-scale, multi-star job. The rooms are
comfortable and many have terraces offer-ing stunning views out to sea.

Eating

Victòria (☎ 972 34 01 66; Passeig del Mar 23; meals
€20-25) This is an eternal waterfront favour-ite that's popular for its no-nonsense sea-food cuisine. Try for a table with windows
looking out to sea. Several other cheerful
restaurants line this esplanade.

La Cuina de Can Simon (☎ 972 34 12 69; Carrer
del Portal 24; meals €45-50; ☙ Wed-Mon) Tossa's
culinary star (Michelin says so!) nestles
by the old walls in a former fisherman's
stone house. It serves an imaginative array
of Med cuisine mixed in with traditional
Catalan seaside cooking. Expect an enticing
parade of *amuse-gueules* followed by exqui-sitely prepared main dishes and good wines
from around Spain to wash it down.

Castell Vell (☎ 972 34 10 30; Carrer del Abat Oliva 1;
meals €20-25; ☙ Tue-Sun, Easter-Oct) This rustic
house lurks within the walls of the old
town. Take your meal, which ranges from
local cuisine to more-international fare, on
the terrace.

Entertainment

Many of the old town's lively bars, some
with music, are along and near Carrer de
Sant Josep. **Bodega La Parra** (Carrer de Sant Josep 26;
☙ 9pm-3am Apr-Oct) manages to maintain
an old-fashioned wine-cellar atmosphere,
while **Bounty** (Carrer de l'Església 6; ☙ 9pm-3am Apr-Oct) is a lively watering hole specialising in
Spanish rock and long mixed drinks.

Disco Ely (☎ 972 34 00 09; Carrer de Pola; ☙ 10pm-5am Apr-Oct), one of a handful of clubs in town,
puts on a wide range of mainstream dance
music with the odd bit of house thrown
in. **Paradís Club** (☎ 972 34 07 55; Passeig del Mar;
☙ 11pm-6am Apr-Oct) is in much the same
category.

Getting There & Away

BOAT

From April to October **Dolfi-Jet** (☎ 972 37 19 39)
runs boats several times a day between

Calella, Blanes, Lloret de Mar and Tossa de
Mar (one to 1½ hours), with stops at a few
in-between points. You could catch one of
the *rodalies* from Barcelona's Catalunya
station to Calella or Blanes, then transfer
to the boat. The return trip to Tossa from
Calella costs €19 (€11 one way). In many
places the boats simply pull up at the beach
(in Tossa, at Platja Gran) and tickets are
sold at a booth there. From June to Septem-ber a couple of other companies also kick
in, some extending the route as far north-east of Tossa as Sant Feliu de Guíxols.

BUS

Sarfa (☎ 902 302025; www.sarfa.com) runs to/
from Barcelona's Estació del Nord up to
11 times daily via Lloret de Mar (€8.05, 1¼
hours). Otherwise there is only a handful
of summer connections to Girona and Sant
Feliu de Guíxols.

CAR & MOTORCYCLE

From Barcelona, the C32 *autopista*, which
takes you almost to Blanes, saves a weary
trudge on the toll-free A2. To the north, the
23km stretch of the GI682 to Sant Feliu de
Guíxols is a great drive, winding its way up,
down and around picturesque bays.

Getting Around

Jimbo Bike (☎ 972 34 30 44; Avinguda de Pau Casals 12;
☙ 9am-9pm mid-Jun–mid-Sep, 10.30am-1.30pm & 4-7.30pm Mon-Sat mid-Sept–Nov & Easter–mid-June) rents
out mountain bikes for €17.50 to €21 (de-pending on the type) per day.

SANT FELIU DE GUÍXOLS
pop 18,500

A snaking road hugs the spectacular ups
and downs of the Costa Brava for the 23km
from Tossa de Mar to Sant Feliu de Guí-xols. On this road Rose Macaulay, author
of *Fabled Shore* (1950), 'met only one mule
cart, laden with pine boughs, and two very
polite *guardias civiles*'. Along the way are
several enticing little inlets and largely hid-den beaches.

Sant Feliu itself has an attractive water-side promenade and a handful of curious
leftovers from its long past, the most im-portant being the so-called **Porta Ferrada**
(Iron Gate): a wall and entrance, which is
all that remains of a 10th-century mon-astery, the **Monestir de Sant Benet**. A couple

Cala Estreta on the Costa Brava (p328), Catalonia

Waterfront homes on the Riu Onyar in Girona (p336), northern Catalonia

Salvador Dalí's Teatre-Museu Dalí (p346), Figueres, Catalonia

Estany de Certascan (2236m, p362), the largest glacial lake in the Pyrenees, Catalonia

Monasterio de San Juan de la Peña (p430), Aragón

CHRISTOPH

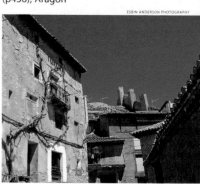

The remote medieval town of Albarracín (p436), Aragón

ESBIN ANDERSON PHOTOGRAPHY

INGRID RODDIS

Cascada de la Cola del Caballo (p425), Parque Nacional de Ordesa y Monte Perdido, Aragón

Circo de Soaso (p425) in the Parque Nacional de Ordesa y Monte Perdido, Aragón

INGRI

of nice-enough beaches can be found on either side of the town.

Sarfa buses call in here frequently (up to 16 in summer) from Barcelona, on the way to Palafrugell (€10.15; one hour 20 minutes). They do *not* follow the coast road.

PLATJA D'ARO & PALAMÓS

These spots mark the two ends of one of the Costa Brava's party spots. The beaches are OK, the high-rises are standard issue and the nightlife is busy. The area tends to attract more Spanish tourism than foreign. Around the main broad beaches and their resorts are some magnificent stretches of coast with enticing coves. Both are stops on the frequent Barcelona–Palafrugell Sarfa bus route (€10.60 and €11.35 respectively, 1½ hours to Platja d'Aro and 15 minutes more to Palamós).

The 2km-long **Platja d'Aro** beach is big and sandy but for something more secluded you could head north along the GR92 coastal walking path, which winds along the high leafy coastline for about 4km to Sant Antoni de Calonge. The first beach you hit is **Platja Rovira**, and soon after, the smaller and more enchanting **Sa Cova**. A little further on again are two small nudist coves, **Platja d'en Ros** and **Platja d'es Canyers**.

If you should end up in Palamós and wonder how it happened, all is not lost. Again you can pick up the GR92 trail and head north for **Platja del Castell**, a virtually untouched strand. If you don't fancy the walk, drive out of Palamós heading for Palafrugell and look for the signs that lead right to the beach. Two kilometres of partly unsealed road get you there. The northern end of the beach is capped by a high wooded promontory that hides the 'castle' (the remains of a 6th- to 1st-century-BC Iberian settlement) after which the beach is named.

Hostal Vostra Llar (☎ 972 31 42 62; www.vostra llar.com; Avinguda del President Macià 12, Palamós; s/d €63.65/72.55; 🅿), a graceful hostal that backs on to a tranquil and leafy courtyard (and with its own restaurant), is a good choice. Airy rooms with timber floors, and in some cases balconies, are relaxing, and you can dine in the courtyard on balmy nights.

PALAFRUGELL & AROUND

North of Palamós begins one of the most beautiful stretches of the Costa Brava. The town of Palafrugell, 5km inland, is the main access point for a cluster of enticing beach spots. Calella de Palafrugell, Llafranc and Tamariu, one-time fishing villages squeezed into small bays, now constitute three of the Costa Brava's most charming, low-key resorts.

Begur (see p335), 7km northeast of Palafrugell, is an interesting village with a cluster of less developed beaches nearby. Inland you should search out the charming villages of Pals and Peratallada.

Palafrugell
pop 17,670

Palafrugell is the main transport, shopping and service hub for the area but is of little interest in itself. The C66 Palamós–Girona road passes through the western side of Palafrugell, a 10-minute walk from the central square, Plaça Nova. The **tourist office** (☎ 972 30 02 28; www.palafrugell.net/turisme; Carrer del Carrilet 2; 🕑 9am-9pm Mon-Sat, 11am-1pm Sun Jul & Aug; 10am-1pm & 5-8pm Mon-Sat, 10am-1pm Sun May-Jun & Sep; 10am-1pm & 4-7pm Mon-Sat, 10am-1pm Sun Oct-Apr) is beside the C66 highway. The **bus station** (Carrer de Torres Jonama 67-69) is a five-minute walk from the tourist office.

Sarfa runs to Palafrugell from Barcelona up to 16 times daily (€12.15, two hours). Loads of buses also run between Girona and Palafrugell (€4, one hour).

Calella de Palafrugell
pop 760

The southernmost of the Palafrugell resorts, Calella is also the most spread out. Its low buildings are strung Aegean-style around a bay of rocky points and small beaches, with a few fishing boats still hauled up on the sand. The **tourist office** (☎ 972 61 44 75; Carrer de les Voltes 4; 🕑 10am-1pm & 5-8pm Jul-Aug; 10am-1pm & 5-8pm Mon-Sat, 10am-1pm Sun Apr-Jun & Sep–mid-Oct) is near the seafront.

SIGHTS & ACTIVITIES

Apart from plonking on one of the beaches, you can stroll along nice coastal footpaths northeast to Llafranc (20 or 30 minutes), or south to Platja del Golfet, close to Cap Roig (about 40 minutes). Atop Cap Roig, the **Jardí Botànic de Cap Roig** (☎ 972 61 45 82; admission €2.50; 🕑 8am-8pm Jul & Aug, 9am-6pm Sep-Jun) is a beautiful garden of 1200 Mediterranean species, set around the early-20th-century castle-palace of Nikolai Voevodsky. He was a tsarist colonel with expensive tastes, who felt out of place in his homeland after the Russian Revolution.

FESTIVALS & EVENTS

Calella stages the Costa Brava's biggest summer **cantada de havaneres** (singsong). *Havaneres* are melancholy Caribbean sea shanties that became popular among Costa Brava sailors in the 19th century, when Catalonia maintained busy links with Cuba. *Havaneres* are traditionally accompanied by the drinking of *cremat* – a rum, coffee, sugar, lemon and cinnamon concoction that you set alight briefly before quaffing. Traditionally, Calella's *cantada* is held in August.

SLEEPING & EATING

Camping Moby Dick (☎ 972 61 43 07; www.camping mobydick.com; Carrer de la Costa Verde 16-28; 2-person tent & car €19; ⏰ Apr-Aug; 🏊) Set in a pine-and-oak stand about 100m from the seaside, this camping ground is in an ideal location. The people running it offer the chance to do a little scuba diving in the area, and they have tennis courts.

Hotel La Torre (☎ 972 61 46 03; www.hotel-latorre .com; Passeig de la Torre 28; s/d €57.80/111.80; ⏰ Jun-Sep; 🅿) Dominating a high point on the road leading north out of Calella, and in a leafy spot near an old watchtower, this hotel offers 28 rooms, most with extensive sea views and cheery balconies. The hotel has its own restaurant, bars and terrace gardens.

Restaurant Tragamar (☎ 972 61 51 89; meals €25; ⏰ Wed-Mon, closed 1 month Jan-Feb & 2 weeks Nov) A few hundred metres north of the arcaded seaside Plaça de Port Bo, on a separate beach, Platja Canadell, the Tragamar serves up tapas and seafood. The *escarmalans gratinats amb pasta fresca* (crayfish with a light cheese crust and fresh pasta) is typical of their original approach to dishes.

GETTING THERE & AWAY

Buses from Palafrugell run to Calella, then Llafranc, then back to Palafrugell, which takes 30 minutes (€1.10). They leave every half-hour or so between 7.40am and 8.30pm in July and August; the service is progressively reduced to three or four buses a day from November to February.

Llafranc

pop 310

Barely 2km northeast of Calella de Palafrugell, and now merging with it along the roads back from the rocky coast between them, Llafranc has a smaller bay but a longer stretch of sand and gets more crowded. The **tourist office** (☎ 972 30 50 08; Carrer de Roger de Llúria; ⏰ 10am-1pm & 5-8pm Jul-Aug, 10am-1pm & 5-8pm Mon-Sat, 10am-1pm Sun Apr-Jun & Sep–mid-Oct) is a kiosk just back from the western end of the beach.

From the **Far de Sant Sebastià** (a lighthouse) and **Ermita de Sant Sebastià** (a chapel now incorporated into a luxury hotel), up on Cap de Sant Sebastià (east of the town), there are tremendous **views** in both directions along the coast. It's a 40-minute walk up: follow the steps from the harbour and the road up to the right. You can walk on to Tamariu.

SLEEPING & EATING

Camping Kim's (☎ 972 30 11 56; www.campingkims .com; Camí de la Font d'en Xeco; 2-person tent & car €39.60, bungalow d from €60; ⏰ Apr-Sep; 🏊) is about 750m back from the beach and in a pine wood. It offers a pool, a market and restaurant facilities.

Hotel Montecarlo (☎ 972 30 04 04; www.hotel montecarlollafranc.com; Carrer de Cesárea 14; s/d with bathroom €51/100; ⏰ Apr–early Dec) This bright hotel boasts sparkling rooms, most of which have views out to sea, or back to the hills behind the settlement.

Hotel Far de Sant Sebastià (☎ 972 30 16 39; www.elfar.net; d €284; 🅿 🏊) A fine old 18th-century hostelry, with a chapel and a defence tower, has been converted into a startling and elegant luxury hotel with magnificent sea views. The best of the rooms come with a spacious terrace. Grand stone arches and sunny courtyards add a romantic touch and the fine dining in the hotel restaurant is another draw.

Casamar (☎ 972 30 01 04; Carrer de Nero 3; meals €30; ⏰ Wed-Mon Mar–mid-Jan) The best waterfront hotel restaurant offers all sorts of culinary wonders, from peach ravioli to succulent lamb's ribs.

GETTING THERE & AWAY

See Calella de Palafrugell for information on bus services (p333). The Llafranc bus stop is on Carrer de la Sirena, up the hill on the Calella side of town.

Tamariu
pop 140

About 3.5km north up the coast from Llafranc, as the crow flies, Tamariu is a small crescent cove surrounded by pine stands and other greenery – a real haven. Its beach has some of the cleanest waters on Spain's Mediterranean coast. The **tourist office** (☎ 972 62 01 93; Carrer de la Riera; ☼ 10am-1pm & 5-8pm Mon-Sat, 10am-1pm Sun Jun-Sep) is in the middle of the village.

Hotel Es Furió (☎ 972 62 00 36; Carrer del Foraió 5-7; d with breakfast €114), just back from the beach, has spacious, cheerfully decorated rooms.

The beachfront is lined with seafood eateries. **Restaurant Royal** (☎ 972 62 00 41; Passeig Marítim; meals €20; ☼ Mar-Nov) is one of the best and serves a reasonable seafood *fideuá* (paella made with noodles instead of rice).

Sarfa buses from Palafrugell run to Tamariu (€1.10, 15 minutes) three or four times daily, from mid-June to mid-September only. A rough road leads to the beach of Aiguablava (below).

Begur
pop 2520

The **castell** (castle), dating to the 10th century and towering above the village, is in much the same state in which it was left by the Spanish troops who wrecked it to impede the advance of Napoleon's army in 1810. Dotted around the village are half-a-dozen towers built for defence against 16th- and 17th-century pirates. The **tourist office** (☎ 972 62 45 20; Avinguda del Onze de Setembre 5; ☼ 9am-2pm & 5-8pm Mon-Sat, 10am-1pm Sun) has loads of information.

Hotel Rosa (☎ 972 62 30 15; Carrer de Pi i Ralló 19; s/d €75/82; ☒ ☐), a few steps towards the castle from the central church, is a little surprise package with well-kept, spacious rooms. You can get some sun upstairs on the terrace, relax in the hydro-massage baths, and opt for bigger doubles with lounge area (€113).

Fonda Caner (☎ 972 62 23 91; Carrer de Pi i Ralló 10; meals €25; ☼ Sat & Sun, dinner only Mon-Fri Apr-Oct), a cosy hostelry, combines a love for local cuisine with a playful flexibility. The emphasis is on a wide variety of tempting seafood but the occasional surprise, such as duck in fig sauce, keeps you on your toes.

Sarfa buses run up to four times a day from Barcelona (€12.90, 1¾ to 2¼ hours) via Palafrugell. On weekdays one Sarfa bus runs to Girona (€5.05, 1½ hours).

Around Begur

You can reach a series of smallish beaches, on an enticing stretch of coast, by turning east off the Palafrugell road 2km south of the centre of Begur. About 2km down is a turn-off to the black-sand **Platja Fonda** (1km). Half a kilometre further on is the turn-off to **Fornells** (1km), a small village on one of the most picturesque bays of the whole Costa Brava, with a marina, a beach and incredibly blue water.

One kilometre on from the Fornells turn-off is **Aiguablava**, with a slightly bigger and busier beach, and the **Parador Nacional de la Costa Brava** (☎ 972 62 21 62; www.parador .es; s/d €108/135), a modern luxury hotel enjoying lovely views back across the Fornells bay.

Another road from Begur leads 2km east to **Aiguafreda**, a beach on a lovely cove backed by pine-covered hills, and, a bit further south, the slightly more built-up **Sa Tuna** beach.

Three kilometres west of Begur is the inland medieval hamlet of **Regencós**, which is known for its ceramics and is also the site of a wonderful accommodation option. **Hotel del Teatre** (☎ 972 30 62 70; www.hoteldelteatre.com; Plaça Major; s/d €181.90/342.40; ☐ ☒ ☐ ☒) is a combination of two adjacent and carefully restored stone houses, decorated in classic Catalan country-manor style (with plenty of fragrant timber, warm brown floor tiles and solid wooden furnishings). Room décor is light and more modern, and the pool is half covered, half open.

GETTING THERE & AWAY

A *bus platges* (beach bus) service runs from Plaça de Forgas in Begur between late June and mid-September.

Pals
pop 1010

About 6km inland from Begur is the pretty walled town of Pals. The main monument is the 15m **Torre de les Hores** (clock tower) but what makes the trip worthwhile is simply wandering around the uneven lanes and poking your nose into one medieval corner or another. From the **Mirador del Pedró** you can see northeast across the coastal plains to the sea, with the Illes Medes in the background. Up to four Sarfa buses come here from Barcelona (€13.25, two hours) en route to L'Escala.

Peratallada

The warm stone houses of Peratallada have made this village a favourite day trip for Catalans. Its narrow streets and fine old 11th-century castle-mansion (now a luxury hotel and restaurant) have been supplemented by several other places to stay, enticing restaurants and a sprinkling of low-key boutiques.

Ca l'Àliu (☎ 972 63 40 61; www.ruralplus.com/cala liu; Carrer de la Roca 6; d €55) is an 18th-century village home, where the old stone-and-timber frame has been teamed with modern comforts to create an atmospheric place for an overnight stop.

Peratallada is on the Begur–Girona bus line (once daily Monday to Friday).

CASTELL DE PÚBOL

The **Castell de Púbol** (☎ 972 48 86 55; www .salvador-dali.org; La Pera; adult/student/senior €5.50/4/4; ⏰ 10.30am-7.15pm mid-Jun–mid-Sep, 10.30am-5.15pm Tue-Sun mid-Mar–mid-Jun & mid-Sep–end Oct) is at La Pera, just south of the C66 and 22km northwest of Palafrugell. It forms the southernmost point of northeastern Catalonia's 'Salvador Dalí triangle', whose other elements include the Teatre-Museu Dalí in Figueres and the Cadaqués area, where the artist spent much of his life.

In 1968 Dalí bought this Gothic and Renaissance mansion, which includes a 14th-century church, and gave it to his wife, Gala, who lived here without him until her death. Local lore has it that the notoriously promiscuous Gala was still sending for young village men almost right up to the time she died in 1982, aged 88.

The castle was renovated by Dalí in his inimitable style, with lions' heads staring from the tops of cupboards, statues of elephants with giraffes' legs in the garden, and a stuffed giraffe staring at Gala's tomb in the crypt. In the garage is the blue Cadillac in which Dalí took Gala for a last drive round the estate – after she died.

Sarfa buses between Palafrugell and Girona run along the C66.

GIRONA

pop 77,130

Northern Catalonia's largest city, Girona (Gerona in Castilian) sits in a valley 36km inland from Palafrugell. Its impressive medieval centre, which struggles uphill above the Riu Onyar, is a powerful reason for making a visit.

The Roman town of Gerunda lay on Via Augusta, the highway from Rome to Cádiz (Carrer de la Força in Girona's old town follows part of Via Augusta). Taken from the Muslims by the Franks in AD 797, Girona became capital of one of Catalonia's most important counties, falling under the sway of Barcelona in the late 9th century. Its wealth in medieval times produced many fine Romanesque and Gothic buildings, which have survived repeated attacks and sieges through the centuries.

Orientation

The narrow streets of the old town climb above the eastern bank of the Riu Onyar and are easy to explore on foot. Several road bridges and footbridges link it to the new town across the river. The train station is 1km southwest, on Plaça d'Espanya, off Carrer de Barcelona, with the bus station behind it on Carrer de Rafael Masó i Valentí.

Information

Hospital de Santa Caterina (☎ 972 18 26 00; Plaça de l'Hospital 5).

Policía Municipal (Municipal Police; Carrer de Bernat Bacià 4)

Policía Nacional (National Police; Carrer de Sant Pau 2) At the northern end of the old town.

Tourist office (☎ 972 22 65 75; www.ajuntament .gi/turisme; Rambla de la Llibertat 1; ⏰ 8am-8pm Mon-Fri, 8am-2pm & 4-8pm Sat, 9am-2pm Sun) Towards the southern end of the old town.

Sights

CATEDRAL

The fine baroque façade of the **cathedral** stands at the head of a majestic flight of steps rising from Plaça de la Catedral. Most of the building, however, is much older than its exterior. Repeatedly rebuilt and altered down the centuries, it has Europe's widest Gothic nave (23m). The cathedral's **museum** (☎ 972 21 44 26; admission €3; ⏰ 10am-2pm & 4-6pm Tue-Sat Oct-Apr, to 7pm Tue-Sat May-Sep, to 2pm Sun & holidays year-round), through the door marked 'Claustre Tresor', contains the masterly Romanesque *Tapís de la Creació* (Tapestry of the Creation) and a Mozarabic illuminated *Beatus* manuscript, dating from AD 975.

The fee for the museum also admits you to the beautiful 12th-century Romanesque

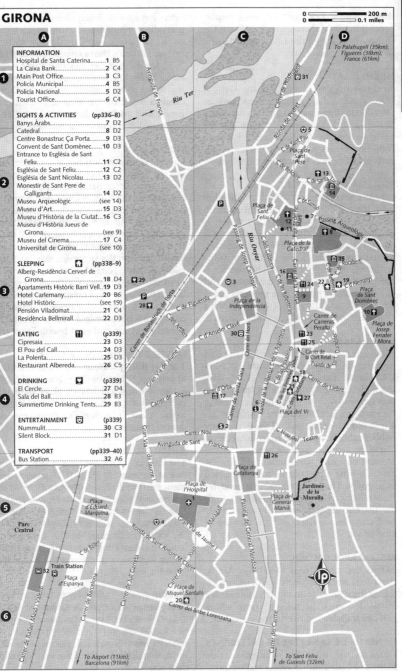

GIRONA

0	200 m
0	0.1 miles

INFORMATION
Hospital de Santa Caterina......................1 B5
La Caixa Bank..2 C4
Main Post Office.......................................3 C3
Policía Municipal......................................4 B5
Policía Nacional..5 D2
Tourist Office...6 C4

SIGHTS & ACTIVITIES (pp336–8)
Banys Àrabs..7 D2
Catedral..8 D2
Centre Bonastruc Ça Porta.......................9 D3
Convent de Sant Domènec......................10 D3
Entrance to Església de Sant
   Feliu..11 C2
Església de Sant Feliu.............................12 C2
Església de Sant Nicolau.........................13 D2
Monestir de Sant Pere de
   Galligants..14 D2
Museu Arqueològic...........................(see 14)
Museu d'Art..15 D3
Museu d'Història de la Ciutat.................16 C3
Museu d'Història Jueus de
   Girona..(see 9)
Museu del Cinema...................................17 C4
Universitat de Girona........................(see 10)

SLEEPING 🏠 (pp338–9)
Alberg-Residència Cerverí de
   Girona...18 D4
Apartaments Històric Barri Vell..............19 D3
Hotel Carlemany......................................20 B6
Hotel Històric...................................(see 19)
Pensió Viladomat...................................21 C4
Residència Bellmirall..............................22 D3

EATING 🍴 (p339)
Cipresaia 23 D3
El Pou del Call..24 D3
La Polenta...25 D3
Restaurant Albereda...............................26 C5

DRINKING 🍷 (p339)
El Cercle...27 D4
Sala del Ball..28 B3
Summertime Drinking Tents...................29 B3

ENTERTAINMENT 🎭 (p339)
Nummulit...30 C3
Silent Block...31 D1

TRANSPORT (pp339–40)
Bus Station...32 A6

cloister, whose 112 stone columns display some fine, if weathered, carving. From the cloister you can see the 13th-century Torre de Carlemany bell tower.

MUSEU D'ART

Next door to the cathedral, in the 12th- to 16th-century Palau Episcopal, the **art museum** (☎ 972 20 38 34; www.museuart.com; Plaça de la Catedral 12; admission €2; 🕑 10am-6pm Tue-Sat Oct-Feb, 10am-7pm Tue-Sat Mar-Sep, 10am-2pm Sun & holidays year-round) collection ranges from Romanesque wood-carvings to early 20th-century paintings.

ESGLÉSIA DE SANT FELIU

Girona's second great church is downhill from the cathedral. The 17th-century main façade, with its landmark single tower, is on Plaça de Sant Feliu, but the entrance is around the side. The nave has 13th-century Romanesque arches but 14th- to 16th-century Gothic upper levels. The northern-most of the chapels, at the far western end of the church, is graced by a masterly Catalan Gothic sculpture, Aloi de Montbrai's alabaster *Crist Jacent* (Recumbent Christ).

BANYS ÀRABS

Although modelled on earlier Muslim and Roman bathhouses, the **'Arab baths'** (☎ 972 21 32 62; Carrer de Ferran Catòlic; admission €1.50; 🕑 10am-8pm Tue-Sat Jul-Aug, 10am-7pm Tue-Sat Apr-Jun & Sep, 10am-2pm Tue-Sat Oct-Mar, 10am-2pm Sun & holidays year-round) are a 12th-century Christian affair in Romanesque style. This is the only public bathhouse discovered from medieval Christian Spain, where, in reaction to the Muslim obsession with water and cleanliness, washing almost came to be regarded as ungodly. The baths contain an *apodyterium* (changing room), followed by a *frigidarium* and *tepidarium* (with respectively cold and warm water), and a *caldarium* (a kind of sauna).

PASSEIG ARQUEOLÒGIC

Across the street from the Banys Àrabs, steps lead up into lovely gardens, which follow the city walls up to the 18th-century Portal de Sant Cristòfol gate, from where you can walk back down to the cathedral.

MONESTIR DE SANT PERE DE GALLIGANTS

Down across little Riu Galligants, this 11th- and 12th-century Romanesque monastery has another lovely cloister with some marvellous animal and monster carvings on the capitals of its pillars. The monastery houses Girona's **Museu Arqueològic** (☎ 972 20 26 32; admission €1.80; 🕑 10.30am-1.30pm & 4-6pm Tue-Sat Oct-Apr, 10.30am-1.30pm & 4-7pm Tue-Sat May-Sep, 10am-2pm Sun & holidays year-round), whose exhibits date from prehistoric to medieval times, and include Roman mosaics and some medieval Jewish tombstones.

THE CALL

Until 1492, Girona was home to Catalonia's second-most important medieval Jewish community (after Barcelona), and its Jewish quarter, the Call, centred on Carrer de la Força. For an idea of medieval Jewish life and culture, visit the **Museu d'Història dels Jueus de Girona** (Centre Bonastruc Ça Porta; ☎ 972 21 67 61; Carrer de la Força; admission €2; 🕑 10am-8pm Mon-Sat May-Oct, 10am-6pm Mon-Sat Nov-Apr, 10am-3pm Sun & holidays year-round). Named after Jewish Girona's most illustrious figure, a 13th-century cabbalist philosopher and mystic, the centre – a warren of rooms and stairways around a courtyard – hosts limited exhibitions and is a focal point for studies of Jewish Spain.

MUSEU D'HISTÒRIA DE LA CIUTAT

The **City History Museum** (☎ 972 22 22 29; Carrer de la Força 27; admission €2; 🕑 10am-2pm & 5-7pm Tue-Sat, 10am-2pm Sun) has displays covering everything from the city's Roman origins to the *sardana* (Catalonia's national round-dance) tradition.

MUSEU DEL CINEMA

The Casa de les Aigües houses Spain's only **cinema museum** (☎ 972 41 27 77; www.museudel cinema.org; Carrer del Perill 5; admission €3; 🕑 10am-8pm Tue-Sun May-Sep; 10am-6pm Tue-Fri, 10am-8pm Sat, 11am-3pm Sun Oct-Apr). The Col·lecció Tomàs Mallol includes not only displays tracing the history of cinema, but also a parade of hands-on items for indulging in shadow games, optical illusions and the like – it's great for kids.

Sleeping

Alberg-Residència Cerverí de Girona (☎ 972 21 80 03; Carrer dels Ciutadans 9; adult/student & under 26 Jul & Aug €19.40/17, rest of year €17.20/14.80; 🖳) A modern youth hostel, well placed in the old town, doubles for most of the year as a student residence.

Pensión Viladomat (☎ 972 20 31 76; Carrer dels Ciutadans 5; s/d €17/32, d with bathroom €55) This is one of the nicest of the cheaper *pensiones* scattered about the southern end of the old town.

Residència Bellmirall (☎ 972 20 40 09; Carrer de Bellmirall 3; s/d €33/58; 🔀) An attractive little place in a lovely medieval building. Rooms with shared bathroom are marginally cheaper.

Apartaments Històric Barri Vell (☎ 972 22 35 83; http//:historic.go.to; Carrer de Bellmirall 4; s/d €62.50/96.30) These small studio apartments are set in the heart of the old town and have the advantage of their own kitchen.

Hotel Històric (☎ 972 22 35 83; http//:historic .go.to; Carrer de Bellmirall 4; s/d €109/122; 🔀 🖳) Located in the same building as the Apartaments Històric Barri Vell, the owners have opened a bijou hotel with a handful of pretty rooms. Exposed stonework and timber ceilings are combined with modern comforts such as satellite TV and soundproofing.

Hotel Carlemany (☎ 972 21 12 12; www.carlemany .es; Plaça de Miquel Santaló; s/d €107/118.70; 🅿 🔀) In this, the city's top (if somewhat impersonal) hotel, spacious, carpeted and soundproofed rooms come with all the mod cons you would expect.

Eating

La Polenta (☎ 972 20 93 74; Carrer de la Cort Reial 6; meals €15-20; 🕑 Mon & Wed-Sat, lunch only Tue) For vegetarian goodies, this cheerful little place is a good option.

El Pou del Call (☎ 972 22 37 74; Carrer de la Força 14; meals €20; 🕑 Mon-Sat & lunch only Sun) This charming restaurant faces partly onto a little square off the main street in the heart of medieval Girona and serves up a mix of Franco-Catalan dishes.

Cipresaia (☎ 972 22 24 49; Carrer de Blas Fournàs 2; meals €25-30; 🕑 dinner only Fri-Sat, lunch only Mon-Wed & Sun) This tranquil, romantic option is one of the town favourites for the house specialities of paella and *fideuá*. Candle-lit dinners for two in the heart of the old town are on the menu too.

Restaurant Albereda (☎ 972 22 60 02; Carrer de l'Albereda 9; meals €35-40; 🕑 Tue-Sat & lunch only Mon) The elegant Albereda, Girona's most senior restaurant, serves classic Catalan cuisine with some rather interesting twists, such as the frogs' legs.

Entertainment

Students make the nightlife here, so in summer things calm down. Thursday is the big night of the week, as most people head for the coast on weekends.

El Cercle (☎ 972 22 45 29; Carrer del Ciutadans 8; 🕑 8-3am) Carved out of a medieval warren of stone arches and timber beams, this centuries-old house has been nicely converted into the perfect spot for a morning coffee or a late-night tipple.

Nummulit (☎ 972 21 51 68; Carrer del Nord 7; 🕑 10pm-3am) For mixed music and clientele, this is one of the most attractive bars in the centre of town. On some nights it warms up a little for dancers. Thursday is house night.

You can keep going until 3am near the river north of the old town, where streets such as Carrer de Palafrugell and Ronda de Pedret harbour several lively and varied music bars. **Silent Block** (☎ 972 22 74 62; Carrer de Palafrugell 20; 🕑 10.30pm-3am) is a good one. Tropical cocktails are the drink theme and you never know when you might run into an evening of alternative theatre or live music.

In summer (May to September), a series of **drinking tents** (*las carpas*) goes up in the park, west of the railway line. Across the road, the cybertechno **Sala del Ball** (Carrer del Riu Güell 2; 🕑 midnight-5am Thu-Sat) is Girona's Thursday-night disco-dance destination.

Getting There & Away
AIR
Girona's **airport** (☎ 972 18 66 00), 11km south of the centre, just off the AP7 and A2, has become Ryanair's Spanish hub for Barcelona. A couple of other airlines have followed suit. Barcelona Bus runs direct buses to/from Barcelona (see p317). Sarfa runs a couple of buses a day in summer, from the airport to coastal destinations, including Tossa de Mar (€8, one hour) and Roses (€13, one hour 20 minutes), as well as Figueres (€13, 55 minutes).

BUS
There are three to six daily services run by **Barcelona Bus** (☎ 902 130014) to/from Barcelona's Estació del Nord (€9.50, one hour 20 minutes) and Figueres (€3.90, one hour). **Teisa** (☎ 972 20 02 75; www.teisa-bus.com) runs up to eight services daily (four on Sunday) to Besalú (€3.80, 50 minutes) and Olot (€4.90, 1¼ hours).

TRAIN

Girona is on the railway line between Barcelona, Figueres and Portbou on the French border. There are more than 20 trains per day to Figueres (€2.15 to €2.50, 30 to 40 minutes) and Barcelona (€5.10 to €5.85, 1½ hours), and about 15 to Portbou and/or Cerbère (€3.30 to €3.80, 50 minutes to one hour).

Getting Around

Barcelona Bus services run into Girona from the airport (€1.75, 20 minutes) in connection with flights. A **taxi** (☎ 972 20 33 73, 972 22 23 33) to/from the airport costs around €15.

VERGES

pop 1150

About 15km east of Girona, this town has little to offer, but if you happen to be in the area on Holy Thursday (Easter) make an effort to see the rather macabre evening procession of the **Dansa de la Mort**. People dressed up as skeletons dance the Dance of Death through the streets as part of a much bigger procession enacting Christ's way to Calvary. The fun usually starts at about 10pm. Girona–Torroella buses pass through here.

TORROELLA DE MONTGRÍ

pop 6970

On the Riu Ter, about 30km northeast of Girona and 15km north of Palafrugell, the agreeable old town of Torroella de Montgrí is the funnel through which travellers to L'Estartit must pass.

Sights & Activities

Overlooking the town from the top of the 300m limestone Montgrí hills to the north, the impressive-but-empty **Castell de Montgrí** was built between 1294 and 1301 for King Jaume II, in his efforts to bring to heel the disobedient counts of Empúries, to the north. There's no road, and by foot it's a 40-minute climb from Torroella. Head north from Plaça del Lledoner along Carrer de Fàtima, at the end of which is a sign pointing the way.

In town itself, the **Centre Cultural de la Mediterrània** (☎ 972 75 51 80; Carrer d'Ullà 31; admission free; ☻ 11am-2pm & 5-8pm Wed-Sat & Mon, 11am-2pm Sun) is a local museum and cultural centre housed in the Can Quintana mansion.

The permanent exhibition on the 1st floor concentrates on local history, culture and music.

Getting There & Away

Ampsa (☎ 972 75 82 33; Plaça d'Espanya 19) runs buses about hourly (€1.10) to L'Estartit from June to September, and about half as often during the rest of the year. Sarfa has three or four daily buses to/from Barcelona's Estació del Nord (€14.40, up to 2½ hours).

L'ESTARTIT & THE ILLES MEDES

pop 2430

L'Estartit, 6km east of Torroella de Montgrí, has a long, wide beach of fine sand but nothing over any other Costa Brava package resort – except for the Illes Medes (Islas Medes). The group of rocky islets barely 1km offshore are home to some of the most abundant marine life on Spain's Mediterranean coast.

The main road in from Torroella de Montgrí is called Avinguda de Grècia as it approaches the beach; the beachfront road is Passeig Marítim, at the northern end of which is the **tourist office** (☎ 972 75 19 10; www .estartit.org; Passeig Marítim; ☻ 8am-9pm Mon-Sat, 10am-2pm Sun Jul-Aug; 9.30am-2pm & 4-8pm Mon-Sat, 10am-2pm Sun Jun & Sep; 9am-1pm & 3-6pm Mon-Fri, 10am-2pm Sat & Sun Oct-May).

Illes Medes

The shores and waters around these seven islets, an offshore continuation of the limestone Montgrí hills, have been protected since 1985 as a *reserva natural submarina* (underwater nature reserve), which has brought a proliferation in their marine life and made them Spain's most popular destination for snorkellers and divers. Some 1345 plant and animal species have been identified here. There's a big bird population too; one of the Mediterranean's largest colonies of yellow-legged gulls (8000 pairs) breeds here between March and May.

Kiosks by the harbour, at the northern end of L'Estartit beach, offer snorkelling and glass-bottomed boat trips to the islands. Other glass-bottomed boat trips go to a series of caves along the coast to the north, or combine these with the Medes. A two-hour snorkelling trip to the Illes Medes costs anything up to €20 per person. There are frequent daily trips, from June to

DIVING OFF THE COSTA BRAVA

The range of depths (down to 50m) and the number of underwater cavities and tunnels around the Illes Medes contribute much to their attraction. On and around rocks near the surface are colourful algae and sponges, as well as octopuses, crabs and various fish. Below 10m or 15m, cavities and caves harbour lobsters, scorpion fish and large conger eels and groupers. Some groupers and perch may feed from the hand. If you get down to the sea floor, you may see angler fish, thornback rays or marbled electric rays.

At least half a dozen outfits in L'Estartit can take you out scuba diving, at the Medes or off the mainland coast – the tourist office has lists of them. It's worth shopping around before taking the plunge. If you're already a qualified diver, a single two-hour trip usually costs between €25 and €27 per person. Full gear rental can cost €16 a day. Night dives are possible too (usually about €28.50). If you're a novice, you can do an introductory dive for around €45 or a full, five-day PADI Open Water Diver course for between €330 and €375 depending on the company and the time of year.

September and, depending on demand, in April, May and October. Snorkelling, diving and other activities all tend to cost more in the peak months of July and August.

Sleeping

Les Medes (☎ 972 75 18 05; www.campinglesmedes .com; Paratge Camp de l'Arbre; 2-person tent & car €25; ☼ Dec-Oct) Of the eight camping grounds in and around town, this is one of the better ones. It's in a leafy location nor far from the seaside and has its own pool and sauna. Even massages are available.

Hotel Les Illes (☎ 972 75 12 39; www.hotelle silles.com; Carrer de Les Illes 55; s/d with half-board €46/78) A decent place with comfortable, if unspectacular, rooms, all with sparkling bathroom and balcony. This is basically a divers' hangout that's in a good spot just back from the port.

Eating

The northern end of Passeig Marítim, by the roundabout, is swarming with eateries.

These places are all pretty similar, presenting a mix of basic Spanish fare and chicken-and-chips-style meals.

La Gaviota (☎ 972 75 20 19; Passeig Marítim 92; meals €20-25; ☼ Tue-Sun mid-Dec–mid Nov) In this no-nonsense sea-salty eatery – the local classic for great seafood – the chunky *sopa de peix* (fish soup) is the flagship dish.

Getting There & Around

Sarfa runs to/from Barcelona once daily (€14.40, 2¾ hours), rising to four times in peak season (July to August).

L'ESCALA
pop 6930

L'Escala, 11km north of Torroella de Montgrí, is a pleasant medium-sized resort on the southern shore of the Golf de Roses. It's close to the ancient town of Empúries (Ampurias in Castilian) and, about 10km further north, the wetlands of the Parc Natural dels Aiguamolls de l'Empordà.

Orientation & Information

If you arrive by Sarfa bus, you'll alight on L'Escala's Plaça de les Escoles, where you'll find the **tourist office** (☎ 972 77 06 03; Plaça de les Escoles 1; ☼ 8am-8.30pm Mon-Fri, 10am-2pm & 4-7pm Sat, 10am-1pm Sun Jul-Aug; 9am-8pm Mon-Fri, 10am-2pm & 4-7pm Sat, 10am-1pm Sun Jun & Sep; 9am-1pm & 4-7pm Mon-Sat, 10am-1pm Sun Oct-May). Empúries is 1km around the coast to the northwest of the town centre.

Empúries

Empúries was probably the first, and certainly one of the most important, Greek colonies on the Iberian Peninsula. Early Greek traders, pushing on from a trading post at Masilia (Marseille in France), set up a new post around 600 BC at what is now the charming village of Sant Martí d'Empúries, then an island. Soon afterwards they founded a mainland colony nearby, which came to be called Emporion (Market) and remained an important trading centre, and conduit of Greek culture to the Iberians, for centuries.

In 218 BC, Roman legions landed here to cut off Hannibal's supply lines in the Second Punic War. About 195 BC they set up a military camp and by 100 BC had added a town. A century later it had merged with the Greek one. Emporiae, as the place was then known, was abandoned in the late 3rd century AD, after raids by Germanic tribes. Later, an early Christian basilica and a cemetery stood on the site of the Greek town, before the whole place, after over a millennium of use, disappeared altogether, only to be discovered by archaeologists at the turn of the 20th century.

Many of the ancient stones now laid bare don't rise more than knee-high. You need a little imagination – and perhaps the aid of a taped commentary (€1.50 from the ticket office) – to make the most of it.

THE SITE

During spring and summer there's a pedestrian entrance to the **site** (☎ 972 77 02 08; adult/student/child under 7 & senior €2.40/1.80/free; ☼ 10am-8pm Jun-Sep, 10am-6pm Oct-May) from the seafront promenade in front of the ruins; just follow the coast from L'Escala to reach it. At other times the only way in is the vehicle approach from the Figueres road, about 1km from central L'Escala.

The **Greek town** lies in the lower part of the site, closer to the shore. Main points of interest include the thick southern defensive walls, the site of the Asklepion (a shrine to the god of medicine) with a copy of his statue found here, and the Agora (town square), with remnants of the early Christian basilica and the Greek *stoa* (market complex), beside it.

A small **museum** (Barcelona's Museu d'Arqueologia de Catalunya, p295) has a bigger and better Empúries collection) separates the Greek town from the larger Roman town on the upper part of the site. Highlights of the **Roman town** include the mosaic floors of a 1st-century-BC house, the Forum and ancient walls. Outside the walls are the remains of an oval amphitheatre.

A string of brown-sand beaches stretch along in front of the site. On one of them, 1.2km from L'Escala, stands a Greek stone jetty. Nearby is where the 1992 Olympic flame was landed in a remake of an ancient Greek vessel amid great theatrical circumstance.

Another few hundred metres north along the beaches from Empúries brings you to a wonderful and unexpected gem, the tiny 15th-century seaside hamlet of **Sant Martí d'Empúries**, all bright stone houses and cobbled lanes, right on the seaside. On Plaça Major four restaurant-bars compete for your attention under the watchful gaze of the strange, squat façade of the local church.

Sleeping

Hostal El Roser (☎ 972 77 02 19; Carrer de l'Església 7; s/d €32.10/49.60; P ☼) This is one of the best bets at the lower mid-range level in the heart of town. A cheerful corner block with restaurant and rooms upstairs, it is a friendly place. Rooms are straightforward but clean and welcoming. You can sun yourself on the terrace and there is wheelchair access.

Hotel Voramar (☎ 972 77 01 08; Passeig de Lluís Albert 2; s/d €51.70/92.90; ☼) This is a strikingly ugly building but the rooms are comfortable and the better ones offer sea views. It also has a little swimming pool across the road.

Eating

L'Escala is famous for its *anchoas* (anchovies) and fresh fish, both of which are likely to crop up on menus. Plenty of eateries are scattered along the waterfront parade of Port d'En Perris.

Restaurant El Roser II (☎ 972 77 11 02; Passeig Lluís Albert 1; meals €25-30; ☼ Thu-Tue) This is a good waterfront seafood eatery, ideal for a hearty lunch of grilled catch of the day and *suquet* (a fish-and-potato hotpot).

Getting There & Away

Sarfa has one bus from Barcelona (via Palafrugell) on weekdays (€14.40, up to 2¾ hours), and three on Sunday (four daily July to August). Buses also run to/from Girona.

PARC NATURAL DELS AIGUAMOLLS DE L'EMPORDÀ

This *parc natural* (nature park) preserves the remnants of marshes that once covered the whole coastal plain of the Golf de Roses, an important site for migrating birds. Birdwatchers have spotted over 100 species a day in the March to May and August to October migration periods, which bring big increases in the numbers of wading birds and even the occasional flamingo, glossy ibis, spoonbill or rare black stork. There are usually enough birds around to make a visit worthwhile at any time of year.

The best place to head for is the **El Cortalet information centre** (☎ 972 45 42 22; ☼ 9.30am-2pm & 4.30-7pm mid-Jun–mid-Sep, 9.30am-2pm & 3.30-6pm mid-Sep–mid-Jun), 1km east off the Sant Pere Pescador–Castelló d'Empúries road. Marked paths lead to a 2km stretch of beach and several *aguaits* (hides) with saltwater-marsh views. From the top of the **Observatori Senillosa**, a former silo, you can see out across the whole park. The paths are always open, but morning and evening are the best times for birds (and mosquitoes!).

The nearest places to El Cortalet that can be reached by bus are Sant Pere Pescador, 6km south (served by four or five Sarfa buses daily from L'Escala and Figueres), and Castelló d'Empúries, 4km north.

CASTELLÓ D'EMPÚRIES
pop 3490

This old town was the capital of Empúries, a medieval Catalan county that maintained a large degree of independence up to the 14th century. The finest monument here is the **Església de Santa Maria** (Plaça de Jacint Verdaguer), a large 13th- and 14th-century Gothic church with a fine Romanesque bell tower remaining from an earlier church on the site.

Hotel Canet (☎ 972 25 03 40; www.hotelcanet.com; Plaça del Joc de la Pilota 2; s/d with bathroom €48.15/64.20; P 🗐 🟦) is a modernised 17th-century mansion in the centre, with elegant rooms, low-slung stone arches and a sundeck. A soothing swimming pool glistens within the stone walls of the interior courtyard. They also run a decent restaurant offering mostly Catalan fare.

Sarfa runs from about 12 (fewer on Sundays and up to 28 in July and August) buses a day from Figueres (€1.10, 15 minutes), three or four (more in July and August) from Cadaqués (€2.75, 50 minutes) and up to two from Barcelona's Estació del Nord (€13.75, 1¾ hours).

ROSES & AROUND
pop 14,720

Some believe Roses is the site of an ancient Greek settlement, Rodes, although nothing remains to confirm the hypothesis. The town does boast the impressive seaward wall of its 16th-century citadel. Although this middling holiday town's beaches are OK, Roses is, above all, a handy base for going elsewhere.

With a vehicle, you can get well beyond the crowds of Roses into the southern end of Parc Natural del Cap de Creus. About 6km east of Roses, a road runs up into the hills and along the rugged coast to **Cala Montjoi**, with a pebbly beach and possibly Spain's most renowned restaurant, El Bulli (below).

Le Rachdingue (☎ 972 53 00 23; www.rachdingue .com; admission €10-15), about 8km northwest of Roses on the road to Vilajuïga, is one of the Costa Brava's club meccas. Big name DJs from around Europe are wheeled in to this *masia* (country house) to spin their sets of house, jungle and the like. Clubbers from all over the continent make a special effort to get here. It is especially active in summer (the pool comes in handy!), but opens on Saturday nights in winter too. The best way to find out what's happening is to call.

Sarfa buses from Barcelona run one to four times a day to Roses, depending on the day and season (€14.80, 1¾ hours). Plenty run between Roses and Figueres (€2.20, 30 minutes).

CADAQUÉS & AROUND
pop 2610

If you have time for only one stop on the Costa Brava, you can hardly do better than Cadaqués. A whitewashed village around a rocky bay, it and the surrounding area have a really special magic – a fusion of wind, sea, light and rock – that isn't dissipated even by the throngs of mildly fashionable summer visitors.

A portion of that magic owes itself to Salvador Dalí, who spent family holidays in Cadaqués during his youth, and lived much of his later life at nearby Port Lligat. The empty moonscapes, odd-shaped rocks and

CATALONIA

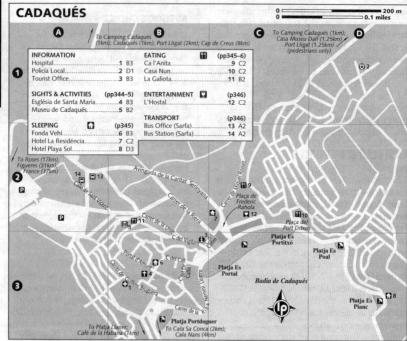

CADAQUÉS

INFORMATION
Hospital.........................1 B3
Policía Local...................2 D1
Tourist Office.................3 B3

SIGHTS & ACTIVITIES (pp344–5)
Església de Santa Maria....4 B3
Museu de Cadaqués........5 B2

SLEEPING (p345)
Fonda Vehí...................6 B3
Hotel La Residència.........7 C2
Hotel Playa Sol..............8 D3

EATING (pp345–6)
Ca l'Anita.....................9 C2
Casa Nun....................10 C2
La Galiota...................11 B2

ENTERTAINMENT (p346)
L'Hostal.....................12 C2

TRANSPORT (p346)
Bus Office (Sarfa)...........13 A2
Bus Station (Sarfa).........14 A2

barren shorelines that litter Dalí's paintings weren't just a product of his fertile imagination. They're strewn all round the Cadaqués area in what Dalí termed a 'grandiose geological delirium'.

The country here is drier than further south. The sparseness continues to dramatic Cap de Creus, 8km northeast of Cadaqués, lending itself to some coastscapes of almost (ahem) surreal beauty.

Thanks to Dalí and other luminaries, Cadaqués pulled in a celebrity crowd for decades. One visit by the poet Paul Éluard and his Russian wife, Gala, in 1929 caused an earthquake in Dalí's life: he ran off to Paris with Gala (who was to become his lifelong obsession and, later, wife) and joined the surrealist movement. In the 1950s the crowd he attracted was more jet-setting – Walt Disney, the Duke of Windsor and Greek ship-owner Stavros Niarchos. In the 1970s, Mick Jagger and Gabriel García Márquez popped by. Today the crowd is neither so creative, nor so famous – though a lot bigger – but Cadaqués' atmosphere remains.

Information
Hospital (☎ 972 25 88 07; Carrer de Guillem Bruguera) Just west of the church.
Policía Local (Local Police; ☎ 972 15 93 43; Carrer de Barcelona) Out of town, off the road to Port Lligat.
Tourist office (☎ 972 25 83 15; Carrer del Cotxe 2; 9am-2pm & 4-9pm Mon-Sat, 10.30am-1pm Sun Easter-Sep; 9.30am-1pm & 4-7pm Mon-Sat Oct-Easter) Just back from the waterfront.

The Town
Cadaqués is perfect for wandering, either around the town or along the coast. The 16th- and 17th-century **Església de Santa Maria**, with a gilded baroque *retablo* (altarpiece), is the focus of the older part of town with its narrow hilly streets.

The **Museu de Cadaqués** (☎ 972 25 28 77; Carrer de Narcís Monturiol 15; 10am-1.30pm & 4-8pm Sat-Thu) includes Dalí among other local artists. The admission fee depends on the temporary exhibition being held.

Beaches
Cadaqués' main beach, and several others along the nearby coast, are small, with more

pebbles than sand, but their picturesqueness and beautifully blue waters make up for that. Overlooking Platja Llaner, to the south of the town, centre is Dalí's parents' holiday home; out the front is a statue by Josep Subirachs, dedicated to Federico García Lorca, and in memory of his 1920s stay.

Port Lligat

Port Lligat, a 1.25km walk from Cadaqués, is a tiny settlement around another lovely bay, with fishing boats pulled up on its beach. Its **Casa Museu Dalí** (☎ 972 25 10 15; www .salvador-dali.org; Port Lligat; adult/student & senior €8/5; ⏱ 10.30am-9pm mid-Jun–mid-Sep; 10.30am-6pm Tue-Sun mid-Sep–mid-Jan & mid-Mar–mid-Jun) began as a fisherman's hut and was steadily altered and enlarged by Dalí, who lived here from 1930 to 1982, apart from a dozen or so years abroad during and around the Spanish Civil War. It's the house with a lot of little white chimney-pots and two egg-shaped towers, overlooking the western end of the beach. You must book ahead, sometimes several days in advance.

Cap de Creus

Cap de Creus is the most easterly point of the Spanish mainland and a place of sublime, rugged beauty. With a steep, rocky coastline indented by dozens of turquoise-watered coves, it's an especially wonderful place to be at dawn or sunset. Atop the cape stand a lighthouse and a good, mid-priced eatery Bar Restaurant Cap de Creus (p346) that also has accommodation (see below).

Walking

There are infinite possibilities for walking: out along the promontory between Cadaqués and Port Lligat; to Port Lligat and beyond; along the southern side of the Cadaqués Bay to the Far de Cala Nans; or over the hills south of Cadaqués to the coast east of Roses.

Sleeping

Camping Cadaqués (☎ 972 25 81 26; Carretera de Port Lligat 17; 2-person tent & car €22; ⏱ Apr-Sep; ⌨) About 1km from central Cadaqués, on the road to Port Lligat, is this fairly straightforward place to pitch a tent; it can get crowded in summer. For relief from the heat, jump into the pool.

Fonda Vehí (☎ 972 25 84 70; Carrer de l'Església 5; s without bathroom €20, d with/without bathroom €45/32) Near the church in the heart of the old

town, this simple but engaging *pensión* tends to be booked up for July and August. It is easily the cheapest deal in town, and popular because of its position and decent restaurant.

Hotel La Residència (☎ 972 25 83 12; www .laresidencia.net; Avinguda de la Caritat Serinyana 1; s/d €96.30/112.35; P ✖) Right in the heart of the town, with just a dozen good-sized rooms, this hotel oozes history. It opened its doors in 1904 and Picasso stayed here six years later. Nowadays the place has a studied, classy air. A beautiful stained-glass ceiling creates a light well in the main staircase, and decorative details range from Dalí to rococo. The best rooms look directly out to sea. For those with more-elastic bank accounts there are a few suites.

Hotel Playa Sol (☎ 972 25 81 00; www.playasol.com; Platja Es Pianc 3; s/d €116.60/182; P ✖ ⌨) Located on the eastern side of the bay, this sprawling hotel offers spacious rooms with cable TV and a tree-lined pool. Room prices vary according to position (those with sea views are the dearest) and, predictably, season. The hotel hires out mountain bikes.

Bar Restaurant Cap de Creus (☎ 972 19 90 05; Cap de Creus; apartments €85) These apartments, which sleep four people, are upstairs from the mid-range eatery. They're fairly simple, but have attached bathrooms. What makes the place special is its privileged position at the edge of the country's easternmost cape.

Eating

Casa Nun (☎ 972 25 88 56; Plaça del Port Ditxos 6; meals €25-30; ⏱ Fri-Mon, dinner only Tue-Thu Easter-Oct; Fri-Mon, dinner only Thu Nov-Easter) Head for the cute little upstairs dining area or take one of the few tables outside overlooking the port. Try the *lluç farcit de gambes* (hake stuffed with prawns).

Ca l'Anita (☎ 972 25 84 71; Carrer de Miquel Roset 16; meals €20-25) This busy, ebullient place, where customers often find themselves elbow to elbow with perfect strangers, has built a name for its tasty grilled fish and other seafood delights.

La Galiota (☎ 972 25 81 87; Carrer de Narcís Monturiol 9; meals €25-30; ⏱ Thu-Tue Jun-Sep; Sat & Sun Easter-May, Oct & Nov) Hidden away upstairs in a cosy house, this place was a favourite with Dalí and writer Josep Pla. You can indulge in a wide range of local cooking, encompassing seafood and meat dishes.

CATALONIA

Bar Restaurant Cap de Creus (☎ 972 19 90 05; Cap de Creus; meals €15) Bizarrely, at this good mid-range eatery, you can get a fine curry or settle for cheesecake.

Entertainment
L'Hostal (Passeig; ☺ Mar-Oct) Facing the beachfront boulevard, this classic has live music on many nights. One evening, in the 1970s an effusive Dalí called L'Hostal the *lugar más bonito del mundo* ('the most beautiful place on earth').

Café de la Habana (☎ 972 25 86 89; Carrer de Dr Bartomeus, Punta d'En Pampa; ☺ 9pm-2.30am Easter-Oct, 9pm-2.30am Fri-Sun Nov-Easter) One kilometre south of town, this icon of Cadaqués' nightlife can get lively with Latin-music nights, art exhibitions and cool cocktails.

Getting There & Away
Sarfa buses to/from Barcelona (€16.20, 2¼ hours) leave two times daily (sometimes more frequently in July and August). Buses also run to/from Figueres (€3.65, one hour) up to seven times daily (three in winter) via Castelló d'Empúries.

CADAQUÉS TO THE FRENCH BORDER
If you want to prolong the journey to France, **El Port de la Selva** and **Llançà** are pleasant-enough minor beach resorts-cum-fishing towns, and both have a range of accommodation. **Portbou**, on the French frontier, is less enticing. From El Port de la Selva you can undertake a wild and woolly walk along the rugged coast. The trail, which is awkward at some points, leads east to Cap de Creus.

A more spectacular stop is the **Monestir de Sant Pere de Rodes** (☎ 972 38 75 59; adult/student €3.60/2.40, admission free Tue; ☺ 10am-8pm Tue-Sun Jun–end Sep; 10am-5.30pm Tue-Sun end Sep–May), a classic piece of Romanesque architecture looming 500m up in the hills southwest of El Port de la Selva, with great views. Founded in the 8th century, it later became the most powerful monastery between Figueres and Perpignan in France. The great triple-naved, barrel-vaulted basilica is flanked by the fine square Torre de Sant Miquel bell tower and a two-level cloister.

Getting There & Away
The monastery is on a back road over the hills between Vilajuïga, 8km to its west, and El Port de la Selva, 5km northeast. Each town is served by at least one Sarfa bus from Figueres daily, but there are no buses to the monastery. Vilajuïga is also on the railway between Figueres and Portbou.

FIGUERES
pop 36,010

Twelve kilometres inland from the Golf de Roses, Figueres (Figueras in Castilian) is a humdrum town (some might say a dive) with a single, very big attraction: Salvador Dalí. In the 1960s and '70s Dalí created here, in the town of his birth, the extraordinary Teatre-Museu Dalí. Whatever your feelings about old Salvador, this is worth every minute you can spare.

Information
Tourist office (☎ 972 50 31 55; Plaça del Sol; ☺ 9am-9pm Mon-Sat, 9am-3pm Sun Jun–mid-Sep; 9am-2pm & 4.30-8pm Mon-Fri, 10am-2pm & 3.30-6.30pm Sat, 10am-2pm Sun mid-Sep–May) Has information on the city and surrounding area.

Policía Nacional (Carrer de Pep Ventura 8) Handily located near the centre.

Creu Roja (Red Cross; ☎ 972 50 17 99; Carrer de Santa Llogàia 67) For medical emergencies; near the post office.

Hospital (☎ 972 67 50 89; Ronda del Rector Aroles)

Sights
TEATRE-MUSEU DALÍ
Salvador Dalí was born in Figueres in 1904. Although his career took him to Madrid, Barcelona, Paris and the USA, he remained true to his roots and lived well over half his adult life at Port Lligat, east of Figueres on the coast. Between 1961 and 1974 Dalí converted Figueres' former municipal theatre, ruined by a fire at the end of the civil war in 1939, into the **Teatre-Museu Dalí** (☎ 972 67 75 00; www.salvador-dali .org; adult/student incl Dalí Joies €9/6.50, night sessions €11; ☺ 9am-7.45pm Jul-Sep, 10.30am-5.45pm Tue-Sun Oct-Jun, night sessions 10pm-1am Jul-Sep). 'Theatre-museum' is an apt label for this multidimensional trip through one of the most fertile (or disturbed) imaginations of the 20th century. It's full of surprises, tricks and illusions, and contains a substantial portion of his life's work. Readers have reported that queues can get so long, that opening hours have been extended, on an ad hoc basis. There is a limit of 500 people for night sessions.

Even outside, the building aims to surprise, from the collection of bizarre sculptures outside the entrance, on Plaça de Gala

FIGUERES

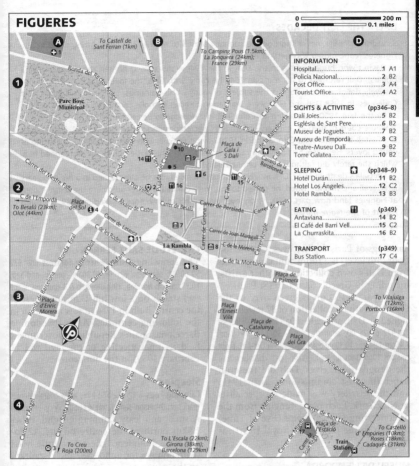

i Salvador Dalí, to the pink wall along Pujada del Castell, topped by a row of Dalí's trademark egg shapes and what appear to be female gymnast sculptures, and studded with what look like loaves of bread.

Inside, the ground floor (1st level) includes a semicircular garden area on the site of the original theatre stalls. In its centre is a classic piece of weirdness called *Taxi Plujós* (Rainy Taxi), composed of an early Cadillac – said to have belonged to Al Capone – and a pile of tractor tyres, both surmounted by statues, with a fishing boat balanced precariously above the tyres. Put a coin in the slot and water washes all over the inside of the car. The **Sala de Peixateries** (Fish Shop Room) off here holds a collection of Dalí oils, including the famous *Autoretrat Tou amb Tall de Bacon Fregit* (Self-Portrait with Fried Bacon) and *Retrat de Picasso* (Portrait of Picasso). Beneath the former stage of the theatre is the crypt, with Dalí's plain tomb.

If proof were needed of Dalí's acute sense of the absurd, *Gala Mirando el Mar Mediterráneo* (Gala Looking at the Mediterranean Sea) on the 2nd level would be it. With the help of coin-operated viewfinders, the work appears, from the other end of the room, to be a portrait of Abraham Lincoln.

One floor up (3rd level) the **Sala de Mae West** is a living room whose components, viewed from the right spot, make up a portrait of Ms West: a sofa for her lips, twin fireplaces for the nostrils, impressionist

DALÍ – THE LAST DECADES

Salvador Dalí's life, never short on the surreal, seemed to tip over the edge during the time the Figueres *teatre-museu* was getting under way.

Having won huge success in the USA in the 1940s (and earned himself the anagram Avida Dollars), Dalí returned to his roots. In 1948 he came with Gala, the lover to whom he was obsessively devoted and who was the subject of many of his paintings, to live at Port Lligat near Cadaqués. In 1958 Dalí and Gala were married in a secret Catholic ceremony.

By the late 1960s, according to Colm Tóibín's *Homage to Barcelona* (1990), the couple had 'a whole court of helpers, hangers-on, advisers, secretaries and sexual performers'. Dalí bought the Castell de Púbol near Girona and in 1970 gave it to Gala, who was now enjoying a string of young lovers. He masochistically contracted never to visit the castle unless she summoned him, which she rarely did (although she phoned daily).

On Gala's death in 1982, Dalí moved into Púbol himself, but he almost died in a fire two years later. Frail and malnourished, he retired to the Torre Galatea, a tower adjoining the *teatre-museu* at Figueres (and now part of it), hardly ever leaving his room before he died in 1989. His tomb is part of the *teatre-museu*.

---

paintings of Paris for her eyes. On the top floor (5th level) is a room containing works from Dalí's own collection by other artists, including El Greco's *Sant Pau* (St Paul).

A separate section is given over to the Owen Cheatham collection of 37 jewels, designed by Dalí, and called **Dalí Joies** (Dalí Jewels; ☎ 972 67 75 00; adult/student €4.50/3.50; ☯ 9am-7.45pm Jul-Sep, 10.30am-5.45pm Tue-Sun Oct-Jun, night sessions 10pm-1am Jul-Sep). Also on display are the designs themselves. Dalí did these on paper (his first commission was in 1941) and the jewellery was made by specialists in New York. Each piece, ranging from the disconcerting *Ull del Temps* (Eye of Time) through to the *Cor Reial* (Royal Heart), is unique.

MUSEU DE L'EMPORDÀ

This local **museum** (☎ 972 50 23 05; La Rambla 2; adult/student €2/1, admission free with a Teatre-Museu Dalí ticket; ☯ 11am-7pm Tue-Sat, 11am-2pm Sun & holidays) combines Greek, Roman and medieval archaeological finds with a sizable collection of art, mainly by Catalan artists, but there are also some works on loan from the Prado in Madrid.

MUSEU DE JOGUETS

Spain's only **toy museum** (☎ 972 50 45 85; www .mjc-figueres.net; La Rambla 10; adult/student €4.70/3.80; ☯ 10am-1pm & 4-7pm Tue-Sat, 11am-1.30pm Sun & holidays Oct-May; 10am-1pm & 4-7pm Tue-Sat, 11am-1.30pm & 5-7pm Sun & holidays Jun-Sep) has more than 3500 Catalonia- and Valencia-made toys from the pre-Barbie 19th and early 20th centuries.

CASTELL DE SANT FERRAN

The sprawling 18th-century **fortress** (☎ 972 50 60 94; admission €2; ☯ 10.30am-8pm Jul-mid-Sep, 10.30am-2pm Nov-Feb, 10.30am-2pm & 4-6pm rest of the year) stands on a low hill 1km northwest of the centre. Built in 1750, it saw no action in the following centuries. After abandoning Barcelona, Spain's Republican government held its final meeting of the civil war (1 February 1939) in the dungeons.

Sleeping

Camping Pous (☎ 972 67 54 96; www.androl.internet -park.net; 2-person tent & car €21.50; ☯ year-round) A small and leafy camping ground, it lies 1.5km north of the centre on the A2 towards La Jonquera. There is a little hotel (with doubles for up to €48) and restaurant on the same site.

Hotel Los Ángeles (☎ 972 51 06 61; www.hotelan geles.com; Carrer de la Barceloneta 10; s/d €35.50/47.80; **P** ☒ ☐) Rooms are all much the same in this spick-and-span place. White walls, brown floor tiles and sparkling attached bathroom are standard throughout. Parking costs €6.

Hotel Rambla (☎ 972 67 60 20; www.hotelrambla .net; La Rambla 33; s/d up to €75/85; **P** ☒ ☐) Hiding behind an 1860 façade right in the heart of town on the central boulevard, this hotel has pleasant rooms with crisp décor in blues and beiges. Parking costs €6.

Hotel Durán (☎ 972 50 12 50; www.hotelduran.com; Carrer de Lasauca 5; s/d €62/87.75; **P** ☒) Tradition marks out this other key central option. With one of the best restaurants in town on the premises, it has an advantage over much of the competition. It has been going since the late 19th century (on the site, it is said, of a wayside inn as far back as the 17th century) and offers comfortable, old-world rooms.

Eating

Hotel Durán (☎ 972 50 12 50; Carrer de Lasauca 5; meals €30-40) More than a century of tradition has not tired the Durán clan of serving up fine traditional food. Frequently the stage of gastronomic events, it serves up such Catalan affairs as *conill rostit amb cargols* (roast rabbit with snails).

La Churraskita (☎ 972 50 15 52; Carrer Magre 5; meals €15) This is the place for South American style big-as-your-head servings of slabs of meat with tangy accompanying sauces.

Antaviana (☎ 972 51 03 77; Carrer de Llers 5; meals €20-25; ☽ Tue-Sun) For a good mix of Mediterranean cooking, with some enticing seafood options and light meals, this is a tasty bet.

El Café del Barri Vell (☎ 972 50 57 76; Plaça de les Patates 7; ☽ Tue-Sun) A quick stroll away from the tourist hordes on Carrer de la Jonquera (where several cheapie eateries line up), this is a pleasant café on 'Potatoes Square'.

Getting There & Away

Sarfa serves Castelló d'Empúries (€1.10) 10 to 20 times daily and Cadaqués (€3.65, one hour) up to eight times daily.

Figueres is on the railway line between Barcelona, Girona and Portbou on the French border, and there are regular connections to Girona (€2.05 to €2.40, 30 to 40 minutes) and Barcelona (€7.05 to €8.05, 2¼ hours) and to Cerbère and the French border (€1.60 to €1.85, 25 minutes).

AROUND FIGUERES

It's hard to imagine that just a few kilometres outside Figueres, such pleasant country should soothe the eyes. Take the C252 road northeast out of town for a refreshing excursion.

In **Vilabertran**, 2.5km northeast of central Figueres, there is what started life as an Augustinian **convent** (☎ 972 50 87 87; admission €2.40, free Tue; ☽ 10am-1.30pm & 3-6.30pm Tue-Sun Jun-Sep, 10am-1.30pm & 3-5.30pm Oct-May). The 11th-century Romanesque church, with its three naves and fine Lombard bell tower is outstanding. Also of great charm is the cloister.

AUTHOR'S CHOICE

Five kilometres southwest of Figueres on the road to Olot, and near the village of Avinyonet de Puigventós, is the breathtaking country hotel and restaurant, **Mas Pau** (☎ 972 54 61 54; www.maspau.com; s/d €89.90/102.75; P ☒ ☲). With its stone and ochre plaster walls, shady timber verandah and peaceful gardens, it makes a perfect rural getaway. Rooms are immaculate, with antique furnishings and art on the walls. There are some more luxurious suites too. The **restaurant** (meals €60-80; ☽ lunch & dinner Wed-Sat, lunch Sun, dinner Tue) is a paradise of delicate flavours, with local products lovingly arranged into *haute cuisine* masterpieces.

Five kilometres up the road, the pretty town of **Peralada** is known for the 16th-century **Castell-Palau dels Rocabertí**. The castle with its round towers has a rather French air and is given over to a casino and restaurant. The only way in, if you're not eating or gambling, is to turn up for a classical-music performance during the annual **Festival del Castell de Peralada** (☎ 93 503 86 46; www.festivalperalada.com; Carrer de Sant Joan s/n; ☽ Jul-Aug) in summer.

BESALÚ
pop 2070

In the 10th and 11th centuries, pretty Besalú was the capital of an independent county that stretched as far west as Cerdanya before it came under Barcelona's control in 1111.

Most picturesque of all is the view of the village across the tall, crooked 11th-century **Pont Fortificat** (Fortified Bridge), with its two tower gates, from the southern side of the Fluvià.

The **tourist office** (☎ 972 59 12 40; Plaça de la Llibertat; ☽ 10am-2pm & 4-7pm) is on the arcaded central square. It has a decent map-brochure, sells €1 tickets for the **Miqvé** (a 12th-century Jewish ritual bath by the river) and offers worthwhile guided visits to the Miqvé, the bridge and the Romanesque **Església de Sant Vicenç**, which is otherwise normally closed. Have a look at the 11th-century Romanesque church of the **Monestir de Sant Pere**, with an unusual ambulatory (walkway) behind the altar, and the 12th-century Romanesque **Casa Cornellà**.

Sleeping & Eating

There are a couple of cheap *pensiones* in town. Otherwise try **Els Jardins de la Martana** (☎ 972 59 00 09; www.lamartana.com; s/d with breakfast €77/114; P ⊠ 🖳), a charming mansion set on the out-of-town end of the grand old bridge. It offers well-appointed rooms, many with views from little balconies across the bridge to the town, comfortable sitting rooms and peaceful garden terraces.

Els Fogons de Can Llaudes (☎ 972 59 08 58; Prat de Sant Pere 6; meals €35) Opposite the Monestir de Sant Pere awaits this fine restaurant set in an elegant stone former chapel. Try the *solomillo*, a tender loin slab of beef bathed in a raisin-based sauce. It is best to book 24 hours in advance.

Getting There & Away

The N260 road from Figueres to Olot meets the C66 from Girona at Besalú. See the Girona section (p339) and Olot (p351) for information on Teisa bus services to Besalú.

THE PYRENEES

The Pyrenees in Catalonia aren't as high as those in neighbouring Aragón, but they still encompass some awesomely beautiful mountains and valleys. Above all, the Parc Nacional d'Aigüestortes i Estany de Sant Maurici, in the northwest, is a jewel-like area of lakes and dramatic peaks. The area's highest peak, the Pica d'Estats, also makes for a spectacular hike past pretty lakes to arrive at a privileged point with 360-degree views over France and Spain.

Aside from the natural beauty of the mountains, and the obvious attractions of walking, skiing and other sports, the Catalan Pyrenees and their foothills also have a rich cultural heritage, notably many lovely Romanesque churches and monasteries, often tucked away in surprisingly remote valleys. These are mainly the product of a time of prosperity and optimism in these regions in the 11th and 12th centuries, after Catalonia had broken ties with France in AD 988 and as the Muslim threat from the south receded.

WEST CATALAN PYRENEES

OLOT

pop 26,710

The hills around Olot are little more than pimples, but those pimples are the volcanoes of the Parc Natural de la Zona Volcànica de la Garrotxa. Admittedly they're either extinct or dormant, but one erupted as recently as 11,500 years ago.

Information

Casal dels Volcans (☎ 972 26 62 02; Avinguda de Santa Coloma de Farners; ☼ 9am-2pm & 4-6pm Mon-Fri, 10am-2pm & 4-6pm Sat, 10am-2pm Sun) For information about the Parc Natural de la Zona Volcànica de la Garrotxa. It's in the Jardí Botànic, 1km southwest of Plaça de Clarà.

Patronat Municipal de Turisme (☎ 972 26 01 41; Carrer del Bisbe Lorenzana 15; ☼ 10am-2pm & 5-8pm Mon-Fri, 10am-2pm Sat & Sun late Jun–late Sep; 9am-2pm & 5-7pm Mon-Fri, 10am-2pm & 5-7pm Sat, 11am-2pm Sun late Sep–late Jun) Opposite the bus station; it has a decent town map.

Sights

The **Museu Comarcal de la Garrotxa** (☎ 972 27 91 30; Carrer de l'Hospici 8; adult/senior/student & child combined with Museu dels Volcans €3/1.50/free; ☼ 11am-2pm & 4-7pm Mon & Wed-Sat, 11am-2pm Sun & holidays) covers Olot's growth as an early textile centre and includes a collection of local 19th-century art.

The **Jardí Botànic**, a botanical garden of Olot-area flora, contains the interesting **Museu dels Volcans** (☎ 972 26 67 62; adult/senior/student & child combined with Museu Comarcal de la Garrotxa €3/1.50/free; ☼ 10am-2pm & 4-6pm Mon & Wed-Sat, 10am-2pm Sun & holidays), which covers local flora and fauna as well as volcanoes and earthquakes.

Four **volcanoes** stand sentry on the fringes of Olot. Head for Volcà Montsacopa, 500m north of the centre, or Volcà La Garrinada, 1km northeast of the centre. In both cases paths climb to their craters.

Sleeping & Eating

Torre Malagrida (☎ 972 26 42 00; Passeig de Barcelona 15; dm adult/under 26 €18/14.90) This youth hostel is set in an unusual early 20th-century Modernista building surrounded by gardens. The accommodation is unadorned dorm-style and you can purchase meals and rent bicycles.

Aparthotel Perla D'Olot (☎ 972 26 23 26; www.turismegarrotxa.com/hperla; Avinguda de Santa Coloma de Farners 97; s/d €33.90/56.80; P ✄) The rooms in this comfortable hotel come with their own kitchenette.

Els Ossos (☎ 972 26 61 34; meals €25-30; ☼ Fri-Tue, lunch only Wed) About 2.5km out of town on the road to Santa Pau, this is one of the locals' favourite spots for good old-fashioned hearty Catalan cooking. The *ànec amb peres* (duck cooked in pears) is typical of the kind of country dishes to expect.

Getting There & Away

Teisa (☎ 972 26 01 96) runs buses to/from Barcelona, up to seven times a day (€12.70, two to 2½ hours) and Girona via Besalú up to eight times a day (€4.90, 1¼ hours). The easiest approach by car from Barcelona is by the AP7 and C63.

PARC NATURAL DE LA ZONA VOLCÀNICA DE LA GARROTXA

The park completely surrounds Olot but the most interesting area is between Olot and the village of Santa Pau, 10km southeast.

Volcanic eruptions began here about 350,000 years ago and the most recent one, at Volcà del Croscat, happened 11,500 years

OUT & ABOUT IN THE PYRENEES

The Catalan Pyrenees provide magnificent walking and trekking. You can undertake strolls of a few hours, or day walks that can be strung together into treks of several days. Nearly all of these can be done without camping gear, with nights spent in villages or *refugis* (mountain shelter).

Most of the *refugis* mentioned in this chapter are run by two Barcelona alpine clubs, the **Federació d'Entitats Excursionistes de Catalunya** (FEEC; ☎ 93 412 07 77; www.feec.org) and the **Centre Excursionista de Catalunya** (CEC; ☎ 93 315 23 11; www.cec-centre.org). A night in a *refugi* costs around €12. Normally FEEC *refugis* allow you to cook, CEC ones don't. Moderately priced meals are often available.

The coast-to-coast GR11 long-distance path traverses the entire Pyrenees from Cap de Creus on the Costa Brava to Hondarribia on the Bay of Biscay. Its route across Catalonia goes by way of La Jonquera, Albanyà, Beget, Setcases, the Vall de Núria, Planoles, Puigcerdà, Andorra, south of Catalonia's highest peak, Pica d'Estats (3143m), over to the Parc Nacional d'Aigüestortes i Estany de Sant Maurici, then on to the southern flank of the Val d'Aran and into Aragón.

The best season for walking in the high Pyrenees is from late June to early September. Earlier than that, snow can make things difficult, and avalanches are possible. Later, the weather can turn poor. It can get very hot even at high altitudes in midsummer, but nowhere in the Pyrenees is the weather reliable; even in July and August you can get plenty of rainy days and cloud – and cold at high altitude.

For detailed route descriptions and advice on equipment and preparation, get a hold of Lonely Planet's *Walking in Spain*. Local advice from tourist offices, park rangers, mountain *refugis* and other walkers is also invaluable and you should look out for hiking maps of the kind mentioned in the Directory (p841).

There's boundless scope for **climbing** – Pedraforca in the Serra del Cadí offers some of the most exciting ascents. For more information on walking and trekking in Spain, see the Spain Outdoors chapter (p78).

ago. In the park there are about 30 volcanic cones, up to 160m high and 1.5km wide. Together with the lush vegetation, a result of fertile soils and a damp climate, these create a landscape of unusual beauty. Between the woods are crop fields, a few hamlets and scattered old stone farmhouses.

The main information office for the park is the **Casal dels Volcans** in Olot. Another is the **Centre d'Informació Can Serra** (☎ 972 19 50 74), beside the GI524 Olot–Banyoles road 4.5km from the centre of Olot.

The old part of **Santa Pau** village, picturesquely perched on a rocky outcrop, contains a porticoed plaza, the Romanesque Església de Santa Maria, and a locked-up baronial castle.

Castellfollit de la Roca, on the N260 about 8km northeast of Olot, stands atop a crag composed of several layers of petrified lava – it's most easily viewed from the road north of the village.

Several good marked **walks**, which you can complete in less than a day, allow you to explore the park with ease. Inquire at the park information offices about routes.

Just off the GI524, and close to the most interesting parts of the park, are some pleasant, small country camping grounds. Wild camping is banned throughout the Garrotxa district, which stretches from east of Besalú to west of Olot, and from the French border to south of Sant Feliu de Pallerols. **Camping La Fageda** (☎ 972 27 12 39; www .campinglafageda.com; Batet de la Serra; 2-person tent & car €16.90; 🏊), 4km east of the centre of Olot, is a leafy ground with a pool, picnic areas and a children's playground.

RIPOLL
pop 9590

Ripoll, 30km west of Olot and in the next valley, is a shabby industrial town. However, it can claim, with some justice, to be the birthplace of Catalonia. At its heart, in the Monestir de Santa Maria, is one of the finest pieces of Romanesque art in Spain.

In the 9th century, Ripoll was the power base from which the local strongman, Guifré el Pilós (Wilfred the Hairy), succeeded in uniting several counties of the Frankish March along the southern side of the

Pyrenees. Guifré went on to become the first Count (Comte) of Barcelona. To encourage repopulation of the Pyrenees valleys, he founded the Monestir de Santa Maria, the most powerful monastery of medieval Catalonia.

Orientation & Information

The **tourist office** (☎ 972 70 23 51; Plaça del Abat Oliba; ✆ 9.30am-1.30pm & 4-7pm Mon-Sat, 10am-2pm Sun) is by the Ribes de Freser–Sant Joan de les Abadesses road, which runs through the north of town. The Monestir de Santa Maria is virtually next door.

Monestir de Santa Maria

Following its founding in AD 879, the monastery grew rapidly rich, big and influential. From the mid-10th to mid-11th centuries it was Catalonia's spiritual and cultural heart. A five-naved basilica was built, and adorned in about 1100 with a stone portal that ranks among the high points of Romanesque art. Two fires had left the basilica in ruins by 1885, after which it was restored in a rather gloomy imitation of its former glory. The most interesting feature inside is the restored tomb of Guifré el Pilós.

You can visit the basilica and its great **portal** (admission free; ✆ 8am-1pm & 3-8pm), now protected by a wall of glass. A chart near the portal (in Catalan) helps to interpret the feast of sculpture: a medieval vision of the universe, from God the Creator, in the centre at the top, to the month-by-month scenes of daily rural life on the innermost pillars.

Down a few steps, to the right of the doorway, is the monastery's beautiful **claustre** (cloister; admission €2; ✆ 10am-1pm & 3-7pm). It's a two-storey affair, created in the 12th to 15th centuries.

Sleeping & Eating

Hostal Paula (☎ 972 70 00 11; Carrer de Berenguer 8; s/d €22.50/53.50) This friendly family establishment is barely a stone's throw from the Monestir de Santa Maria. It has modern rooms with sparkling bathrooms.

Hostal del Ripollès (☎ 972 70 02 15; www.el ripolles.com/hostaldelripolles; Plaça Nova 11; s/d €32/51) The renovated rooms in this central hostal, overlooking a town square, all have bathrooms, and are light and spotless.

Can Nerol (☎ 972 70 18 94; Carrer del Pla d'Ordina 11; meals €30; ✆ lunch only Sun-Fri, dinner only Sat) In a lovely house surrounded by gardens, this restaurant serves a mix of Catalan and French cooking. You'll need to ask for directions at the tourist office: from Carretera de Ribes follow the winding lane of Carrer dels Hortolans down to the Riu Freser and cross the bridge. Turn right and head upstream to the highway overpass – the restaurant is just beyond it.

Getting There & Away

The bus and train stations are almost side by side on Carrer del Progrés, 600m southeast of the centre. Connections with Barcelona, Ribes de Freser and Puigcerdà are all better by train than bus (although problems on the line have meant on occasion that trains are replaced by buses anyway!). About 12 trains a day run to/from Barcelona (€5.10, two hours), up to nine to Ribes de Freser (€1.20, 20 minutes) and five to Puigcerdà (€2.70, 1¼ hours).

AROUND RIPOLL

A short way north of Ripoll, the GI401 branches west from Campdevànol, passes through Gombrèn and then proceeds in twisting and turning fashion on to **La Pobla de Lillet**, set a short way below the source of one of Catalonia's more important rivers, the Llobregat.

The grey stone village started life as a Roman outpost and grew to some importance as a local agricultural centre. People still cross its beautiful 12th-century Romanesque bridge and the town is also known for its delightful **Jardins Artigas**, a Modernista landscaped garden spread out along the river.

Follow the road up into the mountains from La Pobla de Lillet to the source of the Llobregat. Just half a kilometre on and you reach the charming mountain hamlet of **Castellar de n'Hug**, over the shoulder from the La Molina ski resort (see p358). The hamlet was founded in the 13th century under the lords of Mataplana (based in Gombrèn). A tight web of alleys is bundled around the Romanesque **Església de Santa Maria** (much remodelled over the centuries), and from the square by the church you look north across a valley to the bare mountains beyond.

Six simple *pensiones* are gathered about the hamlet, three of them on Plaça Major. Most have a bar attached, where you can get something to eat.

One **Transports Mir** (☎ 972 70 30 12) bus a day (except Sunday) runs between Ripoll and Bagà via Campdevànol, Gombrèn, Castellar de N'Hug and La Pobla de Lillet. The whole journey takes 1½ hours.

VALL ALTO DEL TER

This upper part of the Riu Ter valley reaches northeast from Ripoll to the small pleasant towns of Sant Joan de les Abadesses and Camprodon, then northwest to the modest **Vallter 2000 ski centre** (☎ 972 13 60 75; www.vallter 2000.com), just below the French border and at 2150m. It has 12 pistes of all grades, nine lifts and a ski school, but snow can be unreliable. A day's lift pass is €23. The area makes a more pleasant overnight stop than Ripoll, and from the upper reaches there are some excellent walks to the Vall de Núria. Get the Editorial Alpina *Puigmal* map-guide.

The C38 road leaves the Ter valley at Camprodon to head over the 1513m Collado d'Ares into France.

Sant Joan de les Abadesses
pop 3600

In Sant Joan de les Abadesses the restored 12th-century **bridge** over the Ter, and the **Museu del Monestir** (☎ 972 72 00 13; Plaça de l'Abadessa; admission €1; ☉ 10am-2pm & 4-6pm Oct-Apr, 10am-2pm & 4-7pm May-Jun & Sep, 10am-7pm Jul & Aug) are worth a look. This monastery, another founded by Guifré el Pilós, began life as a nunnery but the nuns were expelled in 1017

for alleged licentious conduct. Its elegant 12th-century church contains the marvellous *Santíssim Misteri*, a 13th-century polychrome woodcarving of the descent from the cross, composed of seven life-size figures. Also remarkable is the Gothic *retablo* of Santa Maria La Blanca, carved in alabaster. The elegant 15th-century late-Gothic cloister is charming.

Hostal Janpere (☎ 972 72 00 77; Carrer del Mestre Andreu 3; s/d with bathroom €20/40), a simple family hostal in Sant Joan de les Abadesses, has good if somewhat clinical rooms. Prices haven't budged in years!

Teisa (☎ 972 70 20 95) operates up to seven buses daily from Ripoll to Sant Joan de les Abadesses (€1, 15 minutes). One daily bus runs from Barcelona (Carrer de Pau Claris 117) at 7.15pm to Camprodon via Ripoll (€7.85, two hours).

Beget

Capping the end of a winding mountain lane that trails off here into a heavily wooded valley, this hamlet is a joy. The 12th-century Romanesque church is accompanied by an implausible array of roughly hewn houses, all scattered about stone-paved lanes. Through it gushes a mountain stream. Beget is on the GR11 walking route.

El Forn (☎ 972 74 12 31; Carrer de Josep Duñach 9; full board per person €57), a well-kept cosy stone-and-timber house in the heart of the hamlet,

---

THE LEGEND OF COMTE ARNAU

Sant Joan de les Abadesses is one of many places in the country north of Ripoll associated with perhaps the strangest of Pyrenean legends: that of Comte Arnau, the wicked medieval Count of Mataplana, who cheated his workers of their due payments of wheat and had more than his quota of lust for local womanhood. The insatiable count, it seems, came by tunnel to Sant Joan from Campdevànol, 10km west, for covert trysts with the abbess and other nuns. When his favourite abbess died, her pious replacement barred him from the convent, but, thanks to some help from the devil, he still got in – and carried on.

Eventually, Arnau fell in love with a local lass, whose only refuge was the nunnery at Sant Joan. Arnau forced his way into the convent to find his beloved dead – from fear and misery, it's surmised. Her corpse, however, revived just long enough to give the count a good ticking-off. Overcome by remorse, Arnau retired to Serra de Mogrony, where, condemned to eternal misery for his sins, his tortured soul still wanders, returning on thundery nights (and, some say, under a full moon) to the convent: a horrific vision on horseback with a pack of balefully howling dogs.

If you visit Sant Joan or other villages in the region during summer, you might be lucky enough to catch one of the occasional re-enactments of bits of the Arnau legend. Or you can look at his supposed residence, the Castell de Mataplana, at Gombrèn, about 11km northwest of Ripoll on the Gl401.

is the best of the handful of accommodation and eating options.

There is no public transport to Beget.

VALL DE NÚRIA & RIBES DE FRESER

Around AD 700, the story goes, Sant Gil (St Giles) came from Nîmes in France to live in a cave in an isolated mountain valley 26km north of Ripoll, preaching the Gospel to shepherds. Before he left, four years later, apparently fleeing Visigothic persecution, Sant Gil hurriedly hid away a wooden Virgin-and-child image he had carved, a cross, his cooking pot and the bell he had used to summon the shepherds. They stayed hidden until 1079, when an ox led some shepherds to the spot. The statuette, the *Mare de Déu de Núria*, became the patron of Pyrenean shepherds and Núria's future was assured. The first historical mention of a shrine was made in 1162.

Sant Gil would recoil in shock if he came back today. The large, grey sanctuary complex squatting at the heart of the valley is an eyesore and the crowds would make anyone with hermitic leanings run a mile. But otherwise Núria remains almost pristine, a wide, green, mountain-ringed bowl that is the starting point for numerous walks. Getting there is fun too, either on foot up the Gorges de Núria – the green, rocky valley of the thundering Riu Núria – or from Ribes de Freser town, by the little *cremallera* (rack-and-pinion railway), which rises over 1000m on its 12km journey up the same valley.

Orientation

Unless you're walking across the mountains to Núria, you must approach from the small town of Ribes de Freser, on the N152 14km north of Ripoll. The *cremallera* to Núria starts at Ribes-Enllaç station, just off the N152 at the southern end of Ribes. There's a road from Ribes to Queralbs, but from there on it's the *cremallera* or your feet.

Information

Núria's **tourist office** (☎ 972 73 20 20; www .valldenuria.com; ☷ 9am-6pm Oct-Jun, 9am-8pm Jul-Sep) is in the sanctuary complex.

Santuari de Núria

The large 19th- and 20th-century building that dominates the valley contains a hotel,

restaurants and exhibition halls as well as the *santuari* (sanctuary) itself and its sacred *símbols de Núria*. The *santuari* has the same opening hours as the information office. The Mare de Déu de Núria sits behind a glass screen above the altar and is in the Romanesque style of the 12th century, so either Sant Gil was centuries ahead of his time or this isn't his work! Steps lead up to the bell, cross and cooking pot (which all date from at least the 15th century). To have your prayer answered, put your head in the pot and ring the bell while you say it.

Skiing & Walking

In winter, Núria is a small-scale ski resort with 10 short runs. A day pass for the lifts costs €23.

Get Editorial Alpina's *Puigmal* mapguide before you come to Núria, if you plan on doing some walking.

If you want to walk up to Núria, you can avoid the first unexciting 6km from Ribes de Freser by taking the *cremallera* (or road) to Queralbs, and thus saving your energies for the steepest and the most spectacular part of the approach, which is about three hours' walk up. Or take the *cremallera* up and walk down!

From the Vall de Núria, you can cap several 2700m-to-2900m peaks on the main Pyrenees ridge in about 2½ to four hours' walking for each (one way). The most popular is **Puigmal** (2913m).

Sleeping & Eating

Wild camping is banned in the whole Ribes de Freser–Núria area.

NÚRIA

Behind the sanctuary there's a basic **zona d'acampada** (bookings ☎ 972 73 20 20; camping per person/tent €1.80/1.80), a camping area with limited facilities.

Alberg Pic de l'Àliga (☎ 972 73 20 48; dm under/ over 26 Dec-Mar & May-Sep €18.10/21.60, rest of year €15.90/19.40) The youth hostel is at the top of the cable car (*telecabina*) on the eastern side of the valley. Dorm rooms sleep from four to 14, and the price includes breakfast. The cable car runs 9am to 6.35pm daily (to 8.15pm July to September) and also 9.30pm to 10pm Friday and Saturday.

Hotel Vall de Núria (☎ 972 73 20 00; half-board per person €74.60) Housed in the sanctuary building, the hotel has comfortable rooms with bathroom and satellite TV. It has apartments that are available year-round.

In the sanctuary building, Autoservei self-service cafeteria and Bar Finistrelles both have starters in the €6 region and main courses for around €10. La Cabana dels Pastors specialises in fondue and braised meats. A shop in the sanctuary building sells food. The bar and restaurant are closed during slow periods, but the Autoservei is generally open daily.

RIBES DE FRESER

Hotel Els Caçadors (☎ 972 72 70 77; Carrer de Balandrau 24; s/d €25/50, half-board per person €33.80) A family-run business, this small hotel offers simple-enough rooms with bathroom and TV. The buffet breakfast is grand – loads of cold meats, cheeses, juice, cereal and sweet pastries. If you want something nicer, try their three-star across the road (half-board €44 to €50), where the best rooms are spacious, with parquet and timber, and, in some cases, a hydromassage bathtub.

QUERALBS

This delightful hamlet of stone houses with slate roofs makes a prettier base. Try for a room at **Pensió L'Avet** (☎ 972 72 73 63; Carrer Major 7; d €39). It's a pleasant old house that is the only option (often open only at weekends and hard to get a hold of). A couple of restaurants open up on weekends and during holiday periods too.

Getting There & Away

Transports Mir runs between Ripoll and Ribes de Freser, with two or three buses a day on weekdays, and one on Saturday.

About six trains a day run to Ribes-Enllaç from Ripoll (€1.20, 20 minutes) and Barcelona (€5.60, 2¼ hours).

The **cremallera** (☎ 972 73 20 20) is a narrow-gauge electric-powered rack-and-pinion railway that has been operating since 1931. It runs from Ribes-Enllaç to Núria and back six to 12 times a day; depending on the season (one way/return €9.05/14.50, 45 minutes one way). All trains stop at Ribes-Vila and Queralbs (1200m). It's a spectacular trip, particularly after Queralbs, as the train winds up the Gorges de Núria. Some services connect with Renfe trains at Ribes-Enllaç.

CERDANYA

Cerdanya, along with French Cerdagne across the border, occupies a low-lying basin between the higher reaches of the Pyrenees to the east and west. Although Cerdanya and Cerdagne, once a single Catalan county, were divided by the Treaty of the Pyrenees in 1659, they still have a lot in common. Walkers should get a hold of Editorial Alpina's *Cerdanya* map and guide booklet (scaled at 1:50,000).

Puigcerdà

pop 6060

Just 2km from the French border, Puigcerdà (puh-cher-*da*) is not much more than a way station, but it's a jolly little one, particularly in summer and during the ski season. A dozen Spanish, Andorran and French ski resorts lie within 45km. At a height of just over 1200m, Puigcerdà is the capital of Cerdanya.

ORIENTATION & INFORMATION

Puigcerdà stands on a small hill, with the train station at the foot of its southwest side. A few minutes' climb up some flights of steps takes you to Plaça de l'Ajuntament, off which is the **tourist office** (☎ 972 88 05 42; Carrer de Querol 1; ☯ 9am-1pm & 4-7pm Mon-Fri, 9am-1.30pm & 4.30-8pm Sat, 10am-1pm Sun).

The **Hospital de Puigcerdà** (☎ 972 88 01 50; Plaça de Santa Maria 1) is up the road from the tourist office.

SIGHTS

The town was heavily damaged during the civil war and only the tower remains of the 17th-century **Església de Santa Maria** (Plaça de Santa Maria). The 13th-century Gothic **Església de Sant Domènec** (Passeig del 10 d'Abril), was also wrecked but later rebuilt. It contains 14th-century Gothic murals that somehow survived (opening times are erratic). The *estany* (lake) in the north of town, created back in 1380 for irrigation, is surrounded by turn-of-the-20th-century summer houses, built by wealthy Barcelona families.

SLEEPING

The town is home to 17 varied hotels and *pensiones*.

Camping Stel (☎ 972 88 23 61; www.stel.es; 2-person tent & car €28.50; ☯ Jun-Sep) Out along the road to Llívia, this is the only nearby

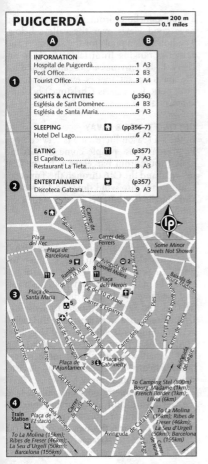

camping option and a pleasant one, with a pool, basketball and a football pitch. You can also rent camping spaces by the month between October and May.

Hotel del Lago (☎ 972 88 10 00; www.hotellago .com; Avinguda del Dr Piguillem 7; s/d €74.90/101.65; P 🖳 🖭) Near the *estany* (lake), this hotel has old-fashioned style and a nice leafy garden. The rooms vary greatly: some have heavy timber beams, while corner ones have windows opening in several directions out to the leafy exterior. The best doubles have hydromassage bathtubs.

EATING
Restaurant La Tieta (☎ 972 88 01 56; Carrer dels Ferrers 20; meals €30-35; 🕑 daily in high season, Thu-Sun

Jul-May) One of the best choices in town, this understated restaurant offers a creative range of dishes, from *magret d'ànec* (slices of duck) through to cod in a creamy garlic sauce.

El Capritxo (☎ 972 88 06 62; Carrer Major 55; meals €25; 🕑 Fri-Wed) A long-standing family business, this is one of the better eateries in town. The paella is fine, and they do a range of tapas too.

ENTERTAINMENT
Discoteca Gatzara (☎ 972 88 09 01; Rambla de Josep Martí 1; 🕑 10pm-5am Tue-Sun) This club has been keeping Puigcerdà's après-ski set dancing into the wee hours for years now. It remains a classic and is easy to roll home from.

GETTING THERE & AWAY
Bus
Alsina Graells runs two daily buses (one at weekends) from Barcelona (€13.05, three hours) via the 5km Túnel del Cadí and two or three to La Seu d'Urgell (€4.45, one hour). They stop at the train station.

Car & Motorcycle
From Barcelona, the C16 approaches Puigcerdà through the Túnel del Cadí. Bicycles are not allowed in the tunnel, which is a tollway.

The N152 from Ribes de Freser climbs west along the northern flank of the Rigard valley, with the pine-covered Serra de Mogrony rising to the south, to the 1800m Collado de Toses (pass), then winds down to Puigcerdà.

The main crossing into France is at Bourg-Madame, immediately east of Puigcerdà, from where roads head to Perpignan and Toulouse.

Train
Six trains a day run from Barcelona to Puigcerdà (€7.30, 3¼ hours) via Ripoll and Ribes de Freser. Five in each direction make the seven-minute hop over the border to Latour-de-Carol in France, where they connect with trains from Toulouse or Paris, and with the narrow-gauge Train Jaune ('yellow train') down the Têt Valley to Perpignan.

Llívia
Six kilometres northeast of Puigcerdà, across flat farmland, Llívia is a piece of

Spain within France. Under the 1659 Treaty of the Pyrenees, Spain ceded 33 villages to France, but Llívia was a 'town' and so, together with the 13 sq km of its municipality, remained a Spanish possession.

The interest of Llívia's tiny medieval nucleus, near the top of the town, centres on the **Museu Municipal** (Carrer dels Forns 4; admission €1; ☒ 10am-7pm Tue-Sat, 10am-2pm Sun) and the 15th-century Gothic **Església de Nostra Senyora dels Àngels**, just above the museum. The museum is in what's claimed to be Europe's oldest pharmacy, the Farmacia Esteva, founded in 1415. From the church you can walk up to the ruined **Castell de Llívia** where, during the short-lived period of Islamic dominion in the Pyrenees, the Muslim governor Manussa enjoyed a secret dalliance with Lampègia, daughter of the Duke of Aquitaine (or so legend has it).

Dine on the balconies of **Restaurant Can Ventura** (☎ 972 89 61 78; Plaça Major 1; meals €24-30; ☒ Tue-Sun), a ramshackle building dating from 1791. The food is delightful – traditional Catalan fare that comes from a discreetly hidden modern kitchen.

Two or three buses a day run from Puigcerdà train station to Llívia. Otherwise, it's not a long walk, and the road is flat and quiet. You only cross about 2km of France before entering the Llívia enclave.

La Molina & Masella
These ski resorts lie either side of Tosa d'Alp (2537m), 15km south of Puigcerdà, and are linked by the Alp 2500 lift, which opened in 2000. The two resorts have a combined total of 84 runs (day lift pass for the whole area €32.50) of all grades at altitudes of 1600m to 2537m. Information, rental equipment and ski schools are available at both **resorts** (☎ 972 89 20 31; www.lamolina .com, www.masella.com).

SLEEPING
Many skiers stay in Puigcerdà or further afield.

Alberg Mare de Déu de les Neus (☎ 972 89 20 12; beds under/over 26 incl breakfast €18.10/21.60; ℗) At the bottom part of La Molina, near the train station, this is a handy youth hostel. Rooms range from doubles to eight-bed dorms. Many of the rooms have a bathroom.

Hotel Adserà (☎ 972 89 20 01; www.hoteladsera .com; half-board per person from €62; ℗ ☒) This is

a mountain hotel from whose rooms you have good views over the valleys below. The hotel has a pool (for the summer) and activities ranging from table tennis to archery. Kids' activities are organised and for the après-ski set there's even a disco. In peak periods (such as Christmas) booking is essential.

GETTING THERE & AWAY
In the ski season there's a bus service from Puigcerdà. Most people come by car; the easiest route from Barcelona is by the C58 toll road and the C16 through the Túnel del Cadí. Roads also wind down to La Molina and Masella from the N152 west of the Collado de Toses.

Northern Cerdanya
The N260 highway runs southwest from Puigcerdà along the Riu Segre valley towards La Seu d'Urgell. It cuts its path between the main Pyrenees chain to the north and the range made up mainly of the Serra del Cadí and Serra de Moixeró to the south. Up to three buses a day run along this valley between Puigcerdà and La Seu d'Urgell.

About 6km from Puigcerdà, **Bolvir** has a little Romanesque church and, more importantly, a luxurious and characterful place to stay, Torre del Remei (see below).

Another kilometre on from Bolvir, take the Ger turn-off for an excursion into the mountains. A minor asphalted road winds its way west and north through the broad, arid Valltova Valley to **Meranges**, a dishevelled, stone farming village that makes few con-

---

AUTHOR'S CHOICE

Torre del Remei (☎ 972 14 01 82; www .torredelremei.com; Camí Reial s/n, Bolvir; d €221-342.40; ℗ ☒ ☒) A tastefully decorated Modernista mansion (which during the civil war was requisitioned as a school and later as a hospital by the Republican government) sitting majestically amid tranquil gardens, this is a romantic and stylish getaway. The rooms, all exquisitely furnished and each one different from the other, are superb and the dining is equally tempting. You can go to gastronomic heaven for around €70 a head. Big spenders could try the main tower suite (€588.50).

cessions to the passing tourist trade. You can stay in the charming **Can Borrell** (☎ 972 88 00 33; www.canborrell.com; Carrer de Retorn 3; s/d from €71.70/91), a rustic hideaway that has been tastefully redecorated for a modestly discerning clientele. The rooms are all different, loaded with timber beams and high ceilings, and there is also a fine restaurant.

Those with cars can proceed along a sliver of road that worsens as it approaches the **Refugi de Malniu** (☽ daily Jun-Sep, Sat & Sun rest of year), at 2130m. Right behind the *refugi* is the reed-covered **Estany Sec** (the misnamed Dry Lake). The *refugi* is on the path of the long-distance GR11 walk, which approaches from Guils de Cerdanya (also reachable by car) in the east, and continues west to Andorra.

SERRA DEL CADÍ

The N260 runs west along the wide Riu Segre valley from Puigcerdà to La Seu d'Urgell, with the Pyrenees climbing northwards towards Andorra, and one of the finest pre-Pyrenees ranges, the Serra del Cadí, rising steep and high along the southern flank. Although this face of the Cadí – rocky and fissured by ravines known as *canales* – looks daunting enough, the range's most spectacular peak is **Pedraforca** (2497m), a southern offshoot with probably the best rock-climbing in Catalonia. Pedraforca and the main Cadí range also offer some excellent mountain walking for those suitably equipped and experienced.

Orientation

The Pedraforca area is most easily reached from the C16, then along the B400, which heads west 1.5km south of Guardiola de Berguedà. Pedraforca looms mightily into view about halfway to the village of Saldes, which sits 1215m high at its foot, 15km from the C16. The main Cadí range runs east–west, about 5km north of Saldes. The Refugi Lluís Estasen (see p360) is under the northern face of Pedraforca, 2.5km northwest of Saldes. You can reach it by footpath from Saldes or by a partly paved road that turns north off the B400 about 1km west of Saldes. Park at the Mirador de Gresolet, from where it's a 10-minute walk up to the refuge.

Information

The Parc Natural del Cadí-Moixeró's main **Centre d'Informació** (☎ 93 824 41 51; Carrer de la Vinya 1;

☽ 9am-1.30pm & 3.30-6.30pm Mon-Fri, 10am-2pm & 4-6.30pm Sat, 10am-2pm Sun & holidays) is in Bagà, a pleasant little village (walk down to the stone bridge that crosses the stream) 4km north of Guardiola de Berguedà on the C16.

In Saldes, the **Centre d'Informació Massís del Pedraforca** (☎ 93 825 80 05; ☽ 11am-1pm & 5-7pm daily Jun-Sep, Sat & Sun rest of year) has information on the Saldes and Pedraforca area only.

Walking
PEDRAFORCA

The name means 'stone fork' and the approach from the east makes it clear why. The two separate rocky peaks, the northern Pollegó Superior (2497m) and the southern Pollegó Inferior (2400m), are divided by a saddle called L'Enforcadura. The northern face, rising near vertically for 600m, has some classic rock climbs; the southern has a wall that sends alpinists into raptures.

Pedraforca is also possible for walkers. From Refugi Lluís Estasen you can reach the Pollegó Superior summit in about three strenuous hours – either southwards from the refuge, then up the middle of the fork from the southeastern side (a path from Saldes joins this route); or westwards up to the Collada del Verdet, then south and east to the summit. The latter route has some hairy precipices and requires a good head for heights. It's not suitable for coming down: you must use the first route.

Gósol, Tuixén & Beyond

The B400 is paved from Saldes to the pretty stone village of Gósol, 6km further west. The original Gósol (the Vila Vella), which dated back to at least the 9th century, is now abandoned on the hill south of the present village.

A road west from Gósol climbs the 1625m Coll de Josa pass, then descends past the picturesque hamlet of Josa del Cadí to Tuixén (1206m), another attractive village on a small hill. From Tuixén, scenic paved roads lead northwest to La Seu d'Urgell (36km) and south to Sant Llorenç de Morunys (28km), which is on a beautiful cross-country road from Berga to Organyà.

Sleeping & Eating
SALDES & AROUND

There are at least four **camping grounds** along the B400 between the C16 and Saldes, some open year-round. In Saldes you'll find a handful of *pensiones* and a larger hotel.

Refugi Lluís Estasen (☎ 93 822 00 79; ☼ daily Jun-Sep; Sat, Sun & holidays rest of year) Run by the Federació d'Entitats Excursionistes de Catalunya FEEC, and near the Mirador de Gresolet, this *refugi* has 87 places, meals and a warden in summer. In winter it has about 30 places. When it's full you can sleep outside, but not in a tent.

GÓSOL & TUIXÉN

Cal Fusté (☎ 973 37 00 83; Plaça Major 9, Gósol; d with bathroom €35) A charming, renovated house is gathered around a patio on the main square. Rooms are spotless and bright.

Forn Cal Moixó (☎ 973 37 02 74; Carrer del Canal 2, Gósol; meals €15-18; ☼ lunch daily, dinner only Fri & Sat) This bakery doubles as a homey restaurant. Tuck into filling and tasty local food, such as a tender *filet de vedella* (filet of beef). The house wine is a little rough though!

Can Farragetes (☎ 973 37 00 34; www.calfarragetes .com; Carrer del Coll 7, Tuixén; d with bathroom €28.80; P) This is a big, friendly stone place set over two floors around a sprawling courtyard.

It's cosy, with smallish but immaculate rooms featuring iron bedsteads and wood panelling. There's also a restaurant and an intriguing shop with everything from home-made jams to *cava* (sparkling wine).

Getting There & Around

You need your own vehicle to get to Saldes, Gósol or Tuixén.

LA SEU D'URGELL

pop 10,370

The lively valley town of La Seu d'Urgell (la *se*-u dur-*zhey*) is Spain's gateway to Andorra, 10km to the north. It's a pleasant place to spend a night, with a fine medieval cathedral.

When the Franks evicted the Muslims from this part of the Pyrenees, in the early 9th century, they made La Seu a bishopric and capital of the counts of Urgell. It has been an important market and cathedral town since the 11th century.

Information

Hospital (☎ 973 35 00 50) At the southern end of Passeig de Joan Brudieu.

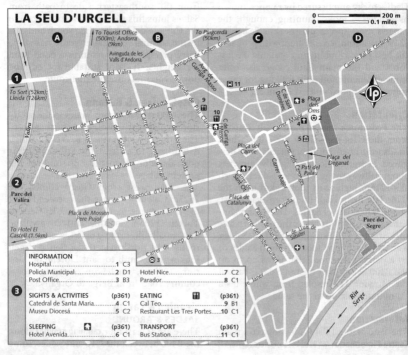

LA SEU D'URGELL

0 ————— 200 m
0 ————— 0.1 miles

CATALONIA

Policía Municipal (☎ 973 35 04 26; Plaça dels Oms 1) In the Casa de la Ciutat (Town Hall).

Tourist office (☎ 973 35 15 11; www.laseu.org /turisme; Avinguda de les Valls d'Andorra 33; 🕑 9am-9pm Jul-Aug, 10am-2pm & 4-6.30pm Mon-Sat Sep-Jun) At the northern entrance to town.

Catedral de Santa Maria & Museu Diocesà

Looming on the southern side of Plaça dels Oms, the 12th-century **seu** (cathedral; admission free; 🕑 10am-1pm & 4-6pm Mon-Sat, 10am-1pm Sun) is one of Catalonia's outstanding Romanesque buildings despite various remodellings. It is one of more than a hundred Romanesque churches lining what has come to be known as the Ruta Románica, from Perpignan (France) to the Urgell district.

The fine western façade, through which you enter, is decorated in typical Lombard style. The inside is dark and plain but still impressive, with five apses, some murals in the southern transept, and a 13th-century Virgin-and-child sculpture in the central apse.

From inside the cathedral you can enter the **Museu Diocesà** (☎ 973 35 32 42; www .museudiocesaurgell.org; admission €2.50; 🕑 10am-1pm & 4-6pm Mon-Sat Jul-Aug; noon-1pm Mon-Fri, 11am-1pm Sat & Sun Sep-Jun). This good museum encompasses the fine cloister and the 12th-century Romanesque **Església de Sant Miquel**, as well as some good medieval Pyrenean church murals, sculptures and altarpieces, and a rare 10th-century Mozarabic Beatus (illustrated manuscript of the Apocalypse).

On Sunday morning the cloister, but not the museum, is open. You can enter the cloister and Església de Sant Miquel for €1, if you don't have time to visit the worthwhile museum.

Sleeping

Hotel Avenida (☎ 973 35 01 04; www.avenhotel.com; Avinguda de Pau Claris 24; s/d €31.50/53.50) This hotel has a range of mostly sunny rooms. Though not overly characterful, the rooms are big enough and kept spick-and-span.

Hotel Nice (☎ 973 35 21 00; www.hotelnice.net; Avinguda de Pau Claris 4-6; s/d €43.80/59.70; P ⊠) With timber floors and furniture, rooms here have a warmer, less-clinical feel.

Parador (☎ 973 35 20 00; Carrer de Sant Domènec s/n; s/d €94.20/117.70; P ⊠ ⊠) Built around the restored cloister of the 14th-century Sant Domènec convent, this is a fairly modern establishment that was fully refurbished in 2003. Rooms are comfortable without being luxurious. What makes this place is the setting, and extra touches such as the pool and sauna.

Hotel El Castell (☎ 973 35 00 00; www.hotelel castell.com; Castellciutat; s/d €250/380; P ⊠ ⊡ ⊠) Set in a castle in a hilltop jumble of lanes about 1.5km west of central La Seu, this spa hotel is a world of its own. Run by the Relais & Châteaux team, it is the classiest hotel for miles around, with soothing gardens, a gym, a sauna and a fine restaurant (below).

Eating

Restaurant Les Tres Portes (☎ 973 35 29 07; Carrer de Garriga i Massou 7; meals €20-25; 🕑 Thu-Sun) This is a homely little place, where you can chow down on a mixed Spanish cuisine in the peaceful garden.

Cal Teo (☎ 973 35 10 29; Avinguda de Pau Claris 28; meals €15-20; 🕑 Tue-Sat, lunch only Sun) Specialists in grilled meats, the cooks of Cal Teo enjoy a good reputation with the local clientele. Locals crowd in especially for a big weekend lunch, washed down with lots of house wine and boisterous humour. On the menu are Catalan classics such as *botifarra amb mongetes* (pork sausage with white beans).

Hotel El Castell (☎ 973 35 00 00; www.hotelcastell .com; Castellciutat; meals €45) The restaurant lives up to the luxury standards set by the hotel. The cuisine is a mix of traditional Catalan and modern. Duck and other meats feature prominently.

Getting There & Away

BUS

The bus station is on the northern edge of the old town. **Alsina Graells** (☎ 973 35 00 20) runs four or five buses daily to Barcelona (€18.70, 3½ hours): two each via Solsona and Ponts, and one, which does not run on Sunday, via the Túnel del Cadí; three to Puigcerdà (€4.55, one hour); and two to Lleida (€12.75, 2½ hours).

CAR & MOTORCYCLE

The N260 heads 6km southwest to Adrall, then turns off west over the hills to Sort. The C14 carries on south to Lleida, threading the towering Tresponts gorge about 13km beyond Adrall.

VALL DE LA NOGUERA PALLARESA

The Riu Noguera Pallaresa, running south through a dramatic valley about 50km west of La Seu d'Urgell, is Spain's best-known white-water river. The main centres for white-water sports are the town of Sort and the villages of Rialp and Llavorsí. You'll find companies that will take you rafting, hydrospeeding, canoeing and kayaking or canyoning, climbing, mountain biking, horse riding and ponting (basically bungee jumping from bridges).

The main **tourist office** (☎ 973 62 10 02; Avinguda dels Comtes del Pallars 21; ☺ 10am-2pm & 3-7pm Mon-Sat, 10am-1pm Sun Jun-Sep; 10am-2am & 3-7pm Mon & Thu-Sat, 10am-2pm Tue & Sun Oct-May) for the area is in Sort.

White-Water Rafting

The Riu Noguera Pallaresa has no drops of more than grade 4 (on a scale of 1 to 6), but it's exciting enough to attract a constant stream of white-water fans between April and August. It's usually at its best in May and June.

The best stretch is the 14km or so from Llavorsí to Rialp, on which the standard raft outing lasts one to 1½ hours and costs €30 to €33 per person depending on the company and season. A quicker surge down the same stretch on a hydrospeed costs from €32 (5km) up to €57 (14km). Longer rides down to Sort and beyond will cost more.

At least one company, **Yeti Emotions** (☎ 973 62 22 01; www.yetiemotions.com; Carrer de Borda Era d'Alfons s/n, Llavorsí), organises a number of high-grade trips, for experienced rafters only, further upstream. Two other rafting companies also operate from Llavorsí and you will find still more companies based in places such as Sort. Canoeing trips on the same river start at €32 per hour.

For all trips you need to bring your own swimming costume, towel and a change of clothes. All other gear is usually provided.

Sleeping

Llavorsí is the most pleasant base, much more of a mountain village than Rialp or Sort, with a couple of camping grounds and four hotels.

Camping Aigües Braves (☎ 973 62 21 53; 2-person tent & car €17.80; ☺ Mar-Sep; ☒) About 1km north of Llavorsí proper, this pleasant riverside camping ground has a pool, restaurant and minimarket.

Hotel Riberies (☎ 973 62 20 51; Camí de Riberies s/n; r per person €46; P ☒) This is by far the most pleasant choice. Timber ceilings and polished wooden floors give the spacious rooms a warm feel, and the price includes breakfast. Add the verdant site away from the main road, a good restaurant and a swimming pool, and you have the picture.

Getting There & Away

Alsina Graells runs one daily bus (at 7.30am) from Barcelona to Sort, Rialp, Llavorsí (€22.50, 5½ hours) and Esterri d'Àneu (€25.40). From June to October it continues to Vielha (€29.55) and the Val d'Aran. The return bus leaves Llavorsí at 1.56pm.

NORTHWESTERN VALLEYS

North of the highway that leads northwest from Llavorsí towards the Port de Bonaigua pass, stretch a series of verdant valleys leading up to some of the most beautiful sights in the Catalan Pyrenees.

The Vall de Cardós and Vall Ferrera, heading back into the hills northeast of Llavorsí, lead to some remote and, in parts, tough mountain walking country along and across the Andorran and French borders, including Pica d'Estats, the highest peak in Catalonia. Editorial Alpina's *Pica d'Estats* and *Montgarri* maps will help.

Vall de Cardós

Heading north into the hills along the L504 road from Llavorsí, this pretty valley leads to some challenging mountain-walking possibilities. Editorial Alpina's *Pica d'Estats* map-guide is useful here. There is no public transport up the valley.

Lladrós and **Lladorre**, the latter graced with a charming Romanesque church, are pretty stone hamlets oozing bucolic charm. Tavascan marks the end of the asphalt road. It's a huddle of well-kept houses and a launch pad for numerous excursions. The most stunning item of scenery is a crystal-blue glacial lake (the largest in the Pyrenees), **Estany de Certascan**, about 13km away along a tough road best negotiated by 4WD. Just out of view of the lake is the **Refugi de Certascan** (☎ 973 62 13 89; ☺ daily early Jun–mid-Sep, most weekends & holidays rest of year), which has room for 30 people, showers and offers meals. More trails and lakes await in this frontier mountain territory. The valley's towns are littered with charming *cases de pagès* (country guesthouses).

Vall Ferrera

Greener than the Vall de Cardòs, this valley is another pleasant surprise, hiding several pretty villages and bringing even more good walking country within reach. The ascent of the Pica d'Estats (3143m), the region's highest peak, is generally undertaken from here. Get hold of Alpina's *Pica d'Estats* map. There is no public transport.

The prettiest hamlet, **Àreu**, is a popular base for walkers. It is divided into two separate settlements, each with a Romanesque church: Sant Climent is in the lower part and Sant Feliu de la Força up the road. The ascent of and return from the Pica d'Estats is an all-day affair and only for the fit. You need to be at the **Refugi de Vall Ferrera** (☎ 973 62 07 54; Jun–mid-Oct), 10km to the north of Àreu, at dawn. On the way up you will pass glacial lakes, high pastures and ever-changing scenery, before ascending the bare rocky summit.

There are several *cases de pagès* in Àreu. **Casa Gallardó** (☎ 973 62 43 44; Carrer La Força s/n; d €19.20), in the upper part of the village, is hard to beat. Rooms are spotless, if in some cases a little small, and the family is extra friendly.

Valls d'Àneu

To proceed to the next valleys west, you return to Llavorsí and the C13 highway, along which you proceed north. After 12km you pass the turn-off on the left for Espot – this is the most popular way into the Parc Nacional d'Aigüestortes i Estany de Sant Maurici.

Six kilometres further on from the turn-off, after passing an artificial lake on the right where you can hire rowing boats and canoes to potter about in, you'll arrive at **Esterri d'Àneu**, a popular, if distant, base for the ski fields of Baqueira-Beret (p368) in the Val d'Aran. Of the various valleys that make up the Valls d'Àneu, the **Vall d'Isil** is the most intriguing. Follow the C13 directly north through Esterri d'Àneu and it will lead you over a bridge across the Riu Noguera Pallaresa. You then follow this back road (which is now known as the C147) up into a mountain valley, passing through the villages of **Borén**, **Isil** and the half-abandoned **Alós d'Isil**.

PARC NACIONAL D'AIGÜESTORTES I ESTANY DE SANT MAURICI & AROUND

Catalonia's only national park extends 20km east to west, and only 9km from north to south, but packs in more beauty than most areas 100 times its size. The product of glacial action over two million years, it's essentially two east–west valleys at 1600m to 2000m altitude lined by jagged 2600m to 2900m peaks of granite and slate. Against this backdrop, pine and fir forests, and open bush and grassland, bedecked with wildflowers in spring, combine with some 200 small *estanys* (lakes) and countless streams and waterfalls to create a wilderness of rare splendour.

The national park, whose boundaries cover 141.2 sq km, lies at the core of a wider wilderness area, whose outer limit is known as the *zona perifèrica* and includes some magnificent high country to the north and south. The total area covered by the wilderness area is 408.5 sq km and is monitored by park rangers.

Orientation

APPROACHES

The main approaches are via the village of Espot (1320m), 4km east of the park's eastern boundary, and Boí, 5.5km from the western side.

THE PARK

The two main valleys are those of the Riu Escrita in the east and the Riu de Sant Nicolau in the west. The Escrita flows out of the park's largest lake, the 1km-long **Estany de Sant Maurici**. The Sant Nicolau's main source is **Estany Llong**, 4km west of Estany de Sant Maurici across the 2423m Portarró d'Espot pass. Three kilometres downstream from Estany Llong, the Sant Nicolau runs through a particularly beautiful stretch known as **Aigüestortes** (Twisted Waters).

Apart from the valley openings at the eastern and western ends, virtually the whole perimeter of the park is mountain crests, with numerous spurs of almost equal height reaching in towards the centre. One of these, from the south, ends in the twin peaks **Els Encantats** (2746m and 2733m), towering over Estany de Sant Maurici.

MAPS & GUIDES

Editorial Alpina's map guides are adequate, although they don't show every single trail.

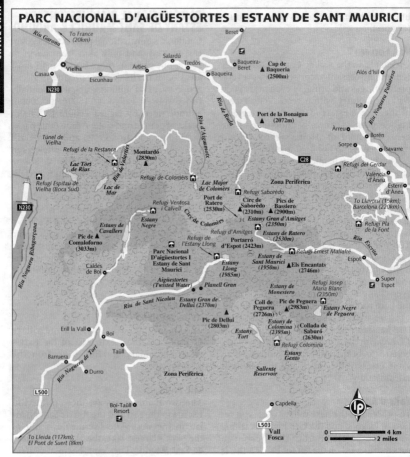

PARC NACIONAL D'AIGÜESTORTES I ESTANY DE SANT MAURICI

Sant Maurici – Els Encantats covers the eastern half of the park and its approaches; *Vall de Boí* covers the western half and its approaches; *Montsent de Pallars* covers the northern Vall Fosca; and *Val d'Aran*, naturally, covers the Val d'Aran. A better map of the whole area is the Institut Cartogràfic de Catalunya's *Parc Nacional d'Aigüestortes i Estany de Sant Maurici*, scaled at 1:25,000 – but even it is not perfect. The help of guides can be enlisted at the Espot and Boí information offices.

Information
TOURIST INFORMATION
There are **national park information offices** in Espot (☎ 973 62 40 36; ◷ 9am-1pm & 3.30-6.45pm)

and Boí (☎ 973 69 61 89; ◷ 9am-1pm & 3.30-6.45pm). The **tourist office** (☎ 973 69 40 00; ◷ 10am-2pm & 4-7pm Mon-Sat) in Barruera, on the L500, 10km north from the N230, is a good source of information on the area around the western side of the park. There are also other tourist offices south of the park in **El Pont de Suert** (☎ 973 69 06 40) and **La Pobla de Segur** (☎ 973 68 02 57).

PARK RULES
Private vehicles cannot enter the park. Wild camping is not allowed, nor is swimming or other 'aquatic activities' in the lakes and rivers. Hunting, fishing, mushroom-picking and just about every other kind of potentially harmful activity are banned.

Romanesque Churches

The Vall de Boí southwest of the park is dotted with some of Catalunya's loveliest little Romanesque churches, which together were declared a Unesco World Heritage site in 2000. Two of the finest are at Taüll, 3km east of Boí. **Sant Climent de Taüll**, at the entrance to the village, with its slender six-storey bell tower, is a gem, not only for its elegant, simple lines but also for the art that once graced its interior until the works were transferred to museums in the 20th century. The central apse contains a copy of a famous 1123 mural that now resides in Barcelona's Museu Nacional d'Art de Catalunya (see p295). At the church's centre is a *Pantocrator* (Christ figure), whose rich Mozarabic-influenced colours, and expressive but superhuman features, have become a virtual emblem of Catalan Romanesque art. Other art from this church has found its way to museums as far away as Boston in the USA!

Santa Maria de Taüll (admission free, ⏰ 10am-3pm), up in the old village centre and possessing a five-storey tower, is also well represented in the Barcelona museum but lacks the *in situ* copies that add to the interest of Sant Climent.

Other worthwhile Romanesque churches in the area are at Boí (Sant Joan), Barruera (Sant Feliu), Durro (Nativitat) and Erill la Vall (Santa Eulàlia). The latter has a slender six-storey tower to rival Sant Climent's and slopes upwards to the altar. Next door is the **Centre d'Interpretació del Romànic** (☎ 973 69 67 15; ⏰ 9am-2pm & 4-7pm Mon-Sat, 10am-2pm Sun), which has a small Romanesque art collection, and it's also where you can organise guided tours of the above churches.

You can visit all the above churches (with the exception of Santa Maria de Taüll) from 11am to 2pm and 4pm to 7pm daily (admission €1 each).

Walking

The park is crisscrossed by plenty of paths, ranging from well marked to unmarked, enabling you to pick suitable routes.

EAST–WEST TRAVERSE

You can walk right across the park in one day. The full Espot-to-Boí (or vice versa) walk is about 25km and takes nine hours, but you can shorten this by using Jeep-taxis to/from Estany de Sant Maurici and/or Aigüestortes (3km downstream from Estany Llong). Espot (1300m) to Estany de Sant Maurici (1950m) is 8km (two hours). A path then climbs to the Portarró d'Espot pass (2423m), where there are fine views over both of the park's main valleys. From the pass you descend to Estany Llong and Aigüestortes (1820m; about 3½ hours from Estany de Sant Maurici). Then you have around 3.5km to the park entrance, 4km to the L500 and 2.5km south to Boí (1260m) – a total of about three hours.

SHORTER WALKS

Numerous good walks of three to five hours' return will take you up into spectacular side valleys from Estany de Sant Maurici or Aigüestortes.

From the eastern end of Estany de Sant Maurici, one path heads south 2.5km up the beautiful Monastero valley to **Estany de Monastero** (2171m), passing Els Encantats on the left. Another goes 3km northwest up by Estany de Ratero to **Estany Gran d'Amitges** (2350m). From **Planell Gran** (1850m), 1km up the Sant Nicolau valley from Aigüestortes, a path climbs 2.5km southeast to **Estany Gran de Dellui** (2370m). You can descend to **Estany Llong** (3km); it takes about four hours from Aigüestortes to Estany Llong.

Skiing

The **Boí-Taüll ski resort** (☎ 902 304430; day pass €28) is one of Catalonia's more promising areas, with 40 pistes (most fairly easy) covering 39km. You can also ski around **Espot** (☎ 973 62 40 58; day pass €27), which gives you a further 31 pistes over 38km.

Sleeping

CAMPING

There are four camping grounds in and around Espot. **Camping Vorapark** (☎ 973 62 41 08; www.voraparc.com; Prat del Vedat; 2-person tent & car €18.80; ⏰ Apr-Sep; 🐾) is about the best camping option in Espot, about 1.5km out of town towards the park entrance. It has a pleasant swimming pool, as well as a pool hall, a bar and a minimarket.

MOUNTAIN REFUGIS

Five *refugis* in the park and seven more inside the *zona perifèrica* provide accommodation for walkers. In general they tend to be staffed from early or mid-June to September, and for some weeks in the first half of the year for skiers. At other times several of them leave a section open where you can stay overnight; if you are unsure, call ahead or ask at the park information offices. Most charge €12 per person to stay overnight.

In the Park
You don't usually need to book for these except in August. The Espot park office can contact the Refugi Ernest Mallafré, Refugi d'Amitges and Refugi Josep Maria Blanc for you, to check on availability.

Refugi Ernest Mallafré (☎ 973 25 01 18) Near the eastern end of Estany de Sant Maurici (1950m) and run by the FEEC. It has meals but no showers.

Refugi d'Amitges (☎ 973 25 01 09) At Estany Gran d'Amitges (2380m), in the north of the park, it's run by the Centre Excursionista de Catalunya (CEC). Meals and showers are available.

Refugi de l'Estany Llong (reservations ☎ 629-374652) Near Estany Llong (1985m) and run by the national park; there's a kitchen and showers.

Refugi Josep Maria Blanc (☎ 93 423 23 45) Near Estany Tort (2350m) and run by the CEC; meals available when staffed.

Refugi Ventosa i Calvell (☎ 973 29 70 90) Run by the CEC, in the northwest of the park (2220m), has a kitchen and showers.

Zona Perifèrica
Refugi Colomina (☎ 973 68 10 42) South of the park, by Estany de Colomina (2395m), meals are available, when staffed.

The following places are run by the FEEC.

Refugi de Colomèrs (☎ 973 64 05 92) North of the park in the lovely Circ de Colomèrs (2135m), with a kitchen, showers and meals (when staffed).

Refugi de la Restanca (☎ 608-036559) Has showers.

Refugi Saborèdo (☎ 973 25 30 15) Also north of the park, but in the lake-strewn Circ de Saborèdo (2310m).

HOSTALES & HOTELS
The villages of Espot, Boí and Taüll have a range of accommodation options. There are hostales and/or cases de pagès in Barruera, El Pont de Suert, Capdella and La Torre de Capdella.

Espot
Residència Felip (☎ 973 62 40 93; s/d with bathroom €15/30, Jul-Aug €20/36) A friendly, family-run

place in the heart of the village, this spot has clean rooms, and rates include breakfast. Nothing, including the prices, has changed in years. It is one of three country homestays here.

Taüll
Three kilometres uphill from Boí, Taüll is by far the most picturesque place to stay on the west side of the park. It has no less than nine cases de pagès and over a dozen hotels and pensiones, either in the village itself or in the area surrounding it.

Pensión Santa Maria (☎ 973 69 61 70; www.taull .com; Plaça Cap del Riu 3; d €87) Through a shady entrance a grand stone archway leads into the quiet courtyard of this rambling country haven, with rose-draped balcony. The rooms are tastefully furnished and the whole building, all stonework, timber and slate roof, oozes character.

Eating
Note that throughout the area many places close mid-week and in the off-season. Most of the towns have one or two fairly basic restaurants. In Espot, **Restaurant Juquim** (☎ 973 62 40 09; meals €15-20), on the main square, has a varied menu concentrating largely on hearty country fare, with generous winter servings of escudella (steaming hotpot) and lots of sausage and river trout on hand. Also in Espot, the **Hotel Roya** (☎ 973 62 40 40; meals €20-25) offers a similar range of food in a slightly more upmarket setting.

In Taüll, where there are a handful of eateries, you could try **Sant Climent** (☎ 973 69 60 52; meals €15-20) for a piping-hot onion soup.

Getting There & Away
BUS
Daily buses from Barcelona, Lleida and La Pobla de Segur to Esterri d'Àneu (and in summer to the Val d'Aran) will stop at the Espot turning on the C13. From there you have an 8km uphill walk (or hitch) to Espot.

Alsina Graells buses from Barcelona to La Pobla de Segur (€19.90, three to 4½ hours) run up to three times a day all year. From July to mid-September, a connecting bus runs daily from La Pobla de Segur to El Pont de Suert and from there to Barruera and the Boí turn-off (el Cruce de Boí) on the L500 (1km short of Boí).

Getting Around

Once you're close to the park, the easiest way of getting inside it is by Jeep-taxi from Espot or Boí. They run a more or less continuous shuttle service between Espot and Estany de Sant Maurici, and between Boí and Aigüestortes, saving you, respectively, 3km and 10km. The one-way fare for either trip is €4 per person and the services run from outside the park information offices in Espot and Boí (from July to September 8am to 7pm, other months 9am to 6pm).

VAL D'ARAN

pop 7300

This lush green valley, Catalonia's northernmost outpost, is surrounded by spectacular 2000m-plus mountains. Its only natural opening is northwards to France, to which it gives its river, the Riu Garona (Garonne), flowing down to Bordeaux. Thanks in part to its geography, Aran's native language is not Catalan but Aranese (aranés), which is a dialect of Occitan or the langue d'oc, the old Romance language of southern France.

Despite this northward orientation, Aran has been tied politically to Catalonia since 1175, when Alfonso II took it under his protection to forestall the designs of rival counts on both sides of the Pyrenees. A major hiccup came with the Napoleonic occupation from 1810 to 1815.

For all its intriguing past, the Val d'Aran is in danger of being overrun by tourism, which, since the 1964 opening of the Baqueira-Beret ski resort, has replaced farming and herding as the economic mainstay. That said, many villages retain an old-fashioned core and, from Aran's pretty side valleys, walkers can go over the mountains in any direction, notably southwards to the Parc Nacional d'Aigüestortes i Estany de Sant Maurici.

The Val d'Aran is some 35km long and is considered to have three parts: Naut Aran (Upper Aran), the eastern part, aligned east–west; Mijaran (Middle Aran) around Vielha; and Baish Aran (Lower Aran), where the Garona flows northeast to France.

Vielha

pop 2830

Vielha is Aran's junction town, and the Aranese spelling of its name is more common than the Catalan and Castilian version, Viella.

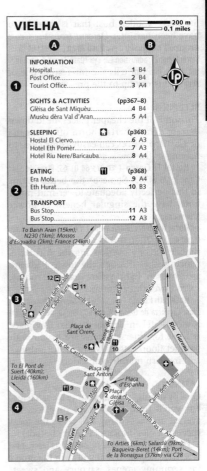

VIELHA

0 — 200 m
0 — 0.1 miles

INFORMATION
Hospital.................................1 B4
Post Office.............................2 B4
Tourist Office........................3 A4

SIGHTS & ACTIVITIES (pp367–8)
Glèisa de Sant Miquèu..........4 B4
Musèu dèra Val d'Aran..........5 A4

SLEEPING (p368)
Hostal El Ciervo.....................6 A3
Hotel Eth Pomèr....................7 A3
Hotel Riu Nere/Baricauba.......8 A4

EATING (p368)
Era Mola.................................9 A4
Eth Hurat..............................10 B3

TRANSPORT
Bus Stop...............................11 A3
Bus Stop...............................12 A3

To Baish Aran (15km);
N230 (1km); Mossos
d'Esquadra (2km); France (24km)

To El Pont de
Suert (40km);
Lleida (160km)

Plaça de
Sant Orenç

Plaça de
Sant Antoni

Plaça
d'Espanha

Plaça
dèra
Glèisa

To Arties (6km); Salardú (9km);
Baqueira-Beret (14km); Port
de la Bonaigua (37km) via C28

INFORMATION

Hospital (☎ 973 64 00 04; Carrèr deth Espitau)
Mossos d'Esquadra (Catalan regional police;
☎ 973 64 09 02) Two kilometres north of the centre along the N230 to France.
Tourist office (☎ 973 64 01 10; Carrèr de Sarriulèra 5;
⏰ 9am-9pm)

SIGHTS

The small old quarter is around Plaça dèra Glèisa and across the little Riu Nere, just west of the square. The **Glèisa de Sant Miquèu** (Plaça déra Glèisa) is a church that displays a mix of 12th- to 18th-century styles, with a 13th-century main portal. It contains some notable medieval artwork, especially the 12th-century *Crist de Mijaran*, an almost life-sized wooden bust that is thought to have been part of a *Descent from the Cross* group. The **Musèu dèra Val d'Aran** (☎ 973 64 18 15; Carrèr Major 11; admission €2; ☻ 10am-1pm & 5-8pm Tue-Sat, 10am-1pm Sun) tells the interesting tale of Aran's history up to the present.

SLEEPING

For some of the cheaper places, head down Passeig Llibertat, north off Avenguda de Castièro. Prices can easily come close to halving in the low season.

Hostal El Ciervo (☎ 973 64 01 65; Plaça de Sant Orenç 3; s/d €47/75) Some of the better rooms in this perfectly adequate lower-mid-range hotel have the singular benefit of power showers.

Hotel Riu Nere/Baricauba (☎ 973 64 01 50; Carrèr Major 4; s/d €72/102; P) Go for a room with a timber balcony overlooking the Riu Nere, which gushes through the town. Beds are spacious in light yellow-painted rooms, spread over three storeys.

Hotel Eth Pomèr (☎ 973 64 28 88; www.hotelpomer .com; Carretera de Gausac 4; s/d €73/96.30; P ▲ 🖵) A new hotel in central Vielha, this place is ideal for skiers. Rooms are bright with parquet floors, attractive wood furnishings and modern marble bathrooms.

EATING

Quality dining is hard to come by in Vielha, but you'll find no shortage of places for average meals – many will serve the local speciality, *olla aranesa* (a hearty hotpot).

Eth Hurat (☎ 973 64 02 10; Passeg dèra Llibertat 14; crepes €7-9) Stop in here if you're in the mood for scrummy crepes, savoury and sweet. They also specialise in fondue and *raclette*, for that Swiss Alpine touch.

Era Mòla (☎ 973 64 24 19; Carrèr de Marrèc 8; meals €30-35; ☻ mid-Jul–Sep & Dec-Apr) Easily the best restaurant in town, located in a fine, low-slung house in the heart of the old town. Expect carefully prepared local and more international cuisine. The desserts, with a French leaning, rate a special mention.

Arties
pop 445

Six kilometres east of Vielha, this pretty village on the southern side of the highway also sits astride the confluence of the Garona and the Valarties rivers. Among its cheerful stone houses is the Romanesque

Glèisa de Santa Maria, with its three-store belfry and triple apse.

Another reason for coming to Arties i to stay at **Hotel Valarties** (☎ 973 64 43 64; Carrè Major 3; s/d €90/164; P ▲) and/or enjoy a mea at its renowned restaurant, **Casa Irene** (meal €40-55, ☻ Wed-Sun, dinner only Tue, closed Oct & May) The hotel is a tasteful mansion with a slat roof set in a broad, verdant garden. Th food at Casa Irene is sublime, featuring tempting mix of sturdy local dishes and in ternational flair.

Salardú
pop 1200

Three kilometres east of Arties, Salardú' nucleus of old houses and narrow streets ha largely resisted the temptation to sprawl. I May, June, October or November, however you will find only a few hotels open. I the apse of the village's 12th- and 13th century **Sant Andreu** church, you can admir the 13th-century *Crist de Salardú* crucifix ion carving.

The town is a handy base for the Baqueira Beret ski resort, just 4km further on.

Alberg Era Garona (☎ 973 64 52 71; Carretera d Vielha s/n; dm student & under 26/over 26 €18.10/21.60) a large youth hostel built in local stone and slate, has rooms of up to four beds, each with a bathroom.

Hotel deth Pais (☎ 973 64 58 36; Plaça dera Pica, s/d €71.70/86.70), in the middle of the origi-nal village, is a pleasant little hotel with straightforward rooms.

Baqueira-Beret

Baqueira (Vaquèira in Aranese), 3km east of Salardú, and Beret, 8km north of Baqueira, form Catalonia's premier **ski resort** (☎ 973 63 90 00; www.baquiera.es; day lift pass €35), favoured by the Spanish royal family, no less! Its good lift system gives access to 73 varied pis-tes totalling 104km (larger than any other Spanish resort), amid fine scenery at be-tween 1500m and 2510m.

There's nowhere cheap to stay in Baqueira, and nowhere at all at Beret. Many skiers stay down the valley in Salardú, Arties or Vielha.

North of Vielha

The hills on either side of the highway up to the French frontier hide some exquisite countryside with fine walking trails and an assortment of curious villages.

AUTHOR'S CHOICE

El Raconet (☎ 973 64 17 30; Carrèr de Crestalhera 3, Arròs; meals €20; ☽ Mon-Fri mid-Jul–Sep, plus Sat & Sun ski season; otherwise weekends only) Regulars keep coming back to this cosy stone-walled house that's been converted into a charming country restaurant. The setting alone makes it worthwhile. Solid country cooking is on offer and the cooks have a special penchant for *bacalao* (dried and salted cod).

ARRÒS, VILA & OTHER VILLAGES

Turn off the highway at Eth Pònt d'Arròs and climb a few kilometres into **Arròs**. This sleepy village makes a better choice of place to stay than the valley towns. Try **Casa Mariun** (☎ 973 64 03 41; Carrèr del Centre 13; d €28). This charming village house, all stone and dark wood shutters, is typical of the Val d'Aran.

PLAN DERA ARTIGA DE LIN

Branch west, off the main highway at **Es Bòrdes**, a typical Aranese village, and keep following the road as it twists its way up into heavily wooded country. The drive alone is a delight: follow the course of the Joèu stream, as you gain altitude, to reach the high mountain pastures of the Plan dera Artiga de Lin plain. Walking trails lead off into the tall forbidding mountains of the Aragonese Pyrenees, capped by the Pic d'Aneto (see p423).

Getting There & Around

BUS

Two Alsina Graells buses run daily between Barcelona and Vielha (€25, 5¼ hours) via Lleida and El Pont de Suert. Lleida to Vielha (€10) takes three hours. From June to October a daily Alsina Graells bus connects Barcelona and Vielha (€30) via La Pobla de Segur, Llavorsí, the Espot turning on the C13, Port de la Bonaigua and Salardú (the total journey time is about seven hours).

A local bus service runs from four (at weekends) to nine times daily along the valley from Baqueira to Les or Pontaut (for Eth Pont de Rei) via Vielha and the intervening villages. Several others run from Vielha either to Baquiera or to Les/Pontaut. The trip from one end of the valley to the other takes up to an hour. A single ticket for any destination is €0.80 (or €7.20 for a book of 10 tickets).

CAR & MOTORCYCLE

The N230 from Lleida and El Pont de Suert reaches Aran through the 5.25km Túnel de Vielha, then heads north from Vielha to the French border at Eth Pont de Rei.

From the Vall de la Noguera Pallaresa, the C28 crosses the Port de la Bonaigua pass (2072m) – which is sometimes closed in winter – into Naut Aran, meeting the N230 at Vielha.

CENTRAL CATALONIA

Away from the beaches and mountains that captivate the bulk of roamers in Catalonia is a host of little-visited gems splashed across the Catalan hinterland. About halfway between Barcelona and the Pyrenees lies the pretty town of Vic, with its grand Plaça Major. Northwest of the capital, you can strike out for the towns of Manresa (just beyond Montserrat), Cardona (with its windy castle complex) and Solsona, en route to Lleida. An alternative route to Lleida takes you further south through the Conca de Barberà, littered with grand medieval monasteries.

VIC

pop 35,350

Vic, with its attractive historic centre and some fine restaurants, dominates the flatlands of La Plana de Vic to the south of the Pyrenees, and was one of Catalonia's leading religious centres. The power of the bishops of Vic stretched far and wide and explains the surprising number of churches crammed into the old town today.

Information

Tourist office (☎ 93 886 20 91; Carrer de la Ciutat 4; ☽ 10am-2pm & 4-8pm Mon-Sat, 10am-1pm Sun).

Sights

Plaça Major, the largest of Catalonia's central squares, is lined with medieval, baroque and Modernista mansions. It is still the scene of regular markets, hence its other name, Plaça del Mercadal.

The **Catedral de Sant Pere** (admission €2; ☽ 10am-1pm & 4-7pm) is a neoclassical Goliath of rather gloomy taste, and flanked by a stout Romanesque bell tower. Inside, the dark, square-based pillars are lightened somewhat by murals by Josep Maria Sert (he had to do them twice because the first set was destroyed by fire in 1936). It is worth the admission fee to enter the Romanesque crypt, see the treasury rooms and, above all, wander into the stone lace-work splendour of the Gothic cloister. Entry is from the left side of the altar.

Across Carrer de Cloquer, the **Museu Episcopal** (☎ 93 886 93 60; Plaça del Bisbe Oliba 3; adult/child, student & senior €4/2; ☺ 10am-7pm Tue-Sat, 10am-2pm Sun Apr-Sep; 10am-1pm & 3-6pm Tue-Fri, 10am-7pm Sat, 10am-2pm Sun Oct-Mar) holds a marvellous collection of Romanesque and Gothic art, among other things. In Catalonia it is probably second only to the Museu Nacional d'Art de Catalunya collection in Barcelona (p295). The Romanesque collection includes the vivid *Davallament*, a scene depicting the taking down of Christ from the cross. The Gothic collection contains works by such key figures as Lluís Borrassà, Bernat Martorell and Jaume Huguet.

Sleeping & Eating

Vic is an easy day trip from Barcelona. It has are a couple of cheap *pensiones* and several rather more expensive hotels. The city is known for its disproportionate density of high-quality restaurants, and it's close enough to Barcelona for people from the big city to have an agreeable getaway.

Ca l'U (☎ 93 889 03 45; Plaça de Santa Teresa 4; meals €20-25; ☺ Tue-Sat, lunch only Sun) This big old hostal is in an all-purpose location with a long history. Sit down in the dining hall, where you can tuck into good Catalan home cooking.

Jordi Parramón (☎ 93 886 38 15; Carrer de Cardona 7; meals €50-60; ☺ Tue-Sun) The chef, Mr Parramón has carved out a name for himself for his avant-garde style. Like many of his Catalan colleagues, he has taken the best of local tradition and given it some zest. Simple dishes such as *arròs amb boletus* (mushroom rice) are exquisitely prepared.

Getting There & Away

Regular *rodalies* (line C3) run from Barcelona (€3.50, up to 1½ hours).

AROUND VIC
Rupit
pop 240

An enchanting excursion northeast of Vic takes you 31km along the C153 to Rupit, a splendid old village set amid rugged grazing country – the flat-top mountains around here come as quite a surprise. You cross a suspension footbridge made in the 1940s to reach the village, which is full of quaint 17th-century houses, a baroque church and tucked-away squares. Especially enticing is Carrer del Fossar, which climbs the spine of the hill, along which part of the village is spread-eagled. Rupit is a good base for rambles in the area.

Getting here without your own vehicle is problematic. **Pous** (☎ 93 889 25 77) buses leave Carrer de Casp 30 in Barcelona at 6pm Monday to Friday and at 11am on Saturday, and return at 8am (with an extra service at 5pm on weekends and holidays). Change buses in Vic. The trip (€7.50) takes about two hours from Barcelona.

MANRESA
pop 64,760

A big commercial centre in the Catalan heartland, Manresa was the scene of the first assembly of the nationalist Unió Catalanista (1897), which published the *Bases de Manresa*, a political manifesto for an autonomous Catalan state.

Not a great deal of the old town remains but you can't miss the great bulk that is the **Basílica de Santa Maria**, atop the Puig Cardener hill in the centre of town. Its huge Gothic nave is second in size only to that of the cathedral in Girona (p336). The unique Romanesque **Pont Vell**, whose eight arcs span the rather less-impressive Riu Cardener, was rebuilt after destruction in the civil war.

Rodalies from Barcelona (€3.50, 1¼ hours) via Terrassa run here regularly.

CARDONA
pop 4730

Long before arrival, you espy in the distance the outline of the impregnable 18th-century fortress high above the town of Cardona, which itself lies next to the Muntanya de Sal (Salt Mountain). Until 1990 the salt mines were an important source of income to the people of Cardona.

The castle (follow the signs uphill to the Parador) was built over an older predecessor. The single most remarkable element of the buildings is the lofty and spare Romanesque **Església de Sant Vicenç** (☎ 93 868 41 69; adult/child €2.40/1.80, admission free on Tue; ☺ 10am-1.30pm &

3-6.30pm Tue-Sun Jun-Sep, 10am-1.30pm & 3-5.30pm Tue-Sun Oct-May). To get in, stop at the guardian's office on the right as you enter the castle (and now hotel) courtyard. The bare stone walls were once covered in bright frescoes, some of which can be contemplated in the Museu Nacional d'Art de Catalunya in Barcelona (see p295).

A couple of modest *pensiones* offer relatively cheap digs for an overnight stay. If you can afford it, the place to be is the magnificent **Parador Ducs de Cardona** (☎ 93 869 12 75; cardona@parador.es; s/d €97/121.20). It's your chance to follow in ducal splendour and be king of the castle for a night or two.

Cardona is served by the Alsina Graells Barcelona–Manresa–Solsona bus route. Up to four run daily from Barcelona (€9.80, 1¾ hours) and nine from Manresa (€3.35, 40 minutes). Up to four buses proceed to Solsona (€1.65, 25 minutes).

SOLSONA
pop 7930

They call the people of Solsona *matarucs* (donkey-killers), which seems an odd tag until you hear what the townsfolk's favourite festive activity used to be.

Every February the high point of Solsona's carnival fun was the hoisting of a donkey, by the neck, up the town bell tower (Torre de les Hores). The donkey, literally scared to death, not unreasonably, would shit and

---

AUTHOR'S CHOICE

Can Boix (☎ 973 470266; www.canboix .com; Carrer Afores, Peramola; s/d €133.75/ 203.30; P 🐾 🖭) About 35km west of Solsona, bang up against the tree-laden lower slope of a couple of modest mountains, hides this splendid country retreat on the edge of the hamlet of Peramola. This rambling country estate has been in the same family's hands since the mid-18th century. Rooms have been furnished with iron bedsteads and lots of wood, as you would expect in a country lodge. The extensive, manicured gardens contrast with the dense green wilderness beyond. The hotel restaurant is known across Catalonia for its impeccable quality. And they'll prepare picnic lunches for the keen hikers among you.

---

piss on its way up, much to the delight of the drink-addled crowd below. To be hit by a glob of either substance was, they say, a sign of good fortune for the coming year. Animal rights people have put an end to this particularly bizarre form of entertainment and the donkey nowadays is a water-spraying fake.

The **Catedral de Santa Maria** (admission free; ⏰ 10am-1pm & 4-8pm) boasts Romanesque apses, a Gothic nave and a pretty cloister. Behind the cathedral is the 18th-century neoclassical **Palau Episcopal** (Plaça del Palau; adult/child & senior €2/1; ⏰ 10am-1pm & 4-6pm Tue-Sat, 10am-2pm Sun Oct-May; 10am-1pm & 4.30-7pm Tue-Sat, 10am-2pm Sun Jun-Sep), which houses a considerable collection of medieval art gathered from churches in the surrounding district.

Hotel Sant Roc (☎ 973 48 00 06; www.hotelsant roc.com; Plaça de Sant Roc 2; s/d €60/100; P 🐾) has recently been completely renovated, and is the best spot in town – it's quite a surprise. Modern rooms feature huge low beds with stark black-and-white décor, modern art on the walls and glistening bathrooms. Some of the top-floor rooms feature sloping, wood-beam ceilings.

La Cabaña d'En Geli (☎ 973 48 29 57; Carretera de Sant Llorenç 35; meals €25-30; ⏰ Tue-Sat, lunch only Sun), just outside town on the road that leads north to Sant Llorenç de Morunys, is a classic Catalan diner, where you can expect good, hearty local cooking and fine local wines.

Two to four Alsina Graells buses run daily from Barcelona (€11.50, two hours) via Manresa (€5.05, 65 minutes) and Cardona to Solsona.

CONCA DE BARBERÀ

This hilly, green, wine-making district comes as a refreshing surprise in the otherwise drab flatlands of southwest Catalonia and makes an alternative route from Barcelona (or Tarragona) to Lleida and beyond. Vineyards and woods succeed one another across rolling green hills, studded by occasional medieval villages and monasteries.

Reial Monestir de Santa Maria de Poblet

The jewel in the crown is doubtless this imposing fortified **monastery** (☎ 977 87 00 89; adult/student €4.20/2.40, plus Santes Creus & Vallbona monasteries €6; ⏰ 10am-12.30pm & 3-5.30pm), founded by Cistercian monks from southern France in 1151.

CATALAN TIPPLES

Avid tipplers all over the world will have come across a playful, relatively inexpensive bubbly called Freixenet. They know it comes from Spain but generally don't give it much more thought. One of the country's flagship exporters of *cava*, Freixenet is based at the heart of Catalonia's Penedès wine region, which alone produces the bulk of all Spain's sparkling white wines (see the Barcelona chapter, p325).

But Freixenet and bubbly are only the tip of the Catalan wineberg. Catalonia hosts 11 DO *(denominación de origen)* wine-producing zones and a remarkable variety of tipples. Although perhaps less well known than wines from the Rioja area, Catalan wines are full of pleasant surprises. Indeed, the heavy, deep-coloured red wines of El Priorat have gained the much-desired DOC *(denominación de origen calificada)* status long held by Rioja wines alone. To further investigate El Priorat's wines, and wines from the adjacent Montsant DO region, head for the tourist office in **Falset** (☎ 977 83 10 23; www.priorat.org; Carrer de Sant Marcel 2; ☺ 9am-3pm & 4-7pm Mon-Fri, 10am-2pm Sat, 11am-2pm Sun) for information on local wine cellars. Falset, the capital of the Priorat area, offers some fine restaurant options too.

Catalonia's other DO wines come from points all over the region, spread as far apart as the Empordà area around Figueres in the north, and the Terra Alta zone around Gandesa in the southwest. The Penedès region pumps out almost two million hectolitres a year and thus doubles the combined output of the remaining DO regions.

Most of the grapes grown in Catalonia are native to Spain and include the White Macabeo, Garnacha and Xarel.lo (for white wines), and the Black Garnacha, Monastrell and Ull de Llebre (Hare's Eye) red varieties. Increasingly, foreign varieties (such as Chardonnay, Riesling, Chenin Blanc, Cabernet Sauvignon, Merlot and Pinot Noir) are also grown.

Freixenet, Codorniu and Torres are the big names in the Penedès region, but there is plenty to discover beyond that region. Raïmat, in the Costers del Segre DO area in Lleida province, produces some fine reds and a couple of notable whites. Good fortified wines come from around Tarragona; some pleasing fresh wines are also produced in the Empordà area in the north by Cellers Santamaria and Cooperativa de Mollet de Perelada.

The walls of this abbey devoted to Santa Maria (a Unesco World Heritage site), were a defensive measure and also symbolised the monks' isolation from the vanities of the outside world. A grand portal gives access to a long uneven square, the Plaça Major, flanked by several dependencies including the small Romanesque **Capella de Santa Caterina**. The nearby **Porta Daurada** is so called because its bronze panels were overlaid with gold to suitably impress the visiting emperor Felipe II in 1564.

Once inside the **Porta Reial** (Royal Gate), flanked by hefty octagonal towers, you will be led through a worn Romanesque entrance to the grand cloister, of Romanesque origins but largely Gothic in style. With its peaceful fountain and pavilion, the two-level cloister is a marvellous haven. You will be led from the cloister to the head of the church, itself a typically tall and austere Cistercian Gothic creation, to witness the sculptural glory in alabaster that is the *retablo* and Panteón de los Reyes (Kings'

Pantheon). The raised alabaster coffins, restored by Frederic Marès (see p283), contain such greats as Jaume I (the conqueror of Mallorca and Valencia) and Pere III.

Of six **Vibasa buses** (☎ 902 101363) from Tarragona to Montblanc and L'Espluga de Francolí, three also stop at the monastery (one of two on weekends). Regular trains from Barcelona (Ca4 regional line) stop at Montblanc (€5.60) and L'Espluga de Francolí (€6.10) – the monastery is a 40-minute walk from the latter.

Around Reial Monestir de Santa Maria de Poblet

It is worth spending time exploring the vicinity. **L'Espluga de Francolí**, 2.5km from the monastery along a pleasant tree-lined country road that makes walking tempting, is a bright little town with several small hotels.

More interesting still is **Montblanc**, 8km away. Still surrounded by medieval battlements, this one-time royal residence is jammed with medieval jewels, including a

Gothic royal mansion and churches, as well as some vestiges of its Romanesque origins. The winding cross-country drive to **Prades** also takes you through lovely country.

If monasteries are your thing, the less imposing **Monestir de Santes Creus** (☎ 977 63 83 29; Plaça de Jaume el Just s/n; adult/child €3.60/2.40, plus Poblet & Vallbona monasteries €6, admission free Tue; ☑ 10am-1.30pm & 3-5.30pm Tue-Sun mid-Sep–mid-Mar, 10am-1.30pm & 3-7pm Tue-Sun mid-Mar–mid-Sep), about 28km east of Montblanc, and **Vallbona de les Monges** (☎ 973 33 02 66; adult/child €2.50/2, plus Santes Creus & Poblet monasteries €6; ☑ 10.30am-1.30pm & 4.30-6.45pm Tue-Sat, noon-1.30pm & 4.30-6.45pm Sun & holidays Mar-Oct; 10.30am-1.30pm & 4.30-5.30pm Tue-Sat, noon-1.30pm & 4.30-5.30pm Sun & holidays Nov-Feb) to the north, are also worth searching out.

See p372 for transport details.

LLEIDA
pop 111,260
Much of western Catalonia is flat and drab, but if you're not in a hurry Lleida (Lérida) is a likable place with a long and varied history. It's also the starting point of several routes towards the Pyrenees.

Information
Centre d'Informació i Reserves (☎ 902 250050; http://turisme.paeria.es; Carrer Major 31bis; ☑ 10am-8pm Mon-Sat, 10am-1.30pm Sun) Turisme de Lleida provide information about the city.
Oficina Turisme de la Generalitat (☎ 973 27 09 97; Avinguda de Madrid 36; ☑ 9am-2pm & 3-7pm Mon-Fri, 10am-2pm Sat) For tips on the rest of Lleida province.
Policía Nacional (☎ 973 24 40 50; Carrer de Sant Martí s/n)
Post office (Rambla de Ferran)

La Seu Vella
Lleida's 'old cathedral', **La Seu Vella** (☎ 973 23 06 53; admission €2.40; ☑ 10am-1.30pm & 3-5.30pm Tue-Sat, 10am-1.30pm Sun Oct-May; 10am-1.30pm & 4-7.30pm Tue-Sat, 10am-1.30pm Sun Jun-Sep) towers above all else in position and grandeur. It stands within a *recinte* (compound) of defensive walls erected between the 12th and 19th centuries.

The main entrance to the **recinte** (admission free; ☑ 8am-9pm daily) is from Carrer de Monterey on its western side, but during the cathedral's opening hours you can use the extraordinarily ugly **ascensor** (lift; admission €0.40; 10am-1.30pm & 4-8pm Tue-Sat, 10am-1.30pm Sun Jun-Sep; 10am-1.30pm & 3-5.30pm Tue-Sat, 10am-1.30pm Sun Oct-May) from above Plaça de Sant Joan.

The cathedral was built in sandy-coloured stone in the 13th to 15th centuries on the site of a former mosque (Lleida was under Muslim control from AD 719 to 1149). It's a masterpiece of the Transitional style, although it only recently recovered from 241 years' use as a barracks, which began as Felipe V's punishment for the city's opposition in the War of the Spanish Succession.

A 70m octagonal bell tower rises at the southwest end from the cloister, whose windows have exceptionally fine Gothic tracery. The spacious although rather austere interior, used as stables and dormitories during the military occupation, has a veritable forest of slender columns with carved capitals.

Above the cathedral are remains of the Islamic fortress and residence of the Muslim governors, known as the Castell del Rei or La Suda.

Carrer Major & Around
A 13th-century Gothic mansion **La Paeria** has housed the city government almost since its inception. The 18th-century neoclassical **La Seu Nova** (Plaça de la Catedral) was built when La Seu Vella was turned into a barracks.

Opposite is the Hospital de Santa Maria, with a Gothic courtyard. It now houses the **Sala d'Arqueologia** (☎ 973 27 15 00; Plaça de la Catedral; admission free; ☑ 10am-2pm & 6-9pm Tue-Fri, 11am-2pm & 7-9pm Sat, 11am-2pm Sun Jun-Sep; 10am-2pm & 5.30-8.30pm Tue-Fri, noon-2pm & 5.30-8.30pm Sat, noon-2pm Sun Oct-May), which includes Iberian and Roman finds from the Lleida region.

Carrer dels Cavallers and Carrer de la Palma climb from Carrer Major up through the old part of town. The Antic Convent del Roser, featuring an unusual three-storey cloister, houses the **Museu d'Art Jaume Morera** (☎ 973 70 04 19; Carrer dels Cavallers 15; admission free; ☑ 10am-1pm & 6-9pm Tue-Sat, 10am-1pm Sun mid-Jun–mid-Sep; 11am-2pm & 5-8pm Tue-Sat, 11am-2pm Sun mid-Sep–mid-Jun) and its collection of work by Lleida-associated artists.

Sleeping
Hotel Ramon Berenguer IV (☎ 973 23 73 45; Plaça de Ramon Berenguer IV 2; s/d with bathroom €32.50/41; P ⊠) These somewhat dog-eared digs are quite all right and handy for the train station. Rooms are all decent if unexciting. Those on the higher floors enjoy a bit of a view.
Hotel Principal (☎ 973 23 08 00; www.hotelprincipal.net; Plaça de la Paeria 8; s/d €43.90/53.50; P ⊠)

CATALONIA

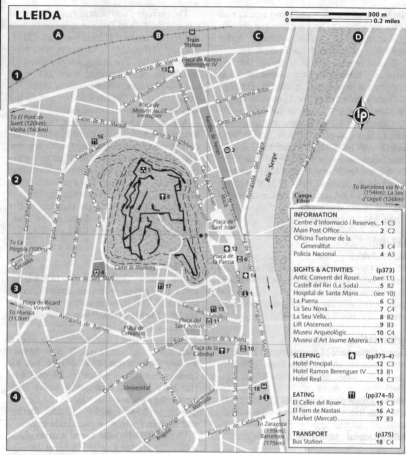

LLEIDA

| 0 | | 300 m |
| 0 | | 0.2 miles |

INFORMATION
Centre d'Informació i Reserves...**1** C3
Main Post Office.....................**2** C2
Oficina Turisme de la
Generalitat.........................**3** C4
Policía Nacional.......................**4** A3

SIGHTS & ACTIVITIES (p373)
Antic Convent del Roser........(see 11)
Castell del Rei (La Suda)...........**5** B2
Hospital de Santa Maria........(see 10)
La Paeria................................**6** C3
La Seu Nova..........................**7** C4
La Seu Vella..........................**8** B2
Lift (Ascensor).......................**9** C3
Museu Arqueològic...............**10** C4
Museu d'Art Jaume Morera.....**11** C3

SLEEPING (pp373–4)
Hotel Principal.......................**12** C3
Hotel Ramon Berenguer IV.....**13** B1
Hotel Real.............................**14** C3

EATING (pp374–5)
El Celler del Roser.................**15** C3
El Forn de Nastasi..................**16** A2
Market (Mercat).....................**17** B3

TRANSPORT (p375)
Bus Station...........................**18** C4

This hotel is one of the city's few good central accommodation options, if you're looking for marginally more style. Although it's aimed rather more at a business clientele, the hotel is perfectly located for touring the city. The rooms are spacious and well maintained in a building that has a somewhat faded glory.

Hotel Real (☎ 973 23 94 05; www.hotelreallleida .com; Avinguda de Blondel 22; s/d €62/81.30; P ⚒ ▯) A modern mid-rise place with a pleasant garden, Hotel Real is also mostly aimed at business visitors and offers various classes of room. All of the rooms are bright and clean, and many also have generous-sized balconies. A couple of rooms have wheelchair access.

Eating

Lleida is Catalonia's snail-eating capital. So many *cargols* are swallowed during the annual **Aplec del Cargol** (Snail Festival) held on a Sunday in early May, that some have to be imported.

El Celler del Roser (☎ 973 23 90 70; Carrer del Cavallers 24; meals €25-30; ☾ Tue-Sat, lunch only Sun) This is one place that delights in serving up the slithering things *a la llauna* (baked on tin over hot coals), as well as other Catalan fare. The big house specialty is *bacallà* (cod) prepared in oh-so-many ways.

El Forn de Nastasi (☎ 973 23 45 10; Carrer de Salmerón 10; meals €30-35; ☾ Tue-Sat, lunch only Sun) This remains a reference point of local dining. Dishes can range from ostrich to traditional *cargols*. What about *solomillo con salsa de Oporto* (sirloin bathed in a port sauce)?

La Pèrgola (☎ 973 23 82 37; Passeig de Ronda 123; meals €40-50; ☾ Mon & Tue, Thu-Sat) The chefs in this unlikely shady house (one of several on this strip – a surprise given the horrible high-rises), take the business of cooking seriously. Such Catalan mixes as pig trotters with lobster are among the unforgettable offerings.

Getting There & Away
BUS
For general bus-timetable information, call ☎ 973 26 85 00. Daily services by **Alsina Graells** (☎ 973 27 14 70) include up to 13 buses (three on Sunday) to Barcelona (€14.05, 2¼ to 2¾ hours); two to El Pont de Suert and Vielha (€9.65, 2¾ hours); one (except Sunday) to La Pobla de Segur, Sort, Llavorsí and Esterri d'Àneu (€15, three hours); and two to La Seu d'Urgell (€11.95, 2½ hours).

CAR & MOTORCYCLE
The quickest routes to Barcelona, Tarragona and Zaragoza are by the AP2, but you can avoid tolls by taking the A2 to Zaragoza or Barcelona or the N240 to Tarragona. The main northward roads are the C14 to La Seu d'Urgell, the N230 to Vielha and the N240 to Barbastro and Huesca (in Aragón).

TRAIN
Lleida is on the Barcelona–Zaragoza–Madrid line. Around 15 to 20 trains daily run to/from Barcelona, with most taking about two hours (although some dawdle along and take four). Second-class fares range from €8.25 to €19. A similar number of trains head to Zaragoza (€10.50 to €24, up to two hours), including high-speed ones, taking just under one hour. About 10 high-speed trains head to Madrid (€54, 2¾ hours).

MONTSEC
This hilly range 65km north of Lleida is the main stage for hang-gliders and ultra-lights in Catalonia. It is also a popular area for walking, caving and climbing.

The focal point is **Àger**, a village in the valley of the same name. If coming via Balaguer, you'll see it to the northeast as you reach the top of **Coll d'Àger** (912m). The village is draped like a mantle over a hill, protruding from the top of which is the intriguing ruin of the **Església de Sant Pere**.

Montsec has a half-dozen take-off points, including one at the Sant Alís peak (1678m), the highest in the range. **Volàger** (☎ 973 32 02 30; www.volager.com; Camí de Castellnou s/n), based in Bellpuig, offers hang-gliding courses here and provides all the equipment. Introductory weekend courses in hang-gliding cost €150, while a full six-day course comes to €400.

A choice location for walkers and climbers is the stunning **Congost de Mont-Rebei**, a narrow gorge of 80m-high rock walls at the western end of the Montsec range. The Riu Noguera Ribagorçana flows into the gorge from the north, along the border with Aragón. Caves along the foot of the gorge, and around the dam to the south, attract speleologists.

You can stay at one of a handful of *cases de pagès* or a hostal. About the only way to get into and around the area is with your own wheels.

COSTA DAURADA

South of Sitges (p321) stretches the Costa Daurada (Golden Coast), a series of quiet resorts with unending broad beaches along a mainly flat coast, capped by the delta of the mighty Riu Ebre (Ebro), which protrudes 20km out into the Mediterranean. Along the way is the old Roman capital of Tarragona, and the modern extravaganza of Universal Mediterrànea – Catalonia's answer to EuroDisney.

VILANOVA I LA GELTRÚ
pop 57,300
Six minutes' west of Sitges by train, Vilanova is home to the culinary delicacy of *xató* (an almond-and-hazelnut sauce used on various dishes, particularly seafood), the much sought-after actor Sergi López, and a fine trio of broad beaches. Much of the sprawling town itself is, however, of little interest.

Information
Tourist office (☎ 93 815 45 17; www.vilanova.org; Passeig del Carme; ☾ 10am-1pm & 5-8pm Tue-Fri, 10am-2pm & 5-8pm Sat, 10am-2pm Sun & holidays Jul-Sep; 10am-1pm Tue-Fri, 10am-2pm & 5-8pm Sat, 10am-2pm Sun & holidays Oct-Jun)

Sights
A few blocks inland from the beaches is Vilanova's main attraction, the **Museu del**

Ferrocarril (Railway Museum; ☎ 93 815 84 91; Plaça d'Eduard Maristany; adult/child €4.30/3; ☉ 4.30-8.30pm Tue-Fri, 10am-1pm & 4.30-8.30pm Sat, Sun & holidays mid-Jul–mid-Sep; 10am-3pm Tue-Fri & Sun, 10am-3pm & 4.30-8.30pm Sat mid-Sep–mid-Jul), located in the 19th-century installations for the maintenance of steam trains, next to the train station. It is claimed that the collection of steam locomotives is the biggest in Europe, and it attracts kids of all ages.

Festivals
Vilanova i la Geltrú stages a riotous *carnaval* (carnival) in February that lasts for 13 days. One of the highpoints is the **Batalla dels Caramels** (Battle of the Sweeties), when townsfolk in costume launch more than 100,000 kilos of sweeties at one another!

Sleeping & Eating
It's easy enough to pop down for the day from Barcelona or Sitges but there is one serious reason for hanging out a little longer…

Hotel César (☎ 93 815 11 25; www.hotelcesar.net; Carrer d'Isaac Peral 4-8; s/d €90-160; ✄ ▯ ▣) The town's top hotel is set in a leafy, tranquil part of town just back from the waterfront. It offers a series of double rooms and suites. The top rooms have their own computers with ADSL Internet access. Saunter off to the sauna, or opt for a massage. Or just chill in the garden a day at the nearby beach. Prices halve in low season. The hotel is also home to **La Fitorra** (meals €20-25; ☉ Tue-Sat, lunch only Sun), one of the senior denizens of local cooking.

Getting There & Away
The town is just down the *rodalies* (line 2) from Sitges. From Barcelona the fare is €2.25.

ALTAFULLA
pop 3610
Once a Roman holiday resort for the affluent citizens of Tarragona, this town about 10km east of Tarragona, was converted into a fortified settlement in the wake of the Muslim invasion. The original medieval core of Altafulla is small but charming, all cream and whitewashed walls with rose-coloured stone portals and windows. It is topped by a 13th-century **castle**.

Altafulla's broad **beach** (about 2km away on the other side of the freeway) is backed

by a row of cheerful single-storey houses known as the **Botigues de Mar** (Sea Shops). Until well into the 19th century they served as warehouses but have since been converted into houses – many up for holiday let through **Europ Service** (☎ 977 650308; Carrer de Llevant 12, Altafulla) – as well as seafood and tapas restaurants.

Sleeping & Eating
Alberg Casa Gran (☎ 977 65 07 79; Plaçeta 12; dm student & under 26/over 26 €17/19.40) In the old part of town, this is one of the region's more enchantingly placed youth hostels. Occupying a fine old mansion with a terrace, it even incorporates a tower belonging to the old town walls.

Getting There & Away
A host of local trains run to Altafulla from Tarragona (€1.25 to €1.45, 10 minutes).

TARRAGONA
pop 121,080
Tarragona was first occupied by the Romans, who called it Tarraco, in 218 BC. In 27 BC Augustus made it the capital of his new Tarraconensis province (roughly all modern Spain) and stayed until 25 BC, directing campaigns in Cantabria and Asturias. Tarragona was abandoned when the Muslims arrived in AD 714, but reborn as the seat of a Christian archbishopric in 1089. Today its rich Roman remains and fine medieval cathedral make it an absorbing place.

Orientation
The main street is Rambla Nova, which runs roughly northwest from a cliff-top overlooking the Mediterranean. A couple

TARRAGONA

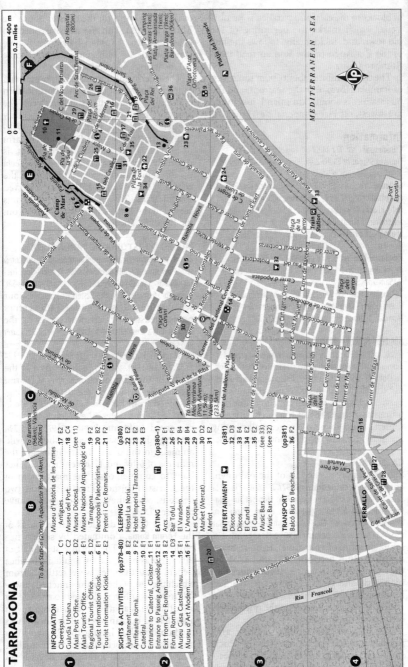

To Bus Station (200m); Aqüeducte Romà (4km);

To Barcelona (96km); Valencia (260km)

INFORMATION		
Ciberespai	1	C1
Guàrdia Urbana	2	C2
Main Post Office	3	D2
Main Tourist Office	4	E1
Regional Tourist Office	5	D2
Tourist Information Kiosk	6	E1
Tourist Information Kiosk	7	E2

SIGHTS & ACTIVITIES	(pp378–80)	
Ajuntament	8	E2
Amfiteatre Romà	9	F2
Catedral	10	E1
Entrance to Catedral, Cloister	11	E1
Entrance to Passeig Arqueològic	12	E1
Exit from Circ Romà	13	E2
Fòrum Romà	14	D3
Museu Casa Castellarnau	15	E1
Museu d'Art Modern	16	F1

Museu d'Història de les Armes		
Antigues	17	E2
Museu del Port	18	C4
Museu Diocesà	(see 11)	
Museu Nacional Arqueològic de		
Tarragona	19	F2
Necròpolis Paleocristians	20	B2
Pretori i Circ Romans	21	F2

SLEEPING	(p380)	
Hostal La Noria	22	E2
Hotel Imperial Tàrraco	23	F2
Hotel Lauria	24	E3

EATING	(pp380–1)	
Arcs	25	E1
Bar Toful	26	F1
El Varadero	27	B4
L'Àncora	28	B4
Les Coques	29	F1
Market (Mercat)	30	D2
Merlot	31	E2

ENTERTAINMENT	(p381)	
Discos	32	D3
Discos	33	E4
El Candil	34	E2
El Cau	35	E2
Music Bars	(see 33)	
Music Bars	(see 32)	

TRANSPORT	(p381)	
Balcó Bus to Beaches	36	F2

MEDITERRANEAN SEA

To Hospital (800m)

To Camping Las Palmeras (1km); Platja Arrabassada (1km); Platja Llarga (3km); Barcelona (90km)

To Universal Mediterrània (Port Aventura; 11.5km); Valencia (233.5km)

Riu Francolí

SERRALLO

of blocks to the east, and parallel, is Rambla Vella, which marks the beginning of the old town and, incidentally, follows the line of the Via Augusta, the Roman road from Rome to Cádiz.

The train station is about 500m southwest of Rambla Nova, near the seafront, and the bus station is about 2km inland, just to the northwest, off Plaça Imperial de Tàrraco.

Information

Ciberespai (☎ 977 24 57 64; Carrer d'Estanislau Figueres 58; per hr €1.80-2.40; ☉ 9am-midnight Mon-Fri, 10am-midnight Sat & Sun)

Guàrdia Urbana (☎ 977 24 03 45; Carrer de Pare Palau 7)

Hospital (☎ 977 23 27 14; Passeig de Torroja)

Info kiosks (☉ 10am-2pm Sat & Sun Apr-Sep) These are scattered about town.

Main post office (Plaça de Corsini; ☉ 8am-8pm Mon-Fri)

Regional tourist office (☎ 977 23 34 15; Carrer de Fortuny 4; ☉ 9.15am-2pm & 4-6.30pm Mon-Fri, 9.15am-2pm Sat)

Tourist office (☎ 977 25 07 95; www.tarragona turisme.com; Carrer Major 39; ☉ 10am-2pm & 4-7pm Mon-Sat, 10am-2pm Sun & holidays)

Sights & Activities

Pick up the handy *Ruta Arqueològica Urbana* brochure from the main tourist office. It details more than 30 locations throughout the old town where Roman remains can be viewed, some of them in shops and restaurants. If they are not too busy with customers, shop owners are generally happy for individuals to drop by and take a look.

CATEDRAL

Sitting grandly at the top of the old town, Tarragona's **cathedral** (☎ 977 23 86 85; Pla de la Seu; admission €2.40; ☉ 10am-7pm Mon-Sat Jul–mid-Oct, 10am-5pm Mon-Sat mid-Oct–mid-Nov, 10am-2pm Mon-Sat mid-Nov–mid-Mar, 10am-1pm & 4-7pm Mon-Sat mid-Mar–Jun) is a treasure house deserving 1½ hours or more of your time, if you're to do it justice. Built between 1171 and 1331 on the site of a Roman temple, it combines Romanesque and Gothic features, as typified by the main façade on Pla de la Seu. The entrance is by the cloister on the northwestern side of the building.

The cloister has Gothic vaulting and Romanesque carved capitals, one of which shows rats conducting what they imagine to be a cat's funeral…until the cat comes back

to life! The rooms off the cloister house the Museu Diocesà, with an extensive collection extending from Roman hairpins to some lovely 12th- to 14th-century polychrome woodcarvings of a breastfeeding Virgin.

The interior of the cathedral, over 100m long, is Romanesque at the northeastern end and Gothic at the southwestern. The aisles are lined with 14th- to 19th-century chapels and hung with 16th- and 17th-century tapestries from Brussels. The arm of St Thecla, Tarragona's patron saint, is normally kept in the Capella de Santa Tecla on the southeastern side. The choir in the centre of the nave has 15th-century carved walnut stalls. The marble main altar was carved in the 13th century with scenes from the life of St Thecla.

MUSEU D'HISTÒRIA DE TARRAGONA

This **museum** (www.museutgn.com; adult/student & senior per site €2/1, all sites €8/4; sites ☉ 9am-9pm Tue-Sat, 9am-3pm Sun & holidays Easter-Sep; 9am-7pm Tue-Sat, 10am-3pm Sun & holidays Oct-Easter) comprises four separate Roman sites and a 14th-century noble mansion, which now serves as the **Museu Casa Castellarnau** (☎ 977 24 22 20; Carrer dels Cavallers 14).

Start with the **Pretori i Circ Romans** (☎ 977 24 19 52; Plaça del Rei), which includes part of the vaults of the Roman circus, where chariot races were held. The circus, 300m long, stretched from here to beyond Plaça de la Font to the west. Near the beach is the well-preserved **Amfiteatre Romà** (☎ 977 24 25 79), where gladiators battled each other, or wild animals, to the death. In its arena are the remains of 6th- and 12th-century churches built to commemorate the martyrdom of the Christian bishop Fructuosus and two deacons, who, they say, were burnt alive here in AD 259.

East of Carrer de Lleida are remains of the **Fòrum Romà**, dominated by several imposing columns. The northwestern half of this site was occupied by a judicial basilica (where legal disputes were settled), from which the rest of the forum stretched downhill to the southwest. Linked to the site by a footbridge is another excavated area with a stretch of Roman street. This forum was the hub of public life for the Roman town but was less important, and much smaller, than the provincial forum, the navel of all Tarraconensis province.

OF GIANTS, DRAGONS & HUMAN CASTLES

Catalans get up to all sorts of unusual tricks at *festa* (festival) time. Fire and fireworks play a big part in many Spanish festivals, but Catalonia adds a special twist with the *correfoc* (fire-running), in which devil and dragon figures run through the streets spitting fireworks at the crowds. (Wear protective clothes if you intend to get close!) *Correfocs* are often part of the *festa major* – a town or village's main annual festival. Many of these take place in July or August.

Also usually part of the *festa major* fun are the *sardana* (Catalonia's national round-dance) and *gegants*, which are splendidly attired and lifelike 5m-high giants that parade through the streets or dance in the squares to the sound of old-fashioned instruments. Giants usually come in male-female pairs: a medieval king and queen, a Muslim sultan and a Christian princess. Almost every town and village has its own – sometimes just one pair, sometimes five or six. They're usually accompanied by an entourage of grotesque 'dwarfs' (otherwise known as *capgrossos*, or 'big heads').

On La Nit de Sant Joan (23 June), big bonfires burn at crossroads and on town squares in a combined midsummer and St John's Eve celebration. Fireworks go off all night. But Catalonia's supreme fire festival is the Patum in the otherwise unexceptional Pyrenean foothill town of Berga. An evening of dancing and firework-spitting angels, devils, mule-like monsters, dwarfs, giants and men covered in grass culminates in a kind of mass frenzy of fire and smoke that has been likened to a medieval vision of hell. The 'real' Patum happens on Corpus Christi (the Thursday following the eighth Sunday after Easter Sunday) although there are watered-down versions over the next two or three days.

An activity demanding rather more calm and order, but still emotive, is the building of *castells* – human castles. This tradition is strongest in southern and central Catalonia: Valls, Vila-franca del Penedès and Terrassa have three of the most famous groups of *castellers*. The golden age was the 1880s, when castells of *tres de nou* and *quatre de nou* ('three of nine' and 'four of nine', ie nine storeys of three people and nine storeys of four people) were achieved. Such castles have only occasionally been raised in the past few years.

There are all sorts of permutations in the construction of the *castell*: those built without a *pinya*, *folre* or *manilles* (extra rings of support for the first, second and third storeys) are particularly tricky and termed *net* (clean). A completed *castell* is signalled by the child at the top (the *anxaneta*) raising their arm – a cue for tumultuous applause and cheering from the onlookers. A *castell* that manages to dismantle itself without collapsing is *descarregat*. Especially difficult is a *pilar*, a tower of one person per storey. The best *pilar* ever done was eight storeys – a *pilar de vuit*.

The two teams of the town of Valls have a long and venerable history in this odd branch of the construction industry. The Vilafranca del Penedès team are also in the top league. Every two years a championship competition is held in Tarragona's bullring – the next one will be in October 2006. Otherwise, these and many other teams turn up at *festes* all over Catalonia.

The **Passeig Arqueològic** is a peaceful walk around part of the perimeter of the old town between two lines of city walls; the inner ones are mainly Roman, while the outer ones were put up by the British during the War of the Spanish Succession.

MUSEU NACIONAL ARQUEOLÒGIC DE TARRAGONA

This carefully presented **museum** (☎ 977 23 62 09; www.mnat.es; Plaça del Rei 5; admission €2.40; ☺ 10am-8pm Tue-Sat, 10am-2pm Sun & holidays Jun-Sep; 10am-1.30pm & 4-7pm Tue-Sat, 10am-2pm Sun & holidays Oct-May) gives further insight into Roman Tarraco, although most explanatory material is in Catalan or Castilian. Exhibits

include part of the Roman city walls, frescoes, sculpture and pottery. A highlight is the large, almost complete *Mosaic de Peixos de la Pineda*, showing fish and sea creatures. In the section on everyday arts you can admire ancient fertility aids including an outsized stone penis, symbol of the god Priapus.

Admission entitles you to enter the museum at the **Necròpolis Paleocristians** (☺ 10am-1.30pm & 4-7pm Tue-Sat, 10am-2pm Sun Jun-Sep; 10am-1.30pm & 3-5.30pm Tue-Sat, 10am-2pm Sun Oct-May). This large Christian cemetery of late-Roman and Visigothic times is on Passeig de la Independència on the western edge of town and boasts some surprisingly elaborate tombs. Unfortunately only its small museum is open at present.

MUSEU D'ART MODERN

This modest **art gallery** (☎ 977 23 50 32; Carrer de Santa Anna 8; admission free; ⏲ 10am-8pm Tue-Fri, 10am-3pm & 5-8pm Sat, 11am-2pm Sun & holidays) is at its most interesting when temporary exhibitions take place.

MUSEU D'HISTÒRIA DE LES ARMES ANTIGUES

If you are into old swords, lances and pistols this **museum** (☎ 977 22 41 84; Carrer de la Nau 12; admission €3; ⏲ 11am-1pm & 4-7pm Mon-Sat, 10am-1pm Sun) is an interesting stop.

MUSEU DEL PORT

Down by the waterfront, this curious **museum** (☎ 977 25 94 42; Refugi 2 Moll de la Cost; adult/ student €1.80/1.20; ⏲ 10am-2pm & 5-8pm Tue-Thu, 11am-2pm Sun & holidays Jun-Sep; 10am-2pm & 4-7pm Tue-Thu, 11am-2pm Sun & holidays Oct-May) is housed in a dockside shed. There's not a lot to it – some displays tracing the history of the port from Roman times (in Catalan and Castilian only), a few models boats and one or two other seafaring items.

PONT DEL DIABLE

The so-called Devil's Bridge is actually the **Aqüeducte Romà** (admission free; ⏲ 9am-dusk), yet another of the marvels the Romans left behind. It sits, somewhat incongruously, in the leafy rough just off the AP7 freeway, which leads into Tarragona (near where it intersects with the N240). It is a fine stretch of two-tiered aqueduct (217m long and 27m high), along which you can totter to the other side. Bus No 5 to Sant Salvador from Plaça Imperial de Tàrraco, running every 10 to 20 minutes, will take you to the vicinity, or park in one of the lay-bys marked on either side of the AP7, just outside the freeway toll gates.

BEACHES

The town beach, **Platja del Miracle**, is reasonably clean but can get terribly crowded. **Platja Arrabassada**, 1km northeast across the headland, is longer, and **Platja Llarga**, beginning 2km further out, stretches for about 3km. Bus Nos 1 and 9 from the Balcó stop on Via Augusta go to both (€1.10). You can get the same buses from along Rambla Vella and Rambla Nova.

Sleeping

Camping Las Palmeras (☎ 977 20 80 81; www .laspalmeras.com; 2-person tent & car €34.25) This cheerful camping ground lies at the far end of Platja Llarga (3km northeast of Tarragona) and is one of the better of eight camping grounds scattered behind the beaches northeast of the city. A big pool stretches out amid leafy parkland just back from the beach. The camping ground enjoys a 1.5km stretch of seaside frontage.

Hostal La Noria (☎ 977 23 87 17; Plaça de la Font 53; s/d €26/42) For a position right on the old town's main square, you can't do much better than these corner digs. Rooms are simple enough but have their own attached clean bathroom, and those with a balcony assure you a window on old Tarragona's street life.

Hotel Lauria (☎ 977 23 67 12; www.hlauria.es; Rambla Nova 20; s/d €36/64; P ✖ ☎) With its dignified façade along the city's nicest boulevard, the hotel has a whiff of another era. The rooms are a little on the functional side, but the best have parquet floors, leatherbacked furniture and the occasional nice touch such as fresh flowers.

Hotel Imperial Tàrraco (☎ 977 23 30 40; www .hotelhusaimperialtarraco.com; Passeig de les Palmeres s/n; s/d €110.25/147.70; P ✖ ☎) It's the position that makes this fairly outsized international business-style hotel. Grab a room with a balcony and you'll have limitless vistas out to sea. The rooms are spacious and fairly standard for this level. A buffet breakfast is included.

Eating

Bar Toful (☎ 977 21 42 16; Arc de Sant Bernat 4; meals €15-20; ⏲ 8am-6pm Mon-Thu, 8am-midnight Fri-Sat) Since the 1940s this knockabout bar just off the Roman forum has been a mecca for locals in search of good ol' tapas over a beer or two. During the day people drop by for a tipple, and on weekend evenings others crowd in for a steak in mushroom sauce, or fish – a cheap, cheerful and good value dinner.

Les Coques (☎ 977 22 83 00; Carrer del Nou Patriarca 2bis; meals €40-50; ⏲ Mon-Sat) In the shadow of the cathedral, this tranquil restaurant offers a panoply of meat dishes. Why not some *manetes de porc desosades amb bolets* (boned pig's trotters with mushrooms)? The desserts are homemade and delicious.

Arcs (☎ 977 21 80 40; Carrer de Misser Sitges 13; meals €45-50; ⏲ Mon-Sat) Behind a heavy old-town stone façade lies this den of gastronomic pleasure. After choosing from a fusion menu, let your eyes wander over the contemporary art on the walls. Dishes here have those predictably long names associated with modern eating, eg *tronc de rap rostit a la crema de Gorgonzola i pipes caramelitzades* (trunk of monkfish roasted in Gorgonzola cream with caramelised sunflower seeds)!

Merlot (☎ 977 22 06 52; Carrer dels Cavallers 6; meals €40; ☺ Tue–Sat, dinner only Mon) Merlot pioneered the way for stylish eating in the once rundown old town of Tarragona and remains a key culinary stop. All sorts of inventive dishes, starting with Catalan classics as a base, are served. The bare stone walls are lightened by paintings and other decorations.

The quintessential Tarragona seafood experience can only be had in Serrallo, the town's fishing port. About a dozen bars and restaurants here sell the day's catch, and on summer weekends in particular the place is packed. Most of the restaurants close their kitchens fairly early, by 10.30pm.

L'Ancora (☎ 977 24 28 06; Carrer de Trafalgar 25; meals €25) and its sister establishment **El Varadero** (☎ 977 24 28 06; Carrer de Trafalgar 13; meals €25) brim with mouthwatering seafood. Go for a selection of dishes (they're all good) at anything from €3 to €6 each, and wash them down with house white. Or try the *parrillada*, a mixed-fish grill (€19). You can sit inside or, in the summer, take up a seat at one of the outdoor tables. On weekends and other busy days the kitchens run until 2am. Their renown has spread far and wide – hour-long queues at midnight are not unheard-of.

Entertainment

El Candil (Plaça de la Font 13; ☺ daily) This is a popular, relaxed bar-café with a student clientele on the main square in the old town.

El Cau (☎ 977 23 12 12; www.elcau.net; Carrer de Trinquet Vell; ☺ daily) Set in one of the vaults of the Roman circus, this is the best place for dancing in central Tarragona. Various DJs and acts perform on weeknights, ensuring that no two nights are the same.

The main concentration of nightlife is the **bars** and **discotecas** along the waterfront behind the train station, and in some of the streets in front of it, such as along Carrer de la Pau del Protectorat.

Getting There & Away

Lying on main routes south from Barcelona, Tarragona is well connected. The train is generally the much easier option.

BUS

Bus services run to Barcelona, Valencia, Zaragoza, Madrid, Alicante, Pamplona, the main Andalucian cities, Andorra and the north coast. As a rule though, you are better off with the train.

TRAIN

Up to 50 regional and long-distance trains per day run to/from Barcelona's Passeig de Gràcia station via Sants. The cheapest fares range from €4.35 to €4.95, and the journey takes one to 1½ hours. Long-distance trains are faster but more expensive (up to €16 in *turista* class) than the regional ones.

Up to 15 trains a day run south to Valencia (€13.65 to €29, two to 3½ hours) and several proceed down the coast and into Andalucía. Up to seven head northwest to Lleida (€4.95 to €13.50, one to two hours).

UNIVERSAL MEDITERRÀNEA

Spain's biggest and best funfair-adventure park is **Universal Mediterrànea** (☎ 902 202041 or ☎ 902 202220; www.portaventura.es; adult/senior & child 5-12 yrs €35/28 mid-Sep–mid-Jun 33/26.50, night tickets €23/18.50, 2-day tickets €51/40.50; ☺ 10am–midnight mid-Jun–mid-Sep; 10am-7pm Mon-Fri 10am-10pm Sat & Sun mid-Mar–mid-Jun, mid-Sep–Oct), 7km west of Tarragona. Most people still know it as Port Aventura, the original core of the park (which retains its name). It makes an amusing day out, especially if you have children in tow. The park has plenty of spine-tingling rides and other attractions, such as the Temple del Foc (Temple of Fire), spread across themed areas ranging from the Wild West to Polynesia.

The nocturnal tickets are valid from 7pm to midnight and available between mid-June and mid-September. Opening days and hours from November to March vary greatly. The park usually opens on weekends and holidays but it is wise to call ahead to check.

In addition to Port Aventura, the Universal Mediterrànea complex includes two hotels and **Universal Costa Caribe** (adult/child & senior €18/14.50 mid-Jun–Sep, €9/7.50 remaining days when only the heated areas are open; ☺ 10am-7pm Jun-Sep, 10am-6pm Sep–early Nov, 11am-5pm early Nov–May), a waterworld with all sorts of wet rides.

Trains run to Universal Mediterránea's own station, about a 1km walk from the site, several times a day from Tarragona (€1.10 to €1.40, 10 to 15 minutes) and Barcelona (from €4.95 to €19, one to 1½ hours). By road, take exit 35 from the AP7, or the N340 from Tarragona.

REUS & AROUND
pop 92,410

Reus was, for much of the second half of the 19th century, the second most important city in Catalonia and a major export centre of textiles and brandy. Birthplace of Gaudí, it boasts a series of Modernista mansions. The **tourist office** (☎ 977 77 81 49; Carrer de Sant Joan s/n; ☒ 9.30am-1.30pm & 4-7pm Mon-Sat) can provide a map guiding you to 30-odd Modernista mansions around the town centre. Regular trains connect Reus with Tarragona (€1.30 to €1.50, 15 to 20 minutes).

About 35km northwest of Reus, above the pretty mountain village of **Siurana**, stand the remains of one of the last Muslim castles to fall to the reconquering Christians. To its west rise the rocky walls of the Serra de Montsant range. The area attracts rock-climbers and walkers; and in Siurana you could stay in **Can Roig** (☎ 977 82 14 50; Carrer Major 6; d €35), a charming, refurbished stone house in the middle of the village.

From Cornudella de Montsant, 9km from Siurana, a narrow and picturesque road (the TV7021) hugs the rugged southern face of the Montsant westwards to **Escaladei**, located in a valley below the mountain range, which produces some fine El Priorat reds. The evocative ruins of the **Cartoixa d'Escaladei** (☎ 977 82 70 06; adult/student & senior €2.40/1.80; ☒ 10am-1.30pm & 4-7.30pm Tue-Sun Jun-Sep, 10am-1.30pm & 3-5.30pm Tue-Sun Oct-May), a 12th-century monastery complex, are a 1km walk out of the village.

To the southeast, stands the **Castell-Monestir de Sant Miquel d'Escornalbou** (☎ 977 83 40 07; adult/student & senior €2.40/1.80; ☒ 10am-1.30pm & 4-7.30pm Tue-Sun Jun-Sep, 10am-1.30pm & 3-5.30pm Tue-Sun Oct-May) on a high windy point, 4km west of the village of **Riudecanyes**. Dating from 1153, much of the castle-monastery complex is in ruins; parts have been rebuilt but hardly to exacting historical criteria. The most interesting elements are the church (from the 12th and 13th centuries), cloister and chapterhouse. You will be taken on a compulsory guided tour, probably in Catalan, of about half an hour.

There is no public transport to Siurana, Escaladei or Castell-Monestir de Sant Miquel d'Escornalbou.

TORTOSA
pop 29,450

Home to Iberian tribes some 2000 years ago, Tortosa has seen them all come and go: Greeks, Romans, Visigoths and Muslims. The town was on the northern front line between Christian and Muslim Spain for four centuries.

There's a **tourist kiosk** (☎ 977 44 25 67; Avinguda de la Generalitat; ☒ 10am-1.30pm & 4-7pm Mon-Fri, 10am-1pm Sat & Sun), and another on Carrer de Ferran Arasa that's open similar hours.

The old town, concentrated at the western end of the city, north of the Ebro, is watched over by the imposing **Castell de la Suda**, where a small medieval Arab cemetery has been unearthed and in whose grounds there now stands a fine **parador** (☎ 977 44 44 50; s/d €83.15/103.90; P ☒). The **Gothic catedral** (Seu; ☒ 9am-1pm & 4-8pm) dates back to 1347 and contains a pleasant cloister and some baroque additions. Other attractions include the **Palau Episcopal** and the lovely **Jardins del Príncep**, perfect for a stroll.

Hostal Virginia (☎ 977 44 41 86; Avinguda de la Generalitat 139; s/d €40/60; ☒ ☒) is a cheerful, central stop with modern rooms and wheelchair access. Prices drop considerably out of season.

The train and bus stations are opposite each other on Ronda dels Docs. Trains to/from Barcelona, Lleida and Tarragona are more regular than the buses. Two to four buses run into the Delta de l'Ebre area.

EBRO DELTA

The delta of the Río Ebro (Delta de l'Ebre in Catalan), formed by silt brought down by the river, sticks out 20km into the Mediterranean near Catalonia's southern border. Dotted with reedy lagoons and fringed by dune-backed beaches, this flat and exposed wetland is northern Spain's most important water-bird habitat. The migration season (October and November) sees the bird population peak, with an average of 53,000 ducks and 15,000 coots, but they're also numerous in winter and spring: 10% of all water birds wintering on the Iberian Peninsula choose to park themselves here.

Nearly half the delta's 320 sq km are given over to rice-growing. Some 77 sq km, mostly along the coasts and around the lagoons, form the **Parc Natural Delta de l'Ebre**.

Orientation

The delta is a seaward-pointing arrowhead of land with the Ebro flowing eastwards across its middle. The town of Deltebre straggles about 5km along the northern bank of the river at the centre of the delta. Deltebre's western half is called Jesús i Maria and the eastern half La Cava. Facing Deltebre on the southern bank is Sant Jaume d'Enveja. Roads crisscross the delta to Deltebre and beyond from the towns of L'Ampolla, Amposta and Sant Carles de la Ràpita, all on the N340. Three ferries (*transbordadors*), running from early morning until nightfall, link Deltebre to Sant Jaume d'Enveja (two people and a car €2.50).

Information

There's a **Centre d'Informació** (☎ 977 48 96 79; Carrer de Martí Buera 22, Deltebre; ☒ 10am-2pm & 3-6pm Mon-Fri, 10am-2pm & 3.30-6pm Sat, 10am-1pm Sun). Adjoining is an **Ecomuseu** (admission €1.50; ☒ 10am-2pm & 3-6pm Mon-Fri, 10am-1pm & 3.30-6pm Sat, 10am-1pm Sun), with displays describing the delta environment and an aquarium-terrarium of delta species.

There's another **information office** (admission €1.50; ☒ 10am-2pm & 3-6pm Tue-Sun) with a permanent exposition on the delta's lagoons at La Casa de Fusta, beside L'Encanyissada lagoon, about 10km southwest of Deltebre. Other offices are in Sant Carles de la Ràpita, Amposta and L'Ampolla.

Sights & Activities

A good way to explore the delta is by bicycle and you can rent one for about €10 per day from several places in Deltebre. **Lloguer de Bicicletes Torné** (☎ 977 48 00 17; Avinguda Goles de l'Ebre 184), in the heart of town, is open for bicycle hire (€10 per day) year-round.

Early morning and evening are the best times for **bird-watching**, and good areas include L'Encanyissada and La Tancada lagoons and Punta de la Banya, all in the south of the delta. L'Encanyissada has two observation towers and La Tancada one (others are marked on a map you can pick up at the Centre d'Informació). La Tancada

and Punta de la Banya are generally the best places to see the **greater flamingos**, the delta's most spectacular birds. Almost 2000 of the birds nest here, and since 1992 the delta has been one of only five places in Europe where they reproduce. Punta de la Banya is joined to the delta by a 5km sand spit with the long, wide and sandy Platja de l'Eucaliptus at its northern end.

Olmos (☎ 977 48 05 48) is just one of a couple of companies that run daily tourist **boat trips** (1½ hours, €6 to €10 per person) from Deltebre to the mouths of the Ebro and the Illa de Buda at the delta's tip. Boats go daily, but the frequency depends on the season.

Sleeping

Camping Mediterrani Blau (☎ 977 47 90 46; 2-person tent & car €15.45; ☒ Mar-Oct) This camping ground is in a small eucalyptus grove on Platja de l'Eucaliptus. It has a restaurant, a bar and a minimarket. There are two more camping grounds at Riumar, 10km east of Deltebre.

Delta Hotel (☎ 977 48 00 46; www.dsi.es/delta-hotel; Avinguda del Canal, Camí de l'Illeta s/n; s/d €49.25/81.35; [P] [X]) On the northern edge of Deltebre, by the road to Riumar, this delightful hotel has modern rooms and a good restaurant. It has a leafy courtyard and gardens in which some of what you eat in the restaurant is grown.

There are several places to stay in Sant Carles de la Ràpita, a pleasant fishing town with a marina.

You'll find several eateries by Riumar and the mouth of the river. In La Cava, try **Nuri** (☎ 977 48 01 28; Carretera de les Goles; meals €25-30). Located right by the mighty Ebro, much of what you eat, ranging from frog's legs through eel to seafood-and-rice dishes, comes from the river or around about it. Ask the owners also about their boat restaurant, the **Santa Susana** (☎ 629-204117), tied up on the river a little further along.

Getting There & Away

The delta is easiest to get to and around with your own wheels, but it is possible to reach Tortosa by bus or a train-bus combination.

Autocars Hife (☎ 902 119814) runs buses to Jesús i Maria and La Cava from Tortosa (€2.45, 50 minutes) up to four times daily (twice on Saturday, Sunday and holidays), and from Amposta (30 minutes) once or twice daily.

Andorra

Andorra

Slip Andorra into the conversation and people will tell you, with either horror or joy, that it's all skiing and shopping. They'll also probably add that it's a one-road, one-town mini-state. And that its only highway, which links Spain and France, cuts a swathe through its only town, Andorra la Vella – which in turn is little more than a vast traffic jam bordered by cut-price temples to human greed.

They're right to some degree, but also very wrong. Shake yourself free of Andorra la Vella's tawdry embrace to purr along one of the state's only three secondary roads and you'll be led to villages as unspoilt as any in the Pyrenees. Although Andorra, with a resident population of less than 70,000 and an area of only 464 sq km, absorbs more than 11 million visitors each year (most of whom just pop in to shop), there are still areas where you can be completely alone. And the principality's small, friendly tourist offices offer support that's second to none.

Tucked into the Pyrenees between Spain's Catalonia region and France, Andorra has the distinction of being the only country in the world where Catalan is the official language. Though short on historical interest and monuments of consequence, this tiny, political anomaly, rucked and buckled with scarcely a flat square metre to its name, has some of the most dramatic scenery and by far the best skiing in all the Pyrenees. And, once the snows have melted, there's great walking in abundance, ranging from leisurely family strolls to challenging day hikes in the higher, more remote, parts of the principality.

ANDORRA

HIGHLIGHTS

- Cross the spectacular **Port d'Envalira**, the highest road pass in the Pyrenees (p398)
- Pack your (ice) pick and **trek** just about anywhere in the principality
- Drop in on quaint **Casa de la Vall** (p389), the parliament building of one of the world's smallest nations
- Steep yourself in the warm mineral waters of the space-age **Caldea** (p390)

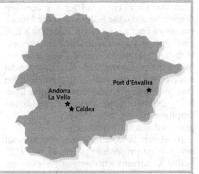

Andorra la Vella ★
★ Caldea
Port d'Envalira ★

| ■ AREA: 464 SQ KM | ■ POP: 67,100 | ■ AVE SUMMER TEMP: HIGH 22°C, LOW 12°C |

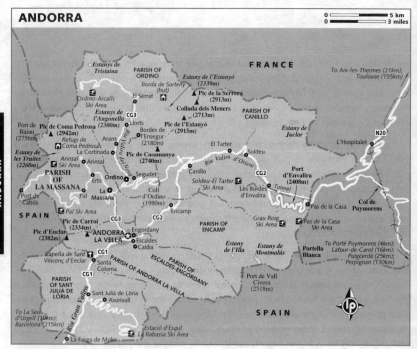

History

By tradition, Andorra's independence is credited to Emperor Charlemagne, who captured the region from the Muslims in AD 803. In 843 his grandson, Charles II, granted the Valls d'Andorra (Valleys of Andorra) to Sunifred, Count of Urgell, whose base was La Seu d'Urgell, in adjacent Catalonia. From the counts, Andorra later passed to the bishops of Urgell, also based in La Seu.

In the 13th century, after a succession dispute between the bishops and the French counts of Foix to the north, Andorra's first constitutional documents, the Pareatges, established a system of shared sovereignty between the two rivals. This originally feudal setup created a peculiar political equilibrium that, over the centuries, saved Andorra from being gobbled up by its powerful neighbours despite recurrent tension between the co-princes down the centuries.

In March 1993, after seven centuries of being a 'co-princedom', 75% of the 9123 native Andorrans who were eligible to vote (less than one-sixth of the actual population at the time) opted in a referendum to establish Andorra as an independent, democratic 'parliamentary co-princedom'. The new constitution placed full sovereignty in the hands of the Andorran people, although the co-princes continue to function as joint heads with much reduced powers. The country retains its full name of Principat (Principality) d'Andorra.

Since the 1950s Andorra has developed as a centre for skiing and duty-free shopping, the latter a legitimate progression from the more dubious smuggling of French goods to Spain during the Spanish Civil War and Spanish goods to France in WWII (Andorra remained conveniently and profitably neutral in both). These activities have brought not only wealth, foreign workers and more than 11 million visitors a year to the country, but also some unsightly development and heavy traffic in the capital, Andorra la Vella.

Environment

Andorra, in the heart of the Pyrenees, is essentially a pair of major valleys and the steep mountains that hug them. It

CHARLEMAGNE AND THE THISTLE

As Emperor Charlemagne's army was passing through the Pyrenees, on its way to do battle with the Arab occupiers of Spain, the plague struck. When the emperor prayed to God for help, says the legend, an angel appeared and instructed him to fire an arrow into the air – whichever plant it pierced would prove to be an effective remedy. The arrow fell upon a kind of ground-hugging thistle, still common in the Pyrenees and still used as a natural remedy. It's called 'carlina' in both Catalan and Spanish, after Carlomagno – Charlemagne to us.

measures a mere 25km from north to south at its maximum, and 29km from east to west. Most of its 40 or so towns and hamlets – some with just a few dozen people – are in the valleys. The main river, the Riu Gran Valira, is formed near the capital, Andorra la Vella, by the confluence of the Valira d'Orient and the Valira del Nord.

Pic de Coma Pedrosa (2942m) in western Andorra is the highest mountain, while the lowest point, on the Spanish frontier at La Farga de Moles, is still a healthy 838m above sea level.

Population & People

A mere 38% of Andorra's 67,100 inhabitants (well over half of whom live in Andorra la Vella and the contiguous parish of Escaldes-Engordany) are Andorran nationals. The rest are Spanish (39.5%), Portuguese (10%), French (6.5%) and others. While 67,100 is fairly trifling and may fit comfortably into a suburb of your home town, bear in mind that, no more than 50 years ago, Andorra's population was only around 6000 souls.

The state language, enforced by a 1999 law of the Andorran parliament, is Catalan, but nearly everyone can speak Spanish fluently. Local lore has it that everyone speaks Catalan, Spanish and French, but plenty of Andorrans know only a smattering of French and many Spanish residents have little Catalan. Young people and those working in tourism speak basic to good English.

Government & Politics

In 1993 the country's elected parliament, the Consell General (General Council), took over from the Consell de la Terra (Land Council), which had run the show since 1419. The Consell General has 28 members – four from each of the seven parishes – who meet three or four times a year. It appoints a *cap de govern* (prime minister), who chooses ministers whose programmes in turn have to be approved by the Consell. The liberal Marc Forné Molné, *cap de govern* since 1994, was re-elected in 2001.

Women gained suffrage as late as 1970 and all Andorran citizens over 18 can now vote. Andorra is a member of the UN and of the Council of Europe, but not a full member of the European Union (EU).

Of Andorra's seven *parròquie* (parishes), six have existed since at least the 9th century. The seventh, Escaldes-Engordany, was created in 1978 by dividing the fast-growing parish of Andorra la Vella.

Economy

The Andorran economy is based on cheap tax-free shopping; banking and tourism alone account for some 80% of the country's GDP. Of the 11.6 million annual visitors (many drive in, shop hard and drive out the same day), 72% are Spanish and 23% French.

The most important components of the agricultural sector, which makes up only around 1% of total economic activity, are tobacco growing and cattle raising.

MIND HOW YOU GO

A law passed in 1999 makes Catalan obligatory for all signage, publicity, restaurant menus, announcements and the like. However, since massive tourism is Andorra's lifeblood, most notices are also in Spanish, English and sometimes French.

But not always; even though Catalan is opaque to the vast majority of visitors, we came across the following monolingual signs, to which, for your safety, we append the English translation!

■ Perill: Zona Voladures = Beware: Falling stones

■ Caiguda de Neu = Watch out for snow sliding from roofs

■ Risc Allaus = Risk of avalanche

Alternatively, just jump when the locals jump!

Getting There & Away

The only way into Andorra – unless you choose to trek across the mountains – is by road. One route climbs in from La Seu d'Urgell in Spain, 20km south of Andorra la Vella. The other enters Andorra at Pas de la Casa, which is on the eastern border with France.

Petrol in Andorra is about 15% cheaper than in Spain and a good 25% cheaper than in France.

AIR

The nearest major airports are in Barcelona (225km south) and Toulouse (180km north). Both cities and their airports are linked to Andorra by bus or a train–bus combination.

An agreement has recently been signed with Spain to upgrade a small airport near La Seu d'Urgell, enabling it to take commercial flights.

BUS & TRAIN

Some of the bus and train services listed here may vary seasonally, so always check with the company or any Andorran tourist office.

Spain

La Hispano Andorrana (☎ 821 372) runs hourly buses between La Seu d'Urgell and Andorra la Vella (€2.40, 40 minutes).

Autocars Nadal (☎ 805 151; www.autocarsnadal .com, in Spanish & French) runs four to six buses daily to/from Barcelona's airport (€25, 3¾ hours), calling by the city's Estació Sants train station (€20, 3¼ hours).

Alsina Graells (☎ 827 379) has five buses daily (€19.50, 3½ hours) running between Barcelona's main bus station (Estació del Nord) and Andorra la Vella's **bus station** (Avinguda de Tarragona 42). Three of the buses are nonstop.

Minibuses of **Novatel Autocars** (☎ 803 789) do four runs daily between Andorra la Vella's bus station and Barcelona airport (€25).

Viatges Montmantell (☎ 807 444) runs three buses daily to/from Lleida (Catalonia) (€15, 2¾ hours) to connect with the Madrid-bound high-speed AVE train.

From Barcelona, take the train (five daily) to the frontier terminus of Latour-de-Carol in France. From there, La Hispano Andorrana buses leave for Andorra at 10.45am and 1.15pm daily.

France

Autocars Nadal (☎ 805 151) has two buses a day (€21, 3½ to four hours) on Wednesday, Friday and Sunday to/from Toulouse's *gare routière* (bus station).

Novatel Autocars (☎ 803 789) operates two minibuses daily (€28, 3½ hours) to/from Toulouse airport.

By rail, you can take a train from Toulouse to L'Hospitalet (2¼ hours, three to eight daily), but onward bus connections are few, except on Saturday, when as many as five buses run from L'Hospitalet to Pas de la Casa.

It's also possible to drop to the Mediterranean. From Latour-de-Carol (see To/From Spain) trains go to Perpignan (€20.30, four hours, two to four daily).

Getting Around

BUS

Buses run along the principality's three main roads. Ask at a tourist office for the free leaflet giving current timetables for the eight bus routes radiating from the capital, all run by **Cooperativa Interurbana** (☎ 806 555).

CAR & MOTORCYCLE

The speed limit is 40km/h in populated areas and 90km/h elsewhere. Two problems are the recklessness of local drivers and Andorra la Vella's horrendous traffic jams. It's possible to bypass the worst of the latter by taking Avinguda de Salou, which becomes Avinguda de Tarragona, around the southern side of town. If you're driving between the parishes of Ordino or La Massana and those of Encamp or Canillo, avoid this motorist's nightmare by taking the scenically striking route over the Coll d'Ordino. However, snow blocks this alternative for most of winter.

ANDORRA LA VELLA

pop 25,500 / elevation 1030m

Andorra la Vella (Vella, pronounced 'vey-yah', means 'old'), surrounded by mountains of up to 2400m, is the capital and only real town of the principality. Its main preoccupation is retailing duty-free electronics and luxury goods.

ORIENTATION

Andorra's capital is strung out along one main street, the name of which changes from Avinguda del Príncep Benlloch to Avinguda de Meritxell to Avinguda de Carlemany. The little Barri Antic (Historic Quarter) around Antic Carrer Major (Old High Street) is split by this heavily trafficked artery. The town merges with the once-separate villages of Escaldes and Engordany to the east, and Santa Coloma to the southwest.

INFORMATION

Bookshops

Llibreria Jaume Caballé (☎ /fax 829 454; Avinguda Fiter Rossell 31) A splendid collection of antiquarian and new travel books in Spanish, French and Catalan, plus a comprehensive range of walking and travel maps.

Emergency

Main police station (☎ 821 222; Carrer del Prat de la Creu 16)

Internet Access

Future@point (☎ 828 202; Carrer de la Sardana 6; per hr €2.80; ☻ 10am-11pm Mon-Sat, 10am-10pm Sun)

E-Café (☎ 865 677; Carrer de l'Alziranet 5; per hr €3; ☻ 9am-midnight Mon-Fri, 10am-midnight Sat)

Medical Services

Hospital Nostra Senyora de Meritxell (☎ 871 000; Avinguda Fiter i Rossell)

Post

La Poste (Carrer de Pere d'Urg 1; ☻ 8.30am-2.30pm Mon-Fri, 9am-noon Sat) The French post office.

WHEN TO VISIT

The ski season (December to April) is the high season for visitors, along with late July, August and September.

Correus (Correos) i Telègrafs (Carrer de Joan Maragall 10; ☻ 8.30am-2.30pm Mon-Fri, 9.30am-1pm Sat) The Spanish post office.

Tourist Information

Municipal tourist office (☎ 827 117; turisme@comuandorra.ad; Plaça de la Rotonda; ☻ 9am-9pm Jul-Aug, 9am-1pm & 3.30-7pm Mon-Sat, 9am-1pm Sun Sep-Jun) Also carries pan-Andorra information.

National tourist office (☎ 820 214; sindicatdiniciativa@andorra.ad; Carrer del Doctor Vilanova s/n; ☻ 9am-1pm & 3-7pm Mon-Sat, 9am-1pm Sun Jul-Sep; 10am-1.30pm & 3-7pm Mon-Sat, 10am-1pm Sun Oct-Jun) Just off Plaça de Rebés.

SIGHTS

Barri Antic

The small Barri Antic (Historic Quarter), intrusively and artificially bisected by heavily trafficked Avinguda Príncep Benlloch, was the heart of Andorra la Vella when the principality's capital was little more than a village. The narrow cobbled streets around the Casa de la Vall are flanked by attractive stone houses.

Andorra la Vella's parish church, **Església de Sant Esteve**, these days aligned north–south, dates from the 11th century. Apart from the Romanesque apse on its eastern side, it's mainly modern and has little interest apart from some wonderfully warm, glowing stained-glass windows.

Casa de la Vall

The Casa de la Vall (House of the Valley; Carrer de la Vall), constructed in 1580 as the home of a wealthy family, has served as Andorra's parliament building since 1702. Downstairs is **El Tribunal de Corts**, the country's one and only courtroom. The **Sala del Consell**, upstairs, has to be one of the cosiest parliament chambers in the world. **L'Armari de les Set Claus** (the Cupboard of the Seven Keys) once held Andorra's most important official documents. Security was guaranteed because it could only be opened if a key-bearing representative from each of the seven parishes was present. There are **guided tours** (reservations ☎ 829 129; admission free; ☻ 9.15am-1pm & 3-7pm Mon-Sat year-round, 10am-2pm Sun Jun-Nov) in several languages, including English. Book at least a week ahead in summer to ensure you get a place – though individuals can often be squeezed in at the last minute.

ANDORRA LA VELLA

INFORMATION	
E-Café	1 C1
French Consulate	2 D1
French Embassy	3 D1
French Post Office	4 E2
Future@point	5 E2
Hospital Nostra Senyora de Meritxell	6 G1
Llibreria Jaume Caballé	7 H1
Municipal Tourist Office	8 E2
National Tourist Office	9 C2
Police Station	10 D2
Spanish Embassy	11 D2
Spanish Post Office	12 D2
Telephones	13 F2

SIGHTS & ACTIVITIES	(pp389–90)
Caldea Spa Complex	14 H1
Casa de la Vall	15 B2
Església de Sant Esteve	16 C2

SLEEPING	(pp390–1)
Hostal del Sol	17 C1
Hotel Flora	18 B2
Hotel Florida	19 C1
Hotel Pyrénées	20 B2
Hotel Sasplugas	21 E1

Plaça del Poble

This large public square, just south of Plaça de Rebés, occupies the roof of the Edifici Administratiu Govern d'Andorra, a modern government office building. Giving good views of the valley and mountains, it's a popular local gathering place, especially in the evening. The lift in the southeastern corner whisks you down to the car park below on Carrer del Prat de la Creu.

Caldea Spa Complex

In Escaldes, the **Caldea spa complex** (☎ 800 995; Parc de la Mola 10; adult/child €26/19.60; ⏰ core hr 10am-11pm, last admission 9pm) is Europe's largest. Looking like some futuristic cathedral, it's a wonderful place for some soothing relaxation after exertions in the mountains. Fed by hot springs, its heart is a 600-sq-metre lagoon kept at a constant 32ºC. A series of other pools, plus Turkish baths, saunas, spas and hydromassage, are all included in the three-hour entrance ticket. For an extra €3.40, you can experience *Helimoció*, a virtual-reality flight above Andorra. Caldea is

a 10-minute walk upstream from Plaça de la Rotonda.

SLEEPING

Most hotels, except those in the budget category, hike their prices by 20% or more in the high season (essentially August and major Spanish and French public holidays), when advance reservations are essential.

Camping Valira (☎ /fax 722 384; Avinguda de Salou; camping per person/tent/car €4.50/4.50/4.50; 🅿) Just west of town, this place has a small indoor swimming pool.

Hostal del Sol (☎ 823 701; fax 822 363; Plaça de Guillemó 3; s/d with shower €13.50/27) This friendly, family-run place has 12 spruce, excellent-value rooms. It's set back on the northern side of a semi-pedestrian square, so noise is no problem and there are several cheap eateries just below.

Hotel Sasplugas (☎ 820311; hotelsasplugas@andorra.ad; Carrer de la Creu Grossa 15; s/d with breakfast €46/65; 🅿) You can lord it over the din and haggling in the valley way below at Hotel Sasplugas, where every room has a bathtub and balcony overlooking the town or

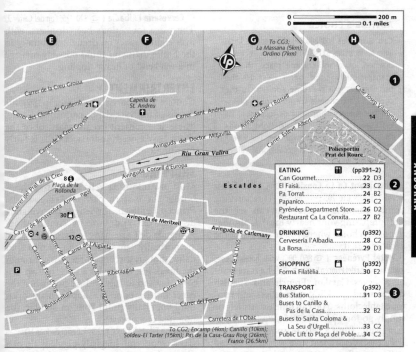

EATING 🍴 (pp391–2)
Can Gourmet.....................22 D3
El Faisà............................23 C2
Pa Torrat..........................24 B2
Papanico...........................25 C2
Pyrénées Department Store...26 D2
Restaurant Ca La Conxita......27 B2

DRINKING 🍷 (p392)
Cerveseria l'Albdia...............28 C2
La Borsa............................29 D3

SHOPPING 🛍 (p392)
Forma Filatèlia....................30 E2

TRANSPORT (p392)
Bus Station........................31 D3
Buses to Canillo &
 Pas de la Casa..................32 B2
Buses to Santa Coloma &
 La Seu d'Urgell.................33 C2
Public Lift to Plaça del Poble...34 C2

mountain behind. Rates are constant year-round and represent great value. If you're on foot, take the steep steps up to Carrer de la Creu Grossa from the northwest corner of Plaça de la Rotonda.

Hotel Florida (☎ 820 105; www.hotelflorida.ad; Carrer de la Llacuna 15; s/d from €36.50/44) This delightful, modern hotel sits on a quiet side street. If you stagger in after a hard day's skiing or hiking, relax in the sauna and *hammam* (bathhouse), free to guests, or steep yourself in the bathtub that's a feature of all rooms, then tone yourself up for the morrow in the mini-gym. All rooms are attractively furnished in blue and with mock-parquet flooring.

Nearby is a pair of good upmarket choices, owned by two brothers. They share a common tennis court, swimming pool and private garage (€9 to €11 per night).

Hotel Pyrénées (☎ 860 006; www.hotelpyrenees .com; Avinguda del Príncep Benlloch 20; s/d €35/56; 🏊) After the Casa de la Vall and a Romanesque church or two, Hotel Pyrénées, constructed in 1940 and speaking style, ranks among the most venerable buildings in the principality. Rooms have plenty of appealing dark wood-

work and are attractively furnished. Ask for one at the rear, well away from the traffic-clogged main artery. In high season, you have to take half-board (€50 per person).

Hotel Flora (☎ 821 508; flora@andornet.ad; Antic Carrer Major 25; s/d with breakfast €47/60; 🏊) Younger sibling of Hotel Pyrénées and close by, though shorter on tradition, four-star Hotel Flora has 45 large, immaculate rooms, all with safe and bathtub.

EATING
In the heart of Barri Antic there's a quartet of great little restaurants specialising in local cuisine.

Pa Torrat (☎ 865 065; Carrer de la Vall 18; mains €8-17) A splendid place for hearty meat dishes, including 11 varieties of home-made *butifarra* (thick Catalan sausage). The menu's only in Catalan, but the friendly staff are happy to provide a glossary.

El Faisà (☎ 823 283; Cap del Carrer 4; mains €6-20) 'The Pheasant' is just as popular and equally Andorran in flavour as Pa Torrat. Trim, with crisp white tablecloths, its mains offer something for all pockets and preferences.

ANDORRA

Restaurant Ca La Conxita (☎ 829 948; Placeta Monjó 3; meals €16-20; ☽ Mon-Sat) This bustling family business, where you can see the staff preparing your hearty meal, is another tempting choice where you're sure to come away satisfied.

Hotel Pyrénées (☎ 860 006; www.hotelpyrenees .com; Avinguda del Príncep Benlloch 20) The restaurant here serves Catalan, French and Spanish dishes amid sparkling chandeliers and two-tone tablecloths. You can dine exquisitely or simply go for a *plato combinado* (combination plate), from a very reasonable €5.

Pyrénées department store (Avinguda de Meritxell 21) The top-floor cafeteria and restaurant of this megastore offers great fare at very reasonable prices. Pile your salad plate (€4.20) high at the self-service buffet and follow it with the dish of the day (a mere €4.25) or select from one of the seven varieties of *plato combinado* (€6). One floor down, self-caterers will enjoy picking here and there from the aisles of the well-stocked supermarket.

Papanico (☎ 867 333; Avinguda del Príncep Benlloch 4; mains €8-18) This cheery place does tasty tapas from €2.45 and a range of sandwiches, *platos combinados* (from €6.40) and mains. Fun at midday and vibrant at night, it's also a place to see and be seen.

DRINKING

La Borsa (The Stock Exchange; ☎ 827 657; Avinguda de Tarragona 36) Like a drink now and again? Enjoy a little flutter? Here you can indulge in both. Keep a weather eye on the electronic, computer-controlled screen, because the price of each drink varies according to the night's consumption so far. Some you win, some you lose. It's like life, really, only rather more fun as the evening wears on…

Cervesería l'Albadia (☎ 820 825; Cap del Carrer 2) The place for serious beer drinkers, with over eight classics on draught and more in the bottle than you could possibly manage in a weekend of heavy tippling.

ENTERTAINMENT

Contact the tourist office (see p389) for details of festivals, dance performances etc. These intermittent events apart, once the shops have closed Andorra la Vella is fairly moribund.

SHOPPING

Most of Andorra la Vella's duty-free shops border the eastern part of Avinguda del Príncep Benlloch, the length of Avinguda de Meritxell and into its continuation, Avinguda de Carlemany in Escaldes. Hours are normally 9am to 1pm and 4pm to 8pm daily, though the big stores work through the break lest they miss a buck or two. On Saturday and in July and August, when the eager hordes pour in, shops remain open until 9pm daily (until 7pm on Sunday, the nominal day of rest).

Forma Filatèlia (☎ 822 894; Carrer de Joan Maragall 4) is a wonderful, higgledy-piggledy tip of a place, where stamp-, coin- and phonecard-collectors will find themselves in heaven.

GETTING THERE & AROUND

Buses to La Seu d'Urgell via Santa Coloma and Sant Julià call by the stop on Plaça Guillemó. Those for all other destinations within Andorra and for train stations just over the border in France (see p388) pass by the bus stop on Avinguda del Príncep Benlloch.

Long-distance buses arrive and depart from the main bus station on Avinguda de Tarragona.

Call ☎ 863 000 to order a taxi.

Andorra la Vella is compact, and is a traffic nightmare; you're much better off walking. Stick your car in the multistorey car park beneath Plaça del Poble or, at less cost, in the huge open-air park just north of the bus station.

AROUND ANDORRA LA VELLA
Església de Santa Coloma

The pre-Romanesque form of the Church of Santa Coloma mentioned in documents from the 9th century, and Andorra's oldest church, has been much modified over the centuries. The four-storey, freestanding circular bell tower was raised in the 12th century. All the church's 12th-century Romanesque murals, except one entitled *Agnus Dei* (Lamb of God), were taken to Berlin for conservation in the 1930s and still languish there. The church is 2.5km southwest of Plaça de Guillemó along the main road to Spain.

NORTHWESTERN ANDORRA

La Massana, 6km north of Andorra la Vella, is the gateway to the ski centres of Arinsal and Pal. From it, the CG3 continues north into the mountainous Parròquia d'Ordino, for us the country's most beautiful parish, with slate and stone farmhouses, gushing streams and picturesque old bridges. Up there is the ski area of Ordino-Arcalís and, in summer, soul-stirring walking.

LA MASSANA
pop 3000 / elevation 1250m
La Massana is much less attractive than its smaller neighbours a few kilometres north and deeper into the valleys. The **tourist office** (☎ 835 693; ☺ 9am-1pm & 3-7pm Mon-Sat, to 6pm Sun), at the base of the brand-new cabin lift, covers both Arinsal and Pal.

Sights & Activities
In Sispony, 1km off the CG3 at the entry to La Massana, is **Casa Rull** (☎ 836 919; Carrer Major, Sispony; adult/student/child €2.40/1.20/free; ☺ 9.30am-12.45pm & 3-6.30pm Tue-Sat, 10am-2pm Sun), a mostly 17th-century restored farmhouse and rural museum.

Year-round, for a magnificent bird's-eye view of the Pyrenees and Andorra in its entirety, you can take a 10-minute helicopter flight from La Massana with **Heliand** (☎ 837 929). At €45 per person, a chopper doesn't come cheap; it seats five and requires a minimum of four people.

Eating
Just outside La Massana on the road to Arinsal are two restaurants offering quality Andorran cuisine and good wine selections.

Borda de l'Aví (☎ 835 154; Carretera de Arinsal Km0.5; mains €15-23) Low-beamed and popular,

this stylish upmarket choice, while specialising in grills and roasts, offers an ample selection of more subtle fare.

La Borda Raubert (☎ 835 420; Carretera de Arinsal Km1.5) Smaller, less expensive and more informal, La Borda Raubert also specialises in mountain cuisine and grills and is equally tempting.

Getting There & Away
Buses between Andorra la Vella and Ordino pass through La Massana about every half-hour from 7am to 9pm.

ARINSAL & PAL SKI AREAS
Arinsal (☎ 737 020), 5km northwest of La Massana, has good skiing and snowboarding for beginners and intermediates, and a lively après-ski scene. The smaller ski station of **Pal** (☎ 737 000), 7km from La Massana, has gentler slopes, which make it ideal for families. Both the more exposed Pal and Ordino-Arcalís ski areas can be considerably colder than those of eastern Andorra.

Skiing
The combined stations, which share a website (www.palarinsal.com), are linked by a cabin lift and have 63km of pistes with a vertical drop of 1010m.

Lift passes at both resorts cost €23.50/60.50 per day/three days (€28/72 in high season).

Walking
The parishes of La Massana and Ordino have jointly produced an excellent walking booklet, *Thirtysix Interesting Itineraries on the Paths of the Vall d'Ordino & the Parish of La Massana* (€2). It's available from either parish's tourist office – and walk descriptions are altogether tauter than the title!

From Aparthotel Crest at Arinsal's northern extremity, a trail leads northwest then west to **Estany de les Truites** (2260m). **Refugi de Coma Pedrosa** (☎ 327 955; per person €7; ☺ Jun-late Sep), Andorra's only staffed mountain refuge, is just above this natural lake and does snacks and simple meals for all comers.

The steepish walk up to the lake takes around 1½ hours from Arinsal. From here, it's a further 1½ to two hours of vigorous walking to **Pic de Coma Pedrosa** (2942m), Andorra's highest point.

Other Activities

In July and August, the long La Serra chairlift (€5.90 return) at Pal operates. Here you can hire **mountain bikes** (€15 per day) and go **horse riding** (€15 per hour).

Sleeping

Camping Xixerella (☎ 836 613; www.campingxixer ella.com; per person/tent/car €4.20/4.20/4.20; ☽ Nov-Sep; ☐) Between Pal and Arinsal, this large, well-equipped site has an outdoor pool.

All accommodation is in Arinsal (Pal has none); each of the places we recommend here is on the main drag.

Hotel Coma Pedrosa (☎ 737 950; fax 737 951; d €44, half-board per person €38; closed 4 weeks Jun or Jul) This is another welcoming place, popular with both skiers and summer walkers. Most rooms have a bathtub, there's free public parking just behind and you can relax in the cosy bar.

Hotel Solana (☎ 737 999; hotelsolana@andorra.ad; half-board per person €42-49; ☐ ☐) This is a very comfortable choice – if you're lucky enough to get a bed – with a covered, heated pool and sauna, free to guests. All 95 rooms have a balcony; those facing the front have attractive views, while from the rear ones all you see is a wall of hillside. Reservation well in advance is essential in the ski season. The Solana normally insists upon half-board, year-round.

Eating

Refugi de la Fondue (☎ 839 599) As a change from the plentiful snack and sandwich joints in Arinsal, try this restaurant, on its own up the hill towards the main chairlift. Its speciality is cheese and meat fondue dishes (€13.50) and in summer it does outdoor barbecues on the small terrace.

AUTHOR'S CHOICE

Hostal Pobladó (☎ 835 122; hospoblado@ andornet.ad; B&B per person in basic room €20, with bathroom €25; ☽ Dec-Oct; ☐) Hostal Pobladó sits right beside the cabin lift, handy for skiing in winter and for taking off on summer day walks. Though no longer the bargain it once was, it's friendliness itself, and is a great place to make contact with other skiers or walkers. It has a lively bar and an Internet point (€3.60 per hour), and rents skis.

Restaurant el Molí de la Plaça (☎ 835 281; ☽ Jul-May) This popular place bills itself as Italian – and indeed offers the usual staple pastas and pizzas (both €7 to €9.40). But it also has more exotic fare such as Szechaun chicken (€11.50) and Thai green coconut chicken curry (€12).

Entertainment

In winter Arinsal fairly throbs after sunset; in summer it can be almost mournful. When the snow's around, call by **Surf**, near the base of the cabin lift. Pub, dance venue and restaurant, it also specialises in Argentinian dishes of juicy grilled meat (€7 to €13.20). **Quo Vadis** seethes with British skiers and also stays open until the wee hours. For somewhere congenial and quieter, call by **El Café Gourmet d'Arinsal** (☽ mid-Jun–mid-May; ☐), which does delightful snacks and also has an **Internet point** (per hr €4).

Getting There & Away

Five buses daily leave Andorra la Vella for Arinsal via La Massana. There are also around 15 local buses daily between La Massana and Arinsal and five between La Massana and Pal.

In winter a special ski bus runs six times daily between La Massana and Arinsal.

ORDINO

pop 1000 / elevation 1300m

Despite all the ongoing development (holiday homes and English-speaking residents abound), Ordino is a charming little village. All new buildings are constructed in local stone, its main square is pedestrian only and a chuckling stream sluices through it.

The **tourist office** (☎ 737 080; www.vallordino .com; ☽ 8am-7pm Mon-Sat, 9am-5pm Sun Jul-Sep, 9am-1pm & 3-7pm Mon-Sat, 9am-1pm Sun Oct-Jun) is within the Centre Esportiu d'Ordino sports complex beside the CG3. It hires out mountain bikes (€7/24 per hour/day).

Museums

The ancestral home of one of Andorra's great families, the Areny Plandolits, was built in 1633. Modified in the mid-19th century, it's now the **Museu d'Areny i Plandolit** (☎ 836 908; adult/child €2.40/1.20; ☽ 9.30am-1.30pm & 3-6.30pm Tue-Sat, 10am-2pm Sun), which offers half-hour guided visits, in Spanish or Catalan, of its richly furnished interior.

In the same grounds, the **Museo Postal de Andorra** (adult/child €2.40/1.20; ☾ 9.30am-1.30pm & 3-6.30pm Tue-Sat, 10am-2pm Sun) is far from nerdy. It has a 15-minute audiovisual presentation (available in English), and set upon set of stamps issued by France and Spain specifically for Andorra.

The **Centre d'Interpretació de la Natura** (Nature Interpretation Centre; ☎ 837 939; adult/student/child €3.70/1.85/free; ☾ 9.30am-1pm & 3.30-6pm Tue-Sat, 9.30am-1.30pm Sun) is a good multimedia introduction to Andorra's flora and fauna. A guided visit follows a 10-minute slide/video presentation (both with English option).

Walking
From the hamlet of Segudet, 1km east of Ordino, a path goes up through fir woods to the **Coll d'Ordino** (1980m), reached in about 1½ hours. **Pic de Casamanya** (2740m), where you can enjoy expansive panoramas, is some two hours north from the *coll* (mountain pass).

Sleeping & Eating
Camping Borda d'Ansalonga (☎ 850 374; www.campingansalonga.com; per person/tent/car €4/4/4; ☾ mid-Jun–Sep & Nov-Apr; ☒) This place enjoys an attractive valley site just outside the village.

Hotel Santa Bàrbara de la Vall d'Ordino (☎ 738 100; santabarbara@andorra.ad; Plaça d'Ordino; s/d €45/60; ℗) Just above the main square and facing the church, this 22-room family-run hotel with its small, attractive bar is excellent value for money.

Hotel Coma (☎ 736 100; www.hotelcoma.com; per person with breakfast €33-60, with half-board €42-64; ☾ Dec-Oct; ℗ ▯ ☒) Curling around the hillside like a boomerang, this spacious 48-room hotel has attractive rooms, all with parquet flooring and a spa. All except the top-floor eyries have a balcony giving fine views. Not least of the Coma's pleasures is its superb **restaurant** (menú del día €16, menús €27 & €45), much favoured by wealthy Andorrans for weddings and other rites of passage.

Restaurant Armengol (☎ 835 977; ☾ Jun-Apr) offers *menús* for €10.50 and €15 and also does a wide range of plentiful à-la-carte meat and fish dishes (€9 to €17). **Bar Restaurant Quim**, next door, friendly and more snacky, has a great range of tapas and does a filling midday *menú*.

Getting There & Away
Buses to/from Andorra la Vella run every half-hour from 7am to 9pm.

VALL D'ORDINO
The tiny, partly Romanesque **Església de Sant Martí** (☾ Jul-Aug) in **La Cortinada** has some well-preserved 12th-century frescoes and four finely wrought gilded altarpieces. Opposite is a small working water-powered **flour and sawmill** (adult/child €2/1; ☾ in principle, 10am-1.30pm & 3.30-6.30pm Tue-Sun Jun-Nov).

Walking
For an excellent walking guide in English, get a copy of *Thirtysix Interesting Itineraries on the Paths of the Vall d'Ordino & the Parish of La Massana* (€2) from the tourist office. Exhilarating trails lead from the small settlements that nestle beside the CG3, north of Ordino.

A track leads west from **Llorts** (1413m) up the Riu de l'Angonella valley to a group of lakes, the **Estanys de l'Angonella**, at about 2300m. Count on three hours to get there.

From slightly north of the even smaller settlement of **El Serrat** (1600m), a secondary road leads 4km east to the Borda de Sorteny mountain hut (1969m). From there a trail goes southeast to **Estany de l'Estanyó** (2339m). Another heads east up to the Collada dels Meners pass (2713m, about 1½ hours), from where you can go north to **Pic de la Serrera** (2913m, 30 minutes) or a couple of hours south and west via **Pic de la Cabaneta** (2863m) to **Pic de l'Estanyó** (2915m), Andorra's second-highest summit. In about eight hours of tough trekking from Borda de Sorteny you could bag all three peaks and continue via the Coll d'Arenes pass (2539m) and Pic de Casamanya to the **Coll d'Ordino**, enjoying great views along the way.

From **Arans** (1385m), a trail goes north-eastward to **Bordes de l'Ensegur** (2180m), where there is an old shepherd's hut.

Sleeping
Camping Mitxeu (☎ /fax 850 022; per person/tent/car €3/3/3; ☾ Jul–mid-Sep) Some 200m north of Llorts, this place is basic but it's one of Andorra's most beautiful camping grounds, with its own spring.

Pensió Vilaró (☎ 850 225; basic s/d €18/31, half-board per person €29; ☾ Dec-Oct; ℗) This simple, friendly place, 300m south of the village, is a favourite with both walkers and skiers and does copious meals for guests.

Getting There & Away
Buses to El Serrat leave from Andorra la Vella at 7.15am, 1pm and 8.30pm. The small communities in the valley are also served by buses linking Ordino and Arcalís.

ORDINO-ARCALÍS SKI AREA
The slopes of the **Ordino-Arcalís ski area** (☎ 739 600), in Andorra's far northwestern corner, are better for beginner and intermediate skiers. A number of the rugged peaks in this beautiful area reach 2700m and provide challenging and spectacular summer walking. There's no accommodation in Arcalís.

Restaurant La Coma (2200m) at the end of the paved road (closed in winter) is a useful landmark. From there, the **Creussans chairlift** (adult/child one way €5.30/3.25, return €7/4.30; ☼ Dec-Apr & Jul-Sep) whisks you up to 2625m.

Skiing
In winter, Ordino-Arcalís has enough snow and a decent selection of runs, but can be cold and windy. There are 14 lifts covering 26km of pistes at elevations between 1940m and 2640m. A lift pass costs €23.50/59.50 for one/three days (€27.50/70 in high season).

Walking
The trail behind Restaurant La Coma leads eastwards across the hill, then north and over the ridge to a group of beautiful mountain lakes, **Estanys de Tristaina**. The walk to the first lake takes about 30 minutes.

Eating
Restaurant La Coma (☼ 10am-6pm) functions from December to early May and late June to early September, offering both snacks and a full menu.

Getting There & Away
In the ski season there are eight buses daily between Ordino and the ski station (€0.80), and six in summer.

EASTERN ANDORRA

In eastern Andorra lies the principality's best skiing (see the boxed text, p397), while in the quiet of summer walks around Sol-

deu and Canillo rival those of northwest Andorra for beauty and grandeur.

ENCAMP
Encamp is really little more than a sprawl on either side of the CG2. The **tourist office** (☎ 731 000; www.encamp.ad; ☼ 9am-1pm & 3.30-7.30pm Mon-Fri, 10am-1pm & 4-7pm Sat year-round, 10am-2pm Sun Dec-Mar & Jul-Sep) is beside the CG2, 100m south of Encamp's town hall, a striking smoked-glass cube.

Sights & Activities
The **Museu Nacional de l'Automòbil** (National Automobile Museum; ☎ 832 266; adult/child €2.40/1.20; ☼ 9.30am-1.30pm & 3-6pm Tue-Sat, 10am-2pm Sun), beside the CG2, displays about 80 vintage cars plus antique motorcycles and over 100 bicycles from old bone-rattlers to sleek racers.

Most of the **Església Sant Romà de les Bons**, about 1km north of Encamp, dates from the 12th century. The Romanesque frescoes in the apse are reproductions of the originals, now in Barcelona's Museu Nacional d'Art de Catalunya (see p295).

To the right of the CG2, 3km north of Encamp, the austere **Santuari de Nostra Senyora de Meritxell** (admission free; ☼ 9.15am-1pm & 3-6pm Wed-Mon) looms over the highway. Designed by the internationally renowned Catalan architect Ricardo Bofill, it replaces the original shrine to Andorra's patron, destroyed by fire in 1972.

Funicamp (adult/child return €10/7; ☼ operates Dec-Mar & Jul-Aug), the long bubble lift at the northern end of Encamp, hauls you from 1300m to 2500m, giving access to the Grau Roig and Pas de la Casa snowfields.

Getting There & Away
Buses run from Andorra la Vella to Encamp every 15 minutes between 7am and 9.30pm.

CANILLO
elevation 1500m
Canillo is a pleasant, expanding ski village, small by comparison with Soldeu-El Tartar 7km to its east, yet ideal if you're looking for a quiet family winter holiday spot.

Once the snows melt, Canillo adopts an even gentler pace and is a delightful base for a summer activity holiday. It offers canyon clambering, guided walks, four *vía ferrata* climbing routes and a climbing wall, the year-round Palau de Gel with its ice rink and swimming pool, and endless possibilities for walking (including La Ruta del Gallo, an easy 6.5km, signed nature walk that follows the valley downstream from Soldeu).

The helpful **tourist office** (☎ 751 090; www vdc.ad; ☽ 8am-8pm Mon-Sat, 8am-4pm Sun), on the main road at the east end of the village, also covers Soldeu and El Tarter. A little beyond is the splendid 11th-century Romanesque **Esglesià de Sant Joan de Caselles** (☽ Jul-Aug). Year-round, you can collect the key from Hostal Aina (see Sleeping & Eating, below). Inside is a rare, stucco *Christ in Majesty* and a fine 16th-century altarpiece.

Sleeping & Eating

Camping Santa Creu (☎ 851 462; per person/tent/car €3.10/3.10/3.10; ☽ mid-Jun–Sep) The greenest of Canillo's five camping grounds and, since it's the furthest from the highway, the quietest.

Hostal Aina (☎ 851 434; colonies.aina@andorra ad; dm €12, half-board €18.05; ☽ Sep–mid-Jun) This place functions as a children's holiday camp in summer and as a youth hostel for the rest of the year. Ring ahead during the ski season, as it's often full. Dormitories sleep six and you need your own sleeping bag.

Hotel Canigó (☎ 851 024; hotelcanigo@hotmail com; s/d €35/45) On the main street, this modest little hotel with a popular bar beneath offers good value. Ask for a room overlooking the mountain behind.

Hotel Bonavida (☎ 851 300; hotel.bonavida@ andorra.ad; Plaça Major; per person with breakfast Dec-Apr €34.70-49.30, Jun-Oct €31.30-40.50, closed May & Nov; P ☒) Only a well-cast snowball from Canillo's telecabin, the Bonavida couldn't be better placed for skiers, and there's a mini-gym with sauna and spa to relax the muscles at day's end. Most of its cosy rooms each has balcony overlooking the river and mountain beyond. The copious buffet breakfast has real espresso coffee and dinners are ample too.

Cal Lulu (☎ 851 427; menú €11.45, mains €10-16, pizzas €6.45-9; ☽ closed Mon & Tue except high season) Full of character and normally packed to the gills, Cal Lulu serves up excellent Catalan and French dishes in generous quantities.

The **restaurant** (reservations ☎ 800 840) of the Palau de Gel sports complex isn't the kind of place you'd automatically associate with good cuisine. But both its weekday *menú* (€9.60) and gourmet mains (€8.40 to €10) are excellent value. The bar is a good spot for a snack – and for entertainment you can watch the swimming and skating below.

SOLDEU-EL TARTER SKI AREA

Soldeu and El Tarter, both popular with British skiers, are separate villages 2km apart whose ski-lift systems interconnect. Soldeu has the bulk of the accommodation and facilities. For general information, www.soldeu .ad gives a rundown on the resort and, in winter, the latest snow conditions, including a see-for-yourself webcam if you don't trust the official weather forecast.

Skiing

Twenty-eight lifts connect 92km of runs with a vertical drop of 850m from 2560m. Skiing here is similar to that at Pas de la Casa (with which it is nowadays interconnected) except that here black runs into the villages are steeper and more picturesque. Also, the slopes, wooded in their lower reaches, are often warmer than the exposed ski areas of Pas de la Casa and Grau Roig, where the wind can lash.

Lift passes for one/three days cost €29/74.25 (€31.50/80.25 high season). For skiing information call ☎ 890 555.

Other Activities

You'll find a week's worth of walks around Canillo and Soldeu in Lonely Planet's *Walking in Spain*.

The telecabins in Canillo and Soldeu (adult/child €10/7 both) also operate in July and August, whisking you up to the higher reaches, from where you can walk or mountain bike down.

SNOW MATES

In the winter of 2003, the ski resorts of Soldeu-El Tarter and Pas de la Casa-Grau Roig, after decades of jealously eyeing each other's slopes and fortunes, agreed to install a short, umbilical lift and join forces. The result is the combined snowfields of **Grandvalira** (☎ 808 900; www.grandvalira. com), far and away the most extensive in all the Pyrenees, with 192km of runs and a combined lift system that can shift 90,000 skiers per hour. Lift passes, valid for the combined area for one/three days, cost €33.50/87 (€35/90.75 in the high season).

Centre d´Equitació Calbo (☎ 852 101; per hr/3 hr €20/35), at the western end of the village, does horse rides.

You can hire mountain bikes (€18/42 per day/three days) from Sport Hotel Village.

Sleeping

Most hotels are in thrall to the tour operators throughout winter. There are, however, two splendid exceptions at each end of the price spectrum.

Hotel Roc de Sant Miquel (☎ 851 079; www .hotel-roc.com; s/d winter €39/58, summer €21/32, all with breakfast) The pleasant young Anglo-Andorran owners here, both of them ski instructors and experienced walkers, can arrange nature walks and hikes. It's a relaxed, laid-back hotel (the owner also plays lead guitar in a local band) that also hires mountain bikes to guests for a nominal fee.

Sport Hotel (☎ 870 600; www.sporthotelcomplex .com; half-board per person €74-95 Dec-Apr, €41-61 May-Nov) and **Sport Hotel Village** (☎ 870 500; half-board per person Dec-Apr €86-111, May-Nov €46-66) Imagine a pair of Alpine chalets on the scale of a department store, where woodwork predominates and the vast open spaces are broken down into more intimate lounges and bars. The brand-new **Centre Lúdico** offers guests a range of aquatic and fitness activities. At Sport Hotel Village, with its internal atrium, soaring upwards for four storeys, all rooms have balconies overlooking the ski slopes.

If you're prepared to push just 2.5km eastward to Les Bordes d'Envalira, equidistant between the Soldeu-El Tartar and Grau Roig-Pas de la Casa ski fields, prices drop significantly. Both hotels have restaurants, so you aren't obliged to drop down to Soldeu to eat.

Hotel Austria (☎ 735 555; www.soldeuhotels .com – Spanish only; per person with breakfast May-Jul & Nov €22-30, compulsory half-board per person Dec-Apr & Aug €44-60; P) This friendly, English-speaking place has 60 rooms, including four for the handicapped, plus 30 apartments that can accommodate up to eight just across the road.

Hotel Confort (☎ 852 288; hotelconfort-b.env@ Andorra.ad; s/d €37/40) Next door to Hotel Austria, the Confort is also a family hotel, with 26 rooms. It too requires half-board (€58/70 for singles/doubles) during the ski season.

Eating

Hotel Bruxelles (☎ 851 010) This hotel has a cheerful restaurant with a small open-air terrace overlooking the pistes. It does well-filled sandwiches, whopping burgers and a tasty *menú* (€9.90).

Restaurant Fontanella (☎ 871 750; mains €6.75-11.50) This restaurant does a range of very reasonably priced Italian specialities, plus the usual pizzas and pastas (€6.60 to €7.80).

Borda de l'Horto (☎ 851 622; mains €12-15; ☽ Tue-Sun) This upmarket restaurant, 1km west of El Tarter, is one of not too many places in the valley where you can be sure to find Andorrans dining. With its low beams and white-washed walls, it's a congenial, attractively restored farmhouse with good cuisine.

El Mosquit (☎ 851 030) Off the main highway and in the village of El Tarter, 'The Mosquito' is at once intimate bar, restaurant and, below, heaving pub. The restaurant, run by a young Belgian pair, has robust wood furnishings; its chairs and benches as heavy as church pews. It does fondues (€13 to €14), large and lavishly topped pizzas and Tex-Mex.

Entertainment

The night scene at Soldeu-El Tarter gets hopping in winter. **Pussy Cat** and its neighbour **Fat Albert**, both one block from the main drag, rock until far too late to allow any impressive skiing the next day. **Avalanche** (☎ 852 282) and, three doors away, **Aspen** (☎ 851 974) feature music every day and a live band performance at least twice a week.

Getting There & Around

Hourly buses run from Andorra la Vella to Canillo and on to El Tarter and Soldeu between 8am and 8pm. In winter, there are free shuttle buses (just flash your ski pass) between Canillo, El Tarter, Soldeu and Les Bordes d'Envalira, running approximately hourly (with a break from noon to 3pm) until 11pm. A telecabin also links Canillo directly with the ski slopes.

All four villages are also on the route of buses travelling between Andorra la Vella, Pas de la Casa and the French railhead of Latour-de-Carol or the Franco-Spanish one at L'Hospitalet (see p388).

PAS DE LA CASA-GRAU ROIG SKI AREA

The linked ski stations of Pas de la Casa and Grau Roig lie on either side of the Port d'Envalira pass. Grau Roig, with just one hotel, is on the western side of the *coll*, 2km south of the CG2. Pas de la Casa, on the French border and largest of the Andorran ski resorts, is a fairly tawdry, architecturally bleak place, catering principally to French visitors and day trippers on a duty-free shopping orgy. In high season, especially the French winter school holiday from mid-February to early March, it's near impossible to get a bed and lift queues can be frustratingly long.

Pas de la Casa's **tourist office** (☎ 855 292; fax 856 275; ☉ 9am-1pm & 3-7pm Mon-Sat) is in a kiosk opposite the Andorran customs station. For local information, consult www pasgrau.com.

Skiing

There's more than decent skiing and snowboarding for all levels. The combined **ski area** (☎ 871 900) has a network of 24 lifts and 100km of pistes. Lift passes cost €29.50/75 for one/three days (€31.50/80 in high season).

Other Activities

The **Centre Esportiu** (☎ 856 830) is an architecturally striking leisure complex with swimming pools, solarium, hydromassage, sauna, squash, a climbing wall and more.

The **Centre Outdoor** (☎ 872 900) in Grau Roig runs a variety of fun snowy activities, including snowshoe treks (from €12), igloo building (from €20) and dog sledding (from €30).

During the ski season, **Helitrans** (☎ 871 900) does 10-minute helicopter flights from Grau Roig.

Sleeping

During the ski season and, to a lesser extent, July and August, it's almost impossible to find reasonably priced accommodation in Pas de la Casa because so many hotels are occupied partially or fully by tour companies.

Hotel Central (☎ 855 375; www.hotelcentraland .com; Carrer Abelletes 5; s/d Apr-Nov €22/34, compulsory half-board per person Dec-Mar €30-46) Open year-round, the vast concrete Hotel Central has bland, unexceptional, rooms, and the same could go for the cuisine. That said, it does represent, in Pas de la Casa currency, good value for your euro.

Hotel la Muntanya (☎ 855 318; fax 855 898; Carrer Catalunya 12; per person with breakfast €27-51, half-board

€39-63) Also open year-round is this welcoming place, recently under new ownership. During the ski season, half-board is compulsory at weekends and during French school holidays.

Eating

In Pas de la Casa, you can eat sandwiches and burgers until they ooze out of your ears. For more substantial fare, try the battery of restaurants around the base of the ski slopes.

Restaurant La Cabanya (☎ 855 574; Carrer Bearn 18; mains €7.50-12.50, menús €11-13.50) Easily missed – go up a flight of steps and turn right – this is one place that offers something more subtle, in a pleasant, informal environment.

La Belle Époque (☎ 855 173; Carrer de Catalunya 12) This place, which also styles itself **Si-Ski-Klan**, does a bargain lunch *menú* at €10 and offers an imaginative range of dishes based on French and Spanish cuisine.

El Racó d'en Sorolla (☎ 856 657; Carrer Bearn 26; mains €9.50-14; ☉ Nov-Apr) Intimate, low-beamed and with bare brick walls, this attractive restaurant, which serves until midnight, has recently been taken over by a French team and oh, how it shows in the imaginative, creative menu. Early days to judge, but all the indications are that it will be a welcome player within Pas de la Casa's limited gastronomic repertoire.

Entertainment

What Pas de la Casa lacks in places to sleep or eat, it compensates for in its ski-season nightlife, which pounds from sunset onwards. Dance away your bruises at **West End** and **Billboard**. **Milwaukee** (Carrer Bearn; ☉ 5pm-1am), a favourite of the British snow crowd, also packs in the après-skiers, as do **Kyu** (Plaça dels Vaquers; ☉ 5pm-3am) and, nearby, **Underground** (☉ 8pm-3am).

Vertigo (Carrer Solana 9; ☉ 5pm-3am), next door to Underground, is on a smaller scale and altogether more versatile. There's the hip pub with its resident DJ. Penetrate more to a quieter bar with its three Internet points (€5 per hour), then deeper still to its pleasant restaurant (mains €10 to €15), which also does takeaway pizzas and tapas.

Getting There & Away

From Andorra la Vella, there are eight buses daily to/from Pas de la Casa. Of the four run by Hispano Andorrana, two continue to the French train station of L'Hospitalet and two to the railhead at Latour-de-Carol (see p388).

Drivers can avoid Port d'Envalira by taking the 2.8km toll tunnel (€5.60) between Pas de la Casa and Grau Roig. But unless you're pushed for time or the weather's poor, you'll be missing out on the spectacular drive up and over Port d'Envalira, at 2408m the highest road pass in the Pyrenees.

ANDORRA DIRECTORY

ACCOMMODATION

Andorra, which survives on 'touroeuros', is low on budget accommodation. Most visitors come as members of an organised group. Indeed, if you're happy to stay in one place, the cheapest option, especially during the ski season, is to sign up for a package. All major tour operators in Britain, for example, offer Andorra as a destination.

Hotels are fullest from December to March and in July and August. During these months, some places put prices up substantially, sometimes wildly, or insist on half-board, while others simply don't take in independent travellers. They also sometimes fail to post their prices.

There are no youth hostels in Andorra. In compensation there are several great camping grounds, many beautifully situated.

You don't need to reserve at any of Andorra's 26 *refugis* (huts). All are some distance from the road and all but one are unstaffed and free. Most have bunks, fireplaces and drinkable water, but no cooking facilities.

Tourist offices stock a free booklet, *Guia d'Allotjaments Turístics*, but it's far from a comprehensive listing and, while the rest of the information is reliable, the prices it quotes are merely indicative.

ACTIVITIES
Skiing
DOWNHILL

Andorra, with five *estacióis d'esquí* (downhill ski resorts), boasts the best skiing and snowboarding in the Pyrenees and its ski passes work out cheaper than those of many other European resorts. Tourist offices and **Ski Andorra** (☎ 864 389; www.skiandorra.ad) offer up-to-the-minute information.

The biggest and best are the linked resorts of Pas de la Casa-Grau Roig and Soldeu-El Tarter in the east. Arinsal, Pal and Ordino-Arcalís – more limited, often windier yet less expensive – are in the northwest.

Skiing is good for all levels – especially so for beginners and intermediates – and the season normally runs from December to mid-April.

You can get a five-day pass, valid for all resorts, for €127 (€144 high season).

Ski school costs around €32 per hour for one-on-one tuition (much cheaper per head if you're in a small group) and €75 to €92.50 for 15 hours of group classes, prices varying according to resort and season.

Downhill ski gear hire varies between €8 and €11 per day, while snowboards go for €17 to €20 per day.

CROSS-COUNTRY SKIING & SKI TOURING

There's a cross-country skiing centre with 15km of marked forest trails at La Rabassa near Andorra la Vella.

Walking

The best walking map is *Andorra & Cadí* (1:50,000), produced by the French company Rando Éditions with input from the Institut Cartogràfic de Catalunya. Close on its heels comes *Andorra* (1:40,000), by the Spanish map company Alpina (make sure you pick up the 2002 edition, which is a distinct improvement upon its predecessor). Another alternative is the *Mapa de Refugis i Grans Recorreguts d'Andorra* (1:50,000) which pinpoints all of Andorra's 26 mountain refuges and network of marked trails.

Andorra's unspoiled back country, where more than 50 *estanys* (lakes) lie hidden among the soaring mountains, begins only a few hundred metres from the bazaar-like bustle of the capital.

The best season for walking is June to September, when temperatures climb well above 20°C, dropping to around 10°C at night. June can be wet. Ordino in the northwest and Canillo or Soldeu in eastern Andorra (here, Lonely Planet's *Walking in Spain* has suggestions for a week's worth of walking) make excellent bases for day walks.

The GR11 trail, which traverses the Spanish Pyrenees from the Mediterranean to the Atlantic, enters Andorra by the Port de Vall Civera pass (2518m) in the southeast and crosses to the challenging Port de Baiau pass (2756m) in the northwest.

Walkers and cross-country skiers can sleep for free in any of Andorra's 26 mountain refuges dotted around the high country.

CUSTOMS

Tourist offices carry a leaflet outlining duty-free allowances for goods entering Spain, France or any EU country from Andorra. These include 5L of still wine, either 1.5L of spirits or 3L of lighter spirits or sparkling wine, and 300 cigarettes. Spot checks for smugglers are fairly rigorous on both Spanish and French borders.

DANGERS & ANNOYANCES

Roads follow the floor of the tight valleys and long traffic jams can clog Andorra la Vella's main arteries. Andorran drivers must rank among Europe's most reckless, hurtling around the tight mountain bends as if propelled by some collective death wish.

EMBASSIES & CONSULATES
Andorran Embassies & Consulates

Andorra has embassies in France and Spain:

France (☎ 01 40 06 03 30; 30 Rue d'Astorg, 75008 Paris)

Spain (Map pp106-8; ☎ 91 431 74 53; Calle Alcalá 73, 28001 Madrid)

Embassies & Consulates in Andorra

France and Spain maintain reciprocal missions in Andorra:

France (Map pp390-1; ☎ 869 396; Carrer de les Canals 38-40, Andorra la Vella)

Spain (Map pp390-1; ☎ 800 030; Carrer del Prat de la Creu 34, Andorra la Vella)

HOLIDAYS

Public holidays fall on 1 January (Año Nuevo), 14 March (Constitution Day), Good Friday (Viernes Santo), 8 September (Día de Meritxell, patron saint of Andorra) and 25 December (Christmas Day).

INTERNET RESOURCES

Plenty of general and specific background information on the principality can be found online at www.andorra.ad.

MEDIA

The principality's two daily papers, both in Catalan, are *Diari d'Andorra* and *Periòdic d'Andorra*. You can watch Spanish and French TV, along with the local Andorra Televisión (ATV).

A selection of radio stations can be found on the following frequencies: Ràdio Nacional Andorra (RNA; 91.4MHz & 94.2MHz); Andorra 7 (101.5MHz); Ràdio Valira (93.3MHz & 98.9MHz); and Andorra Uno (96.0MHz).

MONEY

Though not a full member of the EU, Andorra uses the euro. For exchange rates, see the inside front cover. Banks and ATMs abound in this commercially minded country.

POST

Andorra has no postal service of its own. France and Spain each operate a separate postal system with their own Andorran stamps. They're valid only for items posted within Andorra – and needed only for international mail, since letters for destinations within the country go free. You can't use regular French or Spanish stamps.

International mail (except letters to Spain) is better routed through the swifter and more reliable French postal system. There are two kinds of post boxes, but if you use the wrong one your letter will be transferred.

The best way to get a letter to Andorra (except from Spain) is to address it to 'Principauté d'Andorre via FRANCE'.

SHOPPING

With low customs duties and no sales tax, Andorra is an Aladdin's cave of cheap electronic goods, sports gear, photographic equipment, shoes, clothing, perfume, petrol and, above all, alcohol, cigarettes and French dairy products. Shops selling these goods cluster in Andorra la Vella, Pas de la Casa and near the Spanish border. The majority of visitors from Spain and France come for the shopping, although potential savings are no longer what they were.

Some warranties are valid only in the country of purchase, so read the fine print.

TELEPHONE

Andorra's country code is ☎ 376. To call Spain from Andorra, dial ☎ 00-34 followed by the local number. To call France, dial ☎ 00-33 then the local number.

Directory assistance (☎ 111 for numbers within Andorra, ☎ 119 for international information) has multilingual operators. Cheap rates for international calls apply between 9pm and 8am Monday to Saturday, plus all day Sunday. During off-peak hours, a three-minute call to Europe costs €0.60 (€0.92 to the US or Australia). You can't make reverse-charge (collect) calls from Andorra.

Euros or an Andorran *teletarja* (phonecard) can be used for calls. These phonecards are widely sold at tourist offices and tobacconists for €3 and €6.

TOURIST INFORMATION

There's a municipal and a national tourist office in Andorra la Vella and several other smaller ones around the country. Most carry information about the whole of the principality and sell both stamps and phonecards.

Andorra's tourist offices or tourism representatives abroad include:

France (☎ 01 42 61 50 55; 26 Ave de l'Opéra, 75001 Paris)

Spain Madrid (Map pp106-8; ☎ 91 431 74 53; Calle Alcalá 73, 28001) Barcelona (☎ 93 508 84 48; World Trade Center, Moll de Barcelona, Edificio Nord, Planta Baja 27, 08039)

UK (☎ 020-8874 4806; 63 Westover Rd, London SW18 2RF)

VISAS

Visas are not necessary; the authorities figure that if Spain or France lets you in, that's good enough for them. But bring your passport or national ID card.

Aragón

ARAGÓN

Aragón is flanked by several worlds: France, Catalonia, Valencia, Basque Navarra and the northeastern reaches of Spain's Castilian heartland. If you love mountains, castles and ancient stone villages, this place is for you. Its major rewards come from exploring the smaller towns and sparsely populated back-country areas.

Aragón's beautiful northern strip, taking in the highest and some of the most awesome parts of the Pyrenees, offers a wealth of walking and skiing that you could easily extend over to the French side of the range. Along the valleys and down into the lower pre-Pyrenees hills is an intriguing mix of canyons, pretty villages, lonely castles and venerable monasteries with some outstanding Romanesque architecture.

The one big city, Zaragoza (Saragossa), has warmth and a collection of monuments and sights that may make you linger longer than you planned.

Central Aragón consists mainly of treeless depressions and forlorn plateaus. Further south, you reach other, thinly populated mountain regions, sprinkled with picturesque, mysterious villages. The towers of Teruel, the south's biggest town, are among the masterpieces of Spanish Mudéjar architecture.

ARAGÓN

HIGHLIGHTS

- Savour lusty Cabernets from the **Somontano area** (p421)
- Feast on cured hams from **Teruel** (p433)
- Revel at **Fiestas de Pilar** (p410), Zaragoza's October blow out
- Be charmed by the Pyrenean valleys of **Echo** and **Ansó** (p431)
- Explore **Albarracín** (p437), an ancient kingdom hewn from a red-rock hilltop
- Ski the slopes of **Candanchú** (p430) and **Cerler** (p422)
- Be awed by the Romanesque monastery of **San Juan de la Peña** (p430)
- Marvel at the Mudéjar towers of **Teruel** (p433) and Zaragoza's magnificent **Aljafería palace** (p409)
- Walk the trails of the **Parque Nacional de Ordesa y Monte Perdido** in the Pyrenees (p424)
- Feel the surreal spirit at Calanda's **Luis Buñuel Centre** (p439)

| ■ AREA: 47,720 SQ KM | ■ POP: 1,230,090 | ■ AVE SUMMER TEMP: HIGH 31°C, LOW 17°C |

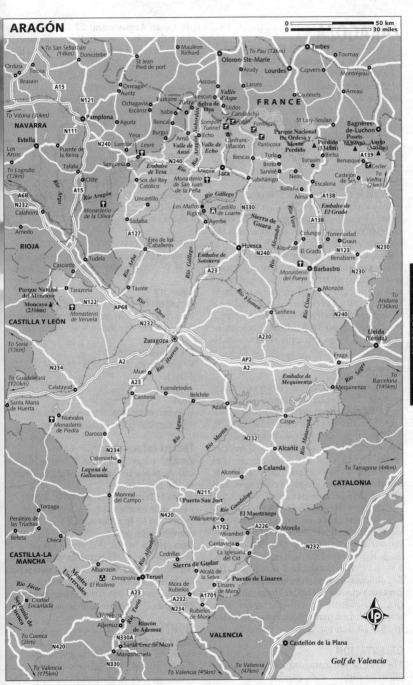

ARAGÓN

0 ———— 50 km
0 ———— 30 miles

To San Sebastián (14km)
Ordizia
Tolosa
Beasain
A15
To Vitoria (30km)
NAVARRA
N121
Doneztebe
Mauléon Richard
St Jean Pied de port
Orreaga Auritz
Ochagavía
Escároz
Euzkarre
Zuriza
Isaba
Selva de Oza
N111
Pamplona
Agoitz
Roncal
Burgui
Ansó
Echo
N240
Lumbier
Leyre
Valle de Ansó
Valle de Echo
Estella
Puente de la Reina
Sanguesa
Embalse de Yesa
Yesa
Río Aragón
Jaca
Los Arcos
Tafalla
Olite
Sos del Rey Católico
Monasterio de San Juan de la Peña
A68
Río Arga
Monasterio de la Oliva
Uncastillo
Los Mallos Riglos
Castillo de Loarre
N330
N232
Calahorra
Sádaba
Ayerbe
Sierra de Guara
RIOJA
Arnedo
Ejea de los Caballeros
A127
To Logroño (12km)

FRANCE

To Pau (12km)
Tarbes
Oloron-Ste-Marie
Arudy
Lourdes
Capvern
Tournay
Montréjeau
Accous
Laruns
Arreau
Vallée d'Aspe
Lescun
Urdos
Candanchú
St Lary-Soulan
Cauterets
Somport Tunnel
Astún
Formigal
Bagnères-de-Luchon
Canfranc-Estación
Panticosa
Parque Nacional De Ordesa y Monte Perdido
Perdido (3348m)
Posets (3369m)
Aneto (3404m)
Biescas
Torla
Broto
Bielsa
Benasque
Cerler
Sarvisé
Nerín
Escuaín
Sabiñánigo
Escalona
Castejón de Sos
To Vielha (2km)
Boltaña
Aínsa
A138
Río Gállego
Embalse de El Grado
A138
Colungo
Torreciudad
Huesca
Alquézar
El Grado
Graus
N240
N123
N230
Barbastro
A23
Monasterio del Pueyo
Monzón
N230
N240
To Andorra (136km)
Embalse de Sotonera
Río Cinca
Sariñena
Lleida (Lérida)
Río Flumen
N232
Río Ebro
Zaragoza
Fraga
To Barcelona (145km)
Río Segre
Muel
Río Huerva
AP2
A2
Fuendetodos
Belchite
Embalse de Mequinenza
Mequinenza
To Tarragona (44km)
CATALONIA
Azaila
Caspe
Río Martín
N232
Alcañiz
Calanda
Alcorisa
Calanda
N211
Puerto San Just
El Maestrazgo
Villarluengo
Río Guadalope
A1702
Mirambel
Morella
A226
Cantavieja
La Iglesuela del Cid
N232
Cedrillas
Sierra de Gúdar
Puerto de Linares
Albarracín
Dinópolis
Teruel
Alcalá de la Selva
Linares de Mora
El Rodeno
Mora de Rubielos
A232
A1701
A23
Rubielos de Mora
N234
Torrebaja
Ademuz
Rincón de Ademuz
N330A
Santa Cruz de Moya
Manzanaruela
N330
VALENCIA
Castellón de la Plana
To Valencia (45km)
To Valencia (47km)
Golf de Valencia

Río Arba
Tudela
Cascante
Tarazona
Parque Natural del Moncayo
Moncayo (2316m)
Monasterio de Veruela
N122
AP68
Tauste
Río Arba
N232
CASTILLA Y LEÓN
To Soria (13km)
N234
To Guadalajara (120km)
Calatayud
Santa Maria de Huerta
Nuévalos
Monasterio de Piedra
Daroca
N234
Calamocha
Laguna de Gallocanta
Monreal del Campo
Terzaga
Peralejos de las Truchas
Beteta
Checa
CASTILLA-LA MANCHA
To Soria
Río Júcar
Montes Universales
Ciudad Encantada
Serranía de Cuenca
To Cuenca (2km)
N420
To Valencia (175km)
Río Turia
Río Alfambra
Cariñena
A2
A23
A230

ARAGÓN

ZARAGOZA

pop 597,472 / elevation 200m

The regional capital is home to over half of Aragón's population, the result of an intense country-to-city drift that began in the 19th century. Set on the Río Ebro, Spain's fifth-largest city has long been an important crossroads, and its centre rewards exploration. Intriguing archaeology, fine art and architecture, and dozens of lively bars and restaurants are just a few of the attractions.

Outside the city centre, Zaragoza is primarily a series of grey 20th-century apartment blocks lining straight streets. On a bad day it can get blowy, and locals call the biting north wind 'El Cierzo'.

Despite its multicultural past, Zaragoza has become synonymous with provincialism. The recent arrival of high-speed trains and the inauguration of a massive new train station herald a period of change, and local leaders are currently lobbying hard for their city to host Expo 2008, whose theme, most appropriately for this arid region, will be water use.

HISTORY

The Romans founded the colony of Caesaraugusta (from which 'Zaragoza' is derived) in 14 BC. As many as 25,000 people migrated to the prosperous Roman city. In Muslim times Zaragoza was capital of the Upper March, one of Al-Andalus' frontier territories. In 1118 it fell to Alfonso I 'El Batallador' (The Battler), ruler of the expanding Christian kingdom of Aragón, and immediately became its capital.

Centuries later Zaragoza put up unusually stiff resistance under the Napoleonic siege, although it capitulated in 1809. Industrial growth late in the 19th century made it a centre of militant trade unionism, but in 1936, when the civil war began, the Republicans had no time to organise and Zaragoza quickly fell under Nationalist control. The country's main military academy was established here under General Franco in 1928 (still in use, north of town).

ORIENTATION

The core of old Zaragoza lies south of the Ebro, its former walls marked by Avenida de César Augusto and El Coso. Much of what there is to see, and a good choice of hotels, restaurants and bars, lie within these old city limits.

The vast Plaza del Pilar, dominated by Zaragoza's great churches, gives way southward to a labyrinth of lanes and alleys whose heart is known as El Tubo. The Estación Intermodal Delicias train station is about 2km west of the old centre.

INFORMATION
Bookshops
Librería General (☎ 976 22 44 83; Paseo de la Independencia 22) Good stocks of road and walking maps and guidebooks, as well as some English- and French-language novels.

Internet Access
Conecta-T (☎ 976 20 59 79; Murallas Romanas 4; per hr €1.20; ☽ 10am-11pm Mon-Fri, 11am-11pm Sat & Sun)

Laundry
Lavandería Casa (☎ 976 21 75 67; Calle de Pedro María Ric 37; wash & dry per 3kg load €9; ☽ 9.30am-1.30pm & 4.30-8.30pm Mon-Fri, 9.30am-1.30pm Sat)

Medical Services
Hospital Clínico Universitario (☎ 976 35 75 01; Calle de San Juan Bosco 15)

Post
Main post office (Paseo de la Independencia 33; ☽ 8.30am-8.30pm Mon-Fri, 9.30am-2pm Sat)

Tourist Information
Zaragoza has two helpful central tourist offices, plus a branch in the Estación Intermodal Delicias.

Oficina de Turismo de Aragón (☎ 902 47 70 00; www.turismodearagon.com; Avenida de César Augusto; ☽ 9am-2pm & 5-8pm, from 10am Sat & Sun) Stop by for information on the region.

Plaza del Pilar (☎ 976 39 35 37; www.turismo zaragoza.com; ☽ 10am-8pm) Opposite the basilica.

Torreón de la Zuda (☎ 976 20 12 00; Glorieta de Pío XII; ☽ 10am-2pm & 4.30-8pm 7 Jan-Easter, 10am-8pm rest of year) In a 15th-century Mudéjar tower by the Roman walls. Climb the tower for panoramic views (free).

SIGHTS
Plaza del Pilar
Plaza del Pilar and its eastward continuation, Plaza de la Seo, form a 500m open space, lined by important buildings.

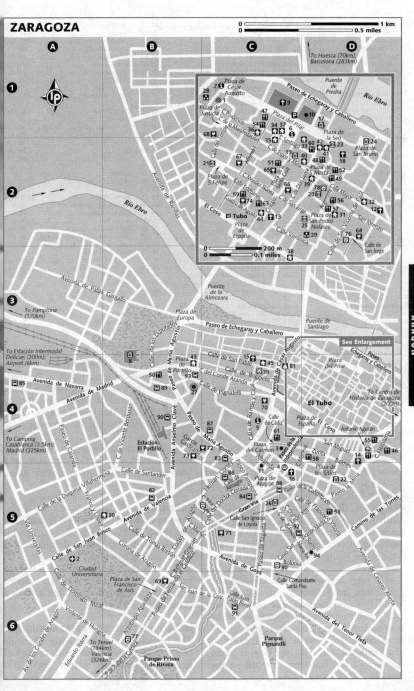

ARAGÓN

BASÍLICA DE NUESTRA SEÑORA DEL PILAR

On 2 January AD 40, Santiago (St James the Apostle) supposedly beheld here a vision of the Virgin Mary, descended from the heavens atop a marble *pilar* (pillar). A chapel was later built around the remaining pillar, then a series of ever-grander churches. At least that's the story behind Zaragoza's enormous baroque **basílica** (☎ 976 39 74 97; admission free; ⌚ 6.45am-9pm), designed in 1681 by Felipe Sánchez y Herrera and heavily modified in the 18th century by Ventura Rodríguez. The towers weren't finished until the early 20th century. Today the main dome is accompanied by 10 smaller ones, decorated with tiles of blue, green, yellow and white, with an unusual Byzantine effect.

The legendary **pilar** is hidden in the Capilla Santa, inside the east end of the basílica. A tiny oval-shaped portion of the *pilar* is accessible on the chapel's outer west side, and busloads of pilgrims arrive daily to kiss it. Attached to a square white column at the northeast corner of the Capilla Santa are two bombs that were dropped on the basílica early in the civil war.

The basílica's single greatest piece of fine art is a 16th-century alabaster altarpiece by Damián Forment from Valencia. It stands roughly in the middle of the basílica, facing west. Goya painted *La Reina de los Mártires* (Mary, Queen of Martyrs) in a cupola above the north aisle, outside the Sacristía de la Virgen.

You can ascend the northwest tower by taking the **lift** (admission €1.50; ⌚ 9.30am-2pm & 4-6pm Sat-Thu), then climbing a steep spiral staircase.

LA LONJA

Now an **exhibition hall** (☎ 976 39 72 39; admission free; ⌚ 10am-2pm & 5-9pm Tue-Sat, 10am-2pm Sun), this plain but finely proportioned Renaissance-style building, east of the basílica, was constructed in the 16th century as a trading exchange. The medallions on its exterior depict kings of Aragón and other historical personages.

MUSEO DEL FORO DE CAESARAUGUSTA

The unassuming trapezoid on Plaza de la Seo is the modern entrance to part of Roman Caesaraugusta's **forum** (☎ 976 39 97 52; Plaza de la Seo 2; admission €2; ⌚ 10am-2pm &

5-8pm Tue-Sat, 10am-2pm Sun), now well below ground level.

What you see underground are the remains of porticoes, shops, a great *cloaca* (sewer) system, and a limited collection of artefacts dating from between 14 BC and about AD 15. Sections of lead pipes used to channel water to the city demonstrate the Romans' genius for engineering. A good audiovisual show, presented on the hour in Spanish, breathes life into the old crockery.

MUSEO DEL TEATRO DE CAESARAUGUSTA

Discovered during the excavation of a building site in 1972, the ruins of Zaragoza's Roman theatre are the focus of this interesting **museum** (☎ 976 20 50 88; Calle de San Jorge 12; admission €2; 🕑 10am-9pm Tue-Sat, 10am-2pm Sun), opened in 2003. Although the ruins aren't particularly impressive, great efforts have been made to help visitors reconstruct the edifice's former splendour, including evening projections of a virtual performance on the stage (Friday and Saturday only; consult the museum for times). The exhibit culminates with a boardwalk tour through the theatre itself.

LA SEO

Rising at the eastern end of Plaza del Pilar is the Catedral de San Salvador, also known as **La Seo** (☎ 976 29 12 38; Plaza de la Seo; admission €2; 🕑 10am-2pm & 4-7pm Tue-Fri, 10am-noon & 4pm-7pm Sat & Sun summer; 10am-2pm & 4-6pm Tue-Fri, 10am-noon & 4-6pm Sat & Sun rest of year). You must enter at the eastern end, dodging skateboarders on Plaza de San Bruno en route.

La Seo, built between the 12th and 17th centuries, displays a smorgasbord of architectural styles from Romanesque to baroque. It stands on the site of Muslim Zaragoza's main mosque (which in turn stood upon the temple of the Roman forum). The northwest façade is a Mudéjar masterpiece, deploying classic dark brickwork and colourful ceramic decoration in eye-pleasing geometric patterns. The interior is essentially Gothic, though many of the chapels are baroque, the artistic highlight being the 15th-century altarpiece in polychrome alabaster.

La Seo's **Museo de Tapices** (admission €2; 🕑 10am-2pm & 4-6pm or 7pm Tue-Sat, 10am-2pm Sun) has a large collection of 14th- to 17th-century Flemish and French tapestries.

Other Roman Remains

The small **Museo del Puerto Fluvial** (☎ 976 39 31 57; Plaza de San Bruno 8; admission €2; 🕑 10am-2pm & 5-8pm Tue-Sat, 10am-2pm Sun) displays the Roman city's river-port installations, with an audiovisual programme every half-hour. The **Museo de las Termas Públicas** (☎ 976 29 72 79; Calle San Juan y San Pedro 3-7; admission €2; 🕑 10am-2pm & 5-8pm Tue-Sat, 10am-2pm Sun) houses the old Roman baths.

Aljafería

Despite centuries of changes, the **Aljafería** (☎ 976 28 96 84; Calle de los Diputados; adult/student & pensioner/child under 12 €3/1/free, Sun free; 🕑 10am-2pm Sat-Wed & 4-6.30pm Mon-Wed & Fri-Sat Nov-Mar; 10am-2pm Sat-Wed & 4.30-8pm Fri-Wed Apr-Jun & Sep-Oct; daily Jul & Aug) remains Spain's finest Muslim-era edifice outside Andalucía, though it's not in the league of Granada's Alhambra or Córdoba's Mezquita.

A 20-minute walk west from Plaza del Pilar (or seven-minute ride on bus No 32 or 36 from Plaza Españá), the Aljafería was built as a pleasure palace for Zaragoza's Muslim rulers, chiefly in the 11th century. From the 12th century Zaragoza's Christian rulers made alterations, and in the 1490s the Catholic Monarchs, Fernando and Isabel, tacked on their own palace. Later the Aljafería served as a hospital and barracks, when it was allowed to decay. From the 1940s to 1990s restoration was carried out, and in 1987 Aragón's regional parliament, the Cortes de Aragón, established itself here.

Inside the main gate, cross the unexciting first courtyard into a second, the **Patio de Santa Isabel**, once the central courtyard of the Muslim palace. Here you are confronted to the north and south by the opulence and geometric mastery of Muslim architecture, with lovely interwoven arches. The innermost hall at the northern end was the throne room, now with reproductions of its delicate plaster and alabaster wall carvings. Also opening off the northern porch is a small, octagonal **oratorio** (prayer room), with a magnificent horseshoe-arched doorway leading into its *mihrab* (prayer niche indicating the direction of Mecca). The finely chiselled floral motifs, Arabic inscriptions from the Quran and pleasingly simple cupola are impressive examples of Muslim art.

Moving upstairs, you pass through rooms of the **Palacio Mudéjar**, added by Christian

ARAGÓN

rulers in the 12th to 14th centuries, then to the Catholic Monarchs' **palace**, which, as though by way of riposte to the Muslim finery below, contains some exquisite Mudéjar coffered ceilings, especially that of the **Salón del Trono** (Throne Room).

Churches

Several other Zaragoza churches are well worth a look. The **Iglesia de San Pablo** (Calle de San Pablo, cnr Miguel de Ara; ☽ 9am-1pm) has a delicate 14th-century Mudéjar tower and an early 16th-century *retablo* (altarpiece) by Damián Forment. The **Iglesia de La Magdalena**, **Iglesia de San Miguel** and **Iglesia de San Gil** sport further fine 14th- and 15th-century Mudéjar towers – at their prettiest when floodlit at night. The 16th-century **Iglesia de Santa Engracia** has an underground crypt containing the bones of the eponymous saint and other Zaragozan early Christian martyrs.

Museums
MUSEO DE ZARAGOZA

Devoted to archaeology and fine arts, the **city museum** (☎ 976 22 21 81; Plaza de los Sitios 6; admission free; ☽ 10am-2pm & 5-8pm Tue-Sat, 10am-2pm Sun) displays artefacts from prehistoric to Muslim times, and an important collection of Gothic art, as well as a dozen Goya paintings.

MUSEO CAMÓN AZNAR

This eclectic **collection** (☎ 976 39 73 28; Calle de Espoz y Mina 23; admission €1, ID required; ☽ 9am-2pm & 6-9pm Tue-Sat, 11am-2pm Sun) of Spanish art through the ages features a room of Goya etchings (on the top floor) and half a dozen paintings attributed to El Greco. It spreads over the three storeys of the Palacio de los Pardo, a Renaissance mansion.

PATIO DE LA INFANTA

This **exhibition** (☎ 976 76 76 76; Calle San Ignacio de Loyola 16; admission free; ☽ 8.30am-2.30pm & 6-9pm Mon-Fri, 11am-2pm & 6-9pm Sat) is the Ibercaja bank's collection of Goya paintings, displayed in a lovely Plateresque courtyard.

MUSEO DE PABLO GARGALLO

Within the 17th-century Palacio Argillo is a representative **display** (☎ 976 72 49 23; Plaza de San Felipe 3; admission free; ☽ 10am-2pm & 5-9pm Tue-Sat, 10am-2pm Sun) of sculptures by Pablo Gargallo (1881–1934), probably Aragón's most gifted artistic son after Goya.

CENTRO DE HISTORIA DE ZARAGOZA

The old convent of San Agustín (only the neoclassical façade remains) is the site of this **museum** (Zaragoza History Centre; ☎ 976 20 56 40; Plaza San Agustín 2; admission adult/child €3.25/free; ☽ 10am-8pm Tue-Sat, 10am-2pm Sun). Each of the eight exhibit rooms focuses on a different aspect of the city's heritage, from trade and transport to popular celebrations. Of particular interest is a series of models depicting Zaragoza's physical transformation through four key phases of its development. Take bus No 22 or 30. Catch bus No 22 going east along Coso. Catch bus No 30 at Plaza de Espana.

WALKING TOUR

Although only fragments of Roman Zaragoza remain, they form the centrepiece of a quartet of well-designed museums (a €6 combination ticket admits you to all four). Start the tour (see map opposite) with a glimpse of the **Roman walls** (1), stretching from the Mercado Central to the Torreón de la Zuda. Next head east parallel to the Ebro, taking the first right to enter Plaza del Pilar. At the far end of the plaza, just short of the cathedral, is the Roman forum, **Museo del Foro de Caesaraugusta** (2; p408). Continue east another 100m to the Plaza de San Bruno to find the remains of Zaragoza's river port at the **Museo del Puerto Fluvial** (3; p409). Circle around behind the cathedral, La Seo, perhaps stopping for tapas on Plaza Santa Marta, then head south on Refugio, turning left at the sign for the **Museo de las Termas Públicas** (4; p409). After the baths, continue in the same direction to the Plaza de San Pedro Nolasco and the **Museo del Teatro de Caesaraugusta** (5; p409).

FESTIVALS & EVENTS

Zaragoza's biggest event is the **Fiestas del Pilar**, a week of full-on celebrations (religious and otherwise) peaking on 12 October, the **Día de Nuestra Señora del Pilar**. On 5 March, Zaragozans celebrate **Cincomarzada**, commemorating the 1838 ousting of Carlist troops by a feisty populace. Thousands head for Parque Tio Jorge, north of the Ebro, for concerts, games, grilled sausage and wine.

SLEEPING

At the time of writing, there was no camping ground operating in the area. A new

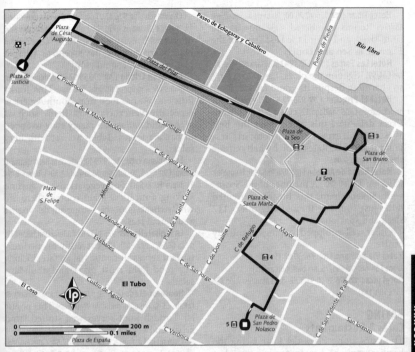

one was being planned, but tourism personnel could not say when it would open, nor where it would be located.

Budget

Hostal El Descanso (☎ 976 29 17 41; San Lorenzo 2; s/d with shared bathroom €15/22) Facing a pretty plaza near the Roman theatre, this family-run guesthouse offers 20 clean, bright rooms. It's often full.

Hotel San Jorge (☎ 976 39 74 62; Calle Mayor 4; s/d €29/36) This good-value option features simple but decent-sized rooms, a small café and friendly staff.

Pensión Holgado (☎ 976 43 20 74; Calle de Conde de Aranda 126; s/d €22/35) Near the Aljafería, this is a straightforward choice, with bright, well-tended rooms on three floors.

Posada de Las Almas (☎ 976 43 97 00; Calle San Pablo 22; s/d €31/39) Though housed in a three-century-old mansion, beyond the lobby it's an ordinary frayed-at-the-edges guesthouse.

Albergue Juvenil Baltasar Gracián (☎ 976 30 66 92; Franco y López 4; HI ID under 26/other incl breakfast €8.60/11.55) Doubling as a student residence during the school term, this HI hostel has

room for 50 in quads. It's a 2km hike from El Tubo, or a quick ride on bus No 22 or 38.

Other decent, reasonably priced places in or near the old city:

Hostal Navarra (☎ 976 29 16 84; Calle de San Vicente de Paúl 30; s/d €25/32)

Hostal Santiago (☎ 976 39 45 50; Calle Santiago 3-5; s/d €25/40)

Pensión La Peña (☎ 976 29 90 89; Cinegio 3; s/d with shared bathroom €10/20)

Mid-Range & Top End

There are plenty of large top-end hotels on the fringes of the city centre, but also a number of good, smaller places around Plaza del Pilar. Most offer parking for approximately €9 per day.

Hotel Sauce (☎ 976 20 50 50; www.hotelsauce.com; Calle de Espoz y Mina 33; s/d €46/63) This excellent-value, small hotel has modern but cosy rooms; bookings are advisable Monday to Thursday.

Hostal Plaza (☎ 976 29 48 30; Plaza del Pilar 14; s/d with bathroom €40/50) Some of the bright and neatly trimmed rooms look directly out onto Plaza del Pilar. Singles are small but OK.

Hotel Tibur (☎ 976 20 20 00; Plaza de la Seo 2; s/d €57/70) Rooms numbered -03 and -04 are suite-sized, and afford the best views of the Plaza de la Seo and Lonja.

Hotel Las Torres (☎ 976 39 42 50; Plaza del Pilar 11; s/d €44/59) Right on the plaza, Las Torres isn't so charming despite its grand façade.

Hotel El Príncipe (☎ 976 29 41 01; www.hotel-el principe.com; Calle Santiago 12; r €141) A block from Plaza del Pilar, this place bears the Best Western seal; expect modern comforts, restaurant and bar. Rates drop by half outside the high season.

Hotel Reino de Aragón (☎ 976 46 82 00; El Coso 80; s/d 92/105; ☐ Ⓟ ✗) A member of the Spain-wide Silken chain, this business-oriented hotel just south of the old city offers 117 sleek and spacious units.

Other well-equipped lodgings in the city centre:

Hotel Vía Romana (☎ 976 39 82 15; Calle de Don Jaime I 54-56; s/d €55/75 incl buffet breakfast)

Hotel Inca (☎ 976 39 00 91; Calle de la Manifestación 33; s/d €108/133)

EATING
Cafés & Restaurants
The cafés along Plaza del Pilar facing the basilica can't be beaten for location, but tend to do pretty ordinary fare, with *menús del día* (daily set menus) for around €6/7.25 indoors/outdoors.

Casa Emilio (☎ 976 43 58 39; Avenida Madrid 5; menú from €6.50; ✪ closed Sun night; ✗) Near the Aljafería, this long-standing establishment serves excellent, moderately priced, home-cooked meals. You'll find few tourists here.

La Migueria (☎ 976 20 07 36; Calle Estébanes 4; migas €3.60, salads €6.50) This El Tubo locale specialises in *migas* (breadcrumbs drenched in olive oil, and topped with sausage, egg and pineapple) and other *aragonese* comfort food. Great for an evening snack.

AUTHOR'S CHOICE

Parrilla de Albarracín (☎ 976 15 81 00; Plaza del Carmen 1; mains €9-12, menú 12.30; ✪ Tue-Sun; ✗) Usually buzzing with families and groups of friends, this traditional dining hall offers classic *aragonese* cuisine, including attractively presented lamb and mushroom dishes, salads with Teruel ham and fantastic desserts.

Churrasco (☎ 976 22 91 60; Calle de Francisco Vitoria 19; menú €10, mains €17; ✗) A popular tavern offering all manner of seafood. Check the blackboard for the day's *centros* (shared platters of ham, squid etc).

El Rincón Criollo (☎ 976 39 92 86; Antonio Agustín 1; mains €6; ✪ 8pm-midnight Tue-Sun) This funky little enclave has food from South America, especially Venezuela, with items such as *arepas* and *hallacas*, a meaty stew wrapped in banana leaves. Tables are set with fiery salsas.

La Retama (☎ 976 39 79 10; Calle de la Reconquista 4; menú €9; ✪ 1.30-3.30pm Mon-Thu, 1.30-3.30pm & 9-11.30pm Fri & Sat) For vegetarians or anyone seeking a meatless main course, there are wholewheat gnocchi, home-made yogurt and herbal teas.

La Tagliatella (☎ 976 39 27 66; Calle de Don Jaime I 43; pizza €8.50, pasta €10) This recently opened restaurant serves authentic Italian fare, including good light-crust pizza and abundant salads.

House of Medusa (☎ 976 29 30 33; Argensola 8; kebabs €3-4; ✪ 8pm-midnight Wed-Mon) This popular Turkish joint serves well-stuffed lamb kebab and vegetarian sandwiches.

Churrería La Fama (☎ 976 39 37 54; Calle Prudencio 25; 3 churros for €1; ✪ 8am-1pm & 5-9.30pm) Stop by morning or evening for fresh *churros* (long, deep-fried doughnut) and chocolate.

Tapas Bars
The narrow streets and small plazas south of La Seo harbour some brilliant tapas bars – ideal for cooling off with a beer on a warm evening. On Plaza Santa Marta, **Cervecería Marpy** and **Vitorinos II** are appealing, while **Casa Domino** offers hams and *montados* (toasted baguette slices topped with Cabrales cheese, among other tantalising spreads). Nearby, the tight little **Casa Amadico** (Calle Jordán de Urries 3) provides seafood *raciones* (meal sized serving of tapas) for as little as €3. **La Calzorras** (Plaza de San Pedro Nolasco) has tantalising larger-than-*tapa* specialities for around €3.50.

There's another string of tapas bars towards the southern end of Calle Heroísmo (most open until midnight), including the atmospheric **Alta Taberna Pantagruel** (Calle Heroísmo 35), with nine varieties of paté and a well-stocked wine rack. Around El Tubo, **Taberna Doña Casta** (☎ 976 20 58 52; Calle Estébanes 6; ✪ Tue-Sun) and **Casa Juanico** (☎ 976 39 72 52;

Plaza Santa Cruz 21;) do 'artisan tapas'. Still more snacking options cram Calle Moneva, east of Paseo de la Independencia, where **El Calamar Bravo** does a brisk business in fried squid sandwiches (€2.20) and **La Mejillonería** goes through buckets of mussels nightly.

DRINKING

The old city and environs abound with cafés suitable for lingering away the morning.

Gran Café de Zaragoza (Alfonso I 25) The picture windows at this elegant old-world salon are perfect for viewing the strollers on Alfonso I.

Café Praga (☎ 976 20 02 51; Plaza de la Santa Cruz 13) A minimalist blue space sprawling onto the plaza in early evening.

Café Barrio Sur (Calle San Jorge 29) A smoky alternative hang-out serving organic coffee and tea, as well as quiche and cake.

An evening stroll along Calle de Espoz y Mina and Calle Mayor, a stone's throw from Plaza del Pilar, presents dozens of varied bars to choose from, even before you explore the side streets.

Chastón (Plaza Ariño 1) A relaxed little bar playing recorded jazz.

Rock & Blues Café (Cuatro de Agosto 5-7; from 5pm) Rock 'n' roll paraphernalia set the tone for this baby-boomer bastion, with live music Wednesday and Thursday.

Zaragoza is awash with faithful reproductions of Irish and Scottish pubs.

Loch Ness Scottish Pub (☎ 976 56 16 28; Calle Baltasar Gracián 31) This pub does a roaring trade in Scottish and English beers at €3 to €4 a *pinta* – worth the trip just for the corny décor. Bus No 30 or 40 from Plaza de España.

Morrissey Tavern (☎ 976 23 96 88; Gran Vía 33) A large pub with DJs Thursday to Sunday nights.

Bar Corto Maltés (Calle del Temple 23) and **La Cucaracha** (Calle del Temple 25) are among a string of raucous disco-pubs on a lane near the Mercado Central. This area is popular with Zaragoza's students: nothing much moves before midnight.

Several gay clubs are close to the old El Portillo train station. **Paradys** (García Galdeano 6) is a friendly, stylish place, where red satin curtains separate the bar from crowded dance floor. Across the street is the lesbian-oriented **Pub Essencia** (García Galdeano 13). Closer to the old city, **Mick Havanna** (Calle de Ramón

Pignatelli 7; from 5pm) is a pleasantly subdued lounge, frequented by a mature crowd.

ENTERTAINMENT

The tourist office puts out the bimonthly *Agenda Cultural*, covering theatre, art, music and film events.

Filmoteca de Zaragoza (☎ 976 72 18 53; Plaza San Carlos 4; screenings €2; Wed-Sat night) One of the few cinemas showing films in their original language (subtitled in Spanish).

La Casa del Loco (☎ 976 39 67 71; Calle Mayor 10; cover €6-8 for live music; from 9.30pm Thu-Sat) This intimate rock 'n' roll pub hosts touring bands towards the weekend.

Oasis (☎ 976 43 95 34; Calle de Boggiero 28; cover €10; from midnight Fri & Sat) A few streets west of the old centre, Oasis began life long ago as a variety theatre. It's currently going strong as a disco with varied shows, including highly popular drag queen extravaganzas.

Further south, towards the university, Calle del Doctor Cerrada and side streets between Calle Fita and Calle Marcial have more pubs, discos and disco-pubs, some full of adolescents, others with Latin sounds, and a 20s and 30s crowd.

El Cantor de Jazz (☎ 976 23 89 24; Calle Dato 18) Not a jazz club, but a Caribbean and African dance venue with occasional live music.

For house sessions at weekends, check out **Roxy Club Zgz** (Calle Comandante Santa Pau 4; 2-8am Fri-Sat), then around dawn head for **Kitsch Experimental Club**(☎ 976 46 74 40; Paseo de Fernando El Católico 70; 6-10am Sat-Sun; cover €8 incl drink), where they're still shakin' well past breakfast time.

GETTING THERE & AWAY
Air

The **Zaragoza airport** (☎ 976 71 23 00) has direct Iberia flights to/from Madrid daily, to Barcelona daily except Sunday and to Frankfurt (Germany) most days. Air Europa flies to/from Palma de Mallorca.

Bus

Randomly scattered around town, Zaragoza's dozen or so bus lines will eventually be consolidated at the new Estación Intermodal Delicias train station, but nobody can say just when. Until that time, the most useful bus station is **Ágreda Automóvil** (Paseo de María Agustín 7), where **ALSA** (☎ 902 42 22 42; www.alsa.es) operates at least 15 buses a day

ARAGÓN

to/from Madrid (€11.75, 3¾ hours) and Barcelona (€11.10, 3¾ hours), and **Alosa** (☎ 976 22 93 43; www.alosa.es) runs at least eight buses to/from Huesca (€5, one hour), half of which continue to Jaca (€10.40, 2¼ hours). Other services operating from here include Linecar (Soria, León), Hife (Valencia, Tarragona) and Suroeste (Badajoz, Mérida).

Other bus stations and the destinations they serve include:

Abasa & Agreda Automóvil (☎ 976 55 45 88; www.agredasa.com; Avenida de Valencia 20)
Destinations: Alcañiz, Belchite, Cariñena, Daroca, Fraga, Lleida (Lérida), Muel.

Autobuses Conda (☎ 976 33 33 72; Avenida de Navarra 1) Destinations: Pamplona, San Sebastián, Tudela.

Automóviles Zaragoza (☎ 976 21 93 20; www .automovileszaragoza.com; Calle de Almagro 18)
Destinations: Calatayud, Monasterio de Piedra.

Samar Buil (☎ 976 43 43 04; Calle de Borao 13) Fuendetodos (buses depart from in front of the Museo Pablo Serrano, Paseo de María Agustín 20) Destination: Andorra.

Sanguesa (Car park below Estación El Portillo, Avenida Anselmo Clavé) Destination: Sos del Rey Católico.

Tezasa (☎ 976 27 61 79; Calle Juan Pablo Bonet 13)
Destinations: Burgos, Logroño, Teruel, Valencia.

Therpasa (☎ 976 22 57 23; Calle del General Sueiro 22)
Destinations: Soria, Tarazona.

Viaca Viajes (☎ 976 28 31 00; Calle de Pignatelli 120)
Destinations: Bilbao, León, Oviedo, Santander, Santiago de Compostela, Vitoria.

Train
The opening of the impressive **Estación Intermodal Delicias** (Calle Rioja 33) in 2003 coincided with the arrival of high-speed trains from Madrid.

Services include Madrid (€19 to €43, 1¾ to 3¾ hours, approximately 13 daily); Barcelona (€20 to €34, one to 4½ hours, approximately 12 daily); Valencia (€17, 5½ hours, two daily); Huesca (€5.40, one hour, approximately four daily); Jaca (€11.50, 3½ hours, three daily); and Teruel (€9.15, three hours, three daily).

GETTING AROUND
There are **airport buses** (☎ 976 22 93 43) to/from Gran Via 4 (the stop for municipal bus No 30) that link with flights.

Most city bus routes (€0.70) go through Plaza de España on the southern edge of El Tubo. Bus No 51 to/from Estación Intermodal Delicias begins/ends at Paseo de la Constitución, one block from Plaza de Aragón.

SOUTH OF ZARAGOZA
The following places can all be reached by bus, but having your own transport is ideal.

Muel & Cariñena
The N330 south towards Teruel passes through Cariñena country – Aragón's premier wine-producing region. Along the way, peek into the **Ermita de la Fuente** in Muel, 19km before Cariñena, with paintings of saints by Goya.

Bodegas (cellars) dot the main road into Cariñena, and in town there's a **Museo del Vino** (☎ 976 79 30 31; Calle de la Platera 7; admission €1.50; ⏱ 11am-2pm & 5-7pm or 8pm Tue-Sun except Sun afternoon).

Hostal Iliturgis (☎ 976 62 04 92; Plaza de Ramón y Cajal 1; s/d with bathroom €30/32) Should you linger in Cariñena, this refurbished 17th-century home is a comfortable option.

Fuendetodos
Some of the greatest start small. One such was Francisco José de Goya y Lucientes, born in this insignificant hamlet, 24km east of Cariñena, in 1746. The **Casa Natal de Goya** (☎ 976 14 38 30; Zuloaga 3; admission €1.80 incl Museo del Grabado de Goya; both ⏱ 11am-2pm & 4-7pm Tue-Sun) stayed in his family until the early 20th century, when the artist Ignacio Zuloaga found and bought it. Partly destroyed during the civil war, the three-storey abode, which is less humble than legends make out, has since been restored. Down the road, the **Museo del Grabado de Goya** contains a seminal collection of the artist's engravings.

Samar Buil buses leave Zaragoza for Fuendetodos (one hour) at 10am and 6pm Monday to Saturday.

Belchite
The town, or rather the twin towns, of Belchite are perhaps the most eloquent of reminders of the destruction wrought in the civil war. The ruins of the old town, which have been replaced by an adjacent new village, stand as a silent memorial (see Lest We Forget, opposite). Abasa buses (€3.30, 45 minutes) arrive from Zaragoza three times daily.

A few kilometres west of Belchite stands the 18th-century baroque **Santuario de Nuestra Señora del Pueyo**.

LEST WE FORGET

In the summer of 1937 the Republican forces fought a savage battle with Franco's troops for the small town of Belchite. By the time they had finished, the elegant houses on Calle Mayor, along with the town's two churches, mostly built of the narrow bricks typical of Mudéjar architecture, had been thoroughly blasted. The Torre del Reloj (Clock Tower) was left leaning precariously, its clock face blown away. In March the following year Nationalist forces marched back in as the seesaw war in this heavily fought-over part of Spain swung back in Franco's favour. By now the town's populace was living in a labyrinth of wreckage, struggling to keep life going in the midst of disaster. The Franco government judged the town too far gone to be rebuilt, and decided to build it afresh next door. That plan was not completed until 1954 – a long wait for people living in such misery. Today it's an eerie experience to wander past the shell-shocked buildings down silent streets, where for a time life and death led a tragic coexistence.

WEST OF ZARAGOZA
Tarazona
pop 10,500 / elevation 480m

West of Zaragoza on the N122, the serpentine streets of Tarazona's crumbling old town are a remarkable reminder of the Middle Ages. In an even earlier age, Turiaso, as it was then known, was the scene of a famous victory by a small band of Roman soldiers over a far greater Celtiberian army.

The enthusiastic **tourist office** (☎ 976 64 00 74; www.tarazona.org; Plaza San Francisco 1; ⏰ 9am-1.30pm & 4.30-7pm Mon-Fri, 10am-1.30pm & 4-6pm or 7pm Sat & Sun) has lots of material on the town and area.

SIGHTS

The **cathedral**, a fetching concoction of Romanesque, Gothic, Mudéjar and Renaissance styles, closed for restoration in 1997 and shows no sign of reopening soon. Lacking proper foundations in a spring-fed orchard zone, it has tended to drift precariously, but without sufficient funding rebuilding efforts have proceeded slowly.

Nearby, the octagonal **Plaza de Toros Vieja**

(Old Bullring) is made up of 32 houses built in the 1790s as a private housing initiative – with entertainment thrown in.

A signposted walking route takes you round the twisting cobbled ways of the medieval 'high part' of the town, north of the Río Queiles. Unfortunately you can't enter any of the main monuments. From all around you can see the slender Mudéjar tower of the **Iglesia de Santa María Magdalena**. The **Palacio Episcopal** (Bishop's Palace), next door, was a Muslim fortified palace. Further northeast, on Plaza de España, is the 16th-century **ayuntamiento** (town hall). Its detailed frieze depicts the 1530 coronation of Carlos V in Bologna. Tarazona's medieval *judería* (Jewish area) is exceptionally well preserved. A multimedia programme on the quarter is presented at the **Centro Moshé de Portella** (☎ 976 64 28 61; Plaza de los Arcedianos; admission free; ⏰ 11am-2pm & 5-8pm Sat & Sun).

SLEEPING & EATING

Hostal Palacete de los Arcedianos (☎ /fax 976 64 23 03; Plaza de los Arcedianos 1; s/d €22.50/31) The least expensive lodging is in the *judería*.

Hostal Santa Águeda (☎ 976 64 00 54; www.santa agueda.com; Calle Visconti 26; s/d from €50/66; 🐾 🖳) Just off Plaza San Francisco, this 200-year-old home has 11 meticulously restored rooms. The *comedor* (dining room) features a gallery dedicated to Raquel Meller, Aragón's queen of popular song.

Hotel Condes de Visconti (☎ 976 64 49 08; www .condesdevisconti.com; Calle Visconti 15; r from €72 incl breakfast; 🅿) Quite luxurious is this 16th-century palace. The renaissance patio is now a lounge, with original Tuscan-stone columns.

El Galeón (☎ 976 64 29 65; Avenida de la Paz 1; menu €9) This down-to-earth dining hall is a good place to try *ternasco*.

GETTING THERE & AWAY

Up to six **Therpasa** (☎ 976 64 11 00; Avenida de Navarra 17) buses run daily to/from Zaragoza (1¼ hours) and Soria (one hour). **Autobuses Conda** (☎ 948 82 03 42; Parque de la Estación) goes to Tudela. Both stops are a minute's walk from Plaza de San Francisco.

Around Tarazona

The fortified walls of the **Monasterio de Veruela** (☎ 976 64 90 25; admission €1.80; ⏰ 10am-2pm & 4-7pm Tue-Sun Apr-Sep, 10am-1pm & 3-6pm

DANCING IN THE DESERT

Few stops suggest themselves along the de-forested steppes between Zaragoza and Va-lencia, but the rural town of Fraga is famous among dance fans as the home of **Florida 135** (☎ 974 47 02 50; www.florida135.com; Calle Sotet 2; admission around €12; ☾ from 11.30 Sat), the temple of Spanish techno. The window-less 3000-sq-metre, graffiti-strewn space is just the most recent incarnation of a dance-hall that's been going since 1942. Busloads of ravers arrive every Saturday (the only night the club is open) for its legendary raves. One night back in 1994 the action boiled over to the desert, giving birth to the Mone-gros Desert Festival (www.monegrosfestival .com), formerly called the Groove Parade. Dozens of Spanish and internationally re-nowned DJs demonstrate their skills on vari-ous stages at the event, which takes place in mid-July at Finca Les Peñetes, about 18km west of Fraga. The most recent festival was attended by 30,000 people, three times the population of Fraga.

Tue-Sun Oct-Mar), founded in the 12th century, are more reminiscent of a Castilian castle than a monastery. Once inhabited by Jesu-its, it now belongs to Zaragoza's provincial government. The cold Gothic church is flanked by a charming cloister, which has a lower, Gothic level surmounted by a Renais-sance upper gallery. Inside the complex is a small **wine museum**. The monastery is 13km southeast of Tarazona and 1km from Vera de Moncayo. Just two of Therpasa's daily Zaragoza–Tarazona buses stop in Vera it-self; the others stop at the Vera turn-off on the N122, 4km from the monastery.

In Vera, accommodation includes **Camp-ing Vera de Moncayo** (☎ 976 64 91 54; per person/tent/car €3/3/3; ☾ mid-June–mid-Oct) and **La Casa del Carpintero** (☎ 976 64 65 65; Calle Moncayo 6; r with bathroom €31), a charming country home.

Those with a vehicle can visit the **Parque Natural del Moncayo**, with several walking trails on the flank of the 2300m-plus Sierra del Moncayo.

Calatayud

pop 17,300 / elevation 530m

This dusty town just off the Zaragoza–Madrid A2 highway has an atmospheric centre of narrow streets and enough points of interest to merit a stop. Head for the labyrinthine old town and search out the Mudéjar towers of the **Colegiata de Santa María**, **Iglesia de San Andrés** and the 14th-century **Iglesia de San Pedro** (Rua de Eduardo Dato), which looks as though it's about to topple into the street. The baroque **Parro-quia de San Juan El Real** (Calle Valentín Gómez 3) features four Goya paintings of the fathers of the church, housed in the angles below its dome.

Places to stay include **Pensión La Perla** (☎ 976 88 13 40; Calle de San Antón 17; s/d with shared bathroom €11/21), with big sparkling rooms, and the charming **Hospedería El Pilar** (☎ 976 89 70 20; www.hospederiaelpilar.com; Calle Baltasar Gracián 15; s/d €25/45), in a restored 17th-century inn near the Colegiata de Santa María. Both have restaurants serving all meals.

Calatayud's bus station is hidden in a building off the central Plaza del Fuerte. Automóviles Zaragoza runs four or more buses daily to/from Zaragoza (€5.70, one hour), while ALSA runs at least three buses to/from Madrid. Three trains run to/from Zaragoza, one of which continues to/from Madrid.

Monasterio de Piedra

This one-time Cistercian **monastery** (ad-mission to both monastery & park adult/child €10/6.50; ☾ 9am-dusk) and the surrounding park, 28km southwest of Calatayud, make a tranquil and soothing retreat. Founded in 1194 and moved to its present site in 1218, the monastery was ultimately abandoned in the 1830s. Now in private hands and partially restored, it is home to the posh **Hotel Monasterio de Piedra** (☎ 976 84 90 11; www.monasteriopiedra.com; r incl breakfast €129). The park, known for its waterfalls, woodlands and caves, is undeniably pretty, but the whole experience somehow tends towards the Disneyesque.

Of several lodgings in the lakeside vil-lage of **Nuévalos**, 3km north, a good choice is **Hostal Las Rumbas** (☎ 976 84 91 12; r €43), with balconies for lounging and a cheerful res-taurant.

On Tuesday, Thursday, Saturday and Sunday (or daily in summer), Automóviles Zaragoza runs a 9am bus to the monastery from Zaragoza (€7.80, 2½ hours) via Cala-tayud, returning at 5pm.

THE NORTH

As you turn north from parched Zaragoza province, a hint of green tinges the landscape. Although the town of Huesca lies in a basin, the Pyrenees foothills are not too far off.

Aragón's portion of the Pyrenees is the most rewarding on the Spanish side of the range, with magnificent scenery, several decent ski resorts and great walking. There are many ways to approach the area, with several routes clawing up through the valleys and some crossing into France.

Activities
SKIING

Aragón is well endowed with ski slopes, especially in the Pyrenees, with resorts at Cerler, Formigal, Panticosa, Astún and Candanchú. Most accommodation in and near the resorts offers packages that include ski passes and some meals.

WALKING

Aragón's mountains are more popular in summer than in winter. Some 6000km of long-distance trails (Grandes Recorridos, or GRs) and short-distance trails (Pequeños Recorridos, PRs) are now marked in all parts of Aragón. The coast-to-coast GR11 traverses the most spectacular Aragón Pyrenees, but there are plenty of other routes.

The optimum time to lace up your walking boots is mid-June to early September, though the more popular parks and paths can become crowded in midsummer. Even then, the weather can be unpredictable, so walkers must prepare for most contingencies. Ask ahead about path conditions, water sources and shelter along your route.

This chapter mentions several mountain *refugios* (refuges). Some are staffed and serve meals, while others are empty shacks providing nothing but shelter. At holiday times refuges are often full, so unless you have booked ahead, be prepared to camp. The **Federación Aragonesa de Montañismo** (FAM; ☎ 976 22 79 71; www.fam.es; Calle Albareda 7, Zaragoza) can provide some information, and a FAM card will get you substantial discounts on *refugio* stays.

The *aragonese* publisher Prames produces some of the best maps for walkers in the Aragón Pyrenees. Editorial Alpina maps are an acceptable substitute, although they have their inaccuracies. Lonely Planet's *Walking in Spain* is a good companion if you plan any serious outings in the Pyrenees.

See also the boxed text Out & About in the Pyrenees (p352).

HUESCA
pop 54,634 / elevation 488m

Huesca has an interesting medieval centre, and is an excellent starting point for exploring the north.

Known to the Romans as Osca and to its Muslim masters of nearly four centuries as Wasqa, Huesca was conquered by Christian Aragón in 1096. As in many places across Spain, the decision to expel the Jews in 1492 and the subsequent dispersal of the Muslims struck a blow from which the flourishing trading town never recovered. During the civil war Huesca was long besieged by Republican forces but never taken.

Orientation & Information

The old part of Huesca sits on a slight rise, with the bus and train stations sharing the modern Estación Intermodal, 500m south. Several banks with ATMs are found on Plaza de Navarra.

Hospital General San Jorge (☎ 974 21 11 21; Avenida Martínez de Velasco)

Osc@.com (☎ 974 21 21 58; San José de Calasanz 13; per hr €2; ☼ 4pm-1am)

Post office (Calle del Coso Alto 14)

Tourist office (☎ 974 29 21 70; www.huescaturismo .com; Plaza López Allué 1; ☼ 8am-8pm Jul & Aug, 9am-2pm & 4-8pm rest of year) Inside the market building; Huesca Turismo also operates a summer info kiosk on Plaza de Navarra.

Sights
PLAZA DE LA CATEDRAL & AROUND

Tranquil Plaza de la Catedral, at the heart of the old town, is presided over by a venerable Gothic **cathedral** (☎ 974 22 06 76; admission free; ☼ 8am-1.30pm & 4-7.30pm summer, 8am-1pm & 4-6.30pm rest of year), built between the 13th and 16th centuries. The richly carved main portal dates from 1300; the 14 figures on either side of the doorway represent the apostles (minus Judas) and the city's three patron saints. The stately interior features a large, 16th-century alabaster *retablo* (altarpiece) by Damián Forment. The adjoining

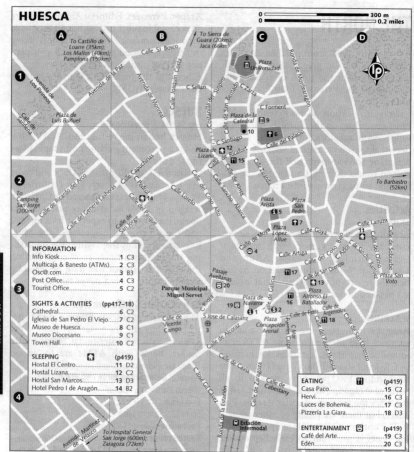

HUESCA

INFORMATION
Info Kiosk....................................1 C3
Multicaja & Banesto (ATMs).....2 C3
Osc@.com...................................3 B3
Post Office..................................4 C1
Tourist Office.............................5 C2

SIGHTS & ACTIVITIES   (pp417–18)
Cathedral....................................6 C2
Iglesia de San Pedro El Viejo.....7 C2
Museo de Huesca......................8 C1
Museo Diocesano......................9 C1
Town Hall.................................10 C2

SLEEPING   (p419)
Hostal El Centro.......................11 D2
Hostal Lizana...........................12 C2
Hostal San Marcos...................13 D3
Hotel Pedro I de Aragón..........14 B2

EATING   (p419)
Casa Paco................................15 C2
Hervi..16 C3
Luces de Bohemia....................17 C3
Pizzería La Giara.......................18 D3

ENTERTAINMENT   (p419)
Café del Arte............................19 C3
Edén..20 C3

Museo Diocesano (admission €2; 🕑 10am-1.30pm &
4-7.30pm Mon-Sat summer, 10.30am-1.30pm & 4-6pm
Mon-Sat rest of year) exhibits religious art and
artisanship from the Huesca diocese. The
16th-century **town hall** across the square is
another *aragonese* gem. A little way north,
the octagonal **Museo de Huesca** (☎ 974 22 05 86;
Plaza Universidad 1; admission free; 🕑 10am-2pm & 5-
8pm Tue-Sat, 10am-2pm Sun) has a well-displayed
collection covering the archaeology and art
of Huesca province, including works by
Goya. The temporary exhibition rooms are
the halls of an old *aragonese* palace.

IGLESIA DE SAN PEDRO EL VIEJO
Another of the city's historical and architectural gems stands 250m southeast of

Plaza de la Catedral. The church of **San
Pedro** (adult/child €2/1; 🕑 10am-1.30pm & 4-7.30pm
Jun-Sep, 10am-1.30pm rest of year) is an understated 12th-century Romanesque masterpiece. Worth a close look is its cloister,
with beautiful Romanesque capitals that
have been attributed to the same maestro who carved those at the Monasterio de
San Juan de la Peña (see p430). The fourth
and fifth monarchs of Aragón, Alfonso I El
Batallador (1104–34) and Ramiro II (1134–
37), lie here in the Panteón Real, a chamber
off San Pedro's cloister. (Most subsequent
aragonese monarchs were buried at the
Monestir de Poblet in Catalonia, following Aragón's union with the neighouring
region.)

Tours

The tourist office gives guided tours of the historic centre (€4) in Spanish, English and French at 10am, 11am and 5pm daily in July and August, and 11am daily from Semana Santa (Easter) to June and in September and October.

Tours by vintage bus are offered daily in summer to the Castillo de Loarre (p419), Los Mallos (p420), the Sierra de la Guara, and other destinations of historical interest or natural beauty. Buses depart at 9am daily from the Estación Intermodal; get tickets at the tourist office.

Sleeping

Camping San Jorge (☎ 974 22 74 16; www.camping sanjorge.com; Calle de Ricardo del Arco s/n; per person/ tent/car €3.75/3.75/3.75; ☼ Apr–mid-Oct) 1km west of the old town centre.

Hostal Lizana (☎ 974 22 07 76; lizana2@teleline .es; Plaza Lizana 6; s/d €27/48; **P**) This humble guesthouse and the slightly pricier Lizana 2 overlook a pleasant little plaza near the cathedral.

Hostal El Centro (☎ 974 22 68 23; Calle de Sancho Ramírez 3; s/d with bathroom €21/34) This homely, welcoming place is on a narrow lane just outside the old town.

Hostal San Marcos (☎ 974 22 64 49; Calle de San Orencio 10; s/d €26/47; **✷** **P**) In the heart of town, the San Marcos has 29 modern units above a popular bar.

Hotel Pedro I de Aragón (☎ 974 22 03 00; Calle del Parque 34; s/d €89/128) Overlooking leafy Parque Municipal Miguel Servet, this is the place for top-end comfort.

Eating & Drinking

Hervi (☎ 974 24 03 33; Calle Santa Paciencia 2; menú €9; ☼ closed Thu) A lunch-time crowd pleaser, Hervi offers four or five choices per course, including superb salads, stews and desserts.

Pizzería La Giara (☎ 974 23 16 60; Calle de Argensolas; pizza €7; ☼ 8pm-midnight Thu-Tue) Aragón's finest pizzas are baked in La Giara's wood-fired oven and topped with fresh ingredients.

Casa Paco (☎ 974 22 14 70; Calle de Ricafort 2; menú €10) This bar/*comedor* serves hearty home-style fare made with whatever's in season.

Luces de Bohemia (☎ 974 24 19 90; Calle del Coso Bajo 6) Everyone pops into this busy main street café at some point. Fresh pastries and *bocadillos* (bread roll with filling) are among the offerings.

Entertainment

Ask the tourist office for a copy of *Radar*, which has a rundown of the month's music, theatre and arts events, or see its website www.huescacultura.com.

Eden (☎ 974 22 76 25; Pasaje Avellanas; ☼ 4pm-3am) Huesca's hippest pub hosts live rock and electronica on Friday night.

Café del Arte (Plaza de Navarra; ☼ closed Tue) Downstairs from the senior centre, the local alternative space hosts live music from around 10.30pm on Thursday night.

Getting There & Away

BUS

The bus company **Alosa** (☎ 974 21 07 00; www .alosa.es) runs at least eight daily buses to/from Zaragoza (€5, one hour), and around five each to/from Jaca (€5.40, 1¼ hours), Barbastro (€3.30, 50 minutes), Lleida (Lérida; €7.75, two hours) and Barcelona (€13.25, 4¼ hours). There's also daily service to Benasque and Pamplona.

TRAIN

Five to seven trains a day run to/from Zaragoza (€5.40, one hour), with one each to/from Madrid, Teruel and Valencia. Three trains daily head north to Jaca (€5.40, 2½ hours), two continuing to Canfranc-Estación (€6.65, three hours).

AROUND HUESCA

Castillo de Loarre

Rambling and haughty on its rocky perch, this **castle** (☎ 974 38 26 27; admission €2; ☼ 10am-4.30pm Tue-Sun Jan–mid-Mar; 10am-1.30pm & 4-7pm Tue-Sun mid-Mar–Jun & Sep–mid-Oct; 10am-8pm Jul & Aug) was perfectly placed to watch for Muslim raiders racing across the wheat plains to the south. Raised in the 11th century by Sancho III of Navarra and Sancho Ramírez of Aragón, it's uncannily reminiscent of crusader castles in the Middle East.

A labyrinth of dungeons, tunnels and towers, in and around the living rock, has been left in a state of partial restoration, giving it a suitably untamed feeling. Some parts are so dark that a torch (flashlight) would be useful. You can climb two towers for magnificent views.

If it all looks familiar, you may have seen it in the Ridley Scott film *Kingdom of Heaven* (2005). The medieval fortress served as a backdrop for much of the

ARAGÓN

action (though the film is set in 12th-century France), and the banquet scenes were shot in the Iglesia de San Pedro.

The castle is a 5km drive, or a 2km, one-hour, uphill walk by the PR-HU105 footpath, from the village of Loarre, 35km from Huesca.

Camping Castillo de Loarre (☎ 974 38 27 22; www .campingloarre.com; per person/tent/car €3.10/3.10/3.10; ❍ Apr-Oct) It's halfway from village to castle, by road or footpath.

Hospedería de Loarre (☎ 974 38 27 06; www.hospe deriadeloarre.com; Plaza Miguel Moya; s/d incl breakfast €50/62) This charming small hotel occupies a converted 16th-century mansion on Loarre village square. It has an excellent, medium-to-expensive restaurant.

Two buses run to Loarre village from Huesca (€2.20, 40 minutes) Monday to Friday; there's just one bus on Saturday.

Los Mallos
After a rather unexciting patch along the Huesca–Pamplona road, you come to a pretty stretch along the Río Gállego north of Ayerbe. On the eastern bank, bizarre rock formations known as Los Mallos (The Mallets) rise up – they wouldn't look out of place in the Grand Canyon. For a closer look, head for **Riglos**.

ALQUÉZAR
pop 310 / elevation 670m
The dramatic canyons of the Río Vero and other rivers cutting through the Sierra de Guara north of the Huesca–Barbastro road are Europe's prime location for the sport of **canyoning** (descenso de barrancos in Spanish), which involves following canyons downstream by whatever means are appropriate – walking, abseiling, jumping, swimming, even diving.

The main base is the picturesque village of Alquézar, 20km northwest of Barbastro. Alquézar is well worth a detour even if you don't want to get wet in a canyon. The rocky hill on which the village stands is topped by the **Colegiata de Santa María** (☎ 974 23 10 99; admission €2; ❍ 10.30am-1.30pm & 4-7.30pm Mon-Fri, morning only Sat), a large castle-monastery. Originally built by the Arabs in the 9th century, it was conquered around 1060 by Sancho Ramírez. Remnants of the Augustinian monastery he established here in 1099 are still visible. The columns within its delicate cloister are

crowned by perfectly preserved carved capitals depicting biblical scenes, and the walls are covered with spellbinding murals. On the upper level is a museum of sacred art. Visits are by guided tour only.

A **tourist office** (☎ 974 31 89 40; Calle Arrabal) operates in summer.

Several agencies, such as **Vertientes** (www .vertientesaventura.com) at Casa Tintorero (see p420), offer guided canyoning trips costing €35 to €50 a day per person. The main season is mid-June to mid-September.

Sleeping & Eating
Camping Alquézar (☎ 974 31 84 34; www.alquezar .com; per person/tent/car €3.80/3.80/3.50) Just outside the village, this camping ground offers guide service and equipment rental.

Casa Tintorero (☎ 974 31 83 54; www.vertientes aventura.com; Calle San Gregorio 5; bunks incl breakfast €13) This is the best of several albergues (hostels) in the village, with two- to six-person rooms and great views from the upper floors.

Casa Jabonero (☎ 974 31 89 08; Calle Mayor; r without/with bathroom €22/28) This charming, six-room casa rural (country house) is in a Mudéjar building in the village centre.

Hotel Villa de Alquézar (☎ /fax 974 31 84 16; Calle Pedro Arenal Cavero 12; s/d incl breakfast €40/48; Ⓟ) Practically next door to Casa Jabonero is this larger hotel, with modern, tastefully decorated rooms.

Fonda Narbona (☎ 974 31 80 78; Calle Baja 19; d without/with bathroom €27.50/30.50; ❍ weekends only in winter) You'll find simple, pleasant rooms here and a restaurant with a great terrace for warm weather.

Mesón del Vero (☎ 974 31 80 74; dishes €5-10) On the plaza, this upstairs comedor serves hearty peasant fare, including scrumptious grilled sausages.

Getting There & Away
Autocares Cortés (☎ 974 31 15 52) runs a bus to Alquézar from Barbastro at 2.30pm daily, except Sunday.

North of Alquézar, the road through Colungo to Aínsa is a fantastic drive through pre-Pyrenean canyons.

BARBASTRO & AROUND
pop 15,400 / elevation 341m
Ancient Barbastro spent some 350 years as one of Muslim Spain's most northerly outposts. Today it's a shabby spot, although

ARAGÓN

the area around Plaza del Mercado retains some atmosphere and the 16th-century **cathedral** has a main altarpiece partly done by the Renaissance master Damián Forment. In more recent times the founder of the Catholic movement Opus Dei, Josemaría Escrivá (1902–75), grew up at Plaza del Mercado 11.

The **tourist office** (☎ 974 30 83 50; www.barbastro.org; Avenida de la Merced 64; ☼ 10am-2pm & 4.30-8pm Tue-Sat Sep-Jun, daily Jul & Aug), by the bullring, is combined with a **wine museum** devoted to the local Somontano vintages. The central **Hostal Pirineos** (☎ 974 31 00 00; hspirineos@eresmas .net; Calle General Ricardos 13; s/d €38/48; **P**) has a cheerful décor and the town's coolest café.

Six kilometres west of Barbastro on the main highway from Huesca, the hilltop **Monasterio del Pueyo** commands unlimited vistas, with the Pyrenean peaks of Monte Perdido, Posets and Aneto to the north. For that alone it's worth a stop if you're motorised, but there are also a quaint chapel and a good restaurant.

Enemies riding against **Monzón** (population 14,650), 19km southeast of Barbastro, must have been fazed by the impregnable **castle** (☎ 974 34 90 07; admission €2; ☼ 10am-1pm & 5-8pm Tue-Sun except Sun afternoon Jul-Sep; 11.30am-1pm & 3-5pm Tue-Fri, 11.30am-1pm & 4-6pm Sat, 10am-2pm Sun rest of year), rising proudly above its jumbled streets. The Muslims built Monzón's first great fortress, later taken for Aragón by Sancho Ramírez. The Knights Templar took it over in 1143, but after the order of knights fell, the fortress decayed under several sieges in the 16th to 19th centuries. It has now been partly restored, as has the 12th-century church, the **Colegiata de Santa María del Romeral**.

Getting There & Away

Departures from Barbastro's **bus station** (☎ 974 31 12 93) most days include four buses to Barcelona; 11 to Huesca and Monzón, half of which continue to Lleida (Lérida); two to Benasque; and one or two to Aínsa. Several trains stop in Monzón on their way from Zaragoza to/from Lleida or Barcelona.

BENASQUE

pop 1388 / elevation 1140m

The highest peaks in the Pyrenees rise in the northeastern corner of Aragón, and even in midsummer they can be covered in

a blanket of snow and ice. The area, much of which is protected as the Parque Natural Posets-Maladeta, offers walkers almost limitless options and climbers a wide choice of peaks. The happening nerve centre of the district is the growing village of Benasque (Benás in the local dialect), set in a broad, green valley with rocky mountains rising on three sides. Walkers, climbers and skiers flock here not only as a jumping-off point for fresh-air activities but also for a spot of after-dark bar-hopping.

The approach from the south gets exciting as the A139/N260 threads through the Congosto de Ventamillo, a narrow defile carved by the crystalline Río Ésera. North of the defile, the village of Castejón de Sos is a paragliding centre with accommodation.

Information

Lavandería Ecológica (☎ 974 55 15 04; Carretera de Francia; ☼ 10am-2pm & 4-8pm Mon-Fri, morning only Sat) Wash and dry duds here.

Telecomunicaciones S&Z (Los Huertos 5; per hr €2) Benasque's Internet connection.

Tourist office (☎ 974 55 12 89; www.turismobenasque .com; Calle San Sebastián 5; ☼ 9.30am-1.30pm & 4.30-8.30pm) Offers copious information on shorter walking routes.

Plenty of outfitters offer guides and instruction for climbing, skiing and other activities; most sell or rent clothing and equipment for the hills:

Barrabés (☎ 974 55 16 81; Avenida de Francia) Stocks a truly vast array, including maps and guidebooks.

Casa de la Montaña (☎ 974 55 20 94; Avenida de los Tilos)

Compañía de Guías Valle de Benasque (☎ 974 55 13 36; www.guiasbenasque.com; Avenida Luchón 19)

Gradodiez (☎ 629 18 24 82; www.grado-diez.com; Avenida Luchón) Local branch of Cerler ski shop.

Sleeping

There are several camping grounds along the A139 north of Benasque.

Camping Aneto (☎ 974 55 11 41; www.camping aneto.com; per person/tent/car €4.10/4.10/4.10) This is the closest camping ground to town (3.5km).

Camping Plan de Senarta (per person/tent/car €2/1.80/1.80; ☼ year-round, staffed Jul-Sep) Another 2.5km north, this is a more bucolic site with primitive facilities.

In town you'll find a dozen hotels and *hostales* (budget hotels). During the ski season most offer packages with *media pensión* (half-board).

Hotel Avenida (☎ 974 55 11 26; www.h-avenida .com; Avenida de Los Tilos 14; s/d €49/61) Benasque's best value is also more cordial than most. Rooms are handsomely furnished and the top-floor rooms are especially nice.

Hostal Valero (☎ 974 55 10 61; www.hotelesvalero .com; Carretera de Anciles; s/d with shared bathroom €18/32; ⏰ mid-Dec–Sep; 🖳 🛒) Designed for groups, this place features a gym, sauna and dining hall.

Hotel San Marsial (☎ 974 55 16 16; www.hotelsan marsial.com; Carretera Francia s/n; s/d incl buffet breakfast €60/100) At the north end, this is a comfort-able, well-run hotel, with an old-fashioned touch.

La Fonda de Vescelia (☎ 974 55 16 54; vescelia@ terra.es; Calle Mayor 5; bunks €8, s/d with shared bathroom €25/40; 🖳) Although friendly and central, accommodation at this place is very basic, with up to 30 bunks sharing the same toilet and showers. You'll need a sleeping bag for the slumber party–style dorms. Vegie burgers and such are served in the café.

Eating & Drinking

The best pickings are along Avenida de los Tilos and its continuation, Calle Mayor.

Restaurante El Fogaril (☎ 974 55 16 12; Calle Mayor 5; mains €16-25) Worth the splurge, this elegant country dining room serves outstanding *aragonese* fare. It's speciality is *cozal* (small deer) and other kinds of game.

Taberna del Ixarso (☎ 974 55 28 32; Calle Mayor 12) This lively little bar does tasty tapas.

Pastelería Flor de Nieve (☎ 974 55 10 27; Calle Mayor 17) For coffee and something cream-filled, settle into a booth at this traditional bakery.

La Pizzería (☎ 974 55 15 76; Calle Los Huertos; pizza & pasta €5-9) Benasque's favourite.

Bar La Compañía (☎ 974 55 13 36; Avenida Luchón 19; ⏰ 2-11pm, closed Wed) Mountain lovers will enjoy the shelves of reading matter at this convivial café.

Getting There & Away

Two buses operate Monday to Saturday, and one runs on Sunday, from Barbastro to Benasque (€6.30, two hours) and back. Buses to/from Huesca, Lleida (Lérida) and Barcelona connect with these buses at Barbastro.

AROUND BENASQUE
Skiing

Aragón's easternmost **ski resort** (☎ 974 55 10 12; www.cerler.com) has two centres: one at **Cer-ler** itself, at 1500m altitude, 6km southeast of Benasque, and another at **Ampriu**, 8km beyond Cerler, at 1900m. On offer are 45 varied runs, totalling 52km at altitudes up to 2630m, plus ski and snowboard schools and equipment rentals. With limited ac-commodation available, many people prefer to stay in Benasque. A bus service connects Benasque and the ski stations dur-ing ski season.

Walking & Climbing

From mid-June to mid-September, bus services link Benasque with La Besurta (one way/return €5/8), 16km north in the upper Ésera valley, and with the Re-fugio Pescadores (one way/return €9/12), which is in the Valle de Vallibierna, 11km northeast of Benasque. The buses stop at camping grounds on the A139 north of Benasque – you can use them to reach many of the walks mentioned in this section. Check current timetables at Benasque's tourist office (see p421).

Good maps for northeast Aragón are *Aneto-Maladetas* and *Llardana-Posets* in Prames' 1:40,000 Mapa Excursionista series.

NEAR BENASQUE

Plenty of marked trails, ranging from an hour to a day long, start from Benasque itself or from nearby villages, such as Eriste and Sahún.

VALLE DE VALLIBIERNA

This valley runs southeastwards up from the A139 about 5.5km north of Benasque. On foot, take the track towards Camping Ixeia, which leaves the A139 just before the Puente de San Jaime (or Chaime) bridge, 3km out of Benasque. You're now on the GR11 coast-to-coast trail, which after a couple more kilometres diverges into Valle de Vallibierna. It's then about a 6km (2½-hour) walk, ascending nearly 600m, to the **Refugio Pescadores** or the **Refugio Coronas**, small fishers' shelters with no facilities. Three groups of mountain lakes, the Lagos (or Ibons) de Coronas, Llosás and Valli-bierna, can each be reached in under two hours from the refuge.

ARAGÓN

GR11 TO BIELSA

Westbound, the GR11 leaves the A139 just after the Puente de San Jaime. It's an easy three-hour walk (600m ascent) up the Valle de Estós to **Refugio de Estós** (☎ 974 55 14 83; bunks €11.50; dinner €12.10). This good 115-bunk refuge is attended year-round, but it's essential to ring ahead. A further five or so hours bring you, via the 2592m Puerto de Gistaín (or Chistau) pass and some superb views of the Posets massif, to the excellent **Refugio de Viadós** (☎ 974 50 61 63; bunks €7, half-board €21; ☺ staffed Jun-Sep, Sat & Sun Semana Santa-May). Viadós is a base for climbs on **Posets** (3369m) – to the summit it's a tough six hours often requiring crampons and an ice axe. The GR11 continues some six hours west to the hamlet of Parzán in the Bielsa valley, before heading into the Parque Nacional de Ordesa y Monte Perdido (p424). Bielsa, 4km south of Parzán, has several *hostales* and hotels.

Autocares Bergua (☎ 974 50 00 18) runs a bus from Bielsa to Aínsa at 6am Monday, Wednesday and Friday (daily, except Sunday in July and August).

UPPER ÉSERA VALLEY & MALADETA MASSIF

North of Benasque, the A139 continues paved for about 12km. About 10km from Benasque, a side-road leads 6km east along the pretty upper Ésera valley, ending at a spot called La Besurta, with a hut serving drinks and some food.

Llanos del Hospital (☎ 974 55 20 12; www.llanosdel hospital.com; bunks €28, s/d incl breakfast from €69/83) A little under halfway from the A139 to La Besurta, in a great rural location, this place has a bar, restaurant, and a variety of accommodation from bunks to comfy rooms. From Benasque, a summer bus makes six trips a day here (€6 return, 30 minutes); another shuttles back and forth between here and La Besurta.

An exacting trail from Llanos del Hospital heads northeast and upwards to Peña Blanca, and from there winds steeply up to the 2445m Portillón de Benasque pass on the French frontier. This should take fit walkers about 2½ hours. You could return via a visit to the Puerto de la Picada, another pass to the east – or another 3½ hours north would take you down past the Boums del Port lakes to the French town of Bagnères-de-Luchon.

South of La Besurta towers the great Maladeta massif, a superb challenge for experienced climbers. This forbidding line of icy peaks, with glaciers suspended from the higher crests, culminates in Aneto (3404m), the highest peak in the Pyrenees.

Refugio de la Renclusa (☎ 974 55 21 06; bunks €11.50, half-board €28) Staffed and serving meals from about June to mid-October and weekends from March to June, this refuge is a 40-minute walk from La Besurta. Climbers can reach the top of Aneto from here in a minimum of five hours.

The massif offers other peaks, including Maladeta (3308m). From La Besurta or La Renclusa, walkers can follow paths southeast beneath the Maladeta massif, leading ultimately into Catalonia.

AÍNSA

pop 1650 / elevation 589m

The wide, cobbled, hilltop Plaza Mayor of the medieval village of Aínsa (L'Aínsa in the local dialect) draws a disconcerting number of tourists each day – with reason. Aínsa is one of the prettiest places in Aragón, definitely worth a stop en route to/from France or the Parque Nacional de Ordesa y Monte Perdido.

The helpful **tourist office** (☎ 974 50 07 67; ainsa@pirineo.com; Avenida Pirenaica 1; ☺ 9am-9pm Jul & Aug, 10am-2pm & 4-8pm Sep-Apr, closed Sun & Mon Nov-Mar) is by the crossroads in the lower, newer part of the village. In addition, there's an excellent **regional tourist office** (☎ 974 500 512; info@turismosobrarbe.com; Plaza del Castillo 1, Torre Nordeste; ☺ 10am-2pm & 4-7pm Tue-Sun, closed Sun afternoon) within the castle walls.

The restored Romanesque **Iglesia de Santa María**, on the southeastern corner of Plaza Mayor, has a pleasing little Gothic cloister; climb the **belfry** (admission €1; ☺ approx 11am-1.30pm & 4-7pm) for great views of the mountains to the north. The **castle** and fortifications off the far end of the plaza mostly date from the 1600s, though the main tower, which contains an **eco-museum** (☎ 976 29 96 67; ☺ 10.30-2pm & 5-8.30pm Wed-Sun Semana Santa–Oct) on Pyrenean fauna, is from the 11th century.

Sleeping

Accommodation in the old part of town is limited: book ahead.

Habitaciones La Botiga (☎ /fax 974 50 07 50; Calle del Arco del Hospital; r €42) Opposite the south door of the church, this charmingly renovated old house has six comfortable rooms with brass beds.

Hotel Posada Real (☎ 974 50 09 77; www.posadareal.com; Plaza Mayor; r from €60) The six rooms in this 11th-century structure have antique-style furnishings and views. Inquire at Restaurant Bodegón de Mallacán on the plaza.

Hotel Los Arcos (☎ 974 50 0016; www.hotellosarcosainsa.com; Plaza Mayor 23; r €100; 🖳 🖂) Right on the plaza, this recently renovated structure offers luxury chambers with canopied beds and huge bathrooms.

Otherwise, half a dozen *hostales* and hotels stand within a short walk of the crossroads in the lower town.

Eating

About half the houses around Plaza Mayor function as restaurants and most have outside tables – a magnificent place to eat in the cool of a summer evening.

Bodegas del Sobrarbe (☎ 974 50 09 37; Plaza Mayor 2; mains from €12, menú €19.25) Just off the plaza, this is recommended if you feel like splashing out on a traditional *aragonese* meal.

Bar Fes (☎ 974 50 08 99; Calle Mayor 22; menú €10; 🕑 closed Tue) Less tourist-oriented, the Fes has hearty fare and good views from its stone-walled dining room.

Getting There & Away

From Barbastro bus station, **Autocares Cortés** (☎ 974 31 15 52) runs buses to Aínsa (one hour) at 11am Monday and Saturday during July to August, and at 7.45pm Monday to Saturday year-round. Buses return from Aínsa at 7am and 3.10pm.

PARQUE NACIONAL DE ORDESA Y MONTE PERDIDO

This national park and adjacent areas contain the most spectacular scenery in the Spanish Pyrenees, and afford several days' fine walking at most levels. The park's 'spine' is a chain of limestone peaks skirting the French border, with a southeastward spur that includes Monte Perdido (3348m), the third-highest peak in the Pyrenees. From these heights descend a series of deep valleys, most of which were gouged out by glaciers and are now headed by bowl-like glacial *circos* (cirques). Chief among the valleys are Pineta (east), Escuaín (southeast), Bellos (south), Ordesa (southwest),

Bujaruelo (west) and Gavarnie (north, in France).

The depth of the valleys gives rise to a range of vegetation at different altitudes. Lush green forest gives way higher up to pines, some clinging to the sheer cliffs that rise to the high mountain zone above, where edelweiss, gentians and other wildflowers add colour.

Chamois (*rebeco* in Spanish but often called *sarrio* in Aragón) hop around the park's upper reaches in herds of up to 50. In the skies fly the rare and ugly lammergeier or *quebrantahuesos* (bearded vulture) and the more common golden eagle. But in some seasons, the most numerous beast in the 156-sq-km park is *Homo sapiens*. So popular are the more accessible zones that severe restrictions have been placed on vehicle access in summer.

Orientation

The main jumping-off point is the village of Torla, 3km south of the southwest corner of the national park. From Torla a paved road leads to the Pradera de Ordesa, in the Valle de Ordesa, with a big car park, 5.5km inside the national park (see Getting There & Away, p427, for seasonal vehicle restrictions). If you don't have a vehicle and the shuttle bus isn't running, it's a walk of about 7km from Torla to Pradera de Ordesa starting by Hostal Bella Vista.

The Valle de Bujaruelo, outside the park's western boundary, is accessed by an unpaved road veering north at the Puente de los Navarros on the road north of Torla.

From Escalona, 11km north of Aínsa on the A138, a minor paved road heads northwest across to Sarvisé, a few kilometres south of Torla. This road crosses the park's southern tip, with a narrow, sinuous section winding up the dramatic Bellos valley and giving access to walks in the spectacular Cañón de Añisclo (the upper reaches of the Bellos valley).

From Bielsa, a 12km paved road runs up the Valle de Pineta.

MAPS

Ordesa y Monte Perdido Parque Nacional (1:25,000), published by the Ministerio de Fomento in 2000, costs around €7 and comes with a booklet detailing 20 walks. It's available in Torla shops.

PARQUE NACIONAL DE ORDESA Y MONTE PERDIDO

ARAGÓN

Information

The **Centro de Visitantes El Parador** (☎ 974 48 64 21; ⏰ 9am-1.30pm & 3-6pm Easter-Oct), with worthwhile displays and helpful staff, is 2km inside the park along the Torla–Pradera de Ordesa road. A second visitors centre operates the same hours at Tella in the Escuaín sector. There's also a **park information office** (☎ 974 48 64 72; ⏰ 8am-3pm Mon-Fri) in Torla, towards the north end of the village, opposite the Guardia Civil, and **park information centres** (⏰ 9am-1.30pm & 3-6pm Easter-Oct, 8am-3pm Mon-Fri rest of year) in Escalona and Bielsa. In addition, summer **tourist offices** operate in Torla, Broto, Fanlo and Bielsa.

If you need to use an ATM, or change money, you can do so in Torla.

Camping is allowed only above certain altitudes (1800m to 2500m), in small tents pitched at sunset and taken down at sunrise. Swimming in rivers or lakes, mountain biking, fishing and fires are banned.

Activities
WALKING & CLIMBING

If you fancy crossing the whole park, Lonely Planet's *Walking in Spain* will guide you from the Valle de Bielsa to the Valle de Bujaruelo in three to four days.

Circo de Soaso

A classic day walk follows the Valle de Ordesa to the Circo de Soaso, a rocky balcony whose centrepiece is the **Cola del Caballo**

(Horsetail) waterfall. From the eastern end of the Pradera de Ordesa, take the path that crosses the Río Arazas and climbs steeply up through woods on the valley's south side. This hardest part, called the Senda de los Cazadores (Hunters' Path), in which you ascend 600m, takes an hour. Then it's level or downhill all the way along the high Faja de Pelay path to the *circo*. Return by the path along the bottom of the valley, passing several waterfalls. The whole circuit takes about seven hours.

Refugio de Góriz & Monte Perdido

Fit walkers can climb a series of steep switchbacks (part of the GR11) to the top of the Circo de Soaso and up to the **Refugio de Góriz** (☎ 974 34 12 01; bunks €11), at 2200m. This 72-place refuge, attended and serving meals year-round, makes an obvious base for ascents of Monte Perdido. For July and August, book a month ahead. A lot of people end up simply camping nearby. You'll need an ice axe and crampons to make the peak.

Faja Racón, Circo de Cotatuero & Faja Canarellos

This walk takes you along spectacular high-level paths on the north flank of the Valle de Ordesa. It takes about five or six hours, or an hour less if you omit Faja Canalleros. Avoid it in winter and spring, when you'll encounter ice and possibly falling rocks or even an avalanche.

From Pradera de Ordesa head 600m west back along the paved road to a stone building, Casa Oliván, and take the path signed 'Tozal del Mallo, Circo de Carriata'. About 1½ hours up this fairly steep, zigzag path, diverge eastward along the path signed 'Faja Racón': this high-level route of about 3km brings you out below the Circo de Cotatuero's impressive 200m **waterfall**. From here head a few minutes' downhill to a wooden shelter. Here you can either continue down the Cotatuero *circo* to a path junction 600m east of Pradera de Ordesa or, if you're still energetic, cross a bridge opposite the shelter to follow another high-level path of 3km to 4km, Faja Canarellos. This brings you down to the Valle de Ordesa at Bosque de las Hayas, from which it's 4km westward, gently downhill, back to Pradera de Ordesa.

Brecha de Rolando

The sturdy-hearted may climb the wall of the Circo de Cotatuero by the **Clavijas de Cotatuero**, a set of 32 iron pegs installed back in 1881 (no special equipment is needed, except an unshakeable head for heights). From here you are about 2½ hours' march from **La Brecha de Rolando** (Roldán; 2807m), a dramatic, often windy gap in the mountain wall on the French frontier. You can also reach the Brecha by a 3½-hour path from the Refugio de Góriz. From the Brecha it's a steep 500m descent to the French **Refuge des Sarradets** (☎ 00-33 (0) 683 381 324). Ask beforehand about conditions between the Brecha and the refuge.

Puerto de Bujaruelo

The GR11 describes a 6km arc up the very pretty Valle de Bujaruelo to San Nicolás de Bujaruelo. From there an east-northeastward path leads in about three hours (with a 950m ascent) up to the Puerto de Bujaruelo pass on the border with France. You are now in the French Parc National des Pyrénées, and in about two hours can descend to **Gavarnie** village. Alternatively you can head southeast and upwards for about 2½ hours to the **Refuge des Sarradets** and from there back into Spain via the **Brecha de Rolando** (p426).

Southern Gorges

The **Cañón de Añisclo** is a gaping wound in the earth's fabric, carved out, unlike the glacial valleys further north, by the erosive action of water on limestone. Energetic walkers can start from the Refugio de Góriz and descend the gorge from the north, but if you have a vehicle you can take a day walk from the southern end. Some 12km from Escalona on the road to Sarvisé, a broad path leads down to the dramatic **Puente de San Úrbez**, then up the canyon. You can walk as far north as La Ripareta and back in about five hours, or to Fuen Blanca and back in about eight hours.

The **Gargantas de Escuaín** is a smaller-scale but still dramatic gorge on the Río Yaga, further east. You can descend into the gorge in about an hour from the semi-abandoned hamlet of Escuaín, reached by a minor road off the Escalona–Sarvisé road.

Sleeping & Eating

Although Torla is the obvious base, there are many other villages near the park that offer accommodation. Broto, Escalona and Biescas each has a dozen or so hotels, *hostales* or *casas rurales*, and even tiny Nerín has a *hostal* and *albergue*.

TORLA

Standing above the Río Ara with a backdrop of the national park's mountains, the stone village of Torla has not yet lost too much charm to holiday building. Getting a bed is tricky only in the monster July–August season, when booking ahead is mandatory. There are three **camping grounds** within 2km north of Torla (all closed from mid- or late October till Easter).

Hostal Alto Aragón (☎ /fax 974 48 61 72; Calle de Capuvita; r €37) This is about the cheapest alternative, with plain, clean rooms.

Hotel Ballarín (☎ /fax 974 48 61 55; Calle de Capuvita 11; s/d €30/46) Under the same ownership as the Alto Aragón, this place provides just that little bit more comfort.

The following are French-managed refuge-style places in the village:

Refugio L'Atalaya (☎ /fax 974 48 60 22; Calle de Francia; bunks €8.50; ☼ Apr–mid-Oct)

Refugio Lucien Briet (☎ 974 48 62 21; www
.refugiolucienbriet.com; Calle de Francia; bunks €8.50, d with bathroom €34)

All the above have restaurants. You can stock up on supplies in small supermarkets seven days a week.

VALLE DE BUJARUELO

Camping Valle de Bujaruelo (☎ 974 48 63 48; www
.campingvalledebujaruelo.com; per person/tent/car €3.40/
3.40/3.40, d/tr/quads in refuge €28.50/38/43; ☼ Easter–
Oct) Located 3.5km up the Valle de Bujaruelo, this camping ground features a refuge with bunks, a restaurant and a supermarket.

Mesón de Bujaruelo (☎ 974 48 64 12; dm €12, half-board €26) At San Nicolás, 3km further up the valley, this old hostelry provides bunks and meals in a particularly pretty spot by the Puerto de Bujaruelo.

SOUTH OF TORLA

The nicest place in Broto, nestled in the Río Ara valley 3km south of Torla, is the stone **Casa O'Puente** (☎ 974 48 60 72; Calle Porches 7; r incl breakfast €40), beside a piece of the old bridge.

Among a handful of lodgings in Sarvisé, the next village south, is the cosy **Casa Frauca** (☎ 974 48 63 53; www.casafrauca.com; r from €39;

☼ Mar–Dec), with a dozen delightfully decorated rooms, a dining room and fireplace.

In Nerín, 3km from the Cañón de Añisclo, **Albergue Añisclo** (☎ 974 48 90 10; dm €7.50; ☼ Easter-Nov) offers meals as well as cheap lodging, and **Hotel Palazio** (☎ 974 48 90 02; www
.hotelpalazio.com; r incl breakfast €70), perched on a cliff, has spacious rooms with terraces.

EAST OF THE PARK

Escalona, a roadside village at the park's southeastern corner, boasts several attractive lodgings, including **Hotel Revestido** (☎ 974 50 50 42; www.hotelrevestido.com; Avenida Pineta; s/d €35/50), with guide services, and the **Casa Carpintera** (☎ 974 50 51 69; b.ponz@wanadoo.es; Avenida Pineta; half-board €35), with seven comfortably crafted rooms and lavish breakfasts.

Bielsa, too, has plenty of accommodation, but you'd be better off heading up the steep-sided Valle de Pineta, which is crowned by an impressive cirque. Along the way you'll find the shady **Camping Pineta** (☎ 974 50 10 89; per person/tent/car €3.80/3.80/3.80; ☼ Apr–mid-Oct), a *zona de acampada*, the always-attended **Refugio de Pineta** (☎ 974 50 12 03), with meals, and the luxurious **Parador de Bielsa** (☎ 974 50 10 11; r €91/114).

Getting There & Away
BUS

A daily **Hudebús** (☎ 974 21 32 77) bus runs at 11am from Sabiñánigo, on the N330 between Huesca and Jaca, to Torla (noon), Broto, Sarvisé and Aínsa (1pm). It heads back from Aínsa at 2.30pm. In addition, in July and August a 6.30pm bus makes the Sabiñánigo–Sarvisé (but not Aínsa) run daily, returning at 8pm.

A daily Alosa bus leaves Zaragoza (Paseo de María Agustín 7) at 8.30am, and arrives in Sabiñánigo at 10.20am, in time to connect with the Torla bus. From Jaca, there's a 10.15am bus to Sabiñánigo daily, except Sunday (€1.25, 20 minutes).

PARK ACCESS

See Orientation (p424) for details of road approaches to the park. The following scenario has remained unchanged for several years. Private vehicles may not drive from Torla to Pradera de Ordesa during Easter week and July to mid-October. During these periods a shuttle bus (€2.10/3.10 one way/return) runs between Torla car park

ARAGÓN

and Pradera de Ordesa. On the upward run, the bus's only stop is at the Centro de Visitantes El Parador; on the way back, it will stop if requested at the Puente de los Navarros and three hotels or camping grounds between there and Torla. The last run back is at 10pm in July and August, 9pm in September. A maximum of 1800 people are allowed in the park at any one time.

During the same periods, a one-way system is enforced on part of the Escalona–Sarvisé road. From the Puyarruego turn-off, 2km out of Escalona, to a point about 1km after the road diverges from the Bellos valley, only northwestward traffic is allowed. Southeastward traffic uses an alternative, more southerly road.

JACA

pop 14,700 / elevation 820m

Jaca is a busy and amiable town with plenty of remnants of its illustrious past: it was capital of the nascent Aragón kingdom for a few decades in the 11th century. Tourism and skiing further north have brought Jaca a degree of prosperity in recent years. On winter weekends it becomes an après-ski-cum-lager-lout fun town.

Information

There are plenty of banks, including a couple on Calle Mayor.

Ciberciva (Avenida del Regimiento de Galicia 2; per hr €1.90) Internet access next door to the tourist office.

Post office (Avenida del Regimiento de Galicia 13)

Tourist office (☎ 974 36 00 98; Avenida del Regimiento de Galicia 2; ⏰ 9am-1.30pm or 2pm & 4.30-7.30pm or 8pm Mon-Sat)

Sights & Activities

The 11th-century **cathedral** is a fine building, although tinkering has obscured much of its original French-style Romanesque grace. Worth a look is the side chapel dedicated to Santa Orosia, the city's patron saint, whose martyrdom is depicted in a series of mysterious murals. Overhead the vaulted ceiling is studded with gold stars. In the cloister, the **Museo Diocesano** has a remarkable collection of frescoes and sculpture from churches throughout the region, but the museum was undergoing restoration at the time of writing.

The star-shaped, 16th-century **Ciudadela** (Citadel; adult/child €4/2; ⏰ 11am-noon year-round;

4-5pm Nov-Mar, 5-6pm Apr-Jun & Sep-Oct, 6-8pm Jul & Aug) now houses an army academy, but the soldiers briefly drop their guard to permit visits, with interesting 40-minute guided tours (in English, Spanish or French). Deer graze in the surrounding moat.

As an alternative to skiing, you might perform some figure eights at the **ice-skating rink** (☎ 974 35 51 92; Avenida Perimetral; admission €8; ⏰ 7-9.30pm Mon-Fri, 5.30-8.30pm Sat, 4.30-7.30pm Sun), south of the old town.

Festivals & Events

Jaca puts on its party gear for the week-long **Fiesta de Santa Orosia**, which starts on 25 June. To see displays of medieval archery, make sure you visit on the first Friday of May, when Jaca celebrates a **Christian victory** over Muslims in 760. The **Festival Folklórico de los Pirineos**, held in late July and early August, provides 1½ weeks of international music, dance, crafts and theatre. It's held on odd-numbered years in Jaca and even-numbered years in Oloron-Ste-Marie, France.

Sleeping

The town can fill up at peak periods, including ski-season weekends.

Hostal París (☎ 974 36 10 20; Plaza de San Pedro 5; s/d €19.50/31) This central option offers 20 ample-sized rooms and state-of-the-art shared bathrooms. Everything is spotless – even the floorboards really shine! The affable manager is a veritable font of information.

Hostal Somport (☎ /fax 974 36 34 10; Calle de Echegaray 11; s/d with shared bathroom €18/30) Though the Somport lacks the character of Hostal París, at least it's friendly and the rooms are clean.

Hotel Mur (☎ 974 36 01 00; Calle de Santa Orosia 1; s/d incl breakfast €44/60) This long-established, large hotel provides above-average comfort and style. Balconies overlook the Ciudadela or old town.

Several other places cater to the slopes trade, with ski racks and fireplace dens:

Hotel La Paz (☎ 974 36 07 00; Calle Mayor 41; s/d €34/47)

Hotel Ciudad de Jaca (☎ 974 35 64 24; Calle de Sancho Ramírez; s/d incl breakfast €30/52)

Eating

La Cadiera (☎ 974 35 55 59; Calle de Domingo Miral 19; menú €9.20; ⏰ closed Wed afternoon & Mon) More

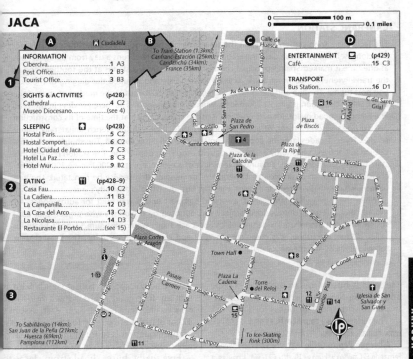

JACA

INFORMATION
Ciberciva............................1 A3
Post Office..........................2 B3
Tourist Office......................3 B3

SIGHTS & ACTIVITIES (p428)
Cathedral............................4 C2
Museo Diocesano...............(see 4)

SLEEPING (p428)
Hostal París........................5 C2
Hostal Somport...................6 C2
Hotel Ciudad de Jaca...........7 C3
Hotel La Paz.......................8 C3
Hotel Mur...........................9 B2

EATING (pp428–9)
Casa Fau............................10 C2
La Cadiera..........................11 B3
La Campanilla.....................12 D3
La Casa del Arco.................13 C2
La Nicolasa........................14 D3
Restaurante El Portón.......(see 15)

ENTERTAINMENT (p429)
Café..................................15 C3

TRANSPORT
Bus Station........................16 D1

than a restaurant, this is a sort of upper Aragón cultural centre. The emphasis is on traditional northern fare. Sure-fire bets include the garlic soup, *ternasco* (lamb) and *migas* (shepherd's breadcrumbs).

La Campanilla (☎ 974 36 14 48; Calle Escuelas Pías 8; menú €8) For a hearty, good-value lunch, join the crowds here.

La Casa del Arco (Calle de San Nicolás 8; 2/3-course menú €10/12) Those seeking alternatives to ham and lamb will find filling vegetarian meals here.

Restaurante El Portón (☎ 974 35 58 54; Plaza l la Cadena 1; menú €18) A classy locale, El Portón serves *haute-cuisine* versions of *aragonese* fare. Reservations are a must.

For awesome tapas, head to **Casa Fau** (☎ 974 36 15 94; Plaza de la Catedral) or **La Nicolasa** (☎ 974 35 54 12; Calle Escuelas Pías 3; ☒ closed Tue).

Entertainment

A bevy of youthful nocturnal bars lines Calle de Gil Berges and trickles off into the neighbouring lanes. **Café** (Plaza Marqués de la Cadena 2), a small lounge with big speakers, is frequented by local hipsters.

Getting There & Away

The **bus station** (☎ 974 35 50 60; Plaza de Biscós) is handily located. Five buses go to Huesca (€5.40, 1¼ hours) and Zaragoza (€10.40, 2¼ hours) most days, and two to Pamplona (€6, 1¾ hours).

The **train station** (☎ 974 36 13 32) is a half-hour walk northeast of the town centre, with three trains daily south to Huesca and Zaragoza, and two north to Canfranc-Estación.

AROUND JACA
Canfranc-Estación
pop 535 / elevation 1200m

Not to be confused with Canfranc-Pueblo to the south, Canfranc-Estación is, as they say, at the end of the line. Trains (two a day to/from Zaragoza via Huesca and Jaca) don't go beyond its massive train station (see Canfranc Station, p430). Located 25km north of Jaca via the pretty Río Aragón valley, Canfranc serves as a gateway to the ski resorts of Candanchú and Astún, and is the point of entry for the recently finished Somport tunnel to the French Pyrenees.

ARAGÓN

CANFRANC STATION

The fact that a train station figures in the town's name shows how important it is to Canfranc-Estación's self-image. These days the station only sees a couple of runs a day from Zaragoza, but at one time it marked Spain's principal connection with France. It stands at the southern end of the trans-Pyrenean link, which took 20 years to complete and required the digging of the 8km Somport tunnel. The line and station were inaugurated in 1928. Built in the modernist style of the day, Canfranc's station is almost 250m long, with as many windows as there are days in the year. The French railroad maintained its operations at the station, which at the time of its construction was Europe's second largest. After an accident in 1970, however, the French unilaterally halted service. Three decades later the people of Canfranc are still bitter about it. The shutdown led to a decline in Canfranc's economy and a consequent drop in its population. The station remains in a state of semi-abandonment, a haunting reminder of a glorious past. In 2003 some 3000 protesters formed a human chain around its perimeter demanding that service be reinstated. The two countries have finally agreed to reopen the line, but just when is anybody's guess.

While the railway line languished, a second Somport tunnel was built for automobiles. Although this European Union–aided project was opposed by ecologists, who argued that construction of the tunnel and widening of its approach roads would disfigure France's beautiful Vallée d'Aspe, the tunnel was completed in 2003 and is now open to traffic. The parallel train tunnel serves as an emergency exit.

Three daily buses cross to the Vallée d'Aspe and Oloron-Ste-Marie in France, connecting there with trains or buses for Pau.

The village has a **tourist office** (☎ 974 37 31 41; www.canfranc.com; Plaza del Ayuntamiento 1).

Albergue Pepito Grillo (☎ 974 37 31 23; Avenida Fernando El Católico 2; bunks €10, d/tr €27/36) This is a good hostel north of the train station.

Casa Marieta (☎ 974 37 33 65; Plaza Aragón 4; s/d incl breakfast €25/39) One of a pair of *casas rurales* in the same vicinity, offering wood-panelled lodging with shared bathroom.

Ski Resorts

To help with booking accommodation in any of these resorts, you can contact the resort information numbers and websites given below. All of the following resorts have ski and snowboard schools, as well as equipment for hire. You can also rent gear in Jaca.

CANDANCHÚ & ASTÚN

Aragón's westernmost and longest-established ski resort, **Candanchú** (☎ 974 37 31 94; www.candanchu.com) is 28km north of Jaca. Some 42km of widely varied pistes make it appealing to most grades of skiers. Accommodation in Candanchú includes three hotels, one *pensión*, two sets of apartments, and four cheap *albergues* or refuges. The small town is reasonably well equipped with general stores and ski-hire shops.

One advantage of visiting Candanchú is that another good resort, **Astún** (☎ 974 37 30 88; www.astun.com), is just 3km east. Astún's 42km of pistes are largely for capable skiers; accommodation is more limited and generally more expensive than in Candanchú.

Five daily buses head from Jaca to Candanchú and Astún (45 minutes), via Canfranc-Estación.

PANTICOSA & FORMIGAL

The comparatively small resort of **Panticosa** (☎ 974 48 72 48; www.panticosa-loslagos.com), northeast of Biescas in the Gállego valley, has a bigger counterpart, Formigal, which is about 10km further north. The runs in Panticosa aren't too difficult and the nearly 2km Mazaranuala ski run is a must for adept skiers.

A livelier place with far more infrastructure than Panticosa, **Formigal** (☎ 974 49 00 00; www.formigal.com) is a regular host for ski competitions. Here you have the full range of facilities, including restaurants, bars, discos and saunas, as well as 57km of ski runs and 22 lifts.

From Jaca, one or two daily buses wind over to Panticosa and Formigal (€4.40, two hours).

Monasterio de San Juan de la Peña

High in a mountain eyrie 21km southwest of Jaca, this is Aragón's most fascinating monastery – but it's not reachable by public transport. You might be able to cover the first 11km by a Jaca–Pamplona bus, getting off at the turn-off for **Santa Cruz de la Serós**, a quaint village 4km south of the N240 and gathered in under the skirts of its tall, 11th-century Romanesque **Iglesia de Santa María**.

Bar Restaurante Santa Cruz (☎ 974 36 19 75; www.santacruzdelaseros.com; Calle Ordana; r with bathroom & breakfast €49), near the church, has eight pleasant rooms and serves reasonably priced food.

From Santa Cruz, a road winds up the Sierra de la Peña. It's nearly 7km to the **Monasterio Viejo** (☎ 974 35 51 19; www.monasterio sanjuan.com; admission €3.50 incl Iglesia de Santa María; 🕑 10am-2pm & 4-7pm 16 Mar-31 May & 1 Sep-15 Oct; 10am-2.30pm & 4-8pm Jun-Aug; 11am-2pm & 4-5.30pm Tue-Sun 16 Oct-15 Mar), tucked under an overhanging lip of rock at a bend in the road. For walkers, a 4km marked path (the GR65.3.2) leads up from Santa Cruz to the monastery in about 1¼ hours, with an ascent of 350m. Drivers can park on the roadside near the Monasterio Viejo (Old Monastery) at most times of year, but during Semana Santa, July and August you must use the car park near the Monasterio Nuevo (New Monastery), 1.3km further up the hill. At these times a shuttle bus (€1.50) runs between the Monasterio Nuevo and Monasterio Viejo.

The rock shelter where the Monasterio Viejo is built, perhaps used by Christian hermits as early as the 8th century, became a monastery in the 10th century, when the Mozarabic lower church was constructed. The monastery emerged as the early spiritual and organisational centre of the medieval kingdom of Aragón. A Romanesque church was built above it in the late 11th century.

The first three kings of Aragón – Ramiro I (1036–64), Sancho Ramírez (1064–94) and Pedro I (1094–1104) – were among those buried at the Monasterio Viejo. The chalice believed to be the Holy Grail, which now resides in Valencia cathedral, was kept there for some time until 1399. The monastery's **Panteón Real** (Royal Mausoleum), constructed in 1770, dislodged some of the tombs of those it was supposed to honour, but you can see the original tombs from another room. The greatest highlight is the Romanesque **cloister**, with marvellous carved 12th- and 13th-century capitals depicting Genesis and the life of Christ.

A fire in 1675 led the monks to abandon the old monastery and build a new one in brick further up the hill. **Monasterio Nuevo** (🕑 same as Monasterio Viejo) was closed in 1835 after the monks misguidedly supported the Carlists. At the time of writing, it was undergoing extensive restoration. By early 2006 its three buildings should have *parador*-style accommodation, a large visitors centre devoted to the *aragonese* kings and an archaeology museum. Nearby are a café-kiosk and the **Balcón del Pirineo**, a lookout with panoramas of the Pyrenees and, usually, members of the local vulture and eagle population.

VALLES DE ECHO & ANSÓ

Though less spectacular than the territory further east, the verdant Echo and Ansó valleys boast some charming old stone villages and beautiful forests, with 2000m-plus peaks rising around their upper reaches. Most places to stay can furnish information on walks. It's good to come equipped with a reasonable map/guide, such as Prames' *Ansó-Echo Aragués-Jasa* or Alpina's *Ansó-Echo*.

A bus to Jaca leaves Ansó at 6.30am, Siresa at 6.53am and Echo at 7am, Monday to Saturday, returning from Jaca at 6.50pm. There are no buses further up either of the valleys. A narrow, pot-holed but driveable road links the two villages, a distance of about 9.5km.

Echo
pop 670 / elevation 833m

The biggest village in its valley, Echo (also spelt Hecho) is a surprising warren of solid stone houses with steep roofs and flowery balconies. It was briefly the seat of the County of Aragón in the 9th century. The only 'sight' is the **Museo Etnológico Casa Mazo** (Calle Aire), with displays on rural life.

Casa Blasquico (☎ 974 37 50 07; Plaza de la Fuente 1; r €50; 🕑 usually closed 1st half Sep) has a half-dozen charming rooms resting above the highly proclaimed Restaurante Gaby. You couldn't do better.

Otherwise there's **Hotel de la Val** (☎ 974 37 50 28; Cruz Alta 1; s/d €25/48), a big chalet-type lodging, and, south of town, **Camping Valle de Echo** (☎ 974 37 53 61).

Siresa & Around
pop 130 / elevation 850m

A couple of kilometres north of Echo, Siresa is dominated by the formidable, 11th-century

Iglesia de San Pedro (admission €1.50; ⊕ 11am-1pm & 3-5pm, closed Wed afternoon), which originally comprised part of one of Aragón's earliest monasteries.

Albergue Siresa (☎/fax 974 37 53 85; www.refugio syalbergues.com/siresa; Calle Reclusa s/n; bunks incl break-fast €12, sheets €1.50; ✗) This hotel provides bunk-and-breakfast accommodation in clean conditions, with other meals available. It also rents mountain bikes and has a library.

Hotel Castillo d'Acher (☎ 974 37 53 13; www .castillodacher.com; Plaza Mayor; s/d €30/36) Offering rooms with bathroom and TV, this place can also provide doubles for €24 in *casas rurales* in the village.

Hotel Usón (☎ 974 37 53 58; www.hoteluson.com; r incl breakfast €29) Standing in splendid isolation 5km north of Siresa on the road to the Selva de Oza, this hotel has fine rooms and a restaurant.

Selva de Oza
This top end of the Valle de Echo is particularly beautiful, with the road running parallel to the Río Aragón Subordán as it bubbles its way through thick woodlands. About 14km from Siresa the paved road ends, shortly after it connects with the GR11 path en route between Candanchú and Zuriza. At least half a dozen mountain peaks sit in an arc to the north for strenuous day assaults.

Ansó
pop 540 / elevation 860m
The rough-hewn stone houses here repeat the pretty picture of Echo, but on a smaller scale. Ansó could make an ideal base for exploring the region, especially if you have your own transport.

Posada Magoria (☎ 974 37 00 49; Calle Milagros 32; s/d €30/45) Sitting just below the church, this *posada* is a beautifully renovated early-20th-century house. There are just six rooms. In the *comedor* you can savour good vegetarian cooking made with home-grown ingredients.

Casa Baretón (☎ 974 37 01 38; zabalcoch@hotmail .com; Calle Pascual Altemir 16; s/d €27/41) A lovingly restored stone house, in a niche off the main street.

Bar Zuriza (☎ 639 28 45 90; Mayor 71) A great old drinking establishment, with a wide selection of beer, tapas and local cider.

Zuriza
Fifteen kilometres north of Ansó, Zuriza is little more than a camping ground and walkers' refuge.

Camping Zuriza (☎ 974 37 01 96; per person/tent/car €3.50/3/3.50, dm from €8.50) Popular – it's worth booking ahead at busy times. It also has a restaurant.

Refugio Linza (☎ 974 37 01 12) A 100-bunk place that serves meals. A rough but driveable track leads up to it, 5km further north of Camping Zuriza.

Walks of varying duration and difficulty abound, as do climbing and caving opportunities. The GR11 passes right through Zuriza. You could follow it west to Isaba (Navarra), about 9km away via a stiff climb over 2050m Ezkaurre. Eastwards, it's a bit further to the Selva de Oza via the 1958m Collado de Petraficha pass. Two peaks on the French border, Sobarcal (2249m) and Petrechema (2360m), attract a lot of attention (the latter is a trickier ascent than the former). Both can be done as day excursions from Refugio Linza, or even from Zuriza.

SOS DEL REY CATÓLICO
pop 610 / elevation 625m
This village, 80km west of Jaca, takes its name from a son of whom any place would be proud: Fernando II of Aragón, born here in 1452. He married Isabel I of Castilla and together, as the Catholic Monarchs (Los Reyes Católicos), the couple finished off the Reconquista and united Spain. The old medieval town is a fascinating spider's web of twisting, cobbled lanes and claustrophobic houses atop a hill on the rim of the *aragonese* wheat plains.

The keep of the **Castillo de la Peña Feliciano** crowns the hilltop, and the Gothic **Iglesia de San Esteban** (admission €1; ⊕ 10am-1pm & 3.30-5.30pm) below it, with a Romanesque portal and crypt, is worth a peek.

Fernando is said to have been born in the **Palacio de Sada**, now an **interpretive centre** (adult/child €2.40/1.20; ⊕ 10am-1pm or 2pm & 4-7pm or 8pm Jun-Aug, closed Mon-Tue rest of year), with fine exhibits on the history of Sos and the life of the king. The tour includes an audiovisual programme in the San Martín de Tours chapel, incorporating the murals that grace the far wall. The palace also serves as a tourist information centre.

Sleeping & Eating

Fonda Fernandina (☎ 948 88 81 20; Plaza del Mesón
s/n; s/d €15/30, half-board €25/50) Ensconced in a
large, well-preserved old house, the *fonda*
(basic eatery and inn combined) provides
simple lodging and feeds its guests hearty
country fare.

Albergue Juvenil Sos del Rey Católico (☎ 948
88 84 80; Calle Meca; per person under/over 26 €14.50/17)
Housed in a medieval tower beyond the Ig-
lesia de San Esteban, this new youth hostel
has 32 bunks and a salon with a fireplace.
Bicycle rental is available, and all meals are
served.

Parador de Sos del Rey Católico (☎ 948 88 80 11;
Calle Arquitecto Sainz de Vicuña 1; s/d €91/113) At the
northern end of town, the *parador* blends
well into the Sos architectural landscape
despite its recent vintage.

Getting There & Away

A bus from Zaragoza to Sos del Rey Católico
departs from below the old El Portillo train
station at 7pm Monday to Friday (€8). It
returns from Sos at 7am.

THE SOUTH

Vast sweeps of the countryside immediately
south of Zaragoza are either dreary plains
or bald, uninviting ridges; however, head
further south or southeast and you'll encounter a more dramatic landscape, along
with some intriguing towns and villages.
Among these are Teruel, a storehouse of
some of the best Mudéjar architecture you'll
find anywhere in the country, and nearby
Albarracín, a medieval treat built above the
Río Guadalaviar.

DAROCA
pop 2250

Daroca lies in a valley just below the
N234 Calatayud–Teruel Hwy. On the hills
on either side of town rise the crumbling
remnants of its once extensive walls, which
originally had 114 towers. Calle Mayor,
the main street, is marked at either end
by monumental gates. About midway
along and up to the west lies the main
square, Plaza de España, dominated by
the large Romanesque-cum-Mudéjar-cum-
Renaissance **Iglesia Colegiata de Santa María**.

La Posada del Almudí (☎ 976 80 06 06; Grajera 5;
s/d €42/55) Its 13 rooms are arranged around
the courtyard of a restored 16th-century
palace in Daroca's historic core. It also has
one of the best restaurants in town.

Buses stop outside the Mesón Félix bar,
at Calle Mayor 104. Two or three buses run
daily to/from Zaragoza and one to/from
Teruel Monday to Friday.

LAGUNA DE GALLOCANTA

Some 20km south of Daroca and a similar
distance west of Calamocha on the N234,
this is Spain's largest natural lake, with
an area of about 15 sq km (though it can
almost dry up in summer). It's a winter
home for some 70,000 cranes and many
other water fowl. A **Centro de Interpretación**
(☎ 978 72 50 04; ⏰ 10am-2pm & 4-8pm Nov & Feb,
Sat & Sun only rest of year), with information and
exhibitions, is on the Tornos–Bello road
near the southeast corner of the lake where
the cranes gather. Take binoculars.

TERUEL
pop 29,970 / elevation 917m

This compact provincial capital contains
a handful of the most ornate and striking
Mudéjar monuments in Spain. Its hilltop
casco viejo (old part of town) merits a few
hours of your time at least, and Teruel
makes a good stopover between Zaragoza
and Valencia, or indeed between northeast
Castilla-La Mancha and the coast.

History

During the 11th century Teruel was briefly
part of a Muslim *taifa* (small kingdom)
based in nearby Albarracín. Taken for
Christendom by Alfonso II of Aragón in
1171, it became an operational base for
Jaume I of Aragón in his 1230s campaign

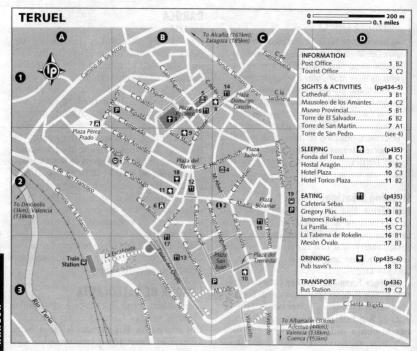

TERUEL

ARAGÓN

to wrest Valencia from Muslim hands. When the Christians got round to building monumental churches in the 13th and 14th centuries, they adorned several with the beautiful Mudéjar towers for which Teruel is now famous.

Orientation & Information

The train station is downhill on the western edge of the old town, and the bus station on the eastern edge. From either it's a short walk into the town centre, where you'll find the **tourist office** (☎ 978 60 22 79; http://turismo .teruel.net; Calle de Tomás Nogués 1; ☑ 9am-2pm & 5-7.30pm).

Sights

CATHEDRAL

From outside, Teruel's **cathedral** (☎ 978 61 99 50; admission €1.80; ☑ 11am-2pm & 4-8pm) looks like a brick wedding cake, decorated with colourful ceramic tiles – a rich example of the Mudéjar imagination at work. Building began in 1176, and the most appealing exterior feature is the Mudéjar bell tower, tinged with Romanesque. Inside, the roof

of the nave is covered with paintings that add up to a medieval cosmography – from musical instruments and hunting scenes to coats of arms and Christ's crucifixion.

OTHER MUDÉJAR MONUMENTS

The most impressive of Teruel's three other Mudéjar towers is the **Torre de El Salvador** (☎ 978 60 20 61; admission €2.50; ☑ 11am-2pm & 4.30-7.30pm Tue-Sun), an early 14th-century fantasy of brick and ceramics built around an old Muslim minaret. You can climb up by stairways occupying the gap between the inner and outer towers. Along the way, you'll find exhibits on Mudéjar art and architecture. Even if you don't go inside, you'll likely pass through its grand arch during your wanders. The similar **Torre de San Martín** was undergoing restoration at the time of writing.

The other tower is the **Torre de San Pedro**, to which is attached the celebrated **Mausoleo de los Amantes** (Mausoleum of the Lovers). The latter holds the mummified remains of Isabel and Diego, star-crossed 13th-century lovers who supposedly died of grief at

TERUEL EXISTS, OK?

Since 1897 the population of the very rural province of Teruel has shrunk from 240,000 to 136,000, and these days it's struggling to avoid economic oblivion. In recent years its people and the provincial government have resorted to the slogan 'Teruel Existe' ('Teruel Exists') for demonstrations attempting to win more central government attention and money. Efforts have focused on trying to get a planned high-speed Tren de Alta Velocidad Española (AVE) railway line directed through Teruel en route between Cuenca and Valencia.

seeing their love frustrated; they lie in modern alabaster tombs, sculpted by Juan de Ávalos with the lovers' heads tilted towards each other. (The mausoleum was also being restored with no fixed date for reopening.)

MUSEO PROVINCIAL

Teruel's **Provincial Museum** (☎ 978 60 01 50; Plaza Polanco; admission free; ☟ 10am-2pm & 4-7pm Tue-Fri, 10am-2pm Sat & Sun) is housed in the 16th-century Casa de la Comunidad, a fine work of Renaissance architecture. The archaeological sections are a highlight, but the extensive displays range from a re-creation of an 18th-century pharmacy to exhibits of contemporary art.

DINÓPOLIS

If you're travelling with kids, plan on visiting this large, modern **dinosaur theme park** (☎ 902 44 80 00; www.dinopolis.com; adult/child €17/13; ☟ 10am-8pm Jul–mid-Sep, Wed-Sun only May & Jun, Fri-Sun Mar-Apr & Sep–mid-Oct). It's 3km from the town centre, well signposted just off the Valencia road. A highlight is 'El Ride', a motorised trip through time spiced up with animated dinosaur robots.

Festivals & Events

On the weekend closest to 14 February, thousands of Teruel's inhabitants don medieval dress for a gala event and a **re-enactment of the Diego and Isabel legend**. The **Día de San Cristóbal** (St Christopher's Day, held on 10 July) is the hub of the week-long **Feria del Ángel**, which commemorates the founding of Teruel.

Sleeping

Fonda del Tozal (☎ 978 60 10 22; Calle del Rincón 5; s/d without bathroom €18/24, d with bathroom €35) This may be the oldest inn in Spain – documents prove it's been going since at least 1568. Today it offers 17 wood-beamed rooms with loads of character. The lower floors tend to be better maintained.

Hostal Aragón (☎ 978 61 18 77; Calle Santa María 4; s/d with bathroom €21.50/36.50) Located on a narrow side street, this is a friendly place, with clean, wood-panelled rooms.

Going upmarket in the central area, you'll find a couple of modern business-oriented hotels, with balconies overlooking their respective plazas:

Hotel Plaza (☎ 978 60 86 55; Plaza del Tremedal 3; s/d €52/76; ☒)

Hotel Torico Plaza (☎ 978 60 86 55; Calle de Yagüe de Salas 5; s/d incl breakfast €77/96; ☒)

Eating

Teruel is pretty obsessed with all things porcine, going to great lengths to promote its local jamón (ham).

La Taberna de Rokelin (☎ 978 78 60 60; Calle El Tozal 33; tapa/ración of ham €3/12) A narrow bar with a beautiful rack of smoked pig hocks, this is one of the best places to try Teruel ham. It's linked to a shop just up the street, **Jamones Rokelin** (Calle del Rincón 2), where you can load up with smoked meats, sausages and cheeses for a week's worth of picnics.

Mesón Óvalo (☎ 978 60 98 62; Paseo del Óvalo 8; menú €11, main dishes €12; ☟ closed Mon) Here the emphasis is on regional cuisine and ingredients, with dishes from throughout the province.

Cafetería Sebas (Calle Ramón y Cajal 4) Try the torrejas (French toast slices) at this bustling breakfast spot.

Gregory Plus (☎ 978 60 80 63; Paseo del Óvalo 5; menú €10) Gregory offers a solid three-course lunch with promenade views. The branch just down the way is more of a tapas joint.

La Parrilla (☎ 978 60 59 17; Calle San Esteban 2; grilled meats €7-15) Pork and lamb chops are kept sizzling at this traditional dining hall.

Drinking

Fonda del Tozal (Calle del Rincón 5) The cavernous ground-floor bar is a good place to unwind. Formerly the stables of the inn upstairs – note the rings for tying up horses – it hosts bands on Friday night.

Pub Isavis's (Plaza de Torico 14) For a relaxed drink or coffee, this pub at the lower end of the plaza has some outdoor tables.

Most of the late-night excitement takes place in the youthful bars on and around Plaza Bolamar.

Getting There & Away

From Teruel's **bus station** (☎ 978 61 07 89), Tezasa runs up to five buses daily to/from Zaragoza (€7.70, 2½ hours). Samar runs five buses to/from Valencia (€7.65, 2¼ hours) most days, and four buses to/from Madrid (€16.50, 4½ hours). La Rápida offers service to/from Barcelona (€21.50, six hours) and Cuenca (€7.90) daily, except Sunday. For more local services see destination sections.

Teruel is on the railway between Zaragoza (€9.15, three hours) and Valencia (€8.25, 2½ hours), with three trains each way daily.

RINCÓN DE ADEMUZ

The 'Ademuz Corner' is a mountainous detached piece of Valencia province sandwiched between the provinces of Teruel and Cuenca (Castilla-La Mancha). It makes a picturesque alternative route between Teruel town and the provinces of Valencia or Cuenca. The most spectacular stretch is the rough and winding 17km of the old N330A, south of the town of Ademuz (a steep but unremarkable place) to Santa Cruz de Moya. Starting along the deepening gorge of the upper Río Turia, the road crosses into Castilla-La Mancha in quite spectacular fashion. This section (and Ademuz town itself) is bypassed by the main N330, so you need to head into Ademuz via Torrebaja – or from the south through Manzaneruela to Santa Cruz de Moya.

The N420 west from the Rincón de Ademuz skirts the southern hills of the Serranía de Cuenca en route to Cuenca. The first 15km or so are a bit of an adventure owing to the road's poor condition.

Hostal Casa Domingo (☎ 978 78 20 30; www .galeon.com/casadomingorincon; Avenida Valencia 1; s/d €21.50/35) A large place on the N330A in Ademuz, Casa Domingo has decent rooms with bathroom and TV, and a restaurant. It's also the stop for buses to/from Teruel (one a day, except Sunday and holidays) and Valencia (twice daily).

ALBARRACÍN

pop 1060 / elevation 1180m

The crenellated walls climbing above the remote medieval town of Albarracín, 38km west of Teruel, dramatically announce its proximity as you approach. Built on a steep, rocky height carved out by a meander of the Río Guadalaviar, Albarracín was, from 1012 to 1104, the seat of a tiny Islamic state ruled by the Berber Banu Razin dynasty. From 1170 to 1285 it was an independent Christian kingdom sandwiched between Castilla and Aragón. With its tall, aged buildings clinging to steep hillsides in an isolated setting, this is the most impressive of Aragón's ancient hill towns, even if tourists seem to outnumber locals at times. Albarracín's narrow streets are even today in the best tradition of the Arab medina, with the centuries-old buildings leaning alarmingly over them.

Information

You'll find the post office and a couple of banks with ATMs on or just off Plaza Mayor.

The **tourist office** (☎ 978 71 02 51; www.albar racin.org; Calle Diputación 4; ◷ 10am-2pm & 4-7pm Tue-Sun except Sun afternoon), too, is just off Plaza Mayor.

Sights

The **cathedral** (admission free; ◷ 10.30am-2pm & 4-6pm except Sun afternoon, until 8pm Jul-Sep), with its cupola typical of the Spanish Levant, has an elaborate gilded altarpiece. The Palacio Episcopal (Bishop's Palace), to which it's connected, houses the **Museo Diocesano** (admission €2; ◷ same as cathedral), with 16th-century paintings, tapestries, and religious *objets d'art*.

The **Museo de Albarracín** (Calle San Juan; admission €2; ◷ 10.30am-1pm & 4-5.30pm except Sun afternoon), in the old city hospital, is devoted to the town's Islamic heritage.

The castle, near the southern end of town, and the **Torre del Andador** (Walkway Tower), at the top of the walls at the north, both date from the 9th century, when Albarracín was already an important Muslim military post. Walk up to the Torre del Andador for fine panoramas, then just enjoy exploring the streets. Nearly every brick, stone, slab of concrete and slap of mortar in the place is in some earthy shade of red or pink, making for wonderful plays of colour, particularly in the evening.

Tours

El Andador (☎ 978 70 03 81) conducts 1½ walks through Albarracín's medieval core for €3.50, departing from outside the tourist office at 11am, 12.45pm and 5pm (except Sunday).

Sleeping & Eating

Camping Ciudad de Albarracín (☎ 978 71 01 97; per person/tent/car €2.90/2.90/2.90; ☺ Apr-Oct) Pleasant, small and shaded, the camping ground is 2km from the heart of town, off the Bezas road.

There are many places to get a bed, but during holiday times it's worth booking ahead or arriving early.

Casa de Santiago (☎ 978 70 03 16; Subida a las Torres 11; s/d €42/58) A few steps up from Plaza Mayor in the heart of the old town is this cosy place, with eight charming rooms.

Posada del Adarve (☎ 978 70 03 04; Calle Portal de Molina 23; r €63) Alongside the Portal de Molina (Molina Gateway), this is another lovingly restored place, with just five rooms.

Hotel Mesón del Gallo (☎ 978 71 00 32; Calle de los Puentes 8; s/d €27/40) Though less charming than some of the central places, these rooms over a restaurant, just before the tunnel entrance, are comfortable enough and have balconies overlooking the river.

Besides the hotel restaurants, there are more eateries in the streets off Plaza Mayor.

La Taberna (Plaza Mayor 6; platos combinados €5-7) The kitchen sets up hearty combinations, or for the adventurous, wild boar and other game.

Near La Taberna, Bar Aben Razin is an atmospheric place for a drink.

AUTHOR'S CHOICE

Habitaciones Los Palacios (☎ 978 70 03 27; www.montepalacios.com; Calle Los Palacios 21; s/d €20/36) Perhaps the best value of all, the spotless rooms here have balconies and gorgeous views. It's about 250m from Plaza Mayor, starting along Calle de Santiago and exiting through Portal de Molina; (from the Teruel direction), pass through the tunnel under the town and take the first road up to the right.

Getting There & Away

Autotransportes Teruel buses leave daily, except Sunday, from Teruel for Albarracín (30 minutes) at 3.30pm, and from Albarracín for Teruel at 8.30am.

EL RODENO

The back road leading southeast from Albarracín towards Bezas passes near a series of Neolithic rock paintings known as the **Conjunto de Arte Rupestre del Rodeno**, among boulder-strewn countryside. There are 12 lots of paintings in total, in five groups. The whole circuit takes about 2½ hours to explore. A small **information centre** (☺ Sat & Sun) at a turn-off 4km from the edge of Albarracín provides background and shows routes, and there are explanatory plaques along the way. The clearest paintings, showing bulls, horses and deer, are at the Abrigo del Navazo.

No buses run this way, but if it's not too hot you can walk by part of the GR10 long-distance path. This diverges (unmarked) to the left from the Bezas road on the south edge of Albarracín, about 100m south of a fork with GR10 information panels and a 'Pinturas Rupestres' sign.

The rock paintings are enveloped within the **Pinares de Rodeno** protected area, a 3335-hectare pine forest upon a layer of characteristic pink sandstone. Five key trails, varying in distance from 2.2km to 15km, traverse the zone; the tourist office in Albarracín gives out maps.

ALBARRACÍN TO CASTILLA-LA MANCHA

For those with a vehicle, a couple of routes suggest themselves across the hill country stretching from Albarracín into Castilla-La Mancha.

A left turn signed 'Royuela' off the A1512, 7km west of Albarracín, leads across the varied and pretty Montes Universales and on across the Serranía de Cuenca towards Cuenca via the dramatic Río Júcar gorge.

The A1512 continues across the Sierra de Albarracín into Guadalajara province. Perhaps the most scenic of several possible routes is that via Checa, Terzaga, Peralejos de las Truchas and the Hoz de Beteta (Beteta Gorge) towards the Alcarria area of Cuenca and Guadalajara provinces (see p254).

ARAGÓN

THE SOUTHEAST

The sparsely populated ranges stretching east of Teruel into the Valencia region present a smorgasbord of bleak rocky peaks and dramatic gorges, among which the quiet and ancient stone pueblos seem to be left to their own devices. This is wonderful country for exploring well off the beaten track, but unless you have a lot of time, you need a vehicle. Buses serve most places, but rarely more than once daily and often not at all on weekends.

The following route is one that drivers might take from Teruel. Start by heading 43km southeast to **Mora de Rubielos** in the foothills of the Sierra de Gúdar. A massive 14th-century **castle** (admission €1.20; ☼ 10am-2pm & 5-8pm Tue-Sun) towers over the village amid a sea of red and pink stone. Across the way is the Gothic **Ex-Colegiata de Santa María**, notable for its single very broad nave.

Another 14km southeast along the A232 is pretty **Rubielos de Mora**, a quiet web of narrow streets adorned with typically small *aragonese* balconies. **Hotel Los Leones** (☎ 978 80 44 77; hotelleones@sierradegudar.com; Plaza Igual y Gil 3; d €80) is friendly and atmospheric, and has a fine restaurant with an €18 *menú*.

The A1701 northeast of Rubielos crosses beautiful, wild country of stony, pine-clad hillsides, deep valleys, isolated, crumbling farmsteads and just a few villages of old stone houses with speckled red-tile roofs. Shortly before one of the highest passes, Puerto de Linares (1720m), is dusty **Linares de Mora**, where you could stay at the **Hostal La Venta** (☎ 978 80 20 18; Calle El Regajo 13; d €40), by the church.

It's 40km from Linares to **La Iglesuela del Cid**. Here you have entered El Maestrazgo, a medieval knightly domain centred on Sant Mateu in Castellón province (see p595). The landscape is now a little gentler. La Iglesuela is worth a quick visit to see its church and old town hall, sharing a tight little medieval plaza with the classy **Hospedería de la Iglesuela del Cid** (☎ 964 44 34 76; Ondevilla 4; s/d €82/117) in an 18th-century mansion.

Casa Amada (☎ 964 44 33 73; Fuentenueva 10; s/d with bathroom €23/35) here you'll find simple accommodation and a good restaurant.

Cantavieja, 13km northwest of La Iglesuela, was reputedly founded by Hannibal. It later became a seat of the Knights Templar. The best-preserved (and partly restored) part of town is the porticoed Plaza Cristo Rey.

Pensión Julián (☎ 964 18 50 05; Calle García Valiño 6; d with shared/private bathroom €20/24) This place is much better than it looks from outside, with cosy wood-beamed rooms and home-cooked meals.

Hotel Balfagón (☎ 964 18 50 76; Avenida Maestrazgo 20; s/d €35/49; ✗ 🖳 P) Comfortable accommodation is on offer here, with a restaurant serving local specialities.

If you're heading for Morella in the Valencian Maestrazgo, the A226 northeast of Cantavieja will take you there via **Mirambel**, a fine example of a small, walled medieval town without the usual modern-day additions.

Hostal Guimerá (☎ 964 17 82 69; Calle Pastor 28; d with shared/private bathroom €24/28) Simple rooms, as well as meals.

Back to the west of Cantavieja, the A1702 tacks north for an attractive drive past the precariously located **Villarluengo** and, a few kilometres further on, it travels past the weird rock formations of the **Órganos de Montoro**, which form the valley walls of the Río Guadalope.

If you'd like to explore the area at a relaxed pace, La Iglesuela, Cantavieja, Mirambel and Villarluengo are all connected by marked footpaths as well as roads.

Getting There & Away

One of the more useful bus services is the 3pm Monday-to-Friday bus from Teruel to La Iglesuela del Cid (€7.20, two hours) via Cantavieja. In the opposite direction, the bus departs from La Iglesuela at 6.15am. Another Monday-to-Friday bus leaves Cantavieja at 5.45am bound for Morella via Mirambel. Yet another early morning weekday bus journeys from Cantavieja to Villarluengo and Alcorisa, where you can connect for Alcañiz (see p439).

CALANDA

Northeast of Teruel, the N420 traverses rugged mountainous terrain, reaching the foggy heights of the 1400m San Just pass before descending to meet the east-west N211. If you take this road east, you'll enter the Bajo Aragón (Lower Aragón) district. The first significant town is Alcorisa, set amid red-shelved cliffs. Another 15km further on is Calanda, at the confluence of the

LUIS BUÑUEL & THE DRUMS OF CALANDA

Luis Buñuel's earliest memories were of the drums of Calanda. In the centuries-old ritual of the lower Aragón town, the film director's birthplace, Good Friday noon marks the *rompida de la hora* (breaking of the hour). At that moment thousands commence banging on *tambores* (snare drums) and *bombos* (bass drums), together producing a thunderous din. The ceremony goes on for the next 24 hours, only ceasing for the passage of the standard Easter processions.

'The drums, that amazing, resounding, cosmic phenomenon that brushes the collective subconscious, causes the earth to tremble beneath our feet', Buñuel recalls in his memoir, *Mi Ultimo Suspiro* (My Last Sigh). 'One has only to place his hand on the wall of a house to feel the vibrations. Nature follows the rhythm...which goes on all night. Anyone who manages to fall asleep, lulled by the banging, awakes with a start when the sound trails off. At dawn, the drum skins are stained with blood: hands bleed after so much banging. And these are the rough hands of peasants.'

This clamour worked its way into Buñuel's dreams and nightmares, and eventually into his surreal films. Even though young Luis' family moved to Zaragoza before the end of his first year of life, the drums left their imprint, along with a taste for ritual, costumes and disguises. These motifs show up in films throughout his career, from *La Edad de Oro* to *Nazarín*, as demonstrated at the Centro Buñuel Calanda museum (see below).

Buñuel continued to feel an attachment to the Aragonese town throughout his life, and returned on occasion to grab a pair of sticks and join in.

Guadalope and Guadalopillo Rivers. The chief reason to visit Calanda is the recently opened **Centro Buñuel Calanda** (☎ 978 84 65 24; admission €3; Calle Mayor 48; ☽ 11am-2pm & 4-8pm Wed-Sun Jul-Sep, 3-6.30pm rest of year), a museum devoted to the life and films of Luis Buñuel. The museum tries to remain faithful to the surrealist spirit of the Calanda native (see Luis Buñuel & the Drums of Calanda, above), cleverly weaving images from his oeuvre into the tour. (Anyone who has seen *The Phantom of Liberty* will be delighted – or perhaps scandalised – to find that one of the film's most outrageous scenes is recalled in the seating arrangements for a video on *Un Chien Andalou*, Buñuel's notorious debut film made in collaboration with Dalí.) For true aficionados, a filmography room has computers with details of all 32 of Buñuel's films, accompanied by screenings of key scenes and commentary by the director.

The museum is 500m from the bus stop on the edge of town. Look for the Plaza de España and follow Calle Mayor three or four blocks east.

Calanda is served by buses from Teruel and Alcañiz.

ALCAÑIZ

An oversized castle popping out of a flat, treeless landscape heralds your arrival in Alcañiz, the administrative centre for lower Aragón. Now a *parador*, the castle was for centuries the *aragonese* base of the Knights of Calatrava. A series of vivid, intricately detailed murals dating from the 14th century cover the walls of the **keep** (admission €4; ☽ 10am-1.30pm & 4-6pm, later in summer), which can be ascended for views.

The town unfolds in a web of narrow lanes around the skirts of the castle. Of equally exaggerated dimensions is the **Iglesia de Santa María La Mayor**, dwarfing Plaza de España with its huge baroque portal.

A **tourist office** (☽ 10am-2pm & 4-6pm except Sun afternoon) is adjacent to the Gothic Lonja (granary) on the plaza's west side.

Of a dozen lodgings, **Hostal Aragón** (☎ 978 87 07 17; Calle Espejo 3; s/d with bathroom €24/36) is an excellent, central choice – a tall, old house with sturdy balconies. **Hotel Guadalope** (☎ 978 83 07 50; Plaza España 8; s/d €27/52) is on the plaza, with one of the more popular cafés.

Up to four buses travel daily to/from Zaragoza, and two stop here en route between Teruel and Barcelona.

Basque Country, Navarra & La Rioja

This region of Spain has it all – one of Europe's premier wine regions, a green, mountainous interior, a rugged, beautiful coast and cosmopolitan cities of sophistication.

Wine lovers should make haste to La Rioja and then linger in its charming villages, sample the fruits of its countless bodegas (wineries), and revel in the tranquillity of its lush countryside of rolling hills and riverbank vistas. Those for whom fine food is a priority should look no further than the seaside city of San Sebastián, with the finest *pintxos* (tapas or bar food) in Spain and restaurants in the vanguard of the internationally renowned Basque *nouvelle cuisine*. Art appreciation takes on a whole new meaning in Bilbao, where the iconic and breathtaking Museo Guggenheim is merely one example of a city at the cutting edge of cultural life. The more active among you will love the opportunities to surf some of the most exhilarating breaks in Spain, hike in the quiet, rural splendour of the Pyrenees of Navarra, or run for your life during the (in)famous festivities at the running of the bulls in Pamplona.

In this part of Spain, it all comes with an intriguing twist. The Basque people have become one of Europe's most prominent yet least understood minorities. According to some theories, the Basque presence here predates even the earliest prehistoric invasions of Europe. The Basques have retained a language, and with it a separate identity, whose origin still puzzles linguists. And yet, in recent years, this ancient people has driven some of the most dynamic urban regeneration projects on the continent, transforming cities like Bilbao from industrial relics to lively cultural capitals.

It is without doubt that the Basque Country (País Vasco in Spanish), Navarra and La Rioja are among Spain's richest rewards for the visitor.

Throughout this chapter, hotel prices are for rooms with private bathroom unless stated otherwise, and restaurants are open daily for lunch and dinner.

BASQUE COUNTRY, NAVARRA & LA RIOJA

HIGHLIGHTS

- Savour the experience of **La Rioja** (p485) with some of the world's finest wines
- Linger in **San Sebastián** (p445) for its beauty, beaches, the best tapas bars in Spain and superb restaurants
- Explore Bilbao's spectacular and state-of-the-art **Museo Guggenheim** (p460)
- Keep alive the spirit of Hemingway in Pamplona, home of the world's best-known **encierro** (running of the bulls; p471)
- Get lost amid the lush alpine countryside of the **Navarran Pyrenees** (p479)

★ Bilbao   ★ San Sebastián

Pyrenees ★

Pamplona ★

La Rioja ★

AREA: 22,670 SQ KM	POP: 2,977,804	AVE SUMMER TEMP: HIGH 28°C, LOW 12°C

BASQUE COUNTRY, NAVARRA & LA RIOJA

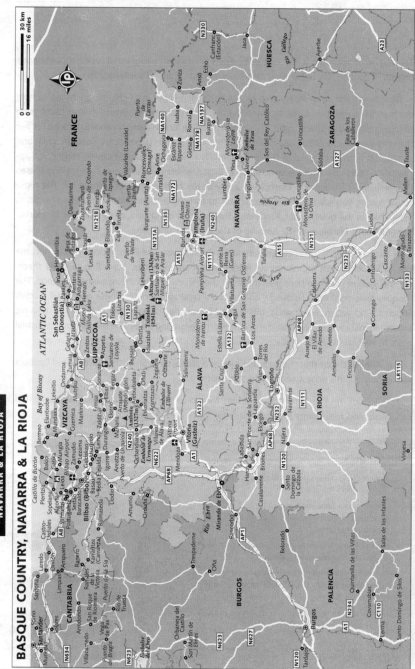

BASQUE COUNTRY

Although the Basque Country historically referred to four provinces of Spain (including Navarra) and three in southwestern France, the Comunidad Autónoma Vasca (CAV) now refers to the provinces of Guipúzcoa (Basque: Gipuzkoa), Álava (Basque: Araba) and Vizcaya (Basque: Bizkaia). In the Basque language, the Basque Country is known as Euskadi, a term coined by nationalists at the end of the 19th century, although some prefer the classic term Euskal Herria (Land of the Basque-speakers).

Throughout this guide Castilian names for towns have been used, but Basque names also appear with the name's first usage in the text.

History

No-one quite knows where the Basque people came from (they have no migration myth in their oral history), but their presence here is believed to predate even the earliest known migrations.

During the Middle Ages (1000–1450), the expanding Castilian crown gained sovereignty over Basque territories with considerable difficulty; Navarra constituted a separate kingdom until 1512. Even once they came within the Castilian orbit, Navarra and the three provinces extracted broad autonomy arrangements, known as the *fueros* (the ancient laws of the Basques), from Madrid. These were first repealed by Napoleon in the early 19th century. During the Carlist wars (see p38) many conservative Basques supported the reactionary Don Carlos. The colour red, associated with the Carlists, came to symbolise Basque assertions of separateness.

At the close of the Second Carlist War in 1876 all provinces except Navarra were stripped of their coveted *fueros*, thereby alienating the many Basques who had sided with liberal Madrid and fuelling the nascent Basque nationalism. Although the Basque Nationalist Party (Partido Nacionalista Vasco; PNV) was established in 1894, support was never uniform, as all Basque provinces included a considerable Castilian contingent.

When the Republican government in Madrid proposed the possibility of home rule (self-government) to the Basques in 1936, both Guipúzcoa and Vizcaya took up the offer. When the Spanish Civil War erupted, conservative rural Navarra and Álava supported Franco, while Vizcaya and Guipúzcoa sided with the Republicans, a decision they paid a high price for in the four decades that followed.

ETA & BASQUE NATIONALISM

In 1961 a small group of Basque separatists known as Euskadi Ta Askatasuna (ETA; the name stands for Basque Homeland and Freedom) carried out its first terrorist attack. Its goal was to carve out an independent Basque state from the Basque territories in northern Spain and southern France. Thus began a cycle of violence and repression that continues to this day, despite the granting of wide-ranging autonomy in the early 1980s and 1990s.

In the last 40 years ETA's grisly war has killed more than 800 people. The main targets have been Basque Partido Popular politicians and members of the Guardia Civil. The worst violence took place in the 1980s, ushered in by 118 deaths in 1980. In September 1998 ETA announced a 'unilateral and indefinite ceasefire'. It only lasted 14 months, foundering on the unwillingness of both sides to make major concessions. President Aznar's government alienated many Basques for its decision in June 2002 to outlaw Batasuna, the party widely considered to be ETA's political wing, and its refusal to even discuss proposals by the Basque regional government for greater autonomy. Relations reached their nadir in March 2004 when the government blamed ETA for the 11 March bombings.

Although calls for an independent homeland remain strong, precise figures are unknown and the majority of Basques who support independence would prefer to achieve it through peaceful and democratic means. Nationalist parties regularly gain about 70% of the Basque vote and the Partido Nacionalista Vasco (PNV) has ruled the Basque Country in coalition with other nationalist groupings since autonomy was granted.

Language

In the modern autonomous region of the Basque Country the *ikurriña* (Basque flag) flies everywhere, and pride in Basque identity has thankfully not only expressed itself in violence but also in language. This is one of Europe's oldest and most quixotic languages, with no known relationship to the Indo-European family of languages. Suppressed by Franco, Basque was subsequently recognised as one of Spain's official languages.

Although Franco's repression meant that many older Basques are unable to speak their native tongue, it has now become the hip language of choice (and resistance) among a growing number of young Basques, fuelling a dynamic cultural renaissance and a resurgence of cultural identity. There are now Basque-language radio and TV stations and newspapers. In Guipúzcoa province especially, you'll find that street signs are increasingly in both Castilian and Basque.

For more information on the Basque language, see p867.

Sport

The Basques indulge in an odd assortment of sports, ranging from grass-cutting and log-chopping to caber-tossing and tug-of-war. The most famous is *pelota vasca* (*jai-alai* in Basque), a form of handball played on a walled court known as a *frontón*. There's also a version involving the use of a *txistera,* a kind of hand-held basket that allows the ball to be slung with disconcerting velocity at the wall. You can often see local teams whacking away at the town *frontón,* especially in Vitoria. The traditional game, with teams of two players each, is played with the bare hand, but there are up to 20 variants of the sport, now played all over the world.

Cycling is also popular, as is football; the successful Athletico de Bilbao team is known for its policy of only signing Basque players.

Food & Drink

Basque cuisine is generally regarded as Spain's finest; if you can wangle your way into one of the private Basque gastronomic societies (which are traditionally all-male affairs and known as *txokos* in Basque), you'll certainly find yourself in foodie heaven.

San Sebastián has Spain's greatest tapas (often known as *pintxos* in the Basque Country; see p451) – just entering some bars is enough to get you salivating. Apart from beer and cider (see the boxed text Basque Cider House Rules, p455), the traditional drink of the region is a slightly tart but eminently drinkable young white wine called *txacoli.*

The central tenets of Basque gastronomy are deceptively simple: take the finest and freshest ingredients, interfere with them as little as possible and enjoy the result in convivial company. Seafood is the staple ingredient, although the region is also renowned for its high-quality beef. Some of the most famous dishes include *bacalao al pil pil* (salt cod cooked with garlic and chillies), *merluza a la vasca* (hake in green sauce), *chipirones en su tinta* (squid cooked in its own ink) and *chuletas de buey* (enormous beef chops), but there are hundreds more. Other important, distinctive ingredients include mushrooms, *pimientos* (red peppers or capsicum), *gulas* (tiny baby eels) and *alubias* (black beans).

Led by such master-chefs as Juan Mari Arzak and Pedro Subijana, the Basque Country's contribution to *nouvelle cuisine*

SIGNS IN BASQUE

Basque words that commonly appear on signs include:

Basque	English	Spanish
AIREPORTUA	airport	*aeropuerto*
ERDIA	centre	*centro*
ERDIALDEA	city centre	*centro de la ciudad*
JATETXEA	restaurant	*restaurante*
KALEA	street	*calle*
KALE NAGUSIA	main street	*calle mayor*
KOMUNA/K	toilet/s	*servicios*
KONTUZ!	caution/beware!	*¡atención!*
NEKAZAL	agrotourism homes	*casa rural*
ONGI ETORRI	welcome	*bienvenido*
TURISMOA/TURISMO	tourism	*turismo*
TURISMO BULEGO	tourist office	*oficina de turismo*

has become internationally famous with what is commonly called the *nueva cocina vasca*, a world-class 'school' of innovation.

An essential companion for food lovers should be the excellent *Guide to Basque Cuisine* (free), which details the regional specialities throughout the Basque Country. It's available from tourist offices across the region.

SAN SEBASTIÁN

pop 178,534

Forming a half-moon around the beautiful Bahía de La Concha, San Sebastián (Basque: Donostia) is at once the most Basque of Basque cities and a captivating crossroads. A beautiful and sophisticated seaside resort surrounded by the green hills of Guipúzcoa province, San Sebastián's stunning setting is supplemented by a vibe that's hard to resist.

With its graceful avenues and chic inhabitants, you may be forgiven for thinking you've arrived in an elegant vestige of the *belle époque*. Scratch the surface though, and you'll soon discover that there's nothing old hat about the action in San Sebastián's Parte Vieja (Old Town), which boasts possibly the greatest concentration of bars per square metre in Spain. Old and new similarly co-exist in the city's world-famous cuisine.

History

Although the earliest written evidence of settlement here dates from 1014, San Sebastián was for centuries little more than a fishing village. By 1174 San Sebastián was granted self-governing status by the kingdom of Navarra for whom the bay was their principal outlet to the sea. Whale and cod fishing – historical staples of Basque cooking – were the primary industries, along with a prosperous role in the export of Castilian products to European ports, later benefiting from burgeoning commerce with the Americas. In the 18th century San Sebastián yielded twice to French invaders, but disaster came with the Peninsular War, during which Anglo-Portuguese forces razed the city in 1813 after wresting it from French hands. After the fire, the Parte Vieja was built and the city you see today is largely a product of the years following the withdrawal of Napoleon's troops from Spain. In the 19th century San Sebastián became a popular summer retreat for the Spanish royal family and aristocracy.

Orientation

San Sebastián has three main centres of activity. The busy and modern centre surrounds the Catedral del Buen Pastor, while the heart of San Sebastián beats in the Parte Vieja, squeezed below Monte Urgull Parque on the eastern spur of the superb Bahía de la Concha. Bars, restaurants and *hostales* (budget hotels) are bunched up in this narrow grid of car-free lanes. The third area is Gros, east across the Río Urumea, which also has a sprinkling of eating and accommodation options, not to mention a good beach, and is home to the Renfe train station. The main bus station is about 1km south of the cathedral.

Information

BOOKSHOPS

Newsstands on Avenida de la Libertad stock the previous day's issue of many foreign newspapers.

Caxton English Bookshop (☎ 943 31 20 95; Paseo de Ondarreta 10; ☺ 10am-1pm & 3.30-7.30pm Mon-Fri, 10am-1pm Sat) Located not far from the funicular railway and a great place to seek out reading matter.

Librería Graphos (☎ 943 42 63 77; Alameda del Blvd at Calle Mayor; ☺ 10am-1.30pm & 4-7.30pm Mon-Fri, 10am-2pm Sat) Excellent for travel books and maps, with a good stock of Lonely Planet guidebooks.

EMERGENCY

Medical Emergency ☎ 112
Policía Nacional ☎ 091

INTERNET ACCESS

Donosti-Net (☎ 943 42 94 97; Calle de Narrica 3; per 10 min/hr €0.90/3.30; ☺ 9am-11pm) The best place for Internet access. Also doubles as a super-savvy travellers' information centre, offering everything from a left-luggage service to money transfers and car hire.

Click in D@ House (Calle de San Martín 41; per 1/6 hr €3/6; ☺ 9.30am-2pm & 4-9.30pm Mon-Sat, 10.30am-2pm & 4-9.30pm Sun)

Zarranet (Calle San Lorenzo 6; per hr €3; ☺ 10am-10pm Mon-Sat, 4-10pm Sat)

LAUNDRY

Wash'n Dry (☎ 943 29 31 50; Calle de Iparragirre 6; ☺ 8am-10pm) Just across the river in the Gros district, this is one of the best self-service laundries in Spain, primarily because the Australian owner, Amaia, runs the place like a defacto tourist office. The full wash-and-dry treatment for an 8kg load costs €10, the left-luggage service costs €3 per day, and the book exchange and the benefits of local knowledge come free.

SAN SEBASTIÁN

A

INFORMATION
Casa de Socorro	1 F4
Caxton English Bookshop	2 A5
Centro de Atracción y Turismo	3 F3
Click in D@ House	4 E5
Donosti-Net	5 D5
Librería Graphos	6 C5
Main Post Office	7 G4
Wash'n Dry	8 H4
Zarranet	9 D4

SIGHTS & ACTIVITIES (pp448–50)
Aquarium	10 D3
Iglesia de San Vicente	11 D4
Iglesia de Santa María del Coro	12 E3
Museo de San Telmo	13 E3
Museo Naval	14 E3
Peine de Vientos	15 B4
Pukas	16 H3
Pukas	17 C5

SLEEPING (pp450–1)
Albergue Ondarreta	18 A5
Hostal Alemana	19 E5
Hostal La Concha	20 E5
Hotel de Londres e Inglaterra	21 E5
Pensión Aida	22 H4
Pensión Amaiur Ostatua	23 C4

B

Pensión Aussie	24 C4
Pensión Donostiarra	25 F5
Pensión Edorta	26 E3
Pensión Itxasoa	27 F3
Pensión Kursaal	28 G3
Pensión La Perla	29 F5
Pensión Larrea	30 D4
Pensión Loinaz	31 D5
Pensión San Lorenzo	32 D4
Pensión San Martin	33 F5
Pensión Urkia	34 F5

EATING (pp451–2)
Alotza Jatetxea	35 D4
Arraitxiki	36 E3
Bar Aloña Berri	37 H3
Bar Aralar	38 C4
Bar Bergara	39 H3
Bar Ganbara	40 C4
Bar La Cepa	41 D4
Bar Txepetxa	42 D4
Bar-Patio de Ramuntxo	43 G3
Café Kursaal	44 G3
Caravanserai	45 F5
Casa Urbano	46 C4
Casa Valles	47 F6
Izkiña	48 D4
Juantxo Taberna	49 D5

C

Koskol	50 D4
La Rampa	51 D3
La Zurri	52 G3
Martinez	53 D4
Plaza Café	54 F5
Restaurante Pollitena	55 F5
Restaurante Portaletas	56 C4
Restaurantes Mariñela & Sebastián	57 E3
Zeruko	58 D4

D

ENTERTAINMENT (pp452–3)
Altxerri Jazz Bar	59 F3
Bar Akerbeltz	60 E3
Bar Urbia	61 C4
Be Bop	62 F3
Bibbido	63 D4
Cervecería Garagar	64 D5
El Blue	(see 64)
Hotel Niza	65 E5
Molly Malone's	66 E5
Ostertz	67 E3
Sagardotegia Itxaropena	68 C5
Soho	69 E5
Tas Tas	70 C5
Truk	71 C4
Udaberri-berri	72 F5
Zuripot	73 F5

Monte Igueldo

Faro de Igeldo

Paseo del Faro

To Akelarre (2km)

Mar Cantábrico (Kantauri Itsasoa)

Punta Torrepea

Isla de Santa Clara

Plaza de la Trinidad

Plaza de la Constitución

C de 31 de Agosto
C Juan de Bilbao
C de Narrica
C del Puerto
C Mayor
Calle de San Vicente
Calle de Iñigo
Calle de la Pescadería
Calle de San Juan
Calle de San Lorenzo
Calle de Fermín Calbetón
C de Esterlines
C de San Jerónimo
Plaza Sarriegui
Calle de Embeltrán
Alameda del Boulevard

0   100 m
0   0.1 miles

Avenida de Satrústegui
Paseo de Igueldo

Playa de Ondarreta

Ondarreta

Calle de Brunet
Calle de Pamplona

To Camping Igueldo (1km)

Paseo de Ondarreta
Calle de Vitoria-Gasteiz
Avenida de Tolosa
Calle de Zumalkárregi

Antiguo

Calle de Matía

Plaza de Alfonso XIII

Pico del Loro

Playa de la Concha

Paseo de la Concha
Paseo de Miraconcha

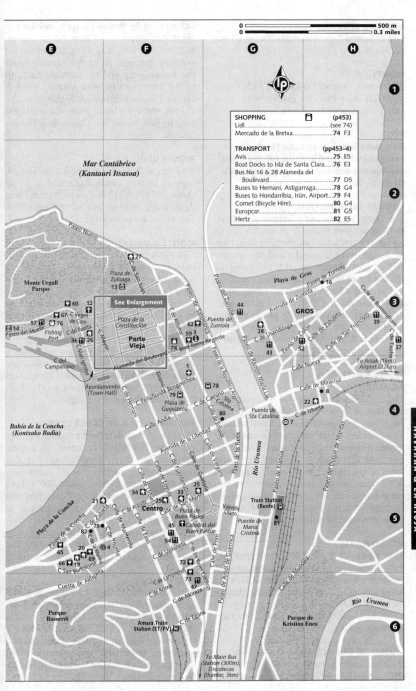

0   500 m
0   0.3 miles

*Mar Cantábrico
(Kantauri Itsasoa)*

Paseo Nuevo

Plaza de San Juan

Plaza de
Zuloaga

See Enlargement

Monte Urgull
Parque

Plaza de la
Constitución

**Parte
Vieja**

C Virgen
de Coro

Fishing
Port

Paseo del Muelle

C del Puerto

Mari Jantzat

Alameda del Boulevard

C del
Campanario

Ayuntamiento
(Town Hall)

*Bahía de la Concha
(Kontxako Badia)*

C de Hernani

C Peñaflorida Bengoechea

Plaza de
Guipúzcoa

Calle Andía

Playa de la Concha

Avenida de la Libertad

Centro

Plaza de
Buen Pastor

Catedral del
Buen Pastor

C de Urdaneta

C de Larramendi

Cuesta de Aldapeta

C San Bartolomé

Parque
Basoerdi

Amara Train
Station (ET/FV)

C de Egaña

To Main Bus
Station (300m);
Discotecas
(Ilumbe; 3km)

Playa de Gros

Paseo de Zurriola

GROS

Avenida de Zurriola

Puente de
Zurriola

Blvd Reina Regente

Paseo de la República Argentina

Calle Nueva

Puente de
Sta Catalina

C de Iztueta

Paseo de Ramón María Lili

Río Urumea

Paseo de Francia

Paseo del Dique de Mandas

Train Station
(Renfe)

Valentín
Olano

Puente de
María
Cristina

Paseo de Árbol de Guernica

Calle de Mundáiz

Parque de
Kristina Enea

Río Urumea

To Arzak (1km);
Airport (22km)

Calle de Miracruz

**BASQUE COUNTRY,
NAVARRA & LA RIOJA**

MEDICAL SERVICES
Casa de Socorro (Calle Peñaflorida Bengoechea 4) Free medical care.

MONEY
There are plenty of banks with ATMs scattered all over the city centre, with most along Avenida de la Libertad.

POST
Main post office (Paseo de Francia) This office may be moving back to its original location on Calle de Urdaneta once restoration works have been completed, so check at the tourist office.

TOURIST INFORMATION
The **Centro de Atracción y Turismo** (CAT; ☎ 943 48 11 66; Blvd Reina Regente 3; ☺ 8am-8pm Mon-Sat Jun-Sep, 9am-2pm & 3.30-7pm Mon-Sat Oct-May, 10am-2pm Sun year-round) is friendly and offers comprehensive information on the city and the remainder of the Basque country.

Two **tourist kiosks** (☺ 9am-9pm Jun-Sep) operate at the train and bus stations in summer.

A couple of good private places offering information for travellers include **Donosti-Net** (see Internet Access p445) and **Wash 'n Dry** (see Laundry p445).

Sights & Activities
AQUARIUM
The city's **aquarium** (☎ 943 44 00 99; www.aquariumss .com; Paseo del Muelle 34; adult/student €9/6; ☺ 10am-9pm Jul-Aug, 10am-8pm Apr-Jun & Sep, 10am-7pm Mon-Fri & 11am-8pm Sat & Sun Oct-Mar) houses a reasonable museum about the Bay of Biscay and numerous tanks that re-create the habitats of hundreds of species of tropical fish. The highlight is the glass underwater tunnel where you come face to face with rays and sharks. Shark feedings (if that's your thing) take place at 11am and 4pm Monday to Friday.

MUSEO NAVAL
This **museum** (☎ 943 43 00 51; www.gipuzkoa.net /kultura/untzimuseoa; Paseo del Muelle 24; admission €1.20, free Thu; ☺ 10am-1.30pm & 4-7.30pm Tue-Sat, 11am-2pm Sun) offers an in-depth look into the Basque seafaring tradition, but will be best appreciated by those with at least basic Spanish-language skills.

MUSEO DE SAN TELMO
Housed in a former 16th-century monastery with an attractive cloister, this **museum**

(☎ 943 42 49 70; Plaza de Zuloaga 1; admission free; ☺ 10.30am-1.30pm & 4-7.30pm Tue-Sat Sep-Jun, 10.30am-8.30pm Mon-Sat Jul & Aug, 10.30am-2pm Sun year-round) features paintings ranging from the Renaissance and the baroque through to the 19th century, with a heavy emphasis on Basque painters. A highlight is the chapel, whose walls are decorated with frescoes by José María Sert chronicling Basque history.

MONTE URGULL
You can walk to the top of Monte Urgull, topped by low castle walls and a grand statue of Christ, by taking a path from Plaza de Zuloaga or from behind the aquarium. The views are wonderful.

MONTE IGUELDO
The views from the summit of Monte Igueldo, just west of town, are better still – a breathtaking aerial panorama of the Bahía de la Concha and the surrounding coastline and mountains of Guipúzcoa. The best way to get there is via the old-world **funicular railway** (€1.80 return; ☺ 10am-8pm Sep-Jun, 10am-10pm Jul & Aug) to the **Parque de Atracciones** (amusement park; ☎ 943 21 02 11; ☺ 11am-6pm Mon-Tue & Thu-Fri, 11am-8pm Sat & Sun). The best views are from the **torreón** (tower; admission €1.80) right on the summit, which also has a good collection of old photos of the region.

BEACHES & ISLA DE SANTA CLARA
The placid **Playa de la Concha** and its westerly extension, the **Playa de Ondarreta**, are among the best city beaches in Europe. For this reason, both get rather crowded in summer. The Isla de Santa Clara, about 700m from the beach, is accessible by boats that run to the island every half-hour from June to September (€2).

The **Playa de Gros** (Playa de la Zurriola), east of the Río Urumea, is popular (though less crowded) with both swimmers and surfers.

SURFING
Surf bums should drop by **Pukas** (☎ 943 542 72 28; shop@pukassurf.com; Calle Mayor 5; ☺ 10am-1.30pm & 4-8pm Mon-Sat), which rents surfboards (€20 per day), as well as wetsuits, boogie boards and fins. In summer it also offers a week-long beginners' surfing course (€60) from its seasonal surf club, **Pukas** (☎ 943 32 00 68; Paseo de Zurriola; ☺ 10am-7.30pm Mon-Sat Jun-Oct).

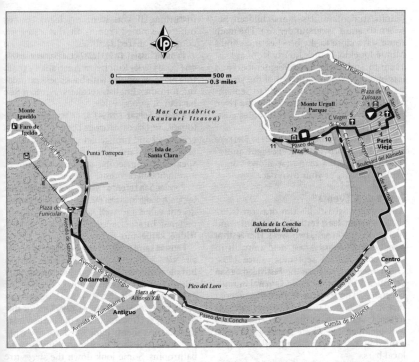

Walking Tour

San Sebastián is a wonderful city to explore on foot and the following itinerary could easily take up to four hours.

Begin in the northeastern corner of the wonderful **Parte Vieja** at the **Museo de San Telmo** (**1**; p449). Not far away is the 16th-century **Iglesia de San Vicente** (**2**; Calle de San Vicente; 9am-1pm & 6.30-8pm), the city's oldest standing church. Opposite the church is the entrance to **Calle Juan de Bilbao** (**3**), which has the highest concentration of bars popular among ETA sympathizers; it should probably be avoided, although is usually fine during the day. An alternative route to the east takes you across the colonnaded **Plaza de la Constitución** (**4**). After that, wander at will, stopping off for a *pintxo* and a glass of cider or *txakoli* from time to time. Don't miss the **Iglesia de Santa María del Coro** (**5**; Calle Mayor; 8am-2pm & 4-8pm), which stands out for its churrigueresque façade.

From the Parte Vieja, make your way to the waterfront promenade overlooking the supremely beautiful **Playa de la Concha** (**6**), San Sebastián's world-famous arc of splendid sand. A pleasant walk west will bring you to the **Playa de Ondarreta** (**7**). From there, take the **funicular** up **Monte Igueldo** (**8**; p448) for breathtaking vistas. Upon your return to sea level, follow the beach around to its western headland to see Eduardo Chillida's intriguing abstract sculpture **Peine de Vientos** (**9**; Wind Combs), best appreciated on stormy days when waves lash the iron sculpture and a haunting wind whistles through subterranean blowholes.

From there, follow the arc of the bay all the way around to the gritty **fishing port** (**10**), with its **aquarium** (**11**; p448), **Museo Naval** (**12**; p448) and exceptional views en route, especially at sunset. After that, you'll be hungry and there's no better place in Spain to satisfy that hunger than by returning to the Parte Vieja.

Tours

Donosti Tour is a one-day bus tour that allows you to hop on and off as often as you wish. Tickets, which include headphones for commentary in your choice of language, are sold on the bus and cost €9/8/4/free

BASQUE COUNTRY, NAVARRA & LA RIOJA

(adults/students and seniors/children between six and 12 years/under six). The main route stays close to the beaches and climbs Monte Igueldo. It runs hourly from at least 11am to 8pm from July to September, and less often throughout the rest of the year. A second route operates from July to September, heading further inland along the river. A combined ticket for the two routes costs €10/9/5/free.

The **CAT tourist office** (☎ 943 48 11 66; Blvd Reina Regente 3) also provides an excellent audioguide (€10) with a map that allows you to explore the city at your own pace.

Festivals & Events

Among San Sebastián's top drawcards are the **International Jazz Festival**, held in July, and the world-renowned, two-week **Film Festival** (www.sansebastianfestival.ya.com), held annually in the second half of September since 1957. Other major fiestas are the **Festividad de San Sebastián** on 20 January and **Carnaval** in mid-February. The **Regatta de Traineras**, a boat race in which local teams of rowers race out to sea, takes place on the first two Sundays in September. The whole shebang is accompanied by raucous drinking and betting in local bars.

Sleeping

Accommodation in San Sebastián is generally excellent, but prices rise considerably in July and August (at some places from May to September), a time when advance reservations are highly recommended. High season prices follow.

BUDGET
Camping & Hostels

Camping Igueldo (☎ 943 21 45 02; Paseo del Padra Orkolaga 69; per person/car with light, water & electricity €12/23.80) The nearest camping ground is west of the city, served by bus No 16 from Alameda del Blvd (€0.80).

Albergue Ondarreta (☎ 943 31 02 68; odarreta@ donostia.org; Paseo de Igueldo 25; dm under/over 25 incl breakfast €14.40/16) San Sebastián's HI hostel is not far from Playa de Ondarreta. Its midnight curfew extends to 2am on weekends.

Hostales & Pensiones

The Parte Vieja is almost as replete with *pensiones* (small private hotels) as it is with bars – great for stumbling home, but

disturbing if you want to sleep. Unless otherwise noted, rooms in this category come with shared facilities.

Pensión Aussie (☎ 943 42 28 74; Calle San Jerónimo 23; dm €15, s/d €18/30) Run by an Australian expat, this place is popular with backpackers looking for other English speakers. For San Sebastián, it's good value.

Pensión Loinaz (☎ 943 42 67 14; pensionloinaz@ telefonica.net; Calle de San Lorenzo 17; d €45; 💻) Modern, small and immaculate, Pensión Loinaz is very pleasant, with friendly English-speaking proprietors, spotless bathrooms and light-filled rooms.

Pensión San Lorenzo (☎ 943 42 55 16; Calle de San Lorenzo 2; d with bathroom €48; 💻) Its rooms are decent value and well kept. Assets include metered Internet access in the hall, and a fridge, kettle and TV in each room.

Pensión Larrea (☎ 943 42 26 94; Calle de Narrica 21; s/d €24/45) Also recommended. Quite simple but pleasant, with polished floorboards and (almost) soundproof windows.

Pensión La Perla (☎ 943 42 81 23; www.pension laperla.com; Calle de Loyola 10; s/d €30/45) One of the best budget choices outside the Parte Vieja, this has excellent, light-filled rooms with balconies, polished floorboards and private bathrooms. Some look down the street towards the cathedral. The owner is friendly, but takes no nonsense from her guests.

Pensión Urkia (☎ 943 42 44 36; www.pensionurkia .com; Calle de Urbieta 12; s/d €30/45) Run by the sister of La Perla's proprietor, the nearby Pensión Urkia is similarly good value.

MID-RANGE

Rooms in this category all have private bathrooms and TV.

Pensión Edorta (☎ 943 42 37 73; www.pension edorta.com; Calle del Puerto 15; s/d €50/80; 💻) Pensión Edorta is excellent. Recently opened, its rooms are filled with character and charmingly decorated. It's also a friendly place and ideal for those who don't wish to stray too far from the Parte Vieja.

Pensión Itxasoa (☎ 943 42 01 32; itxasoa@pension esconencanto.com; Calle de San Juan, 14; s/d €45.80/65.30) Just beyond the Parte Vieja, this place has attractive rooms, many of which come with great views over Playa de la Gros. Highly recommended.

Pensión Aida (☎ 943 32 78 00; aida@pensiones conencanto.com; Calle de Iztueta 9; s/d €45.80/65.30) Away (but just a 10-minute walk) from the noise of the Parte Vieja, Pensión Aida has lovely renovated rooms that are spacious, excellent value and tastefully decorated.

Pensión Kursaal (☎ 943 29 26 66; kursaal@pension esconencanto.com; Calle de Peña y Goñi, 2; s/d €45.80/65.30) A good choice, just a stone's throw from the Parte Vieja, this place has well-kept, light-filled rooms.

Hostal La Concha (☎ 943 45 03 89; www.hostal laconcha.com; Calle de San Martín 51; d €55; ☐) This is a very good option. The rooms at this friendly, well-run place aren't huge, but they're nicely decorated, very comfortable, and come with minibar and music system. The location, close to Playa de la Concha, is also a winner.

Hostal Alemana (☎ 943 46 25 44; www.hostal alemana.com; Calle de San Martín 53; s/d from €48/60; ☐) An excellent choice, lovingly decorated with great attention to detail, not to mention spacious, semi-luxurious and well-equipped rooms (if you have your own computer, high-speed Internet connection is free). It also serves a buffet breakfast for €4.75.

Pensión San Martín (☎ 943 42 87 14; Calle de San Martín 10; s/d €43/52.80) This tiny place has just six squeaky-clean, good-sized doubles, all with TV, and some come with a few nice touches. The location is good: central but with less noise than some.

Pensión Donostiarra (☎ 943 42 61 67; www.pension donostiarra.com; Calle de San Martín 6; s/d €52/80) Close to the cathedral, this place has good rooms with polished floorboards and a few nice period touches.

TOP END

Hotel de Londres e Inglaterra (☎ 943 44 07 70; reservas@hlondres.com; Calle de Zubieta 2; s/d with sea view €169/202, without sea view €143/175) Ask any

---

AUTHOR'S CHOICE

Pensión Amaiur Ostatua (☎ 943 42 96 54; www.pensionamaiur.com; Calle de 31 de Agosto 44; s/d €30/50; ☐) Set in one of the city's oldest buildings, this charming place is as pretty as a picture. Rooms are wonderfully Bohemian, with period furnishings and loads of character. The bathrooms are shared, but plentiful and as well cared for as the rooms. The owners are friendly, there's a great kitchen and Internet access, and credit cards are accepted. Outstanding value.

Spaniard for their favourite hotel in Spain and many will choose this hotel. Oozing old-world charm and with a wonderful waterfront location, this is undoubtedly San Sebastián's premier address.

Hotel Niza (☎ 943 42 66 63; www.hotelniza.com; Calle de Zubieta 56; s/d €94/118) This three-star hotel is an excellent choice by the water. The rooms are more modern than those at Hotel Londres, but it's a charming, family-run place. Ask for a room facing the sea as they cost no extra. There are some singles without views for €54, but they're still very good value.

Eating

San Sebastián has a growing reputation as a world leader in gastronomic innovation of the highest order – it has the highest number of *Michelin* stars of any city in Spain. Whether it's Spain's finest restaurant, or more varieties of the humble *pintxo* than you thought possible, San Sebastián is Spain's culinary capital.

SNACKS

Juantxo Taberna (Calle de Embeltrán 6; bocadillos from €3) Famous for its cheap, super-sized *bocadillos* (filled rolls) this *taberna* (tavern) also has some good *pintxos*. It's the sort of place where suits, construction workers and teens all rub shoulders.

Caravanserai (☎ 943 47 54 18; Calle San Bartolomé 1; bocadillos from €2.50, meals from €7) Just west of the cathedral, this trendy, buzzy place has stylish North African-inspired décor and an extensive menu, which runs the gamut from burgers and sandwiches to pasta.

Plaza Café (☎ 943 44 57 12; Plaza del Buen Pastor, 14; breakfast €2-5) This pleasant place is popular with locals for a mid-morning breakfast. It also has a *menú del día* (daily set meal available at lunchtime) in French and English.

TAPAS BARS

San Sebastián is *pintxo* heaven. The choice of venues seems limitless and it's here that the art of the bar snack has been refined to perfection, with tray after tray of mouth-watering goodies lining the bars. Tapas generally cost €1 to €4, depending on their size and quality. Heated *pintxos* usually cost more than the cold, ready-to-eat variety.

You'll quickly find your personal favourite, but here are a few places to get you started.

Bar Txepetxa (Calle de la Pescadería 5) Txepetxa has won numerous awards for its *anchoa* (anchovy) *pintxos*, listed on a board behind the bar and made to order.

Bar Aralar (Calle del Puerto 10) Produces good *pintxos*, which are very popular with French visitors.

Bar La Cepa (Calle de 31 de Agosto 7) With wooden tables and hams hanging from the ceiling, La Cepa deals up some of the best *jamón jabugo* (top-quality ham) in town.

Martinez (Calle de 31 de Agosto 11) A very popular choice, it can be hard to push your way to the bar but well worth the wait. When we were there, it was doing great things with zucchini and crab.

Bar Ganbara (Calle de San Jeronimo 24) A small bar that's a local favourite with high quality offerings.

Casa Valles (Calle de los Reyes Católicos 10) South of the cathedral, this is an unpretentious place where *pintxos*, *raciones* (meal-sized tapas) and substantial *bocadillos* are consumed at communal tables.

Across the river in Gros are some outstanding choices, including **Bar Bergara** (Calle de Bermingham s/n), **Bar Aloña Berri** (Calle de Bermingham 24) and **Bar-Patio de Ramuntxo** (Calle de Peña y Goñi 10); the latter has won numerous nationwide awards for its *pintxos*.

RESTAURANTS

Casa Urbano (☎ 943 42 04 34; Calle de 31 de Agosto 17; mains around €15, menú €19) An upmarket choice, this place is an old favourite, with a well-established reputation for quality seafood.

Restaurante Portaletas (☎ 943 42 42 72; Calle del Puerto 8; mains €10) A popular place with locals, dining takes place beneath heavy timber beams and the food is consistently good.

Restaurante Pollitena (Calle de San Jeronimo 3) Pollitena is notable for its *menú de degustación* (tasting menú; €41.50 for two), which is a great way to sample local specialities at a reasonable price.

Arraitxiki (☎ 943 43 13 02; Calle del Campanario 3; mains €10-15) Vegetarians are also invited to the San Sebastián feast. This cool place has quality food and creative cooking.

La Zurri (☎ 943 29 38 86; Calle de Zabaleta 9; menú €7.30) In Gros, La Zurri is great value, with Basque home cooking, a friendly owner and a stream of locals (always a good sign in this discerning food city). You'll sometimes have to queue for lunch, but it's worth the wait.

AUTHOR'S CHOICE

Arzak (☎ 943 27 84 65; www.arzak.es; Avenida Alcalde Jose Elosegui 273; meals €80-100) With three *Michelin* stars, Arzak is regarded by some as the best restaurant in Spain, due to the acclaimed chef Juan Mari Arzak, who cooks up his world-renowned Basque nouvelle cuisine. Reservations are obligatory.

Akelarre (☎ 943 31 12 09; www.akelarre.net; Paseo del Padre Orcolaga 56; menú €88) Claimed by some locals to be Arzak's equal, the two-starred chef, Pedro Subijana, offers similarly inventive and high-class Basque nouvelle cuisine. The dining room also has superb views over the Cantabrian Sea. Akelarre is about 2km west along the coast from Monte Igueldo, just past the village of Igueldo.

Café Kursaal (☎ 943 00 31 62; Paseo del Zurriola 1; menú €13, mains €18-30) Located in the striking, modern Kursaal building that overlooks Playa de la Gros, the café of this expensive restaurant has creative dishes that are available in the *menú del día*, which is a bargain.

For seafood by the sea, a handful of places have set up by the fishing harbour. Open from March until September, they include the following:

Restaurante Mariñela (☎ 943 42 73 83; Paseo del Muelle; mains €9-15)

Restaurante Sebastián (☎ 943 42 58 62; Paseo del Muelle; mains €9-15)

La Rampa (☎ 943 42 16 52; Paseo del Muelle; mains €12-22; ◷ closed Tue night & Wed)

In the Parte Vieja, **Izkiña** (☎ 943 42 25 62; Calle de Fermín Calbetón 4) and **Alotza Jatetxea** (☎ 943 42 07 82; Calle de Fermín Calbetón 7), across the street, both have consistently good *menús* (around €12), as well as respectable *pintxos* selections.

For large portions, relatively simple home cooking and liberal servings of wine, try **Zeruko** (Calle de la Pescadería 10; lunch menú €8, dinner menú €12) and **Koskol** (Calle de Iñigo 5; lunch €8); the latter is a tiny, low-key place that feels a bit like your *abuela's* (grandmother's) kitchen.

Entertainment
BARS & DISCOTECAS
San Sebastián has three main areas for bar activity. Nights usually start in the Parte Vieja, then move on to the area near the

corner of Calle de los Reyes Católicos and Calle de Larramendi around midnight or 1am. By *madrugada* (early morning) most of those who intend to last the distance have headed south to the Illumbe area where there are loads of *discotecas* that keep going until the break of dawn.

Walk around the Parte Vieja on a Friday and Saturday night and you'll soon discover that the old town is crawling with all sorts of bars and plenty of people to occupy them. In fact, the area comes alive from about 8pm virtually every night of the week, with Calle de la Pescadería and Calle de Fermín Calbetón two of the busier streets. You could easily take your pick, but the following should get you going:

Altxerri Jazz Bar (Calle Reina Regente 2) A super cool jazz bar.

Bar Akerbeltz (Calle Virgen de Coro 10) Tiny but utterly hip hang-out perfect for a *zurito* (small beer) to kick off the evening.

Bar Urbia (Calle del Puerto 7) Thudding dance bar that attracts a mixed crowd.

Be Bop (Paseo de Salamanca 3) Very cool jazz joint that's packed until dawn.

Bibbibo (Plaza Sarriegi 8) Always packed to the doors and loads of energy.

Cervecería Garagar (Alameda del Blvd 22; ⏳ till 4am) Irish pub-cum-Austrian beer cellar with Guinness on tap and some dark, inviting booths. Upstairs, open till dawn, is El Blue, a cool, laid-back techno hang-out with inhouse DJ.

Ostertz (Paseo del Muelle s/n) Great spot for a late-afternoon beer.

Sagardotegia Itxaropena (Calle de Embeltrán 16) Ideal if you need a swig of cider.

Tas Tas (Calle de Fermin Calbetón 35) A buzzy place where you wonder how the neighbours sleep.

Truk (Calle del Puerto 2) An infectious, tightly packed place.

The following places are located around Calle de los Reyes Católicos:

Molly Malones (Calle de San Martín 55) Great Irish bar that's popular with students.

Soho (Calle de San Martín 49) Funky music and décor attracting a crowd that doesn't watch the clock.

Udaberri-berri (Calle de Larramendi) A cool ground-floor bar, with a somewhat more boisterous scene downstairs.

Ziripot (Calle de Larramendi 9) Small and smoky, with a distinctly anarchistic vibe.

Shopping

If you want to stock up to make your own meals, go where the locals go: the underground Mercado de la Bretxa in the Parte Vieja, which also has a cheap Lidl supermarket open until 9pm.

Getting There & Away
AIR
The city's **airport** (☎ 943 64 12 67) is 22km out of town, near Hondarribia. There are regular flights to Madrid and occasional charters to major European cities.

BICYCLE
You can rent bicycles and mountain bikes at **Comet** (☎ 943 42 23 51; Avenida de la Libertad 6; per day/week €18/84).

BUS
The main bus station, a 20-minute walk south of the Parte Vieja, is between Plaza de Pío XII and the river. Local bus No 28 connects the bus station with the city centre.

Continental Auto (☎ 943 46 9074) buses travel to Madrid up to 12 times daily (€25.84, 5¾ hours), with 10 going via Vitoria (€6.35, 1½ hours) and seven via Burgos (€12.59, 3½ hours).

La Roncalesa (☎ 943 46 10 64) has up to 10 buses daily to Pamplona (€6.10, one hour).

PESA (☎ 902 10 12 10) runs half-hourly services to Bilbao along the A8 *autopista* (tollway) from 6.30am to 10pm (€8, one hour). It also sends a few buses to Durango (€2.30), Elorrio (€2.65) and Oñati (€4.30), plus twice-daily buses to Hendaye (€10.40), St Jean de Luz (€12.55) Biarritz (€15) and Bayonne (€16) in France.

Interbus services to Hondarribia (€1.45), Irún and the airport depart from Plaza de Guipúzcoa; bus Nos A1 and G1 travel to Hernani and Astigarraga (€0.80) from the stop on Calle de Echaide.

CAR & MOTORCYCLE
The A8 *autopista* heads to Bilbao in the west and into France (where it becomes the A63) to the east. You can avoid the toll on the virtually parallel N634. The main route south is the A1, which runs to Madrid via Vitoria.

Car Hire
Several major car-hire companies are represented by agencies in San Sebastián, including **Avis** (☎ 943 46 30 13; Calle del Triunfo 2), **Europcar** (☎ 943 32 23 04) in the Renfe train station and **Hertz** (☎ 943 46 10 84; Calle de Zubieta 5). A good

place to ask for the best deal is the Internet facility **Donosti-Net** (☎ 943 42 94 97; Calle de Narrica 3; ⌚ 9am-11pm).

TRAIN

The main Renfe train station is just across the Río Urumea on Paseo de Francia, on a line linking Paris to Madrid. There are seven services daily to Madrid (€32, six hours) and two to Barcelona (from €33.50, eight hours).

There's only one direct train to Paris, but there are plenty more from the French border town of Hendaye (€1.25, 35 minutes), which is served by the private company **Eusko Tren/Ferrocarril Vasco** (ET/FV; ☎ 902 54 32 10) on a railway line nicknamed 'El Topo' ('the Mole'). Trains depart every half-hour from Amara train station, about 1km south of the city centre, and also stop in Pasajes (€0.90, 12 minutes) and Irún (€1.15, 25 minutes). Another ET/FV railway line heads west to Bilbao (€5.70, 2¾ hours, hourly) via Zarautz, Zumaia and Durango.

EAST OF SAN SEBASTIÁN

Pasajes
pop 16,145

Pasajes (Basque: Pasaia), where Río Oiartzun empties into the Atlantic, is the largest port in the province of Guipúzcoa. While the new part of town is asphyxiated by a clot of highway bypasses, the Pasai de San Juan maintains a great degree of charm. Victor Hugo spent the summer of 1843 here and you can still see the house where he stayed at Calle de San Juan 63. The single street and the area immediately around the central square are lined with pretty houses and colourful balconies; it's accessible by road via the town of Lezo. Pasajes is on the El Topo railway line from San Sebastián (€0.80, 12 minutes, every half-hour) and is also served by regular buses from San Sebastián.

Irún
pop 57,133

A more nondescript introduction to Spain you could hardly get; you're better off continuing to Hondarribia or San Sebastián.

GETTING THERE & AWAY

The half-hourly El Topo train runs to Hendaye (€0.85) in France, from where up to 10 trains daily leave the SNCF station for Paris

and from the ET/FV station on Paseo de Colón for San Sebastián (€1.15).

Frequent buses connect Irún with San Sebastián (Plaza de Guipúzcoa) and Hondarribia. Long-distance trains from the Renfe train station run to Madrid and Barcelona. Long-distance buses also depart from here.

Hondarribia
pop 15,493

Hondarribia (Castilian: Fuenterrabía), founded by the Romans and the scene of several sieges throughout its history, has managed to preserve its charming *casco antiguo* (old city). Although it has a character all its own, the whiff of France, lying just across the bay, is also perceptible in the reserved orderliness of the place.

You can enter the partly intact old town walls through the **Puerta de Santa María**. Past the Gothic **Iglesia de Santa María de la Asunción** you arrive in the pretty Plaza de Armas, dominated by the sumptuous Parador El Emperador (see Sleeping & Eating below). Cross the plaza and work your way downhill to the **tourist office** (☎ 943 64 54 58; Calle de Javier Ugarte 6; ⌚ 9.30am-1.30pm & 4-7pm Mon-Fri, 10am-2pm Sat) and La Marina, Hondarribia's most picturesque quarter. Its main street, Calle San Pedro, is flanked by typical fisherfolk houses, with façades painted bright green or blue and wooden balconies gaily decorated with flower boxes.

SLEEPING & EATING

Camping Faro de Higuer (☎ 943 64 10 08; Paseo del Faro 58; per person/small tent €3.50/3.50) This camping ground has a pool, restaurant and bar, and is located about 6km west of the town centre.

Albergue Juan de Elkano (☎ 943 64 15 50; juv .hondarribia@gazteria.gipuzkoa.net; Foroko Igoera; dm under/over 30 incl breakfast €9/14) About 500m west of the centre, this place offers discounts for HI cardholders.

Hostal Txoko Goxoa (☎ /fax 943 64 46 58; Calle Murrua 22; s/d €33.50/45) This sweet, family-run establishment offers clean rooms. Prices drop in the low season.

Hotel San Nikolás (☎ /fax 943 64 42 78; Plaza de Armas 6; d €64) This is a very good choice in the heart of the old town.

Parador El Emperador (☎ 943 64 55 00; s/d €135.45/ 169.30) This imposing 12th-century edifice was turned into a palace by Carlos V. Behind the foreboding battle-scarred façade, a breezy inner courtyard, festooned with flowers, gives access to luxurious rooms.

Bar Maitane (Calle Arana Goiri; platos combinados €6) In the new part of town just behind the tourist office, this bar is popular with locals and has good bar snacks.

There are loads of restaurants along Calle de San Pedro and the quieter Calle de Santiago, one block west.

GETTING THERE & AWAY

Buses leave every 20 minutes from near the post office for Irún (€1, 10 minutes), San Sebastián (€1.45, 45 minutes) and occasionally across the border to Hendaye in France.

SOUTH OF SAN SEBASTIÁN
Museo Chillida Leku

This open-air **museum** (☎ 943 33 60 06; www.eduardo-chillida.com; admission €6; ⊙ 10.30am-3pm Tue-Sat Sep-Jun, 10.30am-7pm Tue-Sat Jul & Aug, 10.30am-3pm Sun year-round) is the most engaging museum in rural Basque country. Amid the beech, oak and magnolia trees, you'll find 40 sculptures of granite and iron conceived by the renowned Basque sculptor Eduardo Chillida. Many more of Chillida's works appear inside the renovated 16th-century farmhouse.

To get here, take the G2 bus for Hernani from Calle de Okendo in San Sebastián and get off at Zabalaga. If you're driving, take the A1 south from San Sebastián. After 7km, take the turn-off southwest for Hernani (GI3132). The museum is 600m along on your left.

Walking in the Hills

Thirty kilometres south of San Sebastián and served by frequent buses, **Ordizia** is the best base from which to visit the hills to the east. A popular 1½-hour walk leads up to the top of Monte Txindoki, one of the highest peaks (1341m) in the Sierra de Aralar, and begins from the village of **Larraitz**, about 8km to the east (follow the signs for Zaldibia). A few buses make the run from Ordizia to Larraitz on weekends only.

More-ambitious walkers head for other peaks further into the chain and even make for the Santuario de San Miguel de Aralar (p477), a good day's strong walking to the southeast in Navarra. Along the way, look out for **dolmens** (prehistoric megalithic tombs).

Push on south from Ordizia to Zegama and the hamlet of **Otzaurte** just beyond, and you can pick up a stretch of the GR12 trail heading 5km westwards to the **Refugio de San Adrián** and a **natural tunnel** of the same name (higher up from the *refugio*). This medieval pilgrim route once linked the heart of Spain with the rest of Europe. Traces of an early medieval highway can still be seen on the approach to the tunnel, inside which rests a small chapel. The road then emerges from the tunnel and continues southwards.

BASQUE CIDER HOUSE RULES

The lush green hinterland just in from the coast has long been home to a liquid tradition most pleasing to the palate. The cider produced here looks deceptively like apple juice – flat and slightly bitter – but with a fierce alcoholic kick. Most *sagardotekis* (cider houses) stay open only during cider production (January to April); they then bottle the surplus, and most close the doors to their bars and restaurants.

If you happen to be in town during those months, treat yourself to a ritual cider house dinner, a culinary extravaganza built around a giant beef chop, preceded by a *bacalao* (cod) omelette, and capped off by a dessert of cheese, quince jelly and walnuts. Dinners start around 10pm and cost about €20 per head, including all the cider you can sip.

When drinking the cider, it's important to keep in mind the local etiquette: '*gutxi eta maiz*', which translates as 'little and often'. Rather than filling up the entire glass, pour only a small amount and drink it right away (you do this yourself from the giant barrels inside the cider house). Letting the cider sit spoils the fresh taste.

A well-signposted series of half a dozen *sagardotekis* lie along a 2km winding, hilly road off the narrow highway connecting Hernani to Astigarraga (3km apart). One of the more popular places is **Sidreria Petritogi**. Getting to the area from San Sebastián is easy, with buses A1 and G1 departing frequently from Calle de Echaide (€0.80). Services back into town cease at about 9pm, so you'll need to catch a taxi.

A daily train serves Otzaurte from Vitoria (€3.18, 40 minutes) and San Sebastián (€5.05, one hour). The *refugio* is supposedly open on weekends and in summer, but it's a little unreliable.

The Interior

The hills rising to the south between San Sebastián and Bilbao offer a number of appealing towns nestled into a luxuriant green backdrop reminiscent of Tuscany – but much more affordable. There's plenty of accommodation, with an abundance of *nekazal turismoas* (agrotourism homes – family homes in rural areas with rooms to rent).

SANTUARIO DE LOYOLA

Just outside Azpeitia (12km south of the A8 motorway along the GI631) lies the portentous **Santuario de Loyola** (admission free; 10am-noon & 4-7pm), dedicated to St Ignatius, the founder of the Jesuit order. The sumptuous baroque façade gives way to a circular basilica laden with dark grey marble and plenty of carved ornamentation. The house where the saint was born in 1490 is preserved in one of the two wings of the *santuario* (shrine).

OÑATI

Continue southwest from Azpeitia, along the Río Urola and a delightful back road (GI3750), which winds through the hills to the rather scraggly town of Bergara. Push on down the GI627 to one of the most enticing towns in rural Basque Country. Oñati contains a Renaissance gem in the **Universidad de Sancti Spiritus**, where for 350 years alumni were schooled in philosophy, law and medicine until its closure in 1902. Highlights are the Plateresque façade and Mudéjar courtyard. Nearby is the **Iglesia de San Miguel**, a late-Gothic confection whose cloister was built over the river. The church faces onto the main square, Foruen Enparantza, dominated by the eye-catching baroque **ayuntamiento** (town hall).

The **tourist office** (943 78 34 53; 10am-1pm & 3.30-7pm Mon-Fri, 10am-1pm & 4.30-6.30pm Sat, 11am-2pm & 4.30-6.30pm Sun Apr-Sep) is nearby and open shorter hours in winter.

Hostal Echeverria (943 78 04 60; Zuazola 15; s/d with washbasin €16/24) has fairly simple, functional rooms, but if you stretch just a bit more you can stay in rural luxury at **Arregi**

(/fax 943 78 08 24; Garagaltza 19; d with bathroom €36.50), the splendid agrotourism home 2km south of town. There are also several good restaurants in town.

There are daily buses to/from San Sebastián, Vitoria and Bilbao.

ARANTZAZU

About 10km south of Oñati, the **Santuario de Arantzazu**, with its richly textured façade, is a Franciscan-run religious complex where the patron saint of Guipúzcoa is worshipped. Considered the most important example of modern architecture in the rural Basque Country, it's a collaboration of major regional architects and sculptors, including Eduardo Chillida, who designed the entrance doors.

The road up and the setting are worth the trip themselves, and the whole area lends itself to some nice walks – the Oñati tourist office can sell you a collection of route maps.

THE CENTRAL BASQUE COAST

The coast road out of San Sebastián snakes its way past some spectacular ocean scenes, with cove after cove stretching west and verdant fields suddenly dropping away in rocky shafts to the sea. Fairly regular buses from San Sebastián run as far as Lekeitio, and agrotourism homes and camping grounds are plentiful and well signposted.

Getaria

pop 2494

If surfing's your thing, you may want to stop in the resort town of **Zarautz**, 23km west of San Sebastián, which hosts a round of the **World Surfing Championship** every September.

Otherwise, continue on to Getaria, a small medieval fishing settlement huddled in the shadow of El Ratón ('the Mouse'), the distinctive islet watched over by the sober mass of the 14th-century Gothic **Iglesia de San Salvador**.

In 1522 this port saw the return of its most illustrious son, Juan Sebastián Elcano, after more than three years spent on Magellan's expedition in 1519. The expedition's aim was to find a passage to India across the Atlantic and Pacific Oceans. Magellan and most of the fleet perished, but Elcano crawled back to Spain with just

18 survivors, the first known explorers to circumnavigate the globe.

A couple of local homes offer cheap beds, and there's **Pensión Guetariano** (☎ 943 14 05 67; Calle Herrieta 3; s/d €28/42). Several harbour-front restaurants grill up the fresh catch of the day, which washes down well with a glass of crisp, locally produced *txakoli*.

Zumaia
pop 8320

A few kilometres west of Getaria, Zumaia sprawls out to accommodate summer beach goers aplenty. The **Playa de Itzurun** is wedged in among cliffs, while the **Playa de Santiago** is a more open strand a couple of kilometres east of the town centre. Next to the latter stands the surprising and richly rewarding **Museo de Zuloaga** (admission €4; ☼ 4-8pm Wed-Sun), housed in the one-time studio of Basque artist Ignacio Zuloaga (1870–1945). It contains some of his important works, as well as a handful by other headliners, including El Greco and Zurbarán.

Mutriku
pop 4188

The picturesque fishing village of Mutriku is clamped by a steep rocky vice cut into the coast, its streets winding tortuously down to a small harbour. Four **camping grounds** surround the town, largely because of the fine beach of **Saturrarán**, a few kilometres west, which has a fine rocky headland.

Inland to Markina

A few kilometres west of Saturrarán, the BI633 turns south just before Ondarroa to reach, after about 10km, the pretty town of Markina, whose main claim to fame is as the home of *pelota* (see p444) – the local *frontón* is even known as the Universidad de la Pelota!

Another 5km south lies the birthplace of Simón Bolívar, the great early-19th-century South American independence fighter. The **Museo Simón Bolívar** (☎ 946 16 41 14; Calle Beko 4; admission free; ☼ 10am-1pm Tue-Fri, noon-2pm Sat & Sun) is dedicated to his exploits. Hourly buses between Ondarroa and Bilbao stop at Iruzubieta, from where it's a 2km walk.

If you're travelling around the area, a good place to stay is the **Arrigorri Itsas Ostatua** (☎ 946 13 40 45; www.arrigorri.net; Calle de Arrigorri 3; s/d from €21/29). Run by friendly folk,

it has a great location overlooking the beach, and clean, pleasant rooms (you pay more for rooms with a view). It also serves good food.

Lekeitio
pop 7354

Back on the coast, travelling another 12km west of Ondarroa brings you to this attractive fishing town. Of the two beaches here, the one just east of the river is nicer. The harbourside is dominated by the late-Gothic **Iglesia de Santa María de la Asunción**.

Unfortunately, accommodation is scarce, driving prices up. In summer advance bookings are mandatory. **Camping Endai** (☎ 946 84 24 69; per person/tent €3.15/3.25; ☼ summer) is a smallish camping ground with a bar and a shop on Playa Mendexa, a few kilometres back east.

The waterfront and back streets of the old town teem with bars and snack joints.

Elantxobe
pop 460

The tiny hamlet of Elantxobe is seemingly glued onto almost-perpendicular rock walls cascading down to the sea. A couple of buses run from Guernica daily, except Sunday.

Urdaibai Reserva de la Biosfera

Just west of Elantxobe, the Río Oka spills into the Bay of Biscay, its last 10km forming an estuary that was given biosphere reserve status by Unesco in 1984. Home to hundreds of bird species, it's also a stop on the migratory route between Europe and Africa for birds, including barnacle geese and eiders. Sprawling over 220 sq km, the reserve encompasses 22 towns and villages, including Guernica, Mundaka and Bermeo. On its eastern and northern edges, respectively, are the expansive and sandy beaches of **Laga** and **Laida**.

Mundaka
pop 1686

The legend of one of the world's longest left-handers still attracts surfers the world over to this pretty but pretentious little estuary town, 10km north of Guernica; surfers may want to track down Craig, who came in the early 1980s and hasn't been able to drag himself away since, at his Mundaka Surf Shop. Craig rents out gear and gives surfing lessons.

BASQUE COUNTRY, NAVARRA & LA RIOJA

There's a small **tourist office** (☎ 946 17 72 01; www.mundaka.org; Calle Kepa Deuna), but food and accommodation are hopelessly overpriced in this town, even out of season.

Camping Portuondo (☎ 946 87 77 01; recepcion@ campingportuondo.com; per person/tent/car €4.75/9.50/ 9.50, 4-person bungalows from €52) is your best bet, with lovely terraced grounds, a pool and restaurant. It also has several nice bunga-lows with fully equipped kitchens.

Buses and ET/FV trains connecting Bil-bao with Bermeo stop here.

Bermeo
pop 16,092

A stone's throw up the coast, this fishing port looks appealing at first but turns out to be a rather sprawling and gritty place.

The **tourist office** (☎ 946 17 91 54; Askatasun Bidea 2) is on the waterfront. Those interested in commercial fishing could poke their noses into the **Museo del Pescador** (☎ 946 88 11 71; Plaza Torrontero 1; admission free; ☽ 10am-1pm & 4-7pm Tue-Sat, 10am-1pm Sun).

The coast road west of Bermeo offers some tantalising glimpses of the rugged, and at times forbidding, Basque coast. A few kilometres beyond Bermeo, the **Ermita de San Juan de Gaztelugatxe** juts out to sea on an odd lick of land. The minor fishing village of **Bakio**, 12km around the tip, has a lovely beach.

Half-hourly buses and ET/FV trains run from Bermeo to Bilbao (€2.70, 1¼ hours).

BILBAO
pop 353,567

No other city in Spain has reinvented itself quite like Bilbao. Hip, frenzied and cul-turally dynamic, it's hard to believe that less than two decades ago Bilbao seemed a doomed fossil of the postindustrial age. It's now one of the most exciting cities in Spain and considered one of the coun-try's premier cultural capitals, home to the extraordinary Museo Guggenheim and a wonderful gallery of modern art. The city also boasts excellent restaurants and crack-ling nightlife.

The Basque country's biggest and busi-est city, Bilbao (Bilbo in Basque) is also known by locals as the 'Botxo' (Basque: hole), wedged as it is into the green hills of Vizcaya province and sliced in two by the murky waters of the Ría de Bilbao. But this is a hole with attitude: hang around for a weekend evening and you'll find yourself immersed in a whirlwind of frenetic party-ing in Las Siete Calles, the nucleus of the medieval *casco viejo* (old town). Here the Spanish propensity for raucous all-night revelry is taken for a serious spin.

History

Bilbao was granted the title of villa (a city state) in 1300, and medieval *bilbaínos* (resi-dents of Bilbao) went about their business in the bustle of Las Siete Calles and on the wharves of San Antón and Abando. As busi-ness and the city grew, the quays moved fur-ther towards the coast. The conquest of the Americas stimulated trade, and Basque fish-ers, merchants and settlers soon built strong links to the Americas, particularly Boston. By the late 19th century the area's skyline was dominated by the smoke stacks of steelworks, shipbuilding yards and chemical plants.

From the Carlist wars in the 1830s through to the Spanish Civil War, Bilbao was always considered the greatest prize in the north, largely for its industrial strength. After the devastating attacks by Franco-German forces on Guernica (see p465) and other Basque towns, there was open talk among Franco's generals about laying waste to Bilbao. The city's defenders withdrew from the city after a long siege in order to save it, and it was taken by Franco in late spring 1937. Reprisals against Basque na-tionalists were massive and long lasting.

Orientation

Bilbao's old quarter, the *casco viejo*, lies bundled up on the east bank of the Ría de Bilbao. Hotels, restaurants and bars clus-ter in Las Siete Calles, while the sights and services in the newer part of town are also within walking distance of the river. The main train stations are alongside the river near the Puente de Arenal in an area known as El Ensanche. The bus stations are scat-tered across the western part of town.

Information
BOOKSHOPS

Librería Camara (Calle de Euskalduna 6) Excellent bookshop, with huge selection of international newspapers and magazines.

Tintas (☎ 944 44 95 41; Calle del Generál Concha 10) Travel bookshop with topographical maps for trekkers.

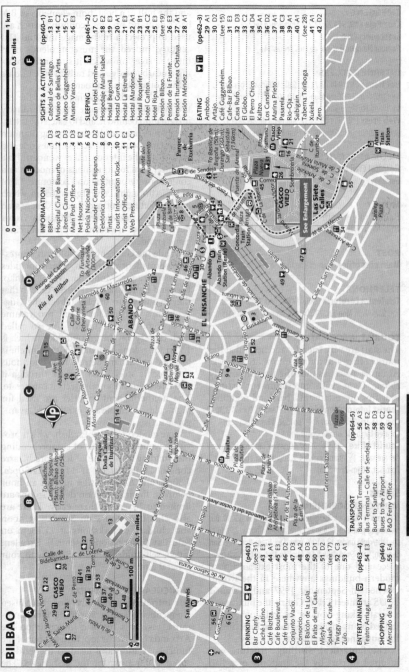

BILBAO

INFORMATION
BBK...1 D3
Hospital Civil de Basurto............2 A3
Librería Camara............................3 D3
Main Post Office..........................4 D3
Net House....................................5 E2
Policía Nacional...........................6 A3
Santander Central Hispano.........7 D2
Telefónica Locutorio...................8 E2
Tintas..9 C3
Tourist Information Kiosk...........10 C1
Tourist Office............................11 E2
Web Press.................................12 C1

SIGHTS & ACTIVITIES   (pp460-1)
Catedral de Santiago................13 B1
Museo de Bellas Artes..............14 C2
Museo Guggenheim..................15 C1
Museo Vasco.............................16 E3

SLEEPING   (pp461-2)
Gran Hotel Domine....................17 C1
Hospedaje María Isabel.............18 E2
Hostal Begoña...........................19 E3
Hostal Gurea.............................20 A1
Hostal La Estrella......................21 E3
Hostal Mardones......................22 A1
Hostal Roquefer........................23 B1
Hotel Carlton............................24 C2
Hotel Ripa.................................25 D2
Pensión de la Fuente...............(see 19)
Pensión Iturrienea Ostatua.......26 E3
Pensión Iturrienea Ostatua.......27 A1
Pensión Méndez........................28 A1

EATING   (pp462-3)
Amboto.....................................29 A1
Artajo.......................................30 D2
Café Guggenheim....................(see 15)
Café-Bar Bilbao.........................31 E3
Casa Rufo.................................32 D3
El Globo....................................33 C2
El Perro Chico............................34 D4
Kaltzo.......................................35 A1
Los Candiles..............................36 D2
Marina Prieto............................37 A1
Pasarela....................................38 C3
Rio-Oja.....................................39 A1
Saibigain...................................40 A1
Taberna Txiriboga.....................41 A1
Xukela......................................(see 28)
Zero...42 D2

DRINKING   (p463)
Bar Charly...............................(see 31)
Caché Latino..............................43 E3
Café Bizitza................................44 A1
Café Boulevard..........................45 E3
Café Iruña..................................46 D2
Conjunto Vacío..........................47 D3
Consorcio...................................48 A2
El Balcón de la Lola...................49 D3
El Patio de mi Casa...................50 D1
Mistyk.......................................51 D1
Splash & Crash........................(see 7)
Twiggy......................................52 C3
Zulo...53 A1

ENTERTAINMENT   (pp463-4)
Teatro Arriaga............................54 E3

SHOPPING   (p464)
Mercado de la Ribera.................55 E4

TRANSPORT   (pp464-5)
Bus Station Termibus.................56 A3
Bus Terminal – Calle de Sendeja...57 E2
Buses to Santurtzi......................58 D3
Buses to the Airport...................59 C2
P&O Ferry Office........................60 D1

EMERGENCY
Cruz Roja (☎ 944 22 22 22) Ambulance service.
Emergency (☎ 112)
Policía Nacional (Calle de Luis Briñas 14)

INTERNET ACCESS
Net House (☎ 944 23 71 53; Calle Villarías 6; per hr €3;
⏰ 10.30am-10.30pm Mon-Fri, 10.30am-11.30pm Sat,
11.30am-10.30pm Sun)
Web Press (☎ 944 23 39 37; Alameda de Recalde 12;
per hr €2.40; ⏰ 10am-10pm Mon-Fri, 4-10pm Sun)

MEDICAL SERVICES
Hospital Civil de Basurto (☎ 944 41 87 00; Calle de
Gurtubay)

MONEY
Banks, many with ATMs, abound in central
Bilbao, particularly around Plaza de España.

POST
Main post office (Alameda de Urquijo 19)

TELEPHONE
Telefónica Locutorio (Calle de Barroeta Aldámar 7;
⏰ 9am-9pm Mon-Fri, 10.30am-1.30pm & 5-9pm Sat)

TOURIST INFORMATION
The staff are very friendly and helpful at the
tourist office and tourist information kiosk.
At either place, ask for the free bimonthly
Bilbao Guía, with entertainment listings
plus tips on restaurants, bars and nightlife.
Tourist information kiosk (⏰ 11am-2.30pm & 3.30-
6pm Tue-Fri, 11am-3pm & 4-7pm Sat, 11am-2pm Sun)
Located by the Museo Guggenheim.
Tourist office (☎ 944 79 57 60; www.bilbao.net; Paseo
del Arenal 1; ⏰ 9am-2pm & 4-7.30pm Mon-Fri, 9am-
2pm Sat, 10am-2pm Sun)

Sights
MUSEO GUGGENHEIM
Bilbao's **Museo Guggenheim** (☎ 944 35 90 00;
www.guggenheim-bilbao.es; Ave Abandoibarra 2; adult/
student/child under 12 €10/6/free; ⏰ 10am-8pm Tue-Sun
Sep-Jun, 9am-9pm daily Jul & Aug) is the city's show-
piece and one of the most extraordinary
modern buildings anywhere in the world.
Opened in September 1997 and designed
by US architect Frank Gehry, the building is
a breathtaking work of art in its own right;
indeed many visitors see the architecture as
the outstanding highlight.

The fantastical, swirling structure was
inspired in part by the anatomy of a fish

and the hull of a boat, both elements of Bilbao's past and present economy, which are
used to project a fresh image into the 21st
century. Indeed, the museum blends right
into the river on which it sits, incorporating a nearby bridge and railway line into its
sphere of aesthetic influence.

It's well worth wandering around the entire building to appreciate the extraordinary
imagination behind it, and to catch the different colours reflected by the rippling titanium
(meant to resemble fish scales), limestone and
glass shell. The interior makes wonderful use
of space, ideal for its exhibits of modern and
contemporary painting and sculpture. Light
pours in through a central glass atrium, which
has the loftiness of a cathedral. There's an
emphasis on organic lines, so that the visitor
doesn't feel overwhelmed by its hallucino-
genic grandeur.

While the Guggenheim holds an impressive permanent collection, which includes
Picasso, Braque, Mondrian, Miró, Rothko,
Klee and Kandinsky, that doesn't mean that
they're always on display (check the Guggenheim's website for a full programme
of upcoming exhibitions). The so-called
'Fish Gallery' on the ground floor, which is
130m long, longer than a football pitch, is
bisected by Richard Serra's 1996 enormous
site-specific steel *Snake* – walk through it
and check out the aural effects it can create.
The nonpermanent galleries are used for
high-calibre temporary exhibits of avant-
garde artists.

Free guided tours in English, which provide a wonderful means of comprehending
the building and some of its more bizarre
contents, take place at 11am, 12.30pm,
4.30pm and 6.30pm; sign up half an hour
before at the information desk. Groups are
limited to 20, so get there early. There are
also children's tours on Sunday at noon
and children's workshops at 11.15am on
Saturday (reservations essential). Excellent
taped, self-guided tours are free with your
general admission.

FUNICULAR DE ARTXANDA
For intriguing perspectives of the Museo
Guggenheim and a sweeping city panorama, take this historic funicular up the
Artxanda hill. At the top, turn left out of the
funicular station and head to the gardens
about 150m away for the best views. The

funicular operates daily every 15 minutes from 7.15am until 10pm, and until 11pm on summer weekends (€0.80 one way).

MUSEO DE BELLAS ARTES
Just 300m up the street from the Museo Guggenheim, Bilbao's **Fine Arts Museum** (☎ 944 39 60 60; www.museobilbao.com; Plaza del Museo 2; adult/student €4.50/3, free Wed; ☒ 10am-8pm Tue-Sat, 10am-2pm Sun) is an excellent complement to the Guggenheim, with a surprisingly wide-ranging and impressive collection that includes everything from Gothic sculptures to 20th-century pop art. Major highlights include classic Spanish artists, such as Goya, El Greco and Zurbarán, as well as international masters, such as Van Dyck and Gauguin. Basque artists, including the sculptor Chillida, are represented as well.

CASCO VIEJO
Bilbao's old town, loaded with bars and restaurants, is an attraction in itself. While wandering, take note of the **Teatro Arriaga**, the arcaded **Plaza Nueva** and the recently spiffed-up Gothic **Catedral de Santiago**, with its lovely Renaissance cloister. The **Museo Vasco** (☎ 944 15 54 23; Plaza Unamuno 4; adult/student/child under 10 €3/1.50/free, free Thu; ☒ 11am-5pm Tue-Sat, 11am-2pm Sun) is a proud and well-executed display of archaeological findings from the Basque region, enhanced by exhibits on local livelihoods.

Festivals & Events
Held in February, **Carnaval** is celebrated with vigour, but Bilbao's grandest fiesta begins on the first Saturday after 15 August and is known as the **Aste Nagusia** (Big Week). Traditional parades and music mix with a full programme of cultural events over 10 days.

About 25km north of Bilbao, Getxo hosts a week-long **international jazz festival** in July, as well as smaller **blues** (June) and **folk** (September) music festivals.

Sleeping
BUDGET
Camping Sopelana (☎ 946 76 21 20; per person/tent/car €3.75/3.75/3.75) A pleasant spot by the beach in the town of the same name; it's on the Metro line, 15km from Bilbao.

Albergue Bilbao Aterpetxea (☎ 944 27 00 54; aterpe@albergue.bilbao.net; Carretera Basurto-Kastrexana

Errep 70; dm/s €11.60/18.50; ☒) This youth hostel is a 10-minute bus ride (bus No 58 from Plaza Arriaga) from the town centre. Meals, Internet access, bike hire, money exchange and laundry facilities are some of the extras on offer.

The *casco viejo* brims with budget lodging options, although things get noisy on weekends. Ask for a room facing away from the street or bring ear plugs.

Hospedaje María Isabel (☎ 944 24 85 66; Calle de la Amistad 5; s/d with shared bathroom €15/30) Just out of the *casco viejo* west of the river, this fairly characterless place has functional rooms. It's central nonetheless and one of Bilbao's cheapest, habitable options.

Pensión de la Fuente (☎ 944 16 99 89; Calle Sombrerería 2; s/d with shared bathroom €20/28, d with bathroom €40) A family-run place on the 2nd floor of a large old building, this is a good, central budget choice with spacious rooms, many with balconies.

Hostal Gurea (☎ /fax 944 16 32 99; Calle de Bidebarrieta 14; s/d with shared bathroom €28/35, s/d with bathroom €30/40) A slight step-up in quality, this is a reasonable choice, with friendly management and generally good rooms.

Hostal Roquefer (☎ 944 15 07 55; Calle de la Lotería 2; s/d with washbasin €25/35, d with bathroom €45) Very good value is to be found here where the rooms have high ceilings, and stripey wallpaper; most have balconies and it's all presided over by a motherly owner.

MID-RANGE
Hostal La Estrella (☎ 944 16 40 66; fax 944 16 70 66; Calle de María Múñoz 6; s/d €30/48) This is excellent value, with comfortable rooms in a charming building. The rooms have a touch less character than the entrance, but most have balconies and are quieter than others in this area.

Hostal Mardones (☎ 944 15 31 05; Calle Jardines Victor 4; s/d with washbasin €33/34, with bathroom €40/43) A lovely 18-room *pensión*, whose chatty owners rent out clean, spacious rooms with wooden floors, beams and balconies.

Pensión Méndez (☎ 944 16 03 64; www.pension mendez.com; Calle de Santa María 13; s/d with shared bathroom €25/35, s/d/tr with bathroom from €37/50/65) On the 1st and 4th floors of a fabulous, centrally located, lofty building, this place offers good rooms in the lower mid-range category.

Pensión Bilbao (☎ 944 24 69 43; www.pension bilbao.com; Calle de la Amistad 2; s/d €35/45) For simple

---

AUTHOR'S CHOICE

Pensión Iturrienea Ostatua (☎ 944 16 15 00; fax 944 15 89 29; Calle de Santa María 14; s/d with bathroom €54.10/60.10) This place is hard to beat, with loads of atmosphere. The whole place is filled with natural wood, stone and antiques, and each room (all different) is very comfortable and spacious. It also serves a good breakfast (€4) till noon.

Hostal Begoña (☎ 944 23 01 34; www .hostalbegona.com; Calle de la Amistad 2; s/d from €48.00/57.10) Central without the noise, this exceptionally well-run place offers colourful rooms decorated with modern artworks, and all come with funky tiled bathrooms, mini-bar, cable TV and fabulous wrought-iron beds. Bonuses include free Internet access and drinks; English is also spoken. Outstanding value.

---

comfort in a central location and for a reasonable price, Pensión Bilbao is well worth trying.

Hotel Ripa (☎ 944 23 96 77; hotelripa@teleline.es; Calle de Ripa 3; s/d €42/58) A consistently popular choice with tourists, Hotel Ripa has decent, good-sized rooms, some of which have balconies and views across the river. The attached bathrooms are smallish and in need of renovation.

TOP END

Hotel Carlton (☎ 944 16 22 00; carlton@aranzazu -hoteles.com; Plaza de Federico Moyúa 2; s/d Fri-Sun €85/107) With soothing marble interiors, vaulted ceilings and graceful rooms, the Carlton has a patrician air and is a landmark in its own right. It's also well situated near the Guggenheim. Prices rise during the week.

Gran Hotel Domine (☎ 944 25 33 00; www.gran hoteldominebilbao.com; Alameda Mazarredo 61; d from €145) A breathtakingly chic hotel a stone's throw from the Guggenheim, this place is a great choice. Luxurious and stylish, some rooms (from €190) and the rooftop terrace have views of the Guggenheim.

Eating

Bilbao is a great place to sample excellent Basque food. Many of Bilbao's bars, including some of those listed under Drinking opposite, have a restaurant attached, usually out the back.

TAPAS BARS

Although not quite San Sebastián, Bilbao has a great range of *pintxos* to satisfy most tastes. Check out the following places in the *casco viejo*.

Saibigain (☎ 944 15 01 23; Calle Barrenkale Barrena 16) This friendly place is a minor temple to Athletic Bilbao Football Club and it's always got a good selection of *pintxos* on offer; it also does wonderful things with mushrooms.

Café-Bar Bilbao (☎ 944 15 16 71; Plaza Nueva 6) With some of the most creative *pintxos* in town, you'll be lucky to elbow your way in here on a Saturday night.

Xukela (Calle de Perro 2) Choices like salmon, eggplant and goat's cheese make this atmospheric place a winner.

Other good places to try include **Taberna Txiriboga** (Calle de Santa María 13), which is always popular, even on quiet weekend nights, and **Bar Charly** (☎ 944 15 01 27; Plaza Neuva 8), which is good for *pulpo* (octopus), *rabo* (bull's tail) and pizza.

Don't restrict your search for the perfect *pintxo* to the *casco viejo*. The El Ensanche area also has some good options.

Los Candiles (☎ 944 24 14 79; Calle de Diputación 1) It might be small, but Los Candiles has a host of great *pintxos* and is well known for its seafood, especially fried calamari and *erizo de mar* (sea hedgehog).

El Globo (☎ 944 15 42 21; Calle de Diputación 8) Large but with an intimate feel, this popular place has an innovative selection of *pintxos* that locals swear by; the *morcilla* (blood sausage) is particularly well loved.

Artajo (☎ 944 24 85 96; Calle de Ledesma 7) An atmospheric place, Artajo is renowned for it's *tigres* (mussels in spicy sauce).

RESTAURANTS

Rio-Oja (Calle de Perro 6) A good place for a cheap meal, Rio-Oja doesn't have the most inspiring décor, but it's usually packed with locals swilling €0.60 glasses of wine and chowing down on *cazuelitas* (small stews) of, among other things, salted cod with peppers.

Kaltzo (Calle Barrenkale Barrena 7; menú €12.50; closed Sun night & Mon) With its comfortable upstairs dining room, Kaltzo is less frenetic than Rio-Oja, but the food (standard Basque fare) is equally good.

Amboto (☎ 944 15 61 48; Calle de Jardines 2; meals around €30) A rustic establishment with traditional Basque dishes, this place comes highly recommended for preserving the old way of preparing Basque food in the midst of all the innovative cuisine offered elsewhere.

Marina Prieto (☎ 944 15 44 08; Calle Barrenkale Barrena 16; entrées €4-6, mains €9-15; ☟ closed Sun night & Mon) Super stylish, reasonably priced and serves high-quality Galician food, with an emphasis on fish and seafood.

Café Guggenheim (☎ 944 23 93 33; set lunch €12.60, restaurant meals from €60; ☟ Tue-Sun) On the top floor of the Museo Guggenheim, this café is perfect for refuelling after a morning of art and architecture. You can eat pastries at the bar or the sit-down café serves up a fabulous set lunch from 1pm to 3.30pm enabling you to enjoy creative Basque cooking without the usual price tag. The attached restaurant is one of Bilbao's best, so reservations and fat wallets are essential.

Pasarela (☎ 944 10 05 04; Alameda de Urquijo 30; mains from €5) Pasarela is a great spot for those who can't face another plate of exotic Basque fare; pasta, burgers and pizza in a fun setting are the order of the day. It's popular among young *bilbaínos* too.

El Perro Chico (☎ 944 15 05 19; Calle de Aretxaga 2; meals around €33) Propelled into the trendy stratosphere when it was 'discovered' by Frank Gehry, this place mixes theatrical décor and high-quality cooking. Reservations are a good idea.

Zero (☎ 944 35 41 15; Calle de Henao 3; entrées €9-16.50, mains €11-17) Stylishly minimalist in its décor, this trendy place does a superb *chuleton de buey con pimientos asados* (T-bone steak with roasted peppers) for €32.

Drinking
BARS
On weekends, Las Siete Calles can be extremely crowded, infectiously rowdy, if a

touch adolescent. Indeed, on a Saturday night, Calle de Barrenkale is probably the most concentrated scene of drinking and post-tipple lunacy in the country.

Taberna Txiriboga (Calle de Santa María 13) A traditional, noisy Basque bar, where the action often spills onto the street outside.

Café Bizitza (Calle de Torre 1) For a Bohemian atmosphere and clientele, this is a cheerful place with colourful surroundings that is very popular with students.

Other very popular places include the delightful **Xukela** (Calle de Perro 2) and the earthier **Zulo** (Cnr Calle Barrenkale Barrena & Calle de Torre), which is small, smoky and perfect for lovers of loud music.

Along the river, there's a line of bars along Calle de Ripa, between the Puente del Ayuntamiento and the Puente del Arenal. For something a little more discerning, the eclectic and very fun **Twiggy** (Alameda de Urquijo 35) or the small and intimate **El Patio de mi Casa** (Calle de Cosme Echevarrieta 13) are both good; the latter kicks off after midnight.

CAFÉS
The porticoed Plaza Nueva is a good spot for coffee and people watching, especially in summer.

Café Boulevard (Calle del Arenal 3) Bilbao's oldest coffeehouse (1871) has carried an old-world charm into the 21st century and, apart from its wonderful décor, it serves breakfast specials (from €1.80), *platos combinados* (literally, combined plates; a largish serve; €6 to €7) or *pintxos* (€1.15).

Café Iruña (cnr Calle de Colón de Larreátegui & Calle Berástegui) Going strong since 1903, this is probably the most celebrated old café in town. Its fairy-tale, Mudéjar-style décor was inspired by Granada's Alhambra, making it an evocative place to have a coffee.

Entertainment
CLUBS & DISCOTECAS
Consorcio (Calle de Barrenkale Barrena) In the *casco viejo*, this is a good place to start (ie around midnight).

El Balcón de la Lola (Calle Bailén 10) One of Bilbao's most popular mixed/gay clubs, this is the place to come if you're looking for hip industrial décor and a packed Saturday-night disco.

Mistyk (Alameda Mazarredo 21) A colourful late-night hang-out that hosts occasional

BASQUE COUNTRY, NAVARRA & LA RIOJA

live music, Mistyk is always home to lots of *marcha* (action) on weekends.

Conjunto Vacío (Muelle de la Merced 4; ☺ 9pm-9am Fri & Sat) If you make it to closing time here, you'll wonder why you booked a hotel; it's the ever-popular haunt of the young *bacalao* (techno) set.

Caché Latino (Calle de Ripa 3) An energetic place to go 'Cubano', you'll find fiery salsa and merengue dominating the turntables. It also has free dance lessons on Friday night.

Splash & Crash (Alameda de Mazarredo 61) All curves and super chic. From Thursday to Saturday, the DJs do the full range from chill-out to jazz, funk, soul and house, depending on the crowd.

THEATRE
Bilbao is a good place to catch a stage show or concert, with several theatres, including the opulent **Teatro Arriaga** (☎ 944 16 33 33; Plaza Arriaga 1) and its own symphony orchestra. Available from tourist offices, *Bilbao Guía* has the latest events schedule.

Shopping
To pack your own lunch, try the Mercado de la Ribera in the *casco viejo* – it's allegedly the largest food market in Europe, with three storeys of meat, fish, cheese and produce.

Getting There & Away
AIR
Bilbao's new **airport** (☎ 944 86 96 63), a futuristic ensemble of glass and steel that brings to mind a stealth bomber about to take flight, has regular services to/from Madrid, Barcelona, Seville, Las Palmas and other European cities.

BOAT
P&O ferries (☎ 944 23 44 77; www.poportsmouth.com; Calle de Cosme Echevarrieta 1) leave twice weekly, except November to March, for Portsmouth, England, from Santurtzi, about 14km northwest of Bilbao's city centre. Tickets cost €120 to €260 for passengers, €18/252/378 per bicycle/motorcycle/car, and departures from Portsmouth/Bilbao take 35/29 hours.

BUS
Most companies are based at the Termibus bus station in the southwestern corner of town (Metro: San Mamés), with regular

services operating to/from Madrid (€22.50 4¾ hours), Barcelona (€34.80, seven hours) Burgos (€10.10, two hours), Vitoria (€4.80, 5(minutes), Pamplona (€10.85, 1¾ hours), Logroño (€10, two hours), Irún and the French border (€7.26, two hours), Santander (€5.80 1½ hours) and Oviedo (€17.05, five hours)

Pesa (☎ 902 10 12 10) operates services every 30 minutes to one hour to San Sebastián (€8, one hour) and also serves Durango-Elorrio and Oñati.

Bizkaibus (☎ 902 22 22 65) travels to destinations throughout the rural Basque Country, including coastal communities such as Lekeitio and Bermeo, and mostly uses the terminal at Calle de Sendeja, northeast of town. Some of its buses, including the one to the port of Santurtzi (€1.05), leave from Calle de Lutxana, near the main post office.

TRAIN
Renfe's Abando train station has two trains daily to Madrid (€30, 6¼ hours) and Barcelona (€34.50, nine hours). Other cities served include Valladolid (€20, four hours) and Burgos (€14.50, three hours).

Next door is the rather fancy Concordia train station used by the FEVE private rail company for trains west into Cantabria and Asturias.

ET/FV offers regional services from Atxuri train station, east of the *casco viejo*. Trains run every half-hour to Bermeo (€2.70, 1¼ hours) via Guernica (€2.20/3.40 one way/return) and Mundaka, and hourly to San Sebastián (€5.70, 2¾ hours) via Durango, Zumaia and Zarautz.

Getting Around
TO/FROM THE AIRPORT
Bizkaibus No 3247 runs to the airport from Plaza de Federico Moyúa every 40 minutes (€1.10). A taxi from the airport should cost about €15 and take 20 minutes.

METRO
Designed by British star architect Sir Norman Foster (and dubbed 'Fosterito' by locals), Bilbao's Metro opened in 1997 and is the most modern underground (subway) system in the world. It runs to the north coast from a number of stations on both sides of the river and makes getting to the beaches closest to Bilbao quite simple. The Metro also connects the city centre with

the bus station. Tickets within the central area are €1.10.

TRAM
Bilbao also has a super-modern and efficient tram system that connects the Guggenheim with Atxuri train station. Tickets cost €1.10.

AROUND BILBAO
Beaches
For swimming, **Azkorri** is a good bet, while Ereaga is popular with surfers. **Sopelana** is nice, too; its Playa Salvaje section is set aside for nudists. Even better beaches can be found east of Plentzia (the Bilbao Metro services Plentzia and costs €1.20). Also good is the sheltered beach at **Gorliz**, which also has a pretty lighthouse and some fine views from the Astondo end of the beach where there are some well-signposted tracks for walkers.

A worthwhile stop enroute to the beaches is the newly restored **Puente Colgante**, the world's first transporter bridge at its opening in 1893 – it links Getxo and Portugalete. A platform, suspended from the actual bridge high above, is loaded with up to six cars plus foot passengers; it then silently glides over the Río Nervión to the other bank. Rides are €1 per person each way. You can also take a lift up to the superstructure at 46m, and walk across the river and back (not for those prone to vertigo) for some great views (€3). The nearest Metro stop is Areeta (€1.10).

Castillo de Butrón
This sugary fortified pile with crenellated towers, surrounded by a moat and set in a dreamy park, is the quintessential fairy-tale **castle** (☎ 946 15 11 10; adult/child €5/3, with guided tour €6; ☼ 10.30am-5pm Mon-Fri, 11am-6pm Sat & Sun Oct-Feb, 10.30am-8pm daily Mar-Sep). Located a few kilometres west of the village of Gatica (Basque: Gatika), about 20km north of Bilbao, it was built in the 14th century as the bastion of the Basque Butrón clan. Groups of rowdy school kids romp past sickly looking wax mannequins of soldiers, prisoners and fair damsels, and the scene is completed with audiovisual tall tales and a tacky souvenir stall. If you've got children, this could be just the ticket.

To get there, take the Metro to Larrabasterra, then the bus in the direction of Mungía, which leaves from Calle de Akilino

Arriola 71, about 500m from the Metro station, every 90 minutes.

Guernica
pop 15,454
Guernica (Basque: Gernika) occupies a special place in Basque history for many reasons. It was here that, until 1876, a Basque parliament held its legislative meetings beneath an ancient oak tree. But it became a place of infamy as the target of the massive systematic bombing by Hitler's Legión Condor, at the request of Franco, on 26 April 1937. Almost 2000 people died and much of the town was destroyed in the attack, which took place during the busy Monday afternoon market, still held today. The massacre was later immortalised in Picasso's nightmare vision *Guernica* – the painting is housed in Madrid's Centro de Arte Reina Sofía.

INFORMATION
The helpful **tourist office** (☎ 946 25 58 92; Artekale 8; ☼ 10am-7pm mid-Jun–mid-Sep, 10am-2pm & 4-7pm Mon-Sat, 10am-2pm Sun mid Sep–mid-Jun) has staff who speak English. They can organise guided tours of the city sights at 11am (€2, 1½ hours). They also sell a combined entry ticket for the town's sights (€3).

SIGHTS
The highly recommended **Museo de la Paz de Gernika** (Gernika Peace Museum; ☎ 946 27 02 13; Plaza Foru 1; admission €4; ☼ 10am-2pm & 4-7pm Tue-Sat, 10am-2pm Sun) contains fascinating displays on subjects related to world peace. The centrepiece is a detailed photographic and written chronology of the 1937 bombing of Guernica, including an evocative audiovisual display. Other highlights include the displays on the Spanish Civil War, a balanced discussion of the campaign for Basque sovereignty, and a host of photographs, documents and scale models. Display panels are in Spanish and Basque, but the ticket office hands out good English and French translations of almost all the captions.

A couple of blocks north, on Calle Allende Salazar, is a ceramic-tile version of Picasso's *Guernica*.

Further west along Calle Allende Salazar is the **Euskal Herriko Museoa** (☎ 946 25 54 51; admission free; ☼ 10am-2pm & 4-7pm Tue-Sat, 10am-3pm Sun), housed in the 18th-century Palacio de Montefuerte. The comprehensive exhibitions on Basque history and culture are well worth a look, with fine old maps, engravings, and a range of other documents and portraits.

The open area in front of the museum used to be the town **market** and it was here that the bombs of 1937 took their most devastating toll.

The pleasant **Parque de los Pueblos de Europa** (10am-7pm, until 9pm in summer) behind the museum contain a couple of typically curvaceous **sculptures** by Henry Moore and other works by Eduardo Chillida, and leads to the attractive **Casa de Juntas**, where the provincial government has met since 1979. Inside the intimate chamber is a monumental, modern stained-glass window (235 sq metres). In the garden is the famous **Oak Tree**, now a mere stump sheltered by a neoclassical gazebo, while another tree was recently planted in the rear courtyard as a symbol of the ongoing ties that the Basques maintain with their past.

SLEEPING & EATING
There are a few hotels dotted around town. Central and worth trying are the comfortable **Hotel Boliña** (☎ 946 25 03 00; www.hotelbolina.net; Calle de Barrencalle 3; s/d €34.60/43), which has a recommended restaurant (menús cost €10), and the well-run **Pensión Akelarre** (☎ 946 27 01 97; Calle de Barrencalle 5; s/d from €33/40). Both are good value but prices rise on weekends.

GETTING THERE & AWAY
Guernica is an easy day trip from Bilbao by ET/FV train from Atxuri train station, where trains run every half-hour (€2.20/3.40 one way/return, one hour).

Cueva de Santimamiñe
The grotto of Santimamiñe is a crowd pleaser for its impressive stalactites, stalagmites and well-preserved prehistoric cave paintings. Free guided tours (with a maximum of 15 people) start at 10am, 11.15am, 12.30pm, 4.30pm and 6pm Monday to Friday. They're very popular, so arrive early or inquire about organised trips at the Guernica tourist office.

There's no public transport, although the Guernica–Lekeitio bus can drop you off at Kortezubi (€1), from where it's a 3km walk. If you're driving, take the BI638 to Kortezubi, then turn off to the BI4244 just before town.

El Bosque Pintado de Oma
Near the grottoes is one of the region's most unusual attractions, the 'Painted Forest' of Basque artist Agustín Ibarrola. Aided by several of his students, he has adorned dozens of trees in the Oma Valley with rainbows, outlines of people and colourful abstract shapes. While at first they seem rather disjointed, a closer look reveals an intentional composition, with several trees together forming a complete picture. Each visitor is invited to recompose the images and to discover their own visions. See if you can spot the two motorcyclists!

The Bosque is accessible by bike, car or on foot. Follow the directions to the Cueva de Santimamiñe, but turn off the BI4244 onto a marked forest road before reaching the caves.

Durango & Elorrio
The industrial town of Durango has few drawcards, although the **Iglesia de Santa Ana** has an interesting blend of Renaissance, Gothic and Herrerian styles. Under construction while we were there was the new Euskotren train station, the latest in a series of ambitious urban regeneration projects in the Basque Country. The real attraction is the **Duranguesado**, the mountainous area around the city. The drive south to the **Puerto de Urquiola** pass is festooned with spectacular lookouts. Climbers make for the summit of Amboto (1327m), 5km east of the pass. For more information, contact the Durango **tourist office** (☎ 946 03 00 30; Calle de Bruno Mauricio Zabala 2).

It seems that at one stage just about everyone in nearby Elorrio was a VIP, if the number of mansions bearing family crests is anything to go by. Calle de San Balentin Berrio-Otxoa in particular is loaded with the impressive façades of past greatness; it spills out onto the delightful **Plaza Gernikako Arbola**, which is dominated by the austere 15th-century Basílica de la Purísima Concepción. Opposite the church is the local frontón.

Regular buses and the ET/FV train, coming from either Bilbao or San Sebastián, stop in Durango, from where buses run every hour or so to Elorrio.

VITORIA

pop 218,604 / elevation 512m

Capital not only of the southern Basque province of Álava (Basque: Araba) but of the entire Basque Country, Vitoria (Basque: Gasteiz) is a strange mix of businesslike city and ebullient student enclave. This cocktail is given that special Basque twist, with enough ETA posters and graffiti to remind you of its presence, alongside friendly games of *pelota* down at the *frontón* on Plaza de los Fueros.

History

Nueva Vitoria was founded in 1181 by Navarran king Sancho VI (El Sabio) on the site of an old Basque village, Gasteiz; it later swapped between the Castilian and Navarran crowns. The expansion that began in the 18th century picked up in the 20th century with the growth of industry. The city was named capital of the Basque Country in 1979.

Orientation

The *casco viejo* is composed of narrow lanes arranged more or less in a series of concentric circles around a slight hill-top swell. A 10-minute walk south brings you to the Renfe train station, while the bus station lies a few blocks to the east of the city centre.

Information

There's a **tourist office** (☎ 945 16 15 98; www.vitoria -gasteiz.org/turismo; Plaza General Loma s/n; ✆ 10am-7pm Mon-Sat, 11am-2pm Sun) opposite the Basque Parliament Building.

Banks abound in the newer part of town, between the train station and Plaza de España, and the **main post office** is on Calle de las Postas.

The **Hospital de Santiago** (☎ 945 25 36 00; cnr Calle de la Paz & Calle de Olaguíbel) is near the Policía Nacional. For emergencies dial ☎ 112.

Sights

As the Basque capital, there are some important buildings of great symbolic significance, including the **Basque Parliament Building** (1853; Calle de General Alava), in the Parque de la Florida, and the **Palacio de Ajuria-Enea** (1920), residence of the *lehendakari* (president of the regional government).

ART GALLERIES

The city's new gallery of modern art, the **Artium** (☎ 945 20 90 20; Calle de Francia 24; adult/student

€3/1.50, free Wed; ✆ 11am-8pm Tue-Fri, 10.30am-8pm Sat & Sun) hosts some fine temporary and permanent exhibits. It's no Guggenheim, but the well-designed subterranean space is fresh, modern and filled with some great works by Basque, Spanish and international artists. Big names include Picasso, Dalí and Miró. Keep your eyes peeled for the 45m-high iron sculpture by Miguel Navarro in the courtyard and the magnificent crystal semi-sphere by Javier Pérez as you enter the gallery.

Another worthwhile stopping-off point for art lovers is the **Museo de Bellas Artes** (☎ 945 18 19 18; Calle Fray Francisco de Vitoria), with Basque paintings and sculpture from the 18th and 19th centuries.

CHURCHES

At the base of Vitoria's medieval *casco viejo* is the delightful **Plaza de la Virgen Blanca**, which is lorded over by the **Iglesia de San Miguel** and anchored by a monument to Wellington's victory over the French in 1813.

The 14th-century **Iglesia de San Pedro** (Calle Herrería) is the city's oldest church and has a fabulous Gothic frontispiece on its eastern façade.

On the summit of the old town and dominating its skyline is the **Catedral de Santa María** (☎ 945 25 51 35; 3-hr guided tour €2; ✆ 11am & 5pm), a veritable gallery of classical art (including works by Caravaggio and Rubens). Alas, it's closed for restoration for several years. You can ogle at its magnificent Gothic portico, but if you're keen to get inside, three-hour guided tours are offered.

MUSEUMS

Vitoria has a sprinkling of moderately interesting **museums** (admission free; ✆ 10am-2pm & 4-6.30pm Tue-Fri, 10am-2pm Sat, 11am-2pm Sun), notably the brick-and-timber **Museo de Arqueología** (☎ 945 18 19 22; Calle de la Correría 116), which is housed in a former armoury. Also worth a quick visit is the **Museo de Ciencias Naturales** (Natural Science Museum; ☎ 945 18 19 24; Siervas de Jesús 24), in the Torre de Doña Oxtanda; the **Museo Fournier de Naipes** (Card Museum; ☎ 945 18 19 20; Calle de la Cuchillería 54), in the 16th-century Palacio de Bendaña, and with an impressive collection of historic presses and playing cards, including some of the oldest European decks; and the **Museo de Armería** (☎ 945 18 19 25; Calle Fray Francisco de Vitoria) for those interested in suits of armour and weapons.

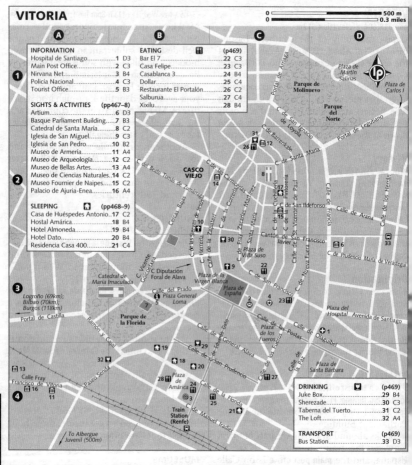

VITAORIA

0 — 500 m
0 — 0.3 miles

INFORMATION	
Hospital de Santiago	**1** D3
Main Post Office	**2** C3
Nirvana Net	**3** B4
Policía Nacional	**4** C3
Tourist Office	**5** B3

SIGHTS & ACTIVITIES	(pp467–8)
Artium	**6** D3
Basque Parliament Building	**7** B3
Catedral de Santa María	**8** C2
Iglesia de San Miguel	**9** C3
Iglesia de San Pedro	**10** B2
Museo de Armería	**11** A4
Museo de Arqueología	**12** A4
Museo de Bellas Artes	**13** A4
Museo de Ciencias Naturales	**14** C2
Museo Fournier de Naipes	**15** C2
Palacio de Ajuria-Enea	**16** A4

SLEEPING	(pp468–9)
Casa de Huéspedes Antonio	**17** C2
Hostal América	**18** B4
Hotel Almoneda	**19** B4
Hotel Dato	**20** B4
Residencia Casa 400	**21** C4

EATING	(p469)
Bar El 7	**22** C3
Casa Felipe	**23** C3
Casablanca 3	**24** B4
Dollar	**25** C4
Restaurante El Portalón	**26** C2
Salburua	**27** C4
Xixilu	**28** B4

DRINKING	(p469)
Juke Box	**29** B4
Sherezade	**30** C3
Taberna del Tuerto	**31** C2
The Loft	**32** A4

TRANSPORT	(p469)
Bus Station	**33** D3

Festivals & Events

Vitorianos, who are otherwise conservative, let their hair down for the **Fiestas de la Virgen Blanca**, held from 4 to 9 August with a typically frenzied range of fireworks, bullfights, concerts and street dancing. All of this is preceded by the symbolic descent of Celedón, a Basque effigy that flies down on strings from the Iglesia de San Miguel into the plaza below.

A **jazz festival** is held in July.

Sleeping

Albergue Juvenil (☎/fax 945 14 81 00; cnr Calle de Escultor Isaac Diéz & Calle Salvatierrabide; junior/senior dm €9/14) About 600m southwest of the train station, this is the cheapest deal in town.

Plenty of *pensiones* in and around the *casco viejo* offer decent rates.

Casa de Huéspedes Antonio (☎ 945 26 87 95; Calle de la Cuchillería 66; s/d with shared bathroom €11/22) A bit seedy from the outside, the dingy staircase gives way to comfortable and clean rooms.

Residencia Casa 400 (☎ 945 23 38 87; Calle de la Florida 46; s/d €36/45) This friendly place has recently been renovated, and offers spacious studios with TV, kitchen and bathroom. A good choice if you're staying a few days.

Hotel Dato (☎ 945 14 72 30; info@hoteldato.com; Calle de Eduardo Dato 28; s/d €28.90/41.70) This charming place is splendid value, crammed with Art Deco designs and stained-glass windows. Rooms have all the mod cons, and the location is central.

Hostal Amárica (☎ 945 13 05 06; fax 945 13 05 48; Calle de la Florida 11; s/d with breakfast €35.35/51.45) A comfy option, with pleasant rooms (some of the singles are quite small), including TV and phone. There's also a buzzing little café downstairs.

Hotel Almoneda (☎ 945 15 40 84; www.hotel almoneda.com; Calle de la Florida 7; s/d Mon-Thu €58/92, Fri-Sun €48/69) This high-quality hotel has attractive rooms and excellent service. It's particularly good value on weekends.

Eating

The cafés around Plaza de España and the adjacent Plaza de la Virgen Blanca are the most atmospheric for a leisurely coffee.

Casablanca 3 (Calle de Eduardo Dato 38; breakfast from €3.20) This much-loved café has snug booths and attentive bar staff, ideal for a leisurely breakfast over the newspapers.

You can get *pintxos* and *menús del día* at many of the bars in the *casco viejo*. Good places to start include **Bar El 7** (☎ 945 27 22 98; Calle de la Cuchillería 3; menú €9.20), a popular local stamping ground that serves no-fuss tapas, and **Salburua** (☎ 945 28 64 60; Calle de los Fueros 19), which has picked up several awards for its *pintxos*. Also a cool place, **Dollar** (Calle de la Florida 26) does good *pintxos* and is popular for an early evening glass of wine.

Xixilu (☎ 945 23 00 68; Plaza Amárica 2; meals €23) One of the few places in Vitoria that gets crowded on weekdays as well as weekends, Xixilu is famous for its *litiruelas* (crisply fried lamb sweetbreads) and unpretentious atmosphere.

Casa Felipe (☎ 945 13 45 54; Calle de los Fueros 28; full meals €20) This bastion of Vitoria's culinary scene serves up classic Basque fare, and prepares especially good *raciónes* of *caracoles* (snails), mushrooms and *jamón jabugo* (top-quality ham).

Restaurante El Portalón (☎ 945 14 27 55; Calle Correría 151) Arguably the city's best restaurant, El Portalón offers quality Basque cuisine in splendid timbered and vaulted surrounds, but expect to drop €50 or more for a three-course meal. Reservations are essential.

Drinking

Wall-to-wall bars abound in the *casco viej*, creating an intense, largely student nightlife. Calle de la Cuchillería and Calle Herrería are particularly vibrant.

Taberna del Tuerto (Calle de la Correría 151) In El Portalón, this is a dark den with pirate-ship décor and a dance floor at the back.

Sherezade (Calle Correría 42) For a different theme entirely, sip tea or coffee over a game of chess in this *Arabian Nights* setting.

Juke Box (Calle de San Prudencio 10) An American-style bar, this is the hip hang-out where you'll get eyed-up over your drinks.

The Loft (Paseo Senda s/n; admission €9; ☽ 11pm-late Thu-Sat) For later in the night, this is where house-music DJs ensure a packed dancefloor on weekends.

Getting There & Away

There's an **airport** (☎ 945 16 35 00) at Foronda, about 9km northwest of the city, with connections to Madrid and Barcelona. It's €15 to Vitoria by taxi.

Vitoria's **bus station** (☎ 945 25 84 00; Calle de los Herrán) has regular services to Madrid (€19.50, five hours, up to 13 daily), Barcelona (€32, 6¾ hours), Pamplona (€6.25, 1½ hours), San Sebastián (€6.35, 1½ hours) and Bilbao (€4.80, 50 minutes).

Trains go to Madrid (€27.50, 5½ hours, eight daily), Barcelona (€32, seven hours, one daily), San Sebastián (€7.65, 1¾ hours, up to 10 daily) and to Pamplona (€3.80, one hour, four daily).

NAVARRA

Several Spains intersect in Navarra (Basque: Nafarroa). The soft greens and bracing climate of the Navarran Pyrenees lie like a cool compress across the sunstruck brow of the south, which is all stark plains, cereal crops and vineyards, sliced up by high, forbidding sierras. Navarra is pilgrim territory: for centuries the faithful have used the pass at Roncesvalles to cross from France on their way to Santiago de Compostela (see Camino de Santiago, p83).

Although many associate Navarra exclusively with the running of the bulls in Pamplona, the region's real charm is its small towns, many with fine monuments ranging from the Romanesque to the Renaissance.

PAMPLONA
pop 190,937 / elevation 456m
Pamplona (Basque: Iruña), capital of the fiercely independent Navarrese, is an

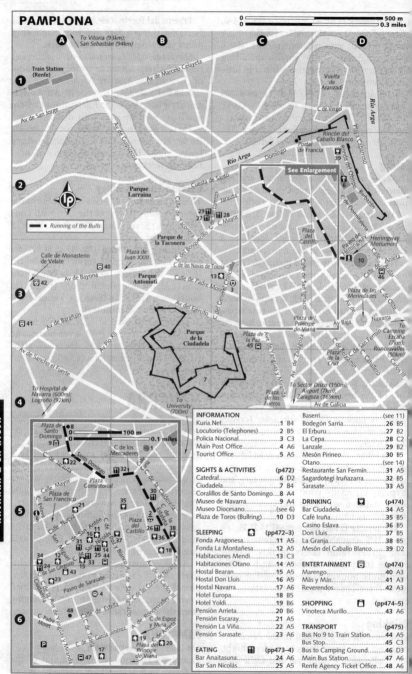

PAMPLONA

0   500 m
0   0.3 miles

Running of the Bulls

See Enlargement

To Vitoria (93km);
San Sebastián (94km)

Train Station (Renfe)

Av de Marcelo Celayeta

Vuelta de Aranzadi

C de Vergel

Río Arga

Av de San Jorge

Av de Guipúzcoa

Río Arga

Domingo

Portal de Francia

Rincón del Caballo Blanco

39

Portal del Obispo Barbazán

6

Cuesta de Santo

Jarauta

Parque Larraina

Calle de Tacorera

C del Bosquecillo

C de Curia

C Mayor

29 28
27

Plaza del Castillo

Hemingway Monument

Paseo de Hemingway

Calle de Arrieta

10

Parque de la Taconera

Plaza de Juan XXIII

C de las Navas de Tolosa

Calle de Padre Moret

13

Parque Antoniuti

C de General Chinchilla

Av del Ejército

Calle de San Ignacio

Plaza de las Merindades

C de Oitte

Navarra

To Camping Excaba (7km); Roncesvalles (50km)

Calle de Monasterio de Velate

40

42

Av de Bayona

Plaza del Príncipe de Viana

Av Baja

Plaza de la Cruz

C de San Fermín

41

Av de Barañáin

Av Pío XI

Parque de la Ciudadela

7

Plaza de Ave de Yanguas y Miranda

Plaza de la Paz

45

Plaza de la Cruz

C de San Fermín

C Caballero

Carlos III

Av de Sancho el Fuerte

To University (700m)

Plaza de los Fueros

To Sector Disco (150m); Airport (7km); Zaragoza (169km)

To Hospital de Navarra (600m); Logroño (92km)

Av de Galicia

Plaza de Santo Domingo

8

9

100 m
0.1 miles

C de los Mercaderes

1

C de Jarauta

22

32

Santo Domingo

Plaza Consistorial

Calle Mayor

Plaza de San Francisco

21

30

35

Plaza del Castillo

26 38

36

18

C de la Cuidadela

Calle Nueva

C de San Antón

11 16

31 2 37

19 44

33

34

23

Paseo de Sarasate

C de San Gregorio

43

4

48

C de Estella

C de Roncesvalles

C de las Cortes de Navarra

C de Espoz y Mina

C de Arieta

17

20

Plaza del Príncipe de Viana

P

47

C de Tudela

C de García Jiménez

C de Yanguas y Miranda

C de Navarrería

INFORMATION

Kuria.Net..................................**1**	B4
Locutorio (Telephones)...........**2**	B5
Policía Nacional........................**3**	C3
Main Post Office......................**4**	A6
Tourist Office..........................**5**	A5

SIGHTS & ACTIVITIES (p472)

Catedral...................................**6**	D2
Ciudadela.................................**7**	B4
Corralillos de Santo Domingo..**8**	A4
Museo de Navarra....................**9**	A4
Museo Diocesano..............(see 6)	
Plaza de Toros (Bullring).......**10**	D3

SLEEPING (pp472–3)

Fonda Aragonesa....................**11**	A5
Fonda La Montañesa...............**12**	A5
Habitaciones Mendi.................**13**	C3
Habitaciones Otano................**14**	B5
Hostal Bearan.........................**15**	A5
Hostal Don Lluis.....................**16**	A5
Hostal Navarra.......................**17**	A6
Hotel Europa..........................**18**	B5
Hotel Yoldi.............................**19**	B6
Pensión Arrieta.......................**20**	B6
Pensión Escaray......................**21**	A5
Pensión La Viña.......................**22**	A5
Pensión Sarasate....................**23**	A5

EATING (pp473–4)

Bar Anaitasuna.......................**24**	A6
Bar San Nicolás.......................**25**	A5

Baserri..............................(see 11)	
Bodegón Sarria.......................**26**	B5
El Erburu...............................**27**	B2
La Cepa..................................**28**	C2
Lanzale...................................**29**	B2
Mesón Pirineo........................**30**	B5
Otano...............................(see 14)	
Restaurante San Fermín.........**31**	A5
Sagardotegi Iruñazarra...........**32**	B5
Sarasate.................................**33**	A5

DRINKING (p474)

Bar Ciudadela.........................**34**	A5
Café Iruña..............................**35**	B5
Casino Eslava.........................**36**	B5
Don Lluis................................**37**	B5
La Granja................................**38**	B5
Mesón del Caballo Blanco.......**39**	D2

ENTERTAINMENT (p474)

Marengo.................................**40**	A3
Más y Más...............................**41**	A3
Reverendos............................**42**	A3

SHOPPING (pp474–5)

Vinoteca Murillo.....................**43**	A6

TRANSPORT (p475)

Bus No 9 to Train Station.......**44**	A5
Bus Stop................................**45**	C3
Bus to Camping Ground..........**46**	D3
Main Bus Station....................**47**	A6
Renfe Agency Ticket Office.....**48**	A6

attractive array of centuries-old middle-class wellbeing set behind the remains of its city walls. A fine cathedral is the jewel in the crown, but the footloose wanderer will get pleasure from simply meandering along narrow streets or relaxing in the vast green belt on the western edge of the inner city.

On 6 July, all hell breaks loose as Spain's best-known bull fest, **Sanfermines** (Fiesta de San Fermín), kick starts the city into a frenzy of drinking and mayhem. El Encierro (the running of the bulls), which was made famous by Hemingway in his 1926 novel *The Sun Also Rises*, is accompanied

THE RUNNING OF THE BULLS

One of Spain's best-known fiestas, **Sanfermines** (Fiesta de San Fermín) is an almost nonstop cacophony of music, dance, fireworks, processions and bullfights (taking place at 6.30pm daily) from 7 to 14 July. The day starts early: at 6.45am bands march around town with the aim of waking everyone from their slumber to launch them into another onslaught of festivity and bacchanalian abandon. Although the festivities begin on 6 July, the first running of the bulls doesn't take place until the following morning.

The running of the bulls always preceded the day's bullfights for the simple reason that you had to get the bulls to the ring somehow. Today in most cities the bulls are transported by truck to the *plaza de toros* (bullring), but some Spanish towns still celebrate *el encierro* (running of the bulls) as an integral part of the fiesta.

In Pamplona, every morning from 7 to 14 July, six bulls are let loose from the Coralillos de Santo Domingo to charge across the square of the same name (a good vantage point). They continue up the street, veering onto Calle de los Mercaderes from Plaza Consistorial and sweeping right onto Calle de la Estafeta for the final charge to the ring. *Mozos* (the brave or foolish, depending on your point of view) race madly with the bulls, aiming to keep close – but not too close. The total course is some 825m long and lasts little more than three minutes.

Every year people are hurt, gored and sometimes killed in *encierros* across the country. At last count, 13 people had died during the history of Pamplona's bull run, a figure that dramatically understates the risk you face if you participate. The majority of those who run are full of bravado (and/or drink), but have little idea of what they're doing. It's difficult to recommend this activity, but plenty of people (mostly Spaniards) participate anyway. Try to run with someone experienced, and above all don't get caught near bulls that have been separated from the herd – a lone, frightened 500kg bull surrounded by charging humans makes for an unpredictable and dangerous animal. Keeping ahead of the herd is the general rule. As part of your preparation, familiarise yourself with the course.

To participate you must enter the course before 7.30am from Plaza de Santo Domingo and take up your position. Around 8am two rockets are fired: the first announces that the bulls have been released from the corrals; the second lets you know they're all out and running. The first truly dangerous point is where Calle de los Mercaderes leads into Calle de la Estafeta. Here many of the bulls crash into the barriers because of the sheer speed at which they attempt to take the turns, and this is where at least some are likely to be separated from the herd. Another particularly treacherous stretch comes towards the end, where Calle de la Estafeta slopes down into the final turn to Plaza de Toros.

A third rocket goes off when all the bulls have made it to the ring, and a final one when they have been rounded up in the stalls where they will await the fight. If you want to watch a fight and fail to get tickets in advance, you'll usually find scalpers selling cheap seats for around €8.

The whole shebang winds up at midnight on 14 July with a candle-lit procession, known as the Pobre de Mí, which starts from Plaza Consistorial.

During the 2004 running of the bulls 300 protesters from the People for the Ethical Treatment of Animals conducted a widely reported protest against the cruelty of the fiesta. They marched only in their underwear (city officials refused permission for a naked protest). Protests were also held in Madrid and elsewhere around the country, although it was unclear how many of the protesters were foreigners and how many were Spanish. The 2004 fiesta was one of the most dangerous in recent years with dozens of injuries, but no deaths.

by a stampede of visitors from all over the world, hellbent on having such a good time they are unlikely to remember much of it. For more details, see The Running of the Bulls, p471.

History

The Romans called the city Pompaelo, after its founder Pompey the Great. They were succeeded by the Visigoths and briefly by the Muslims, but by the 8th century Pamplona formed the nucleus of an independent power, the future kingdom of Navarra. It reached the height of its glory under Sancho III in the 11th century, and its position on the Camino de Santiago assured its prosperity.

Orientation

The compact old city centre is marked off to the north and east by the Río Arga and what remains of the old defensive wall. To the west it's bordered by parks and Ciudadela, the former citadel. The main square, Plaza del Castillo, roughly marks the division between old and new. Everything, including the bullring, is a short walk away. The train station is less central, northwest of the city centre.

Information

There are several banks with exchange services and ATMs along Paseo de Sarasate. During the Sanfermines, they're open in the morning only.

Emergency (☎ 112)

Hospital de Navarra (☎ 948 42 21 00; Calle de Irunlarrea)

Kuria.Net (☎ 948 22 30 77; Calle Curia 15; per hr €3; ☼ 10am-10pm) Savvy place.

Main post office (Cnr Paseo de Sarasate & Calle de Vínculo)

Policía Nacional (Calle del General Chinchilla)

Telephone Locutorio (Plaza de Castillo; ☼ 9am-11pm)

Tourist office (☎ 948 20 65 40; oit.pamplona@cf navarra.es; Calle de Esclava 1; ☼ 10am-2pm & 4-7pm Mon-Sat, 10am-2pm Sun) This excellent tourist office has English-speaking staff and stacks of information about Navarra.

Sights
CATEDRAL

Pamplona's main **catedral** (☎ 948 21 08 27; www .cultura5.com; guided tours adult/student €3.85/2.25) stands on a rise just inside the city ram-

parts. Its single most outstanding feature is the Gothic cloister in the French style inside the church, Carlos III of Navarra (the Noble) and his wife Doña Leonor are buried in splendour. The **Museo Diocesano** oc cupies the former refectory (dining room) and kitchen, and houses the usual assort ment of religious art, including some fine Gothic woodcarvings.

The cathedral, cloister and museum can be visited on three-hour guided tours at 10am and 4pm daily, except Saturday afternoon and Sunday. The cathedral gates are open just before and after Mass, allowing you to sneak a free look inside.

MUSEO DE NAVARRA

Housed in a former medieval hospital this **museum** (☎ 948 42 64 92; admission €2, free Sa afternoon & Sun; ☼ 9.30am-2pm & 5-7pm Tue-Sat, 11am 2pm Sun) contains a mildly interesting and eclectic collection of archaeological finds (including a Roman mosaic), as well as a selection of art (including a Goya).

CIUDADELA & PARKS

The walls and bulwarks of the grand fortified citadel, the star-shaped **Ciudadela** (admission free ☼ 7.30am-9.30pm Mon-Sat, 9.30am-9.30pm Sun), can barely be made out for all the grass and trees in what now constitutes a park. Just north of here are three more parks, allowing ample room for relaxing and strolling.

Sleeping

During Sanfermines all hotels raise their rates – some even triple their normal prices – and it can be impossible to get a room without booking ahead. Touts may greet you at the train station at this time, offering rooms in private houses.

Otherwise, you can join the throngs sleeping in the parks. People choosing this option should be aware that they are a prime target for thieves who are expert at slitting sleeping bags and whipping out anything from inside, apart from yourself. It's best to leave most belongings in the *consigna* (left-luggage office) at the bus or train stations.

BUDGET

Ezcaba (☎ 948 33 03 15; per person/tent/car €3.75/3.75/ 3.75) On the banks of the Rió Ulzama, about 7km north on the N121, this is the nearest camping ground. A bus service runs four times daily from near the Plaza de Toros; look for the Montañesa bus to Arre/Oricain.

You'll find plenty of cheap *fondas* (inns) and *pensiones* around Pamplona's old centre. All places in this category have basic rooms with shared bathroom.

Pensión La Viña (☎ 948 21 32 50; Calle de Jarauta 8; s/d €12/24) This place is hard to beat for its combination of central location, simple but pleasant rooms and rock-bottom prices.

Pensión Escaray (☎ 948 22 78 25; Calle Nueva 24; s/d €18/36) Pensión Escaray is excellent value with polished floorboards, high ceilings, and very clean rooms and bathrooms, although some rooms are on the small side.

Fonda La Montañesa (☎ 948 22 43 80; Calle de San Gregorio 2; s/d €14/28) This creaky old building has ageing rooms; they're simple but clean and adequate for a night. Try to get one with a balcony.

Fonda Aragonesa (☎ 948 22 34 28; Calle de San Nicolás 32; d €28) Not a bad choice, the rooms here are simple if in a little better condition than those at Fonda La Montañesa.

MID-RANGE & TOP END

All of the following places have private bathrooms unless state otherwise.

Habitaciones Mendi (☎ 948 22 52 97; Calle de las Navas de Tolosa 9; s/d €30/36) Mendi is one of the best places in Pamplona for its price. The building has loads of character and enough of it spills over into the rooms, which are large and come with TV. There are some larger doubles with a sitting area and balcony for €45, which are a steal.

Pensión Sarasate (☎ /fax 948 22 30 84; Paseo de Sarasate 30; s/d €30/37) This is a good choice, as the rooms are well priced and come with a few pretty touches in a renovated 19th-century building.

Hostal Bearan (☎ /fax 948 22 34 28; Calle de San Nicolás 25; s/d from €31/37) If you want to be right in the heart of the action, you'd do well to choose Hostal Bearan, with its comfortable rooms that come with TV and phone. It's a pity the service is at times indifferent.

Habitaciones Otano (☎ 948 22 50 95; Calle de San Nicolás 5; s/d with shared bathroom €13/30, with private bathroom €30/42) Unfortunately, the rooms lack the character of the attached restaurant (see Eating, p474), but they're comfy, clean and come with TV and polished floorboards.

Pensión Arrieta (☎ 948 22 84 59; Calle de Arrieta 27; s/d with shared bathroom €32/38, d with private bathroom €45) One of the best (and friendliest) of the options near the bus station, Pensión Arrieta has attractive rooms that come with TV and ceiling fans.

Hostal Don Lluis (☎ 948 21 04 99; Calle de San Nicolás 24; s/d from €35/40) A good central choice, Hostal Don Lluis has pleasant rooms and some of the doubles have sofas.

Hotel Yoldi (☎ 948 22 48 00; www.hotelyoldi.com; Avenida de San Ignacio 11; s/d €53/78) A Pamplona institution since the 1920s, Hotel Yoldi has hosted celebs from Hemingway to Charlton Heston. Don't be put off by the uninspiring exterior – the rooms are very agreeable with all the mod cons (including a CD player in some rooms).

Hotel Europa (☎ 948 22 18 00; www.hreuropa.com; Calle de Espoz y Mina 11; s/d €49/112.50) Good levels of comfort await you here in this very central location. Some rooms carry a touch of old-world flair (the singles are small, though comfortable). Ask about its weekend packages.

Eating

Bar Anaitasuna (☎ 948 22 79 56; Calle de San Gregorio 58; menú €7.50) This bar is one of those one-size-fits-all places attracting the newspaper-reading breakfast crowd to those in search of late-night *marcha* (action). The décor's nothing to write home about, but the place has a buzz.

Baserri (☎ 948 22 20 21; Calle San Nicolás 32) This is the bar to belly up to for the most innovative and creative *pintxos* in town. For €15 you can get a selection of nine *pintxos*, including new creations, and the wine selection here is tops, too.

BASQUE COUNTRY, NAVARRA & LA RIOJA

Otano (☎ 948 22 26 38; Calle de San Nicolás 5) Really outstanding *patatas bravas* (sautéed potatoes) are the best choices here, are some of the most creative *pintxos* in Pamplona. The upstairs restaurant of the same name (☎ 948 22 50 95; menú €11, mains €11-15) is a good upmarket place amid a pleasant high-beamed setting.

Restaurante San Fermín (☎ 948 22 21 91; Calle de San Nicolás 44; menú €12) An upmarket place, this is a Pamplona classic, with excellent *alcachofas* (artichokes) for €7.50.

Bar San Nicolás (Calle de San Nicolás 13) A popular place serving Spanish standards, such as paella and *bacalao* (salted cod), as well as a Basque menú (€9).

Sarasate (☎ 948 22 57 27; Calle de San Nicolás 21; menú weekday/weekend €10/16) This bright, uncluttered vegetarian restaurant on the 1st floor is consistently good. It also does a refreshing apple and carrot juice (€1.40).

Bodegón Sarria (Calle de la Estafeta 50; mains from €7.90, menú €11.50) An excellent choice, this place draws an older crowd with its substantial, mostly meat-based meals. It's an atmospheric place, with a great collection of B&W photos of Hemingway and the bulls gracing the walls.

Mesón Pirineo (☎ 948 22 20 45; Calle de la Estafeta 41; menú €11.50) Similar to Bodegón Sarria, Mesón Pirineo has a varied menu from which, if you pick carefully, you could eat well (three courses) for about €15.

For more options, wander west to the more downmarket Calle de San Lorenzo.

El Erburu (☎ 948 22 51 69; Calle de San Lorenzo 19) Churning out reliable home-made cooking this the much-loved place has a *menú* for €9. It's unassuming and frequented by a local elbow-on-the-table crowd.

Lanzale (☎ 948 22 10 71; Calle de San Lorenzo 31) Next door to El Erburu and very similar, Lonzale charges just €8.50.

La Cepa (☎ 948 21 31 45; Calle de San Lorenzo 2; menú €9) This high-ceilinged eatery with red walls and wooden tables pulls in a hip, young crowd, and it's a good bet for meals or just drinks and snacks.

Sagardotegi Iruñazarra (☎ 948 22 51 67; Calle de los Mercaderes 15) You don't have to venture out into the Navarran countryside to enjoy the cider house experience (see the boxed text Basque Cider House Rules, p455). Here you'll get the full traditional meal (including huge plates of beef) for €20 to €25.

Included in the price, of course, is as much cider as you can drink.

Drinking
CAFÉS & BARS
Thanks to a student population of about 20,000, Pamplona has a lively after-dark scene year-round.

The cafés on Plaza del Castillo, with their French-style awnings, are a great place to start or end the day. **Café Iruña** (Plaza del Castillo 44), with frilly *belle époque* décor, is one of Pamplona's grande dames and a perennial favourite for coffees or aperitifs, while **Casino Eslava**, at the other end of the plaza, has more reservedly modern chic and an older crowd.

Other good bars nearby include the intimate **Don Lluis** (Cnr Calle de San Nicolás & Calle de Pozo Blanco) or the more modern **La Granja** (Calle de la Estafeta 71), which is a popular place early in the evening.

Bar Ciudadela (Calle de la Ciudadela 3) An upstairs bar where you can sip a drink on little balconies in summer, this is one of our favourites.

Mesón del Caballo Blanco (Ronda del Obispo Barbazán) An enduring favourite in an old church just inside the city wall north of the cathedral. It's mostly outdoors with fantastic views, making it ideal for a summer's afternoon.

Calle de Jarauta is wall-to-wall bars (of the loud and late variety). It can be slightly adolescent here in the early evening, but it quickly fills up with 20- and 30-somethings after midnight.

Entertainment
CLUBS & DISCOTECAS
Most of Pamplona's dance venues are a walk or short taxi ride south and west of the old city centre in the general direction of the university.

Reverendos (Calle de Monasterio de Velate 5) and **Más y Más** (Avenida Bayona 45) pull in the dance and techno fiends, while **Marengo** (Avenida de Bayona 2) gets the crowds going with Latin rhythms. Doors at these places are usually open after 11pm Thursday to Saturday, and the cover charge tends to be around €6 to €10, depending on the night.

Shopping
Vinoteca Murillo (☎ 948 22 10 15; cnr Calle de San Gregorio & Plaza de San Nicolás; ☼ 9am-1.45pm & 4-8pm Mon-Sat) A wine shop that fills 5L containers

of good Navarran wine for €5.38, this is a good place to stock up on local wines and other delicacies. It's also a great place to buy a *bota*, the traditional Navarran wine skin.

Getting There & Away

AIR

Pamplona's **airport** (☎ 948 16 87 00), about 7km south of the city, has regular flights to Madrid and Barcelona. To get there take bus No 16 from Plaza de La Paz (€0.85).

BUS

From the **main bus station** (Avenida de Yanguas y Miranda) buses leave for most towns throughout Navarra, although service is restricted on Sunday.

Regular buses run to Bilbao (€10.85, 1¾ hours), Vitoria (€6.25, 1½ hours), Logroño (€6.55, 1½ hours), San Sebastián (€6.10, one hour), Soria (€10.70, two hours), Madrid (€22.20, five hours) and Barcelona (€31.20, five hours). Regional destinations include Olite (€2.50, 40 minutes, 16 daily), Javier (€3.70, one hour, two daily), Estella (€3.05, one hour, 10 daily), Tudela (€5.75, 1¼ hours, eight daily) and Puente La Reina (€1.55, 30 minutes, 10 daily).

CAR & MOTORCYCLE

The A15 *autopista* connects Pamplona with San Sebastián, although the N121 is a more scenic – and free – alternative. The N135 leads east into the Pyrenees, while the N240 heads west to Vitoria and Burgos and east to Aragón. For Logroño take the N111.

TRAIN

Although Pamplona's train station is north of town, it's connected to the city centre by bus No 9 from Paseo de Sarasate every 15 minutes. Tickets are also sold at the **Renfe agency** (☎ 948 22 72 82; Calle de Estella 8; ☼ 9am-1.30pm & 4.30-7.30pm Mon-Fri, 9.30am-1pm Sat).

Trains run to/from Madrid (€45.50, 4½ hours, three daily), Barcelona (€29.50, six hours, three daily) and San Sebastián (from €12.50, two hours, three daily).

EAST OF PAMPLONA

Southeast along the road to Aragon (N240), there are a handful of interesting towns and the grand Monasterio de Leyre in the foothills of the Pyrenees which offer worthwhile stopovers.

Sangüesa

pop 4750 / elevation 430m

The biggest town in eastern Navarra and once an important stop on the pilgrim route to Santiago de Compostela for those crossing from France, Sangüesa retains a keen sense of its past, including one of the premier examples of Romanesque religious art in Navarra, the **Iglesia de Santa María** with its octagonal tower, alongside the Río Aragón. Entry is through an exquisite 12th-century portal.

Immediately opposite is the **tourist office** (☎ 948 87 14 11; oit.sanguesa@cfnavarra.es; Calle Mayor 2; ☼ 10am-2pm & 4-7pm Mon-Sat, 10am-2pm Sun).

Sangüesa is not a bad place to spend the night, since it has more life than any of the nearby pueblos (villages).

Cantolagua (☎ 948 43 03 52; www.mardelpirineo .com; Camino de Cantolagua s/n; per person/tent €3.30/3.30; ☼ mid-Feb–Oct) is a well-equipped camping ground, while the most comfortable place in town is **Hostal JP** (☎ 948 87 16 93; jphostal@ciberwebs .com; Paseo Raimundo Lumbier 3; s/d €30/44), opposite the Iglesia de Santa Maria. **Pensión Las Navas** (☎ 948 87 00 77; Calle de Alfonso el Batallador 7; s/d €18/36) has cheap rooms and also does good food, including a special *asado* (grilled meat) menu for €15.

Regular buses run daily to/from Pamplona (€3.15, 45 minutes).

Javier

pop 77 / elevation 448m

Javier (Xavier), 11km northeast of Sangüesa, is where the patron saint of Navarra, San Francisco Xavier, was born in 1506. The unattractive town lies downhill from the quaint, Jesuit-owned **Castillo de Javier** (☎ 948 88 40 00; admission free; ☼ 9am-12.40pm & 4-6.40pm Apr-Sep, 9am-12.40pm & 4-5.40pm Oct-Mar), an evocative piece of medieval architecture that houses a small museum dedicated to the life of the patron saint, who was a missionary in the Far East.

Hotel El Mesón (☎ 948 88 40 35; d with bathroom €53.50), about 200m from the Castillo, is the best place to rest your head, although it's a touch overpriced.

A daily bus passes through from Pamplona and Sangüesa enroute for Huesca; another heads up the Valle de Roncal.

Yesa & the Monasterio de Leyre

pop 219 / elevation 559m

About 5km north of Yesa lies the **Monasterio de Leyre** (☎ 948 88 41 50; admission €1.80;

☻ 10.15am-2pm & 3.30-7pm), set in the shadow of the Sierra de Leyre. A religious community was first established here in the 9th century. In 1836 the monks were evicted and, over the next 100 years, shepherds used the monastery to shelter their flocks. In 1954, when the Benedictines moved in, they found themselves confronted with the enormous task of restoration.

The early-Romanesque crypt is the most fascinating part of the complex. It's a three-nave structure with a low roof; its squat columns and vaguely horseshoe-shaped arches are unique to the monastery. The Romanesque cloister was destroyed after the expulsion of the Cistercians, but the 12th-century main portal of the church is a fine example of Romanesque artistry at its most challenging, and is rich in symbolism.

The monks sell recordings of themselves performing Gregorian chants, but you can hear the real thing if you can make it to the 9am Mass or 7pm vespers service.

The most imaginative choice of accommodation is the **Hospederia de Leyre** (☎ 948 88 41 00; www.monasteriodeleyre.com; s/d €30.38/54.07), which is housed in part of the monastery complex. After the day visitors trickle away, it's wonderfully silent, the rooms are comfortable and there's a reasonable restaurant.

There's an early morning bus from Yesa to Pamplona, as well as one to Huesca. Virtually no buses run on Sunday, and none at all from Yesa to the monastery.

Museo Oteiza

Around 9km northeast of Pamplona in the town of Alzuza, this impressive new **museum** (☎ 948 33 20 74; www.museooteiza.org; Calle de la Cuesta 7; adult/student/child €3/1.50/free, free Fri; ☻ 10am-8pm Tue-Sun) contains almost 3000 pieces by the renowned Navarran sculptor, Jorge Oteiza. As well as his workshop, this beautifully designed gallery incorporates the artist's former home in a lovely rural setting.

Rio Irati (☎ 948 22 14 70) has at least one bus a day to Alzuza from Pamplona's bus station. If you're driving, Alzuza is signposted north off the NA150, just east of Huarte.

WEST OF PAMPLONA

The N111 is the main route west out of Pamplona, winding gently to Logroño along the Camino de Santiago. Dotted with a handful of charming villages and especially

bursting with colour after the spring rains, it's one of the more enticing stretches for those walking the Camino. Buses travel between Pamplona and Logroño along this route.

Puente la Reina
pop 2520 / elevation 421m

It's at Puente la Reina (Basque: Gares) that pilgrims approaching from Roncesvalles to the north and Aragón to the east have for centuries joined together to take the one main route west to Santiago de Compostela. Their first stop here was at the late-Romanesque **Iglesia del Crucifijo**, erected by the Knights Templar and still containing one of the finest Gothic crucifixes in existence. From here the narrow Calle Mayor leads to the **Iglesia de Santiago**, sporting an eroded Romanesque portal with Mudéjar touches; inside is an especially beautiful sculpture of the saint. The town's bridge, the six-arched medieval **Puente la Reina** at the end of Calle Mayor, remains the nicest way to cross the Río Arga and continue along the Camino.

Estella
pop 13,449 / elevation 483m

The attractive town of Estella (Basque: Lizarra), huddled on the bend of the tree-shaded Río Ega, makes a good base for excursions in the vicinity.

Seat of the Carlists in the 19th century, the village of Lizarra later became the primary reception point for the growing flood of pilgrims along the Camino.

The helpful **tourist office** (☎ 948 55 63 01; oit .estella@cfnavarra.es; Calle de San Nicolás 1; ☻ 10am-2pm & 4-7pm Mon-Sat Sep & Easter-Jun, 10am-8pm Mon-Sat Jul & Aug, 10am-5pm Mon-Sat Oct-Easter, 10am-2pm Sun year-round) is on the southwestern bank of the river.

The most important monument, opposite the tourist office, is the 12th-century, cliff-top **Iglesia de San Pedro de la Rúa**, whose fortified tower lords over the town. Guided visits leave from the tourist office seven times a day (€2.20, 30 minutes) or you can view the cloister by climbing the steps further along the street. Guided tours of the entire town, along with an English commentary, cost €3.50 and last for 1½ hours.

Adjacent to the tourist office is the **Palacio de los Reyes**, a rare example of Romanesque civil construction, containing a small art museum. Across the river and overlooking the town is the **Iglesia de San Miguel**. Its most interesting feature is the Romanesque north door.

Every year from 31 July to 8 August, Estella hosts a **feria** (fair) with its own running of the bulls – not nearly as hyped as Pamplona's but equally exhilarating.

Estella has many hotels, among the better of which are **Pensión San Andrés** (☎ 948 55 41 58; Plaza Santiago 58; s/d with washbasin from €12/24, with private bathroom €23/32), with simple, clean rooms; **Hostal Cristina** (☎ 948 55 07 72; Calle Baja Navarra 1; d €42.07), which overlooks the main square and has good rooms; and central **Hotel Yerri** (☎ 948 54 60 34; fax 948 55 50 81; Avenida de Yerri 35; s/d €30.05/50), which is very comfortable.

Around Estella

There are some fascinating monasteries in the vicinity of Estella. About 3km southwest of Estella, near Ayegui, the **Monasterio de Irache** (☎ 948 55 44 64; admission free; 9.30am-1.30pm Tue, 9.30am-1.30pm & 5-7pm Wed-Fri, 8.30am-1.30pm & 4-7pm Sat & Sun, closed 1 Dec-7 Jan) is an ancient Benedictine monastery that has undergone many changes over the centuries. Its most alluring features are the 16th-century Plateresque **cloister** and the **Puerta Especiosa**, decorated with delicate sculptures.

Set in quieter country, the **Monasterio de Iranzu** (☎ 948 52 00 47; www.monasterio-iranzu.com; admission €2.40; 10am-2pm & 4-8pm May-Sep, 10am-2pm & 4-6pm Oct-Apr) is backed by a wooded hillside about 10km north of Estella, near Abárzuza.

The Road to Logroño

The road to Logroño continues past **Los Arcos**, with the **Iglesia de Santa María** and its impressive Gothic cloister, before winding through rolling country to **Torres del Río**, whose octagonal 12th-century Romanesque **Iglesia del Santo Sepulcro** is a little gem. Only about 10km short of Logroño, **Viana** is a quiet spot with the mansions of noble families peppered around its old centre; the town's Gothic **Iglesia de Santa María** has an outstanding Renaissance doorway.

NORTH OF PAMPLONA

Sierra de Aralar

The scenic Sierra de Aralar was much beloved by Hemingway, an avid trout fisherman. From **Lekunberri**, the area's main town,

NAVARRA'S CASAS RURALES

Navarra has a particularly well organised set of *casas rurales* (village houses or farmsteads with rooms to let) and are often beautifully looked-after houses in mountain villages. They are popular in peak periods and reservations are recommended. The standards are often higher and rates lower than in your average *hostal*. You can recognise the *casas rurales* by one of two small plaques: one has 'CR' in white on a dark-green background; the more modern one, in brown, olive-green and white, displays the letter 'C' and the outline of a house.

A copy of the *Guía de Alojamientos*, is available free from most tourist offices in Navarra, and it lists all the private homes and farmsteads that rent out rooms.

which also has a **tourist office** (☎ 948 50 72 04; oit .lekunberri@cfnavarra.es; Calle de Plazaola 21), the NA1510 leads southwest through the most scenic countryside, culminating (after 21km) in the austere 9th-century **Santuario de San Miguel de Aralar** (☎ 948 39 60 28; 10am-2pm & 4-7pm), which lies in the shadow of Monte Altxueta (1343m) and has attractive circular naves and a 12th-century *retablo* (altarpiece).

Lekunberri has a number of hotels and restaurants. The best choice is **Hostal Ayestarán** (☎ 948 50 41 27; hotelayestaran@terra.es; Calle de Aralar 27; r €48.05).

Most buses between Pamplona and San Sebastián stop in Lekunberri, but you'll need your own vehicle to explore the sierra.

Valle del Baztán

This is rural Basque country at its best with minor roads taking you through charming little villages, such as **Arraioz** (known for the fortified **Casa Jaureguizar**), **Ziga**, with its 16th-century church, and about 1km further north, a beautiful lookout point and **Irurita**, with another fine church.

Just beyond Irurita on the N121B is the valley's biggest town, **Elizondo**. Although not the prettiest of the Baztán pueblos, it makes a convenient base for exploring the area, and there's plenty of accommodation. Among these, you'll find the comfortable **Hotel Bastán** (☎ 948 58 00 50; www.hotelbaztan .com; s/d €52/64;), which has well-equipped rooms, two swimming pools and a children's playground. If you prefer a more rural setting, **Casa Jaén** (☎ 948 58 04 87; d €25) is a *casa rural* with two delightful little doubles in a chalet-style building, while **Casa Urruska** (☎ 948 45 21 06; urruxka@terra.es; d €41) is another tranquil choice about 10km out of town.

Buses go to Pamplona up to four times daily (€3.70), stopping in many of the smaller villages up and down the valley.

Beyond Elizondo, a particularly lovely road climbs eastwards through the enchanting villages of **Arizkun** and **Erratzu** to the French border-pass of **Puerto de Izpegui**. You'll find at least 10 well-priced *casas rurales* in Arizkun. There are more choices in Erratzu, as well as **Camping Baztan** (☎ 948 45 31 33; per person/tent €3.80/7.20).

The N121B continues northwards to the Puerto de Otxondo and the border crossing into France at Dantxarinea. Just before the border a minor road veers west to **Zugarramurdi**, home to the **Cuevas de Las Brujas** (Witches' Caves; admission €2.40; ☺ 9am-dusk); a trail snakes around and through a huge rock tunnel. A few kilometres away are more caves, this time with the odd stalactite and stalagmite, at **Urdazubi-Urdax**.

At last count, there were 11 *casas rurales* in Zugarramurdi, with doubles starting from €25. One bus daily (except Sunday) goes to Elizondo.

From Zugarramurdi you could follow a tiny back road south to Mugairi (Basque: Oronoz), putting you back on the N121A where the first worthwhile stop is a few kilometres off to the east at **Etxalar**. The churchyard is sprinkled with traditional tombstones in the shape of small discs. A little further north and off to the west, **Lesaka** is noted for its **Iglesia de San Martín de Tours** and the so-called *casherna*, a medieval tower in the village centre. All these towns have *casas rurales*.

SOUTH OF PAMPLONA

The roads south of Pamplona aren't the most inspiring in Navarra, but this only makes the towns of Olite and Tudela even more of a surprise.

Olite

pop 3265 / elevation 365m

Olite is a delight, with quiet streets and an exceptional medieval defensive castle complex known as the **Palacio Real** (Castillo de Olite; ☎ 948 74 00 35; adult/child €2.70/1.80; ☺ 10am-2pm & 4-7pm Apr, May, Jun & Sep; 10am-2pm & 4-8pm Jul & Aug; 10am-2pm & 4-6pm Oct-Mar), which completely dominates the town. Built by Carlos III of Navarra on the site of what was originally a fortified Roman *praesidium* (garrison), it served as the residence of the Navarran kings until the union with the kingdom of Castile in 1512. The centrepiece of the rambling crenellated structure is the **Gran Torre**, one of a straggle of round towers and annexes that offer fine views. Integrated into the castle is the **Iglesia de Santa María la Real**, with its astonishingly detailed Gothic portal.

Another wonderful reason to visit is the state-of-the-art **Museo del Vino** (☎ 948 74 07 54; museodelvino@congresosnavarra.com; Plaza de los Teobaldos 10; admission €3.50; ☺ 10.30am-2pm & 4.30-8pm Wed-Sun, 4.30-8pm Mon & Tue). This excellent museum starts with a display of the major wine labels of Navarra, then takes you in detail through the processes of grape growing (1st floor), wine making (2nd floor) and finishes with a discussion of wine appreciation (basement). There are interactive displays, and all descriptions are in English, French and Spanish. The entrance ticket to the Palacio Real entitles you to a €1 discount.

Olite has a helpful **tourist office** (☎ 948 74 17 03; oit.olite@cfnavarra.es; Calle Mayor 1; ☺ 10am-2pm & 4-7pm Mon-Sat, 10am-2pm Sun Easter-12 Oct; 10am-5pm Mon-Fri & 10am-2pm Sat & Sun 13 Oct-Easter).

Olite is a pleasant place to spend a night. **Hotel Merindad de Olite** (☎ 948 74 02 13; Rúa de la Judería 11; s/d from €51.10/60.10) is particularly charming, while **Hotel Casa Zanito** (☎ 948 74 00 02; Rúa Revillas s/n; s/d from €45.10/54.10) is also good for a bit less. As with all paradors, the **Principe de Viana** (☎ 948 74 00 00; olite@parador.es; Plaza de los Teobaldos 2; s/d €93.80/109.80) is in a sumptuous, atmospheric class of its own.

Casa del Preboste (☎ 948 71 22 50; Rúa de Mirapies 8; menú €8.25) is a fun pizzeria-grill in a vaulted building – pizza starts at €6.60.

Hourly buses run between Olite and Pamplona (€2.50, 40 minutes).

Around Olite

Some 18km east of Olite, the tiny medieval village of **Ujué** balances atop a hill overlooking the plains of southern Navarra. The village itself is quiet and pretty with steep, narrow streets tumbling down the hillside, but what gives it something special is the hybrid **Iglesia de Santa María**, a fortified church of mixed Romanesque–Gothic style. The heart of Carlos II is preserved here. If you stop 1.5km before town, there are exceptional views.

Monasterio de la Oliva

Off another side road to the east of the main Pamplona–Zaragoza highway lies the quiet backwater of Carcastillo. Two kilometres further on, the formidable Monasterio de la Oliva was begun by the Cistercians in the 12th century. Its austere church gives onto a particularly pleasing Gothic cloister. There are two or three buses daily between Pamplona and Carcastillo.

Tudela

pop 31,228 / elevation 243m

An ancient city that was in Muslim hands for some 400 years, Tudela is well worth a wander, with its twisting street layout serving as a reminder of its Islamic past. There's a **tourist office** (☎ /fax 948 84 80 58; oit.tudela@cfnavarra .es; Calle de Juicio 4; ⊙ 10am-2pm & 4-7pm Mon-Sat, 10am-2pm Sun Easter–12 Oct; 10am-5pm Mon-Fri, 10am-2pm Sat & Sun 13 Oct–Easter) opposite the catedral.

The brightly decorated, 17th-century **Plaza de los Fueros** is a great place to start your exploration of the town. A short distance away is the **catedral**, a sober 12th-century Gothic structure built of stone and brick. The western Puerta del Juicio is particularly striking, with its many sculpted figures looking decidedly uneasy about their participation in the Last Judgment. At the time of writing the cathedral was closed for a long restoration.

Perhaps the quirkiest of Tudela's attractions is its 13th-century **bridge** over the Río Ebro. It's east and downhill from the cathedral, past the 12th-century **Iglesia de la Magdalena**. Devoid of uniformity, it's what Spaniards call a *chapuza* (botched job). Seven centuries later, it still works fine!

Of the other churches in Tudela, the **Iglesia de San Nicolás** still sports a fine Romanesque tympanum featuring lions above one of its doors; it's at the end of Calle Rúa. Take time to wander the streets as there are some fine old mansions, many with Aragónese-style *aleros* (awnings) jutting out from the roof – the **Palacio del Marqués de San Adrián** (Calle de Magallón 10) is an impressive example.

Hostal Remigio (☎ 948 82 08 50; Calle de Gaztambide 4; s/d €22.50/38), with a venerable old dining room and very good-value rooms, is just off Plaza de los Fueros.

At least five trains run daily to/from Pamplona (€10.80, 1¼ hours). Buses (€5.75, 1¼ hours, eight daily) operate from next to the train station, southeast of the town centre.

THE PYRENEES

The Navarran Pyrenees are hugely rewarding for nature lovers, outdoor enthusiasts and pilgrims on the Camino de Santiago. Trekkers and skiers alike should note a couple of emergency numbers in case they get into serious trouble in the mountains: ☎ 112 in Navarra or ☎ 17 in Aquitaine (France).

Walking

In addition to numerous local walking trails, the GR12 long-distance trail from Burguete leads eastward for five days (80km) through some of the best scenery Navarra has to offer. You'll need a sleeping bag and all-weather gear, even in summer. Further information can be obtained from the **Federación Navarra de Deportes de Montaña y Escalada** (☎ 948 22 46 83; www.fedme.es) in Pamplona.

Starting in Burguete, head north to Roncesvalles, cross the Puerto de Ibañeta and steer eastward to Fábrica de Orbaitzeta. You may need to head south to the town of Orbaitzeta proper to get a bed (there are three *casas rurales*).

The next day will take you through the Bosque de Irati to Las Casas de Irati; you may be able to stay in the *casa del guarda* (a kind of warden's house) but be prepared to camp (free). The following stage sees you climbing to the bare heights of the Puerto de Larrau (ask at the restaurant-bar, 4km south of the French border, about bunk beds). The trail then cuts across the Sierra de Abodi; you can reach the Belagua *refugio* (shelter) in about five hours.

The final trek takes you to the highest mountain in Navarra, La Mesa de los Tres Reyes (2438m), from where the easiest thing to do is descend to the town of Zuriza at the top end of the Valle de Ansó in Aragón (see p471).

To France via Roncesvalles

As you bear northeast out of Pamplona on the N135 and ascend into the Pyrenees, the yellows, browns and olive-greens of lower Navarra begin to give way to more luxuriant vegetation.

BURGUETE

Burguete (Basque: Auriẓtz), a spotless mountain village straddling the main road, was a favourite getaway for Hemingway – it's worlds apart from its dusty counterparts further south.

There's a supermarket, bank and a fair spread of accommodation.

Camping Urrobi (☎ 948 76 02 00; per person/tent €3.30/3.30; ☺ Apr-Oct) is a few kilometres south. In the town itself and apart from a sprinkling of *casas rurales*, **Hostal Juandeaburre** (☎ 948 76 00 78; Calle de San Nicolas 38; s/d with washbasin €14/25) is good value, with its immaculate polished floorboards, while **Hotel Loizu** (☎ 948 76 00 08; hloizu@cmn.navarra.net; s/d from €36.10/45.10) is the most comfortable choice and also has a good restaurant.

Restaurante Txikipolit (☎ 948 76 00 19; Calle de San Nicolas 52; menú €14), on the main drag, has tasty mains and specialises in *foie gras*.

RONCESVALLES

A few kilometres further north, Roncesvalles (Basque: Orreaga) is little more than a **monastery complex** (admission to cloister, chapterhouse & museum €2.10, guided tours €3.60; ☺ 10am-1.30pm & 3.30-7pm, shorter hrs Oct-Mar) sitting within an atmospheric mountain pass, which for centuries has been a major Pyrenees crossing point for pilgrims on the Camino de Santiago. The 13th-century Gothic church **Real Colegiata de Santa María** (admission free; ☺ 10am-8.30pm) contains a much-revered, silver-covered statue of the Virgin. Also of interest is the **cloister** (rebuilt in the 17th century), and more particularly the **chapterhouse**, with its beautiful star-ribbed vaulting. This contains the tomb of King Sancho VII (El Fuerte) of Navarra, the apparently 2.25m-tall victor in the Battle of Las Navas de Tolosa fought against the Muslims in 1212. Also nearby is the 12th-century **Capilla de Sancti Spiritus**.

A few steps away in an old millhouse is the **tourist office** (☎ 948 76 03 01; ☺ 10am-2pm & 4-7pm Mon-Sat, 10am-2pm Sun).

Albergue de la Juventud (☎ 948 76 03 02; dm under/over 29 €7/9) is a possibility for HI members. It's housed in an 18th-century hospital where pilgrims used to take respite.

Hostal La Posada (☎ 948 76 02 25; s/d with bathroom €38.50/45) is highly recommended.

The morning bus, which travels from Pamplona via Burguete daily, except Sunday, stops here (€4.10) and returns in the late afternoon.

PUERTO DE IBAÑETA & VALCARLOS

From Roncesvalles the road climbs to the Puerto de Ibañeta, from where you have magnificent views across into France. The last town before the frontier is Valcarlos (Basque: Luzaide), a sleepy but quite pretty spot. Of the numerous *casas rurales* in town, **Casa Etxezuria** (☎ 948 79 00 11; d €30), on the main road heading towards France, has delightful doubles.

THE ROADS TO OCHAGAVÍA

If little villages and quiet country roads are an attraction, there's plenty of scope for losing yourself in the area east of the main Roncesvalles road. A couple of kilometres south of Burguete, the NA140 branches off east to Garralda. Push on to **Arive**, a charming hamlet, from where you could continue east to the Valle del Salazar, go south along the Río Irati past the fine Romanesque church near **Nagore**, or perhaps take a loop northeast through the **Bosque de Irati** forest, which again would eventually bring you to the Valle del Salazar, at Ochagavía. The forest, full of elms, beeches and lime trees, is one of Europe's most extensive, inviting you to ditch your vehicle and head off for a hike. If you stick to the NA140 between Arive and Ochagavía, **Abaurregaina** and **Jaurrieta** are particularly picturesque. Most villages along the route have *casas rurales*.

Ochagavía

This charming Pyrenean town lying astride the narrow Río Zatoya sets itself quite apart from the villages further south. Grey stone, slate and cobblestones dominate the old centre, which straddles a bubbling stream (crossed by a pleasant medieval bridge). The town's sober dignity is reinforced by the looming presence of the **Iglesia de San Juan Evangelista**.

As this is a popular base for walkers and even skiers, many local families have opened up their homes as *casas rurales* – there are no fewer than 27 of them. For a list of options and hiking opportunities in the region, visit the **Centro de Interpretación de la Naturaleza** (☎ 948 89 06 41; oit.ochagavia@cfnavarra.es; ☷ 10am-2pm Mon-Thu & Sun, 10am-2pm & 4.30-7.30pm Fri & Sat). There's also **Camping Osate** (☎ 948 89 01 84; per person/tent €3.50/3.50).

A lively place for a meal or drink is Iratxo Bar, the first place to the left on the main road when you arrive from the south.

HEADING NORTH

To reach France, take the N140 northeast from Ochagavía into the Sierra de Abodi and cross at the Puerto de Larrau (1585m), a majestically bleak pass. Four kilometres short of the border there's a seasonal restaurant and bar for skiers.

Valle del Salazar

If you've made your way to Ochagavía, a good choice for heading south is the Valle de Salazar, many of whose hamlets contain gems of medieval handiwork with quiet cobbled streets and little plazas. **Esparza**, with its mansions, medieval bridge and restored Iglesia de San Andrés, is particularly rewarding, while **Ezcároz**, **Sarriés**, **Güesa** and nearby **Igal** (off the main road) are also worth an amble. A daily bus runs the length of the Valle de Salazar between Pamplona and Ochagavía.

If you're looping back to ·Pamplona, the NA178 veers southwest towards the N240. En route, don't miss the precipitous **Foz de Arbayún**, which can be viewed from a platform that affords splendid vistas. A few kilometres further on is the sleepy town of **Lumbier**, the last stop before your return to a more clamorous world. It has a medieval bridge and the beautiful *foz* (gorge) of the same name.

For details of *casas rurales* in the towns of the valley, visit www.roncal-salazar.com.

Valle del Roncal

An alternative route for leaving or entering the Navarran Pyrenees, this easternmost valley is also the most attractive. Its mountain territory is Navarra's most spectacular, although for skiing and alpine splendour, the neighbouring Aragónese Pyrenees have more to offer. One bus leaves Pamplona at 5pm Monday to Friday (1pm on Saturday), passing through all the Valle de Roncal towns on its way to Uztárroz. It returns early in the morning. For details of *casas rurales* in the valley, visit www.roncal-salazar.com.

BURGUI

The gateway to this part of the Pyrenees is Burgui. Its Roman bridge over the Río Esca, combined with its huddle of stone houses straddling the river, is an evocative introduction to the rural Pyrenean towns further upstream. **Hostal El Almadiero** (☎ 948 47 70 86; almadiero@jet.es; Plaza Mayor; d with breakfast €51) has bright, pleasant rooms in the heart of the village.

RONCAL

This brooding, tightly knit village boasts a 16th-century parish church, but it's the cobblestone alleyways twisting between dark stone houses that lend the place its charm. This enchanting village is also renowned for its Queso de Roncal, a sheep's cheese that's sold in the village.

The **tourist office** (☎ 948 47 51 36; ☷ 10am-2pm & 4.30-8.30pm Mon-Sat mid-Jun–mid-Sep, 10am-2pm Mon-Thu, 10am-2pm & 4.30-7.30pm Fri & Sat mid-Sep–mid-Jun, 10am-2pm Sun year-round), on the main road towards the Isaba exit from town, can provide photocopies of walking maps. There's one bank and even a ski-hire outlet here.

Although Isaba, further north, makes a better base, you could do a lot worse than to choose **Hostal Zantua** (☎ 948 47 50 08; Calle de Castillo 23; s/d €24.05/30.05), which is central and some rooms have good views over the valley.

ISABA

The village of Isaba is another popular base for walkers and skiers, lying above the confluence of the Río Belagua and the Río Uztárroz, which together flow into the Río Esca. There are a few banks with ATMs and a **tourist office** (☎ 948 89 32 51; ☷ 10am-2pm & 4.30-8.30pm Mon-Sat mid-Jun–mid-Sep, 10am-2pm Mon-Thu, 10am-2pm & 4.30-7.30pm Fri & Sat mid-Sep–mid-Jun, 10am-2pm Sun year-round).

Its popularity is reflected in a wealth of accommodation options, starting with the modern, comfortable, three-star **Hotel Isaba** (☎ 948 89 30 00; hotel_isaba@ctv.es; s/d from €39/60). Slightly less comfortable but with more character, **Casa Catalingarde** (☎ 948 89 31 54; s/d with shared bathroom €15/29, d with bathroom €40) is possibly the pick of the 10 *casas rurales* in the village. **Camping Asolaze** (☎ 948 50 40 11; per person/tent/car €3.75/3.75/3.75) is at Km6 on the road to France. At **Tapia** (☎ 948 89 30 13), just out of the old centre on the road to Roncal, you can eat well for €10.

NORTH OF ISABA

The **Belagua refugio**, 19km north of Isaba, is a handy base for trekkers in summer and skiers in winter. It operates a restaurant and bar, and has some bunks to throw a sleeping bag onto. There's no bus up this way.

LA RIOJA

Mention the word Rioja and thoughts dreamily turn to some of the best red wines produced in Spain. The bulk of the vineyards line the Río Ebro around the town of Haro, extending into neighbouring Navarra and the Basque province of Álava. A lesser-known fact is that La Rioja was also a major stomping ground of dinosaurs, with much fossilised evidence still in existence (see the boxed text In the Footsteps of Big Feet, opposite). The Camino de Santiago also passes through La Rioja.

LOGROÑO

pop 137,614

Many Spaniards speak of Logroño with great fondness. There's not a lot to see in terms of monuments, but the town's old quarter somehow gets the mix right between plentiful, high-quality La Rioja wines and a pleasant, lively atmosphere in which to enjoy them. It's the sort of place that you'll leave with a good feeling.

Orientation

If you arrive at the train or bus station, head up Calle del General Vara de Rey until you reach the Espolón, a large, park-like square. The tourist office is here and the *casco viejo* starts just to the north.

Information

The friendly **tourist office** (☎ 941 29 12 60; ✆ 9am-2pm & 5-8pm Mon-Fri, 10am-2pm & 5-8pm Sat, 10am-2pm Sun) is in Espolón square, while the **main post office** (Plaza de San Agustín 1) is in the old town. There are Internet terminals at **Café Yimar** (Calle Chile 4; per hr €2.40; ✆ 8am-2am), but the equipment's a bit ropey.

Sights

The **Catedral de Santa María Redonda** (✆ 8am-1pm & 6.30-7.30pm Mon-Sat) started life as a Gothic church, a fact easily overlooked when your gaze is held by the voluptuousness of the

---

IN THE FOOTSTEPS OF BIG FEET

Dinosaurs seem to have taken a particular liking to La Rioja. Hikers looking for something a little different could do worse than head for the GR93 (long-distance walking route), between the villages of Enciso (about 10km south of Arnedillo) and Cornego (about 22km southeast of Enciso) which has eight fossil prints of dinosaurs signposted along the way, with explanations posted in Spanish. In Valdecevillo (2km southeast of Enciso), you can see footprints left by an enormous carnivorous biped. Other fossils are scattered about the area along different tracks, including those known as Virgen del Campo, Poyales, Navalsaz and Cornego itself. You'll be accompanied overhead by Leonado (griffon) vultures along the way. The most attractive place to stay around here is Arnedillo (p487).

If you've a particular interest, before setting out stop off in the **Centro Paleontológico de Enciso** (☎ 941 39 60 93), or get the excellent *Footprints and Dinosaurs in La Rioja* (free) from any tourist office. Buses are rare in these parts, so it's best to explore the area with your own vehicle.

---

churrigueresque towers added in the 18th century. Take a look at the impressive main entrance to the 13th-century **Iglesia de San Bartolomé**, too.

A stroll around the old town and down to the river is a pleasant diversion, or you could pop in to the **Museo de la Rioja** (☎ 941 29 12 59; Plaza de San Agustín; admission free; ✆ 10am-2pm & 4-9pm Tue-Sat, 11.30am-2pm Sun), housed in a grand, 18th-century building. Among the Gothic horrors on show is a rather lovely 12th-century wooden statue of Christ.

Festivals & Events

Logroño's week-long **Fiesta de San Mateo** starts on 21 September and is a great time to be in town. Doubling as a harvest festival, all of La Rioja comes to town to watch the grape-crushing ceremonies in the Espolón and to drink ample quantities of the end product.

Sleeping

Most of Logroño's accommodation is in the somewhat unappealing new part of town, but there are some choices in the old town.

Hostal Marqués de Vallejo (☎ 941 24 83 33, fax 941 24 02 88; Calle del Marqués de Vallejo 8; s/d €51/74) Definitely the pick of the hotels in the old town, this well-run *hostal* promises high-standard, recently renovated rooms that come with good-sized bathrooms, TV and phone.

Eating

Of the unpretentious stand-up tapas bars, **Lorenzo** (Travesía de Laurel) is a good choice, serving great *pinchos morunos* (the Spanish version of kebabs) at €0.65 a stick, as well as cheap *crianza* (€1.10 a glass) and young Rioja wines (€0.75). Also good, **Bar Angel** (Calle Laurel 6) fries up the best garlic mushrooms in town, while **La Taberna del Laurel** (Calle Laurel 9) serves great *patatas bravas*. **La Taberna de Baco** (Calle de San Agustín 12) has more pleasant surroundings, and serves good *cazuelitas*, *bocadillos* and fried green tomatoes.

The sit-down restaurant, **Las Cubanas** (☎ 941 22 00 50; Calle de San Agustín 17; mains €7.35-13), is noisy and popular in a rustic setting of red-checked tablecloths and beamed ceilings. You'll eat very well for about €20,

Pensión Bilbaína (☎ 941 25 42 26; Calle de Capitán Gallarza 10; s/d €18/26) As central as you'll get, this *pensióne* offers decent doubles in a peeling old building.

Hostal La Numantina (☎ 941 25 14 11; fax 941 25 16 45; Calle de Sagasta 4; s/d €30/44) For a little more comfort, this place has revamped rooms with TV and phone.

BASQUE COUNTRY, NAVARRA & LA RIOJA

but it also does a good *menestre de verduras* (vegetable stew) for €7.05.

Other good choices for a sit-down meal in Logroño's busy restaurant district include the following:

Lorenzo (☎ 941 21 01 46; Calle de San Agustín 8; entrées mostly €4.80-9, mains €12-18) Serves fish and meat dishes.

Carabanchel (☎ 941 20 50 03; Calle de San Agustín 2; entrées €5-7, mains €6-14) Extensive wine list.

Casa Taza (☎ 941 22 00 39; Calle Laurel 5; menú €10) Popular lunchtime spot with locals.

Drinking

Café/Bar Moderno (Plaza de Franco Martínez Zaporta 9) is something of a local institution, with old men playing dominoes and drinking wine amid B&W photos of the good old days.

The bars along Calle Laurel are a great place to start your evening, as most offer good local wines for bargain prices. To keep your night rolling on, follow the crowds from here. Chances are that quite a few of them will be heading for the lively **Café Eldorado** (Calle de Portales 80), which sometimes offers live music.

Noche y Día (Calle de Portales 63; ☯ 8am-2am) is a trendy, friendly café-bar that's popular at any time of day, while **Café-Bar Traz Luz** (Calle de Portales 71; ☯ 8am-10pm) is run by the same owners and has a similarly cool vibe.

Shopping

Mercado San Blas has fresh fruit and vegetables. For irresistible pastries and breads, head to **Panadería El Paraíso** (Calle de San Agustín).

To round out your picnic hamper, there are two excellent wine shops, ideal for picking up wines that can be difficult to find outside La Rioja. Of the two, **Vinos de Rioja** (Plaza San Agustín 4; ☯ 11am-2pm & 6-9pm Tue-Sat) is a touch dustier and more traditional, while **Vinos El Peso** (☎ 941 22 82 54; cnr Calle Laurel & Calle de Capitán Gallarza; ☯ 9am-9pm Mon-Fri, 9am-4pm Sat, 9am-2pm Sun) also has a knowledgeable owner.

Getting There & Away

Up to five buses leave daily for Burgos (€5.75, two hours), Bilbao (€10, two hours), Pamplona (€6.55, 1½ hours) and Madrid (€17.15, 4½ hours). There are frequent connections to/from Vitoria (€7.15, 1½ hours), Haro (€2.30, one hour), Calahorra (€2.90, one hour) and Santo Domingo de la Calzada (€2.40, 45 minutes).

By train, Logroño is regularly connected to Zaragoza (€9.45, two hours), Madrid (€45.50, 3½ hours), Bilbao (€15, three hours) and Burgos (€14.50, 2½ hours).

WINE REGION

Spain's best-known wines come from La Rioja (where the vine has been cultivated since Roman times), with vineyards covering the hinterland of the Río Ebro. On the river's north bank, the region is part of the Basque Country and known as La Rioja Alavesa.

Haro

pop 9813 / elevation 426m

Haro is the capital of La Rioja's wine-producing region. With a compact old quarter leading off **Plaza de la Paz**, the intriguing alleyways with bars and wine shops are a good base from which to scoot out into the vineyards.

The **tourist office** (☎ 941 30 33 66; Plaza de Florentino Rodríguez; ☯ 10am-2pm & 4.30-7.30pm Mon-Sat Jul-Sep; 10am-2pm Tue-Fri, 10am-2pm & 4-7pm Sat Oct-Jun) is downhill from Plaza de la Paz and has a list of wineries open to the public.

The **Museo del Vino** (☎ 941 31 05 47; Calle de Cira Anguciana; admission €2, Wed free; ☯ 10am-2pm & 4-8pm Mon-Sat, 10am-2pm Sun), near the bus station, houses a detailed display on how wine is made.

The winery **Bodega Muga** (☎ 941 31 04 98), just after the railway bridge on the way out of town, gives guided tours and tastings at 11am and 4.30pm Monday to Thursday (€3). You can also pick up local wines at shops like **Vinoteca Rodriguez Alonso** (☎ 941 30 32 72; Calle Conde de Haro 7), which offers tasting sessions for €2. There are more wine shops on Calle de Santo Tomás.

FESTIVALS & EVENTS

On 29 June, the otherwise mild-mannered citizens of Haro go temporarily berserk during the **Batalla del Vino** (Wine Battle), squirting and chucking wine all over each other in the name of San Juan, San Felices and San Pedro.

SLEEPING & EATING

Pensión La Peña (☎ 941 31 00 22; Calle de Arrabal s/n; s/d with washbasin €21/30, d with bathroom €36) A great choice in the town centre, La Peña is a maze of bright, clean rooms with TV, some overlooking Plaza de la Paz.

Hostal Higinia (☎ 941 30 43 68; Calle de Virgen de la Vega; s/d €44.90/52.90) For more comfort in an attractive building, Hostal Higinia has spacious, carpeted rooms with TV, phone and private bathroom.

Restaurante Beethoven II (☎ 941 31 11 81; Calle de Santo Tomás 5; mains €9-14) The place to try for a classy meal washed down with fine Rioja wines.

Terete (☎ 941 31 00 23; Calle Lucrecia Arana 17; menú €10.20) Highly recommended, this is a rustic place serving traditional fare on butcher-block tables.

GETTING THERE & AWAY

Regular trains connect Haro with Logroño (€2.30, 45 minutes), and buses additionally serve Vitoria, Bilbao, Santo Domingo de la Calzada and Laguardia.

Laguardia

pop 1289 / elevation 557m

Medieval Laguardia, the prettiest of the Rioja wine-growing towns, surveys the wine region from its dramatic hilltop perch in La Rioja Alavesa. The area has been inhabited since the Iron Age, and the old walled town is filled with the houses of noble families. Look for the **Iglesia de Santa María de los Reyes** and its rare example of a grand Gothic doorway (with the polychrome colouring intact). Virtually every house in town has a basement wine cellar, and bars and bodegas serve local drinks for as little as €0.35 a glass.

The **tourist office** (945 60 08 45; Paseo Sancho Abarca s/n; ☉ 9am-1.30pm & 3-7pm Mon-Fri, 10am-2pm Sat & Sun) has a list of bodegas that can be visited in the local area.

SLEEPING & EATING

There aren't many places to stay, but this is a lovely town that's well worth lingering in.

Camas (☎ 945 60 01 14; Calle Mayor 17; s/d €14/26) Within the town walls, this is far and away the cheapest option. The take-no-prisoners landlady rents out basic but clean rooms with shared facilities.

Hostal Pachico Martinez (☎ 945 60 00 09; hotel@pachico.com; Calle Sancho Abarca 20; s/d €39/51) In a historic building, this hostal has comfortable doubles with TV and bathroom.

IN SEARCH OF THE FINEST DROP

To fully appreciate a wine tour of La Rioja requires a bit of advance preparation, although none of it is the least bit onerous.

The best place to start your research is at the exceptional **Museo del Vino** (p478) in Olite, which covers wine growing from planting to tasting, focusing on wines from Navarra (an important wine-growing region in its own right) and La Rioja. Also excellent are the **Museo del Vino** (p484) in Haro and **Quaderna Via** (☎ 948 55 40 83; fax 948 55 65 40; admission free; ☉ 8am-2pm & 3-7pm Mon-Fri, 10am-2pm Sat & Sun), around 4km west of Estella, near Igúzquiza. It's also worth picking up the concise *Wine & Gastronomy in La Rioja* (free) from any tourist office in the region.

Wines produced around Laguardia, on the Basque side, are fruity and soft, and can only be grown in this part of La Rioja because of its unique microclimate. Protected from the worst of the bitter northern cold by the Sierra de Cantabria, and blessed with an ochre soil made from the red earth of the south bank, vines here produce a result quite distinct from elsewhere in the region.

The bulk of Rioja reds are designed to be aged and experts have developed a classification system for the years where the wine was particularly good. Years for which five stars (the maximum) have been awarded include 1982, 1994, 1995 and 2001, although some regard it as too soon to say for sure with the latter. Four-star years include 1981, 1987, 1991, 1996 and 1998.

Most of the La Rioja wine is bought up and marketed by big concerns and, traditionally, wine tasting for passing tourists is not common in Spain; most bodegas reserve these activities for people in the business. That said, things are changing, with small family bodegas reasserting themselves. The tourist offices in Haro, Laguardia and Logroño are among those that have lists of bodegas that can be visited throughout the region, although it usually requires ringing in advance to arrange a time. One exception is **Bodega Muga** (p484), which has set times for guided tours and tastings.

If time is tight, there are particularly good wine shops in Logroño and Haro.

Ask for a room at the back with sweeping views of the Riojan mountains.

Vinoteca Mayor de Migueloa (☎ 945 62 11 75; Calle Paganos 13) Drop by to sample some great *vino tinto* (red wine) and a plate of manchego cheese dipped in olive oil (€4.50). They also do good *cazuelitas* (small stews).

GETTING THERE & AWAY

Six slow daily buses connecting Vitoria and Logroño pass through Laguardia.

Around Laguardia

You'll find plenty of interesting little villages if you have your own vehicle. Heading for Haro, the road west from Laguardia passes through the pretty village of **San Vicente de la Sonsierra**, whose remaining castle walls spill off their hilltop perch.

It's here, during Easter week, that a curious sect of flagellants known as Los Picaos perform a nasty but mesmerising ritual. Dressed in hooded white robes, they whip their backs and then press balls of wax splintered with glass into the wounds till the blood flows.

Views across the plains are marvellous and an impressive medieval bridge spans the Río Ebro below. Continuing on, **Labastida** straggles up a small hillside capped by the Ermita del Cristo, with a fine Romanesque portal.

MONASTERIES WEST OF LOGROÑO

Nájera

pop 7287 / elevation 506m

The main attraction of this town is the Gothic **Monasterio de Santa María la Real** (☎ 941 36 36 50; admission €2; ☺ 10am-1pm & 4-5.30pm Tue-Sun), in particular its fragile-looking early-16th-century cloisters. Inside the church you can see splendid choir stalls with imaginative carvings, and a pantheon of tombs containing the remains of various kings of Castile, León and Navarra. It closes a little earlier in winter. Buses between Logroño and Santo Domingo de la Calzada stop in Nájera.

San Millán de Cogolla

pop 266 / elevation 733m

About 16km southwest of Nájera are the two remarkable monasteries in the hamlet of San Millán de Cogolla, framed by a beautiful valley. The **Monasterio de Yuso** (☎ 941 37 30 49; admission €3.50; ☺ 10.30am-1.30pm & 4-6.30pm Tue-Sun), sometimes presumptuously called El Escorial de La Rioja, contains numerous

treasures in its museum. Highlights are the remains of the 6th-century hermit San Millán – contained within a shrine whose delicate ivory carvings depict scenes from the saint's life – the lavishly decorated, barrel-vaulted sacristy, the library, with its rare manuscripts, and the church with paintings by Juan Rizzi.

A short distance away is the **Monasterio de Suso** (admission €3; ☺ 10.30am-1.30pm & 4-6pm Tue-Sun). Built above the caves where San Millán once lived, the monastery was consecrated in the 10th century. Much of the original Mozarabic architecture survives. It's believed that in the 13th century, a monk named Gonzalo de Berceo penned the first Castilian words here. He is buried in one of the chapels.

Santo Domingo de la Calzada

pop 5904 / elevation 630m

This fascinating little town with its enchanting pedestrian old quarter gets its name from a feisty 11th-century hermit who, having been rejected by two local monasteries, simply built his own hermitage on the site of the present-day town.

THE MIRACLE OF THE ROOSTER

The most curious 'decoration' in the cathedral of Santo Domingo is that of a live white rooster and hen kept in a special niche. They owe their presence to a legend that, once upon a time, a young German pilgrim overnighting at the local inn snubbed the advances of the innkeeper's daughter. To get back at him, she hid a piece of silver in his satchel, then denounced him to the authorities. The poor man was quickly convicted and hanged, but when his parents came to say farewell to their dead child, they found him still alive: he had been saved by the intercession of Santo Domingo. When told of this, the disbelieving local *corregidor* (ruler) exclaimed that the lad was about as alive as the roast chook he was about to tuck into, upon which the hen and rooster leapt off his plate and started to crow. An amusing ditty is now recited about the town: *Santo Domingo de la Calzada, que canto la gallina despues de Asada* (Santo Domingo de la Calzada, where the hen crows after being roasted).

Watching a steady stream of pilgrims struggle through here along a worn Roman path enroute to Santiago de Compostela inspired him to construct a new road, a bridge and a hospital (now a parador – a state-owned luxury hotel). The king rewarded his efforts by constructing a church, which became a cathedral in 1232.

At the **cathedral** (admission €1.50, free Sun; ☿ 10am-6.30pm), turn your attention to the oldest section, the Romanesque eastern end, which has some particularly nice carved sandstone pilasters. Their expressive simplicity contrasts with the overwhelming detail of the main altar by Damián Forment, and the elaborate mausoleum of the saint topped by an alabaster canopy. The actual remains of Santo Domingo are buried in the crypt beneath. Also of note is the cloister, with exhibits on the Camino de Santiago and artwork. For more on the cathedral, see the boxed text The Miracle of the Rooster, opposite.

Pilgrims should feel comfortable in **Hospedería Cisterciense** (☎ 941 34 07 00; Calle Pinar 2; s/d €22/38), a religious-run hostel, with clean, comfortable rooms. Another choice is the palatial **Parador** (☎ 941 34 03 00; sto.domingo@parador.es; Plaza del Santo 3; s/d €90.65/113.30), which occupies a former hospice built by Santo Domingo himself. Even St Francis of Assisi is said to have stopped here once.

Jiménez (☎ 941 23 12 34) buses run to Burgos (€3.50, 1¼ hours, five daily) and Logroño (€2.40, 45 minutes, up to 13 daily on weekdays, less on weekends). The Logroño buses travel via Nájera (€1.10, 30 minutes). There are also two daily buses to Haro (€1, 25 minutes).

SOUTH OF LOGROÑO

A couple of picturesque routes suggest themselves if you're heading south for Soria. One is along the N111 which, after a boring start, picks up as it follows deep canyon walls along the Río Iregua into the sierras marking Soria province off from the flatlands of central La Rioja. Several pretty villages, including **Villanueva de Cameros**, line the lower half of the route. About halfway to Soria you could turn west for **Montenegro de Cameros**, and then drop south for **Vinuesa** and the Laguna Negra near Soria.

Another good route to Soria is to head southeast of Logroño to **Calahorra**, on the N232. Of Roman origin, Calahorra overlooks the Río Ebro and its tributary Río Cidacos, upon which dwells a moderately interesting Gothic **cathedral**. The sacristy, chapterhouse and museum are all worth a look. Free guided tours operate daily from 9am to 1pm and 5pm to 8pm. **Hostal Teresa** (☎ 941 13 03 32; Calle de Santo Domingo 7; s/d €14/22) has worn but adequate rooms. For far greater levels of comfort, there's a typically elegant **Parador** (☎ 941 13 03 58; calahorra@parador.es; s/d €85.60/107).

From Calahorra, head southwest towards Arnedo, and then follow the Río Cidacos through dramatic country. The small, traditional spa town of **Arnedillo**, gathered up in a fold of the valley, is a pretty location and ideal for a night or two if you plan to do a spot of walking in the area. **Hostal Purras** (☎ 941 39 40 34; Joaquin Velasco 11; s/d with washbasin €15/30, with bathroom €18/36) has friendly owners and airy rooms.

The road starts to climb after entering Soria province and is frequently blocked by snow during winter.

Cantabria & Asturias

CONTENTS

Together with the Basque Country to their east and Galicia to their west, the neighbouring regions of Cantabria and Asturias form the greenest part of Spain, with a verdure similar to the greener parts of the British Isles.

The two regions share a beautiful coastline along the Bay of Biscay, alternating between sheer cliffs, tiny protected coves, small fishing and resort towns, and scores of sandy beaches, long and short. From the coast a patchwork of green and often misty meadows, pastures and hills, dotted with stone villages, rises to the chainmail strip of mountains that forms the regions' natural southern boundary, the Cordillera Cantábrica – beyond which the landscape changes with amazing abruptness to the parched plains of the *meseta* (tableland). The mountains reach their greatest heights and grandeur in the Picos de Europa, a northern spur of the cordillera straddling southeast Asturias, southwest Cantabria and the north of Castilla y León. The Picos are allotted a section to themselves at the end of this chapter.

The only drawback to 'green Spain' is what makes it green: the rain. Even in August you might endure a week of grey skies and showers, especially inland. But what Cantabria and Asturias may lack in sunshine, they certainly make up for in beauty and history. There's a thriving cultural and nightlife scene, too, in cities such as Santander, Oviedo and Gijón.

HIGHLIGHTS

- Connect in the convivial *sidrerías* (cider bars) of **Asturias** (p495)
- Savour the tangy blue-green **Cabrales cheese** (p525)
- Travel by train along the Santander–Oviedo coastal corridor
- Walk the **Garganta del Cares** (Cares Gorge; p524) in the Picos de Europa
- Be enchanted by the medieval town of **Santillana del Mar** (p498)
- Bathe at secluded **Playa del Silencio** (p514)
- Admire the paintings at **Cueva de Altamira** (Altamira Cave; p499) and **Puente Viesgo** (p496)
- Canoe down the **Río Sella** for an adrenaline rush (p521)
- Marvel at the pre-Romanesque churches of **Oviedo** (p503)
- Tour the tapas bars and clubs of **Santander** (p494)

- AREA: 15,925 SQ KM
- POP: 1,625,070
- AVE SUMMER TEMP: HIGH 22°C, LOW 14°C

CANTABRIA

The Romans reported having a hard time dealing with Cantabrians, a people of obscure origins who inhabited coastal and mountain areas extending beyond the limits of modern Cantabria. From 29 to 19 BC the fortunes of war fluctuated, but in the end Rome carried the day and the subdued coastal tribes were absorbed into imperial Hispania.

In more recent centuries Cantabria was long regarded simply as a coastal extension of Castilla and as its direct gateway to what was confidently known as the Mar de Castilla (Castilian Sea). Cantabria, therefore, gained more recognition when Spain's 1978 constitution made it into an autonomous region.

Cantabria's chief attractions are natural, from the eastern flank of the Picos de Europa through the evergreen rural hinterland, to the rippled coastline and its sprinkling of pretty beaches and coastal towns.

Santander, the capital, boasts fine beaches and a thumping nightlife, while Santillana del Mar, to the west, near the Cueva de Altamira, with its famous cave paintings, is a perfectly preserved medieval gem.

SANTANDER

pop 150,030

Most of modern Santander, with its bustling centre, clanking port and shapeless suburbs, stands in drab contrast to its pretty beaches, particularly the old-world elegance of El Sardinero, which is reminiscent of the French resort of Biarritz, albeit without much of the ritz.

A huge fire raged through the city in 1941, but what's left of the 'old' centre is certainly a lively source of entertainment for the palate and liver, and has an atmosphere well worth stopping to savour. All up, however, Santander is a good deal more staid than its resort cousin, San Sebastián.

History

When the Romans landed here in 21 BC, they named the place Portus Victoriae (Victory Harbour) and, indeed, within two years they had vanquished the Cantabrian tribes that had given them such strife.

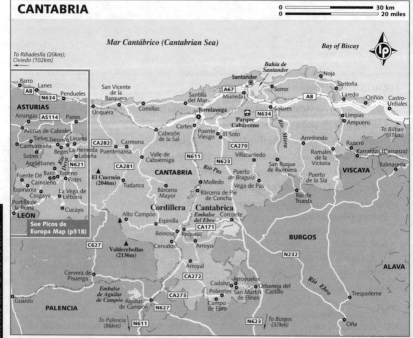

CANTABRIA

See Picos de Europa Map (p518)

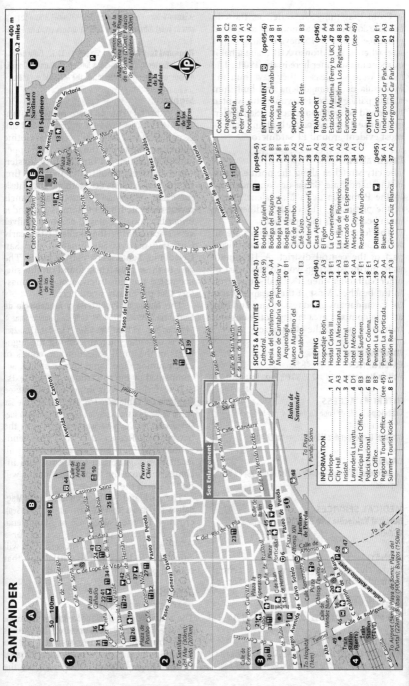

SANTANDER

0 — 0.2 miles / 400 m

To Peninsula de la
Magdalena (50m); Playa
de Bikinis (20cm); Palacio
de la Magdalena (500m)

To Camping; 17
Cabo Mayor (2.5km)

To Santillana
del Mar (30km);
Oviedo (207km)

To Airport (5km); Playa del Somo; Playa del
Puntal (22km); Bilbao (100km); Burgos (750km)

Bahía de
Santander

To Playa
Puntal; Somo

To UK

INFORMATION
Ciberlope..............................1 A1
City Hall...............................2 A3
Insistel.................................3 A4
Lavandería Lavatu.................4 D1
Municipal Tourist Office.......5 B3
Policía Nacional....................6 B3
Post Office............................7 B3
Regional Tourist Office....(see 45)
Summer Tourist Kiosk...........8 E1

SIGHTS & ACTIVITIES (pp492–3)
Cathedral..............................9 A4
Iglesia del Santísimo Cristo....(see 9)
Museo de Cantabria de Prehistoria y
    Arqueología......................10 B1
Museo Marítimo del
    ....11 E3

SLEEPING (p494)
Hospedaje Botín...................12 A3
Hostal Carlos III...................13 E1
Hostal La Mexicana..............14 A3
Hotel Central........................15 B3
Hotel México........................16 A4
Hotel Sardinero....................17 E1
Pensión Coloma....................18 E1
Pensión La Corza..................19 A2
Pensión La Porticada............20 A4
Pensión Real.........................21 A3

EATING (pp494–5)
Bodega Cigaleña..................23 A1
Bodega El Riojano................23 B3
Bodega Fuente De................24 B1
Bodega Mazón......................25 B1
Café de Pombo......................26 A2
Café Suizo.............................27 A2
Cafetería/Cervecería Lisboa...28 E1
Casa Ajero............................29 A2
El Figón................................30 A3
La Conveniente.....................31 A1
Las Hijas de Florencio............32 A2
Mercado de la Esperanza.......33 A3
Mesón Goya..........................34 A1
Restaurante Marucho............35 C2

DRINKING (p495)
Blues....................................36 A1
Cervecería Cruz Blanca.........37 A2

Cool.......................................38 B1
Dragón..................................39 C2
La Floridita............................40 B3
Peter Pan...............................41 A1
Rocambole............................42 A2

ENTERTAINMENT (pp495–6)
Filmoteca de Cantabria.........43 B1
Sala Indian............................44 B1

SHOPPING
Mercado del Este..................45 B3

TRANSPORT (p496)
Bus Station...........................46 A4
Estación Marítima (Ferry to UK) 47 B4
Estación Marítima Los Reginas 48 B3
Europcar...............................49 A4
National...........................(see 49)

OTHER
Gran Casino..........................50 E1
Underground Car Park...........51 A3
Underground Car Park...........52 B4

From that time Santander, as the city became known, led a modestly successful existence as a port. Its heyday came rather late, when King Alfonso XIII made a habit of spending summer here in the 1900s. The locals were so pleased they gave him the Península de la Magdalena and built him a little palace there. Everyone who wanted to see and be seen converged on Santander, giving rise to a *belle époque* building boom – most evident around El Sardinero.

Orientation

The city stretches along the northern side of the handsome Bahía de Santander out to the Península de la Magdalena. North of the peninsula, Playa del Sardinero, the main beach, faces the open sea.

The ferry, train and bus stations are all within 300m of each other in the southwest part of the central district. A 10-minute walk northeast brings you to the heart of older Santander, then it's a half-hour stroll to the beaches. Most of the cheaper places to stay and many good restaurants and bars are in a compact area taking in the bus and train stations and the old quarter.

Information

EMERGENCY
Policía Nacional (☎ 942 35 90 00; Plaza Porticada)

INTERNET ACCESS
Ciberlope (Calle de Lope de Vega 14; per hr €2; till midnight)
Insistel (Calle Méndez Núñez 8; per hr €2.40)

LAUNDRY
Lavandería Lavatu (Avenida de los Castros 29; €9 per 3kg load)

MEDICAL SERVICES
Hospital Valdecilla (☎ 942 20 25 20; Avenida de Valdecilla)

MONEY
Banks cluster in the newer part of central Santander around Avenida de Calvo Sotelo.

POST
Post office (☎ 942 36 55 19; Plaza Alfonso XIII 2)

TOURIST INFORMATION
Municipal tourist office (☎ 942 20 30 00; www.ayto-santander.es; Jardines de Pereda; 9am-9pm Jul-Aug,

9.30am-1.30pm & 4-7pm Mon-Fri, 9.30am-1.30pm Sat rest of year) A branch office in El Sardinero, opposite Plaza Italia, operates in summer.
Regional tourist office (☎ 901 11 11 12; Calle de Hernán Cortés 4; 9am-9pm Jul-Sep, 9.30am-1.30pm & 4-7pm rest of year) Located inside the Mercado del Este.

Sights

The **cathedral** (Plaza del Obispo Eguino; 10am-1pm & 4.30-7.30pm Mon-Sat, 8am-2pm & 5-8pm Sun) is composed of two 13th-century Gothic churches, one above the other. The upper church, off which is a 14th-century cloister, was extensively rebuilt after the 1941 fire. In the lower **Iglesia del Santísimo Cristo** (Calle Somorrostro; 8am-1pm & 5-8pm) glass panels reveal excavated bits of Roman Santander under the floor. Displayed nearby are silver vessels containing the skulls of the early Christian martyrs San Emeterio and San Celedonio, Santander's patron saints. The care of these holy relics, found on this site, prompted the construction of the monastery that previously stood here.

The **Museo de Prehistoria y Arqueología de Cantabria** (☎ 942 20 71 09; Calle de Casimiro Sainz 4; admission free; 10am-1pm & 4-7pm Tue-Sat, 11am-2pm Sun) is of some interest. Among the highlights of the small collection are copies of cave paintings and some Roman stellae, accompanied by interpretations of their texts.

If seafaring is your thing, visit the **Museo Marítimo del Cantábrico** (☎ 942 27 49 62; Calle San Martín de Bajamar s/n; admission €6; 10am-9pm Tue-Sun summer, 10am-6pm Tue-Sun rest of year), near the bay beaches. Reopened in 2003 after renovations, the four-floor museum covers all facets of navigation in Cantabria, and includes an aquarium. Only aficionados will find it worth the steep fee.

The parklands of the **Península de la Magdalena** (8am-8.30pm Oct-May, 8am-10pm Jun-Sep), crowned by the Palacio de la Magdalena, the former royal palace, are perfect for a stroll and popular with picnickers. Kids will enjoy the sea lions and the little train that choo-choos around the headland.

Activities

BEACHES & BOAT TRIPS
The beaches on the **Bahía de Santander** are more protected than **Playa del Sardinero**. The latter is a hike from the city centre, so catch bus No 1, 2 or 3 from outside the post office. **Playa del Puntal**, a finger of sand jutting out from the

Views of Olite from the Gran Torre of the Palacio Real (p478), an extensive medieval defensive complex in the Basque Country

Pintxos (tapas) bar in San Sebastián (p451), Basque Country

The spectacular central Basque coast (p456) between San Sebastián and Bilbao

STEPHEN SAKS

Oviedo's outstanding Gothic Catedral de San Salvador (p503), Asturias

OLIV

Castro Urdiales (p497), near Bilbao in eastern Cantabria

Descent from Fuente Dé (p528) in the jagged Picos de Europa

INGR

eastern side of the bay roughly opposite Playa de la Magdalena, is idyllic on calm days (but beware the currents). Boats sail there every 15 to 30 minutes between 10am and 8pm June to August, from the Estación Marítima Los Reginas (€2.60 return). From the same boat station there are one-hour bay tours (€6.20) daily in summer (on weekends in May and June) and a year-round passenger ferry to Somo (with another sandy beach), just beyond Playa del Puntal.

SURFING
Surfers emerge in force along El Sardinero when the waves are right. Playa de Somo, across the bay, can also be good. Three or four shops on Calle de Cádiz and Calle Méndez Núñez sell boards, wetsuits and other surfing gear. The **Escuela de Surf Santander** (☎ 669 48 80 15; www.escueladesurfsantander.com; Calle de Cádiz 19) is a surf school with boards for rent.

Walking Tour
The tour begins within the stately **Plaza Porticada** (**1**), which is surrounded by 64 porticoes. Proceed down past the post office to the **cathedral** (**2**, opposite). Below it, amid a traffic circle, a poignant **sculpture** (**3**) recalls the devastation of the 1941 fire. To the east spread the lovely **Jardines de Pereda** (**4**), named after the Cantabrian writer José María de Pereda, whose seminal work, *Escenas Montañeses*, is illustrated in bronze and stone here. Opposite the park you'll

see the 1950s **Banco de Santander** building (**5**), a sort of monument to Spanish banking. Going through its grand archway you enter the old quarter. Proceed through the delightful **Plaza de Pombo** (**6**), turning north (left) at the far end to reach the lively **Plaza de Cañadio** (**7**, p495), brimming with bars. Follow Calle de Daoiz y Velarde east, grabbing a few tapas along the way. At the end, you'll find the **Museo de Prehistoria y Arqueología de Cantabria** (**8**, opposite). Afterwards, head down to the Puerto Chico (Marina). Beside it, standing on stilts in the bay, is the **Real Club Marítimo** (**9**), the surprisingly austere yacht club. Those boys you see diving into the bay after coins are actually another bit of public sculpture, **Los Raqueros** (**10**). Stroll the bay-front promenade back, noting on your right the row of opulent buildings with their glassed-in galleries, fruits of early 20th-century boom times. Finally, catch the ferry at the **Palacio del Embarcadero** (**11**), itself a gem, over to Somo for a seafood lunch.

Festivals & Events
Santander's big summer fiesta is the **Semana Grande**, a week of fun around 25 July. Right through summer, the Palacio de la Magdalena hosts the **Universidad Internacional Menéndez Pelayo** (www.uimp.es), a global get-together for specialists in all sorts of disciplines. The **Festival Internacional de Santander** is a sweeping musical review in August that covers everything from jazz to chamber music.

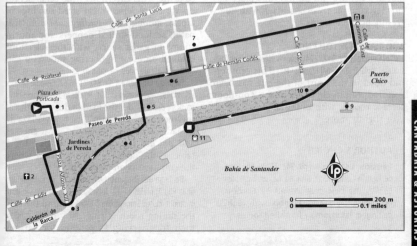

Sleeping

Loads of budget spots can be found around the train and bus stations. Down by fashionable Playa del Sardinero, the cheaper places tend to close during the low season.

BUDGET

Camping Cabo Mayor (☎ 942 39 15 42; www.cabo mayor.comc; Avenida del Faro s/n; per adult/tent/car €4.25/4.25/3.85) This place is out towards the Cabo Mayor lighthouse, beyond Playa del Sardinero. Take bus No 9 from Jardines de Pereda. Within easy reach of the beach, this 500-site camping ground provides a super-market and laundry facilities.

Pensión La Porticada (☎ 942 22 78 17; Calle de Méndez Núñez 6; r with washbasin/bathroom €34/45) Though it's basic, here the staff make you feel at home. Rooms overlooking the bay are nice if you don't mind the traffic.

Hospedaje Botín (☎ 942 21 00 94; www.hospedaje botin.com; Calle de Isabel II No 1; s/d with shared bathroom €29/43) A little closer to the city centre, the homey Botín has some spacious rooms with *galerías* (Galician glassed-in balconies), though bathroom space is limited. Gregari-ous manager Aurelio is only too happy to suggest activities.

Pensión Real (☎ 942 22 57 87; Plaza de la Esperanza 1; s/d with shared bathroom €32/38) Facing the mar-ket, this is a basic, hospitable place, often booked up in the high season.

Pensión Coloma (☎ 942 27 06 36; Avenida de Anto-nio Maura 23; r €45 with shared bath; ☽ Apr-Sep) On a sidestreet above the Casino, this place has no views but plenty of character, with huge, freshly painted rooms.

MID-RANGE & TOP END

Hotel Central (☎ 942 22 24 00; www.elcentral.com; Calle General Mola 5; s/d €76/117; ☒ ℗) This century-old hotel in the heart of the city has been restored with its character intact. Top-floor terrace rooms, with unbeatable bay views, cost slightly more.

AUTHOR'S CHOICE

Pensión La Corza (☎ 942 21 29 50; Calle de Hernán Cortés 25; r with washbasin/bathroom €39/42) The best deal around, La Corza is on pleasant Plaza de Pombo, with high-ceilinged, handsomely furnished rooms.

Hostal La Mexicana (☎ 942 22 23 54; Calle Juan de Herrera 3; s/d €40/54) This cordially managed place near the city hall has several floors of bright rooms and a charming lounge.

Hotel México (☎ 942 21 24 50; mexico@abbahotels .com; Calle Calderón de la Barca 3; r €125) This promi-nent hotel opposite the train station boasts comfortable, attractively decorated rooms, many facing the bay.

The following two places to stay are located in El Sardinero.

Hostal Carlos III (☎ /fax 942 27 16 16; Avenida de la Reina Victoria 135; s/d €50/66; ☽ Easter-Oct) Frosted-glass fixtures and painted moldings adorn this vintage, turreted structure, often booked with returning guests.

Hotel Sardinero (☎ 942 27 11 00; www.grupo sardinero.com; Plaza de Italia 1; s/d €96/131) This grand old seaside hotel evokes the area's golden age. Substantial discounts are available for low-season weekends.

Eating

BODEGAS

Atmospheric old bodegas (wine cellars) ac-count for many of the best places to eat.

Bodega Fuente Dé (☎ 942 21 30 58; Calle del la Peña Herbosa 5; ☽ closed Sun) An enormous help-ing of soulful *cocido montañés* (mountain stew), served here Tuesday, Thursday and Friday, costs just €5. Follow it with a pot of tea spiked with *orujo* (grape-based liquor) and herbs from the Picos de Europa.

Bodega Mazón (☎ 942 21 57 52; Calle de Hernán Cortés 57; raciones €4-10; ☽ 11am-3pm & 6pm-midnight, closed Wed) This cavernous wine cellar serves up varied *raciones* (meal-sized servings of tapas), among them *puding cabracho* (fish paté), seafood-stuffed peppers and mush-rooms in garlic sauce, with the selections chalked on great lumbering vats. You can order half serves of *raciones*.

Bodega Cigaleña (☎ 942 21 30 62; Calle de Daoiz y Velarde 19; pinchos from €1.50; ☽ closed Sun) The wine racks creak under the load of dusty bottles at this tiled 'wine museum', just below Plaza de Cañadío. You can munch on great cheeses and *pinchos* (snacks) while waiting for a table in the adjacent dining room, where the emphasis is on fresh seafood.

Bodega del Riojano (☎ 942 21 67 50; Calle del Río de la Pila 5; mains €7-12, fish dishes €12-14.40; ☽ until midnight, closed Sun evening & Mon) Behind the bar, the dining room is ringed by huge casks, their tops serving as palettes for various artists. Dishes are straightforward but tasty, particularly the day's catch.

Mesón Goya (☎ 942 21 30 66; Calle de Daoíz y Velarde 25; dishes €6-12; ⊙ closed Mon) The focus here is a bit more on food than wine, with expertly grilled fish and meat.

CAFÉS
Santander's waterfront promenades brim with cafés.

Café Suizo (☎ 942 21 58 64; Paseo de Pereda 28; sandwiches & desserts €3.60) With a sleek coffee machine behind a long pink counter, the Suizo bears a seaside charm that's conducive to lingering.

Café de Pombo (☎ 942 22 32 24; Calle de Hernán Cortés 21) On the plaza of the same name, this is a classy and soothing spot for breakfast, crepes, tea or sandwiches.

Cafetería/Cervecería Lisboa (☎ 942 27 10 20; Plaza de Italia) Below the Gran Casino Sardinero, this Santander institution has a very large *terraza* (terrace).

TAPAS BARS
Casa Ajero (☎ 942 21 83 86; Calle de Daoíz y Velarde 18; raciones €5-10; ⊙ 1pm-midnight) One of many wonderful places to *picotear* (snack) along this street, the lively Casa Ajero has tiled counters arrayed with tempting trays of seafood salads, varied tortillas, stuffed mushrooms and so on. The desserts are amazing.

Las Hijas de Florencio (☎ 942 31 04 75; Paseo de Pereda 23; tostas €2) This busy bar gives you plenty to nibble on with your wine, including *tostas* topped with things such as brie and smoked salmon. The terrifically social atmosphere spreads outdoors on warm evenings.

La Casa del Indiano (Calle de Hernán Cortés 4; brochettes €4-6) In the Mercado del Este, this pseudo-bodega serves tasty tapas, brochettes and cold beer.

RESTAURANTS
Restaurante Marucho (☎ 942 27 30 07; Calle Tetuán 21; fish dishes €10-12) One of a few modest seafood eateries on a seedy street east of the old centre, Marucho is often packed – testimony to the quality of its fresh fish.

El Figón (☎ 942 23 53 66; Calle de Cisneros 7; menú €7) If you're just after a cheap meal, this friendly neighbourhood joint offers a generous *menú del día* (daily set meal available at lunch time), which includes home-made flan, and a chance to watch the game.

Drinking
Plaza de Cañadío is home to several *bares de copas,* where you can enjoy an outdoor beer in the evening.

Blues (Calle Gómez Oreña 15) A 30s to 40s crowd frequents this slick, lively gathering place, where the music tends towards funk and soul.

Peter Pan (Calle de Daoiz y Velarde 21) This rowdy drinking hall overflows with young folks, most downing *cachis de calimocho* (wine and Coca-Cola) from big plastic cups.

La Floridita (☎ 942 22 33 09; Calle Bailén 4) A tropically themed nightspot attracting a broad age group, Floridita is a place to get close – real close – to your friends in Santander. If it gets too crowded, you can enjoy your *mojitos* (a rum concoction) outdoors on the plaza.

Cervecería Cruz Blanca (☎ 942 36 42 95; Calle de Hernán Cortés 24) A possible port of call in your after-dark investigations, this beer hall has 29 mostly non-Spanish brews in bottles and a few more on tap.

Cool (Calle de San Emeterio 3) Despite the beyond-capacity crowds, this small hash-infused club stays pretty relaxed, with everyone getting their dose of funky music.

Calle del Río de la Pila and its immediate neighbourhood also teem with bars of all descriptions.

Entertainment
The municipal tourist office produces a summer what's-on guide.

Filmoteca de Cantabria (☎ 942 31 93 10; Calle Bonifaz 6; admission €2) The cinema club puts together an excellent series, with films screened in their original languages.

Rocambole (☎ 942 36 49 61; Calle de Hernán Cortés 37) The action often goes on till dawn at this dimly lit, block-length rock-music bar, with live blues on Thursday night.

Sala Indian (☎ 687 70 35 64; http://club.telepolis .com/elevador; Calle de Casimiro Sainz 10) Touring bands perform here several times a month. Check its website for upcoming events.

Dragón (☎ 942 22 10 63; www.discodragon.8m.com; Calle Tetuán 32; cover €10 Fri-Sun) A gay men's club where women are welcome, Dragón features drag shows at 12.30am and 2.30am.

Getting There & Away
AIR
The **airport** (☎ 942 20 21 00) is about 5km south at Parayas. A handful of daily flights serve Madrid and Barcelona.

BOAT
From Plymouth in the UK, **Brittany Ferries** (☎ UK 0870 366 5333, Spain 942 36 06 11; www.brittany ferries.co.uk) operates a twice-weekly car ferry to Santander (18 hours' sailing time) from mid-March to mid-November. Two people with a car pay return fares of UK£580 to UK£730 seated, and UK£759 to £UK950 in a cabin.

BUS
From the **bus station** (☎ 942 21 19 95; www.santan dereabus.com), Continental-Auto runs at least six buses daily to/from Madrid (€22.50, 5½ hours), plus five or six to/from Burgos (€9.20, three hours). ALSA runs frequent buses east to Bilbao (€5.40, 1½ hours) and at least six to San Sebastián (€11.30, three hours), Irún and the French border. ALSA also runs to Oviedo (€10.70 to €18.25, three hours), with most buses stopping in Llanes, but only two daily to Arriondas and Ribadesella.

Daily ALSA group buses also serve the cities of Valladolid, Salamanca, Zaragoza and Barcelona.

CAR & MOTORCYCLE
Heading west, take the A67 for Torrelavega for a quick getaway. The N623 to Burgos – a pretty route – is the main road south. All traffic heads out of the city along the south side of the train station.

Hertz (☎ 942 36 28 21) has a car-hire office inside the Estación Marítima; **Europcar**

(☎ 942 21 78 17) and **National** (☎ 942 22 29 26) are beside the Renfe train station.

TRAIN
There are two train stations. **Renfe** (☎ 942 28 02 02) has three trains daily to/from Madrid (€33 to €43.50, 5½ to 8½ hours) via Palencia and Ávila. Six trains also run daily to/from Reinosa, two of which continue on to Valladolid.

FEVE (☎ 942 20 95 22; www.feve.es), next door, operates two trains daily to/from San Vicente de la Barquera, Llanes and Oviedo (€11.40, 4½ hours), and three to/from Bilbao (€6.25, 2½ hours).

Getting Around
Santander buses cost €1 per ride. Purchase a 10-ride ticket for €4.50 at tobacco stands throughout the city.

AROUND SANTANDER
Puente Viesgo
pop 550 / elevation 70m
The valley town of Puente Viesgo, 25km south of Santander on the N623 towards Burgos, is 1.5km downhill from the impressive **Cuevas del Castillo** (☎ 942 59 84 25; adult/child each cave €3/1.50; ⏱ 10am-2pm & 4.15-8.30pm May-Sep, 9.30am-5pm Wed-Sun Oct-Apr). The two caves on view here, El Castillo and La Moneda, contain a series of prehistoric wall paintings of varied animals that are just as breathtaking as those at Cueva de Altamira (p499), but these are the genuine article rather than copies. In between the art, there's a labyrinth of stalactites and stalagmites in an astounding array of shapes. You'll find art and geologic formations in both caves, but El Castillo has more paintings.

Visits to the caves are by guided tour only (in Spanish), departing every half-hour; the last tour is given an hour before closing. In summer it's advisable to book a day ahead.

Southeast of town, by the tranquil Río Pas, **Posada La Anjana** (☎ 942 59 85 26; www .posadalaanjana.com) offers spacious rooms and meals.

Seven buses run to Puente Viesgo from Santander on Monday to Friday, (€1.70, 45 minutes), fewer on weekends.

EASTERN CANTABRIA
The 95km stretch of coast between Santander and Bilbao offers jaded citizens of

ART PRE-HISTORY

Some of Spain's greatest works of art don't hang in a museum. The paintings inside the Cueva de Altamira, near Santillana del Mar, and at dozens of other caves in Cantabria and Asturias, hold an undeniable power and mystery, enhanced perhaps by the anonymity of their creators.

The region's relatively mild climate and limestone caves provided a convenient habitat for Paleolithic settlers, when ice still covered much of the earth's surface. Ensconced in this environment, some of these early inhabitants felt the need to express themselves using the materials at hand.

Around 50 sites have been revealed throughout Cantabria, though only a few are open for visits. The most spectacular, covering the ceiling of the Cueva de Altamira, are thought to be the work of a single artist. Witnessing the level of artistic skill displayed in this tableau, archaeologists at the time of its discovery in 1879 dismissed it as a hoax.

Most of the thousands of paintings found at Altamira and elsewhere are stylised depictions of animals, usually deer, bison, boars and bulls, rendered in red, black and ochre tones. But other motifs appear. At Monte de Castillo cave near Puente Viesgo, for example, there are 53 negative handprints (produced by what was surely the world's first air-brush), and a series of crimson discs that one theory (among many) suggests could have been used as a lunar calendar. The painters, whose work dates back as far as 20,000 years, showed a fair degree of sophistication in their use of the canvas – in this case the cave walls – for example, by blending the shapes and fissures of the rock into the images.

both cities several seaside escape hatches. Some, such as Noja, are little more than beaches fronted by rows of holiday flats. The pick of the bunch is undoubtedly Castro Urdiales, 35km short of Bilbao.

Santoña

The fishing port of Santoña is dominated by two forts, **Fuerte de San Martín** and, further north, the abandoned **Fuerte de San Carlos**. You can take a pleasant walk around both forts, or plonk yourself down on sandy Playa de San Martín. Otherwise, head north along the C141 to **Playa Berria**, a magnificent sweep of sand on the open Mar Cantábrico. The **Hostal de Berria** (☎ 942 66 08 47; s/d €43/49) is the oblong white block at the west end.

Seven or more buses a day run to/from Santander (€2.60, one hour), and a passenger ferry crosses the estuary to the western end of Laredo beach (€1.50). Hourly buses link Santoña with Playa Berria.

Playa de Oriñón

One of the nicer beaches along this coast is at Oriñón, 14km east of Laredo. Popular on summer weekends, the broad sandy strip is set deep behind protective headlands, making the water calm and *comparatively* warm. In contrast, you'll find a chilly sea and some surfable waves on the windward side of the western headland. There's just one

place to stay, **Hostal El Conde** (☎ 942 87 86 24; s/d €70/75), on the beach's western end. Up to 10 buses a day head from Castro Urdiales to Oriñón (30 minutes).

Castro Urdiales

pop 19,670

The haughty Gothic **Iglesia de Santa María de la Asunción** (☑ 10am-1.30pm & 4-7pm Jul & Aug, 4-6pm rest of year) stands out above the harbour and the tangle of narrow lanes that make up the medieval centre of Castro Urdiales. The church shares its little headland with the ruins of what was for centuries the town's defensive bastion, now supporting a lighthouse. Of the two beaches, the westerly **Playa de Ostende** is the more attractive.

Find out about other beaches in the area at the **tourist office** (☎ 942 87 15 12; Avenida de la Constitución; ☑ 9am-9pm Jul–mid-Sep, 9am-2pm & 5-9pm rest of year), by the waterfront.

Several small places to stay are scattered about the old centre.

Hostal La Mar (☎ 942 87 05 24; Calle de la Mar 27; s/d €32/50) is located on the east side of the old centre and has freshly painted, functional rooms.

Traditional fare, such as *sopa de pescado* (fish soup) and *pudín de cabracho* (seafood paté), abounds in *mesones* (old-style eateries) and *tabernas* (taverns) along Calle La Mar and Calle Ardigales.

CANTABRIA & ASTURIAS

ALSA (☎ 902 42 22 42; Calle Leonardo Rucabado 2) runs at least nine buses daily to/from Santander (€4.50, one hour). Bizkaibus has frequent buses to/from Bilbao (€2, one hour), stopping at Bar La Ronda, on the corner of Calle La Ronda and Calle Benito Pérez Galdós.

Eastern Valleys

Short on specific sights but rich in unspoiled rural splendour, the little-visited valleys of eastern Cantabria are great for exploring in a vehicle. Plenty of routes suggest themselves: what follows is an example only.

From El Soto, on the N623 just south of Puente Viesgo, take the CA270 southeast towards Vega de Pas. The town is of minimal interest, but the drive is quite something. The views from the **Puerto de la Braguía pass** in particular are stunning. From Vega de Pas you could continue southeast, briefly crossing into Castilla y León, before turning north again at Río de Trueba, then following the Río Miera down through San Roque de Riomiera towards Santander.

Another option from Río de Trueba is to take the BU571 road up over the Puerto de la Sía pass towards Arredondo. This road is full of switchbacks, a couple of mountain passes and isolated little farmhouses.

SOUTHERN CANTABRIA

Wonderful views of high peaks and deep river valleys flanked by patchwork quilts of green await the traveller penetrating the Cantabrian interior. Every imaginable shade of green seems to have been employed to set this stage, strewn with warm stone villages and held together by a network of narrow country roads.

Reinosa (population 10,780), the main town in southern Cantabria, is drab, with little to stop for, except perhaps to look at the mansions and other buildings around the central Plaza de España. But the **Colegiata de San Pedro** in Cervatos, 5km south, is one of Cantabria's finest Romanesque churches.

Inquire at Reinosa's **tourist office** (☎ 942 75 52 15; Avenida del Puente de Carlos III 23) for information on *senderos* (walking routes) if a little rambling in the area appeals to you (see Western Valleys, p501 for one possibility).

If you get stuck in Reinosa, **Hostal Sema** (☎ 942 75 00 47; Calle de Julióbriga 14; s/d with bathroom €25/30) is conveniently close to the train and bus stations.

Five or six trains a day (€3.40, 1½ hours), and up to 11 buses (€3, 1¾ hours), head to/from Santander.

Along the Río Ebro

The Río Ebro (from whence 'Iberia' stems) rises about 6km west of Reinosa, fills the Embalse del Ebro reservoir and then meanders south and east into Castilla y León. You can follow the river's course along minor roads out of Reinosa.

Head first along the CA171 towards Corconte, then turn right at Requejo to cross over to the reservoir. Follow the southern shore towards Arroyo (you'll pass the ruins of Roman **Julióbriga**). Just before Arroyo, turn right (south). Along this exceedingly narrow route, you encounter the **Monasterio de Montes Claros**, dating from the 9th century. Next, descend to Arroyal and finally hit a T-junction where the CA272 meets the CA273. About 13km east is **Polientes**, where you'll find banks, a petrol station and four places to stay. Along or just off the road, several medieval chapels hewn from the rock can be visited. The best example, the **Iglesia de Santa María de Valverde**, is actually about 10km *west* of the T-junction. Eastwards, there are chapels at **Campo de Ebro** and, beyond Polientes, **Cadalso** and **Arroyuelos**.

Across the Ebro from Arroyuelos, **San Martín de Elines** has a fine Romanesque church and marks the end of the line for a daily bus from Reinosa via Polientes. With your own transport you can push on for Orbaneja del Castillo.

WESTERN CANTABRIA
Santillana del Mar
pop 3956

You could easily pass through this medieval jewel and never know what lies off the main road. Thanks to strict town planning rules first introduced back in 1575, Santillana has preserved its lovely old stone buildings and cobbled streets so well that it appears almost like a film set. Combined with the proximity of Cueva de Altamira, this makes Santillana a major tourist attraction. Along the old streets, shops hawk everything from Asturian cider to rabbit-fur footwarmers.

There are banks, a post office, telephones and a bookshop all on or just off the handsome Plaza Mayor. You'll find an informative **tourist office** (☎ 942 81 88 12; Calle Jesús Otero 20;

(🕑 9am-9pm Jul-Sep, 9.30am-1.30pm & 4-7pm rest of year) at the main car park.

SIGHTS

A stroll along the cobbled main street past solemn nobles' houses from the 15th to 18th centuries leads you to the lovely 12th-century Romanesque **Colegiata de Santa Juliana** (admission €2.50; 🕑 10am-1.30pm & 4-7.30pm Apr-Oct, 10am-1.30pm & 4-6.30pm Tue-Sun rest of year). The drawcard in this former monastery is the cloister, a formidable storehouse of Romanesque artisanry, with the capitals of its columns carved into a huge variety of figures. The sepulchre of Santa Juliana, a 3rd-century Christian martyr from Turkey (and the real source of the name Santillana), stands in the centre of the church. The monastery and town grew up around the saint's relics, which arrived here after her death.

Admission to the Colegiata includes entry to the **Museo Diocesano** (🕿 942 84 03 17; Calle Cruce; 🕑 see Colegiata) at the other end of town. The former Dominican monastery contains a fascinating collection of 'popular' polychrome wooden statuary, some of it quite bizarre.

Santillana also hosts an eclectic bunch of museums, cultural foundations and exhibitions. The **Museo El Solar** (🕿 942 84 02 73; Calle Jesús Otero 1; adult/child €3.60/2.40; 🕑 10am-10pm Jul & Aug, 10.30am-8pm rest of year) houses a permanent exhibit on the Inquisition, displaying over 70 instruments of torture, while the **Fundación Santillana** (🕿 942 81 82 03; Plaza Mayor; admission free) and the **Palacio Caja Cantabria** (🕿 942 81 81 71; Calle Santo Domingo 8; adult/child €2.50/free) stage excellent temporary exhibitions from around the world.

SLEEPING

There are dozens of places to stay, from large hotels designed for tour groups to small guesthouses in old mansions, scattered about the old part of town and along the roads towards Cueva de Altamira and Santander. Some close from about November to February.

Camping Santillana (🕿 942 81 82 50; per person/tent/car €5.30/4.20/5.15) Just west of town on the Comillas road, this camping ground has good facilities, including bungalows.

La Casa del Organista (🕿 942 84 03 52; www.casa delorganista.com; Camino de Los Hornos 4; s/d €43/87; 🅿) Rooms at this elegant 18th-century house

are particularly attractive, with wood-rail balconies, Persian rugs and plenty of antique furniture.

Casa Angélica (🕿 942 81 82 38; Camino de los Hornos 2; d with shared/private bathroom €35/45) Located over a tapestry shop just off Plaza Mayor, its three old-fashioned rooms (two sharing a bathroom) are lovely, with embroidered bedspreads.

Parador Gil Blas (🕿 942 02 80 28; santillana gb@parador.es; Plaza Ramón Pelayo 11; s/d €119/149; 🆘 🅿) A fine choice if you're in the luxury bracket, this 17th-century mansion is on the main square.

Along the main street are two rustic-style but comfortable little places offering rooms with bathroom:

Posada El Cantón (🕿 942 84 02 74; Calle Carrera 2; r €51) Inquire at Restaurant La Viga next door.

Posada Santa Juliana (🕿 942 84 01 06; Calle Carrera 19; r €54) Inquire at Bodega Los Nobles across the way.

There are another half-dozen lodgings around Campo Revoglo park, across the main road from the old town, most in remodelled stone farmhouses or stables:

Posada Araceli (🕿 942 84 01 94; www.posadaaraceli .com; Calle La Robleda 20; s/d €43/49)

Casa de Labranza González (🕿 942 81 81 78; Calle La Robleda 13; r €43)

EATING

Santillana has a lot of humdrum eateries catering to the passing tourist trade, but one or two offer better fare.

Casa Cossío (🕿 942 81 83 55; Plaza del Abad Francisco Navarro 13; fish dishes €6-14; 🕑 closed Tue) The nearest restaurant to the Colegiata grills up succulent seafood and sausages.

Restaurante La Viga (Calle Carrera 2; menú €9) This place's suitably ancient, wood-beamed *comedor* (dining room) is a nice setting for a platter of Tresviso cheese or Santoña anchovies.

GETTING THERE & AWAY

Four times a day Monday to Friday, three on weekends, **Autobuses La Cantábrica** (🕿 942 72 08 22) has buses from Santander to Santillana (€1.80, 45 minutes), and on to Comillas and San Vicente de la Barquera. They stop on Avenida Santonio Sandí, opposite the medical centre.

Museo & Cueva de Altamira

Until a few years ago, Spain's finest prehistoric art, in the Cueva de Altamira, 2km southwest of Santillana, was off-limits to all but 20-odd visitors daily – a maximum imposed in the 1980s to protect the world-famous cave paintings from further damage by too much human breath.

In 2001, however, the **Museo Altamira** (☎ 942 81 80 05; adult/child €2.40/1.20, free Sun & from 2.30pm Sat; ☾ 9.30am-5pm Tue-Sun Oct-May, 9.30am-7.30pm Tue-Sat, 9.30am-5pm Sun Jun-Sep) was opened near the cave. Now everyone can view the inspired, 14,500-year-old depictions of bison, horses and other beasts (or rather, their replicas) in the museum's full-size re-creation of the cave's most interesting chamber, the Sala de Polícromos (Polychrome Hall). The viewing is enhanced by excellent interactive exhibits on prehistoric humanity and cave art around the world, from Altamira to Australia.

But despite the astounding feat of reproducing not just the painting, but the also irregular cave walls that served as a canvas, the experience can't really compare with seeing the original artwork *in situ*, which you can do at Ribadesella and Puente Viesgo, among other places (see Art Pre-History, p497).

Visits to the replica cave, called the Neocueva, are guided; you're assigned a tour time with your ticket. Tours are in Spanish only, though there's explanatory text in English along the way. During Easter and from July to September it's worth purchasing tickets in advance at branches of **Banco Santander** (☎ 902 24 24 24; www.bancosantander.es), or by phoning or else by visiting its website. Those without vehicles must walk or take a taxi the 2km from Santillana.

Comillas

pop 1780

Comillas offers the attractive combination of a charming old centre, a handful of interesting monuments and a couple of good nearby beaches. One result is that you can all but forget about finding a bed here in high summer without a reservation.

The **tourist office** (☎ 942 72 07 68; Plaza Joaquín del Piélagos; ☾ 9am-9pm Jul & Aug, 10.30am-1.30pm & 4.30-7.30pm Mon-Sat, 10.30am-1.30pm Sun rest of year) is behind the town hall.

SIGHTS

Antoni Gaudí left few reminders of his genius beyond Catalonia, but of those that he did, the 1885 **Capricho de Gaudí** (Gaudí's Caprice)

in Comillas is easily the most flamboyant, if modest in stature. The brick building, originally a summer house for the Marqués de Comillas and now an expensive restaurant, is liberally striped with ceramic bands of alternating sunflowers and green leaves.

The Capricho was one of several buildings commissioned for Comillas from leading Catalan Modernista architects by the first Marqués de Comillas, who was born here as plain Antonio López, made a fortune in Cuba and returned to beautify his home town. In the same hillside parklands stand the wonderful neo-Gothic **Palacio de Sobrellano** (admission €3; ☾ 10am-9pm 1 Jul-9 Sep, 10.30am-2pm & 4-7.30pm 10-30 Sept, 10.30am-2pm & 4-7.30pm Wed-Sun Oct-Jun) and **Capilla Panteón de los Marqueses de Comillas** (admission €3; ☾ see palacio), both designed by Joan Martorell. With the *palacio*, Martorell truly managed to out-Gothic real Gothic. Visits to both buildings are by guided tour.

Martorell also had a hand in the **Universidad Pontificia** on the hill opposite, but it was Lluís Doménech i Montaner, another Catalan Modernista, who contributed the medieval flavour to this elaborate building, a former seminary, whose grounds you can stroll.

Comillas' compact medieval centre is full of its own little pleasures. **Plaza de la Constitución** is its focal point, a sloping, cobbled square flanked by the town hall, the Iglesia de San Cristóbal and old sandstone houses with flower-bedecked balconies.

Comillas boasts a fine beach, and it's just a 10-minute walk from the Plaza de la Constitución.

SLEEPING

Camping Comillas (☎ 942 72 00 74; per person/car & tent €3.85/11.25; ☾ Jun-Sep) A grassy spot on the eastern edge of town, the camping ground spreads to a clifftop area over the road in July and August.

Pensión Fuente Real (☎ 942 72 01 55; Fuente Real 19; s/d with shared bathroom €20/33; P) In a lane just behind the Capricho de Gaudí (some rooms have views of it), this makes a very pleasant budget choice.

Pensión La Aldea (☎ 942 72 10 46; La Aldea 5; s/d with separate bath €28/30) This homely guesthouse offers simple rooms with hardwood floors, and there's a little *comedor* downstairs. It also runs a second, slightly fancier place over on Calle Díaz de la Campa.

Hostal Esmeralda (☎ 942 72 00 97; fax 942 72 22 58; Calle Antonio López 7; s/d with bathroom €56/73) A short distance east of the town centre, this handsomely restored *hostal* (budget hotel) contains large, old-fashioned rooms and a moderately priced restaurant.

Casal del Castro (☎ 942 72 00 36; Calle San Jerónimo s/n; s/d €64/91) This period-furnished 17th-century mansion could compete with the best *paradors*.

EATING & DRINKING

The obvious place for morning coffee is the Plaza de la Rabia, behind the cathedral.

Restaurante El Pirata (☎ 942 72 21 05; Calle del Marqués de Comillas 6; menú €10) A cute little place on the street below the Palacio de Sobrellano, El Pirata offers tasty home cooking. Try for a table by the window upstairs.

Restaurante Gurea (☎ 942 72 24 46; Calle Ignacio Fernández de Castro; mains €11-15; ☒ closed Sun afternoon & Mon) Behind Hostal Esmeralda, this elegant restaurant dishes up great Basque and *montañés* (Cantabrian-style) fare. The *sopa de mariscos* (seafood soup) is especially delicious.

GETTING THERE & AWAY

Comillas is served by the same buses as Santillana del Mar. The main stop is on Calle del Marqués de Comillas, near the driveway to the Capricho de Gaudí.

Around Comillas

Out of several beaches around Comillas, the long, sandy **Playa de Oyambre**, 5km west, is decidedly superior. There are two year-round camping grounds behind the beach.

A little further west, the wilder, less crowded and clothing-optional **Playa de Merón** and its continuation **Playa del Rosal** stretch 3km to the estuary at San Vicente de la Barquera. Heed the warning signs about currents here.

San Vicente de la Barquera

pop 3360

San Vicente was an important fishing port throughout the Middle Ages and later became one of the so-called Cuatro Villas de la Costa – converted by Carlos III into the province of Cantabria in 1779.

Coming in from the east you cross over the low arches of the 15th-century Puente de la Maza, then skirt the waterfront Parque

Municipal to reach the central Plaza de José Antonio. Towering above is the craggy outcrop between two estuaries that supports what remains of the old town.

San Vicente has a central **tourist office** (☎ 942 71 07 97; www.sanvicentedelabarquera.org; Avenida del Generalísimo 20; ☒ closed Sun afternoon), which doubles as an agent for *casas rurales* in the area.

The old part of town has a castle and some remnants of the old city walls, but its outstanding monument is the largely 13th-century **Iglesia de Santa María de los Ángeles**. Though Gothic, it sports a pair of impressive Romanesque doorways. In one of the chapels, the lifelike statue of 16th-century Inquisitor Antonio del Corro (reclining on one elbow, reading) is deemed to be the best piece of Renaissance funerary art in Spain.

Located near the beach, **Camping El Rosal** (☎ 942 71 01 65; www.campingelrosal.jazztel.es; per person/tent/car €4.20/3.70/3.70) is just across San Vicente's eastern estuary.

The friendly little **Pensión Liébana** (☎ 942 71 02 11; Calle Ronda 2; s/d €37/40), up some steps from Plaza de José Antonio, features cosy stone-walled rooms, some with skylights.

Hostería La Paz (☎ 942 71 01 80; Calle del Mercado 2; s/d without bathroom €18/29) is just off the plaza, in an ancient but well-preserved structure that boasts large, comfortable rooms with high ceilings.

El Pescador (☎ 942 71 00 05; Calle Antonio Garrelly; raciones €3-8; ☒ closed Mon) This is about the liveliest of a string of seafood restaurants with tables overlooking the estuary.

The unpretentious **Mesón Madrid** (☎ 942 71 21 60; Plaza San Antonio; menú €9; ☒ closed Wed) is a great place to sample grilled sardines or paella.

San Vicente bus station, by the Puente de la Maza, is served by the same buses as Santillana del Mar, plus half a dozen ALSA services linking Oviedo, Ribadesella, Santander, Bilbao and beyond. Autobuses Palomera also stop here en route between Santander and Potes (see Picos de Europa, p520). Two FEVE trains stop here daily en route between Santander (€3.60, 1½ hours) and Oviedo.

Western Valleys

Generally ignored by holidaymakers, who concentrate their attention on the Picos de Europa further west, the valleys of the Río Saja and, next west, the Río Nansa, make a soft contrast to the craggy majesty of the Picos.

A beautiful drive if you're starting from the Picos is the CA282, which snakes up high and eastwards from La Hermida on the Río Deva. The village of **Puentenansa** (with banks and bars) forms a crossroads. The CA281 southwards follows the Río Nansa upstream: along the way, a short detour east leads to the attractive hamlet of **Tudanca**, where accommodation includes the *casa rural* (village or country house or farmhouse with rooms to rent) **La Cotera** (☎ 942 72 90 69; d €35). The CA281 eventually meets the C627, on which you can head south to Cervera de Pisuerga (see Montaña Palentina, p208) or turn northwest back to the Picos.

Proceeding east from Puentenansa takes you through **Carmona**, with many fine stone mansions. When you reach the village of Valle de Cabuérniga and the Río Saja, head south towards Reinosa. The views are magnificent. The hamlet of **Bárcena Mayor**, about 9km east of the main road, is a popular spot with a couple of *casas rurales* to stay in and great *mesones,* where you should try *cocido montañés,* the local bean, cabbage, meat and sausage stew.

ASTURIAS

'Ser español es un orgullo', the saying goes, 'ser asturiano es un título'. 'If being Spanish is a matter of pride, to be Asturian is a title', or so some of the locals would have you think.

Like neighbouring Galicia, Asturias was exclusively Celtic territory before the arrival of the Romans. It's also the sole patch of Spain never conquered by the Muslims. Ever since King Pelayo warded them off in the Battle of Covadonga in AD 722 and laid the foundations of Christian Spain's 800-year comeback, Asturians have thought of themselves – or have been peceived to think of themselves – as a cut above the rest of the peninsula's inhabitants. Asturias, they say, is the real Spain; the rest is simply *tierra de la reconquista* (reconquered land).

Nevertheless, the Reconquista's slow southward progress left Asturias increasingly a backwater. As a concession, Juan I of Castilla y León made Asturias a *principado* (principality) in 1388, and to this day the heir to the Spanish throne holds the title Príncipe de Asturias. Annual awards handed out by the prince to personalities of distinction are Spain's equivalent of the Nobel prizes.

Although Oviedo and other towns have their moments, Asturias' real beauty lies beyond the cities. Much of the Picos de Europa are on Asturian territory, and towns such as Llanes and Cudillero make great bases for exploring the lovely coast. For the architecture buff, Asturias is the land of the pre-Romanesque – modest but unique survivors of early medieval building and decoration.

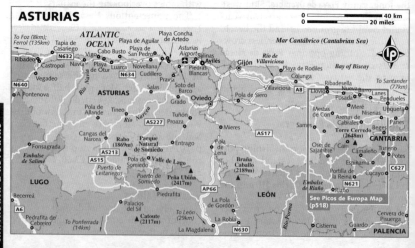

Bucolically green though much of it is, Asturias also has its gritty industrial side. The Oviedo–Gijón–Avilés triangle is the heart of industrial Asturias.

Traditional Asturian food is simple peasant fare. Best known is the *fabada asturiana*, a hearty bean dish jazzed up with meat and sausage. The region is also renowned for its earthy cheeses, many produced in the Picos de Europa (see Say Cheese, p525).

Asturias' regional tourism office maintains an excellent website, www.infoasturias.com, which is well worth exploring before or during your visit.

OVIEDO

pop 207,700 / elevation 232m

The elegant parks and modern shopping streets of Asturias' capital are agreeably offset by what remains of the *casco antiguo* (old town). Out on the periphery, the hum and heave of factories is a strong reminder that Oviedo is a key producer of textiles, metal goods, sugar and chocolate.

History

When Asturian king Alfonso II El Casto (the Chaste; AD 791–842) defeated a Muslim detachment that had all but destroyed the small town of Oviedo, he was sufficiently impressed by the site to rebuild and expand it, and move his court here from Pravia. It stayed until 910 when it was moved to León. By the 14th century, with the declaration of Asturias as a principality and the construction of the cathedral, Oviedo had secured its place as an important religious and administrative centre. The university opened its doors around 1600, and industry took off in the 19th century. A miners' revolt in 1934 and a nasty siege in the first months of the Spanish Civil War led to the destruction of much of the old town.

Orientation

From the train station, Oviedo's main drag, Calle de Uría, leads southeast straight to the Campo de San Francisco, a large leafy park, and the old town. The new ALSA bus station is 300m east of the train station on Calle Pepe Cosmen, the continuation of Avenida de Santander. A good collection of restaurants, cafés and bars waits to be discovered in and near the narrow, mainly pedestrianised streets of the historic old town.

Information

EMERGENCY

Policía Nacional (☎ 985 96 71 00; Calle de General Yagüe)

INTERNET ACCESS

Café Oriental (Calle de Jovellanos 8; per hr €2.40) Log on here by pre-paid card.

L@ser (Calle de San Francisco 9; per hr €3; ☷ 24hr) Check email here.

MEDICAL SERVICES

Farmacia Nestares (☎ 985 22 39 25; Calle de Uría 36; ☷ 9am-midnight)

Hospital Central de Asturias (☎ 985 10 61 00; Avenida de Julián Clavería)

MONEY

Calle de Uría is lined with banks, most equipped with ATMs.

POST

Main post office (Calle de Alonso Quintanilla 1)

TOURIST INFORMATION

Oficina Municipal de Turismo (☎ 985 22 75 86; Calle Marqués de Santa Cruz; ☷ 10.30am-2pm & 4.30-7.30pm) Occupying a kiosk off Campo de San Francisco.

Regional tourist office (☎ 985 21 33 85; Calle de Cimadevilla 4; ☷ 9am-2pm & 4.30-6.30pm Mon-Fri, 10am-2pm & 4-7pm Sat & Sun) Stop here for lots of useful brochures and maps.

Sights

CATEDRAL DE SAN SALVADOR

In a sense, the mainly Gothic edifice you see today forms the outer casing of a many-layered history in stone of Spanish Christianity. Its origins lie in the Cámara Santa, a chapel built by Alfonso II to house holy relics. The chapel is now the inner sanctuary of the **cathedral** (☎ 985 20 31 17; admission incl Cámara Santa, Museo Diocesano & cloister €3, Thu free; ☷ 10am-1pm & 4-8pm Mon-Fri, 10am-1pm & 4-6pm Sat mid-May–Sep; 10am-1pm & 4-6pm or 7pm Mon-Sat rest of year), which was chiefly built between the 14th and 16th centuries.

The **Cámara Santa** contains some key symbols of medieval Spanish Christianity. Alfonso II presented the Cruz de los Ángeles (Cross of the Angels) to Oviedo in 808, and it is still the city's emblem. A century later Alfonso III donated the Cruz de la Victoria (Cross of Victory), which in turn became the sign of Asturias.

CANTABRIA & ASTURIAS

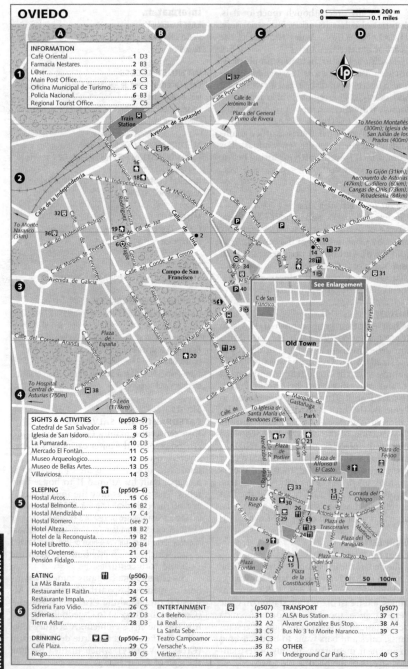

OVIEDO

| 0 | 200 m |
| 0 | 0.1 miles |

INFORMATION
Café Oriental..1 D3
Farmacia Nestares................................2 B3
L@ser..3 C3
Main Post Office..................................4 C3
Oficina Municipal de Turismo..............5 C3
Policía Nacional....................................6 B3
Regional Tourist Office.........................7 C5

To Mesón Montañés
(300m); Iglesia de
San Julián de los
Prados (400m)

To Gijón (31km);
Aeropuerto de Asturias
(47km); Cudillero (60km);
Cangas de Onís (73km);
Ribadesella (84km)

To Monte
Naranco
(3km)

**Campo de San
Francisco**

See Enlargement

Old Town

To Hospital
Central de
Asturias (750m)

To León
(118km)

To Iglesia de
Santa María de
Bendones (5km)

SIGHTS & ACTIVITIES (pp503–5)
Catedral de San Salvador.....................8 D5
Iglesia de San Isidoro..........................9 C5
La Pumarada......................................10 D3
Mercado El Fontán.............................11 C5
Museo Arqueologico...........................12 D5
Museo de Bellas Artes.........................13 D5
Villaviciosa..14 D3

SLEEPING (pp505–6)
Hostal Arcos.......................................15 C6
Hostal Belmonte................................16 B2
Hostal Mendizábal..............................17 C4
Hostal Romero...........................(see 2)
Hotel Alteza.......................................18 B2
Hotel de la Reconquista.......................19 B2
Hotel Libretto.....................................20 B4
Hotel Ovetense..................................21 C4
Pensión Fidalgo.................................22 C3

EATING (p506)
La Màs Barata.....................................23 C5
Restaurante El Raitàn...........................24 C5
Restaurante Impala.............................25 C5
Sidrería Faro Vidio..............................26 C5
Sidrerías..27 D3
Tierra Astur.......................................28 D3

DRINKING (pp506–7)
Café Plaza..29 C5
Riego...30 C5

ENTERTAINMENT (p507)
Ca Beleño..31 D3
La Real...32 A2
La Santa Sebe....................................33 C5
Teatro Campoamor.............................34 C3
Versache's..35 B2
Vértize...36 A3

TRANSPORT (p507)
ALSA Bus Station................................37 C1
Alvarez Gonzàlez Bus Stop..................38 A4
Bus No 3 to Monte Naranco................39 C3

OTHER
Underground Car Park.........................40 C3

Plaza de
Porlier

Plaza de
Alfonso II
El Casto

Plaza de
Feijoo

Plaza de
Riego

Corrada del
Obispo

Plaza de
Trascorrales

Plaza del
Paraguas

Plaza
Fontán

Plaza
del Sol

Plaza
de la
Constitución

0   50   100m

CANTABRIA & ASTURIAS

These and other items can be viewed from the Sala Apostolar, whose remarkable sculptures of the apostles are the work of Maestro Mateo, creator of the Pórtico de la Gloria in the cathedral of Santiago de Compostela. Turning to leave, you'll see three heads sculpted out of a single block of stone above the doorway. This strikingly simple work depicts, from left to right, the Virgin Mary, Christ and St John on Calvary.

The **cloister** is pure 14th-century Gothic, rare enough in Asturias, and just off it the sala capitular (chapter house) contains some well-restored Flemish-Gothic choir stalls. The **Museo Diocesano** houses some interesting ecclesiastical artefacts.

One vestige of the original 9th-century structure is a Romanesque tower on the south side, best approached via the Tránsito de Santa Barbara.

AROUND THE CATHEDRAL

Plaza de Alfonso II El Casto and neighbouring Plaza de Porlier are fronted by elegant palaces dating from the 17th and 18th centuries. The nearby **Museo de Bellas Artes de**

Asturias (Calle de Santa Ana 1; admission free; 11am-2.30pm & 5-9pm Tue-Sat, 11am-2.30pm Sun Jul & Aug; 10.30am-2pm & 4.30-8.30pm Tue-Fri, 11.30am-2pm & 5-8pm Sat, 11.30am-2.30pm Sun Sep-Jun) is well worth a visit: its collection includes paintings by Goya, Murillo and other Spanish greats, and plenty by Asturians, such as Evaristo Valle, plus a roomful of El Grecos. Behind the cathedral, the 16th-century Benedictine Monasterio de San Vicente houses the **Museo Arqueológico** (closed indefinitely for restorations).

PLAZAS

It's enjoyable to indulge in a little exploration of the old town's nooks and crannies. **Plaza de la Constitución** occupies a barely perceptible rise close to the heart of old Oviedo, capped at one end by the **Iglesia de San Isidoro**, and fronted by an eclectic collection of old shops, cafés and the 17th-century *ayuntamiento* (city hall). To the south, past the **Mercado El Fontán** food market, arcaded **Plaza Fontán** is equipped with a couple of *sidrerías* and has passages leading under the houses to surrounding streets.

PRE-ROMANESQUE ARCHITECTURE IN ASTURIAS

More or less cut off from the rest of Christian Europe by the Muslim invasion, the small kingdom that emerged in 8th-century Asturias gave rise to a style of art and building unique in Europe.

The 14 buildings, mostly churches, which survive from the two centuries of the Asturian kingdom take some inspiration from other sources, but have no real siblings. Typical of all are the straight lines of their profiles and floor plans – no apses or cylinders here – though their semicircular arches are obvious forerunners of the style that would later triumph in northern Spain and across much of Europe – Romanesque. Another precursor to the Romanesque style is the complete vaulting of the nave.

Roman and Visigothic elements *are* visible. In many cases the bases and capitals of columns, with their Corinthian or floral motifs, were simply cannibalised from earlier structures. Another adaptation, which owes something more to developments in Muslim Spain, was the use of lattice windows. They appear purely as a design effect, since their eastern progenitors were inspired by the desire to maintain privacy from the outside world – hardly an issue in a church.

Some of the best representatives of the pre-Romanesque style are found in or near Oviedo. The **Iglesia de San Julián de los Prados** (admission €1.20, Mon free; 10am-1pm Mon, 10am-1pm & 4-6pm Tue-Fri, 9.30-11.30am & 3.30-5.30pm Sat May-Sep, shorter hr rest of year) in Oviedo, just above the Gijón Hwy, is the largest remaining pre-Romanesque church, and one of the oldest, built under Alfonso II. It is flanked by two porches – another very Asturian touch – and the inside is covered with frescoes. The **Iglesia de Santa María de Bendones** (closed to visitors at the time of writing), southeast of Oviedo, is unique for its extra-wide nave, a result of Roman influence. On the slopes of Monte Naranco, 3km northwest of central Oviedo, the tall, narrow **Palacio de Santa María del Naranco** and the **Iglesia de San Miguel de Lillo** (admission to both €2.20, Mon free; 9.30am-1pm Sun & Mon, 9.30am-1pm & 3.30-7pm Tue-Sat Apr-Sep, shorter hr rest of year) were built by Ramiro I (842–50), Alfonso II's successor, and mark an advance in Asturian art. An outstanding feature of the decoration in the former is the *sogueado*, the sculptural motif imitating rope used in its columns.

Other little squares include **Plaza de Trascorrales**, **Plaza de Riego** and **Plaza del Paraguas**. The last got its name from its inverted-umbrella design, which once accommodated an open-air market. Today it sports a big umbrella to protect visitors from the elements.

You can't fail to notice the many bronze sculptures scattered about town. The most comment-provoking is **Culis monumentalibus**, a 4m-high representation of a female bottom by Eduardo Úrculo, which adorns the street outside the Teatro Campoamor.

Festivals & Events
Oviedo's biggest fiesta is that of **San Mateo**, celebrated in the third week of September and climaxing around 21 September.

Sleeping
BUDGET & MID-RANGE
Hostal Arcos (☎ 985 21 47 73; Calle de Magdalena 3; s/d with bathroom €32/42) The only lodging in the old town has 12 simple, clean rooms and is ideally located within stumbling distance of some of Oviedo's best watering holes.

Pensión Fidalgo (☎ 985 21 32 87; Calle de Jovellanos 5; s/d with bathroom €36/47) This family-run place on the northern edge of the old town has eight homely rooms and well-scrubbed facilities.

Hotel Ovetense (☎ 985 22 08 40; info@hotelovetense .com; Calle de San Juan 6; s/d €36/50) Located 100m northwest of the cathedral, this modern lodging boasts neat little rooms at a good price. There's a popular late-night coffee shop downstairs.

Hostal Mendizábal (☎ 985 22 01 89; Calle de Mendizábal 4; s/d with bathroom €30/35) Conveniently located off Plaza de Porlier, this modest, second-floor guesthouse is often full.

Calle de Uría below the train station is a veritable gallery of inexpensive lodgings, all within easy walking distance of the old town. Traffic noise is an issue, however.

Hotel Alteza (☎ 985 24 04 08; Calle de Uría 25; s/d €35/ 48) The nicest of the bunch, with spacious rooms and a café.

Hostal Belmonte (☎ 985 24 10 20; calogon@teleline .es; Calle de Uría 31; s/d with bathroom €28/46)

Hostal Romero (☎ 985 22 75 91; hostalromero@ telecable.es; Calle de Uría 36; s/d €42/48)

TOP END
Hotel Libretto (☎ 985 20 20 04; www.librettohotel .com; Calle Marqués de Santa Cruz 12; s/d €92/118; 🖳 P) Music lovers will appreciate this new, opera-inspired hotel in a Modernista-style building facing the Campo de San Francisco. The 15 sleekly furnished rooms include CD players; in one, an oversized portrait of Maria Callas overlooks the antique bathtub.

Hotel de la Reconquista (☎ 985 24 11 00; www.hotel delareconquista.com; Calle de Gil de Jaz 16; s/d €179/221; ❌ 🖳 P) The top of the heap. Ironically, this 18th-century building started off as a poorhouse!

Eating
Restaurante Impala (☎ 985 22 01 56; Calle de Cabo Noval 10; menú €6) Head here for good Asturian food at reasonable prices.

La Más Barata (☎ 985 21 36 06; Calle de Cimadevilla 2; dishes €6-10) This place specialises in rice-based dishes originating from Spain's Mediterranean seaboard, highlighted by *arroz a banda* (rice and seafood/chicken/game).

Restaurante El Raitán (☎ 985 21 42 18; Plaza Trascorrales 6; mains €14-20) The *menú asturiano* (from €14) lets you sample a range of regional favourites without breaking the bank. Next door is Raitán's classy version of a *chigre* (traditional tavern).

Mesón Montañés (☎ 985 28 00 68; Calle Isla de Cuba 8; menú €6-10) After visiting the Iglesia San Julián de los Prados, try this nearby joint, preparing classics such as *fabada de mariscos* (bean and shellfish stew) and *bacalao al horno* (baked cod).

More is said under Drinking (see below) about *sidrerías*, but it is definitely worth noting that you can get a square meal in most of them. Those on Calle de la Gascona serve *raciones* from €4 to €15.

Tierra Astur (☎ 985 21 56 79; Calle de la Gascona 1; dishes €9-20) A particularly atmospheric *sidrería*/restaurant, Tierra Astur is famed for its grilled meats. Start off with a plate of Asturian sausage, cheese or ham.

Sidrería Faro Vidio (☎ 985 22 86 24; Calle de Cimadevilla 19; fish dishes €18-24; ❌) This upmarket cider-and-seafood option provides a palatial setting for a plate of eel or a sea urchin scramble.

Drinking
If you're after no-frills drinking Asturian-style, don't miss the *sidrerías*. Calle de la Gascona is a classic street lined with eight lively, no-nonsense cider houses, but you'll

soon start finding them all over town. Those listed here are among the bubbliest:

La Pumarada (☎ 985 20 02 79; Calle del Gascona 8)
Villaviciosa (☎ 985 22 70 61; Calle de la Gascona 7)

The lacework of squares around the old town is loaded with cafés to suit all tastes.

Riego (Plaza de Riego) Riego is for coffee aficionados, with lots of tables on the square.

Café Plaza (Plaza de Riego) This nighttime haunt is for music lovers.

Café Oriental (☎ 985 20 28 97; Calle de Jovellanos 8) An Arabesque tiled fantasy where Moroccan mint tea is served on traditional silver trays, the Oriental is a very popular gathering place.

Entertainment

The narrow pedestrian streets of the old town are thronged with people having a great time inside and outside dozens of bars on weekends. Calle de Mon has many of the rowdier, later-opening spots. Other streets to explore are Calle San Antonio, Calle Ildefonso Martínez and Calle de la Canóniga.

Ca Beleño (☎ 985 21 53 06; Calle de Martínez Vigil 4) A well-established venue for Celtic music, whether of Asturian, Galician or Irish extraction, Ca Beleño hosts jam sessions on Wednesday and Thursday nights.

La Real (☎ 985 24 38 93; www.lareal.org; Calle de Cervantes 19; cover €6; ☽ Sat) La Real's three dance floors (house, techno and progressive) can accommodate up to 1800 people. There are two Saturday sessions: from 6pm to 11pm for youth aged 16 to 24, and from 2am for a more mature crowd.

Vértize (Calle del Matemático Pedrayes 18; cover €5-8; ☽ Fri & Sat) This large club leads a double life: Friday night it's a Latin dance hall with live combos, on Saturday it becomes a gay disco.

Other gay-oriented nightlife options are found in the old town and up by the train station.

La Santa Sebe (Calle de Altamirano 6) A cavernous space for dancing and occasional theatre, this gay and lesbian club is open to all.

Versache's (Calle de Campoamor 24) This mostly male disco offers a mirror-ball dance floor.

Getting There & Away

AIR

The **Aeropuerto de Asturias** (☎ 985 12 75 00) is at Santiago del Monte, 47km northwest of Oviedo and 40km west of Gijón. Iberia has daily nonstop flights to/from Madrid and Barcelona, and flights a few days a week direct to/from London and Paris. Spanair also serves Madrid.

BUS

From the massive new **ALSA bus station** (☎ 902 49 99 49; Calle Pepe Cosmen), direct services charge up the motorway to Gijón (€1.75, 30 minutes) every 10 or 15 minutes from 6am to 10.30pm.

Other daily buses head to/from Galicia, Cantabria and elsewhere. Three buses travel daily to A Coruña (€22, four to six hours), at least nine go to León (€7, 1¾ to two hours), 11 to Madrid (€26.35 to €41.50, five to 5½ hours), five to San Sebastián (€22.60 to €38.50, five to 6½ hours), at least seven to Santander (€11 to €18.70, 2¼ to 3½ hours) and four to Santiago de Compostela (€26 to €33, 4½ to 6¾ hours). Still others travel to Valladolid, Salamanca, Barcelona and Seville. Buses to Cangas de Onís (p520) and Covadonga (p520) also run from Oviedo.

TRAIN

One train station serves both rail companies, Renfe and FEVE, the latter located on the upper level. For Gijón, it's best to use the Renfe *cercanías* (local trains that serve large cities; €2.15, 35 minutes), which run until after 10pm. Half a dozen daily Renfe trains travel to León (€6.10 to €16.50, 2½ hours), some continuing to other cities, such as Burgos, Pamplona, Madrid and Barcelona.

FEVE (☎ 985 29 76 56) runs four daily trains to/from Arriondas (€3.60, 1½ hours), Ribadesella (€4.65, two hours) and Llanes (€6, 2½ hours), with two continuing to Santander (€11.40, 4¼ hours) and one to Bilbao. Westbound, FEVE trains link up with trains from Gijón at Pravia, with three daily runs to Cudillero (€2.10, 1¼ hours) and Luarca (€5.20, 2¼ hours). Two of these continue to Tapia de Casariego, Ribadeo (€8.65, 3½ hours), Viveiro and Ferrol (€16.70, 6½ hours).

Getting Around

Up to eight buses daily run between the ALSA bus station and the Aeropuerto de Asturias (€5.25, 45 minutes).

GIJÓN

pop 258,200

Bigger, busier and gutsier than Oviedo, Gijón (khi-*hon*) produces iron, steel and chemicals, and is the main loading terminal for Asturian coal. But more than an industrial centre, Gijón has emerged as a popular travellers' destination by pedestrianising old streets, creating new parks and seafront walks, and opening museums. Allied to its people's *joie de vivre* and vast summer entertainment programme, this makes the place well worth your time.

Information

In addition to the two tourist offices mentioned here, summer information booths open at Playa de San Lorenzo and elsewhere in town.

Asturias regional tourist office (☎ 985 34 60 46; Calle del Marqués de San Esteban 1; ☷ 9am-2pm & 4.30-6.30pm Mon-Fri, 9am-2pm & 4-7pm Sat & Sun)

Ciber Capua (Calle de Capua 4; per hr €2; ☷ 10am-2am) Check email here.

English Bookshop (☎ 985 33 83 26; Calle de Ezcurdia 58) Stocks a fair selection of novels.

Hospital de Cabueñes (☎ 985 18 50 00) Four kilometres east of the city centre.

Municipal tourist office (☎ 985 34 17 71; www .gijon.info; Espigón Central de Fomento; ☷ 8am-8pm) On a pier of the Puerto Deportivo (Marina).

Policía Local (☎ 985 18 11 00; Calle San José 2) South of the centre of town.

Post office (Plaza de Seis de Agosto)

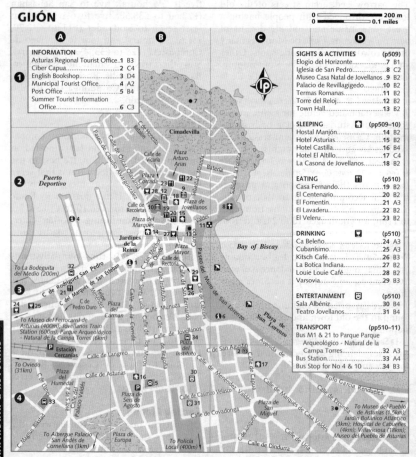

GIJÓN

INFORMATION	
Asturias Regional Tourist Office..1	B3
Ciber Capua.............................2	C4
English Bookshop......................3	D4
Municipal Tourist Office............4	A2
Post Office...............................5	B4
Summer Tourist Information Office....6	C3

SIGHTS & ACTIVITIES	(p509)
Elogio del Horizonte...................7	B1
Iglesia de San Pedro..................8	C2
Museo Casa Natal de Jovellanos .9	B2
Palacio de Revillagigedo............10	B2
Termas Romanas......................11	B2
Torre del Reloj.........................12	B2
Town Hall...............................13	B2

SLEEPING	(pp509–10)
Hostal Manjón..........................14	B2
Hotel Asturias.........................15	B2
Hotel Castilla..........................16	B4
Hotel El Altillo.........................17	C4
La Casona de Jovellanos............18	B2

EATING	(p510)
Casa Fernando........................19	B2
El Centenario..........................20	B2
El Fomentín............................21	A3
El Lavadero............................22	B2
El Veleru................................23	B2

DRINKING	(p510)
Ca Beleño..............................24	A3
Cubanísimo.............................25	A3
Kitsch Café.............................26	B3
La Botica Indiana......................27	B2
Louie Louie Café......................28	B2
Varsovia................................29	B3

ENTERTAINMENT	(p510)
Sala Albéniz...........................30	B4
Teatro Jovellanos....................31	B4

TRANSPORT	(pp510–11)
Bus M1 & 21 to Parque Parque Arqueológico - Natural de la Campa Torres....32	A3
Bus Station............................33	A4
Bus Stop for No 4 & 10 34	B3

Sights & Activities

The ancient core of Gijón is concentrated on the headland known as **Cimadevilla**. At the top of this, what used to be a fortified military zone has been converted into an attractive park. At the edge of the promontory stands the **Elogio del Horizonte**, a monumental concrete sculpture by Basque artist Eduardo Chillida that has become a symbol of the city. Wrapped around the landward side is a fine web of narrow lanes and small squares.

Plaza de Jovellanos is dominated by the home of 18th-century Enlightenment politician Gaspar Melchor de Jovellanos, now housing the **Museo Casa Natal de Jovellanos** (☎ 985 34 63 13), devoted mainly to Asturian art and Jovellanos himself.

To the east, underneath Campo Valdés, are the town's **Termas Romanas** (Roman Baths; ☎ 985 30 16 82), built in the 1st to 4th centuries AD. West of here is the harmonious **Plaza Mayor**, with porticoes on three sides and the *casa consistorial* (town hall) on the fourth. Further west, the impressive 18th-century **Palacio de Revillagigedo** (☎ 985 34 69 21; Plaza del Marqués 2) is now a lively cultural centre, hosting modern art exhibitions and the occasional play or concert. The **Torre del Reloj** (Clock Tower; ☎ 985 18 13 29; Calle Recoletas 5), just behind it, houses a six-floor exhibition on Gijón's history, with a viewing platform at the top.

The **Museo del Ferrocarril de Asturias** (☎ 985 30 85 75; Plaza de la Estación del Norte), in Gijón's old Renfe train station, a few minutes' walk west of the city centre, explores the role of railways in Asturian history, with 50 locomotives and carriages, and plenty of choo-choo paraphernalia.

The **Museo del Pueblo de Asturias** (☎ 985 33 22 44; Paseo Dr Fleming 877; admission free), on a large woodland site 2km east of the city centre, is a regional ethnographic museum with several traditional buildings, one containing the **Museo de la Gaita**, with bagpipes from Asturias and elsewhere. Take bus No 10 from Plaza del Instituto to the Grupo Cultura Covadonga stop, about 400m from the museum.

Parque Arqueológico-Natural de la Campa Torres (☎ 985 30 16 82), on the Cabo Torres headland 6km northwest of the city centre, is Gijón's birthplace – a Roman and pre-Roman site where you can examine remains of dwellings and cisterns. Take bus No M1 or 21 from in front of the marina.

> ### GIJÓN MUSEUMS
>
> All Gijón museums are closed on Monday. Opening hours on other days vary by place and season, but the typical timetable is 10am to 1pm and 5pm to 8pm Tuesday to Saturday, 11am to 2pm and 5pm to 8pm Sunday. Tourist offices have lists of current hours. Most museums are free, the exceptions being the Termas Romanas, Museo del Ferrocarril de Asturias and Parque Arqueológico de la Campa Torres, which cost €2.20 each (€1.30 for students, under-16s and seniors), or €3.90 (€1.90) for all three. There's no charge on Sunday.

The **Jardín Botánico Atlántico** (Atlantic Botanical Garden; ☎ 985 13 07 13; adult/senior & student €5/2.50; ☼ 10am-9pm Tue-Sun Jun-Sep, 10am-6pm Tue-Sun Oct-May), 3km east of the city centre, provides an excellent introduction to Cantabrian flora. The grand finale is the Jardín de la Isla, a landscaped park laced with pools and streams, based on the plans of 19th-century industrialist Florencio Valdés. Take bus No 4 from Plaza del Instituto.

For swimming, **Playa de San Lorenzo** is a surprisingly good, clean city beach, but rather thin when the tide comes in. **Playa de Poniente**, west of the Puerto Deportivo, has imported sand and is much broader.

Festivals & Events

Throughout the summer, Gijón finds some excuse for a fiesta almost every week, from the **Semana Negra** (Black Week) arts festival in early July, focusing on detective novels, to the **Fiesta de la Sidra Natural** (Natural Cider Festival) in late August. Varied musical programmes and plenty of partying accompany all these events. The biggest week of all is **Semana Grande** (early to mid-August).

Sleeping

The old part of the city has just two hotels.

La Casona de Jovellanos (☎ 985 34 20 24; hotel@lacasonadejovellanos.com; Plaza de Jovellanos 1; s/d €62/81; P) This antique-furnished mansion is on one of Cimadevilla's nicest squares.

Hotel Asturias (☎ 985 35 06 00; hotelasturias@fade.es; Plaza Mayor 11; s/d €59/78) Touched with elegance, Hotel Asturias' spacious rooms overlook Gijón's main square. Watch out for low-season discounts.

CANTABRIA & ASTURIAS

Plenty of places of most standards are scattered about the central zone.

Hostal Manjón (☎ 985 35 23 78; Plaza del Marqués 1; s/d with bathroom €36/45) Though basic, this is in a good spot, with some rooms overlooking the marina, others facing the Palacio de Revillagigedo.

Hotel El Altillo (☎ 985 34 33 30; Calle de Capua 17; s/d with bathroom €50/60; 💻 Ⓟ) Not far from Playa de San Lorenzo, this modest guesthouse over a restaurant was planning an upgrade at the time of writing.

Hotel Castilla (☎ 985 34 62 00; http://welcome.to /hcastillagijon; Calle de la Corrida 50; s/d 54/80) Standing beside the lively Plaza Seis de Agosto, the Castilla is old but cosy, with friendly service and good-sized rooms on seven floors.

Albergue Palacio San Andrés de Cornellana (☎ 985 16 06 73; www.alberguegijon.com; dm under 26 years/26 and over €10.50/12.50; 💻) This large youth hostel in a late 17th-century palace is quite a way out, in the Contrueces neighbourhood, but it's a quick ride on the No 12 bus.

Eating

The newer part of the city centre offers many options, but the most atmospheric area is Cimadevilla. Just off Plaza Mayor is a series of lively *sidrerías*, most with outside tables, including **Casa Fernando** (☎ 985 34 59 13; Plaza del Marqués 5) and **El Centenario** (☎ 985 34 35 61; Plaza Mayor 7). Among more exotic local specialities are *oricios* (sea urchins), *llámpares* (limpets) and *centollos* (spider crabs). *Raciones* go for around €5 to €12, cider for €2 per bottle.

Other *sidrerías* are found a bit further up.

El Lavaderu (☎ 985 35 93 80; Plaza Arturo Arias; menú €7.20) This popular spot has an excellent four-course *menú* and tables spread over a broad, often rowdy, plaza.

El Veleru (☎ 985 31 94 43; Calle Rosario 2) Crates of fresh shellfish arrive here regularly.

El Fomentín (☎ 985 35 86 76; Calle de Rodríguez San Pedro 21; menú €7; 🕑 closed Tue; 🔀) Below the marina, this smoky, working-class place is often packed at lunch time, when great quantities of squid and potatoes are consumed.

Drinking

La Botica Indiana (☎ 985 35 02 00; Plaza Mayor) On the main square, this café in a former chemist's shop makes a perfect spot for your morning dose.

Gijón can be a lively place after dark. The *sidrerías* mentioned under Eating are fun, and further up in Cimadevilla, a youthful music-bar scene flourishes in spots around Plaza Corrada and down Calle Vicaría. The coolest is **Louie Louie Café** (Calle Vicaría 13), with a voluminous recorded rock collection.

A more mature crowd descends upon the string of varied bars and clubs along Calle de Rodríguez San Pedro – ranging from salsa dens **Cubanísimo** (☎ 985 17 25 17; No 35) and **La Bodeguita del Medio** (☎ 985 35 21 46; No 43) to **Ca Beleño** (☎ 984 29 22 53; No 39), with jazz and Celtic sounds.

Varsovia (Calle Cabrales 18) is a particularly popular spot facing Playa de San Lorenzo; you can dance downstairs and chat upstairs. Nearby, **Kitsch Café** (Calle Rectoría 8) provides a suitably low-lit ambience before or after clubbing.

Entertainment

Teatro Jovellanos (☎ 985 18 29 29; www.teatrojovellanos.com; Calle de Casimiro Velasco 23) Pick up an events programme, published quarterly, at the municipal tourist office.

Sala Albéniz (☎ 985 35 65 13; Calle de San Bernardo 62; cover €6-10) This large nightclub is a venue for touring bands; on Friday night from around 1.30am it doubles as a dance club.

Getting There & Away
BUS

Frequent buses to Oviedo travel from the **ALSA bus station** (☎ 985 34 27 11; Calle Magnus Blikstad), plus about nine daily to León (€8.85, 2¼ hours), 13 to Madrid (€28 to €42, six hours) and two to Barcelona (€45, 13½ hours). Heading east, there are hourly buses to Villaviciosa (€2.15, 45 minutes) and up to eight daily to Ribadesella (€5.72, 1¾ hours). A similar number go to Llanes, continuing to Santander (€12.50 to €21, 2¾ to four hours) and San Sebastián. Westward, four or more go to Cudillero (€4, 1½ hours) and one or more to Luarca (€7.75, 1½ hours). Four or more go to Santiago de Compostela (€26, five to 7½ hours) and other Galician cities. Other buses head as far south as Seville.

TRAIN

The main train station is **Estación Cercanías** (Plaza del Humedal), though it isn't only used by suburban trains. The other station, Jovellanos, is 600m west.

Renfe provides frequent *cercanías* to/from Oviedo (€2.15, 35 minutes), and long-distance trains two or three times daily to/from Madrid (€35.50, 6¼ to nine hours) and twice daily to Barcelona. All of the long-distance trains stop at León. The overnight Madrid train uses Jovellanos station only; all others stop at both stations.

FEVE (☎ 985 34 24 15), using Estación Cercanías only, runs *cercanías* to/from Cudillero (€2, 1½ hours) hourly on weekdays, half as often on weekends. Two each day connect in Pravia with FEVE trains to/from Luarca (€5.75, 2½ hours from Gijón), Viveiro and Ferrol (€17.20, 6½ hours).

EASTERN COAST

With the magnificent Picos de Europa rising up as close as 15km inland, Asturias' eastern coast attracts many Spanish holidaymakers over the summer. A string of pretty beaches and coves provides a tempting counterpoint to the mountains.

A BLESSING FROM ON HIGH

Asturias' climate is great for growing apples – many of which are put to very good use in the production of excellent *sidra* (cider). Cider-drinking for Asturians is a particularly gregarious activity – and if Asturias has a national sport, it has to be pouring cider. In *sidrerías* throughout Asturias you'll see drinkers, waiters and bartenders pouring cider from bottles held high overhead into glasses held close to horizontal near ground level. The object of this drinks appears to be to instil some fizz into drinks, and the essence of the activity is to do it with maximum nonchalance, preferably while looking in another direction entirely and holding a slurred conversation with someone in yet a third direction. The quantities of cider that actually enter the glass or are splashed over people's clothes are, by comparison, of slight importance. The Fiesta de la Sidra Natural, staged in August in Gijón, gives serious cider-tippers the chance to compete for the title of champion *escanciador* (pourer).

When drinking cider, it is customary to down the entire contents of the glass at a single go, shortly after it's poured, to fully appreciate the fizz factor.

Villaviciosa & Around
pop 5139 / elevation 16m

Apart from the Iglesia de Santa María, a late-Romanesque structure, Villaviciosa's pretty centre is mostly a child of the 18th century. Calle García Caveda, the main street, is lined with noble houses. There's a helpful **tourist office** (☎ 985 89 17 59; summer only) in Parque Vallina.

The surrounding area is sprinkled with often diminutive churches bearing Romanesque features. Many are for aficionados only, but one that shouldn't be missed is the pre-Romanesque **Iglesia de San Salvador de Valdediós** (☎ 985 89 23 24; admission €1; 11am-1pm & 4.30-6.30pm Tue-Sun Apr-Sep, 11.15am-1pm Tue-Fri, 4pm-5.30pm Sat & Sun Oct-Mar), about 9km southwest, off the road to Pola de Siero. It was built in AD 893 as part of a palace complex for Alfonso III El Magno in what Asturians dubbed 'God's Valley', but archaeologists have failed to find any remnant beyond this simple church. Next door is the Romanesque **Iglesia y Monasterio de Santa María** of the Cistercian persuasion, open for guided tours. Oviedo-bound buses from Villaviciosa can drop you at Ambás, a 2km walk to the site.

Another fine Romanesque church is the **Iglesia de San Juan de Amandi**, 1.5km south of Villaviciosa.

Facing the open sea on the western side of the Ría de Villaviciosa is the minute port of **Tazones**, where Carlos I supposedly first landed in Spain in 1517. It's quite a popular spot with some pricey seafood restaurants. The eastern side of the estuary is covered by the golden sands of the **Playa de Rodiles**. Surfers might catch a wave here in late summer.

SLEEPING & EATING
Camping La Ensenada (☎ 985 89 01 57; per person/tent/car €3/3/3) Open year-round at Playa de Rodiles, this beachfront camping ground has laundry facilities and a restaurant. Pets are allowed.

Café del Sol (☎ 985 89 11 30; Calle del Sol 27; s/d with bathroom €18/36) This best-value option has lovely wood-floored rooms with decorative touches.

There are several mid-range places on Calle García Caveda and more along Calle del Carmen, but for a real treat try **La Casona de Amandi** (☎ 985 89 01 30; s/d €96/120), a 19th-century farmhouse in Amandi, 1.5km south of Villaviciosa. Rooms have their original Isabelline furnishings.

Hotel Imperial (☎ 985 89 71 16; r €48) In Tazones, this place is a reasonable option right on the waterfront.

Sidrería Campomanes (Calle General Campomanes; menú €7.25; ☾ closed Sun) This is where everyone eats, with outstanding *fabadas* (rich stew of beans) and tables dressed with chequered cloths.

GETTING THERE & AWAY

ALSA provides six buses daily to/from Oviedo (€3.10, one hour) and Ribadesella (€2.80, one hour), as well as an hourly service to/from Gijón (€2.15, 45 minutes). From early July to early September a 12.45pm bus runs to Playa de Rodiles, returning six hours later.

Lastres

Apart from a few sandy beaches, the only worthwhile stop along the 40km stretch between Villaviciosa and Ribadesella is the precarious cliffside fishing village of Lastres, a scruffier version of Cudillero (see Western Coast, p514), with a couple of 16th-century churches thrown in.

Ribadesella

pop 3195

Unless you've booked in advance, stay away from here on the first weekend after 2 August when the place goes mad for the **Río Sella canoe festival** (see Arriondas, p521). Otherwise, Ribadesella is a low-key resort. Its two halves, split by the Sella's estuary, are joined by a long, low bridge. The western half has a good, expansive beach, Playa de Santa Marina, while the older part of town and fishing harbour are on the eastern side.

The **tourist office** (☎ 985 86 00 38; www.ribadesella.com; ☾ 10am-10pm Jul & Aug, 10am-1pm & 4-8pm Tue-Sat, 11am-2pm Sun Sep-Jun) is at the eastern end of the Sella bridge.

SIGHTS & ACTIVITIES

To see some real cave paintings (as opposed to the copies at Altamira in Cantabria), plan on visiting the **Cueva de Tito Bustillo** (☎ 985 86 11 20; adult/child €3/1, Wed free; ☾ 10am-4.30pm Wed-Sun Apr-8 Sep only). The cave drawings here, mostly of horses, are roughly 14,000 years old.

The site is a short distance south of the western end of the Sella bridge. Groups enter

the cave every 25 minutes. The hour-long 1500m tour includes some slippery stretches, and is not recommended for children under 11. There's a limit of 360 visitors daily, so turn up early in August, or book ahead on ☎ 902 19 05 08 or http://tematico.princast.es /cultura/yacimientos/entradas.php.

Several companies can set you up with canoe trips on the Río Sella (see Arriondas, p521), hire bikes, take you canyoning and so on. **Turaventura** (☎ 985 86 02 67; www.turaventura .com; Calle Manuel Caso de la Villa 50) is one company that has been around for a few years.

SLEEPING & EATING

Camping Ribadesella (☎ 985 85 82 93; www.camping-ribadesella.com; per adult/tent/car €4.50/4.25/3.85; ☾ Easter–mid-Sep; ☒) Set amid peaceful pastures at Sebreño, 1km inland from the Gijón road, this fully-equipped site has barbecue grills, launrdry facilities, tennis courts, TV, game rooms and a store.

Albergue Roberto Frassinelli (☎ 985 86 11 05; www.albergueribadesella.com; Calle Ricardo Canga; per person under/over 29 years with hostelling card €11.50/13.50; ☒) Housed in a *palacio de indianos* (mansion built by a returnee from the Americas), this REAJ hostel backs onto Playa de Santa Marina. It has two- and four-bed rooms.

Hotel Covadonga (☎ 985 86 01 10; Calle Manuel Caso de la Villa 9; r with shared/private bathroom €55/68) In the older part of town, the Covadonga is worn, but boasts character, as well as a reasonable *sidrerías*.

There are plenty of more expensive places on Playa de Santa Marina.

Hotel Villa Rosario (☎ 985 86 00 90; www.hotelvilla rosario.com; Calle Dionisio Ruisánchez 6; s/d €128/160) This magnificently restored *palacio de in-diano* would be a good choice for a honeymoon or anniversary celebration. (Rates fall by more than half in winter.)

Hotel Don Pepe (☎ 985 85 78 81; fax 985 85 78 77; Calle Dionisio Ruisánchez 12; s/d €70/86; ☒ Ⓟ) More of a standard holiday lodging, Don Pepe is right in front of the waves.

For food, the busy waterfront *sidrerías* on the eastern side of the river are a good bet.

El Tarteru (☎ 985 85 76 39; Calle Marqueses de Argüelles; raciones €5-12; ☾ closed Tue) At the far end, this *sidrería* offers a change from fish with the *revueltos de oricios y gambas* (eggs scrambled with sea urchins and prawns).

Café Capri (Plaza Nueva) A popular gathering place and Parcheesi-playing venue.

GETTING THERE & AWAY

The **bus station** (☎ 985 86 13 03; Avenida Palacio Valdés) is about 300m south of the bridge. There are regular services to/from Arriondas (€1.30, 25 minutes), Oviedo (€5.80, 1¼ hours) and Gijón, and eastward to/from Llanes (€2, 35 minutes), San Vicente de la Barquera and Santander. In July and August a couple of daily buses run to/from Cangas de Onís.

FEVE (☎ 985 86 05 18) provides at least three trains daily to/from Llanes and Oviedo, and two to/from Santander.

Ribadesella to Llanes

Several little beaches and coves await discovery between Ribadesella and Llanes by those with transport and time. About 10km short of Llanes, **Playa de San Antolín** is a vast, unprotected beach where you might pick up the odd wave.

About 7km west of Llanes is the village-cum-understated holiday resort of **Barro**. Its main beach is a bit bigger than the average cove and not too crowded. Stay at the pretty little **Hostal La Playa** (☎ 985 40 07 66; r €66).

Llanes

pop 4110

Inhabited since ancient times, Llanes was for a long period an independent-minded town and whaling port with its own charter awarded by Alfonso IX of León in 1206. Today, with a small medieval core and bustling harbour, it's one of northern Spain's more popular holiday destinations – a handy base for some very pretty beaches and with the Picos de Europa close at hand.

The **tourist office** (☎ 985 40 01 64; llanes turismo@ctv.es; Calle Alfonso IX; ⏱ 10am-2pm & 5-9pm except Sun afternoon mid-Jun–mid-Sep, 10am-2pm & 4-6.30pm Mon-Fri, 10.30am-1.30pm Sat rest of year) is in La Torre, a tower left over from Llanes' 13th-century defences. **Cafetería Travelling** (Calle Genaro Riestra) provides Internet access.

SIGHTS & ACTIVITIES

Of the three town beaches, **Playa de Toró** to the east is easily the best. Westward along a 2.5km clifftop path, the **Paseo de San Pedro** leads to the village of Poo.

The Gothic church **La Basílica** (Plaza de Cristo Rey), begun in 1240, is worth a look.

Strewn alongside the far end of the pier like a set of children's blocks are the **Cubes of Memory**, painter Agustín Ibarrola's playful

public artwork using the port's breakwater as his canvas.

If you're interested in canoeing or canyoning, see what **Vindius Aventura** (☎ 985 40 01 31; www.vindiusaventura.com; Calle Mercaderes 11) has to offer.

SLEEPING

Camping Entreplayas (☎ 985 40 08 88; per person/car/tent €4/4/4; ⏱ Easter-Sep) Located near Playa de Toró, this seaside spot offers campers hot showers, tennis courts and a store.

Albergue Juvenil Juventudes (☎ 985 40 07 70; Calle Celso Amieva 7; per person under/over 30 years incl breakfast €8/11, HI card required; ⏱ check-in 9.30am-1pm & 6-8pm) This HI hostel has 35 twin rooms and meals available.

Pensión La Guía (☎ 985 40 25 77; Plaza de Parres Sobrino 1; r €55) Just west of the river, this 300-year-old house has plenty of charm, with glassed-in balconies overlooking the plaza.

Hospedaje Casa del Río (☎ 985 40 11 91; Avenida de San Pedro 3; s/d with washbasin €23/40, d with bathroom €53; **P**) This best budget choice is set amid gardens and has huge rooms with hardwood floors.

La Posada del Rey (☎ 985 40 13 32; http://laposada delrey.iespana.es; Calle Mayor 11; r €103) This is a beautifully remodelled little mansion in the old town centre.

EATING

A trio of lively *marisquerías* (seafood raciones €7 to €15) face the Río Carrocedo, just upstream from the main street.

Marisquería La Marina (☎ 985 40 00 12; seafood *raciones* €6-12; ⏱ Easter-Sep) Towards the sea end of the port, this friendly family-run place serves great paella.

Restaurante Siete Puertas (☎ 985 40 27 51; Calle de Manuel Cué 7; mains €12-20; 🔀) The kitchen dares to depart from tradition, with dishes such as mushroom-stuffed sea bass (€18).

El Bodegón (☎ 985 40 01 85; Calle Mayor 14; ⏱ closed Thu) If it's just cider and tapas you want, try this big old *sidrería*.

GETTING THERE & AWAY

The **bus station** (☎ 985 40 23 22; Calle La Bolera) is east of the river. ALSA's Gijón–Santander buses (except the express Supras) stop in Llanes en route, with seven buses travelling daily in both directions (€7.35, two hours), and up to nine daily to/from Oviedo (€7.25, 1¾ hours).

Three or four FEVE trains come here daily from Oviedo and Ribadesella, two of them continuing to Santander.

East of Llanes

The 350m-long **Playa La Ballota** is a particularly attractive beach a few kilometres east of Llanes, hemmed in by green cliffs and accessible by dirt track; part of it is for nudists. **Playa de la Franca**, further towards Cantabria, is also nice and has a summer camping ground.

WESTERN COAST
Cudillero
pop 1745

Cudillero is the most picturesque fishing village on the Asturian coast, and it knows it. The houses, painted varying pastel shades, cascade down to a tiny port on a narrow inlet. Despite its touristy feel, Cudillero is cute and remains reasonably relaxed, even in mid-August when almost every room in town is occupied. For a good map of area beaches, stop by the **tourist information office** (☎ 985 59 13 77; www.cudillero.org; 10am or 11am-9pm Jul-Sep, 10am-2pm & 5-8pm Mon-Sat, 11am-2pm Sun rest of year) by the port, which is also the only place to park.

The main activity is watching the fishing boats come in (between 5pm and 8pm) and unload their catch, then sampling fish, molluscs and urchins at the *sidrerías*.

BEACHES

The coast around here is a particularly appealing sequence of cliffs and beaches. The nearest beach is the fine, sandy **Playa de Aguilar**, a 3km drive or walk east. Those to the west include **Playa Concha de Artedo** (4km) and the pretty **Playa de San Pedro** (10km).

Playa del Silencio (also called El Gavieiru), 15km west of Cudillero, could certainly qualify as one of Spain's most beautiful beaches: a long sandy cove backed against a natural rock amphitheatre. Take the exit for Novellana and follow signs to Castañeras.

SLEEPING

Accommodation in the village of Cudillero is limited, especially during the low season when some places shut down.

La Casona de Pío (☎ 985 59 15 12; www.arrakis .es/~casonadepio; Calle Riofrío 3; r €61.50) Just back from the port area is this stone house, fea-

turing 11 very comfortable rooms with a rustic touch, and a good restaurant.

Hotel Casa Prendes (☎ 985 59 15 00; Calle San José 4; r €74) Cudillero's most recent addition, this hotel is a neatly restored structure that got all the details right.

Apartamentos La Lula (☎ 985 59 15 00; Calle San José 8; 4-person apt €86) Behind Hotel Casa Prendes and under the same ownership, these apartments are self-catering.

Hotel Isabel (☎ 985 59 17 06; Calle Suárez Inclán 36; s/d incl breakfast €49/75; ☾ Jun–mid-Sep) This sturdy 14-room lodging is in the centre of town and has a nice café downstairs.

A couple of small good-value lodgings are about 500m back from the harbour along Cudillero's single street. Both are open July to September only, though the first has one room available year-round:

Pensión Álver (☎ 985 59 00 05; Calle García de la Concha 8; s/d €37/40)

Pensión Campillo (☎ 626 12 65 04; Calle García de la Concha 3; r €40) Beside the 13th-century Capilla del Humilladero.

Plenty of hotels, *casas de aldea*, *pensiones* and apartments are scattered around the countryside within a few kilometres. The tourist information office can give you an up-to-date list.

Camping L'Amuravela (☎ 985 59 09 95; www.la muravela.com; per person/tent/car €4.25/4/4.25, bungalows

2/3 persons €69/78; 🕙 Mar-Nov; 🏊) At the village of El Pito, about 1.5km southeast (uphill) from the town centre, this is the closest camping ground to town. Facilities include a big playground, hot showers, washing machines, a store and café, plus bungalows for up to five people.

EATING

There's no shortage of eateries down towards the port: a meal with drinks is likely to cost you upwards of €20 in most places. Sidrería El Remo is the most popular seafood and cider spot, with tables out on the harbour-front plaza.

Bar Santiago (☎ 985 59 12 01; Plaza de La Marina 3) This is a lively gathering place, where *necoras* (small crabs) go for €3.50 apiece and shrimp-mushroom scrambles are €10.

Sidrería La Marina (☎ 985 59 13 58; Plaza de La Marina 4) La Marina serves great grilled fish; many come for the *parrillada de mariscos* (seafood grill) at €25 per person.

GETTING THERE & AWAY

The bus station is at the top of the hill, 800m from the port, and the FEVE train station is 1km further inland. Three to five buses come here from Gijón and one or two from Oviedo (€4.25, 1¼ hours), all via Avilés. From Monday to Friday, FEVE trains arrive about once an hour from Gijón (€2, 1½ hours), the last returning at 8.30pm. There are three FEVE trains running daily from Oviedo, continuing to Luarca; two continue westward along the coastal line as far as Ferrol (Galicia).

Luarca

pop 4780

More dishevelled than Cudillero, Luarca has a similar setting in a deep, narrow valley running down to a harbour full of small fishing boats. Though getting a little smarter as the years pass, it will still appeal to lovers of seaside decay. It's a base for some good nearby beaches.

The **tourist office** (☎ 985 64 00 83; Calle Caleros 11; 🕙 11am-2pm & 4-7pm Tue-Sat, 11am-2pm Sun) is behind the town hall.

Kids will not want to miss the **Aula del Mar** (☎ 985 47 03 70; Calle Villar; admission €3; 🕙 11am-1pm & 4-9pm), which features a collection of giant squid, along with some 700 other marine species.

BEACHES

Sandy, 600m-long **Playa de Cueva**, 7km east, is one of the best beaches in the district, with cliffs, caves and occasional decent surf. Nearby **Cabo Busto** (Cape Busto) will give you some sense of the Asturian coast's wildness. **Playa de Otur**, 8km west of Luarca, and **Playa de Barayo**, 2km further, are good sandy beaches in pretty bays. Barayo is a protected natural reserve at the mouth of a river winding through wetlands and dunes. To reach it, turn off the N634 at Puerto de Vega and head for the village of Vigo, then follow signs (painted on the road) for the beach. From the car park, it is accessible by a well-marked 30-minute nature hike.

SLEEPING & EATING

At least five hotels and *hostales* are on or just off the central Plaza de Alfonso X.

Pensión Moderna (☎ 985 64 00 57; Calle Crucero 2; s/d with shared bathroom €13/25) Though it doesn't live up to its name – witness the jugs and buckets required for use of the tapless washbasins – the Moderna is clean, friendly and central.

Hotel Rico (☎ 985 47 05 85; Plaza de Alfonso X 6; r €55) This hotel features a café and plain bright rooms, some with balconies and *galerías* overlooking the plaza.

Hotel Villa La Argentina (☎ 985 64 01 02; www.villa laargentina.com; s/d €83/90) This 1899 *casa de indianos*, now a comfy 12-room hotel amid lovely gardens, drips with *belle époque* elegance. Between meals, play tennis or billiards, or dip in the pool. It's in the Villar district about 1.5km southeast (uphill) from the town.

El Ancla (☎ 985 64 14 48; Paseo del Muelle 14) By the harbour, this humble *sidrería* serves good seafood. Try a *media-ración* (a larger serve of tapas, but smaller than a *ración*) of about 16 *mejillones picante* (chillied mussels) for €3.40, or a generous *tabla de queso* of Asturian cheeses (€12).

Mesón de la Mar (☎ 985 64 09 94; Paseo del Muelle 35; raciones €4-12), Further up is this large and popular shellfish eatery, with tables right on the waterfront.

GETTING THERE & AWAY

Seven daily ALSA buses run to/from Oviedo (€7.15, 1½ hours) and along the coast as far as Ribadeo (Galicia). A couple come from Gijón, too. A daily bus (two in summer) runs to/from Madrid via Lugo and Ponferrada. The FEVE train station is 800m south of the town centre: three trains run daily to/from Cudillero and Oviedo, and two along the coast to/from Ferrol (Galicia).

Coaña & Río Navia

The small town of Coaña lies about 4km inland of the port of Navia, west of Luarca. A couple of kilometres beyond is the **Castro de Coaña** (☎ 985 97 84 01; admission €1.50, Wed free; ⏱ 11am-2pm & 4-7pm Tue-Sun Apr-Sep, 11am-2.30pm Tue-Sun Oct-Mar), one of the best-preserved Celtic settlements in northern Spain.

From the *castro* (Celtic-fortified village), a poor road snakes its way high above the cobalt-blue Río Navia, through classic Asturian countryside – meadows alternating with rocky precipices – to Lugo in Galicia, crossing some of Galicia's least-visited and wildest territory, around the town of **Fonsagrada**.

Tapia de Casariego

pop 2386

This welcoming fishing haven makes a pleasant lunch stop if you're driving, but little more. Beaches along the next few kilometres west, such as **Playa Anguileiro**, **Playa La Paloma**, **Playa de Serantes** and **Playa de Santa Gadea**, all boast surfable waves, and there are several surf shops in Tapia.

Hotel San Antón (☎ 985 62 80 00; www.hotelres taurantesananton.com; Plaza San Blas 2; s/d €43/62) A few blocks up from the small harbour, this is the best of several mid-range places in Tapia de Casariego.

Among the more popular seafood houses are **Sidrería La Cubierta** (☎ 985 47 10 16; Travesía Médico Enrique Álvarez; platos combinados €6) and, down by the harbour, **La Marina** (☎ 985 62 84 88; seafood raciones €10).

Castropol & Around

pop 460

The Ría de Ribadeo marks the frontier between Asturias and Galicia. Spanning the broad mouth of this, the first of the many grand estuaries that slice into Galicia's coast, is the Puente de los Santos.

Whitewashed Castropol village, on a rise a few kilometres up the eastern side of the *ría* (estuary), is a tranquil alternative to Ribadeo, Galicia, the town on the other side. From Castropol, the N640 southwest to Lugo forms a little-travelled back route into Galicia.

One of a couple of hotels at the northern entrance into Castropol, **Hotel Casa Vicente** (☎ 985 63 50 51; Carretera General; s/d €25/43) has 14 just-restored rooms, half of which give matchless views of the *ría*.

A lovely Art Deco mansion standing amid English gardens studded with palms and magnolias, **Palacete Peñalba** (☎ 985 63 61 25; www.hotelpalacetepenalba.com; r from €74) is in Figueras, 4km north of Castropol and a mere 200m from the beach.

Camping Playa Penarronda (☎ 985 62 30 22; per person/tent/car €4/4/3.60; ⏱ Semana Santa-Sep) is set on the fringe of the broad, open Playa de Penarronda beach, 7km northeast of Castropol, and offers a café and shop as well as bicycle hire.

The village of Castropol is served by at least six daily ALSA buses to/from Oviedo (€11, 2½ hours).

INLAND WESTERN ASTURIAS

Although it's mostly difficult to reach unless you're driving, there's some gorgeous country in southwest Asturias. Even just passing through on alternative routes into Castilla y León, such as the AS227 via the 1486m **Puerto de Somiedo**, or the spectacular 1525m **Puerto de Leitariegos** on the AS213, can be rewarding.

Salas

pop 1526

Drivers between Oviedo and Luarca could take, instead of the standard highways, the pretty N634, which snakes up and down lush valleys northwest of Oviedo. At Salas, 48km from Oviedo, it soon becomes clear that the town's most famous son was Grand Inquisitor Fernando de Valdés Salas, who also founded Oviedo's university in the 16th century. His **castle** has been converted into a hotel (see below), and his elaborate alabaster tomb is inside the nearby **Colegiata de Santa María**.

Hotel Castillo de Valdés Salas (☎ 985 83 01 73; www.castillovaldesalas.com; Plaza Campa; r €64/80) makes an attractive stop; its restaurant is the best choice, too.

Regular ALSA buses run to/from Oviedo.

Senda del Oso

Between the villages of Tuñón and Entrago, southwest of Oviedo, the Senda del Oso is a 20km concrete walking and cycling path that follows the course of a former mine railway through fields, riverbank woodlands and canyons. About 5km south of Tuñón, the path passes the **Monte del Oso** (Bear Mountain), where Paca and Tola, two Asturian brown bears orphaned by a hunter in 1989, live in semi-liberty in a 40,000-sq-metre compound. Each day around noon, except during their hibernation from about December to February, the bears are fed at a spot where their compound borders the path and you stand an excellent chance of seeing them. One kilometre southwest of this spot, near Proaza village, is the **Casa del Oso** (☎ 985 76 10 53; admission free; 10am-2pm & 4-7pm Jul–mid-Sep, 10am-2pm & 4-6pm year-round), with a restaurant, shop and interesting exhibits on Spanish bears, which, apart from a small handful in the Pyrenees, survive only in the Cordillera Cantábrica, where they number around 80.

In Proaza, **Hotel Peñas Juntas** (☎ 985 76 14 63; Plaza de la Abadía; d with bathroom €50) has cosy rooms. In San Martín de Teverga, 1.5km south of Entrago, is the hostel **Albergue San Martín** (☎ 985 76 43 54; Calle Nueva 2; bunks with sheets €10). Both places serve meals.

GETTING THERE & AROUND
The bear feeding spot is a 15-minute walk from the AS228 Trubia–Tuñón–Entrago road, 2km north of Proaza: watch for the 'Cercado Osero' sign and car park. **Álvarez González** (☎ 985 11 93 86) runs three or more daily buses from Oviedo to Tuñón (€1.70), Proaza (€2.10) and Entrago (€3.20). During the main visitor periods, you can hire bicycles at various points along the Senda del Oso.

Parque Natural de Somiedo
If you fancy exploring some dramatic mountain country that few foreigners know of, consider this 300-sq-km protected area on the northern flank of the Cordillera Cantábrica. Composed of five valleys descending from the cordillera's 2000m-plus main ridge, the park is characterised by lush woodlands and high pastures dotted with thatched shepherds' shelters. It's also the major bastion of Spain's remaining brown bear population.

Each of the valleys has a number of marked walking trails, which you can find out about at the park's **Centro de Recepción** (☎ 985 76 37 58; 10am-2.30pm & 4-9pm mid-Jun–mid-Sep, 10am-2pm & 4-7pm rest of year) in the small village of **Pola de Somiedo**. Pola also has a bank, supermarket, and half-a-dozen budget and mid-range places to stay. One of the best walking areas is the **Valle de Lago**, whose upper reaches contain a number of glacial lakes and high summer pastures. There is a camping ground, *hostal* and hotel in Valle de Lago hamlet, a good starting point for walks, 8km southeast of Pola de Somiedo.

ALSA runs two daily buses (one on Sunday) from Oviedo to Pola de Somiedo.

PICOS DE EUROPA

These jagged, deeply fissured mountains straddling Asturias, Cantabria and the northeast of Castilla y León province amount to some of the finest walking country in Spain, offering plentiful short and long outings for striders of all levels, plus lots of scope for climbers and cavers, too.

Beginning only 15km from the coast, and stretching little more than 40km from east to west and 25km north to south, the Picos still encompass enough spectacular mountain and gorge scenery to ensure a continual flow of Spanish and international visitors. They comprise three limestone massifs: the eastern Macizo Ándara, with a summit of 2444m; the western Macizo El Cornión, rising to 2596m; and the particularly rocky Macizo Central or Macizo Los Urrieles, reaching 2648m. The 647-sq-km **Parque Nacional de los Picos de Europa** covers all three massifs and is Spain's second-biggest national park.

Virtually deserted in winter, the area is full to bursting in August and you should always try to book ahead, whether you are heading for a hotel or a mountain *refugio* (refuge).

Orientation
The main access towns for the Picos are Cangas de Onís in the northwest, Arenas de Cabrales in the central north, and Potes in the southeast. Paved roads lead from Cangas southeast up to Covadonga, Lago de Enol and Lago de la Ercina; from Arenas south up to Poncebos then east up to Sotres and Tresviso; and from Potes west to Fuente Dé. The mountains are roughly bounded on the western side by the Río Sella and the N625 Cangas de Onís–Riaño road; on the north by the AS114 Cangas de Onís–Arenas de

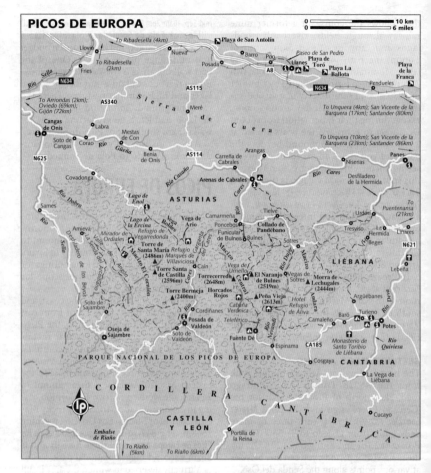

Cabrales–Panes road; and on the east by the Río Deva and the N621 Panes–Potes road.

MAPS & GUIDEBOOKS

The best maps of the Picos, sold in shops in Cangas de Onís, Potes and elsewhere for €4 to €5 each, are Adrados Ediciones' *Picos de Europa* (1:80,000), *Picos de Europa Macizos Central y Oriental* and *Picos de Europa Macizo Occidental* (1:25,000). Lonely Planet's *Walking in Spain* describes, in far more detail than we have room for here, a multiday circuit through much of the Picos' finest scenery, which can be joined or left at several points. In Spanish, the walking and climbing guides by Miguel Ángel Adrados are recommended.

Information

The national park's main information office, in Cangas de Onís, is **Casa Dago** (☎ 985 84 86 14; Avenida de Covadonga 43; ☒ 9am-2pm & 4-6.30pm Mon-Sat, 9am-3pm Sun Semana Santa–mid-Oct; 9am-2pm & 4-6.30pm Mon-Fri rest of year). Other park information offices are at **Urbanización La Molina** (☎ 942 73 05 55), just outside Potes on the Fuente Dé road; and on Travesía de los Llanos, **Posada de Valdeón** (☎ 987 74 05 49). Basic information on walks and accommodation is available at these offices. Local tourist offices can usually provide information on nearby sections of the park, as well as on their own towns.

Cangas de Onís, Arenas de Cabrales and Potes all have banks, ATMs and good supermarkets. Cangas and Potes are the best places to buy walking boots, waterproof clothing and other outdoor equipment.

Camping within the national park is permitted only above 1600m and only overnight: tents can only be erected in the evening and must be taken down in the morning.

WHEN TO GO
The weather across northern Spain is similar to what you'd find in the UK, Ireland or Brittany, and in the Picos it's notoriously changeable. You could begin a walk in brilliant sunshine, only to be enveloped in a chilly pea-soup fog a few hours later. On the whole, the southeast parts of the Picos are drier than further north and west.

In August most of Spain is taking its holidays and finding rooms anywhere near the Picos is hard. July is not far behind. May, June and September are the best times to visit – more tranquil and just as likely to be sunny as August. Most serious walkers and climbers choose September, as it tends to be the driest month – an important consideration in the mountains. Drivers should also beware of bad weather. Conditions can become extremely dangerous, especially in winter, when chains are often needed.

WHAT TO BRING
For the walks mentioned here, you don't need special equipment. But sun protection (hats, sunscreen, sunglasses, adequate covering of clothes) is essential, as is a water bottle – sources of drinkable water are

irregular. Walking boots are advisable, if not absolutely necessary on every route, and even on a sunny day you should take some items of warmer and waterproof clothing. For any treks or climbs off established tracks, you'll need the appropriate gear and experience.

GUIDED WALKS
The national park offers free guided walks of between three and six hours daily in July, August and September. Routes vary according to the day of the week; pick up a programme at an information office. Most guides speak Spanish only.

FAUNA
Although some wolves and the odd brown bear still survive in the Picos, you're highly unlikely to see either. Far more common is the *rebeco* (chamois), a kind of cross between antelope and mountain goat. Around 6500 of them skip around the rocks and steep slopes. Deer, foxes, badgers, wild boar, hedgehogs, squirrels and martens, in various quantities, inhabit the more wooded areas.

A variety of eagles, hawks and other raptors fill the Picos' skies, but you'd be lucky to catch sight of the majestic *águila real* (golden eagle) or the huge scavenging *buitre leonado* (griffon vulture) or Egyptian vulture. Choughs, with their unmistakable caws, accompany walkers at the highest altitudes.

Getting There & Around
Trying to taste the main delights of the Picos by public transport can be a frustrating matter, if you're not hanging around long enough to crisscross them on foot. Just a few bus and train services – mostly summer only – will get you into the hills or to the edge of them.

An alternative to the buses for getting around the Picos area is taxis. Apart from regular taxis that stick to the better roads, such as **Taxitur** (☎ 985 84 87 97) in Cangas, there are also 4WD taxi services that can manage some of the mountain tracks. One of the latter is operated by Casa Cipriano (see Sotres, p525). A regular taxi costs around €25 from Cangas de Onís to the Lagos de Covadonga, and about €18 from Arenas de Cabrales to Sotres or Potes to Fuente Dé.

CANTABRIA & ASTURIAS

BUS & TRAIN

Details of the following bus and train services change from time to time but the broad outlines described below are likely to be maintained.

Oviedo–Panes

From Oviedo, ALSA has up to 22 buses daily to Arriondas (€4.50, 50 minutes to 1¼ hours) and 12 to Cangas de Onís (€5, 1½ hours). About half of the Cangas buses continue to Arenas de Cabrales (€7.15, two hours), and one or two go on to Niserias and Panes. Frequencies in the opposite direction are similar. At Panes you can switch to/from buses running between Santander and Potes (but make sure you get the timetables right!). The last bus (some days the only bus) from Panes back towards Oviedo leaves at 5.25pm.

Arriondas is also on the FEVE railway line between Oviedo, Ribadesella, Llanes and Santander.

Covadonga

Up to seven ALSA buses daily run to Covadonga from Cangas de Onís (€0.95, 20 minutes). In July, August and early September services are more frequent. On weekends and holidays year-round, three buses run from Oviedo to Covadonga (€5.80); in summer there are two on weekdays as well; otherwise, change in Arriondas or Cangas. The last bus down from Covadonga is at 8pm in summer, and 7.15pm in other seasons.

Covadonga–Lago de Enol

In July, August and early September four or five buses a day travel from Covadonga up to Lago de Enol (€1.65, 30 minutes) and return. The first one up leaves Covadonga at 10am and the last one down leaves from the lake at 6.30pm (4.45pm Saturday, Sunday and holidays).

Picos–Madrid

An ALSA bus travels from Llanes to Madrid and return daily in July, August and the first half of September (and on Sunday southbound, Friday northbound in other months), stopping in Ribadesella, Arriondas, Cangas de Onís, Oseja de Sajambre and Valladolid. The Cangas–Madrid trip (€26.26) takes seven hours.

Cangas–Ribadesella/Llanes

To travel just between Cangas and Ribadesella or Llanes you normally need to change buses at Arriondas, which is linked with the pair of coastal towns by up to 12 buses daily and four FEVE trains. In July, August and early September, however, up to three daily buses run from Cangas to Ribadesella and return.

Cangas–Oseja de Sajambre

There's a Cangas–Oseja service on weekdays year-round, and on weekends, too, in summer.

Poncebos & Garganta del Cares

In July, August and early September three buses run between Arenas de Cabrales and Poncebos on Monday to Friday (but only one on weekends). In the same period a daily ALSA bus runs in the morning from Oviedo to Cangas de Onís and Posada de Valdeón, then in the afternoon/evening from Poncebos back to Cangas and Oviedo. The idea is that people can walk the 8km road along the Cares valley from Posada de Valdeón to Caín, then along the Garganta del Cares to Poncebos, and be picked up at the end. Buses to/from Llanes, Ribadesella and Gijón connect with this service at Cangas de Onís. Contact local bus stations or **ALSA** (☎ 902 42 22 42) for current details.

There's also a daily bus from León to Posada de Valdeón (year-round), but no buses go to Caín.

Arenas de Cabrales–Llanes

ALSA buses link Arenas de Cabrales with Llanes daily in the morning and afternoon (€2, 45 minutes).

Santander–Picos

From Santander, **Autobuses Palomera** (☎ 942 88 06 11) travels via San Vicente de la Barquera to Panes, Urdón, La Hermida, Lebeña and Potes (€5.80, 2½ hours), and return, two or three times daily.

Santander–Fuente Dé

In July and August the 10.30am Palomera bus from Santander (1pm from Potes) continues to Fuente Dé (50 minutes from Potes). During this period Palomera also has buses from Potes to Fuente Dé at 8.15am on weekdays. Buses leave Fuente Dé for Potes at 9am and

5pm Monday to Friday, 5pm on weekends, continuing to Santander. These schedules are, as always, subject to change.

WESTERN PICOS
Arriondas
pop 2489 / elevation 40m

Arriondas is the starting point for easy and popular **canoe trips** down the pretty Río Sella to various end points between Fries and Llovio (13km to 16km).

At least a dozen agencies in town will rent you a canoe, paddle, life jacket and waterproof container, show you how to paddle and bring you back to Arriondas at the end. Try these agencies:

Astur Aventura (☎ 985 84 10 02; Calle Río Piloña)

Jaire (☎ 985 84 14 64; www.canoasdelsella.com; Calle Juan Carlos I No 7)

The standard charge, including a picnic lunch, is €23 per person. Excursions set off around 11am. Bring a change of clothes. Agencies in Cangas de Onís and nearby coastal towns offer much the same deal, including transport to Arriondas and return.

This stretch of the Sella has a few entertaining minor rapids, but it's not a serious white-water affair, and anyone from about eight years can enjoy this outing, which for most people lasts four or five hours. In summer you can halt at a couple of temporary riverside cafés.

The river is easily at its busiest on the first Saturday after 2 August when 1500 canoes head downriver from Arriondas to Ribadesella, in the **Descenso Internacional del Sella**, a major international canoeing event.

Arriondas has a range of accommodation, including **Camping Sella** (☎ 985 84 09 68; per adult/tent/car €3.90/3.50/3.25; ◷ mid-Jun–mid-Sep), and **Hotel La Estrada** (☎ 985 84 07 67; www.laestrada hotel.com; Calle Inocencio del Valle 1; s/d €45/70 incl breakfast; P).

Cangas de Onís
pop 3390 / elevation 87m

Good King Pelayo, after his victory at Covadonga, moved about 12km down the hill to settle the base of his nascent Asturian kingdom at Cangas in AD 722. Cangas' big moment in history lasted 70 years or so, until the capital was moved elsewhere. Its second boom time arrived in the late 20th century with the invasion of Picos de Europa tourists.

In August, especially, the largely modern town is full to bursting with trekkers, campers and holidaymakers, many desperately searching for a room – a common story throughout eastern Asturias in high summer.

Cangas makes a reasonable base, but those seeking tranquility should push on eastwards.

INFORMATION
The **tourist office** (☎ 985 84 80 05; www.cangasdeonis .com; Jardines del Ayuntamiento 2; ◷ 10am-10pm Jul & Aug, 10am-2pm & 4-7pm Tue-Sat, 10am-2pm Sun Sep-Jun) is just off the main street, Avenida de Covadonga. Casa Dago (see Information, p518) provides national park information. Cangas has a fair smattering of banks with ATMs.

SIGHTS
The so-called **Puente Romano** spanning the Río Sella is almost certainly medieval rather than Roman, though it remains pretty impressive nonetheless. From it hangs a copy of the Cruz de la Victoria, the symbol of Asturias, which resides in Oviedo's cathedral.

Not far off, on Avenida Contranquil, the tiny **Capilla de Santa Cruz** (◷ 10am-1pm & 3-6.30pm Tue-Sun Jul–mid-Sep, Sat & Sun rest of year) marks the site of a millennia-old shrine, though the chapel itself was placed there in the 1940s. Within the crypt is a megalithic tomb.

Parque de la Naturaleza La Grandera (☎ 985 94 00 17; ◷ 11am-8pm, closed Mon Oct-Semana Santa) at Soto de Cangas, 3km east on the Covadonga road, offers the chance to observe captive bears, wolves, birds of prey and other Spanish wildlife that you'd be lucky to see on the trail.

ACTIVITIES
Many agencies offer a range of activities, including canoeing on the Río Sella, horse riding (€15 per hour), canyoning (€36 for two to three hours) and caving (€25 for two to three hours). There are several agencies:

Cangas Aventura (☎ 985 84 85 76; Avenida de Covadonga 17)

Frontera Verde (☎ 985 35 84 14 57; www.frontera verde.com; El Portazgo)

Los Cauces (☎ 985 94 73 18; www.loscauces.com; Avenida de Covadonga 23)

SLEEPING
Cangas has loads of hotels and a few *pensiones*, and there are plenty more of both,

plus numerous *casas rurales,* in villages within 10km to 15km of town. Along the road towards Soto de Cangas, Mestas de Con, Benia de Onís and Arenas de Cabrales all have several options. Most places in town can also inform you of apartments available for rent.

Hostal de Casa Fermín (☎ 985 84 84 91; Paseo de Contranquil 3; d €40) Located 500m past the Capilla de Santa Cruz, in a more rural zone, this brick structure has bright, simple rooms and a good restaurant.

Hotel Santa Cruz (☎ 985 84 94 17; www.hotelsanta cruz.net; Avenida Constantino González 11; s/d incl breakfast €64/83) Between the Capilla de Santa Cruz and a big riverside playground, this modern hotel goes for the rustic look.

Hotel Los Lagos (☎ 985 84 92 77; www.loslagos.as; Jardines del Ayuntamiento 3; s/d €48/96) This makes a good choice for somewhere more comfortable.

Hospedaje Principado (☎ 667 98 31 85; Avenida de Covadonga 6; d with bathroom €36) One of a handful of *pensiones* near the Puente Romano, this 3rd-floor residence is friendly and has clean rooms, but the traffic noise may get on your nerves.

Pensión El Chófer (☎ 985 84 83 05; Calle de Emilio Laria 10; s/d with shared bathroom €24/35) The 'Driver' is another reasonable-value place in the centre of town, with a dozen rooms above a popular *comedor.*

Several one-star hotels offer comfy if plain rooms with bathroom and TV at fair prices:

Hotel Los Robles (☎ 985 94 70 52; Calle San Pelayo 8; s/d €48/64)

Hotel Monteverde (☎ 985 84 80 79; www.hotel -monteverde.net; Calle Sargento Provisional 5; d incl breakfast €60) Acts as a headquarters for an activities outfitter.

EATING

Sidrería Restaurante Casa Mario (☎ 985 84 81 05; Avenida de Covadonga 19; mains €8.50-18) On the main street just off Jardines del Ayuntamiento, this *sidrería* has good *raciones* under €10 – try the fish in sea-urchin sauce! – plus exotic salads.

Meson Puente Romano (☎ 985 84 81 10; tablas €6-9) The terrace is just below the bridge, and a great spot to enjoy a board of Asturian cheeses and a bottle of cider.

Sidrería El Casín (☎ 985 84 83 31; Avenida de Castilla 2; menu €8) A block up from the Puente Romano is this local favorite. Regulars

recommend the smoked anchovies and *chuletilla de lechazo* (suckling lamb chops).

The restaurant at **Hostal de Casa Fermín** (see left) has a friendly local atmosphere and, specialises in stewed and grilled meats: a good choice is the *cachopo* (breaded veal cutlets).

GETTING THERE & AWAY

You will find the bus stop and office of **ALSA** (☎ 985 40 24 85; Avenida de Covadonga) opposite Jardines del Ayuntamiento.

Covadonga

The importance of Covadonga, 11km southeast of Cangas de Onís, lies in what it represents rather than what it is. Somewhere hereabouts, in approximately AD 722, the Muslims received their first defeat in Spain at the hands of King Pelayo, who set up the Asturian kingdom considered to be the beginning of the Reconquista – a mere 800-year project.

The place is an object of pilgrimage, for in a cave here, the **Santa Cueva**, the Virgin supposedly appeared to Pelayo's warriors before the battle. On weekends and in summer the queues at the cave, now with a chapel installed, are matched only by the line of cars crawling past towards the Lagos de Covadonga. The **Fuente de Siete Caños** spring, by the pool below the cave, is supposed to ensure marriage within one year to women who drink from it.

Landslides destroyed much of Covadonga in the 19th century and the main church here now, the **Basílica de Covadonga**, is a neo-Romanesque affair built between 1877 and 1901. Opposite the basilica is the **Museo de Covadonga** (☎ 985 84 60 96; admission €2; ☯ 10.30am-2pm & 4-7.30pm Tue-Sun), filled with all sorts of items, mostly donations by the illustrious faithful.

Hospedería del Peregrino (☎ 985 84 60 47; s/d €27/34) is located 500m before the basilica, and offers a dozen rooms sharing five bathrooms, as well as a restaurant.

Lagos de Covadonga

Don't let summer traffic queues deter you from continuing the 10km uphill from Covadonga to these two beautiful little lakes. Most of the day-trippers don't get past patting a few cows' noses near the lakes, so walking here is as enjoyable as anywhere else in the Picos. Some days in August the road is closed for an hour or two when the car parks near the lakes can't accept anymore vehicles.

Lago de Enol is the first lake you reach. It's linked to Lago de la Ercina, 1km away, not only by the paved road but also by a footpath via the **Centro de Visitantes Pedro Pidal** (☼ 10am-6pm Semana Santa-early Dec), which has information and displays on the Picos and a bookshop. There are rustic restaurants near both lakes, closed in winter. Bathing in the lakes is banned.

When mist descends, the lakes, surrounded by the green pasture and bald rock that characterise this part of the Picos, take on an eerie appearance.

WALKS FROM THE LAKES

Two classic and relatively easy trails begin and end at the lakes. The first leads about 5km southeast, with an ascent of 600m, from Lago de la Ercina to the **Vega de Ario**, where the **Refugio Marqués de Villaviciosa** (Refugio Vega de Ario; ☎ 639 81 20 69; bunks €7.50), attended and with meal service daily from Semana Santa to early December, has sleeping space for 40 people. The reward for about 2½ hours' effort is magnificent views across the Garganta del Cares (Cares Gorge) to the Macizo Central of the Picos.

The alternative walk takes you roughly south from Lago de Enol to the **Refugio de Vegarredonda** (☎ 985 92 29 52; www.vegarredonda .com; bunks €7.50) and on to the **Mirador de Ordiales**, a lookout point over a 1km sheer drop into the Valle de Angón. It's about a 3½-hour walk (one way) – relatively easy along a mule track as far as the Refugio de Vegarredonda, then a little more challenging on up to the mirador. The 68-place *refugio* is attended, with meals available year-round.

Desfiladero de los Beyos

The N625 south from Cangas de Onís follows the Río Sella upstream through one of the most extraordinary defiles in Europe. The road through the Desfiladero de los Beyos gorge is a remarkable feat of engineering. Towards the southern end of the defile, you cross from Asturias into Castilla y León.

Hotel Puente Vidosa (☎ 985 94 47 35; www .puentevidosa.com; r €60) Gloriously perched on a bend in the Sella by a waterfall, this hotel is 20km south of Cangas. The converted stone

house contains 19 lovely rustic-style rooms with gorge views.

Oseja de Sajambre

pop 132 / elevation 650m

Once inside the province of Castilla y León you'll soon strike Oseja de Sajambre, an average place with magnificent views across the gorge.

The **Hostal Pontón** (☎ 987 74 03 48; Carretera General; s/d with bathroom €33/37) is located on the main road. You'll probably also be able to find someone who rents rooms privately. There are a couple of restaurants and grocery shops.

Soto de Sajambre

pop 80 / elevation 930m

A better base for walking is this much prettier village by a freshwater stream, 4km north of Oseja de Sajambre.

Walks from Soto de Sajambre include La Senda del Arcediano, a very scenic trip of five or six hours north to Amieva, manageable by most walkers, and a more difficult trail eastward to Posada de Valdeón.

Offering meals and comfortable beds **Hostal Peñasanta** (☎ 987 74 03 95; s/d €25/31, d with bathroom €37), is housed in an attractive old stone structure.

Next door to Hostal Peñasanta and under the same management, **Albergue Peñasanta** (bunk €6.50) has 30 bunk beds (a sleeping bag is required).

CENTRAL PICOS

A star attraction of the Picos' central massif is the gorge that divides it from the western Macizo El Cornión. The popular Garganta del Cares trail can be crowded in summer, but the walk is worthwhile. This part of the Picos also has plenty of less heavily tramped paths and climbing challenges once you've 'done' the Cares.

You can approach the area from several directions, but for many it will be easiest to come from the north. Arenas de Cabrales and Poncebos are obvious bases.

Arenas de Cabrales

pop 800

Arenas de Cabrales (or just plain Arenas), lies at the confluence of the Río Cares and Río Casaño, 30km east of Cangas de Onís. The busy main road is lined with hotels, restaurants and bars, and just off it lies a little tangle of quiet squares and back lanes.

ORIENTATION & INFORMATION

Buses stop next to the **tourist office** (☎ 985 84 64 84; ☺ 10am-2pm & 4-8pm Easter, Jul & Aug), which is a kiosk in the middle of town at the junction of the Poncebos road.

Another valuable (and English-speaking) source of information is Ascatur, an association of local businesses, which maintains its own **kiosk** (☎ 985 84 67 47; 9am-10pm mid-Jun–Aug, 10am-1pm & 5-9pm Tue-Sun mid-Apr–mid-Jun & Sep–mid-Oct) across the road.

You'll find a post office, bank and ATM on the main street. Maps of the Picos are available at newsstands.

SNP Viajes (☎ 985 84 64 55; www.snptravel.com; Plaza del Castañedo) is an English- and Dutch-speaking agency that can set you up with guides for walking and cycling treks.

SLEEPING

Camping Naranjo de Bulnes (☎ 985 84 65 78; per person/tent/car €4.80/4.50/4.25) This large and efficiently run camping ground sits within a chestnut grove, 1.5km east of the town centre on the Panes road.

Arenas has about 10 other accommodation options, plus holiday apartments.

Pensión La Covadonga (☎ 985 84 65 66; r with private/shared bathroom €30/24) This family-run place is just off the main road opposite the tourist office. Rooms are immaculate, and there are great views of the valley from the upper floors. Outside August, rates drop by as much as half.

AUTHOR'S CHOICE

Hotel Torrecerredo (☎ 985 84 67 05; www .fade.es/torretours/home.htm; s/d €43/59) Taking its name from the Picos' tallest peak (which can sometimes be glimpsed from the dining room), the Torrecerredo is a relaxed place to spend a few days. Hosted by a friendly Anglo-Spanish couple who also leads excursions, it has 19 solar-powered rooms and a delightful terrace, plus all-you-can-eat breakfasts. Arriving from Cangas, you'll see a sign pointing left: follow an unpaved track 250m to the hotel, standing alone on a hillside.

Pensión El Castañeu (☎ 985 84 65 73; r with private/shared bathroom €30/24) Just behind the Covadonga, this *pensión* has decent homely rooms with extra blankets.

Hotel Rural El Torrejón (☎ 985 84 64 28; www .eltorrejon.com; r incl breakfast €49) An excellent mid-priced choice, this sturdy eight-room house enjoys a blissfully serene location beside the Río Casaño, a short walk from the town centre.

If you have no luck finding rooms in Arenas, there are a few reasonable places in Carreña de Cabrales, an unassuming village on the Río Casaño, 3km west along the AS114:

Hostal Cabrales (☎ 985 84 50 06; r €40)

Pensión Casa Corro (☎ 985 84 51 62; s/d €27/36) Inquire at the market across the bridge.

EATING

Restaurante Cares (☎ 985 84 66 28; menú €11) On the western approach into town, this atmospheric eatery offers country comfort food.

Café Santelmo (☎ 985 84 65 05; platos combinados €5.60-7.20) This locally popular spot, 100m east of the Poncebos junction, is good for breakfast or a Cabrales cheese *bocadillo*.

Garganta del Cares

Nine kilometres of well-maintained path high above the Río Cares between Poncebos and Caín constitute, perhaps unfortunately, the most popular mountain walk in Spain; in August the experience is akin to London's Oxford St on a Saturday morning. If you do arrive with the holiday rush, try not to be put off – the walk is a spectacular excursion between two of the Picos' three massifs. If you're feeling fit (or need to get back to your car), it's quite possible to walk the whole 9km and return as a (somewhat tiring) day's outing; it takes about seven hours plus stops.

PONCEBOS & FUNICULAR DE BULNES

Poncebos, a straggle of buildings at the northern end of the gorge, set amid already spectacular scenery, is exclusively dedicated to Picos tourism. A road turning uphill just above the Pensión Garganta del Cares leads 1.5km up to the hamlet of **Camarmeña**, where there's a lookout with views to El Naranjo de Bulnes in the Macizo Central.

A few metres up the Sotres road, just below Poncebos, is the lower end of the

Dining under medieval arches in Santiago de Compostela (p533), Galicia

OLIVER STREWE

Pulpo a la gallega (boiled octopus), a typical
Galician dish, Santiago de Compostela (p539)

OLIVER STREWE

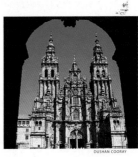

DUSHAN COORAY

Catedral del Apóstol (p535),
Santiago de Compostela

Vineyards and *vinicultor* (wine grower) in Ourense (p565), Galicia

OLIVER STREWE

Oceanogràfic (p578) in the Ciudad de las Artes y las Ciencias, Valencia

Las Fallas spring festival (p582), in the city of Valencia

Guadalest (p610), in the Valencia region

SAY CHEESE

Northern Spain, with its damp climate supporting herds of dairy cattle (rare elsewhere in the country), makes greater quantities of, and more varied, cheese than other regions. The Picos de Europa region produces a particularly high number of traditional cheeses, and the Cabrales *concejo* (municipality), running up into the mountains from the central northern rim of the Picos, is home to one of the most celebrated of all Spanish cheeses, a powerful bluey-green creation much appreciated by connoisseurs. The basic raw material of *queso de Cabrales* is untreated cow milk, particularly when obtained in May, June and July. Traditionally, this is mixed with lesser quantities of goat and/or sheep milk, though these are included in less than 20% of cheeses today. The cheese is matured for up to six months in mountain caves.

It's the penicillium fungus that gives the cheese its characteristic hue and creamy consistency – not to mention a rather strong odour. In this case, the bite is every bit as powerful as the olfactory bark, as a good Cabrales cheese tends to have considerable kick.

You can learn more about Cabrales cheese-making at the **Cueva El Cares** (☎ 985 84 67 02; adult/child €2.50/1.50; ⏰ 10am-2pm & 4-8pm Apr-Sep, Sat & Sun only rest of year), an exhibition cave south of Arenas along the Poncebos road.

Cabrales goes to town over its cheese on the last Sunday of August, with Arenas hosting cheese-making demonstrations, a cheese judging (with the winning cheese being auctioned for as much as €1200), a folklore festival and thousands of free Cabrales *bocadillos*.

You can distinguish a genuine Cabrales cheese from imitators by its label, which will show a five-pointed green leaf along with the crucial wording 'Denominación de Origen Protegida Cabrales'.

Funicular de Bulnes (☎ 985 84 68 00; adult/child return €16/4.75; ⏰ 10am-8pm Easter & Jul-Sep, 10am-12.30pm & 2-6pm rest of year), a tunnel railway that climbs 2km inside the mountain to the hamlet of Bulnes, which is inaccessible by road. The funicular functions year-round, making the seven-minute trip every half-hour in either direction.

Hotel Garganta del Cares (☎ /fax 985 84 64 63; s/d/tr incl breakfast €36/60/72; menú del día €7; ⏰ closed 10 Dec-15 Jan; **P**) offers beds and meals that are the closest to the Garganta del Cares trail.

Next door to Hotel Garganta del Cares, **Hotel Mirador de Cabrales** (☎ 985 84 66 73; www .hotelmirador.com; r €74; ⏰ Easter–mid-Oct; **P**) is a classier place. There's a minimum three-night stay from mid-July to mid-September.

GARGANTA DEL CARES WALK

By doing the walk from north to south, you save the best till last. Follow the 'Ruta de Cares' sign pointing uphill about 700m along the road from the top end of Poncebos. The beginning involves a steady climb upwards in the wide and mostly bare early stages of the gorge. After about 3km you'll reach some abandoned houses and probably a makeshift drinks' stand. A little further and you're over the highest point of the walk. Within 1km or so you should encounter another drinks' stand (they lug the stuff up on horseback).

As you approach the regional boundary with Castilla y León, the gorge becomes narrower and its walls thick with vegetation, creating greater contrast with the alpine heights above. The last stages of the walk are possibly the prettiest, and as you descend nearer the valley floor, you pass through a series of low, wet tunnels to emerge at the end of the gorge among the meadows of Caín. Along the way, there are several paths – most of them on the slippery side – leading down to the river, which you can follow for stretches.

CAÍN

If you're coming from the south, the trail-head of the walk is at Caín, where the rickety (and picturesque) road from Posada de Valdeón ends.

Casa Cuevas (☎ 987 74 27 20; r with/without bathroom €33/20) has basic rooms. There are at least two fancier places to stay, plus a couple of bars and restaurants. You'll find further lodgings in the string of villages south of Caín, including Cordiñanes and Posada de Valdeón.

Sotres

A side road heads up from Poncebos to little Sotres, the highest village in the Picos at 1045m and starting point for a number of good walks. Casa Cipriano (below) offers a professional mountain-and-caving guide service.

A long-established mountaineers' haunt is **Casa Cipriano** (☎ 985 94 50 24; www.casacipriano .com; s/d/tr incl breakfast €40/50/65).

Across the road from Casa Cipriano, **Pensión La Perdiz** (☎ 985 94 50 11; hotel.laperdiz@ terra.es; d/tr €35/50) has decent rooms: best are the the two top ones, which have balconies and wonderful views.

Hotel Peña Castil (☎ 985 94 50 49; www.hotel .penacastil.com; r incl breakfast €50) is a new establishment in a restored stone house.

Albergue Peña Castil (☎ 985 94 50 70; albergue@ penacastil.com; bunks incl breakfast €10; ⏱ Semana Santa-early Dec) is located uphill from the central square, and offers good, well-maintained bunk rooms.

All four places have restaurants, and there's a shop. No public transport runs here.

WALKS AROUND SOTRES

A popular route goes east to the village of **Tresviso** and on to **Urdón**, on the Potes–Panes road. As far as Tresviso (10km) it's a paved road, but the final 6km is a dramatic foot-only trail, the **Ruta de Tresviso**, snaking 850m down to the Desfiladero de la Hermida. Doing this in the upward direction, starting from Urdón, is at least as popular. An alternative track winds off the Sotres–Tresviso road and down via the hamlet of Beges to La Hermida, also in the Desfiladero de la Hermida.

Many walkers head west from Sotres to the **Collado de Pandébano**, about 90 minutes' away up on the far side of the Duje valley. From Pandébano it's possible to see the 2519m rock finger called **El Naranjo de Bulnes** (Pico Urriello), an emblem of the Picos de Europa and a classic challenge for climbers.

Few walkers can resist the temptation to get even closer to El Naranjo. It's possible to walk in around three hours from Pandébano to the **Vega de Urriello**, at the foot of the northwestern face of the mountain, where the 96-place **Refugio de la Vega de Urriellu** (☎ 985 92 52 00; www.picuurriello.com; bunks €7) is attended, with meal service, year-round.

Otherwise, you can descend for about an hour west to **Bulnes** (see Poncebos, p524). Bulnes is divided into two parts, the upper Barrio del Castillo and the lower La Villa. All amenities are in La Villa, including the six-room *casa rural* **El Chiflón** (☎ 985 84

59 43; bulneschiflon@terra.es; d/tr/q with bathroom €42.50/ 49.50/56.50; ⏱ Mar-Nov, Sat & Sun by reservation rest of year) and **Bar Bulnes** (☎ 985 84 59 34), with good home cooking. You can also get to Bulnes by walking southeast up from Poncebos (about 1¼ hours).

South from Sotres, you can walk to Vegas de Sotres (which from afar looks like a village, but is only used for animal shelter) and the Teleférico de Fuente Dé (cable car) or Espinama. This track is also suitable for 4WD vehicles.

Niserias

East of Arenas de Cabrales, the AS114 follows the attractive Río Cares valley downstream towards Panes. About 15km from Arenas is the peaceful hamlet of Niserias, at a particularly pretty bend in the Cares.

Casa Julián (☎ 985 41 57 79; www.casajulian.com; s/d €51/64) has just four rooms, all with broad terraces facing the river. The restaurant does great fish dishes.

The owners of Casa Julián have a more modest **hostal** (s/d €32/45) across the road.

La Tahona de Besnes (☎ 985 41 57 49; latahona@ctv .es; d €66) comprises a beautifully renovated set of old stone bakery buildings in a leafy river valley 1.75km north of Niserias (take the Alles road and follow the signs). It has attractive double rooms, a few apartments and a good restaurant. You can go horse riding here, too.

EASTERN PICOS
Panes

Panes is where the AS114 from Cangas and Arenas meets the N621 running from the coast south to Potes. It has a range of accommodation. Hotel Trespalacios on the main street is the main bus stop.

Desfiladero de la Hermida

The N621 south from Panes follows the Río Deva and enters the impressive Desfiladero de la Hermida gorge. You cross into Cantabria here at Urdón, the bottom end of the Ruta de Tresviso path, 2km before the hamlet of **La Hermida**. There's not much at La Hermida, but the bubbling Deva, the Picos looming to the west and a couple of *pensiones*.

Lebeña

About 8.5km south of La Hermida, there is a spot that warrants visiting. A kilometre east of the N621 stands the fascinating little 9th-century **Iglesia de Santa María de Lebeña** (until 7pm Tue-Sun). The horseshoe arches in the church are a telltale sign of its Mozarabic style – rarely seen this far north in Spain. The floral motifs on the columns are Visigothic, while below the main *retablo* (altarpiece) stands a Celtic stone engraving. They say the big yew tree outside was planted 1000 years ago.

Casa de Labranza El Agero (942 74 43 37; Calle Allende 3; s/d €20/39) is on the N621 just north of the Lebeña turn-off, and has eight good doubles with bathroom in a charmingly restored farmhouse.

Across from Casa de Labranza El Agero is the Restaurant Desfiladero.

Potes

pop 1590 / elevation 291m

Fairly overrun in peak periods, but with some charm in the old centre (restored in attractive traditional stone and slate after considerable damage during the civil war), Potes is a popular staging post on the southeastern edge of the Picos. Spanned by the medieval San Cayetano bridge, the Río Quiviesa joins the Río Deva at the heart of the village, with the Macizo Oriental (also called Macizo Andara) rising close at hand.

INFORMATION

Potes has a few banks with ATMs, two cybercafés on Calle Doctor Encinas in the town centre, and a couple of big supermarkets.

The **tourist office** (942 73 07 87; Plaza de la Serna; 10am-1.30pm or 2pm & 4-7pm or 8pm) shares a building with the bus station on the west side of town.

SIGHTS

Right in the centre of town, the squat **Torre del Infantado** was built as a defensive tower in the 15th century and is now the town hall, having long served as a prison. A bit farther down the river, the 14th-century **Iglesia de San Vicente**, deconsecrated in the 19th century, is a nice example of rustic Gothic architecture.

ACTIVITIES

Several activities' outfits are based in Potes. **Turismo Activo La Liébana** (942 73 10 00; www .laliebanaaventura.com), next door to the park information office on the way out to Fuente Dé, will hire you a bicycle (€25 per day), take you canoeing (€22 for three hours), canyoning (€36 for 2½ hours), horse riding (€26 for two hours) or on walking trips in the Picos. One possible itinerary combines Fuente Dé and the Garganta de Cares walk in one day.

SLEEPING & EATING

Camping La Viorna (942 73 20 21; per person/tent/car €3.40/3.40/3.40; Apr-Oct;) Just 1km from Potes on the road to the Monasterio de Santo Toribio de Liébana, this bucolic camping ground includes a restaurant.

La Antigua (942 73 00 37; eltarugu@mixmail .com; Calle Cántabra 9; s/d €38/48;) Around the corner from Casa Cayo, this stone-house lodging offers similarly rustic style, though minus the views.

Hostal Lombraña (942 73 05 19; Calle del Sol 2; d with/without bathroom €32/28) Some of the spacious, if basic, rooms here face the Torre del Infantado.

Hostal Picos de Europa (942 73 00 05; www .europicos.com; Calle San Roque 6; d incl breakfast €68) A sound fall-back, this large establishment houses an outfitter running 4WD tours of the Picos.

Bar Los Camachos (942 73 00 64; Calle San Cayetano) A football-watching bar with hams and chilies hanging overhead, Los Camachos is good for a plate of bacon and eggs chased by a shot of *orujo*. Nightly specials include *fabada* (Tuesday) and *cocido lebaniego* (spiced pork and bean stew; Thursday). It also has a few rooms for rent.

Around Potes

MONASTERIO DE SANTO TORIBIO DE LIÉBANA

Liébana valley, of which Potes is in a sense the 'capital', lies between the southeastern

---

AUTHOR'S CHOICE

Casa Cayo (942 73 01 50; www.casacayo.com; Calle Cántabra 6; s/d €25/45) This is the pick of the bunch, with helpful service and attractive, comfy, wood-beamed rooms, some overlooking the river. You'd be very lucky to get a room here in July or August, though. There's an excellent restaurant where you can eat well for about €15.

side of the Picos de Europa and the main spine of the Cordillera Cantábrica. The valley was repopulated in the 8th century with Christians from Spain's *meseta* by Alfonso I of Asturias, putting it on the front line between Muslim Spain and what little there was at that stage of its Christian opponent.

The settlers brought with them the Lígnum Crucis, a purported piece of Christ's cross supposedly transported from Jerusalem by Bishop Toribio of Astorga in the 4th century. The holy relic has been housed ever since in this **monastery** (⌚ 9am-1pm & 3.30-7pm or 8pm), 3km west of Potes (signposted off the Fuente Dé road).

The relic, which according to tradition features the hole made by the nail that passed through Christ's left hand, is an extraordinary magnet for the faithful. It's kept inside a crucifix of gold-plated silver, which is housed in a lavish 18th-century baroque chapel off the monastery's austere Gothic church (dating from 1256).

Potes to Fuente Dé

The 23km CA185 from Potes to Fuente Dé is a beautiful trip, with several places to stay along the way. At **Turieno**, 2.5km from Potes, are **Camping La Isla** (☎ /fax 942 73 08 96; per person/tent/car €3.30/3/3.30; ⌚ Apr-Oct; 🐕), with a leafy, riverside site, and a few small *hostales*. At **Camaleño**, 4km past Turieno, is the **Hostal El Caserío** (☎ 942 73 30 48; s/d €23/39), housed in a cluster of beautifully restored old structures, including what used to be the town's *cantina*. **Cosgaya**, 13km southwest of Potes, is a nice spot to relax, with the **Hotel del Oso** (☎ 942 73 30 18; www.hoteldeloso.com; s/d €53/66; 🐕) comprising two very solid stone-built lodges facing each other across a stream.

ESPINAMA

This is the last stop of any significance before Fuente Dé, and probably makes a more appealing base if you have your own transport. A 4WD track from here leads about 7km north and uphill to the Hotel Refugio de Áliva and on to Sotres.

There's a surprising choice of decent places to stay in Espinama, all with restaurants – you can't miss them. The family-run **Hostal Remoña** (☎ 942 73 66 05; s/d €22/43), the only one that isn't by the roadside, has large units, some with balconies over the rushing Río Nevandi. Other options include the

Hotel Máximo (☎ 942 73 66 03; s/d incl breakfast €39/45), with a 4WD excursion service, and **Hostal Puente Deva** (☎ 942 73 66 58; s/d €23/35).

Fuente Dé & the Teleférico

At 1078m, Fuente Dé lies at the foot of the stark southern wall of the Macizo Central. In four minutes the **Teleférico de Fuente Dé** (Cable Car; ☎ 942 73 66 10; adult/child return €10/3; ⌚ 9am-8pm Easter & Jul-Sep, 10am-6pm rest of year, closed 7 Jan-Feb) here whisks people 762m to the top of that wall, from where walkers and climbers can make their way deeper into the central massif.

Be warned that during the high season (especially August) you can wait for hours at the bottom to get a seat. Coming down, you simply join the queue and wait – OK on a sunny day, but a little unpleasant if the queue's long.

ACTIVITIES
Walking & Climbing

It's a walk of 3.5km from the top of the *teleférico* to the Hotel Áliva, or you might catch one of the private 4WD shuttles that do the trip for €3 per person. From the hotel, two trails descend into the valley that separates the central massif from its eastern cousin. The first winds its way some 7km south down to Espinama, while the other will get you north to Sotres via Vegas de Sotres. If there is a demand, 4WDs cover the Sotres and Espinama routes.

Other possibilities for the suitably prepared include climbing Peña Vieja (2613m) and making your way across the massif to El Naranjo de Bulnes. This requires proper equipment and experience – Peña Vieja has claimed more climbers' lives than any other mountain in the Picos. Less exacting is the route of about two hours leading northwest from the *teleférico*, passing below Peña Vieja by marked trails to the tiny (three-place) Refugio Cabaña Verónica at 2325m near Horcados Rojos.

Eagle Show

If it looks like you'll have a long wait for the *teleférico* in summer, check to see when the **Águilas de Fuente Dé** (☎ 629 40 75 28; adult/child €5/3) are flying. At the time of writing, this 40-minute performance by low-flying eagles, buzzards and other birds of prey, a short distance up the road from the lower *teleférico* station, was taking place at 1pm, 4pm and 6.30pm between mid-July and mid-September. It's a rare chance to see these trained birds, including the majestic golden eagle, swooping in over the audience and picking up their reward of meat. The organisers are also involved in rehabilitating injured wildlife.

SLEEPING & EATING

El Redondo (☎ 942 73 66 99; per person/car & tent €5.40/5.40; ☼ Jun-Sep) About 400m along the road from the bottom *teleférico* station, this camping ground has adequate sites, as well as *refugio*-style accommodation for 16 people.

Otherwise, Fuente Dé has two hotels, both offering 4WD trips into the mountains.

Hotel Rebeco (☎ 942 73 66 01; hotelrebeco@mun divia.es; s/d €45.50/59; **P**) This handsome stone lodge is the better-value option. Eleven of the 30 rooms include loft levels that are suitable for kids.

Parador de Fuente Dé (☎ 942 73 66 51; s/d €75/93.50; **P**) One of the less attractive members of the national network, the *parador's* modern upper storey has all the charm of a high school cafeteria.

Hotel Refugio de Áliva (☎ 942 73 09 99; d €63, half-board €16; ☼ mid-Jun–mid-Oct) Set 1700m high, this 27-room *refugio* features a restaurant, café and even a solarium.

Dining options are limited to the hotel restaurants and cafés, and the reasonable-value **cafeterías** (platos combinados €6.60-9) at both *teleférico* stations.

Galicia

CONTENTS

If the regions of Spain were identified by colour, Galicia's might well be green tinged with grey. Just as Andalucía wears its dazzling whitewash and Castilla-La Mancha bathes in the burnt red and dusty olive green of its sun-scorched plains, so granite walls and slate rooftops on a verdant rural background seem symbolic of Galicia. Without doubt, the often inclement weather contributes to the impression. You've *always* got to be ready for rain here.

Galicia's wild coastline, battered by the Atlantic, is frayed up and down its length by a series of majestic *rías* (inlets or estuaries). In the south, the Río Miño divides Galicia from Portugal, and in the east, Galicia is separated from Spain's *meseta* (central tableland) by the western end of the Cordillera Cantábrica and associated ranges. Frenetic deforestation has unfortunately stripped much of Galicia of its indigenous trees, mostly replaced by eucalyptus.

Many travellers in Galicia make a beeline for Santiago de Compostela and no one can blame them. This medieval city-shrine is one of Spain's most engaging urban centres. Beyond it, however, lies plenty more. The popular Rías Baixas and less well known Costa da Morte and Rías Altas are peppered with coves, great sandy beaches, bays and fishing villages, and you'll see some of Spain's wildest coast towards Cabo Ortegal in the northwest. Of the numerous other towns that could go on a must list, Pontevedra stands out.

HIGHLIGHTS

- Taste refreshing Albariño whites from **Cambados** (p554)
- Dive into **pulpo a la gallega** (p540): octopus straight up
- Watch the wild-horse round-ups of the **Serra de Capelada** (p548)
- Absorb the splendour of the **Gargantas del Sil** (p567), north of Ourense
- Relax at **Cedeira** (p547) and the **Rías Altas** (p546)
- See **Lugo** (p568) from atop the Roman walls
- Indulge yourself and stay at the divine **Parador dos Hostal Reis Católicos** (p539)
- Be thrilled at **Punta da Estaca de Bares** (p548), Spain's northernmost cape
- Listen to gaiteros (bagpipers) at Galicia's summer **music festivals** (p541)
- View the magnificent cathedral at **Santiago de Compostela** (p535)

- AREA: 29,574 SQ KM
- POP: 2,751,090
- AVE SUMMER TEMP: HIGH 24°C, LOW 13°C

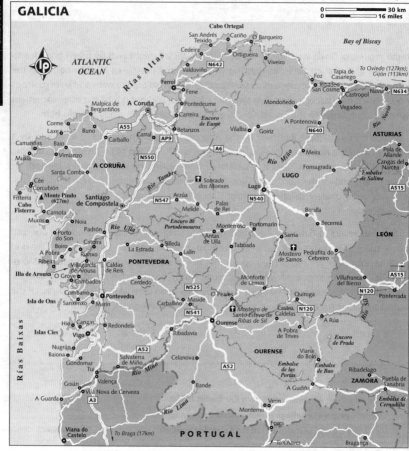

GALICIA

0 — 30 km
0 — 16 miles

History

Inhabited since at least 3000 BC, by the Iron Age Galicia was populated by Celts living in *castros*, villages of circular stone huts surrounded by defensive perimeters. The Romans, who mingled reasonably well with the locals, gave the area its name, initially Gallaecia. Galicia was then ruled by a Germanic tribe, the Suevi, for most of the 5th and 6th centuries AD, before the Visigoths asserted themselves. Little touched by the 8th-century Muslim invasion, Galicia was under the control of the Christian kingdom of Asturias by 866.

The big event in the area's medieval history was the 'rediscovery' of the grave of Santiago Apóstol (St James the Apostle)

in 813, at what would become Santiago de Compostela. The site became a rallying symbol for the Reconquista, but by the time this was completed in 1492, Galicia had become an impoverished backwater in which the centralist-minded Catholic Monarchs, Fernando and Isabel, had already begun to supplant the local tongue and traditions with Castilian methods and language.

The Rexurdimento, a reawakening of the Galician consciousness, did not surface until late in the 19th century, and then suffered a 40-year interruption during the Franco era.

Rural, with its own language, and still much ignored by the rest of Spain, Galicia is in many aspects another country.

Rather than hope for any good from the nation's centre, Galicians have traditionally looked outwards. Fishing and emigration (to Latin America and, more recently, other European countries) have long been their mainstays. Galicia is home to half of Spain's fishing fleet, and its boats cast their nets far and wide. With world fish stocks falling, however, Galician fishing communities find themselves staring at an uncertain future. A further blow came in November 2002 when the oil tanker *Prestige* sank, leaking massive oil slicks towards the coast and inflicting serious damage on hundreds of kilometres of coastal habitat (see The Big Spill, p551).

SANTIAGO DE COMPOSTELA

pop 76,270 / elevation 260m

There can be few cities in the world as beautiful as Santiago that are founded on the basis of so preposterous a story. The corpse of Santiago Apóstol (St James), the myth relates, was transported in a stone boat from the Holy Land to the far side of Spain by two disciples after his execution in Jerusalem in AD 44. They landed at Padrón and buried Santiago in a spot 17km inland.

In 813 the grave was supposedly rediscovered by a religious hermit following a guiding star (hence 'Compostela', a corruption of the Latin *campus stellae*, field

of the star). The saint's purported grave became a welcome rallying symbol for Christian Spain and work began on building a church above its remains. The myth gained strength in the following centuries and Santiago de Compostela became a goal for Christian pilgrims from all over Western Europe. It has since improved with both age and the various architectural additions made after the initial peak of enthusiasm for the pilgrimage around the 12th century. For more on the pilgrimage, past and present, see Camino de Santiago (p83).

Apart from the undisputed splendour of its gold-tinged monuments and the charm of its medieval streets, Santiago de Compostela is a lively city with a sizable student population during term.

HISTORY

The story begins with Santiago Apóstol, but the region had long been inhabited by Visigoths, Romans and Celts. Once the holy site had been identified, it wasn't long before Alfonso II, the Asturian king, turned up to have the first church erected.

By 1075 when the Romanesque basilica was begun and the pilgrimage was becoming a major European phenomenon, Santiago de Compostela had already been raided on various occasions by the Normans and Muslims. Bishop Diego Gelmírez added numerous churches to the city in the 12th century, when homage paid to its saint brought in a flood of funds.

TRAVELLING IN TONGUES

Long suppressed during the Franco years (strange, since Franco was born in Galicia), the Galician language (*galego* or, in Castilian Spanish, *gallego*) sounds like a cross between Portuguese and Castilian. Basically a Romance language (ie a latter-day version of Latin), it also contains elements of Celtic and Germanic tongues from peoples who inhabited Galicia before and after the Romans.

Galician is widely spoken and in recent years has been strongly pushed as the main local language. The Galician versions of city, town and village names are now pretty well universal on signposts in Galicia (and starting to appear beyond its borders, too).

In this chapter we use the names you're likely to encounter during your travels. By and large, this means Galician spellings for cities, villages and geographical features. Beaches tend to be *praia* rather than *playa*, islands *illa*, not *isla* and mountain ranges *serra* instead of *sierra*. Streets (Galician: *rúa*/Castilian: *calle*), squares (*praza/plaza*), churches (*igrexa/iglesia*), monasteries (*mosteiro/monasterio*) and the like are given whichever name is most prominently used.

A few clues to those who know Castilian Spanish: 'x' in Galician generally replaces 'j' (so Junta becomes Xunta and Juan is Xoán) and is pronounced like the 's' in pleasure; 'o' replaces 'ue' (*puente* becomes *ponte*); while the ending 'eiro' replaces 'ero' and 'erio'. Three very useful but not obvious words are *saída* (exit), *caixa* (the bill) and *pechado* (closed)!

SANTIAGO DE COMPOSTELA

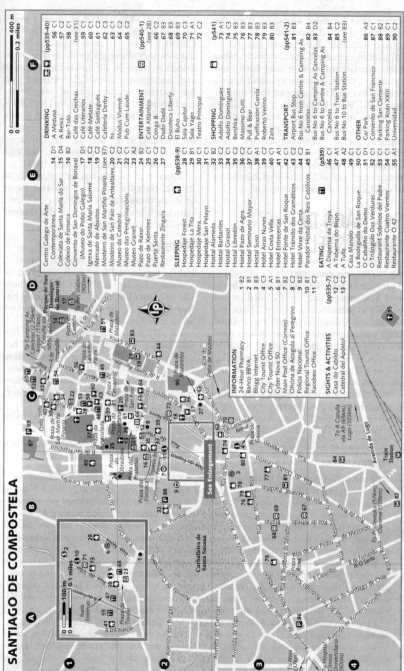

The following centuries were marked by internecine squabbling between rival nobles, damped down by Fernando and Isabel after the conclusion of the Reconquista. After misguidedly siding with the Carlists in the 1830s, Santiago de Compostela slipped into the background. Only since the 1980s, as capital of the autonomous region of Galicia and a rediscovered tourist target, has the city re-emerged.

ORIENTATION

Santiago's compact old town, focused on the cathedral and its surrounding squares and virtually completely pedestrianised, contains most of the monuments and places to stay and eat. Praza de Galicia marks the boundary between the old town and the modern shopping area to its south.

The train station is about a 15-minute walk downhill from the city centre, and the bus station is marginally further, to the northeast of the city centre.

INFORMATION

Emergency

Policía Nacional (☎ 981 58 19 44; Avenida de Rodrigo de Padrón 101)

Internet Access

Bbigg Internet (Rúa da Senra 19; per hr €1.75)
Cyber Nova 50 (Rúa Nova 50; per hr €1.20)

Medical Services & Emergency

24-hour pharmacy (☎ 981 58 58 95; Cantón do Toural 1)
Hospital Clínico Universitario (☎ 981 95 00 00; Travesa da Choupana)

Money

Banks and ATMs are dotted about the centre. A handy one is **Banco BBVA** (Rúa do Vilar 33).

Oficina de Acogida al Peregrino

People who have covered at least the last 100km of the Camino de Santiago (p83) on foot, or the last 200km by bicycle, with a Christian intention (the term is interpreted broadly) can obtain their 'Compostela' certificate to prove it at the **Pilgrims' Reception Office** (☎ 981 56 24 19; www.archicompostela.org; Rúa do Vilar 1; ⊗ 9am-9pm).

Post

Main post office (Travesía de Fonseca)

Tourist Offices

Rúa do Vilar is home to three information centres.

City tourist office (☎ 981 55 51 29; www.santiago turismo.com; Rúa do Vilar 63; ⊗ 9am-9pm Jun-Sep, 10am-3pm & 5-8pm Oct-May) A branch office, on Praza de Galicia, is handy if you're coming from the train station.

Regional tourist office (☎ 981 58 40 81; www.tur galicia.es; Rúa do Vilar 43; ⊗ 10am-2pm & 4-7pm Mon-Fri, 11am-2pm & 5-7pm Sat, 11am-2pm Sun)

Xacobeo office (☎ 981 57 20 04; Rúa do Vilar 32; ⊗ 8.30am-2.30pm & 4.30-6.30pm) Offers information on the Camino de Santiago.

SIGHTS

Catedral del Apóstol

Those who have journeyed along the Camino de Santiago will hardly be disappointed on finally entering Praza do Obradoiro to behold the lavish baroque western façade of the **Catedral del Apóstol** (admission free; ⊗ 7am to 9pm). Before this was built in the 18th century, the less-overwhelming but artistically unparalleled **Pórtico de la Gloria** (Galician: Porta da Gloria) – now behind the baroque façade – was the first scene to greet weary pilgrims. The bulk of the cathedral was built between 1075 and 1211, in Romanesque style, and the Pórtico de la Gloria was its original façade. Much of the 'bunting' (the domes, statues and endless flourishes) came later.

The baroque icing on the Romanesque cake undoubtedly muted the impact of the Pórtico de la Gloria, but it has also been something of a blessing, protecting the sculptures of Maestro Mateo – the master architect and sculptor placed in charge of the cathedral-building programme in the late 12th century by King Fernando II – from the elements. The main figure in the portico's central archway is Christ risen. At his feet and hands are the four Evangelists, and beside them are angels with the crown of thorns and other instruments connected with Jesus' passion. In an arc above are the 24 musicians said in the Apocalypse to sit around the heavenly throne. Below Christ's feet Santiago is represented and a popular belief has it that below him is the figure of Maestro Mateo. Bump your head on it three times and you're supposed to acquire some of his genius; the problem is that Mateo's statue is the one on the other side, kneeling facing the altar, while the popular but mistaken head probably belongs to Hercules (holding open the mouths of two lions). Some people bump both heads to cover all options. Another tradition calls for a brief prayer as you place your fingers in the five holes created above Hercules' head by the repetition of this very act by millions of faithful over the centuries.

The remarkably lifelike figures that dominate the columns on the right side of the portico are apostles, while those to the left represent Old Testament prophets.

Approaching the churrigueresque **Altar Mayor** (Main Altar), you'll notice an opening and stairs on the right side. Follow the crowds to embrace the 13th-century statue of Santiago. You emerge on the left side and proceed underground down some steps to contemplate what you are assured is the tomb of Santiago.

You may catch one of the special Masses where the greatest dispenser of incense in the world, the *botafumeiro*, is swung heftily across the transept by an expert team using an ingenious pulley system – an unforgettable sight.

The cathedral's many artistic and architectural riches fill guidebooks of their own. To do the place justice, make more than one visit to try to absorb it all.

A special pilgrims' Mass is celebrated at noon daily. Others are at 10am, 6pm and 7.30pm daily, with an extra service at 1.30pm Sunday.

MUSEO DA CATEDRAL

To the right of the cathedral's Praza do Obradoiro entrance is the main entrance to the **Cathedral Museum** (☎ 981 56 05 27; admission €5; ☑ 10.30am-2pm & 4-8pm Mon-Sat, 10.30am-2pm Sun). The museum includes the cathedral's cloister (*claustro*, inside this entrance), treasury and crypt, and the Pazo de Xelmírez on the north side of the cathedral.

The **cloister** is a successful mix of late-Gothic and Plateresque styles. Rooms on several floors around it contain displays on the cathedral's development from early shrine to the complex structure of today, an impressive collection of religious art, tapestries and the lavishly decorated 18th-century chapter house (*sala capitular*). Maestro Mateo's original stone **choir** (*coro*) has been reconstituted and is on view beside the main entrance.

The **crypt**, entered from the foot of the cathedral's Praza do Obradoiro steps, is notable for its 12th-century architecture.

The **Pazo de Xelmírez** was built for Bishop Diego Gelmírez in 1120. Worth seeking out in this Gothic adjunct is the **Sala de Ceremonias**, the main banquet hall. The exquisite little busts around the walls depict feasters and musicians, plus the odd king and juggler. Bishop Gelmírez's biggest contribution to Santiago de Compostela was to resuscitate the myth of the Battle of Clavijo. Supposedly Santiago had joined Ramiro I in this fiesta of Moor-slaying in 844, for which the grateful king promised to dedicate the first fruits of every harvest to the saint. Few historians believe the battle ever took place, but for centuries Gelmírez turned the myth into one of his city's biggest revenue sources.

Around the Cathedral

However much the cathedral dominates the heart of Santiago, the area around it is rich in other architectural jewels. The northern end of Praza do Obradoiro is closed off by the Renaissance **Hostal dos Reis Católicos**. Built to shelter the poor and infirm by Fernando and Isabel, with some of the loot from Granada, it now shelters the well off instead, as a luxury *parador*. Along the western side of the square is the elegant 18th-century **Pazo de Raxoi**, now housing the city hall.

A stroll around the cathedral takes you through some of Santiago's most inviting squares. To the south is **Praza das Praterías** (Silversmiths' Square), with the **Fuente de los Caballos** (1829) at its centre. The cathedral's south façade, up the steps, is an original, if weathered, Romanesque masterpiece. Facing it from the lower side of the square is the ornamental 18th-century **Casa do Cabildo**, a residence for the cathedral clergy.

Following the cathedral walls you enter **Praza da Quintana**. Facing it is the cathedral's **Puerta Santa** (Holy Door), opened only in years of grace, when the Feast of Santiago (25 July) falls on a Sunday. Across the plaza is the long, stark wall of the **Mosteiro de San Paio de Antealtares** (Vía Sacra 5; ☑ 11am-1.30pm or 2pm & 4-7pm Mon-Sat), founded by Alfonso II as a monastery for Benedictine monks to look after St James' relics, and converted to a nunnery in 1499. Climbing the steps at the top of the plaza, you'll find the entrance to the convent, above which stands the beatific figure of the child saint San Paio, his throat being slashed in remembrance of his martyrdom in Córdoba. Within is a **museum of sacred art** (admission €1.50). Nuns recite Benedictine chants at Mass, nightly at 7.30pm.

Keep following the cathedral walls northwards to reach Praza da Inmaculada. Rising up on the far side is the huge Benedictine **Mosteiro de San Martiño Pinario**. The classical façade hides two 17th-century cloisters, behind which (but entered from Praza de San Martiño Pinario) is the monastery's church, an elaborate piece of baroque architecture begun in 1611. The church's towers were never finished, their construction apparently blocked by cathedral officials averse to seeing any shadows cast on its greater glory.

Other Sights

Museums worth seeking out include the **Museo das Peregrinacións** (☎ 981 58 15 58; Rúa de San Miguel 4; admission free; ☿ 10am-8pm Tue-Fri, 10.30am-1.30pm & 5-8pm Sat, 10.30am-1.30pm Sun), devoted to the Camino de Santiago phenomenon over the centuries, and the **Museo Granell** (☎ 981 57 21 24; Praza do Toural; admission €2; ☿ 11am-2pm & 4-9pm Wed-Mon, except Sun afternoon) with an impressive collection of surrealist art.

Northeast of the old town, the former Convento de San Domingos de Bonaval houses the **Museo do Pobo Galego** (Museum of the Galician People; ☎ 981 58 36 20; Rúa San Domingos de Bonaval; admission free; ☿ 10am-1pm & 4-8pm Mon-Sat, 11am-2pm Sun), with exhibits on Galician life and arts, from the fishing industry to music and crafts to traditional costumes. The most singular feature is the triple spiral staircase. The monastery's Gothic church is part of the visit. Facing the museum is the contrasting **Centro Galego de Arte Contemporánea** (☎ 981 54 66 19; admission free; ☿ 11am-8pm Tue-Sun), hosting exhibitions of modern art.

About 1km south of the old town along Rúa do Patio de Madres stands, precariously (it suffers a pronounced tilt), the Romanesque **Colexiata de Santa María do Sar** (☎ 981 56 28 91; admission €0.60; ☿ 10am-1pm & 4-7pm Mon-Sat). Part of the beautiful cloister can still be admired and there's a small museum, mainly of Romanesque sculpture.

WALKING TOUR

Any tour of Santiago inevitably begins with the **Catedral del Apóstol** (**1**; p535), and

many hours can be devoted to this alone. Exit onto the Praza do Obradoiro, which aside from the mind-boggling western façade of the cathedral is bordered by the opulent **Hostal dos Reis Católicos** (**2**; p536) and **Pazo de Raxoi** (**3**; p536). Proceed south to the Praza de Fonseca, with the **Colexio de Fonseca** (**4**; ☎ 981 57 20 04; admission free; ☿ 10am-2pm & 4-9pm Tue-Sun) containing the university library and a gallery for exhibitions. Cross this plaza and loop back to the cathedral, bearing right to the **Praza das Praterías** (**5**; p536). Continuing around the cathedral, you reach the **Praza da Quintana** (**6**; p536). Climb the steps at the top end to enter the **Mosteiro de San Paio de Antealtares** (**7**; p536). Turn right onto Rúa de San Paio; a little way down you'll find the **Praza de San Paio** (**8**; p539), with half a dozen inviting cafés and bars. At the end of the street, go right, down Rúa de Conga, then left at the café Conga 8. Follow Rúa Nova with its quaint stone-pillared pavement arcades, along the way consulting the upcoming programme at the **Teatro Principal** (**9**; p541) and stopping to admire the **Santa María Salomé chapel** (**10**). A right on the narrow Ruela de Entrerrúas takes you to Rúa do Vilar. Go left on Vilar to reach the Praza do Toural, where there's likely to be a concert going on. Otherwise, pop into the surreal **Museo Granell** (**11**; p537). A short distance down Rúa dos Bautizados, exit the old town into the greenery of the **Carballeira de Santa Susana** (**12**).

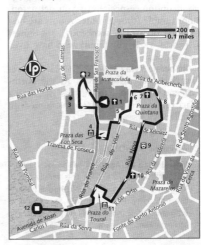

FESTIVALS & EVENTS

July is a fine month to be in Santiago. The **Feast of Santiago** is on 25 July and is simultaneously Galicia's 'national' day. The night before, Praza do Obradoiro comes alight with the *fogo do Apóstolo*, a spectacular fireworks display that culminates in the incineration of a mock façade erected in front of the cathedral.

SLEEPING

Santiago is bursting with accommodation. In the old town, signs announce *habitaciones* (rooms) or *camas* (beds), and the number of *hospedajes* (hostelries) and *casas de huéspedes* (guesthouses) is reassuring. But even so, your first choices may fill up in July or August, so ring ahead. Other options are around Praza de Galicia.

Budget

Camping As Cancelas (☎ 981 58 02 66; Rúa Vintecinco de Xullo 35; per person/tent/car €4.90/5.10/5.10) About 2km northeast of the city centre is this amply shaded camping ground. Bus No 6 from Rúa do Hórreo or Rúa da Virxe da Cerca stops on Rúa de San Lázaro, from where it's a 200m uphill walk to the site.

Hostal Suso (☎ 981 58 66 11; Rúa do Vilar 65; s/d €20/40) In the heart of the old town, this guesthouse has large, comfortable units. A facelift was planned at the time of writing.

Hospedaje Forest (☎ 981 57 08 11; Rúa de Abril Ares 7; s with shower/d with bathroom €15/25) A good option, especially if you get a top-floor double (though outer rooms are best avoided on rowdy weekends), the Forest is run by a friendly family who have lived in London.

Hospedaje Mera (☎ 981 58 38 67; Rúa da Porta da Pena 15; s/d with bathroom €28/38) At the northern end of the old town, this welcoming place offers clean, simple rooms, some with excellent views.

AUTHOR'S CHOICE

Hostal Pazo de Agra (☎ 981 58 35 17; Rúa da Caldeirería 37; s/d €23/36) This family-run lodging occupies a stately old house near the university. Rooms are big and bright with balconies. Inquire around the corner at Restaurante Zíngara.

Hospedaje La Tita (☎ 981 58 39 81; Rúa Nova 46; s/d with shared bathroom €15/24) A central over-a-bar place, La Tita is basic but fine.

Hospedaje San Pelayo (☎ 981 56 50 16; Rúa San Paio de Antealtares 2; s/d with shared bathroom €20/30) Though overpriced and needing an upgrade, the rooms have great balconies and there's a guest kitchen.

Mid-Range

Hostal Alameda (☎ 981 58 81 00; www.hostal-alameda .net; Rúa de San Clemente 32; s/d with private bathroom €30/49) This relaxed lodging has a good position just below the city gardens, and there's a large car park nearby.

Hostal Seminario Mayor (☎ 981 57 28 80; incoming@viajesatlantico.com; Praza da Inmaculada 5; s/d incl breakfast €30/47; ☻ Jul-Sep) Conditions are spartan, but it offers the rare experience of staying inside a Benedictine monastery. With 126 rooms, it's a good bet when everywhere else is full.

A number of charming small hotels occupy renovated old-town mansions.

Hotel Airas Nunes (☎ 981 55 47 06; www.pousadas decompostela.com; Rúa do Vilar 17; s/d €64/80) The hotel's 10 rooms sport ancient stone walls and cosy modern comforts, on one of Santiago's most atmospheric streets.

Hotel Tránsito dos Gramáticos (☎ 981 57 26 40; hotel@transitodosgramaticos.com; Tránsito dos Gramáticos 1; s/d €54/65) This attractive new addition graces pleasant Praza Mazarelos, with luxurious rooms and an innovative restaurant.

A few more hotels of this type are north of the old town:

Hotel Entrecercas (☎ 981 57 11 51; Rúa Entrecercas 11; s/d €45/65 incl breakfast)

Hotel Costa Vella (☎ 981 56 95 30; www.costavella .com; Rúa da Porta da Pena 17; s/d €47/66; ☒)

Hotel Fonte de San Roque (☎ 981 55 44 47; Rúa do Hospitalillo 8; s/d €39/60)

Hostal Libredón (☎ 981 57 65 20; www.libredon .com; Praza de Fonseca 5; s/d with bathroom €40/45)

Hostal Barbantes (www.barbantes.com; Rúa do Franco 3; s/d with bathroom €45/60) This pair, both under the same management, have small, ordinary rooms but great locations on either side of a lively little square. Reception for both is in the Libredón.

Top End

Hotel Virxe da Cerca (☎ 981 56 93 50; www.pousadas decompostela.com; Rúa da Virxe da Cerca 27; s/d from €80/91) Opposite the Mercado de Abastos and backed by tranquil gardens, this large, elegant hotel was once a Jesuit residence.

Parador Hostal dos Reis Católicos (☎ 981 58 22 00; santiago@parador.es; Praza do Obradoiro 1; r €178) This building is one of Santiago's prime monuments. In keeping with its exalted past, guests pay exalted prices – but it' a splendid place to stay!

EATING

There are countless places to eat to suit all pockets. Do-it-yourselfers should visit the handsome Mercado de Abastos, above Rúa da Virxe da Cerca.

Rúa do Franco and parallel Rúa da Raiña, south of the cathedral, are packed with restaurants displaying boatloads of live seafood. Prime time is around 9pm.

Restaurante Ó 42 (☎ 981 58 10 09; Rúa do Franco 42; mains €5-10) Ó 42 is often recommended for traditional Galician fare in a charming setting.

Restaurant Sobrinos del Padre (☎ 981 58 35 66; Rúa da Fonte de San Miguel 7) Octopus rules here: a *media-ración* (a larger serve of tapas but smaller than a *ración*) of *pulpo a la gallega* (bite-sized pieces of boiled octopus) goes for €4.60.

A Dispensa da Troya (☎ 981 58 19 09; Rúa da Troia 9; tabla for one/two €3/6) This little bodega is a delightful spot to enjoy a *tabla* (board) of sausage/meats or cheese accompanied by a Ribeiro wine.

Casa Manolo (☎ 981 58 29 50; Praza de Cervantes; menú €6; ☽ closed Sun night) Nothing but a daily three-course *menú* here – but it's cheap and filling, and there's a wide choice – hence the lunchtime queues.

A Tulla (☎ 981 58 08 89; Ruela Entrerúas 1; vegetarian/regular menú €8.50/11; ☽ closed Sun) One of a pair of restaurants sharing a tiny square hidden along Santiago's narrowest street, this cheerful locale turns out tasty tapas, including a few meatless options. Try the mushroom cutlets!

La Bodeguilla de San Roque (☎ 981 56 43 79; Rúa de San Roque 13; mains €6-10) Northeast of the old town, this often busy spot serves an eclectic range of excellent dishes. We recommend, among other things, the *boliños de tenreira en prebe de espinacas* (meatballs in spinach sauce, €6.60).

O Triángulo Das Verduras (☎ 981 57 51 81; Praciña das Peñas 2; dishes €6, menú €10.50; ☽ 1.30-3.30pm & 9-11.30pm Mon-Sat) Almost opposite La Bode-guilla de San Roque, these folks prepare some good vegetarian dishes with organic ingredients.

O Cabaliño do Demo (☎ 981 58 81 46; Rúa Aller Ulloa 7; mains €4.50-5.50; ☽ 2-4pm & 9pm-midnight Mon-Sat) This is a recommended vegetarian restaurant, where an American owner-chef prepares exotic dishes like Thai curries.

Santiago is full of bakeries proffering tempting pastries. Don't even think about leaving without trying a *tarta de Santiago*, an almond-based cake with a sword-cum-cross emblem etched from the top layer of powdered sugar.

DRINKING
Cafés

The cafés on Praza da Quintana have a prime location and a captive clientele: you may get served quicker at **Café Santiagués** at the bottom of the square than at **Café Literarios** at the top.

Cafetería Derby (☎ 981 58 64 17; Rúas das Orfas 29) On the border of the old and new towns, this is something of an institution.

Café Metate (☎ 981 58 19 16; Travesa de San Paio de Antealtares) At one time a chocolate factory, this plaza locale serves luscious hot chocolate, straight or spiked.

Bars

Santiago's liveliest central bars lie in a sort of arc east of Praza da Quintana. From the top of the steps, Rúa de San Paio de Antealtares runs southeast to Praza de San Paio, where at least half a dozen bars form a single boisterous entity, with good music playing into the early hours.

Borriquita de Belém (Rúa de San Paio 12) On the far side of the plaza, this is a particularly inviting little jazz club serving *mojitos*.

Modus Vivendi (Praza de Feixoo 2) At the bottom end of the street, you'll find this classic Santiago haunt, with nightly musical variations.

GALICIAN FOOD FARE

When stomachs grumble in Galicia, thoughts turn to seafood. Galician seafood is plentiful, fresh, relatively cheap – and may well be the best you have ever tasted. Adventurous eaters will dive into *pulpo a la gallega,* the region's signature dish, with tender pieces of octopus sprinkled with olive oil and paprika, or *pulpo á feira* with chunks of potato added. Along similar lines are *chipirones,* a type of small squid served whole, or *chocos,* a larger member of the squid family. Mollusc mavens will enjoy the variety of *ameixas* (clams) and *mexillons* (mussels). Some of the special shellfish of the region include *vieiras* (scallops), *berberechos* (cockles), *navajas* (razor clams) and the tiny barnacles known as *percebes,* with a curious resemblance to fingernails. Other delicacies include various crabs, from little *necoras* to the great big *buey del mar* – the 'ox of the sea.' Also watch for *bogavante,* a large, lobster-like creature with two enormous claws.

If you prefer seafood that swims, sample *xoubiñas* – sardines, tastiest when grilled – or *caldeirada,* a hotpot of potato and fish. *Marraxo,* a sort of shark generally served *a la plancha* (lightly grilled) is surprisingly tasty. Many people like *anguilas* (small eels from the Río Miño). More familiar items include *gambas* – prawns that are most commonly served *al ajillo* (with garlic) or the much larger *langostino* (king prawn).

If you just want to cleanse your palate before the next sea feast, order a hearty bowl of *caldo gallego* (broth with cabbage or turnip, potato and usually a bit of meat) or a plate of *lacón con grelos* (boiled pork shoulder, potatoes and greens). And to spice things up a bit, bite into some *pimientos de Padrón* (small green peppers fried with lots of garlic).

Since the 13th century pilgrims on the Camino de Santiago have looked forward to the *empanadas* of Galicia. Something like pasties, they're most commonly filled with tuna and tomato; an *empanadilla* is the bite-size snack version.

Galicia produces some fine wines, too. The Ribeiro wines, mostly from around Ribadavia, count among their number a clean, crisp white and a decent red. Mencia is also a pleasing red. For a robust white, the Condado label from the lower Río Miño is recommended. Rosal is a more expensive drop from A Guarda, while the white Albariño from Cambados is considered the prince of Galician tipples.

North of the cathedral, two happening spots dominate the Praza de San Miguel.

Café Atlántico (Fonte de San Miguel 9) This multi-level bar pulls in a hip, attractive 20s set, with Zeppelin and T Rex setting the mood.

Bar-Tolo (Fonte de San Miguel 8) This dimly lit place cultivates a punk attitude.

hs (Rúa da Troia; ⊙ from 10pm Mon-Sat) A highly spirited gay club.

A Reixa (Rúa Tras de Salomé 3) A popular rock-and-roll den, with a heavy '60s influence and occasional live music.

A Medusa (Praza de Salvador Parga 1) This place exudes a tribal feel, with cutting-edge funk and hip-hop.

ENTERTAINMENT
Live Music
Some of the best music can be heard free on Santiago's streets and plazas; groups often perform on Praza da Quintana or Praza do Toural, and you're bound to run into a few *gaiteros* (bagpipers) and street combos in your wanderings.

Café das Crechas (Vía Sacra 3) *The* place for Celtic music. Jam sessions (called *foliadas*) are held Wednesday night in the cellar; other nights guest DJs work the club. Check here for posters announcing live music elsewhere.

Sala Capitol (☎ 981 57 43 99; www.salacapitol.com; Rúa Concepción Arenal 5; cover €12-24; ⊙ from 11pm Tue-Sat) The Capitol is a major venue for touring bands; check its website for upcoming events.

Dado Dadá (☎ 981 59 15 74; Rúa de Alfredo Brañas 19; ⊙ from 10pm Mon-Sat) Jazz fans should head for this Santiago mainstay, featuring Tuesday-night jam sessions.

Dance Clubs & Discotecas
Conga 8 (Rúa da Conga 8) Upstairs is a casual café, downstairs a mirror-ball–enhanced dance floor for salsa enthusiasts.

Pub Cum Laude (Rúa da Conga 6) This pub plays Latin pop and always has a bit of a party atmosphere.

More drinking and dancing goes on in the new town. Make for Rúa da República

Arxentina and, especially, rowdy Rúa Nova de Abaixo, with an equal smattering of pubs and discos.

Discoteca Liberty (Rúa de Alfredo Brañas 4; €4 minimum; ☾ from 1am) This cavernous club doesn't tend to get going until 4am or so on weekends.

El Buho (Rúa de Alfredo Brañas 11) From Discoteca Liberty, people head across the street to this *rockero* haven. Enter through the garage door.

Theatre & Film
Teatro Principal (☎ 981 58 29 28; Rúa Nova 21) Ask the city tourist office for a programme of events.

Sala Yago (☎ 981 58 92 88; www.salayago.com; Rúa do Vilar 51) This alternative theatre stages a varied programme of plays and puppet shows, and screens a steady diet of classic and Galician films.

SHOPPING
Santiago's old town is littered with shops selling handicrafts, including the characteristic local jet or jet-and-silver jewellery, which is beautiful and ornate. You'll find plenty of traditional Galician lace here, too. Southwest of Praza de Galicia, stylish shoppers can explore sleek boutiques or browse through the designer outlets of Adolfo Domínguez, Purificación García and Roberto Verino, or those of Amancio Ortega,

such as Zara, Bershka, Massimo Dutti and Pull & Bear.

GETTING THERE & AWAY
Air
Santiago de Compostela's **Lavacolla airport** (☎ 981 54 75 00) is 11km east of the city. Iberia flies up to seven times daily to Madrid, three times to Barcelona, twice to Bilbao, and once each to London, Amsterdam and Brussels. Air Europa and Spanair also serve Madrid.

Bus
From Santiago's bus station, **Castromil** (☎ 981 58 97 00) has buses running hourly north to A Coruña (€5.95, one hour), west to Noia (€2.85, 45 minutes) and Muros (€5.55, two hours), and up to nine times daily south to Pontevedra (€4.70, one hour) and Vigo (€6.85, 1½ hours). Castromil buses also go up to 11 times daily southeast to Ourense (€8.90, two hours), and up to five times southwest to Cambados and O Grove (€5.85, two hours).

Intercar/ALSA/Dainco (☎ 902 42 22 42) operates up to six buses daily to Madrid (€35.50, seven to nine hours). They also have two or more going to Oviedo (€26 to €33, 5½ to 6½ hours), two or three each to Zamora (from €18, six hours), Salamanca (€20, 7½ hours), Cáceres and Seville, and one to Barcelona (€58.40, 15 hours).

DANCING TO THEIR OWN TUNE

Perhaps it is in their rich musical tradition that Galicians' Celtic strains come most vividly to the fore. Although the sounds and rhythms differ noticeably from those played by their cousins in Brittany, Ireland and Scotland, the links between them all are impossible to deny. Most readily recognisable is the *gaita* (Galician bagpipes). Summer in Santiago is a good time to catch buskers playing traditional Galician tunes, on quite an inventory of instruments. In addition to the standard *gaita*, *bombo* (big drum) and *violín*, there is a range of simple wood instruments, including the *pito* (whistle) and *pandereita* (tambourine); the *castañolas* and *tarrañolas* (both variations on castanets); and the *zanfona*, a string and key instrument vaguely similar to an accordion.

Bagpipe ensembles feature in many Galician festivals and the leading *gaiteros* (bagpipers) are major popular heroes in Galicia. If you get the chance to hear contemporary stars, such as Carlos Núñez, Xosé Manuel Budiño or Susana Seivane, don't pass it up. Many practitioners experiment with instruments and influences from well beyond the confines of Galician folk. The shaven-headed Mercedes Peón, whose music is perhaps best characterised as neo-pop-folk, puts on particularly dramatic stage shows.

Possibly the best internationally known Galician traditional music group is the polished Milladoiro. Other prominent ensembles are Luar Na Lubre, Berroguetto and Fía Na Roca. Uxía is a powerful female vocalist and interpreter of traditional popular song.

Further daily services head for Lugo, Santander, San Sebastián and Burgos.

On Friday and Sunday (and daily, except Saturday, from June to September), an ALSA bus heads to Lisbon (€37, 7½ hours) via Porto (€21, 2¼ hours) and Coimbra. ALSA also travels to Paris, London, Brussels, Amsterdam and Zurich.

Car & Motorcycle
Tolls on the A9 *autopista* (tollway) are €4.22 to A Coruña (64km) and €3.62 to Pontevedra (57km). Parallel to the A9, slower and free of cost is the N550.

Train
You can travel to/from Madrid (Chamartín station; €38.50) on a daytime Talgo (seven hours) or an overnight *trenhotel* (nine hours).

Trains run almost hourly north to A Coruña (€3.30 to €4.25, one hour), and south to Pontevedra and Vigo (€5.10 to €6.50, two hours). There are three trains most days to Ourense (from €6.10, two hours) and one to Irún, on the French border, via Burgos and San Sebastián. For Portugal you need to make a connection at Redondela, outside Vigo.

GETTING AROUND
Santiago de Compostela is walkable, although it's a bit of a hike from the train and bus stations.

To/From the Airport
Up to 22 **Empresa Freire** (☎ 981 58 81 11) buses run daily between Lavacolla airport and the bus station (€1.55). About half depart from the corner of Rúa do Xeneral Pardiñas and Rúa da República do Salvador, southwest of Praza de Galicia, passing the train and bus stations en route. Taxis charge around €15.

Bus
Bus No 6 runs every 20 to 30 minutes from Rúa do Hórreo near the train station to Rúa da Virxe da Cerca on the eastern edge of the old town. Bus No 10 runs every 20 to 30 minutes between Praza de Galicia and the bus station, via Rúa da Virxe da Cerca. Coming from the centre to the train station, the bus stops on Rúa de Santiago Leon de Caracas.

A CORUÑA & THE RÍAS ALTAS

Often more intemperate and certainly much less visited than the west-facing coast of Galicia, the northern coast is peppered with pleasant surprises. A Coruña is a busy and surprisingly attractive port city with decent beaches. There are plenty of smaller towns and fishing villages worth exploring too – plus some of the most impressive coast in all Galicia.

A CORUÑA
pop 226,580
A Coruña (Castilian: La Coruña) has only in recent years been rivalled by Vigo as Galicia's biggest city. It remains the region's most outward-looking urban centre, with a liberal-republican tradition at variance with the conservative remainder of Galicia. Its port was the gateway through which hundreds of thousands of Galician emigrants left for new lives in the Americas.

In the 2nd century AD the Romans built the lighthouse known as the Torre de Hércules here. Nothing much is known of A Coruña's subsequent history until 991, when the port was put under control of the church in Santiago.

Britain looms large on A Coruña's horizon. In 1588 the ill-fated *Armada* weighed anchor here, and the following year Sir Francis Drake tried to occupy the town, but was seen off by María Pita, a heroine whose name lives on in the town's main square. Napoleon's troops occupied A Coruña for the first six months of 1809. Their British opponents were able to 'do a Dunkirk' and evacuate, but their commander, General Sir John Moore, died in the Battle of Elviña and was buried here.

Orientation
The train and bus stations are a couple of kilometres southwest of the city centre. A Coruña gets interesting along a fairly narrow isthmus and the large headland to its east and north. The old town (*ciudad vieja*) huddles in the southern tip of the headland, while the Torre de Hércules caps its northern extreme. Most hotels, restaurants and bars are in the newer, predominantly 19th-century part of

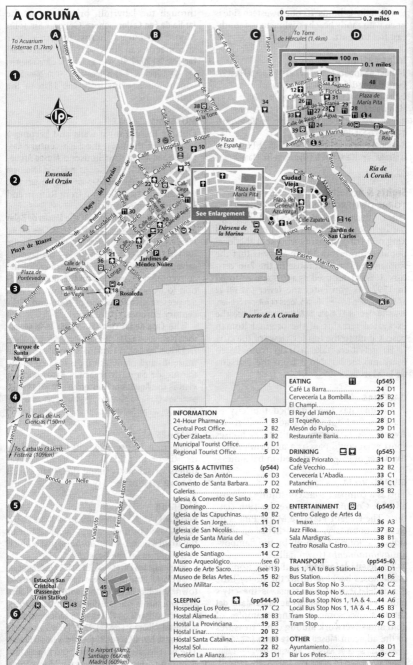

A CORUÑA

town on the isthmus. Its northwestern side is lined with sandy beaches, while to the southeast lies the port.

Information

24-hour pharmacy (☎ 981 22 21 34; Calle del Real 92)
Central Post Office (Avenida de la Marina)
Cyber Zalaeta (Calle de Zalaeta 7; per hr €1.20)
Municipal tourist office (☎ 981 18 43 44; www .turismocoruna.com; Plaza de María Pita; ◷ 10am-2pm & 4-8pm Mon-Sat, 10am-2pm Sun)
Regional tourist office (☎ 981 22 18 22; Dársena de la Marina; ◷ 10am-2pm & 4-7pm Mon-Fri, 11am-2pm Sat & Sun)

Sights & Activities
TORRE DE HÉRCULES

One myth says that Hercules built the original lighthouse here after slaying the cruel king of a tribe of giants who kept the local populace in terror. All we *know* is that the Romans built a lighthouse in the 2nd century. It was later used as a fort and destroyed in 1792. As you enter the **tower** (☎ 981 22 37 30; admission €2; ◷ 10am-5.45pm or 6.45pm Sep-Jun, 10am-10.45pm or 11.45pm Jul & Aug), you'll see the excavated remains of the original Roman base. Climb to the top for views of the city.

To get there take a tram from Paseo Marítimo, or bus No 3 from the Dársena de la Marina.

GALERÍAS

A Coruña has been dubbed the 'city of glass'; to find out why, head to waterfront Avenida de la Marina. Multistorey houses sport what could pass as a uniform protective layer of *galerías* (glassed-in balconies).

CIUDAD VIEJA

This is a compact zone constituting almost all of A Coruña built before the 19th century. The elegant Plaza de María Pita is its western boundary, with porticoes on three sides, the fourth taken up by the flamboyant *ayuntamiento* (town hall).

The **Iglesia de Santiago**, with three Romanesque apses backing on to the pretty little Plaza del General Azcárraga, is the city's oldest church. The **Iglesia de Santa María del Campo** shows some dazzling examples of gold and silverwork among other treasures in the adjacent **Museo de Arte Sacro** (☎ 981 20 31 86; Rúa Puerta de Aires 23; admission free; ◷ 10am-1pm & 5-7pm Mon-Fri, 10am-1pm Sat). A short walk

through the labyrinth brings you to the **Jardín de San Carlos**, where General Sir John Moore lies buried. Across the street, war aficionados can look over the **Museo Militar** (☎ 981 20 67 91; Plaza de Carlos I; admission free; ◷ 10am-2pm & 4-7pm Mon-Sat, 10am-2pm Sun), which houses arms from the 18th to the 20th centuries.

MUSEUMS

Outside the old town walls and keeping a watch over the port, the 12th-century **Castelo de San Antón** now houses a **Museo Arqueológico** (☎ 981 18 98 50; admission €2; ◷ 10am-7pm Tue-Sat, 10am-2.30pm Sun Sep-Jun, later in summer), with an eclectic collection from Roman and Visigothic times onwards.

The innovative design of the **Museo de Belas Artes** (Fine Arts Museum; ☎ 981 22 37 23; Calle Zalaeta; admission €2.40, free Sat & Sun; ◷ 10am-8pm Tue-Fri, 10am-2pm & 4.30-8pm Sat, 10am-2pm Sun) manages to salvage something of the atmosphere of the convent that once stood on the site. In addition to works by Rubens and Goya, it holds a representative collection of 16th- and 17th-century European paintings.

The **Casa de las Ciencias** (☎ 981 18 98 44; museum/planetarium €2/1; ◷ 11am-9pm Jul & Aug; 10am-7pm or 8pm Sep-Jun), A Coruña's popular science museum and planetarium, is located in the Parque de Santa Margarita. Also worth a visit is the **Aquarium Finisterrae** (☎ 981 18 98 42; admission €8; Paseo Marítimo; ◷ 10am-9pm Jul & Aug, 10am-7pm or 8pm Sep-Jun).

BEACHES

Aside from the protected city beaches, Playa de Riazor and Playa del Orzán, several others stretch away along the 30km sweep of coast west of the city.

Sleeping

Hostal Sol (☎ 981 21 03 62; Calle del Sol 10; s/d €36/72; P) Beyond its nondescript façade is one of the town's better-value *hostales*, just a block and a half from the beach.

Hospedaje Los Potes (☎ 981 20 52 19; Calle Zapatería 15; s/d €25/40) One of the few options in the old town, this has large rooms with wood floors and *galerías* (Galician glassed-in balconies). Inquire at Bar Los Potes, two blocks west.

Hostal Alborán (☎ 981 22 65 79; www.meiganet .com/hostalalboran; Calle de Riego de Agua 14; s/d €24/37) The best-located budget bet, the functional Alborán is steps from Plaza de María Pita.

Hostal Alameda (☎ 981 22 70 74; Calle de la Alameda 12; s/d with private bathroom €28/48) West of the old centre is this dependable option, with neat, pleasant rooms over a busy café.

Hostal La Provinciana (☎ 981 22 04 00; Rúa Nueva 9; s/d €34/45) A homey place with polished furniture, this is a grade up from the budget *hostales*.

Hostal Linar (☎ 981 22 78 37; Calle de General Mola 7; s/d €25/45) Don't expect luxury, but you'll get a good night's rest here and the location is convenient.

Eating

The narrow lanes stretching west of Plaza de María Pita are the first place to head for. Calle de la Franja in particular is lined with options. Calle Estrella and Calle de los Olmos are also rich hunting grounds.

El Champi (☎ 981 22 70 03; Calle de la Franja 50) Don't miss its signature chomp – a little shrimp on a big sautéed mushroom.

Mesón do Pulpo (☎ 981 20 24 44; Calle de la Franja 9; half/full ración €5.50/8.50; ☿ closed Sun) Go for the octopus, as the name suggests, classically prepared with paprika, rock salt and olive oil.

El Tequeño (☎ 981 22 00 38; Plaza de María Pita 21; tapas €0.90) Named after its specialty, a twisty cheese-filled pastry of Venezuelan origin, El Tequeño is an obligatory stop.

El Rey del Jamón (☎ 981 22 74 85; Calle de la Franja 45; raciónes €4; ☿ closed Sun night) Enjoy *tablas* of fine hams here.

Restaurante Bania (☎ 981 22 13 01; Calle de Cordelería 7; mains €7.50; ☿ closed Sun, Mon night) Tofu scallops, natural juices and all kinds of salads are a few of the tasty items offered by this vegetarian eatery.

Drinking

Although you pay extra for your coffee, the cafés on Plaza de María Pita are unbeatable for people-watching.

Café La Barra (☎ 981 22 73 82; Calle Riego de Agua 33) Stop by this lively social hall for a double espresso and a game of Parcheesi.

AUTHOR'S CHOICE

Cervecería La Bombilla (Calle de Galera 7; raciónes €4.50) The 'lightbulb,' an unpretentious corner locale, serves fresh, retropriced tapas: a slab of tortilla and a cold beer will get you change from €2.

You'll find plenty to drink with your tapas in the central streets already mentioned.

Cervecería L'Abadía (☎ 981 22 97 02; Calle de Franja 49; ☿ closed Mon) This wood-trimmed beer hall has Estrella de Galicia on tap.

Bodega Priorato (Calle de la Franja 16; ☿ 10.30am-2.30pm & 5.30-midnight or later) Sawdust and peanut shells litter the floor of A Coruña's oldest bodega, where wine is poured by the *porrón* (jug with a long, thin spout through which you pour wine into your mouth).

Dozens of watering holes cram the streets off Playa del Orzán, party central towards the weekend.

xxele (Calle del Orzán 9) A punky ambience pervades this small pub, with as much action outside as inside.

Jazz Filloa (Calle del Orzán 31; ☿ 9pm-3am) Jazz connoisseurs will appreciate the great musical selection at this cavernous hang-out.

A little northwest of Plaza de María Pita, Calle de Orillamar caters to the considerable alternative scene.

Patanchín (☎ 981 22 43 62; Calle de Orillamar 16; ☿ from 5pm) Rootless cosmopolitans can plant themselves here for the evening.

Entertainment

For non-mainstream films in their original language, see what's playing at the **Centro Galego de Artes da Imaxe** (☎ 981 20 34 99; www .cgai.org; Durán Loriga 10; admission €1.20).

Teatro Rosalía Castro (☎ 981 22 47 75; Calle de Riego de Agua 37) Classical concerts and other cultural events are held here.

Sala Mardigras (☎ 981 20 38 77; www.salamardigras.com; Calle de la Torre 8; variable cover) This dark little club can get pretty crowded, especially on weekends when touring bands perform here.

Getting There & Away

AIR

A Coruña's **Alvedro airport** (☎ 981 18 73 15) is located 8km south of the city centre. Iberia has at least five flights daily to/from Madrid, plus services to Barcelona, Bilbao and Paris. There are also flights to Lisbon by Portugalia.

BUS

The bus company **Castromil** (☎ 981 24 91 92) frequently services Santiago de Compostela, Pontevedra and Vigo. **Arriva** (☎ 981 23 90 01) heads to Ferrol (€5.95, one hour), Betanzos

(€1.75), Viveiro, Ribadeo, Lugo and Ourense, and to the Costa da Morte.

ALSA runs east to Asturias, Cantabria
and the Basque Country, and to Madrid
(€35, 8½ to 10½ hours).

CAR & MOTORCYCLE
The A9 tollway towards Santiago de Compostela is the quickest southeastward route.
Before Betanzos another tollway heads north
to Fenne, just short of Ferrol (A Coruña–
Fenne costs €3.05). The N550 to Santiago is
prettier and there's no charge.

TRAIN
From 6.15am to 10.30pm (more or less
hourly), trains head south to Santiago de
Compostela (from €3.30), Pontevedra and
Vigo (from €8.25). There are two trains
daily to Madrid (Chamartín station; €38, 10
hours), and two to Barcelona via Zaragoza.
Three or four trains travel daily to Ferrol
(€3.30, 1¼ hours) via Betanzos.

Getting Around
Nine buses a day travel from the bus station
to the airport (€1) on Monday to Friday; on
weekends you'll have to take a taxi (€12).

Local bus No 5 links the train station
with central A Coruña; it stops diagonally
opposite the train station. Bus Nos 1, 1A
and 4 stop outside the bus station en route
to the city centre.

In summer, trams (€1) run daily (weekends only the rest of the year) along Paseo
Marítimo around the large headland to the
north of the city centre, convenient for
reaching the Torre de Hércules and the
Aquarium Finisterrae.

RÍAS ALTAS
Although the Rías Altas and surrounding
countryside east of A Coruña are less visited than the Rías Baixas, in many respects
they have an edge over their more popular
counterpart. They are far less populated,
retaining a greater natural attraction, and
many beaches on this stretch are every bit
as good as those to the south. A handful
of enticing towns, such as medieval Betanzos and Pontedeume, are accompanied by
some of the most dramatic coast in all of
Galicia.

Regular buses ply the main road to
Ribadeo, and Asturias-bound trains follow a similar route. Buses are rarer off
the main roads but many destinations are
reachable.

Betanzos
pop 9920 / elevation 38m
Just 24km east of A Coruña, Betanzos can
be seen as a small-scale Toledo of the north,
with its multistorey houses glassed in by
classic *galerías*. Re-sited here in 1219, medieval Betanzos was long a busy port until
eclipsed by A Coruña. Lately it has made
valiant efforts to stave off the tangible effects of economic depression.

A **tourist information module** (☎ 981 77 01 00;
www.betanzos.net; Rúa de Emilio Romay; ☒ 10am-2pm &
4-8pm Mon-Fri, 10.30am-1pm Sat) shares a building
with the Museo das Mariñas. Banks are on
or near the sprawling main square, Praza
dos Irmáns García Naveira.

The Celtic settlement that predated the
town stood on what is now Praza da Constitución, flanked by the neoclassical **Casa do
Concello** and Gothic **Iglesia de Santiago**. More
interesting is the small Praza de Fernán
Pérez de Andrade, with the Gothic churches
of **Santa María do Azogue** and **San Francisco**
(☒ 9.30am-1pm & 4.30-7.30pm). Inside the latter,
the tomb of Fernán Pérez de Andrade, the
noble who founded a monastery in nearby
Ferrol in the 14th century, is supported by
the family emblems in stone – a bear and
a wild boar.

The **Museo das Mariñas** (admission €1.20; ☒ 10am-
2pm & 4-8pm Mon-Fri, 10am-1pm Sat) contains many
curios, including medieval funerary sculpture and traditional Galician costumes.

The **Fiesta de San Roque**, on 16 August, is
marked at midnight by the releasing of a
huge, decorated paper hot-air balloon from
the tower of Santo Domingo church.

SLEEPING & EATING
Accommodation is limited. There's **Hospedaje Universal** (☎ 981 77 00 55; Avenida Linares
Rivas 18; s/d €15/22), a shabby town-centre
guesthouse, and the unremarkable **Hotel Los
Ángeles** (☎ 981 77 15 11; Rúa dos Ánxeles 11; s/d with
bathroom €40/52).

Culinary life focuses on Travieso do
Progreso, a lane off the main square: O'
Pote and O Rabel are popular watering
holes serving tapas and *bocadillos* (bread
rolls with fillings). The parallel lane, Venela
do Campo, has more tapas bars, while the

cafés on the main square are popular for breakfast. You can quench your thirst at Cervecería Old Inn with an Irish or German beer, just off the small Praza Domingo Etcheverría.

GETTING THERE & AWAY

Frequent Arriva buses to/from A Coruña operate from Praza dos Irmáns García Naveira. Up to four Arriva buses head daily to Viveiro, and six go to Lugo and Ferrol.

The closest of the two train stations, Betanzos Cidade, is north of the old town, across the Río Mendo. Three trains go daily to Ferrol and A Coruña.

Pontedeume

pop 4730

Founded in 1270, this hillside feudal bastion, while scruffier than Betanzos, is an appealing stop with a **beach** close to its fishing port. Rúa Real, the porticoed main street leading off the roundabout at the entry to town from Betanzos, climbs past a cheerful little square up to the 18th-century **Iglesia de Santiago**. Down on the waterfront, opposite the market, rises the **torreón** (main tower) of what was once the Palacio de Andrade, named after the local feudal lord.

Fonda Martís (☎ 981 43 06 37; Rúa Real 23; s/d €12/18) has spartan rooms in the heart of town. A more comfortable option is **Hostal Allegue** (☎ 981 43 00 35; Calle Chafaris 1; r €38.50), the best of three similar restaurant/guesthouses around Plaza del Convento.

Rúa Real is lined with taverns and eateries. **Bar/Restaurante Compostela** (☎ 981 43 01 61; Rúa Real 19; raciones €3.50-8.50) is popular. For something different, try **Taberna Tostaky** (☎ 981 43 44 45; Rúa Real 34; raciones €7; closed Sun night & Mon), where a Frenchman prepares dishes such as vegetarian lasagne and scrambled *zamburiñas* (sea scallops).

Ferrol

pop 70,550

For a town with leftist leanings, it's no small irony that Franco was born here (at Calle María 136) in 1892. His equestrian statue dominated Plaza de España until 2002, when it was removed to the naval dockyards. Ferrol has a substantial maritime heritage and a lively centre.

The **city tourist office** (☎ 981 44 67 00; Praza Porta Nova; 10am-2pm & 5-8pm Mon-Fri, 10.30am-2pm

Sat) is a 10-minute walk east of the bus and train stations.

Should you choose to explore the city centre, head down to busy Praza de España. Join the evening crowds strolling along pedestrianised Rúa Real, lined with cafés and shops, and admire some of the older, more elegant buildings scattered along parallel Rúa Magdalena.

Half a block beyond the Praza de Armas you'll find **Hostal Real** (☎ 981 36 92 55; www .hostalrealferrol.com; Rúa de Dolores 11; s/d €36/45;), with modern units facing a pedestrian thoroughfare. There are cheaper *hospedajes* on Rúa Pardo Baixo.

Restaurante Coté (Rúa Pardo Baixo 19; menú 7.80) is one of several similarly priced places on this street where you can survey the seafood offerings through the window.

Hourly buses run to A Coruña (€5.50, 50 minutes), and there are good services to Santiago de Compostela (€7.55), most via Pontedeume, Pontevedra and Vigo. Four buses go daily to Viveiro and two to Madrid. Three Renfe trains connect Ferrol daily with A Coruña (from €3.30) via Betanzos, and four FEVE trains head east to Viveiro and Ribadeo.

Cedeira

pop 4720

You could give Ferrol a miss and head for Cedeira, 38km up the coast. En route, after about 16km, is **Valdoviño**, with the beautiful Praia Frouxeira. Just beyond Valdoviño, **Praia de Pantín** hosts an international surfing competition in early September.

Cedeira sits at the inland end of the pretty Ría de Cedeira. The older nucleus fronts the river with traditional *galerías*, while across two parallel bridges on the modern side of town is the pleasant Praia da Magdalena. Around the headland to the south is the more appealing **Praia de Vilarrube**, a protected dunes/wetlands area.

Cedeira's **tourist office** (☎ 981 48 21 87; Calle Ezequiel López 17; 10.30am-1.30pm & 5-8pm Mon-Fri, 10.30am-2pm Sat Apr-Sep) is in the old town.

For a nice hour or two's stroll, walk oceanward along the waterfront to the fishing port, climb up beside the old fort above it and then walk out onto the headland overlooking the mouth of the Ría de Cedeira. The rockier sections of the coast here produce rich harvests of *percebes* (barnacles), a much-coveted (and expensive) delicacy throughout Spain.

SLEEPING & EATING
You should phone ahead in August for bookings.

Habitaciones El Puente (☎ 981 48 00 87; Calle Ortigueira 1; s/d €15/20) By the western bridge, this is clean and quiet, and upper rooms have outstanding *ría* views.

Hostal Brisa (☎ 981 48 10 54; Arriba da Ponte 19; s/d €25/35) On the other side of the same bridge, this affably managed place offers rooms of variable size and ventilation, but all are in good shape.

Hostal Chelsea (☎ 981 48 23 40; Praza Sagrado Corazón 9; d €40) Steps from the town beach, this apartment block has cheerful rooms.

Mesón Muiño Kilowatio (☎ 981 48 26 90; Rúa do Mariñeiro 12; raciónes €6-10) Stop by this popular locale, on the waterfront of the old town, for a large portion of *marraxo* (a type of shark) and a cold beer.

Restaurante A Revolta (☎ 981 48 07 64; Calle Fraga Iribame; menú €7.20) Down by the beach, this is a good place to sample *percebes* (ración €12) or whatever else was netted earlier in the day.

Taberna do Puntal (☎ 981 48 05 32; tortillas €4; ☢ closed Tue) Along the road towards Vilarrube beach is this lively tavern, serving exquisitely gooey tortillas and a superior selection of Ribeiro wines.

Cafetería Plaza (☎ 981 48 20 35; Praza de Galicia 1) One of many establishments backing onto Praza Sagrado Corazón on the newer side of town, this café does breakfasts, juices and pastries year-round.

Café A Marina (Rúa do Mariñero 5) On the other side of the *ría* towards the port, fishermen gather here for news and the best cup of coffee in town.

GETTING THERE & AWAY
By bus, you'll need to change in Ferrol, from where Rialsa runs up to eight buses daily (€2.60).

Serra da Capelada
North of Cedeira it only gets better. On the road to San Andrés de Teixido you exchange the ever-changing horizons of the *rías* for higher, wilder ground. The Serra da Capelada is heavily wooded and, instead of milestones, the winding road is regularly

marked by spectacular *miradores* (lookouts) over some of the sheerest Atlantic coast in Europe. Windy even on a hot summer day, this territory can be downright fear-inspiring in a winter storm.

Wild horses still mingle here with cattle and late June tends to be the time for the *curro*, the festive roundup and breaking in of these free-spirited animals.

SAN ANDRÉS DE TEIXIDO
Along a particularly pretty stretch of coast, this hamlet is renowned as a sanctuary of relics of St Andrew. Spaniards flock to the sanctuary and fill up bottles with spring water from the **Fonte do Santo**. Anyone with a vehicle should take this route just for the views.

CABO ORTEGAL
Another 20km northeast is Cabo Ortegal, the mother of Spanish capes. Great stone shafts drop sheer into the ocean from such a height that the waves crashing onto the rocks below seem pitifully – and deceptively – benign. The cape, which marks the meeting of the Atlantic Ocean and Cantabrian Sea, is 3.5km beyond the workaday town of **Cariño**. Buses run to Cariño from Ferrol, Cedeira and Ortigueira, and there are three **hostales**.

Cariño to Viveiro
From Cariño the road roughly follows the Ría de Ortigueira southwards to the Río Mera. The area is rich in bird life and the only town of any consequence is **Ortigueira**, a fishing town on the bus route and FEVE railway line between Ferrol and Viveiros, and the site of a major Celtic music festival held in July (see Galicia's Top Five Festivals, p549).

Otherwise, you'd be better off continuing northeast to **O Barqueiro**, a Galician fishing village as you might imagine one, again on the Ferrol–Viveiro bus route and railway line. White houses with slate-tile roofs cascade down to a small protected port. There's little to do but watch the day's catch come in, but that's the point – this is the real thing. There are three places to stay and eat on the waterfront. Try **Hostal O'Forno** (☎ 981 41 41 24; r €42).

Campers should push on to the smaller **Porto de Bares**, 2km past Vila de Bares, boasting a lovely crescent beach. **Restaurante La Marina** (☎ 981 41 40 01) does a superb paella (€12 per person). A side road leads to the **Punta da**

Estaca de Bares, Spain's most northerly point. From the lighthouse, a trail follows the spine of the serpentine outcrop almost to its end.

The coast eastwards to Viveiro is broken up by several decent **beaches**. Choose one at least 5km from Viveiro, before the built-up stretch of beach begins.

Viveiro
pop 6460
Behind the grand **Puerta de Carlos V** (the most impressive of Viveiro's three remaining medieval gates) lies a straggle of cobbled lanes and plazas where little has changed since the town was rebuilt after a fire in 1540. Directly up the road past Praza Maior is the **Iglesia de Santa María do Campo**, displaying Romanesque and Gothic features. Nearby is a bad-taste reproduction of Lourdes, while to the north the 14th-century **Iglesia de San Francisco** features an extraordinary apse with tall, slender stained-glass windows.

GALICIA'S TOP FIVE FESTIVALS

Perhaps the best setting in which to enjoy Galicia's musical heritage is at its myriad summer folk festivals. These summits bring together players of Celtic traditional music from within the region and from beyond its borders, with groups from Asturias, Brittany, Ireland and as far away as Nova Scotia sharing their roots.

■ **Ortigueira International Celtic Music Festival** (☎ 981 40 00 00; www.festival deortigueira.com) Rías Altas; second weekend in July.

■ **Morrazo-Moaña Inter-Celtic Music Festival** (☎ 986 31 01 00) Peninsula de Morrazo between the Rías of Pontevedra and Vigo; last weekend in July.

■ **Festa da Carballeira** (☎ 981 70 83 03) Zas, Costa de Morte region, 40km northwest of Santiago de Compostela; first weekend in August.

■ **Festival Celta de Pardiñas** (☎ 982 37 01 09) Guitiriz, midway between A Coruña and Lugo; first weekend in August.

■ **Festival Celta dos Irmandiños** (☎ 607 73 54 24) Moeche, 20km northeast of Ferrol; second-last weekend in August.

A **tourist kiosk** (☎ 982 56 08 79; Avenida Benito Galcerán; ◷ 10.45-2pm & 5-8pm) is opposite the small bus station (north along the waterfront from the Puerta de Carlos V).

Just below Santa María church, **Fonda Nuevo Mundo** (☎ 982 56 00 25; Rúa de Teodoro de Quirós 14; s/d with shared bathroom €13/25) is a modest and clean hostelry. Try for a room in one of the *galerías*.

Hotel Vila (☎ 982 56 13 31; Calle Nicolás Cora Montenegro 57; s/d €37/43) is located about 300m up the main street from the port and is a functional place to stay.

There are more **hostales** and a couple of **camping grounds** on the beaches outside town, particularly at Praia de Covas.

Marisquería Serra (☎ 982 71 55 62; Rúa de Antonio Bas 2; raciónes €4.20-9) is the place for a decent seafood meal.

Rúa Pastor Díaz presents a few appealing options: try **El Café** (17 Rúa Pastor Díaz) for coffee or **Fragata** (32 Rúa Pastor Díaz) for pizza.

For a nightcap, Rúa Pérez das Mariñas and Rúa Almirante Chicarro have bars.

FEVE trains between Ferrol, and Oviedo stop at Viveiro. Six buses operate on most days to A Coruña (€11.30, 3¼ hours), Ferrol and Lugo and a couple go on weekdays to Ribadeo (€4.35).

Mondoñedo
pop 2090 / elevation 139m
Compared with the natural spectacles of northwestern Galicia's Atlantic coast, the offerings east of Viveiro cut a poor figure. For much of the trip towards Asturias the road lies well inland, and what beaches there are pale before their cousins further west and east.

By contrast, a detour inland from Foz up the Río Masma to Mondoñedo is rewarding. First settled in the 5th century by restless migrants from Brittany, Mondoñedo became a religious centre and provincial capital in the medieval kingdom of Galicia. Its down-at-heel appearance today in no way diminishes its interest.

The **tourist office** (☎ 982 50 71 77) is just off Praza de España, near the impressive **cathedral**. Also fronting the old square is the **Palacio Episcopal**. The **Fonte Vella** (Old Fountain), a short walk south, was built in 1548.

Hostal Central (☎ 982 52 10 50; Rúa Andrés Baamonde 3; r €36) occupies the upper floors of an attractive building across from the town hall. For more unusual and historic lodging, try the **Hospedaje Seminario** (☎ 982 52 10 00; Praza do Seminario; s/d €19.25/32), housed in the 18th-century Santa Catalina seminary, with spartan but OK rooms.

There are several buses operating to Lugo, Ribadeo and Viveiro.

Ribadeo

The best thing about this frontier town is its broad *ría*. The impressive **Ponte dos Santos** crosses the waterway that, becoming the Río Eo further inland, marks the regional border with Asturias for some 30km south. A busy little place, Ribadeo has a tranquil, palm-studded central square, the Praza de España, highlighted by the modernist Torre de los Moreno with a glazed ceramic dome. The area around this plaza is awash with hotels: **Hotel Mediante** (☎ 982 13 04 53; mediante@interbook.net; Praza de España 16; r €60) is recommended for its rooms and its restaurant.

Two daily FEVE trains run along the Asturian coast to/from Oviedo; four run to/from Ferrol. Half a dozen daily buses head to/from Oviedo and Luarca, and a few to/from Lugo, and (except weekends) Viveiro.

COSTA DA MORTE

On one of those rare, hot sunny days you could be forgiven for thinking that the tales of danger surrounding this stretch of the Atlantic seaboard – the 'Death Coast' – are exaggerated. But the idyllic landscape can undergo a rapid transformation when ocean mists blow in and envelop the whole region.

The A55 tollway from A Coruña bypasses the beginning of the Costa da Morte, running inland to Carballo. From there, a reasonable road heads northwest to Malpica de Bergantiños, passing through Buño, which is known for its ceramics. The minor coastal road out of A Coruña skirts a few beaches, such as Playa de Barrañán and Playa de Sorrizo, where you must be mindful of the currents. The Costa da Morte begins at unassuming Caión.

Arriva (☎ 902 27 74 82) runs buses from Santiago de Compostela and A Coruña to many places on the Costa da Morte.

MALPICA DE BERGANTIÑOS

pop 3210

Malpica has a sandy beach on one side and a busy port on the other. The village centre is lively, and some bars and eateries face the beach. Off the coast you can see the **Illas Sisargas**, where gulls nest, at least those that managed to survive the *Prestige* oil spill.

Hostal JB (☎ 981 72 19 06; Rueiro da Praia 3; s/d €22.50/38.50) has lovely rooms, some overhanging the beach.

Hostal Panchito (☎ 981 72 30 07; Praza de Villar Amigo 5; d €36.05) is upstairs from a busy fishermen's café near the end of the main street.

For seafood, try **Restaurante Isidoro** (☎ 981 72 00 04; Plaza Santa Lucía), in the alley next to Café Panchito, serving generous tapas, or **O'Burato** (☎ 981 72 00 57), across the way, specialising in *caldeirada* (€12), simmered fish in a spicy red sauce.

Up to seven daily buses come here from A Coruña (€5.35), but just one from Santiago de Compostela on Saturday and Sunday.

LAXE, CAMELLE & AROUND

If you're driving down the coast, make first for **Ponteceso**, a local crossroads. Nearby **Laxe** (population 1830) has a sweeping beach, though unfortunately its diminutive historic core is overshadowed by modern buildings.

Hostal Bahía (☎ 981 72 82 07; www.bahialaxe .com; Avenida Generalísimo 24; s/d €30/40) has 22 well-maintained rooms; the more expensive ones have stupendous terraces overlooking the port. Owner Manuel is a mine of information about the best walks in the district. **Restaurante Sardiñera** (☎ 981 72 80 29; Rosalía de Castro 51) serves heaped helpings of flavoursome local fare.

Up to five buses run daily to/from A Coruña (€6.50), with a change in Carballo; there's also a bus Monday to Friday from Santiago de Compostela with Aucasa (€5.80).

One lovely two-day, 40km walk, outlined in Lonely Planet's *Walking in Spain*, takes you southwest along the coast to Camariñas. Along the way are **Praia de Traba**, a 2km sweep of sand that remains virtually deserted even in mid-August, and the laid-back fishing village of **Camelle**, where you can spend the night: **A Molinera** (☎ 981 71 03 28; Rúa Principal 79; apt from €40) has excellent self-catering apartments.

Towards the end of Camelle's pier you'll find what's left of the **Museo do Alemán**, a

---

THE BIG SPILL

On 13 November 2002 the ageing, single-hull tanker *Prestige*, en route to delivering 77,000 tonnes of low-grade oil to Singapore, hit stormy seas some 200km west of Vigo. One of the ship's tanks ruptured, spilling 5000 tonnes of cargo into the Atlantic. Six days later, the *Prestige* split in two and sank, and oil continued leaking at the rate of 125 tonnes per day. It wasn't until July 2003 that the fissures in the hull were sealed (by robots). In all, around 60,000 tonnes of oil escaped, over three times as much as initial estimates by the government, which assured the leak would cease after the ship sank.

Initially worst hit was the Costa da Morte, with its many fishing villages. Two 'black tides' left the coast from A Coruña to Fisterra smothered in black sludge, along with extensive stretches north of A Coruña. Galicia's scenic Rías Altas, with their rich shellfish beds, managed to escape the worst. The oil spread into the Bay of Biscay to strike the coasts of Asturias, Cantabria and as far as the southwest coast of France, leaving more than 3000km of coastline affected and long-term damages estimated at 4.5 billion euros. Some 300,000 seabirds of over 70 species were among the casualties.

It was Spain's worst ecological disaster in history. The government's deception and lackadaisical response gave birth to a grassroots political movement, Nunca Máis (Never Again), which mobilised spontaneously to clean up the coast, aided by volunteers from all over Europe.

Government compensation somewhat lessened the blow to fishermen, who went back to work in spring 2003, although environmentalists claimed that the fishing ban had been lifted too soon.

Two years later many Galicians would like to put the disaster behind them. The effects on Costa da Morte and Rías Baixas beaches have been seemingly erased, though concerns linger over remaining seabed deposits, and consequent destruction of shellfish habitat and risks to consumers of Galician seafood. Most fishermen will tell you that seafood stocks are back to normal, while marine scientists continue to warn that carcinogenic traces could remain for up to a decade.

---

garden of quirky sculpture created by an eccentric, German, long-time resident. Local inhabitants say the sculptor, known simply as Man, was so devastated by the *Prestige* spill, which splotched his fanciful figures black, that he died shortly afterwards, apparently sapped of his will to live. The museum has been left to decay.

Just west of Camelle is **Arou**, a little-visited fishing village with a couple of pleasant swimming areas.

A passable dirt track leads off from near Arou towards **Ensenada de Trece**, a quiet beach, and eventually to the Camariñas–Cabo Vilán road. After 10km the track passes the **Cemiterio dos Ingleses** (English Cemetery), the burial ground for the few bodies recovered from an 1890 shipwreck in which 170 British cadets drowned.

CAMARIÑAS
pop 2760

The fishing village of Camariñas is a place of simple charms: cobblestoned lanes wind past cubist houses, and elderly inhabitants

gather at the port like seagulls. You'll see women making the traditional *encaixe* (lacework) in the streets. The **Museo de Encaixe** (☎ 981 73 63 40; Praza Insuela; admission €1.20; ☑ 11am-2pm & 4-8pm Tue-Sun Jun-Oct) is by the town hall.

While you're here, take a look at **Cabo Vilán**, an impressive cape with a 25m lighthouse, 5km northwest of the town.

Hostal Scala (☎ 981 73 71 09; Tras Playa 6; r €36), over a burger bar, is bright and clean.

Hostal Dársena (☎ 981 73 63 31; Calle Alcalde Noguera Patiño 20; r €30) has well-scrubbed, decent-sized units with balconies facing the docks, and a restaurant that serves good seafood.

Up to three buses run daily to/from Santiago de Compostela (two hours, €8.25), with a change in Baio, and two to four daily from A Coruña (two hours, €8.60).

MUXÍA & AROUND

Getting to/from Camariñas you'll pass through Ponte do Porto, on the Río Grande. The coastal road south for Os Muiños (Molinos) passes the pretty hamlet of **Cereixo** and heads down a narrow, shaded road.

Along this enchanting route, near Leis, you'll find one of the most inviting beaches along the Costa da Morte, **Praia do Lago**. The sand fronts the ocean and also a quiet river. There are a couple of camping grounds and a *hostal*.

Muxía itself (population 1670) is nothing special, but you can head out to **Punta da Barca**, which affords good views of the coast. The rocks in front of the baroque **Santuario de Nuestra Señora de la Barca** are the scene of a popular *romería* (festive pilgrimage) in mid-September.

Hostal La Cruz (☎ 981 74 20 84; Avenida López Abente 44; s/d €43.50/53.50) has bright rooms, great views and a restaurant.

Two or three buses travel daily to/from A Coruña, with a change at either Vimianzo or Laxe.

FISTERRA & AROUND

Those wandering about the Costa da Morte will probably want to make it to Galicia's version of England's Land's End, **Cabo Fisterra** (Castilian: Cabo Finisterre), where Spain stops and the Atlantic begins. Although this is *not* mainland Spain's westernmost point (Cabo Touriñán, 18km north, has that distinction), it's certainly an impressive spot.

From the town of Fisterra it's 3.5km to the cape. To the right on the way out is the 12th-century **Iglesia de Santa María das Areas**, a mix of Romanesque, Gothic and baroque. The best views of the coast are to be had by climbing up the track, beginning about 600m from the church, to **Monte Facho** and **Monte de San Guillerme**. The area is laced with myth and superstition, and they say childless couples used to come up here to improve their chances of conception.

Just off the main square in the older part of Fisterra, **Pensión Casa Velay** (☎ 981 74 01 27; Rúa La Cerca 1; r with/without bathroom €24/30) has simple rooms, some facing the harbour. The gregarious owners also run a pleasant sea-view restaurant. Otherwise, you could go round the corner to **Mesón O Fragón** (☎ 981 74 04 29; mains €15), where good choices include *kokotxas a la cazuela* (cod chin stew) and *zorza* (spiced pork over potatoes).

Up to six buses daily come from A Coruña (€10.35), and up to seven come from Santiago de Compostela (€10), some requiring a change in Baio.

TOWARDS THE RÍAS BAIXAS

The southernmost stretch of the Costa da Morte has its moments. From the village of **Ézaro**, 25km southwest of Fisterra, a 2.5km side-road leads up to a *mirador* (lookout point) with breathtaking views over the Atlantic.

O Pindo is a cute fishing village set back on a shallow, tranquil bay. Here you'll find **Hospedaje La Morada** (☎ 981 76 48 70; s/d €20/30), with a restaurant.

Another 10km south you reach the long, sandy Playa de Carnota – usually not too crowded and fine if the wind isn't up. Towards the southern end, **Carnota** town is renowned as home to Galicia's longest *hórreo* (grain store) – 34.5m long, it was built late in the 18th century.

RÍAS BAIXAS

The four great estuaries of Galicia's south, the Rías Baixas (Castilian: Rías Bajas), are the grandest of all the *rías* that indent the length of the Galician coast and are justifiably well known. There are plenty of beaches and several relatively low-key resorts, and in summer good weather is a better bet here than further north. You may be a little disappointed with the dull, built-up stretches to be found along every *ría*, and by the traffic and 'House Full' signs in summer, but there are enough pretty villages and expanses of beautiful shore to keep most of us happy. Throw in the Islas Cíes, lovely old Pontevedra and bustling Vigo, and you have a travel cocktail that's hard to beat.

Getting around the Rías Baixas is, as usual, easiest with your own wheels, but buses do enable you to reach most places, occasionally with the aid of a bit of footwork. Santiago de Compostela is a good enough stepping-off point for the northern *rías*; Pontevedra and Vigo are the main hubs for the south.

The following sections start at the inland end of each *ría* and work outwards, but if you have a vehicle an appealing option is simply to follow the coast around from one *ría* to the next: the coastal C550 road runs 400km from Cée on the Costa da Morte to Tui on the Portuguese border – a straight-line distance of just 110km!

RÍA DE MUROS Y NOIA
Noia
pop 7690

Noia's old centre preserves a few reminders of its glory days, in particular, the Gothic **Igrexa de San Martiño** (Praza do Tapal). Near the old centre, the former **Igrexa de Santa María A Nova** (☎ 981 82 41 69; Carreiriña do Escultor Ferreiro; admission free; 10.30am-1.30pm & 4-6pm Mon-Sat), together with its cemetery, forms a unique museum of headstones and funerary art.

Hotel Elisardo (☎ 981 82 01 30; Costa do Ferrador 15; r €42) is a small, comfortable lodging near the palm-lined Alameda.

For food and drinks, you can't beat **Tasca Típica** (☎ 981 82 18 42; Rúa Cantón 15), right in the 14th-century Pazo de Costa, up the street from the Igrexa de San Martiño.

Buses run here hourly from Santiago de Compostela, continuing to Muros.

Muros
pop 1950

Founded in the 10th century towards the western end of the *ría*, en route to the Costa da Morte, Muros was long an important port for Santiago de Compostela. It has no great surviving monuments and apart from enjoying a beer or meal on the waterfront, there's not much to detain you, though there's a couple of nice beaches west of town.

South Shore

The main attraction here is the long series of beaches – such as **Praia de Aguieira**, 2km past Portosín. The village of **Porto do Son**, 2km beyond, makes a relaxed stop. On a picturesque headland, 4km southwest, are the remains of a Celtic settlement, the **Castro de Baroña**. The **Centro de Interpretación do Castro de Baroña** (Calle de Fernando Fariña; admission €0.60; 11am-2pm & 7-9pm mid-Jun–mid-Sep), in Porto do Son, provides background. Stretching south from the *castro*, **Praia Area Longa** is the first of a small string of surfing beaches down this side of the *ría*.

Hostal O Chinto (☎ 981 76 70 86; Avenida de Galicia 20; r with shared/private bathroom €18/30), overlooking Porto do Son's little harbour, has 12 small, clean rooms.

Hotel Villa del Son (☎ 981 85 30 49; Rúa Trincherpe 11; s/d €32/51; P), just back from the harbour, is a little more comfortable.

Drivers could detour to the **Dolmen de Axeitos**, a well-preserved megalithic monu-

ment, signposted between Xuño and Ribeira; and on to **Corrubedo** at the tip of the peninsula, with beaches either side of town, a lighthouse at the end of the road and a few relaxed bars around its small harbour.

RÍA DE AROUSA
Padrón
pop 2800

The hottest thing to come out of Padrón is peppers. That's right, *pimientos de Padrón* – shrivelled little green things that taste very good, but beware the odd *very* hot one. Franciscan friars imported them from Mexico in the 16th century and the whole area now grows them to meet the demand.

This town where Santiago's corpse supposedly arrived in Galicia also prides itself as the former home of Galician poet Rosalía de Castro, who died here in 1885. The **Casa Museo Rosalía de Castro** (☎ 981 81 12 04; 10am-1.30pm & 4-7pm Tue-Sat Sep-Jun, 10am-1.30pm Sun), just behind the train station, is the prime stop in the so-called Ruta Rosaliana that has been mapped out around this region.

Hostal del Jardín (☎ 981 81 09 50; Rúa de Salgado Araujo 3; r €40), a pretty place with spacious rooms, is opposite the park on the road to the train station.

Buses run hourly on weekdays to/from Santiago de Compostela, Pontevedra and Vigo, less often on weekends, and a few travel daily to/from Noia, Cambados and O Grove.

Catoira

About 15km from Padrón down the southern side of the Río Ulla, which shortly afterwards widens into the Ría de Arousa, stand the **Torres do Oeste** at Catoira. These towers are what remains of Castellum Honesti, the medieval castle that was the key in protecting (not always successfully) Santiago de Compostela against Norman landings. On the first Sunday of August, a Viking landing is staged here as part of a boisterous fiesta, the **Romería Vikinga**.

Illa de Arousa

Southwest of Catoira you could head straight past **Vilagarcía de Arousa** and **Vilanova de Arousa** and make for the Illa de Arousa, an island connected to the mainland by a 2km-long bridge. The small town on the island lives mainly from fishing and the whole place has a low profile. Some of the beaches facing the mainland are very pleasant and protected, with comparatively warm water. A walking trail runs around the 29km coastline. The southern part of the island forms the **Parque Natural Carreirón**, where you'll find dunes, marshlands and abundant bird life.

Camping Salinas (☎ 986 52 74 44; per person/tent/car €4.10/4/4; ☼ Jun-Sep) and **Camping El Edén** (☎ 986 52 73 78; per person/tent/car €4.10/3.75/3.40; ☼ Jun-Sep) are on Playa de Salinas, facing the mainland, and there are a couple of mid-range hotels in the town.

Monbus (☎ 902 15 87 78) has a few daily buses that link the island with Vilanova and Vilagarcía, either of which has connections for Santiago de Compostela, Cambados and O Grove. The José Núñez Barros railway line operates to/from Pontevedra up to five times daily.

Cambados
pop 6310

Founded by the Visigoths and a victim of constant harrying by Vikings in the 9th and 10th centuries, Cambados is today a peaceful seaside town. At the north end of the town centre is the magnificent **Praza de Fefiñáns**, bordered on two sides by a grand 16th-century *pazo* (mansion) and on another by the 15th-century **Igrexa de San Bieito**. The **tourist information kiosk** (☎ 986 52 07 86; Avenida de Galicia; ☼ 10am-2pm & 4.30-6pm or 7pm), near the bus station. will give you a map of Albariño wineries, many of which are open for visits daily.

You could incorporate a winery or two into a pretty inland excursion to **San Salvador de Meis**, with a Romanesque church, and the Cistercian **Mosteiro de Armenteira**, founded in 1162.

SLEEPING & EATING
Hostal Pazos Feijoo (☎ 986 54 28 10; Rúa de Curros Enríquez 1; r €37) One street inland from the bus station, this is a no-frills option.

Hotel A Traíña (☎ 986 52 46 84; www.atraina.com; Rúa Triana 2; r €60 incl breakfast) One of a pair of lovely wine-tasting salon/lodgings by the waterfront bordering the old town.

For food, take a walk beside the *parador* up cobbled Rúa Príncipe and Rúa Real towards Praza de Fefiñáns. Here you'll find various *vinotecas* (wine shops) and res-

taurants flogging what can be a very fine drop of wine.

Vinoteca As Pias (☎ 629 86 20 79; Albergue 1) Off Praza das Rodas, this is a particularly attractive *vinoteca*, also serving tasty tapas and *tostas*.

Los Amigos (☎ 986 52 06 76; Rúa Real 7; platos combinados €5-12) This is one of the cheaper eateries in the zone. If you're on the move, grab one of its big takeaway *bocadillos* (filled rolls) from €2.

GETTING THERE & AWAY
Up to five buses a day run to/from Santiago de Compostela (€4.30, one hour), up to 10 to/from Pontevedra (€2.15) and up to seven to/from O Grove (some via Sanxenxo).

O Grove
pop 7400

How you react to O Grove may depend on the weather. It's a strange mix of England's Blackpool and some of Italy's Adriatic 'family' resorts. In summer you'll find little more than hotel blocks, mediocre nightclubs and Galicia's unpredictable climate. In winter most of the above is closed and the weather is worse.

The **tourist office** (☎ 986 73 14 15, www.turism ogrove.com; Praza do Corgo 1; ☼ 10am-2pm & 4-7pm Mon-Sat, 11am-2pm Sun) is located beside the marina.

Nature enthusiasts can enjoy a visit to the **Centro de Visitantes A Siradella** (☎ 986 68 02 84; ☼ 10am-2pm & 4-8.30pm Mon-Fri, 11am-2pm Sat & Sun), above the town in a forested area, with excellent displays on the district's plentiful marine and bird life. There's also **acquarium-galicia** (☎ 986 73 15 15; admission €9; ☼ 10am-8pm Mon-Fri, 10am-9pm Sat & Sun) at Punta Moreiras on the northwest side of the O Grove peninsula, with sea creatures mainly from the Galician coasts.

In steady weather, numerous companies run *ría* cruises, chiefly to look at the **bateas** – platforms where mussels, oysters and scallops are cultivated. Tours, including mussel tastings, cost €12 per person and run for 1½ hours.

The best beach in the area is **Praia A Lanzada** (p558), on the isthmus linking O Grove to the mainland.

SLEEPING & EATING
There are half a dozen camping grounds on the west side of the O Grove peninsula,

north of Praia A Lanzada. In town, accommodation is spread along Rúa Castelao and by the bridge to A Toxa island.

Hostal Montesol (☎ 986 73 09 16; Rúa Castelao 160; r €40) On the waterfront, this *hostal* offers comfy beds and panoramic *ría* views.

Hostal María Aguiño (☎ 986 73 30 07; Rúa de Pablo Iglesias 26; r €30) Family-run, offers small but homey rooms.

Of the slew of large seafood houses along Beiramar, **O Crisol** (☎ 986 73 00 99; Rúa de Hospital 10; fish dishes €14) is most warmly recommended, while **Restaurante Dorna** (☎ 986 73 18 42; Rúa de Castelao 150; mains €6-14), near the bridge, is renowned for its traditional kitchen.

GETTING THERE & AWAY

Buses run to/from Cambados, Pontevedra, Santiago de Compostela and elsewhere. The bus station is on Beiramar, by the port.

PONTEVEDRA

pop 55,530 / elevation 290m

Galicia's smallest provincial capital has managed to preserve intact a classic old centre backing on to the Río Lérez – ideal for simply wandering around and poking one's nose into all sorts of nooks and crannies.

History

Known to the Romans as Ad Duos Pontes (Two Bridges), Pontevedra reached the height of its glory in the 16th century, when it was the biggest city in Galicia and an important port. Columbus' flagship, the *Santa María*, was built here, and a local legend that the Genoese explorer was born in Pontevedra persists to this day. In the 17th century the city began to decline in the face of growing competition in the *ría* and the silting up of its port. Nevertheless, Pontevedra was made provincial capital in 1835 and today tourism is proving a healthy boon.

Orientation & Information

The historic centre is clearly confined within a rough circle drawn by the former city walls. Inside this area you'll find several places to stay, all your eating and drinking options, and much of what you'll want to see.

Banks and other offices lie on or near Rúa de Michelena, the main drag of the newer town.

Ambulatorio Virgen Peregrina (☎ 986 85 27 99; Rúa de Maestranza) Emergency medical clinic.
Ciber Las Ruinas (Rúa do Marqués de Riestra 21; per hr €1.80)
Municipal tourist information kiosk (☎ 986 84 85 52; Praza de España; ☾ 10.30am-1.30pm & 4.30-7.30pm Mon-Sat Jun-Oct)
Regional tourist office (☎ 986 85 08 14; Rúa Xeneral Gutiérrez Mellado 3; ☾ 10am-2pm & 4-6pm Mon-Fri, 10am-12.30pm Sat Oct-Jun, 10am-2pm & 4-7.30pm Jul-Sep)

Sights

HISTORIC CENTRE

Starting at the southeastern edge of the old town, you can't miss the distinctive curved façade of the **Santuario da Virxe Peregrina**, an 18th-century caprice with a distinctly Portuguese flavour. Virtually across the street is the broad **Praza da Ferrería**, colonnaded on one side and displaying an eclectic collection of buildings dating as far back as the 15th century. Set back from Praza da Ferrería in its own gardens is the **Igrexa de San Francisco**, believed to have been founded personally by St Francis of Assisi when on pilgrimage to Santiago de Compostela. What was the adjacent convent is now the local tax office.

Head down Rúa da Pasantería and you emerge in **Praza da Leña**, one of Pontevedra's most enchanting niches, partly colonnaded and with a *cruceiro* (wayside crucifix) in the middle. Just off it lies the **Museo Provincial** (☎ 986 85 14 55; Rúa Pasantería 10; admission free; ☾ at least 10am-1.30pm & 5-8pm Tue-Sat, 11am-2pm Sun), two 18th-century palaces joined by an arch. The collection ranges from Bronze Age finds to Renaissance painting. A third building, around the corner on Rúa de Padre Sarmiento, houses contemporary Galician art, as well as touring exhibitions.

Further west, the area known as **As Cinco Rúas** is a hub of Pontevedra nightlife. The tiny Praza das Cinco Rúas, where five lanes converge, is marked by a *cruceiro*.

West of Praza das Cinco Rúas, up Rúa de Isabel II, stands the **Basílica de Santa María** (☾ 10am-1pm & 5-9pm), a mainly Gothic church with a whiff of Plateresque and Portuguese Manueline influences. Signposted on the way up is the **Santuario das Aparicións**, a chapel and lodgings where the Virgin Mary is said to have appeared to Lucía of Fátima, the early-20th-century child visionary from Fátima in Portugal.

PONTEVEDRA

| | 0 | 200 m |
| | 0 | 0.1 miles |

INFORMATION
Ambulatorio Virgen Peregrina............1 A4
Ciber Las Ruinas.............................2 B4
Municipal Tourist Information Kiosk...3 B4
Post Office....................................4 C5
Regional Tourist Office.....................5 B4
Summer Tourist Information Kiosk......6 C4

SIGHTS & ACTIVITIES (pp555-6)
Basílica de Santa María.....................7 B3
Igrexa de San Bartolomeu.................8 D3
Igrexa de San Francisco...................9 D4
Mercado....................................10 D3
Museo Provincial Sarmiento Building..11 D4
Museo Provincial...........................12 D4
Ruínas de San Domingos..................13 B4
Santuario da Virxe Peregrina............14 C5
Santuario das Aparicións.................15 B3

SLEEPING (p557)
Casa Alicia..................................16 B3
Hospedaje Casa Maruja..................17 B3
Hospedaje Margó..........................18 B5
Hospedaje Penelas.........................19 B3
Hotel Rúas..................................20 D4
Parador Casa del Barón...................21 C2

EATING (p557)
Bar Chiruca.................................22 C4
Casa Fidel - O'Pulpeiro...................23 C4
Casa Filgueira..............................24 D4
El Masón....................................25 D3
O'Noso Bar.................................26 C3

DRINKING (p557)
Gloria...................................(see 16)

ENTERTAINMENT (p557)
Carabas.....................................27 D5
Madrila.....................................28 D5

TRANSPORT (p557)
Bus No 2 to Train Station................29 B4

OTHER
Concello.....................................30 B4
Teatro Principal...........................31 B3

NEW TOWN

The elegant Alameda and Xardíns de Vicenti spread southwest of the historic centre and together form modern Pontevedra's green lung. Opposite one end of the Alameda are the **Ruínas de San Domingos**, a ruined 14th-century church now housing part of the Museo Provincial's archaeological collection.

Festivals & Events

The **Festas da Peregrina**, held for a week in mid-August, features a big fun fair on the Alameda and concerts in Praza da Ferrería. In late July, the **Festival Internacional de Jazz de Pontevedra** (www.jazzpontevedra.com) attracts top-notch jazz musicians from around the world.

Sleeping

There are just five lodgings within the historic core of town.

Hospedaje Casa Maruja (☎ 986 85 49 01; Avenida de Santa María 12; s/d €25/37) The best budget bet has 10 spotless rooms, all with private bathroom, and balconies over a tranquil plaza.

Hotel Rúas (☎ 986 84 64 16; hotelruas@terra.es; Rúa de Padre Sarmiento 20; s/d €42/61; 🕮) Flanked by two plazas, Hotel Rúas is a sleek, comfortable place to spend the night.

Parador Casa del Barón (☎ 986 85 58 00; pontevedra@parador.es; Rúa do Barón 19; s/d €97/121) Housed in a large Renaissance/neoclassical mansion, this is one of Spain's more appealing paradors.

Casa Alicia (☎ 986 85 70 79; Avenida de Santa María 5; d with shared bathroom €30) Across from Casa Maruja is this recently refurbished place on the upper levels of a fine old stone building.

Hospedaje Penelas (☎ 986 85 57 05; Rúa Alta 17; s/d with shared bathroom €18/30) Never mind the funky entryway: upstairs are four perfectly good rooms with views.

Hospedaje Margó (☎ 986 85 26 94; Rúa do Marqués de Riestra 4; r with shared/private bathroom €15/18) Despite the creaky floors and poorly lit stairwell, this low-rent guesthouse just outside the old town isn't bad. Inquire at the bakery next door (closed after 10pm).

Eating

Praza da Leña and Rúa Figueroa harbour a cluster of popular eateries, most doling out serves of seafood for €2.50 to €10.

Casa Filgueira (☎ 986 85 88 15; Eirado da Leña) Among other items from its delectable tapas list, you'll want to try the *filloas* (€2.75) – crepes stuffed with oyster mushrooms, salt cod and so on.

Bar Chiruca (Rúa Figueroa 17; 🕮 closed Sun) A good place to sample Galician *empanadas* (pies).

El Masón (☎ 986 89 66 10; Rúa Alta 4; mains €6-9) A stylish gathering place, El Masón serves delicious, though reasonably priced, food and plenty of Rías Baixas wines.

The Cinco Rúas area is another Pontevedra eating and drinking hub.

Casa Fidel – O' Pulpeiro (☎ 986 85 12 34; Rúa de San Nicolás 7; pulpo a la gallega €7) The zone's octopus specialist: look for the boiling tubs of chopped-up cephalopod.

O' Noso Bar (Rúa de San Nicolás 5; raciónes €4.50-5.50) You can eat cheaply and abundantly here,

except on Saturday night when it becomes a rowdy music bar.

Drinking

The best places for coffee and people-watching are the cafés along the squares. Praza da Ferrería probably wins on this score.

Gloria (☎ 986 85 12 40; Avenida Santa María 5) This airy, brick-walled space makes a pleasant hang-out between strolls.

For nocturnal drinking, head for the pocket of bars on Rúa do Barón, and then, for some heftier *marcha* (action), up the road to Rúa de Charino – you'll soon get a feel for what's right for you. Much of the activity takes place outside the bars, especially the Praza de Pedreira, whose stately porticoes become the scene of major partying after dark.

For a more bohemian atmosphere, head for **Bar Cabaña** (☎ 986 85 28 24; García Flórez 22; 🕮 from 10.30pm), a subterranean jazz den.

Entertainment

If it's nightclubs you're after, try **Estarlux** (Rúa Cruz Vermella 6; 🕮 from midnight Thu-Sat), with eclectic programming over a 6000-watt system, or check out the cutting-edge discotheques **Madrila** (Rúa de Benito Corbal 14; 🕮 from 4.30am Sat) and **Carabas** (Rúa de Cobián Raffignac 4; 🕮 from 1am Thu-Fri, 3am Sat), southeast of the town centre.

Getting There & Away

The **bus station** (☎ 986 85 24 08; Rúa Calvo Sotelo) is about 1.5km southeast of the town centre. Frequent services link Pontevedra with Vigo (€2.20, 30 minutes). Up to nine buses travelling daily along the A9 motorway stop in Pontevedra en route between Vigo, Santiago de Compostela (€4.70, one hour) and A Coruña; other Santiago-bound buses stop in Padrón. Buses also go to/from Tui, Ourense, Lugo and Madrid. **Monbus** (☎ 902 15 87 78) runs roughly hourly to/from Combarro, Sanxenxo and O Grove (€3.25, one hour).

The **train station** (☎ 986 85 13 13) is across the street from the bus station. Pontevedra is on the Vigo–Santiago de Compostela line, with almost hourly trains to those cities and A Coruña.

Getting Around

Local circle line buses run from the bus and train stations to Praza de España, in front of the Concello (Town Hall) building.

RÍA DE PONTEVEDRA
Mosteiro de Poio

Just northwest of Pontevedra (in fact barely separated from it now) and 3km short of Combarro, the town of Poio is dominated by its grand **monastery** (admission €1.50; ☼ 10am-1.30pm & 4.30-8pm Apr-Oct, 10am-1pm & 4-6pm Nov-Mar). This was long a Benedictine stronghold – the first church here may have been built in the 7th century – but the Benedictines abandoned the site in 1835, to be replaced 55 years later by the Mercedarios (roughly translated, the Fathers of Mercy). The gardens of the 16th-century **Claustro de las Procesiones** are gathered around a baroque fountain.

Hospedería Monasterio de Poio (☎ 986 77 00 00; d with/without bathroom €26/40) offers straightforward lodgings inside the monastery.

Combarro
pop 1150

The fishing village of Combarro, though hardly indifferent to the tourist dollar, has managed to retain some measure of its original character. It possesses a very quaint area of old stone houses and a picturesque string of *hórreos* down near the waterfront.

Hotel Xeito (☎ /fax 986 77 00 39; Avenida da Cruz 35; per person €18), up on the congested main road, is a very friendly place; the rooftop deck alone merits a stay.

O Peirao (☎ 986 77 23 01; Rúa do Mar 6; seafood raciónes €5-10) is the best of several spots among the waterfront *hórreos* where you could enjoy a leisurely meal. The women here bake some amazing *empanadas de berberecho* (cockles) and dessert pies, and in summer they stoke up the sardine grill.

The road west towards Sanxenxo is liberally laced with **hostales**.

Monbus buses between Pontevedra, Sanxenxo and O Grove stop at Combarro.

Sanxenxo
pop 2030

Sanxenxo (Castilian: Sangenjo), 10km west of Combarro, is about as close as Galicia comes to emulating the holiday coast on the Mediterranean. It's a little more stylish than its resort cousin, O Grove, around the coast, and its best beach, **Praia de Silgar**, is fine and sandy, if crowded in summer. There's a **tourist office** (☎ 986 72 02 85; Rúa de Madrid s/n; ☼ 10.30am-1.30pm & 4-8pm Mar-Nov).

Rúa de Carlos Casas, running uphill just east of Praia de Silgar, has a few places offering decent rooms with bathroom at relatively decent prices, the best being **Hotel Casa Román** (☎ 986 72 00 31; www.hotelcasaroman.com; Rúa de Carlos Casas 2; r €45).

For a beachfront location, try **Hotel Minso** (☎ 986 72 01 50; Avenida do Porto 1; s/d €55/99) at the eastern end of Praia de Silgar. Rooms ending in -04 give the best views.

For food and drink, trek a couple of kilometres west to **Portonovo**, where you'll find many **tapas bars** and **seafood eateries**.

Buses between Pontevedra and O Grove (over 20 a day in summer) stop in Saxenxo.

Praia A Lanzada

The coastal road beyond Portonovo is dotted with hotels, *hostales* and camping grounds all the way around to the longest beach in the Ría de Pontevedra – the 2.3km-long, dune-backed A Lanzada, along the west side of the isthmus leading to the O Grove promontory. The beach is free of the resort feel, but it's *not* deserted and remote! O Grove-bound buses will drop you here.

Isla de Ons

One possible diversion from Sanxenxo in summer is to take a boat beyond the mouth of the *ría* to the Isla de Ons, with sandy beaches, cliffs, ruins, walking trails, rich bird life and a **camping area** (☎ 986 68 76 96; camping free). Call at 8pm to book for the next day.

Weather permitting, **Cruceros Rías Baixas** (☎ 986 73 13 43; www.crucerosriasbaixas.com) sails to/from Isla de Ons several times daily (adult/child return €10) from Sanxenxo and Portonovo from July to mid-September. In Sanxenxo, buy tickets at the port, just east of Praia de Silgar. From June to September you can sail to the Isla de Ons up to nine times daily from Bueu on the south side of the *ría*, with **Cruceros Isla de Ons** (☎ 986 32 09 53; www.crucerosillasdeons.com) or **Naviera Illa de Ons** (☎ 986 32 00 48; www.isladeons.net).

South Shore

Don't be put off by the road from Pontevedra to Marín. It's an ugly business that bears little resemblance to what lies beyond.

HÍO & AROUND

Just west of the C550 towards the end of the *ría*, the peaceful little village of Hío has its focal point in Galicia's most remarkable **cruceiro**. This was sculpted during the 19th century from a single block of stone and key passages of Christian teaching, from Adam and Eve's sinful errors through to the taking down of Christ from the cross, are narrated up its length.

About 2.5km north of Hío by paved road is a fairly tranquil sandy beach, **Praia Areabrava**. Another paved road heads 5km roughly southwest from Hío to **Cabo de Home**, where you can ramble over rocky crags and enjoy great views of the Islas Cíes and the Atlantic. Along the way are turn-offs for **Praia de Nerga**, **Praia de Barra** and **Praia de Melide** on the Ría de Vigo.

Hostal Stop (☎ 986 32 94 75; Rúa Igresiario 71; r €40), near the famous *cruceiro*, has pleasant rooms if you want to halt in Hío.

Autobuses Cerqueiro runs a few buses from Cangas to Hío Monday to Friday, and a more frequent Cangas–Bueu service that stops at Vilariño, 1.5km east of Hío on the C550.

RÍA DE VIGO

It's enjoyable to drive along the northern bank of the *ría*. You can see serried ranks of *bateas* and observe Vigo in the distance. But except for the far western area around Hío, there's not much to stop for. If you have your own transport, head a few kilometres inland from Moaña to the **Mirador de Cotorredondo**, a lookout commanding magical views over the Ría de Vigo, with its imposing suspension bridge, the Puente de Rande and the Ría de Pontevedra.

Drivers passing the head of the *ría* on the old N550 could make a quick diversion east to the well-preserved **Castelo de Soutomaior**.

VIGO

pop 207,640

Vigo's traffic and urban assault on the senses can come as a bit of a shock if you're arriving from anywhere else in Galicia. The city's long port – home to, among other things, Europe's biggest fishing fleet – is protected from Atlantic disturbances by the Islas Cíes and once boasted a busy passenger terminal. These days, the furthest you'll get from Vigo by sea is the Islas Cíes, though big cruise liners drop in. The small, tangled nucleus of old Vigo is interesting enough for a stroll and a meal, and hanging

about the port and nearby cafés on a sunny afternoon is not unpleasant, but overall this city may disappoint given its wonderful setting.

People only started to notice Vigo in the Middle Ages as it began to overtake Baiona as a major port. Sir Francis Drake thought it sufficiently interesting to take control for a few days in 1589.

Orientation

The Renfe train station is 800m southeast of the old centre. The bus station is on Avenida de Madrid, about 1.4km beyond. From near the train station, Rúa do Urzáiz and its pedestrianised continuation, Rúa do Príncipe, lead down to Praza da Porta do Sol, the gateway to the old centre and port area. The town's modern business centre focuses on the thoroughfares between Rúa do Príncipe and the waterfront.

Information

The two tourist offices are within a block of each other, just up from the ferry landing. There's no shortage of banks and ATMs, particularly along Avenida de García Barbón.

Ciberstation (Plaza da Princesa 3; per hr €2; ☺ until 1am)

Hospital Xeral-Cíes (☎ 986 81 60 00; Rúa do Pizarro 22)

Main post office (Avenida de García Barbón 50)

Municipal tourist office (☎ 986 22 47 57; www .turismodevigo.org; Rúa de Teófilo Llorente 5; ☺ 10am–2pm & 4.30-8pm)

Policía Nacional (emergency ☎ 091; Rúa de García Olloqui 2)

Regional tourist office (☎ 986 43 05 77; Rúa Cánovas del Castillo 22; ☺ 9.30am-2pm & 4.30-6.30pm or 7.30pm Mon-Fri, 10am-2pm & 5-7pm Sat & Sun Jul-Sep, closed Sat afternoon & Sun Oct-Jun)

Sights & Activities

The entrance to the **Casco Vello** (Old Town) from the bustling thoroughfares of central Vigo is marked by Praza da Princesa. A narrow alley leads through to elegant Praza da Constitución, a pleasant spot for a morning coffee. Head north down Rúa dos Cesteiros, lined by wicker shops, and you'll come upon the **Igrexa de Santa María**, built in 1816 – a considerable time after its Romanesque predecessor had been burnt down by Sir Francis Drake. Nearby **Praza da Almeida** is home to a number of art galleries, while **Rúa Real** is the old town's main street.

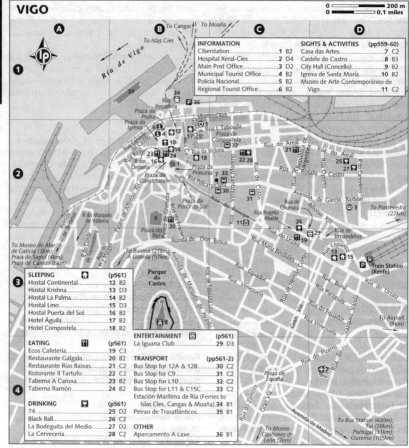

VIGO

| 0 | 200 m |
| 0 | 0.1 miles |

INFORMATION
Ciberstation	1 B2
Hospital Xeral-Cíes	2 D4
Main Post Office	3 D2
Municipal Tourist Office	4 B2
Policía Nacional	5 B2
Regional Tourist Office	6 B2

SIGHTS & ACTIVITIES (pp559-60)
Casa das Artes	7 C2
Castelo do Castro	8 B3
City Hall (Concello)	9 B2
Igrexa de Santa María	10 B2
Museo de Arte Contemporáneo de Vigo	11 C2

SLEEPING (p561)
Hostal Continental	12 B2
Hostal Krishna	13 D3
Hostal La Palma	14 B2
Hostal Lino	15 D3
Hostal Puerta del Sol	16 B2
Hotel Águila	17 B2
Hotel Compostela	18 B2

EATING (p561)
Ecos Cafetería	19 C3
Restaurante Gálgala	20 B2
Restaurante Rías Baixas	21 C2
Ristorante Il Tartufo	22 C2
Taberna A Caruxa	23 B2
Taberna Ramón	24 B2

DRINKING (p561)
74	25 D2
Black Ball	26 C2
La Bodeguita del Medio	27 D2
La Cervecería	28 C2

ENTERTAINMENT (p561)
La Iguana Club	29 D3

TRANSPORT (pp561-2)
Bus Stop for 12A & 12B	30 C2
Bus Stop for C9	31 C2
Bus Stop for L10	32 C2
Bus Stop for L11 & C15C	33 C2
Estación Marítima de Ría (Ferries to Islas Cíes, Cangas & Moaña)	34 B1
Peirao de Trasatlánticos	35 B1

OTHER
Aparcamento A Laxe	36 B1

Opened in 2002, the **Museo de Arte Contemporánea de Vigo** (Marco; ☎ 986 11 39 00; Rúa Príncipe 54; admission €3; ⏰ 11am-9pm Tue-Sun) covers the full range of modern artistic expression. At the time of the building's construction in 1861, the former penitentiary was considered at the forefront of architectural design.

Directly south (and uphill) of the old town you can wander in the verdant **Parque do Castro**, and inspect the **Castelo do Castro** that formed part of the city's defences built under Felipe IV.

English and French gardens surround the **Museo Quiñones de León** (☎ 986 29 50 70; Parque de Castrelos; admission free; ⏰ 9am-7pm or 8pm Tue-Sat, 10am-2pm Sun), 3km south of the city centre. Housed in a 17th-century palace, the museum contains two major collections of European painting. Bus No L20 from Porto do Sol heads there via Paseo Alfonso XII.

The brand-new **Museo do Mar de Galicia** (☎ 986 24 77 50; Avenida Atlántida 160; ⏰ 10am-2pm & 5-10pm Mon-Sat, 10am-10pm Sun), on the way out to Praia de Samil (see below), features innovatively arranged exhibits on Vigo's maritime heritage.

The best beaches within reach are southwest of the city centre at **Praia de Samil** and, further on, **Praia de Canido**. Local bus No C15C goes to Praia de Samil; bus Nos L10 and L11 go to Praia de Canido. Catch bus No C15C or L11 going westbound on Policarpo Sanz or southbound on Paseo Alfonso XII, or bus No L20 westbound along Praza de Compostela.

Sleeping

BUDGET

Hostal La Palma (☎ 986 43 06 78; Rúa Palma 7; s/d €22/24) This humble old-town option offers decent-sized rooms with balconies facing the Igrexa de Santa María.

Hotel Águila (☎ 986 43 13 98; www.hotelaguila.com; Rúa da Victoria 6; s/d €30/44 incl breakfast; 🖳 P) East of the old town, the Águila has been thoughtfully renovated to make the most of its big old-fashioned rooms, which include sofas.

Hostal Continental (☎ 986 22 07 64; Bajada a la Fuente 3; s/d €36/42; Jul-Sep; 🖳) A student residence most of the year, this affably managed place just above the port is open to all in summer.

Hostal Lino (☎ 986 44 70 04; Rúa Lepanto 26; from €36/42) The closest *hostal* to Renfe has a good deal more character than the rest, with wraparound balconies and tastefully furnished rooms.

MID-RANGE

Hostal Puerta del Sol (☎ 986 22 23 64; www.vigonet .com/puertadelsol; Porta do Sol 14; s/d €47/60; P) Just renovated, its charming rooms have CD players and terrific views over the Praza da Princesa.

There's a host of places to stay near the train station, not distressingly far from the city centre.

Hostal Krishna (☎ 986 22 81 61; Rúa do Urzáiz 57; s/d with bathroom €33/45) You won't hear any sitars playing, but this family-run lodging is friendly and comfortable, and willing to negotiate rates.

Eating

Restaurante Gálgala (☎ 986 22 14 17; Rúa do Pracer 4; meals around €12; 1-4pm Tue-Sat, 8.30-11.30pm Fri & Sat) A few minutes' walk uphill from the old town, this vegetarian restaurant serves a variety of reasonably priced dishes.

AUTHOR'S CHOICE

Restaurante Rías Baixas (☎ 986 22 30 41; Rúa República de Argentina 2; menu €7, fish dishes €8-10; closed Sun afternoon & Wed) Rarely visited by tourists, this lively dining hall is the place to head for fresh fish, traditionally prepared. Try the *bacalao a la gallego* (Galician-style salt cod), steamed till it flakes off and drizzled with oil.

Ristorante Il Tartufo (☎ 986 22 20 25; Praza de Compostela 16; pasta & pizza €8.50) Il Tartufo is hard to beat for quality Italian food; the pasta is made on the premises.

The winding lanes and blind alleys of old Vigo are laced with tapas bars and eateries of all descriptions. **Taverna Ramón** (Rúa dos Cesteiros 2A; closed Mon) is a cheap, spit-and-sawdust place off Praza da Constitución. Across the way, **Taverna A Caruxa** (Rúa dos Cesteiros 2; closed Wed) is another no-nonsense locale.

Rúa Pescadería is perhaps the old city's most atmospheric street – an entire pedestrian block jammed with people tucking into fresh seafood. It's definitely aimed at the tourist trade, though, and tends to be overpriced. Your best bet might be the oyster shuckers at the far end of the street selling oysters for €5/8 per half-dozen/dozen.

Drinking & Entertainment

On weekends, in particular, the taverns around Rúa Real in the old town can get quite lively.

The *zona de marcha* (nightlife area) centres around Rúa de Churruca and Rúa Rogelio Abalde, a few blocks west of the train station. You might start your investigations at the retro lounge-style **Black Ball** (Rúa de Churruca 8), then stop into **La Iguana Club** (☎ 986 22 01 90; Rúa de Churruca 14; from midnight), a rock-and-roll enclave where bands take the stage on weekends.

La Cervecería (Praza de Compostela 7) This is the place to quaff Estrella de Galicia beer (five varieties on tap), along with burgers and other comfort food.

Northwards, down towards the waterfront, is a zone that attracts a more mature crowd. At **La Bodeguita del Medio** (Rúa do Canceleiro 6) you can groove the night away to Latin rhythms (sometimes live) in a bodega ambience. **74** (Rúa do Areal 74; Thu-Sat), around the corner, is another late-night drinking place attracting a mixed crowd.

For clubs and pubs where you can dance after the other bars have closed, head to Gran Vía.

Getting There & Away

AIR

Vigo's **Peinador airport** (☎ 986 26 82 00) is about 10km east of the old town. Iberia flies to/from Bilbao, Barcelona and Madrid daily; it also flies to Valladolid and Paris daily, except Saturday. Spanair and Air Europa also serve Madrid, and the latter has flights to Mallorca and the Canary Islands.

BOAT
Ferries to Cangas sail about every half-hour from 6.30am to 10.30pm year-round, and Moaña ferries go hourly (€2.15 to either place). For details on ferries to the Islas Cíes, see opposite.

BUS
From the **bus station** (☎ 986 37 34 11; Avenida de Madrid) there are frequent services to Pontevedra (€2.20, 30 minutes), Santiago de Compostela (€6.85, 1½ hours), A Coruña (€12.50, 2½ hours), Ourense, Lugo, Baiona, Tui and A Guarda. La Unión/Monbus runs a few daily buses to Sanxenxo and O Grove. AutoRes goes six or seven times daily to Madrid (€29.50 to €34, 6½ hours), and other buses head for Oviedo, Santander, Bilbao, Pamplona, Barcelona, Salamanca, Seville and elsewhere.

Autna operates buses twice daily Monday to Friday (once daily on weekends) to/from Porto, Portugal (€8.65, 2½ hours), with connections there for Lisbon (€22.15, six hours). ALSA runs to Porto (€14) and Lisbon (€30) four times weekly (six in summer), as well as to Paris, Brussels, Amsterdam and Germany.

CAR & MOTORCYCLE
The A9 tollway runs to A Coruña via both Pontevedra (€2.50) and Santiago de Compostela.

TRAIN
Trains run approximately hourly to Pontevedra (€1.70 to €2.15, 30 minutes), Santiago de Compostela (€5.10 to €6.55, 1½ to 1¾ hours) and A Coruña, and four times daily to Ourense. There are daily trains to Madrid, Barcelona, San Sebastián and Irún (on the French border). Trains to Porto, Portugal (€13.35, three hours) depart at 8.25am and 7.08pm.

Getting Around
Vigo has a decent local bus system. The city centre (Rúa Policarpo Sanz) is linked to the airport by bus No C9, the bus and train stations by bus Nos 12A and 12B, among others.

ISLAS CÍES
The best beaches in the Rías Baixas aren't really in the *rías* at all. Rather, you need to head out to the Islas Cíes. Two of the three main islands, Illa do Faro and Illa de Monteagudo, are linked by a white sand crescent that also forms a lagoon known as Lago dos Nenos. The rocky little archipelago, reaching 197m above sea level at its highest point, forms a 6km breakwater for Vigo and its *ría* from the Atlantic's fury. The Islas Cíes, together with the Isla de Ons, Sálvora and Cortegada further north, constitute the **Parque Nacional de las Islas Atlánticas de Galicia**, declared in 2002 as a vital nesting sanctuary for seabirds. Almost immediately afterwards, oil slicks from the ill-fated *Prestige* wiped out hundreds of thousands of the birds.

You can only visit the islands during Semana Santa, on weekends from May to mid-June and daily from mid-June to mid-September. To stay overnight you must book for **Camping Illas Cíes** (per person/tent €5/5) through the **camping ground's office** (☎ 986 43 83 58) at the Islas Cíes boat terminal in Vigo. The camping ground has a restaurant, bar and shop, and a capacity of 800 people – often filled in August.

Boats to the islands are operated by the **Naviera Mar de Ons** (☎ 986 22 52 72; www.mardeons .com). During the season, weather permitting, up to nine daily trips are made from Vigo, and beginning in July, up to five from Baiona and four from Cangas. Wherever you start, return tickets cost €14.50 .

Baiona
pop 2750
On 1 March 1493, the caravel *Pinta* came into view off Baiona (Castilian: Bayona), bearing the remarkable news that Columbus had made it to the Indies. (In fact, he and his band had bumped into the Americas.) Then an important trading port, Baiona was later eclipsed by Vigo, and in the 17th century its population dropped to 150 people. Today it is one of Galicia's premier summer resorts, but understated compared with its Mediterranean counterparts, and has a small *casco antiguo* (old city) that's worth a wander.

There is a **tourist information booth** (☎ 986 68 70 67; www.baiona.org; Paseo Ribeiro; ✆ 10am-2pm & 4-8pm Jun-Oct) on the approach to the Monte Boi promontory.

The pine-covered Monte Boi promontory supports the **Fortaleza de Monterreal** (pedestrian/car €1/4; 10.30am-9.30pm), erected between the 11th and 17th centuries, and protected by a mighty 3km circle of walls. Also within the precinct today is a luxurious **parador**.

For beaches, head eastwards on the C550 towards Vigo. About 1.5km from the centre of Baiona is **Praia Ladeira**, but better (though still with an urban background) is the magnificent sweep of **Praia América** at Nigrán, about 4km north. Most buses between Baiona and Vigo call in at these beaches.

SLEEPING & EATING

Camping Bayona Playa (986 35 00 35; camping bayona@campingbayona.com; per person/tent/car €5.50/3.50/5.75) This large camping ground is on a spit of land fronting straight on to Praia Ladeira.

The harbour front drive, and, one block inland, Rúa de Ventura Misa, offer at least half-a-dozen places to stay.

Hospedaje Kin (986 35 56 95; Rúa de Ventura Misa 27; r with shared/private bathroom €35/50; Jun-Sep) Its rooms are among the least expensive in town.

Hotel Tres Carabelas (986 35 54 41; www.hotel trescarabelas.com; Rúa de Ventura Misa 61; s/d €48/62) If comfort is your priority, you won't find a cosier place than this sturdy old inn. Breakfast is served downstairs.

The cobbled lanes in the centre of town, including Rúa do Conde and Rúa de Ventura Misa, are full of restaurants, tapas bars and watering holes.

GETTING THERE & AWAY

Frequent **ATSA** (986 35 53 30) buses run north to Vigo (€1.90) every 30 minutes till 9pm most days, and a couple a day run south to Oia and A Guarda, from in front of the *lonja* (fish market) by the harbour. In summer boats sail to the Islas Cíes (see p562).

Oia

pop 100

The coast road between Baiona and A Guarda is a beautiful ride. The shore is fringed by rocks all the way, so it is quite undeveloped. About 20km south of Baiona, a small cove giving shelter to some fishing boats is presided over by the majestic **Mosteiro de Oia**. Although the present baroque façade was erected in 1740, the monastery church dates from the 16th century.

A Guarda

pop 6190

The fishing port of A Guarda (Castilian: La Guardia) sits just north of where Galicia's longest river, the Río Miño, enters the Atlantic. The formerly ramshackle harbour now has a pedestrian *paseo* (promenade) right around it, but the treat here is to head 4km up from the town to **Monte de Santa Trega** (admission per person €0.80 if you drive up, free Mon). On the way up you can inspect a Celtic *castro*, where a couple of the primitive circular dwellings have been restored, and at the top is a small **museum** with a few archaeological finds. But best of all are the magnificent views up the Miño, across to Portugal and out over the Atlantic.

A few kilometres south of A Guarda you'll find a beach at **Camposancos**, just inside the heads of the Río Miño, although you'd be better off across the river and on an ocean beach in Portugal.

SLEEPING & EATING

Hotel Pazo de Santa Tecla (986 61 00 02; fax 986 61 10 72; s/d €32/49) Up on top of the mountain, this ageing hotel has a restaurant and average rooms; its best feature is the view.

Hotel Eli-Mar (986 61 30 00; fax 986 61 11 56; Rúa Vicente Sobrino 12; s/d €46/63) In the centre of town, this newer place offers nicely decorated accommodation and a cheerful café.

Hotel Convento de San Benito (986 61 11 66; www.hotelsanbenito.com; Praza de San Beiito; s/d €51/75) A Guarda's top choice is housed in a former monastery down by the harbour.

A dozen bars and restaurants by the harbour serve tapas and meals; most fish and seafood will have been caught the same day you eat it.

Porto Guardés (986 61 34 88; Rúa do Porto 1; fish dishes €5-9) Possibly the best choice is the first in line, where reasonably priced swordfish, tuna, cod and other seafood are served upon chequered tablecloths.

GETTING THERE & AWAY

Most **ATSA** (986 61 02 55) buses to/from Vigo (€4.20) run via Tui, but a few go via Baiona. On Monday to Friday services are frequent, while on Sunday buses make only half a dozen trips.

GALICIA

A ferry (transbordador) runs from Camposancos to Caminha in Portugal, from where you can get to the first of a string of sandy ocean beaches on the way south to Viana do Castelo. Departures are every hour or less between 9.30am and 8.30pm from September to June, and between 9.30am and 10.30pm from July to August. Fares are €0.60/2.49/0.75 per person/car/bicycle.

RÍO MIÑO
Tui

pop 5440 / elevation 58m

Tui (Castilian: Tuy) is a gem: a pretty old town sitting on the Río Miño. Especially popular in summer when its little bars come alive, it's ideally situated by a bridge across to Portugal's equally interesting Valença. A fair crowd of Portuguese day-trippers fill Tui on weekends and Spaniards reciprocate in Valença.

Tui briefly hosted the court of the Visigothic king Witiza (r AD 702–10). It was subsequently attacked several times by Spain's Muslim invaders and Norman raiders. Later still it found itself on the front line during various wars between Spain and Portugal.

There's a **regional tourist office** (☎ 986 60 17 89; Rúa Colón 2; ☽ 10.30am-1.30pm & 4.30-6pm Mon-Fri, 10am-noon Sat Sep-Jun, plus Sat afternoon & Sun Jul & Aug) opposite the Hotel Colón.

SIGHTS

The brooding, fortress-like **cathedral** (☎ 986 60 05 11; ☽ 9.30am-1.30pm & 4-8pm) dominates Tui's small old town. Completed in 1225, the cathedral was much altered in the 15th century and the extra stone bracing was added after the Lisbon earthquake in 1755. Entry to the main body of the cathedral costs nothing, but it's well worth getting the €2.50 ticket that admits you to the Gothic cloister, Romanesque chapter house, the tower and gardens with views over the river, the cathedral museum and the **Museo Diocesano** (☽ Jun-early Sep only), across the street, with its archaeology collection.

The surrounding narrow lanes hold a pair of cruceiros (standing crucifixes found at many crossroads in Galicia) and chapels, including the **Iglesia de San Telmo**, containing relics of the patron saint of sailors.

Beyond the old town centre, a riverside walk from the **Iglesia de San Domingo** is en-

ticing. The baroque façade of this monastery church hides a largely 14th-century interior.

While here, take a look at the charming Portuguese fortress town of **Valença**, just across the century-old Puente Internacional.

SLEEPING

Hotel Colón (☎ 986 60 02 23; colonhot@jet.es; Colón 11; s/d €40/77; ☒ [P]) This modern hotel is 500m up the main drag from the old town. There are duplex apartments available.

Hostal San Telmo (☎ 986 60 30 11; Avenida de la Concordia 84; s/d €30/40) A comfortable if unremarkable mid-range option, the San Telmo is opposite the Renfe train station, a 15-minute walk from the old town.

Hostal La Generosa (☎ 986 60 00 55; Paseo de Calvo Sotelo 37; s/d €20/24) This ancient inn is convenient to the old town. Bathrooms are down the hall, though some rooms feature showers.

EATING & DRINKING

There are several inviting places near the cathedral.

O Vello Cabalo Furado (☎ 986 60 19 88; Rúa Seixas 2; mains €5-12; menú €8; ☽ closed Tue) Not to be confused with the inferior Novo Cabalo Furado around the corner, this large inviting dining hall puts together a very hearty lunch. Check out the cocido gallego (Galician stew; €10).

Mesón Jaqueyvi (Praza do Concello 4; tapas & tablas €5-15; ☽ closed Tue) This humble tavern serves some unusual snacks (sea urchin caviar, fried asparagus), though most patrons just order a helping of Serrano ham.

On Friday to Sunday nights, the quaint cobblestoned streets behind the cathedral are the scene of some major partying. Entrefornos sees the most activity, with half a dozen pubs.

GETTING THERE & AWAY

Frequent ATSA buses to Vigo (€2.75) and A Guarda stop on Paseo de Calvo Sotelo, opposite Librería Byblos. Autna buses between Vigo and Portugal stop at the Puente Internacional.

The two daily trains each way between Vigo and Porto stop at Tui train station, 700m north of the town centre. More trains run to Porto from Valença. A few trains to other destinations, such as Ribadavia, Ourense, Madrid and León, go from Guillarei, a couple of kilometres northeast.

Ribadavia

pop 3170 / elevation 100m

About 80km up the Miño from Tui towards Ourense, Ribadavia is in the heart of Ribeiro wine country. It was once Galicia's most important Jewish settlement. Even after Fernando and Isabel, the Catholic monarchs, decided to expel Jews in 1492, most managed to hang on, either converting to Christianity or fleeing temporarily to Portugal, and returning after the hue and cry had died down.

The enthusiastic **tourist office** (☎ 988 47 12 75; www.ribadavia.com; Praza Maior) is in a 17th-century palace on the main square. Upstairs is the **Centro de Información Xudía** (admission €1), with an exposition on the Jews of Galicia.

It is a pleasure to wander around the medieval town centre, characterised by a patchwork of uneven little cobbled squares, lined with heavy stone arcades and *galerías*. The **Barrio Xudío** (Jewish Quarter) occupies the zone between the south wall and the Praza Magdalena, where a house once served as the community synagogue. The **Casa da Inquisición** fronts the nearby Praza de García Boente. The coats of arms on its façade belonged to the Ribadavia families who served as local officials for the Inquisition.

Of the several churches dotted about the town, the Romanesque **Igrexa de Santiago** and **Igrexa de San Xoán** stand out. The **Museo Etnolóxico** (admission free; ◷ 10am-2.30pm & 4-8pm Tue-Sat, 11am-2.30pm Sun), just down the street from the Igrexa de Santiago, is well worth a look, too. The remains of the **Castelo dos Condes de Ribadavia** date from the 15th century.

Ribeiro white wines are considered among the best on the peninsula. The tourist office can set up visits to the bodegas.

Hostal Plaza (☎ 988 47 05 76; Praza Maior; s/d €18/80) offers cosy, well-kept rooms with tub, TV and balcony, and one of the old town's better restaurants.

La Tafona de Herminia (Travesía Porta Nova de Arriba 2) is one of several little bakeries selling poppy-seed cookies and other traditional Jewish pastries.

You can sample Ribeiro wines, along with a bit of ham or sheep's cheese, at **Vinoteca Olgar** (Merelles Caula 1), on the plaza.

Up to 10 buses and three trains run daily to Ourense and Vigo from stations in the east of town, just over the Río Avia.

THE EAST

With the notable exception of the well-trodden Camino de Santiago, Galicia's deep interior is little visited. Of its cities, Ourense has a surprisingly attractive, compact centre, while Lugo's main claim to fame is its Roman walls. Away from the towns, nothing human-made can match the natural splendour of the Gargantas del Sil (Sil Gorge).

OURENSE

pop 101,680

Ourense (Castilian: Orense) may well be the first Galician city encountered by travellers arriving from neighbouring Castilla y León. First impressions are of an unexciting sprawl of apartment blocks, but give it a chance, for at Ourense's core is a wonderful old town bursting with life.

History

Ourense was a Roman settlement of some importance. The Visigoths took over and raised a cathedral here, but the Muslims destroyed it during several raids. After it was repopulated by Sancho II of Castile in 1071, the town eventually began to take off as a trade centre. Ourense's considerable Jewish population, having contributed generously to the campaign against Granada, was promptly rewarded in 1492 with expulsion. Essentially an ecclesiastical town, it declined for centuries until the arrival of the railway in 1882.

Orientation

The train station is 500m north of the Río Miño and the bus station is a further 1km northwest. On foot you can approach the city centre across the Ponte Romano, which is actually a medieval bridge constructed in place of an older Roman one. Head for the Catedral do San Martiño, around which unfolds the old town.

Information

For banks, look along Rúa do Paseo and Rúa Curros Enríquez.

GALICIA

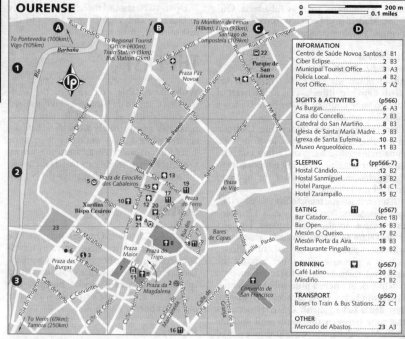

OURENSE

INFORMATION
Centro de Saúde Novoa Santos..1 B1
Ciber Eclipse...............................2 B3
Municipal Tourist Office............3 A3
Polícia Local.............................4 B3
Post Office...............................5 A2

SIGHTS & ACTIVITIES   (p566)
As Burgas................................6 A3
Casa do Concello......................7 B3
Catedral do San Martiño...........8 B3
Iglesia de Santa María Madre.....9 B3
Igrexa de Santa Eufemia..........10 B2
Museo Arqueolóxico................11 B3

SLEEPING   (pp566-7)
Hostal Cándido.......................12 B3
Hostal Sanmiguel....................13 B2
Hotel Parque.........................14 C1
Hotel Zarampallo....................15 B3

EATING   (p567)
Bar Catador..........................(see 18)
Bar Open...............................16 B3
Mesón O Queixo......................17 B2
Mesón Porta da Aira...............18 B3
Restaurante Pingallo...............19 B2

DRINKING   (p567)
Café Latino...........................20 B2
Mindiño...............................21 B2

TRANSPORT   (p567)
Buses to Train & Bus Stations...22 C1

OTHER
Mercado de Abastos.................23 A3

Centro de Saúde Novoa Santos (☎ 988 38 55 80; Rúa de Juan XXIII 10) Handiest medical clinic.

Ciber Eclipse (Rúa Monte Cabeza de Manzaneda 2; per hr €2) Coin-operated Internet access.

Municipal tourist office (☎ 988 36 60 64; www .turismoourense.com; Rúa As Burgas 12; ☒ 10am-2pm & 5-7pm Mon-Fri, noon-2pm Sat & Sun)

Polícia Local (☎ 988 39 17 00; Praza de San Martiño 1)

Regional tourist office (☎ 988 37 20 20; ☒ 9am or 10am-2pm & 4.30-8.30pm Mon-Fri) On the Ponte Romano.

Sights

The main feature of the rather gloomy 13th-century **Catedral do San Martiño** is the Pórtico do Paraíso, a Gothic copy of Santiago de Compostela's Pórtico de la Gloria. The cathedral **museum** (admission €1; ☒ noon-1pm & 4.30-7pm) displays ecclesiastical relics dating from as far back as 1200.

Around the cathedral spreads a web of charming little squares and alleyways, inviting exploration by day or night. The sloping **Praza Maior** is the grandest plaza, hemmed in by arcaded walkways. At one end of the plaza are the dignified **Casa do Concello** (Town Hall) and, next door, Ourense's **Museo Arque-**oloxico (Archaeological Museum), which was closed for renovations at the time of writing. About 50m northwest of the cathedral stands the **Igrexa de Santa Eufemia**. Its magnificent concave façade is an archetypal example of Gallego baroque.

As Burgas, Ourense's steaming mineral waters, have been a blessing for the sick, tired and sore-footed since at least Roman times. They still gush out in fountains on Praza das Burgas and the water is still used for heating surrounding houses.

Sleeping

First head for Praza de Eirociño dos Cabaleiros, about 100m north of Praza Maior.

Hotel Zarampallo (☎ 988 23 00 08; Rúa dos Irmáns Villar 19; s/d €26/45) The smartest of the bunch features all exterior rooms and an elegant restaurant.

Hostal Sanmiguel (☎ 988 23 92 03; Rúa San Miguel 12; s/d with bathroom €18/24) This basic inn contrasts surprisingly with the fancy restaurant below, but it's still a good deal.

Hostal Cándido (☎ 988 22 96 07; Rúa dos Irmáns Villar 15; s/d with bathroom €18/26) Almost next door to the Zarampallo, this budget choice atop a *chocolatería* (chocolate shop) offers worn-at-the-edges accommodation.

Hotel Parque (☎ 988 23 36 11; Parque de San Lázaro 3; s/d with bathroom €20/39) This large old hotel could use some work, but has nice park views and will probably have room if the others are full.

Eating

The streets and squares around the cathedral, particularly Rúa Viriato and Rúa dos Fornos, are bursting with restaurants and watering holes.

Mesón Porta da Aira (☎ 988 25 07 49; Rúa dos Fornos 2; dishes €7-14; ☒ closed Mon) Locals flock here for the generous platters of *huevos rotos*, lightly fried eggs over a bed of thinly sliced potatoes, served alongside various sausages, steaks and chops.

Bar Catador (Rúa dos Fornos 4; raciónes €4.50-6) Galician-style eels, squid and octopus are served at this lively neighbourhood tapas bar.

Restaurante Pingallo (☎ 988 22 00 57; Rúa San Miguel 6; mains €5-10) *Lacón con grelos* (boiled pork shoulder with greens) is one of the traditional favourites available daily at this long-standing establishment.

Mesón O Queixo (Praza de Eirociño dos Cabaleiros) This jolly spot on an attractive old-town square specialises in great cheese tapas.

Drinking & Entertainment

Rúa Pizarro and neighbouring lanes are awash with late-opening bars and pubs purveying a multitude of musical styles. The Igrexa Santa Eufemia vicinity has a few more refined locales, including **Mindiño** (☎ 988 24 55 36; Rúa Arcediagos 13) playing Celtic music, and **Café Latino** (☎ 988 22 67 21; Rúa Coronel Ceano 7), which hosts a spring jazz festival.

Getting There & Away

Ourense's **bus station** (☎ 988 21 60 27; Carretera de Vigo 1) has service to Galicia's main cities, with at least 14 departures to Santiago de Compostela (€8.90, two hours) vía Lalín. Daily buses also go to most other regions of Spain, including six to Madrid (€25, 6¼ hours). Empresa Villalón heads to Feces, on the Portuguese border south of Verín, where you can get buses to Chaves, a hub for many Portuguese destinations.

Six trains a day run to Santiago de Compostela (1½ to two hours, €6.10 to €14),

three of which continue to A Coruña. Up to eight trains daily serve Vigo (€6.65 to €17, two hours), and a few go to Pontevedra, León, Madrid and Barcelona.

Getting Around

Local bus Nos 1, 3, 6A, 8, 12, 15 and 33 run between the train station and Parque de San Lázaro in the city centre. Bus Nos 6A and 12 also serve the bus station.

CASTELO DE MONTERREI

The A52 southeast of Ourense crosses several low ranges on the way to Castilla y León. Outside Verín the N532 diverges south to Feces on the Portuguese border. If you have transport, it's worth detouring to the **Castelo de Monterrei** (admission free; ☒ 10.30am-1.30pm & 4-7pm), in a commanding position just west of Verín.

RÍO SIL

The N120 northeast of Ourense follows the Río Miño, a pretty stretch but nothing compared to what's in store if you turn off east at Os Peares, where the Río Sil joins the Miño. The ensuing 15km make for a spectacular drive along the upper levels of the **Gargantas del Sil** (Sil Gorge). The Ourense–Monforte railway also follows the gorge for a few kilometres.

About 7km from Os Peares, you come to a spectacular arched bridge over the gorge, where the railroad turns north for Monforte de Lemos. After another 3km, you reach a boat landing, from which 95-seat catamarans speed up the gorge. Reservations are advisable in summer: contact **Hemisferios** (☎ 902 10 04 03; www.hemisferios.es).

The road leaves the gorge here, ending in a T-junction at the village of Loureiro. If you turn right (west) here, after 4km you'll reach the **Mosteiro de Santo Estevo de Ribas de Sil**. Established in the 6th century, the huge complex has three cloisters, each from a different period in history. At the time of writing the monastery was set to open as a Parador Nacional, though anyone will be able to have a look around.

Two daily buses (one on Saturday, none on Sunday) from Ourense to Parada do Sil, via Luintra, stop at the monastery.

From the monastery those with a their own transport have the option of heading back eastwards past the T-junction and on

GALICIA

towards Castilla y León. It's a picturesque route through woods and across high, windswept heath, with the Gargantas del Sil never far away. **Castro Caldelas** has a castle and a couple of **hostales**. Twenty-seven kilometres northeast of Pobra de Trives, your road meets the N120 again.

MONFORTE DE LEMOS
pop 16,180 / elevation 363m

Inhabited before the Romans appeared and later converted into the medieval Mons Forti, this dishevelled but interesting place, northeast of Ourense, has been Galicia's principal rail junction since 1883.

Long before you reach the centre of town you'll see the **Torre del Homenaje** (admission €1.20; ☺ noon-2pm & 4-6pm or 7pm), the most intact part of the 13th-century castle that sits at the top of the *monte forte* (mountain) and gives the town its name. For the obligatory photo opportunity, you can climb the 30m to the summit. A sumptuous Parador Nacional has been installed in the adjacent former Benedictine **Monasterio de San Vicente del Pino**.

The area south of the town centre is dominated by the proud **Colexio de Nosa Señora da Antiga**, erected by Cardinal Rodrigo de Castro in 1593. A pair of El Greco paintings highlights its **art gallery** (admission free by guided tour, consult tourist office for schedules). Nearby is the **municipal tourist office** (☎ 982 40 47 15; ☺ 10am-2pm & 4.30-8.30pm).

Should you decide to stay, head for the 16th-century bridge over the Río Cabe. **Hotel Puente Romano** (☎ 982 41 11 68; www.hpuenteromano .com; Paseo del Malecón; d €26/41) has great river views. The best bet for meals is **Restaurante Polar** (☎ 982 40 00 01; Rúa do Cardenal 13; mains €6-11), a nice informal joint, with dozens of dinner options and tables on the promenade.

Many trains crossing Galicia call in here. Buses head north to Lugo and southwest to Ourense about once an hour on weekdays, and a few travel east to Ponferrada and León. Both stations are north of the castle.

LUGO
pop 82,170 / elevation 475m

Lugo's impressive Roman walls are reason enough for a visit, but within them is a beautifully preserved and lively historic centre worthy of exploration.

The Romans established Lucus Augusti over a Celtic *castro* in the 1st century BC. The walls went up three centuries later, but failed to keep out the Suevi in 460, or indeed the Muslims 300 years later. Until well into the 19th century the city gates were closed at night and tolls were charged to bring in goods from outside.

Orientation & Information
Whether you arrive in Lugo by train or bus, you will end up not too far outside the circuit of Roman walls.

You'll find several banks and ATMs on nearby Rúa da Raíña and Praza de Santo Domingo.

Futura (Rúa Vilalba 6; per 15 min €0.60) Internet access outside the walls.

Hospital Xeral Calde (☎ 982 29 60 00; Rúa Doutor Ochoa) About 500m west of the old town.

Policía Municipal (☎ 982 29 71 10; Praza da Constitución)

Regional tourist office (☎ 982 23 13 61; Praza Maior 27; ☺ 10am-2pm & 4-7pm Mon-Sat Oct-Jun, plus Sun in Jul & Aug) Located in a shopping corridor opposite the *ayuntamiento*.

Sights
ROMAN WALLS
More than 2km round, up to 15m high and studded by 82 stout turrets, the Roman walls enclosing Lugo are the best preserved of their kind in the whole of Spain, if not the world. You can climb on top of the walls – one convenient access point is the **Porta de Santiago** (Gate of Santiago) near the cathedral – and walk all the way round the town.

CATHEDRAL
Inside the Porta de Santiago, the **cathedral**, with its grey symmetrical façade, might not at first glance seem that ancient, but it was in fact begun in 1129, inspired by the cathedral in Santiago de Compostela. Work continued until the 14th century and the neoclassical front was added later still. The northern doorway, which is protected by a formidable portico, remains obviously Romanesque. In an oval frame amid the archway is a majestically seated figure of Christ; beneath his bare feet, a Last Supper scene has been carved into an unsupported capital. Inside, the walnut choir stalls are a baroque masterpiece.

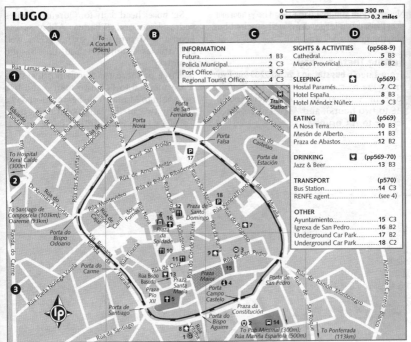

LUGO

INFORMATION		SIGHTS & ACTIVITIES	(pp568-9)
Futura.....................1 B3		Cathedral.................5 B3	
Policía Municipal...........2 C3		Museo Provincial..........6 B2	
Post Office................3 C3			
Regional Tourist Office.....4 C3		SLEEPING	(p569)
		Hostal Paramés............7 C2	
		Hotel España..............8 B3	
		Hotel Méndez Núñez........9 C3	
		EATING	(p569)
		A Nosa Terra..............10 B3	
		Mesón de Alberto..........11 B3	
		Praza de Abastos..........12 B2	
		DRINKING	(pp569-70)
		Jazz & Beer...............13 B3	
		TRANSPORT	(p570)
		Bus Station...............14 C3	
		RENFE agent..............(see 4)	
		OTHER	
		Ayuntamiento..............15 C3	
		Igrexa de San Pedro.......16 B2	
		Underground Car Park......17 B2	
		Underground Car Park......18 C2	

MUSEO PROVINCIAL

Lugo's **museum** (☎ 982 24 21 12; Praza da Soidade; admission free; ⏱ 11am-2pm & 5-8pm Mon-Fri, 10am-2pm Sat Jul & Aug, 10.30am-2pm & 4.30-8.30pm Mon-Sat, 11am-2pm Sun Sep-Jun) includes what remains of the Convento de San Francisco – a Gothic cloister and the convent kitchen and refectory. The collections range from pre-Roman gold jewellery and Roman mosaics to Galician art from the 15th to 20th centuries.

Sleeping

Just two lodgings are located within Lugo's walls.

Hotel Méndez Núñez (☎ 982 23 07 11; Rúa da Raíña 1; s/d €45/56) Run by the same family since the 19th century, this large hotel has been completely redone, with brand-new bathrooms.

Hostal Paramés (☎ 982 22 62 51; Rúa do Progreso 28; s/d €18/28) This humble choice is on a quiet street. Ask for a room with a *galería*.

Hotel España (☎ 982 23 15 40; Rúa Vilalba 2; s/d €28/36) Just outside the Porta do Bispo Aguirre, this easy-going establishment offers comfortable beds, and you might be able to bargain down the rate.

Eating

Head to the **Praza de Abastos** (Rúa Quiroga) for picnic supplies: fruit, local cheeses (*tetilla, San Simón*) and cured meats.

Head down Rúa de Cruz or Rúa Nova, where the restaurant windows are filled with sea creatures.

Mesón de Alberto (☎ 982 22 83 10; Rúa da Cruz 4; tapas €2.50-6) The *menú de la tapería* (€12) lets you sample several of its original tapas, plus dessert: try the *filloas gallegas* (chocolate or cream-filled crepes).

A Nosa Terra (☎ 982 22 92 35; Rúa Nova 8; mains €9) The street's most popular spot doles out good tapas (free with a drink). The downstairs bodega is a good place to try *pulpo a la gallega* or *lacón con grelos*.

Drinking & Entertainment

Lugo has a relatively subdued nightlife area around the cathedral, with half a dozen pubs offering a varied musical menu, including the self-explanatory **Jazz & Beer** (☎ 982 25 09 51; Rúa Bispo Basurto 2). *Chundas* (electronica dance clubs) are strung along Rúa Mariña Española, south of the walls.

Nearby, **Pub Minimal** (Rúa Galicia 11; ☯ from midnight Thu-Sat) is a large, dim, well-stocked bar playing good rock and roll.

Getting There & Away

From Lugo's **bus station** (☎ 982 22 39 85), Empresa Freire runs at least six buses daily to/from Santiago de Compostela (€6.20, 1½ to two hours), and Arriva offers direct service to A Coruña.

Six buses head daily for Ourense, Pontevedra, Vigo and Ribadeo. ALSA serves León and Madrid (€29, six hours), as well as Asturias, Cantabria and the Basque Country.

Three or more trains run northwest to A Coruña (€6 to €16, two hours) and five run south to Monforte de Lemos most days. One or two of the latter continue across Castilla y León to Madrid or Barcelona.

Valencia

VALENCIA

When you visit the Comunidad Valenciana (Valencia region) you won't be alone. Each year, well over four million visitors descend upon its thin coastal ribbon. Most stay sprawled on the beaches – except, perhaps, for a day trip to Valencia city. But with a little planning and cash set aside to rent a bike or car, you can leave behind the frantic coastal hedonism and explore the region's rich interior.

Valencia is both of Spain and distinct from Spain. In Muslim hands for five centuries, its Christian European history has been shaped as much by Catalonia as by Castile. The region's flag bears the red and yellow stripes of Catalonia and the mother tongue of many, particularly in the hinterland, is Valenciano, a dialect of Catalan.

Valencia city, the region's capital, is famed for its exuberant nightlife, the wild Las Fallas spring festival and, lately, for its Ciudad de las Artes y las Ciencias, a breathtaking piece of modern architecture.

To the north, along the Costa del Azahar (Orange Blossom Coast), is a string of low-key resorts plus the historic site of Sagunto and Peñíscola's castle, stuck out to sea on its promontory.

Southwards along the Costa Blanca (White Coast) stretch some of Spain's finest sandy beaches. You can party around the clock and calendar in international resorts such as Benidorm, Torrevieja and the lively provincial capital of Alicante. Others, such as Denia, still retain a much more Spanish flavour.

Inland, west of the coastal motorway, lies another world where mountains buckle and castles abound. Hilltop Morella; Xàtiva, with its own splendid castle running the ridge; Elche and Europe's most extensive endless palm groves – each beckons to enterprising travellers.

HIGHLIGHTS

- Party long and strong through Valencia's **Las Fallas** (p582), Europe's wildest spring festival

- Join the 45,000 marine creatures at the **Oceanogràfic** (p578), Europe's largest and most exciting aquarium

- Gasp at the daring architecture of Valencia city's **Ciudad de las Artes y las Ciencias** (p577)

- Savour your first glimpse of the medieval fortress town of **Morella** (p594) from afar

- Wander the streets of **Guadalest** (p610), again at peace once the last tourist bus pulls out

Morella ★

Valencia ★

Guadalest ★

| ■ AREA: 23,255 SQ KM | ■ POP: 2,216,300 | ■ AVE SUMMER TEMP: HIGH 32°C, LOW 19°C |

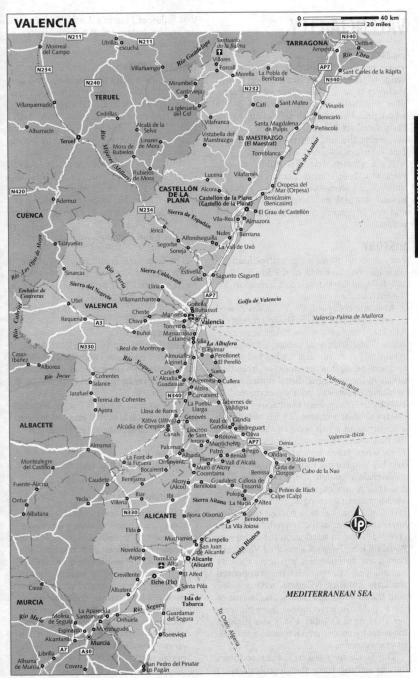

VALENCIA CITY

pop 738,400

Valencia, Spain's third-largest city and venue of the 2007 America's Cup extended yachting regatta, is the place where paella, now multinational, first simmered over a wood fire. The city also lays claim to the Holy Grail, is blessed with great weather and hosts the mid-March festival of Las Fallas, Europe's wildest street party.

It's a vibrant, friendly, mildly chaotic place that boasts an outstanding fine arts museum, an accessible old quarter, Europe's newest cultural and scientific complex – and one of Spain's most exciting nightlife scenes.

HISTORY

Pensioned-off Roman legionaries founded 'Valentia' on the banks of the Río Turia in 138 BC and first developed irrigation for the surrounding regions.

As Rome collapsed, the Visigoths moved in, only to be expelled by Muslim cohorts in AD 711. The Arabs made Valencia an agricultural and industrial centre, establishing ceramics, paper, silk and leather industries, and extending the network of irrigation canals in the rich agricultural hinterland.

Muslim rule was briefly interrupted in 1094 by the triumphant rampage of the legendary Castilian knight El Cid, but almost a century and a half were to elapse before the Christians definitively retook the city in 1238, when Jaime I incorporated the area into his burgeoning Catalan kingdom.

Valencia's golden age was in the 15th and 16th centuries, when it was one of the Mediterranean's strongest trading centres. Like Catalonia, Valencia backed the wrong horse in the War of the Spanish Succession (1702–13) and in retribution the victorious Bourbon king Felipe V abolished Valencia's *fueros*, the autonomous privileges the city had enjoyed. The Spanish Civil War proved similarly unlucky; Valencia, having sided with the Republicans (and acting as seat of the Republican government from November 1936 until October 1937) was slighted for years by successive victorious nationalist governments.

The *fueros* may not have been restored, but, benefiting from the decentralisation that followed Franco's death, Valencia and its region today enjoy a high degree of autonomy.

ORIENTATION

The 'action' part of the city is an oval area bounded by the old course of the Río Turia, long ago diverted, and the sickle-shaped inner ring road of Calles de Colón, Xàtiva and de Guillem de Castro. These trace the walls of the old city, demolished in 1865 as a job-creation project.

Within the oval are three major squares: Plazas del Ayuntamiento, de la Reina (also known as Plaza de Zaragoza) and de la Virgen. The oldest quarter of the city, the Barrio del Carmen (or El Carmé), is delimited by the Plaza de la Virgen, the Torres de Quart and Serranos, and the Turia riverbed.

The train station, Estación del Norte, is 250m south of Plaza del Ayuntamiento. The main bus station is beside the riverbed on Avenida Menéndez Pidal.

INFORMATION
Bookshops

Casa del Llibre (Map pp576-7; ☎ 96 353 00 80; www.casadellibro.com; Passeig Russafa 11) Offspring of the giant Madrid mother store, with a reasonable stock of books in English.
English Book Centre (Map pp576-7; ☎ 96 351 92 88; Calle Pascual y Genís 16)
Librería Patagonia (Map pp576-7; ☎ 96 393 60 52; Calle Santa Amalia 2) An excellent travel bookshop with some guides in English, including Lonely Planet titles.

Emergency
EU standard emergency number ☎ 112

CREEPING CATALAN

More and more, town halls are replacing street signs in Spanish (Castilian) with the Valenciano/Catalan equivalent (though some broader-minded local authorities still sign in both) and, while the difference between the two versions is often minimal, this can sometimes be a source of confusion for visitors. Occasionally we use the Valenciano version, where it's clearly the dominant one, but since Spanish, for the moment at any rate, remains fairly common – and is the version every local understands – we've elected to stick with it in most cases.

VALENCIA CITY

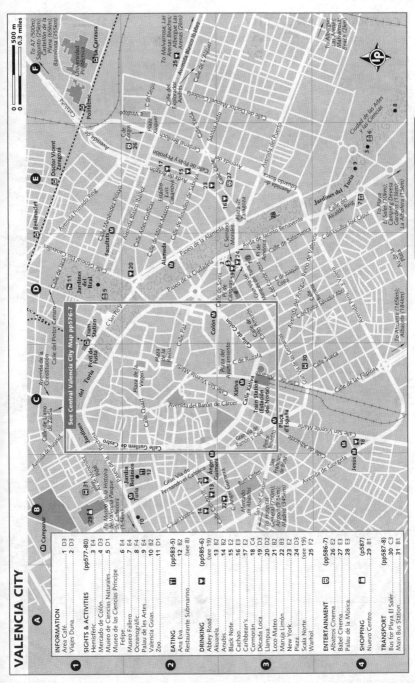

Ⓐ

INFORMATION
Area Café............................	1 D3
Viajes Duna........................	2 D3

SIGHTS & ACTIVITIES (pp577-80)
Hemisféric............................	3 E4
Mercado de Colón................	4 D3
Museo de Ciencias Naturales...	5 D1
Museo de las Ciencias Príncipe	
Felipe.................................	6 E4
Museo Fallero......................	7 F4
Oceanogràfic.......................	8 F4
Palau de les Arts..................	9 E4
Valencia Guías.....................	10 B2
Zoo......................................	11 D1

Ⓑ

EATING 🍴 (pp583-5)
Ana Eva..............................	12 B2
Restaurante Submarino.........	(see 8)

DRINKING 🍷 (pp585-6)
Abbey Road.........................	13 B2
Akuarela..............................	14 B2
Anubis.................................	15 E2
Black Note...........................	16 E3
Cachao................................	17 E2
Caribbean's.........................	18 C4
Cormorán............................	19 D3
Década Loca........................	20 D2
Llampuа..............................	21 B2
Loco Mateo.........................	22 B3
Maruja Limón......................	23 D3
Plaza..................................	24 D3
Scala Norte.........................	(see 19)
Warhol................................	25 F2

ENTERTAINMENT 🎭 (pp586-7)
Albatros Cinema..................	26 E2
Babel Cinema......................	27 E3
Palau de la Música..............	28 E3

SHOPPING 🛍 (p587)
Nuevo Centro......................	29 B1

TRANSPORT (pp587-8)
Bus for Playa El Saler..........	30 C3
Main Bus Station.................	31 B1

VALENCIA

VALENCIA

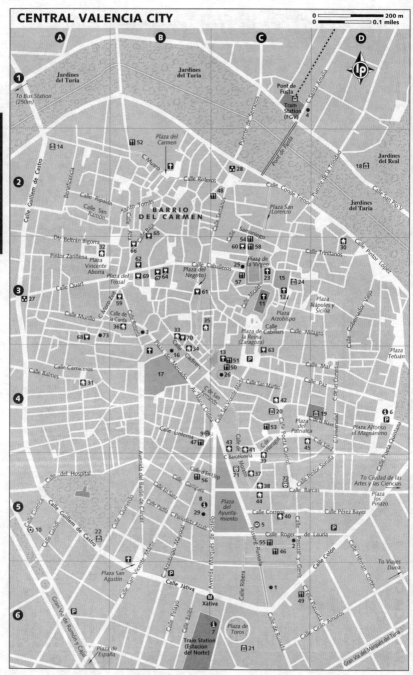

CENTRAL VALENCIA CITY

0   200 m
0   0.1 miles

Jardines del Turia

Jardines del Turia

To Bus Station (250m)

Pont de Fusta

Tram Station (FGV)

Calle Amalia

Jardines del Real

14

52

Plaza del Carmen

C. Museo

28

Calle Roteros

Calle Conde Trenor

18

BARRIO DEL CARMEN

Beneficencia

Calle Guillem de Castro

Calle Ripalda

Calle San Ramón

Santo Tomás

Alta

48

Plaza San Lorenzo

Dtor Beltrán Bigorra

Pintor Zariñena

Plaza Vincente Aborra

32

66

65

62

Samaniego

54

60 58

Calle Trinitarios

30

Calle San Pío V

Jardines del Real

Calle Pintor López

Calle Quart

Plaza del Tossal

69

67 64

Calle Caballeros

Plaza del Negrito

25

Plaza de la Virgen

23

57

15

24

Plaza Nápoles y Sicilia

27

Calle Murillo

Calle de la Carda

36

59

C. Moro Zeid

61

Calle Micalet

11

12

Plaza Arzobispo

Calle Gobernador Viejo

68 73

3

33

35

Plaza de Cabillars

Calle Milagro

Plaza Tetuán

16

70

34

13

51

50

Plaza de la Reina (Zaragoza)

63

P

Calle Mar

Calle Balmes

Calle Carniceros

31

17

Av. María Cristina

Cadirers

26

Calle San Martín

Calle Paz

C de las Comedias

C de San Fernando

42

Calle del Hospital

Avenida del Barón de Cárcer

Calle Linterna

9

47

20

53

Plaza de la Navedad

19

Universidad

Plaza del Patriarca

45

Plaza Alfonso el Magnánimo

6

Calle Poeta Quintana

43

41

39

C de Vilaragut

C de Poeta Querol

Calle Quevedo

Calle En Sans

Calle Pielta

C Periodista Azzati

Calle d'En Llop

66

8

29

71

37

72

Calle Pintor Sorolla

To Ciudad de las Artes y las Ciencias

Calle Guillem de Castro

Calle Cuenca

Calle Gracia

10

22

Abadía Mayor

Avenida Marqués de Sotelo

Plaza del Ayunta-miento

38

44

Calle Barcas

Plaza los Pinazo

Calle Correos

40

5

Calle Pérez Bayer

Plaza San Agustín

P

Calle San Vicente Mártir

55

46

2

Pasaje de Russafa

Calle Roger de Lauria

Calle Colón

Calle Hernán Cortés

To Viajes Duna

Calle Játiva

1

C Pizarra

49

Plaza de España

Gran Vía de Ramón y Cajal

Calle Pelayo

Calle Bailén

M Xàtiva

7

Train Station (Estación del Norte)

Plaza de Toros

21

Calle Ribera

Calle Russafa

Calle Cirilo Amorós

Gran Vía del Marqués del Turia

Internet Access

Area Café (Map pp576-7; Calle de Salamanca 37; per hr €3; 🕑 11am-2am Mon-Thu, 4pm-2am Sat, 4pm-midnight Sun)
Ono (Map p575; Calle San Vicente Mártir 22; 🕑 10am-1am; per hr €3)

Internet Resources

www.landofvalencia.com – English version of the Valencia tourism authority's excellent official site.
www.comunitatvalenciana.com – Multilingual (including English) version of the above.

Laundry

Laundrette (Map pp576-7; Plaza del Mercado 12) Near the Mercado Central.

Medical Services

Hospital General (☎ 96 386 29 00; Avenida del Cid, junction with Avenida Tres Cruces)

Money

Viajes Duna (Map p575; ☎ 96 374 15 62; Calle de Cirilo Amorós 88) Represents American Express.

Post

Main post office (Map pp576-7; Plaza del Ayuntamiento) A splendid neobaroque building.

Tourist Information

Call ☎ 902 123212 throughout the comunidad for tourist information (at pre-

mium rates). To email any tourist office in the Valencia region, type *name of town*@touristinfo.net.
Main regional tourist office (Map pp576-7; ☎ 96 398 64 22; Calle Paz 48; 🕑 9am-6.30pm Mon-Sat)
Municipal tourist offices train station (Map pp576-7; ☎ 96 352 85 73); town hall (Map pp576-7; ☎ 96 352 58 12); Teatro Principal (Map pp576-7; ☎ 96 351 49 07; Calle Poeta Querol s/n)

SIGHTS

From medieval monuments to the spectacular 21st-century Ciudad de las Artes y las Ciencias, Valencia offers its rich heritage.

Ciudad de las Artes y las Ciencias

Southeast of the city centre and occupying a massive 350,000-sq-metre swath of the old Turia riverbed is the aesthetically stunning **Ciudad de las Artes y las Ciencias** (City of Arts & Sciences; Map p575; reservations ☎ 902 100031; www.cac.es; Calle Arzobispo Mayoral 14; combined ticket for all three attractions adult/child €28/21). Pulling in well over four million visitors annually – a figure outstripped in Spain only by the Prado museum in Madrid – the 'city' is mostly the work of local architect Santiago Calatrava, designer of, among many other exciting creations around the world, the dome for the Athens 2004 Olympic Games' main stadium.

VALENCIA

The **Hemisfèric** (Map p575; adult/child €7/5.50) is a planetarium, IMAX cinema and laser show in one, all with optional English commentary.

The **Museo de las Ciencias Príncipe Felipe** (Map p575; adult/child €7/5.50; ☯ 10am-8pm) is an interactive science museum where each section has a pamphlet in English summarising its contents.

Highlight of the complex, especially if you have young children, will probably be the **Oceanogràfic** (Map p575; adult/child €20.50/15.50; ☯ 10am-6pm Sun-Fri, 10am-8pm Sat Sep–mid-Jul, 10am-midnight mid-Jul–Aug). This watery world, largest of its kind in Europe, has, among much else, polar zones, a dolphinarium, Red Sea aquarium, Mediterranean seascape – and a couple of underwater tunnels, one 70m long, where the fish, including sharks, giant eels and rays, swim all around you.

The **Palau de les Artes** (Map p575), an auditorium and multifunctional arts complex, looking for all the world like some giant mollusc, is destined for completion in 2005.

Take bus No 14, 15 or 35 from Calle Játiva and No 95 from Torres de Serranos or Plaza de América.

Museo de la Historia de Valencia

Valencia's newest museum, **Museo de la Historia de Valencia** (Map p575; ☎ 96 370 11 05; Calle Valencia; admission free; ☯ 9.15am-2pm & 5.30-8pm Tue-Sat, 9.15am-2pm Sun), above the equally new riverbed Parque de Cabecera, plots more than 2000 years of the city's history. Hands-on and very visual, it's great fun even if your Spanish isn't too hot. Take bus No 3 (via the Gran Vías), 81 (from Plaza del Ayuntamiento) or 95 (follows the Turia riverbank), or get off at the Nou d'Octubre metro stop.

Museo de Bellas Artes

The **Museo de Bellas Artes** (Fine Arts Museum; Map pp576-7; ☎ 96 360 57 93; Calle San Pío V 9; admission free; ☯ 10am-8pm Tue-Sun), on the north side of the former riverbed of the Río Turia, ranks among Spain's best, with works by El Greco, Goya, Velázquez, Ribera, Ribalta and artists such as Sorolla and Pinazo of the Valencian impressionist school.

IVAM (Instituto Valenciano de Arte Moderno)

IVAM (pronounced 'ee-bam') (Map pp576-7; ☎ 96 386 30 00; Calle Guillem de Castro 118; adult/student €2/1, admission free Sun; ☯ 10am-8pm Tue-Sun) houses an impressive permanent collection of 20th-century Spanish art, and hosts excellent temporary exhibitions.

Cathedral

The **cathedral** (Map p577; ☯ 7.30am-1pm & 5-8.30pm) is a microcosm of the city's architectural history: the **Puerta del Palau** on Plaza de la Virgen is Romanesque; the dome, tower and **Puerta de los Apóstoles** are Gothic; the presbytery and main entrance on Plaza de la Reina are baroque; and there are a couple of Renaissance chapels inside.

In the flamboyant Gothic **Capilla del Santo Cáliz**, right of the main entrance, is what's claimed to be the **Holy Grail**, the chalice from which Christ sipped during the Last Supper. Beyond it is the cathedral **museum** (adult/child €2/1; ☯ 10am-1pm & 4.30-7pm Mon-Fri, 10am-1pm Sat & Sun). The next chapel north, **La Capilla de San Francisco de Borja**, has a pair of particularly sensitive Goyas.

Left of the main portal is the entrance to the **Miguelete bell tower** (adult/child €2/1; ☯ 10am-12.30pm & 4.30-6.30pm). Clamber up the 207 steps of its spiral staircase for great 360-degree city and skyline views.

As for the past thousand years, the **Tribunal de las Aguas** (Water Court) meets every Thursday at noon outside the cathedral's Plaza del Palau. Here, local farmers' irrigation disputes are settled in Valenciano.

Plaza de la Virgen & Around

The **Plaza de la Virgen** (Map pp576-7) occupies the site that was once the forum of Roman Valencia, on the very spot where its main north–south and east–west highways intersected. Beside the cathedral is the church of **Nuestra Señora de los Desamparados** (Map pp576-7; ☯ 7am-2pm & 4-9pm Mon-Sat, 9.15am-2pm Sun). Above the altar is a highly venerated statue of the Virgin, patron of the city. Opposite is the handsome 15th-century Gothic – and much amended – **Palau de la Generalitat** (Map pp576-7), seat of government for the Valencia region. The reclining figure in the central fountain represents the Río Turia, while the eight maidens with their gushing pots symbolise the main irrigation canals flowing from it.

The **Cripta de la Cárcel de San Vicente Mártir** (Map pp576-7; ☎ 96 394 14 17; Plaza del Arzobispo; admission free; ☯ 9.30am-2pm & 5.30-8pm Tue-Sat, 9.30am-2pm Sun) was reputedly used as a prison for the

4th-century martyr San Vicente. Although the crypt of this Visigoth chapel isn't particularly memorable in itself, it's well worth taking in the free 25-minute multimedia show that presents Valencia's history and the saint's life and gory death. Make reservations either by phone or at the **Palacio del Marqués de Campo** (Map pp576-7), just opposite, and ask for a showing in English.

Immediately north of the crypt is the archaeological site of **La Almoina** (Map pp576-7), the heart of 'Valentia', the Roman town, which has yielded rich findings.

Palacio del Marqués de Dos Aguas

A pair of wonderfully extravagant rococo caryatids prop up the main entrance surround of the **Palacio del Marqués de Dos Aguas** (Map pp576-7). Inside, the **Museo Nacional de Cerámica** (☎ 96 351 63 92; Calle Poeta Querol 2; admission €2.40, admission free Sat afternoon & Sun; ☑ 10am-2pm & 4-8pm Tue-Sat, 10am-2pm Sun) displays ceramics from around the world – and especially the renowned local production centres of Manises, Alcora and Paterna.

Plaza del Mercado

Facing each other across **Plaza del Mercado** (Map pp576-7) are two magnificent buildings, each a masterpiece of its era. Pop into the 15th-century Gothic **Lonja** (Map pp576-7; admission free; ☑ core hrs 9.15am-2pm & 5-8pm Mon-Sat, 9.15am-2pm Sun), an early Valencian commodity exchange, now a Unesco World Heritage site, with its striking colonnaded hall. And set aside time to prowl the **Mercado Central** (Map pp576-7; ☑ 7.30am-2.30pm Mon-Sat), Valencia's Modernista covered market, constructed in 1928 and a swirl of smells, movement and colour. An even finer Modernista building is the **Mercado de Colón** (Map p575; Calle de Cirilo Amorós), also a market in its time and now occupied by boutiques and cafés.

Torres de Serranos & Torres de Quart

Two imposing, twin-towered stone gates are all that remain of the old city walls. Once the main exit to Barcelona and the north, the well-preserved, 14th-century **Torres de Serranos** (Map pp576-7; admission free; ☑ 9.15am-2pm & 5.30-7pm Tue-Sat, 9.15am-2pm Sun) overlook the bed of the Río Turia. Further west, the 15th-century **Torres de Quart** (Map pp576-7) face towards Madrid and the setting sun. Up high, you can still see the pockmarks caused by

French cannonballs during the 19th-century Napoleonic invasion.

Parks & Gardens

The **Jardines del Turia** (Map p575 & pp576-7) in the former riverbed are a 9km-long lung of green, a glorious mix of playing fields, cycling, jogging and walking paths, fountains, lawns and playgrounds (see Lilliputian kids scrambling over a magnificent, ever-patient **Gulliver** east of the Palau de la Música).

Reaching down to the gardens are the **Jardines del Real** (Royal Gardens; Map pp576-7), also known as Los Viveros, another lovely spot for a stroll. Within them are the **Museo de Ciencias Naturales** (Natural Science Museum; Map p575; admission free; ☑ 9.15am-2pm & 5.30-9pm Tue-Sat, 9.15am-2pm Sun) and a small **zoo** (Map p575; adult/child €4/2; ☑ 10am-sunset). Call by Boris, a drop-dead gorgeous orang-utan.

The **Jardín Botánico** (Map p575; Calle Quart 80; admission €0.30; ☑ 10am-dusk Tue-Sun), established in 1802, is Spain's first botanic garden. With mature trees and plants and an extensive cactus garden, it's a shady, tranquil place to relax.

Beaches

Valencia city's beach is the broad **Playa de la Malvarrosa**, east of the town centre, running into **Playa de las Arenas**, each bordered by the **Paseo Marítimo** promenade and a string of restaurants. One block back, lively bars and discos thump out the beat in summer. Take bus No 19 from Plaza del Ayuntamiento, No 1 or 2 from the bus station or the Gran Vías, or the high-speed tram from Pont de Fusta or the Benimaclet Metro junction. Bus No 21, running along Avenidas Primado Reig and Blasco Ibañez, and No 22, which passes along the Gran Vías and Avenida del Puerto, are additional summer-only services.

Playa El Salér, 10km south, is backed by shady pine woods. **Autocares Herca** (☎ 96 349 12 50; www .autocaresherca.com) buses run hourly (half-hourly in summer). They stop (look for the Herca sign at the bus stop) at the junction of Gran Vía de las Germanias and Calle Sueca, beside Plaza de Cánovas and in front of the Ciudad de las Artes y Las Ciencias. Get off at El Salér village (€0.90, 30 minutes).

Other Attractions

Off Plaza de la Reina is **Iglesia de Santa Catalina** (Map pp576-7), its striking 18th-century baroque belfry one of the city's best-known landmarks. Nearby, stalls in the small circular **Plaza Redonda** (Map pp576-7) sell bits and bobs, buttons and bows, clothes and locally made crafts and ceramics. On Sunday, the plaza becomes a pet market selling caged birds and mournful puppies and kittens.

South of here, the **Estación del Norte** (Map pp576-7) is another impressive Modernista building. Opened in 1917, the train station's main foyer is decorated with ceramic mosaics and murals – and mosaic 'bon voyage' wishes in all major European languages.

The bijou **Museo del Colegio del Patriarca** (Map pp576-7; Calle de la Nave 1; admission €1.20; ⏰ 11am-1.30pm), a fine arts museum, has works by El Greco, Juan de Juanes and Ribalta.

The small **Museo Taurino** (Map pp576-7; Pasaje Doctor Serra 10; admission free; ⏰ 10am-2pm & 4-8pm Tue-Sun, 10am-2pm Mon), behind the Plaza de Toros just south of the centre, holds a collection of bullfighting memorabilia.

The **Museo Fallero** (Map p575; Plaza Monteolivete s/n; admission €1.80; ⏰ 9.15am-2pm & 5.30-9pm Tue-Sat, 9.15am-1.30pm Sun) is dedicated to the festival of Las Fallas. *Ninots* are the near-life-size

figurines that strut and pose at the base of each *falla* (papier-mâché sculpture). And the *ninot indultat* ('reprieved' or 'exempted') is the only one from among thousands to be saved from the flames each year.

The **Museo Valenciano de la Ilustración y la Modernidad** (MUVIM; Map pp576-7; ☎ 96 388 37 30; Calle Guillem de Castro 8; admission free; ⏰ 10am-2pm & 4-8pm Tue-Sat, 10am-2pm Sun), the Museum of the Enlightenment, presents the history of ideas and thought through images, dioramas and dialogue. Hour-long tours start every half-hour. Ask for the English version of the audio and just go with the flow of the images.

WALKING TOUR

Refer to the map below for this walking tour of old Valencia. From **Plaza de la Virgen (1**; 578) – the point where the north-south and east–west arteries of Roman Valentia met – head briefly west along Calle Caballeros, 'Street of the Knights' and the main thoroughfare of medieval Valencia. Turn right into Calle Serranos and continue to **Plaza de los Fueros (2)** and the massive **Torres**

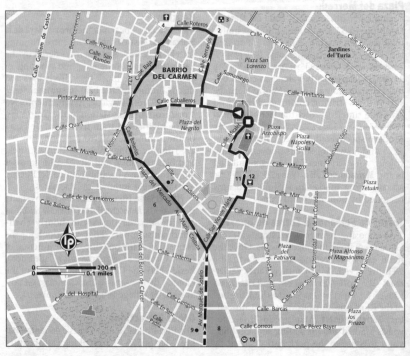

de Serranos (3; 581), through which travellers used to set out on the long journey northwards to Barcelona. Go left into Calle Roteros, sleepy by day but a buzz of restaurants and bars after dark, and continue to **Plaza del Carmen (4)**, where the baroque façade of the old convent and the Palacio de Pineda stare each other out. Turn left (south) into Calle Baja (Low Street) which, together with its twin, Calle Alta (you've guessed it: High St), were also important medieval streets. At **Plaza del Tossal (5**; Square of the Hill, though the gradient's all but imperceptible) you can take a drink in one of the swanky bars then either short-cut eastwards back along Calle Caballeros (admiring the fine mansions as you go) or continue down Calle Bolserías (halting, perhaps, at the earthy Asturian cider café on the left). Bear left into Avenida Maria Cristina and allow yourself time to browse around the **Mercado Central (6**; p579) and **Lonja (7**; p579), each a gem of its kind.

Bear right at the junction with Calle San Vicente Mártir to detour briefly and take in **Plaza del Ayuntamiento (8)**, where the neoclassical **town hall** (9) looks across to the neobaroque splendour of Valencia's **main post office (10**; 577). Pop inside to savour its freshly renovated interior – more like a theatre foyer than a place to post a letter – and raise your eyes to the magnificent leaded-glass dome). Returning, head north up Calle San Vicente Mártir to **Plaza de la Reina (11)**, once a jumble of shops and houses but now wide, functional and a bit soulless – something that can't be said for **Finnegan's bar (12**; 585), where, with the walk's end almost in sight, you might want to reward yourself with a Guinness. Otherwise, slip up the lane that runs to the left (west) of the cathedral to rejoin your starting point.

VALENCIA FOR CHILDREN

Beaches (p579), of course: nearest is the combined beach of Malvarrosa and Las Arenas (the latter meaning 'sand'), a shortish bus or tram ride from the centre. The high-speed tram is for fun: feel the G-force as it surges along. The other great playground, year-round, is the diverted Río Turia's former 9km **riverbed** (p579). Of its play areas, Gulliver just asks to be clambered all over.

Within the **Jardines del Real** (Los Viveros gardens) (p579), there's a miniature road system, complete with traffic signs and bridges. You have to take your own bike, trike or pedal car, but it's great fun – and a learning experience too. The **Jardín Botánico** (p579) is altogether more peaceful; mind the cactuses, play hide and seek among the trees and look for frogs in the fountain.

Of the Ciudad de las Artes y las Ciencias' diversions (p577), the Oceanogràfic, with more than 45,000 aquatic beasts and plants, has something for all ages. The science museum, reasonably documented in English, is more for over-12s (we've seen primary-school kids innocently and casually wrecking the hands-on exhibits), while the IMAX cinema offers thrills for all. The fun is far from free, however, so do research the range of family and combined tickets.

TOURS
Bicycle Tours
On Saturday at 10am, **Valencia Guías** (☎ 96 385 17 40; www.valenciaguias.com; Paseo de la Pechina 32) 3½-hour guided visits (in Spanish and English) of Valencia by bike (€22 including rental; reserve in advance), leaving from their premises, and also two-hour multilingual walking tours of the historic heart of town (adult/child €10/5), departing from the town hall in Plaza del Ayuntamiento.

Bus Tours
Valencia Bus Turístico (☎ 96 341 44 00) runs 90-minute **city tours** (adult/child €12/6; half-hourly, 10.30am-9pm Apr-Oct, hourly 10.30am-7.30pm Nov-Mar) with a recorded commentary in eight languages. Buses leave from Plaza de la Reina, tickets are valid for 24 hours and you can hop off and on at four of the city's most significant sites: IVAM, Ciudad de las Artes y las Ciencias, Oceanogràfic and Museo de Bellas Artes.

It also does a similar multilingual tour of La Albufera (adult/child €12/6; two hours). The tour includes a half-hour boat trip on the Albufera lagoon (p588).

Walking Tours
Valencia Walking Tours (www.valenciawalkingtours .com; 2-hr tour Mon-Sat, May-Sep €12) does a laid-back two-hour walking tour in English, leaving the Lounge (p585) at 7pm. The fee includes a free glass of *horchata* and *agua de Valencia* back at the Lounge.

FESTIVALS & EVENTS

MARCH/APRIL
Semana Santa The suburb of La Malvarrosa celebrates Holy Week with elaborate processions.
Fiesta de San Vicente Ferrer On the Sunday after Easter, colourful parades and miracle plays are performed around town.

MAY
On the second Sunday in May, the effigy of the Virgen de los Desamparados, patron of the city, makes the short journey across the Plaza de la Virgen to the cathedral, hemmed in by fervent believers struggling to touch her.

JUNE
Festival of Corpus Christi This festival, held in early June, was first celebrated in Valencia City way back in 1355 and is another excuse for a procession.
Día de San Juan (Midsummer's Day) Each 24 June thousands spend the evening on the Playa de la Malvarrosa, taking part in a traditional cleansing ceremony where you wash your feet in the ocean and write your bad habits on a piece of paper, which you throw onto a bonfire.

JULY
Feria de Julio Features a packed programme of performing arts, brass band competitions, free concerts, bullfights, a jazz festival, fireworks and a 'battle of the flowers' – when decorated, horse-drawn floats parade down the Paseo de la Alameda as their occupants and spectators pelt each other with tens of thousands of orange marigolds.

OCTOBER
Every October Valencia hosts a **festival of Mediterranean cinema**, while 9 October marks the **Día de la Comunidad**, commemorating the city's 1238 liberation from the Arabs.

SLEEPING
Budget
There are three related budget alternatives, each hugely welcoming and jazzily designed with self-catering facilities, a cosy lounge, Internet access and corridor facilities:

Hôme Backpackers (Map pp576-7; ☎ 96 391 37 97; www.likeathome.net; Calle Santa Cristina s/n; dm €12-14, d/tr/q €32/48/64; 🖳) This place has nearly 100 beds (some bunks) and a vast roof terrace.

Hôme Youth Hostel (Map pp576-7; ☎ 96 391 62 29; www.likeathome.net; Calle Lonja 4; dm/s/d €14/21/32; 🖳) More intimate than Hôme Backpackers.

Hôme Deluxe Hostel (Map pp576-7; ☎ 96 391 46 91; www.likeathome.net; Calle Cadirers 11; d with breakfast €40; 🖳) Has 10 bright doubles, each individu-

ally – sometimes eccentrically – designed. All three alternatives are true hômes from home.

Albergue Ciudad de Valencia (Map pp576-7; ☎ 96 392 51 00; www.alberguedevalencia.com; Calle Balmes 17; dm under/over 26 €12/15) Affiliated to Hostelling International, this *albergue* is in an attractive, recently renovated building. Mind how you go, as it's on the fringe of the red-light district.

Hostal El Rincón (Map pp576-7; ☎ 96 391 79 98; Calle de la Carda 11; basic s/d €10/18, with bathroom & air-con €13/24) This is one of Valencia's oldest and best-known *hostales* (budget hotels). The basic rooms are a bit poky and dim but more than acceptable, while its 14 renovated rooms with bathroom and air-con represent outstanding value.

Two other good budget choices, both family-run, are:

Pensión París (Map pp576-7; ☎ /fax 96 352 67 66; 1st & 3rd fl, Calle de Salvá 12; basic s/d/tr €19/28/41, d/tr

---

LAS FALLAS

The exuberant, anarchic swirl of **Las Fallas de San José** – fireworks, music, festive bonfires and all-night partying – is a must if you're in Spain between 12 and 19 March.

The *fallas* themselves are huge sculptures of papier-mâché on wood (with, increasingly, environmentally damaging polystyrene), built by teams of local artists. Each neighbourhood sponsors its own *falla*, and when the town wakes to the *plantà* (overnight construction of the *fallas*) on the morning of 16 March, more than 350 have been erected. Reaching up to 15m in height, with the most expensive costing more than €120,000 (oh yes, we've got those eurozeros right!), these grotesque, colourful effigies satirise celebrities, current affairs and local customs.

Around-the-clock festivities include street parties, paella-cooking competitions, parades, open-air concerts, bullfights and nightly free firework displays. Valencia considers itself the pyrotechnic capital of the world and each day at 2pm from 1 to 19 March a *mascletà* (over five minutes of deafening thumps and explosions) shakes the window panes of Plaza del Ayuntamiento.

After midnight on the final day each *falla* goes up in flames – backed by yet more fireworks.

with shower €32/45) Welcoming, with spotless rooms and corridor bathrooms.

Hostal-Residencia Universal (Map pp576-7; ☎ /fax 96 351 53 84; 2nd-4th fl, Calle Barcas 5; s/d/tr €19/28/41, d with shower €32) Run by the same family to a similarly high standard.

Around 12km south of town, **Devesa Gardens** (Map p575; ☎ 96 161 11 36; www.devesagardens .com/camping; Carretera el Salér; camping per person/tent/ car €4.50/4.50/4.50) is a 15-minute walk from El Salér beach; this the nearest camping ground to Valencia.

Mid-Range & Top End (Map pp576-7)

Since Valencia is a business centre, big hotels struggle to fill rooms at weekends and most offer fat weekend and high summer discounts of up to one-third.

Hostal Antigua Morellana (☎ 96 391 57 73; www.hostalam.com; Calle En Bou 2; s/d €33/48; ☒) This friendly, family-run 18-room hotel is tucked away near the central market. Occupying a renovated 18th-century building on a quiet street, it has cosy, good-sized rooms, most with balconies, and is warmly recommended.

Hostal Moratín (☎ 96 352 12 20; www.hmoratin .com; 4th-5th fl, Calle de Moratín 15; s/d with shower €24/39, d/tr with bathroom €51/75) Another central option, Hostal Moratín is tidy and tranquil and the staff are courteous and welcoming. With 19 rooms, it's relatively small, so do book in advance. Leave your vehicle in the multilevel car park just next door.

Hotel Continental (☎ 96 353 52 82; www.contitel .es; Calle Correos 8; s/d with breakfast €49/74, mid-Jul–mid-Aug with breakfast €46/60; ☒) The Continental, a favourite with business visitors, is bright, modern and an equally friendly choice.

Hotel Londres (☎ 96 351 22 44; fax 96 352 15 08; Calle Barcelonina 1; s with shower €32, d/tr with bathroom & air-con €58/79; ☒) Beside Plaza del Ayuntamiento, the family-run Londres couldn't be more central. Rooms are attractive and cosy; some have a balcony and others overlook the square. Ask for room 803, on the top, eighth floor, which has both – and a gorgeous view.

Ad Hoc (☎ 963 91 91 40; www.adhochoteles.com; Calle Boix 4; s/d €87/115; ☒) Rooms at this charming intimate hotel, converted with great taste from a 19th-century mansion, have stencilled ceilings, balconies and attractive exposed brickwork adorned with richly coloured fabrics.

Hotel Excelsior (☎ 96 351 46 12; www.hoteles-cata lonia.com; Calle Barcelonina 5; s/d with breakfast €85/97; ☒) The spacious rooms at this recently renovated hotel have gleaming parquet flooring and lavish marble bathrooms. Central and welcoming, it also has a small, pleasant downstairs bar area.

Hotel Reina Victoria (☎ 96 352 04 87; www.husa .es; Calle Barcas 4; s/d €105/127, Fri-Sun & Jul-Aug r €70; ☒ ☒) This grand old place, comprehensively renovated, harmoniously blends old-world charm with contemporary efficiency and facilities.

Hotel Inglés (☎ 96 351 64 26; www.solmelia.es; Calle Marqués de Dos Aguas 6; s/d €98/115, d with breakfast €82 Fri-Sun & Jul-Aug; ☒ ☒ ▣) In a stylishly renovated 18th-century mansion, the long-established Hotel Inglés has rooms with character, some exclusively for nonsmokers. The café and some bedrooms overlook the glorious rococo main entrance to the Palacio del Marqués de Dos Aguas.

Hotel Astoria Palace (☎ 96 398 10 00; www.hotel -astoria-palace.com; Plaza Rodrigo Botet 5; s/d €110/142, d with breakfast €94 Fri-Sun; ℗ ☒ ☒) More self-consciously modern, the well-established Astoria Palace, with its 214 rooms, runs a good restaurant. It's a firm favourite with visiting dignitaries and bullfighters – not many of whom opt for a room on the whole floor that's dedicated to nonsmokers.

EATING

Valencia is the capital of *la huerta*, a fertile coastal agricultural plain that supplies the city with delightfully fresh fruit and vegetables.

AUTHOR'S CHOICE

Restaurante Submarino (Map pp576-7; ☎ 96 197 55 65; Oceanogràfic; mains €16.20-25.80, rice dishes €10.50-20) OK, so it's not strictly speaking submarine, not literally underwater, but the illusion of this very classy restaurant, implanted into the heart of the Oceanogràfic aquarium complex (p578), is almost complete. Instead of wallpaper at this circular restaurant, over 1000 silvery bream and sardines slowly gyrate around. The food is superb; if you feel uncomfortable eating fish with all those glaucous eyes staring reproachfully, there are meat alternatives and good, less expensive rice dishes too.

VALENCIA

Rice is the staple of much Valencian cuisine – and the basis of the dish Valencia exported to the world: paella. Other local favourites include *arroz a banda* (rice simmered in a fish stock), *arroz negro* (rice with squid, including its ink) and *arroz al horno* (rice baked in the oven). Then there's *fideuá*, a paella made with noodles instead of rice. Valencianos normally eat rice only at lunch time, when locals in their hundreds head for Las Arenas, just north of the port.

Quick Eats (Map pp576-7)

En Bandeja (☎ 96 394 06 95; Calle San Vicente Mártir 24; ☺ to 9pm Mon-Sat Oct-May, Mon-Fri Jun-Sep) This relaxed self-service place does excellent-value continental breakfasts (€3.50) and lunches (€7.90 including drink and coffee).

FrescCo (☎ 96 310 63 88; Calle Felix Pizcueta 6; buffet meal €6.90; ☺ lunch Mon-Fri, €8.80 dinner & Sat & Sun) With its all-you-can eat buffet, FrescCo is much more than a fill-you-to-the-brim joint; there's a veritable kitchen garden of salad items and a choice of main dishes. With its bare, mellow brickwork, it's also a very agreeable place to be eating in, though you're not encouraged to linger once dessert's over.

Restaurants (Map pp576-7)

In Las Arenas, a long line of restaurants overlooking the beach all serve up the real stuff in a three-course meal costing around €12.

La Pepica (☎ 96 371 03 66; Paseo Neptuno 6) Larger and more expensive than its competitors, this is where Ernest Hemingway, among many other luminaries, once strutted. Between courses, browse through the photos and tributes that plaster the walls and see how many you recognise.

La Lonja del Pescado Frito (☎ 96 355 35 35; Calle Eugenia Viñes 243; meals around €15; ☺ dinner Tue-Fri, lunch & dinner Sat & Sun Mar-Oct, Sat & Sun only Nov-Feb) Right beside the Eugenia Viñes tram stop, this informal place in what's little more than an adorned tin shack offers unbeatable value for fresh fish. Grab an order form as you enter and fill it in at your table.

There are several excellent restaurants within easy striding distance of Plaza de la Virgen.

Seu-Xerea (☎ 96 392 40 00; Calle Conde Almodóvar 4; meals around €25; ☺ Mon-Fri, dinner Sat) This welcoming restaurant is favourably quoted in just

about every English-language press article about Valencia. It has a creative and regularly changing *à la carte* menu featuring dishes both international and rooted in Spain, and does a warmly recommended lunch-time *menú del día* (daily set menu) at €14.

There are several other good choices around the square:

S'Horabaixa (☎ 96 391 21 77; Calle Conde Almodóvar 2; ☺ dinner Tue-Sun) Offers cuisine with a Mallorcan slant. With its cosy décor, it's popular for its salads and open sandwiches. Count on €12-15 for a fulfilling and feel-fulling combination of salads and sammos.

Las Cuevas (☎ 96 391 71 96; Calle Samaniego 9; tapas €2-7) Aptly named 'The Caves', this low-ceilinged, semi-basement place carries a huge range of tapas.

Restaurante El Generalife (☎ 96 391 78 99; Calle Caballeros 5; menú €9) Does a *menú* that's considerably more imaginative than most. Arrive early to avoid having to wait.

Around Plaza del Ayuntamiento you'll find a couple of attractive yet economical alternatives:

Pizzeria La Vita é Bella (☎ 96 352 21 31; Calle d'En Llop 4; mains €4.50-7.50) Occupying a tastefully restored draper's shop, this cosy café-bar does good pizzas and pastas, and mouth-watering home-made ice creams.

La Utielana (☎ 96 352 94 14; Plaza Picadero dos Aguas 3; meals around €10; ☺ lunch Mon-Sat, closed dinner Sat & Sun) Tucked away off Calle Prócida and not easy to find, the Utielana is excellent value and merits a few minutes' sleuthing.

There's a cluster of superb upmarket seafood restaurants along pedestrianised Calle Mosén Femades, including **Palacio de la Bellota** (☎ 96 351 53 61; Calle Mosén Femades 7; ☺ Mon-Sat) and **Civera Centro** (☎ 96 352 97 64; Calle Mosén Femades 10; ☒), which comes with a strong reader recommendation. For both, count on at least €50 per head, including wine, so pack your plastic.

HORCHATA

Horchata is a sweet, opaque local drink made from pressed *chufas* (tiger nuts), into which you dip large finger-shaped buns called *fartons*; both name and taste are to savour. Two traditional places to sample it in the heart of town are **Horchatería de Santa Catalina** and **Horchatería el Siglo**, both on Plaza Santa Catalina.

Self-Catering

A visit to the magnificent central covered market, the **Mercado Central** (Map pp576-7; Plaza del Mercado; ⏲ 7.30am-2.30pm Mon-Sat), is a must, even if you only browse.

Vegetarian

Erba Cipollina (Map pp576-7; ☎ 96 392 04 96; Calle Padre Tosca 7; midday menú €10.50; ⏲ Thu-Tue Oct-Jun, daily Jul-Sep) This intimate restaurant serves mainly tasty, imaginative vegetarian dishes, while making the odd concession to carnivores, and is excellent value, particularly its €8.50 lunch buffet.

La Tastaolletes (Map pp576-7; ☎ 96 392 18 62; Calle Salvador Giner 6; menú €8; ⏲ lunch Tue-Sun, closed dinner Sun & Mon) This tiny place does a creative range of vegetable tapas. Pleasantly informal, it's worth visiting for the friendly atmosphere and good, wholesome food created from quality prime ingredients – not least the fresh brown bread.

Ana Eva (Map p575; ☎ 96 391 53 69; Calle Turia 49; meals €12-15; ⏲ Tue-Sat, lunch Sun) More sophisticated and rather more pricey, Ana Eva has tasteful décor, a delightful patio and some very imaginative dishes.

DRINKING

Fuelled by a large student population and an overdeveloped sense of competitiveness with Madrid and Barcelona, Valencia has a justified reputation for having one of Spain's best nightlife scenes.

The **Barrio del Carmen** has both the grungiest and grooviest collection of bars. The other major area is around the **university**; Avenidas de Aragón and Blasco Ibáñez and surrounding streets have enough bars and *discotecas* to keep you busy beyond sunrise.

Two other zones worth checking out are around the **Mercado de Abastos** and **Plaza de Cánovas**, while in summer, **Malvarrosa**, north of the port, comes alive with disco fever.

The action usually doesn't begin until about 11pm and continues until well towards dawn.

Bars & Pubs
BARRIO DEL CARMEN (MAP PP576-7)

'El Carmé' has everything from designer bars and yuppie pubs to grungy thrash-metal haunts and punk bars. On weekends, Calle Caballeros, the main street, seethes with revellers seeking *la marcha* (the action).

Plaza del Tossal is rimmed by sophisticated bars. At **Café Bolsería** a cool crowd gathers on the ground floor while house music pounds upstairs. By contrast, the 1st floor of **San Jaume**, a converted pharmacy and all quiet crannies and poky passageways, is altogether more intimate.

Carmen Sui Generis (Calle Caballeros 38; admission €8) Built around a huge hunk of Valencia's Arab city wall, each of its three levels offers different music.

Johnny Maracas (Calle Caballeros 39) A suave salsa place with fish tanks on the bar.

Fox Congo (Calle Caballeros 35) This place has a cool marble bar, patchwork suede benches, scrap-metal montage ceilings – and glass-walled toilets.

Cafe-Bar Negrito (Plaza del Negrito), A block south of Calle Caballeros, the crowd and music spill out onto the square here.

John Silver (Calle Alta 8) Low, dark and named after the monopod old pirate himself (his wooden leg hangs behind the bar), this place is typical of the cheaper bars north of Plaza del Tossal, with tables on the street.

OTHER AREAS

Café de las Horas (Map pp576-7; Calle Conde de Almodóvar 1) Just north of Plaza de la Virgen, this café is wonderfully baroque, with tapestries, classical music and candelabras dripping wax.

Finnegan's (Map pp576-7; Plaza de la Reina) The longest established of Valencia's several Irish bars, this is a popular meeting place for English speakers.

The Lounge (Map pp576-7; ☎ 96 391 80 94; Calle Estameñaría Vieja 2) A true Irish bar without a false fiddle or unread copy of James Joyce in sight, this is a friendly place, with deep sofas and an Internet terminal. It's popular with both Valencianos and visitors, and does a great-value vegetarian lunch *menú* (€5). It also shakes and stirs some wicked cocktails; happy hour is from 8pm to 10pm.

Near the **Mercado de Abastos** (Map p575), just west of the town centre, Calle Juan Lloréns and surrounding streets are very much the 'in' area. Drop into modish **Akuarela** at No 49; the smaller **Maruja Limón** at No 54, which is strong on Spanish pop; or, for a little Pharaonic frenzy, **Anubis**, with its ancient Egyptian theme at No 34.

Just east of the centre, **Plaza de Cánovas** (Map p575), tamer and more upmarket, attracts a younger crowd. **Plaza** is a stylish corner bar on the square itself. Around the corner on Calle Serrano Morales, a trio of neighbours waits to pull you in: **Scala Norte**, **Abbey Road** – and **Década Loca,** with karaoke and a weekend go-go dancer.

ENTERTAINMENT
There are several good resources for keeping abreast of what's on in this lively city. *La Turia* and *Que y Donde* (both €1.20, weekly, in Spanish) are sold at kiosks and news agents. 24-7 *Valencia* (free in bars, clubs etc, in English) also has an informative, regularly updated website (www.24-7valencia. com). *Cool Carmen* (www.coolcarmen.com) is another worthwhile freebie available in bars and tourist offices. It provides informed tip-offs about places around the where-it-happens Barrio del Carmen.

Cinemas
The **Filmoteca** (Map pp576-7; ☎ 96 399 55 77; Plaza del Ayuntamiento; admission €1.50), on the 4th floor of the Teatro Rialto building, screens undubbed classic, art-house and experimental films.

Valencia has two multiscreen cinemas showing exclusively undubbed films: **Albatros** (Map p575; ☎ 96 393 26 77; Plaza Fray Luis Colomer) and **Babel** (Map p575; ☎ 96 362 67 95; Calle Vicente Sancho Tello 10). Admission prices are lower on Monday.

Football
Valencia, as football crazy as any other corner of the Mediterranean, has an extraordinarily successful soccer team. The trophy cabinet of Valencia Club de Fútbol has probably been strengthened recently to bear the fruits of recent achievements: European Cup runners-up, 2000 and 2001; Spanish League Champions 2003 and 2004; and UEFA cup holders in 2004. You can pick up a scarf, woolly hat, shirt or other memento from the club's **shop** (Calle Pintor Sorolla 24).

In 2004 the city's other professional football club, Levante, a minnow by comparison, won promotion to the Spanish first division for the first time in more than 20 years. Should they still be up there by the time you hit town, do take in a game; they'll be needing all the support they can get.

Live Music
Black Note (Map p575; ☎ 96 393 36 63; Calle de Polo y Peyrolón 15) This place has live jazz, blues and soul Monday to Thursday.

Jimmy Glass (Map pp576-7; Calle Baja 28) Plays cool jazz from the owner's vast CD collection and puts on live performers fortnightly.

Loco Mateo (Map p575; ☎ 96 326 05 26; Calle Erudito Orellena 12) Until recently Valencia's prime flamenco venue, Loco Mateo has broadened its repertoire – some would say lost its focus – and nowadays serves up a bit of everything. Choose your night according to your music then, the concert over, dance on until throwing-out time.

Cormorán (Map p575; ☎ 96 380 38 52; Calle San Vicente Mártir 200) South of the train station, Cormorán has the pulling power to bring in the big names of pop and rock.

Nightclubs
At weekends, **Radio City** (Santa Teresa 19; ⏲ 11pm-late) has a free disco that's good for post-bar dancing to salsa, house and sometimes cheesy pop. There's live flamenco on Tuesday.

For more life after 3am, head for the university area along and around **Avenida Blasco Ibáñez** and **Avenida de Aragón** (Map p575), where new bars are opening by the month. Most *discotecas* have cover charges of around €6 to €9, although discounted passes are often available from local bars.

Of the bars, **New York** (NY; Avenida de Aragón 28) plays funky music, while **Caribbean's** (Calle Bélgica 5; ⏲ Tue-Sat) has a mix of salsa and merengue. **Cachao** (Calle Periodista Ros Belda 5) is another salsa bar that offers free lessons.

Rumbo 144 (Avenida Blasco Ibáñez 146; ⏲ Thu-Sat Sep-Jul) This is a funky, large-floored place with a light show.

Warhol (Avenida Blasco Ibáñez 111; ⏲ Wed-Sat) Across the road, this is a smallish venue playing eclectic music that attracts a predominantly student crowd.

Llampua (Plaza Legión Española 12) Another small, fun club that plays a blend of house, pop and techno.

Bananas (☎ 96 178 17 06; Carretera Valencia-Alicante, El Romani; from midnight Fri & Sat) Just about the maxiest maxidisco you'll ever party at, Bananas packs in dancers by the thousand. Forget taxi lines: take the special train that leaves Estación del Norte at 1.15am, go Bananas and return on the early bird at 6.15am.

Theatre & Opera
The **Teatro Principal** (Map pp576-7; ☎ 96 351 00 51; Calle Barcas 15) is Valencia's main venue for opera and the performing arts.

The **Palau de la Música** (Map p575; ☎ 96 337 50 20; Paseo de la Alameda 30), a huge, glass-domed concert hall above the Jardines del Turia, hosts mainly classical music recitals. Downstream, the new **Palau de les Artes** (p578) is due to open its doors within the lifetime of this edition of this guidebook.

GETTING THERE & AWAY
Air
Valencia's **Aeropuerto de Manises** (☎ 96 159 85 00) is 10km west of the centre. Regular flights connect the city with Madrid, Barcelona, Ibiza and Palma de Mallorca; daily scheduled flights go to London, Paris, Milan and Lisbon. Of the budget carriers, Thomson (www.fly thomson.com) flies to/from Coventry airport in the UK. Check British Airways too, since it offers comparable or better deals to/from London (Gatwick). Hapag Lloyd (www.hlx .com) and Air Berlin (www.airberlin.com) cover a number of German destinations and Air Europa offers bargain flights to Paris (Orly). EasyJet (www.easyjet.com) flies daily to/from Bristol & London (Gatwick & Stansted). Ryanair too has a daily flight to/from London (Stansted). Vueling (www.vueling .com) flies to both Paris (Charles de Gaulle) and Brussels for as little as €35 one way.

Boat
In summer, **Trasmediterránea** (☎ 902 454645) operates car and passenger ferries to Mallorca (Monday to Saturday) and Ibiza (Tuesday, Thursday, Saturday and Sunday). During the rest of the year, sailings are less frequent (p617). Buy your ticket at the passenger terminal of the **Muelle de Poniente** (☎ 96 316 48 59) or any travel agency.

Bus
The **bus station** (Map p575; ☎ 96 349 72 22; Avenida de Menéndez Pidal) is beside the riverbed. Bus No 8 connects it to Plaza del Ayuntamiento.

AutoRes (☎ 902 020999) runs more than 10 buses daily to/from Madrid (€21, four hours). **Alsa** (☎ 902 422242) has more than 10 daily buses to/from Barcelona (€22, 4¼ to five hours) and Alicante (€15.25, 2½ hours), most passing by Benidorm (€11.20, 1¾ hours).

Train
From Valencia's Estación del Norte (Map pp576-7), seven to 10 Alaris express trains

travel daily to/from Madrid (€37, 3½ hours), going via Albacete.

A dozen trains daily make the three- to five-hour haul north to Barcelona via Tarragona, including the high-speed Euromed (€34.35, up to seven daily) and the slightly slower Arco (€29). Up to eight trains head daily to Alicante, (€10.50 to €23, 1½ to 2 hours).

Most of the frequent northbound trains stop at Sagunto (€2.20, 30 minutes) and Castellón (€3.40, up to one hour).

GETTING AROUND
Valencia has an integrated bus, tram and metro network. EMT buses ply town routes, while MetroBus serves outlying towns and villages. Tourist offices stock maps for both services.

To/From the Airport
MetroBus (€1.10, 45 minutes) takes a roundabout route to/from the bus station, departing every 10 minutes. Trains (€1.15, 20 minutes) run from Estación del Norte every 20 minutes (hourly at weekends), leaving you with a 300m walk to the airport. A taxi into the centre costs €12 to €15 (there's a supplement of €2.50 for journeys originating at the airport).

Bicycle
Orange Bikes (Map pp576-7; ☎ 963917551; www.orange bikes.net; Calle Santa Teresa 8), opposite Radio City, rents mountain bikes (€12/24/72 per day/ weekend/week) and town bikes (€14/28/84). The initiative of a young Anglo-Valenciano couple, this is also a good place to buy a second-hand cycle.

Car & Motorcycle
Street parking can be a real pain. There are large subterranean car parks beneath Plazas de la Reina and Alfonso el Magnánimo and, biggest of all, near the train station, covering the area between Calle Xàtiva and the Gran Vía.

Major car-hire companies include **Europcar** (airport ☎ 96 152 18 72; train station/town ☎ 96 351 90 55) and **Avis** (airport ☎ 96 152 21 62; train station/town ☎ 96 352 24 78).

Reliable local companies operating from Valencia airport include **Javea Cars** (☎ 96 579 3312; www.javeacars.com), **Solmar** (☎ 96 646 10 00; www.solmar.es) and **Victoria Cars** (☎ 96 579 27 61;

www.victoriacars.com). They are usually substantially less expensive than the major companies.

Public Transport

Most **EMT** (☎ 96 352 83 99) buses run until about 10pm, with night services continuing on seven routes until around 1am. A single journey costs €0.95, a T1 (one-day pass) is €3 and a 10-trip Bonobus is €4.90.

The smart high-speed tram is a pleasant way to get to the beach, paella restaurants of Las Arenas and the port. Pick it up at Pont de Fusta or where it intersects with the Metro at Benimaclet.

Metro lines serve the outer suburbs. The closest stations to the centre are Ángel Guimerá, Xàtiva (for the train station), Colón and Pont de Fusta.

Taxi

Call **Radio-Taxi** (☎ 96 370 33 33) or **Valencia Taxi** (☎ 96 357 13 13).

AROUND VALENCIA CITY

LA ALBUFERA

About 15km south of Valencia, La Albufera is a huge freshwater lagoon separated from the sea by a narrow strip of sand dunes and pine forests known as La Devesa. The lake and surrounding areas are a breeding ground and sanctuary for migrating and indigenous birds. Keen bird-watchers flock to the **Parque Natural de la Albufera**, where around 90 species regularly nest while more than 250 use it as a staging post on their migrations.

The sunsets can be spectacular. You can take a boat trip on the lagoon, joining the local fisherfolk, who use distinctive flat-bottomed boats and nets to harvest fish and eels from the shallow waters.

Surrounded by rice fields, La Albufera was the birthplace of paella. The villages of **El Palmar** and **El Perellonet** boast some excellent restaurants that specialise in paella and other rice and seafood dishes.

Autocares Herca buses for Playa El Saler (p579) are also good for La Albufera and continue to either El Palmar (five to seven daily) or El Perellonet (hourly), further down the coast.

SAGUNTO
pop 56,500

Sagunto (Valenciano: Sagunt), 25km north of Valencia, was a thriving Iberian community as early as the 5th century BC, when the settlers fortified their hill town with stone walls and traded with Greeks and Phoenicians. It's usually visited as a day or half-day excursion from Valencia.

In 219 BC Hannibal besieged the town for eight months. The inhabitants were eventually wiped out and their town destroyed, sparking the Second Punic War

---

LA TOMATINA

Buñol? It'll make you see red.

If you're in Valencia on the last or penultimate Wednesday in August (the date varies), you can participate in one of Spain's messiest and most bizarre festivals. Held in the town of Buñol, an otherwise drab industrial town about 40km west of Valencia city, La Tomatina is a tomato-throwing orgy.

The festival's origins, though relatively recent, are obscure, but who cares? And while it mightn't last long, it attracts up to 30,000 visitors to a town of just 9000 inhabitants.

Just before noon on this very red-letter day, truckloads of ripe, squishy tomatoes (125,000kg is one estimate) are tipped out to the waiting crowd, and for the next hour or so everyone joins in a frenzied, cheerful, anarchic tomato battle. The most enthusiastic participants chant '*tomate, tomate, queremos tomate!*' ('tomato, tomato, we want tomato!').

After being pounded with pulp, expect to be sluiced down with hoses by the local fire brigade. The mayhem takes place on the town's main square and Calle del Cid.

At 1pm an explosion signals the end and the drenched participants don their stash of fresh clothes. Most people come for the day, arriving on the morning train from Valencia and heading back in the afternoon.

You can watch the spectacle in comfort on Canal 9, Valencia's local TV channel.

between Carthage and Rome. Rome won, named the town Saguntum and set about rebuilding it.

From the train station it's a 10-minute walk to the **tourist office** (☎ 96 266 22 13; Plaza del Cronista Chabret; ☷ 8am-3pm & 4-6.30pm Mon-Fri, 9.30am-1.30pm Sat, 9am-2pm Sun). A further 15-minute uphill walk through narrow streets (passing beside the Judería, the former Jewish quarter) brings you to the Roman theatre and castle.

The **Roman theatre** was built into the hillside during the 1st century AD. Centuries of use and disuse had left it in poor shape, but the controversial modern 'restoration' is in questionable taste. Still, the acoustics remain outstanding and the theatre is the main venue for Sagunto's three-week, open-air August **arts festival**.

Higher up, the stone walls of the **castle complex** (admission free; ☷ 10am-dusk Tue-Sat, 10am-2pm Sun) wind around the hillside for almost a kilometre. Mostly in ruins, the rambling complex's seven sections each speak of a different period in Sagunto's long history.

Getting There & Away

There are frequent trains between Valencia and Sagunto (€2/3.70 one way/return) and AVSA runs a half-hourly service (€2) from Valencia's bus station.

SEGORBE

pop 7910 / elevation 395m

Segorbe, 33km northwest of Sagunto, has a fine **cathedral** with a delicate, tranquil cloister. At the western corner of the old town is a pair of cylindrical towers. The **Torre de la Cárcel** for a time served as the town's lockup while the town executioner, for those whose fate was even worse, lived nearby in the **Torre del Botxí**. The **medieval aqueduct**, of which a healthy hunk remains, brought water from the fountain of **La Esperanza** (Hope), from where it still springs eternal.

Segorbe is renowned for its **Entrada de Toros y Caballos** (Entry of Bulls and Horses) where, prompt at 2pm during the second week of September, skilled horsemen guide and prod the bulls down Calle Colón between two human walls of spectators.

The **tourist office** (☎ 964 71 32 54; www.segorbe .org; Calle Marcelino Blasco 3; ☷ 9am-2.30pm & 4-6pm Mon-Sat, 11am-2pm Sun) is beside the municipal car park.

NAVAJAS

About 2km north of the Segorbe turn-off on the main N234, take a signed right to drive beside orchards, almond and olive groves to the lovely little village of Navajas, shaded by cypress and palm trees and spurting with fountains and springs. Savour the charming tiled and pastel-painted **summer villas**, built during the 19th century by rich Valencians, then stretch your legs by following one of the four signed **walking trails**, each about 12km long, that radiate from Plaza del Olmo.

REQUENA

pop 19,200 / elevation 690m

Just off the A3, 71km west of Valencia, Requena is a bustling commercial centre from whose heart rises a little walled medieval town, established by the Muslims in the 8th century. Requena's former wealth came from silk; at one time it had 800 active looms, making this tiny town Spain's 4th-biggest producer. Nowadays it's primarily wine country, producing robust reds and sparkling *cavas* (Spain's rival to champagne).

In late August/early September, Requena's **Fiesta de la Vendimia** attracts revellers eager to participate in this hearty bacchanal celebrating the end of the grape harvest.

The **tourist office** (☎ 96 230 38 51; www.requena .es; Calle García Montés s/n; ☷ 9.30am-2pm Tue-Thu & Sun, 9am-2pm & 4-7pm Fri & Sat) is near the entrance to the old town.

Sights

Enter the old quarter from its northern side, passing by the 10th-century Muslim **Torre del Homenaje**. Within the town walls are the Gothic **Santa María** and **San Salvador** churches, each with a magnificent main portal, and sturdy manorial houses such as the **Casa del Arte Mayor de la Seda** (Silk Guild House), **Casa del Corregidor** (Mayor's House) and **Palacio del Cid**.

The **Museo Municipal** (adult/child €1.80/1.20; ☷ 11am-2pm Tue-Sun) is in the **Convento Carmelito** near Plaza Consistorial in the new town. Possibly more interesting is what lies below ground: **Plaza de la Villa** (Plaza Albornoz; adult/child €1.80/1.20) in the old town hides in its intestines a network of interlinked cellars, once used as storerooms and, during strife, hideouts. **Guided visits** (11am, noon & 1pm Tue-Sun plus 4.15pm, 5.15pm & 6.15pm Fri-Sun) descend from the entrance on the square.

If you can't visit the cellars, dine at **Mesón La Villa** (☎ 96 230 12 75; Plaza de Albornoz 13) and ask your hosts to let you see theirs – briefly used by the local branch of the Inquisition to turn the screws on heretics.

Getting There & Away

Autolineas Alsina (☎ 96 349 72 30) runs more than 12 buses daily to/from Valencia (€3.90, one hour). Eight trains run daily to/from Valencia (€3.40) and there are three frequent stoppers to/from Madrid.

COSTA DEL AZAHAR

The Costa del Azahar – the orange blossom coast – is backed by a mountainous hinterland, its coastal plain a green sea of orange groves, from whose headily scented flowers the region takes its name.

Getting There & Away

The Valencia to Barcelona railway follows this coast and regional trains stop at all main towns. From Valencia, trains run every half-hour to Castellón de la Plana. Up to seven trains daily call at Benicàssim, three at Oropesa and eight at Benicarló/Peñíscola and Vinaròs.

CASTELLÓN DE LA PLANA
pop 147,700

The outskirts of Castellón de la Plana (Valenciano: Castelló de la Plana) are drab, industrial and rambling, so the centre comes as a pleasant surprise to the few tourists who penetrate to the heart of this prosperous commercial and university town.

Orientation & Information

Plaza Mayor and, just to its south, Plaza Santa Clara, are the nucleus of the interesting part of Castellón. The bus and train stations – the one above the other – are around 1km northwest, beyond leafy Parque Ribalta. El Grau de Castellón, the port area, is 4km east of downtown.

TOURIST INFORMATION
Main tourist office (☎ 964 35 86 88; www.castellon turismo.com; Plaza María Agustina 5; ☉ 9am-2pm &

4-7pm Mon-Fri Sep-Jun, 9am-7pm Mon-Fri Jul-Aug, 10am-2pm Sat year-round)
Port tourist office (☎ 902 203130; Paseo Buenavista 28)

Sights

The **Museo de Bellas Artes** (☎ 964 72 75 00; Avenidas Hermanos Bou 28; admission free; ☉ 10am-8pm Mon-Sat, 10am-2pm Sun) occupies award-winning premises. Its displays include a large and impressive ceramics section, reflecting the region's major industry.

Art lovers will enjoy a visit to the chapel of the **Convento de Capuchinas** (Calle Núñez de Arce 11; admission free; ☉ 2-6pm), which houses 10 fine paintings by Zurbarán. Slip €1 into the slot for illumination.

From Plaza Mayor, bordered by the early 18th-century town hall and the bustling covered market, thrusts the long finger of **El Fadrí** (1604), an octagonal bell tower and symbol of the city. Beside the tower is the reconstructed **Concatedral de Santa María**, shattered in the civil war and now restored to its original state.

Four kilometres east of the centre is **El Grau de Castellón**, a harbour that handles this industrial region's exports as well as the local fishing fleet. Castellón's beaches start north of here.

Sleeping & Eating

Hotel Intur Castellón (☎ 964 22 50 00; www.intur .com; Calle Herrero 20; r €73.50 Mon-Thu, €55 Fri-Sun & Aug; P ☒ ☒) Castellón's newest hotel has a bright, spacious central atrium, onto which both restaurant and bar give. Weekend rates are a particular bargain and – rare for Spain – there's a whole floor of rooms for nonsmokers.

Hostal La Esperanza (☎ 964 22 20 31; Calle Trinidad 37; basic s/d/tr €16.50/27/40.50) This hostal has spotless rooms above a cosy, family-run **bar-restaurant** (menú €6.30; ☉ Mon-Sat). The bar carries a great range of tapas.

Julivert (☎ 964 22 37 26; Calle Caballeros 41; ☉ lunch Mon-Fri) This tiny place does a good three-course *menú* with a vegetarian option for €7.60.

Mesón Navarro Calle Amadeo (☎ 964 25 09 66; Calle Amadeo I 8); Calle Sanchis Abella (☎ 964 26 11 33; Calle Sanchis Abella B°); Plaza Tetuán (☎ 964 21 31 15; Plaza Tetuán 26; mains €8.50-12.60) Has three restaurants around town, all busy and all excellent value for meat dishes. The one at Calle Amadeo I 8 also specialises in fresh fish.

Getting There & Around

Long-distance services use the **bus station** (☎ 964 24 07 78). Buses for El Grau and the beaches to its north leave from Plaza Borrull, 300m south of Plaza Mayor. Frequent buses for Benicàssim set out from Plaza Fadrell.

For both Valencia and resorts to the north, except for Benicàssim, trains are both swifter and more frequent than buses.

Local bus No 9 connects bus and train stations with the town centre.

AROUND CASTELLÓN DE LA PLANA
Vilafamés

What draws visitors to Vilafamés, a hillside town 26km north of Castellón de la Plana, is its excellent **Museo de Arte Contemporáneo** (☎ 964 32 91 52; Calle Diputació 20; adult/child €2/free; ☺ 10am-1.30pm & 4-7pm). Within the 15th-century Palacio de la Bailía, which is worth a visit in its own right, is a superb and highly eclectic collection of contemporary paintings and sculpture.

The small old town is an agreeable clutter of whitewashed houses and civic buildings in rust-red stone. From Plaza de la Sangre, stone steps take you up to the ruined **castle**, with its Muslim foundations, rebuilt circular turret and sensational panorama.

Jardín Vertical (☎ 964 32 99 38; www.eljardinvertical.jazztel.es; Carrer Nou 15; r from €90) This small – there are only seven rooms, so reservations are essential – yet spacious hotel is a gem. A mainly 17th-century noble house with five floors, it has been renovated with great taste by the proprietress herself. There's a lovely terrace, all rooms have a balcony and those overlooking the valley – which cost no more – have sweeping views.

More modestly, **Hotel El Rullo** (☎ 964 32 93 84; Calle de la Fuente 2; s/d €20/40), 200m below the museum, is a friendly family hotel that does a good *menú* (€12).

Montanejos
pop 480 / elevation 460m

It's a spectacular drive along the CV20 from Castellón up the Río Mijares gorges to this popular resort and spa village, surrounded by craggy, pine-clad mountains, at the heart of the Sierra de Espadán. The warm springs of the nearby **Fuente de Los Baños**, and the cool, fresh mountain air attract hordes of mainly Spanish visitors in summer. The village, uninteresting in itself, is a popular base for mountain sports.

The **tourist office** (☎ 964 13 11 53; www.montanejos.com, Spanish only) is within the *balneario* (spa) on Carretera Tales.

SLEEPING
Most hotels open only in summer and on weekends.

Hotel Rosaleda del Mijares (☎ 964 13 10 79; fax 964 13 11 36; www.hotelesrosaleda.com; Carretera Tales 28; winter s/d from €27/41.75, summer from €37.85/51.40) is upmarket and barely 100m from the *balneario*.

Refugio de Escaladores (☎ 964 13 13 17; www.albergue-elrefugio.com, Spanish only; half board per person in dm or camping €25, in cabin €35; ☺ Easter–mid-Oct) This is your place if you want to meet friendly outdoor folk. It also has limited camping space and serves tasty home-made pizzas and *platos combinados* (combined dishes), both for around €6, to all comers.

BENICÀSSIM
pop 12,500

Benicàssim (Spanish: Benicasim) vies with Peñíscola for the title of the Costa del Azahar's best coastal playground. It has been a popular resort since the 19th century, when wealthy Valencian families built summer residences here. To this day, a high 80% of visitors are Spanish and many people from Madrid, Valencia and Castellón own summer apartments.

Orientation & Information

Benicàssim's beaches and accompanying development, scarcely a couple of blocks wide, stretch for 6km along the coast.

TOURIST INFORMATION
Main tourist office (☎ 964 30 09 62; www.benicassim.org; Calle Santo Tomás 74; ☺ 10am-2pm & 5-7.30pm Mon-Sat, 10am-1.30pm & 5-8pm Sun) One kilometre inland in the old town.

Tourist kiosks (beside Torre San Vicente & Playa Heliópolis; ☺ Jun–mid-Oct)

Sights & Activities

Those 6km of broad beach are the main attraction. Bordering the promenade at the northeastern end are **Las Villas**, wonderful, exuberant, sometimes frivolous holiday homes built by wealthy Valencians at the end of the 19th century and into the 20th.

VALENCIA

The English version of the tourist office pamphlet *Ruta de las Villas* is a comprehensive guide, complete with photos.

Inland are the **Aquarama water park** (☎ 964 30 33 21; adult/child €14/10; ⊗ 11am-7pm mid-Jun–Aug) and several **golf courses**.

Approximately 6km inland is the **Desierto de las Palmas**, a mountain range – cooler than the coast, on occasion misty – with a Carmelite monastery (1697) at its heart. Nowadays a nature park and far from desert (for the monks it meant a place for mystic withdrawal), it's a green, popular outdoor activities area. From **Monte Bartolo**, its highest point at 728m, there are staggering wraparound views. Ask at the tourist office for the English version of the pamphlet *Parque Natural del Desierto de las Palmas*, which illustrates three splendid, signed walking trails.

Festivals & Events

In early August thousands of young people gather for the annual **Festival Internacional de Benicàssim** (FIB; www.fiberfib.com), one of Europe's top outdoor music festivals, which also embraces short films, dance and alternative theatre.

Sleeping & Eating

Hotel Avenida (☎ 964 30 00 47; www.hotelecoavenida .com; Avenida Castellón 2; d €32 Mar-Jun & Oct, d with compulsory breakfast €49.50 Jul & Sep, €98.50 Aug; ⊗ Mar-Oct; P ✗ ☚) This appealing mid-range hotel, on the old town's main street, has a pool and shady courtyard. It's particularly good value outside the summer season.

Hotel Voramar (☎ 964 30 01 50; www.voramar .net; Paseo Marítimo Pilar Coloma 1; s/d from €42/55, from €63/74 high season; P ✗) Venerable (run by the same family for four generations) and blooded in battle (it functioned as a hospital in the Spanish Civil War), the Voramar has considerably more character than most of Benicàssim's modern upstarts and is the only hotel that gives directly onto the sands. The dining room, where the cuisine is first class, has large windows overlooking the sea.

Hotel Tramontana (☎ 964 30 03 00; www.hotel tramontana.com; Paseo Marítimo Ferrandis Salvador 6; s/d/tr with breakfast from €28/46/64; ⊗ Mar-Oct; P) More in the heart of things and only half a block from the beach, the Tramontana is also family owned and welcoming. All triples overlook the shore.

Albergue Argentina (☎ 964 30 27 09; Avenida Calle Ferrandis Salvador 40), Benicàssim's youth hostel, is closed for renovations until at least 2006.

Plenty of economical **restaurants** line Calle de Santo Tomás and Calle Castellón, the old town's main street.

Benicàssim's seven **camping grounds** are all within walking distance of the beaches. **Camping Azahar** (☎ 964 30 31 96; fax 964 30 25 12; beside Hotel Voramar; person/tent/car €3.55/11.50/3.55 Jul-Aug, €3/6/3 Jan-Jun & Sep-Dec; ☚) is a first-class camping ground, particularly popular in winter with northern Europeans. Its only downside is intermittent noise from the railway that passes close by.

Drinking

During summer and on weekends, Benicàssim has a vibrant nightlife. The eastern end of Calle de los Dolores in the old town has a great collection of small, lively bars including **El Único**, **Bumerang**, **Pedal**, **Campus** and **Resaca** (the perhaps appropriately named 'Hangover').

Getting There & Away

Buses run every half-hour (every 15 minutes in summer) to Castellón, from where train connections are more plentiful.

OROPESA DEL MAR

It's a fine scenic drive from Benicàssim to Oropesa (Orpesa) along a narrow road winding around the rocky coastline. With its two main beaches of **Morro de Gos** and **La Concha**, this small resort is, for the moment, a relatively tranquil high-season alternative to seething Peñíscola and Benicàssim, although it grows increasingly skywards.

The main **tourist office** (☎ 964 31 22 41; Avenida de la Plana 1) is in the old town. A second one operates in summer from Plaza París beside Playa de la Concha.

PEÑÍSCOLA

pop 4800

Peñíscola's old town, all narrow, cobbled streets and whitewashed houses, perches on a rocky, fortified promontory jutting into the sea. It's pretty as a postcard – and just as commercial, with dozens of souvenir and ceramics shops and clothes boutiques catering to the ascending hordes of tourists. In stark contrast, the modern high-rises sprouting northwards along the coast are mostly leaden and charmless. But the **Paseo Marítimo promenade** makes pleasant walking, and the beach, recently extended northwards to meet that of neighbouring Benicarló, is now over 5km long.

The **main tourist office** (☎ 964 48 02 08; www .peniscola.org; ☾ 9am-8pm Mon-Fri mid-Jun–mid-Sep, 9.30am-1.30pm & 4-7pm Mon-Fri mid-Sep–mid-Jun, 10am-1pm & 4-7pm Sat, 10am-1pm Sun year-round) is at the south end of Paseo Marítimo. There are three other kiosks, staffed in summer only.

Sights

The 14th-century **castle** (adult/child €2/free; ☾ 9.30am-2.30pm & 4.30-8.30pm Easter–mid-Oct; 9.30am-1pm & 3.15-6pm mid-Oct–Easter) was built by the Knights Templar on Arab foundations and later became home to Pedro de Luna ('Papa Luna', the deposed Pope Benedict XIII).

The **Museu de la Mar** (Maritime Museum; Calle Principe s/n; admission free; ☾ 10am-2pm & 4pm-dusk daily Apr-Sep, Tue-Sun Oct-Mar) does a fine job of illustrating the town's former preoccupation with all things maritime.

Sleeping & Eating

There are two great alternatives to the beachside concrete towers. Since they're small, do reserve.

Chiki Bar (☎ 964 48 02 84; Calle Mayor 3; d with bathroom €30/42 winter/summer; closed Tue except Jul-Sep) High up in the old town, in addition to its engaging name Chiki Bar has seven spotless, modern rooms with great views and a small, unpretentious restaurant. You might want your earplugs, since the nearby parish church chimes tinnily, on the hour, every hour.

Hotel-Restaurante Simo (☎ 964 48 06 20; www .hotelsimo.com; Calle Porteta 5; s/d €56/70 Aug, €44/55 Jun-Jul & Sep, €33/40 Mar-May; ☾ Mar-Sep) At the base of the castle pile and right beside the sea, the Simo also runs a recommended, highly regarded restaurant with magnificent views. Of its nine rooms, six have balconies and equally impressive views of the setting sun across the bay. Rooms are trim, unfussy and well thought out (savour the sexy shampoo and soap dispensers).

The Paseo Marítimo, the main waterfront promenade, is lined with **restaurants** specialising in local fish and seafood.

Casa Jaime (☎ 964 48 00 30; Avenida Papa Luna 5; mains €14.50-17.50; ☾ daily summer, Mon-Tue & Thu-Sun

winter) The cosy dining room – there's an ample outside terrace too – is like stepping into someone's lounge room. But this family restaurant is very professional indeed. You can see mum and dad (once a fisherman who learnt his trade cooking for the crew) at work in the kitchen. They're renowned for their *suquet de peix* (fish stew; €17.50; minimum two people), and other rice and simmered fish dishes.

Getting There & Around

Local buses run at least every half-hour between Peñíscola, Benicarló and Vinaròs, from where there are trains to Barcelona and, southwards, to Castellón and Valencia.

To patrol the long beach front, hire a bike from **Diver Sport** (☎ 964 48 20 06; Avenida Estación 17; per half-/full day €8/15), beside Hotel Herasu.

VINARÒS

pop 22,100

Unlike its sybaritic neighbours, Vinaròs is a working town whose port is still used commercially and by in-shore fishing boats. A fairly grim place, its redeeming features are the small but sandy beaches and its bustling fishing port, famous for *langostinos* (scampi).

The **Iglesia Arciprestal** (Plaza del Ayuntamiento) is a fine baroque church with a tall bell tower and elaborate main doorway decorated with candy-twist columns. From here, pedestrianised Calle Mayor takes you to the attractive Modernista **covered market**, **tourist office** (☎ 964 45 33 34; Paseo Colón s/n) and **Playa del Fortí** beach.

Hostal Miramar (☎ /fax 964 45 14 00; Paseo Blasco Ibáñez 12; s/d/tr with bathroom €29.50/51.70/59.50), fronting the prom, is a family hotel with an agreeably old-fashioned ambience.

You've plenty of eating choices on the waterfront, most specialising in seafood.

El Faro de Vinaròs (☎ 964 45 63 62; Zona Portuaria s/n; ☾ closed Sun dinner) This restaurant, in a former lighthouse, offers both traditional dishes and more innovative fare, and has desserts that will seduce the most stringent dieter.

EL MAESTRAZGO

Straddling northwestern Valencia and southeast Aragón, El Maestrazgo (Valenciano: El Maestrat) is a mountainous land, a world away from the coastal resorts, that's sprinkled with ancient pueblos huddled on rocky outcrops and ridges.

One such place, Sant Mateu, was chosen in the 14th century by the maestro (hence the name El Maestrazgo) of the Montesa order of knights as his seat of power.

Ask at local tourist offices for the *Guía de Alojamientos del Maestrazgo,* a complete guide to accommodation from four-star hotels to *casas rurales* (country homes) to camping grounds in both the Valencian and Aragonese sectors.

Activities

CYCLING & WALKING

The area is fertile territory for cyclists and walkers. The long-distance GR-7 walking trail crosses the Els Ports and La Tinença de Benifassá districts, near Morella, while the GR-10 and GR-36 pass through the Alto Palancia region. In addition, there are many other shorter signed day and half-day routes.

MORELLA

pop 2700 / elevation 1000m

Morella, the principal town of El Maestrazgo, is an outstanding example of a medieval fortress. Perched on a hilltop, crowned by a castle and enclosed by a wall over 2km long, it's one of Spain's oldest continually inhabited towns.

Orientation & Information

Morella's walls are broken only by their seven entrance gates. The town is a confusing, compact jumble of narrow streets, alleys and steep steps. The main street, running east–west between Puerta San Miguel and Puerta de los Estudios, compounds the confusion by assuming five different names along its length of less than a kilometre.

The **tourist office** (☎/fax 964 17 30 32; Plaza San Miguel 3; ⌚ 10am-2pm & 4-6pm Tue-Sat, 10am-2pm Sun year-round) is just behind the Torres de San Miguel, twin 14th-century towers flanking the main entrance gate.

Sights

Morella's **castle** (adult/child €2/0.60; ⌚ 10.30am-7.30pm Easter-Oct, 9.30am-6.30pm Oct-Easter), though badly knocked about, well merits the strenuous climb up to savour the breathtaking views of town and the surrounding countryside. At its base, work is under way to convert the **Convento de San Francisco** into a Parador hotel.

There are three small museums in the towers of the ancient walls: the **Museo Tiempo de Dinosaurios**, opposite the tourist office, displays dinosaur bones and fossils – the Maestrazgo's remote hills have been a treasure-trove for palaeontologists – and has an informative video (in Spanish); the **Museo Tiempo de Imagen** is a collection of evocative black-and-white photos of Morella; and the **Museo Tiempo de Historia** charts the town's history. The **Museo del Sexenni** in the Sant Nicolau church evokes the atmosphere of this major fiesta. Admission to each costs €1.80/1.20 per adult/child.

The Gothic **Basílica de Santa María la Mayor** (Plaza Arciprestal; ⌚ core hr 12-2pm & 4-6pm) has two elaborately sculpted doorways on its south façade. Inside are a fine choir and altarpiece and the **Museo Arciprestal** (admission €1.20).

Also worth seeing are the 14th-century **town hall** and several impressive manorial houses, such as the **Casa de la Cofradía de Labradores** (House of the Farmers' Guild).

On the outskirts of town stand the arches of a 13th-century **aqueduct**.

Festivals & Events

Morella's major festival is the **Sexenni**, held every six years during August (the next is in 2006) in honour of the Virgen de Vallivana. Visit the Museo del Sexenni to get the flavour of this major celebration with its elaborate compositions in crêpe paper. Annually in August, there's a **baroque music festival**, starring the huge organ in the Basílica de Santa María la Mayor.

Sleeping & Eating

Hotel Cardenal Ram (☎ 964 17 30 85; www.cardenalram.com; Cuesta Suñer 1; s/d €40/60; ❄) This venerable hotel has ancient stone floors, high ceilings and antique furniture, all in a wonderfully transformed 16th-century cardinal's palace. Rooms are attractively decorated with local prints and have sensual power showers. Its **restaurant** (mains €6-13; ⌚ daily Jul-Sep, Tue-Sun Oct-Jun) does a first-class *menú degustación* and a tempting *menú del día* (€14).

Fonda Moreno (☎ 964 16 01 05; Calle San Nicolás 12; basic d €12) Friendly, and Morella's cheapest option, Fonda Morena's price and that of the hearty *menú del día* (€7.20) have stayed constant for almost a decade. The **restaurant** (daily Jul-Sep, Tue-Sun Oct-Jun, closed dinner Sun) also does a *menú típico* (€15.50) and *menú degustación* (€18), both rich in regional dishes.

Other good-value choices include **Hotel El Cid** (964 16 01 25; fax 964 16 01 51; Puerta de San Mateo 3; s/d €23.20/40), with spruce, modern rooms; and **Hostal La Muralla** (/fax 964 16 02 43; Calle de la Muralla 12; s/d with breakfast €21.50/31), just around the corner and just as trim.

Restaurante Casa Roque (964 16 03 36; Cuesta San Juan 1), occupying an attractive 17th-century mansion, does a good-value weekday *menú* (€10). For a selection of typical Els Ports dishes, go for the *menú gastronómico* (€18; minimum two people).

Getting There & Around
On weekdays, **Autos Mediterráneo** (964 22 05 36) runs two daily buses to/from both Castellón (€7.30) and Vinaròs (€4.35). There's also one Saturday bus to/from Castellón.

ELS PORTS
Morella is the ancient capital of Els Ports, the 'mountain passes'. This northeastern corner of Valencia offers some outstanding scenic drives and strenuous cycling excursions, as well as excellent possibilities for walkers and climbers.

Fábrica de Giner
On the Forcall road, 4.5km west of Morella, is the Fábrica de Giner complex, a former textile factory with a pair of choices at each end of the sleeping spectrum:

Hotel Fábrica Giner (964 17 31 42; www.ghihoteles.com; per person with breakfast €33-42; P) occupies the former factory owners' sumptuous dwelling, while the **Youth Hostel** (964 16 01 00; fax 964 16 09 77; dm under/over 26 €7.45/10.60) has been converted from workers housing.

Across the road is a large public swimming pool, liquid heaven on a hot day.

Forcall
Nine kilometres further west, this quiet village is at the confluence of the Ríos Caldés and Cantavieja. On the weekend closest to 17 January, the **Santantonà** (also known as the Fiesta de San Antón), a winter festival celebrating fire, briefly dispels the prevailing calm as local youths sprint through a blazing tunnel.

> ### SANTUARIO DE LA BALMA
> Push northwards beyond Forcall for 15km along the CV14 to experience the extraordinary Santuario de la Balma, set inside a rocky crag. Behind the main altar is a forest of offerings and ex-votos – wax limbs, baby clothes, bridal dresses, military berets and much more – accompanied by notes of thanks to the Virgin for her protection or intercession.

Hotel-Restaurante Palau dels Osset (964 17 75 24; www.ghihoteles.com; 964 14 45 48; per person with breakfast €35-50;) One of two fine, renovated, 16th-century Aragonese palaces on opposite sides of the Plaza Mayor, it has been converted into an elegant hotel with a more than respectable **restaurant** (mains €9-13).

From Forcall, an attractive 20km drive along the CV120, ascending the rugged Río Cantavieja valley, brings you to the charming medieval town of Mirambel (p438).

CATÍ
On the CV128 about 35km southeast of Morella is the village of Catí, famous for its cheeses. One or two well-preserved **Renaissance noble houses**, reminders of the days when Catí enjoyed wealth generated by the wool trade, still flank the main Calle Mayor.

An obligatory stop for those with a sweet tooth is the **Fábrica de Turrones y Mazapanes J. Blasco** at the northern entrance to town. This small factory transforms almonds, the valley's main crop, into marzipan and *turrón*, a Valencian variant upon nougat, which you can sample and buy.

SANT MATEU
pop 1900 / elevation 325m
A drive 5km south from the N232 along the CV132 brings you to Sant Mateu, ancient capital of the Maestrazgo. Its solid mansions and elaborate façades are reminders of the town's more illustrious past and former wealth, based upon the wool trade. Bars and cafés surround the colonnaded Plaza Mayor, from where signposts point to four municipal museums: the **Museo Paleontológico**, **Museo Arciprestal** of religious art (in the parish church), **Museo les Presons** in the former jail and **Museo Histórico-Etnológico**,

entered via the tourist office in the **Palacio Borrull**, a fine 15th-century building.

The **tourist office** (☎ 964 41 66 58; www.sant mateu.com, Spanish only; Calle Historiador Betí 10; ☎ 10am-2pm & 4-6pm Tue-Sat, 10am-2pm Sun mid-Sep–mid-Jul, daily mid-Jul–mid-Sep) is just off the Plaza Mayor.

Hotel-Restaurante La Perdi (☎ 964 41 60 82; Calle Historiador Betí 9; s/d mid-Sep–mid-Jul €18/30, mid-Jul–mid-Sep €24/36) has modern, comfortable rooms and its restaurant does a decent *menú* costing only €7.25.

Getting There & Away

Weekday Autos Mediterráneo buses link San Mateu with Vinaròs (€2.20, one hour, four daily), Castellón (€4.45, up to two hours, three daily) and Morella (€2.90, 1½ hours, two daily). On Saturday, one bus runs from Castellón to Morella via Sant Mateu. The bus stop is 100m east of Hotel Restaurante Montesa.

COSTA BLANCA

The long stripe of the Costa Blanca (White Coast) is one of Europe's most heavily visited areas. If you're after a secluded midsummer beach, stay away. But if you're looking for a lively social life, good beaches and a suntan…

It isn't all concrete and package deals. Although the original fishing villages have long been engulfed by the sprawl of resorts, holiday villas and skyscrapers, a few old town kernels, such as those of Xàbia (Jávea) and Altea, still survive.

In July and August it can be tough finding accommodation if you haven't reserved. Out of season, those places remaining open usually charge far less than in high summer.

Most buses linking Valencia and Alicante head straight down the motorway, making a stop in Benidorm. A few, however, call by other intervening towns. Renfe trains connect Valencia with Gandia, while the FGV narrow-gauge train and tram ply the scenic route between Denia and Alicante, stopping at all pueblos en route.

Inland Trips from the Costa Blanca by Derek Workman describes in detail and with flair 20 one-day car excursions into the interior.

GANDIA

pop 59,900

Gandia, 65km south of Valencia, is a tale of two cities. The main town, once home to a branch of the Borja dynasty (more familiar to most people as the infamous Borgias), is a prosperous commercial centre.

Four kilometres away on the coast, Playa de Gandia has so far avoided the tawdriness of too many Costa Blanca resorts. Its long, broad, sandy beaches are groomed daily by a fleet of tractors and backed by medium-rise hotels and apartments. It's a popular and predominantly Spanish resort, with a well-merited reputation for lively summer nightlife.

Information

INTERNET ACCESS

Intern@ut@ (Calle Magistrado Catalá 5; per hr €2.40; ☎ 9am-11pm Mon-Sat, 4-11pm Sun).

TOURIST INFORMATION

Playa de Gandia tourist office (☎ 96 284 24 07; Paseo de Neptuna s/n; ☎ 10am-2pm & 5-7.30pm Mon-Fri, 10am-1.30pm Sat & Sun mid-Mar–mid-Oct, 10am-1.30pm Sun only mid-Oct–mid-Mar)

Town tourist office (☎ 96 287 77 88; www.gandia excelencia.com; ☎ 9.30am-1.30pm & 4.30-7pm Mon-Fri, 10am-1.30pm Sat) Opposite the bus/train station.

Sights & Activities

Highlights of Gandia's magnificent **Palacio Ducal de los Borja** (☎ 96 287 14 65; Calle Duc Alfons el Vell 1; guided tour adult/child €4/2; ☎ 10am-2pm & 5-8pm Tue-Sat, 10am-2pm Sun), the 15th-century home of Duque Francisco de Borja, include its finely carved *artesonado* ceilings and rich ceramic work – look out for the vivid *mapa universal* floor composition. One-hour guided tours in Spanish, with an accompanying leaflet in English, take place hourly.

There are two excellent Rutas Ecoturísticas (Ecotourism Routes). The 12km **Racó del Duc** walking and cycling trail follows an old railway line through unspoiled countryside between the villages of Vilallonga (8km south of Gandia) and L'Orxa. **Entre Senill i Borró** is a 13km walking trail through coastal marsh and dunes from Gandia town to the coast. Both tourist offices have brochures in English describing the routes.

Sleeping

Albergue Mar i Vent (☎ 96 283 17 48; albergpiles _ivaj@gva.es; dm under/over 26 €7.45/10.60; ☎ year round) This excellent beachfront youth hostel, comprehensively renovated in 2004, is 5km south of Gandia beside Playa de Piles. Take La Amistad bus from the bus station.

Hostal El Nido (☎ 96 284 46 40; fax 96 284 65 71; Calle Alcoy 22; s/d €28/39 Sep-Jun, d €45-56 Jul-Aug) Rooms are as cheerful as the owners at this friendly, warmly recommended place, a block back from the beach. Between June and September, it also runs a small bar for guests.

Hotel Riviera (☎ 96 284 50 42; www.hotelesrh.com; Paseo de Neptuna 28; half-board per person €53-77 Jul-Sep, €33-40 Oct-May; P ✗ ⚮) It's well worth going for half-board – compulsory anyway from May to October – at this large hotel, comprehensively renovated in 2002 and stretching back from the beach. Invest an extra €4.80 for one of the eight sea-view rooms.

Hotel Bayren 1 (☎ 96 284 03 00; www.hoteles bayren.com; Paseo Neptuna 62; s €55.50-85 d €79.50-104; P ✗ ⚮) Rooms are comfortable, the covered pool is open year-round, and there's both a gym and spa at this good, if a little monolithic, hotel. For sea views check in here at the Bayren I, rather than Hotel Bayren II, a block away and a little cheaper.

Camping L'Alquería (☎ 96 284 04 70; www.lalque ria.com; Carretera del Grau de Gandia s/n; per person/tent/ car €4.30/6.20/4.90; ⚮ year-round) About 1km inland, this place has a heated indoor pool.

Eating

The Paseo Marítimo Neptuno abounds in eateries. You'll also find a few longer-established places at the western end of the port and along Calle Verge.

El Charro (☎ 96 284 63 64; Calle Verge 4; ⚮ Wed-Mon, daily Jul-Aug, closed Oct) Spilling onto the street and with an atmospheric interior, El Charro, a modest little place with a good wine list, serves up freshly caught fish – and also rich meats and sausages of Salamanca, from where the owners hail.

As de Oros (☎ 96 284 02 39; Paseo Neptuno 26; fish mains €15-20; ⚮ Tue-Sun, daily Jul-Sep) This famous fish restaurant brings in diners from far and wide for its *menú* (€47.25). For a more modestly priced alternative, try the *fideuà de mariscos* (seafood noodle paella; €13; minimum two people).

Restaurante Emilio (☎ 96 284 07 61; Bloque F-5, Avenida Vicente Calderón; mains €14.50-17; ⚮ Thu-Tue, daily Jun–mid-Sep) Despite a cupboardful of gastronomic accolades, Emilio, his wife and three children manage to preserve a

family atmosphere in this traditionally furnished restaurant, where you'll eat very well indeed.

Drinking

There's great summer and weekend nightlife at Playa de Gandia, with bars, including **Paco Paco Paco**, **Mama Ya Lo Sabe** and **Ke Caramba**, clustered around Plaza del Castell, barely 300m inland from the beach. After they close, head for one of the discos that bop till dawn, such as **Coco-Loco** (cnr Paseo Marítimo & Calle de Galicia) or **Bacarra** (Calle Legazpi 7), both two blocks from the beach.

Getting There & Around

Trains run between Gandia and Valencia (€3.40, one hour) every half-hour (hourly on weekends). The combined bus and train station is opposite the tourist office. La Marina Gandiense buses for Playa de Gandia run every 20 minutes, stopping beside the tourist office.

DENIA

pop 33,300

Denia, a popular, fairly pricey resort, has some good beaches to its north.

Orientation & Information

The **tourist office** (☎ 96 642 23 67; www.denia.net; Glorieta del Oculista Buigues 9; ⚮ 9.30am-2pm & 4.30-8pm daily Jul–mid-Sep, 9.30am-1.30pm & 4-7pm Mon-Sat, 9.30am-1.30pm Sun mid-Sep–Jun) is near the waterfront. Both the train station and ferry terminal are close by.

Activities

To catch the sea breezes, sign on with **Mundo Marino** (☎ 96 642 30 66), which does return catamaran trips to/from Xàbia (€14/7 adult/child), some of which continue to Calpe (€25/12.50) and Altea (€30/15).

Sleeping

Hotel Costa Blanca (☎ 96 578 03 36; www.hotelcosta blanca.com; Calle Pintor Llorens 3; s/d from €30/45; P ✗) In front of the train station, this hotel is an excellent-value mid-range option except in high summer, when prices rocket. Rooms are comfortable and cosily furnished, and the port is but a few steps away.

Hotel la Posada del Mar (☎ 966 43 29 66; www .laposadadelmar.com; Plaza Drassanes s/n; d with breakfast €120-160; P ✗) Full of character, this recently opened and sensitively renovated hotel occupies a 13th-century building that last functioned as Alicante's customs post. Each of its 25 rooms is individually decorated with a nautical theme and light streams through the large windows that overlook the harbour.

Eating

There's a clutch of tempting restaurants for all pockets along harbour-facing Calle Port and its continuation, Plaza del Raset.

Restaurante Drassanes (☎ 96 578 11 18; Calle Port 15; mains €7-12, menús €15-23; ☺ Tue-Sun, closed Nov) Bustling and seething on two levels, the Drassanes is pleasantly informal compared to some of its more expensive and stuffier neighbours.

Asador del Puerto (☎ 96 642 34 82; Plaza del Raset 10-11; mains €16-18.75) This is an excellent choice for either meat or fish dishes. Try the *cochinillo* (suckling pig; €18.75), crispy on the outside, juicy within and roasted to perfection.

Getting There & Away

From the station, seven trains daily follow the scenic route southwards to Alicante (€7.15, 2½ hours; change to the tram in El Campello) via Altea (€3.20) and Benidorm (€3.95).

Balearia Lines (☎ 902 160180; www.balearia.net) runs daily ferries to/from Palma de Mallorca and both Ibiza city and San Antonio, also on Ibiza island. The superfast ferry, the *Garcia Lorca*, whizzes to Ibiza in just two hours and continues to Palma de Mallorca (3½ hours). The normal ferry takes four and nine hours respectively. For more details, see p617.

XÀBIA

pop 18,800

With a third of its resident population and over two-thirds of its annual visitors non-Spanish (every second shop seems to be an estate agent/realtor), Xàbia (Spanish: Jávea) isn't the best place to meet the locals. That said, it's gentle, laid-back and well worth a visit early in the season, when the sun shines but the masses haven't yet arrived.

Xàbia comes in three parts: the attractive old town 2km inland, El Puerto (the port), directly east of the old quarter, and the beach zone of El Arenal, a couple of kilometres south of the harbour. Further

south, the promontory of **Cabo de La Nao** offers spectacular views.

Information

BOOKSHOPS

Bookworld (☎ 96 646 22 53; Avenida Amanecer de España 13, old town)

INTERNET ACCESS

Video Net Xàbia (Avenida Amanecer de España s/n, El Arenal; per hr €4; ☺ 10am-10pm Tue-Sun)

LAUNDRY

Lavandería Los Delfines (Avenida del Pla s/n, El Arenal; ☺ 9am-1pm & 4-6pm Mon-Fri, 9am-1pm Sat)

TOURIST INFORMATION

El Arenal tourist office (☎ 96 646 06 05; Carretera Cabo de la Nao; ☺ 10am-1pm & 5-9pm Mon-Sat Jul-Sep, 9am-1.30pm & 4-7pm Mon-Fri, 10am-1pm Sat Oct-Jun)

Old town tourist office (☎ 96 579 43 56; www.xabia .org; Plaza de la Iglesia; ☺ 10am-1pm & 5-9pm Mon-Sat Jul-Sep, 9am-1.30pm & 4-7pm Mon-Fri, 10am-1pm Sat Oct-Jun)

Port tourist office (☎ 96 579 07 36; Plaza Almirante Bastareche 11; ☺ 10am-1pm & 5-9pm Mon-Sat Jul-Sep, 9am-1.30pm & 4-7pm Mon-Fri, 10am-1pm Sat Oct-Jun, 4-7pm Sat & 10am-1pm Sun year-round).

Activities

To explore the old town, pick up the free tourist office brochure, *Historical Centre of Jávea*. Its *Nature Parks & Trekking Routes* describes six waymarked routes in the area, including an ascent of Montgó, the magnificent craggy mountain that lours over the town. From April to December the tourist office leads free guided walks almost daily.

Sleeping

The pleasant port area has a couple of excellent choices.

Pensión la Favorita (☎ 96 579 04 77; fax 96 579 64 68; Calle Magellanes 4; r €29, with bathroom €32-40, €41-46

CABO DE LA NAO

Head south for 9km from El Arenal, up past the fancy villas through the pine trees to the lighthouse and lookout point of Cabo de la Nao, the most westerly point in the Valencia region. From this rocky promontory you can see the island of Ibiza if the air's clear enough.

Jul-Aug; ⊗ Mar-Nov) Run by a friendly young couple, this popular place is welcoming, used to travellers, clean as a new pin, fresh with flowers and warmly recommended.

Hotel Miramar (☎ /fax 96 579 01 02; Plaza Almirante Bastareche 12; s/d €27/48, Jul-Sep €37/58; ⊗) Hotel Miramar is an imposing building right beside the port, with a bar and restaurant terrace below. It couldn't be nearer the sea and rooms are cosy; those overlooking the bay carry a €10 supplement.

Parador de Jávea (☎ 96 579 02 00; www.paradores .es; Avenida del Mediterráneo 7; d €101-126.20) Architecturally, Jávea's boxy, once-modern Parador ranks among the least exciting of this excellent state-owned chain. But the magnificent site, on a tiny headland overlooking the bay of El Arenal amid lovely gardens, is matched by the comfort and service on offer.

Camping Naranjal (☎ 96 579 29 89; www.camping elnaranjal.com; Camino dels Morers 15; per person/pitch €4.50/12; ⊗ year-round) A 10-minute walk from the beach.

Eating

Cafés and restaurants hug the rim of El Arenal's Paseo Marítimo.

Tasca Tonis (☎ 96 646 18 51; Calle Mayor 2; menú €9; ⊗ Tue-Sun) This modest yet stylish place in the old town has a great selection of bar tapas and turns out some mean rice dishes.

La Bohême (☎ 96 579 16 00; mains €13-19; ⊗ Thu-Tue, daily Jun-Sep) At the beach's northern end, La Bohême has a range of tapas the length of a tall blackboard, serves fine food and also does takeaways.

Cristóbal Colón (Christopher Columbus; ☎ 96 647 09 58; menú €9.50, mains €12-14) Popular with both Spaniards and foreigners, the Christopher Columbus specialises in rice and fresh fish dishes.

La Masía de la Sal (☎ 96 579 58 76; Avenida del Mediterráneo 182; mains €12.20-21.50, menú €11; ⊗ Thu-Tue, daily Jul-Sep) Beside Hotel Sol y Mar and set back from the road 0.5km north of El Arenal, this charming, discreet little restaurant is tastefully furnished in rustic style and there's an equally intimate rear garden. It does a vegetarian option.

Getting There & Around

At least five buses run daily to both Valencia (€8.50) and Alicante (€7.25). They stop on Avenida Óndara, near the unnamed square with a large olive tree at its heart.

You can rent a cycle at **Xàbia's Bike Centre** (☎ /fax 96 646 11 50; Avenida Lepanto 21; from €6/36 per day/week) in the port area.

CALPE

pop 18,900

The Gibraltaresque **Peñon de Ifach**, a giant molar protruding from the sea, dominates the seaside resort of Calpe (Valenciano: Calp).

Two large bays sprawl either side of the Peñon: Playa Arenal on the southern side is backed by the old town, while Playa Levante to the north has most of the more recent development.

Information

BOOKSHOPS

Librería Europa (☎ 96 583 58 24; europa@ctv.es; Calle Oscar Esplá 2) Good stock of titles in English (including major Lonely Planet titles) and other European languages.

INTERNET ACCESS

DIP Digital Center (Calle Benidorm 15; per hr €3; ⊗ 10am-midnight Mon-Sat, 4-11pm Sun)

TOURIST INFORMATION

Main tourist office (☎ 96 583 85 32; www.calpe.es; Plaza del Mosquit; ⊗ 10am-1.30pm & 5-9pm Mon-Sat Jul-Sep, 10am-1.30pm & 4-7pm Mon-Fri, 10am-1.30pm Sat Oct-Jun) In the old town.

Tourist office (Avenida Ejércitos Españoles) On the ring road. There is another office beside the port.

Sights

A fairly strenuous trail – allow 2½ hours for the round trip – climbs from the Peñon's **Aula de Naturaleza** (Nature Centre) towards the 332m summit, offering great seascapes from its limit at the end of a dark tunnel. In July and August numbers on the cliff are limited to 150 at a time, so you may have a short wait.

Sleeping

Pensión Centrica (☎ 96 583 55 28; mjpiffet@telefonica .net; Plaza de Ifach 5; per person €12) This welcoming, recommended place just off Avenida de Gabriel Miró has 13 neat, basic rooms with washbasin.

Hotel Bahía (☎ 96 583 97 02; www.bahiacalpe-hotel .com, Spanish only; Avenida de Valencia 24; d €103, mid-Jul–Aug €131; P ⊗ ⊠) Opened in 2004, the Bahia, overlooking Playa Arenal, is a very stylish newcomer that's handy for both beach and town. Sea-facing rooms (aim high, towards the top of its seven floors) offer good views of the beach and Peñon.

Hotel Esmeralda (☎ 96 583 61 01; www.rocaesmeralda.com, Spanish only; Calle Ponent 1; s €60-91, d €80-160.50) At the northern limit of Playa Levante, the huge Esmeralda, as much leisure complex as hotel, is particularly suited to families with children. If the sea fails to call, there are three outside pools and a heated indoor one too, plus gym, a couple of restaurants and a café.

Camping Levante (☎ 96 583 22 72; camping levante@teleline.es; Avenida de la Marina s/n; per person/tent/car €4.60/4.40/4.50; ☾ Jun-Apr) A brief walk from Playa Levante.

Eating

There are plenty of restaurants and bars around Plaza de la Constitución and along the main Avenida de Gabriel Miró, plus a cluster of good fish restaurants down by the port.

La Cambra (☎ 96 583 06 05; Calle Delfín 2; mains €10-15; ☾ Mon-Sat Jul-Aug, lunch only Mon-Thu Oct-Jun) All agreeably antique wood and tile, La Cambra specialises in rice dishes (€10 to €12) and also has a rich *à la carte* selection.

Los Zapatos (☎ 96 583 15 07; Calle Santa María 7; mains €11-18; ☾ Thu-Mon Dec-Oct) Highly recommended, this German-run restaurant has a short, specialised *à la carte* menu. In season it does a tempting *menú caza y pescado* (hunting and fish menu) with boar and fish of the day.

Getting There & Away

Seven FGV trains travel daily northwards to Denia (€2.45, 40 minutes) and south to Alicante (€4.90, 1¾ hours) via Benidorm (€1.70).

Buses connect Calpe with both Valencia and Alicante. They pull in along Calle Capitán Pérez Jordá beside the Cruz Roja (Red Cross) station.

ALTEA
pop 15,900

Altea, separated from Benidorm only by the thick wedge of the Sierra Helada, could be a couple of moons away. Its beaches are mostly pebbles and rock – and that's what has saved it so far from mass tourism, though the pile-drivers are beginning to pound. The whitewashed old town, perched on a hilltop overlooking the sea, is just about the prettiest pueblo in all the Comunidad Valenciana, despite having been systematically gentrified.

Altea's **tourist office** (☎ 96 584 41 14; Calle San Pedro 9; ☾ 10am-2pm & 5-7.30pm Mon-Fri, closed Sat & Sun) is on the beachfront.

Off Plaza de la Iglesia in the old town, and especially down Calle Major, there's a profusion of cute little **restaurants**, many open for dinner only except in high summer.

BENIDORM
pop 51,900

It's easy to be snobbish about Benidorm, which, with around five million visitors each year – and over 1000 bars – long ago sold its birthright to cheap package tourism. But, while quite a few of the horror tales are true and although you have to poke around among the tawdriness, Benidorm can still throw up a gem or two. The 5km of white sandy beaches are backed by some hideous concrete high-rises. But Benidorm, though violated most summer nights by louts from northern Europe, still manages to retain a certain dignity. The foreshore is magnificent as the twin sweeps of Playa del Levante and the longer Playa del Poniente beach meet beneath Plaza del Castillo, where the land juts into the bay like a ship's prow.

In winter precisely 50% of visitors are over 60, mostly from northern Europe. During summer Benidorm is for all ages – and boasts a nightlife and club scene to rival Ibiza's.

Information
BOOKSHOPS
Books & Books (☎ 630-120776; Calle Sant Roc 17)
New and second-hand books in English.

INTERNET ACCESS
Chat.com (Avenida de Europa s/n; per hr €2.40; ☾ 10am-midnight)
Cyberc@t Cafe (Calle Ruzafa 2; per hr €3; ☾ 10am-1am)
Vic Center (Calle Lepanto 6; per hr €2.40; ☾ 9.30am-11.30pm)

LAUNDRY
Laundrette (Calle Ibiza 14; ☾ 9am-8pm Mon-Fri, 9am-2pm Sat)

TOURIST INFORMATION
Main tourist office (☎ 96 585 13 11; www.benidorm .org; Avenida Martínez Alejos 6; ☾ 9.30am-8.30pm

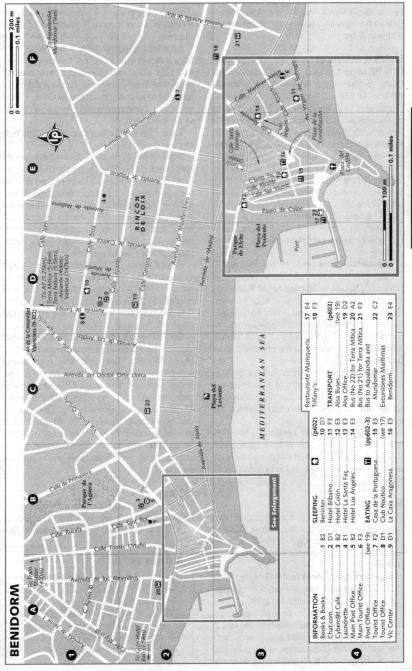

BENIDORM

VALENCIA

INFORMATION	
Books & Books.........................1	B2
Chat.com................................2	D1
Cyber@t Cafe........................3	B2
Laundrette.............................4	E1
Main Post Office.....................5	B2
Post Office.......................(see 19)	
Tourist Office........................6	F3
Tourist Office........................7	F2
Vic Center.............................8	D1
Main Tourist Office.................9	D1

SLEEPING	(p602)
Beninter...............................10	D1
Hotel Bilbaíno.......................11	F3
Hotel Colón..........................12	E3
Hotel La Santa Faç.................13	E3
Hotel Los Ángeles..................14	E3

EATING	(pp602-3)
Casa de la Portuguesa............15	E3
Club Náutico...................(see 17)	
La Cava Aragonesa.................16	D1

Restaurante Marisquería........17	E4
Tiffany's...............................18	F3

TRANSPORT	(p603)
Alsa Buses.....................(see 19)	
Alsa Office...........................19	D2
Bus (No 22) for Terra Mítica....20	A2
Bus (No 21) for Terra Mítica....21	F3
Bus to Aqualandia and	
Mundomar........................22	C2
Excursiones Marítimas	
Benidorm..........................23	E4

Mon-Fri, 10am-1.30pm & 5-8pm Sat, 10am-1.30pm Sun)
There are also tourist office kiosks on Avenida de Europa
and Rincòn de Loix.

Sights & Activities

Terra Mítica (Mythical Land; ☎ 902 020220; adult/child
€32/24; ⏰ 10am-midnight Jun-Aug, 10am-8pm daily Apr-
May & Sep, Sat & Sun only Oct-Dec) is the Costa Blanca's answer to Disneyland and Port Aventura
in Catalonia. A fun day out, especially if
you're with children, it's Mediterranean in
theme, with areas devoted to ancient Egypt,
Greece, Rome, Iberia and the Mediterranean islands. Take bus No 21 or 22.

Terra Natura (☎ 96 681 36 55; adult/child €20/14;
⏰ 10am-8pm summer, 10am-5pm winter), just behind Terra Mítica, is a rival theme park, also
on the grand scale, where animals will live
as nearly as possible in their native habitat. It was being completed at the time of
writing.

Aqualandia (☎ 96 586 01 00; adult/child €21/14;
⏰ 10am-7pm May-Oct), Europe's largest water
park and, beside it, **Mundomar** (☎ 96 586 91 01;
adult/child €18/12; ⏰ 10am-7pm) – with parrots,
dolphins, sea lions and even bats – are
each worth a full day. It's economical to
buy a combined ticket (€28/18 adult/child),
which can be used on different days. Take
bus No 11.

Should Benidorm's frenetic pace get you
down, pick up a free copy of *Routes Across
Sierra Helada* from the tourist office and
stride out into the hills north of town for
superb bay views.

Excursiones Marítimas Benidorm (☎ 965 85
00 52) runs hourly boats (€10/8 adult/child
return) to the Isla de Benidorm and a cruise
up the coast to Calpe (€15/11 adult/child
return).

Sleeping

In all of Europe, only Paris and London have
more hotel beds than Benidorm. Almost
everyone's on a package deal, so accommodation is expensive for the independent
traveller.

Benidorm Reservations Center (Beninter; ☎ 96
586 82 82; www.beninter.com; Calle Ibiza 6) offers discounted hotel and apartment rates.

Hotel La Santa Faç (☎ 96 585 40 63; www.santafaz
hotel.com; Calle Santa Faç 18; s/d/tr €48/72/90; ⏰ Apr-Oct;
🔀) This long-established hotel, up a nar-
row street in the old quarter, is friendly and
full of character. All rooms have a balcony.

Since the street can sometimes be rowdy in
the small hours, you may prefer one facing
the rear.

Hotel Los Ángeles (☎ 96 680 74 33; fax 96 585 31 39;
Calle Los Ángeles 3; s/d from €27/50 Nov-Jun, €42/76 Jul-
Sep) This pleasant, informal family-owned
hotel (the family also runs Pensión del Mar,
just down the road) is in the old town. Fifth-
and sixth-floor rooms have large balconies
at no extra cost.

Larger hotels can be reasonable value out
of season.

Hotel Colón (☎ 96 585 04 12; www.hotelcolon.net;
Paseo Colón 3; s/d €30/42 winter, rising to €56/84 Jul-Aug)
Conveniently positioned where the neck of
the promontory and old town meet Playa
del Poniente, the Colón is great value outside high season. Half-board is only €3
more than the B&B, though don't expect
fine cuisine. East-facing rooms have great
views of the Playa Poniente.

Hotel Bilbaíno (☎ 96 585 08 04; bilbaino@asanza
.es; Avenida Virgen del Sufragio 1; s/d winter €31.60/51,
summer €54/96; ⏰ Mar-Nov) Subsequently remodelled, this was Benidorm's first hotel.
Overlooking the beach, it's a particularly
good winter deal.

Gran Hotel Bali (☎ 96 681 52 00; www.grupobali
.com; Calle Luis Prendes s/n; half-board per person €45-95;
🅿 🔀 🔀) At 186m high, this mammoth,
self-contained complex, as much space-age
village as hotel, is Europe's tallest. Its very
vastness isn't to everyone's taste but, with
23 lifts/elevators (have fun riding one of
the two external ones), 776 rooms and a
pair of restaurants that can accommodate
up to 1000 diners, it's superlative in many
senses – and very reasonably priced in low
season.

Eating

For Benidorm's biggest concentration of
local and Spanish regional restaurants and
tapas bars, take your pick from those lin-

AUTHOR'S CHOICE

We've been dropping into **La Cava Aragonesa** (Plaza de la Constitución) for well
over a decade now. What keeps drawing
us back is its magnificent selection of tapas,
fat canapés, 20 different plates of cold cuts
and good wine by the glass (a decent measure of Catalan bubbly is only €0.80).

ing Calle Santo Domingo at the Plaza de la Constitución end.

Restaurante Marisquería Club Naútico (☎ 96 585 54 25; Paseo de Colón s/n; mains €12-18, menú €21) At this elegant restaurant, designed with flair, you can pick at tapas by the bar or enjoy a full meal on the large terrace, where you can also simply enjoy a drink and the view over Benidorm's small port.

Casa de la Portuguesa (☎ 96 585 89 58; Calle San Vicente 39; mains €9-12) With its tables spilling onto the narrow street in summer, this restaurant, a favourite of Benidorm's movers and shakers, is nevertheless very reasonably priced.

Getting There & Away

Alsa (☎ 96 680 39 55) buses run north and south along the Costa Blanca to/from Valencia (€11.20, 1¾ hours, seven daily) and Alicante (€3.25, at least hourly, one hour). The ticket office (set back in La Nuria shopping mall) and bus stop are at Avenida de Europa 8.

Alternatively, take the FGV train to Alicante (€2.45, 1¼ hours, hourly), Denia (€3.95, 1¼ hours, seven daily) and all stations in between.

ALICANTE

pop 284,600

Alicante (Valenciano: Alacant) is the Valencia region's second-largest town. Dynamic and always brimming with fresh projects, it has managed to transform itself from a somewhat seedy port to an attractive town that improves with every visit. And unlike its coastal neighbours, it's a real town, living for much more than tourism alone. Try to fit in at least one overnight stay to experience its frenetic – and unmistakably Spanish – nightlife.

Orientation

Palm trees shade the pedestrianised Paseo Explanada de España, lined with cafés and running parallel to the harbour. Around Catedral de San Nicolás are the narrow streets of El Barrio (the old quarter), which has most of the cheaper accommodation options and a vibrant nightlife. El Barrio is bordered by the Rambla de Méndez Núñez, the principal north–south artery. The main bus and train stations are west of this avenue.

Information

INTERNET ACCESS

UP Internet (Calle de Ángel Lozano 10; per hr €3; 🕙 10am-2am Mon-Thu, 10am-4am Fri & Sat, 10am-midnight Sun)

POST

Main post office (Calle de Alemania)

TOURIST INFORMATION

Regional tourist office (☎ 96 520 00 00; alicante@touristinfo.net; Rambla de Méndez Núñez 23; 🕙 10am-8pm Mon-Sat Jun-Sep, 10am-7.30pm Mon-Fri, 10am-2pm & 3-7.30pm Sat Oct-May) Largest and best informed.
Town tourist offices (www.alicanteturismo.com; bus & train stations, beach & Plaza del Portal de Elche)

Sights & Activities

MARQ (Museo Arqueológico Provincial; ☎ 96 514 90 06; Plaza Doctor Gómez Ulla s/n; adult/child €3/1.50; 🕙 10am-7pm Tue-Sat, 10am-2pm Sun), nominated as European Museum of the Year in 2004, is very visual and high-tech, and well merits a visit, even though there's little information in English. Bus Nos 2, 6, 9, 20 and 23 pass by.

The new **Museu de Fogueres** (Museo de las Hogueras; ☎ 96 514 68 28; Rambla de Méndez Núñez 29; admission free; 🕙 10am-2pm & 6-8pm Tue-Sat, 10am-2pm Sun) has a great audiovisual presentation of what the Fiesta de Sant Joan (p605), all fire and partying, means to Alecantinos.

From the 16th-century **Castillo de Santa Bárbara** (admission free; 🕙 10am-7pm) there are sweeping views over the city. Inside is the **Collección Capa** (admission free), a permanent display of contemporary Spanish sculpture. A **lift/elevator** (€2.40 return), reached by a footbridge opposite Playa del Postiguet, rises through the bowels of the mountain like a giant endoscope. It's a pleasant walk down through Parque de la Ereta via Calle San Rafael to Plaza del Carmen.

MUBAG (Museo de Bellas Artes Gravina; ☎ 96 514 67 80; Calle Gravina 13-15; admission free; 🕙 10am-2pm & 5-8pm Mon-Sat, 10am-2pm Sun), Alicante's stimulating fine arts museum, is within a fine 18th-century mansion.

Nearby, the **Iglesia de Santa María** (🕙 10.30am-1pm & 6-7.30pm) has a flamboyant, 18th-century façade and ornate, gilded altarpiece, both contrasting with the nave's Gothic simplicity of line.

Kontiki (☎ 96 521 63 96) runs a daily boat (€15 return) from the harbour to the popular **Isla de Tabarca**, 20km south.

VALENCIA

ALICANTE

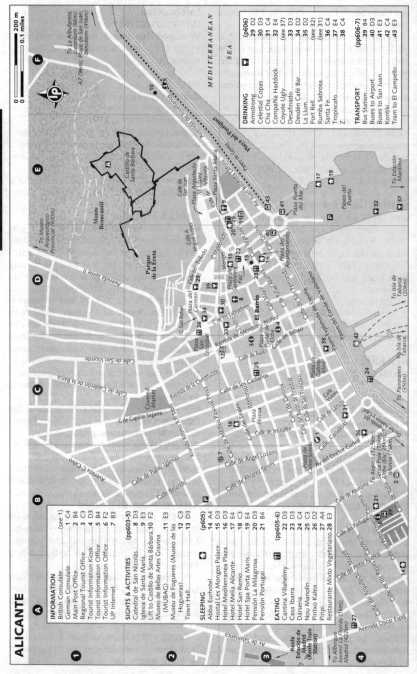

A huge industrial port and ritzy boat harbour take up most of central Alicante's foreshore. On the western mole is **Panoramis**, a vast shopping and leisure complex.

Immediately north of the port is the sandy beach of **Playa del Postiguet**. Larger and less crowded beaches are at **Playa de San Juan**, easily reached by bus No 21 and 22.

Festivals & Events

Alicante's major festival is the **Fiesta de Sant Joan**, spread either side of 24 June, when the city stages its own version of Las Fallas (see the boxed text, p582), with fireworks and satirical effigies (Valenciano: *fogueres*, Spanish: *hogueras*) going up in smoke all over town.

Sleeping
BUDGET

Albergue Juvenil La Florida (☎ 96 511 30 44; Avenida Orihuela 59; under/over 26 €7.45/11.40) Around 2km west of the centre and normally a student residence, La Florida functions as a youth hostel between July and mid-September. Facilities are excellent, with most beds in single rooms. Take bus No 2 or 3, both of which pass by the bus station and Renfe train station.

Pensión La Milagrosa (☎ 96 521 69 18; Calle de Villavieja 8; per person €15) La Milagrosa has decent, basic, no-frills rooms. There's a small guest kitchen and roof terrace, and some rooms overlook Plaza de Santa María.

Pensión Portugal (☎ 96 592 92 44; 1st fl, Calle del Portugal 26; basic s/d €21/30, d with bathroom €36) Opposite the bus station, this slightly old-fashioned place has light, spacious rooms that belie its gloomy public areas.

Camping Costa Blanca (☎ 965 63 06 70; www.campingcostablanca.com; Calle Convento, Campello; per person/tent/car €4.30/6.55/4.30; 🛱) This large camp site is about 10km north of Alicante. The train passes right by.

MID-RANGE & TOP END

Hotel San Remo (☎ 96 520 95 00; fax 96 520 96 68; Calle Navas 30; s €27-33, d €40-55, tr €57-75; 🔲) This friendly, family-run hotel has 27 spruce, well-maintained, if smallish, rooms. Although they don't offer breakfast, there is a coffee machine near reception that dispenses the real brew.

Hotel Mediterranea Plaza (☎ 96 521 01 88; www.hotelmediterraneaplaza.com; Plaza del Ayuntamiento 6; s/d

€96/110, d €85 weekend) Occupying a converted 18th-century mansion in a pedestrian square opposite the town hall, this hotel couldn't come more central. It has large, stylishly furnished rooms, and a sauna and gym.

Hotel Spa Porta Maris (☎ 96 514 70 21; www.hotelspaportamaris.com; Plaza Puerta del Mar 3; s/d €86/99; 🔲 🛱) Each of the 114 rooms here has a balcony overlooking either beach or marina. Among the facilities at this hyperhealthy choice are three pools, sauna, spa, gym and beauty treatment centres. But no one will care if you simply slob around…

Hotel Melia Alicante (☎ 96 520 50 00; www.solmelia.com; Plaza Puerta del Mar 3; s €94-150, d €105-175; 🔲 🔲 🖴 🛱) Next door, this larger (more than 500 rooms), comfortable, long established top-end option operates what must be Spain's most opaque pricing policy. Bang beside Hotel Spa Porta Maris, it's nowadays rather overshadowed by its smart, youthful neighbour.

Abba Eurhotel (☎ 96 513 04 40; www.abbahoteles.com; Calle del Pintor Lorenzo Casanova 33; s/d €82.50/92.50; 🅿 🔲 🔲 🖴) This good mid-range possibility has – so rare in Spain – a few rooms for nonsmokers. Facilities are excellent, though you may find the reception low on warmth. Weekend rates drop to €66 per room.

Eating

Restaurante Mixto Vegetariano (Plaza Santa María 2) This simple low-ceilinged place offers vegetarian and – paradoxically – meat *menús* (€8). You can combine dishes from each.

Casa Ibarra (Calle de Rafael Altamira 19) One of several budget places around Plaza del Ayuntamiento, it does a *menú* (€9) and offers plenty of tapas ('squids to the Roman' and 'mussels to the seafarine' are but two of their engaging English translations) plus fish and grilled-meat options.

Piripi (☎ 96 522 79 40; Avenida Oscar Esplá 30; meals around €25) This highly regarded restaurant |is strong on stylish tapas (head for the shoulder-to-shoulder downstairs bar) and fine rice or seafood dishes. The *mousse de turrón de Jijona* (almond nougat mousse) is to die for.

Nou Manolín (☎ 96 520 03 68; Calle Villegas 3; menú €15, mains €16-22) This mellow bare-brick place does magnificent bar tapas and delightful rice dishes. Book in advance, since it's another favourite among discerning – and well-heeled – Alicantinos.

Dársena (☎ 96 520 75 89; Muelle del Levante 6) With great views over the marina, Dársena is another locally esteemed restaurant. Select from the nearly 150 rice dishes or, for something more meaty, go for the flagship *solomillo de ternera a la sal* (fillet of beef encrusted in a salt casing).

Pintxo Kalea (☎ 96 514 58 41; Plaza San Cristóbal 11; menú €11) Basque music wails and jigs in the background at this modern, stylish bar and restaurant, which does a wonderful selection of juicy *pinchos* (small open sandwiches).

Cantina Villahelmy (☎ 965 21 25 29; Calle Mayor 37; mains €4-8; closed dinner Sun & Mon) Intimate, funky and popular, this place has lots of snacks, excellent salads and a menu that features dishes from couscous to squid.

SELF-CATERING
Browse around Alicante's huge, Art Nouveau twin-storey **covered market** (Avenida Alfonso X El Sabio).

Drinking
The old quarter around Catedral de San Nicolás is wall-to-wall bars. Down by the harbour, the Paseo del Puerto, tranquil by day, is a double-decker line of bars, cafés and discos. Like just about everywhere in Spain, most places hot up around 11pm and stay lively until the sun begins to peek.

Celestial Copas (Calle San Pascual 1) is heavenly (and weird) and has a kitsch collection of religious art/junk and great music. Nearby, **Desafinado** (Santo Tomas 6) is another heaving dance bar that also offers good jazz.

Armstrong (Plaza del Carmen 12) is the Barrio's best venue for jazz, often live and with regu-

lar DJs. Early opener **Desdén Café Bar** (Calle de los Labradores 22) also has live music on weekends, while **La Llum** (cnr Calle Montengon & Calle Padre Maltés) is a tiny sweatbox dance-bar that goes wild late into the night.

The area further west between Rambla de Méndez Núñez and Avenida del Doctor Gadea is an equally hectic option.

Santa Fe (cnr Calle San Fernando & Avenida del Doctor Gadea) is a sophisticated place to kick off the evening. Just down the street, rhythms at **Cha Cha** (Calle Canalejas 6) and its neighbour, **Rumba Sabrosa**, are strictly Latino.

Z (☽ until dawn Tue-Sun), a popular place just off Plaza de Gabriel Miró, is a slick *discoteca* with a dress code. Don't turn up before 3am.

In the port area, if you don't recognise **Compañía Haddock** by the din, you will from the image of Tintin's pipe-smoking companion. Sitting above it – and risking bringing the roof down on a good night – is **Port Rell**.

A couple of doors along, **Tropiscafo** beams out good recorded jazz, while beside it **Coyote Ugly** sometimes has live music.

If you're still on your feet, take the night ferry over to the **Panoramis** complex, where the opportunities for nocturnal action are almost as rich.

During summer the disco scene at Playa de San Juan gets thumping. In fact, there are dozens of discos all along the coast from Alicante to Denia. They are all served by Búhobus (the 'Night Owls Bus'), which runs three night routes, starting from Panoramis and passing by Plaza Puerta del Mar.

Getting There & Away
AIR
Alicante's **El Altet airport** (☎ 96 691 91 00), gateway to the Costa Blanca, is served by charters and scheduled flights from all over Europe.

Two cut-price operators, both with offices at Alicante airport, are **Servitour** (☎ 96 568 26 42; www.servitour.es) and **V. Travel 2000** (☎ 96 691 94 60), which also calls itself **Goflightline**.

BOAT
There's a regular **ferry** (book through Romeu ☎ 96 514 70 10; Romeu office, Puerto Marítimo) to **Oran** (Algeria), but check on the security situation in Algeria before you jump aboard.

BUS

From the **bus station** (☎ 96 513 07 00) there are more than 10 motorway buses daily to Valencia (€15.25, 2½ hours) and others, much slower, that pass through Costa Blanca coastal towns such as Benidorm (€3.25, one hour, at least hourly). Other long-distance destinations include Madrid (€23.15 to €29.25, 4½ hours).

TRAIN

Destinations from the main **Renfe Estación de Madrid** (Avenida de Salamanca) include Murcia (€3.70, 1½ hours, up to 20 daily) via Orihuela and Elche, Valencia (€10.50 to €23, 1½ to two hours, up to eight daily) via Villena and Xátiva, Madrid (€36, 3¾ hours, seven daily) and Barcelona (€39.50, 4½ hours).

Ferrocarriles de la Generalitat Valenciana (FGV) (☎ 900 720472) has a tram and narrow-gauge train service, commonly called the *trenet* (little train), which follows an at times scenically stunning coastal route. The tram (every half-hour) runs northwards as far El Campello, where the *trenet* takes over. It runs to Denia (€6.40) via Playa de San Juan (€0.85), Benidorm (€2.45) and Calpe (€3.95). Trains run hourly as far as Altea and every two hours to Denia (€7.15).

Getting Around

El Altet airport is around 12km southwest of the centre. Bus No C-6 runs every 40 minutes between Plaza Puerta del Mar and the airport, passing by the north side of the bus station.

Reliable and very economical local car-hire companies operating from the airport include: **Javea Cars** (☎ 96 579 33 12; www.javeacars .com), **Solmar** (☎ 96 646 10 00; www.solmar.es) and **Victoria Cars** (☎ 96 579 27 61; www.victoriacars .com).

For a **taxi**, call either ☎ 96 591 05 91 or ☎ 96 510 16 11.

AROUND ALICANTE
Lucentum

The remains of the Roman town of **Lucentum** (☎ 96 526 24 34; adult/child €2/1.50; 🕙 9am-noon & 7-10pm Mon-Sat, 9am-noon Sun Jun-Sep, 10am-2pm & 4-6pm Mon-Sat, 10am-2pm Sun Oct-May), forerunner of Alicante, are nowadays dominated by the high-rise apartment blocks of La Albufareta. Take bus No 9 or 21.

SANTA POLA
pop 19,800

Santa Pola, 20km south of Alicante, sprawls around its harbour, base of the local fishing fleet and haven to hundreds of pleasure vessels. From here **boats** (€11/8 adult/child return) leave for the popular **Isla de Tabarca**, just 4.5km offshore.

There's a helpful **tourist office** (☎ 96 669 22 76; 🕙 10am-2pm & 5.30-7.30pm Mon-Sat) at the entrance to town beside El Palmeral park and another **tourist office** (☎ 96 669 62 39; Calle Astilleros) near the port.

Most of Santa Pola's beaches are backed by jungles of concrete, but sandy **Gran Playa**, **Playa Lisa** and **Santa Pola del Este** are worth spreading your towel on.

In the centre of town on Plaza del Castillo, the well-preserved 16th-century **Castillo-Fortaleza de Santa Pola** fortress stands besieged by 20th-century high-rise architecture. Within its stark courtyard are two small museums: **Museo del Mar** (☎ 96 669 15 32; admission €0.60; 🕙 11am-1pm & 5-8pm Tue-Sat, 11am-2pm Sun), a maritime museum; and **Museo de la Pesca** (☎ 96 541 33 51; adult/child €1.50/0.60, 🕙 11am-1pm & 5-8pm Tue-Sat, 11am-2pm Sun), which commemorates Santa Pola's heritage as a fishing port.

The **Museo de la Sal** (☎ 96 669 35 46; off Avenida Zaragoza; admission free; 🕙 9am-2.30pm Tue-Sun, 4-6pm Tue & Thu), occupying a converted salt mill, tells the story of salt production.

Sleeping

Hostal-Restaurante Michel (☎ 96 541 18 42; fax 96 541 19 42; Calle Felipe II 11; s/d €35/48; 🏖) Norwegian-run and with a pleasant little restaurant where you can get fishy Scandinavian tapas, this tidy option has 20 well-furnished rooms and a roof terrace. In summer request a room with air-con, which comes at no extra cost.

Hotel Polamar (☎ 96 541 32 00; www.polamar .com; s/d €43/68 Sep-Jun, €59/88 Jul-Aug, all with breakfast; 🅿) Ask for a room with sea views at this traditional hotel, well positioned right on the Playa de Levante beachfront. All rooms have balconies.

Camping Bahía (☎ 96 541 10 12; per person/tent/car €4/4/4; 🏖) This well-equipped camp site is on the outskirts of town, just off the N332.

Getting There & Around

Buses run at least hourly to Alicante, every half-hour to Elche and eight times daily to Torrevieja and on to Cartagena.

VALENCIA

TORREVIEJA

pop 51,000

A heavily developed resort with a high proportion of northern European visitors, Torrevieja retains a twinkle or two of its former charm – such as the elegant casino just west of the tourist office – and has good beaches.

The **tourist office** (☎ 96 570 34 33; www.webtorre vieja.com; Plaza de Capdepont; ⏰ 8.30am-8.30pm Mon-Fri, 10am-2pm & 4.30-7.30pm Sat) is near the waterfront. Just to its south is a large parking area and the jetty from which boats leave in summer for the day trip (€18/12 adult/child) to **Isla de Tabarca**.

Sleeping

Hotel Cano (☎ 96 670 09 58; hotelcano@terra.es; Calle Zoa 53; s/d €30/40 mid-Sep–Jun, €40/60 Jul–mid-Sep; P ⌘) Five blocks west of the bus station, the Cano, which has recently doubled its capacity yet preserved its character, has trim, modern rooms.

Hotel Madrid (☎ 96 571 00 38; hmadrid@mundofree .com; Calle Villa Madrid 15; s/d with breakfast €45/63, €60/85 Jul–mid-Sep; P ⌘ 🖳) Smaller, with 16 rooms, and one star up, the Madrid has comfortable, fairly spacious rooms, one of which is equipped for travellers with disabilities. There's also a top-floor spa.

Hotel Masa Internacional (☎ 96 692 15 37; hotel -masa@arrakis.com; Avenida Alfredo Nobel 150; s €51-85, d €71-110; P ⌘ 🖳) This smart clifftop hotel, extensively renovated in 2003, is a lovely top-end choice, east of town and remote from all the downtown frenzy. Rooms overlooking the sea come at no extra cost.

Camping La Campana (☎ 96 571 21 52; per person/pitch €4/10; ⏰ year-round) The nearest camping ground, 4.5km south of town on the Cartagena road.

Eating

Plenty of restaurants around the waterfront offer cheap meals and international menus. On Plaza Isabel II, park yourself on a patio and enjoy great grilled fresh fish.

Restaurante Vegetariano (☎ 96 670 66 83; Calle Pedro Lorca 13; mains €7.50-9, salads €5-7.50; ⏰ Tue-Sun) One block back from the beachfront, this little vegetarian haven, run by a Spanish-Australian couple, offers salads, sandwiches, pizzas and tasty mains.

El Muelle (☎ 96 670 41 72; Paseo Marítimo Juan Aparicio; mains €10-15, pizzas €8-11; ⌘) East of and

set apart from the run-of-the-mill promenade restaurants, the highly regarded 'Jetty' does great house pastas and mains. You can eat on the terrace overlooking the sea or inside in the chill of the air-con.

Getting There & Away

The **bus station** (☎ 96 571 01 46) is on Calle Antonio Machado. There are up to six buses daily to Madrid (€32.25, 4½ hours). Autocares Costa Azul runs eight buses daily to Cartagena (€3.55, 1¼ hours) and Alicante (€3.10, one hour).

INLAND FROM THE COSTA BLANCA

The difference between the holiday *costa* and the interior is, perhaps appropriately, marked by a motorway. Just head west of the A7 and you find yourself in a different world – a truly Spanish one. Those visitors who venture away from the coast are richly rewarded. By far the easiest way to explore the region is with your own transport.

XÀTIVA

pop 25,700

Xàtiva (Spanish: Játiva) sits snug at the base of the Serra Vernissa mountain range 50km south of Valencia, from where it's an easy day trip.

After the Reconquista, Xàtiva became Valencia's second-largest city. Birthplace of the Borgia Popes Calixtus III and Alexander VI, its glory days ended in 1707 when Felipe V's troops torched most of the town.

Information

The **tourist office** (☎ 96 227 33 46; Alameda Jaime I 50; ⏰ 10am-1.30pm & 4-6pm Tue-Fri, 10am-1.30pm Sat & Sun Oct-May, 10am-2.30pm Tue-Sun Jun-Sep) is on the shady main street.

Sights & Activities

What's interesting lies south and uphill from the Alameda (the main avenue). Ask at the tourist office for the English brochure, *Xàtiva: Monumental Town*.

The **Museo del Almudín** (☎ 96 227 65 97; Calle Corretgería 46; admission €2; ⏰ 9.30am-2.30pm Tue-Fri, 10am-2.30pm Sat-Sun mid-Jun–mid-Sep, 10am-2pm & 4-6pm Tue-Fri, 10am-2.30pm Sat-Sun mid-Sep–mid-Jun) has a decent collection of archaeological relics and artworks, including a portrait of Felipe V, hung upside down in retribution for his pyrotechnic assault.

In the heart of town, the 16th-century **Colegiata Basílica** (Collegiate Church) merits a visit primarily for the rich treasures of its **museum** (admission €1; ⏱ 10.30am-1.30pm Tue-Sun).

It's a long climb to the **castle** (adult/child €2/1; ⏱ 10am-6pm Tue-Sun), from where the views are inspiring. On the way up, notice on your left the 18th-century **Ermita de San José** and, to the right, the lovely Romanesque **Iglesia de Sant Feliu** (1269), Xàtiva's oldest church. Alternatively, hop aboard the little tourist train that heads up from the tourist office at 12.30pm and 4.30pm or 5.30pm.

Sleeping & Eating

Hostería Mont Sant (☎ 96 227 50 81; www.mont -sant.com; s/d from €78.15/90.15; P ⛄ ⛄) On the road to the castle and charmingly set amid palm trees and an orange grove, this place offers comfortable rooms in either the main building or garden cabins, and runs a splendid restaurant, agreeably divided up into intimate crannies.

Hotel Huerto Virgen de las Nieves (☎ 96 228 70 58; Avenida Ribera 6; d Sun-Fri €75, Sat €115; ⛄ ⛄) This intimate hotel (it has only six rooms) has recently been restored with very considerable flair. It's a wonderfully spacious place, all mellow brick and woodwork, with a secluded garden. Its **restaurant** (midday menú €12), open to all comers, is equally rich in character.

Pensión Restaurante El Margallonero (☎ 96 227 66 77; Plaza del Mercado 42; basic rooms per person €12) This homely place and its popular, bustling **restaurant** (menú €8/11 weekdays/weekends) recently celebrated its centenary, having been run by three generations of the same family.

Casa la Abuela (☎ 96 228 10 85; Calle de la Reina 17; mains €10-14; ⏱ mid-Aug–mid-Jul) Renowned for its à la carte cuisine, 'Grandmother's House' does a good menú for €12 and is strong on regional dishes.

Getting There & Away

Train and bus stations are on Avenida del Cavaller Ximén de Tovia. The train's by far your best bet. Frequent services connect Xàtiva with Valencia (€2.70, half-hourly) and most Valencia to Madrid trains stop here too. You can also reach Alicante (€7 to €17, five daily).

VILLENA
pop 32,700

Villena, on the N330 between Alicante and Albacete, is the most attractive of the towns that dot the corridor of the Val de Vinalopó.

Plaza de Santiago is at the heart of the old quarter. The **tourist office** (☎ 96 580 38 04; ⏱ 8am-3pm Mon-Fri, 10.30am-1.30pm Sat & Sun) is at No 5. Within the fine 16th-century **Palacio Municipal** (Plaza de Santiago 2) is the **Museo Arqueológico** (admission free; ⏱ 10am-2pm & 5-8pm Tue-Fri, 11am-2pm Sat & Sun). Pride of its collection are 60 gold artefacts weighing over 10kg, dating from around 1000 BC and found by chance in an old riverbed. Perched high above the town, the 12th-century **Castillo de la Atalaya** (admission free; guided visits mornings to 12.30pm Tue-Sun) is splendidly lit at night.

Villena celebrates its **Moros y Cristianos** fiesta from 5 to 9 September (see the boxed text, p610).

Alsa runs hourly buses regularly to/from Alicante (€3.50) via Elda, and up to eight trains run daily to/from Alicante via Elda and Novelda.

ELDA
pop 51,600

Elda vies with Elche for the title of shoemaking capital of Spain. Foot fetishists shouldn't miss the **Museo del Calzado** (Shoe Museum; ☎ 96 538 30 21; Avenida Chapí 32; adult/child €2.40/1.20; ⏱ 10am-1pm & 4-8pm Tue-Sat, to 1pm Sun). Above the mezzanine floor with its row upon row of Heath Robinson drills, stamps and sewing machines, it's wall-to-wall footwear: boots through the ages; shoes and slippers from around the world; fanciful designs that must have been agony to wear; and donated cast-offs from matadors, flamenco dancers, King Juan Carlos, Queen Sofia and other well-shod greats.

NOVELDA
pop 24,800

If you're a fan of Art Nouveau (more often known as Modernisme in Spanish), make the 25km pilgrimage from Alicante to Novelda's wonderful **Casa-Museo Modernista** (☎ 96 560 02 37; Calle Mayor 24; admission free; ⏱ 9am-2pm & 4-7pm Mon-Fri, 11am-2pm Sat). A bourgeois mansion completed in 1903, its stained glass, soft shapes in wood, period furniture and magnificent spiralling wrought-iron staircase take the breath away.

VALENCIA

Peek, too, inside No 6 Calle Mayor – these days the **municipal library** – and admire the exterior of the **Cruz Roja building** (Spanish Red Cross; Plaza del Ayuntamiento).

Novelda's **tourist office** (☎ 96 560 92 28; 9am-2pm & 4.30-7pm Mon-Fri, 10am-2pm Sat) is at Calle Mayor 6.

ALCOY

pop 58,400 / elevation 565m

For 51¾ weeks a year, there's really not a lot to entice you to the lugubrious industrial town of Alcoy (Valenciano: Alcoi), which is located 50km south of Xàtiva. But there's everything to draw you here between 22 and 24 April. These threee days are when Alcoy holds its annual **Moros y Cristianos** festival (see the boxed text below), the region's most colourful event after Valencia city's Fallas.

To get an idea of the splendour of the costumes and a feel for the fiesta, visit the **Casal de Sant Jordi** (☎ 96 554 05 80; Calle San Miguel 62; admission €1.50; 11am-1pm & 5.30-7.30pm Tue-Fri, 10.30am-1.30pm Sat & Sun). Occupying an 18th-century noble mansion, it houses the festival's museum.

Alcoy's **tourist office** (☎ 96 553 71 55; alcoi@touristinfo.net; Calle San Lorenzo 2; 9.30am-1.30pm & 5-7pm Mon-Fri, 10.30am-1.30pm Sat-Sun) is just off the main Plaza de España.

Hostal Savoy (☎ 96 554 72 72; Calle Casablanca 9; s/d/tr with bathroom €35/50/65), a friendly place one block south of the main Plaza de Es-paña, is one of only two accommodation options in town.

There are four to five trains daily to/from Valencia (€6.50, 1¾ hours) via Xàtiva. From the nearby bus station, four to six daily services run to Valencia, at least 10 to Alicante and a couple to Gandia.

GUADALEST

You'll be far from the first to discover the village of Guadalest – the history of which goes back to at least AD 715 – since nowadays coaches, heading up from the Costa Blanca resorts, disgorge more than two million visitors annually. But if you arrive there early, or stay put after the last bus has pulled out, you'll find the place can be almost your own.

Crowds come because Guadalest, reached by a natural tunnel and overlooked by the **Castillo de San José** (adult/child €3/1.50; 10.30am-8pm Jun-Sep, 10.30am-1.45pm & 3.15-5pm Oct-May) is indeed very pretty, and it's a joy to stroll through a traffic-free village.

One little jewel amid so much day-tripper-oriented tackiness is the diminutive **Museo Etnológico** (☎ 96 588 52 38; admission free but donations welcome; 10am-6pm, closed Sat winter), a sensitive presentation of what life in Guadalest was like before the coach parties came along.

There's a small **tourist office** (☎ 96 588 52 98) alongside the parking area on the road that bypasses the village.

FIESTAS DE MOROS Y CRISTIANOS

More than 80 towns and villages in the south of Valencia hold their own Fiesta de Moros y Cristianos (Moors and Christians festival) to celebrate the Reconquista, the region's liberation from Arab rule.

Biggest and best known is Alcoy's (22 to 24 April), when hundreds of locals dress up in elaborate traditional costumes representing different 'factions' – Muslim and Christian soldiers, slaves, guild groups, town criers, heralds, bands – and march through the streets in spectacular and colourful processions with mock battles.

The various processions converge upon Alcoy's main plaza, where a huge, temporary wooden fortress is erected. It's an exhilarating spectacle of sights and sounds: soldiers in shining armour, white-cloaked Muslim warriors bearing scimitars and shields, turban-topped Arabs, scantily clad wenches, brass bands, exploding blunderbusses, firework displays and confetti showering down on the crowds.

Each town has its own variation on the format, steeped in traditions that allude to the events of the Reconquista. For example, Villena's festival (5 to 9 September) features midnight parades, while La Vila Joiosa (24 to 31 July) re-enacts the landing of Muslim ships on the beaches. Other major festivals include those of Bocairent (1 to 5 February), Biar (10 to 13 May), Guardamar (late July) and Ontinyent (end August).

Getting There & Away
Guadalest is ill-served by public transport. One bus daily, Monday to Friday only, leaves Benidorm, passing by its train station at 9am. For the return journey, it departs Guadalest at 12.30pm.

JIJONA
If you love all things sweet, you really ought to pay a pilgrimage to Jijona (Valenciano: Xixona), on the N340 more or less midway between Alicante and Alcoy. This small town has two claims to fame. Nowadays, it's Spain's principal producer of *turrón*, a kind of nougat with both soft and crunchy variants. In the past, the place was also a stopover for porters bearing ice from the high hinterland to assuage the heat of a coastal summer. And so it lent its name to Jijona, a popular brand of ice cream that sells by the hectolitre throughout the land.

ELCHE
pop 194,800
A mere 23km southwest of Alicante, Elche (Valenciano: Elx) is a Unesco World Heritage site twice over: first for the Misteri d'Elx, its annual mystery play (see the boxed text following) and next for its extensive palm groves, Europe's largest and most northerly, originally planted by the Arabs. Muslim irrigation systems converted the region into a rich agricultural district that still produces citrus fruit, figs, almonds and dates – not to mention 85% of Spain's pomegranates.

Orientation
The town is split north–south by the Río Vinalopó. The older quarter and most of the parks and monuments lie on its eastern side.

Train and bus stations are beside each other on Avenida de la Libertad (also called Avenida del Ferrocarril), north of the centre. From either, exit, go left along Avenida de la Libertad then left again down Paseo de la Estación to reach the tourist office and town centre in less than 10 minutes.

Information
INTERNET ACCESS
Entre Acto Cybercafé (Calle Santa Barbara 15; per hr €3; ☯ 9am-midnight Mon-Fri, 3pm-2am Sat & Sun)

TOURIST INFORMATION
Tourist office (☎ 96 545 27 47; www.turismedelx.com; ☯ 10am-7pm Mon-Fri, 10am-2pm Sat & Sun) At the southeast corner of Parque Municipal (Town Park).

Sights & Activities
Palm trees – over 200,000, some shaggy and in need of a haircut, most trim and clipped – make the heart of this busy industrial town (it produces over 80 million pairs of shoes annually) a veritable oasis. A recently signed 3km walking trail leads you through the groves.

Opposite the hotel of the same name, the **Huerto del Cura** (adult/child €4/1.50; ☯ 9am-6pm, to 8.30pm Jul-Sep) is a lovely private garden with tended lawns and colourful flowerbeds.

To get an overview of Elche, call by **Centro de Visitantes** (admission free; ☯ 10am-6.45pm Mon-Sat, 10am-1.45pm Sun). This Arab-style building in the park behind the tourist office runs a 10-minute audiovisual presentation with multilingual commentary.

The 12th-century **Baños Árabes** (Arab Baths; ☎ 96 545 28 87; Plaza Santa Lucia; admission free; ☯ 10am-1.30pm & 4.30-8pm Tue-Sat, 10.30am-1.30pm Sun) runs an enjoyable free audiovisual presentation with optional English soundtrack.

The vast baroque **Basílica de Santa María** is used for performances of the Misteri d'Elx. Climb up its tower (adult/child €2/1; ☯ 11am-6pm) for a pigeon's-eye view over the palms.

At the time of writing, the 15th-century **Palacio de Altamira** and, within it, Elche's **Museo Arqueológico Municipal**, were closed for renovations.

The well-signposted **Alcúdia archaeological site** is 3.5km south of the town centre. Here was unearthed the Dama de Elche, a masterpiece of Iberian art that's now in Madrid's Museo Arqueológico Nacional. Visit the site's excellent **Museo Arqueológico** (☎ 96 661 15 06; adult/child €3/2; ☯ 10am-2pm & 4-8pm Tue-Sat Apr-Sep, 10am-5pm Tue-Sat Oct-Mar, 10am-2pm Sun year-round). The museum displays the rich findings from a settlement that was occupied continuously from Neolithic to late Visigoth times.

Sleeping & Eating
Hotel Faro (☎ 96 546 62 63; Camí dels Magros 24; basic s/d €14/28) This friendly nine-room family place is a little gem, with simple, spotless rooms.

Hotel Huerto del Cura (☎ 96 661 00 11; www .huertodelcura.com; Calle Puerta de la Morera 14; s/d

MISTERI D'ELX

The *Misteri d'Elx*, a two-act lyric drama dating from the Middle Ages, is performed annually in Elche's Basílica de Santa María.

One distant day, according to legend, a casket was washed up on Elche's Mediterranean shore. Inside were a statue of the Virgin and the *Consueta*, the music and libretto of a mystery play describing Our Lady's death, assumption into heaven and coronation.

The story tells how the Virgin, realising that death is near, asks God to allow her to see the apostles one last time. They arrive one by one from distant lands and, in their company, she dies at peace. Once received into paradise, she is crowned Queen of Heaven and Earth to swelling music, the ringing of bells, cheers all round and – hey, we're in the Valencia region – spectacular fireworks.

The mystery's two acts, *La Vespra* (the eve of her death) and *La Festa* (the celebration of her assumption and coronation) are performed in Valenciano by the people of Elche themselves on 14 and 15 August respectively (with public rehearsals on the three previous days).

You can see a multimedia presentation – complete with virtual apostle – in the **Museu Municipal de la Festa** (☎ 96 545 34 64; Carrer Major de la Vila 25; adult/child €3/1.80; ☷ 10am-1pm & 5-8.30pm Tue-Sat, 10am-1pm Sun), about a block west of the basilica. The show lasts 35 minutes and is repeated several times daily, with optional English commentary.

Mon-Thu from €90/106, d Fri-Sun €85) The town's longest-standing luxury hotel sits in its own lush, palm-shaded gardens. During the week it's popular with businesspeople and priced accordingly, but on weekends (and during most of August) it's a bargain. Complete the cosseting by dining in **Els Capellans**, the hotel restaurant, strong on local cuisine.

Carrer Mare de Déu del Carmé (Calle Nuestra Señora del Carmen) has a cluster of good, cheap and cheerful eateries including **Bar Los Extremeños** (Calle Nuestra Señora del Carmen 14), which serves great tapas. On summer evenings almost the whole length of this short street is set with tables.

Restaurante Parque Municipal (☎ 965 45 34 15; mains €8-12, menús €12 & 18) Within the municipal park, this vast emporium to eating can accommodate almost 2000 diners. Even so, the cuisine is far from institutional and it's one of the best places in town to sample local cuisine at reasonable prices.

Getting There & Around
AM Mollá operates buses every half-hour to/from Alicante (€1.60) and Santa Pola (€1). Alsa runs four buses daily to Valencia (€9.70) via Elda and Villena and seven to/from Murcia (€3.40).

Elche is on the Alicante to Murcia railway. Around 20 trains daily rattle through, bound for Alicante (€1.80) or Murcia (€2.50) via Orihuela.

ORIHUELA
pop 54,400

On the banks of the Río Segura and flush with the base of a barren mountain of rock, the historical heart of Orihuela with its Gothic, Renaissance and, especially, baroque buildings well merits a detour.

The **tourist office** (☎ 96 530 27 47; Calle Francisco Die 25; ☷ Mon-Fri 8am-3pm, to 1.30pm Jul–mid-Sep) works jobsworth hours, successfully contriving to be closed when most visitors need it.

Sights
The 16th-century **Convento de Santo Domingo** (Calle Adolfo Claravana s/n; ☷ 9.30am-1.30pm & 5-8pm Tue-Sat, 10am-2pm Sun) has two fine Renaissance cloisters and a refectory rich in 18th-century tilework.

Other splendid **ecclesiastical buildings** (all ☷ – in principle – 10am-1.30pm & 5-7pm Tue-Sat, 10am-1.30pm Sun) include the 14th-century Catalan-Gothic **Catedral de San Salvador** (Calle Doctor Sarget) with three finely carved portals. It houses the **Museo Diocesano**, whose collection includes Velázquez' *Temptation of St Thomas*.

The **Iglesia de las Santas Justa y Rufina** (Plaza Salesas 1) has a Renaissance façade and a Gothic tower graced with gargoyles. Also noteworthy are the sober baroque façade of the **Palacio Episcopal** (Calle Ramón y Cajal), the 14th-century **Iglesia de Santiago Apóstol** (Plaza de Santiago 2) and, crowning the mountain, the ruins of a **castle** originally constructed by the Muslims.

Access to Orihuela's **Museo de la Muralla** (☎ 96 674 31 54; Calle del Río s/n; admission free; ⏲ 10am-2pm & 5-7pm Tue-Sat, 10am-2pm Sun) is through the main door to the Universidad Miguel Hernandez. A 20-minute guided tour in Spanish (ask for the English leaflet) leads you through the vast underground remains of the city walls, Arab baths and domestic buildings.

Sleeping & Eating

Hotel Palacio de Tudemir (☎ 96 673 80 10; www .sh-hoteles.com; Calle Alfonso XIII 1; s €85, d €94-103; ⊠ ⊠ ⊑) 'Palace' is indeed the word for this tastefully renovated 18th-century building. Its weekend rooms, at €75 including breakfast, are excellent value, and there's a pleasant café, too. It's also one of the best places in town to dine (*menú* €15). Some bedrooms are smoke-free.

Hostal-Residencia Rey Teodomiro (☎ /fax 96 674 33 48; 1st fl, Avenida de Teodomiro 10; s/d €30/50; ⊠) This hotel is a tidy option in the more modern part of town.

Cafè Bar Casablanca (☎ 96 530 10 29; Calle Meca 1; tapas from €2.50-3.50) An unpretentious place with a wide selection of tapas.

Ateneo (☎ 96 530 40 18; Calle Cardenal Loaces 1; mains €12-17 menú €17) Also called the Casino, Ateneo is open to the public and serves good food in elegant, 19th-century surroundings.

Getting There & Away

Bus and train stations are combined at the Intermodal, an airy structure at the end of Avenida de Teodomiro. Orihuela is on the Alicante to Murcia train line and has frequent services to each.

VALENCIA

Balearic Islands

Each of these four islands (Islas Baleares, Illes Balears in Catalan), floating serenely in the glittering waters of the Mediterranean, could be said to have a theme. Mallorca (Majorca in English) is the senior island, a place that combines a little of everything, from spectacular mountain scenery and hiking through to the standard sea 'n' sun seaside tourism. Ibiza is synonymous with clubbing; it's the island that gave Europe the rave. Menorca (Minorca to Anglos) is a haven of peace and quiet – splendid isolated beaches and coves, and prehistoric monuments standing as taciturn reminders of how small we are in the grand scheme of things. And tiny Formentera, a chill-out island, where some people lose themselves for the entire summer, needing little more to keep them happy than white beaches and sunset parties.

Each year a massive multinational force invades the islands in search of a piece of this multifaceted paradise. The total population of the isles does not amount to a million, but many times that number are involved in a round-the-clock airlift and disembarkation of sun- and fun-seeking from Easter to October.

Surprisingly, the islands have managed to maintain much of their intrinsic beauty, individuality and links with the past. Beyond the high-rise resort hotels, bars and more popular beaches are Gothic cathedrals, Stone Age ruins, fishing villages, spectacular walks, secluded coves, endless olive and almond groves and orange orchards.

BALEARIC ISLANDS

HIGHLIGHTS

- Cast your eyes skyward at Palma de Mallorca's enormous Gothic **cathedral** (p622)
- Walk in Mallorca's **Serra de Tramuntana** (p626)
- Rave to your faves in **Ibiza's amazing clubs** (p640)
- Chill out at Formentera's sunset parties at **Platja de ses Illetes** (p619)
- Seek out villages such as **Fornalutx** (p629) in Mallorca's northwest
- Gaze out to sea from **Miramar** and **Can Marroig** (p628)
- Peer into prehistory at **Naveta des Tudons** (p657) and Menorca's other ancient monuments
- Slip into Menorca's limpid waters at the beaches of **Cala Macarelleta** and **Cala en Turqueta** (p659)
- Party hard at the Festa de Sant Joan in **Ciutadella** (p651)
- Say three Hail Marys before travelling the spectacular 12km route to **Sa Calobra** (p630)

| AREA: 4992 SQ KM | POP: 947,361 | AVE SUMMER TEMP: HIGH 28°C, LOW 20°C |

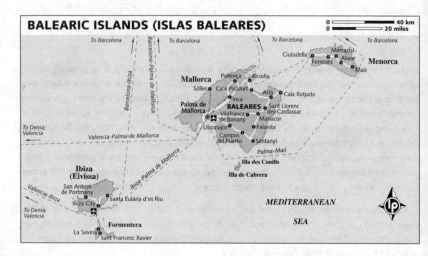

BALEARIC ISLANDS (ISLAS BALEARES)

BALEARIC ISLANDS

History

Archaeologists believe the first human settlements in the Balearic Islands date from around 5000 BC. An abundance of prehistoric relics and monuments uncovered on the islands show that these communities built houses of stone, practised basic agriculture, domesticated animals, performed ritual burials and manufactured pottery, tools and jewellery.

The Balearics were regular ports of call for ancient Phoenician traders. They were followed by the Carthaginians, who founded Ibiza City in 654 BC and made it one of the Mediterranean's major trading ports. Next came those compulsive road builders, the Romans, who, in turn, were overwhelmed by the Visigoths.

Three centuries of Muslim domination ended with the Christian Reconquista, led by Jaume I of Catalonia and Aragón, who took Palma de Mallorca in 1229 and sponsored the invasion of Ibiza in 1235. Menorca was the last to fall: Alfonso III took it in 1287 in a nasty Vietnam-style campaign, completing the islands' incorporation into the Catalan world.

After their initial boom as trading centres and Catalan colonies, the islands had fallen on hard times by the 15th century. Isolation from the mainland, famines and frequent raids by pirates contributed to their decline. During the 16th century Menorca's two major towns were virtually destroyed by Turkish forces and Ibiza City's fortified walls were built. After a succession of bloody raids, Formentera was abandoned.

The Balearics fared poorly in warfare. After backing the Habsburgs in the Spanish War of Succession, Mallorca and Ibiza were occupied by the victorious Bourbon monarchy in 1715. Menorca, on the other hand, was granted to the British along with Gibraltar in 1713 under the Treaty of Utrecht. British rule lasted until 1802, with the exception of the Seven Years War (1756–63), during which the French moved in. In the Spanish Civil War, Menorca was the last of the islands to succumb to Franco's forces.

Tourism since the 1950s has brought considerable wealth. The islanders now enjoy – by some estimates – the highest standard of living in Spain, but 80% of their economy is based on tourism alone. This has led to thoughtless and massive construction on some of the islands' coastlines, and leads to Balearics-wide anxiety attacks whenever a season doesn't meet expectations.

The islands' foreign admirers seem to have their preferences. If the Germans have set their sights on Mallorca, Formentera becomes something akin to little Italy in July and August. The Brits are numerous in Mallorca, but have a special affection for Menorca. Ibiza's clubs, on the other hand, attract a more international brigade of hedonists.

Place names and addresses in this chapter are in Catalan, the main language spoken (with regional variations). The major exceptions are Ibiza and Ibiza City – both are called Eivissa in Catalan but we use the better-known Spanish rendition.

Getting There & Around
AIR

If your main goal in Spain is to visit the Balearic Islands, it makes *no* financial sense to fly via the mainland. If already in Spain, scheduled flights from major cities on the mainland are operated by Iberia, Air Europa and Spanair (see the Transport chapter, p850).

The cheapest and most frequent flights leave from Barcelona and Valencia. Standard one-way fares from Barcelona and Valencia hover around €80 to €100 to Palma de Mallorca and usually more to the other islands. However, it is possible to get a fixed-date return flight, valid for up to a month, for little more than €100 depending on seasonal demand.

Inter-island flights are expensive (given a flying time of less than 30 minutes), with a trip from Palma de Mallorca to Maó or Ibiza easily costing €90 to €100 (depending on season; return flights cost double). There are no direct flights from Ibiza to Maó. If you book far enough in advance, the price comes down. Iberia and Air Europa are the main operators, with up to 10 flights a day between Palma and Ibiza or Maó. Spanair's subsidiary Aebal also operates several daily flights.

Charter flights from Europe are usually sold as a package, including accommodation. If you're looking for a cheap deal, check with travel agencies, as spare seats on charter flights are often sold at discounted prices. In summer masses of charter and regular flights converge on Palma de Mallorca and Ibiza. From the UK, EasyJet and BMI Baby can get you there for as little as UK£30 one way (plus taxes), depending on how far in advance you book, while German budget airlines, such as Air-Berlin and LTU, shuttle in thousands of passengers from cities all over Germany daily. (Typical return fares hover around €150, but can easily hit €300 in July and August.) For more airline details turn to the Transport chapter (p850).

BOAT
The major ferry company is **Trasmediterránea** (☎ 902 454645; www.trasmediterranea.com), which has offices in and runs services between

---

> **YOUR PLACE IN THE SUN**
>
> Renting apartments, studios and bungalows has long been a popular way to stay on the islands. Rural accommodation, often in tranquil spots away from the general hubbub, has become popular in the past few years. Increasingly people are turning to the web to find such places. A few sights to get you started include: www.baleares .com/fincas, www.rusticrent.com, www.top rural.com and www.homelidays.com.

Barcelona and Valencia on the mainland, and Ibiza City, Maó and Palma de Mallorca. Tickets can be purchased from any travel agency or online. Timetables and fares change quite a lot from year to year, but the following will give you an idea of the options. This company also operates in conjunction with Balearia (see p618).

Up to three kinds of service are available: standard ferries, super ferries (larger, faster boasts) and high-speed (*alta velocidad*) services. The latter will either be a catamaran (which can do up to 42 knots) or the Fast Ferry (37 knots). All services transport vehicles.

In the peak summer period scheduled services include: Barcelona–Palma (up to two catamarans and one super ferry a day, 3¾ hours, seven hours respectively); Barcelona–Maó (super ferry or standard ferry, one daily, 5¼ hours and seven hours respectively); Barcelona–Ibiza City (one or two daily, 8½ to 10½ hours); Valencia–Palma (Fast Ferry, one daily, standard ferry, six days a week, 4¼ hours and 7¼ hours respectively); Valencia–Ibiza City (Fast Ferry, one daily, 3½ hours); Palma–Ibiza City (Fast Ferry, one daily, 2½ hours); and Palma–Maó (standard ferry, one weekly). Frequency drops throughout the rest of the year.

Standard summer fares from the mainland (Barcelona or Valencia) to any of the islands cost around €38 to €50 one way for a 'Butaca Turista' (seat) on standard and super ferries. On slower overnight services, beds in cabins of up to four people are also available. The cost of transporting a small car is about €129.

Inter-island services (Palma–Ibiza City and Palma–Maó) both cost from €26.70 one way on standard ferries.

BALEARIC ISLANDS

Baleària (☎ 902 160180; www.balearia.net) operates two daily ferries (one a fast ferry) from Denia to Palma de Mallorca (five to 8¾ hours depending on the ferry) via Ibiza City (two to four hours from Denia). One service a week is direct to Palma. It also has a daily high-speed ferry from Barcelona to Ciutadella (four hours). It then goes on to Alcúdia (on occasion it stops first at Alcúdia). From Barcelona there is a fast ferry up to three times a week to Ibiza City (four hours) and up to two services to Sant Antoni (four to 10 hours, depending on the ferry). Another service links Ibiza to Palma (two to four hours). From the mainland you pay €48/60 one way on the standard/fast ferry. The fares between Palma and Ibiza are €32/43 respectively.

Iscomar (☎ 902 119128; www.iscomarferrys.com) has one to two daily car ferries (depending on the season) between Ciutadella on Menorca and Port d'Alcúdia on Mallorca (€36 per person and €54 per small car one way). It also has one sailing a day between Palma and Valencia (€25 one way seated, nine hours).

Cape Balear (☎ 902 100444; www.capebalear.es) operates two to three fast ferries daily to Ciutadella (Menorca) from Cala Ratjada (Mallorca) in summer for €60 one way (€75 return if you do a day trip). The crossing takes 55 minutes.

BUSIER THAN BEN HUR

The Balearics in high summer (from late June to about halfway into September) can be incredibly busy. Palma de Mallorca alone turns around some 40 inbound and outbound flights a day. It is no coincidence that local bus and taxi drivers occasionally choose to strike around this time. Most of the millions of visitors have pre-booked package accommodation and the strain on local infrastructure can make it tricky for the independent traveller wanting the freedom to choose at the last minute. It is wise to book at least the first couple of nights around this time to avoid getting off to an uncomfortable start. In July and, especially, August, some hotels really push the boat out on prices. This chapter reflects such high-season maxima, which means that in some places you can expect to pay considerably less in quieter times.

With all companies you should ask about student and senior discounts. Such discounts (where they exist) are frequently suspended in the high season (July to September).

For details of ferries between Ibiza and Formentera, see Formentera.

MALLORCA

In 1950 the first charter flight landed on a small airstrip on Mallorca, the largest of the Balearic Islands (3640 sq km). The number of annual visitors today hovers around 10 million – most in search of the three S's: Sun, Sand and Sea, and somewhat swamping the local island populace of some 754,000 people (nearly half of whom live in the capital, Palma de Mallorca).

However, there's much more to the place. Palma de Mallorca (or simply Palma) is the main centre and a charming stop. The northwest coast, dominated by the Serra de Tramuntana mountain range, is a beautiful region of olive groves, pine forests and small villages, with a spectacularly rugged coastline.

Most of Mallorca's best beaches are on the north and east coasts and, although many have been swallowed up by tourist developments, you can still find the occasional exception.

Before setting off for Mallorca, surf some websites such as www.visitbalears.com, www.baleares.com, www.abcmallorca.com and www.newsmallorca.com.

Orientation

The capital, Palma de Mallorca, is on the south side of the island, on a bay famous for its brilliant sunsets.

Locals refer to what lies beyond the capital as the *part forana*, the 'part outside'. A series of rocky coves and harbours punctuate the short southwest coastline. Offshore from the island's westernmost point is the large, uninhabited Illa de Sa Dragonera.

The spectacular Serra de Tramuntana mountain range runs parallel with the northwest coast and Puig Major (1445m) is its highest point. The northeast coast is largely made up of two bays, the Badia de Pollença and the larger Badia d'Alcúdia.

The east coast is an almost continuous string of sandy bays and open beaches,

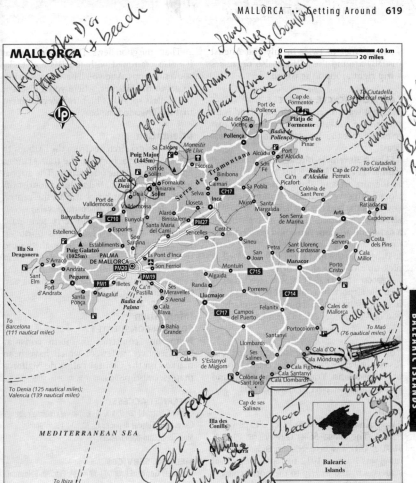

MALLORCA

(Map of Mallorca with handwritten annotations including: "Hotel Costa d'Or & beach", "20 Taxirange", "Picturesque", "Popular/gateway/trams", "Brilliant Drive with cove ahead", "lovely hike coves (busy) area", "Sand beaches + Beaches (running total on island) Bar", "lady cove (clear water)", "Es Trenc", "Best beach hike with some unbeatable water", "good beach", "Most attractive on east coast (coves freshwater)", "Cala Marcal little car", "To Ciutadella (34 nautical miles)", "To Ciutadella (22 nautical miles)")

which explains the densely packed tourist developments. Most of the south coast is lined with rocky cliffs interrupted by often pretty beaches and coves, and the interior is largely made up of the fertile plain known as Es Pla.

Getting Around
BUS

Most of the island is accessible by bus from Palma. All but a handful of buses depart from the Estació d'Autobusos on Carrer d'Eusebi Estada. The remaining services depart from that street itself, nearer the train stations. For information contact **Transport de les Illes Balears** (TIB; ☎ 971 17 71 77; http://tib.caib.es)

One-way fares from Palma include Cala Ratjada (€7.85), Ca'n Picafort (€4.15), Port de Pollença (€4.75) and Port d'Andratx (€3.30). About the most expensive single bus ride you can make is from Ca'n Picafort along the coast to Port de Sóller (€8.45).

BOAT

Palma and the major resorts and beaches around the island are also connected by numerous boat tours and water-taxi services. Some of these are detailed in the *Excursiones En Barca* brochure, available at tourist offices. **Cruceros Iberia** (☎ 971 71 71 90; per person incl lunch & hotel transfers €48; ☻ Tue-Sun Jun-Sep) organises day trips to Port d'Andratx and Sant Elm, leaving at 9.30am and returning at

BALEARIC ISLANDS

4.30pm. Once or twice in July and August (usually around the 15th) it also organises a trip right around the island.

CAR, MOTORCYCLE & BICYCLE

The best way to get around the island is by car or bike, and it's worth renting one just to experience the drive along the northwest coast.

About 30 vehicle-hire agencies operate in Palma. The big league has representatives at the airport and along Passeig Marítim, along with several cheaper companies.

One of the best deals is **Hasso** (☎ 902 20 30 12; www.hasso-rentacar.com). If you can live without a radio and air-con, you could get a Ford Ka for €28 a day, all-inclusive (the price starts to drop after the first three days), as well as pick-up and drop at airport.

Pepecar (☎ 971 26 71 81; www.pepecar.com) is near the airport. Its courtesy bus leaves from in front of the terminal building regularly. If you don't see one, call to arrange pick-up.

TAXI

You can get around the island by taxi, but it's costly. Prices are posted at central points in many towns. You're looking at around €60 from the airport to Cala Ratjada.

TRAIN

Two train lines run from Plaça d'Espanya in Palma. The **Palma–Sóller railway** (☎ 971 75 20 51/902 36 47 11; www.trendesoller.com; €6.50/11 one way/ return) was built in 1912 to replace the local stagecoach, and its trip to the north coast is now one of the island's most popular excursions. Trains leave five or six times daily.

The other **train line** (☎ 971 17 71 77) runs inland to Sa Pobla (€2.65; 53 minutes) via Inca (€1.80; 37 minutes). A secondary line links Inca with Manacor, but was temporarily replaced with a bus service at the time of writing.

PALMA DE MALLORCA

pop 367,300

Palma de Mallorca is the islands' only true city and a highly agreeable one to explore. Central Palma's old quarter is an attractive blend of tree-lined boulevards and cobbled laneways, Gothic churches and baroque palaces, designer bars and slick boutiques. It's a stylish city that buzzes by day and sizzles by night.

That's the good news. The bad news is that it's also crammed with tourists and tacky souvenir shops. And you'll have to take a bus to get to the beaches, where you'll discover the endless sprawl of high-rise development that has engulfed the bay.

Orientation

Central Palma stretches from the harbour to Plaça d'Espanya, home to the train stations and 200m from the bus station. The airport bus stops here, too. It also has a tourist office, and frequent buses run to the central Plaça de la Reina (a 20-minute walk).

From the harbour and ferry terminals, Avinguda d'Antoni Maura runs north up to Plaça de la Reina and through the old quarter. On the west side is Palma's main restaurant and nightlife zone, while on the east side are the Palau de l'Almudaina and the *catedral* (cathedral).

Information

FOREIGN CONSULATES

Numerous countries maintain consular agencies here, a few of which have been marked on the Central Palma de Mallorca map (see also p836).

INTERNET ACCESS

Cyber Central (☎ 971 72 01 68; www.ccpalma.com; Carrer de la Soledat 4; per hr €2.30; ☺ 10am-9pm Mon-Thu, 10am-8pm Fri-Sat)

MEDICAL SERVICES

Hospital General (☎ 971 72 84 84; Plaça de l'Hospital)

MONEY

Mallorca Tours (☎ 971 72 26 06; Carrer de Sant Miquel 52; ☺ 9.30am-1pm & 4.30-7pm Mon-Fri) Represents Amex.

POST

Post office (Carrer de la Constitució 6; ☺ 8am-8.30pm Mon-Fri, 9.30am-2pm Sat) A public telephone office is attached (☺ 10am-11pm Mon-Fri, 11am-midnight Sat, noon-11pm Sun).

TOURIST INFORMATION

Consell de Mallorca tourist office (☎ 971 71 22 16; Plaça de la Reina 2; ☺ 8.30am-8.30pm Mon-Fri, 9.30am-2.30pm Sat) Covers the whole island.

Municipal tourist office (☎ 971 72 40 90; www.a-palma.es; Passeig des Born 3; ☺ 9am-8pm Mon-Fri, 9am-1.30pm Sat)

CENTRAL PALMA DE MALLORCA

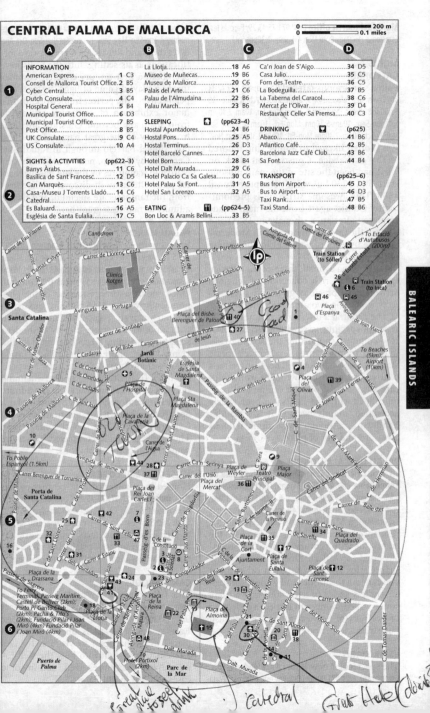

| 0 | 200 m |
| 0 | 0.1 miles |

INFORMATION
American Express................................1 C3
Consell de Mallorca Tourist Office..2 B5
Cyber Central.....................................3 B5
Dutch Consulate................................4 C4
Hospital General................................5 B4
Municipal Tourist Office....................6 D3
Municipal Tourist Office....................7 B5
Post Office...8 B5
UK Consulate.....................................9 C4
US Consulate....................................10 A4

SIGHTS & ACTIVITIES (pp622–3)
Banys Àrabs.....................................11 C6
Basílica de Sant Francesc.................12 D5
Can Marquès....................................13 C6
Casa-Museu J Torrents Lladó..........14 C6
Catedral...15 C6
Es Baluard..16 A5
Església de Santa Eulàlia.................17 C5

La Llotja...18 A6
Museo de Muñecas..........................19 B6
Museu de Mallorca..........................20 C6
Palais del Arte..................................21 C6
Palau de l'Almudaina.......................22 B6
Palau March.....................................23 B6

SLEEPING (pp623–4)
Hostal Apuntadores.........................24 B6
Hostal Pons......................................25 A5
Hostal Terminus...............................26 D3
Hotel Barceló Cannes......................27 C3
Hotel Born.......................................28 B4
Hotel Dalt Murada...........................29 C6
Hotel Palacio Ca Sa Galesa.............30 C6
Hotel Palau Sa Font.........................31 A5
Hotel San Lorenzo...........................32 A5

EATING (pp624–5)
Bon Lloc & Aramis Bellini................33 B5

Ca'n Joan de S'Aigo.........................34 D5
Casa Julio...35 C5
Forn des Teatre................................36 C5
La Bodeguilla...................................37 B5
La Taberna del Caracol....................38 C6
Mercat de l'Olivar............................39 D4
Restaurant Celler Sa Premsa...........40 C3

DRINKING (p625)
Abaco..41 B6
Atlantico Café..................................42 B5
Barcelona Jazz Café Club.................43 B6
Sa Font...44 B4

TRANSPORT (pp625–6)
Bus from Airport..............................45 D3
Bus to Airport..................................46 D3
Taxi Rank...47 B5
Taxi Stand..48 B6

BALEARIC ISLANDS

Municipal tourist office (☎ 971 75 43 29; Parc de les Estacions; ⏰ 9am-8pm Mon-Fri, 9am-1.30pm Sat)

Sights

CATEDRAL

Palma's enormous **catedral** (La Seu; ☎ 971 72 31 30; Carrer del Palau Reial 9; adult/student/child under 10 €3.50/2.80/free; ⏰ 10am-6.30pm Mon-Fri, 10am-2.30pm Sat Jun-Sep; 10am-5.30pm Mon-Fri, 10am-2.30pm Sat May & Oct; 10am-2.30pm Mon-Fri, 10am-2.30pm Sat Nov-Mar) is often likened to a huge ship moored at the city's edge. Construction work on what had been the site of the main mosque started in 1230 but wasn't completed until 1600. This awesome structure is predominantly Gothic, apart from the main façade (replaced after an earthquake in 1851) and parts of the interior (renovated in Modernista style by Antoni Gaudí at the beginning of the 20th century).

Entry is via a small, three-room **museum**, which holds a rich collection of religious artwork and precious gold and silver effects, including two amazing candelabra.

The catedral's interior is stunning in its sense of spaciousness, with a series of narrow columns supporting the soaring ceiling and framing three levels of elaborate stained-glass windows. The front altar's centrepiece, a twisting wrought-iron sculpture suspended from the ceiling and periodically lit with fairy lights, has been widely acclaimed, mainly because it was Gaudí's handiwork, although some think it looks awkward and out of place.

PALAU DE L'ALMUDAINA

In front of the catedral stands the **Palau de l'Almudaina** (☎ 971 21 41 34; Carrer del Palau Reial s/n; adult/student €3.30/2.30; ⏰ 10am-6.30pm Mon-Fri, 10am-2pm Sat Apr-Sep; 10am-2pm & 4-6pm Mon-Fri, 10am-2pm Sat Oct-Mar), a Muslim castle converted into a residence for the Mallorcan monarchs at the end of the 13th century. It is still occasionally used for official functions when King Juan Carlos is in town, but at other times you can join the hordes and wander through an endless series of cavernous and austere stone-walled rooms and inspect a collection of portraits of Spanish monarchs, Flemish tapestries and period furniture.

ES BALUARD

The spectacular new **Museu d'Art Modern i Contemporani** (☎ 971 90 82 00; www.esbaluard.org; Porta de Santa Catalina; adult/student & senior €6/4.50; ⏰ 10am-midnight Tue-Sun May-Sep, 10am-8pm Tue-Sun Oct-Apr) takes the grand Renaissance-era seaward fortifications as its setting. Into the walls have been built a 21st-century concrete complex that is a playful game of light, surfaces and perspective – the perfect framework for this major exhibition of contemporary artists from Spain and beyond. On show are items from many of the great names, from local boy Miquel Barceló through to Kandinsky. Ceramics by Picasso, notes and sketches by Miró and sculptures by the late Basque master Jorge Oteiza await discovery. The views from the ramparts are splendid, and there's a funky terrace restaurant-bar.

PALAU MARCH

For more modern art try this **mansion** (☎ 971 71 35 15; www.march.es/arte/palma; Carrer de Sant Miquel 11; admission with temporary exhibition €3.60; ⏰ 10am-6.30pm Mon-Fri, 10.30am-2pm Sat) near the *catedral*. Once one of several residences of the phenomenally wealthy March family, this extraordinary private palace has now opened with an outdoor terrace display of modern sculpture, including pieces by August Rodin, Henry Moore and Eduardo Chillida. Inside is an extraordinary 18th-century Neapolitan *belén* (Nativity scene) of overwhelming richness and detail; upstairs you can admire the ceiling and wall murals by Josep Maria Sert (better known for his murals in the Catedral de Sant Pere in Catalonia, p369). The scene is usually completed by several parallel temporary exhibitions.

MUSEU DE MALLORCA

Housed in a converted 15th-century palace, this **museum** (☎ 971 71 75 40; Carrer de la Portella 5; adult/student & child €2.40/free; ⏰ 10am-7pm Tue-Sat, 10am-2pm Sun) holds an impressive collection of archaeological artefacts, religious art, antiques and ceramics. Upstairs is a great portrait gallery of local identities and painters.

CAN MARQUÈS

This fine **mansion** (☎ 971 71 11 75; www.casascon historia.net; Carrer de Zanglada 2a; adult/student & senior €6/5; ⏰ 10am-6pm Mon-Sat, 11am-2pm Sun May-Sep, 10am-3pm Mon-Sat Oct-Apr) is one of few such places in Palma open to visitors. It gives a fascinating insight into how the well-to-do of bygone centuries lived (and in some cases still do) in old Palma.

CASA-MUSEU JOAQUIM TORRENTS LLADÓ

This fine old **house** (☎ 971 72 98 35; Carrer de la Portella 9; adult/student & senior €3/1.80; ⏰ 11am-7pm Tue-Fri, 10am-2pm Sat mid-Jun–mid-Sep; 10am-6pm Tue-Fri, 10am-2pm Sat mid-Sep–mid-Jun) with a timber gallery overlooking a courtyard is yet another mansion on show. It once belonged to the Catalan artist of the same name (1946–93) and has been largely preserved as it was, giving a unique glimpse into this kind of old-town mansion and a look at the painter's works. Temporary exhibits complete the picture.

BANYS ÀRABS

The **Arab baths** (☎ 971 72 15 49; Carrer de Serra 7; adult/child €1.50/free; ⏰ 9.30am-8pm Apr-Nov, 9.30am-6pm Dec-Mar) are the only extant monument to the Muslim domination of the island. All that remains are two small underground chambers, one of which has a domed ceiling supported by columns. Interestingly, each of the columns is topped by a different capital: the Muslims were really great recyclers and the capitals came from demolished Roman buildings.

MUSEO DE MUÑECAS

While around the cathedral you might want to pop into this shop-cum-museum dedicated to old dolls, known in Catalan as the **Museu de Nines Antigues** (☎ 971 72 98 50; Carrer del Palau Reial 27; admission €3; ⏰ 10am-6pm Tue-Sun). If you like them enough, you can even buy one.

LA LLOTJA

The gorgeous Gothic **La Llotja** (Plaça de la Llotja s/n), opposite the waterfront, was built as a merchants' stock exchange and is used for temporary exhibitions.

CHURCHES

Two of Palma's oldest churches are the soaring Gothic **Església de Santa Eulàlia** (☎ 971 71 46 25; Plaça de Santa Eulàlia 2; admission free; ⏰ 8am-1pm & 5.30-8pm) and the nearby **Basílica de Sant Francesc** (☎ 971 71 26 95; Plaça de Sant Francesc 7; admission free; ⏰ 9.30am-12.30pm & 3.30-6pm Mon-Sat, 9.30am-12.30pm Sun & holidays). The latter was begun in 1281 in Gothic style and its baroque façade was completed in 1700. Inside are the tomb of, and monument to, the 13th-century scholar Ramon Llull, while at the front of the church is a statue of Junípero Serra, the Franciscan missionary who founded many missions in California.

FUNDACIÓ PILAR I JOAN MIRÓ

Joan Miró's **art foundation** (☎ 971 70 14 20; Carrer de Joan de Saridakis 29; adult/student & senior/child €4.80/2.50/free; ⏰ 10am-7pm Tue-Sat, 10am-3pm Sun & holidays mid-May–mid-Sep; 10am-6pm Tue-Sat, 10am-3pm Sun & holidays mid-Sep–mid-May) in Cala Major (about 4km southwest of the city centre) is housed in the artist's Palma studios and contains a permanent collection of the works stored here at the time of his death. In all, more than 100 paintings, a small collection of sculpture and hundreds of drawings make up the collection. There are also temporary exhibitions and a shop selling Miró souvenirs, prints etc. Take bus No 3 or 6 to get here from the city centre.

OTHER ATTRACTIONS

In the west of the city, **Poble Espanyol** (☎ 971 73 70 75; Carrer del Poble Espanyol 39; adult/student & senior €5/3; ⏰ 9am-7pm Apr-Nov, 9am-6pm Dec-Mar) is a copy of the village of the same name in Barcelona. It contains replicas of famous monuments and other buildings representative of a variety of Spanish architectural styles, not to mention souvenir shops galore, although these are closed on Saturday afternoon, Sunday and on holidays. Further south, the circular **Castell de Bellver** (☎ 971 73 06 57; admission €1.80; ⏰ 8am-8.30pm Mon-Sat Apr-Sep, 8am-7.15pm Mon-Sat Oct-Mar, 10am-5pm Sun & holidays year-round) is an unusual 14th-century castle (with a unique round tower) set atop a pleasant park.

Sleeping

Central Palma is by far the best area to stay. Avoid the string of glossy (and not-so-glossy) tourist hotels around the waterfront west of the city centre – they're a long way from anything (except each other).

BUDGET

Hostal Pons (☎ 971 72 26 58; Carrer del Vi 8; s/d €18/35) This *hostal* (budget hotel) seems unchanged since the 1880s. The downstairs chambers are cluttered with antiques and artworks, and the quaint bedrooms all have timber bedsteads and rickety tiled floors. Amid such dusty charm you can almost overlook the spongy beds and queues outside the (solitary) bathroom.

Hostal Apuntadores (☎ 971 71 34 91; Carrer dels Apuntadors 8; dm €17; s/d from €27/35, d with shower €46) Among the chaos of restaurants and bars in this lively part of town, this place has a

BALEARIC ISLANDS

modern feel about it. It has a great roof terrace for breakfast, and 24-hour reception.

Hostal Terminus (☎ 971 75 00 14; terminus@mail .cinet.es; Plaça d'Espanya 5; s/d to €41.25/51.75) This place has been hosting guests since it opened as Hotel Terminus in 1913. Fan-cooled rooms are spacious and retain a fusty feel, but are very clean. Some with shared toilet cost a little less.

MID-RANGE
Hotel Born (☎ 971 71 29 42; www.hotelborn.com; Carrer de Sant Jaume 3; s €47, d €74-91) A superb place in the heart of the city, this hotel is in an 18th-century palace. The rooms combine elegance and history, with all the mod cons. The best rooms have an engaging view on to the courtyard.

Hotel Barceló Cannes (☎ 971 72 69 43; Carrer del Cardenal Pou 8; s/d to €52/75; 🅿) Close to Plaça d'Espanya, this is a typically mid-level hotel that, while lacking in charm, guarantees comfort and reliability, and is quiet. For just €3 extra, lone travellers can take a double room.

Hotel Palau Sa Font (☎ 971 71 22 77; www.palausa font.com; Carrer dels Apuntadors 38; s/d from €101.95/149.80; 🅿 🅿) Behind the mighty timber doors lies a series of 19 elegant rooms and suites, all varying in size and layout but sharing a simple, light décor. Rose is the primary outdoor colour, much in evidence around the little open-air hotel pool.

Hotel Dalt Murada (☎ 971 42 53 00; www.dalt murada.com; Carrer de la Almudaina 6; d €140, ste to €196) Gathered around a medieval courtyard, this carefully restored old townhouse is a gorgeous if tiny option, with just a handful of doubles and suites. The penthouse suite has a Jacuzzi and views across to the catedral.

Hotel San Lorenzo (☎ 971 72 82 00; www.hotelsan lorenzo.com; Carrer de Sant Llorenç 14; r €107-225;

> ### AUTHOR'S CHOICE
> **Hotel Portixol** (☎ 971 27 18 00; www.portixol .com; Carrer de la Sirena 27; s/d from €120/180; 🅿 🅿) Boasting one of the trendiest seafood restaurants around, Portixol is also one of the hippest hotels in town. It's a fine exercise in cool, streamlined minimalism. The best rooms have sea views, and a drink on the bar terrace is a pleasant way to begin the evening.

🅿 🅿) Tucked away inside the old quarter, this hotel is in a beautifully restored 17th-century building, and has a marvellous Mallorcan courtyard, its own bar, dining room and rooftop terrace with swimming pool. There are just six rooms.

TOP END
Hotel Palacio Ca Sa Galesa (☎ 971 71 54 00; www.palaciocasagalesa.com; Carrer de Miramar 8; s/d to €234.35/297.50; 🅿 🅿 🅿 🅿) Welcome to the classiest act in town. This enchanting 16th-century mansion has five doubles and two singles arranged around a cool patio garden. A genteel air wafts through the elegant rooms, with antiques, artwork and silk bed throws. Head up to the roof and take some sun with cocktail in hand.

Eating
A mess of eateries and bars cater to Palma's visitors in the maze of streets between Plaça de la Reina and the port. Another good area to look around is the *barrio* (district) of Santa Catalina, west of Passeig de Mallorca. For doing-it-yourself, the **Mercat de l'Olivar** (Plaça del Olivar; 🕑 7am-2pm Mon-Sat) is a good, central produce market.

Forn des Teatre (☎ 971 71 52 54; Plaça de Weyler 9; 🕑 8am-8pm Mon-Sat) This pastry shop has the best *ensaimada* (a light, spiral pastry emblematic of the island) in town.

Ca'n Joan de S'Aigo (☎ 971 71 07 59; Carrer de Can Sanç 10; hot chocolate €1.40; 🕑 8am-9pm Wed-Mon) For a hot chocolate in what can only be described as an antique-filled milk bar dating from 1700, you must pop by here and observe the ladies with their fans and the children with their ice cream.

Bon Lloc (☎ 971 71 86 17; Carrer de Sant Feliu 7; meals €15; 🕑 lunch only Mon-Sat) With its mighty timber ceiling, fans and discrete lighting, this is a soothing setting for a good, healthy four-course *menú del día* (daily set meal available at lunch time) that might include a carrot-and-orange soup and a hearty *tarta de verduras* (vegetable pie).

Casa Julio (☎ 971 71 06 70; Carrer de la Previsió 4; 🕑 lunch only Mon-Sat) This is something of a classic workers' local and is packed for the set *menú del día* (€7.50) lunch.

Restaurant Celler Sa Premsa (☎ 971 72 35 29; Plaça del Bisbe Berenguer de Palou 8; menú €15-20; 🕑 daily Sep-Jun, Mon-Fri Jul-Aug) A visit is almost obligatory to this local institution. It's a cavernous tavern filled with huge old wine barrels, and has walls plastered with faded bullfighting posters. The food is hearty and the atmosphere jolly.

La Taberna del Caracol (☎ 971 71 49 08; Carrer de Sant Alonso 2; meals €20-25; ☒ Mon-Sat) Step down into this cool basement, with a pebble encrusted floor and tiny dark-timber tables for four, to settle in for a mix of tapas and *raciónes* (meal-sized serving of tapas).

La Bodeguilla (☎ 971 71 82 74; Carrer de Sant Jaume 1-3; meals €35-45; ☒ 1-11pm Mon-Sat) Formerly the Mesón Salamanca, this has morphed into a gourmet eatery doing lightly creative interpretations of dishes from across Spain (such as the famed *cochinillo*, suckling pig, from Segovia) and a tasting menu of tapas for €21 a head. Wash down with fine wines from its extensive list.

Aramís Bellini (☎ 971 72 52 32; Carrer de Sant Feliu 7; meals €35-45; ☒ dinner Mon-Fri & Sat Sep-Jul) Tucked away off the street, this is a carefully orchestrated gourmet hideaway, with dark-timber floors and art on the walls.

Porto Pí (☎ 971 40 00 87; Avinguda de Joan Miró 174; meals €50-70; ☒ dinner Mon-Fri & Sat) Arguably one of the finest eateries in Palma, this place is loved locally for its beautifully prepared dishes, especially seafood. Service is near perfect and the ambience is carefully casual.

Drinking & Entertainment

The old quarter is the city's most vibrant nightlife zone. Particularly along the narrow streets that lie between Plaça de la Reina and Plaça de la Drassana, you'll find an enormous selection of bars and pubs, ranging from rather flashy tourist haunts to much more stylish *bodegas* (wine cellars). The free fortnightly *Youthing*, available in tourist offices, is a handy guide to what's on.

Barcelona Café Jazz Club (www.barcelonacafe jazzclub.com; Carrer dels Apuntadors 5; admission €4; ☒ 8.30pm-1am Mon-Thu, 8.30pm-3am Fri-Sat) Enter into the liveliest local music scene in the heart of the old quarter. The smallish bar fills up for live jazz and soul most nights in its somewhat cramped upstairs bar.

Atlantico Café (Carrer de Sant Feliu 12; ☒ 8pm-1am Sun-Thu, 8pm-3am Fri-Sat) A few of *mojitos* in this lively Spanish cocktail bar and the graffiti on the walls will soon blur.

Jahfarai (Carrer de Sant Feliu 16; ☒ 8pm-1am Mon-Thu, 8pm-3am Fri-Sat) Here is the place if you're

AUTHOR'S CHOICE

Abaco (☎ 971 71 59 47; Carrer de Sant Joan 1; cocktails €15; ☒ Mon-Sat) Behind a set of ancient timber doors is the bar of your wildest dreams. Inside, a Mallorcan patio and candle-lit courtyard are crammed with elaborate floral arrangements, cascading towers of fresh fruit and bizarre artworks. Bow-tied waiters will fulfil your wishes, while classical music soothes your ears.

after a combo of reggae, ska, dub and dancehall tunes. Pull up a leopard-skin stool.

Sa Font (☎ 971 71 76 28; Carrer de l'Aigua 3; ☒ Mon-Sat) This tranquil Mallorcan drinking establishment is set back from the main nocturnal hubbub and is a great place to sip a *pomada* (Menorcan gin with lemon soft drink), the local poison.

For the city's clubs you have to head west (about 2km from the old quarter) to the area around Passeig Marítim (or Avinguda de Gabriel Roca), Avinguda de Joan Miró and Plaça de Gomila. A popular option is **Garito Club** (☎ 971 73 69 12; Dàrsena de Can Barberà; admission generally free; ☒ 7pm-4.30am). DJs and live performers doing anything from jazz rock through disco classics to electro beats heat up the scene from around 10pm.

Backing on to the nearby square is one of Palma's longest survivors, **Tito's** (Plaça de Gomila 3; ☒ midnight-6am). Spain's big name in clubbing, **Pacha** (☎ 971 45 59 08; Passeig Marítim 42; ☒ 10pm-6am), has a branch here, with two bars and an immense dance floor.

S'Arenal and Magaluf, the amorphous tourist haunts, are full of bars and discos filled to bursting with the lobster-hued package-tourist crowd.

Getting There & Away

The **Sant Joan airport** (☎ 971 78 90 00) is about 10km east of Palma. For trains and buses to other parts of the island, see Getting Around (p619).

Getting Around
TO/FROM THE AIRPORT

If you arrive by air, bus No 1 runs every 15 minutes between the airport and Plaça d'Espanya in central Palma (€1.80, 15 minutes) and on to the ferry terminal. Alternatively, a taxi will cost around €15.

BUS

There are some 23 local bus services around Palma and its bay suburbs with **EMT** (☎ 971 21 44 44). Single-trip tickets cost €1.10, or you can buy a 10-trip card for €7.50. For the beaches at S'Arenal, take bus No 15 from Plaça de la Reina or Plaça d'Espanya.

TAXI

For a taxi call either ☎ 971 75 54 40 or ☎ 971 40 14 14.

SOUTHWEST COAST

A freeway skirts around the Badia de Palma towards Mallorca's southwest coast. Along the way you'll pass the resorts of Cala Major, Illetes and Palma Nova, which are basically a continuation of Palma's urban sprawl. From the inland town of Andratx, two turn-offs lead down to the coast: one goes to Port d'Andratx and the other to Sant Elm.

Port d'Andratx

pop 2630

Port d'Andratx is a glamorous little town set on low hills surrounding a narrow bay. The main road around the waterfront is lined with upmarket seafood restaurants. Several dive schools are based here, and you can rent boats and **scuba diving** equipment at numerous outlets.

SLEEPING & EATING

Hostal-Residencia Catalina Vera (☎ 971 67 19 18; Carrer de Isaac Peral 63; s/d €40/62) A couple of hundred metres back from the harbour, this is a lovely guesthouse retreat with rooms set around a tranquil garden courtyard. The best doubles have balconies.

Restaurante La Gallega (☎ 971 67 13 38; Carrer de Isaac Peral 52; meals €25-30) A couple of blocks inland from the waterfront, this is a popular local seafood restaurant overlooked by most foreigners, who prefer the pricier waterfront alternatives.

Sant Elm

pop 340

The seaside township of Sant Elm is a popular destination for day trips from Palma. The last part of the drive (7km) across from Andratx is a spectacular climb through attractive hills. If you'd rather walk this section, take a bus to Andratx. There are about 20 a day and it takes 30 minutes.

Sant Elm's sandy beach is pleasant, but can get crowded. Just offshore is a small rocky islet – within swimming distance if you've been in training. Further north is a small dock from where you can join a **glass-bottomed boat tour** or take a cruise across to the imposing and uninhabited **Illa Sa Dragonera** (€9), which is crisscrossed with good walking trails. You can also take the boat between Sant Elm and Port d'Andratx (€7). For more details, call ☎ 971 75 70 65 or ☎ 639-617545.

NORTHWEST COAST & SERRA DE TRAMUNTANA

Dominated by the rugged Serra de Tramuntana mountain range, Mallorca's northwest coast and its hinterland make up 'the other Mallorca'. No sandy beach resorts here. The coastline is rocky and largely inaccessible, the towns and villages are mostly built of local stone (as opposed to concrete), and the mountainous interior is much loved by walkers for its beautiful landscapes of pine forests, olive groves and spring wildflowers.

The main road through the mountains (the C710) starts at Andratx and runs roughly parallel to the coast to Pollença. It's a stunning scenic drive and a popular cycling route, especially during spring, when the muted mountain backdrop of browns, greys and greens is splashed with the bright colours of yellow wattles and blood-red poppies. Plenty of *miradores* (lookout points) recommend themselves as stops to punctuate the trip. Unfortunately the journey can be a slow-going traffic nightmare during late spring and summer.

Estellencs

pop 390

Estellencs is a picturesque village of stone buildings scattered around the rolling hills below the **Puig Galatzó** (1025m) peak. It's a

---

MALLORCA'S TOP FIVE BEACHES

- Es Trenc (p643)
- Platja de Formentor (p642)
- Cala Llombards (p642)
- Cala de Sant Vicent (p643)
- Cala de Deià (p644)

A SPORTING LIFE

Time spent in Mallorca doesn't have to mean just lying around on the beach in a puddle of sweat and thickly applied suntan lotion, or tripping the night away in the bars and clubs. You can also get out there and do something…physical.

Mallorca offers some outstanding walking in the mountainous northwest. Spring is the best time for this, as summer is often unbearably hot and dry. The tourist office's *20 Hiking Excursions on the Island of Mallorca* brochure outlines some of the better walks and includes a locator map. For more detailed information, see one of the numerous specialist publications, including Lonely Planet's *Walking in Spain*.

Cycling tours are also popular and the island's tourist offices can supply several route maps on Mallorca.

Water sports are well catered for, and most beach resorts around the islands have a selection of sailboards, catamarans, kayaks and paddle boats for hire. Scuba-diving schools and equipment-hire places are scattered around the island.

popular base for walkers and cyclists, or for simply escaping Palma and relaxing. A rugged walk of about 1km leads down to the local 'beach', a rocky cove with crystal-clear water.

SLEEPING & EATING

Hotel Maristel (☎ 971 61 85 29; Carrer de Eusebio Pascual 10; s/d incl breakfast €51/73; 🅿 🔄) Popular and stylish, this hotel has comfortable rooms with all the mod cons, as well as a pool and a restaurant with fine views from its outdoor terrace.

Restaurant Son Llarg (☎ 971 61 85 64; Plaça de la Constitució 6; meals €25-30; 🕒 Wed-Mon) This excellent restaurant specialises in *cuina mallorquina* (Mallorcan cuisine). Tuck into main courses, such as *calamars amb salsa de ceba* (squid casserole Mallorcan-style).

Banyalbufar
pop 580

Further north, Banyalbufar is slightly larger than Estellencs, but similarly positioned high above the coast. Surrounded by steep, stone-walled farming terraces carved into the hillside, the town is home to a cluster of bars and cafés, and three upmarket hotels.

SLEEPING & EATING

Hotel Baronia (☎ 971 61 81 46; Carrer de Baronia 16; s/d €45/58; 🅿 🔄) Here is a maze of a building with an olde-worlde feel, built in the ruins of a Muslim-era fort (part of the central tower remains). It has modern rooms with fine views, and a great cliffside swimming pool.

Restaurante Son Tomas (☎ 971 61 81 49; Carrer de Baronía 17; meals €30-35; 🕒 Wed-Sun, lunch only Mon)

This is one of the finest restaurants in the area. The dining area is spread over two floors, with stunning views far out to sea.

Valldemossa
pop 1820

Valldemossa is an attractive blend of tree-lined streets, old stone houses and impressive new villas. It owes most of its fame to the fact that the ailing composer Frédéric Chopin and his lover George Sand spent their 'winter of discontent' here in 1838–39.

They stayed in the **Cartuja de Valldemossa** (☎ 971 61 21 06; admission €7.50; 🕒 9.30am-6pm Mon-Sat, 10am-1pm Sun), a grand monastery that was turned into rental accommodation after its monks were expelled in 1835. Their stay wasn't an entirely happy experience and Sand later wrote *Un Hiver à Mallorque* (Winter in Mallorca), which, if nothing else, made her perennially unpopular with Mallorcans (although you will still find copies of it at some souvenir stands).

Tour buses and day-trippers now arrive in droves to visit the monastery. It's a beautiful building with lovely gardens and fine views. In the couple's former quarters are Chopin's piano (which, due to shipping delays, arrived only three weeks before their departure), his death mask and several original manuscripts. Entry includes piano recitals (eight times daily in summer), and entry to the adjacent 14th-century **Palau del Rei Sanxo** (King Sancho's Palace) and local **museum**.

Costa Nord (☎ 971 61 24 25; www.costanord.com; Avinguda de Palma 6; adult/child €7.50/4.50; 🕒 9am-5pm Tue-Sun, 9am-3pm Mon) was dreamed up by part-time Mallorca resident and fan/Hollywood

BALEARIC ISLANDS

SLEEPING IN STYLE

In recent years Mallorcans have switched their attention from mass tourism to attracting a more discerning traveller. Nowhere is this more evident than in the mushrooming of middle and high-end boutique hotels, which are often lovingly carved out of restored mansions and country farmhouses. Several are listed throughout this book, but there are, of course, many more, some of them magnets for the rich and famous. Among those you might like to try are:

- **Finca Ets Abellons**, Binibona (p630)
- **Hotel Dalt Murada**, Palma de Mallorca (p624)
- **Hotel Palacio Ca Sa Galesa**, Palma de Mallorca (p624)
- **La Residencia**, Deià (p629)
- **Son Brull**, Pollença (p631)
- **Es Passarell**, Felanitx (p634)

celebrity Michael Douglas (who owns an estate in Deià and landed a deal in 2003 to represent the island in world tourism fairs). His (what should we call it?) show is made up of two parts. The first is a three-screen 'documentary' on the history of this part of the island – Douglas' tribute to a beautiful island. Next you are ushered into a mock-up of the master's quarters of the good ship *Nixe*. The vessel belonged to Archduke Luis Salvador (or Ludwig to his family), son of the 19th-century Habsburg ruler of Tuscany, Leopoldo II. Luis spent much of his life bobbing around on the Mediterranean in *Nixe* and writing treatises on an astounding range of subjects, including Mallorca, which he came to live on and love. Indeed, he liked it so much that he proceeded to buy as much of it as he could.

From here a tortuous 7km drive leads down to **Port de Valldemossa**, where a dozen or so buildings (including two bar-restaurants) huddle around a rocky cove.

SLEEPING & EATING

Hostal Ca'n Mário (☎ 971 61 21 22; Carrer de Uetam 8; s/d €31.30/50) Nice, central and cheap is this simple but spotless little digs. Overlooking a leafy street, and rooms with balconies at the front have splendid views across a valley.

A sprinkling of cheerful eateries, all offering lunch *menús* of around €8 to €10, decorates the streets. None are of any culinary significance.

Miramar & Can Marroig

Five kilometres north of Valldemossa on the road to Deià is **Miramar** (☎ 971 61 60 73; admission €3; ⏰ 9.30am-7pm Tue-Sun May-Oct, 10.30am-6pm Tue-Sun Nov-Mar), one of Habsburg Archduke Luis Salvador's former residences. The Archduke built this home on the sight of a 13th-century monastery, of which only a small part of the cloister remains. Walk out the back and enjoy the clifftop views.

Two kilometres further on is one of the archduke's other main residences (Douglas bought yet another!), **Can Marroig** (☎ 971 63 91 58; admission €3; ⏰ 9.30am-7.30pm Mon-Sat Apr-Sep, 9.30am-2pm & 3-5.30pm Mon-Sat Oct-Mar). It is a delightful, rambling mansion, jammed with furniture and period items, including many of the archduke's books. The views are the stuff of dreams. Wander down to the **Foradada**, the strange hole-in-the-rock formation by the water. It's about a 3km walk. You can swim, but beware the men o' war. Take the opening times at both places with a pinch of a salt.

Deià
pop 670

Deià is perhaps the most famous village on Mallorca. Its setting is idyllic, with a cluster of stone buildings cowering beneath steep hillsides terraced with vegetable gardens, vines and fruit orchards.

Such beauty has always been a drawcard, and Deià was once a second home to an international colony of writers, actors, musicians and the like. The most famous member was the English poet Robert Graves, who died here in 1985 and is buried in the town's hillside cemetery.

Now somewhat overrun by pretentious expats, travel writers and tourists, Deià still has something special and is worth experiencing, particularly if you can avoid the summer crowds.

SIGHTS & ACTIVITIES

The C710 passes though the town centre, where it becomes the main street and is lined with bars and shops, expensive restaurants and ritzy boutiques. Several pricey **artists' workshops** and **galleries** flog locally produced work. The steep cobbled lanes lead to the parish church and attached **museum**.

On the coast, **Cala de Deià** has some popular swimming spots and a couple of bar-restaurants. The steep walking track from town takes about half an hour; you can drive down, but in the high season this might take almost as long. Some fine walks crisscross the area, such as the gentle **Deià Coastal Path** to the pleasant hamlet of Lluc Alcari (three hours return).

SLEEPING

Fonda Villa Verde (☎ 971 63 90 37; Carrer de Ramon Llull 19; s/d with bathroom €43/58) A charming little *pensión* (small private hotel) in the heart of the hilly village, it offers homely rooms and splendid views from the sunny terrace.

La Residencia (☎ 971 63 90 11; Son Moragues; s/d from €278.20/444; 🛇 🖵 🛋 🅿) 'The Res' to its habitués, this is the place to stay if you want to rub shoulders with the rich and famous. A short stroll from the village centre, this former 16th-century manor house is now a luxurious resort hotel set in 12 hectares of manicured lawns and gardens.

EATING

The diverse collection of eateries along the main street includes a couple of affordable pizzerias and several expensive restaurants that claim to specialise in local cuisine.

Ca'n Quet (☎ 971 63 91 96; Carretera Valldemossa-Deià; meals €40-45; 🕑 lunch only Tue-Sun & Mon) In this hushed, ivy-draped locale 1km out of Deià on the road to Valldemossa, you have a choice of good seafood and meat dishes. Try the *bacalao a la puttanesca* (cod in a spicy Italian sauce).

AUTHOR'S CHOICE

Hotel Costa d'Or (☎ 971 63 90 25; s/d €92.50/179; 🛋 🅿) This secluded spot is on the coast 3km north of Deià, in the captivating hamlet of Lluc Alcari. Beautiful rooms have high ceilings, tiled floors and windows opening onto gardens. It has a restaurant and sun terrace with fine views over the water. A 15-minute walk through a pine forest takes you down to a little pebbly beach with crystal-clear water.

Sóller

pop 7980

Sóller's train station is the terminus for the Palma–Sóller railway, one of Mallorca's most popular and spectacular excursions (see Getting Around, p620).

The town sprawls across a flat valley beneath soaring and jagged outcrops of the Serra de Tramuntana. It's a pleasant place, with attractive old buildings, lush gardens and open plazas, and is a preferred base for walkers.

The main square, Plaça de la Constitució, is 100m downhill from the train station. It's surrounded by bars and restaurants, and is home to the *ajuntament* (town hall). Also here is the large 16th-century **Església Parroquial de San Bartolomé**, with a beautiful Gothic interior and a modernist façade.

Most visitors take a ride on one of Sóller's open-sided old trams, which shuttle 2km down to **Port de Sóller** on the coast (€2). They depart from the train station every 30 minutes between 7am and 9pm.

SLEEPING & EATING

Hotel El Guía (☎ 971 63 02 27; Carrer del Castañer 2; s/d €50/75) Handily located beside the train station, this is a good place to meet fellow walkers. Its bright rooms feature timber trims and modern bathrooms.

Petit Celler Ca's Carreter (Carrer del Cetre 9; meals €20-25; 🕑 lunch only Tue-Sat & Sun) Set in an old cart workshop downhill and west of the tram line, this 'cellar' has a rough and rustic feel. The chef concentrates on mostly local favourites, such as rabbit, or on more national options, like *berenjena rellena* (stuffed aubergine).

Biniaraix & Fornalutx

From Sóller it's a pleasant 2km drive, pedal or stroll through narrow laneways up to the tiny village of Biniaraix. From there, another narrow and scenic route continues north up to Fornalutx, taking you through terraced groves crowded with orange and lemon trees.

Fornalutx is a pretty village of distinctive stone houses with green shutters, colourful flower boxes and well-kept gardens. Many of the homes are owned by expats but it's a far cry from the (comparative) bustle of Sóller. These are the kind of places people dream about and no doubt were just the type to lure Peter Kerr to live on the island – his trials and tribulations settling in to Mallorca have proven a nice little earner in the form of his travel humour tomes *Snowball Oranges, Mañana Mañana* and *Viva Mallorca!*

Hostal Fornalutx (☎ 971 63 19 97; Carrer de l'Alba 22; s/d €85/126.40; ✖ P) A delightfully converted former convent just off the main street, this is a friendly, tranquil place to stay.

Sa Calobra

The 12km road from route C710 across and down to the small port of Sa Calobra is one of the most spectacular and hair-raising scenic drives you'll ever take. The serpentine road has been carved through the weird mountainous rock formations, skirting narrow ridges before twisting down to the coast in an eternal series of hairpin bends.

If you come in summer you won't be alone. NATO would be proud to organise such an operation. Divisions of buses and fleets of pleasure boats disgorge battalion after battalion of tireless tourists. It makes D-Day look like play lunch, and all that's missing are the choppers playing 'The Ride of the Valkyrie'. Instead, a couple of Peruvian musicians keep the tempo going over the ubiquitous loudspeaker system. Sa Calobra must be wonderful on a quiet, bright mid-winter morning…sigh.

From the northern end of the road a short walking trail leads around the coast and through a series of long tunnels to a river gorge, the **Torrent de Pareis**, and a small cove with some fabulous (but crowded) **swimming** spots.

One bus a day (Monday to Saturday) comes from Ca'n Picafort (9am) via Pollença and the Monestir de Lluc. It returns at 3pm. The trip takes 2½ hours (€7.05), with a one-hour stop at the Monestir de Lluc.

Monestir de Lluc

Back in the 7th century, a local shepherd claimed to have seen an image of the Virgin Mary in the sky. Later, a similar image appeared on a rock. 'It's a miracle', everyone cried and a chapel was built near the site to commemorate it.

A monastery was established here after Jaume I conquered Mallorca. Since then thousands of pilgrims have come every year to pay homage to the 14th-century **statue**

of the Virgin of Lluc**, known as *La Moreneta* because of her dark complexion.

The present **monastery** (☎ 971 87 15 25; admission €2; ✆ 10am-1.30pm & 2.30-5.30pm), a huge austere complex, dates from the 18th century. Off the central courtyard is the entrance to the **Basílica de la Mare de Déu**, which contains the statue. There is also a **museum** with archaeological bits and bobs and a modest art collection.

SLEEPING & EATING
Santuari de Lluc (☎ 971 87 15 25; s/d from €16.50/25) The monastery's accommodation section has 97 rooms, and is popular with school groups, walkers and pilgrims. The downstairs rooms are dark and best avoided. Several restaurants and caféterias cater to your tummy's demands.

Finca Ets Abellons (☎ 971 87 50 69; www.albellons .com; Binibona; s/d €82.40/114.50; ✖ 🖥 🛋 P) Just 1km outside the tiny hamlet of Binibona, south of the monastery, is this charming, restored stone farmhouse in the foothills of the Serra de Tramuntana. Rooms have classic brown ceramic floors, timber ceilings and graceful furnishings.

The once near-abandoned Binibona village has been singled out for attention, with several other classy **rural retreats** located in and around it.

GETTING THERE & AWAY
Up to three buses a day run from Ca'n Picafort to Monestir de Lluc via Pollença (€4.95, 1¾ hours).

Pollença
pop 9020

Next stop on the Mallorcan pilgrimage is this attractive inland town. The devout and hardy come here to climb up **Calvari** (Calvary), 365 stone steps leading from the town up to a hilltop chapel and small shrine; the rest of us drive up the back road. Either way, the views from the top are worth it. Otherwise, the central Plaça Major is a good place to relax, with several cafés and restaurants.

SLEEPING & EATING
Santuari del Puig de Maria (☎ 971 18 41 32; s/d €10.80/18) Built during the 14th and 15th centuries, this former monastery is now a somewhat chaotic retreat. Neither the food

nor the accommodation are anything to write home about, but the setting and views are spectacular. Call ahead for bookings. It's a couple of kilometres south of Pollença on the road to Palma.

Restaurant Clivia (☎ 971 53 36 35; Avinguda Pollentia; meals €45-50; ☺ Tue & Thu-Sun, dinner only Mon & Wed) Set in what was once a private house, this spot offers fine food (especially the fish) prepared and presented with panache. The service is attentive and the ambience tranquil.

GETTING THERE & AWAY
Pollença is on the Ca'n Picafort–Sóller bus route.

Cala de Sant Vicent
pop 270
Actually a series of tiny jewel-like *calas* (coves), this is a tranquil little resort in a magnificent setting. Yes, the inevitable English breakfast and German bratwurst problem is in evidence, but it's minimal compared with the big beaches further southeast. And the water is so limpid you feel you could see to the centre of the world.

Hostal Mayol (☎ 971 53 04 40; Carrer de Cerdá i Marroig; s/d €46/56; ☺) A quirkily arranged place run by a British-Mallorcan couple, this spot has bright, simple rooms. The best have balconies and sea views.

Up to four buses run between Pollença and Cala de Sant Vicent (€1, 15 minutes). A similar number of buses also connect Cala de Sant Vicent with Port de Pollença for the same price.

Port de Pollença
pop 5930
On the northern shores of the Badia de Pollença, this resort is popular with British families soothed by fish 'n' chips and pints of ale. Sailboards and yachts can be hired on the beaches. South of town, the bay's shoreline becomes quite rocky and the beaches are less attractive.

Cap de Formentor
A splendid drive (cyclists be warned: it's steep, narrow and often busy) leads from Port de Pollença out along this narrow, rocky promontory.

Hotel Formentor (☎ 971 89 91 00; www.hotel formentor.net; s/d from €235.40/337) Midway along the promontory is this jewel of pre-WWII

days, when hotels of any type were in a strict minority on the island. This ritzy digs, completely modernised in 2002, has played host to the likes of Grace Kelly and Winston Churchill since 1926.

Near the hotel and backed by shady pine forests, the sandy beaches of **Platja de Formentor** are among the island's best. At your disposal are a couple of exclusive beach bars, a golf course and a nearby horse-riding ranch.

From here it's another 11km out to the lighthouse on the cape that marks Mallorca's northernmost tip.

BADIA D'ALCÚDIA
The long beaches of this huge bay dominate Mallorca's northeast coast, its broad sweeps of sand stretching from Port d'Alcúdia to Ca'n Picafort.

Alcúdia
pop 5360
Wedged between the Badia de Pollença and Badia d'Alcúdia, busy Alcúdia was once a Roman settlement. Remnants of the Roman theatre can be seen and the old town is still partly protected by medieval walls. Head for the ruins of the Roman city of **Pollèntia** (☎ 971 54 70 04; Carrer de Sant Jaume 30; admission €2; ☺ 10am-1.30pm & 3.30-5.30pm Tue-Fri, 10.30am-1pm Sat & Sun), just outside one of the town's squat medieval gates.

Port d'Alcúdia
pop 4060
A large harbour dominates the town centre and imparts a slightly chic maritime flavour,

with boat trips leaving daily to Ca'n Picafort, Platja de Formentor and Port de Pollença (€12 to €21.50 per person; inquire directly at the port). Boats leave here for Ciutadella on the island of Menorca (see Getting There & Around p618).

Hostal Vista Alegre (☎ 971 54 73 47; Passeig Marítim 22; s/d €20/35) The friendly managers run a tidy little joint. The singles are pokey and have no air-con, while the doubles have either sea views (and breeze) or air-con. The doubles have their own bathroom.

Ca'n Picafort

A smaller version of Port d'Alcúdia, Ca'n Picafort is a package-tour frontier town, and somewhat raw and soulless, but the beaches are pretty good.

EAST COAST

Most of the fine beaches along Mallorca's east coast have succumbed to the ravages of mass tourism. The northern half of this stretch of coastline is home to a series of concrete jungles that rivals the worst excesses of the Costa del Sol on the mainland. Further south the coastline is corrugated with a series of smaller coves and ports, saving it from the same fate.

Artà

pop 6070

The quiet, ochre inland town of Artà is dominated by a 14th-century hilltop fortress and **Església de San Salvador**, from where you have wonderful views across the town, countryside and even out to sea. A simple restaurant-bar opens for lunch up here.

On the coast 10km southeast are the **Coves d'Artà** (☎ 971 84 12 93; adult/child under 13 €8/4; ◷ 10am-7pm Jul-Sep, 10am-5pm Oct-Jun), rivalling Porto Cristo's Coves del Drac. Tours of the caves leave every 30 minutes.

Hotel Casal d'Artà (☎ 971 82 91 63; Carrer de Rafael Blanes 19; s/d €42.10/78.15; ◪) A wonderful old mansion in the centre of town, this place has real character. It doesn't serve breakfast, though.

Cala Ratjada

pop 5100

Germans seem particularly enamoured with Cala Ratjada, a heavily developed and busy resort. The main streets are wall-to-wall souvenir shops, and the pretty beaches

are carpeted with sizzling flesh. A few kilometres inland, **Capdepera** is marked by the walls of the 13th-century **castle** (☎ 971 81 87 46; admission €2; ◷ 9am-8pm Apr-Oct, 10am-5pm Nov-Mar) above the town.

This is package-tourist territory and it can be hard to find a place to sleep in July and August. For details of daily fast ferries to Ciutadella (Menorca), see Getting There & Around, p618.

Porto Cristo

During the day, this place teems with daytrippers visiting the nearby underground caves. Porto Cristo won't help your claustrophobia, but by late afternoon when the hordes have disappeared it can be quite nice. The town cradles a small sandy beach and boat harbour.

The **Coves del Drac** (Dragon's Caves; ☎ 971 82 07 53; adult/child under 8 €8.50/free; ◷ 10am-5pm Apr-Oct, 10.45am-3.30pm Nov-Mar) are on the southern outskirts of town. One-hour tours are held hourly, the 'highlight' being the classical music played by boat-bound musicians floating across a large subterranean lake. Nearby you can also visit Porto Cristo's large **aquarium** (☎ 971 82 09 71; adult/child under 9 €5/2.50; ◷ 10.30am-6pm Apr-Oct, 11am-3pm Nov-Mar).

Hotel Sol i Vida (☎ 971 82 10 74; Avinguda de Joan Servera 11; s/d with bathroom from €30.70/51.80; ▣) Just opposite the caves is this cheerful hostal, with a pool, bar-restaurant and tennis court.

Portocolom

pop 3630

A tranquil village set on a generous harbour, Portocolom has managed to resist the tourist onslaught with a degree of dignity. Various restaurants dot the long bay, and within a couple of kilometres are some fine beaches, such as the immaculate little cove of **Cala Marçal**.

Pensión Portocolom (☎ 971 82 53 23; Ronda Cristóbal Colón 5; r per person €15) This place is predictably popular with such cheap rates. Good clean rooms with bathroom are snapped up throughout the summer period.

Hotel Estoril (☎ 971 82 51 30; www.inturco.com; Carrer de la Pinta 34; s/d €30/40; ◪ ▣) Just in from the waterfront, this is a fairly typical holiday hotel and popular with the Brits. It's equipped with such extras as a small gym and a pool table by the, er, pool.

Up to six buses run here daily from Palma via Felanitx (€4.70, 1¾ hours).

Cala d'Or to Cala Mondragó

Once a quaint fishing village, Cala d'Or is now an overblown big-dollar resort. Its sleek new marina is lined with glisteningly expensive boats and the surrounding hills are crowded with blindingly whitewashed villas. Plenty of lifestyle, little substance.

Immediately south of Cala d'Or (and virtually joined to it by urban sprawl) is the smaller and more tranquil **Portopetro**. Centred on a boat-lined inlet and surrounded by residential estates, it has a cluster of harbour-side bars and restaurants, and a couple of small beaches nearby.

Two kilometres south of Portopetro, Cala Mondragó is one of the most attractive coves on the east coast. Sheltered by large rocky outcrops and fringed by pine trees, a string of three protected sandy beaches (two with a bar each and one with a restaurant) connected by coast footpaths await you.

Hostal Playa Mondragó (☎ 971 65 77 52; per person €32; 🍴 🍺 P) This five-storey place is barely 50m back from one of the beaches. It's a tranquil option whose better rooms have balconies and fine sea views. It also operates its own restaurant downstairs.

Regular local buses travel Monday to Saturday between Cala d'Or and Cala Mondragó via Portopetro.

Cala Figuera

The fishermen here really still fish, threading their way down the winding inlet before dawn while the predominantly German tourists sleep off the previous night's food and drink. What has probably kept the place in one piece is the fact that the nearest beach, the equally pretty **Cala Santanyí**, is a few kilometres drive southwest. Nicer still is **Cala Llombards**, which you can walk to (scaling endless stairs) from Cala Santanyí or drive to via the town of Santanyí (follow the signs to Llombards and then Cala Llombards).

Hostal-Restaurant Ca'n Jordi (☎ 971 64 50 35; Carrer de la Virgen del Carmen 58; s/d €28/41) Excellent rooms with bathrooms and balconies offer splendid views over the inlet. The owners also rent out a few apartments and villas.

Several restaurants and bars dotted around town will keep hunger and thirst at bay.

On Monday to Saturday, four to six buses a day travel from Palma to Cala Figuera via Es Llombards (town), Cala Santanyí and Santanyí.

Colònia de Sant Jordi

On the southeast coast, the large resort town of Colònia de Sant Jordi is rather unexciting and the local beach is no great shakes either. Some good **beaches** lurk nearby, however, particularly **Ses Arenes** and **Es Trenc** (with a nudist strip), both a few kilometres up the coast towards Palma. The water at the latter, 6km away by road, is an impossible shade of blue and it's so popular that you pay to **park** (car €5, motorcycle €2; 🕙 9am-9pm May-Oct).

From Colònia de Sant Jordi itself you can take full-day **boat trips** (☎ 971 64 90 34; adult/child under 10 €28/14) to the former prison island of **Cabrera**, where more than 5000 French soldiers died after being abandoned in 1809 towards the end of the Peninsular War. Illa Cabrera and its surrounding islets now form the **Parc Nacional Archipiélago de Cabrera**. Take your own lunch or pay the boat people €7 a head for a simple repast. The boats leave the port at 9am and return at 3.30pm – the trip takes an hour each way.

THE INTERIOR

East of the Serra de Tramuntana, Mallorca's interior is a flat and fertile plain. Dominated by farmland and often unremarkable agricultural townships, it holds little of interest to the average beach-obsessed tourist. But for those with time, transport and an interest in discovering the traditional Mallorcan way of life, an exploration of the island's interior is highly rewarding. If you like Mallorcan windmills – you'll feast on them on the initial stretch of the Palma–Manacor road!

PICKING YOUR PEARLS

There's more than one way to make a pearl. Some occur naturally inside oysters, while cultivated ones are helped along artificially, with the minerals injected into the sea critters. Majorica pearls are made by replicating these processes in the factory. You can visit Majorica's huge labs and **showrooms** (☎ 971 55 09 00; Carrer de Majorica s/n; 🕙 9am-7pm Mon-Fri, 10am-1pm Sat & Sun, 10am-6pm holidays) at its main factory in Manacor.

Several of the major inland towns are well known for their specialised products. **Inca** holds a popular market each Thursday and has numerous factory outlets selling locally produced leather goods (check out the places along Gran Via de Colón and Avinguda del General Luque). **Felanitx** has a name for ceramics.

Industrial and melancholy **Manacor** is known for its manufactured pearl industry (including the famous Majorica factory; see Picking Your Pearls, p633) and as home to many of the island's furniture manufacturers. It seems remarkable that a place so prosperous could be so ugly. Mind you, the prosperity is not what it was. Some sour years in the jewellery business have cut heavily into profitability at Majorica, which announced in 2004 that it intended to more than halve its workforce of 400 and move part of its production to cheaper locations in Asia.

Sleeping

If you're interested in experiencing 'the other Mallorca', numerous rural properties, mountain houses and traditional villas around the island operate as upmarket B&Bs. Pick up brochures at tourist offices or take a look at the website of **Agroturismo Balear** (www.baleares.com/fincas).

Many of the properties are historic and often stylish country estates offering outstanding facilities, including swimming pools, tennis courts, and organised activities and excursions. The prices for double rooms (often sleeping three people) cost about €60 to €200 per day (there are a few very expensive exceptions).

AUTHOR'S CHOICE

Es Passarell (☎ 971 18 30 91; www.espassarell .net; Segunda Vuelta s/n, Felanitx; d €80-135; ☼ mid-Dec–Nov; ⚇ ⚈ Ⓟ) The sun-bleached stone walls and tiled roofs of this one-time farmstead are immediately enticing. Modern, spacious rooms decorated with modern art and the occasional antique occupy what were once such areas as the wash house and rooms for drying out sausages. The gardens are alive with fruit trees, and other vivid plants and flowers. Rooms and apartments vary considerably. Some have only a shower, while others have a full bathroom.

Son Mercadal (☎ 971 18 13 07; Camí de Son Pou; s/d to €76/100; ⚇ ⚈ Ⓟ) Five km out of Porreres on the road to Campos and then signposted 2km down a side road, this tastefully restored 19th-century country estate makes a perfect rural halt. Surrounded by 7 hectares of land, the place offers a truly homey atmosphere, with exposed stone walls, dark-timber furnishings and plenty of tranquillity.

IBIZA (EIVISSA)

Ibiza is the most extreme of the islands, in landscape and the people it attracts.

The Greeks called Ibiza and Formentera the Islas Pitiusas (Islands of Pine Trees). The landscape is harsh and rocky, and the island receives little rainfall. Alongside the hardy pines, the most common crops are olives, figs and almonds. Perhaps surprisingly, about half the island (especially the fairly unspoilt northeast) remains covered by thick woods. Indeed, driving around the back roads of the island's north is to plunge into a quiet, largely rural idyll – not what one associates with Ibiza at all!

A rugged coastline is interspersed with dozens of fine sandy beaches, most consumed by intensive tourist developments. A few out-of-the-way beaches remain, but in summer you won't be doing much solitary swimming.

The island's beaches and laid-back attitude first became a major drawcard in the flower-power heyday of the 1960s – while North America's hippies were 'California dreaming', their European counterparts were heading for Ibiza to tune in, turn on and drop out. It's hard to believe that in 1956 the island boasted 12 cars!

Initially for the hip and fashionable, Ibiza soon discovered the financial rewards of bulk tourism and started shipping in summer sun seekers by the thousand. Today the island populace of 105,000 watches several million visitors a year (more than four million passengers were registered through the airport in 2003) – a strange blend of hippies, fashion victims, nudists, clubbers and package tourists – pour through.

Ibiza's nightlife is renowned. The island, birthplace of the rave, is home to some of Spain's biggest and most famous discos, and its great summer club scene is com-

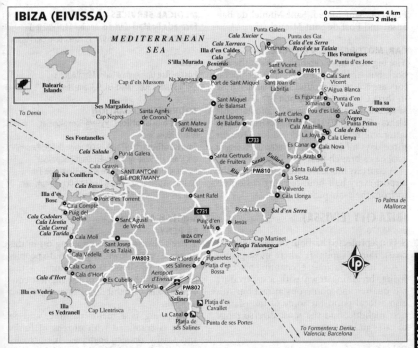

IBIZA (EIVISSA)

plemented by a huge and diverse collection of bars.

Away from the bars are the woods, walking trails (particularly around the coast) and quiet (if not deserted) beaches that allow you to get away from Ministry of Sound-style madness. Places such as Santa Eulària d'es Riu and the small beach resorts and coves of the northeast are ideal for family holidays. The northeast corner is also perfect for a few days' escape from the madding crowds of either Ibiza City (or London), with its pretty coves, high wooded cliffs and coastal walks.

A few interesting websites to browse are www.ibizaholidays.com, www.ibiza-spot light.com and www.ecoibiza.com.

Getting Around
BUS

Four bus companies operate services to different parts of the island. Fares cost €1 to €2.45, so you won't break the bank this way! Get a copy of *Horario y Líneas de Autobuses* (the bus timetable) from tourist offices.

Autobuses Empresas HF Vilas (☎ 971 31 16 01) operates from Ibiza City to Santa Eulària

d'es Riu, Es Canar, Cala Sant Vicent, Portinatx, and other beaches on the east and north coasts. It also does the Santa Eulària d'es Riu–Sant Antoni de Portmany run.

Autobuses San Antonio (☎ 971 34 05 10) operates between Ibiza City and Sant Antoni de Portmany.

Autobuses Voramar El Gaucho (☎ 971 34 03 82) operates from Ibiza City to the airport, Sant Jordi de ses Salines, Platja d'en Bossa, Cala Llonga and Santa Eulària d'es Riu. It also services the south and southwest coasts from Ibiza City and Sant Antoni de Portmany.

Autocares Lucas Costa (☎ 971 31 27 55) operates from Ibiza City to Santa Gertrudis de

---

IBIZA'S TOP FIVE BEACHES

- **Cala Benirràs** (p643)
- **Cala Mastella** (p642)
- **Cala de Boix** (p642)
- **Cala Xarraca** (p643)
- **Cala Codolars** (p644)

Fruitera, Sant Mateu, Sant Miquel de Balansat and Port de Sant Miquel.

CAR, MOTORCYCLE & BICYCLE

The big boys have car-hire desks at the airport, but smaller and often cheaper operators are scattered around the island. Those in Ibiza City include **Valentin** (☎ 971 31 08 22; Avinguda de Bartomeu Vicent Ramón 19) and **Autos Isla Blanca – Sixt** (☎ 971 31 54 07; Carrer de Felipe II). The latter will hire an Opel Corsa for €103 for three days all-inclusive. **Pepecar** (www.pepecar .com) has a branch near the airport.

A courtesy bus leaves from in front of the airport every half-hour ferrying customers to/from their car pick-up point.

IBIZA CITY (EIVISSA)
pop 40,170

Set on a protected harbour on the southeast coast, Ibiza's capital is where most people arrive. It's a vivacious, enchanting place – a living, breathing town with a captivating old quarter and numerous attractions. It's also a focal point for some of the island's best nightlife, and the most diverse range of cafés and restaurants.

Orientation

The old walled town, D'Alt Vila, is perched high on a hilltop overlooking all. Between D'Alt Vila and the harbour lies the Sa Penya area, a jumble of narrow streets and lanes lined with whitewashed shops, bars and restaurants.

The broad Passeig de Vara de Rey is a favourite spot for the traditional sunset promenade. It runs westward from Sa Penya to Avinguda d'Espanya, which in turn takes you out of the city towards the airport, 7km southwest. The new town spreads west of the old centre.

Information

EMERGENCY
Policía Nacional (Avinguda de la Pau s/n)

INTERNET ACCESS
Chill Internet Café (☎ 971 399736; Via Púnica 49; per hr €4; ☻ 10am-midnight Mon-Sat, noon-midnight Sun) Check your email with relaxing chill-out sounds while sipping on a milkshake or munching on vegetarian snacks.
Surf@Net (☎ 971 19 49 20; Carrer de Riambau 8; ☻ 10am-2am; per 30 min €1.80) A bit more clinical than Chill but handily located.

MEDICAL SERVICES
Farmacia Dr Mari (Carrer d' Anníbal 11; ☻ 24hr)
Hospital Can Misses (☎ 971 39 70 00; Barri Can Misses)

POST
Post office (Avinguda d'Isidor Macabich; ☻ 8.30am-8.30pm Mon-Fri, 9.30am-1pm Sat)

TOURIST INFORMATION
Airport tourist office (☻ 9am-9pm Mon-Sat, 9am-2.30pm Sun)
Tourist office (☎ 971 30 19 00; www.cief.es; Passeig des Moll; ☻ 9am-9pm Mon-Fri, 9am-7.30pm Sat Jun–mid-Oct; 9.30am-1.30pm & 5-7.30pm Mon-Fri, 10.30am-1pm Sat Apr-May & 2nd half Oct; 8.30am-3pm Mon-Fri, 10.30am-1pm Sat Nov-Mar)

Sights & Activities
SA PENYA

There's always something going on in this portside part of town. If you're into people-watching you'll be right at home – this pocket must have one of the highest concentrations of exhibitionists and weirdos in Spain.

Shopping is a major pastime, and Sa Penya is crammed with dozens of funky and trashy **clothing boutiques**. It's actually surprisingly good for clothes shopping – the intense competition between the locally made gear and the imports keeps a lid on prices. The so-called **hippie markets**, street stalls along Carrer d'Enmig and the adjoining streets, sell just about everything under the sun. The hippies aren't too numerous, but the stalls that specialise in locally made arts and crafts are worth checking out.

D'ALT VILA & AROUND

From Sa Penya wander up into D'Alt Vila, the old walled town (and Unesco World Heritage site since 1999). The Romans were the first to fortify this hilltop, but the walls you see were raised by Felipe II in the 16th century to protect against invasion by combined French and Turkish forces.

A steep ramp leads from Plaça de sa Font in Sa Penya up to the **Portal de ses Taules** gateway, the main entrance to the old town. Above it hangs a commemorative plaque bearing Felipe II's coat of arms and an inscription recording the 1585 completion date of the fortification, which consists of seven artillery bastions joined by thick protective walls up to 22m in height.

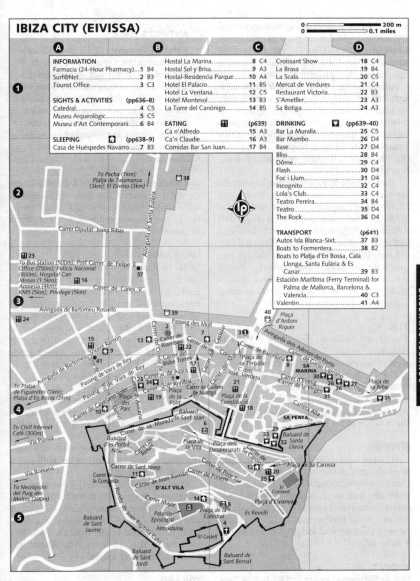

IBIZA CITY (EIVISSA)

INFORMATION	
Farmacia (24-Hour Pharmacy)...**1** B4	
Surf@Net..................................**2** B3	
Tourist Office...........................**3** C3	

SIGHTS & ACTIVITIES	(pp636–8)
Catedral...................................**4** C5	
Museu Arqueològic..................**5** C5	
Museu d'Art Contemporani......**6** B4	

SLEEPING	(pp638–9)
Casa de Huéspedes Navarro......**7** B3	

Hostal La Marina....................**8** C4
Hostal Sol y Brisa..................**9** A3
Hostal-Residencia Parque.......**10** A4
Hotel El Palacio.....................**11** B5
Hotel La Ventana...................**12** C5
Hotel Montesol......................**13** B3
La Torre del Canónigo............**14** B5

EATING	(p639)
Ca n'Alfredo.........................**15** A3	
Ca'n Claudie.........................**16** A3	
Comidas Bar San Juan............**17** B4	

Croissant Show.....................**18** C4
La Brasa................................**19** B4
La Scala................................**20** C5
Mercat de Verdures...............**21** C4
Restaurant Victoria................**22** B3
S'Ametller.............................**23** A3
Sa Botiga..............................**24** A3

DRINKING	(pp639–40)
Bar La Muralla......................**25** C5	
Bar Mambo..........................**26** D4	
Base....................................**27** D4	
Bliss....................................**28** B4	
Dôme..................................**29** C4	
Flash...................................**30** D4	
Foc i Llum............................**31** D4	
Incognito.............................**32** C4	
Lola's Club...........................**33** D4	
Teatro Pereira......................**34** B4	
Teatro.................................**35** D4	
The Rock..............................**36** D4	

TRANSPORT	(p641)
Autos Isla Blanca-Sixt............**37** B3	
Boats to Formentera..............**38** B2	
Boats to Platja d'En Bossa, Cala	
Llonga, Santa Eulària & Es	
Canar...............................**39** B3	
Estación Marítima (Ferry Terminal) for	
Palma de Mallorca, Barcelona &	
Valencia............................**40** C3	
Valentin..............................**41** A4	

Immediately inside the gateway is the expansive **Plaça de la Vila**, with its upmarket restaurants, galleries and shops. Up behind the plaza you can walk along the top of the walls and enjoy great views of the city, its harbour and the coast.

Nearby, the **Museu d'Art Contemporani** (☎ 971 30 27 23; Ronda de Narcís Puget s/n; adult/student & senior

€1.20/free; ⏰ 10am-1.30pm & 5-8pm Tue-Fri, 10am-1.30pm Sat & Sun Apr-Sep, 10am-1.30pm Tue-Sun Oct-Mar) is in an 18th-century powder store and armoury. It features constantly changing exhibitions of contemporary art.

A steep and well-worn route leads from Plaça de la Vila along narrow streets up to the **catedral**, which overlooks all from the

BALEARIC ISLANDS

top of the hill. It elegantly combines several styles: the original structure was built in the 14th century in Catalan Gothic, the sacristy was added in 1592 and a major baroque renovation took place in the 18th century.

Adjoining the cathedral, the **Museu Arqueo-lògic** (☎ 971 30 17 71; Plaça de la Catedral 3; adult/student/child & senior €2.40/1.30/free; ☺ 10am-1pm & 4-6pm Tue-Sat, 10am-2pm Sun Oct-Mar, 10am-2pm & 5-8pm Tue-Sat, 10am-2pm Sun Apr-Sep) houses a fine collection of ancient relics, mainly from the Phoenician, Carthaginian and Roman periods.

The **Necròpolis del Puig des Molins** (Via Romana 31; admission free; ☺ 10am-2pm & 6-8pm Tue-Sat, 10am-2pm Sun mid-Mar–mid-Oct; 9am-3pm Tue-Sat, 10am-2pm Sun mid-Oct–mid-Mar) is an ancient burial ground dating from Phoenician times (as long ago as the 7th century BC), on an olive-tree dotted *puig* (hill). Follow the path around and peer into the north–south oriented burial caverns cut deep into the hill. You can descend into one interlocking series of these *hypogea* (burial caverns).

BEACHES
The closest beach to Ibiza City is **Platja de Figueretes**, about 20 minutes' walk southwest of Sa Penya. In the next bay around to the northeast of Sa Penya is **Platja de Talamanca**. These beaches are all right for a quick dip, although if you have the time you would be much better off heading to the beaches at **Ses Salines**.

Sleeping
You could start your hotel search in Ibiza (and the rest of the island) online at www .ibizahotelsguide.com. The high season is generally mid-June to mid-September, although some places make August ultrahigh. Prices outside this period can fall by a third or more, but even so lodgings here come at a steep price.

BUDGET
Casa de Huéspedes Navarro (☎ 971 31 07 71; Carrer de sa Creu 20; s/d €28/55) Right in the thick of things, this simple place has 10 rooms at the top of a long flight of stairs. The front rooms have harbour views, the interior rooms are quite dark (but cool in summer) and there's a sunny rooftop terrace.

Hostal Sol y Brisa (☎ 971 31 08 18; Avinguda de Bartomeu Vicent Ramón 15; s/d €25/46) One of sev-

eral such places just beyond the old town, the 'Sun & Breeze' has basic, clean rooms with washbasin. Showers and toilets are in the hall, and some of the rooms are airless in summer.

MID-RANGE
Hostal La Marina (☎ 971 31 01 72; www.hostal-la marina.com; Carrer de Barcelona 7; s €62, d €77-150;) Looking onto the waterfront and Carrer de Barcelona, this mid-19th-century building has all sorts of rooms. A handful of singles look onto the street, but you can choose from simple doubles to great attics with terraces and panoramic port and/or town views. It also has a couple of other simpler lodgings options in the same street.

Hostal-Residencia Parque (☎ 971 30 13 58; Carrer de Vicent Cuervo 3; s without bathroom €48, d with private bathroom €100) The best doubles here overlook the pleasant Plaça del Parc from above the café of the same name. They are reasonably spacious and comfortable, although the singles are predictably pokey with views of nothing much at all.

Hotel Montesol (☎ 971 31 01 61; www.hotel montesol.com; Passeig de Vara de Rey 2; s/d to €57/103;) The doubles in this amiable, well-placed and grand-looking hotel are comfortable, if uninspiring, and come with views of the harbour or the old town. The singles are small and nothing special.

TOP END
Hotel El Palacio (☎ 971 30 14 78; www.elpalacio.com; Carrer de la Conquista 2 r from €267.50-374.50; ☺ Easter-Oct;) The 'Hotel of the Movie Stars' is something of a private movie museum, with a collection of signed photos, original movie posters and film awards. Seven rooms each pay homage to a different Hollywood star (from Bogart to Monroe). The

James Dean room, for instance, combines the bedroom and bathroom in a semiopen-plan space, with a separate lounge area and two balconies with views across town to the sea. Indeed the views are great from most vantage points here, and there's a private courtyard with a bar and pool.

La Torre del Canónigo (☎ 971 30 32 57; www.el canonigo.com; Carrer Major 8; apt €210-480; ⊙ Apr-Dec; ☒ ▣) This 14th-century tower houses 10 gorgeous 'apartments' (doubles and suites), all of different size and character. Four-poster beds, lots of timber and classic comfort are the hallmarks of this unique location. Prices almost halve in the low season.

Eating

You can buy fresh fruit and vegies from the small open-air **Mercat de Verdures** (Plaça de la Constitució; ⊙ 7am-7pm Mon-Sat), opposite the entrance to D'Alt Vila.

Croissant Show (☎ 971 31 76 65; Plaça de la Constitució s/n; ⊙ 6am-5am) Opposite the food market, this is where *everyone* goes for an impressive range of pastries and other breakfast, post-partying goodies. It is a quite a little scene all on its own.

Comidas Bar San Juan (☎ 971 31 16 03; Carrer de Guillem de Montgri 8; meals €15-20; ⊙ Mon-Sat) A family-run operation with two small dining rooms, this simple eatery offers outstanding value, with fish dishes for under €10 and many small mains for €6 or less. And for dessert try the *manzana al horno*, a delicious baked caramelised apple.

Restaurant Victoria (☎ 971 31 06 22; cnr Carrer de Riambau & Carrer de Guillem de Montgri; meals €12-15; ⊙ Mon-Sat) The dining room here is stark, with linoleum floors and brown checked tablecloths, but the food is hearty and as cheap as ever.

La Brasa (☎ 971 30 12 02; Carrer de Pere Sala 3; meals €30-35) Clouds of bougainvillea tumble about the entrance and courtyard of

AUTHOR'S CHOICE

Ca' n'Alfredo (☎ 971 31 12 74; Passeig de Vara de Rey 16; meals €30; ⊙ Tue-Sun) Locals have been flocking to Alfredo's place since 1934 for a good square meal. And they still do. Dig into the freshest of seafood and other local cuisine that's so good it's essential to book to get a seat here in the evening.

La Brasa. Sit down to well-prepared food, including some odd combinations, such as *pollo bogavante* (chicken and lobster), in the leafy garden.

La Scala (☎ 971 30 03 83; Plaça de sa Carrossa 6; meals €35; ⊙ dinner Wed-Mon) This candle-lit place serves international cuisine with a Swiss and central European bent, such as meat dishes and even *rösti*, that Swiss potato fave. The clientele is predominantly but not exclusively gay.

For something more earthy, and where you're likely to find mostly locals, venture into the admittedly unattractive grid west of the port and old town.

C'an Claudie (☎ 971 31 70 74; Carrer de Carles V 22; meals €15-20; ⊙ Mon-Sat) With blaring red doors and a sign reading 'Koala' it's hard to know what to expect here. Inside is a crisp, simple eatery crowded with locals and serving dishes such as *quiche de calabacines* (courgette quiche) and *couscous de cordero* (lamb couscous).

S'Ametller (☎ 971 31 17 80; Carrer de Pere Francès 12; meals €15-30; ⊙ Mon-Sat) 'The Almond Tree', resting uneasily next door to a cheap Chinese eatery, offers local cooking with fresh market produce. It offers various set meals, including a good vegetarian one for €15.50, which includes an *ensalada verde con cerezas, mozzarella y almendras* (green salad with cherries, mozzarella and almonds).

Drinking & Entertainment

Sa Penya is the nightlife centre. Dozens of bars keep the port area jumping from around sunset until the early hours. After they wind down, you can continue at one of the island's world-famous discos.

BARS

Carrer de Barcelona, a pedestrian-only street that runs parallel with the harbour, is lined with an impressive collection of funky bars. Most have tall tables and stools out on the street, and all pump out loud music and cold drinks. Don't be surprised if you receive unsolicited invitations from some attractive strangers. The local bar scene is highly competitive and lots of places employ slick and persuasive touts to 'invite' passers-by to join them for a drink, sometimes with the lure of discounted passes to the big discos.

These bars open nightly from early evening until 3am, roughly May to September.

Outside that it's hit-and-miss and depends largely on how much (if any) business there is.

Less in your face are the bars further east along Carrer de Garijo Cipriano, including **Bar Mambo** (☎ 971 31 21 60; Carrer de Garijo Cipriano 10) and **Flash** (Carrer de Garijo Cipriano 9). **The Rock** (Carrer de Garijo Cipriano 13), and its next-door neighbour, **Base** (Carrer de Garijo Cipriano 14), are also good.

Dôme (Via de Alfonso XII 5) Deep inside Sa Penya, this is a largely, but not exclusively, gay haven. Above all, it is glam, and a great, humming spot to hang out before heading for the clubs.

Lola's Club (Via de Alfonso XII 10) Anyone who remembers Ibiza in the '80s will have fond memories of Lola's Club, one of the first on the island. It closed in 1991, but…it's back with a hip happening miniclub in the heart of the old town.

Teatro Pereira (☎ 971 19 14 68; Carrer del Comte de Rosselló 3) Away from the waterfront hubbub, this is a lively bar, packed most nights with a more eclectic crowd than the standard pre-clubbing bunch. It often has live music sessions.

Bliss (Plaça des Parc) With its scintillating rose lights and candles on the outdoor tables, Bliss has become the star bar on this placid drinking square.

KM5 (☎ 971 39 63 49; Carretera de San Jos 5-6; ☽ 8pm-4am May-Sep) The bar named after its highway location is where you go when you want to really glam it up. Head out of town on the road to Sant Josep and dance in the gardens as you gear up for the clubs.

CLUBS (DISCOTECAS)

In summer the island is a continuous party from sunset to sunrise and back again. Fuelled by an overdeveloped sense of competitiveness, the island's entrepreneurs have built a truly amazing collection of clubs – huge, throbbing temples to which thousands of disciples flock nightly to pay homage to the gods of hedonism.

The major discos operate nightly between June and September, from around 1am to 7am. Each has something different to offer, and special theme nights, fancy-dress parties and foam parties (where you are half-drowned in the stuff while you dance) are regular features. Some places go a step or two further, with go-go girls, striptease

acts and even live sex as a climax to the evening (or morning).

Entertainment Ibiza style doesn't come cheaply: most places charge around €50 to €60 admission (and then sting you big-time for drinks). If you hang out around the right bars in Sa Penya, you might score a flier that entitles you to discounted admission handed out by sometimes scantily clad club promoters and touts.

The big names are: **Pacha** (☎ 971 31 36 00; www.pacha.com; ☽ nightly Jun-Sep, Fri & Sat Oct-May), in business on the northern side of Ibiza City's port since 1973 and containing 15 bars (!); **Privilege** (☎ 971 19 81 60), which claims to be the world's largest club (with a mere 20 bars and a pool inside, and capacity for up to 10,000 gyrating clubbers), and **Amnesia** (☎ 971 19 80 41; www.amnesia.es), the latter two 5km and 4km out of Ibiza City, respectively, on the road to Sant Rafel; **Es Paradis** (☎ 971 34 66 00; www.esparadis.com), with its amazing sound system, fountains and outdoor feel (there's no roof, but then in summer it doesn't rain anyway) in Sant Antoni itself; **El Divino** (☎ 971 31 83 38; www.el divino-ibiza.com), across the water from the Ibiza town centre (it organises boats and will refund taxis for groups of three or more); and **Space** (☎ 971 39 67 93), south of Ibiza City in Platja d'en Bossa and a specialist in all-day dancing (although it now opens at night too, meaning 22 hours a day of dancing for those who don't want to change venues!). Regular daytime boats head for Platja d'En Bossa from Ibiza City (€6 return) from May to mid-October.

These are the physical locations, but club teams rotate around the venues. Punters look out for acts such as London's **Ministry of Sound** (www.ministryofsound.com), which play on Friday at Pacha, the 'sexfabulous' **Manumission** (www.manumission.com), on Monday night at Privilege, followed by its Carry On session from 8am on Tuesday at Space, and **Cocoon** (www.cocoon.net), on Monday at Amnesia.

During summer, Ibiza's **Discobus** (☎ 971 31 34 47) operates nightly from midnight until 6am, doing circuits between the major discos, bars and hotels in Ibiza City, Platja d'en Bossa, Sant Rafel, Santa Eulària d'es Riu (and an extension to Es Canar) and Sant Antoni. They leave hourly on the hour or half-hour, depending on where you get on. In Ibiza they leave from the bus station on Avinguda d'Isidor Macabich.

GAY BARS & CLUBS

The gay scene is based towards the eastern end of Sa Penya, particularly along the far end of Carrer de la Virgen. For more on the latest in gay Ibiza check out www.ibigay.net.

Teatro (Carrer de la Virgen 83) has sea views from inside. **Incognito** (Carrer de Santa Lucía 21), in the shadow of the old city walls, is a busy gay bar, while **Bar La Muralla** (☎ 971 30 18 82; Carrer de Sa Carossa 3) is a quieter affair. **Foc i Llum** (☎ 971 19 33 16; Carrer de la Virgen 55) is a bar with terrace, videos and a steamy darkroom.

Down on Platja d'en Bossa, **Pin Up** puts on a gay party, TolerancE (sic) on Tuesday. On the same night **Privilege** stages FxxxHouse (with extreme darkroom action), while **Pacha** puts on Scandal for the gay community on Sunday night.

Getting There & Away

Ibiza's **airport** (Aeroport d'Eivissa; ☎ 971 80 90 00) is 7km southwest of the capital.

Boats for Formentera leave from a separate terminal which is about 300m north of the centre of town. For information on inter-island ferries, see Getting There & Around (p617).

Cruceros Santa Eulalia (☎ 971 33 22 52) runs boats to Cala Llonga, Santa Eulària d'es Riu and Es Canar up to four times daily (€11 return) from May to mid-October.

Buses to other parts of the island depart from a series of stops along Avinguda d'Isidoro Macabich (the western continuation of Avinguda de Bartomeu Rosselló). Tickets can be bought from the bus station booths on the same street or on the buses.

Getting Around

Buses between the airport and Avinguda d'Isidoro Macabich operate hourly between 7.30am and 11.35pm (€1.20, 15 minutes). A taxi from the airport should cost €10 to €12. You can call a taxi on ☎ 971 39 83 40 or ☎ 971 30 66 02.

EAST COAST

A busy highway (C733) speeds you north out of Ibiza City towards Santa Eulària d'es Riu on the east coast. Alternatively, you could take the slower but more scenic coastal road via Cala Llonga – take the turnoff to Jesús a couple of kilometres northwest of Ibiza City. This route winds through low hills and olive groves, with detours along the way to several beaches, including the pleasant **Sol d'en Serra.**

Cala Llonga is set on an attractive bay with high rocky cliffs sheltering a lovely sandy beach, but the town itself has many highrise hotels.

Santa Eulària d'es Riu

pop 6390

Ibiza's third-largest town, Santa Eulària d'es Riu is a bustling and agreeable place with reasonable **beaches**, a large harbour and plenty of 20th-century tourist-resort architecture.

ORIENTATION & INFORMATION

The main highway, known as Carrer de Sant Jaume as it passes through town, is a hectic traffic artery lined with souvenir shops.

The **tourist office** (☎ 971 33 07 28; Carrer de Marià Riquer Wallis 4; �9.30am-1.30pm & 5-7.30pm Mon-Fri, 9.30am-1pm Sat) is just off the highway.

SLEEPING

Modern hotels and apartments crowd the Santa Eulària beachfront, but you'll find a cluster of affordable hostales a couple of blocks inland.

Hostal-Residencia Sa Rota (☎ 971 33 00 22; Carrer de Sant Vincent 59; s/d €33/56) A good-value hostal, this place features bright generous rooms (the doubles in particular) with modern bath or shower.

Ca's Català (☎ 971 33 10 06; Carrer del Sol s/n; s from €45, d €70-85; ⁂ ⁑) A British-run place with 12 rooms, this place is a find. It has the feel of a private villa, with colourful flowerpots, rooms overlooking a garden courtyard and a swimming pool.

EATING

Most of the restaurants and cafés along the beachfront are tacky and overpriced. Four blocks back, there are plenty of decent eateries along Carrer de Sant Vicent.

Restaurante es Rickshaw (☎ 971 33 01 23; Carrer de Sant Vicent 49; meals €30) If the series of generally cheap and cheerful Spanish restaurants on this strip doesn't grab you, pop into this groovy, self-styled 'fusion lounge', where you can start with a crab crepe, follow with wok-fried chicken and finish with pineapple carpaccio.

El Naranjo (☎ 971 33 03 24; Carrer de Sant Josep 31; meals €30-35; ✷ dinner Tue-Sun) Enjoy well-prepared seafood meals in a shady garden at 'The Orange', a tranquil gourmet escape.

ENTERTAINMENT

Guaraná (www.guarana-ibiza.com; Passeig Marítim; ✷ 1am-6am Jun-Sep) Right by the town's marina, this is a cool club away from the Ibiza–Sant Rafel–Sant Antoni circuit, with occasionally mellow tones, as well as live jazz and blues on some nights. It frequently opens on weekends in the low season, too.

GETTING THERE & AWAY

The bus stop is on Carrer de sa Església. Regular buses connect Santa Eulària with Ibiza City, Sant Antoni and the northern beaches.

Santa Eulària d'es Riu to S'Aigua Blanca

Northwest of Santa Eulària d'es Riu is the resort town of **Es Canar**, which is heavily developed and probably best avoided, although a couple of camping grounds are located nearby.

Further north on the main road is the sleepy village of **Sant Carles de Peralta**. Side roads lead off to the pleasant **Cala Llenya** and the serene **Cala Mastella** beaches. Boats run to the former from Santa Eulària fives times daily (€8 return) from June to September. At the latter you could walk around the rocks from the left (northern) end of the pretty beach to reach **Es Bigote** (meals €30; ✷ lunch only May-Sep), a great little eatery perched above the water. Offering fish caught that morning, it is often full – best to wander over from the beach in the morning to book a spot.

The road to Cala Mastella continues a couple of kilometres on up to **Cala de Boix**, the only true black-sand beach in the Balearic Islands. Alternatively, there is another turn-off to Cala de Boix about 1km after Sant Carles.

Back on the main road, the next turn-off leads to the resort area of **Es Figueral**. A little further on a handwritten sign marks the turn-off to the lovely beaches of **S'Aigua Blanca**. Being a bit out of the way and little developed, these beaches are popular with Ibiza's 'young and restless' crowd, most of whom tend to forget to put on their swimsuits. A couple of shacks act as seaside daytime bars.

SLEEPING & EATING

Camping Cala Nova (☎ 971 33 17 74; per 2 people, tent & car €19.90) Just back from the Cala Nova beach and about 1km north of Es Canar, this is the best of the camping grounds here.

Hostal Cala Boix (☎ 971 33 52 24; r per person incl breakfast €24.50; ✷ P) Set uphill and back from the beach, this solitary place could not be further from Ibiza madness. All rooms have bathrooms and some have sea views. It has a restaurant, and there is another one across the road. Down by the beach you'll find a little daytime bar.

Can Curreu (☎ 971 33 52 80; www.cancurreu.com; Carretera de Sant Carles Km12; d €256.80; ✷ ⌨ P) This wonderfully restored Ibizan farmstead lies 1.5km south of Sant Carles, just off the main road from Santa Eulària. Rooms are tastefully decorated and furnished, and the suites are a luxury home in the country, with such extras as a stereo, Jacuzzi and fireplace (for the winter). The restaurant is excellent, and you can use a modest gym and solarium and go horse riding.

Cala Sant Vicent

The package-tour resort of Cala Sant Vicent is built around the shores of a protected bay on the northeast coast, a long stretch of sandy beach backed by a string of modern midrise hotels. It's not a bad place to stop for a swim if you happen to be passing by; you could also join a boat trip to the islet of **Illa sa Tagomago** (☎ 971 32 01 41; return €20; ✷ 3pm daily Jul-Aug), a four-hour excursion entailing a 1½-hour stay on the islet.

NORTH COAST & INTERIOR

This northern part of Ibiza contains some of the island's most attractive landscapes. If you need a break from the beaches, the area's coastal hills and inland mountains are popular with bushwalkers and cyclists.

Cala Sant Vicent to Portinatx

The main road (PM811) heads west from Cala Sant Vicent, passing by the unremarkable village of **Sant Vicent de Sa Cala** before hitting the main north–south highway. From here you can head south to Ibiza City or north to Portinatx.

Portinatx

Portinatx is the north coast's major tourist resort, with phalanxes of hotels around its three adjoining beaches – S'Arenal Petit, S'Arenal Gran and Platja Es Port. The beaches themselves are beautiful but can get crowded.

Cala Xarraca

This beach, just west of Portinatx, is set in a picturesque, partly protected bay with a rocky shoreline and a dark-sand beach. Development is limited to a solitary bar-restaurant overlooked by a couple of private houses.

Sant Miquel de Balansat & Port de Sant Miquel

One of the largest inland towns, Sant Miquel is overlooked by a boxlike 14th-century **church**, but there isn't much else to the place. Several kilometres north, Port de Sant Miquel is dominated by the huge **Hotel Club San Miguel**, which has consumed an entire hillside above the admittedly fine beaches.

A turn-off to the right just before you enter town, coming from the south, takes you around a headland to the entrance to the **Cova de Can Marçà** (☎ 971 33 47 76; adult/child €5.50/3; ◷ 10.30am-7.30pm), a collection of underground caverns spectacularly lit by coloured lights. Tours in various languages take around 30 to 40 minutes.

Beyond the caves, an unsealed road continues 4km around the coast to the unspoiled bay of **Cala Benirrás**. A sealed road to Cala Benirrás leads off the Sant Joan–Sant Miquel road, midway between the towns. High, forested cliffs and a couple of bar-restaurants back the beach. On Sunday at sunset you may well encounter groups of hippies with bongos hanging out to greet the sunset. The word is out, though – the London *Sunday Times* has declared this to be the fourth-best beach in the Mediterranean (possibly a slight exaggeration).

Can Planells (☎ 971 33 49 24; www.canplanells.com; Carrer de Venda Rubió 2; d €160.50-267.50; ❄ ☎ P) This splendid country mansion just 1.5km outside Sant Miquel on the road to Sant Mateu d'Aubarca oozes a relaxed rural luxury in its handful of tastefully arranged doubles and suites. The best suites have private terraces, and the place is set amid delightful gardens and fruit-tree groves. Prices drop more than 30% in the low season.

Ibiza Yoga (☎ 020-7419 0999; www.ibizayoga.com; ❄ ☎) This UK-based centre has installed

itself in a couple of villas a few hundred metres back from the beach at Cala Benirràs and offers week-long, all-inclusive yoga retreats. Villa Palmas is the nicer of the two villas, with a range of rooms (including one at the top with its staircase and terrace) in cool country fashion. Prices are UK£225 to UK£1200 a week per person, which includes twin-share accommodation, breakfast, dinner and six yoga classes for beginners and above.

Hacienda Na Xamena (☎ 971 33 45 00; www.relaischateaux.fr/site/fr/rc_xamena.html; d €205-520, apt to €980; ❄ ☎ P) About 3km west of Port de Sant Miquel is Ibiza's famous clifftop hotel. If you want to rub shoulders with the rich and famous, this is the place to stay. Approaching it, the place seems a discreetly low slung country estate, but it actually has six levels built into the steep cliff facing out to sea. Rooms are furnished in old-fashioned style and in some cases could use a touch up, but the views…

Santa Gertrudis de Fruitera

If you blinked at the wrong time you could easily miss tiny Santa Gertrudis, south of Sant Miquel. Clustered around the central Plaça de l'Església you'll find an unusual collection of **art-and-craft galleries** and antique and bric-a-brac shops, plus several good bars, among which the perennial favourite is **Bar Costa** (11 Plaça de l'Església), with art on the walls and somewhat erratic opening times.

Sant Rafel
pop 1770

Midway between Ibiza City and Sant Antoni de Portmany, Sant Rafel is internationally known as the nearest geographical point to two of Ibiza's biggest and best discos, **Privilege** (☎ 971 19 81 60) and **Amnesia** (☎ 971 19 80 41;

AUTHOR'S CHOICE

El Ayoun (☎ 971 19 83 35; Carre d'Isidor Macabich s/n; meals €30-40; ◷ 8pm-3am) When clubbers are ready to take a breather, some like to chill and feed at this relaxed Moroccan restaurant. The Middle Eastern food is just the beginning. The huge garden terrace is another big attraction, and a (relatively) subdued partying atmosphere builds in the restaurant's Bar Privado towards the end of the evening.

www.amnesia.es). For reviews of these clubs, see p640. By day, the town is known as a craft centre and has a pretty good collection of ceramics workshops, sculpture galleries, shops and markets.

WEST COAST
Sant Antoni de Portmany
pop 14,150

Sant Antoni (San Antonio in Spanish), widely known as 'San An', is big and about as Spanish as bangers and mash. The locals joke that even football hooligans need holidays, and somehow they seem to end up in San An. It's the perfect destination if you've come in search of booze-ups, brawls and hangovers.

Most of the town is on the tacky side, but if you head for the small rock-and-sand strip on the north shore, you can join hundreds of others for sunset drinks at a string of a half-dozen cool bars, the best known of which is **Café del Mar** (☎ 971 34 25 16; Carrer de Vara del Rey s/n; ☒ 5pm-4am). Others include **Café Mambo** (☎ 971 34 66 38; Carrer de Vara del Rey 56; ☒ 2pm-4am), which is a kick-off point for a lot of Pacha's pre-club night shenanigans, and **Savannah Café** (☎ 971 34 80 31; Carrer del General Balanzat 38; ☒ 2pm-4am). The latter plays chill-out music as you munch on Tex Mex and sip sangría. After the sun goes down all of them turn up the rhythmic heat and pound on until 4am, from about June to October. If nothing else, it can be said with confidence that the nightlife here is wild. The town is also home to the club **Es Paradis** (☎ 971 34 66 00; www.esparadis.com), just out of the town centre on the coast road heading west. For its review, see p640.

Not far north of Sant Antoni are several pleasant and undeveloped beaches, such as **Cala Salada**, a wide bay with sandy shores backed by a pine forest. From here, a rough track continues further north to the beach at **Ses Fontanelles**. Closer to Sant Antoni are the cosy little beaches of **Cala Gració** and **Cala Gracioneta**, separated by a small rocky promontory.

Sant Antoni is connected with Ibiza City and the rest of the island by regular bus services. Boats run to local beaches, such as Cala Bassa and Cala Compte.

Camping Sant Antoni (☎ 671-835845; Carretera Sant Antoni Km14.8; per person & tent €12; ☒ Jun-Sep) This busy camping ground, only a few hundred metres outside Sant Antoni, has it all:

pool, bars, restaurant, BBQ facilities and bicycle hire. It can be packed and rowdy in the height of summer.

Hotel Pikes (☎ 971 34 22 22; www.ibiza-hotels.com /pikes; Camí de sa Vorera Km12; d from €192.60; ☒ ☐ ☒ ℗) This is an extraordinary little hotel south of Sant Antoni. It offers a range of doubles and suites (all with varying themes and some with prices reaching for the stars). This stone country mansion has a gym, leafy garden with bar and a translucent pool.

Es Rebost de Ca'n Prats (☎ 971 34 62 52; Carrer de Cervantes 4; meals €15-20; ☒ Wed-Mon) A little worn, but a good spot for decently prepared fish and other local dishes, this is one of the few authentic Ibiza eateries in Sant Antoni. It's a hike from the waterfront bar action.

Cala Bassa to Cala d'Hort

Heading west and south from Sant Antoni, you'll come to the rocky and popular bay of **Cala Bassa**. The next few coves around the coast hide some extremely pretty beaches – **Cala Compte**, with its translucent water, and the popular **Cala Codolars** are among the best. All are accessible by local bus from Sant Antoni. Also, regular boats, such as those of Cruceros Portmany, run to Cala Bassa and Cala Compte at least once an hour from 10am to dusk. Buy tickets at booths in the port and at the beaches.

Further south, **Cala Vedella** is a modest resort with a fine beach in the centre of town, backed by a couple of restaurants. A little further south, **Cala d'Hort** has a spectacular setting overlooking two rugged rocky islets, **Es Vedrà** and **Es Vedranell**. The water here is an inviting shade of blue, and the beach a long arc of sand sprinkled with pebbles and rocks. The developers still haven't ruined this place, and there's nothing here apart from two relaxed bar-restaurants.

SOUTH COAST
Ses Salines
pop 2040

Platja de ses Salines and the adjacent Platja d'es Cavallet, at the southernmost tip of the island, are the best and most popular beaches within easy striking distance of Ibiza City. You can be here in half an hour on the local bus or more quickly with your own transport. The area takes its name from the saltpans that have been exploited here since Carthaginian times and were big business until tourism came along.

If you're taking the bus from Ibiza City, you'll be dropped at the western end of Ses Salines beside a small bar. Across the road, on the other side of the sand dunes, a long crescent-shaped bay stretches away into the distance, with a broad sandy beach broken by patches of rocks. These beaches are popular with Ibiza's party-hard crowd and there are four or five open-air beach bars spread around the bay. Each offers a slightly different vibe and music. The western end is more 'family-oriented' and it seems that swimsuits become less common the further east you go. Stroll on if the *au naturel* look appeals to you: **Platja d'es Cavallet**, the next bay around to the east, is Ibiza's official nudist beach.

SLEEPING & EATING

Hostal Mar y Sal (☎ 971 39 65 84; d to €55; ☼ May-Sep) Handy for the beach, this spot has its own bar and restaurant. It's frequently booked months in advance for July and August.

Sa Trincha, at the eastern end of the beach, is considered the coolest bar on this stretch of sand. It serves burgers, *bocadillos* (filled rolls), salads and fruit smoothies. It also does somewhat stronger drinks, and when the DJ gets into gear things can get kind of wild and crazy.

GETTING THERE & AWAY

Autobuses Voramar El Gaucho runs eight to 10 buses daily to Ses Salines from Ibiza City (€1.20).

FORMENTERA

A short boat ride south of Ibiza, Formentera is the smallest and least developed of the four main Balearic Islands, with a population of 7607 people. This idyllic island boasts fine beaches, and some excellent short walking and cycling trails. It's a popular day trip from Ibiza and gets crowded in midsummer (especially with the Italian contingent, for whom Formentera seems to be what Bali is to the Australians), but most of the time it is still possible to find yourself a strip of sand out of sight and earshot of other tourists.

Formentera's predominantly flat landscape is rugged and at times bleak. The coast is alternately fringed with jagged rocky cliffs

and beaches backed by low sand dunes. A handful of farmers scrape a living from the land in the centre and east, but elsewhere the island is a patchwork of pine plantations, sun-bleached salt beds, low stone walls and vacant fields. The island lives off tourism and little incentive remains to work the unforgiving land.

Orientation & Information

Formentera is less than 20km across from east to west. Ferries arrive at La Savina, a functional harbour town wedged between two large salt lakes, the Estany d'es Peix and Estany Pudent (the aptly named Smelly Lake). Three kilometres south of La Savina is the island's administrative capital, Sant Francesc Xavier, and another 5km southwest is Cap de Barbaria, the southernmost point. Es Pujols, the main tourist resort, is 3km east of La Savina.

The main road (PM820) runs down the middle of the island, passing by the fine beaches of Platja de Migjorn along the south coast and through the fishing village of Es Caló (13km southeast of La Savina) before climbing to Sa Talaia (192m), the island's highest point. The eastern end of the island is marked by the Far de sa Mola lighthouse.

Formentera's **tourist office** (☎ 971 32 20 57; www.visitformentera.com; ☼ 10am-2pm & 5-7pm Mon-Fri, 10am-2pm Sat May-Sep) is in La Savina, hidden behind the row of vehicle-hire agencies that line the port. Opening hours vary seasonally. Most of the banks are in Sant Francesc Xavier. There is a clinic, **Centro Médico** (☎ 971 32 23 69), 3km south of La Savina.

Sights & Activities

Apart from walking, cycling and lying on beaches, activities are limited. Points of interest include a series of crumbling stone **watchtowers** along the coastline, a ruined **Roman fortress** (Fortifició Romá), on the south coast, and 40 minor **archaeological sites** (most signposted off the main roads).

BEACHES

Among the island's best beaches are **Platja de Llevant** and **Platja de ses Illetes** – beautiful strips of white sand that line the eastern and western sides, respectively, of the narrow promontory stretching north towards Ibiza. A 2km **walking trail** leads from the La Savina–Es Pujols road to the far end of

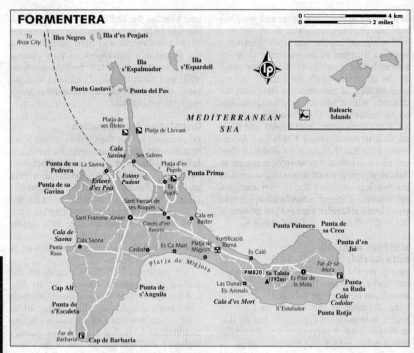

FORMENTERA

the promontory, from where you can wade across a narrow strait to **Illa s'Espalmador**, a tiny uninhabited islet with beautiful, quiet beaches and mud baths. The promontory itself is largely undeveloped. Be careful when wading out – you can easily be caught by |incoming tides. Or better, take the Barca Bahia boat (€10 return) that runs three times daily from La Savina ferry port (via Platja de ses Illetes) to the island and return. You can get to Platja de ses Illetes directly from Ibiza, too. A boat runs daily from Platja Talamanca (3km outside Ibiza City) at 10.15am and returns at 5pm (€13 return).

East of Sant Ferran de ses Roques, towards Es Caló, a series of bumpy roads and unsealed tracks leads to the south coast beaches, known collectively as **Platja de Migjorn**. They are secluded and popular, despite their sometimes rocky and seaweed-strewn shorelines (especially towards the western end). The best are at the eastern end around **Es Arenals**. Most of these beach settlements consist of a handful of houses and apartments, a couple of bar-restaurants and the odd hostal.

Nudism is fairly common on many of the island's beaches. It's not mandatory but no-one bats an eyelid if you shed all your layers.

SANT FRANCESC XAVIER

Formentera's capital and biggest population centre (with 2210 souls), Sant Francesc Xavier is an attractive whitewashed village with some good cafés overlooking small, sunny plazas. The town's older buildings include a 14th-century chapel, an 18th-century **fortress**, and the **Museu Etnològic** (☎ 971 32 26 70; Carrer de Jaume I 17; admission free; ❧ 10am-2pm), a modest ethnological museum devoted to the traditional aspects of predominantly rural island life prior to the arrival of tourism.

CALA SAONA

On the road south of Sant Francesc Xavier, one-third of the way to Cap de Barbaria, you can turn west to the delectable cove of Cala Saona. The beach is one of the island's best, with just one big hotel (see Sleeping, p647) a couple of bar-restaurants overlooking the clear, pale aqua and blue-black waters, and a discreet smattering of a half-dozen houses.

CAP DE BARBARIA

A narrow sealed road heads south out of the capital through stone-walled farmlands to Cap de Barbaria, the island's southernmost point. It's a pleasant ride to the lonely white lighthouse at the road's end, although there ain't much to do once you get there, except gaze out to sea. From the lighthouse *(far)* a track leads east (a 10-minute walk) to the **Torre d'es Cap de Barbaria**, an 18th-century watchtower.

ES PUJOLS

Once a sleepy fishing village, Es Pujols has been transformed by tourism. Rows of sun-bleached timber boat shelters still line the beachfront, but today modern hotels, apartments and restaurants overshadow them. If the beaches are too crowded for your liking, more secluded options lie within easy striking distance (keep walking northwest towards Platja de Llevant).

COVES D'EN XERONI

Beside the main road just east of Sant Ferran are the **Coves d'en Xeroni** (☎ 971 32 87 42; adult/child under 12 €3.50/2; ☺ 10am-1.30pm & 2.30-7pm Mon-Sat May-Oct), an unexceptional series of underground caves with stalactites and all.

EASTERN END

The small fishing settlement of Es Caló is set on a tiny rocky cove ringed by faded timber boat shelters. The coastline here is jagged, but immediately west of Es Caló you'll find some good swimming holes and rock pools with small patches of sand.

From Es Caló, the road twists its way up to the island's highest point. Close to the top, Restaurante El Mirador (see Eating, p648) offers spectacular views along the length of the island. The eastern extremity of the island is an elevated limestone plateau. Most of the coastline is only accessible by boat, and pine stands and farms mainly take up the interior. A road runs arrow-straight to the island's eastern tip, passing through the nondescript hamlet of **Es Pilar de la Mola**. At the end of the road stand the **Far de sa Mola** lighthouse and a **monument** to Jules Verne, who used this setting in one of his novels.

Sleeping

Camping is prohibited on Formentera. Most of the accommodation caters to package-tour agencies, so is overpriced and/or booked out in summer. August and, to a lesser extent, July are the toughest months. Single rooms are as rare as hens' teeth in summer, and rental apartments (a better deal for stays of a week or more) are more common than hostales and hotels (of which there are fewer than 50).

Astbury Formentera (☎ 01642-210163; www .formentera.co.uk; 31 Baker St, Middlesbrough TS1 2LF) is a UK-based specialist in house and apartment rentals in Formentera. Prices per person can start at around UK£175 a week for a four-person bungalow in the low season to UK£630 per person for two-person accommodation in the high season.

SANT FRANCESC XAVIER

Several modest little hostales are scattered about this pleasant town and prices are more realistic than some of the beach locations.

Casa Rafal (☎ 971 32 22 05; Carrer d'Isidoro Macabich; d €60; ☒) Just off sleepy Plaça de sa Constitució, this modest two-storey spot is friendly and offers good, clean rooms with bathroom.

ES PUJOLS

This is the heart of Formentera's tourism efforts and accommodation is particularly expensive in summer.

Hostal Voramar (☎ 971 32 81 19; voramar@inter book.net; s/d €105/125; ☺ May-Oct; ☒ ☒) About 100m inland from the beach, this ochre-fronted hotel has comfortable rooms, most with balcony.

SANT FERRAN DE SES ROQUES

Hostal Pepe (☎ 971 32 80 33; Carrer Major 68; s/d incl breakfast €30/46) Located on the pleasant (and on summer nights quite lively) main street near the village's old sandstone church, this place has 45 simple and breezy rooms with bathroom.

CALA SAONA

Hotel Cala Saona (☎ 971 32 20 30; s/d €107/146; ☺ May-Oct; ☒ ☒ ℗) Something of a white, balcony-lined monolith, this is the only hotel in town, with 116 rooms, a pool, tennis courts and restaurant. From the best rooms the view is straight across the beach and out to sea. Prices halve in low season. The beach bars are perfect for a sunset sangría.

PLATJA DE MIGJORN

A spattering of hostales is spread along Formentera's south beach.

Hostal Ca Marí (☎ 971 32 81 80; Es Ca Marí; s/d incl breakfast €45/70; ❄ ☎) This is actually three comfortable hostales in one: its rooms and apartments all share a central bar, restaurant, pool and grocery shop in the little settlement of the same name.

ES CALÓ

Fonda Rafalet (☎ 971 32 70 16; s/d €50/73) Overlooking a small rocky harbour, this modest guesthouse has good rooms (some with sea views), and also incorporates a bar and popular seafood restaurant.

Eating

Mostly waterfront eateries offer a standard range of seafood and paella-style options. Reckon on an average of €30 a head or more for a full meal in the bulk of restaurants, most of which open from May to October only. Gotta make euros while the sun shines!

SANT FRANCESC XAVIER

Bar Plate (☎ 971 32 23 13; Plaça de sa Constitució; meals €20-25; ❄ Mon-Sat) Set beneath a leafy pergola, this is a charming spot for a lazy breakfast or a simple evening meal.

En Can Vicent (☎ 971 666-167993 Carrer d'Isidoro Macabich 4; meals €25; ❄ Tue-Sun) This place is rather unique on the island, offering such delicacies as sushi and sashimi alongside more workaday tapas.

ES PUJOLS

Luzius (☎ 971 32 84 17; Fonoll Marí 2-6; meals €30-35) The second-to-last of a string of beach-bar restaurants as you head west from the town centre, this is a relaxed and shady option for seafood with a French touch, tapas and a range of refreshing fruit juices.

El Caminito (☎ 971 328106; Carretera La Savina-Es Pujols; meals €40-50; ❄ dinner Apr-Nov) This Argentine meat grill is one of the best restaurants on the island, serving succulent slabs of meat in all its known forms. A touch of the Pampa in the Med, it is barely 1km outside Es Pujols on the road to La Savina.

PLATJA DE SES ILLETES

A 2km partly dirt road winds 2km north of the La Savina–Es Pujols road, just behind the beach and providing access to four beachside restaurants along the way. The best option follows.

Es Molí de Sal (☎ 971 18 74 91; meals €35-50; ❄ Nov-Easter) In a tastefully renovated mill boasting a lovely terrace and magnificent sea views you will discover some of the finest seafood on the island. Try one of the rice dishes or the house speciality, *caldereta de llagosta* (lobster stew).

SOUTH COAST

Flipper (☎ 971 18 75 96; Las Dunas, Platja de Migjorn; meals €25-30) Looking out over one of the nicer stretches at the eastern end of the long southern strand, this is a great place to tuck into some grilled fish. To get there from the main road follow the exit for Las Dunas and Es Arenals.

Restaurante Es Cupiná (☎ 971 32 72 21; Plajta de Migjorn; meals €30-40) At the eastern extremity of the beach, this is a big name on the island, noted especially for the lobster and freshly cooked fish of the day.

ES PILAR DE LA MOLA

Formentera's easternmost town has a handful of bars and restaurants.

Restaurante El Mirador (☎ 971 32 70 37; Carretera de la Mola Km14.3; meals €25-30) The best feature about this fairly average seafood restaurant is the staggering views west across the length of the island, with the Med glittering along its north and south shores.

Pequeña Isla (☎ 971 32 70 68; meals €30) Easily the best restaurant in town, with a shady roadside terrace, the 'Little Island' dishes up hearty meat dishes, fresh grilled fish and paella.

Entertainment

ES PUJOLS

In summer Es Pujols is pretty lively, offering up a cluster of bars along or just off Carrer de Miramar that stay open until 3am or 4am. A favourite with the islanders is **Místic** (Carrer de S'Espardell; ❄ Wed-Mon), one of the few places that stays open throughout the year. On Carrer de sa Roca Plana, a couple of bars worth looking out for are Bananas&co and Bar Coyote, both of which have terraces.

SANT FERRAN DE SES ROQUES

Fonda Pepe (☎ 971 32 80 33; Carrer Major 55; ☺ May-Oct) Welcome to the island classic, a knock-about bar that has been serving *pomades* (gin and lemon) for decades. Haunt of the hippies in the 1970s, it attracts a lively crowd of locals and foreigners of all ages and persuasions, who fill the bar and street with their animated banter.

PLATJA DE SES ILLETES

One of the island beachside rituals is sipping on sangría while observing the sunset.

Bigsurlife (☺ 10.30am-sunset May-Oct), Attracts a good-natured but self-consciously beautiful Italian crowd, and serves nachos all day and Italian dishes at lunch time. About 20m before the turn-off for Platja de ses Illetes from the La Savina–Es Pujols road, a parking area is signposted to the left. Another 30m brings you to the beach and bar.

Tiburón (☎ 659-638945; ☺ 10am-sunset May-Oct) About 200m further up the beach, this is an equally fun beach tavern that tends to attract more locals for fish, salads, sangría and sunset.

PLATJA DE MIGJORN

Blue Bar (☎ 971 18 70 11; Km8; ☺ noon-4am Apr-Oct) This is a Formentera classic, which offers good seafood, paella and spadefuls of *buen rollito* (good vibes). It is the south's chill-out bar par excellence – fair enough on an island that is largely about chilling out.

Getting There & Away

Up to nine ferry services (€10/17 one way/return, one hour) and up to 16 fast ferries (€15.90/29.80, 25 minutes) operate daily between Ibiza City and Formentera with **Baleària** (☎ 902 16 01 80; www.balearia.net). The first ferry leaves Ibiza City at 6.45am and the last returns from Formentera at around 9.45pm (Sunday 8pm).

Fares for vehicles on the slower boats cost €45 for a small car one way, €20 for motorcycles under 250cc and €3.40 for a bicycle.

Mediterranea-Pitiusa SL (☎ 971 32 24 43; www.medpitiusa.com) runs up to eight fast ferries between Ibiza and Formentera (€12 to €15.90 each way, 25 to 35 minutes).

Getting Around

Pedal power is the best way to get around this little island, but **Autocares Paya** (☎ 971 32

31 81) runs a regular bus service connecting the main towns.

You'll find vehicle-hire agencies all over the island, including a string of places opposite the harbour in La Savina. Local agencies include **Moto Rent Migjorn** (☎ 971 32 86 11), **Moto Rent La Savina** (☎ 971 32 27 45) and **Formotor** (☎ 971 32 70 48). Daily rates are around €6 for a bike, €8 to €10 for a mountain bike, €20 to €25 for a motor scooter and up to €37 for a motorcycle. A car is superfluous on this tiny island, but they are available for rent.

MENORCA

Menorca (population 81,000) is the least overrun and most tranquil of the Balearics. In 1993 Unesco declared it a Biosphere Reserve, aiming to preserve environmental areas, such as the Parc Natural S'Albufera d'es Grau wetlands and the island's unique archaeological sites.

The untouched beaches, coves and ravines around its 216km coastline allow the more adventurous the occasional sense of discovery! This must be one of the few places in the Mediterranean where it is possible to have a beautiful beach largely to yourself in summer. Some say the island owes much to Franco for not being overrun with tourist development. While neighbouring Mallorca went over to the Nationalists almost at the outset of the civil war, Menorca resisted for much of the war. Franco later 'rewarded' Mallorca with a construction free-for-all and penalised Menorca by blocking development!

The second-largest and northernmost of the Balearics, Menorca also has a wetter climate and is usually a few degrees cooler than the other islands. Particularly in the low season, the 'windy island' is relentlessly buffeted by *tramuntana* winds from the north.

Check out the tourist information website www.e-menorca.org and the island's official accommodation website, www.visitmenorca.com.

Orientation

The capital, Maó (Mahón in Castilian), is at the eastern end of the island. Ferries from the mainland and Palma de Mallorca arrive

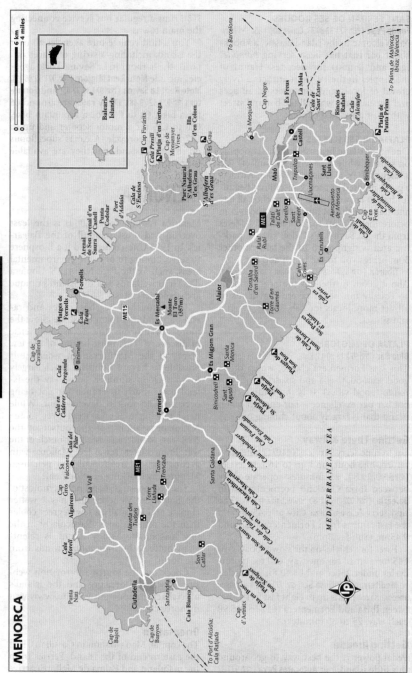

MENORCA

0 ___ 6 km
0 ___ 4 miles

Balearic Islands

To Barcelona

To Palma de Mallorca;
Ibiza; Valencia

Cap Negre
Es Freus
La Mola
Sa Mesquida
Rincó des
Rafalet
Cala
d'Alcaufar
Platja de
Punta Prima
Es
Castell
Maó
Sant
Lluís
Binibèquer
Cap Favàritx
Cala Presili
Platja d'en Tortuga
Cap de Montsenyer
Vives
Illa
d'en Colom
Es Grau
Parc Natural
S'Albufera d'es Grau
S'Albufera
d'es Grau
Cala de
S'Enclusa
Castell
Sanitja
Punta
Codolar
Port
d'Addaia
Trepucó
Cala
d'en Biniancolla
Biniancolla
Binidalí
Llucmaçanes
Cala d'en
Porter
Aeropuerto
de Menorca
ME1
Talatí
de Dalt
Sant
Climent
Torelló
Rafal
Rubí
Arenal
de Son Arenal d'en
Saura
Cala
Tirant
Platges de
Fornells
Fornells
Cap de
Cavalleria
Cala
Pregonda
Binimella
ME15
Es Mercadal
Monte
El Toro
(357m)
Es Migjorn Gran
Santa
Mónica
Alaior
Torralba
d'en Salord
Torre d'en
Gaumès
Es Canutells
Cales
Coves
Cala en
Porter
Ses Penyes
d'Alaior
Cala de
Sant Llorenç
Cala
en Calderer
Cala del
Pilar
Sa
Falconera
Cala
Morell
Cap
Gros
Algairens
La Vall
Ferreries
Binicodrell
Sant
Agustí
Platja
St. Adeodato
Sant
Tomàs
Platges de
Son Bou
Son Bou
Santa Galdana
Santandría
Cala
Macarella
Cala
Mitjana
Cala
Trebalúger
Cala
Escorxada
Cala
Macarelleta
Cala en
Turqueta
Cala
d'es Talaier
Arenal de Son Saura
Torre
Trencada
ME1
Torre
Llucalària
Naveta des
Tudons
Punta
Nati
Ciutadella
Cap de
Bajolí
Santandría
Cala Blanca
Son
Catlar
Cap de
Banyos
Son Xoriguer
Platja
Cala en Bosc
Cap
d'Artrux
To Port d'Alcúdia;
Cala Rajada

MEDITERRANEAN SEA

FESTIVAL TIME

Each town celebrates the feast day of its patron saint. The biggest is the **Festa de Sant Joan**, held in Ciutadella in the third to last week of June; the high point is 23 June, the eve of the saint's feast day, although the atmosphere in the streets builds over preceding evenings. It is one of Spain's best-known and most traditional festivals, featuring busy processions, prancing horses, performances of traditional music and dancing, and lots of partying. The season finishes with the **Festa de Mare de Déu de Gràcia** in Maó on 8 September.

Menorca's festivals are steeped in longheld traditions; jousting tournaments and other medieval games are common fare. The locals pride themselves particularly on their riding skills, and during some fiestas prancing horses are ridden into the crowds, rearing on their hind legs and spinning in circles.

at Maó's busy port, and Menorca's airport is 7km southwest of the city. The main road (ME1) runs along the middle of the island to Ciutadella, Menorca's second town, with secondary roads leading north and south to the resorts and beaches.

The northern half of the island is an undulating area of green rolling hills, with a rugged, rocky coastline. The southern half is flatter and drier, with a smoother coastline and sandy beaches between high cliffs.

Getting Around
TO/FROM THE AIRPORT
Menorca's **airport** (☎ 971 15 70 00) is served by buses to Maó (€1.50, 15 minutes) every half-hour from around 6am to 10pm and then hourly to midnight. The bus stops at the bus station and the Estació Marítima.

BUS
Do not expect to move around the island fast on the buses. You can get to quite a few destinations from Maó, but, with a few exceptions, services are infrequent and sluggish.

CAR, MOTORCYCLE & BICYCLE
In Maó, try **Autos Valls** (☎ 971 35 42 44; Plaça d'Espanya 13) or **Autosmenorsur** (☎ 971 36 56 66; Carrer de la Lluna 23 & Moll de Llevant 35). All the biggies

have reps at the airport. Daily hire can cost €35 to €45 for something like an Opel Corsa or Ford Focus.

MAÓ
pop 24,160
The British have invaded Menorca four times (if you count the modest campaign that began with the first charter flight from London in 1953). As a result Maó, the capital, is an unusual blend of Anglo and Spanish characteristics.

The British made it the capital in 1713, and the influence of their almost 100-year rule (the island reverted to Spanish rule in 1802) is still evident in the town's architecture, traditions and culture. Even today the majority of Maó's visitors come from Britain.

Maó's harbour is its most impressive feature and was the drawcard for the Brits. The deep, well-protected waters handle everything from small fishing boats to tankers. The town is built atop the cliffs that line the harbour's southern shore. Although some older buildings still remain, the majority of the architecture is in the restrained 18th-century Georgian style (note the sash windows!).

Information
Ciber Principal (☎ 971 36 26 89; Carrer Nou 25; per hr €3.50; ☽ 9.30am-10pm Mon-Fri, 11am-2pm & 6-10pm Sat & Sun) Provides Internet access.
Hospital Verge del Toro (☎ 971 15 77 00; Carrer de Barcelona s/n)
Policía Nacional (Carrer de la Concepció 1)
Post office (Carrer del Bon Aire 11-13; ☽ 8.30am-8.30pm Mon-Fri, 9.30am-2pm Sat)
Tourist office (☎ 971 36 37 90; Carrer de sa Rovellada de Dalt 24; ☽ 9am-1.30pm & 5-7pm Mon-Fri, 9am-1pm Sat)
Tourist office branch (Moll de Llevant 2; ☽ 8am-9pm Mon-Fri, 9am-1pm Sat)

Sights & Activities
OLD QUARTER
Maó's main plaza is the large Plaça de s'Esplanada. A **craft and clothing market** is held here every Saturday.

The narrow streets to the east of here comprise the oldest part of Maó. The **Arc de Sant Roc**, a 16th-century archway at the top end of Carrer de Sant Roc, is the only remaining relic of the medieval walls that once surrounded the old city.

The **Església de Santa Maria la Major**, further east on Plaça de la Constitució, was

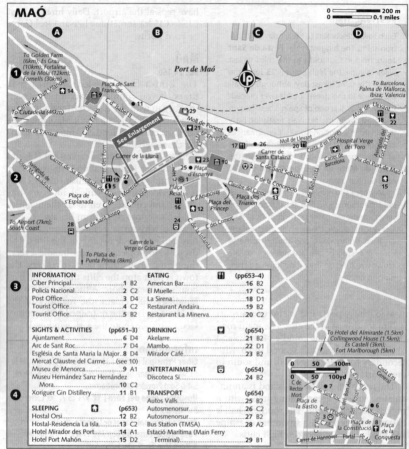

MAÓ

0 ————— 200 m
0 ————— 0.1 miles

Port de Maó

To Golden Farm (6km); Es Grau (10km); Fortalesa de la Mola (12km); Fornells (30km)

Plaça de Sant Francesc

To Ciutadella (46km)

To Barcelona, Palma de Mallorca, Ibiza; Valencia

Moll de Ponent

Moll de Llevant

Hospital Verge del Toro

To Airport (7km); South Coast

To Platja de Punta Prima (8km)

Carrer de la Verge de Gràcia

To Hotel del Almirante (1.5km); Collingwood House (1.5km); Es Castell (3km); Fort Marlborough (5km)

INFORMATION		
Ciber Principal	1	B2
Policia Nacional	2	C2
Post Office	3	D4
Tourist Office	4	C2
Tourist Office	5	B2

SIGHTS & ACTIVITIES	(pp651–3)	
Ajuntament	6	D4
Arc de Sant Roc	7	D4
Església de Santa Maria la Major	8	D4
Mercat Claustre del Carme	(see 10)	
Museu de Menorca	9	A1
Museu Hernández Sanz Hernández Mora	10	C2
Xoriguer Gin Distillery	11	B1

SLEEPING	(p653)	
Hostal Orsi	12	B2
Hostal-Residencia La Isla	13	C2
Hotel Mirador des Port	14	A1
Hotel Port Mahón	15	D2

EATING	(pp653–4)	
American Bar	16	B2
El Muelle	17	C2
La Sirena	18	D1
Restaurant Andaira	19	B2
Restaurant La Minerva	20	C2

DRINKING	(p654)	
Akelarre	21	B2
Mambo	22	D1
Mirador Café	23	B2

ENTERTAINMENT	(p654)	
Discoteca Sí	24	B2

TRANSPORT	(p654)	
Autos Valls	25	B2
Autosmenorsur	26	C2
Autosmenorsur	27	B2
Bus Station (TMSA)	28	A2
Estació Marítima (Main Ferry Terminal)	29	B1

0 ———— 50 ———— 100m
0 ———— 50 ———— 100yd

Plaça de la Constitució

Plaça de la Conquesta

---

completed in 1287, but rebuilt during the 18th century. It houses a massive organ built in Barcelona and shipped across in 1810. At the northern end of this plaza is the **ajuntament** (town hall).

PLAÇA D'ESPANYA

Just off Plaça d'Espanya is the **Mercat Claustre del Carme**, where former church cloisters have been imaginatively converted into a market and shopping centre. Upstairs enjoy temporary art exhibitions and the modest **Museu Hernández Sanz Hernández Mora** (☎ 971 35 05 97; admission free; 10am-1pm Mon-Sat), devoted to Menorcan themes and dominated by art works, maps and decorative items going as far back as the 18th century.

MUSEU DE MENORCA

This former 15th-century Franciscan **monastery** (☎ 971 35 09 55; Plaça de Sant Francesc; adult/child & senior €2.40/free, Sat afternoon & Sun free; 10am-2pm & 6-8.30pm Tue-Sat, 10am-2pm Sun & holidays) has had a chequered history. From the time the Franciscans were obliged to abandon the premises in 1835 after Mendizábal's expropriations, the buildings embarked on a colourful career path – ranging from nautical school and public library to high school and children's home.

The permanent museum collection covers the earliest history of the island, the Roman and Byzantine eras and Muslim Menorca, and includes paintings and other material from more recent times, too.

FORTS & MANSIONS

From the time Great Britain took control of Menorca, Maó's value as a port was clear. And so they built **Fort Malborough** (☎ 971 36 04 62; adult/child under 16 & senior/child under 7 €3/1.80/free; Sun free; 🕑 10am-1pm & 5-8pm Tue-Sat, 10am-1pm Sun) above the charming emerald green inlet, Cala de Sant Esteve (2.5km beyond Es Castell, which to the Brits was Georgetown), southeast of Maó. Most of the fortress was excavated into the rock below surface level, and the 45-minute visit, with videos and sound effects (incoming cannon balls!), is well worth it. On some summer evenings concerts are staged here.

To more fully immerse yourself in the area's British colonial past, stop at **Collingwood House** (Hotel del Almirante; ☎ 971 36 27 00; www.hoteldelalmirante.com; Fonduco, Es Castell; s/d to €60/95.25; 🔲 🅿), once the residence of Nelson's fellow commander-at-sea and now a charming hotel, replete with maritime reminiscences, pool, terrace, bar, restaurant and wonderful views over the port of Maó. With its heavy carpets, dark-timber doors and furniture, and countless paintings and sketches of great vessels and their commanders, you could almost be in a minor museum. It's on the road about halfway between Maó and Es Castell (the two are connected by regular local buses: €1.15, 15 minutes).

In the 19th century Queen Isabel II ordered the construction of a new fortress, the **Fortalesa de la Mola** (☎ 971 36 21 00; admission €4; 🕑 6pm Tue, Wed & Fri, 10am Sun Jul-Sep, 5pm Tue & 10am Sun Jun & Oct, 11am Sun Nov-May) out on the promontory of the same name on the northern shore of the bay. About a 12km drive from Maó and still owned by the military, it can only be visited at limited times – ask at the tourist office. The 2½-hour guided tours take you rambling through galleries, gun emplacements (armed with Vickers guns) and barracks.

On the way back towards Maó you'll notice a rose-coloured stately home surrounded by gardens on a high point near Sant Antoni. **Golden Farm** (Granja Dorada) is private property and can't be visited, but they say Nelson and his lover Lady Hamilton enjoyed a tryst here in 1799. You can also see it across the bay from Collingwood House.

XORIGUER GIN DISTILLERY

On the waterfront, head to the **distillery** (☎ 971 36 21 97; Moll de Ponent 93; 🕑 8am-7pm Mon-Fri, 9am-1pm Sat), where you can try the local gin, another British legacy. At the front is a liquor outlet and souvenir shop where visitors can help themselves to free samples. Menorcan gin is distinctively aromatic and very tasty. You can also try various strange liqueurs and tonics.

BEACHES

The closest decent beaches to the capital are **Es Grau** to the north and **Platja de Punta Prima** to the south. Both are connected to Maó by local bus.

HARBOUR CRUISES

Numerous operators offer glass-bottomed boat cruises around the harbour. These can be a pleasant way to kill an hour or two and generally cost around €8.50/4 (adult/child) for an hour.

Sleeping

Hostal Orsi (☎ 971 36 47 51; Carrer de la Infanta 19; s/d with washbasin €23/38, d with shower €45-47) This is a bright, clean and well-located hostal that's often full to bursting.

Hostal-Residencia La Isla (☎ 971 36 64 92; Carrer de Santa Catalina 4; s/d €26/47) This large, family-run hostal is excellent value, with spacious rooms all with own bathroom.

Hotel Port Mahón (☎ 971 36 26 00; www.sethotels .com; Avinguda del Port de Maó; s/d from €78/132, d with port views €156; 🔲 🔲) This fine hotel's rose façade fronts 72 marble-clad rooms, a pool and pleasant gardens. It also has luxurious suites. Try to get a room fronted by a balcony with a grand view over the port.

Hotel Mirador des Port (☎ 971 36 00 16; www .hoteles-catalonia.es; Carrer de Dalt Vilanova 1; s/d €109/150; 🔲 🔲) The disadvantage of this modern and slightly ageing hotel is that it's out of the town centre, but it makes up for it with comfortable rooms and terrific vistas of the port and back across to the old town.

Eating

American Bar (☎ 971 36 18 22; Plaça Reial 8; mains €8-10) Pull up a seat outside on the terrace in front of this rambling café to linger over breakfast and a newspaper.

BALEARIC ISLANDS

Maó's harbour is lined with restaurants and bars; most offer alfresco dining. Also worth investigating are the many waterfront eateries in Calles Fonts, just 3km away in Es Castell.

El Muelle (Moll de Llevant 33; meals €15; ☺ lunch only Mon-Fri & Sat) The food may look unappetising, but you get well-prepared fish dishes and tapas with none of the pointless frills and spills of more upmarket spots further around the waterfront. It's generally patronised by locals, who also like the *bocadillos*.

La Sirena (☎ 971 35 07 40; Moll de Llevant 199; meals €25; ☺ Wed-Mon) A strong vegetarian slant, with dishes such as vegetable roast, sit a little oddly alongside such meaty treats as hot turkey curry. You could start your meal with a summer Spanish fave, *gazpacho* (cold tomato soup).

Restaurant La Minerva (☎ 971 35 19 95; Moll de Llevant 87; meals €30-35) Dine out on seafood on the boat moored to the waterfront. It may all look a bit cheesy (it is), but this doesn't stop the kitchen from pouring out good fish and seafood – cooked lightly, just as it should be.

Restaurant Andaira (☎ 971 36 68 17; Carrer des Forn 61; meals €30-35; ☺ dinner Mon-Sat Apr-Dec) Away from all the seaside chomping fun, this is a more intimate dining experience. Eat carefully prepared Med cuisine, with the occasional funky twist (eg, beef prepared in yoghurt and parsley) inside or in the shade of a lemon tree out the back.

Drinking & Entertainment

Nightlife in Maó is low key in comparison to Mallorca or Ibiza. Most of the bars are down along the waterfront.

Mirador Café (☎ 971 35 21 07; Plaça d'Espanya 9; ☺ 10am-2am Mon-Sat) In a laneway between the top of Costa de ses Voltes and the Mercat Claustre del Carme, this is a popular little music bar with a cavelike interior carved out of the old walls above the harbour.

Akelarre (☎ 971 36 85 20; Moll de Ponent 41-43; ☺ 8am-5am) Ambient and jazz dance music dominate the wee hours in this place, one of the best late-night options in a small town.

Mambo (☎ 971 35 67 82; www.mambo-menorca .com; Moll de Llevant 209; ☺ 10pm-4am Thu-Sat) Music is a strong point here. A broad range is played, and you can sway inside or opt for a spot on the little terrace instead.

Discoteca Sí (Carrer de la Verge de Gràcia 16; ☺ midnight-6am) If Mambo isn't enough, you can always head uphill for the town's only club, a fairly rough-and-ready disco playing anything from Spanish rock to house.

Getting There & Away

You can catch **TMSA** (☎ 971 36 04 75) buses from the bus station just off the southwest end of Plaça de s'Esplanada. Six go to Ciutadella (€3.90) via Alaior (€1.10), Es Mercadal (€1.90) and Ferreries (€2.40). It also has regular services to the south-coast beaches, including Platje de Punta Prima (€1.15). Occasional services run to Fornells (€2.55, one hour) and Santa Galdana (€3.20, one hour).

THE INTERIOR – MAÓ TO CIUTADELLA

Menorca's main road, from Maó to Ciutadella, divides the island into north and south. It passes through the towns of Alaior, Es Mercadal and Ferreries, and along the way smaller roads branch off towards the beaches and resorts of the north and south coasts.

Many of the island's most significant archaeological relics are signposted off the main road.

Alaior is home to the (run-down) local cheese and shoe industries. You'll find several outlets where you can taste and buy, including **La Payesa** (☎ 971 37 10 72; Carrer des Forn 69-75; ☺ 9am-1pm & 4-7pm Mon-Fri). Sales are across the road at No 64.

In the centre of the island, **Es Mercadal** is perhaps most notable as the turn-off for Fornells. You also turn here to get to **Monte El Toro** (357m), Menorca's highest point. A steep and twisting road leads to the summit, which is shared by a 16th-century **church** and **Augustine monastery**, a cluster of satellite dishes and radio towers, and a statue of Christ (built to honour the dead of the civil war). You can see across the island in all directions and on a clear day as far as Mallorca.

Ferreries is Menorca's highest town. Each Saturday morning the **Mercat de Ferreries** takes place, with stallholders selling fresh produce, along with traditional Menorcan crafts and artworks. On other days, however, there are few reasons to linger. The turn-off to the resort of Santa Galdana is just west of here.

CIUTADELLA

pop 19,360

Founded by Carthaginians and known to the Muslims as Medina Minurqa, Ciutadella was almost destroyed following the 1558 Turkish invasion and much of the city was subsequently rebuilt in the 17th century. It was Menorca's capital until the British arrived.

Known as Vella i Bella (The Old and the Beautiful), Ciutadella is an attractive and distinctly Spanish city with a picturesque port and an engaging old quarter. Its character is quite distinct from that of Maó, and its historic centre is far more appealing.

Information

Policía Nacional (Ajuntament, Plaça d'es Born)
Post office (Plaça d'es Born; ☾ 8.30am-8.30pm Mon-Fri, 9.30am-1pm Sat)
Tourist office (☎ 971 38 26 93; Plaça de la Catedral 5; ☾ 9am-9pm Jun-Sep; 9am-9pm Mon-Fri, 9am-1pm Sat May & Oct; 9am-1.30pm & 5-7pm Mon-Fri Nov-Apr)

Sights & Activities

The main square, Plaça d'es Born, is surrounded by palm trees and gracious 19th-century buildings, including the post office, the **ajuntament** (town hall) and the **Palau Torresaura**. In the centre of the square is an **obelisk**, raised to commemorate those townsfolk who died trying to ward off the Turks on 9 July 1558.

Costa d'es Moll takes you down to the port from Plaça d'es Born. Heading in the other direction, the cobbled laneways and streets between Plaça d'es Born and Plaça d'Alfons III hold plenty of interest, with simple whitewashed buildings alongside ornate churches and elegant palaces. The pedestrian walkway of **Ses Voltes** (The Arches) has a vaguely North African flavour, and is lined with glamorous shops and boutiques, restaurants and smoky bars.

Architectural landmarks worth looking out for include the 14th-century **catedral** (☎ 971 38 07 39; Plaça de la Catedral; ☾ closed for repairs at the time of writing), built in Catalan Gothic style (although with a baroque central façade) on the site of Medina Minurqa's central mosque; the baroque 17th-century churches **Església dels Socors** (Carrer dels Socors), which houses the **Museu Diocesà** (☎ 971 48 12 97;

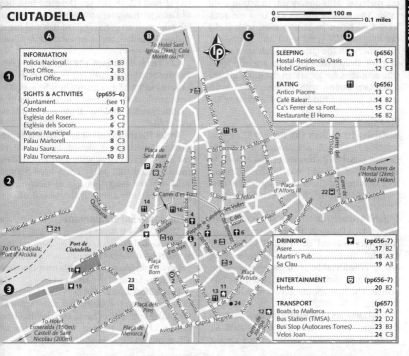

CIUTADELLA

INFORMATION	
Policía Nacional	1 B3
Post Office	2 B3
Tourist Office	3 B3

SIGHTS & ACTIVITIES	(pp655–6)
Ajuntament	(see 1)
Catedral	4 B2
Església del Roser	5 C2
Església dels Socors	6 C2
Museu Municipal	7 B1
Palau Martorell	8 C3
Palau Saura	9 C3
Palau Torresaura	10 B3

SLEEPING		(p656)
Hostal-Residència Oasis	11	C3
Hotel Gèminis	12	C3

EATING		(p656)
Antico Piacere	13	C3
Café Balear	14	B2
Ca's Ferrer de sa Font	15	C2
Restaurante El Horno	16	B2

DRINKING		(pp656–7)
Asere	17	B2
Martin's Pub	18	A3
Sa Clau	19	A3

ENTERTAINMENT		(pp656–7)
Herba	20	B2

TRANSPORT		(p657)
Boats to Mallorca	21	A2
Bus Station (TMSA)	22	D2
Bus Stop (Autocares Torres)	23	B3
Velos Joan	24	C3

adult/student/senior €2.40/1.80/1.20; ☒ 10.30am-1.30pm Tue-Sat), and **Església del Roser** (Carrer del Roser), now used as an occasional exhibition gallery; and impressive noble families' mansions, such as **Palau Martorell** (Carrer del Santíssim 7) and **Palau Saura** (Carrer del Santíssim 2; admission free; ☒ 10am-1pm & 6-9pm Mon-Sat), used for temporary exhibitions.

The **Museu Municipal** (☎ 971 38 02 97; Bastió de sa Font; adult/senior/child under 12 €1.20/0.60/free; ☒ 10am-2pm Tue-Sat) contains displays recounting the island's story from prehistory to medieval times.

West of the town centre, the southern head of the port entrance is dominated by the stout little **Castell de Sant Nicolau** (☎ 971 38 10 50; Plaça del Almirante Ferragut; admission free; ☒ 11am-1pm & 6-8pm Tue-Sat). The views west to Mallorca and south down the coast are lovely.

About 2km east of the town centre is an original 'monument'. The **Pedreres de s'Hostal** (☎ 971 48 15 78, Camí Vell; adult/child under 11 €3/free; ☒ 9.30am-sunset) is an extensive series of stone quarries. The bleached *marés* stone, extracted here and in other quarries around the island, has historically been Menorca's main building material. This quarry was in action until 1994. The bizarre shapes cut into the rock were first hewn by strong men with picks (as long as 200 years ago) and later with machinery. In the latter – which are a series of giant, deep pits – concerts are organised (the acoustics are great). In the older quarry a **botanical garden**, with endemic Menorcan species, grows amid the weird 'sculpture'.

Sleeping

Hostal-Residencia Oasis (☎ 971 38 21 97; Carrer de Sant Isidre 33; d €46-50) Set around a spacious garden courtyard, this quiet place close to the heart of the old quarter has pleasant rooms, some of them done up in the past two years and most with private bathroom. There are no singles.

Hotel Gèminis (☎ 971 38 46 44; Carrer de Josepa Rossinyol 4; s/d €50/80) A friendly, stylish two-star place located on a back street, this graceful, three-storey rose-white lodging offers comfortable if somewhat neutral rooms just a short walk away from the city centre. The best rooms have a nice balcony to boot.

Hotel Esmeralda (☎ 971 43 35 40; www.mac-hotels .com; Passeig de Sant Nicolau 171; s/d €64.25/102.50; ☒ ☒) A somewhat rambunctious tourist three-star hotel, the main advantage of this big, curving corner block is that you will be hard pressed to miss out on a room with views over to the Sant Nicolau fort and west out to the sunset and sea.

Hotel Sant Ignasi (☎ 971 38 55 75; www.sant ignasi.com; Carretera de Cala Morell s/n; rooms per person €107; ☒ ☒ ℗) This tranquil rural hotel is a fine retreat 3km outside Ciutadella. It boasts a pleasant garden, bar and pool.

Eating

Ciutadella's small port is teeming with restaurants and cafés, many of which are set in the old city walls or carved out of the cliffs that line the waterfront.

Café Balear (☎ 971 38 00 05; Plaça de Sant Joan 15; meals €25-30; ☒ lunch only Tue-Sat & Sun Dec-Oct) Sometimes the old timers are the best. Set apart from the town's more frenetic restaurant activity, this remains one of Ciutadella's classic seafood stops. You can eat outside and admire the old quarter towering before you while tucking into local prawns or *navalles* (a strange tubular seafood delicacy).

Restaurante El Horno (☎ 971 38 07 67; Carrer d'es Forn 12; meals €25; ☒ Mon-Sat) Descend into the old quarter basement for wholesome Spanish fare, with an even range of fish and meat dishes, including the seasonal *civet de jabalí* (wild boar stew).

Ca's Ferrer de sa Font (☎ 971 48 07 84; Carrer del Portal de sa Font 16; meals €35; ☒ Tue-Sun Apr-Jan) Located in an 18th-century building, this is a romantic place offering a mix of inventive Mediterranean cooking. It offers a *menú del día* at €16.

Antico Piacere (☎ 971 48 20 72; Carrer de St Pere Alcantara 35; meals €25; ☒ Mon-Sat) For a change, try this Italian eatery with a mix of dishes from around that other Latin Med peninsula. Try the tangy *gnocchi al Gorgonzola* (potato pasta in a strong cheese sauce).

Drinking & Entertainment

Sa Clau (Carrer de la Marina 199; ☒ 7pm-4am) For a post-prandial cocktail, drop by here on the waterfront at the bottom of Costa d'es Moll. Set in the old quarter walls, this hip piano bar sometimes features live jazz and blues.

Martin's Pub (Costa d'es Moll 20; ☒ 9pm-4am) Here they pump out throbbing *bakalao* (Spanish techno) and plenty of beer. The tiny interior fills quickly and punters soon find themselves out on the lane with their tipples.

Asere (Carrer de Capllonch 15; ☉ 10am-5am) As the man behind the bar will tell you, Asere is Cuban for 'mate'. So slip into the Havana mood with a little rum and rhythm.

Herba (Placa de Sant Joan; ☉ 11pm-4am) Lined up with a set of other bars and clubs facing or near the car park, this spot has a funky feel, with a broad range of music and plenty of that Balearic classic, *pomade*, to sip on.

Getting There & Away

Boats for Mallorca (Port d'Alcúdia and Cala Ratjada) leave from the northern side of the Port de Ciutadella. For details, see Getting There & Around, p617.

TMSA (Carrer de Barcelona 8) runs buses between Ciutadella and Maó. **Autocares Torres** (☎ 971 38 64 61) buses serve the coast south of Ciutadella from Plaça dels Pins.

Getting Around

You can hire mountain bikes from **Velos Joan** (☎ 971 38 15 76; Carrer de Sant Isidre 28) for €7 per day, as well as Vespas and scooters (€57 to €72 for two days, depending on the model).

NORTH COAST

Menorca's north coast is rugged and rocky, dotted with small and scenic coves. It's less developed than the south and, with your

---

MENORCA'S PREHISTORIC HERITAGE

Menorca's interior is liberally sprinkled with reminders of its ancient heritage. Many of the most significant sites and monuments are open to the public (with free admission!). These places provide fascinating insights into the past, although many of the minor sites present little but crumbling ruins.

The monuments are linked to three main periods: the Pre-Talayotic Period (or cave era) from 2000 BC to 1300 BC; the Talayotic Period (or Bronze Age) from 1300 BC to 800 BC; and the Post-Talayotic Period (or Iron Age) from 800 BC to around 100 BC. Similarly, there are three types of structures: *navetas*, *talayots* and *taulas*.

Navetas, built from large rocks in the shape of upturned boat hulls, are thought to have been used as either tombs or meeting places – perhaps both.

Talayots, large stone mounds found all over the island, were perhaps used as watchtowers for each settlement.

Unique to Menorca, *taulas* are huge stone tablets precisely balanced in the shape of a 'T'. It has been suggested that they could have been used as sacrificial altars but, as with Stonehenge, nobody is sure how these enormous slabs of stone were moved into position or what they signify.

Off the main road 3km west of Maó, the *talayotic* settlement of **Talatí de Dalt** (adult/student & senior/child under 8 €3/1.50/free; ☉ 10am-sunset) is one of the most interesting sites. It's about five minutes' walk from the car park to the main feature, a well-preserved *taula*.

About 4km further along on the northern side of the road is **Rafal Rubí**, a pair of well-preserved burial *navetas*.

The nearby **Torralba d'en Salord** (☎ 971 37 83 85; adult/student & senior/child under 16 €3/1.50/free; ☉ 10am-8pm Jun-Sep, 10am-1pm & 3-6pm Mon-Sat Oct-May) is another *talayotic* settlement whose outstanding feature is an impressive *taula*.

South of Alaior is the large **Torre d'en Gaumès** (admission €2.40; ☉ 10am-2pm & 5-8pm Tue-Sun) settlement, which includes three *talayots* on a hilltop and a collection of circular dwellings.

Further south on the coast at **Cales Coves**, some 90 caves dug into the coastal cliffs were apparently used for ritual burials. More recently some of the caves have been homes to hippy colonies, and nearby the large **Cova des Xoroi** (adult/child €5/2.50; ☉ 9.30am-7pm) can be visited as a sight by day or as a club by night. The sunset chill-out scene starts around 7pm and the disco gets into action around midnight to 5am. Foreign DJs make regular summer appearances and Ibiza-style foam parties happen on Thursday.

South of Ciutadella, **Son Catlar** (adult/student & senior/child under 16 €3/1.50/free; ☉ 10am-sunset) is the largest *talayotic* settlement in the Balearic Islands. Its five *talayots* and the remains of its dwellings cover around six hectares. East of Ciutadella (near the 40km road marker), the **Naveta des Tudons** is a stone burial chamber.

own transport and a bit of footwork, you'll discover some of the Balearics' best off-the-beaten-track beaches.

Maó to Fornells

North of Maó, head first for **Es Grau**, a plain hamlet on an open bay. The beach is OK and you can kick back at a couple of bar-restaurants.

Inland from Es Grau and separated from the coast by a barrier of high sand dunes is the **Parc Natural S'Albufera d'es Grau**, the largest freshwater lagoon in the Balearic Islands. Home to many species of wetland birds and an important stopover for migrating species, S'Albufera and the surrounding countryside have been designated the 'nucleus zone' of Menorca's Biosphere Reserve, a natural park protected from the threat of development. **Illa d'en Colom**, a couple of hundred metres offshore, is considered part of the park. Boats of the **Viajes Isla Colom company** (☎ 971 35 98 67) splutter across to the island from Es Grau up to four times a day in summer (€14.20 return, 15 minutes).

The drive up to **Cap de Favàritx**, a narrow rocky cape at the top of the Parc Natural S'Albufera d'es Grau zone, is a treat. The last leg is across a lunar-like landscape of black rock. At the end of the road a **lighthouse** stands watch as the sea pounds relentlessly against the impassive cliffs.

South of the cape stretch some fine sandy bays and beaches, including **Cala Presili** and **Platja d'en Tortuga**, reachable on foot.

Fornells

pop 790

This picturesque whitewashed village is on a large, shallow bay popular with windsurfers. Fornells has come to be known for its waterfront seafood restaurants, most of which serve up the local (and rather pricey) speciality, *caldereta de llagosta*.

MENORCA'S TOP FIVE BEACHES

- **Cala Macarelleta** (p659)
- **Cala en Turqueta** (p659)
- **Cala Pregonda** (p658)
- **Cala Presili** (p658)
- **Cala Morell** (p659)

SIGHTS & ACTIVITIES

If the sight of those fishing boats bobbing in the bay stirs the seawolf in your soul, embark on a two-hour catamaran trip with **Catamaran Charter** (☎ 626-486426; www.catamaran charter.net; Passeig Marítim; €55 per person). You will also find a windsurfing school and a couple of diving outfits as you head south out of the village.

At the edge of town stands the squat, round defensive tower, the **Torre de Fornells** (admission €2.40; ☿ 11am-2pm & 5-8pm Tue-Sun Jun-Sep).

A couple of kilometres west at **Platges de Fornells**, the development frenzy has been unleashed on the coastal hills surrounding a small beach. The exclusive villas of the Menorca Country Club resort dominate this ritzy *urbanització* (urban development).

If you want to escape the crowds, continue west to the beach of **Binimella**, from where you can walk around to the unspoilt beaches at **Cala Pregonda**.

SLEEPING

Hostal La Palma (☎ 971 37 66 34; Plaça S'Algaret 3; s/d to €40/75; ☒ ☒) Out the back of this bar-restaurant are cheerful rooms with bathrooms, balconies and views of the surrounding countryside. Singles aren't available in summer.

Hostal Fornells (☎ 971 37 66 76; Carrer Major 17; s/d €84.50/116.70; ☿ Apr-Oct; ☒ ☒) Behinds the typical whitewashed façade on a pedestrian lane sheltering just behind the port, this is a slick option, with a bar and restaurant. A variety of rooms have views of the sea, the courtyard pool or the back country. Rooms without views in October cost less than a third of the above prices!

EATING

The restaurants along the foreshore are all pretty expensive, and if you're here to try *caldereta de llagosta*, you're up for €50 to €60.

Es Cranc (☎ 971 37 64 42; Carrer de Tramuntana 31; meals €35-60; ☿ Thu-Tue) If you're happy to pay, head for this congenial spot on a street a couple of blocks inland. It has a simple dining room and a strong reputation. You can splash out on *caldereta de llagosta* (€60) or even *paella de llagosta* (€120 for two). Fresh delivery of lobster from a half-dozen local fishing vessels is guaranteed.

Es Plá (☎ 971 37 66 55; Passatge Es Pla s/n; meals €30) You can live without lobster but want melt-in-the-mouth seafood? Try this spot, with tables literally at the water's edge. The *lenguado* (sole) is prepared in a rich seafood sauce and vegetables. The *menú del día* (€16) is good value for this town.

Around Ciutadella

North of Ciutadella, **Cala Morell** is a low-key development of whitewashed villas. Steep steps lead to the small port and beach, backed by a couple of bar-restaurants. More intriguing is the **Cala Morell Necropolis**, prehistoric burial caves hacked into the coastal cliffs along a track leading away from the beach.

Before reaching Cala Morell, a right turn to **Algaiarens** leads you to a privately owned **park** (admission €5 per car; ⏰ 10am-7pm), with a parking area, a small lake and pristine beaches.

SOUTH COAST

Menorca's southern flank tends to have the better beaches – and thus the greater concentration of development. The recurring image is of a jagged coastline, occasionally interrupted by a small inlet with a sandy beach and backed by a growing cluster of gleaming white villas. Menorca has largely opted for small-scale developments in the 'Moorish-Mediterranean' style, modelled on the resort of Binibèquer (or Binibeca), near the southeast corner, designed by the architect Antonio Sintes in 1972.

The rugged coastline south of Ciutadella gives way to a couple of smallish beaches at the resorts of **Santandria** and **Cala Blanca**. On the island's southwestern corner looms the large resort of **Cala en Bosc**, a busy boating and diving centre. Not far east are the popular beaches of **Platja de Son Xoriguer**, connected to Ciutadella by frequent buses.

Between Son Xoriguer and Santa Galdana lies some of the least accessible coast in the south. A series of rough tracks and walking trails leads to the beautiful, unspoiled beaches of **Arenal de Son Saura**, **Cala en Turqueta**, **Cala Macarelleta** and **Cala Macarella**.

Southwest of Ferreries is the resort of **Santa Galdana**, which is just the place if karaoke, English pubs and minigolf are your idea of a good holiday. In fairness, the beach is fine and the tack mild. A walking track leads west along the coast to the already mentioned Cala Macarella, which has a few bars. To the east of Santa Galdana, **Cala Mitjana** is another enticing strand.

Camping S'Atalai (☎ 971 37 42 32; per 2 people, tent & car €20.70) This pleasant camping ground, shaded by pine trees, is two-thirds of the way down the Ferreries–Santa Galdana road.

The resort of **Platges de Son Bou**, south of Alaior, boasts the island's longest beach and most depressing development. Just back from the beach are the remains of an ancient **Christian basilica** that dates, by some reckonings, to the 5th century AD.

Most of the coast south of Maó is more intensively developed. Regular buses sidle down to **Platje de Punta Prima**, which has a nice beach (you can even catch the occasional wave here!). West around the coast is **Binibèquer**, touted as a charming old fishing town. It has been given several coats of whitewash and turned into a tourist beehive, but the curious houses and narrow lanes, not to mention the little boat harbour with its transparent water, are attractive. A few kilometres further west lies **Cala de Binidalí**. The village is no big deal and the beach small, but the water is so azure it makes you want to swim out of the inlet and into the open sea.

Not far from Punta Prima is a fine place to stay. **Alcaufar Vell** (☎ 971 15 18 74; www.alcaufar vell.com; Carretera Alcaufar Km7.3; s/d €155/180) is a grand old mansion whipped into modern shape. Inside this white-faced 16th-century edifice, set in a dignified gravel yard, are scattered enticing rooms, with timber beams and a tranquil bucolic feel.

Murcia

Pinched between the more-trodden beaches of Almería to the south and the heaving resorts of Valencia's Costa Blanca to the north, Murcia remains one of Spain's least visited and, La Manga apart, least touristy corners.

The region's name derives from the Latin *murtae* (mulberry). For centuries the mulberry provided a diet for silkworms, exploited workers of a flourishing industry that lasted until well after WWII, when local silk could no longer compete against man-made fibres.

Murcia's coast is called La Costa Cálida (the Hot One), all 250km of it. With beaches that can rival its neighbours' and over 3000 hours of sunshine each year, you're almost guaranteed sunny days, from the tourist pulls of the Mar Menor to quieter, much more Spanish resorts as you follow the Mediterranean coast southwards.

So much sunshine means a dry, semidesert interior. But humankind has toiled over the centuries to put the little rain that falls over the region to its best use. Long occupied by Muslims from North Africa – no strangers to heat – Murcia has inherited their irrigation systems: waterwheels, aqueducts and *acequias* (canals). This network helps to distribute the stingy 300mm of annual rainfall, allowing some land to be cultivated intensively, especially for citrus crops and grapes in the El Guadalentín valley.

Local orchards and the associated canning industry are the main employers of those who live in the busy capital, also called Murcia. Cartagena, the second-largest city and Spain's premier naval port, is excavating, digging down and deep to reveal its rich classical heritage. Inland, Lorca, in its time a frontier town between Christian and Muslim Spain, is famous for its spectacular Semana Santa processions, and the unspoilt Parque Natural de Sierra Espuña draws climbers and walkers.

MURCIA

HIGHLIGHTS

- Dunk yourself in the warm, shallow waters of the **Mar Menor** (p669)
- Crawl the **heaving bars** (p665) of Murcia's university area
- Tag onto one of Lorca's spectacular **Semana Santa processions** (p669)
- Visit a selection of Cartagena's well-documented, freshly revealed **Roman and Carthaginian sites** (p666)
- Walk the trails of the **Parque Natural de Sierra Espuña** (p670)

- AREA: 11,314 SQ KM
- POP: 1,227,000
- AVE SUMMER TEMP: HIGH 34°C, LOW 19°C

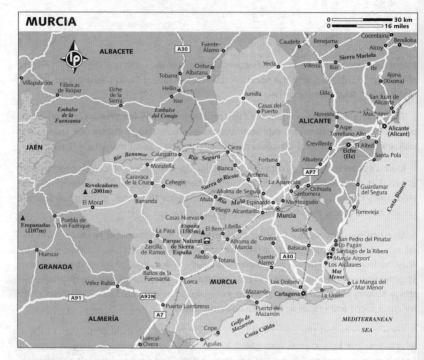

MURCIA CITY

pop 370,700

Murcia, bypassed by most tourists and unjustifiably sneered at by too many Spaniards, well merits a visit. Pass through the industrial outskirts and head straight for the river, cathedral and laid-back, partly pedestrianised heart of this university city.

The Muslims founded 'Mursiya' in AD 825 on the site of a former Roman colony. The town was then reconquered in 1243 by Alfonso X of Castilla and León (who gave his name to one of Murcia's two main thoroughfares).

Enriched by the silk industry and by agricultural prosperity, the city was at its grandest in the 18th century, when the cathedral's magnificent baroque façade was built, along with the urban palaces of the nobility and rising bourgeoisie.

Looted by Napoleonic troops in 1810, then victim of plague and cholera, the city fell into decline during the 19th century. In 1936, during the Spanish Civil War, it was the scene of bitter fighting and many of its churches were burnt down.

ORIENTATION

The city centre spreads north of the Río Segura. The main commercial thoroughfare, Gran Vía del Escultor Francisco Salzillo (usually – and thankfully – abbreviated to 'Gran Vía') runs north from the Puente Viejo (Old Bridge).

From the cathedral, pedestrianised Calle de la Trapería, the main street of medieval and Renaissance Murcia, runs north through the old town.

INFORMATION

L@ Red (Calle Antonio Puig 1; per hr €2; ☺ 10am-2pm & 4-11pm Mon-Sat, 4-11pm Sun)

Main post office (Plaza Circular; ☺ 8am-2pm Mon-Fri)

Tourist kiosk (Calle Maestro Alonso; ☺ as per tourist office)

Tourist office (☎ 968 35 87 49; www.murciaciudad.com; Plaza del Cardenal Belluga s/n; ☺ 10am-2pm & 5-9pm Mon-Sat, 10am-2pm Sun May-Sep, 4-8pm Mon-Sat Oct-Apr)

www.murcia-turismo.com A useful website covering the Murcia region.

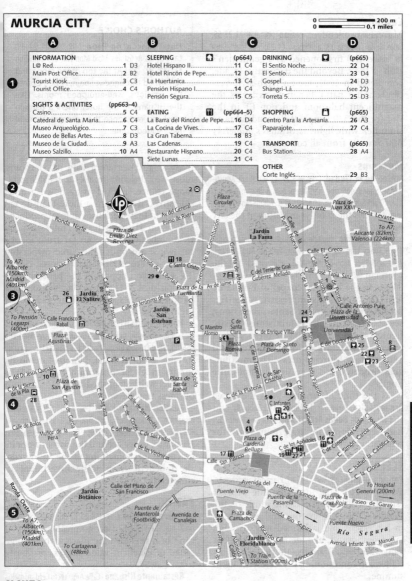

MURCIA CITY

INFORMATION		
L@ Red	1	D3
Main Post Office	2	B2
Tourist Kiosk	3	C3
Tourist Office	4	C4
SIGHTS & ACTIVITIES		(pp663–4)
Casino	5	C4
Catedral de Santa María	6	C4
Museo Arqueológico	7	C3
Museo de Bellas Artes	8	D3
Museo de la Ciudad	9	A3
Museo Salzillo	10	A4

SLEEPING		(p664)
Hotel Hispano II	11	C4
Hotel Rincón de Pepe	12	D4
La Huertanica	13	C4
Pensión Hispano I	14	C4
Pensión Segura	15	C5
EATING		(pp664–5)
La Barra del Rincón de Pepe	16	D4
La Cocina de Vives	17	C4
La Gran Taberna	18	B3
Las Cadenas	19	C4
Restaurante Hispano	20	C4
Siete Lunas	21	C4

DRINKING		(p665)
El Sentío Noche	22	D4
El Sentío	23	D4
Gospel	24	D3
Shangri-Lá	(see 22)	
Torreta 5	25	D3
SHOPPING		(p665)
Centro Para la Artesanía	26	A3
Paparajote	27	C4
TRANSPORT		(p665)
Bus Station	28	A4
OTHER		
Corte Inglés	29	B3

SIGHTS
Catedral de Santa María

Murcia's sumptuous **cathedral** (🕑 10am-1pm & 6-8pm May-Sep, 10am-1pm & 5-7pm Oct-Apr) was raised in 1358 on the site of a mosque. Building began in Gothic style, but alterations were made in the 1500s. From 1748 came dramatic changes, including the addition of the exuberant baroque façade with its tumbling cherubs. A highlight of the interior is the 15th-century flamboyant Gothic Capilla de los Vélez, its flutes and curls like piped icing sugar. For spectacular views of the city, climb the 92m tower, begun in 1519 and not completed until the 18th century (though it was closed for repairs at the time of writing).

Casino

Murcia's resplendent **casino** (☎ 968 21 22 55; Calle de la Trapería 18; admission €1.20; ⏱ 10am-9pm for nonmembers) first opened as a gentlemen's club in 1847. Beyond the decorative façade, completed in 1901, are an Arab-style vestibule and a patio. Penetrate as far as the magnificent ballroom and pop €1 in the slot for the 320 lamps of its candelabra to shimmer with light as Strauss's *Radetsky March* wafts from all corners.

Museums

Museo de la Ciudad (☎ 968 27 43 90; Plaza Agustinas 5-7; admission free; ⏱ 10am-2pm & 5-8pm Tue-Sat, 11am-2pm Sun Sep-Jun, 10am-2pm & 5-8pm Mon-Fri Jul-Aug) follows the 2000-year history of the city of Murcia.

Museo Salzillo (Plaza de San Agustín 1-3; admission €3; ⏱ 9.30am-1pm & 4-7pm Mon-Fri Jul-Aug, 11am-2pm & 5-8pm Mon-Fri Sep-Jun), devoted to the Murcian sculptor Francisco Salzillo (1707–83), is in the baroque chapel of Ermita de Jesús. It displays his impressive *pasos* (figures carried in Semana Santa processions; see p669) and his superb miniature Nativity figures – more than 500 of them clad in an eclectic mixture of Middle Eastern and 18th-century Murcian dress. The multilingual brochure has a section in not-quite English.

At the time of writing, both the **Museo Arqueológico** (Gran Vía de Alfonso X El Sabio 9) and the **Museo de Bellas Artes** (Calle del Obispo Frutos 12) had been closed for over four years for renovations.

SLEEPING

Pensión Segura (☎ 968 21 12 81; Plaza de Camachos 14; s/d €24/35; 🏠) This long-standing *pensión* (small private hotel), 150m south of the Puente Viejo, is courteous and welcoming in a pleasant, old-fashioned way. Though far from grand, it's definitely excellent value, and you'll appreciate the newly installed air-conditioning if you're visiting in summer.

Pensión Legazpi (☎ 968 29 30 81; fax 968 29 91 27; Avenida Miguel de Cervantes 8; s/d €30/40; 🏠) Although Pensión Legazpi, west of the city centre, has an uninspiring exterior and dingy corridors, its bedrooms are clean, cool and good value.

La Huertanica (☎ 968 21 76 68; fax 968 21 25 04; Calle Infantes 3-5; s/d €44/57.50; P 🏠) The rela-

tively small Huertanica with its 31 rooms, most with balcony, makes a reliable midrange choice. Tucked away down a quiet side street, it also runs a more-than-decent restaurant that specialises in local produce.

Pensión Hispano I and Hotel Hispano II, umbilically joined but far from identical twins, are under the same ownership (smile – you're on Hispano II's closed-circuit TV when you approach the pensión's reception desk). The two places also share parking facilities (a thwacking €16.05 per night).

Hotel Hispano II (☎ 968 21 61 52; www.hotelhispano .net, Spanish only; Calle Radio Murcia 3; s/d Mon-Thu €55/65, s & d Fri-Sun €49; P 🏠) This trim, comfortable modern hotel, famous foremostly for its excellent restaurant (see p664) is reliable, well established and popular with business travellers.

Pensión Hispano I (☎ 968 21 61 52; www.hotel hispano.net, Spanish only; Calle Trapería 8; s/d with shower €25/35, with bathroom €29/39; P) The Pensión Hispano I is just around the corner from its fancier sister. Something of the Cinderella, she'd benefit from some investment to smarten her up a bit.

EATING

La Cocina de Vives (☎ 968 21 22 66; Calle San Patricio 7; mains € 5-11) For economical eating, you can't beat this bustling place with its huge range of excellent-value dishes, primarily to take away.

Restaurante Hispano (Calle Arquitecto Cerdán; mains €13-16; ⏱ closed Sun Jul-Aug, closed dinner Sun Sep-Jun) Snug between hotels Hispano I and II, this, like the accommodation, is really two places – the less expensive bar and bar tables and the smart restaurant extending deep into the recesses of the building. They share a fabulous display of fresh fish and a common, creative kitchen. The three-course

AUTHOR'S CHOICE

La Gran Taberna (☎ 968 24 45 22; Avenida de la Libertad 6; mains €14-16) The street address is deceptive; go down Calle Doctor Marañon, opposite the Corte Inglés department store, and La Gran Taberna is in front of you. This is a highly regarded restaurant with impeccable service, and the walls are an attractive clutter of old menus, posters, programmes and calendars. We worked our way through their magnificent *menú tradicional* (€27), where the dishes just kept coming and coming.

lunch *menú* (set meal), eaten at the bar, is, at €10, a great deal.

Siete Lunas (☎ 968 21 89 66; Calle de los Apóstoles 16; mains €12-15, salads €8-10) This light, bright, recently opened restaurant is built around two massive hunks of Arab masonry. Fusion cooking is its theme and the highly creative menu changes radically every two weeks.

Las Cadenas (☎ 968 22 09 24; Calle de los Apóstoles 10; mains €10-16; Mon-Sat) Almost next door to Siete Lunas, Las Cadenas is all low beams and leaded windows. Cosy and friendly, this place offers more traditional but equally tasty fare based on fresh local produce.

The plush 19th-century **restaurant** (Calle de la Trapería 18; mains €11-17; lunch only Tue-Sun) at the casino is showing the cracks a little here and there but is still a wonderful dining experience, and it does an excellent *menú* for €10.

Hotel Rincón de Pepe's **restaurant** (mains €9-18) is justifiably renowned throughout Spain. To really hit the spot and your credit limit, go for its *menú degustación* at €55.

Just around the corner from Hotel Rincón, **La Barra del Rincón de Pepe**, with food from the same kitchen, does an excellent-value *menú del día* (€12).

DRINKING

Pedestrianised Plazas Romea and Santo Domingo plus Calle de la Trapería pack in the crowds at *paseo* time and well into the night. Most through-the-night life buzzes around the university, particularly south of Calle del Doctor Fleming, which pulsates with small elbow-to-elbow bars.

Favourites include **Gospel** (cnr Calle de Enrique Villar & Calle Santo Cristo), **Torreta 5** (Calle Torreta 5), and neighbours **Shangri-Lá** (Calle Trinidad 10) and **El Sentío Noche** (Calle Trinidad 12B).

To wind down later on, award yourself a nightcap at **El Sentío** (Calle Luisa Aledo 14), which is smaller and quieter than most of the alternatives.

SHOPPING

Two good places in Murcia for local handicrafts are the **Centro Para la Artesanía** (Calle Francisco Rabal 6), which is both exhibition and sales outlet, and **Paparajote** (Calle de los Apóstoles 14), near the cathedral.

GETTING THERE & AWAY

Air

Murcia's **San Javier airport** (☎ 968 17 20 00), beside the Mar Menor, is, in fact, much closer to Cartagena. A taxi between the airport and Murcia city costs around €20. There are various daily flights:

Ryanair (www.ryanair.com) to/from London (Stansted) and Birmingham
MytravelLite (www.mytravellite.com) to/from Birmingham
Jet2.com (www.jet2.com) to/from Leeds/Bradford

Bus

For information call ☎ 968 29 22 11. Local services include Cartagena (€3, one hour, at least seven daily via the motorway). For Alicante and Lorca, let the train take the strain.

Alsa has daily buses going to Granada (€19, 3½ hours, five daily), Valencia (€13.10, 3¾ hours, four to seven) and Madrid (€22, five hours, eight).

The bus station is on the western side of town, near Museo Salzillo.

Train

Up to five trains travel daily to/from Madrid (€35.30, 4½ hours). Hourly trains operate to/from Lorca (€3.70) and Alicante (€3.70, 1½ hours), from where options are greater for Valencia and Barcelona.

The train station is south of the Río Segura.

GETTING AROUND

From the bus station, take bus No 3 into town; from the train station hop aboard No 9 or 11.

MULA

It's a bit far for a detour, but the journey to Mula can be a speedy one. Leave Murcia city by the fast, four-lane C415, signed Caravaca de la Cruz and, after 20km, turn off to the little town of Mula. Park your car on the outskirts and simply meander through its narrow lanes, savouring their higgledy-piggledyness and heading eventually for the **Plaza Mayor** with its clock tower. Time allowing, take in the **Museo del Cigarralejo** – not a smoker's dream but a little museum displaying Iberian finds from the necropolis of the same name. On the way back, turn off after a couple of kilometres to **Baños de Murcia**, a tiny thermal station with a cluster of houses, a naturally heated pool and – plan to arrive around lunch time – a meal at Venta de la Magdalena, which is renowned for its tasty rice dishes.

MURCIA REGION

CARTAGENA

pop 184,700

In 223 BC Hasdrubal marched into the Iberian settlement of Mastia at the head of his invading army from Carthage, North Africa. He renamed it Carthago Nova. The town flourished during Roman occupation, and under Muslim rule became the independent emirate of Cartajana. The Arabs improved agriculture and established the town's reputation for building warships before they were expelled in 1242. The extensive defensive walls were built in the 18th century by order of Carlos III.

In the later part of the 20th century, Cartagena fell on hard times. Lead and pyrite mining, a staple of the economy since Roman times, all but ceased. The naval presence – particularly the American Sixth Fleet that periodically disgorged dollar-laden sailors on R&R – was less evident, and the dingy approach to the city centre, closed shops and dilapidated buildings all spoke recession.

But the town is picking itself up. Although Cartagena remains Spain's major naval base, more sedate cruise passengers are replacing roustabout sailors, and the re-dundant military hospital has been recycled as the campus of the Universidad Politécnica. As for tourism, the city is making huge efforts to pull itself up by its seaboot straps, digging deep into its past and stripping back more and more of its old quarter to reveal its long-buried Roman and Carthaginian heritage.

Information

Exit (Plaza del Rey 5; per hr €2; ☉ 11.15am-2.30am Mon-Sat, 3pm-2am Sun)

Post office (Plaza del Rey)

Tourist office (☎ 968 50 64 83; www.marmenor.net; Plaza del Almirante Bastarreche; ☉ 10am-2pm & 5-6pm Mon-Fri, 10am-1pm Sat)

Tourist office kiosk (Paseo del Alfonso XII)

Sights & Activities

Several rich sites from Cartagena's past have recently been restored and opened to the public under the blanket title **Puerto de Culturas** (Port of Cultures). The opening times below apply between June and September. For winter hours (still to be determined at the time of research) ring ☎ 968 50 00 93 or consult the tourist office.

For a start, and for a great panorama of town and the hills that embrace the harbour, make your way up to the **Castillo de la Concepción**, and within its remains, the **History of Cartagena Experience** (adult/child €3.5/2.5; ☉ 10am-2.30pm & 4-8pm Tue-Sun Sep-Jun, daily Jul-Aug), offering a high-tech overview of the city through the centuries. Enjoy the uphill walk or take the lift (€1).

A similar visitors centre, the **Punic Wall Experience** (Calle San Diego; adult/child €3.5/2.5; ☉ 10am-2pm & 4-8pm Tue-Sun Sep-Jun, daily Jul-Aug), built around a section of the old Punic wall, concentrates on the town's Carthaginian and Roman legacy.

Other Roman sites include the below-ground **Augusteum** (Calle de los Quatro Santos; adult/child €2.5/2; ☉ 4-8pm Tue-Sun), the **Decumanus** (off Calle Honda; adult/child €2/1; ☉ 4-8pm Tue-Sun), with the shop-lined remains of one of the town's main Roman streets, and the **Casa de la Fortuna** (Calle de los Quatro Santos; adult/child €2.50/2; ☉ 10.30am-2.30pm Tue-Fri; 10.30am-2.30pm & 4-8pm Sat & Sun), a Roman villa demonstrating daily life of the time.

The **Museum of the Civil War** (Calle Gisbert; adult/child €3.5/2.5; ☉ 10am-2.30pm & 4-8pm Tue-Sun Sep-Jun, daily Jul-Aug), in a former air-raid shelter,

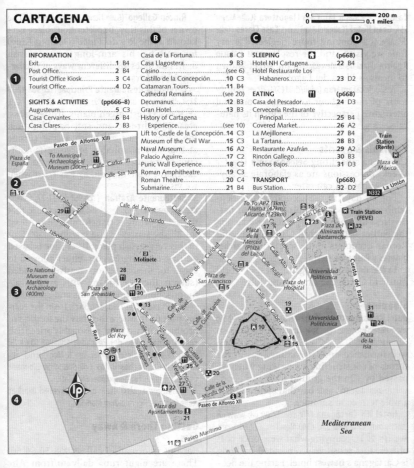

CARTAGENA

0		200 m
0		0.1 miles

INFORMATION
Exit...1 B4
Post Office......................................2 B4
Tourist Office Kiosk.......................3 C4
Tourist Office................................4 D2

SIGHTS & ACTIVITIES   (pp666–8)
Augusteum.....................................5 C3
Casa Cervantes..............................6 B4
Casa Clares....................................7 B3

Casa de la Fortuna.........................8 C3
Casa Llagostera.............................9 B3
Casino..(see 6)
Castillo de la Concepción............10 C3
Catamaran Tours..........................11 B4
Cathedral Remains...................(see 20)
Decumanus..................................12 B3
Gran Hotel...................................13 B3
History of Cartagena
  Experience..............................(see 10)
Lift to Castle de la Concepción....14 C3
Museum of the Civil War..............15 C3
Naval Museum.............................16 A2
Palacio Aguirre.............................17 C2
Punic Wall Experience..................18 B3
Roman Amphitheatre....................19 C3
Roman Theatre.............................20 C4
Submarine....................................21 B4

SLEEPING   (p668)
Hotel NH Cartagena......................22 B4
Hotel Restaurante Los
  Habaneros...............................23 D2

EATING   (p668)
Casa del Pescador.........................24 D3
Cervecería Restaurante
  Principal..................................25 B4
Covered Market............................26 A2
La Mejillonera..............................27 B4
La Tartana....................................28 B3
Restaurante Azafrán......................29 A2
Rincón Gallego.............................30 B3
Techos Bajos................................31 D3

TRANSPORT   (p668)
Bus Station...................................32 D2

presents Cartagena's more recent and more violent history.

The huge grey cigar on Paseo del Alfonso XII is a prototype **submarine** built in 1888 by local inventor Isaac Peral, who, alas, failed to convince the Spanish navy that such a means of propulsion could have a future.

Nearby, to the northeast, are the remains of the 13th-century **cathedral**, devastated by aerial bombardment during the Spanish Civil War and originally constructed from recycled slabs and pillars from the adjacent and now renovated **roman theatre** (admission free; 10.30am-1.30pm & 5-7pm Mon-Sat, to 1.30pm Sun).

The remains of the **Roman Amphitheatre** (admission free; 10am-2pm Tue-Sun, 12.30-1.30pm Mon) lie beneath the former bullring.

The **Municipal Archaeological Museum** (Calle Ramón y Cajal 45; admission free; 10am-2pm & 5-8pm Tue-Fri, 11am-2pm Sat & Sun), built above a late-Roman cemetery, has a rich display of Carthaginian, Roman, Visigoth and Muslim artefacts.

The **National Museum of Maritime Archaeology** (adult/student/child €2.40/1.20/free; 9.30am-3pm Tue-Sun), by the lighthouse on the jetty Dique de la Navidad, has a reconstructed Roman galley and a collection of relics recovered from the sea.

The **Naval Museum** (Calle Menéndez Pelayo 8; admission free; 10am-1.30pm Tue-Sun) has a great collection of maps and charts, plus replicas of boats big and small.

Cartagena is also rich in Modernista buildings: **Casa Cervantes** (Calle Mayor 11), the

Casino (Calle Mayor 13), **Casa Llagostera** (Calle Mayor 25), **Gran Hotel** (Calle del Aire) and **Casa Clares** (Calle del Aire 4) – looking more neglected every time we visit – and the resplendent **Palacio Aguirre** (Plaza de la Merced), on the street known to locals as Plaza del Lago.

A sleek **catamaran** (adult/child €5/4) does hourly tours of the harbour, offering a wonderful alternative perspective of the city in its natural setting.

Festivals & Events

Cartagena's haunting **Semana Santa** (Easter Week) processions are as elaborate as anything Andalucía can offer.

For 10 days in the second half of September, half of town pulls on ancient battle dress and plays war games, re-enacting the battles between rival Carthaginian and Roman occupiers in the spectacular **Carthagineses y Romanos** fiesta.

La Mar de Músicas brings the best of world music to Cartagena throughout July.

Sleeping

Hotel Restaurante Los Habaneros (☎ 968 50 52 50; www.hotelhabaneros.com, Spanish only; Calle de San Diego 60; s/d from €36/51.50; ✂ ✂ ▢) Los Habaneros, well furnished and welcoming, was in the throes of constructing a new wing when we passed by. On the ground floor is a good-value restaurant and bar that spills onto its ample terrace in summer.

Hotel NH Cartagena (☎ 968 12 09 08; www.nh-hotels.com; Calle Real 2; d €140 Mon-Thu, €77 Fri-Sun & Aug; ℗ ✂) Occupying what were once port offices, this sensitively renovated building is Cartagena's newest hotel. Facing the neoclassical town hall, it offers ever better views of the bay the higher your floor.

Eating

There are plenty of bars and restaurants around Plaza del Ayuntamiento and the side streets off Calle Mayor.

La Mejillonera (Calle Mayor 4) This popular place offers fresh, very reasonably priced fish and seafood. Avoid, however, their mass-produced brand-name paella.

La Tartana (Calle Morería Baja) Whether you nibble at the bar or rest your feet in its large restaurant (bypass the terrace tables alongside the hideously noisy street) you'll enjoy their famed tasty tapas. They also do a four-course *menú* for €10.

Rincón Gallego (Calle Honda 3; ☽ Mon-Sat) The owner of this tiny, unpretentious place isn't known as the *Rey del Pulpo* (Octopus King) for nothing; his arm-long menu of fish dishes includes 18 different ways of preparing the suckers.

Cervecería Restaurante Principal (☎ 968 12 30 31; Calle Príncipe de Vergara 2; mains €8-12, menú €10; ☽ Mon-Sat) Fresh green plants, frosted glass, gleaming chrome and soft back lighting: the décor is just as stylish as the cuisine at this very reasonably priced restaurant-cum-beerhouse. Don't let anyone foist an expensive wine on you, as was tried when we visited.

Restaurante Azafrán (☎ 968 52 31 72; Calle la Palma 3; mains €11-15; ☽ Mon-Sat) 'To ensure that the act of eating is transformed into a feast for all the senses' is the mission statement of this very stylish place. Its cuisine is based on first-class ingredients, either allowed to speak for themselves or creatively blended (savour the sea bream with ground almonds, pine kernels, raisins and spinach).

On Plaza de la Isla, set back from the fishing port from where they buy the freshest of produce, are two large, reasonably priced fish restaurants: **Casa del Pescador** (☎ 968 50 63 75; mains €9-14; ☽ closed dinner Sun & Mon) and its neighbour, **Techos Bajos** (☎ 968 50 50 20; mains €4-10; ☽ lunch Tue-Sun, dinner Fri & Sat).

Cartagena also has a big **covered market** (Calle Carlos III; ☽ 7am-2pm Mon-Sat).

Getting There & Away
BUS

For bus information call ☎ 968 50 56 56. There are eight runs daily to/from Alicante (€6.65, two hours) via Los Alcázares (€1.40, 30 minutes), Torrevieja (€3.55, 1¼ hours) and Santa Pola (€5.50, 1¾ hours). At least seven motorway buses go to/from Murcia (€3, one hour) daily and Alsa runs services to/from La Manga (€2.20, one hour, hourly).

The bus station is on the east side of town near Plaza del Almirante Bastarreche.

TRAIN

For Renfe train destinations, change in Murcia (local train €3.30, 50 minutes, three to seven daily) – the Talgo costs €14! FEVE trains make the short run to Los Nietos (€1, 30 minutes, half-hourly) on the Mar Menor.

COSTA CÁLIDA

The Costa Cálida (Warm Coast) stretches either side of Cartagena, from the Mar Menor to Águilas. Tourists, the majority Spanish, are drawn to the **Mar Menor**, a 170-sq-km saltwater lagoon divided from the sea by **La Manga**, a 22km sliver of land.

Averaging 7m deep, the water here is so warm that you can swim virtually year-round. The reputed therapeutic quality of its high salt and iodine content has visitors by the thousand coating themselves in the healing mud of the **Mota de la Calcetera** (close to Lo Pagán) every year.

Los Alcázares is a typical resort, with apartments, restaurants and bars that are hard to squeeze into during the tourist season (when the population swells from a resident 8500 to over 150,000) and empty the rest of the year.

West of Cartagena, on the Golfo de Mazarrón, you'll find the coast much quieter. The main resorts are **Puerto de Mazarrón** and **Águilas**, with little development in between and some beautiful, unspoilt beaches.

For more information and accommodation options visit www.marmenor.net.

LORCA

pop 77,500 / elevation 330m

'Illurco', as this town was previously known, was to the Romans merely a modest stopover on the road between the Pyrenees and Cádiz. For the Visigoths it became a key bastion in the vain attempts to hold off Muslim armies probing northwards. Finally captured by the Arabs around AD 780, it was from then on known as 'Lurka'. On 23 November 1243, the very day his father, Fernando III, captured Sevilla, the future Alfonso X El Sabio reclaimed Lorca from the Muslims.

Nowadays, the town is an urban centre for the arid southwestern corner of the Murcia region.

Orientation & Information

Lorca sits on the banks of the Río Guadalentín. Its old quarter lies between Calle Lope Gisbert and the 13th-century castle that overlooks the town from the north.

Train and bus stations are beside each other, about 200m southwest of the **tourist office** (☎ 968 46 61 57; ofiturismo@ayuntalorca.es; Calle Lope Gisbert 10; ⏲ 10am-2pm & 5-7.30pm Mon-Fri, 11am-2pm Sat & Sun), which occupies part of the Casa de Guevara (see below). You'll probably find the town's **Centro de Visitantes** (☎ 902 40 00 47; www.lorcatallerdeltiempo.com; ⏲ 9.30am-1.30pm & 4-6pm, closed Mon Oct-May) more informative about the town's sights, though you may baulk at some of its overblown prose and be baffled by the eccentric English. Within is a **multimedia exhibition** (adult/child €3/2.30) illustrating Lorca's history. The Centre de Visitantes is in the former Convento de la Merced, beside Puente de la Alberca at the northern end of the old town.

Sights

The Centro de Visitantes sells various combined tickets, offering different packages of visits to Lorca's sights – including a ride on the **tourist train** (adult/child €3/2.30), a painless way of being hauled up to the castle.

Lorca's castle has been turned into a veritable theme park, **La Fortaleza del Sol** (adult/child €9/6.80; ⏲ 10.30am-5pm daily Jun-Sep, Sat-Sun Oct-Dec & Mar-May) with dioramas, actors in costume and plenty of technology.

Behind the baroque façade of the 17th-century **Casa de Guevara** (adult/child €3/2.30) is a harmonious patio and, within it, a restored early 20th-century pharmacy.

There are more splendid baroque buildings around **Plaza de España**, also called Plaza

---

ADDING COLOUR TO SEMANA SANTA

In Lorca, issues are black and white, or rather blue and white, the colours of the two major brotherhoods that have competed every year since 1855 to see who can put on the most lavish Semana Santa display.

Lorca's Easter parades aren't like the slow, sombre processions of Andalucía and elsewhere in Murcia. While still deeply reverential, they're full of colour and vitality, mixing Old and New Testament legend with the Passion story.

If you hail from Lorca, you're passionately Blanco (White) or Azul (Blue). Each of the town's two major brotherhoods has a statue of the Virgin (one draped in a blue mantle, the other in white, naturally), a banner and a spectacular museum. The result of this intense and mostly genial year-round rivalry is just about the most spectacular Semana Santa you'll see anywhere in Spain.

MURCIA

Mayor, in the centre of the old town. These include the **Pósito**, a 16th-century public granary that nowadays houses the town archives, the 18th-century **Casa del Corregidor** and the town hall. Most impressive of all is the **Colegiata de San Patricio** (☉ 11am-1pm & 4.30-6.30pm), a collegiate church with a confident baroque façade and predominantly Renaissance interior.

Peculiar to Lorca are four small, similar and extraordinary museums featuring the magnificent embroidered costumes used in the Semana Santa processions; largest are those of the Azules and the Blancos (see the boxed text Adding Colour to Semana Santa, p669). The **Museo de Bordados del Paso Azul** (Calle de Nogalte 7; adult/child €2/1.50; ☉ 10.30am-2pm & 5-7.30pm Tue-Sat, 10.30am-2pm Sun) competes in splendour, as in everything else, with the **Museo de Bordados del Paso Blanco** (Plaza de Santo Domingo; adult/child €2/1.50; ☉ 10.30am-2pm & 5-7.30pm Tue-Sat, 10.30am-2pm Sun), annexed to the church of Santo Domingo. Opening hours for both are erratic.

Lorca's **Museo Arqueológico** (adult/child €2/1.50; ☉ 10.30am-2pm & 5-7.30pm Tue-Sat, 10.30am-2pm Sun) is in the grand 16th-century Casa de los Salazar, set back from Calle Santo Domingo.

The **Centro de Artesanía** (Calle Lope Gisbert), beside the tourist office, sells local traditional crafts.

Sleeping & Eating

Pensión del Carmen (☎ 968 46 64 59; Rincón de los Valientes 3; per person €15) Spotless rooms all have bathrooms at this cheerful family-run place. It's in a tiny square just off Calle Nogalte, about 150m south of the Museo de Bordados del Paso Azul. The popular, no-frills restaurant, **Rincón de los Valientes** (mains €6-9; ☉ lunch daily, dinner Wed-Sat), serves hearty local fare.

Hotel Alameda (☎ 968 40 66 00; www.hotel-alameda.com; 1st fl Calle Musso Valiente 8; s/d €35.05/48.10;

Ⓟ ⊠) Although a bit on the bland side, this pleasant family hotel in the heart of town compensates with the warmth of its welcome.

Jardines de Lorca (☎ 968 47 05 99; www.hotelesdemurcia.com, Spanish only; Alameda de Rafael Méndez; s/d from €67.60/84.50; Ⓟ ⊠ ▯ ▣) Approximately 200m south of the bullring, this well-equipped four-star hotel, which is popular with business travellers, is in a tranquil residential suburb.

Restaurante Juan de Toledo (☎ 968 47 02 15; Calle Juan de Toledo 14; mains €12-15; ☉ closed dinner Sun & Mon) Here you can pick at tapas in the bar, heavy with hung hams, or dine in the more tranquil rear restaurant.

Getting There & Around

Hourly buses (€4.30) and trains (€3.70) run between Lorca and Murcia.

There's a large **underground car park** (Plaza Colón) 200m west of the tourist office.

PARQUE NATURAL DE SIERRA ESPUÑA

A 40-minute drive southwest of Murcia towards Lorca, just north of the N340, is the Parque Natural de Sierra Espuña, with more than 250 sq km of unspoilt highlands and blazed trails. It beckons to walkers and climbers alike.

Limestone formations tower above its sprawling pine forests. In the northwest of the park are 26 Pozos de la Nieve (Ice Houses). Within them, snow was compressed into ice then transported to nearby towns in summer, a practice that lasted until the early 20th century.

Access to the park is best via Alhama de Murcia. Visit the excellent **Centro de Interpretación** in the heart of the park.

The nearby village of **El Berro** has a couple of restaurants and the friendly **Camping Sierra Espuña** (☎ 968 66 80 38; www.campingsierraespuna .com; person/tent/car €2.75/2.75/2.75).

Andalucía

It's no secret that this most southerly extreme of the European mainland is guaranteed, at least for half the year, to give you a great suntan while reclining on beaches fronted by sparkling seas. As celebrated as Andalucía's sunshine and sand are its full-blooded people. Andalucíans love socialising and partying: either nibbling tasty tapas in their convivial bars or raging all night at one of their innumerable fiestas (festivals). Gregarious, emotional and in love with colour and action, they live life to the fullest of the full. Their intense vivacity reaches its peak perhaps in the passion of Andalucía's own art form, flamenco, an electric combination of dance, song and music. The Seville-Jerez-Cádiz area has always been the greatest hotbed of flamenco and continues to produce many of the finest flamenco artists today (p62).

Andalucía's cities combine modern glitz with an incomparable legacy of Islamic and Christian monuments (Granada's Alhambra and Capilla Real; Seville's Alcázar, Giralda and cathedral; Córdoba's Mezquita), delighting the senses with their interplay of shapes, colours and textures. Away from the cities and coastal resorts, in the white villages and green hills, you enter a different land, one that still moves to the rhythms of the seasons, and nurtures the olive, grape, orange and almond through broiling summers and chilly winters. Andalucía comprises two east–west mountain chains (the rolling Sierra Morena and the rugged Cordillera Bética) separated by the fertile valley of the Río Guadalquivir, plus coastal plains along the Mediterranean and Atlantic. Andalucía's majestic landscapes and seascapes – from long, sandy Atlantic beaches to snowcapped Mulhacén (mainland Spain's highest peak at 3479m), from bottomless gorges where vultures nest to rolling hills covered in cork-oak forests – present ever more possibilities for walkers, climbers, wildlife watchers, windsurfers, paragliders and skiers.

HIGHLIGHTS

- Feast your eyes at Granada's **Alhambra palace** (p759) and **Generalife gardens** (p759)
- Witness the intensity and splendour of **Seville's Semana Santa** (p690)
- Play on the golden-sand beaches of Cádiz's **Costa de la Luz** (p720)
- Try your hand windsurfing or kitesurfing at **Tarifa** (p724)
- Live it up by day and night at the **Feria de Málaga** (p737)
- Get close to deer, wild boar and ibex in the **Parque Natural de Cazorla** (p786)
- Marvel at Córdoba's mesmerizing **Mezquita** (p751)
- Tour the mouthwatering tapas bars of **Seville** (p692)
- Admire the wonderful World Heritage architecture of **Úbeda** (p784) and **Baeza** (p783)
- Climb mainland Spain's highest mountain range, the **Sierra Nevada** (p773), and wend your way along the age-old paths of the beautiful **Alpujarras valleys** (p776)

- AREA: 87,000 SQ KM   - POP: 7.4 MILLION   - AVE SUMMER TEMP: HIGH 37°C, LOW 20°C (SEVILLE)

History

Around 1000 or 900 BC, Andalucía's agricultural and mining wealth attracted early Phoenician trading colonies to coastal sites such as Cádiz, Huelva and Málaga. In the 8th and 7th centuries BC Phoenician influence gave rise to the mysterious, legendarily wealthy Tartessos civilization, somewhere in western Andalucía.

In Roman times (the 3rd century BC to 5th century AD) Andalucía, governed from Córdoba, was one of the most civilized and wealthiest areas of the Roman Empire. Rome imported Andalucian products such as wheat, grapes, olives, copper, silver, lead, fish and garum (a spicy seasoning derived from fish). Andalucía gave Rome two emperors, Trajan and Hadrian, both from Itálica (near Seville).

Andalucía was the obvious base for the Muslim invaders who surged onto the Iberian Peninsula from Africa in AD 711, led by Arab general Tariq ibn Ziyad who landed at Gibraltar with around 10,000 men, mostly Berbers (indigenous North Africans). Córdoba, until the 11th century, then Seville until the 13th and finally Granada until the 15th century, took turns as the leading city of Islamic Spain. At its peak, in the 10th century, Córdoba was the biggest and most dazzling, cultured city in Western Europe, and famed for its 'three cultures' – coexistence between Muslims, Jews and Christians. Islamic civilization lasted longer in Andalucía than anywhere else on the Iberian Peninsula and it's from the medieval name for the Muslim areas of the peninsula, Al-Andalus, that the name Andalucía comes.

The Emirate of Granada, the last bastion of Al-Andalus, finally fell to the Catholic Monarchs, Fernando and Isabel, in 1492. Columbus' landing in the Americas the same year brought great wealth to Seville, and later Cádiz, the Andalucian ports through which Spain's trade with the Americas was conducted. But the Castilian conquerors killed off Andalucía's deeper prosperity by handing out great swaths of territory to their nobles, who set sheep to run on former food-growing lands.

By the late 19th century, rural Andalucía was a hotbed of anarchist unrest. During the Spanish Civil War Andalucía split along class lines and savage atrocities were committed by both sides. Spain's subsequent 'hungry years' were particularly hungry here in the south, and between 1950 and 1970 some 1.5 million Andalucians left to find work in the industrial cities of northern Spain and other European countries.

Tourism, increased agricultural production, some new industries and the overall improvement in the Spanish economy have made a big difference since the 1960s. Andalucía's major cities today are bright cosmopolitan places, its people increasingly well educated, and rural poverty has been dealt a blow by government aid. A construction boom that began in the mid-1990s, primarily along the touristy coasts, still shows no sign of abating.

SEVILLE

pop 710,000 / elevation 30m

Here in Andalucía's capital and biggest city, the Andalucian way of life is lived most intensely. Seville has the most passionate and portentous Semana Santa (Holy Week), the most festive and romantic annual *feria* (fair), the best tapas bars and the most stylish people in Andalucía. It has more narrow, winding, medieval lanes and romantic, hidden plazas soaked in the scent of orange blossom than half of Andalucía's other cities put together. It's the home of those two bulwarks of Andalucian culture, flamenco and bullfighting, and its heritage of art and architecture (Roman, Islamic, Gothic, Renaissance, baroque) is without rival in southern Spain.

But Seville's most developed art form is that of enjoying oneself. To be out at night among the city's relaxed, fun-loving crowds – in the tapas bars, on the streets, in the after-midnight clubs and discos – is an experience you won't forget.

There are a couple of catches, of course: Seville is expensive. You might pay €80 here for a room that would cost €50 elsewhere, and prices go even higher during Semana Santa and the Feria de Abril (April Fair). Also bear in mind that Seville gets *very* hot in July and August: locals, sensibly, leave the city then.

HISTORY

Roman Seville, named Hispalis, was a significant port on the Río Guadalquivir – navigable to the Atlantic Ocean 100km away. Muslim

Seville, called Ishbiliya, became the most powerful of the *taifas* (small kingdoms) into which Islamic Spain split after the Córdoba caliphate collapsed in 1031. Poet-king Al-Mutamid (1069–91) presided over a languid, hedonistic court in the Alcázar palace, but in 1085 had to call in help from the Islamic fundamentalist rulers of Morocco, the Al-moravids, against the growing threat of Christian reconquest from northern Spain. The Almoravids took over all Islamic Spain before being replaced by another strict Moroccan Islamic sect, the Almohads, in the 12th century. Almohad caliph Yacub Yusuf made Seville capital of the whole Almohad realm, building a great mosque where the

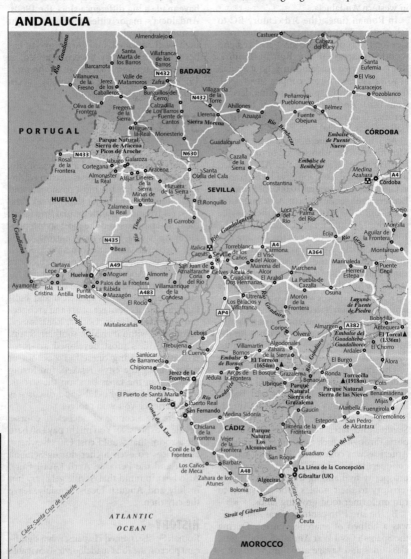

ANDALUCÍA

city's cathedral now stands. His successor, Yusuf Yacub al-Mansur, added the Giralda tower. However, Almohad power crumbled and Seville fell to the Castilian King Fernando III (El Santo, the Saint) in 1248.

By the 14th century Seville was the most important Castilian city. Its biggest break came in 1503, when it was awarded an official monopoly on Spanish trade with the American continent. Seville – *puerto y puerta de Indias* (port and gateway of the Indies) – rapidly became one of the biggest, richest and most cosmopolitan cities on earth, and a magnet for everyone from priests and bankers to beggars and conmen. Lavish Renaissance and baroque buildings

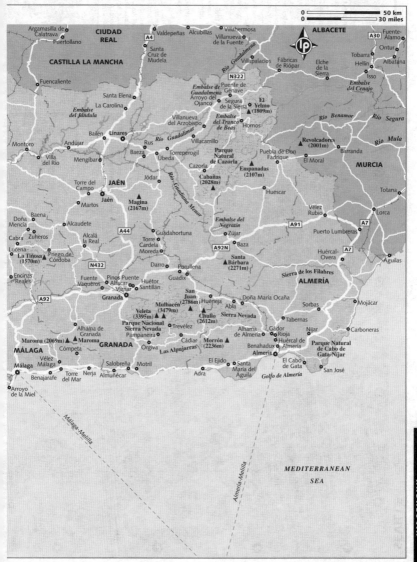

ANDALUCÍA

SEVILLE

See Central Seville map pp680–1

0   500 m
0   0.3 miles

ANDALUCÍA

sprouted, and many stars of Spain's artistic golden age (the late-16th to late-17th centuries) were based here: painters such as Zurbarán, Murillo and Juan de Valdés Leal (though the Seville-born Diego Velázquez left for Madrid), sculptors such as Juan Martínez Montañés and Pedro Roldán.

However a plague in 1649 killed half the city and the Río Guadalquivir became more silted-up and less navigable for the increasingly big ships of the day. In 1717 Casa de la Contratación, the government office controlling commerce with the Americas, was transferred to Cádiz. Another Seville plague in 1800 killed 13,000 people. The beginnings of industry in the mid-19th century brought a measure of prosperity for some, but the majority remained impoverished. Seville fell very quickly to the Nationalists at the start of the Spanish Civil War in 1936, despite resistance in working-class areas (which brought savage reprisals).

Things looked up in the 1980s when Seville was named capital of the new autonomous Andalucía within democratic Spain, and *sevillano* Felipe González, of the left-of-centre PSOE (Partido Socialista Obrero Español), became Spain's prime minister. The Expo '92 international exhibition in 1992 brought the city millions of visitors, eight new bridges across the Guadalquivir and the super-fast AVE (Tren de Alta Velocidad Española) rail link to Madrid. Seville's economy is now steadily improving with a mix of tourism, commerce, technology and industry.

ORIENTATION

Seville straddles the Río Guadalquivir, with most places of interest found on the river's east bank. The central area is a tangle of narrow, twisting old streets and small squares, with the exception of Plaza Nueva and the broad, straight Avenida de la Constitución. Just east of Constitución are the city's major monuments: the cathedral, La Giralda and the Alcázar fortress-palace. The quaint Barrio de Santa Cruz, which lies east of the cathedral and the Alcázar, is a popular place to stay and eat. The true centre of Seville, El Centro, is a little further north, around Plaza de San Francisco and Plaza Salvador. The area between Avenida de la Constitución and the river is called El Arenal.

The bus and train terminals are on the periphery of the central area, and both are served by city buses that circle the centre (p696): Prado de San Sebastián bus station is 650m southeast of the cathedral and within walking distance of the Barrio de Santa Cruz; Plaza de Armas bus station is 900m northwest of the cathedral, within walking distance of El Arenal; and Santa Justa train station is 1.5km northeast of the cathedral.

INFORMATION
Bookshops

Casa del Libro (Map pp680–1; ☎ 954 50 29 50; Calle Velázquez 8; ◷ 9.30am-9.30pm Mon-Sat) Guidebooks in several languages, novels in English, maps, dictionaries.

SEVILLE IN...

Two Days

On your first morning visit the cathedral and the Giralda then wander through the Barrio de Santa Cruz and enjoy lunch at the Corral del Agua or La Albahaca. In the afternoon head over to the Río Guadalquivir then visit one or both of the Plaza de Toros or the Museo de Bellas Artes. Devote the evening to a relaxed tour of a few tapas bars!

Give your second morning to the Alcázar, then enjoy another Barrio de Santa Cruz lunch before heading up to El Centro to visit the Palacio de la Condesa de Lebrija and some of the city-centre shops. In the evening see a flamenco performance.

Four Days

On day three relax with a visit to the leafy Parque de María Luisa and its museums, followed by whichever of the sights you missed on day one. Treat yourself to dinner at a classy restaurant such as the Egaña Oriza or Enrique Becerra. On day four venture out to Santiponce to explore the Roman Itálica and Monasterio de San Isidoro del Campo. If it's the weekend, wind up your visit with a night out enjoying some live music and/or a dance club.

Librería Beta (Map pp680-1) Constitución 9 (☎ 954 56 28 17; Avenida del Constitución 9); Constitución 27 (☎ 954 56 07 03; Avenida de la Constitución 27) Guidebooks in several languages, novels in English, maps.
LTC (Map pp680-1; ☎ 954 42 59 64; Avenida Menéndez Pelayo 42-44; ☻ closed Sat) Best map shop in Andalucía.

Emergency
Ambulance (☎ 061)
Policía Local (Local Police; ☎ 092)
Policía Nacional (National Police; ☎ 091)

Internet Access
First Center (Map pp680-1; Avenida de la Constitución 34; per hr €2; ☻ 9am-10pm Mon-Fri, 10am-9.30pm Sat, noon-9pm Sun)
Internetia (Map pp680-1; Avenida Menéndez Pelayo 46; per hr €2.20; ☻ 10.30-1.30am Mon-Fri, noon-1.30am Sat & Sun)
Sevilla Internet Center (Map pp680-1; ☎ 954 50 02 75; Calle Almirantazgo 2; per min €0.05; ☻ 9am-10pm Mon-Fri, 10am-10pm Sat & Sun)

Internet Resources
Discover Sevilla (www.discoversevilla.com)
Explore Seville (www.exploreseville.com)
Seville Tourism (www.turismo.sevilla.org) The city's official tourism site; its 'Accessible Guide' contains lists of establishments with disabled access.

Laundry
These laundrettes include washing, drying and folding in their prices. Both open 9.30am to 1.30pm and 5pm to 8pm Monday to Friday and 10am to 1.30pm Saturday. It usually takes half a day.
Auto-Servicio de Lavandería Sevilla (Map pp680-1; ☎ 954 21 05 35; Calle Castelar 2C; per load €6)
La Segunda Vera (Map pp680-1; ☎ 954 54 11 48; Calle Alejo Fernández 3; per load €7.80)

Media
El Giraldillo Andalucía-wide what's-on mag, free at tourist offices and some hotels, with a strong Seville emphasis.
The Tourist Free mag for tourists with worthwhile information.
Welcome & Olé Ditto.

Medical Services
Centro de Salud El Porvenir (Map pp680-1; ☎ 955 03 78 17; cnr Avenida Menéndez y Pelayo & Avenida de Cádiz) Public clinic with emergency service.
Hospital Virgen del Rocío (☎ 955 01 20 00; Avenida de Manuel Siurot s/n) The main general hospital, located 1km south of Parque de María Luisa.

Money
There's no shortage of banks and ATMs in the central area. Santa Justa train station, the airport and both bus stations have ATMs. You'll find **exchange offices** on Avenida de la Constitución and at Santa Justa station.

Post
Main post office (Map pp680-1; Avenida de la Constitución 32)

Telephone
There are plenty of pay phones around the centre. The following call centres offer inexpensive international calls:
Ciber Alcázar (Map pp676-7; ☎ 954 21 04 01; Calle San Fernando 35; ☻ 10.15am-10.30pm Mon-Fri, noon-10.30pm Sat & Sun)
First Center (Map pp680-1; Avenida de la Constitución 34; ☻ 9am-10pm Mon-Fri, 10am-9.30pm Sat, noon-9pm Sun)

Tourist Information
Inhfor (Map pp676-7; ☎ 954 54 19 52; Estación Santa Justa; ☻ 8am-10pm Mon-Fri, 8am-2pm & 4-10pm Sat, 8am-2pm & 6-10pm Sun & holidays) Independent tourist office at train station.
Municipal tourist office (Map pp680-1; ☎ 954 22 17 14; barranco.turismo@sevilla.org; Calle de Arjona 28; ☻ 9am-9pm Mon-Fri, 9am-2pm Sat & Sun, reduced hrs during Semana Santa & Feria de Abril)
Regional tourist offices Constitución (Map pp680-1; ☎ 954 22 14 04; otsevilla@andalucia.org; Avenida de la Constitución 21; ☻ 9am-7pm Mon-Fri, 10am-2pm & 3-7pm Sat, 10am-2pm Sun, closed holidays); Santa Justa (Map pp676-7; ☎ 954 53 76 26; Estación Santa Justa; ☻ 9am-8pm Mon-Fri, 10am-2pm Sat & Sun, closed holidays); Airport (☎ 954 44 91 28; Airport; ☻ 9am-8.30pm Mon-Fri, 10am-6pm Sat, 10am-2pm Sun, closed holidays). The Constitución office is well informed but often very busy.
Turismo Sevilla (Map pp680-1; ☎ 954 21 00 05; www.turismosevilla.org; Plaza del Triunfo 1; ☻ 10.30am-7pm Mon-Fri) Information on all Sevilla province.

SIGHTS
Seville's major monuments, the cathedral, the Giralda and the complex of the Alcázar, are all just east of Avenida de la Constitución and south of the city's true centre (El Centro). But you'll find plenty to see and do in El Centro and the neighbouring El Arenal area, as well as in areas to the south, north and west.

ANDALUCÍA

CENTRAL SEVILLE

ANDALUCÍA

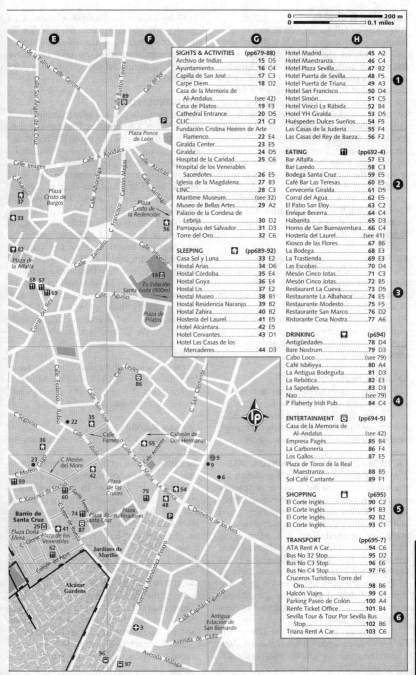

0 / 200 m
0 / 0.1 miles

SIGHTS & ACTIVITIES (pp679-88)
Archivo de Indias...................15 D5
Ayuntamiento.......................16 C4
Capilla de San José................17 C3
Carpe Diem...........................18 D2
Casa de la Memoria de
  Al-Andalus......................(see 42)
Casa de Pilatos.....................19 F3
Cathedral Entrance................20 D5
CLIC....................................21 C3
Fundación Cristina Heeren de Arte
  Flamenco........................22 E4
Giralda Center.......................23 E5
Giralda.................................24 D5
Hospital de la Caridad............25 C6
Hospital de los Venerables
  Sacerdotes......................26 E5
Iglesia de la Magdalena..........27 B3
LINC....................................28 C3
Maritime Museum...............(see 32)
Museo de Bellas Artes............29 A2
Palacio de la Condesa de
  Lebrija...........................30 D2
Parroquia del Salvador............31 D3
Torre del Oro........................32 C6

SLEEPING (pp689-92)
Casa Sol y Luna....................33 E2
Hostal Arias.........................34 D6
Hostal Córdoba.....................35 E4
Hostal Goya.........................36 E4
Hostal Lis............................37 E2
Hostal Museo........................38 B1
Hostal Residencia Naranjo......39 B2
Hostal Zahira.......................40 B2
Hostería del Laurel................41 E5
Hotel Alcántara....................42 E5
Hotel Cervantes....................43 D1
Hotel Las Casas de los
  Mercaderes.....................44 D3

Hotel Madrid........................45 A2
Hotel Maestranza..................46 C3
Hotel Plaza Sevilla.................47 B2
Hotel Puerta de Sevilla...........48 F5
Hotel Puerta de Triana...........49 A3
Hotel San Francisco...............50 D4
Hotel Simón..........................51 C5
Hotel Vincci La Rábida............52 B4
Hotel YH Giralda...................53 D5
Huéspedes Dulces Sueños........54 F5
Las Casas de la Judería...........55 F4
Las Casas del Rey de Baeza......56 F2

EATING (pp692-4)
Bar Alfalfa...........................57 E3
Bar Laredo...........................58 C3
Bodega Santa Cruz................59 E5
Café Bar Las Teresas..............60 E5
Cervecería Giralda.................61 D5
Corral del Agua.....................62 E5
El Patio San Eloy...................63 C2
Enrique Becerra....................64 C4
Habanita..............................65 D3
Horno de San Buenaventura....66 C4
Hostería del Laurel..............(see 41)
Kiosco de las Flores...............67 B6
La Bodega............................68 E3
La Trastienda........................69 E3
Las Escobas..........................70 D5
Mesón Cinco Jotas.................71 C3
Mesón Cinco Jotas.................72 B5
Restaurant La Cueva...............73 D5
Restaurante La Albahaca.........74 E5
Restaurante Modesto..............75 F5
Restaurante San Marco...........76 D2
Ristorante Cosa Nostra............77 A6

DRINKING (p694)
Antigüedades........................78 D4
Bare Nostrum.......................79 D3
Cabo Loco.........................(see 79)
Café Isbiliyya.......................80 A4
La Antigua Bodeguita.............81 D3
La Rebótica..........................82 E3
La Sapotales.........................83 D3
Nao.................................(see 79)
P Flaherty Irish Pub...............84 C4

ENTERTAINMENT (pp694-5)
Casa de la Memoria de
  Al-Andalus......................(see 42)
Empresa Pagés......................85 B4
La Carbonería.......................86 F4
Los Gallos............................87 E5
Plaza de Toros de la Real
  Maestranza......................88 B5
Sol Café Cantante.................89 F1

SHOPPING (p695)
El Corte Inglés......................90 C2
El Corte Inglés......................91 B3
El Corte Inglés......................92 B2
El Corte Inglés......................93 C1

TRANSPORT (pp695-7)
ATA Rent A Car.....................94 C6
Bus No 32 Stop.....................95 D2
Bus No C3 Stop.....................96 E6
Bus No C4 Stop.....................97 F6
Cruceros Turísticos Torre del
  Oro................................98 B6
Halcón Viajes........................99 C4
Parking Paseo de Colón..........100 A4
Renfe Ticket Office................101 B4
Sevilla Tour & Tour Por Sevilla Bus
  Stop...............................102 B6
Triana Rent A Car.................103 C6

ANDALUCÍA

Cathedral & Giralda

After Seville fell to the Christians in 1248 its main mosque was used as a church until 1401 when, in view of its decaying state, the church authorities decided to knock it down and start again. 'Let us create such a building that future generations will take us for lunatics', they reputedly agreed. They certainly got themselves a big church. Seville's **cathedral** (Map pp680-1; ☎ 954 21 49 71; adult/student & senior/disabled & under 12 €7/1.50/free, admission free Sun; ☼ 11am-6pm Mon-Sat, 2.30-7pm Sun Sep-Jun, 9.30am-4.30pm Mon-Sat, 2.30-7pm Sun Jul & Aug) is one of the largest in the world: the main building is 126m long and 83m wide. It was completed by 1507 and was originally all Gothic, though work done after its central dome collapsed in 1511 was mostly in the Renaissance style.

EXTERIOR

The cathedral's bulky exterior gives few hints of the treasures that lie within, apart from the Giralda, its tower on the eastern side (p682), the Puerta del Perdón on Calle Alemanes (two survivors from the Islamic building), and one neo-Gothic and two Gothic doorways on Avenida de la Constitución.

SALA DEL PABELLÓN

Selected treasures from the cathedral's art collection (many of them the work of masters from Seville's 17th-century artistic golden age) are exhibited in this first room, which you reach from the ticket office.

CATHEDRAL CHAPELS & STAINED GLASS

The sheer size of the broad, five-naved cathedral is obscured by a welter of interior decoration that's typical of Spanish cathedrals. The chapels along the northern and southern sides constitute a storehouse of sculpture, stained glass and painting as rich as those of any Spanish church. Near the western end of the northern side is the **Capilla de San Antonio**, with Murillo's large 1666 canvas depicting the vision of St Anthony of Padua; thieves excised the kneeling saint in 1874 but he was found in New York and put back.

Don't forget to look up to admire the Gothic vaulting and rich-hued stained glass. The oldest stained glass, with markedly different colours, was done between 1478 and 1483 by a German, Enrique Alemán. This master artisan takes credit for the glass in the four westernmost bays on either side of the uppermost storey of the nave, and above the five westernmost chapels on both sides of the nave.

COLUMBUS' TOMB

Inside the cathedral's southern door stands the tomb of Christopher Columbus – but the remains inside are probably not those of the great explorer at all. The tomb-monument, dating from 1902, shows four sepulchre-bearers representing the four kingdoms of Spain at the time of Columbus' 1492 voyage: Castile, León, Aragón and Navarra. In 2003, in the face of claims that the Dominican Republic, in the Caribbean, is home to Columbus' remains, investigators began tests on the remains in Seville cathedral. In 2004 international newspapers reported that these remains were those of a man who had died about 15 years younger than Columbus did and were probably those of one of his sons, Hernando, while Columbus himself probably lay in the Dominican Republic.

CORO

In the middle of the cathedral is the large *coro* (choir) with 117 Gothic-Mudéjar carved stalls. Vices and sins are depicted on the misericords.

CAPILLA MAYOR

East of the *coro* is the Capilla Mayor, whose Gothic *retablo* (altarpiece) is the jewel of the cathedral and reckoned to be the biggest altarpiece in the world. Begun by Flemish sculptor Pieter Dancart in 1482 and completed by others by 1564, this sea of gilded and polychromed wood holds more than 1000 carved biblical figures. At the centre of the lowest level is the 13th-century image of the Virgen de la Sede, patron of the cathedral.

SACRISTÍA DE LOS CÁLICES

South of the Capilla Mayor are rooms containing many of the cathedral's art treasures. The westernmost of these is the Sacristy of the Chalices, where Goya's 1817 painting of the Seville martyrs *Santas Justa y Rufina* (a pair of potters who died at the hands of the Romans) hangs above the altar.

SACRISTÍA MAYOR

This large domed room east of the Sacristía de los Cálices is a Plateresque creation of between 1528 and 1547: the arch over its portal has carvings of 16th-century foods. Pedro de Campaña's 1547 *Descendimiento* (Descent from the Cross), above the central altar at the southern end, and Zurbarán's *Santa Teresa*, to its right, are two of the cathedral's masterpieces. In a glass case are the city keys handed to the conquering Fernando III in 1248.

CABILDO

This beautifully domed chapterhouse, in the southeastern corner of the cathedral, was built between 1558 and 1592 to the designs of Hernán Ruiz, architect of the belfry atop the Giralda. High above the archbishop's throne at the southern end is a Murillo masterpiece, *La Inmaculada*. Eight Murillo saints adorn the dome.

GIRALDA

Over 90m high, the Giralda was the minaret of the mosque, constructed in brick between 1184 and 1198. Its proportions, decoration and colour, which changes with the light, make it perhaps Spain's most perfect Islamic building. The topmost parts (from the bell level up) were added in the 16th century, when Christians were busy 'improving on' surviving Islamic buildings. At the very top is **El Giraldillo**, a 16th-century bronze weather vane, which represents Faith and is a symbol of Seville. El Giraldillo was due to be put back in position in 2004 after seven years' absence for repairs (a replica stood in its place).

In the northeastern corner of the cathedral interior you'll find the passage for the climb up to the belfry of the Giralda. The ascent is quite easy, as there's a series of ramps built so that guards could ride up on horseback. The climb affords great views.

PATIO DE LOS NARANJOS

Planted with over 60 orange trees, this was originally the courtyard where Muslims performed ablutions before entering the mosque. On its north side is the beautiful Islamic Puerta del Perdón.

Alcázar

The not-to-be-missed **Alcázar** (Map p684; ☎ 954 50 23 23; adult/under 16, over 65, student & disabled €5/ free; ☯ 9.30am-8pm Tue-Sat, 9.30am-6pm Sun & holidays Apr-Sep, 9.30am-6pm Tue-Sat, 9.30am-2.30pm Sun & holidays Oct-Mar) stands south of the cathedral across Plaza del Triunfo. This intriguing, beautiful complex is intimately associated with the lives and loves of several later rulers, above all the extraordinary Pedro I of Castile (1350–69), who was known as either Pedro El Cruel or Pedro El Justiciero (the Justice-Dispenser), depending on whether you were on the right side of him or not.

Originally founded as a fort for the Cordoban governors of Seville in 913, the Alcázar has been expanded or reconstructed many times in its 11 centuries of existence. This makes it a complicated building to understand, but in the end this has only increased its fascination. Seville's prosperous 11th-century Muslim *taifa* rulers built themselves a palace called Al-Muwarak (the Blessed) in what's now the western part of the Alcázar. The 12th-century Almohad rulers added another palace east of this, around what's now the Patio del Crucero. Christian Fernando III moved into the Alcázar when he captured Seville in 1248 and several later Christian monarchs used it as their main residence. Fernando's son Alfonso X replaced much of the Almohad palace with a Gothic one. Between 1364 and 1366 Pedro I created the sumptuous Mudéjar Palacio de Don Pedro, partly on the site of the old Al-Muwarak palace. The Catholic Monarchs, Fernando and Isabel, set up court here in the 1480s as they prepared for the conquest of Granada. Later rulers created the Alcázar's lovely gardens.

PATIO DEL LEÓN

The Lion Patio was the garrison yard of the Al-Muwarak palace. Off here, the **Sala de la Justicia** (Hall of Justice), with beautiful Mudéjar plasterwork, was built in the 1340s by Alfonso XI, who disported here with his mistress Leonor de Guzmán. Alfonso's dalliances left his heir Pedro I (El Cruel/Justiciero) with five half-brothers and a severe case of sibling rivalry. Pedro had a dozen friends and relatives murdered in his efforts to stay on the throne. One of the half-brothers, Don Fadrique, met his maker right here in the Sala de la Justicia. The room gives on to the pretty **Patio del Yeso**, a 19th-century reconstruction of part of the 12th-century Almohad palace.

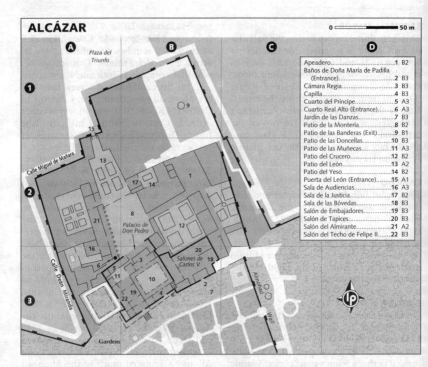

ALCÁZAR

0 ————— 50 m

PATIO DE LA MONTERÍA

The rooms on the western side of this patio were part of the Casa de la Contratación, which was founded by the Catholic Monarchs in 1503 to control American trade. The **Sala de Audiencias** (Audience Hall) contains the earliest known painting on the 'discovery' of the Americas (by Alejo Fernández, 1530s), in which Columbus, Fernando El Católico, Carlos I (Charles I), Amerigo Vespucci and native Americans can be seen sheltered beneath the Virgin in her role as protector of sailors.

PALACIO DE DON PEDRO

Whatever else Pedro I may have done, posterity owes him a big thank you for building his own palace in the Alcázar in the 1360s. His Muslim ally Mohammed V of Granada, the man chiefly responsible for the decoration of the Alhambra's fabulous Palacio Nazaríes, sent along many of his best artisans to help. These artisans were joined by others from Toledo and Seville, and their work, drawing on the Islamic traditions of the Almohads and caliphal Córdoba, is a unique synthesis of Iberian Islamic art.

Inscriptions on the palace's façade on the Patio de la Montería encapsulate the collaborative nature of the enterprise. While one announces in Spanish that the building's creator was 'the very high, noble and conquering Don Pedro, by the grace of God king of Castile and León', another intones repeatedly in Arabic 'There is no conqueror but Allah'.

At the heart of the palace is the wonderful **Patio de las Doncellas** (Patio of the Maidens), surrounded by beautiful arches and exquisite plasterwork and tiling. In 2004 archaeologists uncovered its original sunken garden from beneath a 16th-century marble covering.

The **Cámara Regia** (King's Quarters) on the northern side of the patio has two rooms with stunning ceilings and more wonderful plaster- and tilework. The rear room was probably the king's bedroom. Just west is the small **Patio de las Muñecas** (Patio of the Dolls), the heart of the palace's private quarters, with delicate Granada-style decoration. Its mezzanine and top gallery were built in the 19th century for Isabel II, using plasterwork from the Alhambra. The **Cuarto del Príncipe** (Prince's Quarters), to its north, has superb ceilings and was probably the queen's bedroom.

The spectacular **Salón de Embajadores** (Hall of Ambassadors), off the western end of the Patio de las Doncellas, was Pedro I's throne room and incorporates much earlier caliphal-style door arches from the Al-Muwarak palace. Its fabulous wooden dome of multiple star patterns, symbolising the universe, was added in 1427. The dome's shape gives the room its alternative name, Sala de la Media Naranja (Hall of the Half Orange). On its western side, the beautiful **Arco de Pavones**, with peacock motifs, leads into the **Salón del Techo de Felipe II**, with a Renaissance ceiling (1589–91).

SALONES DE CARLOS V

Reached by a staircase from the Patio de las Doncellas, these are the much-remodelled rooms of Alfonso X's 13th-century Gothic palace. It was here that Alfonso's intellectual court gathered and, a century later, Pedro I installed the mistress he loved, María de Padilla. The **Sala de las Bóvedas** (Hall of the Vault) is adorned with beautiful 1570s tiling, while the **Salón de Tapices** (Tapestry Room) has a collection of huge 18th-century tapestries showing Carlos I's 1535 conquest of Tunis.

PATIO DEL CRUCERO

This patio outside the Salones de Carlos V was originally the upper level of the patio of the 12th-century Almohad palace. At first it consisted only of raised walkways, below which grew orange trees, whose fruit could easily be plucked (at hand height) by the privileged folk strolling along the walkways. María de Padilla must have liked doing this because the patio is also known as the Patio de María de Padilla.

The patio's lower level had to be covered over in the 18th century after earthquake damage.

GARDENS & EXIT

From the Salones de Carlos V you can head out into the Alcázar's large *jardines* (gardens), a perfect place to relax. The gardens in front of the Salones de Carlos

V and Palacio de Don Pedro were mostly brought to their present form in the 16th and 17th centuries, while those to the east, beyond a long Almohad wall, are 20th-century creations. From the little **Jardín de las Danzas** (Garden of the Dances) a passage runs beneath the Salones de Carlos V to the so-called **Baños de Doña María de Padilla**, originally the lower level of the Patio del Crucero, with a grotto that replaced that patio's original pool.

From the new gardens you can leave the Alcázar via the **Apeadero**, a 17th-century entrance hall, and the **Patio de las Banderas** (Patio of the Banners).

Archivo de Indias

On the western side of Plaza del Triunfo, the **Archive of the Indies** (Map pp680-1; ☎ 954 21 12 34; Calle Santo Tomás) is the main archive on Spain's American empire, with 80 million pages of documents dating from 1492 through to the end of the empire in the 19th century. The 16th-century building, designed by Juan de Herrera, was originally Seville's Lonja (Exchange) for commerce with the Americas. It was closed for restoration work at the time of writing.

Barrio de Santa Cruz   Map pp680–1

Seville's medieval *judería* (Jewish quarter), east of the cathedral and Alcázar, is today a tangle of quaint, winding streets and lovely plant-decked plazas, with numerous souvenir shops and popular places to stay, eat and drink. Its most characteristic plaza today is **Plaza de Santa Cruz**, whose central cross, made in 1692, is one of the finest examples of Seville wrought-iron work. **Plaza Doña Elvira** is another pretty spot.

The 17th-century **Hospital de los Venerables Sacerdotes** (☎ 954 56 26 96; Plaza de los Venerables; adult/student & over 65/under 12 €4.75/2.40/free, admission free Sun afternoon; ⊙ 10am-2pm & 4-8pm) was a residence for aged priests. You can visit the lovely central courtyard, several exhibition rooms, and the church with murals by Valdés Leal and fine sculptures by Pedro Roldán.

The **Casa de la Memoria de Al-Andalus** (☎ 954 56 06 70; Calle Ximénez de Enciso 28; admission €1; ⊙ 9am-2pm & 6-7.30pm), an 18th-century mansion on the site of a medieval Jewish house, has an exhibition on Sephardic (Spanish-Jewish) culture.

El Centro
Map pp680–1

The real centre of Seville is the densely packed zone of narrow streets, north of the cathedral, broken up here and there by squares, around which the city's life has revolved for aeons.

PLAZA DE SAN FRANCISCO & CALLE SIERPES

Site of a market in Islamic times, Plaza de San Francisco has been Seville's main public square since the 16th century and was once the scene of Inquisition burnings. The southern end of the **Ayuntamiento** (City Hall) here is encrusted with lovely Renaissance carving from the 1520s and '30s.

Pedestrianised Calle Sierpes, heading north from the plaza, and the parallel Calle Tetuán/Velázquez, are the hub of Seville's fanciest shopping zone. Between the two streets is **Capilla de San José** (Calle Jovellanos; 🕑 8am-12.30pm & 6.30-8.30pm), an 18th-century chapel with breathtakingly intense baroque ornamentation.

The **Palacio de la Condesa de Lebrija** (☎ 954 22 78 02; Calle de la Cuna 8; admission ground fl only €4, whole bldg €7; 🕑 10.30am-1.30pm & 5-7pm Mon-Fri, 10am-1pm Sat), a block east of Calle Sierpes, is a 16th-century noble mansion remodelled in 1914 by the late Countess of Lebrija, an archaeologist, who filled it with her rich collection of art and artisanry and treasures from her travels. There are plenty of remains from Roman Itálica (p697), including a marvellous mosaic in the lovely central Renaissance-Mudéjar courtyard. Upstairs are Arabic, baroque and Spanish rooms.

PLAZA SALVADOR

This plaza, which has a few popular bars, was once the forum of Roman Hispalis. It's dominated by the **Parroquia del Salvador**, a big baroque church that was built between 1674 and 1712, on the former site of Muslim Ishbiliya's main mosque. At the time of writing the church was closed for restoration work and archaeological investigation. Walkways may be installed for viewing the excavations. On the northern side of the church, the mosque's small patio remains, with a few half-buried Roman columns.

CASA DE PILATOS

Another of Seville's finest noble **mansions** (☎ 954 22 52 98; Calle Águilas; whole house €8, lower fl €5, EU citizen 1-5pm Tue free; 🕑 9am-7pm Mar-Sep 9am-6pm Oct-Feb), 500m northeast of the cathedral, is still occupied by the ducal Medinaceli family. This extensive 16th-century building is a mixture of diverse architectural styles, with some beautiful tilework, *artesonado* (Mudéjar wooden ceiling with interlaced beams leaving a pattern of spaces for decoration) and gardens. The Patio Principal, for instance, features intricate Mudéjar plasterwork, 16th-century tiling, a Renaissance fountain and Roman sculpture. The staircase from here to the upper floor has the most magnificent tiles in the building, with a great golden *artesonado* dome above.

If time or money is limited, you could skip the top floor.

El Arenal
Map pp680–1

A short walk west from Avenida de la Constitución brings you to the banks of the Río Guadalquivir, with its pleasant footpath. The district of El Arenal is home to some of Seville's most interesting sights.

TORRE DEL ORO

This 13th-century river-bank Islamic watchtower, which once crowned a corner of the city walls, supposedly had a dome covered in golden tiles, hence its name, 'Tower of Gold'. Inside is a small **maritime museum** (☎ 954 22 24 19; admission €1; 🕑 10am-2pm Tue-Fri, 11am-2pm Sat & Sun, closed Aug).

HOSPITAL DE LA CARIDAD

This **hospice for the elderly** (☎ 954 22 32 32; Calle Temprado 3; admission €4, free Sun & holidays; 🕑 9am-1.30pm & 3.30-7.30pm Mon-Sat, 9am-1pm Sun & holidays) was founded in the 17th century by Miguel de Mañara – by legend a notorious libertine who changed his ways after experiencing a vision of his own funeral procession. For the hospice's church, Mañara commissioned a collection of top-class 17th-century Sevillan art on the theme of death and redemption. Valdés Leal's frightening masterpieces *In Ictu Oculi* (In the Blink of an Eye) and *Finis Gloriae Mundi* (the End of Earthly Glory) face each other across the western end of the church, chillingly illustrating the futility of worldly success.

Four Murillo paintings along the walls illustrate the theme of redemption through mercy. They show Moses drawing water from the rock, the miracle of the 'loaves and fishes', St John of God (San Juan de Dios) caring for an invalid, and Isabel of Hungary curing the sick.

Mañara is buried in the crypt beneath the main altar, on which a masterly sculpture by Pedro Roldán illustrates the final act of compassion, the burial of the dead – in this case, of Christ himself.

PLAZA DE TOROS DE LA REAL MAESTRANZA

Seville's **bullring** (☎ 954 22 45 77; Paseo de Cristóbal Colón 12; tours adult/over-65 €4/3.20; ☒ half-hourly 9.30am-6.30pm, 9.30am-3pm bullfighting days), 300m west of the cathedral, is one of the most handsome in Spain and probably the oldest (building began in 1758). It was here, and in the ring at Ronda, that bullfighting on foot (instead of horseback) began in the 18th century. Interesting guided visits, in English and Spanish, take you into the ring and its museum, with a peep into the mini-hospital for bullfighters who have come off second best.

MUSEO DE BELLAS ARTES

Set in a beautiful former convent, Seville's **fine-arts museum** (☎ 954 22 07 90; Plaza del Museo 9; adult/EU citizen €1.50/free; ☒ 2.30-8.30pm Tue, 9am-8.30pm Wed-Sat, 9am-2.30pm Sun) does full justice to Seville's leading role in Spain's artistic golden age. The 17th-century Seville masters Murillo, Zurbarán and Valdés Leal are particularly well represented here. The museum has lifts, disabled toilets and a wheelchair.

Highlights include Pedro Millán's 15th-century terracotta sculptures (Room I); Pietro Torrigiano's influential Renaissance sculpture *San Jerónimo Penitente* (Room II); paintings by Velázquez and Alonso Cano (Room III); paintings by Murillo including *Inmaculada Concepción Grande* in Room V, formerly the convent church; Ribera's very Spanish-looking *Santiago Apóstol* and Zurbarán's deeply sombre *Cristo Crucificado* (Room VI); and further major works by Zurbarán (Room X).

South of the Centre   Map pp676–7

ANTIGUA FÁBRICA DE TABACOS

Seville's massive former **tobacco factory** (Calle San Fernando; ☒ 8am-9.30pm Mon-Fri, 8am-2pm Sat) – workplace of Bizet's operatic heroine, Car-

men – was built in the 18th century. It had its own jail, stables for 400 mules, 24 patios and even a nursery. Now part of the Universidad de Sevilla, it's a very impressive, if rather gloomy, neoclassical building.

PARQUE DE MARÍA LUISA & PLAZA DE ESPAÑA

A large area south of the tobacco factory was transformed for Seville's 1929 international fair, the Exposición Iberoamericana, when architects spattered it with all sorts of fine, fancy and funny buildings, many of them harking back to Seville's eras of past glory. In its midst, the large **Parque de María Luisa** (☒ 8am-10pm, to midnight Jul & Aug), with 3500 magnificent trees, is a beautiful respite from the hustle of the city.

Plaza de España, one of the city's favourite relaxation spots with its fountains and minicanals, faces the park across Avenida de Isabel la Católica. Around it is the most grandiose of the 1929 buildings, a semicircular brick-and-tile confection featuring Seville tilework at its gaudiest.

On Plaza de América, at the southern end of the park, is Seville's **Museo Arqueológico** (☎ 954 23 24 01; adult/EU citizen €1.50/free; ☒ 3-8pm Tue, 9am-8pm Wed-Sat, 9am-2pm Sun & holidays), whose big collection includes a room of gold jewellery from the mysterious Tartessos culture, and fine collections of Iberian animal sculptures and beautiful Roman mosaics. Facing it is the **Museo de Artes y Costumbres Populares** (☎ 954 23 25 76; adult/EU citizen €1.50/free; ☒ 3-8pm Tue, 9am-8pm Wed-Sat, 9am-2pm Sun & holidays), with mock-up workshops of local crafts and some really beautiful old festival costumes.

Isla Mágica

This large **amusement park** (Map pp676-7; ☎ 902 161716; www.islamagica.es in Spanish; adult/under 13 & over-60 all day mid-Jun–mid-Sep €21/14.50 evening or night €14.50/11, all day rest of season €19/13 evening or night €13/10; ☒ 11am-7pm Tue-Fri, 11am-10pm Sat & Sun Apr–mid-Jun, 11am-10pm Tue-Thu & Sun, 11am-midnight Fri & Sat mid-Jun–mid-Jul, 11am-10pm Sun-Thu, 11am-midnight Fri & Sat 2nd half Jul, 11am-midnight daily Aug, 11am-10pm daily 1st half of Sep, 11am-9pm Fri-Sun 2nd half of Sep, 11am-9pm Sat & Sun Oct, closed Nov-Mar) will provide a great day's fun for kids and anyone who likes white-knuckle rides. It stands on the Isla de La Cartuja, a tongue of land lying between two branches of the Río Guadalquivir, 2km northwest of the cathedral. The theme is 16th-century Spanish colonial adventure, and highlight rides include El Jaguar, a roller coaster with high-speed 360-degree turns, and the Anaconda water roller coaster, which features vertiginous drops.

Isla Mágica uses part of the site of Expo '92. Other parts of the futuristic site have been turned into a technology park called Cartuja 93.

Both Bus Nos C1 and C2 (p696) go to Isla Mágica.

WALKING TOUR

This route will acquaint you with the main central neighbourhoods of Seville as a preliminary to more in-depth investigations.

Start on Plaza del Triunfo, flanked by Seville's two great monuments, the **cathedral (1**; p682) and the **Alcázar (2**; p683). From here take a wander through the narrow streets and pretty plazas of the Barrio de Santa Cruz (p685) – **Plaza Doña Elvira (3)**, **Plaza de los Venerables (4)**, **Plaza de Santa Cruz (5)**, Calle Santa Teresa and Calle Mateos Gago. You'll want

to return to some of the bars, restaurants and shops here later. Calle Mateos Gago brings you out onto **Plaza Virgen de los Reyes (6)**, which is dominated by **La Giralda (7**; p682). Now head up pedestrian Calle Álvarez Quintero to El Centro, the age-old true centre of Seville, for a look at **Plaza de San Francisco (8**; p686) and, 100m further northeast, **Plaza Salvador (9**; p686). Stroll north along Calle Sierpes (p686), a key downtown shopping street. Turn west along Calle Rioja to the **Iglesia de la Magdalena (10**; p690), then follow Calle San Pablo and Calle Reyes Católicos southwest to the Río Guadalquivir. Follow the river southeast along the walking path, passing the **Plaza de Toros de la Real Maestranza (11**; p687) across the road, until you get to the **Torre del Oro (12**; p686), from where it's a short walk east back to the cathedral by Calle Almirante Lobo or Calle Santander.

> **WALKING TOUR**
>
> **Distance** 4km
> **Duration** Two hours plus stops

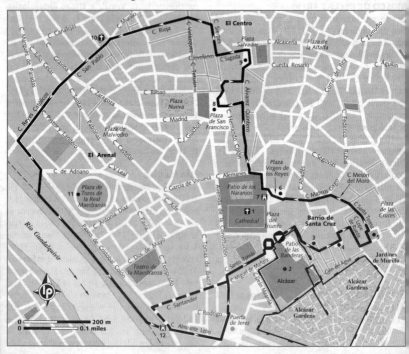

COURSES
Language

Seville is one of the most popular cities in Spain to study Spanish. The best schools offer both short- and long-term courses at a variety of levels:

Carpe Diem (Map pp680-1; ☎ 954 21 85 15; www.carpediemsevilla.com; Calle de la Cuna 13)

CLIC (Map pp680-1; ☎ 954 50 21 31; www.clic.es; Calle Albareda 19)

Giralda Center (Map pp680-1; ☎ 954 21 31 65; www.giraldacenter.com; Calle Mateos Gago 17)

Lenguaviva (Map pp676-7; ☎ 954 90 51 31; www.lenguaviva.es; Calle Viriato 24)

LINC (Map pp680-1; ☎ 954 50 04 59; www.linc.tv; Calle General Polavieja 13)

Flamenco & Dance

Espacio Meteora (Map pp676-7; ☎ 954 90 14 83; http://espaciometeora.com in Spanish; Calle Duque Cornejo 16A) Innovative arts centre.

Fundación Cristina Heeren de Arte Flamenco (Map pp680-1; ☎ 954 21 70 58; www.flamencoheeren.com; Calle Fabiola 1) Academy with long-term courses in all flamenco arts, also one-month intensive summer courses.

Sevilla Dance Centre (Map pp676-7; ☎ 954 38 39 02; Calle Conde de Torrejón 19) Flamenco, classical, hip-hop, contemporary etc.

Tourist offices and *El Giraldillo* (p679) have further information.

SEVILLE FOR CHILDREN

Open spaces such as the banks of the Guadalquivir, **Parque María Luisa** (p687) and the **Alcázar gardens** (p685) are good places for young children to run off some steam. They'll enjoy feeding doves at Plaza de América in Parque María Luisa. **Isla Mágica** (p687) is a huge day of fun: those aged over 10 will get the most out of the rides. Another sure hit is a **city tour** (right) in an open-top double-decker or horse-drawn carriage. On Sunday morning visit the pet market in Plaza de la Alfalfa.

Aquópolis Sevilla (☎ 954 40 66 22; www.aquopolis .es in Spanish; Avenida del Deporte s/n; adult/child under 11 €12.90/8.90; ☽ 11am-7pm or 8pm approx late May–early Sep) provides water slides and wave pools for those who need to get wet in summer. It's in Barrio Las Delicias in the east of the city, off the A92 towards Málaga.

TOURS

Cruceros Turísticos Torre del Oro (Map pp680-1; ☎ 954 56 16 92; adult/children under 14 €12/free) One-hour sightseeing river cruises every half-hour from 11am from the Torre del Oro; last departure can range from 6pm in winter to 10pm in summer.

Horse-drawn carriages These wait around near the cathedral and Plaza de España and Puerta de Jerez, charging €30 for up to four people for a one-hour trot around the Barrio de Santa Cruz and Parque de María Luisa areas.

Sevilla Tour (☎ 902 101081; www.citysightseeing -spain.com) Open-topped double-decker buses and converted trams make one-hour city tours, with ear-phone commentary in a choice of languages. The €11 ticket is valid for 48 hours and you can hop on or off near the Torre del Oro (Map pp680-1), Avenida de Portugal behind Plaza de España (Map pp676-7) or the Isla de La Cartuja (Map pp676-7). Buses typically leave every 30 minutes between 7am and 8pm.

Tour por Sevilla/Guide Friday (☎ 954 56 06 93; www.busturistico.com) Same deal as Sevilla Tour but doesn't start till 10am.

Walking in Seville with Carmen This 90-minute combination of walking tour, street theatre and history lesson is given in English by a lively young woman several days a week, March to October (except July). Look for her flyers around the Barrio de Santa Cruz; pay by donation.

FESTIVALS & EVENTS

Seville's Semana Santa processions (see the boxed text Semana Santa in Seville on p690) and its Feria de Abril, a week or two later, are worth travelling a long way for.

Feria de Abril

The **April Fair**, in the second half of the month, is a kind of release after the solemnity of Semana Santa. The biggest and most colourful of all Andalucía's *ferias*, it takes place on a special site, El Real de la Feria, in the Los Remedios area southwest of the city centre. The ceremonial lighting of the *feria* grounds on the Monday night is the starting gun for six nights of eating, drinking, fabulous flouncy dresses, and music and dancing till dawn. Much of the site is occupied by private *casetas* (enclosures), but there are also public ones, where much the same fun goes on. There's also a huge fairground.

In the afternoon, from about 1pm, those with horses and carriages parade about the *feria* grounds in their finery (horses are dressed up too). It's during the *feria* that Seville's major bullfighting season takes place.

SLEEPING

There's a good range of places to stay in all three of the most attractive areas – Barrio

SEMANA SANTA IN SEVILLE

Nowhere in Spain is Holy Week marked with quite such intense spectacle, anguish and solemnity, and quite such weight of tradition and overriding adoration of the Virgin, as it is in Seville.

Every day from Palm Sunday to Easter Sunday, large, richly bedecked images and life-size tableaux from the Easter story are carried from Seville's churches through the streets to the cathedral, accompanied by processions that may take more than an hour to pass, and watched by vast crowds. These rites took on their present form in the 17th century, when many of the images – some of which are supreme works of art – were created.

The processions are organised by over 50 different *hermandades* or *cofradías* (brotherhoods, some of which include women), each normally with two *pasos* (sculptural representations of events from Christ's Passion).

The first *paso* focuses on Christ; the second is an image of the Virgin. They are carried by teams of about 40 bearers called *costaleros*, who work in relays as each supports a weight of about 50kg. The *pasos* move with a hypnotic swaying motion to the rhythm of their accompanying bands and the commands of their *capataz* (leader), who strikes a bell to start and stop the *paso*.

Each pair of *pasos* has up to 2500 costumed followers, known as *nazarenos*. Many of these wear tall Ku Klux Klan–like capes, which cover their heads (except for eye slits), implying that the identity of the penitent is known only to God. The most contrite go barefoot and carry crosses.

From Palm Sunday to Good Friday, seven or eight brotherhoods leave their churches each day in the afternoon or early evening, arriving between 5pm and 11pm at Calle Campana, at the northern end of Calle Sierpes. This is the start of the *carrera oficial* (official route), which all then follow along Calle Sierpes, Plaza San Francisco and Avenida de la Constitución to the cathedral. They enter the cathedral at its western end and leave at the east, emerging on Plaza Virgen de los Reyes. They get back to their churches some time between 10pm and 3am.

The climax of the week is the *madrugada* (early hours) of Good Friday, when some of the most respected or popular brotherhoods file through the city. The first to reach the *carrera oficial*, at about 1.30am, is the oldest brotherhood, El Silencio, which goes in complete silence. At about 2am comes Jesús del Gran Poder, whose 17th-century Christ is a masterpiece of Sevillan sculpture. Around 3am comes La Macarena, whose passionately adored Virgin is Seville's supreme representation of the grieving-yet-hoping mother of Christ, and is believed to have been sculpted in the mid-17th century by María Luisa Roldán. Then come El Calvario, from the Iglesia de la Magdalena, then Esperanza de Triana and finally, at about 6am, Los Gitanos, the *gitano* (Roma) brotherhood.

On the Saturday evening, just four brotherhoods make their way to the cathedral, and finally, on Easter Sunday morning, only one, the Hermandad de la Resurrección.

Procession schedules are widely available during Semana Santa, and its website, www.semana-santa.org (in Spanish), is devoted to Holy Week in Seville. It's interesting to watch a brotherhood passing through its own neighbourhood or as it leaves or re-enters its church – always an emotional moment. Crowds along most of the official route make it hard to get much of a view, but if you arrive early enough in the evening, you can usually get close enough to the cathedral to see plenty.

If you're not in Seville for Semana Santa, you can get an inkling of what it's about from some of the churches housing the famous images. The **Basílica de La Macarena** (Map pp676–7; ☎ 954 90 18 00; Calle Bécquer 1; museum €3; ☑ 9am-2pm & 5-8pm) and the **Basílica de Jesús del Gran Poder** (Map pp676–7; ☎ 954 91 56 72; Plaza de San Lorenzo 13; ☑ 8am-1.30pm & 6-9pm Sat-Thu, 7.30am-10pm Fri) are both north of the centre of Alameda de Hércules. The **Iglesia de la Magdalena** (Map pp680-1; Calle San Pablo 12; ☑ usually 8am-11.30am & 6.30-9pm) is a few streets south of the Museo de Bellas Artes.

de Santa Cruz (close to the Alcázar and Prado de San Sebastián bus station), El Arenal (convenient for Plaza de Armas bus station) and El Centro.

Room rates in this section are for each establishment's high season – typically from March to June and again from September to October. Just about every room in Seville costs even more during Semana Santa and the Feria de Abril, and sometimes between the two as well. The typical increase is between 30% and 60% over normal high-season rates. It's vital to book ahead at this time.

Renting a tourist apartment here can be good value: a clean, comfortable, well-equipped apartment typically costs under €100 for four people, or between €30 and €70 for two. Try **Apartamentos Embrujo de Sevilla** (☎ 625-060937; www.embrujodesevilla.com) or **Sevilla5.com** (☎ 637-011091; www.sevilla5.com).

Barrio de Santa Cruz   Map pp680–1
BUDGET
Huéspedes Dulces Sueños (☎ 954 41 93 93; Calle Santa María La Blanca 21; s/d €40/50, with shared bathroom €20/40; 🐛) 'Sweet Dreams' is a friendly little *hostal* (budget hotel) with spotless rooms. Those overlooking the street are good and bright. Only the doubles have air-con.

Hostal Arias (☎ 954 22 68 40; www.hostalarias .com; Calle Mariana de Pineda 9; s/d €41/56; 🐛) Floral-print bedspreads and the tiled lobby lend a cute note to the friendly Arias, which has a lift to all floors.

MID-RANGE
Hotel Alcántara (☎ 954 50 05 95; www.hotelalcantara .net; Calle Ximénez de Enciso 28; s/d €64/80; 🐛) This small, friendly, new hotel on a pedestrian street has bright rooms with bathtub, phone, windows on to the hotel's patio, and pretty floral curtains. There's a lift and a room adapted for wheelchair users.

Hostería del Laurel (☎ 954 22 02 95; www .hosteriadellaurel.com; Plaza de los Venerables 5; s/d incl breakfast €71.70/103.80; 🐛) Above a characterful old bar on a small Santa Cruz plaza, the Laurel has simple, spacious and bright rooms with marble floors and good-sized bathrooms.

Hotel Puerta de Sevilla (☎ 954 98 72 70; www .hotelpuertadesevilla.com; Calle Santa María la Blanca 36; s/d €64.20/83.45; P 🐛) This small new hotel is decorated in pleasing, traditional style with flower-pattern textiles and prettily tiled bathrooms. A lift connects the three floors.

Also recommended:
Hostal Córdoba (☎ 954 22 74 98; Calle Farnesio 12; s with/without bathroom €50/40 d €70/60; 🐛)
Hotel YH Giralda (☎ 954 22 83 24; www.yh-hoteles .com; Calle Abades 30; r €69.55; P 🐛 🖳)
Hostal Goya (☎ 954 21 11 70; hgoya@hostalgoya.e.tel efonica.net; Calle Mateos Gago 31; d with bath €70, s/d with shower €43/60)

Las Casas del Rey de Baeza (Map pp680-1; ☎ 954 56 14 96; www.hospes.es; Plaza Cristo de la Redención 2; s/d €162.65/189.40; P 🐛 🖳 🖭) This expertly run and marvellously designed hotel occupies former communal housing patios dating from the 18th century. The large rooms, in tasteful hues, boast attractive modern art, a CD player, DVD and modem line. Public areas include a super-comfortable lounge and reading room, an attractive restaurant featuring Sevillan food, and a gorgeous pool.

Hotel Simón (Map ppp680-1; ☎ 954 22 66 60; www.hotelsimonsevilla.com in Spanish; Calle GarcíadeVinuesa19;s/d€49.65/74.50; 🐛)Acharming small hotel in a fine 18th-century house, with spotless and comfortable rooms, the Simón is extremely popular so book well ahead. It's built around a lovely patio with a fountain, and adorned with antiques and beautiful Sevillan tilework.

TOP END
Las Casas de la Judería (☎ 954 41 51 50; www .casasypalacios.com in Spanish; Callejón Dos Hermanas 7; s/d from €108.10/166.90; P 🐛) This charming hotel is in fact a series of restored houses and mansions based around several lovely patios and fountains. Most of the rooms and suites sport four-poster beds, a bath *and* a shower, and a writing table. An amazing range of art decks the walls. In the evening, relax in the cosy piano bar. Breakfast is available.

El Arenal   Map pp680–1
BUDGET
Hotel Madrid (☎ 954 21 43 07; Calle San Pedro Mártir 22; s/d €40/55; P 🐛) This small friendly hotel offers pretty good value. All rooms have firm little beds, and balconies overlooking quiet streets.

Hostal Residencia Naranjo (☎ 954 22 58 40; Calle San Roque 11; s/d €30/44; 🐛) Colourful bedspreads and pine furniture add a touch of warmth; the rooms are all equipped with TV and phone.

Hostal Zahira (☎ 954 22 10 61; Calle San Eloy 43; s/d/tr €30/50/60; 🐛) The Zahira provides plain, clean rooms with a bright lobby and amiable management; it also happens to be in a good location.

MID-RANGE

Hotel Puerta de Triana (☎ 954 21 54 04; www.hotel puertadetriana.com; Calle Reyes Católicos 5; s/d €64.20/ 85.60; ❄) The cosy rooms here have traditional fittings but modern comforts, and all with windows onto the street or interior patios. Downstairs there are spacious lounge areas.

Hotel Maestranza (☎ 954 56 10 70; www.hotel -maestranza.com; Calle Gamazo 12; s/d €49/87; ❄ 🖳) A small, friendly hotel on a quietish street, the Maestranza has spotless but plain rooms, all equipped with phone and safe. The singles are small.

Also recommended:

Hotel Plaza Sevilla (☎ 954 21 71 49; info@hotel plazasevilla.com; Calle Canalejas 2; s/d incl breakfast €47/67; Ⓟ ❄) Efficiently run hotel with cosy rooms.

TOP END

Hotel Vincci La Rábida (☎ 954 50 12 80; www.vincci hoteles.com in Spanish; Calle Castelar 24; s/d €154.10/ 181.90; Ⓟ ❄ 🖳) A beautiful four-storey columned atrium-lounge greets you in this converted 18th-century palace, now a classy four-star hotel with extremely comfortable rooms. The seasonal rooftop bar-café has magnificent views of the cathedral.

El Centro   Map pp680–1
BUDGET

Casa Sol y Luna (☎ 954 21 06 82; casasolyluna@tele fonica.net; Calle Pérez Galdós 1A; s/tr without bathroom €22/54, d with/without bathroom €48/42) This is a small but first-rate hostal in a characterful, attractively modernised, old town house. Your welcoming young hosts speak fluent English, Italian and Spanish and there's a sociable central lounge. The shared bathrooms (none shared by more than two rooms) are the biggest and most beautiful in Andalucía!

Hostal Lis (☎ 954 21 30 88; www.hostallis.com; Calle Escarpín 10; s/d/tr €21/42/63; 🖳) Once owned by a tile manufacturer, the friendly and well-kept Lis is adorned with colourful old Sevillan tiling throughout. There's a roof terrace and free Internet for guests.

MID-RANGE

Hotel San Francisco (☎ /fax 954 50 15 41; Calle Álvarez Quintero 38; s/d €55/68; ❄) This good-value hotel on a pedestrianised street occupies a recently converted 18th-century family home. Nearly all the good-sized rooms look

out onto the street or an interior patio; all have marble floors and air-con/heating.

TOP END

Hotel Las Casas de los Mercaderes (☎ 954 22 58 58; www.casasypalacios.com; Calle Álvarez Quintero 9-13; s/d €94.20/137; Ⓟ ❄) Classy hotel centred on a lovely two-storey 18th-century patio.

North of the Centre   Map pp680–1
BUDGET

Hostal Museo (☎ 954 91 55 26; www.hostalmuseo .com; Calle Abad Gordillo 17; s/d €42.80/53.50; ❄) The immaculate rooms at the recently opened Museo are endowed with solid wooden furniture and comfortable beds, phone, TV and reading lamps. There's a lift too.

TOP END

Hotel Cervantes (☎ 954 90 02 80; www.hotel-cervantes .com; Calle Cervantes 10; s/d €86/122; Ⓟ ❄) The Cervantes is a charming, modern hotel on a quiet street, in a rather quaint old part of the city. Rooms have pretty furnishings, parquet floors, bright modern art and bathtub. Buffet breakfast is available.

EATING

Seville is one of Spain's tapas capitals, with scores and scores of bars serving all sorts of delectable bites. To catch the city's atmosphere, plunge straight in and follow the winding tapas trail. Most tapas bars open at lunchtime as well as in the evening.

For more conventional dining, classy modern restaurants that prepare Spanish food with some enlivening international touches abound. Don't bother looking for dinner until at least 8pm.

Barrio de Santa Cruz & Around
RESTAURANTS & CAFÉS

Restaurante La Albahaca (Map pp680-1; ☎ 954 22 07 14; Plaza de Santa Cruz 12; mains €18-22, menú €27) Gastronomic invention is the mainstay of this swish restaurant. Try the pork trotter with mushroom, young garlic and mousse of peas!

Restaurant La Cueva (Map pp680-1; ☎ 954 21 31 43; Calle Rodrigo Caro 18; mains €10.75-23.50) This popular eatery cooks up a storming fish casserole (€23.50 for two people) and a hearty *caldereta* (lamb stew; €10.75).

Las Escobas (Map pp680-1; ☎ 954 21 94 08; Calle Álvarez Quintero 62; mains around €15) Touristy though it is, Las Escobas provides good meals with a smile and without delay.

Restaurante Egaña Oriza (Map pp676-7; ☎ 954 22 72 11; Calle San Fernando 41; mains €15-40; ☺ closed lunch Sat & Sun) One of the city's best restaurants, Egaña Oriza cooks up superb Andalucian-Basque cuisine.

Restaurante Modesto (Map pp680-1; ☎ 954 41 68 11; Calle Cano y Cueto 5; mains €7.35-42.60) This classy place presents a full range of fish dishes.

Hostería del Laurel (Map pp680-1; ☎ 954 22 02 95; Plaza de los Venerables 5; mains €10-20) The restaurant and tapas bar here offer charming service, a bustling atmosphere and average fare.

TAPAS BARS

Bodega Santa Cruz (Map pp680-1; ☎ 954 21 32 46; Calle Mateos Gago; tapas €1.40-1.70) A focal point for tapas pilgrims, this bar has a wonderful choice of flavoursome bites. Its popularity speaks volumes.

Cervecería Giralda (Map pp680-1; ☎ 954 22 74 35; Calle Mateos Gago 1; tapas €1.60-2.10) Exotic variations are merged with traditional dishes at this bar in what was once a Muslim bathhouse.

Café Bar Las Teresas (Map pp680-1; ☎ 954 21 30 69; Calle Santa Teresa 2; tapas €1.80-4) Hams dangle proudly from the ceiling and punters are kept happy with plates of authentic tapas.

El Arenal
Map pp680-1

RESTAURANTS & CAFÉS

Horno de San Buenaventura (cnr Avenida Constitución & Calle García de Vinuesa; coffee & ham tostada €2.80) A great

café with a spacious upstairs salon, where you can breakfast in unhurried tranquillity.

Enrique Becerra (☎ 954 21 30 49; Calle Gamazo 2; mains €14.50-20.20; ☺ closed Sun) Adding a smart touch to El Arenal, Enrique Becerra cooks up hearty Andalucian dishes to rave about. The lamb drenched in honey sauce and stuffed with spinach and pine nuts is just one of the delectable offerings.

El Centro
Map pp680-1

RESTAURANTS & CAFÉS

Habanita (☎ 606-716456; Calle Golfo 3; raciones €6-9; ☺ closed Sun evening) This top restaurant serves a winning variety of Cuban, Andalucian and vegetarian food.

Bar Laredo (cnr Calle Sierpes & Plaza de San Francisco) Watch them slap together a variety of *bocadillos* (bread roll with filling; €3) for rapid consumption at this popular breakfast stop.

Restaurante San Marco (☎ 954 21 24 40; Calle de la Cuna 6; pizza around €8, pasta €9-12) Set in an 18th-century palace, this is the grandest of the San Marco batch of pizza-and-pasta eateries.

TAPAS BARS

Plaza de la Alfalfa is the hub of the tapas scene, with a flush of first-rate bars serving tapas from around €1.60 to €3. On Calle Alfalfa just off the plaza, hop from sea-themed La Trastienda to the intimate Bar Alfalfa and on to La Bodega where you can mix head-spinning quantities of ham and sherry.

El Patio San Eloy (Calle San Eloy 9; tapas €1.30-1.60) Hams hang like stalactites at the always-busy Patio San Eloy, where you can feast on a fine array of *burguillos* (small filled rolls).

Triana

RESTAURANTS & CAFÉS

Kiosco de las Flores (Map pp680-1; ☎ 954 27 45 76; Calle del Betis; mains €15-40, media raciones/raciones around €5/9; ☺ closed Sun evening & Mon) Still revelling in the transformation from 70-year-old shack to a glam conservatory (just check the photos), this eatery doles out great *pescaíto frito* (fried fish).

Ristorante Cosa Nostra (Map pp680-1; ☎ 954 27 07 52; Calle del Betis 52; pizzas €5.40-7.50; ☺ closed Mon) Cosa Nostra has an intimate feel that neighbouring pizza-and-pasta joints lack.

TAPAS BARS

Bar Blanca Paloma (Map pp680–1; cnr Calle Pagés del Corro & Calle San Jacinto; tapas €1.50-3.50) The *lomo de novillo*, a slice of juicy steak, is a treat at this always-busy bar.

DRINKING & ENTERTAINMENT

Seville presents a feast of night-time delights, from beer-fuelled bopping and thumping live beats to experimental theatre and steamy flamenco. Bars usually open 6pm to 2am weekdays, 8pm till 4am at the weekend. Drinking and partying get going at midnight on Friday and Saturday (daily when it's hot). In summer, dozens of open-air late-night bars *(terrazas de verano)*, many of them with live music and plenty of room to dance, spring up along both banks of the river.

Get to grips with the latest action by logging onto www.discoversevilla.com or www.exploreseville.com.

Bars

BARRIO DE SANTA CRUZ & AROUND   Map pp680–1

P Flaherty Irish Pub (☎ 954 21 04 15; Calle Alemanes 7) Drench your innards with a Guinness while you watch the TV sport.

Antigüedades (Calle Argote de Molina 40) Blending mellow beats with weird mannequin parts and skewered bread rolls suspended from the ceiling, this is a strange but cool place. Wander past and it'll suck you in.

EL ARENAL   Map pp680–1

Café Isbiliyya (☎ 954 21 04 60; Paseo de Cristóbal Colón 2) Cupid welcomes you to this busy gay music bar, which puts on extravagant drag-queen shows on Thursday and Sunday night.

EL CENTRO   Map pp680–1

Plaza del Salvador throbs with drinkers from mid-evening to 1am and is a great place to down a couple of beers alfresco. Grab a drink from **La Antigua Bodeguita** (☎ 954 56 18 33) or **La Sapotales** next door and sit on the steps of the Parroquia del Salvador.

Calle Pérez Galdós, off Plaza de la Alfalfa, has a handful of pulsating bars: **Bare Nostrum** (Calle Pérez Galdós 26), **Cabo Loco** (Calle Pérez Galdós 26), **Nao** (Calle Pérez Galdós 28) and **La Rebótica** (Calle Pérez Galdós 11). If you're in a party mood, you should find at least one with a scene that takes your fancy.

ALAMEDA DE HÉRCULES   Map pp680–1

The dusty Alameda de Hércules is home to a bohemian and alternative mix of bars and live-music venues.

Bulebar Café (☎ 954 90 19 54; Alameda de Hércules 83; ☽ 4pm-late) This place fills up with young sweaty bodies at night, but is pleasantly chilled in the early evening.

El Corto Maltés (Alameda de Hércules 66) A laid-back saloon by day and boisterous drinking den at night.

La Ilustre Víctima (Calle Doctor Letamendi 35) Buzzing with an international crowd, this place plays good jazzy house music and serves up tasty vegetarian tapas.

TRIANA

The wall overlooking the river along Calle del Betis forms a fantastic makeshift bar. Carry your drink out from one of the following watering holes: Alambique, Big Ben, Sirocca and Muí d'Aquí. They're all clustered at Calle del Betis 54 (Map pp676–7) and open from 9pm.

La Otra Orilla (Map pp676-7; Paseo de Nuestra Señora de la O) Duck through a passage to the river bank to find this buzzing music bar blessed with a great outdoor terrace.

Bullfights

Fights at Seville's ancient and elegant 14,000-seat **Plaza de Toros de la Real Maestranza** (Map pp680–1; Paseo de Cristóbal Colón 12; www .realmaestranza.com) are among the biggest in Spain. The season runs from Easter Sunday to early October, with fights every Sunday, usually at 6.30pm, and every day during the Feria de Abril and the week before it.

From the start of the season until late June/ early July, nearly all the fights are by fully fledged matadors. Seats cost €20 to €100 but only cheap *sol* seats (in the sun at the start of proceedings) may be available to those who don't hold season tickets. Most of the rest of the season, novice bullfights *(novilleras)* are held, with tickets costing €9 to €42. Tickets are sold in advance at **Empresa Pagés** (Map pp680–1; ☎ 954 50 13 82; Calle de Adriano 37), and from 4.30pm on fight days at the bullring itself.

Clubs

Clubs in Seville come and go with amazing rapidity but a few have stood the test of time. The partying starts between 2am and 4am at the weekend.

Boss (Map pp676-7; Calle del Betis 67; admission free with flyer; 8pm-7am Tue-Sun) Make it past the two gruff bouncers and you'll find Boss a top dance spot. The music is a total mix.

Weekend (Map pp676-7; ☎ 954 37 88 73; Calle del Torneo 43; admission around €7; 11pm-8am Thu-Sat) Weekend is one of Seville's top live-music and DJ spots.

Lisboa Music Club (Map pp676-7; Calle Faustino Álvarez 27; admission €6; midnight-6am Wed-Sat) A very hip house and techno club.

Live Music

Fun Club (Map pp676-7; ☎ 958 25 02 49; Alameda de Hércules 86; admission live-band nights €3-6, other nights free; 11.30pm-late Thu-Sun, from 9.30pm live-band nights) With funk, Latino, hip-hop and jazz bands gracing the stage it's not surprising that this little dance warehouse is a music-lovers' favourite. Live bands play Friday or Saturday.

La Imperdible (Map pp676-7; ☎ 954 38 82 19; Plaza San Antonio de Padua 9; sala@imperdible.org; admission €4.80-6) This epicentre of experimental arts stages lots of contemporary dance and a bit of drama and music, usually at 9pm. Its bar, the **El Almacén** (Map pp676-7; ☎ 954 90 04 34; admission free), hosts varied music events from around 11pm Thursday to Saturday.

FLAMENCO

Hotels and tourist offices tend to steer you towards *tablaos* (expensive, tourist-oriented flamenco venues), which can be inauthentic and lacking in atmosphere, though **Los Gallos** (Map pp680-1; ☎ 954 21 69 81; Plaza de Santa Cruz 11; www.tablaolosgallos.com in Spanish; admission incl 1 drink €27; 2hr shows 9pm & 11.30pm) is a cut above the average.

In general, you'll catch more atmosphere – though unpredictable quality – at one of the venues and bars that stage regular flamenco nights:

Casa de la Memoria de Al-Andalus (Map pp680-1; ☎ 954 56 06 70; Calle Ximénez de Enciso 28; adult/child €11/5; 9pm) Authentic nightly shows in a great patio setting.

La Carbonería (Map pp680-1; 954 21 44 60; Calle Levíes 18; admission free) A converted coal yard in the Barrio de Santa Cruz with two large rooms, thronged nearly every night with locals and visitors who come to enjoy the social scene, and live flamenco from about 8pm to 4am.

Sol Café Cantante (Map pp680-1; ☎ 954 22 51 65; Calle del Sol 5; adult/concession incl 1 drink €18/11; 9pm Thu-Sat) Up-and-coming flamenco artists take the stage here.

Well-known flamenco artists appear fairly frequently at theatres and concert halls. Seville also stages the biggest of all Spain's flamenco festivals, the month-long Bienal de Flamenco, in September of even-numbered years.

SHOPPING

The craft shops in the Barrio de Santa Cruz are inevitably tourist-oriented, but many sell excellent local ceramics and tiles.

El Centro has a pretty cluster of pedestrianised shopping streets. Calles Sierpes, Cuna, Velázquez and Tetuán have retained their charm with a host of small shops selling everything from polka-dot flamenco dresses to diamond rings. **El Corte Inglés** department store (Map pp680-1) occupies four separate buildings a little west, on Plaza de la Magdalena and Plaza del Duque de la Victoria. Further north, Calle Amor de Dios and Calle Doctor Letamendi (Map pp676-7) have more alternative shops.

The large Thursday **mercadillo** (flea market; Map pp676-7; Calle de la Feria) north of the city centre, near Alameda de Hércules, is a colourful event that's well worth a visit.

In the traditional **tile-making area** of Triana, a dozen shops and workshops still offer charming, artful ceramics around the junction of Calle Alfarería and Calle Antillano Campos (Map pp676-7).

GETTING THERE & AWAY
Air

Seville's **Aeropuerto San Pablo** (Map pp676-7; ☎ 954 44 90 00) has a fair range of international and domestic flights. **Iberia** (☎ 902 400500; City Avenida de la Buhaira 8; Airport ☎ 954 26 09 15) flies daily nonstop to Valencia, Bilbao, Madrid, Barcelona, London and Paris. **Spanair** (☎ 902 131415; Airport) and **Air Europa** (☎ 902 401501; tickets from Halcón Viajes, Avenida de la Constitución 5) both fly nonstop daily to/from Barcelona. There are further flights to London by **British Airways** (☎ 902 111333; Airport), Paris by **Air France** (☎ 901 112266; Airport), and Brussels by **Brussels Airlines** (☎ 902 901492; Airport). **Air Berlin** (☎ 901 116402; Airport), **LTU** (☎ 954 44 91 99; Airport) and **Hapag-Lloyd Express** (☎ 902 020069; www.hlx.com; Airport) fly to German cities.

Bus

From the **Estación de Autobuses Prado de San Sebastián** (Map pp676-7; ☎ 954 41 71 11; Plaza San

ANDALUCÍA

Sebastián), there are 10 or more buses daily to/from Cádiz (€9.30, 1½ hours), Córdoba (€8.60, 1½ hours), Granada (€15.99, three hours), Jerez de la Frontera (€5.40 to €5.80, 1¼ hours) and Málaga (€13.05, 2½ hours). This is also the station for Arcos de la Frontera (€6.30, two hours, twice daily), Tarifa (€14, three hours, four daily) and other towns in Cádiz province, the east of Sevilla province, Ronda (€8.40, 2½ hours, five or more daily) and destinations along the Mediterranean coast from the Costa del Sol to Barcelona.

From the **Estación de Autobuses Plaza de Armas** (Map pp676–7; ☎ 954 90 77 37; Avenida del Cristo de la Expiración), destinations include Madrid (€15.95, six hours, 14 daily), El Rocío (€4.50, 1½ hours, three to five daily), Huelva (€6.10, 1¼ hours, at least 18 daily) and other places in Huelva province, Mérida (€10.50, three hours, 12 daily), Cáceres (€14.20, four hours, six daily) and northwestern Spain.

This is also the station for buses to Portugal. For Lisbon, there are two daily services by Alsa (€35, 7½ hours, twice daily), one via Badajoz and Évora and the other (overnight) via Faro; three weekly by Damas (€28.25, 4½ hours, three weekly) via Aracena, Serpa and Beja; and three weekly overnight by Anibal (€25, 7½ hours, three weekly) via Badajoz and Évora. Damas also runs buses along Portugal's Algarve to Lagos (€17, 5½ hours, two daily) via Faro and Albufeira.

Car & Motorcycle

Hotels with parking usually charge you €10 to €15 a day for the privilege – no cheaper than some public car parks (p696), but at least your vehicle will be close at hand.

Car rental isn't cheap. Try local firms such as **ATA Rent A Car** (Map pp680–1; ☎ 954 22 17 77; Calle Almirante Lobo 2) or **Triana Rent A Car** (Map pp680–1; ☎ 954 56 44 39; Calle Almirante Lobo 7).

Train

Estación de Santa Justa (Map pp676–7; ☎ 954 41 41 11; Avenida Kansas City) is 1.5km northeast of the city centre. There's also a city-centre **Renfe ticket office** (Map pp680–1; Calle Zaragoza 29).

Fourteen or more super-fast AVE trains, reaching speeds of 280km/h, go daily to/from Madrid (€59 to €65, 2½ hours). The two daily 'Altaria' services are a little cheaper and about one hour slower.

Other destinations include Barcelona (€50 to €77.50, 10½ to 13 hours, three daily), Cáceres (€14.65, 5¾ hours, one daily), Cádiz (€8.40 to €22.50, 1½ to two hours, nine daily), Córdoba (€7 to €24, 40 minutes to 1½ hours, 21 or more daily), Granada (€17.65, 3¼ hours, four daily), Huelva (€6.40 to €15.50, 1½ hours, four daily), Jerez de la Frontera (€5.85 to €19, one to 1¼ hours, nine daily), Málaga (€14.15, 2½ hours, five daily) and Mérida (€11, 3¾ hours, one daily). For Lisbon (€49.65, 16 hours), you must change in the middle of the night at Cáceres.

GETTING AROUND
To/From the Airport

The airport is 7km east of the city centre on the A4 Córdoba road. **Amarillos Tour** (☎ 902 210317) runs buses between the airport and the Puerta de Jerez (€2.30, 30 to 40 minutes, at least 15 daily). A taxi costs about €15.

Bus

Bus Nos C1, C2, C3 and C4 do useful circular routes linking the main transport terminals and the city centre. The C1, departing from in front of Estación de Santa Justa, follows a clockwise circular route via Avenida de Carlos V (close to Prado de San Sebastián bus station and the Barrio de Santa Cruz), Avenida de María Luisa, Triana, Isla Mágica and Calle de Resolana. The C2, heading west from in front of Estación de Santa Justa, follows the same route in reverse. Bus No 32, also from outside Santa Justa, runs to/from Plaza de la Encarnación in El Centro.

The clockwise No C3 will take you from Avenida Menéndez Pelayo (near Prado de San Sebastián bus station and the Barrio de Santa Cruz) to the Puerta de Jerez, Triana, Plaza de Armas bus station, Calle del Torneo, Calle de Resolana and Calle de Recaredo. The C4 does the same circuit anticlockwise except that from Estación de Autobuses Plaza de Armas it heads south along Calle de Arjona and Paseo de Cristóbal Colón to the Puerta de Jerez, instead of crossing the river to Triana.

A single bus ride is €1.

Car & Motorcycle

Parking Paseo de Colón (Map pp680–1; cnr Paseo de Cristóbal Colón & Calle Adriano; per hr up to 10 hr €1.14,

10-24 hrs €11.40) is a relatively inexpensive underground car park.

AROUND SEVILLE

You'll find Andalucía's best Roman ruins at Itálica and, on the rolling agricultural plains east of Seville, fascinating old towns such as Carmona and Osuna that bespeak many epochs of history.

SANTIPONCE

pop 7,000 / elevation 20m

The small town of Santiponce, 8km northwest of Seville, is the location of Itálica and of the historic Monasterio de San Isidoro del Campo.

Itálica (☎ 955 99 65 83; adult/EU citizen €1.50/free; ◷ 8.30am-8.30pm Tue-Sat, 9am-3pm Sun Apr-Sep; 9am-5.30pm Tue-Sat, 10am-4pm Sun Oct-Mar), 8km northwest of Seville on the northern edge of Santiponce, was the first Roman town in Spain. It was founded in 206 BC for veterans of Rome's victory over Carthage at nearby Ilipa. Itálica was also the home town of the 2nd-century-AD Roman emperors Trajan and Hadrian. The partly reconstructed ruins include one of the biggest of all the Roman amphitheatres, broad paved streets, ruins of several houses with beautiful mosaics, and a theatre.

The **Monasterio de San Isidoro del Campo** (☎ 955 99 69 20; admission €2; ◷ 10am-2pm Wed & Thu, 10am-2pm & 5.30-8.30pm Fri & Sat, 10am-3pm Sun & holidays, Fri & Sat afternoons Oct-Mar 4-7pm) is at the southern end of Santiponce (the end nearest Seville), 1.5km from the Itálica entrance. Founded in 1301, the monastery contains a rare set of 15th-century murals, showing saints and Mudéjar geometric and floral designs; and some fine and historically interesting sculpture in its two churches, notably a masterly *retablo* by the great 17th-century Sevillan sculptor Juan Martínez Montañés. It was here that the Bible was first translated into Spanish, by the monk Casiodoro de Reina, in the 1550s.

Casa Venancio (☎ 955 99 67 06; Avenida Extremadura 9; mains €6-13) Located opposite the Itálica entrance, this restaurant has a varied menu. Try the rabbit or partridge with rice (€16.50 for two).

Buses run to Santiponce (€0.80, 30 minutes) from Seville's Plaza de Armas bus sta-

tion, at least twice an hour from 6.30am to 11pm Monday to Friday, and a little less often at weekends. They stop near the monastery and outside the Itálica entrance.

CARMONA

pop 27,000 / elevation 250m

Carmona, fortified since the 8th century BC, is 38km east of Seville, just off the A4 to Córdoba.

The helpful **tourist office** (☎ 954 19 09 55; www.turismo.carmona.org; ◷ 10am-6pm Mon-Sat, 10am-3pm Sun & holidays) is in the Puerta de Sevilla at the main entrance to the old town. Buses from Seville's Prado de San Sebastián bus station (€1.80, 45 minutes, 20 a day Monday to Friday, 10 on Saturday, seven on Sunday) stop 300m west of here, on Paseo del Estatuto.

Sights

Just over 1km southwest of the Puerta de Sevilla is Carmona's impressive **Roman necropolis** (☎ 954 14 08 11; Avenida de Jorge Bonsor 9; admission free; ◷ 9am-2pm Tue-Sat 15 Jun–14 Sep; 9am-5pm Tue-Fri, 10am-2pm Sat & Sun rest of year, closed holidays) You can climb down into a dozen family tombs, hewn from the rock.

The tourist office in the **Puerta de Sevilla**, the impressive fortified main gate of the old town, sells tickets (€2) for the gate's interesting upper levels, called the Alcázar de la Puerta de Sevilla, which include an Almohad patio and traces of a Roman temple.

Up into the old town from here, the 17th-century **Ayuntamiento** (Town Hall; Calle El Salvador; ◷ 8am-3pm Mon-Fri), contains a large, very fine Roman mosaic. The splendid **Iglesia Prioral de Santa María** (Calle Martín López de Córdoba; admission €3; ◷ 9am-2pm & 5.30-7pm Mon-Fri, 9am-2pm Sat, closed 21 Aug–21 Sep) was built mainly in the 15th and 16th centuries in a typical Carmona combination of brick and stone. Its Patio de los Naranjos, originally a mosque's courtyard, has a Visigothic calendar carved into one of its pillars. Behind Santa María, visit the **Museo de la Ciudad** (City History Museum; ☎ 954 14 01 28; Calle San Ildefonso 1; admission €2, free Tue; ◷ 10am-2pm & 4.30-9.30pm Wed-Mon 10am-2pm Tue 16 Jun–31 Aug, 11am-7pm Wed-Mon 11am-2pm Tue rest of year). Its displays provide extensive background for an exploration of the town.

The **Puerta de Córdoba** (Calle Dolores Quintanilla), at the end of the street passing the Iglesia de Santa María, is an original Roman gate, through which there are fine panoramas. South of here is the ruined **Alcázar**, an Almohad fort that Pedro I turned into a country palace. Ruined by earthquakes in 1504 and 1755, it's now the site of the luxurious Parador hotel, a good place to stop for a drink!

Sleeping & Eating

Parador Alcázar del Rey Don Pedro (☎ 954 14 10 10; www.parador.es; s/d €100.05/128.10; P 🍴 🖥 🏊) Carmona's luxuriously equipped *parador* exudes a historic atmosphere, and few Andalucian swimming pools are more spectacularly sited! The refectory-style dining room (*menú del día* €26.78) is one of the best in town.

Casa de Carmona (☎ 954 14 41 51; www.casade carmona.com; Plaza de Lasso 1; r incl breakfast from €160; P 🍴 🏊) A luxury hotel in a beautiful 16th-century palace, the Casa de Carmona has the genuine feel of the aristocratic home that it used to be. Its elegant restaurant (mains €16 to €22, menú €24 to €48) serves *haute cuisine* with an *andaluz* (Andalucian) touch.

Pensión Comercio (☎ 954 14 00 18; Calle Torre del Oro 56; s/d €32/45; 🍴) A lovely old tiled building near the Puerta de Sevilla, this is easily the best bet in its price range, with cosy, clean rooms.

There are several places to eat around Plaza San Fernando, near the Ayuntamiento. **Café Bar El Tapeo** (☎ 954 14 43 21; Calle Prim 9; tapas/raciones €1.50/5, menú €9) is friendly, down-to-earth and popular.

OSUNA

pop 18,000 / elevation 330m

Osuna, 91km from Seville, just off the A92 towards Granada and Málaga, is a relaxed place with some impressive buildings, several of them created by the ducal family of Osuna, one of Spain's richest since the 16th century. On the central Plaza Mayor, the **Oficina Municipal de Turismo** (☎ 954 81 57 32; 🕑 9am-2pm Mon-Sat) and the **Asociación Turístico Cultural Ossuna** (☎ 954 81 28 52; 🕑 10am-2pm & 5-8pm Mon-Fri, 10am-2pm Sat & Sun) both provide tourist information and hand out useful guides.

Sights

Most impressive are the big buildings on the hill overlooking the centre. On the way up from Plaza Mayor, the **Museo Arqueológico** (☎ 954 81 12 07; Plaza de la Duquesa; admission €1.60; 🕑 11.30am-1.30pm & 5-6.30pm Tue-Sun, closed

Sun afternoon Jul & Aug) has a good collection of mainly Iberian and Roman artefacts. Further up the same hill, the 16th-century **Colegiata de Santa María de la Asunción** (☎ 954 81 04 44; Plaza de la Encarnación; admission by guided tour only €2; 🕑 10am-1.30pm & 4-6.30pm Tue-Sun, closed Sun afternoon Jul & Aug), contains a wealth of sacred art, including several paintings by José de Ribera. The visit includes the lugubrious Sepulcro Ducal, the Osuna family vault. Opposite the Colegiata is the **Monasterio de la Encarnación** (☎ 954 81 11 21; admission €2; 🕑 same as Colegiata), now Osuna's museum of religious art, with beautiful tile work and a rich collection of baroque art.

Sleeping

Hotel Palacio Marqués de la Gomera (☎ 954 81 22 23; www.hotelpalaciodelmarques.com in Spanish; Calle San Pedro 20; s/d €77.05/96.30; P 🍴 🖥) This luxury hotel occupies one of Osuna's finest baroque mansions.

Hostal Caballo Blanco (☎ 954 81 01 84; Calle Granada 1; s/d €28.35/44.40; P 🍴) The friendly 'White Horse Inn' is an old coaching inn with courtyard parking and comfy rooms.

Getting There & Away

The **bus station** (☎ 954 81 01 46; Avenida de la Constitución) is 500m southeast of Plaza Mayor. Up to 11 daily buses run to Seville (Prado de San Sebastián; €5.65, 1¼ hours). The **train station** (Avenida de la Estación) is 1km southwest of the centre, with six trains a day to Seville (€6.55, one hour).

HUELVA PROVINCE

Andalucía's westernmost province – an afterthought to most travellers who are not on the way to or from Portugal – is in fact very much worth exploring. Around half the excellent, sandy, Atlantic beaches of the Costa de la Luz lie along Huelva's coast. Also here is most of that hugely important wildlife sanctuary, the Parque Nacional de Doñana, with its vital wetlands. Anyone with an historical leaning will be fascinated by the *lugares colombinos* (Columbus sites) east of Huelva city. And northern Huelva, focused on the town of Aracena, is a beautiful rolling hill–country district that just asks to be discovered on foot.

HUELVA

pop 141,000

The province's likeable but unspectacular capital, a port and industrial city, was probably founded by the Phoenicians as a trading settlement about 3000 years ago. What's here now, however, has almost all been built since the devastating Lisbon earthquake of 1755.

Orientation

Huelva stands between the Odiel and Tinto estuaries. The central area is about 1km square, with the bus station at its western edge, on Calle Doctor Rubio, and the train station at its southern edge on Avenida de Italia. Plaza de las Monjas is the central square; the main street, Avenida Martín Alonso Pinzón (also called Gran Vía), leads southeast from here, eventually becoming Alameda Sundheim.

Information

Policía Local (☎ 959 24 84 22; Avenida Tomás Domínguez 2)

Tourist Office (☎ 959 25 74 03; www.ayuntamiento huelva.es in Spanish; Avenida de Alemania 12; ☯ 9am-7pm Mon-Fri, 9am-2.30pm Sat) A few steps from the bus station.

Sights

The **Museo de Huelva** (☎ 959 25 93 00; Alameda Sundheim 13; admission free; ☯ 3-8pm Tue, 9am-8pm Wed-Sat, 9am-2pm Sun) focuses on the area's prehistoric pedigree, with an interesting exhibition on the Tartessos civilisation, whose origins are thought to be buried somewhere in the floodplains surrounding Huelva.

Take a strange stroll along the **Muelle Río Tinto**, an impressive iron pier curving out into the Odiel estuary about 500m south of the port. It was built in the 1870s by George Barclay Bruce, a disciple of tower specialist Gustave Eiffel, for the British-owned Rio Tinto Company.

Sleeping

Hotel Luz Huelva (☎ 959 25 00 11; Alameda Sundheim 26; s/d €84/99; ℗ ✖) This is the best hotel on offer: it's fairly bland but corporately comfortable in an ugly yellow building with concrete, scallop-shaped balconies.

Hotel Costa de la Luz (☎ 959 25 64 22; Calle José María Amo 8; s/d €27/47.58) Despite its proximity to the fish market and Franco-era taste in furnishings, the Costa de la Luz is reasonable and comfortable with a helpful reception.

Hotel Los Condes (☎ 959 28 24 00; www.hotel loscondes.com; Alameda Sundheim 14; s/d €38.95/56.85; ℗ ✖) Almost next door to Hotel Luz Huelva, Los Condes has air-con rooms at about half the price. The décor is a bit drab but the hotel has good facilities.

Albergue Juvenil Huelva (☎ 959 25 37 93; www .inturjoven.com in Spanish; Avenida Marchena Colombo 14; dm incl breakfast under 26 €11.65-13.75, over 26 €16.20-18.35) This is a good modern youth hostel where all rooms have a bathroom. It's 2km north of the bus station: city bus No 6 (€1) from there stops just around the corner from the hostel, on Calle JS Elcano.

Eating

El Rincon de la Cañada (☎ 959 54 03 21; Calle Garcí-Fernández 5; mains €15) Rustic furnishings disguise a classy and popular place that is heaving for lunch even at 5pm. Choose your own fresh fish from the cold counter. It's just 100m south of Gran Vía.

Taberna El Condado (Calle Sor Ángela de la Cruz 3; tapas €1.50) Just up the street from El Rincon de la Cañada is this atmospheric tapas bar. It's little more than a single room dominated by its ham-heavy bar, but directors' chairs and tables out on the pedestrianised street are great for an evening beer.

Pizzeria Camillo e Peppone (Calle Isaac Peral; pasta & pizza €4.50-7; ☯ closed Wed) Serves up pretty authentic pizza and pasta, and gets very busy at weekends.

Drinking & Entertainment

Late-night crowds flock to the bars and terraces on Avenida Pablo Rada and, to a lesser extent, those around Plaza de la Merced.

Getting There & Away

From the **bus station** (☎ 959 25 69 00) at least 18 daily buses head to Seville (€6.10, 1¼ hours), and three to Madrid (€18.70, seven hours). For Portugal, Damas runs two daily buses (except Sunday) to Faro (€7, 2½ hours), Albufeira (€9, three hours) and Lagos (€12, 4¼ hours). From the **train station** (☎ 959 24 56 14) three daily trains head to Seville (€6.40, 1½ hours).

LUGARES COLOMBINOS

The small towns of La Rábida, Palos de la Frontera and Moguer, three key sites in the

ANDALUCÍA

Christopher Columbus story, lie along the eastern bank of the Río Tinto estuary, east of Huelva. You can visit all three on a day trip from Huelva, the Doñana area, or the coast in between.

La Rábida

Several times while planning his great voyage of discovery, Columbus visited the 14th-century **Monasterio de La Rábida** (☎ 959 35 04 11; admission €2.50, with audio guide €3; ☼ 10am-1pm & 4-7pm Tue-Sat Apr-Sep, 10am-1pm & 4-6.15pm Tue-Sat Oct-Mar, 10am-1pm & 4.45-8pm Tue-Sat Aug, 10.45am-1pm Sun year-round). Columbus won influential support from a monk here, Antonio de Marchena, and abbot Juan Pérez, a former confessor of Queen Isabel La Católica. Absorbing tours of the monastery, which stands among pine trees, are given in simple Spanish every 50 minutes.

On the waterfront below the monastery is the **Muelle de las Carabelas** (Wharf of the Caravels; ☎ 959 53 05 97; admission €3; ☼ 10am-2pm & 5-9pm Tue-Fri, 11am-8pm Sat, Sun & holidays Apr-Sep, 10am-7pm Tue-Sun Oct-May), where you can board replicas of Columbus' tiny ships.

Palos de la Frontera

Columbus set sail from Palos on 3 August 1492; the town also provided two of his three ships and more than half his crew, including cousins Vicente Yañez Pinzón and Martín Alonso Pinzón, captains of the *Niña* and *Pinta*, the two ships that accompanied Columbus' *Santa María*. Palos' access to the Tinto is now silted up.

A short walk uphill from the central plaza, the **Casa Museo Martín Alonso Pinzón** (Calle Colón 24; admission free; ☼ 10am-2pm & 5-7.30pm Mon-Fri) was the home of the *Pinta's* captain. Further along Calle Colón is the 14th-century **Iglesia de San Jorge** (☼ 10am-noon & 7-8pm Tue-Sun), where Columbus and his men took communion before embarking for their great voyage. In a park down the street is **La Fontanilla**, a brick well from which they drew water. A plaque above marks the site of the *embarcadero* (jetty) from which they sailed.

Moguer

This pleasant small town provided many of Columbus' crew. There's a helpful **tourist office** (☎ 959 37 18 98; Calle Castillo s/n; ☼ 10.30am-1.30pm & 6-8pm Mon-Fri, 5-7pm Oct-Mar) a couple of blocks south of the central Plaza del Ca-

bildo, in Moguer's old castle, which is being restored.

The 14th-century **Monasterio de Santa Clara** (☎ 959 37 01 07; Plaza de las Monjas; guided tours €1.80; ☼ 11am-1pm & 5-7pm Tue-Fri) is where Columbus kept a prayerful vigil the night after returning from his first voyage in March 1493. You'll see a lovely Mudéjar cloister, some of the nuns' old quarters and a collection of religious art.

Moguer was also the birthplace of the 1956 Nobel literature laureate Juan Ramón Jiménez, who wrote of childhood wanderings here with his donkey in *Platero y Yo* (Platero and I). His home, the **Casa Museo Zenobia y Juan Ramón** (☎ 959 37 21 48; Calle Juan Ramón Jiménez 10; 1hr guided tours €1.80; ☼ 10.15am-1.15pm & 5.15-7.15pm Tue-Sat, 10.15am-1.15pm Sun) is a five-minute walk from the Monasterio de Santa Clara.

Getting There & Away

At least 10 Damas buses run daily from Huelva bus station to La Rábida (€0.85, 20 minutes) and Palos de la Frontera (€0.90, 25 minutes); some then continue to Mazagón, but most terminate at Moguer (€0.95, 30 minutes).

PARQUE NACIONAL DE DOÑANA

Doñana National Park, one of Europe's most important wetlands, covers 542 sq km in the southeast of Huelva province and neighbouring Sevilla province. This World Heritage site is a vital refuge for such en-

PARQUE NACIONAL DE DOÑANA

ROMERÍA DEL ROCÍO

The Romería del Rocío (Pilgrimage to El Rocío) is a vast cult festivity that pulls people from all over Spain. It all revolves around the tiny image of Nuestra Señora del Rocío, or La Blanca Paloma (White Dove), which was found, so the story goes, back in the 13th century, in a tree in the Doñana marshes by a hunter from Almonte. Carrying it home, the hunter stopped for a rest and the statue miraculously made its own way back to the tree. Before long a chapel was built where the tree had stood (now El Rocío) and pilgrims were making for it. By the 17th century, *hermandades* (brotherhoods) from nearby towns had begun the tradition of making an annual pilgrimage to El Rocío at Pentecost, the seventh weekend after Easter.

Today, over 90 *hermandades*, some comprising several thousand men and women, travel to El Rocío each year on foot, on horseback and in gaily decorated covered wagons pulled by cattle or horses, using cross-country tracks.

Solemn is the last word you'd apply to this quintessentially Andalucian event. The 'pilgrims' dress in bright Andalucian costume and sing, dance, drink and romance their way to El Rocío. The total number of people in the village on this special weekend can reach a million or more.

The weekend comes to an ecstatic climax in the early hours of the Monday. Members of the *hermandad* of Almonte, which claims the Virgin for its own, barge into the church and bear her out on a float. Violent struggles ensue as others battle with the Almonte lads for the honour of carrying La Blanca Paloma. The crush and chaos is immense but somehow good humour survives and the Virgin is carried round to each of the brotherhood buildings, finally being returned to the Ermita in the afternoon.

dangered species as the Iberian lynx and Spanish imperial eagle (with populations here of about 50 and 25, respectively) and a crucial sanctuary for six million other birds that spend part of the year here. It's a unique combination of ecosystems that is well worth the effort of getting to. Visiting the interior of the national park requires booking ahead for a 4WD tour from the Centro de Visitantes El Acebuche (p702) on the western side of the park and from Sanlúcar de Barrameda (p712).

Half the park consists of *marismas* (wetlands) of the Guadalquivir delta. Almost dry from July to October, in autumn the *marismas* fill with water, attracting hundreds of thousands of wintering water birds from the north, including an estimated 80% of Western Europe's wild ducks. As the waters sink in spring, other birds – greater flamingos, spoonbills, storks – arrive, many to nest. The park also has a 28km Atlantic beach, from which the *marismas* are separated by a band of sand dunes up to 5km wide, and 144 sq km of *coto* (woodland and scrub), which harbours many mammals, including deer, wild boar and semi-wild horses.

In addition, there are interesting areas surrounding the national park that you can visit freely, especially the 537-sq-km Parque Natural de Doñana, a separate protected area comprising four distinct zones bordering the national park.

El Rocío
pop 690

El Rocío overlooks a section of the Doñana *marismas*, at the northwestern corner of the national park, that has year-round water. The village's sandy streets bear just as many hoof prints as tyre marks, and they are lined by rows of verandahed buildings that are empty most of the time. But this is no ghost town: most of the houses belong to the 90-odd *hermandades* (brotherhoods) of pilgrim-revellers, who converge on El Rocío every year for the Romería del Rocío (see the boxed text Romería del Rocío above). Indeed, a fiesta atmosphere pervades the village on most weekends as *hermandades* arrive to carry out lesser rituals.

INFORMATION

The **tourist office** (☎ 959 44 26 84; Avenida de la Canaliega s/n; ☼ 10am-2pm) is by the main road at the western end of the village. The **Centro de Visitantes La Rocina** (☎ 959 44 23 40; ☼ 9am-3pm & 4-8pm daily), 1km south on the A483, has national park information as well as short paths to nearby bird-watching hides.

ANDALUCÍA

SIGHTS & ACTIVITIES

The heart of the village is the **Ermita del Rocío** (8.30am-2.30pm & 4.30-8pm), the church housing the celebrated Virgen del Rocío, a tiny wooden image in long, bejewelled robes. Many come to pay their respects every day.

In the **marismas**, deer and horses graze in the shallows and you might see a flock of flamingos wheeling through the sky in a great pink cloud. The Spanish Ornithological Society's waterside observatory, the **Observatorio Madre del Rocío** (959 50 60 93; admission free; 10am-2pm & 4-7pm Tue-Sun), is 150m east of Hotel Toruño (below). The bridge over the river on the A483, 1km south of the village, is another good **viewing spot**. For a longer walk, head across the Puente del Ajolí at the northeastern edge of El Rocío and into the woodland ahead. This is the **Coto del Rey**, a large woodland zone, where in the early morning or late evening you may spot deer or boar.

Discovering Doñana (959 44 24 66; www.discoveringdonana.com; Calle Acebuchal 14) runs daily birdwatching trips with English-speaking guides, heading to the Centro de Visitantes José Antonio Valverde on the edge of the national park about 12km east of El Rocío. A half-day costs €98 to €140 per group, depending on the season and number of participants (maximum six); a full day is €154 to €216. You can hire **horses** at various places in El Rocío.

SLEEPING & EATING

Don't bother even trying for a room at Romería time.

Hotel Toruño (959 44 23 23; hotel-toruno@terra.es; Plaza Acebuchal 22; d incl breakfast €75; P) An attractive villa overlooking the *marismas*, not far from the observatory and only 100m from the church, the Toruño has well-appointed rooms, some with views over the marshland (odd-numbered rooms from 207 to 217).

El Cortijo de los Mimbrales (959 42 22 37; www.cortijomimbrales.com in Spanish; Carretera del Rocío A483 Km20; d €125, 4-person cottages €350; P) This delightful country-estate lodging is between El Rocío and El Acebuche visitor centre. It has an excellent restaurant too.

Pensión Cristina (959 44 24 13; Calle El Real 58; s/d €30/36) Between the Ermita and Hotel Toruño, the Cristina is reasonably comfortable and has a decent restaurant with a *menú* for €9.

There are several cafés, bars and restaurants around the village.

Centro de Visitantes El Acebuche

Twelve kilometres south of El Rocío on the A483, then 1.6km west, El Acebuche (959 44 87 11; 8am-9pm May-Sep, 8am-7pm Oct-Apr) is the national park's main visitor centre. Short footpaths lead to bird-watching hides overlooking a lagoon.

NATIONAL PARK TOURS

Trips in 20-person all-terrain vehicles from El Acebuche are the only way for ordinary folk to get inside the park from the western side. You need to book ahead through **Cooperativa Marismas del Rocío** (959 43 04 32): during spring, summer and holidays, the trips can book out over a month ahead, but otherwise a week or less is usually adequate notice. Bring binoculars if you can and drinking water in summer. Except in winter, cover up against mosquitoes or bring repellent. The four-hour trips (€20 per person) depart at 8.30am year-round, as well as 3pm in winter or 5pm in summer, from Tuesday to Sunday. Most guides speak Spanish only. The tour normally starts with a long beach drive, before moving inland. You can be pretty certain of seeing deer and boar, but ornithologists may be disappointed by the limited bird-observation opportunities.

Matalascañas & Mazagón

These two small resorts on the long, sandy beach running northwest from the national park provide alternative bases. Matalascañas, at the southwestern corner of the national park, has a number of tall hotels and could hardly be in greater contrast to the Doñana wildernesses. Mazagón, 28km up the coast, is more low-key, with a marina. Both places have a handful of *hostales* (budget hotels) and large camping grounds but the two best places to stay are the **Parador de Mazagón** (959 53 63 00; www.parador.es; Playa de Mazagón; s/d €98/123; P), overlooking the beach 6km east of central Mazagón; and **Hotel Albaida** (959 37 60 29; www.hotelalbaida.com; Carretera Huelva-Matalascañas Km18.3; s/d €50/80; P), a comfortable mid-range hotel on the main road, 600m east of Mazagón centre.

Getting There & Away

Three daily buses run between Seville (Plaza de Armas) and Matalascañas (€4.50, two hours) via El Rocío (€4.50, 1½ hours). The El Rocío–Matalascañas road is also covered

ANDALUCÍA

by up to six daily buses each way between Almonte and Matalascañas. All buses stop outside the La Rocina and El Acebuche national park centres on request.

From Huelva, buses go to Mazagón (€1.55, 35 minutes, three or more daily) via Palos de la Frontera, with just one of these (the 2.45pm from Huelva, Monday to Friday only), continuing to Matalascañas (€2.90, 50 minutes). Extra services may run in summer. You can travel between Huelva and El Rocío by changing buses at Almonte.

WEST OF HUELVA

The coast between Huelva and the Portuguese border, 53km west, alternates between estuaries, wetlands, sandy Atlantic beaches, small and medium-sized resorts and fishing ports. A few daily buses run from Huelva to all of these places. From Ayamonte there are buses to the Algarve and Lisbon.

Punta Umbría, Huelva's summer playground, stands on a point of land between the Marismas del Odiel wetlands and a good Atlantic beach. Further west, **La Antilla** fronts a wide beach that runs all the way from the Río Piedras to Isla Cristina. **Isla Cristina** has a sizable fishing fleet; its best beach is Playa Central, about 2km east of the city centre. **Ayamonte** stands beside the broad Río Guadiana, which divides Spain from Portugal. A free road bridge crosses the river 2km north of Ayamonte, but there's also a ferry from the town (€3.50 for a car and driver, €1 for pedestrians).

Sleeping

In La Antilla, at least six hostales are bunched near the beach on Plaza La Parada, with doubles between €50 and €65 in summer (but you'd be lucky to get a room in August).

In Isla Cristina, **Hotel Paraíso Playa** (☎ 959 33 02 35; www.hotelparaisoplaya.com; Avenida de la Playa; s/d €48/85; ❄ ☎), with a seafront site and friendly staff, and the imaginatively refurbished **Hotel Los Geranios** (☎ 959 33 18 00; geraniosh@yahoo.com; Avenida de la Playa; s/d €67/97; P ❄ ☎) are good choices.

Ayamonte's modern **Parador de Ayamonte** (☎ 959 32 07 00; www.parador.es; El Castillito; s/d €77.70/97.10; P ❄ ☎) overlooks the broad Guadiana estuary from a hill 1.5km north of the town.

MINAS DE RIOTINTO

pop 4500m / elevation 420m

This aeons-old mining town, 68km northeast of Huelva, makes an unusual and fascinating stop. Silver was being extracted locally, well before the Phoenicians came here three millennia ago, and iron has been mined since at least Roman times. In the 19th century the British-dominated Rio Tinto Company turned the area into one of the world's great copper-mining centres. The mines returned to Spanish control in 1954.

Sights & Activities

The excellent **Museo Minero** (Plaza Ernest Lluch s/n; adult/under-14 €3/2; ☼ 10.30am-3pm & 4-7pm) covers the geology and history of the mines, with a vivid re-creation of a Roman mine, where slaves worked in appalling conditions, and a big display on the Rio Tinto Company's railways. Pride of place in these goes to the Vagón del Maharajah, a luxurious carriage originally built for a tour of India by Britain's Queen Victoria.

The museum is also the reception centre and main ticket office for guided visits to the awesomely enormous **Corta Atalaya** opencast mine, 1km west of the town; and for rides on the **Ferrocarril Turístico-Minero railway**, a 22km journey in refurbished early-20th-century carriages, pulled by a steam engine through a scarred and surreal landscape. Trips to the 335m-deep, 1.2km-long Corta Atalaya (adult/under 14 €5/4) go from the Museo Minero four or five times daily. The train trips (adult/under 14 €9/8) start and end at Talleres Mina, 2.5km east of Minas de Riotinto, at 1.30pm daily between June and September, with an extra 5pm trip in August. The rest of the year they normally go on Saturday, Sunday and public holidays only. To check the latest schedules, ask a tourist office in the region, or call ☎ 959 59 00 25.

About 1km north of Minas de Riotinto, the Aracena road passes the **Corta Cerro Colorado**, a vast opencast mine that is the centre of the area's mining activity today. A century ago it was a hill.

Sleeping & Eating

Hotel Santa Bárbara (☎ 959 59 11 88; Cerro de los Embusteros s/n; d incl breakfast €52; P ❄ ☎) On a hill-top at the eastern end of town, the Santa Bárbara is a reliable, comfortable option with the best facilities in the town, including its own restaurant.

Hostal Galán (☎ 959 59 08 40; Avenida La Esquila 10; s/d €22.25/35.40) This hostal, with simple, clean rooms and a handy restaurant, is conveniently placed just round the corner from the Museo Minero.

Getting There & Away

Up to six buses run daily from Huelva bus station to Minas de Riotinto (€4.85, 1¼ hours). **Casal** (☎ 954 99 92 90) runs to Minas de Riotinto from Aracena (€2.20, 40 minutes, two daily except Sunday) and Seville (Plaza de Armas; €4, one hour, three daily).

ARACENA

pop 7000 / elevation 730m

The main town of northern Huelva is an appealing, whitewashed place spreading beneath Cerro del Castillo. The **Centro de Visitantes Cabildo Viejo** (☎ 959 12 88 25; Plaza Alta; ☽ 10am-2pm & 6-8pm, 4-6pm Oct-Mar) is the main information centre of the Parque Natural Sierra de Aracena y Picos de Aroche (which covers 1840 sq km of rolling woodlands and hill country in northern Huelva) and also has information on Aracena town. The **Centro de Turismo Rural y Reservas** (☎ 959 12 82 06; Calle Pozo de la Nieve; ☽ 9am-2pm & 4-7pm) is the area's second tourist office.

Sights & Activities

The **Gruta de las Maravillas** (Cave of Marvels; ☎ 959 12 83 55; Calle Pozo de la Nieve; hourly tours adult/under 16 €7.70/5.50; ☽ 10am-1.30pm & 3-6pm) ranks among Spain's most spectacular cave systems, even if it's presented somewhat theatrically. The **Cerro del Castillo** is surmounted by a beautiful church and a ruined castle, both built around 1300.

Sleeping & Eating

Finca Valbono (☎ 959 12 77 11; www.fincavalbono .com; Carretera de Carboneras Km1; d €83.15, 4-person apt €139; [P] [X] [R]) This converted farmhouse 1km north of Aracena is easily the most charming option, with tastefully rustic rooms, a pool, riding stables and a good, medium-priced restaurant.

Hotel Los Castaños (☎ 959 12 63 00; Avenida de Huelva 5; d €50; [P] [X]) The main hotel in town is not very exciting to look at but its rooms are comfortable. The restaurant serves a €12 *menú*.

Casa Manolo (☎ 959 12 80 14; Calle Barbero 6; s/d €12.85/23.50) Just south of the central Plaza del Marqués de Aracena, this tiny little *pensión* (small private hotel) has Aracena's only budget beds. It's friendly but can get very cold in winter.

Restaurante José Vicente (☎ 959 12 84 55; Avenida de Andalucía 53; 3-course menú €15) Aracena's best restaurant is a good place to enjoy the area's specialities such as Jabugo ham, mushrooms, pork loin and even snails.

Café Restaurante Montecruz (☎ 959 12 60 13; Plaza de San Pedro; platos combinados €6-12) The Montecruz does a mean steak and chips, and when everything else in town is shut it's still humming.

Getting There & Away

From the bus stop on Avenida de Andalucía, Damas runs buses to and from Huelva (€6.80, two hours, twice daily) and Lisbon (€24, 3½ hours, 10.30am Monday, Wednesday, Friday); and Casal runs to and from Seville (Plaza de Armas; €5.30, 1¼ hours, three daily) and Minas de Riotinto (p703).

WEST OF ARACENA

The hills, verdant valleys and stone-built villages of Huelva's portion of the Sierra Morena form one of Andalucía's most surprisingly beautiful landscapes. Most of the villages grew up around fortress-like churches, or hilltop castles constructed in medieval times to deter the Portuguese.

Linares de la Sierra, **Alájar**, **Fuenteheridos** and **Almonaster la Real** are all intriguingly old-fashioned places, and Almonaster's 10th-century *mezquita* (mosque) is a miniature gem of Islamic architecture. Ham from **Jabugo** is acclaimed as the best in Spain and the village has a line of bars and restaurants along Carretera San Juan del Puerto waiting for you to sample it. **Cortegana** and **Aroche**, two of the bigger places in the district, have impressive castles and churches. Nearly all these places have **hostales**, with doubles costing between €25 and €50.

There's an extensive web of marked **walking trails** throughout the area, particularly between Aracena and Aroche. Maps and leaflets from the tourist offices in Aracena will help you find your way around.

Casal (Seville ☎ 954 99 92 90) buses connect nearly all these villages with Aracena and Seville (Plaza de Armas).

CÁDIZ PROVINCE

The province of Cádiz (*cad*-i, or even just *ca*-i) possesses perhaps the greatest variety of attractions of any of Andalucía's eight provinces. Its coast – the southern half of the Costa de la Luz – reaches from the mouth of the region's biggest river, the Guadalquivir, to the turbulent Strait of Gibraltar, and is blessed with the best string of beaches in Andalucía, which are surprisingly little developed. As you'd expect, mounds of tasty seafood wait to be sampled along this shore. The cities and towns of Cádiz are among the most fascinating in Andalucía – from the age-old port of Cádiz itself, or Jerez de la Frontera with its sherry wineries, horse displays and flamenco, to historic ports such as El Puerto de Santa María, or small beach towns such as Los Caños de Meca and Bolonia. Inland, Cádiz stretches back to the beautiful, green Sierra de Grazalema with its remote whitewashed towns and villages. The province's natural variety provides opportunities for hosts of activities from windsurfing and kitesurfing along the coasts to hiking, bird-watching and canyoning in the hills.

CÁDIZ

pop 135,000

Once past the coastal marshes and industrial sprawl around Cádiz, you emerge into an elegant, civilized port city of largely 18th- and 19th-century construction. Cádiz is crammed onto the head of a promontory like some huge, overcrowded, ocean-going ship, and the tang of salty air and ocean vistas are never far away. It has a long and fascinating history, absorbing monuments and museums and some enjoyable places to eat and drink – yet it's the people of Cádiz, the *gaditanos*, who make the place truly special. Warm, open, cultured and independent-minded, most *gaditanos* are concerned chiefly to make the most of life – whether simply enjoying each other's company in the city's bars or plazas, or indulging in Spain's most riotous spring carnival.

History

Cádiz may be the oldest city in Europe. Classical sources speak of the founding of the Phoenician trading base called Gadir around 1100 BC.

In less-distant times, Cádiz began to boom after Columbus' trips to the Americas. He sailed from here on his second and fourth voyages. Cádiz attracted Spain's enemies too: in 1587 England's Sir Francis Drake 'singed the king of Spain's beard' with a raid on the harbour, delaying the imminent Spanish Armada. In 1596 Anglo-Dutch attackers burnt almost the entire city.

Cádiz's golden age was the 18th century, when it enjoyed 75% of Spanish trade with the Americas. It grew into the richest and most cosmopolitan city in Spain and gave birth to Spain's first progressive, liberal middle class. During the Napoleonic Wars, Cádiz held out under French siege from 1810 to 1812, and during this time a national parliament meeting here adopted Spain's liberal 1812 constitution, proclaiming sovereignty of the people.

The loss of the American colonies in the 19th century plunged Cádiz into a decline from which it's still recovering.

Orientation

Breathing space between the huddled streets of the old city is provided by numerous squares; the four most important for short-term orientation being Plaza San Juan de Dios, Plaza de la Catedral and Plaza de Topete in an arc in the southeast, and Plaza de Mina in the north. Pedestrianised Calle San Francisco runs most of the way between Plaza San Juan de Dios and Plaza de Mina.

The train station is just east of the old city, off Plaza de Sevilla, with the main bus station (of the Comes line) 900m to its north on Plaza de la Hispanidad. The 18th-century Puertas de Tierra (Land Gates) mark the southern boundary of the old city.

Information

You'll find plenty of banks and ATMs along Calle San Francisco and the parallel Avenida Ramón de Carranza.

Enred@2 (cnr Calle Isabel La Católica & Calle Antonio López; per hr €1.50; ⏰ 11am-11pm Mon-Sat)

Hospital Puerta del Mar (☎ 956 00 21 00; Avenida Ana de Viya 21) The main general hospital, 2.25km southeast of Puertas de Tierra.

Municipal tourist office Main office (☎ 956 24 10 01; Plaza San Juan de Dios 11; ⏰ 9am-2pm & 4-7pm Mon-Fri, 5-8pm 15 Jun–15 Sep); Information kiosk (Plaza San Juan de Dios; ⏰ 10am-1.30pm & 4-6pm Sat, Sun & holidays, 5-7.30pm 15 Jun–15 Sep)

ANDALUCÍA

CÁDIZ

Regional Tourist Office (☎ 956 25 86 46; Avenida Ramón de Carranza s/n; ☺ 9am-7pm Mon-Fri, 10am-1.30pm Sat, Sun & holidays)

Sights & Activities
PLAZA SAN JUAN DE DIOS & AROUND
Broad Plaza San Juan de Dios is surrounded by cafés and dominated by the imposing neoclassical **Ayuntamiento** built around 1800. Between here and the cathedral is the **Barrio del Pópulo**, the kernel of medieval Cádiz and a focus of the city's recent spruce-up programme, now sporting several craft shops and galleries.

CATHEDRAL
Cádiz's yellow-domed **cathedral** (☎ 956 25 98 12; Plaza de la Catedral; adult/child €4/2.50; ☺ 10am-1.30pm & 4.30-7pm Tue-Fri, 10am-12.30pm Sat), fronts a broad, traffic-free plaza. The decision to build the cathedral was taken in 1716, but the cathedral wasn't finished until 1838, by which time neoclassical elements, such as the dome, towers and main façade, had diluted Vicente Acero's original baroque plan. But it's still a beautiful and impressive construction. From a separate entrance on Plaza de la Catedral, climb inside the **Torre de Poniente** (Western Tower; adult/child & over 65 €3/2; ☺ 10am-6pm, to 8pm 15 Jun–15 Sep) for marvellous vistas.

PLAZA DE TOPETE & AROUND
A short walk northwest from the cathedral, this square is one of Cádiz's liveliest, bright with flower stalls and adjoining the large, animated **Mercado Central** (Central Market). Nearby, the **Torre Tavira** (☎ 956 21 29 10; Calle Marqués del Real Tesoro 10; admission €3.50; ☺ 10am-6pm, to 8pm 15 Jun–15 Sep) is the highest and most important of the city's old watchtowers (18th-century Cádiz had no less than 160 of these, built so that citizens could observe the comings and goings of ships without leaving home). It provides great panoramas and has a **camera obscura** projecting live images of the city onto a screen.

The **Museo de las Cortes de Cádiz** (☎ 956 22 17 88; Calle Santa Inés 9; admission free; ☺ 9am-1pm & 5-7pm Tue-Fri, 9am-1pm Sat & Sun) is full of historical memorabilia focusing on the 1812 parliament, including a large marvellous 1770s model of Cádiz, made for King Carlos III. Along the street is the **Oratorio de San Felipe Neri** (☎ 956 21 16 12; Plaza de San Felipe Neri; admission €1.20; ☺ 10am-1pm Mon-Sat), the church where

the Cortes de Cádiz met. This is one of Cádiz's finest baroque churches, with an unusual oval interior, a beautiful dome and a Murillo *Inmaculada* on the altarpiece.

MUSEO DE CÁDIZ
Cádiz's excellent major **museum** (☎ 956 21 22 81; Plaza de Mina; adult/EU citizen €1.50/free, admission free Sun; ☺ 2.30-8pm Tue, 9am-8pm Wed-Sat, 9.30am-2.30pm Sun) faces one of the city's largest and leafiest squares. The stars of the ground-floor archaeology section are two Phoenician marble sarcophagi, carved in human likeness, and a monumental statue of the Roman emperor Trajan, from Baelo Claudia (p722). The fine arts collection, upstairs, has 21 superb canvases by Zurbarán and the painting that cost Murillo his life – the altarpiece from Cádiz's Convento de Capuchinas. The baroque maestro died from injuries received in a fall from scaffolding while working on this in 1682.

COASTAL WALK
This 4.5km walk takes at least 1¼ hours. Go north from Plaza de Mina to the city's northern seafront, with views across the Bahía de Cádiz. Head along the **Alameda** gardens to the **Baluarte de la Candelaria**, then turn southwest to the quirkily clipped **Parque del Genovés**. Continue to the **Castillo de Santa Catalina** (☎ 956 22 63 33; admission free; ☺ 10.30am-6pm, to 8pm approx May-Aug), built after the 1596 sacking; inside there's an historical exhibit on Cádiz and the sea, and a gallery hosting temporary exhibitions. Sandy **Playa de la Caleta** (very crowded in summer) separates Santa Catalina from the 18th-century **Castillo de San Sebastián**. You can't enter San Sebastián but do walk along the airy 750m causeway to its gate. Finally, follow the broad promenade along **Campo del Sur** to the cathedral.

PLAYA DE LA VICTORIA
This lovely, wide, ocean beach of fine Atlantic sand stretches about 4km along the peninsula from its beginning 1.5km beyond the Puertas de Tierra. On summer weekends almost the whole city seems to be out here. Bus No 1 'Plaza España-Cortadura' from Plaza de España will get you there.

Festivals & Events
No other Spanish city celebrates **Carnaval** with the verve of Cádiz, where it turns into

a 10-day singing, dancing and drinking fancy-dress party spanning two weekends. Everyone dresses up and the fun, abetted by huge quantities of alcohol, is infectious. Costumed groups *(murgas)* tour the city on foot or on floats, singing witty satirical ditties, dancing or performing sketches. In addition to the 300 or so officially recognised *murgas*, judged by a panel in the Gran Teatro Falla, there are also the *ilegales* – any group that fancies taking to the streets and trying to play or sing.

Some of the liveliest scenes are in the working-class Barrio de la Viña, and on Calle Ancha and Calle Columela, where *ilegales* tend to congregate.

Rooms in Cádiz get booked months in advance (even though prices can be double their summer rates). If you don't manage to snatch one, you could just visit for the night from anywhere else within striking distance. Plenty of other people do this – many wearing fancy dress.

Sleeping

Hospedería Las Cortes de Cádiz (☎ 956 21 26 68; www.hotellascortes.com in Spanish; Calle San Francisco 9; s/d incl breakfast €98.45/128.40; P ⊠ ⬜) This charming new hotel occupies an elegant 1850s mansion. Each of the period-style rooms is endowed with a specially commissioned oil painting of a figure or place associated with the 1812 Cortes de Cádiz. Three rooms have wheelchair access and to round it all off, the hotel has a good café, a roof terrace, a gym and a Jacuzzi.

Parador Hotel Atlántico (☎ 956 22 69 05; www .parador.es; Avenida Duque de Nájera 9; s €63.70/121.90 d €79.60-152.40; P ⊠ ⬜ ⬛) Cádiz's modern Parador is comfortable and spacious. All of the rooms have a terrace with a sea view of some sort, and the pool is set on a lawn overlooking the ocean.

Hostal Bahía (☎ 956 25 90 61; hostalbahia@terra .es; Calle Plocia 5; s/d €47.05/64.20; ⊠) All rooms are exterior, impeccably looked-after, and have phone, TV and built-in wardrobes.

Hostal Fantoni (☎ 956 28 27 04; www.hostalfantoni .com; Calle Flamenco 5; s €20, d with/without bathroom €40/30) The friendly, family-run Fantoni offers spotless, cool rooms. The roof terrace catches a breeze in summer.

Hostal Centro Sol (☎ /fax 956 28 31 03; www .hostalcentrosolcadiz.com; Calle Manzanares 7; s/d €40/49) This is an efficient and friendly hostal, in

an attractive 1848 house. Rooms are plain and smallish.

Quo Qadis (☎ /fax 956 22 19 39; www.quoqadis.com in Spanish; Calle Diego Arias 1; dm incl breakfast €6-12, d with/without bathroom incl breakfast €30/24; ⊠) Cádiz's independent youth hostel provides basic and sometimes crowded accommodation, but it gets a good clean-out between 11am and 5pm, when the guests have to be out. If you have a sleeping bag, you can sleep under the stars on the roof terrace for €6. Book ahead in summer. The owners rent bicycles for €6 a day and organise bike trips to places around Cádiz province.

Eating

Mesón Cumbres Mayores (☎ 956 21 32 70; Calle Zorrilla 4; tapas €1.50-2, raciones & mains €5-15) Popular, reasonably priced Cumbres Mayores has an excellent tapas bar in the front and a small restaurant in the back. In the bar it's hard to beat the ham and cheese *montaditos* (small toasted sandwiches) or the various *solomillo* (pork sirloin) options. In the restaurant, the endive-and-avocado salad with Roquefort dressing is a meal in itself: if you can, follow up with *guisos* (stews), fish, seafood or barbecued meats.

Taberna San Francisco Uno (Plaza San Francisco 1; raciones €6.50-10) This cosy stone-walled, wood-beamed wine bar, with some tables on the plaza, offers a tempting range of meat, fish, stews, and platters of hams, cheeses and smoked fish.

Cafetería La Marina (☎ 956 25 55 31; Plaza San Juan de Dios 13; breakfast €3) La Marina is a good spot for breakfast or a snack as you watch the life of Cádiz go by on this busy square.

La Cigüeña (☎ 956 25 01 79; Calle Plocia 2; mains €12-16, menúes €20 & €22.50; ⊠ closed Sun) A few steps off Plaza San Juan de Dios, the friendly and relaxed 'Stork' prepares adventurous and excellent food.

El Balandro (☎ 956 22 09 92; Alameda Apodaca 22; tapas €3.50; ⊠ closed Sun evening & Mon) Find a space at the long bar or sit by the picture windows overlooking the bay, and pick from Balandro's huge range of filling seafood, meat and pasta tapas, almost equivalent to restaurant main courses.

Freiduría Las Flores (☎ 956 22 61 12; Plaza de Topete 4; seafood per 250g €2.50-4.50) Cádiz specialises in fried fish and seafood, and Las Flores, resembling a fancy fish-and-chip shop, is one of the best places to sample it. To try a combination, have a *surtido* (mixed fry-up).

El Faro (☎ 956 22 99 16; Calle San Felix 15; mains & raciones €7-15; ✹) Over in Barrio de la Viña, the old fishermen's district, El Faro has a famous and excellent seafood restaurant, decorated with pretty ceramics, and an adjoining less-pricey tapas bar.

Drinking & Entertainment

The Plaza San Francisco–Plaza de España–Plaza de Mina area is the hub of the nocturnal bar scene. Things start to get going around 11pm or midnight at most places, but can be pretty quiet in the first half of the week.

Cambalache (Calle José del Toro 20; ✹ from 8.30pm Mon-Sat) This long, dim, jazz and blues bar occasionally hosts live music.

Medussa (Calle General Luque 8) Local and foreign students converse above loud music in the dimly red-lit interior or spill out into the street.

Café de Levante (Calle Rosario 35; ✹ 8pm-1am) Relaxed gay-mixed bar hung with photos of arts and showbiz icons.

In summer the late-night scene moves to the Paseo Marítimo along Playa de la Victoria, around big Hotel Playa Victoria. You'll find lively music bars and throngs of people standing in the street drinking. Others simply hang out on the beach.

The real late-late zone is the dance bars out along the northern side of the harbour, in the marina area at Punta de San Felipe. Here, **El Malecón** (☎ 956 22 45 19; Paseo Pascual Pery; ✹ from midnight Fri & Sat) is Cádiz's top Latin dance spot.

Peña Flamenca La Perla (☎ 956 25 91 01; Calle Carlos Ollero s/n) Cádiz is one of the true homes of flamenco. This cavern-like club of *aficionados* hosts flamenco nights that are open to the public – the tourist offices have current details.

The **Gran Teatro Falla** (☎ 956 22 08 28; Plaza de Falla) and the **Central Lechera** (☎ 956 22 06 28; Plaza de Argüelles s/n) stage busy programmes of theatre, dance and music.

Getting There & Around

BOAT

See p711 for details of the passenger ferry that leaves from the Estación Marítima (Passenger Port), and heads across the bay to El Puerto de Santa María.

BUS

Most buses are run by **Comes** (☎ 956 80 70 59) from Plaza de la Hispanidad. Destinations include Seville (€9.50, 1¾ hours, 11 daily), El Puerto de Santa María (€1.45, 30 to 40 minutes, 23 daily), Jerez de la Frontera (€2.50, 40 minutes, 23 daily), Tarifa (€7.15, 1½ hours, five daily) and other places down the Cádiz coast, Arcos de la Frontera (€4.80, 1¼ hours, six daily), Ronda (€11.80, 2½ hours, three daily), Málaga (€18.05, four hours, six daily) and Granada (€25.95, 4½ hours, four daily). Some services go less often on Saturday and Sunday.

Los Amarillos operates up to five buses daily to Arcos de la Frontera (€4, 1¼ hours) and El Bosque (€6.35, two hours), plus up to 11 daily to Sanlúcar de Barrameda (€2.75, 1¼ hours), from its stop by the southern end of Avenida Ramón de Carranza. Tickets and information are available at **Viajes Socialtur** (☎ 956 29 08 00; Avenida Ramón de Carranza 31). Take the 12.30pm bus (Monday to Saturday only) for connections to Grazalema.

Secorbus (☎ 956 25 74 15; Avenida José León de Carranza 20) operates up to six buses daily to Madrid (€21.90, six hours). The stop is 3.6km southeast of the Puertas de Tierra.

CAR & MOTORCYCLE

The AP4 motorway from Seville to Puerto Real on the eastern side of the Bahía de Cádiz carries a toll of €6. The toll-free alternative, the A4, is slower.

There is a handily placed **underground car park** (Paseo de Canalejas; per 24hr €6.50) near the port area.

TRAIN

From the **station** (☎ 956 25 10 01) trains run to El Puerto de Santa María (€2.25, 30-35 minutes, 21 daily), Jerez de la Frontera (€2.75, 45 minutes, 21 daily), Seville (€8.40, 1¾ hours, up to 12 daily), Córdoba (€15.75 to €32, three hours, four daily) and Madrid (€56, five hours, two daily).

EL PUERTO DE SANTA MARÍA

pop 76,500

El Puerto, across the bay and 10km northeast of Cádiz (22km by road), is easily and enjoyably reached by ferry. It was here that Columbus met the owner of his flagship (the *Santa María*), Juan de la Cosa, who was his

---

SUNSHINE IN A GLASS

Sherry is a fortified wine that's produced in the towns of Jerez de la Frontera, El Puerto de Santa María and Sanlúcar de Barrameda, plus five other areas in Cádiz province and Lebrija in Sevilla province. A combination of climate, chalky soils that soak up the sun but retain moisture, and a special maturing process called the *solera* system produce this unique wine.

The main distinction in sherry is between *fino* (dry and the colour of straw) and *oloroso* (sweet, dark and with a strong bouquet). An *amontillado* is an amber, moderately dry *fino* with a nutty flavour and higher alcohol content. A manzanilla is an unfortified camomile-coloured *fino* from Sanlúcar de Barrameda; it slips down nicely with seafood and its delicate flavour is reckoned to come from sea breezes wafting into the wineries there.

Harvested sherry grapes are pressed and the resulting must is left to ferment. Within a few months a frothy veil of yeast called *flor* appears on the surface. The wine is transferred to the cellars in big barrels of American oak, which add to its flavour.

Wine enters the *solera* process after one year. The barrels, about five-sixths full, are lined up in rows at least three barrels high: those on the bottom layer, called the *solera* (from *suelo*, floor), contain the oldest wine. Around three times a year, 10% of the wine from these is drawn off. Each layer of barrels is replaced with the same amount of wine from the layer above. The wines are left to age for between three and seven years. A small amount of brandy is added to fortify the wine before bottling, which brings the alcohol content to between 16% and 18%, and this stops fermentation.

Sherry houses (bodegas) are often beautiful buildings in attractive gardens. A tour will take you through the areas where the wine is stored and aged, inform you about the process and the history of the sherry producers, and give you a bit of a tasting. You can also buy sherry at bodegas – or in any supermarket.

---

pilot in 1492. Later, many palaces were built in El Puerto on the proceeds of American trade. Today it's one of Cádiz province's triangle of sherry-making towns, and its beaches, sherry bodegas (wineries) and tapas bars make it a fine outing from Cádiz or Jerez. In summer it's a very lively town.

Orientation & Information

The heart of the town is on the northwestern bank of the Río Guadalete. The ferry *El Vapor* arrives at the Muelle del Vapor jetty, on Plaza de las Galeras Reales. The good **tourist office** (☎ 956 54 24 13; www.elpuertosm.es; Calle Luna 22; 🕙 10am-2pm & 6-7.30pm) is 2½ blocks straight ahead from the Muelle del Vapor.

Sights & Activities

The four-spouted **Fuente de las Galeras Reales** (Fountain of the Royal Galleys), by the Muelle del Vapor, once supplied water to America-bound ships.

The **Fundación Rafael Alberti** (☎ 956 85 07 11; Calle Santo Domingo 25; admission €2.50; 🕙 11am-4pm Tue-Sun), a few blocks inland, has interesting exhibits on Rafael Alberti (1902–99), one of the great poets of the 'Generation of 27', who lived here as a child. The impressive

15th- to 18th-century **Iglesia Mayor Prioral** (🕙 8.30am-12.45pm Mon-Fri, 8.30am-noon Sat, 8.30am-1.45pm Sun, 6.30-8.30pm daily) dominates Plaza de España, a little further inland.

The best-known sherry wineries, **Osborne** (☎ 956 86 91 00; Calle Los Moros) and **Terry** (☎ 956 85 77 00; Calle Toneleros s/n), offer tours (€5) Monday to Friday. It's best to phone ahead. You can visit **Bodegas 501** (☎ 956 85 55 11; Calle Valdés 9; admission €4; 🕙 10am-1pm Mon-Fri) without booking.

Pine-flanked **Playa de la Puntilla** is a half-hour walk southwest of the town centre – or take bus No 26 (€0.60) southwest along Avenida Aramburu de Mora.

Sleeping

Hotel Monasterio San Miguel (☎ 956 54 04 40; www.jale.com/monasterio; Calle Virgen de los Milagros 27; s/d from €144/179; P 🞖 🞔) Tropical garden, pool, valuable artworks and gourmet restaurant await your pleasure, if your pockets are deep enough for this luxurious hotel in a converted 18th-century monastery.

Casa No 6 (☎ 956 87 70 84; www.casano6.com; Calle San Bartolomé 14; r/f incl breakfast €60/100; P) This beautifully renovated 19th-century house provides charming, spacious and spotless rooms.

Hotel Los Cántaros (☎ 956 54 02 40; www.hotellos cantaros.com; Calle Curva 6; s/d €88/105; P 🞬) Classy Los Cántaros has well-equipped rooms and a restaurant looking out onto a verdant little garden.

Budget options:

Hostal Manolo (☎ 956 85 75 25; www.guiadecadiz .com; Calle Jesús de los Milagros 18; s/d €21/35) A block inland from Plaza de las Galeras Reales.

Camping Las Dunas (☎ 956 87 22 10; www.lasdunas camping.com in Spanish; camping per adult/tent/car €4/4/3.40) Well-equipped, leafy camping ground, just behind Playa de la Puntilla.

Eating

Romerijo (☎ 956 54 12 54; Ribera del Marisco s/n; seafood per 250g from €3) A huge, always busy El Puerto institution, Romerijo has two buildings, one boiling the seafood, the other frying it. Choose from the displays and buy by the quarter-kilogram in paper cones: €4.80 to €12.50 for various types of boiled prawns, for example.

Casa Flores (☎ 956 54 35 12; Ribera del Río 9; mains €14-34) For more formal dining, go for tilebedecked Casa Flores across the street from the river. Try the local speciality *urta roteña* (sea bream cooked in white wine, tomatoes, peppers and thyme).

Restaurante TeleShawarma (☎ 956 87 64 23; Ribera del Marisco s/n; falafel roll €3, mains €9) Vegetarians will love this small restaurant next to the Romerijo. The authentic Lebanese-Greek food (with some meat options too) provides a welcome change.

Mesón del Asador (Calle Misericordia; mains €6-14) Come here, to the street just behind the Romerijo, for moderately priced grilled meats, salads, and figs in muscatel sauce to finish.

Calle Misericordia also sports El Puerto's most enticing string of tapas bars. Don't miss **Bodeguita La Antigua** (Calle Misericordia 8; tapas €2.70), which helpfully provides tapas menus in English and French. Try the *serranito*, a bread roll with ham, pork, fried green pepper and a few chips.

Getting There & Away

BOAT

The small ferry **El Vapor** (☎ 956 85 59 06), a decades-old symbol of El Puerto, sails to El Puerto (€3, 45 minutes) from Cádiz's Estación Marítima (Passenger Port) at 10am, noon, 2pm, 4.30pm and 6.30pm daily from

early February to early December (except nonholiday Mondays between early September and May), with an extra trip at 8.30pm from July to early September. Sailings from El Puerto to Cádiz go one hour earlier than all the above times.

BUS

From Monday to Friday, buses run to Cádiz (€1.25 to €1.45, 30 to 40 minutes) about half-hourly, 6.45am to 10pm, from the Plaza de Toros (Bullring), four blocks southwest of Plaza de España, and at least seven times from the train station. Weekend services are less frequent. For Jerez de la Frontera (€1.05, 20 minutes) there are nine or more daily buses from the train station and a few from the bullring. Buses for Sanlúcar de Barrameda (€1.50, 30 minutes, five to 11 daily) depart from the bullring. Buses for Seville (€7.50, 1½ hours, five daily) go from the train station.

TRAIN

The train station is a 10-minute walk northeast of the town centre, beside the Cádiz–Jerez road. Up to 36 trains travel daily to Jerez (from €1.15, 12 minutes) and Cádiz (€2.25, 30 to 35 minutes), and up to 16 to Seville (from €7, 1½ hours).

SANLÚCAR DE BARRAMEDA

pop 62,000

Sanlúcar, 23km northwest of El Puerto de Santa María, is the northern tip of the sherry triangle (see the boxed text opposite) and a likeable summer resort: it looks across the Guadalquivir estuary to the Parque Nacional de Doñana.

Columbus sailed from Sanlúcar in 1498 on his third voyage to the Caribbean. So, in 1519, did the Portuguese Ferdinand Magellan, seeking – as Columbus had – a westerly route to the Asian Spice Islands. Magellan succeeded, thanks to the first known voyage round the bottom of South America, but was killed in the Philippines in 1521. His pilot, Juan Sebastián Elcano, completed the first circumnavigation of the globe by returning to Sanlúcar in 1522 with just one of the five ships, the *Victoria*.

Orientation & Information

Sanlúcar stretches 2.5km along the southeastern side of the estuary and is fronted by a long, sandy beach. Calzada del Ejército (La Calzada), running inland from the seafront Paseo Marítimo, is the main avenue. A block beyond its inland end is Plaza del Cabildo, the central square. The bus station is on Avenida de la Estación, 100m southwest of the middle of La Calzada. The helpful **tourist office** (☎ 956 36 61 10; ⏰ 10am-2pm, variable afternoon hrs) is on Calzada del Ejército.

The old fishing quarter, Bajo de Guía, site of Sanlúcar's best restaurants and boat departures for Parque Nacional de Doñana, is 750m northeast from La Calzada. Here, the **Centro de Visitantes Fábrica de Hielo** (☎ 956 38 16 35; Bajo de Guía s/n; ⏰ 9am-7pm or 8pm) provides displays and information on the Parque Nacional de Doñana.

Sights
From Plaza del Cabildo, cross Calle Ancha to Plaza San Roque and head up Calle Bretones, which becomes Calle Cuesta de Belén and doglegs up to the **Palacio de Orleans y Borbón** (admission free; ⏰ 10am-1.30pm Mon-Fri), a beautiful neo-Mudéjar palace that was built as a summer home for the aristocratic Montpensier family in the 19th century but is now Sanlúcar's town hall. From its entrance at the top of Calle Cuesta de Belén, a block to the left along Calle Caballeros, is the 15th-century **Iglesia de Nuestra Señora de la O** (⏰ 9am-1pm Sun, 7.30-8pm Sun-Fri). Next door is the **Palacio de los Duques de Medina Sidonia** (☎ 956 36 01 61; www.fcmedinasidonia.com in Spanish; Plaza Condes de Niebla 1; admission €3; ⏰ 9.30am-2pm Sun & Mon, café 9am-2pm & 3.30-9pm daily), the large, rambling and ancient home of the aristocratic family that once owned more of Spain than anyone else. The house bursts with antiques and paintings by Goya, Zurbarán and other famous Spanish artists.

Some 200m further along the street is the 15th-century **Castillo de Santiago** (Plaza del Castillo), which is closed to visitors, amid buildings of the Barbadillo sherry company. From here walk downhill to the town centre.

Sherry Bodegas
Sanlúcar produces a distinctive sherry-like wine, manzanilla (see the boxed text Sunshine in a Glass on p710). Three bodegas give tours for which you don't need to book ahead:
La Cigarrera (☎ 956 38 12 85; Plaza Madre de Dios; tours €2.50; ⏰ 10am-2pm Mon-Sat)

Barbadillo (☎ 956 38 55 00; Calle Luis de Eguilaz 11; tours €3; ⏰ in English 11am Tue-Sat, in Spanish noon & 1pm Mon-Sat) Near the castle.
Bodegas Hidalgo-La Gitana (☎ 956 38 53 04; Calle Banda Playa; tours €3; ⏰ 11.30am & 12.30pm)

Parque Nacional de Doñana
From Bajo de Guía, **Viajes Doñana** (☎ 956 36 25 40; tours per person €33; Calle San Juan 20) operates 3½-hour tours into the national park, at 8.30am and 2.30pm on Tuesday and Friday (the afternoon trips go at 4.30pm from May to mid-September). After the river crossing, the trip is by 20-person 4WD vehicle, visiting much the same spots as the tours from El Acebuche (p702). Book as far ahead as you can and either take mosquito repellent, or cover up.

Festivals & Events
The Sanlúcar summer gets going with the spring **Feria de la Manzanilla**, in late May or early June, and blossoms in July and August with jazz, flamenco and classical-music festivals, one-off concerts by top Spanish bands, and Sanlúcar's unique horse races, the **Carreras de Caballo**, in which thoroughbred racehorses thunder along the beach during a couple of three- or four-day evening meetings during August.

Sleeping
Book well ahead at holiday times.
Hotel Posada de Palacio (☎ 956 36 48 40; www .posadadepalacio.com; Calle Caballeros 11; s/d €85/105; P ❄ 🖳) Sanlúcar's most charming and sumptuous lodging is this 18th-century mansion in the upper part of town. Furniture is old-style and heavy.

Hotel Tartaneros (☎ 956 38 53 94; Calle Tartaneros 8; s/d €81/102; P ❄) At the inland end of Calzada del Ejército, this is a century-old industrialist's mansion with solidly comfortable rooms.

Hotel Guadalquivir (☎ 956 36 07 42; www.hotel guadalquivir.com in Spanish; Calzada del Ejército 20; s/d €77/97) The large modern Guadalquivir is opposite the tourist office. Prices nearly halve from January to March.

Hotel Los Helechos (☎ 956 36 13 49; www.hotel loshelechos.com; Plaza Madre de Dios 9; s/d €47/62; P ❄) Off Calle San Juan, 200m from Plaza del Cabildo, the brightly decorated rooms here are mostly set around two plant-filled patios.

Hostal La Bohemia (☎ 956 36 95 99; Calle Don Claudio 5; s/d €20/38) Pretty, folksy-painted chairs dot the corridors of this little hostal, 300m northeast of Plaza del Cabildo; rooms are neat and clean.

Eating

Restaurante Virgen del Carmen (Bajo de Guía s/n; fish mains €6-10) Spain holds few more idyllic dining experiences than tucking into succulent fresh seafood while watching the sun go down over the Guadalquivir at Bajo de Guía, and washing it down with a glass or two of manzanilla. The Virgen del Carmen is one of the best of several restaurants at Bajo de Guía. Decide whether you want your fish *plancha* (grilled) or *frito* (fried), and don't skip the starters: *langostinos* (king prawns) and the juicy *coquines al ajillo* (clams in garlic), both €6, are specialities.

Lots of cafés and bars, many serving manzanilla from the barrel, surround Plaza del Cabildo: **Casa Balbino** (Plaza del Cabildo 11; tapas €1.50) is a must for tapas.

Entertainment

There are some lively music bars on and around Calzada del Ejército and Plaza del Cabildo, and lots of concerts in summer.

Getting There & Away

Buses leave from the terminal on Avenida de la Estación. Destinations include El Puerto de Santa María (€1.50, 30 minutes, up to 10 daily), Cádiz (€2.75, 1¼ hours, up to 10 daily), Jerez de la Frontera (€1.45, 30 minutes, up to 14 daily) and Seville (€7.40, 1½ hours, up to 10 daily).

JEREZ DE LA FRONTERA

pop 185,000

Jerez (heh-*reth*), 36km northeast of Cádiz, is world-famous for its wine – sherry – made from grapes grown in the area's chalky soils. Visitors come to see its sherry bodegas but Jerez is also Andalucía's horse capital and has a large *gitano* (Roma people, formerly known as Gypsies) community that is one of the hotbeds of flamenco. It stages fantastic fiestas with sleek horses, beautiful people and passionate music.

The Muslims called the town Scheris, from which 'Jerez' and 'sherry' are derived. The drink was already famed in England in Shakespeare's time. British money was largely responsible for the development of the wineries from around the 1830s. Jerez high society today is a mixture of *andaluz* and British, due to intermarriage among sherry families over the past 150 years. Though the sherry industry has brought greater prosperity to the town (Jerez brandy, popular in Spain, is another profitable product), it's still a city of extremes: there is 30% unemployment yet also fancy shops, wide and spacious streets, old mansions, many well-heeled residents, and beautiful churches in its interesting old quarter.

Orientation & Information

The centre of Jerez is between Alameda Cristina and Plaza del Arenal, connected by Calle Larga and Calle Lancería (both pedestrianised). The old quarter is west of Calle Larga.

The **tourist offices** (www.webjerez.com; ☾ 10am-2pm & 5-7pm Mon-Fri 9.30am-2pm Sat & Sun 16 Jun–14 Sep, 9.30am-3pm & 4.30-6.30pm Mon-Fri 9.30am-2.30pm Sat & Sun 15 Sep–15 Jun; Plaza del Arenal ☎ 956 35 96 54 Alameda Cristina ☎ 956 33 11 50) have energetic multilingual staff.

There are plenty of banks and ATMs on and around Calle Larga. **Interauto** (Calle Bodegas s/n; per hr €1.50; ☾ 10am-10pm) has speedy Internet connections.

Sights

OLD QUARTER

The obvious place to start a tour of old Jerez is the 11th- or 12th-century Almohad fortress, the **Alcázar** (☎ 956 31 97 98; Alameda Vieja; admission incl/excl camera obscura €3.30/1.30; ☾ 10am-6pm 16 Sep–30 Apr, 10am-8pm 1 May–15 Jun, 10am-8pm Mon-Sat, 10am-3pm Sun 15 Jun–15 Sep). Inside there's a beautiful **mezquita**, converted to a chapel by Alfonso X in 1264; an impressive set of **Baños Árabes** (Arab Baths), and the 18th-century **Palacio Villavicencio**. In the palace's tower, a **camera obscura** provides a live panorama of Jerez, with multilingual commentary. Sessions begin every half-hour until 30 minutes before closing time.

The orange tree–lined promenade around the Alcázar overlooks the mainly 18th-century **cathedral** (admission free; ☾ 11am-1pm daily, 6-8pm Mon-Sat, 11am-2pm Sun), built on the site of Scheris' main mosque.

A couple of blocks northeast of the cathedral is Plaza de la Asunción, with the handsome 16th-century **Antiguo Cabildo** (Old

ANDALUCÍA

JEREZ DE LA FRONTERA

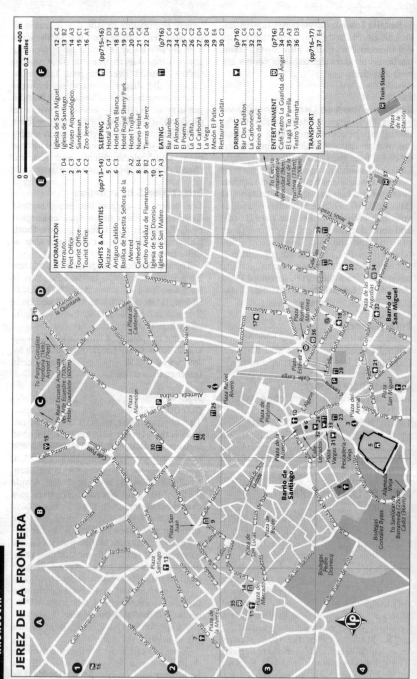

INFORMATION	
Interauto	1 D4
Post Office	2 C3
Tourist Office	3 C4
Tourist Office	4 C2

SIGHTS & ACTIVITIES	(pp713–14)
Alcázar	5 C4
Antiguo Cabildo	6 C3
Basílica de Nuestra Señora de la	
Merced	7 A2
Cathedral	8 B4
Centro Andaluz de Flamenco	9 B2
Iglesia de San Dionisio	10 C3
Iglesia de San Mateo	11 A3
Iglesia de San Miguel	12 C4
Iglesia de Santiago	13 B2
Museo Arqueológico	14 A3
Sandeman	15 C1
Zoo Jerez	16 A1

SLEEPING	(pp715–16)
Hostal Sanvi	17 D3
Hotel Doña Blanca	18 D4
Hotel Royal Sherry Park	19 D1
Hotel Trujillo	20 D4
Nuevo Hotel	21 C4
Tierras de Jerez	22 D4

EATING	(p716)
Bar Juanito	23 C4
El Almacén	24 C4
El Poema	25 C2
La Cañita	26 C2
La Carboná	27 D4
La Vega	28 C4
Mesón El Patio	29 E4
Restaurant Gaitán	30 C2

DRINKING	(p716)
Bar Dos Deditos	31 C4
La Carbonería	32 C3
Reino de León	33 C3

ENTERTAINMENT	(pp716–17)
Café Teatro La Guarida del Ángel	34 D4
El Lagá Tío Parrilla	35 A3
Teatro Villamarta	36 D3

TRANSPORT	(pp716–17)
Bus Station	37 E4

Town Hall) and lovely 15th-century Mudéjar **Iglesia de San Dionisio**.

Northwest of here is the **Barrio de Santiago**, with a sizable *gitano* population and churches dedicated to all four evangelists: the Gothic **Iglesia de San Mateo** (Plaza del Mercado) has Mudéjar chapels. Nearby is the excellent **Museo Arqueológico** (☎ 956 33 33 16; admission €1.75; ☺ 10am-2.30pm Tue-Sun 15 Jun–31 Aug, 10am-2pm & 4-7pm Tue-Fri 10am-2.30pm Sat, Sun & holidays 1 Sep–14 Jun). Pride of the museum's collection is a 7th-century-BC Greek helmet that was found in the Río Guadalete.

Also in this area is the **Centro Andaluz de Flamenco** (Andalucian Flamenco Centre; ☎ 956 34 92 65; http://caf.cica.es; Plaza San Juan 1; admission free; ☺ 9am-2pm Mon-Fri). Jerez is at the heart of the Seville–Cádiz axis, where flamenco began and which remains its heartland today. The centre is a kind of flamenco museum, library and school, with several flamenco videos screened each morning it's open.

Try not to miss what's arguably Jerez's loveliest church, the 16th-century **Iglesia de San Miguel** (Plaza San Miguel; ☺ 8pm for Mass), just southeast of Plaza del Arenal.

SHERRY BODEGAS
For most bodegas, you need to ring ahead to book your visit (it's advisable to confirm hours with the tourist offices, which have full details), but you can turn up without booking at these two places:

Bodegas González Byass (☎ 956 35 70 00; www.gonzalezbyass.es; Calle Manuel María González 12; tours €7; ☺ in English 11.30am-2pm & 3.30-5.30pm Mon-Sat, 11.30am-1.30pm Sun) One of the biggest sherry houses, handily located just west of the Alcázar.

Sandeman (☎ 956 15 17 11; www.sandeman.com; Calle Pizarro 10; tours €5; ☺ 3 or 4 tours in English 10.30am-3.30pm Mon-Fri)

REAL ESCUELA ANDALUZ DEL ARTE ECUESTRE
The famed **Royal Andalucian School of Equestrian Art** (☎ 956 31 80 08; www.realescuela.org; Avenida Duque de Abrantes) trains horses and riders in dressage, and you can watch them going through their paces in **training sessions** (admission €6; ☺ 10am-1pm Mon, Wed & Fri Mar-Jul & Sep-Oct, Mon & Wed Aug, Mon, Tue, Wed & Fri Nov-Feb). At noon on Thursday year-round and noon on Tuesday from March to October (except holidays), plus Fridays in August, there's an official **espectáculo** (show; admission €13-21),

where the handsome white horses show off their tricks to classical music.

ZOO JEREZ
Only a couple of kilometres west of the centre, Jerez's **zoo** (☎ 956 18 23 97; Calle Taxdirt s/n; adult/child €4.20/2.70; ☺ 10am-6pm Tue-Sun, to 8pm Jun-Sep) houses 1300 beasts, well-established gardens and a recuperation centre for wild animals.

Festivals & Events
Festival de Jerez (late Feb/early Mar) Two weeks of music and dance, particularly flamenco.

Feria del Caballo (first half of May) Jerez's week-long Horse Fair is one of Andalucía's biggest festivals, with music, dance and bullfights as well as all kinds of equestrian competitions and colourful horse parades through the Parque González Hontoria fairgrounds in the north of town.

Fiestas de Otoño (September) The three-week Autumn Festivals range from flamenco and horse events to the traditional treading of the first grapes on Plaza de la Asunción.

Sleeping
Most rates go sky-high during the Feria del Caballo and you need to book ahead.

Hotel Royal Sherry Park (☎ 956 31 76 14; www.sherryparkhotel.com; Avenida Álvaro Domecq 11; s/d €109/137; P ⊠ ☐ ☒) A long-standing Jerez favourite, the Sherry Park boasts sound-proofed rooms, excellent indoor and outdoor pools, and verdant park-like grounds.

Hotel Guadalete (☎ 956 18 22 88; Avenida Duque de Abrantes 50; s/d €116/135; P ⊠ ☐ ☒) This spacious, luxurious, modern hotel has an attractive garden with an inviting pool.

Hotel Doña Blanca (☎ 956 34 87 61; www.hoteldonablanca.com in Spanish; Calle Bodegas 11; s/d €79/96; P ⊠ ☐) On a quiet side street, this is an excellent hotel with parquet floors and soothing light-blue paintwork. The buffet breakfast costs €6.

Tierras de Jerez (☎ 956 34 64 00; www.intergrouphoteles.com; Calle Corredera 58; s/d €58/91; P ⊠ ☐) Rooms here are decked out in apricots and pinks, and marbled tiles, and have all mod cons. The location is especially handy. There's a lift (elevator), and buffet breakfast (€6).

Nuevo Hotel (☎ 956 33 16 00; www.nuevohotel.com; Calle Caballeros 23; s/d €21/35; ⊠) In a modernised mansion, Jerez's best budget accommodation provides rooms with TV and winter heating. It's popular, so you need to

ANDALUCÍA

book. A buffet breakfast (€6.50) is served in the bright dining room.

Other good budget options:

Hotel Trujillo (☎ /fax 956 34 24 38; www.hoteltrujillo .com; Calle Medina 36; s/d €22.50/38; P 🕮)

Hostal Sanvi (☎ 956 34 56 24; Calle Morenos 10; s/d €25/36; P)

Eating

Sherry is used to flavour local dishes and the sherry trade has introduced English and French elements into the local cuisine.

Mesón El Patio (☎ 956 34 07 36; Calle San Francisco de Paula 7; fish raciones €6-10, menú €20; 🕑 closed Mon) El Patio combines a touch of refinement with local conviviality. It has high ceilings, warm tones and a collection of old radios. Above all, the food is terrific and there's a huge choice, especially of prawn dishes.

La Carboná (☎ 956 34 74 75; Calle San Francisco de Paula 2; mains €10.50-12.50) This popular, cavernous restaurant, with an eccentric menu and young wait staff, occupies an old winery. Specialities include grilled meats and fresh fish.

Restaurant Gaitán (☎ 956 34 58 59; Calle Gaitán 3; mains €14-16) With a fancy décor of antlers and photos of past clients, Gaitán tempts with dishes such as lamb in honey-and-brandy sauce or hake with squid sauce and pilaff rice. The *menú turístico* (tourist menu) at €16 is a bit easier on the pocket.

La Vega (Plaza Estévez s/n; breakfast €4) Imbibe a dose of local life over breakfast at this noisy, bustling café. You can buy *churros* (doughnuts; €1.50 per 250g) at a kiosk by the adjacent market and bring them here to eat with a coffee or hot chocolate.

TAPAS

Two fine central spots to sample tapas with a sherry are **Bar Juanito** (Pescadería Vieja 8-10; tapas €1.80-2.50) and the cave-like **El Almacén** (Calle Ferros 8; tapas €1.50-3) round the corner.

About 500m north, there are even more brilliant tapas bars surrounding quiet little Plaza Rafael Rivero. Head here after 9.30pm. Don't miss the *montaditos* (€1.50 to €2) at **El Poema** (Calle Porvera). If you've still got room, walk a little further to **La Cañita** (Calle Porvera 11; tapas €1.50-6): the *montaditos* (again) are delicious: try Brie with anchovies.

Drinking & Entertainment

A few bars in the narrow streets north of Plaza del Arenal can get lively with an under-30 crowd late in the evening: try **Bar Dos Deditos** (Plaza Vargas 1), **Reino de León** (Calle Ferros) and **La Carbonería** (Calle Letrados 7). You might also come across some live music at one of these places. Northeast of the city centre, La Plaza de Canterbury, with lots of bars around a central courtyard, attracts a young crowd, as do the music bars a little further northeast on Avenida de Méjico.

For what's-on information, check at the tourist office, visit www.webjerez.com and look out for posters. The **Teatro Villamarta** (☎ 956 3295 07; Plaza Romero Martínez) puts out a seasonal programme. A hip venue for live music, theatre and theatre workshops is **Café Teatro La Guarida del Ángel** (☎ 956 34 91 52; Calle Porvenir 1; 🕑 8pm-late).

Several *peñas flamencas* (flamenco clubs) welcome genuinely interested visitors: ask at the tourist office about events. **El Lagá Tío Parrilla** (☎ 956 33 83 34; Plaza del Mercado; 🕑 10.30pm & 12.30am Mon-Sat) has more tourist-oriented flamenco performances but can still be pretty gusty.

Jerez's **Circuito Permanente de Velocidad** (☎ 956 15 11 00; www.circuitodejerez.com), on the A382 10km east of town, hosts several motorcycle and car-racing events each year, including one of the Grand Prix races of the World Motorcycle Championship, in April or May. This is one of Spain's biggest sporting events, with around 150,000 fans and their bikes swamping Jerez and nearby towns.

Getting There & Away

AIR

Seven kilometres northeast of town on the NIV is **Jerez airport** (☎ 956 15 00 83). Budget airline Ryanair flies here from London Stansted twice daily. **Iberia** (☎ 956 15 00 09) flies direct to/from Madrid and Barcelona every day.

BUS

The **bus station** (☎ 956 34 52 07; Calle Diego Fernández Herrera) is 1km southeast of the centre. Destinations include Seville (€5.60, 1¼ hours, about 15 daily), Sanlúcar de Barrameda (€1.45, 30 minutes, seven or more daily), El Puerto de Santa María (€1.05, 20 minutes, up to 19 daily), Cádiz (€2.55, 40 minutes, up to 21 daily), Arcos de la Frontera (€2.15, 45 minutes, up to 24 daily), El Bosque (€5, 1½ hours, two or more daily) and Ronda (€8.90, 2½ hours, three daily).

SARA-JANE CLELAND

The clear blue water of Ibiza (p634), Balearic Islands

Palma de Mallorca's awesome
catedral (p622), Balearic Islands

NEIL SETCHFIELD

EOIN CLARKE

Inside the Naveta des Tudons (p657),
a stone burial chamber east of Ciutadella on the island of Menorca

Remains of the Roman theatre (p667) in
Cartagena, Murcia

INGRID RODDIS

Row after row of striped arches inside Córdoba's Mezquita (p751), Andalucía

In the oak woods of the Valle de Trevélez in Las Alpujarras (p776), Andalucía

Hooded *nazarenos* in the Easter procession of Seville's Semana Santa (p690), Andalucía

View to Morocco from the Mirador del Estrecho (p723), near Tarifa, Andalucía

TRAIN

Jerez **train station** (☎ 956 34 23 19; Plaza de la Estación) is 300m east of the bus station, with trains to El Puerto de Santa María (€1.15, 12 minutes, up to 36 daily), Cádiz (€2.75, 45 minutes, 21 daily) and Seville (from €5.85, 1¼ hours, nine daily).

ARCOS DE LA FRONTERA

pop 29,000 / elevation 185m

The old town of Arcos, 30km east of Jerez, could not be more dramatically or impregnably sited: it stands on a high ridge with sheer precipices (Peña Vieja and Peña Nueva) dropping away on both sides. The old town is well worth exploring, with a street plan little changed since medieval times and some lovely post-Reconquista buildings.

Always prized for its strategic position, Arcos was briefly, during the 11th century, an independent Muslim kingdom before being absorbed by Seville. In 1255 Alfonso X took the town and repopulated it with Castilians and Leonese. In 1440 it passed to the Ponce de León family, the Duques de Arcos.

When the last duke died in 1780, his cousin, the Duquesa de Benavente, took over his lands. She was partly responsible for replacing sheep farming with cereals, olives, vines and horse breeding as the area's dominant economic activities.

Orientation & Information

From the bus station, it's a 1.5km uphill walk to the old town. Paseo de los Boliches and Calle Debajo del Corral (becoming Calle Corredera) both lead east up to the old town's main square, Plaza del Cabildo.

The **tourist office** (☎ 956 70 22 64; Plaza del Cabildo; ☒ 10am-2pm & 4-7.30pm Mon-Sat) is on the old town's main square. There's also a **tourist information kiosk** (Paseo de Andalucía). Banks and ATMs are along Calle Debajo del Corral and Calle Corredera.

Sights

Wander around Arcos' old town with its narrow cobbled streets, Renaissance mansions and spectacular vistas. Plaza del Cabildo has a vertiginous **mirador** (lookout) with views over the Río Guadalete and

ARCOS DE LA FRONTERA

INFORMATION		Mirador	7 A2	EATING	⊞	(p718)
Post Office	1 B1	Palacio Mayorazgo	8 D2	El Convento		14 B2
Tourist-Information Kiosk	2 A1			Market		15 B2
Tourist Office	3 A2	SLEEPING ⊡	(p718)	Restaurante-Asador		
		Hotel El Convento	9 B2	Los Murales		16 A2
SIGHTS & ACTIVITIES	(pp717–18)	Hotel Los Olivos	10 B1			
Basílica-Parroquia de Santa María	4 A2	Hotel Marqués de Torresoto	11 A2	TRANSPORT		(p718)
Castillo de los Duques	5 A2	La Fonda Hotel	12 B1	Bus Station		17 A1
Iglesia de San Pedro	6 D2	Parador Casa del Corregidor	13 A2			

ANDALUCÍA

countryside. It's also surrounded by fine old buildings, though its crowning glory, the 11th-century **Castillo de los Duques**, is not open to the public. On the plaza's northern side is the Gothic-cum-baroque **Basílica-Parroquia de Santa María** (admission €1; ☺ 10am-1pm & 4-7pm Mon-Fri, 10am-2pm Sat). On the eastern side, the **Parador Casa del Corregidor** hotel is a reconstruction of a 16th-century magistrate's house.

Along the streets east of here seek out lovely buildings such as the **Iglesia de San Pedro** (Calle Núñez de Prado; admission €1; ☺ 10am-1pm & 4-7pm Mon-Sat, 10am-1.30pm Sun), another Gothic-baroque confection, and the 17th-century **Palacio Mayorazgo**, now a senior citizens' centre, with a Renaissance façade and pretty patios.

Tours

One-hour guided tours of the old town's monuments start from the tourist office at 10.30am Monday to Saturday, and 5pm Monday to Friday. Tours of Arcos' pretty patios start 1½ hours later. Each tour costs €5.

Festivals & Events

Semana Santa (Easter) Processions through the narrow old streets are dramatic; on Easter Sunday there's a hair-raising running of the bulls.

Fiesta de la Virgen de las Nieves (early August) Three-day festival includes a top-class flamenco night in Plaza del Cabildo.

Feria de San Miguel (end of September) Arcos celebrates its patron saint, San Miguel, with a four-day fair.

Sleeping & Eating

Parador Casa del Corregidor (☎ 956 70 05 00; www .parador.es; Plaza del Cabildo; s/d €97/120; ✖) Typical Parador luxury with magnificent panoramas. Eight of the rooms have balconies with cliff views. The **restaurant** (mains €18, menú €24) has *andaluz* specialities.

Hotel El Convento (☎ 956 70 23 33; www.webde arcos.com/elconvento; Calle Maldonado 2; s €55, d with/without terrace €80/65) In a beautiful 17th-century convent, this hotel has a large terrace for taking in the stupendous view; six of the tasteful, varied rooms share the view.

Hotel Los Olivos (☎ 956 70 08 11; losolivosdelc@terra .es; Paseo de los Boliches 30; s/d €45/70; Ⓟ ✖) This friendly, attractive, small hotel, with an interior patio, serves breakfast for €6.

Hotel Marqués de Torresoto (☎ 956 70 07 17; hmdetorresoto@terra.es; Calle Marqués de Torresoto 4; s/d

€55.50/66.50; ✖) An old-town mansion with large, comfy rooms in soothing colours and an arcaded courtyard restaurant.

La Fonda Hotel (☎ 956 70 00 57; Calle Corredera 83; s/d €30/50; ✖) A renovated 19th-century inn, La Fonda provides ample rooms with good beds, winter heating and TV.

Restaurante-Asador Los Murales (☎ 956 71 79 53; Calle Marqués de Torresoto; www.restaurantelos murales.com in Spanish; mains €8-14) Come to this slightly classy spot, with mellow music and décor, for its meat and fish prepared *a la brasa* (grilled).

El Convento (☎ 956 70 32 33; Calle Marqués de Torresoto 7; mains €8-15) This fancy restaurant in a 17th-century pillared patio turns out country favourites such as herbed lamb and venison steak.

Getting There & Away

Services from the **bus station** (☎ 956 70 49 77; Calle Corregidores) run to Jerez (€2.15, 45 minutes, 24 daily), Cádiz (€4.80, 1¼ hours, 11 daily), El Bosque (€2.35, 45 minutes, eight daily), Ronda (€7, 1½ hours, four daily) and Seville (€6.35, two hours, two daily). Frequencies to some destinations are reduced on Saturday and Sunday.

PARQUE NATURAL SIERRA DE GRAZALEMA

The mountainous Parque Natural Sierra de Grazalema, in northeastern Cádiz province, is one of Andalucía's greenest and most beautiful areas. The landscape here, dotted with whitewashed villages, ranges from pastoral river valleys to precipitous gorges and rocky summits. Grazalema town has the highest measured rainfall in Spain, at 2153mm per year. This is fine walking country (the best months are May, June, September and October), and there are opportunities for climbing, caving, canyoning, bird-watching and paragliding.

The park extends into northwestern Málaga province, where it includes the Cueva de la Pileta (p747). IGN/Junta de Andalucía's *Sierra de Grazalema* (1:50,000) is a fairly good map.

El Bosque

pop 2000 / elevation 385m

El Bosque, 33km east of Arcos across rolling country, is prettily situated below the wooded Sierra de Albarracín. A pleasant

5km riverside path to Benamahoma starts beside El Bosque's youth hostel.

The natural park's **Punto de Información El Bosque** (☎ 956 72 70 29; Avenida de la Diputación s/n; ⌚ 10am-2pm & 5-7pm Mon-Fri, 9am-2pm & 5-7pm Sat, 9am-2pm Sun) is down a short lane off the A372 at the western end of the village (turn down by the bullring). A new visitors centre beside the bullring is due to open in 2005.

SLEEPING & EATING

Hotel Las Truchas (☎ 956 71 60 61; www.tugasa.com in Spanish; Avenida Diputación s/n; s/d €34.25/56.20; **P** **❄** **♿**) Many of the comfy rooms here have balconies. The terrace of the restaurant (mains €6 to €12) overlooks the village and countryside.

Albergue Campamento Juvenil El Bosque (☎ 956 71 62 12; www.inturjoven.com in Spanish; Molino de Enmedio s/n; under 26 incl breakfast €9.05-13.75, over 26 €12.25-18.35; closed approx 20 Dec–8 Jan; **♿**) El Bosque's modernised youth hostel is pleasantly sited 800m up a side road from Hotel Las Truchas. Accommodation is in double, triple and quadruple rooms; three rooms are adapted for wheelchair access.

Mesón El Tabanco (☎ 956 71 60 81; Calle Huelva 1; mains & menúes €8-12; ⌚ closed Sun evening & 2nd half Jun) Just off the village square, El Tabanco serves excellent meat dishes in a skylit dining room.

Grazalema

pop 2200 / elevation 825m

From El Bosque, the A372 winds east over the Puerto del Boyar (1103m) to Grazalema, a picture-postcard village nestling neatly into a corner of beautiful mountain country: beneath the rock-climbers' crag Peñón Grande. Local products include pure-wool blankets and rugs.

The village centre is the pretty Plaza de España, overlooked by the 18th-century Iglesia de la Aurora. Here you'll find the **tourist office** (☎ 956 13 22 25; ⌚ 10am-2pm & 5-7pm Tue-Sun), with a shop selling local products. Two banks on Plaza de España have ATMs.

Horizon (☎ /fax 956 13 23 63; www.horizonaventura .com; Calle Corrales Terceros 29; per person from €13) is an experienced adventure-tourism firm that can take you climbing, caving, canyoning, walking or bird-watching, with English-speaking guides.

SLEEPING & EATING

Hotel Peñón Grande (☎ /fax 956 13 24 35; Plaza Pequeña 7; s/d €36/52; **❄**) This friendly hotel, just off Plaza de España, has good-sized rooms in a rustic but very comfortable style, with solid stained-wood furnishings.

Casa de las Piedras (☎ /fax 956 13 20 14; www.casa delaspiedras.net in Spanish; Calle Las Piedras 32; s with/without bathroom €34/10, d €42.50/20) A good-value hostal occupying a fine old village house, Casa de la Piedras has plain, well-kept rooms and a hearty, economical restaurant.

Villa Turística (☎ 956 13 21 36; www.tugasa.com in Spanish; El Olivar s/n; s/d €34.25/56.20, 2-person apt €80.90) Overlooking the village from a hillside to the north, the Villa Turística is a comfortable hotel with lawns and pool making the most of a great view.

Camping Tajo Rodillo (☎ 956 13 24 18; Carretera a El Bosque; camping per adult/tent/car €4/4/3.50, 4-person cabins €65; ⌚ daily 20 Jun–10 Sep, holidays & 3pm Fri–noon Sun rest of year; **♿**) Grazalema's camping ground is at the top of the village beside the A372 to El Bosque.

GRAZALEMA RESERVE AREA WALKS

Three of the Parque Natural Sierra de Grazalema's best day walks are the ascent of El Torreón (1654m), the highest peak in Cádiz province; the route from Grazalema to Benamahoma via Spain's best-preserved *pinsapar* (woodland of the rare and beautiful Spanish fir); and the trip into the Garganta Verde, a deep ravine south of Zahara de la Sierra, with a large colony of griffon vultures. All these walks are within a 30-sq-km *área de reserva* (reserve area), with restricted entry, meaning that to do any of them you must obtain a (free) permit from the El Bosque park office (opposite). You can call or visit El Bosque up to 15 days in advance for this and, if you wish, they will forward permits to be collected at the Zahara information office or Grazalema tourist office. Staff at any of these offices may or may not speak a language other than Spanish. It's normally only necessary to book ahead for walking on a weekend or public holiday. In July, August and September, when the fire risk is high, it's obligatory to go with a guide from an authorised local company, such as Horizon (see opposite) or Al-qutun (p720).

ANDALUCÍA

Mesón El Simancón (☎ 956 13 24 21; Plaza Asomadero; mains €5-12) There are plenty of places to eat and drink around Plaza de España, and on Calle Agua, a little street running between the plaza and the large village car park. El Simancón, right by the main car park, is arguably the best eatery of all. Wellprepared local fare (ham, quail, venison and egg dishes) is served in a dining room lined with wine bottles and deer heads.

Zahara de la Sierra
pop 1500 / elevation 550m

Topped by a crag with a ruined castle, Zahara is the most dramatically sited of the area's villages. It feels quite otherworldly, if you've driven through mist from Grazalema via the vertiginous 1331m Puerto de los Palomas (Doves' Pass; but with more vultures than doves). The village centres on Calle San Juan, where you'll find the natural park's **Punto de Información Zahara de la Sierra** (☎ /fax 956 12 31 14; Plaza del Rey 3; ☼ 9am-2pm & 5-7pm Mon-Sat, 9am-2pm Sun).

Zahara's streets invite investigation, with vistas framed by tall palms or hot-pink bougainvillea. To climb to the 12th-century **castle keep**, take the path almost opposite the entrance to Hotel Arco de la Villa – it's a steady 10- to 20-minute climb. The castle's recapture from the Christians, by Abu al-Hasan of Granada in a night raid in 1481, provoked the Catholic Monarchs to launch the last phase of the Reconquista, which ended with the fall of Granada.

Adventure tourism firm **Al-qutun** (☎ 956 13 78 82; www.al-qutun.com), in Algodonales, 7km north of Zahara, will take you canyoning, paragliding, canoeing, caving, climbing, walking and more.

Hostal Marqués de Zahara (☎ /fax 956 12 30 61; www.marquesdezahara.com; Calle San Juan 3; s/d €30/ 39.60), a converted mansion, has comfy rooms with winter heating and a restaurant. Rooms with balcony cost a few euros extra. The **Hotel Arco de la Villa** (☎ 956 12 32 30; www.tugasa.com in Spanish; Paseo Nazarí s/n; s/d €34.25/56.20; ℗ ✿) has spectacular views. **Restaurante Los Naranjos** (☎ 956 12 33 14; Calle San Juan; meat & fish mains €7-12) serves good local dishes, indoors or out, on its *terraza* (terrace).

Getting There & Away
Los Amarillos (☎ 902 210317) runs up to eight buses a day to El Bosque from Jerez (€5,

1½ hours) and Arcos (€2.35, 45 minutes), five from Cádiz (€6.35, two hours) and two from Seville (Prado de San Sebastián; €6.30, 1¾ hours). From El Bosque, buses leave for Grazalema (€1.90, 30 minutes) at 6.45am and 3.15pm Monday to Friday and 7.30pm Friday only. Grazalema–El Bosque buses depart at 5.30am Monday to Friday and 7pm Friday.

Los Amarillos also runs twice daily from Málaga to Grazalema (€9.50, three hours) via Ronda.

Comes (in Ronda ☎ 952 87 19 92) operates two buses each way Monday to Friday between Ronda and Zahara de la Sierra (€3, one hour), via Algodonales (where there are connections for Seville, Arcos, Jerez and Cádiz). There's no bus service between Zahara and Grazalema.

SOUTHERN COSTA DE LA LUZ
The 90km coast between Cádiz and Tarifa can be windy, and its Atlantic waters are a shade cooler than the Mediterranean, but these are small prices to pay for a mostly unspoiled, often wild shore, strung with long, white-sand beaches. Andalucians flock here in July and August, bringing a fiesta atmosphere to the normally quiet coastal settlements; you'll need to phone ahead for rooms at this time. Outside this high season many room prices fall by one-third or so.

Vejer de la Frontera
pop 13,000 / elevation 190m

This old-fashioned white town looms mysteriously atop a rocky hill above the busy N340, 50km from Cádiz. It's experiencing a small influx of foreign residents and is a good base for outdoor activities, with some charming places to stay. Buses stop on Avenida Los Remedios, about 500m below the town centre and next to the **tourist office** (☎ 956 45 17 36; www.turismovejer.com; ☼ 9.30am-2.30pm Mon-Fri, afternoon & weekend hr depending on season).

Vejer's much-reworked **castle** (☼ 10am-9pm) has great views from its battlements and a small museum that preserves one of the black cloaks that Vejer women wore until just a couple of decades ago (covering everything but the eyes). You can rent good mountain bikes (from €12.50 per day) at **Discover Andalucía** (☎ 956 44 75 75; Avenida Los Remedios 45). **Natural Sur** (☎ 956 45 14 19; www.naturalsur.com) will take you trekking, biking or kayaking.

SLEEPING & EATING

Hotel La Casa del Califa (☎ 956 44 77 30; www.vejer .com/califa; Plaza de España 16; s €52-84, d €66-98, incl breakfast; ⊠) This great little place rambles over several floors and has peaceful, comfortable rooms with Islamic décor, and a great Arabic restaurant, **El Jardín del Califa** (mains €7.80-17), extending out into the garden.

El Cobijo de Vejer (☎ 956 45 50 23; Calle San Filmo 7; www.elcobijo.com; r incl breakfast €62-78; ⊠) The rooms and apartments here, some self-catering and with fabulous views, are set around a pretty tiled patio with a fountain and vines. The breakfast is scrumptious and healthy.

Hostal Buena Vista (☎ 956 45 09 69; Calle Machado 4; s/d €18/36 or €21/42; P) Family-run Buena Vista has spotless, spacious rooms.

La Bodeguita (☎ 956 45 15 82; Calle Marqués de Tamarón 9; tapas €1) This tastefully decked-out bar has good vibes, breakfast, excellent tapas and an extensive music collection.

GETTING THERE & AWAY

Buses run to Cádiz (€4.10, 50 minutes) up to 10 times a day. Buses for Tarifa (€3.40, 50 minutes, about 10 daily), Málaga (€13.80, 2¾ hours, two daily) and Seville (€10.80, three hours, five daily) stop at La Barca de Vejer, on the N340 at the bottom of the hill. It's a 15-minute walk up to town from there.

Los Caños de Meca

pop 200

Once a hippie hideaway, Los Caños straggles along a series of sandy coves, beneath

---

TOP 10 ANDALUCIAN BEACHES

---

a pine-clad hill southwest of Vejer. It maintains its laid-back, offbeat air even at the height of summer.

At the western end of Los Caños a side road leads out to a lighthouse on a low spit of land with a famous name – Cabo de Trafalgar. It was off this cape that Spanish naval power was terminated in a few hours one day in 1805 by a British fleet under Admiral Nelson. Wonderful beaches stretch either side of Cabo de Trafalgar. Towards the eastern end of Los Caños, the main street, Avenida Trafalgar, is met by the road from Barbate.

SLEEPING

Casas Karen (☎ 956 43 70 67; www.casaskaren.com; Fuente del Madroño 6; r €85-90, q €102-159; P) This eccentric place, owned by a dynamic young Englishwoman, has seven or so different buildings on a pretty plot, each with a kitchen, lounge, outdoor sitting area and casual *andaluz*-Moroccan décor. Turn off the main road 500m east of the Cabo de Trafalgar, at a tiled 'Apartamentos y Bungalows' sign, go 500m, then turn right at the 'Fuente del Madroño' sign.

Hostal Madreselva (☎ 956 43 72 55; www.madre selvahotel.com; Avenida Trafalgar 102; s/d €62/74; ⊠ closed Oct–late Mar; P ☎) Some of the rooms at this artistically designed and friendly place have their own small garden. The bar area extends outside to the pool. Mountain biking, horse riding and surfing can be arranged.

Hotel Fortuna (☎ 956 43 70 75; www.hotelfortuna .net; Avenida Trafalgar 34; s/d 53/66; P) A short walk east of the Barbate road corner, the Fortuna's excellent rooms all have terraces with sea views.

Hostal Miramar (☎ /fax 956 43 70 24; Avenida Trafalgar 112; s/d €50/60, r with terrace €90, incl breakfast; ⊠ Semana Santa–end Sep; P ☎) This hostal and its pool area are tucked behind a high wall for privacy, about halfway along the main street.

EATING

Bar-Restaurante El Caña (Avenida Trafalgar s/n; seafood dishes from €8.50; ⊠ Semana Santa, Jul & Aug) El Caña has a fine position atop the small cliff above the beach.

El Pirata (seafood media-raciones €5) Overlooking the beach, a couple of hundred metres west of El Caña, El Pirata is usually open when the weather is fine.

ANDALUCÍA

Restaurante El Capi (fish mains €10-14) In winter, when little else is open, El Capi still serves good tapas and fish, and has a welcoming open fire. It's on the main road in Zahora, at the west end of Los Caños.

La Pequeña Lulu (crepes & salads €5-6) At the far eastern end of the village, this cosy creperie opens day and night all year.

ENTERTAINMENT
In the summer season, good bars include the cool Los Castillejos at the eastern end of the village, Café-Bar Ketama opposite El Pirata, and Las Dunas on the road out to Cabo de Trafalgar (with music and busy pool table). La Pequeña Lulu often has live music and even some jammin'.

GETTING THERE & AWAY
Monday to Friday, there are two Comes buses to/from Cádiz (€4.50, 1¼ hours), one to/from Seville (Prado de San Sebastián; €11.55, 2½ hours) and three to/from Barbate (€0.80, 15 minutes), 12km east of Los Caños, which has up to 13 buses a day to/from Cádiz (€4.75, 50 minutes) and Vejer de la Frontera (€0.95, 10 minutes). There may be extra services from Seville and Cádiz from mid-June to early September.

Zahara de los Atunes
Plonked in the middle of nothing, except a broad, 12km, sandy beach, Zahara is an elemental sort of place. At its heart stands the crumbling old Almadraba, once a depot and refuge for the local tuna fishers, who must have been a rugged lot: Cervantes wrote that no-one deserved to be called a *pícaro* (scoundrel) unless they had spent two seasons fishing for tuna at Zahara. Today the nearest tuna fleet is 10km north at Barbate and Zahara has become a fashionable Spanish summer resort, with an old-fashioned core of narrow streets. It's a fine spot to let the sun, wind and sea – and, in summer, a spot of lively nightlife – batter your senses.

SLEEPING & EATING
Hotel Gran Sol (☎ 956 43 93 09; www.hotelgransol .com; Avenida de la Playa s/n; s/d €101/110, d with sea view €121, incl breakfast; P ⚡ ⚟ ⚐) The Gran Sol occupies the prime beach spot, facing the old Almadraba walls on one side and the ocean on the other. It has large, comfortable rooms.

Hotel Doña Lola (☎ 956 43 90 09; Plaza Thompson 1; s/d €90/115; P ⚡ ⚟ ⚐) Only two minutes from the beach, this is a modern place with good rooms in an attractive old-fashioned style, lovely large grounds and open eating and drinking areas.

Hotel Nicolás (☎ 956 43 92 74; www.hotel-nicolas .tuweb.net; Calle María Luisa 13; s/d €39.10/51.10, with half-board €51/80.10; P ⚡) A friendly hotel with simple but attractive rooms. Half-board is obligatory in July and August.

Camping Bahía de la Plata (☎ 956 43 90 40; Avenida de las Palmeras; 2 adults, tent & car €16.35) A good site with plenty of trees, fronting the beach at the southern end of Zahara.

Most restaurants are on or near Plaza de Tamarón, near Hotel Doña Lola, and most offer similar lists of fish, seafood, salads, meat and sometimes pizza. The open-air **Patio la Plazoleta** (Plaza de Tamarón; fish dishes €9, pizza €10) is a good choice.

ENTERTAINMENT
In July and August a line of marquees and shacks, along the beach south of the Almadraba, serves as bars, discos and teahouses. They get busy from about midnight. Some have live flamenco or other music.

GETTING THERE & AWAY
Comes runs four buses daily to and from Cádiz (€6.20, two hours) via Barbate, and one each Monday to Friday to and from Tarifa (€2.85, 45 minutes) and Seville (€13.25, 3½ hours). There are more buses from mid-June to September.

Bolonia
pop 125

This tiny village, hidden on a beautiful bay about 20km up the coast from Tarifa, has a fine white-sand beach, several restaurants and hostales, and the ruins of the Roman town **Baelo Claudia** (☎ 956 68 85 30; adult/EU citizen €1.50/free; ⏰ 10am-2pm Sun, 10am-7pm Tue-Sat, to 8pm Jun-Sep, to 6pm Nov-Feb). The ruins include a theatre, a forum surrounded by temples and other buildings, and workshops that turned out the products that made Baelo Claudia famous in the Roman world: salted fish and *garum*, a prized condiment made from fish entrails. You can walk up the big sand dune at the far end of the beach, or out to Punta Camarinal, the headland protecting the west end of the bay.

The hilly 7km side road to Bolonia heads west off the N340, 15km from Tarifa. You can walk an 8km route along the coast to Bolonia from Ensenada de Valdevaqueros (p724) via Punta Paloma.

SLEEPING & EATING

These three hostales open year-round (a few more open seasonally).

Hostal Lola (☎ 956 68 85 36; www.hostallola.com in Spanish; El Lentiscal 26; r with/without bathroom €50/40; **P**) The pretty garden is flower-filled and the rooms are simple but attractive. There's a little Moroccan-inspired sitting area too. Follow the signs on giant surfboards to find it.

Hostal Bellavista (☎ 956 68 85 53; s/d €40/45; **P**) This reasonable place is in the centre of the village. Some rooms have a terrace and plum sea views.

Hostal Miramar (☎ 956 68 42 04; r €42; **P**) The Miramar has fine views and is run by friendly folk from Tarifa. It's not luxurious but will do.

Bar Restaurante Las Rejas (salad €4, paella per person €8; ☼ year-round) The fish and seafood here are tops. The wait staff suggest which tasty options are best on the day.

TARIFA

pop 16,500

Even at peak times, Tarifa is an attractive, laid-back town. Relatively unknown until 15 or so years ago, it's now a windsurfing and kitesurfing mecca, with some of the very best conditions in Europe for these sports. The beaches have clean, white sand, and inland the country is green and rolling. Then there's the old town to explore, with its narrow streets, whitewashed houses and cascading flowers. A hip international scene with an eclectic bunch of restaurants, bars and places to stay has grown up around the surf crowd. The only negative – though not for the surfers! – is the wind; for much of the year, either the *levante* (easterly) or *poniente* (westerly) is blowing, which is ruinous for a relaxed sit on the beach and tiring if you're simply wandering around. August, however, can be blessedly still.

Tarifa takes its name from Tariq ibn Malik, who led a Muslim raid in 710, the year before the main Islamic invasion of the peninsula.

Orientation

Two roads head into Tarifa from the N340. The one from the northwest becomes Calle Batalla del Salado, ending at Avenida de Andalucía, where the Puerta de Jerez leads through the walls into the old town. The one from the northeast becomes Calle Amador de los Ríos, which meets Calle Batalla del Salado in front of the Puerta de Jerez. The main street of the old town is Calle Sancho IV El Bravo. To the southwest protrudes the Isla de las Palomas, a military-occupied promontory that is the southernmost point of continental Europe.

Information

Centro de Salud (Health Centre; ☎ 956 68 15 15/35; Calle Amador de los Ríos)

Lavandería Acuario (Calle Colón 14; ☼ 10.15am-1.30pm & 7.30-9pm Mon-Fri; wash per 4kg €4, wash, dry & fold €7-8)

Planet (Calle Santísima Trinidad; Internet access per hr €3)

Policía Local (☎ 956 61 41 86; Ayuntamiento, Plaza de Santa María)

Post office (Calle Coronel Moscardó 9)

Tourist office (☎ 956 68 09 93; www.tarifaweb.com in Spanish; Paseo de la Alameda; ☼ 9am-3pm)

Old Town

The Mudéjar **Puerta de Jerez** was built after the Reconquista. Look in at the bustling **market** (Calle Colón) before wending your way to the mainly 15th-century **Iglesia de San Mateo** at the end of Calle Sancho IV El Bravo. The streets south of the church are little changed since Islamic times. The **Mirador El Estrecho**, atop part of the castle walls, has spectacular views across to Africa, only 14km away.

The **Castillo de Guzmán** (Calle Guzmán; admission €1.80; ☼ 11am-2pm & 6-8pm Tue-Sat, 5-7pm Apr-Jun, 4-6pm Oct-Mar) is named after the Reconquista hero Guzmán El Bueno. In 1294, when threatened with the death of his captured son, unless he relinquished the castle to Islamic forces trying to recapture Tarifa, El Bueno threw down his own dagger for the deed to be done. Guzmán's descendants became the Duques de Medina Sidonia, one of Spain's most powerful noble families. The imposing fortress was originally built in 960 on orders of Cordoban caliph Abd ar-Rahman III. Tickets are sold in the stationery shop opposite the castle entrance.

ANDALUCÍA

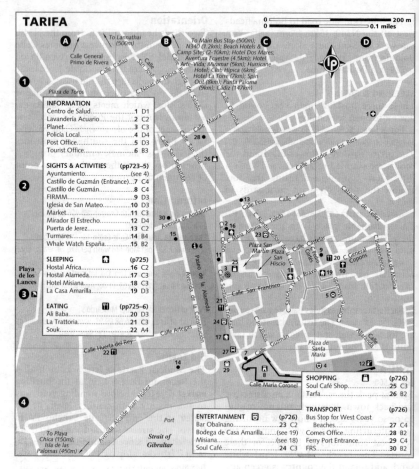

TARIFA

0 ——— 200 m
0 ——— 0.1 miles

To Larinathai (500m)

To Main Bus Stop (500m);
N340 (1.2km); Beach Hotels &
Camp Sites (2-10km); Hotel Dos Mares;
Aventura Ecuestre (4.5km); Hotel
C Arte-Vida; Miramar (5km); Hurricane
Hotel; Club Hípica (6km); Hotel
La Torre (7km); Spin
Out (8km); Punta Paloma
(9km); Cádiz (147km)

Calle General Primo de Rivera

Plaza de Toros

INFORMATION	
Centro de Salud	**1** D1
Lavandería Acuario	**2** C2
Planet	**3** C3
Policía Local	**4** D4
Post Office	**5** D3
Tourist Office	**6** B3

SIGHTS & ACTIVITIES	(pp723–5)
Ayuntamiento	(see 4)
Castillo de Guzmán (Entrance)	**7** C4
Castillo de Guzmán	**8** C4
FIRMM	**9** D3
Iglesia de San Mateo	**10** D3
Market	**11** C3
Mirador El Estrecho	**12** D4
Puerta de Jerez	**13** C2
Turmares	**14** B4
Whale Watch España	**15** B2

SLEEPING	(p725)
Hostal Africa	**16** C3
Hostal Alameda	**17** C3
Hotel Misiana	**18** C3
La Casa Amarilla	**19** D3

EATING	(pp725–6)
Ali Baba	**20** D3
La Trattoria	**21** C3
Souk	**22** A4

SHOPPING	(p726)
Soul Café Shop	**25** C3
Tarfa	**26** B2

TRANSPORT	(p726)
Bus Stop for West Coast Beaches	**27** C4
Comes Office	**28** B2
Ferry Port Entrance	**29** C4
FRS	**30** B2

ENTERTAINMENT	(p726)
Bar Obaínano	**23** C2
Bodega de Casa Amarilla	(see 19)
Misiana	(see 18)
Soul Café	**24** C3

Playa de los Lances

Plaza San Martín

Plaza San Hiscio

Plaza de Santa María

Paseo de la Alameda

Avenida de la Constitución

Avenida Alcalde Juan Núñez

Port

Strait of Gibraltar

To Playa Chica (150m);
Isla de las Palomas (450m)

Beaches

On the isthmus leading out to Isla de las Palomas, **Playa Chica** is sheltered but extremely small. From here the spectacular **Playa de los Lances** stretches 10km northwest to the huge sand dune at Ensenada de Valdevaqueros.

Activities

WINDSURFING & KITESURFING

Most of the action occurs along the coast between Tarifa and Punta Paloma, 10km northwest. El Porro on Ensenada de Valdevaqueros, the bay formed by Punta Paloma, is one of the most popular spots, with easy parking and plenty of space to set up. Kitesurfing is incredibly popular here but kites give way to sails when the wind really gets up.

Buy new or second-hand gear in Tarifa at the shops on Calle Batalla del Salado. For rental or classes try places up the coast such as **Club Mistral** (Hurricane Hotel; ☎ 956 68 49 19; Cortijo Valdevaqueros ☎ 956 23 67 05) or **Spin Out** (☎ 956 23 63 52; El Porro beach). At Spin Out board, sail and wetsuit rental for windsurfing costs €34/66 per hour/day; a six-hour beginner's windsurfing course is €150, a two-hour introduction to kitesurfing €69 and three two-hour sessions €207. It's essential for kitesurfing beginners to take classes, as out-of-control kitesurfers are a danger to themselves and others.

HORSE RIDING

On Playa de los Lances **Aventura Ecuestre** (☎ 956 23 66 32; Hotel Dos Mares) and **Club Hípica**

ANDALUCÍA

(☎ 956 68 90 92; Hurricane Hotel) both rent horses with excellent guides. An hour's ride along the beach costs €25. Four- to five-hour rides, combining beach and inland routes, cost €60 to €80.

WHALE-WATCHING

At least three groups run two-to-three-hour boat trips to track and watch dolphins and whales (most charge over/under 14 €27/18) in the Strait of Gibraltar (or the Bahía de Algeciras, if the strait is too rough). You're highly likely to see dolphins at least.

FIRMM (☎ 956 62 70 08; www.firmm.org; Calle Pedro Cortés 4) Uses every trip to record data.

Turmares (☎ 956 68 07 41; www.turmares.com; Avenida Alcalde Juan Núñez 3; over/under 14 dolphin & whale-watching €25/15, killer whale-watching €40/20) This company has the largest boat.

Whale Watch España (☎ 956 68 22 47; www.whale watchtarifa.org in Spanish; Avenida de la Constitución 6)

BIRD-WATCHING

When the *levante* is blowing or there's little wind, the Tarifa area, including the spectacular Mirador del Estrecho lookout point, 7km east on the N340, is a great spot for watching bird migrations across the Strait of Gibraltar.

Sleeping

It's essential to phone ahead in August. Most places cut prices by 25% to 40% for much of the rest of the year.

IN TOWN

La Casa Amarilla (☎ 956 68 19 93; www.lacasamarilla .net; Calle Sancho IV El Bravo 9; r €64) Right in the centre, the 'Yellow House' is an imaginatively restored 19th-century building, which retains its glass-vaulted patio. Most of the rooms have a kitchenette and all sport bright paintwork and Moroccan features.

Hotel Misiana (☎ 956 62 70 83; www.misiana.com; Calle Sancho IV El Bravo; s/d incl breakfast €86/112) Also very central, the Misiana is almost futuristic in design. Rooms range from lilac and silver to red and turquoise, and passageways can be black with lilac stripes. Some rooms have big views. All have fan and satellite TV.

Hostal Alameda (☎ 956 68 11 81; www.hostal alameda.com; Paseo de la Alameda 4; s/d €30/50; 🖳) Some of the cosy rooms at this excellent-value place have sea views, others overlook the Paseo de la Alameda or Tarifa's pretty roof line.

Hostal Africa (☎ 956 68 02 20; hostal_africa@hotmail .com; Calle María Antonia Toledo 12; s/d €30/45) The well-travelled owners of this revamped old house know just what travellers need. Rooms are bright and attractive, and there's an expansive terrace with wonderful views, plus storage for boards and bicycles.

ALONG THE COAST

Several very attractive hotels are dotted along the beach and the N340 within 10km northwest of Tarifa, but none come cheap.

Hurricane Hotel (☎ 956 68 49 19; www.hurricane hotel.com; land-/ocean-side r incl breakfast €133/150; 🅿 🖳 🖳) This hip Moroccan-style hotel, 6km from town, is the place to go if you're feeling flush. Set in beachside semitropical gardens, it has large, comfy rooms, two pools and two restaurants. The buffet breakfast is probably the best you'll ever have.

Hotel Dos Mares (☎ 956 68 40 35; www.dosmares hotel.com; s/d incl breakfast from €102/127; 🅿 🖳 🖳) Right on the beach, about 4.5km from Tarifa, Dos Mares has a few rooms in the main building, and bungalows in the gardens or on the beachfront. The bar, with tremendous views to Africa, is a popular hang-out. The hotel has a tennis court and its own well-run stables, too.

Hotel Arte-Vida (☎ 956 68 52 46; www.hotelarte vida.com; N340 Km79.3; s/d incl breakfast €118/139; 🅿) The Arte-Vida, 5km from the town centre, combines attractive, medium-sized rooms with an excellent restaurant that has stunning views. Its garden opens on the beach.

La Torre (☎ 956 68 99 90; www.hotel-la-torre -tarifa.com; N340 Km77.2; s/d €60/80; 🅿 🖳) Seven kilometres out, this is a small, neat hotel with comfortable rooms and a high-standard restaurant that prepares local dishes. There's also a garden out the back.

There are six year-round **camping grounds** (www.campingsdetarifa.com in Spanish), with room for more than 4000 campers, on or near the beach, within 10km northwest from Tarifa. The two Torre de la Peña sites are more modern than the others.

Eating

Tarifa tempts your tastebuds with a great array of international cuisines.

Souk (☎ 956 68 07 08; Huerta del Rey 11; mains €9-12; 🕑 closed Tue) Dripping with Moroccan decorations, the dimly-lit Souk has terrific Moroccan- and Asian-inspired food.

Lannathai (☎ 956 68 14 13; Calle Pintor GP Villalta 60; mains €8-12; ✆ closed Wed) On Playa de los Lances beach, about 1km from the centre, the food and ambience are authentically Thai. Owner and cook Sujinda grows some of her own special ingredients.

La Trattoria (☎ 956 68 22 25; Paseo de la Alameda; pasta & pizza €5.50-9) A good location, first-class food and efficient service make this one of the best Italians in town.

Ali Baba (Calle Sancho IV El Bravo; falafel or kebab €2.50-3) Ali Baba serves up cheap, filling and tasty Arabic food made with lovely fresh ingredients. Take away or eat at the benches and stand-up tables outside.

Miramar (☎ 956 68 52 46; Hotel Arte-Vida, N340 Km79.3; mains €8-15) Most of the hotels and hostales up the coast outside town have restaurants. The Miramar's chefs whip up a range of tasty pasta and meat dishes plus fresh local fish and seafood, and some unique salads – and the expansive beach and ocean views double your enjoyment.

Entertainment

Soul Café (Calle Santísima Trinidad 9) This hip, popular bar is run by travel-loving Italians. You may hear guest DJs from Milan play their stuff. Come after 11pm but not in winter, when the owners are travelling.

Bodega de Casa Amarilla (Calle Sancho IV El Bravo 9) A convivial typically Andalucian bar-restaurant that sometimes has live flamenco.

Bar Obaïnano (Calle Nuestra Señora de la Luz) Sip fresh fruit juices and exotic cocktails to cheerful background music and watch surf footage.

Misiana (Hotel Misiana, Calle Sancho IV El Bravo) One of *the* places to be seen in Tarifa, this futuristic bar with blue neon lighting has weekly live music, sometimes flamenco.

Getting There & Away

BOAT

FRS (☎ 956 68 18 30; www.frs.es; Avenida de Andalucía) operates a fast ferry between Tarifa and Tangier, Morocco (passenger/car/motorcycle €24.50/73/23, 35 minutes one-way) up to four times daily, with possibly more sailings in July and August.

Tarifa port is in the process of being upgraded to a full Schengen port with customs facilities, but in the peak months of July and August, travellers without EU passports or residence documents may still have to use other ports such as Algeciras for the crossing to/from Morocco. Check with FRS or the port authority.

BUS

Buses operate from the stop next to the petrol station towards the northern end of Calle Batalla del Salado, about 1km north of the Puerta de Jerez. Buses no longer stop outside the central Comes office.

Comes (☎ 956 68 40 38; Calle Batalla del Salado) runs seven or more buses daily to Cádiz (€6.95, 1¾ hours), Algeciras (€1.55, 30 minutes) and La Línea (€3.25, 40 minutes), six to Barbate (€3.60, 40 minutes), four to Seville (€14, 3½ hours), three to Jerez de la Frontera (€8.25, 2½ hours) and two to Málaga (€10.80, two hours).

In July and August local buses run every 90 minutes west along the coast to Punta Paloma. Some go on to Bolonia. The tourist office will have details. There's a stop at the bottom of the Paseo de Alameda. Another stop is next to the petrol station at the northern end of Calle Batalla del Salado. A timetable and prices should be posted here.

SHOPPING TARIFA

Tarifa's great place to shop, or window shop if you can't afford the prices. Stroll along **Calle Batalla del Salado** to find countless surf shops and boutiques offering the latest fashions in casual wear, jewellery, shoes and accessories. Surf brands such as Tarifa Pirates, Rick Shapes, No Work Team, El Niño and Sons of the Desert are well known names in Spain and most were founded in Tarifa. Rip Curl, Billabong and other international surfwear companies are represented here, too. The **Soul Café Shop** (Plaza San Martín) has the coolest fashions from Italy, Bali and India. There'll be more of this ilk to follow as the town becomes richer. Some glitzy shop fronts are appearing on Calle Batalla del Salado and there's also a lovely Valencian shoe shop.

A few stores sell groovy homewares and even furniture. **Tarfa** (Calle Batalla del Salado 9) is excellent for gifts or that something special for yourself or your home.

ALGECIRAS

pop 109,000

Algeciras, the major port linking Spain with Africa, is also an industrial town, a big fishing port and a centre for drug smuggling. If you have time to kill here, wander up to the palm-fringed main square, **Plaza Alta**, flanked by two old churches.

Algeciras was taken by Alfonso XI from the Merenids of Morocco in 1344, but later razed by Mohammed V of Granada. In 1704 it was repopulated by many of those who left Gibraltar after it was taken by the British.

During summer the port is hectic, as hundreds of thousands of Moroccans working in Europe return home for summer holidays.

Information

If you're going to arrive in Morocco at night, you should have some dirham with you. Exchange rates for buying dirham are best at banks. There are banks and ATMs on Avenida Virgen del Carmen and around Plaza Alta, plus a couple of ATMs inside the port.

Hospital Cruz Roja (☎ 956 65 37 57; Paseo de la Conferencia s/n)

Left Luggage (Estación Marítima; €1.80-2.50; ⌚ 8am-9pm) Bags must be secured. There are lockers (€2.40) nearby and luggage storage at Comes and Portillo bus stations.

Policía Nacional (☎ 956 66 04 00; Avenida de las Fuerzas Armadas 6)

Tourist Office (☎ 956 57 26 36; Calle Juan de la Cierva s/n; ⌚ 9am-2pm Mon-Fri) English-speaking, with a message board.

Dangers & Annoyances

Keep your wits about you in the port, bus terminals and market, and walk purposefully when moving between the Comes and Portillo bus stations in the evening.

Sleeping

Hotel Reina Cristina (☎ 956 60 26 22; www.reina cristina.com in Spanish; Paseo de la Conferencia s/n; s/d €77/116; P ✗ ⊠) If you can afford it, head south from the port to this old colonial-style hotel with olde-worlde rooms, two swimming pools and tropical gardens.

Hotel Al-Mar (☎ 956 65 46 61; Avenida de la Marina 2-3; s/d €46/81; P ✗) Two oversized Moroccan

ALGECIRAS

0 —————— 200 m
0 —————— 0.1 miles

To A7; La Línea de la Concepción (20km); Málaga (132km)

Dársena Pesquera (Fishing Harbour)

Plaza Palma

Train Station

To Hospital Cruz Roja (50m); Hotel Reina Cristina (750m); N340 (3.5km); Tarifa (18km)

lamps decorate the foyer of this large, comfortable hotel, handy for the port. Reception is good on information.

Hotel Marina Victoria (☎ 956 63 28 65; Avenida de la Marina 7; r €47; ✂) A solid choice in a highrise, with excellent views over the port.

Hostal Marrakech (☎ 956 57 34 74; Calle Juan de la Cierva 5; s/d without bathroom €18/25) This is a clean, secure and thoughtfully decorated place, run by a helpful Moroccan family.

Eating

Restaurante Casa Blanca (Calle Juan de la Cierva 1; menú €7.50) Close to the tourist office, the Casa Blanca offers a good-value *menú*, well-priced Moroccan food and good, fresh tapas.

Restaurante Montes (☎ 956 65 42 07; Calle Juan Morrison 27; menú €7.50, mains €10-18) The Montes has a hugely popular lunch *menú* of three courses, bread and wine, and a long list of tempting à la carte seafood.

Pastelería-Cafe La Dificultosa (Calle José Santacana; coffee, toast & juice €2) A good spot for breakfast or a coffee break, near the market.

Getting There & Away

BOAT

Companies such as **Trasmediterránea** (☎ 956 58 34 00, 902 454645; www.trasmediterranea.es) and **Euro-Ferrys** (☎ 956 65 11 78; www.euroferrys.com) operate frequent daily passenger and vehicle ferries to/from Tangier, Morocco (2½-hour ferry passenger/car €25.30/78.80; 1¼-hour fast ferry a few euros more) and Ceuta, the Spanish enclave on the Moroccan coast (35-minute fast ferry passenger/car €21.40/62.70). **Buquebus** (☎ 902 414242) operates a similar Ceuta service at least six times daily. From mid-June to September there are ferries almost round the clock to cater for the Moroccan holiday migration – you may have to queue for up to three hours. Buy your ticket in the port or at the agencies on Avenida de la Marina: prices are the same everywhere.

BUS

Comes (☎ 956 65 34 56; Calle San Bernardo) has buses for La Línea (€1.60, 30 minutes) every half-hour from 7am to 9.30pm Monday to Friday, every 45 minutes from 8am to 7.30pm on weekends. Other daily buses include up to 12 each to Tarifa (€1.55, 30 minutes) and Cádiz (€8.70, 2½ hours), and three to Seville (€14.80, 3½ hours). There's one bus Monday to Friday to Ronda (€8, two to

three hours). **Daibus** (☎ 956 65 34 56; www.daibus .es in Spanish) runs four daily buses to Madrid (€23.55, eight to nine hours), starting from the port then calling at the Comes station. Inside the port, **Viajes Marruecotour** (☎ 956 65 22 00) sells Daibus tickets.

Portillo & Alsina Graells (☎ 956 65 10 55; Avenida Virgen del Carmen 15) runs to Málaga (€9.29, 1¾ hours, five direct daily) and Granada (€17.58, 3½ hours, four daily), plus buses to towns along the Costa del Sol.

Bacoma/Alsa/Enatcar (☎ 902 422242; www.alsa.es), inside the port, runs up to four services daily up Spain's Mediterranean coast, plus buses to Portugal, France, Germany and Holland.

TRAIN

From the **station** (☎ 956 63 02 02), adjacent to Calle San Bernardo, trains run to/from Madrid (€35 to €52.50, six or 11 hours, two daily) and Granada (€15.75, four hours, three daily). All go through Ronda (€5.85 to €15.50, 1¾ hours) and Bobadilla (€9.65 to €27.50, 2¾ hours), where you can change for Málaga, Córdoba or Seville.

LA LÍNEA DE LA CONCEPCIÓN

pop 62,000

La Línea, 20km east of Algeciras, is the unavoidable stepping stone to Gibraltar. A left turn as you exit the bus station will bring you onto Avenida 20 de Abril, which runs the 300m or so from the main square, Plaza de la Constitución, to the Gibraltar border. The slick **Municipal tourist office** (☎ 956 17 19 98; Avenida Príncipe Felipe s/n; ☯ 9am-8pm Mon-Fri, 9am-2pm Sat) faces the border.

Buses run about every 30 minutes to/from Algeciras (€1.60, 30 minutes). Others go to Málaga (€9.30, 2½ hours, four daily), Tarifa (€3.25, 45 minutes, six daily), Cádiz (€10.30, 2½ hours, four daily) and elsewhere.

To save queuing at the border, many visitors to Gibraltar park in La Línea, then walk across. The underground **Parking Fo Cona**, just off Avenida 20 de Abril, charges €1/6.30 per hour/day.

GIBRALTAR

Looming like some great ship off almost the southernmost tip of Spain, the British colony of Gibraltar is a fascinating compound of curiosities. Despite bobbies on the beat, red post boxes and other appearances hinting that you might be in 1960s England, Gibraltar is actually a cultural cocktail with Genoese, Spanish, North African and other elements yielding a unique flavour. And it has quite the most spectacular setting anywhere along the southern Iberian seaboard: Gibraltar's territory is 5km long and up to 1.6km wide, and most of it is one huge lump of limestone, 426m high. To the ancients, this was one of the two Pillars of Hercules, set up by the Greek hero to mark the edge of the known world (the other pillar was the coastal mountain Musa, in Morocco, 25km south). Gibraltar's location and highly defensible nature have attracted the covetous gaze of military strategists ever since.

Gibraltarians (77% of the population) speak both English and Spanish and, often, a curious mix of the two. Signs are in English.

History
In AD 711 Tariq ibn Ziyad, the Muslim governor of Tangier, landed at Gibraltar to launch the Islamic invasion of the Iberian Peninsula. The name Gibraltar is derived from Jebel Tariq (Tariq's Mountain).

Castile wrested the Rock from the Muslims in 1462. Then in 1704 an Anglo-Dutch fleet captured Gibraltar during the War of the Spanish Succession. Spain ceded the Rock to Britain in 1713, but didn't end military attempts to regain it until the failure of the Great Siege of 1779–83. Britain developed it into an important naval base (bringing in a community of Genoese ship repairers, who have made a notable contribution to the Gibraltarian nationality). During the Franco period, Gibraltar was an extremely sore point between Britain and Spain: the border was closed from 1967 to 1985. In 1969, Gibraltarians voted, by 12,138 to 44, in favour of British rather than Spanish sovereignty and a new constitution gave Gibraltar domestic self-government. In 2002 the UK and Spain held talks about a possible future sharing of sovereignty over Gibraltar, but Gibraltarians expressed *their* feelings in a referendum (not recognised by Britain or Spain), which voted resoundingly against any such idea.

The mainstays of Gibraltar's economy are tourism, the port and financial services (including, Spanish police complain, the laundering of proceeds from organised crime). The smuggling of cheap electronics,

alcohol and cigarettes into Spain is another bone of contention.

Orientation
To reach Gibraltar by land you must pass through the Spanish border town of La Línea de la Concepción (opposite). Just south of the border, the road crosses Gibraltar airport runway. Gibraltar's town and harbours lie along the Rock's less steep western side, facing Bahía de Algeciras (Bay of Gibraltar).

Information
BOOKSHOPS
Bell Books (☎ 76707; 11 Bell Lane)
Gibraltar Bookshop (☎ 71894; 300 Main St)

ELECTRICITY
Electric current is the same as in Britain: 220V or 240V, with plugs of three flat pins.

EMERGENCY
Emergency (☎ 199) For police or ambulance.
Police station (120 Irish Town)

INTERNET ACCESS
General Internet Business Centre (☎ 44227; 36 Governor's St; per hr £3; ☷ 10am-10pm Tue-Sat, noon-9pm Sun & Mon)
MEDICAL SERVICES
St Bernard's Hospital (☎ 79700; Hospital Hill) 24hr emergency facilities.

MONEY
The currencies are the Gibraltar pound (£) and pound sterling, which are interchangeable. You can spend euros (except in pay phones and post offices) but conversion rates aren't in your favour. Change any unspent Gibraltar currency before leaving. Banks are generally open from 9am to 3.30pm weekdays. There are several on Main St.

POST
Post office (104 Main St; ☷ 9am-4.30pm Mon-Fri & 10am-1pm Sat, closes at 2.15pm Mon-Fri mid-Jun–mid-Sep)

TELEPHONE
To phone Gibraltar from Spain, precede the five-digit local number with the code ☎ 9567; from other countries, dial the international access code, then the Gibraltar country code (☎ 350) and local number. To phone Spain from Gibraltar, just dial the nine-digit Spanish number.

ANDALUCÍA

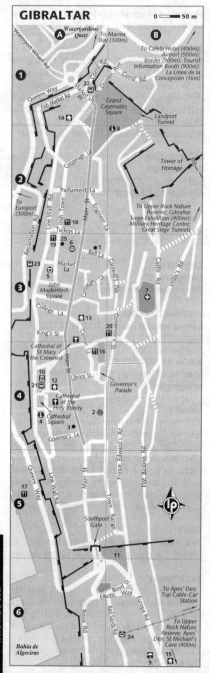

GIBRALTAR

0 — 50 m

TOURIST INFORMATION

Gibraltar has several helpful tourist offices.
Gibraltar Tourist Board (☎ 45000, 74950; www
.gibraltar.gov.uk; Duke of Kent House, Cathedral Square;
🕑 9am-5.30pm Mon-Fri)
Information booth (☎ 73026; Airport; 🕑 Mon-Fri,
for lunchtime flights)
Information booth (☎ 50762; Customs House,
Frontier; 🕑 9am-4.30pm Mon-Fri, 10am-3pm Sat)
Tourist office (☎ 74982; Grand Casemates Square;
🕑 9am-5.30pm Mon-Fri, 10am-3pm Sat, 10am-1pm
Sun & holidays)

VISAS & DOCUMENTS

To enter Gibraltar, you need a passport or
EU national identity card. EU, USA, Canadian, Australian, New Zealand and South
African passport-holders are among those
who do not need visas for Gibraltar. For
further information contact Gibraltar's **Immigration Department** (☎ 71543).

Sights & Activities
THE TOWN

Pedestrianised Main St has an emphati-
cally British appearance, but the Spanish
lilt in the air is a reminder that this is still
Mediterranean Europe. Most Spanish and
Islamic buildings on Gibraltar were destroyed in 18th-century sieges, but the Rock

bristles with British fortifications, gates and gun emplacements.

The **Gibraltar Museum** (Bomb House Lane; adult/ under 12 £2/1; ⊙ 10am-6pm Mon-Fri, 10am-2pm Sat) contains good historical, architectural and military displays, among which are a well-preserved Muslim bathhouse and a copy of a 100,000-year-old female Neanderthal skull, found on Gibraltar in 1848. The **Trafalgar Cemetery** (Prince Edward's Rd; ⊙ 9am-7pm) gives a more poignant history lesson with its graves of British sailors, who died at Gibraltar after the Battle of Trafalgar in 1805. The lush **Alameda Botanic Gardens** (Europa Rd; admission free; ⊙ 8am-sunset) are a short distance south.

UPPER ROCK NATURE RESERVE

The most exciting thing about Gibraltar is, of course, the Rock itself. Most of the upper Rock, starting just above the town, is a **nature reserve** (adult/child incl attractions £7/4, vehicle £1.50, pedestrian excl attractions £0.50; ⊙ 9.30am-7pm), with spectacular views and several interesting spots to visit. A fine way to get up here is by the cable car (p732). During a westerly wind, the Rock is often a fine spot for observing migrations of birds, especially raptors and storks, between Africa and Europe. January to early June is the time for northbound migrations, and late July to early November for southbound migrations. When the wind is calm, or blowing from the east, the Tarifa area is usually better. White storks sometimes congregate in flocks of 3000 to cross the strait.

The Rock's most famous inhabitants are its colony of Barbary macaques, the only wild primates in Europe (probably introduced from North Africa in the 18th century). Some of these hang around the **Apes' Den**, near the middle cable-car station; you'll often see others at the top cable-car station or the Great Siege Tunnels.

In clear weather you can see Morocco from the **top cable-car station**. Down the precipitous eastern side of the Rock is the biggest of the old water catchments (today replaced by desalination plants) that channelled rain into underground reservoirs.

About 20 minutes' walk south down St Michael's Rd from the top cable-car station (or 20 minutes up from the Apes' Den), **St Michael's Cave** is a big natural grotto that was once home to Neolithic inhabitants of the Rock. Today, apart from attracting tourists in droves, it's used for concerts, plays, even fashion shows. There's a café outside.

Princess Caroline's Battery, a half-hour walk north (downhill) from the top cable-car station, houses a **Military Heritage Centre**. From here a road leads up to the impressive **Great Siege Tunnels**, hand-hewn by the British for gun emplacements during the 1779-to-1783 siege. They constitute a tiny proportion of the more than 70km of tunnels in the Rock, most of which are off limits.

On Willis's Rd, which leads down to the town from Princess Caroline's Battery, are the **Gibraltar, A City under Siege** exhibition and the **Tower of Homage**, the last vestige of Gibraltar's Islamic castle, built in 1333.

DOLPHIN-WATCHING

The Bahía de Algeciras has a sizable population of dolphins and, from about April to September, several boats make two or more daily trips out to see them; at other times of the year there's usually at least one in daily operation. You would be unlucky not to get plenty of close-up dolphin contact. Most boats go from Watergardens Quay or adjacent Marina Bay. The trips last about 2½ hours and costs around £20 per adult. Tourist offices have full details.

Sleeping

Caleta Hotel (☎ 76501; www.caletahotel.com; Sir Herbert Miles Rd; d with/without sea view £81/74; P ✕ ☐ ☒) The Caleta has a wonderful location on the edge of a rocky outcrop overlooking Catalan Bay, on the east side of the Rock, five minutes from town. Its cascading terraces have panoramic sea views, and a host of gym and spa facilities make this a truly luxurious option.

Rock Hotel (☎ 73000; www.rockhotelgibraltar.com; 3 Europa Rd; d with/without balcony £175/165; P ✕ ☒) This institution has hosted the likes of Winston Churchill and Noel Coward. Built in the 1930s, it has recently been modernised and the lavish service includes CD players and free parking.

Bristol Hotel (☎ 76800; www.gibraltar.gi/bristol hotel; 10 Cathedral Sq; s/d £49/64, with sea view £53/69; P ✕ ☒) The rooms here are recently refurbished and the hotel has an attractive walled garden and a swimming pool.

Cannon Hotel (☎ 51711; www.cannonhotel.gi; 9 Cannon Lane; s without bathroom £24.50, d with/without bathroom £45/36.50, incl English breakfast) The Cannon is a small, attractive hotel, right in the main shopping area.

Emile Youth Hostel (☎ 51106; Montagu Bastion, Line Wall Rd; dm/s/d £15/17/30) Louche expatriates and old seamen make the hostel an unattractive proposition for lone women travellers, but it's pretty cheap. Conditions are basic and the eight-person dorms are cramped.

Eating

Claus on the Rock (☎ 48686; 14 Queensway Quay; mains £7.50-14; 🕒 closed Sun) This stylish restaurant in the posh Queensway Quays marina has a wonderful array of international cuisine, with influences from the Caribbean to the Middle East – a welcome relief from pub-grub.

The Clipper (☎ 79791; 78B Irish Town; roast £5.95) Most of Gibraltar's pubs serve British pub meals. The Clipper is one of the best and busiest bars, all varnished wood with full-on footie and a cracking Sunday roast. Occasional live music livens things up further on weekends.

House of Sacarello (☎ 70625; 57 Irish Town; daily specials £5.50-6.10; 🕒 closed Sun) A chic place with a good range of vegetarian options. You can linger over a £7.75 afternoon tea for two, between 3pm and 7.30pm.

Cannon Bar (☎ 77288; 27 Cannon Lane; mains around £4.75) The Cannon is justifiably famous for some of the best fish and chips in town – in big portions.

Three Roses Bar (☎ 51614; 60 Governor's St; breakfast £3.50) Gibraltar's unofficial 'Scottish Embassy' does a hefty breakfast of two eggs, sausage, bacon, fried bread, beans, tomato and mushrooms – but it's not for early risers.

There's a line of pleasant waterside eateries at Marina Bay.

Shopping

Gibraltar has lots of British high-street stores, such as Marks & Spencer, Mothercare and the Body Shop (all on Main St) and Safeway (in the Europort development at the northern end of the main harbour). Shops are normally open 9am to 7.30pm weekdays, and until 1pm Saturday.

Getting There & Away

AIR

Flying daily to/from London, **GB Airways** (☎ 79300) has return fares ranging from UK£76 to UK£205, depending on the season and offers. **Monarch Airlines** (☎ 47477) flies daily to/from Luton, with return fares costing from UK£94 to UK£235.

Airline offices are at the airport, but you can book through travel agencies.

BOAT

FRS (in Tarifa, Spain ☎ 956 68 18 30; www.frs.es) operates (at the time of writing) only one ferry a week between Gibraltar and Tangier, departing Gibraltar at 6pm on Friday for the 80-minute crossing. One-way/return fares are: adult £18/30, child £9/15, car £46/92. The ferry takes 80 minutes, departing from the terminal in front of the coach park. Purchase tickets from **Turner & Co** (☎ 78305; 65 Irish Town).

BUS

There are no regular buses to Gibraltar, but La Línea de la Concepción bus station (p728) is only a five-minute walk from the border.

CAR & MOTORCYCLE

Vehicle queues at the border (which is open 24 hours) and congested traffic in Gibraltar often make it less time-consuming to park in La Línea and walk across the border. To take a car into Gibraltar you need an insurance certificate, registration document, nationality plate and driving licence. There is no fee.

Getting Around

The 1.5km walk from the border to the town centre crosses the airport runway. A left turn off Corral Rd takes you through the pedestrian Landport Tunnel into Grand Casemates Square. Alternatively, several bus lines (adult/child/senior 60p/40p/30p) run from the border into town about every 15 minutes (every 30 minutes on Saturday and Sunday), until 8pm or 9pm. Bus No 9 goes to Market Place; No 3 goes to Cathedral Square and the lower cable-car station; and No 10 runs to Europort (stopping at Safeway), then Reclamation Rd near the city centre.

All of Gibraltar can be covered on foot, and much of it (including the upper Rock) by car or motorcycle. You can also ascend, weather permitting, by the **cable car** (Red Sands Rd; adult one-way/return £6/7.50, child £3.50/4; 🕒 every few min 9.30am-5.15pm Mon-Sat; last cable down 4.45pm). For the Apes' Den, disembark at the middle station.

MÁLAGA PROVINCE

Málaga province, in south central Andalucía, is perhaps best known for Málaga Airport, Andalucía's main international airport, and the Costa del Sol, Spain's most densely packed tourist coast. But Málaga also has a vibrant, increasingly cultured capital city; fascinating old towns such as Ronda and Antequera; picturesque rural regions strung with white villages; and some wild hill country. Ever more prosperous thanks to a seemingly never-ending construction boom, the province is providing the tourists, on whom its economy heavily depends, with improving standards of accommodation and restaurants, and an ever wider and better range of things to see and do. The local populace, while increasingly urbane, remains unpretentious and fun-loving.

MÁLAGA
pop 547,000

Emerging from Málaga Airport, you can turn right for the Costa del Sol or left for the city. It's a choice between two different worlds. This exuberant and very Spanish port city, set against a sparkling blue Mediterranean, is both historic and pulsing with modern life. The centre presents the visitor with narrow old streets and wide, leafy boulevards, beautiful gardens and impressive monuments, fashionable shops and a cultural life that is coming to the fore as never before. A major new museum devoted to Málaga-born Pablo Picasso opened in 2003. Its terrific bars and nightlife, the last word in Málaga *joie de vivre*, stay open very late.

History

Probably founded by Phoenicians, Málaga has always had a commercial vocation. It flourished in the Islamic era, especially under the Emirate of Granada, for which Málaga was the chief port. Málaga did not reassert itself as an entrepreneurial centre until the 19th century when a dynamic middle class founded textile factories, sugar and steel mills and shipyards. Málaga dessert wine ('mountain sack') was popular in Victorian England. During the civil war Málaga was initially a Republican stronghold. Hundreds of Nationalist sympathisers were killed before the city fell in February

1937, after being bombed by Italian planes. Particularly vicious reprisals followed.

Málaga has enjoyed a steadily increasing economic spin-off from mass tourism, which was launched on the nearby Costa del Sol in the 1950s and '60s.

Orientation

The tree-lined Paseo del Parque and Alameda Principal run along the southern edge of the old town. The main streets leading north into the old town are Calle Marqués de Larios and Calle Molina Lario. The Gibralfaro hill rising above the eastern half of Paseo del Parque dominates the central area. Avenida de Andalucía continues the Paseo del Parque–Alameda Principal axis west of the often-dry bed of the Río Guadalmedina. The main train and bus stations are around 600m south of Avenida de Andalucía, and the airport is 9km southwest.

Information

There are plenty of banks with ATMs on Calle Puerta del Mar and Calle Marqués de Larios, as well as ATMs in the airport arrivals hall.

Hospital Carlos Haya (☎ 952 39 04 00; Avenida de Carlos Haya) The main hospital, 2km west of the centre.

Librería Alameda (Map p734; Alameda Principal 16) Bookshop with some English and French titles and a good travel section.

Municipal tourist office (Map p736; ☎ 952 13 47 30; www.malagaturismo.com; Avenida de Cervantes 1; ⏰ 9am-2.30pm & 4-7pm Mon-Fri, 9.30am-1.30pm Sat & Sun) Has information booths at the bus station and on Plaza de la Marina and Plaza de la Merced.

Pasatiempos (Map p736; Plaza de la Merced 20; Internet access per hr €1-2; ⏰ 10am-11pm)

Policía Local (Map p734; ☎ 952 12 65 00; Avenida de la Rosaleda 19)

Post office (Map p734; Avenida de Andalucía 1; ⏰ 8.30am-8.30pm Mon-Fri, 8.30am-2pm Sat)

Regional tourist office (Map p736; ☎ 952 21 34 45; Pasaje de Chinitas 4; www.andalucia.org; ⏰ 9am-8pm Mon-Fri, 10am-2pm Sat & Sun) Also has a branch at the airport.

Sights
MUSEO PICASSO MÁLAGA

Málaga's new main attraction is tucked away on a pedestrian street in what was medieval Málaga's *judería*. The **Museo Picasso Málaga** (Map p736; ☎ 902 443377; www.museopicassomalaga .org; Palacio de Buenavista, Calle San Agustín 8; permanent

ANDALUCÍA

ANDALUCÍA

MÁLAGA

collection €6, temporary exhibition €4.50, combined ticket €8, seniors & under-26 students half price; ☉ 10am-8pm Tue-Thu & Sun, 10am-9pm Fri & Sat) has 204 Picasso works, donated and lent by his daughter-in-law Christine Ruiz-Picasso and grandson Bernard Ruiz-Picasso, and also stages high-quality temporary exhibitions on Picasso themes. The Picasso paintings, drawings, engravings, sculptures and ceramics on show (many never previously on public display) span almost every phase and influence of the artist's colourful career – blue period, cubism, surrealism and more. For many the most inspiring will be some of the portraits, such as *Olga Kokhlova with Mantilla*, done in a period when Picasso was looking to return to more traditional forms after the experiments of cubism. The museum is housed in the 16th-century Palacio de Buenavista, beautifully restored at a cost of €66 million. Málaga hopes and anticipates that the Museo Picasso will catalyse a cultural and cultural-tourism boom in the city and area. Picasso was born in Málaga in 1881 but moved to northern Spain with his family when he was nine, and only ever returned for holidays between 1891 and 1900. But he always retained a strong affection for his native region.

CATHEDRAL

Málaga's **cathedral** (Map p736; ☎ 952 21 59 17; Calle Molina Lario, entrance Calle Císter; admission €3; ☉ 10am-6.45pm Mon-Sat, closed holidays) was begun in the 16th century, on the former site of the main mosque. Building continued for two centuries, so while the northern door, **Portada de la Iglesia del Sagrario**, is Gothic, and the interior, with a soaring 40m dome, is Gothic and Renaissance, the façade is 18th-century baroque. The cathedral is known as La Manquita (The One-Armed), since its southern tower was never completed. Of special interest inside are the 17th-century wooden choir stalls, finely carved by the popular Andalucian sculptor, Pedro de Mena.

ALCAZABA

At the lower, western end of the Gibralfaro hill, the **Alcazaba** (Map p734; ☎ 952 22 51 06; Calle Alcazabilla; admission €1.80, with Castillo de Gibralfaro €3; ☉ 9.30am-8pm Tue-Sun Apr-Sep, 8.30am-7pm Tue-Sun Oct-Mar) was the palace-fortress of Málaga's Muslim governors. Dating from 1057, it has two rings of walls, lots of defensive towers,

cobbled ramps, staggered entrance passages, meandering waterways and leafy terraces – a pleasure to visit in the summer heat. A lift (elevator) from Calle Guillén Sotelo (behind the municipal tourist office) brings you out in the heart of the Alcazaba.

Below the Alcazaba, a **Roman theatre** is being excavated.

CASTILLO DE GIBRALFARO

Above the Alcazaba rises the older **Gibralfaro Castle** (Map p734; ☎ 952 22 51 06; admission €1.80; ☉ 9am-8.30pm Apr-Sep, 9am-6pm Oct-Mar), built by Abd ar-Rahman I, the 8th-century Cordoban emir, and rebuilt in the 14th and 15th centuries. Nothing much remains of the interior of the castle, but the walkway around the ramparts affords exhilarating views and there's an interesting little **museum**.

To walk up to the Castillo de Gibralfaro, take the road immediately right of the Alcazaba entrance, and where it bends left into a tunnel, take the steps on the right; or take bus No 35 from Avenida de Cervantes (roughly every 45 minutes).

OTHER MUSEUMS

Casa Natal de Picasso (Map p736; ☎ 952 06 02 15; Plaza de la Merced 15; admission free; ☉ 10am-2pm & 5-8pm Mon-Sat, 10am-2pm Sun) Picasso's birthplace is a centre for exhibitions and research on contemporary art, with a few compelling personal memorabilia.

Centro de Arte Contemporáneo (Map p734; ☎ 952 12 00 55; Calle Alemania; admission free; ☉ 10am-8pm Tue-Sun) Funky new museum of international 20th-century art in skilfully converted 1930s market.

Museo de Artes y Costumbres Populares (Museum of Popular Arts & Customs; Map p734; ☎ 952 21 71 37; Pasillo de Santa Isabel 10; adult/under-16 €2/free; ☉ 10am-1.30pm & 4-7pm Mon-Fri, 10am-1.30pm Sat) Housed in a 17th-century inn, focusing on everyday rural and urban life of the past; note the painted clay figures *(barros)* of characters from Málaga folklore.

Palacio de la Aduana (Map p736; Paseo del Parque; admission free; ☉ 3-8pm Tue, 9am-8pm Wed-Fri, 9am-3pm Sat & Sun) Exhibits part of the good Museo de Málaga art collection, formerly housed in the Buenavista palace now taken over by Picasso; includes great baroque artists such as Zurbarán and Murillo.

BEACHES   Map p734

Sandy city beaches stretch several kilometres in each direction from the port. **Playa de la Malagueta** is handy to the city centre, with several places to eat and drink close

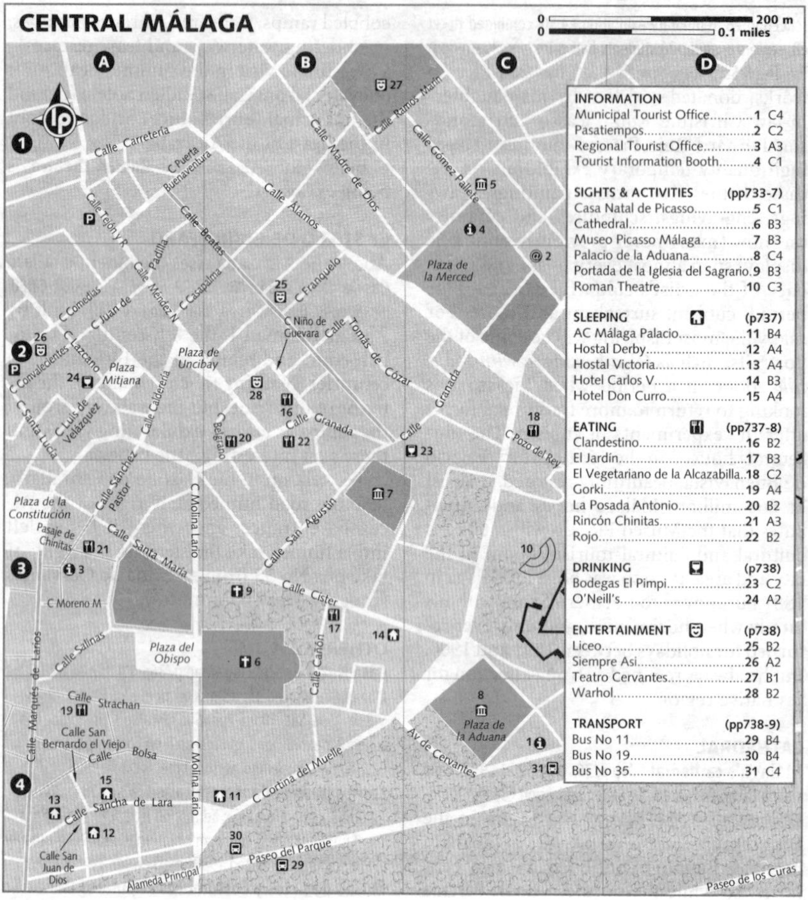
CENTRAL MÁLAGA
0 200 m
0 0.1 miles
A
B
C
D
1
2
3
4
INFORMATION
Municipal Tourist Office 1 C4
Pasatiempos 2 C2
Regional Tourist Office 3 A3
Tourist Information Booth 4 C1
SIGHTS & ACTIVITIES (pp733-7)
Casa Natal de Picasso 5 C1
Cathedral 6 B3
Museo Picasso Málaga 7 B3
Palacio de la Aduana 8 C4
Portada de la Iglesia del Sagrario 9 B3
Roman Theatre 10 C3
SLEEPING (p737)
AC Málaga Palacio 11 B4
Hostal Derby 12 A4
Hostal Victoria 13 A4
Hotel Carlos V 14 B3
Hotel Don Curro 15 A4
EATING (pp737-8)
Clandestino 16 B2
El Jardín 17 B3
El Vegetariano de la Alcazabilla 18 C2
Gorki 19 A4
La Posada Antonio 20 B2
Rincón Chinitas 21 A3
Rojo 22 B2
DRINKING (p738)
Bodegas El Pimpi 23 C2
O'Neill's 24 A2
ENTERTAINMENT (p738)
Liceo 25 B2
Siempre Asi 26 A2
Teatro Cervantes 27 B1
Warhol 28 B2
TRANSPORT (pp738-9)
Bus No 11 29 B4
Bus No 19 30 B4
Bus No 35 31 C4
Calle Carretería
C Puerta Buenaventura
Calle Tejón y R.
Calle Beatas
Calle Madre de Dios
Calle Ramos Marín
Calle Gómez Pallete
Calle Álamos
Calle Padilla
C Casapalma
C Franquelo
Calle Méndez N.
C Juan de
C Comedias
C Convalecientes
C Lazcano
Plaza Mitjana
C Luis de Velázquez
C Santa Lucía
Plaza de Uncibay
Calle Calderería
C Niño de Guevara
Calle Tomás de Cózar
Calle Granada
C Belgrano
Plaza de la Merced
C Pozo del Rey
Plaza de la Constitución
Pasaje de Chinitas
Calle Sánchez Pastor
C Molina Lario
Calle Santa María
Calle San Agustín
Calle Císter
C Moreno M
Calle Salinas
Plaza del Obispo
Calle Cañón
Calle Marqués de Larios
Calle Strachan
Calle San Bernardo el Viejo
Calle Bolsa
Plaza de la Aduana
Av de Cervantes
C Cortina del Muelle
Calle Sancha de Lara
Calle San Juan de Dios
Paseo del Parque
Alameda Principal
Paseo de los Curas

by. **Playa de Pedregalejo** and **Playa del Palo**, about 4km east of the centre, are popular and reachable by bus No 11 from Paseo del Parque.

JARDÍN BOTÁNICO LA CONCEPCIÓN

These largely tropical **gardens** (☎ 952 25 21 48; adult/child €2.80/1.40; 🕑 10am-4pm Tue-Sun Oct-Mar, 10am-6.30pm Apr-Sep), 4km north of the city centre, feature towering trees (including hundreds of palms), 5000 tropical plants, waterfalls, lakes and spectacular seasonal blooms – especially the purple wisteria in spring. Visits are by 1½-hour guided tour in English.

By car, take the N331 Antequera road north to Km166 and follow the signs. On Saturday, Sunday and holidays, bus No 61 leaves Málaga's Alameda Principal for La Concepción hourly from 11am.

Courses

There are many private language schools in Málaga; the main tourist offices have contact lists. The **Universidad de Málaga** (☎ 952 27 82 11; www.uma.es in Spanish) also runs very popular courses.

Tours

To pick up the child-friendly, open-topped **MalagaTour bus** (Map p734; ☎ 902 101081; www.citysightseeing-spain.com; adult/child €12/5.50; 🕑 every 30 min, 9.30am-7pm), head for Avenida Manuel Agustín Heredia or the eastern end of the

Paseo del Parque. This hop-on-hop-off tour does a circuit of the city with stops at all major points of interest. Tickets are valid for 24 hours.

Festivals & Events

Semana Santa (Holy Week) Solemn and spectacular: the platforms bearing the holy images *(tronos)*, are large and heavy, each needing up to 150 bearers. Each night from Palm Sunday to Good Friday, six or seven *tronos* are carried through the city, watched by big crowds. Watch from the Alameda Principal, between 7pm and midnight.

Feria de Málaga (mid to late August) Lasting nine days, this is the biggest and most ebullient of Andalucía's summer fairs. During daytime, especially on the two Saturdays, celebrations take over the city centre, with music, dancing and horses. At night the fun switches to large *feria* grounds at Cortijo de Torres, 4km southwest of the city centre, with fairground rides, music and dancing.

Sleeping

BUDGET

Hostal Derby (Map p736; ☎ 952 22 13 01; Calle San Juan de Dios 1; s/d €27/40) This good-value hostal has spacious rooms, some overlooking the harbour.

Hostal Aurora II (Map p734; ☎ 952 22 40 04; Calle Cisneros 5; s/d €20/36) A recently renovated house with good-sized rooms.

Albergue Juvenil Málaga (☎ 952 30 85 00; www .inturjoven.com in Spanish; Plaza Pío XII No 6; dm under 26 incl breakfast €9.05-13.75, over 26 €12.25-18.35) Málaga's youth hostel, 1.5km west of the centre, has mostly doubles, many with bathroom. There's also a communal sun terrace. Bus No 18 from the Alameda Principal goes most of the way.

MID-RANGE

Hotel Don Curro (Map p736; ☎ 952 22 72 00; www .hoteldoncurro.com; Calle Sancha de Lara 7; s/d €65/92; P ⚒) The busy Don Curro is efficient, comfortable and central, with well-appointed, spacious rooms.

Hostal Victoria (Map p736; ☎ 952 22 42 23; Calle Sancha de Lara 3; d €80; ⚒) Popular for its central location and friendly staff, the Victoria provides clean, comfortable rooms with bathtubs. Doubles come down to €50 in the off-season.

Hotel Venecia (Map p734; ☎ 952 21 36 36; Alameda Principal 9; s/d €58/72; ⚒) On the southern side of the Alameda, Hotel Venecia has very comfortable rooms and helpful English-speaking staff.

Hotel Carlos V (Map p736; ☎ 952 21 51 20; Calle Císter 10; s/d €29.95/62.40; ⚒) Close to the cathedral and Picasso museum, the Carlos V is enduringly popular. It's clean, if basic and a bit gloomy.

TOP END

AC Málaga Palacio (Map p736; ☎ 952 21 51 85; www.ac -hotels.com; Calle Cortina del Muelle 1; d €180; P ⚒ ⚒) Smart, modern design, excellent facilities and sensational views over the busy seafront make this sleek, 15-storey hotel the best luxury option. Room rates come down by one-third in the low season.

Parador Málaga Gibralfaro (Map p734; ☎ 952 22 19 02; www.parador.es; s/d €99/124; P ⚒ ⚒) With an unbeatable location up on the Gibralfaro, Málaga's Parador provides spectacular views and an excellent terrace restaurant.

Eating

Málaga's restaurants are well priced and of a good standard due to the largely local clientele. A speciality here is fish fried quickly in olive oil. *Fritura malagueña* consists of fried fish, anchovies and squid.

Rojo (Map p736; ☎ 952 22 74 86; Calle Granada 44; meals €20; ☾ dinner Tue-Sat) Bang in the middle of the old town, the excellent menu here attracts a youngish professional crowd (reservations are recommended).

Clandestino (Map p736; ☎ 952 21 93 90; Calle Niño de Guevara 3; mains €8) This trendy backstreet joint serves up top meals to hip, house beats. Finish up with a dreamy Doña Blanca ice cream (€2.70).

Mesón Astorga (Map p734; ☎ 952 34 68 32; Calle Gerona 11; meals €15-20; ☾ closed Sun) The excellent meat and fish dishes prepared here have earned this lively little restaurant a well-deserved reputation.

El Yamal (Map p734; ☎ 952 21 20 46; Calle Blasco de Garay 7; mains €8; ☾ lunch) Yamal rustles up excellent Moroccan food in traditional *tajines* (earthenware dishes with pointed lids). Choose from fish, chicken or couscous with vegetables and soak up the relaxed atmosphere.

Restaurante Antonio Martín (Map p734; ☎ 952 22 73 98; Playa de la Malagueta; mains €7-14; ☾ closed Sun night Nov-Apr) Right on the beach and with a large sea-view terrace, Antonio Martín rustles up some of the best fish in town. Celebrities and matadors are rumoured to hang out here: reservations recommended.

Budget spots:

El Vegetariano de la Alcazabilla (Map p736; ☎ 952 21 48 58; Calle Pozo del Rey 5; mains €6-8; ☺ closed Sun) Laid-back veggie restaurant combining friendly service with good food.

El Jardín (Map p736; ☎ 952 22 04 19; Calle Cañón 1; *platos combinados* €4.20-7.50; ☺ closed 2-5pm Fri & Sat, till 5pm Sun) Busy Viennese-style café next to the palm-filled gardens behind the cathedral.

TAPAS

Antigua Casa de Guardia (Map p734; ☎ 952 21 46 80; Alameda Central 18; tapas €1-1.50; raciones €4-6) This venerable old tavern has been serving Málaga's sweet dessert wines since 1840. Try the dark brown, sherry-like *seco* or the romantic *Lágrima Trasañejo* (Very Old Tears), complemented by a plate of monster prawns.

Gorki (Map p736; ☎ 952 22 14 66; Calle Strachan 6; platos €5-7) A popular up-market tapas bar with pavement tables and an interior full of wine-barrel tables and stools.

La Posada Antonio (Map p736; Calle Granada 33; tapas €1.80, mains €8-16) You'll be hard pressed to find a table after 11pm despite the barn-like proportions of this place. It's great for generous helpings of meat.

Rincón Chinitas (Map p736; Pasaje de Chinitas; tapas €2.10, raciones €4.50) Nudge your way into this hole-in-the-wall for the delectable shrimp fritters.

Drinking & Entertainment   Map p736

On weekend nights, the web of narrow old streets north of Plaza de la Constitución comes alive. The best places to look for bars are the areas between Plaza de la Merced and Calle Carretería, and Plaza Mitjana and Plaza de Uncibay.

Bodegas El Pimpi (☎ 952 22 89 90; Calle Granada 62; ☺ 7pm-2am) A Málaga institution with a warren of rooms and mini-patios, El Pimpi attracts a fun-loving crowd with its sweet wine and thumping music.

Siempre Así (Calle Convalecientes 5; ☺ 11pm-3.30am Thu-Sat) Plays flamenco, rumba and rocky Latino to a slightly pretentious 25-to-40 crowd.

Liceo (Calle Beatas 21; ☺ 7pm-3am Thu-Sat) A grand old mansion turned young music bar, the Liceo buzzes with a student crowd after midnight. Go up the winding staircase and you'll find more rooms to duck into.

O'Neill's (☎ 952 60 14 60; Calle Luis de Velázquez 3; ☺ noon-late) A spit-and-sawdust bar that likes

to prove how Irish it is by playing non-stop U2.

Warhol (Calle Niño de Guevara; ☺ 11pm-late Thu-Sat) A stylish haunt for choosy gay clubbers who want funky house beats mixed by dreadlocked DJs.

Teatro Cervantes (☎ 952 22 41 00; www.teatro cervantes.com in Spanish; Calle Ramos Marín s/n) The palatial Cervantes has a fine programme of music, dance and theatre.

Getting There & Away

AIR

Málaga's busy **airport** (☎ 952 04 88 38), the main international gateway to Andalucía, receives flights by dozens of airlines (budget and otherwise) from around Europe (see the list on p850).

For outbound flights, including last-minute and standby seats, try local agencies such as **Flightline** (☎ 902 202240; www.flightline.es), **Servitour** (☎ 902 400069; www.servitour.es), **Travelshop** (☎ 952 46 42 27; www.thetravelshop.com) and **Viajes Mundial Schemann** (☎ 902 100605), all at Málaga Airport.

BOAT

Trasmediterránea (Map p734; ☎ 952 06 12 18, 902 454645; www.trasmediterranea.com; Estación Marítima, Local E1) operates a ferry (except Sunday mid-September to mid-June) to/from Melilla (passenger/car €29/150, 7½ hours, one daily).

BUS

Málaga's **bus station** (Map p734; ☎ 952 35 00 61; www.estabus.emtsam.es; Paseo de los Tilos) is just 1km southwest of the city centre. Frequent buses travel along the coasts, going to both Seville (€13.05, 2½ hours, 12 daily) and Granada (€8.65, 1½ to two hours, 18 daily). Several go daily to inland towns, including Córdoba (€10.45, 2½ hours, five daily), Antequera (€4.55, 50 minutes, 13 daily) and Ronda (€8.35, two hours, eight or more daily). Seven buses also run daily to Madrid (€17.95, six hours) and a few go up Spain's Mediterranean coast. There are services to France, Germany, Portugal and Morocco too.

CAR

Numerous international and local agencies have desks at the airport, many with small cars for €150 or less per week.

TRAIN

The main station, **Málaga-RENFE** (Map p734; ☎ 952 36 02 02; Explanada de la Estación) is round the corner from the bus station. Quick Talgo 200s run to Madrid (€47 to €79, 4½ hours, four daily). A slower, cheaper Intercity train for Madrid (€35, 6½ hours) leaves late morning. Trains also go to Córdoba (€14 to €19, two to 2½ hours, nine daily) and Seville (€13.15, 2½ hours, five daily). For Granada (€12, 2½ hours) there are no direct trains but you can get there with a transfer at Bobadilla. For Ronda (€8.50, 1½ hours minimum) you usually also change at Bobadilla. Trains also run to Barcelona (€44 to €121, 9½ to 13 hours, two daily).

Getting Around
TO/FROM THE AIRPORT

The Aeropuerto train station is a five-minute walk from the airport (follow signs from the departures hall). Trains run about every half-hour from 7am to 11.45pm to Málaga-RENFE station (€1.20, 11 minutes) and the Málaga-Centro station. Trains depart for the airport between 5.45am and 10.30pm.

Bus No 19 to the city centre (€1, 20 minutes) leaves the airport roughly every half-hour from 7am to midnight, stopping at the city bus and train stations en route. Going out to the airport, you can catch it at the western end of Paseo del Parque and outside the stations, from 6.30am to 11.30pm.

A taxi from the airport to the city centre costs around €10.

COSTA DEL SOL

Strewn along the seaboard from Málaga almost to Gibraltar, the Costa del Sol stretches like a wall of wedding cakes. Its recipe for success is sunshine, convenient beaches (of grey-brown sand), cheap package deals and plenty of nightlife and entertainment.

The resorts were once fishing villages, but there's little evidence of that now. The Costa del Sol was launched as a 1950s development drive for impoverished Andalucía and has succeeded admirably on that score, at the cost of turning a spectacular coastline into an unbroken series of untidy, crowded townscapes. The *costa* (coast) is also good for sport lovers, with nearly 40 golf clubs, several busy marinas, tennis courts, riding schools, swimming pools, gyms and beaches offering every imaginable water sport.

In July and August it's a very good idea to ring ahead for a room. Outside these peak months, many room rates drop sharply. The *costa* also has about 15 camping grounds.

A convenient train service links Málaga's Centro, RENFE and Aeropuerto stations with Torremolinos (€1.20), Arroyo de la Miel (€1.20) and Fuengirola (€1.90). Buses from Málaga link all the resorts, and services to places such as Ronda, Cádiz, Seville and Granada go from the main resorts.

The AP7 Autopista del Sol motorway bypasses all the *costa* towns, with tolls amounting to €6.90 (€11.20 from June to September and during Semana Santa) for the full 80km. The old coast road, the N340, is now less beleaguered but you still need to take care on it: don't let other drivers pressurise you into going too fast, and watch out for animals and inebriated pedestrians.

Torremolinos
pop 51,000

'Torrie', which led the Costa del Sol's mass-tourism boom of the 1950s and '60s, is a concrete high-rise jungle designed to squeeze as many paying customers as it can into the smallest possible space. It spruced itself up somewhat in the 1990s.

ORIENTATION & INFORMATION

Torremolinos' main pedestrian artery is Calle San Miguel, running most of the 500m from Plaza Costa del Sol (on the main road through town) down to Playa del Bajondillo. Southwest of Playa del Bajondillo is Playa de la Carihuela, once the fishing quarter.

The **bus station** (☎ 952 38 24 19; Calle Hoyo) is northeast of Plaza Costa del Sol. Buses to Málaga, Benalmádena, Mijas and Fuengirola stop on Avenida Palma de Mallorca, 200m southwest of Plaza Costa del Sol. The **train station** (Avenida Jesús Santos Rein), is off Calle San Miguel.

Tourist Office (☎ 952 37 95 12; www.ayto-torremolinos .org; Plaza Pablo Picasso; ⊗ 9am-1.30pm Mon-Fri) There are also numerous information booths around the town.

SIGHTS & ACTIVITIES

Torrie's **beaches** are wider, longer and a slightly paler shade of grey-brown than most on the *costa*, which helps explain why they get so crowded. The local attractions are mostly child-oriented. In the swish Puerto Deportivo (marina) at Benalmádena

Costa, just southwest of Torremolinos, **Sea Life** (☎ 952 56 01 50; www.sealife.es; adult/child €8/6.60; ⏰ 10am-8pm Jun, 10am-midnight Jul-Aug, 10am-6pm Sep-May) is a good modernistic aquarium of mainly Mediterranean marine creatures, with organised games and shark feeding. **Tivoli World** (☎ 952 57 70 16; www.tivolicostadel sol.com; Avenida de Tivoli; admission excl rides €4.50; ⏰ 6pm-2am Jul-mid-Sep, 4pm-1am May, Jun & 2nd half Sep, 1-10pm Apr & most of Oct, 1-10pm Sun late Oct-Mar), just five minutes' walk from Benalmádena-Arroyo de la Miel train station, is the biggest amusement park on the *costa*. The Supertivolino ticket (€13) gives unlimited access to more than 35 rides.

SLEEPING & EATING

A couple of dozen hostales and hotels are within a few minutes' walk of Torremolinos' train and bus stations. The tourist offices can supply lists.

Red Parrot (☎ 952 37 54 45; www.theredparrot .net; Avenida Los Manantiales 4; s/d €36/42; 🖵) Newly refurbished and centrally located, the Red Parrot offers comfortable balconied rooms, with ceiling fans, around a patio.

Hotel Miami (☎ 952 38 52 55; www.residencia -miami.com; Calle Aladino 14; d €37/57; 🖵 🖵) A lovely villa amid tropical gardens, and only 100m from La Carihuela beach, this small hotel has tasteful rooms.

La Fonda Benalmádena (☎ /fax 952 56 82 73; Calle Santo Domingo 7, Benalmádena Pueblo; s/d €54/73.50; 🖵 🖵) Charming La Fonda has large rooms built around Islamic-style patios with fountains, and an excellent, moderately priced restaurant.

Besides British breakfasts and British beer, Torremolinos has no shortage of good seafood places, many of them lining the Paseo Marítimo in La Carihuela.

ENTERTAINMENT

The weekend nightlife at Benalmádena Costa's Puerto Deportivo pulls a young crowd from all along the coast. The bars start to throb after midnight on Friday and Saturday.

Fun Beach (☎ 952 05 23 97; Avenida Palma de Mallorca 7; ⏰ 8pm-6am) Reputedly the largest club in Europe, Fun Beach has eight huge and packed dance floors on which to lose yourself.

Torrie has a big gay scene; most gay bars are on Calle Nogalera off Avenida Jesús Santos Rein.

Fuengirola
pop 57,000

Fuengirola, 18km down the coast from Torremolinos, has more of a family scene but is just as densely packed. The narrow streets between the beach and Avenida Matías Sáenz de Tejada (where the bus station is) constitute what's left of the old town, with Plaza de la Constitución at its centre. The **train station** (Avenida Jesús Santos Rein) is a block further inland. The **tourist office** (☎ 952 46 74 57; Avenida Jesús Santos Rein 6; ⏰ 9.30am-2pm & 4.30-7pm Mon-Fri, 10am-1pm Sat) is just along from the train station.

The **Hipódromo Costa del Sol** (☎ 952 59 27 00; admission free; Urbanización El Chaparral), Andalucía's only horse-racing track with regular racing, is off the N340 at the southwestern end of Fuengirola. Races start at 10pm every Saturday night from July to September (under floodlights), and at noon on Sunday in other months.

SLEEPING & EATING

Hostal Italia (☎ 952 47 41 93; Calle de la Cruz 1; s/d €40/53; 🖵) A friendly, clean and comfortable budget option in the heart of things, a couple of blocks from the beach.

Hotel Puerto (☎ 952 66 45 03; Calle Marbella 34; s/d €42/59; 🖵 🖵) This towering three-star beach hotel on the beach gives great sea views and has a rooftop pool.

Restaurante Portofino (☎ 952 47 06 43; Paseo Marítimo 29; mains €10.50-30) This is one of Fuengirola's better offerings, with an international menu featuring a host of classic fish dishes.

Lizzaran (☎ 952 47 38 29; Avenida Jesús Santos Rein 1; raciones €4-15) A welcome Spanish relief from the overwhelming number of Chinese and Italian eateries.

Mijas

A white village of winding Muslim-origin streets, in the hills 8km north of Fuengirola, Mijas is now surrounded by villas and *urbanizaciones* (housing estates), and full of busloads up from the *costa*. But it remains a pretty place and the **Casa Museo de Mijas** (☎ 952 59 03 80; Calle Málaga; admission free; ⏰ 10am-2pm year-round, 4-7pm Sep-Mar, 5-8pm Apr-Jun, 6-9pm Jul-Aug) gives a poignant glimpse into life in the area before the 1960s tourist deluge. There are lots of restaurants, cafés and craft shops. Frequent buses run from Fuengirola (€0.90, 25 minutes).

Marbella

pop 116,000

Overlooked by the dramatic Sierra Blanca 28km west of Fuengirola, Marbella has been the Costa del Sol's glossiest resort ever since part-Mexican, part-Austrian Alfonso von Hohenlohe built the exclusive Marbella Club Hotel, just west, in the 1950s. After a decline in the 1980s, Marbella's fortunes revived, sort of, under controversial right-wing mayor Jesús Gil y Gil in the 1990s. Gil cleaned up beaches and streets, encouraged rampant property development and embroiled himself and Marbella town hall in endless corruption and financial scandals. Gil finally resigned as mayor in 2002, having been banned from public office for 28 years. He died in 2004.

ORIENTATION

The N340 through town takes the names Avenida Ramón y Cajal and Avenida Ricardo Soriano. The old town is centred on Plaza de los Naranjos. The bus station is on the northern side of the Marbella bypass, 1.2km from Plaza de los Naranjos. Buses to/from Fuengirola, Puerto Banús and Estepona use stops on Avenida Ricardo Soriano, west of the town centre.

INFORMATION

Hospital Europa (☎ 952 77 42 00; Avenida de Severo Ochoa)

Tourist offices (☺ 9am-8pm; Centre ☎ 952 82 35 50; Plaza de los Naranjos Seafront ☎ 952 77 14 42; Glorieta de la Fontanilla)

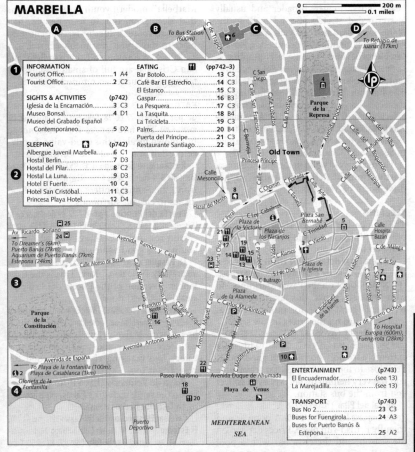

MARBELLA

0 ━━━━ 200 m
0 ━━━━ 0.1 miles

To Bus Station (600m)

To Refugio de Juanar (17km)

INFORMATION	
Tourist Office	1 A4
Tourist Office	2 C2

SIGHTS & ACTIVITIES	(p742)
Iglesia de la Encarnación	3 C3
Museo Bonsai	4 D1
Museo del Grabado Español Contemporáneo	5 D2

SLEEPING	(p742)
Albergue Juvenil Marbella	6 C1
Hostal Berlin	7 D3
Hostal del Pilar	8 C2
Hostal La Luna	9 D3
Hotel El Fuerte	10 C4
Hotel San Cristóbal	11 C3
Princesa Playa Hotel	12 D4

EATING	(pp742–3)
Bar Botolo	13 C3
Café Bar El Estrecho	14 C3
El Estanco	15 C3
Gaspar	16 B3
La Pesquera	17 C3
La Tasquita	18 B4
La Tricicleta	19 C3
Palms	20 B4
Puerta del Príncipe	21 C3
Restaurante Santiago	22 B4

ENTERTAINMENT	(p743)
El Encuadernador	(see 13)
La Marejadilla	(see 13)

TRANSPORT	(p743)
Bus No 2	23 C3
Buses for Fuengirola	24 A3
Buses for Puerto Banús & Estepona	25 A2

Old Town

To Dreamer's (6km); Puerto Banús (7km); Aquarium de Puerto Banús (7km); Estepona (24km)

To Hospital Europa (600m); Fuengirola (28km)

To Playa de la Fontanilla (100m); Playa de Casablanca (1km)

Parque de la Constitución

Parque de la Represa

MEDITERRANEAN SEA

ANDALUCÍA

SIGHTS & ACTIVITIES
Pretty **Plaza de los Naranjos**, with its 16th-century town hall, is the heart of the largely pedestrianised old town. Nearby is the **Iglesia de la Encarnación** (Plaza de la Iglesia), begun in the 16th century. A little further east, the **Museo del Grabado Español Contemporáneo** (Calle Hospital Bazán; admission €2.50; ⏰ 10am-2pm & 5.30-8.30pm Mon-Sat) exhibits prints by Picasso, Miró and Dalí.

The charming **Museo Bonsai** (admission €3; ⏰ 10am-1.30pm & 4.30-7.30pm), devoted to the Japanese art of miniature trees, is in Parque de la Represa in the northeastern part of the old town.

Avenida Ramon y Cajal is peppered with crazed **sculptures** by Salvador Dalí. The central **Playa de Venus** is a standard Costa beach. For a longer, broader and usually less-crowded stretch of sand walk to the 800m-long **Playa de la Fontanilla**, west of Glorieta de la Fontanilla, or even better, **Playa de Casablanca** beyond Playa de la Fontanilla.

Puerto Banús, the Costa del Sol's most ostentatious marina, is 7km west of Marbella. The harbour here, full of huge floating gin palaces, is bordered by glam shops, semiglam eateries and drinkeries, and the **Aquarium de Puerto Banús** (☎ 952 81 87 67; adult/child €4.80/3.60; ⏰ 11am-6pm, closes erratically Mon-Fri winter), similar to Sea Life at Benalmádena Costa (p739).

There are good **walks** in the Sierra Blanca, starting from the Refugio de Juanar, a 17km drive north of Marbella.

SLEEPING
The choice here ranges from some basic old-town hostales to deluxe monsters gobbling up the seafront.

Princesa Playa Hotel (☎ 902 117751; www.princesa playa.com; Avenida Duque de Ahumada s/n; apt €127-160; **P** 🅿 🅐) Right on the Paseo Marítimo and with great sea views, this apartment hotel represents great value for money. Take at least one-third off the prices in low season.

Hostal Berlin (☎ 952 82 13 10, fax 952 82 66 77; Calle San Ramón; s/d/t €35/45/60; 🅐 🖴) This is an extremely friendly hostal, with good facilities, close to the beach. Breakfast is available and the very helpful owner will even collect you from the bus station.

Hostal del Pilar (☎ 952 82 99 36; hostal@marbella -scene.com; Calle Mesoncillo 4; d €40) A popular and friendly British-run place. Prices depend on the season, and there's a bar with a pool table (and log fire for the cooler months) and a roof terrace.

Hotel El Fuerte (☎ 952 86 15 00; www.hotel-el fuerte.es; Avenida El Fuerte s/n; s €125.75, d €181.90-242.90, incl breakfast; **P** 🅐 🅐) This huge complex is almost on the beach, and has a host of facilities including beach access, a gym, gardens, tennis courts and a sauna.

Hostal La Luna (☎ 952 82 57 78; Calle La Luna 7; d €52) Balconied rooms (with fans) overlook an internal patio at this delightful spot.

Hotel San Cristóbal (☎ 952 77 12 50; www.hotelsanc ristobal.com; Avenida Ramón y Cajal 3; s/d €58/90; 🅐) One of the less pricey of the upmarket hotels, with all the requisite facilities.

Albergue Juvenil Marbella (☎ 952 77 14 91; www.inturjoven.com in Spanish; Calle Trapiche 2; dm incl breakfast under 26 €9.05-13.75, over 26 €12.25-18.35) Marbella's modern youth hostel has rooms that sleep from one to four people (half have bathrooms). It's by far the cheapest place to stay and is reasonably central.

Calle San Ramón and the parallel Calle San Cristóbal are full of small hostales offering good budget accommodation.

EATING
Gaspar (☎ 952 77 00 78; Calle Notario Luis Oliver 19; meals €20) The fare ranges from *raciones* to full-blown meals at this good-value, family-run restaurant, just off the seafront.

Restaurante Santiago (☎ 952 77 00 78; Paseo Marítimo 5; 2-course meals €25) Right on the seafront, the Santiago offers gourmet seafood dishes in elegant surrounds.

Puerta del Príncipe (☎ 952 77 49 64; Plaza de la Victoria; mains €10-25; ⏰ 10.30am-1.30pm) This successful restaurant is always packed on account of its good-value steak menu.

La Pesquera (☎ 952 77 53 02; Plaza de la Victoria; mains €10-35; ⏰ 10.30am-1.30pm) This is the fish-fancier's version of the Puerta del Príncipe steakhouse next door.

La Tricicleta (☎ 952 85 76 86; Calle San Lázaro; mains €14-20; ⏰ dinner Mon-Sat, closed Jan) Dine on duck breast with a five-pepper sauce flambéed with Jerez brandy and you'll see why this eatery is a cracking choice. It's good for vegetarians too.

Playa de Venus also has a throng of eateries on the sand, including **Palms** (salads from €6), or **La Tasquita** (seafood mains €8-10).

Café Bar El Estrecho (Calle San Lázaro 12; tapas €1.10), **El Estanco** (☎ 952 92 40 11; Calle Buitrago 24; tapas/raciones €1.50/8) and **Bar Botolo** (☎ 952 82 69 50; Calle

San Lázaro; tapas €1.80) provide varied but good tapas and strong, viscous coffee.

ENTERTAINMENT
On little Calle San Lázaro, bars **El Encuadernador** (Calle San Lázaro 3), with an authentic beerden feel, and **La Marejadilla** (Calle San Lázaro) stay lively late into the evening, even in the low season when the rest of the old town has gone home. Calle Pantaleón has a string of beer bars buzzing late into weekend nights with a young crowd. The Puerto Deportivo, site of many a drinking den, was due to reopen in late 2004 after big renovations.

Dreamer's (☎ 952 81 20 80; www.dreamers-disco .com in Spanish; Carretera de Cádiz 175, Río Verde) Out of town, in nearby Puerto Banús, Dreamer's gives house-lovers a chance to truly let their hair down, with its mix of tribal, vocal and light shows, bongo beats and an ever-changing menu of DJs.

GETTING THERE & AROUND
Half-hourly buses to Fuengirola (€2.05, one hour), Puerto Banús (€0.95, 20 minutes) and Estepona (€1.85, one hour) have stops on Avenida Ricardo Soriano. Other services use the **bus station** (☎ 952 76 44 00) in the north of town. Bus No 7 (€0.85) runs between the bus station and the central **Fuengirola-Estepona bus stop** (Avenida Ricardo Soriano); returning from the city centre to the bus station, take No 2 from Avenida Ramón y Cajal.

Estepona
pop 48,000
Estepona, southwest of Marbella, has controlled its development relatively carefully and remains a fairly agreeable seaside town. The big attraction here is **Selwo Aventura** (☎ 952 79 21 50; www.selwo.es in Spanish; adult/child €18/12; ⊙ 10am-6pm Oct-May, 10am-8pm Jun-Sep), 6km east of town. This 1-sq-km wildlife park has over 200 exotic species. A direct bus runs to Selwo from Málaga via Torremolinos, Fuengirola and Marbella (phone the park for information).

EL CHORRO & BOBASTRO
pop 100 (El Chorro)
Fifty kilometres northwest of Málaga, the Río Guadalhorce and the main railway in and out of Málaga both pass through the awesome **Garganta del Chorro** (El Chorro Gorge), which is 4km long, up to 400m deep and as

little as 10m wide. The gorge is a magnet for rock climbers, with hundreds of routes of almost every grade of difficulty and great variety. Anyone can view the gorge by walking along the railway from the tiny El Chorro village (ask locally for directions).

Swiss-owned **Finca La Campana** (below) is popular with adventure-seekers, and offers climbing courses, climbing, caving and white-water kayaking trips, and mountainbike trips and rentals (€10 per day). One thrilling outing is its five-hour climbing trip along the Camino del Rey (King's Path), a crumbling concrete catwalk clinging to the gorge wall 100m above the river – worth every céntimo of the €40.

Near El Chorro is **Bobastro**, the hill-top redoubt of the 9th-century rebel, Omar ibn Hafsun, a sort of Islamic Robin Hood, who led a prolonged revolt against Cordoban rule. Ibn Hafsun at one stage controlled territory from Cartagena to the Strait of Gibraltar. From El Chorro village, follow the road up the far (western) side of the valley and after 3km take the signed Bobastro turning. Nearly 3km up here, an 'Iglesia Mozárabe' sign indicates a 500m path to the remains of a remarkable little Mozarabic church cut from the rock. It's thought that Ibn Hafsun converted from Islam to Christianity (thus becoming a Mozarab) before his death in 917 and was buried here. When Bobastro was finally conquered in 927, his remains were taken for posthumous crucifixion outside Córdoba's Mezquita. At the top of the hill, 2.5km further up the road and with unbelievable views, are faint traces of Ibn Hafsun's rectangular *alcázar* (fortress).

Sleeping & Eating
Apartamentos La Garganta (☎ 952 49 51 19; infor macion@lagarganta.com; 5-person apt €72; ✕ ☎) A few steps from El Chorro station, this converted flour mill has small apartments and a good restaurant.

Pensión Estación (☎ 952 49 50 04; s/d €21/24) At El Chorro station, this *pensión* has clean rooms, and **Restaurante Estación**, also called Bar Isabel, a renowned climbers' gathering spot, serves *platos combinados* for €3.50 or €4.50.

Finca La Campana (☎ 952 11 20 19; www.el-chorro .com; dm €10, d €24, 2–8-person apt €34-80; ✕ ☎) More than just a great place to stay, this is a club of like-minded adrenaline junkies, with a cult following to show. During the

ANDALUCÍA

climbing season (October to March) the Finca is very busy, so book ahead. To get there follow the signs from behind Apartamentos La Garganta.

Getting There & Away

There's one train daily (except Sunday) to El Chorro from Málaga (€3.10, 45 minutes) and Ronda (€4.95, 1¼ hours). The trip from Ronda to El Chorro to Málaga is in the morning and vice-versa in the evening. No buses run to El Chorro. Drivers can get there via Álora (south of El Chorro) or Ardales (west of El Chorro).

RONDA

pop 35,000 / elevation 744m

Old and new Ronda stand either side of the spectacular 100m-deep El Tajo gorge, in the midst of the beautiful Serranía de Ronda. Though just an hour north of the Costa del Sol, Ronda is a world away from the coastal scene. It attracts its quota of visitors, but many of them return to the coast in the afternoon.

With its spectacular cliff-top setting, quaint old Islamic town and a romantic place in Spanish folklore, Ronda has fascinated travellers from Dumas to Hemingway and beyond. For most of the Islamic period, Ronda was the capital of an independent, or almost-independent statelet. Its near-impregnable position kept it out of Christian hands until 1485.

Orientation

The old Muslim town, called La Ciudad, stands on the southern side of El Tajo. The newer town to the north has most of the places to stay and eat, and the bus and train stations. Three bridges span the gorge, the main one being the Puente Nuevo. Both parts of town end suddenly on their western side, with cliffs plunging away to the valley of the Río Guadalevín.

Information

Banks and ATMs are mainly on Calle Virgen de la Paz and Plaza Carmen Abela.

Municipal tourist office (☎ 952 18 71 19; turismo@ronda-e.com; Paseo de Blas Infante; 🕑 9.30am-6.30pm Mon-Fri, 10am-2pm & 3-6.30pm Sat & Sun)

Regional tourist office (☎ 649-965338; www .andalucia.org; Plaza de España 1; 🕑 9am-7pm Mon-Fri, 10am-2pm Sat)

Sights

PLAZA DE ESPAÑA & PUENTE NUEVO

The majestic Puente Nuevo (New Bridge), spanning El Tajo from Plaza de España, the main square on the north side of the gorge, was completed in 1793. A Ronda tradition claims that its architect, Martín de Aldehuela, fell to his death that year, trying to engrave the date on the bridge's side. Chapter 10 of Hemingway's *For Whom the Bell Tolls* tells how at the start of the Spanish Civil War the 'fascists' of a small town were clubbed and flailed by townspeople 'in the plaza on the top of the cliff above the river', then thrown over the cliff. The episode was based on real events in Ronda, though the perpetrators were apparently a gang from Málaga.

LA CIUDAD

The old Muslim town retains a typical medieval Islamic character of narrow streets twisting between white buildings.

The first street to the left, after you cross the Puente Nuevo, leads down to the **Casa del Rey Moro** (☎ 952 18 72 00; Calle Santo Domingo 17). This 18th-century house, supposedly built over the remains of an Islamic palace, is itself closed, but you can visit its cliff-top **gardens** and climb down **La Mina** (gardens & La Mina adult/child €4/2; 🕑 10am-7pm), a Islamic-era stairway cut inside the rock right down to the bottom of the gorge (take care!).

From the Casa del Rey Moro, head back up towards **Plaza María Auxiliadora**, which has fine views, then continue to the **Palacio de Mondragón** (☎ 952 87 84 50; admission €2; 🕑 10am-6pm Mon-Fri, 10am-3pm Sat & Sun), built for Abomelic, the ruler of Ronda in 1314. Of its three courtyards, only the Patio Mudéjar preserves an Islamic character. A horseshoe arch leads into a small cliff-top garden with splendid views.

A minute's walk beyond is Plaza Duquesa de Parcent, where the **Iglesia de Santa María La Mayor** (☎ 952 87 22 46; admission €2; 🕑 10am-8pm Apr-Oct; 10am-6pm Nov-Mar) stands on the site of Islamic Ronda's main mosque. The tower and the handsome galleries beside it, built for viewing festivities, date from Islamic times. Just inside the entrance is an arch, covered with Arabic inscriptions, which was the mosque's mihrab (prayer niche indicating the direction of Mecca).

Nearby, the **Museo del Bandolero** (☎ 952 87 77 85; Calle de Armiñán 65; admission €2.70; 🕑 10am-8pm

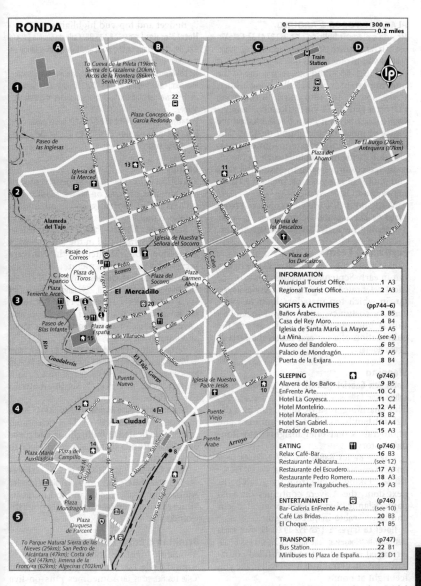

RONDA

0 _____ 300 m
0 _____ 0.2 miles

To Cueva de la Pileta (19km);
Sierra de Grazalema (20km);
Arcos de la Frontera (86km);
Seville (132km)

Plaza Concepción
García Redondo

Train
Station

Avenida de Andalucía

Paseo de
las Inglesas

Calle de San José

Calle Madrid

Calle Lauria

Plaza del
Ahorro

To El Burgo (26km);
Antequera (87km)

Iglesia de
la Merced

Calle Pozo

Calle Infantes

Calle de Sevilla

Calle Doctor Ramón y Cajal

Calle de Montelirio

Alameda
del Tajo

Calle Marina

Calle Mariano Soubirón

Iglesia de Nuestra
Señora del Socorro

Borrego Gómez

C Naranja

C San Antonio

Iglesia de
los Descalzos

Plaza de
los Descalzos

Calle San Vicente de Paul

Pasaje de
Correos

C Pedro
Romero

Carrera del Espinel

C Calvo Asensio

Calle María Cabrera

Calle Sevilla

Plaza
de Toros

Plaza del
Socorro

Plaza
Carmen
Abela

Santa Cecilia

C José
Aparicio

Plaza
Teniente Arce

El Mercadillo

Las Tiendas

Calle Nueva

Calle Ermita

Paseo de
Blas Infante

Plaza de
España

Calle Villanueva

Calle Los Remedios

El Tajo Gorge

Río

Guadalevín

Puente
Nuevo

Iglesia de Nuestro
Padre Jesús

Calle Real

C Tenorio

La Ciudad

Calle Santo Domingo

Puente
Viejo

Plaza María
Auxiliadora

Plaza del
Campillo

Calle de Armiñán

Plaza
Mondragón

C José M Holgado

Puente
Árabe

Arroyo

Plaza
Duquesa
de Parcent

Hoyo San Miguel

C Marqués de Salvatierra

To Parque Natural Sierra de las
Nieves (25km); San Pedro de
Alcántara (47km); Costa del
Sol (47km); Jimena de la
Frontera (62km); Algeciras (102km)

INFORMATION
Municipal Tourist Office...................1 A3
Regional Tourist Office...................2 A3

SIGHTS & ACTIVITIES   (pp744–6)
Baños Árabes...................................3 B5
Casa del Rey Moro...........................4 B4
Iglesia de Santa María La Mayor.......5 A5
La Mina.....................................(see 4)
Museo del Bandolero........................6 B5
Palacio de Mondragón......................7 A5
Puerta de la Exijara..........................8 B4

SLEEPING   (p746)
Alavera de los Baños........................9 B5
EnFrente Arte.................................10 C4
Hotel La Goyesca...........................11 C2
Hotel Montelirio............................12 A4
Hotel Morales................................13 B2
Hotel San Gabriel..........................14 A4
Parador de Ronda..........................15 A3

EATING   (p746)
Relax Café-Bar...............................16 B3
Restaurante Albacara...............(see 12)
Restaurante del Escudero................17 A3
Restaurante Pedro Romero.............18 A3
Restaurante Tragabuches................19 A3

ENTERTAINMENT   (p746)
Bar-Galería EnFrente Arte...........(see 10)
Café Las Bridas.............................20 B3
El Choque.....................................21 B5

TRANSPORT   (p747)
Bus Station...................................22 B1
Minibuses to Plaza de España.........23 D1

Apr-Sep, 10am-6pm Oct-Mar) is dedicated to the banditry for which central Andalucía was renowned in the 19th century.

Beside the museum, steps lead down to an impressive stretch of La Ciudad's old **walls**. Follow them down to the **Puerta de la Exijara**, originally the entrance to Islamic Ronda's Jewish quarter, outside the walls.

A path continues down to the beautiful 13th- and 14th-century **Baños Árabes** (Arab Baths; ☎ 952 87 08 18; Calle San Miguel; admission €2; ⏰ 10am-6pm Mon-Fri, 10am-3pm Sat & Sun). From the northern side of the nearby **Puente Viejo** (1616) you can make your way back up to Plaza de España via a small park along the gorge's edge.

ANDALUCÍA

PLAZA DE TOROS & AROUND

Ronda's elegant **bullring** (☎ 952 87 41 32; Calle Virgen de la Paz; admission €5; ☺ 10am-8pm Apr-Sep, 10am-6pm Oct-Mar) is one of the oldest in Spain – it opened in 1785 – and has seen some of the most important events in bullfighting history. It was here, in the 18th and 19th centuries, that three generations of the Romero family – Francisco, Juan and Pedro – established the basics of modern bullfighting on foot. The bullring's recently expanded museum is crammed with memorabilia such as blood-spattered costumes worn by Pedro Romero, and photos of famous fans, including Hemingway and Orson Welles.

Vertiginous cliff-top views open out from **Paseo de Blas Infante**, behind the Plaza de Toros, and the leafy **Alameda del Tajo** nearby.

Festivals & Events

Ronda's bullring stages relatively few fights, but in early September it holds some of the most celebrated in Spain, the **Corridas Goyescas**, in which top matadors fight in 19th-century costumes, as portrayed in Goya's Ronda bullfighting scenes. These are the culmination of a general fiesta, the **Feria de Pedro Romero**.

Sleeping

Hotel San Gabriel (☎ 952 19 03 92; www.hotelsangabriel.com; Calle José M Holgado 19; s/d 68/82; ☒) This charming, historic hotel, run by a delightful family, is filled with antiques and photographs that offer insights into Ronda's history.

Alavera de los Baños (☎ 952 87 91 43; www.andalucia.com/alavera; Hoyo San Miguel s/n; s/d €50/85; ☒ ☒) Taking its cue from the Arab baths next door, the Alavera continues the Hispanic-Islamic theme, with oriental décor and tasty Arabic-inspired cuisine.

Hotel La Goyesca (☎ 952 19 00 49; www.ronda.net/usuar/hotelgoyesca; Calle Infantes 39; s/d €48/67.50) Arranged around a geranium-filled courtyard, this small tranquil hotel will make you feel right at home.

EnFrente Arte (☎ 952 87 90 88; www.enfrentearte.com; Calle Real 40; s/d incl breakfast, buffet lunch & all drinks €45/90; ☒ ☒ ☒) Funky modern décor combined with a recreation room, a pool, a flowery patio, a bar, a sauna, a film room and fantastic views of the Sierra de la Nieves, make this a great new addition to the scene.

Budget and top-end highlights:

Hotel Morales (☎ 952 87 15 38; Calle de Sevilla 51; s/d €21/39; ☒) Maps on the walls and lots of information on the town and nearby parks.

Hotel Montelirio (☎ 952 87 38 55; www.hotelmontelirio.com; Calle Tenorio 8; s/d €100/150; ☒ ☒) Sensitively converted mansion with magical views of Ronda's gorge.

Parador de Ronda (☎ 952 87 75 00; www.parador.es; Plaza de España s/n; s/d €96/120; ☒ ☒ ☒ ☒) More gorge-side luxury.

Eating

Traditional Ronda food is hearty mountain fare that's strong on stews, trout, game such as rabbit, partridge and quail, and, of course, oxtail.

Restaurante Albacara (☎ 952 16 11 84; Calle Tenorio 8; meals €25-30) Situated in the old stables of gorge-side Hotel Montelirio, the Albacara serves up a sumptuous menu.

Restaurante Tragabuches (☎ 952 19 02 91; Calle José Aparicio 1; mains €15-20; ☺ lunch & dinner Tue-Sat, lunch Sun) Sleek, modern Tragabuches is famous for its creativity. Try venison and sweet potatoes, or pork trotters with squid and sunflower seeds.

Restaurante del Escudero (☎ 952 87 13 67; Paseo de Blas Infante 1; menú €15; ☺ lunch & dinner Tue-Sat, lunch Sun) Tragabuches' sister restaurant, with more-reasonable prices, is set in an attractive garden.

Restaurante Pedro Romero (☎ 952 87 11 10; Calle Virgen de la Paz 18; mains €9-15) This celebrated eatery is dedicated to bullfighting and turns out classic Ronda dishes – a good place to try the oxtail.

Relax Café-Bar (☎ 952 87 72 07; Calle Los Remedios 27; pastas & bakes €5.50; ☺ lunch & dinner Mon-Fri) An oasis of good vegetarian food in meat-hungry Ronda, run by two friendly English-women.

Drinking & Entertainment

A modest nightlife and bar zone centres around Calle Los Remedios. **Café Las Bridas** (Calle Los Remedios 18) sometimes puts on live flamenco or rock. **Bar-Galería EnFrente Arte** (Calle Real 40; www.enfrentearte.com) has a good atmosphere and often stages live music. The café **El Choque** (Calle Espíritu Santo 9; ☺ 9.30-3am Feb-Oct, 1pm-1am Nov-Jan) has fantastic views and Internet screens, and puts on a host of events, from films out on the terrace to live bands.

Getting There & Away

BUS
From the **bus station** (Plaza Concepción García Redondo 2), **Los Amarillos** (☎ 952 18 70 61) goes to Málaga (€7.90, two hours, four daily), Grazalema (€1.95, 35 minutes, two daily) and Seville (€8.40, 2½ hours, four daily); **Comes** (☎ 952 87 19 92) has three or four buses daily to Arcos de la Frontera (€7, two hours), Jerez (€8.89, 2½ hours) and Cádiz (€11.80, 2½ hours), and one Monday to Friday to Algeciras (€8, two hours); and **Portillo** (☎ 952 87 22 62) runs to Málaga (€7.85, 1½ hours, four daily) via Marbella.

TRAIN
The **train station** (☎ 952 87 16 73; Avenida de Andalucía) is on the highly scenic Bobadilla–Algeciras line. Trains run to/from Algeciras (€5.85 to €15, 1¾ hours, six daily), Granada (€10.50, 2½ hours, three daily) via Antequera, Córdoba (€16 to €20.50, 2½ hours, two daily) and Málaga (€7.65, two hours, one daily except Sunday). For Seville, change at Bobadilla or Antequera.

Getting Around
Urban minibuses operate every 30 minutes to Plaza de España from Avenida Martínez Astein, across the road from the train station.

AROUND RONDA
The beautiful green hills of the Serranía de Ronda, dotted with white villages, stretch in all directions from Ronda.

Parque Natural Sierra de las Nieves
This 180-sq-km protected area, southeast of Ronda, offers some good walks. Torrecilla (1918m), the highest peak in the western half of Andalucía, is about a five-hour return walk from Área Recreativa Los Quejigales, which is 10km east by unpaved road from the A376 Ronda–San Pedro de Alcántara road.

Camping Conejeras (☎ 619-180012; 1-person tent & car €7.25; ☼ daily Oct-Jun, Sat & Sun Jul-Sep) located 800m off the A376 on the road to Los Quejigales.

Posada del Canónigo (☎ 952 16 01 85; www.laposadadelcanonigo.com; Calle Mesones 24, El Burgo; s/d €37.30/52) This is a great little hotel in a restored mansion, in the likeable small rural town of El Burgo, which is within striking distance of the park. It has a moderately priced restaurant, and management has information on walking routes and can organise horse riding.

Cueva de la Pileta
Palaeolithic paintings of horses, goats, fish and even a seal, dating from 20,000 to 25,000 years ago, are preserved in this large cave, 20km southwest of Ronda. You'll be guided by kerosene lamp and one of the knowledgeable Bullón family, from the farm in the valley below, one of whom found the paintings in 1905. The **Cueva de la Pileta** (☎ 952 16 73 43; adult/student/child €6.50/3/2.50; hourly tours ☼ 10am-1pm & 4-6pm) is 250m (signposted) off the Benaoján–Cortes de la Frontera road, 4km from Benaoján. Guides speak at least some English and German. If you come on a busy day, you may have to wait, but you can ring ahead to try to book a particular time.

ANTEQUERA
pop 42,000 / elevation 575m

Antequera, set on the edge of a plain 50km north of Málaga, with rugged mountains to the south and east, is one of Andalucía's most attractive old towns. Its 'golden age' was during the 15th and 16th centuries, when dozens of churches and mansions were built.

Orientation & Information
The old heart of town is below the northwestern side of the hill, crowned by the Islamic Alcazaba. The main street, Calle Infante Don Fernando, runs northwest from Plaza de San Sebastián.

Tourist office (☎ 952 70 25 05; www.turismoantequera.com; Plaza de San Sebastián 7; ☼ 10am-2pm & 5-8pm Mon-Sat, 10am-2pm Sun)

Sights
The main approach to the **Alcazaba** (Fortress) passes through the **Arco de los Gigantes**, built in 1585 and incorporating stones with Roman inscriptions. What remains of the Alcazaba affords great views. Just below it is the impressive **Colegiata de Santa María la Mayor** (Plaza Santa María; admission free; ☼ 10am-2pm & 4.30-6.30pm Tue-Fri, 10.30am-2pm Sat, 11.30am-2pm Sun), a 16th-century church with a beautiful Renaissance façade.

The pride of the **Museo Municipal** (Plaza Coso Viejo; tours €3; ☼ 10am-1.30pm Tue-Sat, 11am-1.30pm Sun) is *Efebo*, a beautiful 1.4m bronze Roman

ANDALUCÍA

statue of a patrician's 'toy boy', unearthed near Antequera in the 1950s – one of the finest pieces of Roman sculpture found in Spain.

Only the most jaded would fail to be impressed by the **Iglesia del Carmen** (Plaza del Carmen; admission €1.30; ☼ 10am-2pm daily, 4-7pm Mon-Sat) and its marvellous 18th-century Churrigueresque retable. Carved in red pine by *antequerano* (native of Antequera) Antonio Primo, it's spangled with statues of angels, saints, popes and bishops.

Some of Europe's largest megalithic tombs stand on the fringes of Antequera. The **Dolmen de Menga** and **Dolmen de Viera** (admission free; ☼ 9am-3.30pm Tue, 9am-3pm Wed-Sat, 9.30am-2.30pm Sun) are 1km from the city centre, on the road leading northeast out to the N331. In about 2500 or 2000 BC the local folk managed to transport dozens of huge rocks from nearby hills to construct these earth-covered tombs for their chieftains. Menga is 25m long, 4m high and composed of 32 slabs, the largest weighing 180 tonnes.

Sleeping & Eating

Parador de Antequera (☎ 952 84 02 61; www.parador.es; Paseo García del Olmo s/n; s/d €70/88; Ⓟ Ⓧ) In a quiet area north of the bullring, the *parador* is set amid pleasant gardens with a good view.

Hotel San Sebastián (☎ /fax 952 84 42 39; Plaza de San Sebastián 5; s/d €25/39; Ⓧ) You can't get much more central than the nicely refurbished San Sebastián.

Hotel Castilla (☎ 952 84 30 90; Calle Infante Don Fernando 40; s/d €25/39; Ⓧ) Also central, the Castilla has clean and comfy rooms, a lively bar and a good economical restaurant.

Restaurante La Espuela (Calle San Agustín 1; mains €6-14; ☼ closed Mon) Situated in a charming cul-de-sac off Calle Infante Don Fernando, La Espuela offers traditional dishes such as wild boar, venison and oxtail. Its *menú típico* provides a fine selection of Antequera specialities.

Getting There & Away

The **bus station** (Calle Sagrado Corazón de Jesús) is 1km north of the city centre. Twelve daily buses run to/from Málaga (€4.55, one hour), and three to five each to/from Osuna (€5.55, one hour), Seville (Prado de San Sebastián; €9.90, two hours), Granada (€6.20, 1¼ hours) and Córdoba (€7.45, 1½ hours).

The **train station** (Avenida de la Estación) is 1.5km north of the city centre. Three to five trains a day travel to/from Granada (€6.55, 1½ hours), Seville (€10.60, 1¾ hours) and Ronda (€4.95, 1¼ hours). For Málaga or Córdoba, change at Bobadilla.

AROUND ANTEQUERA
El Torcal

Nature has sculpted this 1336m **mountain**, 16km south of Antequera, into some of the weirdest, most wonderful rock formations you'll see anywhere. Its 12 sq km of gnarled, pillared and deeply fissured limestone began life as sea bed about 150 million years ago.

A 1.5km marked walking trail starts and ends near the **Centro de Recepción** (☎ 952 03 13 89; ☼ 10am-2pm & 4-6pm Jun-Oct, 10am-2pm & 3-5pm Nov-May). You need your own transport to get there: leave Antequera by the C3310 towards Villanueva de la Concepción. The El Torcal turn-off is 12km out.

Laguna de Fuente de Piedra

When not dried up by drought, this shallow lake, close to the A92, 20km northwest of Antequera, is one of Europe's two main breeding grounds for the spectacular **greater flamingo** (the other is France's Camargue). After a wet winter as many as 20,000 pairs of flamingos breed at the lake. They arrive in January or February, with the chicks hatching in April and May, and stay till about August.

The **Centro de Información Fuente de Piedra** (☎ 952 11 17 15; ☼ 10am-2pm & 4-6pm), at the lake, on the edge of Fuente de Piedra village, hires out binoculars (€1.45 for 45 minutes). Four daily buses (€0.90, 30 minutes) run between Antequera bus station and Fuente de Piedra village.

EAST OF MÁLAGA

The coast east of Málaga, sometimes called the Costa del Sol Oriental, is less developed than the coast to the west, but is striving hard to fill in the gaps.

Behind the coast, **La Axarquía**, a region dotted with white villages (of Islamic origin) linked by snaking mountain roads, climbs to the sierras along the border of Granada province. There's good walking here (best in April and May, and from mid-September to late October). Once impoverished and

JOHN NOBLE

Parque Natural de Cazorla (p786), Andalucía

CHRISTOPHER WOOD

The Patio de la Acequia (Court of the Water Channel) in the Alhambra's Generalife (p765), Granada, Andalucía

Patio de los Leones (Courtyard of the Lions, p763), with its fountain of water-spouting lions in the Palacio de los Leones in Granada's Alhambra, Andalucía

DONALD C. & PRISCILLA ALEXANDER EASTMAN

Convent ruins in Trujillo (p814), Extremadura

DUSHAN COORAY

OLIVER STREWE

Cherry-picking season in Cáceres (p809), Extremadura

The Roman Templo de Diana (p821) in Mérida, Extremadura

ESBIN ANDERSON PHOTO

forgotten, La Axarquía has experienced a surge of tourism and an influx of expat residents in recent years.

Nerja

pop 17,000

Nerja, 56km east of Málaga, is older, whiter and marginally more charming than the towns to its west, though still inundated by (mainly British) tourism. The **tourist office** (☎ 952 52 15 31; www.nerja.org; Puerta del Mar; ☺ 10am-2pm & 5.30-8.30pm Mon-Sat, 10am-2pm Sun) is just off the town's focal point, the Balcón de Europa promenade and lookout point, which has fine coastal vistas. The best beach is **Playa Burriana**, on the eastern side of town.

SLEEPING

Rooms in the better hotels tend to be booked two months in advance for the summer period.

Hotel Carabeo (☎ 952 52 54 44; www.hotelcarabeo .com; Calle Carabeo 34; d/ste incl breakfast €66/185; P ✴ ◙) This small family-run hotel is full of stylish antiques and set above manicured gardens right on the seafront.

Hostal Marissal (☎ 952 52 01 99; www.marissal.net; Balcón de Europa; s/d €45/60; ✴) Right by Balcón de Europa, the newly renovated Marissal will delight you with its soothingly clean, quiet and comfortable rooms decked with tasteful art, and a good restaurant.

Hostal Lorca (☎ 952 52 34 26; hostallorca@teleline .es; Calle Méndez Núñez 20; d €47; ◙) This charming place with spotless rooms is run by a friendly Dutch couple who have lots of local information, including details of walking routes.

Hotel Paraíso del Mar (☎ 952 52 16 21; Calle Prolongación de Carabeo; d €94; P ✴ ◙) East of the centre, the Paraíso del Mar has great sea views, spa facilities and private access to the beach.

Hostal Mena (☎ 952 52 05 41; Calle El Barrio 15; s/d €23/36.50) A short distance west of the tourist office, this hostal has immaculate rooms (some with sea views) and a pleasant garden.

EATING

Merendero Ayo (☎ 952 52 12 53; Playa Burriana; mains €5-9) One of the best feeds in town can be had at this always-busy open-air restaurant on Nerja's best beach. You can down a plate of paella, cooked on the spot in great sizzling pans, then go back for a refill.

Casa Luque (Plaza Cavana 2; mains €10) Casa Luque has a prime position on the picturesque Plaza Cavana, and a wonderfully panoramic terrace. With an elegant haute-Med menu, it has a lot more character than most Nerja eateries.

A Taste of India (☎ 952 52 00 43; Calle Carabeo 51; mains €10-12) This fantastic Goan Indian place serves delicious coconut curry cooked on the spot.

ENTERTAINMENT

Nightlife focuses on the aptly named Tutti-Frutti Plaza, with an international clutch of bars and *discotecas*. But check out what's on at the admirable **Centro Cultural Villa de Nerja** (☎ 952 52 38 63; Calle Granada 45).

GETTING THERE & AWAY

On the N340 near the top of Calle Pintada, **Alsina Graells** (☎ 952 52 15 04) runs to Málaga (€3.15, one hour, 14 daily), Almuñécar (€2.05, 25 minutes, eight daily), Almería (€12.50, 2½ hours, five daily) and Granada (€14.25, 1½ hours, three daily).

Around Nerja

The big tourist attraction is the **Cueva de Nerja** (☎ 952 52 95 20; adult/child €5/2.50; ☺ 10am-2pm & 4-6.30pm), 3km east of town and just off the N340. This enormous cavern remains very impressive, like some vast underground cathedral, despite the crowds traipsing continually through it. About 14 buses run daily there from Málaga and Nerja.

Further east the coast becomes more rugged, and with your own wheels you can head out to **Playa El Cañuelo** and other scenic, if stony, beaches that are reached by tracks down from the N340, around 8km to 10km from Nerja.

Cómpeta & Around

pop (Cómpeta) 3000 / elevation 640m

The hill village of Cómpeta, 17km inland, is a popular base for exploring La Axarquía and the mountains, although it's in danger of being overwhelmed by heavy construction traffic and estate agents, as the building boom of the *costa* spreads uncontrolled up the inland valleys. There's a **tourist office** (☎ 952 51 60 06; Avenida de la Constitución; ☺ 10am-2pm Wed-Sun) by the bus stop at the foot of the village. Three buses run daily from Málaga (€3.20, two hours) via Torre del Mar.

ANDALUCÍA

SIGHTS & ACTIVITIES

A few kilometres down the valley from Cómpeta, **Árchez** has a beautiful Almohad minaret next to its church. From Árchez a road winds 8km southwest to **Arenas**, where a steep but drivable track climbs to the ruined Islamic **Castillo de Bentomiz**, which crowns a hill top. **Los Caballos del Mosquín** (☎ 608-658108; www.caballos-mosquin.com), just outside Canillas de Albaida, 2km northwest of Cómpeta, offers horse rides in the mountains lasting from one hour to several days. If you're up for a good long walk, the most exhilarating target is the dramatically peaked **El Lucero** (1779m). From its summit, on a clear day, you can see both Granada and Morocco. This is a demanding full-day return walk from Cómpeta, but it's possible to drive as far up as Puerto Blanquillo pass (1200m) via a slightly hairy mountain track from Canillas de Albaida. From Puerto Blanquillo a path climbs 200m to another pass, Puerto de Cómpeta. One kilometre down from there, past a quarry, the summit path (1½ hours), marked by a signboard, diverges to the right across a stream bed, marked by a signboard.

SLEEPING & EATING

Hotel Balcón de Cómpeta (☎ 952 55 35 35; www.hotel-competa.com; Calle San Antonio 75; s/d €44.60/60.80; 🞰 🞰) The village's only hotel has comfortable rooms with balconies, a good restaurant, a bar, a big pool and a tennis court.

You can book houses, apartments and rooms through **Cómpeta Direct** (www.competadirect.com).

The two best restaurants, both serving excellent and varied Spanish-international food, are **El Pilón** (☎ 952 55 35 12; Calle Laberinto; mains €8-15) and **Cortijo Paco** (☎ 952 55 36 47; Avenida Canillas 6; mains €8-15). In summer ask for an upstairs terrace table at either place.

CÓRDOBA PROVINCE

The big draw here is Córdoba city, which was capital of Al-Andalus when Al-Andalus was at its zenith, and home to the famously cultured and tolerant courts of rulers such as the caliph Abd ar-Rahman III. Córdoba's Mezquita is one of the most magnificent of all Islamic buildings. Beyond the city stretches an essentially rural province with many smaller towns and some attractive hill country, producing some of Andalucía's best olive oil and wine.

CÓRDOBA

pop 319,000 / elevation 110m

Standing on a sweep of the Río Guadalquivir with countryside stretching far in every direction around, Córdoba is both provincial and sophisticated. The best time to visit is between mid-April and mid-June, when the skies are big and blue but the heat is tolerable, and the city's beautiful patios and old lanes are at their best, and dripping with foliage and blooms. This is also the season when, taking advantage of the blissful temperatures, Córdoba stages most of its major fiestas.

History

The Roman colony of Corduba, founded in 152 BC, became capital of Baetica province, covering most of today's Andalucía. This major Roman cultural centre was the birthplace of the writers Seneca and Lucan. In AD 711 Córdoba fell to the Muslim invaders and soon became the Islamic capital on the Iberian Peninsula. It was here in 756 that Abd ar-Rahman I set himself up as the emir of Al-Andalus.

Córdoba's heyday came under Abd ar-Rahman III (912–61), who in 929 named himself caliph and so set the seal on Al-Andalus' de facto independence of the Abbasid caliphs in Baghdad. Córdoba was then the biggest city in Western Europe, with a population somewhere between 100,000 and 500,000. It had dazzling mosques, patios, libraries, observatories and aqueducts, a university and highly skilled artisans in leather, metal, textiles and glazed tiles. Abd ar-Rahman III's multicultural court was frequented by Jewish, Arab and Christian scholars.

At its peak, the Córdoba caliphate encompassed most of the Iberian Peninsula south of the Río Duero, plus the Balearic Islands and some of North Africa. Córdoba became a place of pilgrimage for Muslims who could not reach Mecca or Jerusalem.

Towards the end of the 10th century, Al-Mansour (Almanzor), a fearsome general, took the reins of power and struck terror into Christian Spain with over 50 *razzias* (forays), in 20 years. When he destroyed the cathedral at Santiago de Compostela, home of the Santiago cult, he had its bells carried to Córdoba by Christian slaves and hung upside down as oil lamps in the Mezquita. But after the death of Al-Mansour's son in 1008, the caliphate descended into anarchy. Bands of Berber troops terrorised Córdoba and in 1031 the caliphate collapsed into dozens of *taifas*. Córdoba became part of the Seville *taifa* in 1069.

Its intellectual traditions, however, continued. Twelfth-century Córdoba produced two of the most celebrated of all Al-Andalus' scholars: the Muslim Averroës (Ibn Rushd) and the Jewish Maimonides, polymaths best remembered for their philosophical efforts to harmonise religious faith with reason. Córdoba's intellectual influence was still being felt in Christian Europe many centuries later.

Córdoba was captured in 1236 by Fernando III of Castile and became a provincial town of shrinking importance. The decline began to be reversed only with the coming of industry in the late 19th century.

Orientation

What fascinates visitors is the World Heritage–listed medieval city, a labyrinth of narrow streets focused on the Mezquita, which is immediately north of the Río Guadalquivir. The main square of modern Córdoba is Plaza de las Tendillas, 500m north of the Mezquita.

Information

Most banks and ATMs are around Plaza de las Tendillas and Avenida del Gran Capitán. The bus and train stations have ATMs.

Ch@t (Calle Claudio Marcelo 15; per hr €1.80; ✆ 10am-1pm & 5-9.30pm Mon-Fri, 10am-2pm Sat) Large and efficient Internet access.

Hospital Reina Sofía (☎ 957 21 70 00; Avenida de Menéndez Pidal s/n) Located 1.5km southwest of the Mezquita.

Luque Libros (Calle José Cruz Conde 19) Sells city and Michelin maps at about half the price of the tourist shops near the Mezquita.

Municipal tourist office (☎ 957 20 05 22; Plaza de Judá Leví; ✆ 8.30am-2.30pm Mon-Fri)

Pilar del Potro (Calle Lucano 12; per 30 min €1; ✆ 10am-1pm & 5-10pm) Expensive but convenient Internet access.

Policía Nacional (☎ 95 747 75 00; Avenida Doctor Fleming 2)

Post office (Calle José Cruz Conde 15)

Regional tourist office (☎ 957 47 12 35; Calle Torrijos 10; ✆ 9.30am-7pm Mon-Sat, 10am-2pm Sun,

to 8pm Mon-Sat Apr-Jul) Facing the western side of the Mezquita.

Tourist Information Booth (Train station; ✆ 10am-2pm & 4.30-8pm Mon-Fri)

Sights & Activities

Opening hours for Córdoba's sights change frequently, so check with the tourist offices for updated times. Most places (except the Mezquita) close on Monday. Closing times are generally an hour or two earlier in winter than summer.

MEZQUITA

This wonderful **mosque** (☎ 957 47 05 12; adult/child €6.50/3.25; ✆ 10am-7pm Mon-Sat Apr-Sep, 10am-5.30pm Mon-Sat Oct-May, 1.30-6.30pm Sun year-round), with its shimmering golden mosaics and rows and rows of red-and-white-striped arches disappearing off into infinity, is one of the great creations of Islamic architecture. Abd ar-Rahman I founded the Mezquita in 785 on the site of a Visigothic church that had been partitioned between Muslims and Christians, reputedly purchasing the Christian half from the Christian community. The Mezquita was Córdoba's Friday Mosque, always the most important building in an Islamic city, where men must go for prayers every Friday at noon. As Córdoba's population grew with the passing centuries, the Mezquita was enlarged and embellished by Abd ar-Rahman II in the 9th century, Al-Hakim II in the 960s, and Al-Mansour in the late 10th century. Ultimately it extended over nearly 23,000 sq metres incorporating 1293 columns (856 remain today), some of which had stood in the Visigothic church, in Roman buildings in Córdoba and elsewhere, and even in ancient Carthage.

Architecturally revolutionary, the Mezquita broke away from the verticality of earlier great Islamic buildings, such as the Great Mosque of Damascus and Jerusalem's Dome of the Rock, to recall in a unique way the open yards of desert homes that formed the original Islamic prayer spaces – in this case with a roof over the worshippers' heads, supported by a forest of columns and arches so suggestive of an oasis palm grove.

What we see today is the Mezquita's final Islamic form with two big alterations that make it harder to visualise how it used to be: a 16th-century cathedral plonked right in the middle (which explains the often-used

ANDALUCÍA

CÓRDOBA

INFORMATION
Ch@t	1 E3
Luque Libros	2 D2
Municipal Tourist Office	3 D5
Pilar del Potro	4 F4
Policía Nacional	5 C5
Post Office	6 D2
Regional Tourist Office	7 E5
Tourist Information Booth	8 A2

SIGHTS & ACTIVITIES (pp751–5)
Alcázar de los Reyes Cristianos	9 D6
Casa Andalusí	10 C5
Hammam Baños Árabes	11 E5
Islamic Water Wheel	12 E6
Mezquita	13 E5
Museo Arqueológico	14 F4
Museo de Bellas Artes	15 F4
Museo Julio Romero de Torres	(see 15)
Museo Taurino	16 D5
Patio de los Naranjos	17 E5
Puente Romano	18 E6
Puerta de Almodóvar	19 C5
Puerta del Perdón	20 D5
Roman Temple	21 E3
Sinagoga	22 C5
Torre de la Calahorra	23 F6

SLEEPING (pp755–6)
Hostal La Fuente	24 F4
Hostal Lineros	25 F4
Hostal Maestre	26 F4
Hostal Séneca	27 D5
Hotel Albucasis	28 D4
Hotel Amistad Córdoba	29 D5
Hotel González	30 D5
Hotel Lola	31 D5
Hotel Los Patios	32 D5
Hotel Maestre	33 F4
Hotel Mezquita	34 E5

EATING (pp756–7)
Almudaina	35 D5
Bodega Campos	36 F4
Casa Pepe de la Judería	37 D5
Comedor Árabe-Andalusí	38 E5
El Caballo Rojo	39 D5
El Churrasco	40 D5
Taberna Salinas	41 F3
Taberna San Miguel	42 D3

DRINKING (p757)
Bodega Guzmán	43 C5
Jazz Café	44 F3
Magister	45 D3
Milenium	46 E2
Soul	47 E3
Taberna San Miguel	(see 42)

ENTERTAINMENT (p757)
Filmoteca de Andalucía	48 D5
Gran Teatro de Córdoba	49 D3

SHOPPING (p757)
Meryan	50 E4

TRANSPORT (p757)
Bus No 3 to City Centre	51 A2
Bus No 3 to Train Station	52 E6
Bus Station	53 A2

OTHER
Autobús Turístico	54 D6
Centro de Idiomas Larcos	55 F2
Córdoba Vision	56 D5

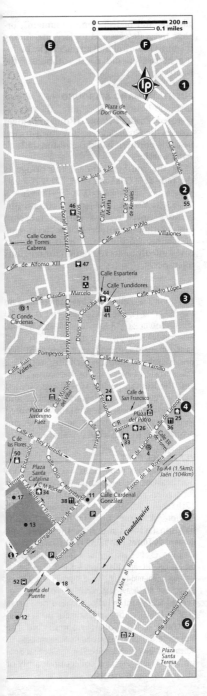

description 'Mezquita-Catedral'); and the closing of the 19 doors that communicated the Mezquita with the outside world, and would have filled it with light.

The main entrance is the **Puerta del Perdón**, a 14th-century Mudéjar gateway on Calle Cardenal Herrero, with the ticket office immediately inside. Beside the Puerta del Perdón is a 16th- and 17th-century tower built around the remains of the Mezquita's minaret. Inside the gateway is the pretty **Patio de los Naranjos** (Courtyard of the Orange Trees), originally the mosque's ablutions courtyard, from which a door leads inside the building itself.

The mihrab is visible straight ahead from the entrance door, in the far (south) wall. The first 12 east–west aisles inside the entrance, a forest of pillars and arches, comprise the original **8th-century mosque**. The columns support two tiers of arches, necessary to avoid the Mezquita having uncomfortably low ceilings.

In the centre of the building is the Christian cathedral, surrounded by Islamic aisles, pillars and arches. Just past its western end, the approach to the mihrab begins, marked by heavier, more elaborate arches. The bay immediately in front of the mihrab and the bay to each side of it form the **maksura**, where the caliphs and their retinues would have prayed (today enclosed by railings). The *maksura* and mihrab were created by Al-Hakim II in the 960s and are the most lavishly decorated sections of the Mezquita. The intricately interwoven arches of the *maksura* and its lavishly decorated domes set it apart from the rest of the Mezquita. The decoration of the **mihrab portal** incorporates 1600kg of gold mosaic cubes, a gift to the Muslim caliph Al-Hakim from the Christian emperor of Byzantium, Nicephoras II Phocas. The mosaics give this part of the Mezquita something of the mysterious aura of a Byzantine church.

Early modifications after the Mezquita was turned into a cathedral in 1236 were carried out with restraint, but in the 16th century its centre was ripped out to allow construction of a cathedral comprising the **Capilla Mayor**, now with a rich 17th-century jasper and marble *retablo*, and the **coro** (choir), with fine 18th-century carved-mahogany stalls. The forests of Islamic arches and pillars provide a magnificent setting for the Christian structures, but if you think of the building in its original terms, you've got to agree with Carlos I, who reputedly exclaimed to the church authorities: 'You have destroyed something that was unique in the world'.

JUDERÍA

Jews were among the most dynamic citizens of Islamic Córdoba, holding posts as administrators, doctors, jurists and philosophers. The medieval *judería*, extending northwest from the Mezquita almost to Avenida del Gran Capitán, is today a maze of narrow streets and small plazas, whitewashed buildings with flowery window boxes, and wrought-iron doorways giving glimpses of plant-filled patios.

The **Museo Taurino** (Bullfighting Museum; ☎ 957 20 10 56; Plaza de Maimónides; admission €3, free Fri; 10am-2pm & 4.30-6.30pm Tue-Sat Oct-Apr, 10am-2pm & 5.30-7.30pm Tue-Sat May-Jun & Sep-Oct, 8.30am-2.30pm Tue-Sat Jul-Aug, 9.30am-2.30pm Sun & holidays year-round) celebrates Córdoba's legendary *toreros*, with rooms dedicated to El Cordobés and Manolete, and even the forlorn, pegged-out hide of Islero, the bull that fatally gored the revered Manolete in 1947.

Just up Calle de los Judíos is the beautiful little 14th-century **Sinagoga** (Calle de los Judíos 20; adult/EU citizen €0.30/free; 9.30am-2pm & 3.30-5.30pm Tue-Sat, 9.30am-1.30pm Sun & holidays), one of Spain's very few surviving medieval synagogues. It retains its upstairs women's gallery, and Hebrew inscriptions and intricate Mudéjar patterns in stucco. The **Casa Andalusí** (Calle de los Judíos 12; admission €2.50; 10.30am-8pm May-Sep, 10.30am-7pm Oct-Apr) is a 12th-century house prettily decked out with exhibits relating to Córdoba's medieval Islamic culture, but also including a Roman mosaic in the cellar.

Just west of the top of Calle de los Judíos is the **Puerta de Almodóvar**, an Islamic gate in the old city walls.

ALCÁZAR DE LOS REYES CRISTIANOS

Just southwest of the Mezquita, the **Castle of the Christian Monarchs** (☎ 957 42 01 51; Campo Santo de Los Mártires s/n; admission €2, free Fri; 10am-2pm & 4.30-6.30pm Tue-Sat mid-Oct–Apr, 10am-2pm & 5.30-7.30pm Tue-Sat May-Jun & Sep–mid-Oct, 8.30am-2.30pm Tue-Sat Jul-Aug, 9.30am-2.30pm Sun & holidays year-round) began as a palace and fort for Alfonso X in the 13th century. From 1490 to 1821 the Inquisition operated from here. Its

gardens, full of fish ponds, fountains, orange trees, flowers and topiary, are among the most beautiful in Andalucía. The building houses an old royal bathhouse, the Baños Califales.

PUENTE ROMANO & AROUND

Just south of the Mezquita, the much-restored **Puente Romano** (Roman Bridge) crosses the Guadalquivir. Just downstream, near the northern bank, is a restored **Islamic water wheel**.

At the southern end of the bridge is the **Torre de la Calahorra** (☎ 957 29 39 29; Puente Romano s/n; adult/child €4/2.50; 10am-2pm & 4.30-8.30pm May-Sep, 10am-6pm Oct-Apr), a 14th-century tower with a curious museum highlighting the intellectual achievements of Islamic Córdoba and focusing rather rose-tintedly on its reputation for religious tolerance.

MUSEO ARQUEOLÓGICO

Córdoba's excellent **archaeological museum** (☎ 957 47 40 11; Plaza de Jerónimo Páez 7; adult/EU citizen €1.50/free; 3-8pm Tue, 9am-8pm Wed-Sat, 9am-3pm Sun & holidays), housed in a Renaissance mansion, provides a real insight into pre-Islamic Córdoba. A reclining stone lion takes pride of place in the Iberian section, and the Roman period is well represented with large mosaics, elegant ceramics and tinted glass bowls. The upstairs is devoted to medieval Córdoba, including a graceful bronze stag from Medina Azahara.

PLAZA DEL POTRO

This attractive, pedestrianised plaza, 400m northeast of the Mezquita, was a hang-out for traders and adventurers in the 16th and 17th centuries and is mentioned in *Don Quijote*. A former hospital houses Córdoba's most visited museum, the **Museo Julio Romero de Torres** (☎ 957 49 19 09; Plaza del Potro 1; admission €3, free Fri; 10am-2pm & 4.30-6.30pm Tue-Sat mid-Oct–Apr, 10am-2pm & 5.30-7.30pm Tue-Sat May-Jun & Sep–mid-Oct, 8.30am-2.30pm Jul-Aug, 9.30am-2.30pm Sun & holidays year-round), devoted to revered local painter Julio Romero de Torres (1880–1930), who specialised in sensual portraits of Cordoban women; and the **Museo de Bellas Artes** (Fine Arts Museum; adult/EU citizen €1.50/free; 3-8pm Tue, 9am-8pm Wed-Sat, 9am-3pm Sun & holidays), with a collection mainly of other Cordoban artists.

ROMAN TEMPLE

A ruined **Roman temple** (Calle Claudio Marcelo) has been partly restored, with 11 columns standing, east of Plaza de las Tendillas.

HAMMAM BAÑOS ÁRABES

Follow the lead of the medieval *cordobeses* (Cordobans) and indulge your senses at the recently renovated **Arab baths** (☎ 957 48 47 46; www.grupoalandalus.com; Calle Corregidor Luis de la Cerda; bath/bath & massage €12/16; ☷ 10am-noon, 2-4pm, 6-8pm & 10pm-midnight), where you pass between baths of different temperatures and can even enjoy an aromatherapy massage, some tea and a visit to the in-house bazaar. Don't forget to bring along your swimming costume.

Courses

Centro de Idiomas Larcos (☎ 957 47 11 03; www.larcos.net; Calle Manchado 9) Good private language school offering a range of Spanish courses; a typical two-week course costs €257, with two weeks in a shared apartment about €156.

Ucoidiomas (☎ 957 21 81 32; www.uco.es/webuco/ceucosa/lenguas in Spanish; Edificio de Servicios Múltiples, 5ª planta, Avenida Menéndez Pidal s/n) Part of Córdoba's university, offering monthly Spanish courses (except August) for €365, with accommodation available from €180 a month.

Festivals & Events

Spring and early summer is the chief festival time for Córdoba.

Concurso & Festival de Patios Cordobeses (Early May) – See the boxed text Córdoba's Patios (below); at the same time there's a busy cultural programme.

Feria de Mayo (Last week of May/first days of June) Ten days of party time for Córdoba, with a giant fair, concerts and bullfights.

Festival Internacional de Guitarra (Late June/early July) Two-week celebration of the guitar, with live classical, flamenco, rock, blues and more; top names play in the Alcázar gardens at night.

Sleeping

Many of Córdoba's lodgings are built around some of the city's charming patios (see the boxed text below). There are plenty of places near the Mezquita, with the cheaper ones chiefly to its east. Booking ahead during the main festivals is essential, and also worth considering any time between March and October. Prices are generally reduced from November to mid-March, and some places also cut their rates during hot July and August. Finding single rooms for a decent price is not easy.

BUDGET

Hostal Lineros (☎ 957 48 25 17; www.hostallineros38.com; Calle de Lineros 38; s/d/ste €30/49/90.15) This hostal has a great location and fantastic Islamic-inspired rooms in a Mudéjar villa. There's a *salon de té* (tearoom) in the courtyard.

Hostal Séneca (☎ /fax 957 47 32 34; Calle Conde y Luque 7; s/d incl breakfast €44/46) The charming, friendly Séneca occupies a rambling house with different-sized rooms and a marvellous pebbled patio that's filled with greenery.

Hostal La Fuente (☎ 957 48 78 27; hostallafuente@terra.es; Calle de San Fernando 51; d €45; ⓟ ⓧ) A refurbished 19th-century house, La Fuente offers compact rooms. There are courtyards

---

CÓRDOBA'S PATIOS

For centuries, Córdoba's beautiful leafy patios have provided shade during the searing heat of summer, a haven of peace and quiet, and a place to talk and entertain. They probably originated in the time of the Romans, for whom they provided a meeting place. The tradition was continued by the Arabs, with the happy addition of a central fountain; the internal courtyard was an area for women to go about family business.

In the first half of May, you'll notice 'Patio' signs in Córdoba's streets and alleys; this means that you're invited to view what is for the rest of the year hidden behind heavy wooden doors or wrought-iron gates. At this time of year, when new blooms proliferate, the patios are at their prettiest. Many patios are entered in the annual Concurso de Patios Cordobéses, a competition with prizes for the best patios. The tourist office can provide a map of patios that are open for viewing. If you don't have a lot of time, those in the vicinity of Calle de San Basilio, about 400m west of the Mezquita, are some of the best.

During the *concurso*, the patios are generally open from 5pm to midnight weekdays, and noon to midnight weekends. Entry is usually free but sometimes there's a container for donations.

for sitting in and a decent breakfast is served for €3.

Hostal Maestre (☎ 957 47 53 95; Calle Romero Barros 4; s/d €30/37) and **Hotel Maestre** (☎ 957 47 24 10; Calle Romero Barros 16; s/d €30/46; P ✗) offer a good number of pleasant rooms, set around neat patios. The hotel rooms have air-con and TV.

MID-RANGE

Hotel Lola (☎ 957 20 03 05; www.hotelconencanto lola.com; Calle Romero 3; d €108; P ✗) A truly charming family-run hotel in the *judería*. Art deco and antiques go hand in hand in the individually decorated rooms. And you can enjoy your minibar drinks up on the roof terrace, overlooking the Mezquita bell tower.

Hotel González (☎ 957 47 98 19; hotelgonzalez@wanadoo.es; Calle Manríquez 3; d €66; ✗) Once home to Córdoba's favourite artist, Julio Romero de Torres, Hotel González now has large air-con rooms. The restaurant serves up in the pretty flower-filled patio and the friendly proprietor speaks fluent English.

Hotel Los Patios (☎ 957 47 83 40; www.lospatios .net; Calle Cardenal Herrero 14; d €59; ✗) Unusually for a hotel opposite the Mezquita, Los Patios has managed to retain its character, as well as offer good value.

Hotel Albucasis (☎ /fax 957 47 86 25; Calle Buen Pastor 11; s/d €45/72; P ✗) Tucked away in the *judería*, away from the tourist circus, this quiet comfortable hotel has spotless, simply furnished rooms around a quaint courtyard.

Hotel Mezquita (☎ 957 47 55 85; hotelmezquita@wanadoo.es; Plaza Santa Catalina 1; s/d €36/69; ✗) Opposite the eastern side of the Mezquita, this hotel offers comfortable rooms in a 16th-century converted mansion.

TOP END

Hotel Amistad Córdoba (☎ 957 42 03 35; www.nh-ho teles.com; Plaza de Maimónides 3; s/d €106/130; P ✗ ▢) Occupying two 18th-century mansions with original Mudéjar patios, the Amistad is part of the modern NH chain with all the requisite facilities including babysitting.

Parador Nacional Arruzafa (☎ 957 27 59 00; www .parador.es; Avenida de la Arruzafa s/n; d €113.30; P ✗ ▨) Situated 3km north of the city centre on the site of Abd ar-Rahman I's summer palace, Córdoba's modern *parador* is set in lush gardens where Europe's first palm trees were planted.

Eating

Dishes common to most Cordoban restaurants include *salmorejo*, a very thick tomato-based gazpacho, and *rabo de toro* (oxtail stew). Fine restaurants feature recipes from Al-Andalus such as garlic soup with raisins, honeyed lamb, or meat stuffed with dates and nuts. The local tipple is wine, similar to sherry, from nearby Montilla and Moriles.

There are lots of places to eat right by the Mezquita – some expensive, some mediocre and some awful. A few better-value places are a short walk west into the *judería*. A longer walk east or north turns up further options.

Bodega Campos (☎ 957 49 75 00; Calle de Lineros 32; tapas/raciones €5/11, mains €13-19; ✗ closed Sun evening) This atmospheric winery-cum-restaurant sports huge oak barrels and its own house Montilla. The restaurant, full of swankily dressed *cordobeses*, serves up a delicious array of meals. For a cheaper but no-less enjoyable evening, try the huge plates of tapas in the bar.

Casa Pepe de la Judería (☎ 957 20 07 44; Calle Romero 1; mains €9-15) Tables are set in rooms around the little patio. Down a complimentary glass of Montilla before launching into the house specials, including Cordoban oxtails or venison fillets. Locals hang out in the bar well into the night.

El Caballo Rojo (☎ 957 47 53 75; Calle Cardenal Herrero 28; mains €10.20-17.70) The 'Red Horse' is busy, big and specialises in Mozarabic specialities from caliphal times. The upstairs terrace overlooks the Mezquita.

El Churrasco (☎ 957 29 08 19; Calle Romero 16; mains €12; ✗ closed Aug) The food is rich, the portions generous and the service attentive. Meaty dishes include *churrasco* (barbecued fillet of pork) with exotic Arabian sauce.

Almudaina (☎ 957 47 43 42; Plaza Campo Santo de los Mártires 1; mains €10-14) An elegant restaurant in a 16th-century mansion, the Almudaina serves excellent traditional food in individual dining rooms including an ivy-clad patio.

Taberna San Miguel (☎ 957 47 01 66; Plaza San Miguel 1; tapas €1.50, media-raciones €3-6; ✗ closed Sun & Aug) Córdoba prides itself on its *tabernas* – busy bars where you can usually also sit down to eat. Taberna San Miguel, going strong since 1880 and known locally as El Pisto (The Barrel), is one of the most atmospheric. You'll find a good range of dishes here and inexpensive Moriles wine ready in jugs on the bar.

Taberna Salinas (☎ 957 48 01 35; Calle Tundidores 3; tapas/raciones €2/8; ☙ closed Sun & Aug) Dating back to 1879, this large patio restaurant fills up fast, gaining a lively atmosphere.

Comedor Árabe Andalusí (Calle Alfayatas 6; bocadillos €2.80) Don't miss this treat of a place, with its dim lighting, Arabian music and mouthwatering falafel *bocadillos*.

Drinking & Entertainment

Most bars in the medieval city close around midnight. Some of Córdoba's liveliest bars, such as **Taberna San Miguel** (☎ 957 47 01 66; Plaza San Miguel 1; ☙ closed Sun & Aug) are in the newer parts of town. More youthful places come alive around midnight on Friday and Saturday.

Bodega Guzmán (Calle de los Judíos 7) Don't miss this atmospheric old-city favourite, with Montilla from the barrel.

Soul (☎ 957 49 15 80; Calle de Alfonso XIII 3; ☙ 9am or 10am-3am) Attracts a hip, arty crowd with its vanguard music.

Jazz Café (☎ 957 47 19 28; Calle Espartería s/n; ☙ 8am-late) This fabulous laid-back bar puts on regular live jazz and jam sessions.

Magister (Avenida del Gran Capitán 2) Attracts maturer drinkers with tasty beers brewed on the spot.

Milenium (Calle Alfaros 33) Popular gay haunt playing a good range of ambient house.

Gran Teatro de Córdoba (☎ 957 48 02 37; www .teatrocordoba.com in Spanish; Avenida del Gran Capitán 3) A busy programme of concerts, theatre, dance and film.

Filmoteca de Andalucía (☎ 957 47 20 18; www .cica.es/filmo; Calle Medina y Corella 5; admission €0.90) This art-house cinema regularly shows subtitled foreign films.

Shopping

Córdoba is known for its *cuero repujado* (embossed-leather) goods, silver jewellery (particularly filigree) and attractive pottery. Craft shops congregate around the Mezquita. **Meryan** (Calleja de las Flores) is the best place for embossed leather.

Getting There & Away
BUS

The **bus station** (☎ 957 40 40 40; Plaza de las Tres Culturas) is 1km northwest of Plaza de las Tendillas, behind the train station. Destinations include Seville (€8.55, 1¾ hours, 10 daily), Granada (€10.35, three hours, eight daily),

Madrid (€10.85, 4½ hours, six daily), Málaga (€10.45, 2½ hours, five daily) and Jaén (€6.70, 1½ hours, five daily).

TRAIN

Córdoba's **train station** (☎ 957 40 02 02; Avenida de América) is on the high-speed AVE line between Madrid and Seville. Rail destinations include Seville (€7 to €24, 45 to 90 minutes, 21 daily), Madrid (€26 to €48, 1¾ to 6¼ hours, 23 daily), Málaga (€14 to €19, two to three hours, nine daily), Barcelona (€48 to €76, 10½ hours, four daily) and Jaén (€7.65, 1½ hours, one daily). For Granada (€14, four hours), change at Bobadilla.

Getting Around

Bus No 3 (€1), from the street between the train and bus stations, runs to Plaza de las Tendillas and down Calle de San Fernando, east of the Mezquita. For the return trip, you can pick it up on Ronda de Isasa, just south of the Mezquita.

Taxis from the bus or train station to the Mezquita cost around €5.

For drivers, Córdoba's one-way system is nightmarish, but routes to many hotels and hostales are fairly well signposted with a 'P' if they have parking. Hotels charge about €8 to €12 per day for parking.

AROUND CÓRDOBA
Medina Azahara

In 936 Abd ar-Rahman III began the building of a magnificent new capital for his new caliphate, 8km west of Córdoba, and by 945 was able to install himself there. However his new city, **Medina Azahara** (Madinat al-Zahra; ☎ 957 32 91 30; adult/EU citizen €1.50/free; ☙ 10am-6.30pm Tue-Sat, to 8.30pm May–mid-Sep, 10am-2pm Sun), was short-lived. Between 1010 and 1013, during the caliphate's collapse, Medina Azahara was wrecked by Berber soldiers.

Though less than one-tenth of the city has been excavated, and only about a quarter of that is open to visitors, Medina Azahara is still fascinating and its rural location adds to the appeal.

The visitor route leads down to the **Dar al-Wuzara** (House of the Viziers), a substantial building with several horseshoe arches, fronted by a square garden. The path leads on downhill, with views over a ruined caliphal **mosque**, to the most impressive building, the painstakingly restored **Salón de Abd ar-Rahman**

III. This was the caliph's throne hall, with beautiful horseshoe arching and carved-stone decoration of a lavishness that was unprecedented in the Islamic world.

Medina Azahara is signposted on Avenida de Medina Azahara, which leads west out of Córdoba onto the A431. Try to visit before 11am to avoid the coaches.

A taxi costs €24 for the return trip, with one hour to view the site, or you can book a coach tour from Córdoba through many hotels, **Córdoba Vision** (☎ 957 23 17 34; Doctor Marañón 1; tours €10) or **Autobús Turístico** (☎ 902 201774; Campo Santo de los Mártires; tours €5).

GRANADA PROVINCE

No other city embodies the romance and mystery of Islamic Spain as does Granada, the final redoubt where a great civilization played out, in diminished but still splendid form, its last 2½ centuries. No other building is so imbued with the exotic aura of sensuous indulgence as the extravagant Alhambra palace. If there's one don't-miss destination in Andalucía, this is it. But Granada the province is more than Granada the city: it's the snow-capped Sierra Nevada, the highest mountain range in mainland Spain; it's the mystically beautiful Alpujarras valleys; and it's the Costa Tropical, Granada's own slice of the Mediterranean coast.

GRANADA
pop 238,000 / elevation 685m
The Alhambra palace-fortress, dominating the Granada skyline from its hill-top perch, and the fascinating, labyrinthine Albayzín, Granada's old Islamic quarter, also rising above the modern city, are highlights of a visit to Spain. But there's more than this to this city: with a large, vibrant Spanish and international student population, Granada boasts a dynamic cultural life, top-notch bars and a riotous nightlife. Its setting, with the often snow-clad Sierra Nevada as backdrop, is magnificent, and its greenness a delight in the often-parched Andalucía. Granada is a traditional hotbed of flamenco too.

History
Granada began life as an Iberian settlement in the Albayzín district. Muslim forces took over from the Visigoths in 711, with the aid

of the Jewish community around the foot of the Alhambra hill in what was called Garnata al Jahud, from which the name Granada derives; *granada* also happens to be Spanish for 'pomegranate', the fruit on the city's coat of arms.

After the fall of Córdoba (1236) and Seville (1248), Muslims sought refuge in Granada, where Mohammed ibn Yusuf ibn Nasr had recently established an independent emirate. Stretching from the Strait of Gibraltar to east of Almería, this 'Nasrid' emirate became the final remnant of Al-Andalus, ruled from the increasingly lavish Alhambra palace for 250 years. Granada became one of the richest cities in medieval Europe, flourishing with its swollen population of traders and artisans. Two centuries of artistic and scientific splendour peaked under emirs Yusuf I and Mohammed V in the 14th century.

But by the late 15th century the economy had stagnated and violent rivalry developed over the succession. One faction supported the emir, Abu al-Hasan, and his harem favourite Zoraya. The other faction backed Boabdil, Abu al-Hasan's son by his wife Aixa.

In 1482 Boabdil rebelled, setting off a confused civil war. The Christian armies that invaded the emirate that year took advantage, besieging towns and devastating the countryside, and in 1491 they finally laid siege to Granada. After eight months, Boabdil agreed to surrender the city in return for the Alpujarras valleys and 30,000 gold coins, plus political and religious freedom for his subjects. On 2 January 1492 the Catholic Monarchs, Isabel and Fernando, entered Granada ceremonially in Muslim dress. They set up court in the Alhambra for several years.

Religious persecution soon soured the scene. Jews were expelled from Spain. Persecution of Muslims led to revolts across the former emirate and eventually to their expulsion from Spain in the 17th century.

Without much of its talented populace, Granada sank into a decline that was only arrested by the interest drummed up by the Romantic movement in the 1830s. This set the stage for the restoration of Granada's Islamic heritage and the arrival of tourism.

When the Nationalists took over Granada at the start of the civil war in 1936, an estimated 4000 *granadinos* (Granadans) with left or liberal connections were killed, among them Federico García Lorca, Granada's most famous writer. Granada still has a reputation for conservatism.

Orientation

The two major central streets, Gran Vía de Colón and Calle Reyes Católicos, meet at Plaza Isabel La Católica. From here Calle Reyes Católicos runs southwest to Puerta Real, an important intersection, and northeast to Plaza Nueva. Cuesta de Gomérez leads northeast up from Plaza Nueva towards the Alhambra on its hilltop. The old Muslim district, the Albayzín, rambles over another hill that rises north of Plaza Nueva.

The bus station (northwest) and train station (west) are both out of the city centre but linked by buses.

Information

BOOKSHOPS

Cartográfica del Sur (Map pp760-1; ☎ 958 20 49 01; Calle Valle Inclán 2) To the south of the city, just off Camino de Ronda. Granada's best map shop; also good for Spanish guidebooks.

Metro (Map pp760-1; ☎ 958 26 15 65; Calle Gracia 31) Stocks an excellent range of English-language novels, guidebooks and books on Spain, plus plenty of books in French.

EMERGENCY

Policía Nacional (Map p762; ☎ 958 80 80 00; Plaza de los Campos) The most central police station

INTERNET ACCESS

Thanks to Granada's 60,000 students, Granada's Internet cafés are cheap (most €1 per hour) and open long hours daily.

Internet Elvira (Map p762; Calle de Elvira 64; per hr €1.60, students per hr €1)

N@veg@web (Map p762; Calle Reyes Católicos 55) A large prominent Internet centre, just off Plaza Isabel La Católica.

INTERNET RESOURCES

www.granada.org (In Spanish) Granada city hall's website. Good, clickable maps and a broad range of information on what to do, where to stay and so on, with plenty of links. For Tourism, click La Ciudad.

www.turismodegranada.org Good website of the provincial tourist office covering Granada City and places of interest in the province.

LAUNDRY

Lavomatique (Map pp760-1; Calle Paz 19) Wash a machine load for €5, dry it for €3.

MEDICAL SERVICES

Hospital Ruiz de Alda (☎ 958 02 00 09, 958 24 11 00; Avenida de la Constitución 100) A central hospital with good emergency facilities.

MONEY

There are plenty of banks and ATMs on Gran Vía de Colón, Plaza Isabel La Católica and Calle Reyes Católicos.

POST

Main post office (Map pp760-1; Puerta Real s/n; ☒ 8.30am-8.30pm Mon-Fri, 9.30am-2pm Sat) Often has long queues.

TOURIST INFORMATION

Provincial tourist office (Map p762; ☎ 958 24 71 28; www.turismodegranada.org; Plaza de Mariana Pineda 10; ☒ 9am-9pm Mon-Fri, 10am-2pm & 4-7pm Sat, 10am-3pm Sun May-Sep, 9am-8pm Mon-Fri, 10am-1pm Sat, 10am-3pm Sun Nov-Apr) Helpful staff; a short walk east of Puerta Real.

Regional tourist office Plaza Nueva (Map p762; ☎ 958 22 10 22; Calle Santa Ana 1; ☒ 9am-7pm Mon-Sat, 10am-2pm Sun & holidays); Alhambra (Map p764; ☎ 958 22 95 75; Ticket-office building, Avenida de Generalife s/n; ☒ 8am-7.30pm Mon-Fri, 8am-2.30pm & 4-7.30pm Sat & Sun Mar-Oct, 8am-6pm Mon-Fri, 8am-2pm & 4-6pm Sat & Sun Nov-Feb, 9am-1pm holidays) Information on all of Andalucía.

Sights & Activities

Most major sights are within walking distance of the city centre, though there are buses to save you walking uphill.

ALHAMBRA

Stretched along the top of the hill known as La Sabika, the **Alhambra** (Map p764; ☎ 902 441211; www.alhambra-patronato.es; adult/EU senior €10/5, disabled & child under 8 free, Generalife only, €5; ☒ 8.30am-8pm daily Mar-Oct, 8.30am-6pm daily Nov-Feb, closed 25 Dec & 1 Jan) is the stuff of fairy tales. From outside, its red fortress towers and walls appear plain, if imposing, rising from woods of cypress and elm, with the Sierra Nevada forming a magnificent backdrop. Inside the marvellously decorated emirs' palace, the Palacio Nazaríes (Nasrid Palace) and the Generalife gardens, you're in for a treat. Water is an art form here and

ANDALUCÍA

GRANADA

To Centro de Interpretación del Sacromonte (450m)

Camino del Sacromonte

See Alhambra Map p764

Vereda de Enmedio

Sacromonte

Cuesta del Chapiz

Cuesta los de Chinos

Paseo de los Tristes

Río Darro

Placeta Fátima

Plaza del Salvador

Pages

Plaza Larga

Camino Nuevo de San Nicolás

Albayzín

To Guadix (56km); Almería (167km)

Carretera de Murcia

To Monasterio de la Cartuja (600m); Víznar (8km); Alfacar (8km)

Calle Cruz de Arqueros

Placeta de San Miguel Bajo

Placeta Cauchiles de San Miguel

Plaza Santa Ana

Cuesta de Gomérez

Realejo

To Camping Sierra Nevada (2km); Bus Station (2km); A44; Northbound (2km); Jaén (99km)

Calle Ancha de Capuchinos

Calle San José

Plaza Nueva

Postigo de la Cuna

Jardines del Triunfo

Calle de Elvira

Plaza del Triunfo

Gran Vía de Colón

Plaza Isabel la Católica

Avenida de la Constitución

Calle San Juan de Dios

C Mano de Hierro

To Train Station (500m); Hospital Ruiz de Alda (650m); Fuente Vaqueros (17km); Airport (17km); Málaga (129km)

Calle San Jerónimo

Plaza Bib-Rambla

Plaza del Carmen

Puerta Real

Parque Fuente Nueva

Calle Duquesa

Plaza de la Trinidad

See Central Granada Map p762

Calle del Gran Capitán

Calle Buensuceso

Calle Paz

Calle Jardines

Calle San Miguel Alta

Carril del Picón

Calle Melchor Almagro

C Pintor López Mezquita

Calle Obispo Hurtado

Plaza de Gracia

Plaza Menorca

Calle Pedro Antonio de Alarcón

Camino de Ronda

Camino de Ronda

To Parque Federico García Lorca (200m); Huerta de San Vicente (400m)

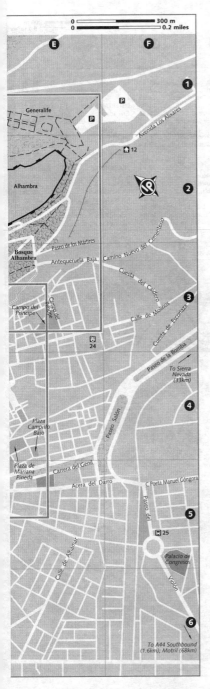

its sounds take you far from the bustle of the city.

The spell can be shattered by the average 6000 visitors who traipse through this Unesco World Heritage site each day, so try to visit first thing in the morning or late in the afternoon, or treat yourself to a magical night visit to the Palacio Nazaríes (p763 for details).

The Alhambra has two outstanding sets of buildings, the Palacio Nazaríes and the Alcazaba (Citadel). Also within its walls are the Palacio de Carlos V, the Iglesia de Santa María de la Alhambra, two hotels, several book and souvenir shops and lots of lovely gardens, including the supreme Generalife.

There's a small café by the ticket office but only the two Alhambra hotels for sit-down dining.

History

The Alhambra, from the Arabic *al-qala'at al-hamra* (red castle), was a fortress from the 9th century. The 13th-and-14th-century Nasrid emirs turned it into a fortress-palace complex adjoined by a small town *(medina),* of which only ruins remain. Yusuf I (1333–54) and Mohammed V (1354–59 and 1362–91) built the Alhambra's crowning glory, the Palacio Nazaríes.

After the Christian conquest the Alhambra's mosque was replaced with a church and the Convento de San Francisco (now the Parador de Granada) was built. Carlos I, grandson of the Catholic Monarchs, had a wing of the Palacio Nazaríes destroyed to make space for a huge Renaissance palace, the Palacio de Carlos V (using Carlos' title as Holy Roman Emperor).

In the 18th century the Alhambra was abandoned to thieves and beggars. During the Napoleonic occupation it was used as a barracks and narrowly escaped being blown up. In 1870 it was declared a national monument as a result of the huge interest stirred by Romantic writers such as Washington Irving, who wrote the entrancing *Tales of the Alhambra* in the Palacio Nazaríes during his brief stay in the 1820s. Since then the Alhambra has been salvaged and very heavily restored.

Admission

Some areas of the Alhambra can be visited at any time without a ticket, but the highlight

ANDALUCÍA

CENTRAL GRANADA

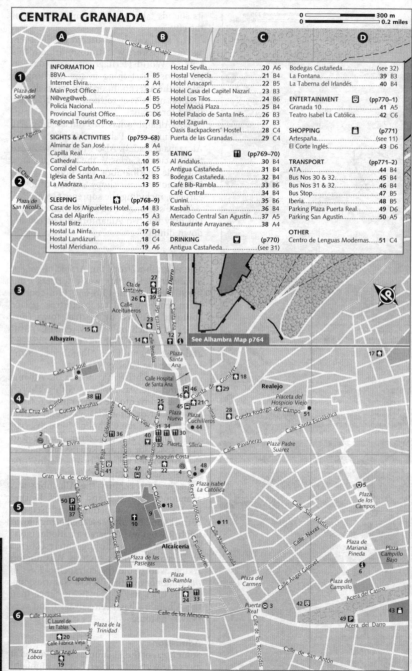

0 — 300 m
0 — 0.2 miles

INFORMATION
BBVA..1 B5
Internet Elvira................................2 A4
Main Post Office...........................3 C6
N@veg@web..................................4 B5
Policía Nacional............................5 D5
Provincial Tourist Office...............6 D6
Regional Tourist Office.................7 B3

SIGHTS & ACTIVITIES (pp759–68)
Alminar de San José.....................8 A4
Capilla Real...................................9 B5
Cathedral....................................10 B5
Corral del Carbón........................11 C5
Iglesia de Santa Ana....................12 B3
La Madraza.................................13 B5

SLEEPING (pp768–9)
Casa de los Migueletes Hotel......14 B3
Casa del Aljarife..........................15 A3
Hostal Britz.................................16 B4
Hostal La Ninfa............................17 D4
Hostal Landázuri..........................18 C4
Hostal Meridiano.........................19 A6

Hostal Sevilla...............................20 A6
Hostal Venecia.............................21 B4
Hotel Anacapri.............................22 B5
Hotel Casa del Capitel Nazarí......23 B3
Hotel Los Tilos............................24 B6
Hotel Maciá Plaza........................25 B4
Hotel Palacio de Santa Inés.........26 B3
Hotel Zaguán...............................27 B3
Oasis Backpackers' Hostel...........28 C4
Puerta de las Granadas................29 C4

EATING (pp769–70)
Al Andalus...................................30 B4
Antigua Castañeda.......................31 B4
Bodegas Castañeda......................32 B4
Café Bib-Rambla..........................33 B6
Café Central................................34 B4
Cunini..35 B6
Kasbah..36 B4
Mercado Central San Agustín......37 A5
Restaurante Arrayanes.................38 A4

DRINKING (p770)
Antigua Castañeda...............(see 31)

Bodegas Castañeda...............(see 32)
La Fontana...................................39 B3
La Taberna del Irlandés................40 B4

ENTERTAINMENT (pp770–1)
Granada 10..................................41 A5
Teatro Isabel La Católica.............42 C6

SHOPPING (p771)
Artespaña.............................(see 11)
El Corte Inglés............................43 D6

TRANSPORT (pp771–2)
ATA...44 B4
Bus Nos 30 & 32.........................45 B4
Bus Nos 31 & 32.........................46 B4
Bus Stop......................................47 B5
Iberia...48 B5
Parking Plaza Puerta Real............49 D6
Parking San Agustín.....................50 A5

OTHER
Centro de Lenguas Modernas......51 C4

areas can only be entered with a ticket. Up to 6600 tickets are available for each day. At least 2000 of these are sold at the ticket office on the day, but in Easter week, July, August and September these sell out early and you need to start queuing by 7am to be reasonably sure of getting one.

It's highly advisable to book in advance (€0.90 extra per ticket). You can book up to a year ahead, in three ways:

Alhambra website (www.alhambratickets.com) In English, Spanish and French.

Banca Telefónica BBVA (☎ 902 224460 within Spain, 00-34-91 537 91 78 from outside Spain; ⏰ 8am-5.55pm) Telephone booking service provided by BBVA bank; English speakers available.

BBVA (Plaza Isabel La Católica; ⏰ 8.30am-2.15pm Mon-Fri year-round, 8.30am-1pm Sat Oct-Mar). Book in person at any of the 4000 BBVA bank branches around Spain.

For Internet or phone bookings you need a Visa card, MasterCard or Eurocard. You receive a reference number, which you must show, along with your passport, national identity card or credit card, at the Alhambra ticket office when you pick up the ticket on the day of your visit.

Every ticket is stamped with a half-hour time slot for entry to the Palacio Nazaríes. Once inside the *palacio*, you can stay as long as you like. Each ticket is also either a *billete de mañana* (morning ticket), valid for entry to the Generalife or Alcazaba until 2pm, or a *billete de tarde*, for entry after 2pm.

The Palacio Nazaríes is also open for **night visits** (⏰ 10pm-11.30pm Tue-Sat Mar-Oct, 8pm-9.30pm Fri & Sat Nov-Feb). Tickets cost the same as daytime tickets: the ticket office opens 30 minutes before the palace's opening time, closing 30 minutes after it. You can book ahead for night visits in the same ways as for day visits.

Alcazaba

The ramparts and several towers are all that remain of the citadel. The most important is the **Torre de la Vela** (Watchtower), with a winding staircase to its top terrace, which has splendid views. The cross and banners of the Reconquista were raised here in January 1492. In the past the tower's bell rang to control the irrigation system of Granada's fertile plain, the Vega.

Palacio Nazaríes

This is the Alhambra's true gem, the most brilliant Islamic building in Europe, with its perfectly proportioned rooms and courtyards, intricately moulded stucco walls, beautiful tiling, fine carved wooden ceilings and elaborate stalactite-like *muqarnas* vaulting, all worked in mesmerising, symbolic, geometrical patterns. Arabic inscriptions proliferate in the stuccowork.

The **Mexuar**, through which you normally enter the palace, dates from the 14th century and was used as a council chamber and antechamber for audiences with the emir. The public would generally not have been allowed beyond here.

From the Mexuar you pass into the **Patio del Cuarto Dorado**, a courtyard where the emirs would give audiences, with the **Cuarto Dorado** (Golden Room) on the left. Opposite the Cuarto Dorado is the entrance to the Palacio de Comares through a beautiful façade of glazed tiles, stucco and carved wood.

Built for Emir Yusuf I, the **Palacio de Comares** served as a private residence for the ruler. It's built around the lovely **Patio de los Arrayanes** (Patio of the Myrtles) with its rectangular pool. Inside the northern **Torre de Comares** (Comares Tower), the **Sala de la Barca** (Hall of the Boat), with a beautiful inverted boat-shaped wooden ceiling, leads into the **Salón de Comares** (Comares Hall), where the emirs would have conducted negotiations with Christian emissaries. This room's marvellous domed marquetry ceiling contains more than 8000 cedar pieces in a pattern of stars representing the seven heavens of Islam.

The southern end of the patio is overshadowed by the walls of the Palacio de Carlos V.

The Patio de los Arrayanes leads into the **Palacio de los Leones** (Palace of the Lions), built under Mohammed V – by some accounts as the royal harem. The palace rooms surround the famous **Patio de los Leones** (Lion Courtyard), with its marble fountain channelling water through the mouths of 12 marble lions. The palace symbolises Islamic paradise, which is divided into four parts by rivers (represented by water channels meeting at the fountain). The patio's gallery, with beautifully ornamented pavilions at its ends, is supported by 124 slender marble columns.

Of the four halls around the patio, the southern **Sala de los Abencerrajes** is the legendary site of the murders of the noble Abencerraj family, whose leader, the story

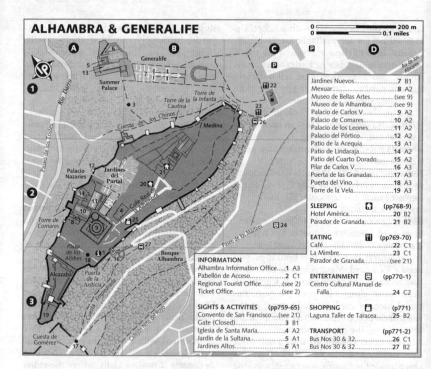

ALHAMBRA & GENERALIFE

Jardines Nuevos	7 B1
Mexuar	8 A2
Museo de Bellas Artes	(see 9)
Museo de la Alhambra	(see 9)
Palacio de Carlos V	9 A2
Palacio de Comares	10 A2
Palacio de los Leones	11 A2
Palacio del Pórtico	12 A2
Patio de la Acequia	13 A1
Patio de Lindaraja	14 A2
Patio del Cuarto Dorado	15 A2
Pilar de Carlos V	16 A3
Puerta de las Granadas	17 A3
Puerta del Vino	18 A3
Torre de la Vela	19 A3

SLEEPING	(pp768-9)
Hotel América	20 B2
Parador de Granada	21 B2

EATING	(pp769-70)
Café	22 C1
La Mimbre	23 C1
Parador de Granada	(see 21)

ENTERTAINMENT	(pp770-1)
Centro Cultural Manuel de Falla	24 C2

SHOPPING	(p771)
Laguna Taller de Taracea	25 B2

TRANSPORT	(pp771-2)
Bus Nos 30 & 32	26 C1
Bus Nos 30 & 32	27 B2

INFORMATION	
Alhambra Information Office	1 A3
Pabellón de Acceso	2 C1
Regional Tourist Office	(see 2)
Ticket Office	(see 2)

SIGHTS & ACTIVITIES	(pp759-65)
Convento de San Francisco	(see 21)
Gate (Closed)	3 B1
Iglesia de Santa María	4 A2
Jardín de la Sultana	5 A1
Jardines Altos	6 A1

goes, dared to dally with Zoraya, Abu al-Hasan's harem favourite. At the eastern end of the patio is the **Sala de los Reyes** (Hall of the Kings), with leather-lined ceilings painted by 14th-century Christian artists. The name comes from the painting on the central alcove, thought to depict 10 Nasrid emirs. On the northern side of the patio is the richly decorated **Sala de Dos Hermanas** (Hall of Two Sisters), probably named after the slabs of white marble at either side of its fountain. It features a fantastic *muqarnas* dome with a central star and 5000 tiny cells, reminiscent of the constellations. This may have been the room of the emir's favourite paramour. At its far end is the **Sala de los Ajimeces**, with low-slung windows through which the favoured lady could look over the Albayzín and countryside, while reclining on ottomans and cushions.

From the Sala de Dos Hermanas a passage leads through the **Estancias del Emperador** (Emperor's Chambers), built for Carlos I in the 1520s, some of them later used by Washington Irving. From here, descend to the **Patio de la Reja** (Patio of the Grille) and

Patio de Lindaraja and emerge into the **Jardines del Partal**, an area of terraced gardens. The small **Palacio del Pórtico**, from the time of Mohammed III (1302–09), is the oldest surviving palace in the Alhambra. Leave the Partal gardens by a gate facing the Palacio de Carlos V, or continue along a path to the Generalife.

Palacio de Carlos V

This huge Renaissance palace was begun in 1527 by Pedro Machuca, a Toledo architect, and was never completed. The imposing building is square but contains a surprising circular, two-tiered courtyard with 32 columns. Were the palace in a different setting, its merits might be more readily appreciated.

On the ground floor, the **Museo de la Alhambra** (☎ 958 02 79 00; admission free; ☿ 9am-2.30pm Tue-Sat) has a wonderfully absorbing collection of Islamic artefacts from the Alhambra, Granada province and Córdoba, with explanatory texts in English and Spanish. A highlight is the elegant **Alhambra Vase**, decorated with gazelles.

Upstairs, the **Museo de Bellas Artes** (☎ 958 22 48 43) was closed for restoration in 2004, but its impressive collection of Granada-related paintings and sculptures should remain unchanged when it reopens.

Other Christian Buildings

The **Iglesia de Santa María** was built between 1581 and 1617 on the site of the former palace mosque. The **Convento de San Francisco**, now the Parador de Granada hotel (p769), was erected over an Islamic palace. Isabel and Fernando were buried in a sepulchre in the patio before being transferred to the Capilla Real (right).

Generalife

The name Generalife means 'Architect's Garden', and this soothing composition of pathways, patios, pools, fountains, trimmed hedges, tall trees and, in season, flowers of every imaginable hue, is the perfect place to end an Alhambra visit. The Muslim rulers' summer palace is in the corner furthest from the entrance. Within the palace, the **Patio de la Acequia** (Court of the Water Channel) has a long pool framed by flowerbeds and 19th-century fountains, and whose shapes sensuously echo the arched porticos at each end. Off this patio is the **Jardín de la Sultana** (Sultana's Garden), with the trunk of a 700-year-old cypress tree, where Abu al-Hasan supposedly caught his lover, Zoraya, with the head of the Abencerraj clan, leading to the murders in the Sala de los Abencerrajes.

Getting There & Away

Bus Nos 30 and 32 both run between Plaza Nueva and the Alhambra ticket office every 5 to 9 minutes from 7.15am to 11pm.

Walking up Cuesta de Gomérez from Plaza Nueva you soon reach the **Puerta de las Granadas** (Gate of the Pomegranates), built by Carlos I. Above this are the Bosque Alhambra woods. If you already have your Alhambra ticket, you can climb the Cuesta Empedrada path up to the left and pass through the austere **Puerta de la Justicia** (Gate of Justice), constructed by Yusuf I in 1348 as the Alhambra's main entrance.

If you need to go to the ticket office, in the **Pabellón de Acceso** (Access Pavilion), continue on for about 900m from the Puerta de las Granadas. From the Pabellón de Acceso you can enter direct into the Generalife,

and move on from there to other parts of the complex.

'Alhambra' signs on the approach roads to Granada direct drivers circuitously to the Alhambra **car parks** (per hr/day €1.35/13.50) on Avenida de los Alixares, above the ticket office.

CAPILLA REAL

The **Royal Chapel** (Map p762; ☎ 958 22 92 39; www.capillareal.granada.com; Calle Oficios; admission €3; ☺ 10.30am-1pm & 4-7pm Mon-Sat 11am-1pm & 4-7pm Sun Apr-Oct, 10.30am-1pm & 3.30-6.30pm Mon-Sat 11am-1pm & 3.30-6.30pm Sun Nov-Mar, closed Good Friday), adjoining the cathedral, is Granada's most outstanding Christian building. Built in elaborate Isabelline Gothic style, it was commissioned by the Catholic Monarchs Isabel and Fernando as their mausoleum, but not completed until 1521 – hence their temporary interment in the Convento de San Francisco.

The monarchs lie in simple lead coffins in the crypt beneath their marble monuments in the chancel, which is enclosed by a stunning gilded wrought-iron screen created in 1520 by Bartolomé de Jaén. The coffins, from left to right, are those of Felipe El Hermoso (Philip the Handsome, husband of the monarchs' daughter Juana la Loca), Fernando, Isabel, Juana la Loca (Joanna the Mad) and Miguel, the eldest grandchild of Isabel and Fernando. The marble effigies of the first four, reclining above the crypt, were a tribute by Carlos I to his parents and grandparents. The representations of Isabel and Fernando are slightly lower than those of Felipe and Juana, apparently because Felipe was the son of the Holy Roman emperor, Maximilian. On the dense Plateresque *retablo,* note the kneeling figures of Isabel (lower right) and Fernando (lower left), attributed to Diego de Siloé, and the brightly painted bas-reliefs below depicting the defeat of the Muslims and subsequent conversions to Christianity.

The sacristy contains a small but impressive **museum** with Fernando's sword and Isabel's sceptre, silver crown and personal art collection, which is mainly Flemish, but does include Botticelli's *Prayer in the Garden of Olives.* Also here are two fine statues of the Catholic Monarchs at prayer by Vigarni.

CATHEDRAL

Adjoining the Capilla Real but entered separately, from Gran Vía de Colón, the cavernous Gothic-Renaissance **cathedral** (Map p762; ☎ 958 22 29 59; admission €2.50; ☺ 10.45am-1.30pm & 4-8pm Mon-Sat 4-8pm Sun Apr-Oct, 10.45am-1.30pm & 4-7pm Mon-Sat 4-7pm Sun Nov-Mar) was begun in 1521, and directed by Diego de Siloé from 1528 to 1563. Work was not completed until the 18th century. The main façade on Plaza de las Pasiegas, with four heavy buttresses forming three great arched bays, was designed in the 17th century by Alonso Cano.

In the gilded and painted Capilla Mayor (de Siloé's work), spot the 17th-century carvings of the Catholic Monarchs at prayer, one above each side of the main altar, by Pedro de Mena. Above the monarchs are busts of Adam and Eve by Cano.

LA MADRAZA   Map p762
Opposite the Capilla Real remains part of the old Islamic university, La Madraza – now with a painted baroque façade, but retaining an octagonal domed prayer room with stucco lacework and pretty tiles. Today the building is part of the university: feel free to look inside whenever it's open.

ALCAICERÍA & PLAZA
BIB-RAMBLA   Map p762
Just south of the Capilla Real, the **Alcaicería** was the Muslim silk exchange, but what you see now is a restoration after a 19th-century fire, filled with tourist shops. Just southwest of the Alcaicería is the large, popular **Plaza Bib-Rambla** with restaurants, flower stalls and a central fountain with statues of giants. This square has been the scene of jousting, bullfights and Inquisition burnings.

CORRAL DEL CARBÓN
You can't miss the lovely Islamic façade with its elaborate horseshoe arch of this **building** (Map p762; Calle Mariana Pineda), which began life as a 14th-century inn for merchants. It was later used as an inn for coal dealers (hence its modern name, meaning Coal Yard) and subsequently a theatre. Today it's under restoration. Hitherto it has housed government offices and the government-run crafts shop, Artespaña.

ALBAYZÍN
A wander round the hilly streets and fascinating alleys of Granada's old Muslim quarter, the Albayzín, on the hill facing the Alhambra across the Darro valley, is a must. The Albayzín's name derives from 1227, when Muslims from Baeza (Jaén province) moved here after their city was conquered by the Christians. It survived as the Muslim quarter for several decades after the Christian conquest in 1492. Islamic ramparts, houses and fountains remain, and many of the Albayzín's churches and *cármenes* (large walled villas with gardens) incorporate Islamic remains. Stay on the more major streets after dark.

Bus Nos 31 and 32 both run circular routes from Plaza Nueva around the Albayzín about every seven to nine minutes from 7.30am to 11pm or later.

Walking Tour
Plaza Nueva extends northeast into Plaza Santa Ana, where the **Iglesia de Santa Ana (1)** has a mosque's minaret in its belltower. Along narrow Carrera del Darro, have a look at the 11th-century Muslim bathhouse, the **Baños Árabes El Bañuelo** (2; Map pp760-1; ☎ 958 02 78 00; Carrera del Darro 31; admission free; ☺ 10am-2pm Tue-Sat). Further along is the **Museo Arqueológico** (3; Archaeological Museum; Map pp760-1; ☎ 958 22 56 40; Carrera del Darro 43; adult/EU citizen €1.50/free; ☺ 3-8pm Tue, 9am-8pm Wed-Sat, 9am-2.30pm Sun), displaying finds from Granada province. It's curious to find ancient

---

WALKING TOUR

Distance 5.5km
Duration 4-5 hours including stops

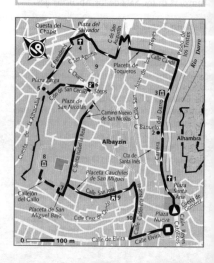

Egyptian amulets (brought by the Phoenicians) so far from home.

Shortly past the museum, Carrera del Darro becomes Paseo de los Tristes. Turn up Calle Candil and climb, via Placeta de Toqueros and Carril de San Agustín, to Plaza del Salvador, near the top of the Albayzín. Plaza del Salvador is dominated by the **Colegiata del Salvador** (4; Map pp760-1; ☎ 958 27 86 44; admission €0.75; ☑ 10am-1pm & 4pm-7.30pm Mon-Sat Apr-Oct, 10.30am-12.30pm & 4.30-6.30pm Mon-Sat Nov-Mar), a 16th-century church on the site of the Albayzín's main mosque, with the mosque's horseshoe-arched patio surviving at its western end. From here head west to Plaza Larga, and go through the **Arco de las Pesas (5)**, an impressive gateway in the Albayzín's 11th-century defensive wall, and turn left along Callejón de San Cecilio. This leads to the **Mirador San Nicolás (6)**, a lookout with unbeatable, fantastic views of the Alhambra and Sierra Nevada. You might like to come back here later for sunset (you can't miss the trail then!) – at any time of day take care: skilful, well-organised wallet-lifters and bag-snatchers operate here.

Take the steps down beside the lookout, turn right and follow the street down to Camino Nuevo de San Nicolás. Turn right and head downhill to **Placeta de San Miguel Bajo (7)**, with its funky café-restaurants. Leave the square by Callejón del Gallo, turn right at the end of this short lane, and you'll come to the 15th-century **Palacio de Dar-al-Horra** (8; Callejón de las Monjas s/n; admission free; ☑ 10am-2pm Mon-Fri), the abode of the mother of Granada's last Muslim ruler, Boabdil, and like a mini-Alhambra.

Return to Placeta de San Miguel Bajo and head down Placeta Cauchiles de San Miguel, which becomes Calle San José, where the lovely little **Alminar de San José (9**; San José Minaret) survives from an 11th-century mosque. Calle San José meets the top of **Calle Calderería Nueva (10)**, which is lined by *teterías* (Middle Eastern–style teahouses) and craft shops. Stop for an *infusión* or head on back to Plaza Nueva.

MONASTERIO DE SAN JERÓNIMO

This 16th-century **monastery** (Map pp760-1; ☎ 958 27 93 37; Calle Rector López Argueta 9; admission €3; ☑ 10am-1.30pm & 4-7.30pm Apr-Oct, 10am-1.30pm & 3-6.30pm Nov-Mar), 500m west of the cathedral, is the burial place of El Gran Capitán

(the Great Captain), Gonzalo Fernández de Córdoba, the military right-hand man of the Catholic Monarchs. It's a treat for lovers of Gothic and Renaissance architecture, and stone carving. Don't miss the two lovely Platesresque doorways in the cloister, carved by the chief architect, Diego de Siloé, or the profusion of brightly painted sculpture inside the monastery church. El Gran Capitán's tombstone is at the foot of the steps before the altar.

MONASTERIO DE LA CARTUJA

Another architectural gem stands 2km northwest of the city centre and is reached by bus No 8 from Gran Vía de Colón. La Cartuja Monastery (☎ 958 16 19 32; Paseo de la Cartuja; admission €3; ☑ 10am-1pm & 4-8pm Mon-Sat 10am-noon & 4-8pm Sun Apr-Oct, 10am-1pm & 3.30-6pm Mon-Sat 10am-noon & 3.30-6pm Sun Nov-Mar) was built between the 16th and 18th centuries. People come to see the lavish monastery church, especially the *sagrario* (sanctuary) behind the main altar, a confection of coloured marbles, golden capitals, profuse sculpture and a beautiful frescoed cupola; and, to the left of the main altar, the *sacristía* (sacristy), the ultimate expression of Spanish late-baroque, in effusive 'wedding-cake' stucco, and brown-and-white Lanjarón marble, resembling a melange of chocolate mousse and cream.

HUERTA DE SAN VICENTE

This **house** (☎ 958 25 84 66; Calle Virgen Blanca s/n; admission €1.80, free Wed; admission only by guided tour in Spanish every 45 min; ☑ 10am-12.30pm & 4-7pm Tue-Sun Oct-Mar, 10am-1pm & 5-8pm Apr-Jun, 10am-3pm Jul-Aug), where Federico García Lorca spent summers and wrote some of his best-known works, is a 15-minute walk south of the city centre. It was once surrounded by orchards. Today the modern **Parque Federico García Lorca** separates it from whizzing traffic.

The house contains some original furnishings, including Lorca's writing desk and piano, some of his drawings and other memorabilia, and exhibitions connected with his life and work. To get there, head 700m down Calle de las Recogidas from Puerta Real, turn right along Calle del Arabial, then take the first left into Calle Virgen Blanca.

Courses

Granada is a great place to study Spanish. It also has several schools of Spanish dance.

The provincial tourist office has lists of schools, or check out www.granadaspanish.org and www.spanishcourses.info.

Centro de Lenguas Modernas (Modern Languages Centre; Map p762; ☎ 958 21 56 60; www.clm-granada.com; Placeta del Hospicio Viejo s/n) Granada University's modern-language department offers a variety of popular Spanish-language and culture programmes. Intensive language courses, at all levels, start at 10 days (40 hours of classes) for €328.

Escuela Carmen de las Cuevas (Map pp760-1; ☎ 958 22 10 62; www.carmencuevas.com; Cuesta de los Chinos 15, Sacromonte) This private school gets good reports. It teaches Spanish language and culture, and flamenco dance and guitar. A 2-week intensive language course (30 hours) costs €273.

Tours

Granavisión (☎ 958 53 58 72) Offers guided tours of the Alhambra and Generalife (€38) and Historic Granada tours (€43). Phone direct or book through a travel agent.

City Sightseeing Granada (☎ 902 101081) Operates Granada's double-decker city tour bus. It has 15 stops outside the main sights. You hop on and off where you like; the ticket (€10) is valid for 24 hours.

Festivals & Events

Semana Santa (Holy Week) This, and Feria de Corpus Christi, are the big two. Benches are set up in Plaza del Carmen to view the Semana Santa processions.

Día de la Cruz (Day of the Cross; 3 May) Squares, patios and balconies are adorned with floral crosses (Cruces de Mayo). These become the focus for typical *andaluz* revelry – drinking, horse riding, polka-dot dresses and *sevillanas* (traditional Andalucian dances with high, twirling arm movements).

Feria de Corpus Christi (Corpus Christi Fair; late May 2005, mid-June 2006) Features fairgrounds, bullfights, more drinking and *sevillanas*.

Festival Internacional de Música y Danza (2½ weeks from late June to early July) Features mainly classical performances, some free, many in historic locations.

Sleeping

Granada is almost oversupplied with hotels – the ones reviewed here are just a tiny selection. However, it's definitely worthwhile booking ahead from March to October, and especially during Semana Santa and Christmas.

BUDGET

At busy times, prime-location rooms tend to fill up before noon, especially on Cuesta de Gomérez.

Plaza Nueva & Around   Map p762

Oasis Backpackers' Hostel (☎ 958 21 58 48; reservation@oasisgranada.com; Cuesta Rodrigo del Campo 13; dm €16.70; 🖵) This top-notch rest stop is designed for serious backpackers. Word spreads fast, so book ahead to enjoy its little luxuries: happy staff, free Internet access, a rooftop terrace, personal safes, tapas tours and a tip-top central location.

Hostal Landázuri (☎ /fax 958 22 14 06; Cuesta de Gomérez 24; s with/without bathroom €28/20 d €45/28, tr/q with bathroom €50/60; P) This folksy place boasts a terrace with Alhambra views. The rooms have been updated and the triples are large, bright and comfortable. There's a 1am curfew.

Hostal Britz (☎ /fax 958 22 36 52; Cuesta de Gomérez 1; s with/without bathroom €32/19 d €42/29) Friendly, efficient Britz has clean, good-sized rooms with central heating. There's a lift.

Hostal Venecia (☎ 958 22 39 87; trevisovenecia@jazzfree.com; Cuesta de Gomérez 2; r €32; s/d/tr/q without bathroom €15/28/39/52) An exceptionally welcoming place, whose owners bring you a soothing herbal drink each morning.

Plaza de la Trinidad & Around   Map p762

Hostal Meridiano (☎ /fax 958 25 05 44; hostalmeridiano@telefonica.net; Calle Angulo 9; r €37, s/d without bathroom €18/30, 4-/6-person apt €35/40; P 🐾 🖵) This modernised former student residence is run by a helpful couple, who are tuned in to travellers' needs. Six of the attractive rooms have bathrooms; there's also free Internet.

Hostal Sevilla (☎ 958 27 85 13; Calle Fábrica Vieja 18; r €32, s/d without bathroom €16/25) This friendly, clean hostal, run by a young family, has some attractive tilework and lampshades.

CAMPING

Camping Sierra Nevada (☎ 958 15 00 62; Avenida de Madrid 107; camping per adult/tent/car €4.80/5.45/5.45; 🐾) Just a short walk from the bus station, 2.5km northwest of the centre, this camping ground has big clean bathrooms and a laundrette. Bus No 3 runs between here and the centre.

MID-RANGE

Hotel América (Map p764; ☎ 958 22 74 71; www.hotelamericagranada.com; Calle Real de la Alhambra 53; s/d €70/106; 🏵 Mar-Nov; 🐾) Within the Alhambra grounds, this is in an early 19th-century building. Reserve well in advance, as there is a limited number of rooms.

Hotel Guadalupe (Map pp760-1; ☎ 958 22 34 23; www.hotelguadalupe.es; Avenida Los Alixares s/n; s/d €76/104; ⓟ ❊) Almost on the Alhambra's doorstep, the Guadalupe has spacious, beautifully fitted-out rooms with Alhambra or olive-grove views.

Puerta de las Granadas (Map p762; ☎ 958 21 62 30; www.hotelpuertadelasgranadas.com; Calle Cuesta de Gomérez 14; s/d €72/90, superior r €100-180; ❊ 💻) This 19th-century building, renovated in a modern minimalist style, has wooden shutters and elegant furnishings. The more-expensive luxury rooms have Alhambra or cathedral views.

Hostal La Ninfa (Map p762; ☎ 958 22 79 85; Campo del Príncipe s/n; s/d €45/65; ❊) A rustic place covered in brightly painted ceramic stars, both outside and in, it has clean, cosy rooms and friendly owners.

There are hotels in beautiful renovated Albayzín mansions.

Hotel Casa del Capitel Nazarí (Map p762; ☎ 958 21 52 60; www.hotelcasacapitel.com; Cuesta Aceituneros 6; s/d €73/91; ❊ 💻) Quiet décor and ambience, focussing on a 16th-century patio with wooden balconies and ancient pillars.

Casa del Aljarife (Map p762; ☎/fax 958 22 24 25; www.granadainfo.com/most; Placeta de la Cruz Verde 2; r €95; ❊) Beautifully restored 17th-century house has helpful hosts, just four spacious and characterful rooms, and an outdoor patio.

Hotel Zaguán (Map p762; ☎ 958 21 57 30; www.hotelzaguan.com; Carrera del Darro; s €50, r €64-100; ❊ 💻) Restored 16th-century Albayzín house, which was almost a complete ruin. The rooms, some fronting the Río Darro, are all different.

These are good city-centre hotels:

Hotel Anacapri (Map p762; ☎ 958 22 74 77; www.hotelanacapri.com; Calle Joaquín Costa 7; s/d €78/105; ❊) The Anacapri has pretty rooms with floral bedspreads, cork floors and satellite TV. Its friendly reception is in an attractive 18th-century patio which is fitted out with cane chairs and palm trees.

Hotel Maciá Plaza (Map p762; ☎ 958 22 75 36; www.maciahoteles.com; Plaza Nueva 4; s/d €50/73; ⓟ ❊ 💻) One of four Maciá hotels in Granada, the Maciá Plaza has comfortable rooms with bright-enough décor but its top location is its major drawcard. Try for a double overlooking the plaza.

Hotel Los Tilos (Map p762; ☎ 958 26 67 12; Plaza Bib-Rambla 4; s/d €41/65; ❊) The Los Tilos offers further comfortable rooms with the doubles at least being a good size. Some rooms overlook the characterful plaza and there's a small roof terrace.

TOP END

Parador de Granada (Map p764; ☎ 958 22 14 40; www.parador.es; Calle Real de la Alhambra s/n; s/d €182/228; ⓟ ❊) The most expensive *parador* in Spain can't be beaten for its location within the Alhambra and its historical connections. Book ahead.

The small hotels in renovated 15th-to-17th-century Albayzín mansions in this price bracket are sumptuous:

Casa de los Migueletes Hotel (Map p762; ☎ 958 21 07 00; www.casamigueletes.com; Calle Benalúa 11; r €129-499; ❊ 💻 ✖) This gorgeous, elegant hotel retains an interior patio with carefully restored wooden balconies. It has some surprising views.

Casa Morisca Hotel (Map p760-1; ☎ 958 22 11 00; www.hotelcasamorisca.com; Cuesta de la Victoria 9; interior s/d €90/119, exterior €120/150; ❊) Occupies a late-15th-century mansion, with atmospheric rooms, centred on a patio with an ornamental pool and wooden galleries.

Hotel Palacio de Santa Inés (Map p762; ☎ 958 22 23 62; www.palaciosantaines.com; Cuesta de Santa Inés 9; r €80-105, ste €128-225; ❊) Some of the highly attractive rooms have original Islamic décor and all have wonderful bathrooms. Reception is installed in the Renaissance patio. Park first and walk, or take a cab.

Eating

With tapas bars and restaurants teeming with life, it's clear that food is a highlight of any visit. Free tapas are available in many bars at night. Hearty local dishes include the typical *rabo de toro* (oxtail stew), *habas con jamón* (broad beans with ham) and *tortilla Sacromonte*, a tasty omelette (traditionally made with calf brains and bull testicles!).

NEAR PLAZA NUEVA Map p762

Café Central (☎ 958 22 97 06; Calle de Elvira; tapas €1.95, raciones €4.20-8.50) Perk up with a strong morning coffee (€1.60) at this no-nonsense café opposite Plaza Nueva.

Al Andalus (☎ 958 22 67 30; Calle de Elvira; mains €3-6) Scurry off with a neatly wrapped parcel of falafel in pitta (€3) from Al Andalus and indulge in an Arabic fast-food feast.

Delicious food in a more *típico* setting can be had at the back-to-back **Bodegas Castañeda** (Calle Almireceros) and **Antigua Castañeda** (Calle de Elvira). Both have tapas for between €1.20 and €1.80, and a variety of more-substantial offerings. At Bodegas, try the filling *tortilla* *española* (Spanish omelette) or a *tabla* piled with cheeses and meats. The Antigua does delicious *montaditos* (open sandwiches with toppings such as smoked salmon with avocado and caviar) for €1.95, and both bars have barrels of potent *costa* wine from the Sierra de la Contraviesa.

For fresh fruit and veg, head for the large covered **Mercado Central San Agustín** (Calle San Agustín; 8am-2pm Mon-Sat), a block west of the cathedral.

ALHAMBRA   Map p764
Parador de Granada (958 22 14 40; Calle Real de Alhambra s/n; 11am-11pm; sandwiches from €5.05) The effortlessly charming Parador de Granada has a swanky restaurant and a terrace bar, where you can contemplate the Alhambra's magnificence.

La Mimbre (958 22 22 76; Cnr Paseo del Generalife & Cuesta de los Chinos; *menú turístico* €17.50) Positioned under the sheer walls of the Alhambra, La Mimbre has outdoor tables in a leafy garden.

ALBAYZÍN
The labyrinthine Albayzín holds a wealth of eateries. Find one with a terrace and be rewarded with mesmerising Alhambra views. Calle Calderería Nueva is a muddle of *teterías* and Arabic-influenced takeaways.

Terraza las Tomasas (Map pp760-1; 958 22 41 08; Carril de San Agustín 4; mains €16-20; lunch Mon-Tue, lunch & dinner Wed-Sat) Ring the little bell, descend the stairs and be awed by the Alhambra views in this classy restaurant. Service is impeccable and the food commendable.

El Agua (Map pp760-1; 958 22 33 58; Plaza Aljibe de Trillo 7; fondues per person, minimum 2 €13.95-18.80; lunch & dinner Wed-Mon, dinner Tue) Wild fondue feasts are the mainstay of this first-rate restaurant, which also offers fabulous views of the Alhambra.

Restaurante Arrayanes (Map p762; 958 22 84 01; Cuesta Marañas 4; mains €7-17; from 8pm) This much-applauded Moroccan favourite cooks up a delicious lamb *tajine* with prunes and almonds (€10) in authentic surrounds. Also authentic – no alcohol!

Kasbah (Map p762; Calle Calderería Nueva 4; tea €1.80-2.40) Duck into this candlelit tea den and absorb the aroma of incense and herbal infusions. Select your tea and maybe try a calorie-laden chocolate-and-cream crepe (€2.30).

PLAZA BIB RAMBLA & AROUND
Café Bib-Rambla (Map p762; 958 71 00 76; Plaza Bib-Rambla 3; mains from €8.00) Fragrant flower stalls and no traffic make pedestrianised Plaza Bib-Rambla a peaceful option for alfresco dining. Pick a pew at this café and opt for a fluffy *tortilla española* (€9.50).

Cunini (Map p762; 958 25 07 77; Plaza de Pescadería 14; menú del día €17.85) The terrace at this swanky seafood restaurant buzzes with the sound of clanking cutlery and chatty diners with deepish pockets.

Poë (Map pp760-1; Calle Paz; drink & tapa €1.50) Hearty free tapas dishes, such as chicken stew with polenta, are served in small earthenware bowls at this trendy bar.

Om-Kalsum (Map pp760-1; Calle Jardines 17; drink & tapa €1.80) Decamp from Poë to Om-Kalsum in a flash and start on the Arabic-influenced tapas served here. All the dishes are unbelievably good and they're free.

Drinking
Granada buzzes with heel-clicking flamenco dancers, bottle-clinking travellers and grooving students out on the pull. The best street for drinking is Calle Elvira but other chilled bars line the Río Darro at the base of the Albayzín.

Bodegas Castañeda (Calle Almireceros) and **Antigua Castañeda** (Calle de Elvira) are the most inviting, with swaying crowds and slopping drinks. Other entertaining bars can be found on Placeta Sillería and Calle Joaquín Costa.

La Taberna del Irlandés (Map p762; Calle Almireceros) This hybrid Spanish/Irish bar melds local tipples with international flavours. Whether you choose Tetley's Bitter or *costa* wine, you're likely to leave legless.

Café Bar Elvira (Map pp760-1; Calle de Elvira 85; from noon) Every man and his dog packs into this trendy joint, where spirit measures are large and mixers are splashed almost everywhere.

La Fontana (Map p762; Carrera del Darro 19; from noon) Huddle around the pool table and listen to rock ballads at this popular joint, opposite the first bridge over the Río Darro, with the Alhambra looming above.

Entertainment
The excellent monthly *Guía de Granada* (€0.85), available from kiosks, lists entertainment venues and places to eat, including tapas bars.

CLUBS & DISCOS

Look out for posters and leaflets around town advertising live music and nontouristy flamenco. The biweekly flyer *Yuzin* lists many live-music venues, some of which also double as dance clubs where DJs spin the latest tracks.

Granada 10 (Map p762; Calle Cárcel Baja; admission €6; ☼ from midnight) Stay wide awake with a riotous bunch late into the night at the ever-popular Granada 10. The added appeal, apart from the skimpy outfits, is that it's housed inside a plush cinema.

Planta Baja (Map pp760-1; Calle Horno de Abad 11; ☼ 12.30-6am Tue-Sat) Deprived acid-jazz and lounge lovers can indulge in a well-needed music fix here. Catch DJ Toner and DJ Vadim going back to the old school with their hip-hop and funk sessions too.

Morgan (Map pp760-1; Calle Obispo Hurtado 15; ☼ from 1am Tue-Sat) House-hunters can find what they're looking for at Morgan, where deep house, funky house and soulful house spar on the decks.

El Camborio (Map pp760-1; ☎ 958 22 12 15; Camino del Sacromonte 47; admission €6; ☼ from 11pm weekends) Mixing modern sounds with prehistoric surroundings, El Camborio has two dance floors, one of them at cave level.

FLAMENCO

El Eshavira (Map pp760-1; ☎ 958 29 08 29; Postigo de la Cuna 2; www.eshavira.com; ☼ from 10pm) Duck down the spooky alley, off Calle Azacayas, to this dark, smoky haunt of sultry flamenco and cool jazz.

Peña de la Platería (Map pp760-1; ☎ 958 21 06 50; Placeta de Toqueros 7) Buried deep in the Albayzín warren, Peña de la Platería is a popular flamenco haunt with a large outdoor patio. Catch a 9.30pm performance on Thursday or Saturday.

The Sacromonte caves harbour a string of touristy flamenco haunts for which you can pre-book through hotels and travel agencies. Some of them even offer free transport. Try the Friday or Saturday midnight shows at **Los Tarantos** (Map pp760-1; ☎ 958 22 45 25 day, 958 22 24 92 night; Camino del Sacromonte 9; admission €21) for a lively experience.

Flamenco dancers and singers also perform in some of Granada's more highbrow venues, such as the Teatro Isabel le Católica (Map p762; see Other Entertainment, opposite).

OTHER ENTERTAINMENT

The foyer of **La Madraza** (Calle Oficios), opposite the Capilla Real, has large posters listing forthcoming cultural events.

Centro Cultural Manuel de Falla (Map p764; ☎ 958 22 00 22; Paseo de los Mártires s/n) A haven for classical-musical lovers, this venue near the Alhambra presents weekly orchestral concerts.

Teatro Alhambra (Map pp760-1; ☎ 958 22 04 47; Calle de Molinos 56) and the more central **Teatro Isabel La Católica** (Map p762; ☎ 958 22 15 14; Acera del Casino) have ongoing programmes of theatre and concerts (sometimes flamenco).

Shopping

A distinctive local craft is *taracea* (marquetry), used on boxes, tables, chess sets and more – the best have shell, silver or mother-of-pearl inlays. Marquetry experts can be seen at work in **Laguna Taller de Taracea** (Map p764) opposite the Iglesia de Santa María in the Alhambra. Other *granadino* crafts include embossed leather, guitars, wrought iron, brass and copper ware, basket weaving, textiles and, of course, pottery. Look out for Granada handicrafts in the Alcaicería, the Albayzín and on Cuesta de Gomérez. Also try the government-run **Artespaña** (Map p762) in the Corral del Carbón.

The Plaza Nueva area is awash with jewellery vendors, selling from rugs laid out on the pavement, and ethnic-clothing shops.

For general shopping, trendy clothes and ever-delightful Spanish shoes, try pedestrianised Calle de los Mesones or **El Corte Inglés** (Map p762; Acera del Darro).

Getting There & Away

AIR

Iberia (Map p762; ☎ 958 22 75 92; Plaza Isabel La Católica 2) flies daily to/from Madrid and Barcelona.

BUS

Granada's **bus station** (Carretera de Jaén) is nearly 3km northwest of the city centre. All services operate from here, except those going to a few nearby destinations, such as Fuente Vaqueros (p772). **Alsina Graells** (☎ 958 18 54 80) runs to Córdoba (€10.65, three hours direct, nine daily), Seville (€16.45, three hours direct, 10 daily), Málaga (€8.30, 1½ hours direct, 16 daily), Las Alpujarras (p776 for details), Guadix (€4.05, one hour, up to 14 daily), Baza (€7.15, two hours, up to eight daily) and Mojácar (€14.65, four hours, two daily).

Alsina also handles buses to destinations in Jaén province and on the Granada, Málaga and Almería coasts, and to Madrid (€13.40, five to six hours, 10 to 13 daily).

Alsa (☎ 902 422242; www.alsa.es) operates buses up the Mediterranean coast as far as Barcelona (€58.10 to €69.35, seven to 10 hours, five daily) and to many international destinations too.

CAR

Car rental is expensive. **ATA** (Map p762; ☎ 958 22 40 04; Plaza Cuchilleros 1) has small cars for €71/83/219 for one/two/seven days.

TRAIN

The **train station** (☎ 958 20 40 00; Avenida de Andaluces) is 1.5km west of the centre, off Avenida de la Constitución. Four trains run daily to/from Seville (€17.65, three hours) and Almería (€11.80, 2¼ hours) via Guadix, and six to/from Antequera (€5.85 to €6.55, 1½ hours). Three go to Ronda (€10.50, three hours) and Algeciras (€15.75, 4½ hours). For Málaga (€12, 2½ hours) or Córdoba (€14, four hours) take an Algeciras train and change at Bobadilla (€7, 1½ hours). Five trains go to Linares-Baeza daily (€9.45 to €18, three hours), and one or two each go to Madrid (€28.50 to €45, six hours), Valencia (€40 to €62, 7½ to eight hours) and Barcelona (€49 to €125, 12 to 14½ hours).

Getting Around
TO/FROM THE AIRPORT

The **airport** (☎ 958 24 52 23) is 17km west of the city on the A92. **Autocares J González** (☎ 958 13 13 09) runs buses between the airport and a stop near the Palacio de Congresos (€3, five daily), with a stop in the city centre on Gran Vía de Colón, where a schedule is posted at the outbound stop, opposite the cathedral. A taxi costs between €18 and €20.

BUS

City buses cost €0.90. Tourist offices give out a leaflet showing routes. Bus No 3 runs between the bus station and Gran Vía de Colón in the city centre. To reach the city centre from the train station, walk ahead to Avenida de la Constitución and pick up bus No 4, 6, 7, 9 or 11 going to the right (east).

CAR & MOTORCYCLE

Vehicle access to the Plaza Nueva area is restricted by red lights and little black posts known as *pilonas*, which block certain streets during certain times of the day. If you are going to stay at a hotel near Plaza Nueva, press the button next to your hotel's name beside the *pilonas* to contact reception, which will be able to lower the *pilonas* for you.

Many hotels, especially in the mid-range and above, have their own parking facilities. Central underground public car parks include **Parking San Agustín** (Calle San Agustín; per hr/day €1/16) and **Parking Plaza Puerta Real** (Acera del Darro; per hr/day €1/10).

TAXI

If you're after a taxi, head for Plaza Nueva, where they line up. Most fares within the city cost between €4.50 and €7.50.

AROUND GRANADA

Granada is surrounded by a fertile plain called La Vega, planted with poplar groves and crops ranging from melons to tobacco. The Vega was an inspiration to Federico García Lorca, who was born and died here. The **Parque Federico García Lorca**, between the villages of Víznar and Alfacar (about 2.5km from each), marks the site where Lorca and hundreds, possibly thousands, of others are believed to have been shot and buried by the Nationalists, at the start of the civil war.

Fuente Vaqueros

The house where Lorca was born in 1898, in this village 17km west of Granada, is now the **Casa Museo Federico García Lorca** (☎ 958 51 64 53; www.museogarcialorca.org in Spanish; Calle Poeta Federico García Lorca 4; admission €1.80; guided visits hourly 10am-1pm & 5-7pm Tue-Sun Apr-Jun, 10am-2pm & 6-8pm Tue-Sun Jul-Sep, 10am-1pm & 4-6pm Tue-Sun Oct-Mar). The place brings his spirit alive, with numerous charming photos, posters and costumes from his plays, and paintings illustrating his poems. A short video captures him in action with the touring Teatro Barraca.

Buses to Fuente Vaqueros (€1.10, 20 minutes) by **Ureña** (☎ 958 45 41 54) leave from Avenida de Andaluces in front of Granada train station. Departures from Granada at the time of research were at 9am and 11am then hourly from 1pm to 8pm except at 4pm, Monday to Friday, and at 9am, 11am,

1pm and 5pm on Saturday, Sunday and holidays.

GUADIX

pop 20,000 / elevation 915m

The A92 northeast from Granada starts off through forested, hilly country before entering an increasingly arid landscape. Guadix (gwah-*deeks*), 55km from Granada, is famous for its cave dwellings – not prehistoric remnants but the homes of about 3000 modern-day townsfolk. The typical 21st-century cave has a whitewashed wall across the entrance, and a chimney and TV aerial sticking out of the top. Some have many rooms and all mod cons.

Guadix's **tourist office** (☎ 958 66 26 65; Carretera de Granada s/n; ⏰ 9am-3pm Mon, 9am-4pm Tue-Fri, 10am-2pm Sat) is on the Granada road leaving the town centre.

Sights

At the centre of Guadix is a fine sandstone **cathedral** (admission €2; ⏰ 10.30am-1pm & 2-7pm Mon-Sat, 9.30am-1pm Sun), built between the 16th and 18th centuries in a succession of Gothic, Renaissance and baroque styles.

A short distance south is the 11th-century Islamic castle, the **Alcazaba** (Calle Barradas 3; admission €1.20; ⏰ 11am-2pm & 4-6.30pm Tue-Sat, 10am-2pm Sun). From the Alcazaba there are views south to the main cave quarter, the Barriada de las Cuevas, where the **Cueva Museo Municipal** (Plaza de Padre Poveda; admission €1.35; ⏰ 10am-2pm & 4-6pm Mon-Sat, 10am-2pm Sun) recreates typical cave life.

Sleeping & Eating

Cuevas Pedro Antonio de Alarcón (☎ 958 66 49 86; www.andalucia.com/cavehotel; Barriada San Torcuato; s/d/q €36.91/55.63/88.27; **P** 🏊) Sleep in a cave at this comfy, modern apartment-hotel that has a pool and a restaurant. It's 3km from the centre, along the Murcia road.

Hotel Comercio (☎ 958 66 05 00; www.hotelcomercio.com in Spanish; Calle Mira de Amezcua 3; s €42.80, d €54.55-64.20; 🍴) This very comfy central hotel has a fine restaurant with a wide variety of medium-priced Spanish fare.

Getting There & Away

Guadix is about one hour from Granada (bus €4.05, train €5.55) and 1½ hours from Almería (bus €6.85, train €6.15 to €14) by at least nine buses and four trains daily in each direction.

SIERRA NEVADA

The Sierra Nevada, which includes mainland Spain's highest peak, Mulhacén (3479m), forms an almost year-round snowy southeastern backdrop to Granada. The range stretches about 75km from west to east, extending into Almería province. All its highest peaks (3000m or more) are towards the Granada end. The upper reaches of the range form the 862-sq-km **Parque Nacional Sierra Nevada**, Spain's biggest national park, with a rare high-altitude environment that is home to about 2100 of Spain's 7000 plant species. Andalucía's largest ibex population (about 5000) is here too. Surrounding the national park at lower altitudes is the 848-sq-km **Parque Natural Sierra Nevada**. The mountains and the Alpujarras valleys (p776) along their southern flank comprise one of the most spectacular areas in Spain, and the area offers not only wonderful walking but also horse riding, climbing, mountain biking and, in winter, good skiing at Europe's most southerly ski station.

The **Centro de Visitantes El Dornajo** (☎ 958 34 06 25; ⏰ 10am-2pm & 6-8pm Apr-Sep, 10am-2pm & 4-6pm Oct-Mar), about 23km from Granada, on the A395 towards the ski station, has plenty of information on the Sierra Nevada. The best overall maps of the area are Editorial Alpina's *Sierra Nevada, La Alpujarra* (1:40,000) and Editorial Penibética's *Sierra Nevada* (1:50,000). Both come with booklets, in English or Spanish, describing walking, biking and skiing routes.

Estación de Esquí Sierra Nevada

The **Sierra Nevada Ski Station** (☎ 902 708090; www.sierranevadaski.com), at Pradollano, 33km southeast of Granada, is one of Spain's biggest and liveliest ski resorts. It can get very crowded at weekends and holiday times. The ski season normally lasts from December to April.

The resort has 67 marked downhill runs (four black, 31 red, 24 blue and eight green) totalling 76km. Some runs start almost at the top of Veleta, the Sierra Nevada's second-highest peak. A one-day ski pass costs between €23 and €33, depending on when you go. Skis, boots and stocks can be rented for €21 per day; snowboards are available too. The resort also has several ski and snowboard schools.

WESTERN SIERRA NEVADA & LAS ALPUJARRAS

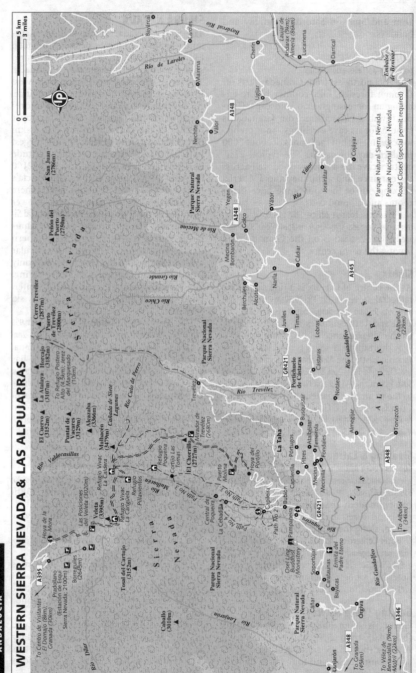

Nonskiers can ride cable cars up from Pradollano (2100m) to Borreguiles (2645m) for €10 return, and then ice-skate, dogsled or snowshoe. One cable car has wheelchair access. Outside the ski season **Sierra Nevada Activa** (www.sierranevadaactiva.com in Spanish) lays on a host of warmer-weather activities, such as mountain biking, trekking, horse riding and canyoning.

SLEEPING
The ski station has around 20 hotels, hostales and apartment-hotels. None is cheap (double rooms start at €80) and reservations are always advisable. Ski packages, which can be booked through the station's website or phone number, start at around €150 per person for two days and two nights, with half board and lift passes. Book two weeks ahead, if you can.

Hotel Ziryab (☎ 958 48 05 12; www.cetursa.es; Plaza de Andalucía; r from €118.35; ☿ late Nov–early May; ☐ ☐) This top-end hotel, near the foot of the resort, is reasonably attractive, and built a lot of stone and wood.

Albergue Juvenil Sierra Nevada (☎ 958 48 03 05; Calle Peñones 22; dm under 26 incl breakfast €9.05-13.75,

over 26 €12.25-18.35) The youth hostel near the top of the ski station has rooms that sleep from two to four, including six doubles with wheelchair access.

The less-expensive hotel or hostal options include **Hostal El Ciervo** (☎ 958 48 04 09; www .eh.etursa.es; Edificio Penibético; r €84; ☿ Dec-Apr) and **Hotel Apartamentos Trevenque** (☎ 958 48 08 62; www.cetursa.es; Plaza de Andalucía 6; r €105; ☐).

Getting There & Away
In the ski season **Autocares Bonal** (☎ 958 46 50 22) runs three daily buses (four at weekends) from Granada bus station to the ski station (one way/return €3.60/6.60, one hour). Outside the ski season there's just one bus daily (9am from Granada, 5pm from Pradollano). A taxi from Granada to the ski station costs about €40.

A road climbs right over the Sierra Nevada from the ski station to Capileira village in Las Alpujarras, on the southern side of the range, but it's closed to private motor vehicles between Hoya de la Mora (2550m), 3km up from Pradollano, and Hoya del Portillo (2150m), 12.5km above Capileira. From about late June to the

---

WALKING THE SIERRA NEVADA

The Sierra Nevada's two highest peaks, Mulhacén (3479m) and Veleta (3395m), rise to the south-east of the ski station and above the head of the Poqueira valley in Las Alpujarras to their south. In the warmer seasons the mountains and Las Alpujarras offer wonderful walking, but the best conditions in the high mountains (early July to early September) unfortunately don't coincide with the most comfortable months down in the Alpujarras. In the Sierra Nevada – which are serious mountains – be prepared for cloud, rain or strong, icy winds *any* day, and come well equipped.

Many exciting walks start where the national park shuttle bus routes drop you (above). The park information offices have leaflets summarising them. From the Posiciones del Veleta it's about 4km to the top of Veleta, an ascent of some 370m (1½ hours), 14km to the top of Mulhacén (four to five hours), or about 15km (six hours) all the way over to the Mirador de Trevélez. From the Mirador de Trevélez it's around three hours to the top of Mulhacén (6km, 800m ascent), or you could reach the Cañada de Siete Lagunas, a lake-dotted basin below the eastern side of Mulhacén, in about 1½ to two hours.

If you want to make more than a day of it, you can sleep in high-mountain refuges. **Refugio Poqueira** (☎ 958 34 33 49; dm €8.20), a modern place with bunks, hot showers and breakfast/dinner €3.50/10, is towards the top of the Poqueira valley at 2500m, a 4km walk from the Mirador de Trevélez. Phone ahead if possible. Two *refugios vivac* (stone shelters with boards to sleep on) are free but reservations are not possible. **Refugio Vivac La Caldera** is below the west flank of Mulhacén, a 1½-hour walk up from Refugio Poqueira; **Refugio Vivac La Cariguela** is a 2½-hour walk west along the road from Refugio La Caldera, at the 3200m Collado del Veleta pass below the summit of Veleta.

You can of course reach the high altitudes without using the summer bus service. A straight-forward route is path No 3 (shown on the Editorial Alpina map), with yellow marker posts, from Capileira – about five hours' walk to the Refugio Poqueira.

end of October the national park shuttle-bus services, called the Servicio de Interpretación Ambiental Altas Cumbres (High Peaks Environmental Interpretation Service), run about 6km up the road from Hoya de la Mora (to the Posiciones del Veleta, at 3020m), and some 21km up from Capileira (to the Mirador de Trevélez, at 2680m). Tickets (one way/return €4/6 on either route) and further information are available from the national park information posts at **Hoya de la Mora** (☎ 630-959739; ⏳ during bus-service season approx 8.30am-2.30pm & 3.30-7.30pm) and **Capileira** (☎ 958 76 34 86, 686-414576; ⏳ year-round approx 9am-2pm & 4.30-7.30pm).

LAS ALPUJARRAS

Below the southern flank of the Sierra Nevada lies one of the oddest crannies of Andalucía, the 70km-long jumble of valleys known as Las Alpujarras. Arid hillsides split by deep ravines alternate with oasis-like white villages set beside rapid streams and surrounded by gardens, orchards and woodlands. An infinity of good walking routes link valley villages, and head up into the Sierra Nevada: the best times to visit are between April and mid-June, and mid-September and early November.

Despite tourism and a recent wave of northern European settlers (chiefly British), Las Alpujarras remains a world apart, with a rare sense of timelessness and mystery. Its bizarre history saw a flourishing Muslim community replaced en masse by Christian settlers in the 16th century. The Berber-style villages, with houses similar to those in Morocco's Atlas Mountains, and the terraced and irrigated hillsides are ubiquitous reminders of the Islamic past.

History

In the 10th and 11th centuries the Alpujarras was a great silkworm farm for the silk workshops of Almería. This activity had arisen hand in hand with a wave of Berber settlers in the area. Together with irrigated agriculture, it supported at least 400 villages and hamlets by the late 15th century.

On his surrender to Fernando and Isabel in 1492, Boabdil, the last Granada emir, was awarded the Alpujarras as a personal fiefdom. He soon left for Africa, however, and as Christian promises of tolerance gave way to forced conversions and land expro-

priations, Muslims rebelled in 1500 across the former Granada emirate, with the Alpujarras in the thick of things. When the revolt failed, Muslims were given the choice of exile or conversion. Most converted but the change was barely skin-deep. A new repressive decree by Felipe II (Philip II) in 1567, forbidding Arabic names, dress and language, sparked a new Alpujarras revolt the following year. Two years of vicious guerrilla war ended only when Felipe's half-brother, Don Juan of Austria, came to quash the insurrection. The Alpujarras population was deported to Castile and western Andalucía, and most of the villages were resettled with Christians from the north. The rest were abandoned. Over the succeeding centuries, the silk industry fell by the wayside.

South From Granada by Gerald Brenan, an Englishman who lived in the Alpujarras village of Yegen in the 1920s and 1930s, is a fascinating picture of what was then a very isolated, superstitious corner of Spain. Another Englishman, Chris Stewart, settled here more recently, as a sheep farmer near Órgiva. His entertaining best-selling *Driving over Lemons* tells of life as a foreigner in Las Alpujarras in the 1990s.

Órgiva

pop 5000 / elevation 725m

The western Alpujarras' main town, Órgiva, is a scruffy but bustling place. On Thursday mornings locals and the area's international populace (which has a big hippy–New Age element) gather to buy and sell everything from vegetables to bead necklaces at a colourful market in the upper part of town, the Barrio Alto. The landmark 16th-century twin-towered **Iglesia de Nuestra Señora de la Expectación** (Plaza García Moreno) stands beside Órgiva's central traffic lights.

Hotel Taray (☎ 958 78 45 25; www.turgranada.com/hoteltaray; A348 Km18.5; r from €72.45; P ✗ ✗), in a rural setting about 1.5km south of the centre, is Órgiva's best hotel, with pleasant pastel rooms in Alpujarras-style buildings, a good restaurant and a lovely big pool at the end of a grassy garden.

Hotel & Hostal Mirasol (☎ 958 78 51 08/59; Avenida González Robles 5 & 3; s €17.10-32.10 d €27.80-42.80) provide plain but adequately comfortable rooms with tiled floors and all-white walls.

Pampaneira, Bubión & Capileira
pop 1270 / elevation 1050-1440m

These small villages clinging to the side of the deep Barranco de Poqueira valley, 14km to 20km northeast of Órgiva, are three of the prettiest, most dramatically sited (and most touristed) in Las Alpujarras. Their whitewashed stone houses seem to clamber over each other in an effort not to slide down into the gorge, while streets decked with flowery balconies wriggle between.

Capileira is the best base for walks.

INFORMATION
You'll find ATMs outside the car-park entrance in Pampaneira, and in Capileira at **La General** (Calle Doctor Castilla).

Ciber Monfí Café Morisco (☎ 958 76 30 53; Calle Alcalde Pérez Ramón 2, Bubión) Internet café in Bubión.

Punto de Información Parque Nacional de Sierra Nevada (☎ 958 76 31 27; Plaza de la Libertad, Pampaneira; ☷ 10am-3pm Sun & Mon, 10am-2pm & 5-7pm Tue-Sat, 10am-2pm & 4-6pm Tue-Sat approx mid-Oct–Easter) Plenty of information about Las Alpujarras and Sierra Nevada; maps and books for sale.

Servicio de Interpretación de Altos Cumbres (☎ 958 76 34 86, 686-414576; ☷ approx 9am-2pm & 4.30-7.30pm) By the main road in Capileira; information mainly about the national park, but also on Las Alpujarras.

SIGHTS & ACTIVITIES
All three villages have solid 16th-century **Mudéjar churches** (☷ Mass times). They also have small **weaving workshops**, descendants of a textile tradition that goes back to Islamic times, and plentiful **craft shops**. In Bubión, get a marvellous glimpse of bygone Alpujarras life at the excellent little folk museum, **Casa Alpujarreña** (Calle Real; admission €1.80; ☷ 11am-2pm Sun-Thu, 11am-2pm & 5-7pm Fri, Sat & holidays), beside the church.

Eight **walking trails,** ranging from 4km to 23km (two to eight hours), are marked out in the beautiful Barranco de Poqueira with little colour-coded posts. Their starting points can be hard to find, but they are marked and described on Editorial Alpina's *Sierra Nevada, La Alpujarra* map. Most start from Capileira. Path No 4 (8km, 3½ hours) takes you from Capileira up to the hamlet of La Cebadilla, then down the western side of the valley and back up to Capileira. To start, walk down Calle Cubo from Plaza Calvario, at the northern end of Capileira, turn right where the street takes its second turn to the left, and follow the street out into the countryside. Fork to the right 125m after the last village building on your right.

Nevadensis (☎ 958 76 31 27; www.nevadensis.com), at the information office in Pampaneira, offers hikes and treks with knowledgeable guides, including a combined 4WD and foot ascent of Mulhacén for €35 per person, plus horse riding (around €30 for two hours), mountain biking, climbing and canyoning.

SLEEPING & EATING
It's worth booking ahead for rooms around Easter, and from July to September. Many villages have apartments and houses for rent; ask in tourist offices or check websites such as **Turgranada** (www.turgranada.com) or **Rustic Blue** (www.rusticblue.com).

Alpujarras food is basically hearty country fare, with good meat and local trout. Trevélez is famous for its *jamón serrano* (mountain-cured ham), but many other villages produce good hams too. A *plato alpujarreño* consists of fried potatoes, fried eggs, sausage, ham and maybe a black pudding, usually for between €5 and €6.

Pampaneira
Two good-value hostales face each other at the entrance to the village: **Hostal Pampaneira** (☎ 958 76 30 02; Avenida Alpujarra 1; s/d €25/36), with a friendly local owner; and **Hostal Ruta del Mulhacén** (☎ 958 76 30 10; www.rutadelmulhacen.com; Avenida Alpujarra 6; s €25-35, d €30-45), where some rooms have terraces with views down the valley. **Restaurante Casa Diego** (☎ 958 76 30 15; Plaza de la Libertad 3; mains €5-9), along the street, has a pleasant upstairs terrace; trout with ham, and local ham and eggs, are good bets towards the budget end of the menu.

Bubión
Below the main road, **Hostal Las Terrazas** (☎ 958 76 30 34; www.terrazasalpujarra.com; Plaza del Sol 7; s/d €21.40/28.90, 2-/4-/6-person apt €48.15/58.85/77.05) has neat little rooms with folksy textiles, and apartments nearby.

Ciber Monfí Café Morisco (☎ 958 76 30 53; Calle Alcalde Pérez Ramón 2; www.cibermonfi.com; light dishes €3-4; ☷ closed Tue & Wed) serves drinks and great Arabic food to cool background music. With Internet, and live music on weekend nights, it's the Poqueira valley's hippest hang-out.

Capileira

Cortijo Catifalarga (☎ 958 34 33 57; www.catifalarga
.com; s €48.15, d €64.20-92, apt from €7; P) This
charmingly renovated old farmstead is the
choicest base in the Poqueira valley. The
driveway begins 750m up the Sierra Nevada
road from the top of Capileira. You can
dine indoors or out, and the food (mains
€6 to €12) and views are fabulous.

Hostal Atalaya (☎ 958 76 30 25; www.hostalat
alaya.com; Calle Perchel 3; s/d with view incl breakfast
€22/34, without view €17/30) The Atalaya is geared
to budget travellers, with simple rooms and
plenty of information.

Finca Los Llanos (☎ 958 76 30 71; www.hotelfinca
losllanos.com; Carretera de Sierra Nevada; s/d €45/72;
P) At the top of the village, Los Llanos
has tasteful rooms, a good restaurant, a
pool and a library.

Campileira (☎ 958 76 34 19; Carretera de Sierra
Nevada; dm €11.77, d €26.75, camping per person/site
€3.40/6.40; P) Some 500m up the Sierra
Nevada road from the top of the village,
Campileira provides clean dorms, camping
on a grassy terrace, wonderful views and
breakfast/dinner (€2.15/8.55).

Restaurante Ibero-Fusión (☎ 958 76 32 56; Calle
Parra 1; salads €5-8.50, mains €7-10; dinner) You'll
get a change from the regular Alpujarras
fare at this restaurant just below the
church – an *andaluz*, Arabic and Indian fusion, with plenty of vegetarian specialities.

Pitres & La Taha

pop 800

Pitres (elevation 1245m) is almost as pretty
as the Poqueira Gorge villages but less
touristed. The beautiful valley below it,
with five tranquil hamlets (Mecina, Meci-
nilla, Fondales, Ferreirola and Atalbéitar)
all grouped with Pitres in the *municipio*
called La Taha, is particularly fascinating
to explore. Its ancient pathways, wending
their way through lush woodlands to the
ubiquitous tinkle of gently running water,
are a walker's delight.

SLEEPING & EATING

Sierra y Mar (☎ 958 76 61 71; www.sierraymar.com;
Calle Albaicín, Ferreirola; s/d incl breakfast €28/48) This
charming guesthouse has just nine indi-
vidual rooms, set around multiple patios
and gardens. You couldn't hope for more
helpful or knowledgeable hosts than the
welcoming, multilingual Danish and Ital-

ian owners, especially when it comes to
planning walks.

L'Atelier (☎ 958 85 75 01; www.ivu.org/atelier; Calle
Alberca 21, Mecina; s/d €28.50/42, incl breakfast €30/45;
dinner Wed-Mon) A welcoming little French-
run guesthouse, in an ancient village house,
L'Atelier also serves gourmet vegetarian
meals and has an art gallery.

Hotel Albergue de Mecina (☎ 958 76 62 41, fax 958
76 62 55; Calle La Fuente s/n, Mecina; r €64.20; P) A
tasteful hotel that's modern and comfortable,
with touches of traditional Alpujarras style.

El Jardín (☎ 689-633529; Calle Escuelas Viejas, Pitres;
mains €6.50-8; dinner Tue-Sun, lunch Sat & Sun, approx Semana Santa–Oct) This excellent British-
run vegetarian restaurant occupies a lovely
shady garden 200m east of Pitres' plaza.

Trevélez

pop 800 / elevation 1476m

Trevélez, in a valley almost as impressive as
the Poqueira Gorge, claims to be the highest
village in Spain (but Valdelinares, Aragón,
reaches above 1700m) and produces famous
jamón serrano. Along the main road, you're
confronted by a welter of *jamón* and souvenir shops, but a wander into the upper parts
reveals a lively Alpujarran village.

SLEEPING & EATING

Hotel La Fragua (☎ 958 85 86 26; Calle San Antonio 4;
s/d €23/35) Popular with walking groups, this
hotel towards the top of town provides comfortably pine-furnished rooms. It's a 200m
walk (signposted) from Plaza Barrio Medio.
Its restaurant, **Mesón La Fragua** (mains €6-9), a
few doors away, is one of the best in town,
with a menu ranging from partridge in walnut sauce to some good vegetarian dishes.

Camping Trevélez (☎ /fax 958 85 87 35; www
.campingtrevelez.org; Carretera Trevélez-Órgiva Km1; camping per adult/tent/car €3.50/3/3; P) On a leafy,
terraced hillside 1km out of Trevélez, the
camping ground has ecologically-minded
owners and a good-value restaurant with
vegetarian options.

Hotel Pepe Álvarez (☎ 958 85 85 03; www.anda
lucia.co.uk; Plaza Francisco Abellán s/n; s/d €23/41) By
the main road at the foot of the village;
some rooms have terraces overlooking the
busy plaza.

East of Trevélez

East of Trevélez the landscape becomes
barer and more arid, yet there are still oases

of greenery around the villages. The central and eastern Alpujarras have their own magic, but see far fewer tourists than the western villages.

BÉRCHULES

Seventeen kilometres from Trevélez, Bérchules is in a green valley stretching far back into the hills, with attractive walks. **Hotel Los Bérchules** (☎ 958 85 25 30; www.hotel berchules.com; Carretera s/n; s/d €30/41; mains €6-11; **P**), by the main road, has good, clean, bright rooms, helpful English-speaking hosts who can help you set up all manner of activities, and an excellent restaurant (try the local lamb with mint).

CÁDIAR

Down by the Río Guadalfeo, 8km south of Bérchules, Cádiar (population 1600) is one of the bigger Alpujarras villages. Nearby you will find what is perhaps the whole charming place to stay in the whole Alpujarras. The **Alquería de Morayma** (☎ /fax 958 34 32 21; www.alqueriamorayma.com; d €57-67, 4-person apt €88-98; **P** **⏺**), 2km south (just off the A348 towards Órgiva), is one of the most charming places to stay in the Alpujarras – an old farmstead lovingly renovated and expanded to provide unique, comfortable rooms and apartments. There's excellent, moderately priced food, a library of Alpujarras information, fine walking, and fascinating art and artefacts everywhere.

YEGEN

Gerald Brenan's home in the 1920s is 12km east of Bérchules, just off the main plaza with the fountain. Parts of the valley below Yegen have a particularly moon-like quality. Several walking routes have been marked out locally including a 2km 'Sendero de Gerald Brenan'. **El Rincón de Yegen** (☎ 958 85 12 70; www .aldearural.com/rincondeyegen; s/d €25/36; mains €7-13; **P** **⏺**), on the eastern edge of the village, has comfortable rooms and an excellent, medium-priced restaurant. Succumb to the pears in local wine and hot chocolate!

Getting There & Away

Alsina Graells (☎ 958 18 54 80) runs three daily buses from Granada to Órgiva (€3.60, 1½ hours), Pampaneira (€4.40, two hours), Bubión (€4.80, 2¼ hours), Capileira (€4.80, 2½ hours) and Pitres (€4.80, 2¾ hours).

Two of these continue to Trevélez (€5.65, 3¼ hours) and Bérchules (€6.70, 3¾ hours). The return buses start from Bérchules at 5am and 5pm, and from Pitres at 3.30pm. Alsina also runs twice-daily buses from Granada to Cádiar (€6.15, three hours) and Yegen (€6.95, 3½ hours).

THE COAST

Granada's rugged, cliff-lined, 80km coast has a few reasonably attractive beach towns, linked by several daily buses to Granada, Málaga and Almería.

Salobreña

pop 11,000

Salobreña's huddle of white houses rises on a crag between the N340 and the sea. The helpful **tourist office** (☎ 958 61 03 14; Plaza de Goya; ⏰ 9.30am-1.30pm & 4-7pm Tue-Sat) is 200m off the N340. Up at the top of the town is the impressive 13th-century **Castillo Árabe** (admission €2.55; ⏰ 10.30am-1.30pm & 4-8pm). The ticket also includes the nearby **Museo Arqueológico**, which is open the same hours. Below all this is a long, dark-sand **beach**, extremely popular with *granadinos* in August.

A fine place to stay is the spick-and-span **Hostal San Juan** (☎ 958 61 17 29; www.hotel-san-juan .com in Spanish; Calle Jardines 1; d €42; ⏺), on a quiet street about 400m from the tourist office. **Pensión Mari Carmen** (☎ 958 61 09 06; Calle Nueva 30; s/d €20/39; ⏺), a 10-minute uphill walk from Plaza de Goya, has beautifully bright and clean pine-furnished rooms, some with their own terraces. There are loads of restaurants and beachside *chiringuitos* (small open-air bars), and a spot of nightlife on and near the beachfront.

Almuñécar

pop 23,000

From the highway Almuñécar seems an uninviting agglomeration of apartment blocks, but it has a more attractive older heart around the 16th-century castle. Popular with Spanish holidaymakers, it's a not-too-expensive resort with pebbly beaches. The **bus station** (☎ 958 63 01 40; Avenida Juan Carlos I 1) is just south of the N340. There's a **tourist information kiosk** (☎ 958 63 11 25; Avenida Fenicia; ⏰ 10am-2pm & 5-8pm, 10am-2pm & 4-7pm approx Oct-Apr) along the street; the **main tourist office** (☎ 958 63 11 25; www.almunecar.info; Avenida Europa s/n) is 1km southwest, just back from Playa de San Cristóbal, and has the same opening hours.

SIGHTS & ACTIVITIES

Just behind Playa de San Cristóbal is a tropical-bird aviary, **Parque Ornitológico Loro-Sexi** (☎ 958 63 02 80; adult/child €2/1.40; ⏰ 11am-2pm & 5-7pm, 11am-2pm & 4-6pm approx Oct-Apr). Atop the hill above is the post-Reconquista **Castillo de San Miguel** (☎ 958 63 12 52; adult/child incl Museo Arqueológico €2/1.40; ⏰ 10.30am-1.30pm & 5-7.30pm Tue-Sat, 10.30am-1.30pm Sun, 10.30am-1.30pm & 4-6.30pm approx Oct-Apr), with great views and an interesting little **museum**. The castle ticket includes the worthwhile **Museo Arqueológico** (Calle Málaga) a few streets northeast in a set of Roman underground galleries called the Cueva de Siete Palacios. It's open the same hours as the castle.

You can paraglide, windsurf, dive, sail, ride a horse or descend canyons in and around Almuñécar and nearby La Herradura. The tourist office and its website have plenty of information.

SLEEPING

Hotel California (☎ 958 88 10 38; www.hotelcaliforniaspain.com; Carretera N340 Km313; s/d €33/48; [P]) With rooms and a restaurant overlooking the town and sea, from an elevated position just off the N340, the California provides colourful touches of Moroccan style and tasty food, including vegetarian offerings. The hotel offers special packages for paragliders.

Hotel Casablanca (☎ 958 63 55 75; www.almunecar.info/casablanca; Plaza de San Cristóbal 4; s/d €44.95/64.20; [P] [⚡]) Just off Playa de San Cristóbal, the Casablanca has spacious rooms with beautiful and distinctive hand-made furnishings.

JAÉN PROVINCE

Set on Andalucía's border with Castilla–La Mancha, Jaén alternates between impressive mountain ranges and rolling country covered with olive trees (it produces about 10% of the world's olive oil). The Desfiladero de Despeñaperros pass, a gap in the Sierra Morena on Jaén's northern border, has, from time immemorial, been the most important gateway into Andalucía from the plains of central Spain. The rout of the Almohad Muslim army by Christian forces

in 1212 at Las Navas de Tolosa, just south of the pass, was a key event of the Reconquista, opening the doors of Andalucía to the Christians. Today the A4 from Madrid enters Andalucía by this same route.

In eastern Jaén, the Parque Natural de Cazorla is perhaps the most beautiful of all Andalucía's mountain regions. The province's urban highlight is the marvellous Renaissance architecture of Andrés de Vandelvira – born in 1509 at Alcaraz in Albacete province – in Úbeda, Baeza and Jaén city.

The Jaén diet is pretty traditional but varied, with plenty of game (partridge, venison, wild boar), especially in the mountains. Many bars still have the endearing habit of serving free tapas with drinks.

The Jaén website (www.promojaen.es) has lots of interesting information about the province.

JAÉN

pop 116,000 / elevation 575m

The provincial capital is a likeable university city and well worth some of your time.

Orientation

Old Jaén, dominated by the huge cathedral, huddles beneath the high, castle-topped Cerro de Santa Catalina. The focal point of the newer part of town is Plaza de la Constitución, 200m northeast and downhill from the cathedral. From here the main artery of the new city, Calle Roldán y Marín, and its continuation Paseo de la Estación, heads northwest to the train station, 1km away.

Information

There's no shortage of banks or ATMs around Plaza de la Constitución.

Cyber Cu@k (Calle Adarves Bajos 24; per 30min €1; ⏰ 10.30am-12.30pm & 5.30pm-midnight)

Librería Metrópolis (Calle del Cerón 17) Good for maps.

Tourist Office (☎ 953 19 04 55; otjaen@andalucia.org; Calle de la Maestra 13; ⏰ 10am-8pm Mon-Fri, to 7pm Oct-Mar, 10am-1pm Sat, Sun & holidays) Helpful, multilingual staff with plenty of free information about the city and province.

Sights

Jaén's huge **cathedral** (☎ 953 23 42 33; ⏰ 8.30am-1pm & 4-7pm Mon-Sat, 8.30am-1pm & 5-8pm Apr-Sep, 9am-1pm & 5-7pm Sun & holidays) was built mainly in the 16th and 17th centuries, and mainly to the designs of Andrés de Vandelvira.

JAÉN

INFORMATION	
Cyber Cu@k..........................	1 F3
Librería Metrópolis................	2 D4
Tourist Office.......................	3 D4

SIGHTS & ACTIVITIES	(pp780–2)
Baños Árabes........................	(see 7)
Castillo de Santa Catalina......	4 B4
Cathedral.............................	5 E4
Museo de Artes y Costumbres	
Populares............................	(see 7)
Museo Internacional de Arte Naïf...	6 D1
Museo Provincial...................	7 C2
Palacio de Villardompardo......	

SLEEPING	🏠
Hostal La Española................	8 D4
Hotel Rey Fernando...............	9 E2
Hotel Xauen.........................	10 E3
Parador Castillo de Santa Catalina...	11 A4

EATING	🍴
Casa Vicente........................	12 D4
Mesón Río Chico...................	13 E2
Taberna La Manchega............	14 D4

DRINKING	🍷
Bar del Pósito......................	15 E3
Iroquai...............................	16 F3

TRANSPORT	(p783)
Bus Station..........................	17 E2

The southwestern façade on Plaza de Santa María sports a dramatic array of 17th-century statuary, much of it by Seville's Pedro Roldán.

The Renaissance **Palacio de Villardompardo** (☎ 953 23 62 92; Plaza de Santa Luisa de Marillac; admission free with passport; ⏱ 9am-8pm Tue-Fri, 9.30am-2.30pm Sat & Sun, closed holidays) houses three excellent attractions: the **Museo Internacional de Arte Naïf**, with a large international collection of colourful naive art; the beautiful 11th-century **Baños Árabes** (Arab Baths), one of Spain's biggest Islamic bathhouses; and the **Museo de Artes y Costumbres Populares**, devoted to the lifestyle of pre-industrial Jaén province.

The **Museo Provincial** (☎ 953 25 06 00; Paseo de la Estación 27; adult/EU citizen €1.50/free; ⏱ 3-8pm Tue, 9am-8pm Wed-Sat, 9am-3pm Sun) has the finest collection of 5th-century-BC Iberian sculptures in Spain. Found in Porcuna, they show a clear Greek influence in their fluid form and graceful design.

Jaén's most exhilarating spot is the top of the Cerro de Santa Catalina, where the **Castillo de Santa Catalina** (☎ 953 12 07 33; admission €3; ⏱ 10am-2pm & 5-9pm Tue-Sun, afternoons Oct-Mar 3.30-7pm) was surrendered to Fernando III in 1246 by Granada after a six-month siege.

MASS FERVOUR IN THE SIERRA MORENA

On the last Sunday of every April, around half a million people converge on a remote shrine in the Sierra Morena in the northwest of Jaén province for one of Spain's biggest religious gatherings, the festive pilgrimage known as the Romería de la Virgen de la Cabeza. The original 13th-century Santuario de la Virgen de la Cabeza, 31km north of Andújar, was destroyed in the civil war, when Francoist troops occupying it were besieged by the Republicans for eight months, but the shrine has since been rebuilt. The annual festivities see a tiny statue of the Virgin Mary, known as La Morenita (the Little Brown One), being carried around the Cerro del Cabezo for about four hours from about 11am. It's a festive and emotive occasion, with children and items of clothing being passed over the heads of the crowd to priests who touch them to the Virgin's mantle.

Audiovisual gimmicks add fun to the visit to the castle's keep, chapel and dungeon. The castle is a circuitous 4km drive from the city centre (€6 by taxi), but you can walk up in 45 minutes using a steep path almost opposite the top of Calle de Buenavista. If you walk, treat yourself to a drink in the *parador* next to the castle!

Sleeping

Parador Castillo de Santa Catalina (☎ 953 23 00 00; www.parador.es; d €113.30; Ⓟ ⓧ ⓡ) Next to the castle at the top of the Cerro de Santa Catalina, this hotel has an incomparable setting and theatrical vaulted halls. Rooms are incredibly comfortable with four-post beds, tiled Islamic details and all mod cons, and there is also an excellent restaurant.

Hotel Rey Fernando (☎ 953 25 18 40; Plaza Coca de la Piñera 5; s/d €48/61; Ⓟ ⓧ) Modern, comfortable and nicely furnished, the Rey Fernando also has a lovely tiled tapas bar and a huge restaurant.

Hotel Xauen (☎ 953 24 07 89; www.hotelxauenjaen .com; Plaza del Deán Mazas 3; s/d €40/55; Ⓟ ⓧ ⓠ) The Xauen has good facilities and spacious, well-appointed rooms, making it popular with businessfolk.

Hostal La Española (☎ 953 23 02 54; Calle Bernardo López 9; s/d €26/32) Near the cathedral and some good tapas bars, La Española is grimly Gothic with its creaking spiral staircase, drab furnishings and lukewarm welcome. Mosquitoes can be a nuisance in the cheaper Jaén hotels.

Eating

Casa Vicente (Calle Francisco Martín Mora; menú €30) Set in a restored old-town mansion with a patio, the Casa Vicente is one of the best restaurants in town. Take tapas in the bar or sit down for specialities such as *cordero mozárabe*, lamb with honey and spices.

Taberna La Manchega (☎ 953 23 21 92; Calle Bernardo López 12; platos combinados €4; ⏱ lunch & dinner Wed-Mon) A terrific old-town bar, more than a century old, with an atmospheric cellar restaurant. The ambience is boisterous and unpretentious and the food cheap and tasty.

Mesón Río Chico (☎ 953 24 08 02; Calle Nueva 2; menú €8) The downstairs *taberna* serves delicious tapas and *raciones* of meat, *revueltos* (scrambled-egg dishes) and fish. There is a more expensive restaurant upstairs.

Drinking & Entertainment

Cool drinking spots include the artsy **Bar del Pósito** (Plaza del Pósito 10) and **Iroquai** (☎ 953 24 36 74; Calle Adarves Bajos 53), which plays good music (usually live on Thursday).

Getting There & Away

The **bus station** (☎ 953 25 01 06; Plaza de Coca de la Piñera) is 250m north of Plaza de la Constitución. Destinations include Granada (€6.25, 1½ hours, 14 daily), Baeza (€3.15, 45 minutes, up to 13 daily), Úbeda (€3.75, 1¼ hours, up to 13 daily), Córdoba (€6.70, 1½ hours, eight daily), Cazorla (€6.50, two hours, two daily) and Madrid (€19.20, four hours, up to five daily).

Most days there are only five departures from the **train station** (☎ 953 27 02 02). One, at 8am, goes to Córdoba (€7.65, 1½ hours), Seville (€14.70, three hours) and Cádiz (€22, 4¾ hours). Four go to Madrid (€19.90, four hours).

BAEZA

pop 15,000 / elevation 790m

This country town, 48km northeast of Jaén, is replete with gorgeous Gothic and Renaissance buildings from the 16th century, when local nobility ploughed much of their wealth from grain-growing and textiles into monumental construction.

Orientation & Information

The heart of town is Plaza de España and the adjacent Paseo de la Constitución. The **tourist office** (☎ 953 74 04 44; Plaza del Pópulo; ⏱ 9am-7pm Mon-Fri, 10am-1pm & 5-7pm Sat, to 6pm Oct-Mar, 10am-1pm Sun) is just west of Paseo de la Constitución.

Sights

Opening times of some buildings vary unpredictably.

In the centre of beautiful **Plaza del Pópulo** is the **Fuente de los Leones** (Fountain of the Lions), topped by an ancient statue believed to represent Imilce, a local Iberian princess who was married to Hannibal. The southern side of the plaza is lined by the Plateresque Casa del Pópulo from about 1540 (housing Baeza's tourist office).

Now a high university, Baeza's **Antigua Universidad** (Old University; Calle Beato Juan de Ávila; admission free; ⏱ 10am-1pm & 4-6pm Thu-Tue) was founded in 1538 and closed in 1824. The main patio

has two levels of elegant Renaissance arches. Round the corner is the early-16th-century **Palacio de Jabalquinto** (Plaza Santa Cruz; admission free; ⏱ 10am-2pm & 4-6pm Thu-Tue), a mansion with a flamboyant Isabelline-Gothic façade and lovely Renaissance patio. Across the square, the 13th-century **Iglesia de la Santa Cruz** (⏱ 11am-1.30pm & 4-6pm Mon-Sat, noon-2pm Sun) may be the only Romanesque church in Andalucía.

Baeza's eclectic **cathedral** (Plaza de Santa María; ⏱ 10.30am-1pm & 5-7pm, 10.30am-1pm & 4-6pm Oct-Mar) is chiefly in 16th-century Renaissance style, with an interior designed by Andrés de Vandelvira and Jerónimo del Prado. The grille on the **antiguo coro** (old choir) is a masterpiece by Jaén's 16th-century wrought-iron supremo, Maestro Bartolomé.

A block north of Paseo de la Constitución, the **Ayuntamiento** (Town Hall; Paseo del Cardenal Benavides 9) has a marvellous Plateresque façade.

Sleeping & Eating

Hotel Puerta de la Luna (☎ 953 74 70 19; www.hotel puertadelaluna.com in Spanish; Calle Canónigo Melgares Raya s/n; d Mon-Thu €95, Fri-Sun €110; P ⓧ ⓧ) This is a fantastically luxurious mansion hotel with real character and wonderful facilities. The rooms are kitted out with lush damask sheets and antiques.

Hotel Palacete Santa Ana (☎ 953 74 16 57; info@palacetesantaana.com; Calle Santa Ana Vieja 9; s/d €42/66; ⓧ) A stylish hotel in a restored 16th-century mansion: the rooms are beautifully furnished and the public rooms are veritable galleries of fine art.

Hospedería Fuentenueva (☎ 953 74 31 00; www .fuentenueva.com; Paseo Arco del Agua s/n; s/d incl breakfast €43/72; ⓧ ⓧ) This former women's prison is now a beautifully restored small hotel, with large, comfortable, bright rooms sporting marble bathrooms.

Hostal Comercio (☎ 953 74 01 00; Calle San Pablo 21; d €30-35) Atmospherically gloomy and creaky, this friendly family-run hostal gives a gracious welcome and has decent, old-fashioned rooms.

Restaurante Vandelvira (☎ 953 74 81 72; Calle de San Francisco 14; meal €30; ⏱ closed Sun night & Mon) The classy Vandelvira, installed in part of the restored Convento de San Francisco, has bags of character. Spoil yourself with the partridge-pâté salad or the *solomillo al carbón* (char-grilled steak).

Restaurante Palacete Santa Ana (☎ 953 74 16 57; Calle Escopeteros 12; menú €15) This large restaurant and bar complex serves up regional specialities that are usually complemented by the local olive oil. Reservations are advised. It also stages excellent flamenco nights.

Mesón (☎ 953 74 29 84; Portales Carbonería 13, Paseo de la Constitución; mains €8-14) Adding to the terrific local atmosphere are the glowing woodburning grill, cheerful service and good food. Try *patatas baezanas*, a huge vegetarian delight of sautéed potatoes and mushrooms.

Getting There & Away

From the **bus station** (☎ 953 74 04 68; Paseo Arco del Agua), 700m east of Plaza de España, buses go to Jaén (€3.15, 45 minutes, 11 daily), Úbeda (€0.75, 30 minutes, 15 daily), Cazorla (€3.40, 2¼ hours, two daily) and Granada (€9.10, 2¼ hours, five daily).

Linares-Baeza train station (☎ 953 65 02 02) is 13km northwest. Buses connect with most trains Monday to Saturday.

ÚBEDA

pop 33,000 / elevation 760m

Just 9km east of Baeza, Úbeda has an even finer heritage of marvellous buildings. In the 16th century, an Úbeda gent named Francisco de los Cobos y Molina became first secretary to Carlos I; his nephew, Juan Vázquez de Molina, succeeded him in the job and kept it under Felipe II. Much of the wealth that they brought to Úbeda was spent on a profusion of Renaissance mansions and churches that remain its glory today. Many were designed by Andrés de Vandelvira.

Orientation & Information

Most of the fine architecture is in the southeastern old part of town, a web of narrow streets and expansive plazas. Budget accommodation and the bus station are in the drab new town in the west and north.

The **tourist office** (☎ 953 75 08 97; Calle Baja del Marqués 4; 🕒 9am-2.45pm & 4-7pm Mon-Fri, 10am-2pm Sat) is in the 18th-century Palacio Marqués de Contadero in the old town.

Sights

PLAZA VÁZQUEZ DE MOLINA

This plaza, Úbeda's architectural crown jewel, is almost entirely surrounded by quite beautiful 15th- and 16th-century stone buildings.

The **Capilla de El Salvador** (admission €2.25; 🕒 10am-2pm & 4.30-7pm) faces the eastern end of the plaza. Founded in the 1540s by Francisco de los Cobos y Molina as his family funerary chapel, it was Vandelvira's first commission in Úbeda. The basic concept is by Diego de Siloé, architect of Granada cathedral, but Vandelvira added plenty of his own touches, including the elaborate main façade, an outstanding piece of Plateresque design. The sacristy by Vandelvira, has a portrait of Francisco de los Cobos y Molina. The richly decorated chancel is modelled on Siloé's Capilla Mayor in Granada cathedral, with a frescoed dome. The Cobos family crypt lies beneath the nave.

Next to the Capilla de El Salvador stands what was the abode of its chaplains – in fact one of Vandelvira's finest palaces, the **Palacio del Deán Ortega**. It's now Úbeda's *parador* and its elegant courtyard is a very fine spot for refreshments.

The harmonious proportions of the Italianate **Palacio de Vázquez de Molina** (🕒 10am-2pm & 5-9pm), at the western end of the plaza make it one of the most magnificent buildings in the town. Now Úbeda's town hall, it was built around 1562 by Vandelvira for Juan Vázquez de Molina, whose coat of arms surmounts the doorway.

PLAZA 1° DE MAYO & AROUND

Plaza 1° de Mayo used to be Úbeda's market square and bullring, and the Inquisition burnt heretics where its kiosk now stands. Worthies would watch the merry events from the gallery of the elegant 16th-century **Antiguo Ayuntamiento** (Old Town Hall) in the southwestern corner. Along the top (northern) side of the square is the **Iglesia de San Pablo** (🕒 7-9pm), with a fine late-Gothic portal from 1511.

The **Museo de San Juan de la Cruz** (☎ 953 75 06 15; Calle del Carmen; admission €1.20; 🕒 11am-1pm & 5-7pm Tue-Sun) is devoted to the mystic and religious reformer St John of the Cross, who died here in 1591. Even if you can't understand the Spanish-speaking monks who guide all visits, you'll still get to see a couple of the saint's fingers and some of his bones, preserved in cabinets, and other memorabilia.

HOSPITAL DE SANTIAGO

Completed in 1575, Andrés de Vandelvira's last **building** (Calle Obispo Cobos; admission free; 🕒 8am-

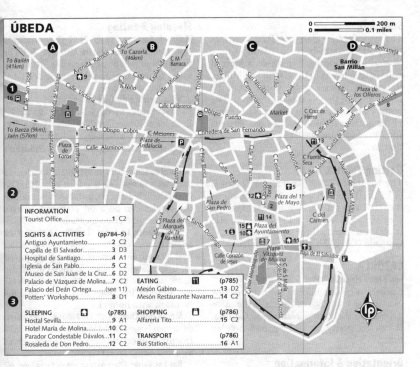

ÚBEDA

0 ——— 200 m
0 ——— 0.1 miles

To Bailén
(41km)

To Cazorla
(46km)

Barrio
San Millán

To Baeza (9km);
Jaén (57km)

INFORMATION	
Tourist Office	1 C2

SIGHTS & ACTIVITIES	(pp784–5)
Antiguo Ayuntamiento	2 C2
Capilla de El Salvador	3 D3
Hospital de Santiago	4 A1
Iglesia de San Pablo	5 C2
Museo de San Juan de la Cruz	6 D2
Palacio de Vázquez de Molina	7 C2
Palacio del Deán Ortega	(see 11)
Potters' Workshops	8 D1

SLEEPING	(p785)
Hostal Sevilla	9 A1
Hotel María de Molina	10 C2
Parador Condestable Dávalos	11 C2
Rosaleda de Don Pedro	12 C2

EATING	(p785)
Mesón Gabino	13 D2
Mesón Restaurante Navarro	14 C2

SHOPPING	(p786)
Alfarería Tito	15 C2

TRANSPORT	(p786)
Bus Station	16 A1

3pm & 4-10pm Mon-Fri, 11am-3pm & 6-10pm Sat & Sun) is on the western side of town. This sober, grand-scale, late-Renaissance masterpiece has been dubbed the 'Escorial of Andalucía'. Off the classic Vandelvira two-level patio are a chapel, now restored as an auditorium (the hospital is now a cultural centre), and a staircase with colourful frescoes.

Sleeping & Eating

Parador Condestable Dávalos (☎ 953 75 03 45; www .parador.es; Plaza Vázquez de Molina; s/d €106/119; Ⓟ 🅧) Úbeda's fabulous *parador* overlooks the wonderful Plaza Vázquez de Molina. The hotel is an historic monument: it was previously the Palacio del Deán Ortega. Now, of course, it is comfortably modern and appropriately luxurious. The restaurant here is deservedly the most popular in town, serving up delicious and elegant dishes (around €25). Even in the off-season the dining room is always happily buzzing in the evening.

Hotel María de Molina (☎ 953 79 53 56; www.hotel -maria-de-molina.com in Spanish; Plaza del Ayuntamiento; s/d €52/83.50; 🅧) This attractive hotel occupies

a 16th-century *palacio* on picturesque Plaza Ayuntamiento. Well-appointed rooms are arranged around a typical patio and the hotel has an excellent restaurant. Room rates are cheaper Monday to Thursday.

Rosaleda de Don Pedro (☎ 953 79 51 47; www .husa.es; Calle Obispo Toral 2; d €57; Ⓟ 🅧 🅡) The Don Pedro offers good three-star facilities in a central old-town location. It has the only pool in this part of town.

Hostal Sevilla (☎ 953 75 06 12; Avenida Ramón y Cajal 9; s/d €20/33) Úbeda's *hostales*, all near each other in the modern part of town, are rather grim in appearance. The pleasant, family-run Sevilla is the best of the bunch, offering good-value rooms with winter heating.

Mesón Restaurante Navarro (☎ 953 79 06 38; Plaza del Ayuntamiento 2; raciones €4-9, mains €8-14) Popular, smoky and noisy, the Navarro is a cherished local favourite. In summer it's nice to sit out on the plaza.

Mesón Gabino (☎ 953 75 75 53; Calle Fuente Seca; mains €6-10) This atmospheric cellar restaurant is a good, solid spot to eat, if you have been wandering in the potters' quarter.

ANDALUCÍA

Shopping

The typical green glaze on Úbeda's attractive pottery dates back to Islamic times. Several workshops on Cuesta de la Merced and Calle Valencia in the Barrio San Millán, the potters' quarter, in the northeast of the old town, sell their wares on the spot. The potters are often willing to explain some of the ancient techniques they use. **Alfarería Tito** (Plaza del Ayuntamiento 12) has a large selection too.

Getting There & Away

The **bus station** (☎ 953 75 21 57; Calle San José 6) is in the new part of town. Destinations include Baeza (€0.75, 30 minutes, 15 daily), Jaén (€3.75, 1¼ hours, 13 daily), Cazorla (€2.95, one hour, three to five daily) and Granada (€9.70, 2¾ hours, seven daily).

CAZORLA

pop 8200 / elevation 885m

Cazorla, a quaint hillside town of narrow old streets, 45km east of Úbeda, is the main gateway to the Parque Natural de Cazorla. It can get pretty busy at Spanish holiday times.

Orientation & Information

Three plazas delineate the town's central axis. Plaza de la Constitución is the main square of the northern, newer part of town. Plaza de la Corredera is 150m further south along Calle Doctor Muñoz. Plaza de Santa María, downhill through narrow, winding streets another 300m southeast, is the heart of the oldest part of town.

The **Oficina de Turismo Municipal** (☎ 953 71 01 12; Paseo del Santo Cristo 17; ⏰ 10am-1pm & 5.30-8pm) is 200m north of Plaza de la Constitución. **Quercus** (☎ 953 72 01 15; Calle Juan Domingo 2), just off Plaza de la Constitución, provides some tourist information, as well as selling maps, souvenirs and park excursions.

Sights

At one end of lovely **Plaza de Santa María** is the large shell of the **Iglesia de Santa María**, built by Andrés de Vandelvira in the 16th century but wrecked by Napoleonic troops. A short walk up from here, the ancient **Castillo de la Yedra** houses the **Museo del Alto Guadalquivir** (adult/EU citizen €1.50/free; ⏰ 3-8pm Tue, 9am-8pm Wed-Sat, 9am-3pm Sun & holidays), with art and relics of past local life.

Sleeping & Eating

Molino la Farraga (☎ 953 72 12 49; www.molinolafarraga.com; Calle Camino de la Hoz s/n; d €64; ☒) The tranquil old mill of La Farraga is just up the valley from Plaza Santa María. Understated comfort is the theme.

Villa Turística de Cazorla (☎ 953 71 01 00; Ladera de San Isicio; 2-/4-person villa €70/120; ℗ ☒ ☒) Each of the comfortable villas has a living room and a terrace, and they share a good-sized swimming pool and a children's play area.

Hotel Guadalquivir (☎ 953 72 02 68; www.hguadalquivir.com in Spanish; Calle Nueva 6; d €42; ☒) The Guadalquivir has comfortable pine rooms: the singles can be a bit cramped but it's good value in a good location.

Restaurante La Sarga (☎ 953 72 15 07; Plaza del Mercado s/n; menú €18; ⏰ closed Sep) Cazorla's best restaurant serves up well-prepared local specialities, many of them involving game, such as the *caldereta de gamo* (venison stew) or the *lomos de venado con miel* (venison with honey).

Mesón Don Chema (☎ 953 72 00 68; Calle Escaleras del Mercado 2; mains €7-9) Down a lane off Calle Doctor Muñoz, this cheerful place serves up good-value local fare.

Bar Las Vegas (Plaza de la Corredera 17; raciones €6) Several bars on Cazorla's three main squares serve good tapas and *raciones*. At Las Vegas you can try *gloria bendita* (blessed glory), a tasty prawn-and-capsicum *revuelto*.

Getting There & Away

Alsina Graells runs buses to/from Úbeda (€2.95, one hour, three to five daily), Jaén (€6.50, two hours, two daily) and Granada (€11.85, 3½ hours, two daily). The main stop in Cazorla is Plaza de la Constitución; the tourist office has timetables.

PARQUE NATURAL DE CAZORLA

The 2143-sq-km **Parque Natural de las Sierras de Cazorla, Segura y Las Villas** is the biggest protected area in Spain. It's a memorably beautiful region of several rugged mountain ranges, divided by high plains and deep, forested valleys. You stand a good chance of seeing wild boar, red or fallow deer, mouflon (a large wild sheep) or ibex if you do a spot of walking here. The ibex lives mainly on rocky heights and the others prefer forests, but you may even come across deer or boar on some of the main roads.

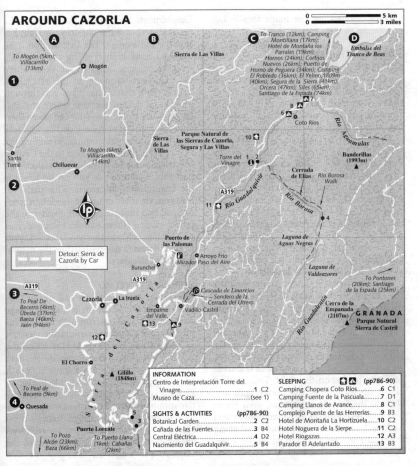

AROUND CAZORLA

INFORMATION	
Centro de Interpretación Torre del Vinagre	1 C2
Museo de Caza	(see 1)

SIGHTS & ACTIVITIES	(pp786-90)
Botanical Garden	2 C2
Cañada de las Fuentes	3 B4
Central Eléctrica	4 D2
Nacimiento del Guadalquivir	5 B4

SLEEPING	(pp786-90)
Camping Chopera Coto Ríos	6 C1
Camping Fuente de la Pascuala	7 D1
Camping Llanos de Arance	8 C1
Complejo Puente de las Herrerías	9 B3
Hotel de Montaña La Hortizuela	10 C2
Hotel Noguera de la Sierpe	11 C2
Hotel Riogazas	12 A3
Parador El Adelantado	13 B3

The Guadalquivir, Andalucía's longest river, rises in the south of the park and flows north into the Embalse del Tranco de Beas reservoir, then west towards the Atlantic.

To make the most of the park, you need wheels to reach some of the most spectacular areas and walks. The best times to visit are between late April and June, and September and October, when the vegetation is at its most colourful and the weather at its best. In spring, the flowers are magnificent. The park boasts 2300 plant species. Peak visitor periods are Semana Santa, July and August.

Orientation & Information

Entering the park from Cazorla, the A319 winds over the 1200m Puerto de las Palomas pass and down to the Empalme del Valle junction, where it turns north and follows the Guadalquivir valley.

The main information centre is the **Centro de Interpretación Torre del Vinagre** (☎ 953 71 30 40; ⏰ 11am-2pm & 5-8pm, 11am-2pm & 4-7pm Oct-Mar), 16km north of Empalme del Valle on the A319. The **Museo de Caza** (Hunting Museum) with stuffed park wildlife, is in an adjoining building; a more-cheerful **botanic garden** is just along the road.

Editorial Alpina's 1:40,000 *Sierra de Cazorla*, which covers the south of the park and is available in English, and *Sierra de Segura*, which covers the north, are the best maps, showing selected walks that are described in accompanying booklets. You

ANDALUCÍA

may be able to get the maps locally but don't count on it.

Sights & Activities

SIERRA DE CAZORLA DRIVE

For those with wheels, this itinerary of about 60km is a good introduction to the parts of the park nearest Cazorla, with a couple of stops to stretch your legs. It's all passable for ordinary cars, if bumpy in places.

Head first up to La Iruela, 1km east of Cazorla, and turn right along Carretera Virgen de la Cabeza. About 12km along here, during which the road ceases to be paved, is **El Chorro**, a gorge that's good for watching vultures. Just beyond El Chorro, ignore another dirt road forking down to the right. Your track winds round over the **Puerto Lorente** pass and down to a junction after 12km. Fork right here, and after about 200m a 'Nacimiento del Guadalquivir' sign to your left points down to the official **source of the Guadalquivir**.

The road heads a short distance past the Nacimiento to the **Cañada de las Fuentes** picnic area, a convenient stop. From here head back northward down the beautiful valley of the infant Guadalquivir. At a T-junction after 14km, about 1km beyond the northern end of the **Complejo Puente de las Herrerías**, go left; after 400m the **Sendero de la Cerrada del Utrero** begins on the right. This marked 2km-loop walk takes you under imposing cliffs to the **Cascada de Linarejos**, then above a narrow reservoir on the Guadalquivir and back to the road. Another 3.5km west along the road and you're at Empalme del Valle, from which it's 17km back to Cazorla.

RÍO BOROSA WALK

Though it gets busy at weekends and holiday times, this walk of about seven hours return (plus stops) is the park's most popular for good reason. It follows the exuberantly vegetated course of the Río Borosa upstream to two beautiful mountain lakes: an ascent of 500m in the course of 12km from Torre del Vinagre. Using the bus to Torre del Vinagre, you can normally do it as a day trip from Cazorla (but confirm latest bus schedules before setting off). You can top up your water bottle at good, drinkable springs along the walk; the last is at the Central Eléctrica hydroelectric station.

A road signed 'Central Eléctrica', opposite Torre del Vinagre, soon crosses the Guadalquivir and, within 1km, reaches the marked start of the walk, on your right beside the Río Borosa. The first section is an unpaved road, criss-crossing the tumbling river on bridges. After about 4km, where the road starts climbing to the left, take a path forking right. This takes you through a beautiful 1.5km section, where the valley narrows to a gorge (the **Cerrada de Elías**) and the path takes to a wooden walkway to save you from swimming. Rejoining the main track, continue for 3km to the Central Eléctrica, a small hydroelectric station. Just past this, a sign points you on up towards the Laguna de Valdeazores. This path will lead you, via some dramatic mountain scenery and two tunnels supplying water to the power station (there's room to stay dry as you go through), to the two lakes – **Laguna de Aguas Negras** (a reservoir), then the natural **Laguna de Valdeazores**.

HORNOS & EL YELMO

Overlooking the northern end of the Embalse del Tranco, Hornos is a small village atop a high rocky outcrop with a small, ruined Islamic castle and panoramic views.

About 10km northeast of Hornos on the A317 is the Puerto de Horno de Peguera pass and junction. One kilometre north from here, a dirt road turns left to the top of El Yelmo (1809m), one of the most distinctive mountains in the north of the park. It's 5km to the top, an ascent of 360m – drivable, but better as a walk, with superb views and griffon vultures wheeling around the skies. At a fork after 1.75km, go right.

SEGURA DE LA SIERRA

The most spectacular and interesting village inside the park, Segura sits 20km north of Hornos, atop a 1100m hill crowned by a castle dominating the countryside for far around. When taken in 1214 by the Knights of Santiago, Segura was one of the very first Christian conquests in Andalucía.

As you reach the upper part of the village, there's a **tourist office** (☎ 953 12 60 53; ☽ 10.30am-2pm & 6.30-8.30pm) beside the Puerta Nueva arch. Segura's two main monuments are normally left open all day every day, but you should check this before proceeding.

The **Baño Moro** (Muslim Bathhouse; Calle Caballeros Santiaguistas), built about 1150, has three elegant rooms (for cold, tepid and hot baths) with horseshoe arches and barrel vaults studded with skylights. The **castle**, at the top of the village, has Islamic (or maybe even earlier) origins. From its three-storey keep there are great views across to El Yelmo and far to the west.

Tours

A number of operators offer trips to some of the park's less accessible areas, plus other activities. Hotels and camping grounds in the park can often arrange for them to pick you up.

The highest-profile operator is **Quercus**, with offices in Cazorla (p786) and at Torre del Vinagre (p788). The firm offers 4WD trips from these centres to *zonas restringidas* (areas where vehicles are not normally allowed) for €19/33 per person per half/full day, as well as guided walks and photographic outings. Some guides speak English or French.

Sleeping & Eating

There's plenty of accommodation in the park, much of it dotted along the A319 north of Empalme del Valle. At peak times it's worth booking ahead. Most restaurants in the park – except small, casual roadside café's – are part of hotels or hostales.

Hotel Riogazas (☎ 953 12 40 35; www.riogazas .com in Spanish; Carretera La Iruela–El Chorro Km4.5; s/d €45.50/61.75; P ⊠ ⊉) The Riogazas is an old hunting lodge that's been converted into an attractive little hotel, along the road between La Iruela and El Chorro. It has a good restaurant.

Hotel de Montaña La Hortizuela (☎ 953 71 31 50; www.turismoencazorla.com/hortizuela.html in Spanish; Carretera del Tranco Km53; s/d €33/55; P ⊠ ⊉) This cosy hotel has a tranquil setting, 1km along a signed track off the A319, 2km north of Torre del Vinagre. The restaurant serves a *menú* at €9.

Los Enebros (☎ 953 72 71 10; www.lfhoteles.com in Spanish; Arroyo Frío; s/d €48/78, 4-person apt €93; P ⊠ ⊉) At the northern end of Arroyo Frío village, on the A319, this complex has a hotel, apartments, chalets and a small campsite. The accommodation is a bit rough and ready, but it has two pools and a playground, and a huge range of activities can be arranged here.

El Parral (☎ 953 72 72 65; Arroyo Frío; 4-person apt €40.30; P ⊠ ⊉) Attractive, spacious apart-

ments with well-equipped kitchens and scenic terraces.

Hotel Noguera de la Sierpe (☎ 953 71 30 21; www.lfhoteles.com in Spanish; Carretera del Tranco Km51; s/d €63/97; P ⊠ ⊉) This curious hotel, overlooking a picturesque little lake 5km north of Arroyo Frío, is a favourite of the hunting fraternity and decked out with trophies, including a strangely alert-looking stuffed lion in the lobby (clearly not a local catch). The rooms are comfortable, if not exactly cosy. You can arrange riding sessions at the hotel's stables and there is a good rustic restaurant.

Parador El Adelantado (☎ 953 72 70 75; www .parador.es; s/d €80.90/97.10; P ⊠ ⊉) This isn't one of the finest *paradors* but its lovely pine forest setting, grassy garden and good pool go some way to compensate. Only nine of the rooms have views. It's at the end of the JF7094, near Vadillo Castril.

Los Huertos de Segura (☎ 953 48 04 02; anton peer@arrakis.es; Calle Castillo 11, Segura de la Sierra; 2-/4-person apt €54/60; P ⊠) Excellent apartments, whose friendly owners are a good source of information about tours and walking in the area.

CAMPING

Camping is not allowed outside the organised camping grounds. From October to April you should check ahead that these are open.

Complejo Puente de las Herrerías (☎ /fax 953 72 70 90; near Vadillo Castril; camping per adult/tent/car €4/3.60/3.60, 2-person cabin €43.60; P ⊠ ⊉) This is the largest camping ground in the park, with room for about 1000 people, plus a restaurant and a pool. You can arrange horse riding, canoeing, canyoning and climbing.

Just off the A319, between 3km and 7km north of Torre del Vinagre, are three medium-sized camping grounds beside the Guadalquivir, all charging between €12 and €15 for two people with a tent and car:

Camping Chopera Coto Ríos (☎ 953 71 30 05)
Camping Llanos de Arance (☎ 953 71 31 39)
Camping Fuente de la Pascuala (☎ 953 71 30 28)

Getting There & Away

Carcesa (☎ 953 72 11 42) runs two daily buses (except Sunday) from Cazorla's Plaza de la Constitución to Empalme del Valle (€1.20, 30 minutes), Arroyo Frío (€1.60, 45 minutes), Torre del Vinagre (€3.05, one hour) and Coto Ríos (€3.05, 70 minutes). Pick up the latest timetable from the Cazorla tourist office or Quercus.

ALMERÍA PROVINCE

Andalucía's easternmost province is the most parched part of Spain, with large expanses of rocky semidesert. The Cabo de Gata promontory is arguably the most dramatic corner of the Andalucian coast, and its beaches are definitely the best in Mediterranean Andalucía. Remote and long impoverished, Almería has used its main resource, sunshine, to stage an economic comeback in recent decades, through tourism and intensive horticulture in ugly plastic greenhouses, where much of the labour is done by thousands of migrant Moroccan workers.

ALMERÍA

pop 177,000

The hefty, cliff-ringed Alcazaba fortress dominating Almería is a dramatic reminder of past glories. As the chief port of the Córdoba caliphate and, later, capital of an 11th-century *taifa*, Islamic Almariya grew wealthy weaving silk from the silkworms of the Alpujarras. Devastated by an earthquake in 1522, Almería is today a likeable and lively port and the hub of a mining and horticultural region.

Orientation

The city centre lies between the Alcazaba and the Rambla de Belén, a broad *paseo* (promenade or boulevard) created from a dry riverbed. Paseo de Almería, cutting northwest from Rambla de Belén to the Puerta de Purchena intersection, is the main city-centre artery. The bus and train stations are together on Plaza de la Estación, east of Rambla de Belén.

Information

There are numerous banks on Paseo de Almería.

El Libro Picasso (☎ 950 23 56 00; Calle Reyes Católicos 17 & 18) Excellent book and map shop.

Hospital Torrecárdenas (☎ 950 01 61 00; Pasaje Torrecárdenas) Four kilometres northeast of the centre.

Municipal tourist office (☎ 950 28 07 48; Rambla de Belén; ⊙ 10am-1pm & 5.30-7.30pm Mon-Fri, 10am-noon Sat)

Policía Local (☎ 950 21 00 19; Calle Santos Zárate)

Regional tourist office (☎ 950 27 43 55; Parque de Nicolás Salmerón s/n; ⊙ 9am-7pm Mon-Fri, 10am-2pm Sat & Sun)

Sights & Activities

ALCAZABA

Founded in 955 by the Córdoba caliph Abd ar-Rahman III, the **Alcazaba** (☎ 950 27 16 17; Calle Almanzor s/n; adult/EU citizen €1.50/free; ⊙ 10am-2pm & 5-8pm May-Sep, 9.30am-1.30pm & 3.30-7pm Oct-Apr) still rises triumphantly from impregnable cliffs and commands exhilarating views, though earthquakes and time have spared little of its internal splendour.

The lowest of the Alcazaba's three compounds, the Primer Recinto, originally served as a military camp and a refuge in times of siege. The Segundo Recinto was the heart of the Alcazaba. At its eastern end is the **Ermita de San Juan** chapel, which was converted from a mosque by the Catholic Monarchs, who took Almería in 1489. On its northern side are the remains of the Muslim rulers' palace, the **Palacio de Almotacín**. The Ventana de la Odalisca (Concubine's Window) here gets its name from a slave girl, who, legend says, leapt to her death from the window after her imprisoned Christian lover had been thrown from it. The Tercer Recinto, at the top end of the Alcazaba, is a fortress added by the Catholic Monarchs.

CATHEDRAL

Almería's weighty **cathedral** (Plaza de la Catedral; admission €2; ⊙ 10am-5pm Mon-Fri, 10am-1pm Sat) is at the heart of the old part of the city below the Alcazaba. Begun in 1524, its fortress-like appearance, with six towers, was the inevitable result of pirate raids from North Africa.

The spacious interior has a Gothic ribbed ceiling and uses jasper and local marble in its trimmings. The chapel behind the main altar contains the tomb of Bishop Villalán, the cathedral's founder, whose broken-nosed image is a work of Juan de Orea, who also created the Sacristía Mayor with its fine carved stonework.

BEACH

A long, grey-sand beach fronts the palm-lined Paseo Marítimo, east of the city's centre.

ALMERÍA

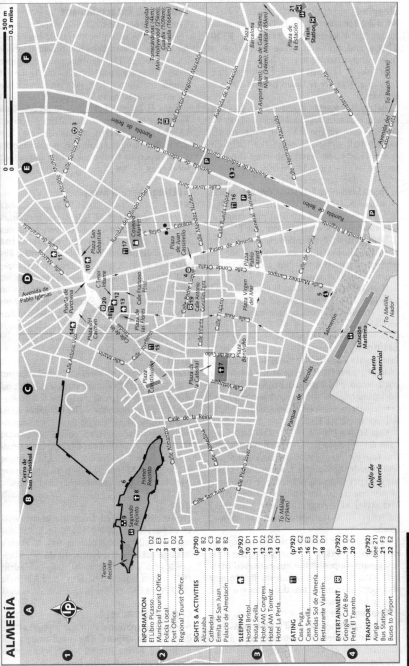

INFORMATION
El Libro Picasso.............	1 D2
Municipal Tourist Office....	2 E3
Policía Local................	3 E1
Post Office.................	4 D2
Regional Tourist Office......	5 D4

SIGHTS & ACTIVITIES (p790)
Alcazaba...................	6 B2
Cathedral..................	7 C3
Ermita de San Juan........	8 B2
Palacio de Almotacín.......	9 B2

SLEEPING 🏠
Hostal Bristol..............	10 D1
Hostal Sevilla..............	11 D1
Hotel AM Congress.........	12 D2
Hotel AM Torreluz.........	13 D2
Hotel La Perla.............	14 D1

EATING 🍴
Casa Puga..................	15 C2
Casa Sevilla................	16 E3
Comidas Sol de Almería.....	17 D2
Restaurante Valentín........	18 D1

ENTERTAINMENT 🎭
Georgia Café Bar...........	19 D2
Peña El Taranto............	20 D1

TRANSPORT (p792)
Auriga.....................	(see 21)
Bus Station................	21 F3
Buses to Airport...........	22 E2

Sleeping

Hotel AM Torreluz (☎ 950 23 49 99; www.amtorre luz.com; Plaza de las Flores 5; s/d €68.80/91.45; P ⊠) This grand four-star place sports lots of brass and marble, and a huge sweeping staircase. A favourite with business clientele, its prices are reduced by up to 40% at weekends.

Hotel AM Congress (☎ 950 23 49 99; www.amtor reluz.com; Plaza de las Flores 5; s/d €55.50/59.60; P ⊠) An offshoot of the AM Torreluz, on the same small square (though the main entrance is on Calle Tenor Iribarne), the Congress provides a good level of service, again with a rather corporate flavour.

Hostal Sevilla (☎ 950 23 00 09; Calle de Granada 23; s/d incl breakfast €32.10/48.15; ⊠) This best budget bet is a cheerful and efficient place that offers clean rooms with air-con and TV.

Hostal Bristol (☎ 950 23 15 95; Plaza San Sebastián 8; s/d €30/40) Though more ramshackle than the Sevilla, the Bristol still has a comfortable, old-fashioned charm.

Hotel La Perla (☎ 950 23 88 77; Plaza del Carmen 7; s/d €45/60; ⊠) The refurbished La Perla provides comfortable, reasonable-value accommodation.

Eating

Restaurante Valentín (☎ 950 26 44 75; Calle Tenor Iribarne 19; mains €10-15; ⊠ closed Mon & Sep) The dark wood and exposed brickwork create an intimate atmosphere and the food and service are good too, although the lobster will set you back €52.

Casa Sevilla (☎ 950 27 29 12; Calle Rueda López; meals €24; ⊠ closed Sun & 1-15 Aug) You'll find this *tour de force* of Andalucian cuisine and wine inside the Galería Almericentro shopping centre. Specialities include *bacalao a la almeriense* (dried and salted cod Almería-style) and Argentine beef, and there are over 8000 bottles of wine to choose from.

Comidas Sol de Almería (Calle Circunvalación, Mercado Central; menú €8.30; ⊠ closed Sun) A fun little restaurant, opposite the busy covered market, with a large patio behind it. Hungry shoppers stream in for the extensive and hearty lunch *menú*.

Casa Puga (Calle Jovellanos 7; tapas €1) Casa Puga has few rivals as Almería's best tapas bar. Shelves of ancient wine bottles and a traditional wall of *azulejo* (glazed blue tiles) set the tone.

Drinking & Entertainment

Georgia Café Bar (☎ 950 25 25 70; Calle Padre Luque 17 ⊠ 8pm-late) A dozen or so music bars cluster in the streets between the post office and cathedral. The Georgia, going for more than 20 years, has terrific ambience. It stages occasional live jazz and even the piped music is great.

Peña El Taranto (☎ 950 23 50 57; Calle Tenor Iribarne 20) In the renovated Aljibes Árabes (Arab Water Cisterns), this is Almería's top authentic flamenco club. Live performances (€20), open to the public, often happen at weekends.

Getting There & Away

AIR

Almería **airport** (☎ 950 21 37 00) receives charter flights from several European countries and also scheduled services by **My Travel Lite** (☎ 902 020191) from Birmingham, **British Airways** (☎ 950 21 38 98) from London Gatwick, **LTU** (☎ 950 21 37 80) and **Hapag-Lloyd** (☎ 902 480500) from Germany, **Transavia** (☎ 902 114478) from Holland, and **Iberia** (☎ 950 21 37 90) from Barcelona, Madrid and Melilla. For one-way international fares leaving Almería, try **Viajes Cemo** (airport ☎ 950 21 38 47).

BOAT

Trasmediterránea (☎ 950 23 61 55; Estación Marítima) sails to/from Melilla six days a week, and three times daily from mid-June to late August or early September. The trip takes up to eight hours. The cheapest passenger accommodation, a *butaca* (seat), costs €29 one way; the fare for a car starts at €122.50 for a small vehicle. Three Moroccan lines sail to/from Nador, the Moroccan town neighbouring Melilla, with similar frequency and prices.

BUS

Destinations served from the clean, efficient **bus station** (☎ 950 26 20 98) include Granada (€9.40 to €16.80, 2¼ hours, 10 daily), Málaga (€13.55, 3¼ hours, 10 daily), Murcia (€14.65, 2½ hours, 10 daily), Madrid (€21, seven hours, five daily) and Valencia (€30.20 to €37.35, 8½ hours, five daily).

CAR & MOTORCYCLE

Several international rental companies have desks at the airport. The good-value local company **Auriga** (☎ 902 206400; www.aurigacar .com) has an office in the bus station.

ANDALUCÍA

TRAIN

Four daily trains run to Granada (€11.80, 2¼ to three hours) and Seville (€28.25, 5½ hours) and two to Madrid (€31 to €36.50, 6¾ to 10 hours).

Getting Around

The airport is 9km east of the city; the No 20 'Alquián' bus (€0.80) runs from Calle Doctor Gregorio Marañón to the airport every 30 to 45 minutes from 7am to 10.30pm (but less frequently on Saturday and Sunday). The last bus from the airport to the city leaves at 10.08pm (11.03pm Saturday and Sunday).

AROUND ALMERÍA
Mini Hollywood

Beyond Benahadux, north of Almería, the landscape becomes a series of canyons and rocky wastes that look as though they are straight out of the Arizona badlands, and in the 1960s and '70s movie-makers shot around 150 Westerns here. Locals played Indians, outlaws and cavalry, while Clint Eastwood, Raquel Welch, Charles Bronson and co did all the talking bits.

The movie industry has left behind three Wild West town sets that are open as tourist attractions. **Mini Hollywood** (☎ 950 36 52 36; adult/child €17/9; ☾ 10am-9pm Apr-Oct, 10am-7pm Tue-Sun Nov-Mar), the best known and the best preserved of these, is 25km from Almería on the Tabernas road. Parts of more than 100 movies, including classic 'spaghetti westerns' (so called because their director was the Italian Sergio Leone) such as *A Fistful of Dollars* and *The Good, the Bad and the Ugly*, were filmed here. At noon and 5pm (and 8pm from mid-June to mid-September) a hammed-up bank hold-up and shoot-out is staged. Rather bizarrely, the ticket also includes entry to the adjoining **Reserva Zoológica** with lions, elephants and numerous other species of African and Iberian fauna. You will need your own vehicle to visit from Almería.

Níjar

Attractive and unusual glazed pottery and colourful striped cotton rugs, known as *jarapas*, are made and sold in this small town that lies 34km northeast of Almería. It's well worth a little detour if you're driving this way.

CABO DE GATA

Some of Spain's most beautiful and least crowded beaches are strung between grand cliffs and capes around this arid promontory east of Almería city. Though Cabo de Gata is not undiscovered, it still has a wild, elemental feel and is far enough from the beaten track to seem empty compared with most Andalucian beach areas. With a couple of exceptions in July and August, its scattered villages remain very low-key.

You can walk along, or not far from, the coast right round from Retamar in the northwest to Agua Amarga in the northeast (61km), but in summer there's little shade.

It's worth calling ahead for accommodation over Easter and in July and August.

The **Parque Natural de Cabo de Gata-Níjar** covers Cabo de Gata's 60km coast plus a slice of hinterland. The park's main information centre is the **Centro de Interpretación Las Amoladeras** (☎ 950 16 04 35; ☾ 10am-2pm & 5.30-9pm daily mid-Jul–mid-Sep, 10am-3pm Tue-Sun mid-Sep–mid-Jul), about 2.5km west of Ruescas.

El Cabo de Gata Village

Fronted by a long straight beach, this village (officially San Miguel de Cabo de Gata) is composed largely of holiday houses and apartments, but has an old nucleus, with a small fishing fleet, at the southern end. The **Oficina de Información** (☎ 950 38 00 04; Avenida Miramar 88; ☾ 10am-2.30pm & 5.30-9pm) rents out bicycles (€13 per day, €4 for two hours).

South of the village stretch the **Salinas de Cabo de Gata**, which are salt-extraction lagoons. In spring many greater flamingos and other birds call in here while migrating to breeding grounds further north. Some stay on to breed, then others arrive in summer: by late August there can be 1000 flamingos here. There's a public viewing hide just off the road, 3km south of the village. You should see a good variety of birds any time except winter, when the *salinas* (salt-extraction lagoons) are drained.

SLEEPING & EATING

Blanca Brisa (☎ 950 37 00 01; www.blancabrisa.com; Las Joricas 49; s/d €38.50/64.50; ℗) A big, peach-coloured, modern hotel at the entrance to the village, with comfortable, if cold-looking, rooms. Its large, decent restaurant (one of the few) serves *platos combinados* for about €5.

CABO DE GATA

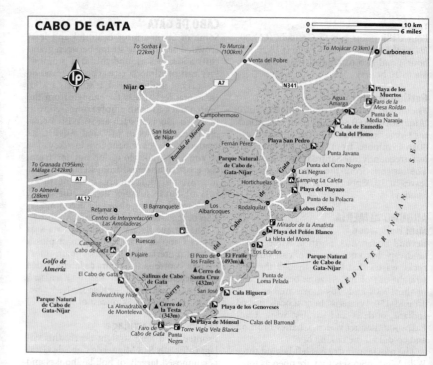

Camping Cabo de Gata (☎ /fax 950 16 04 43; camping per person/site €4/7.35, bungalows €76; **P** **⊠**) This extremely well-run campsite, 1km from the beach, has all the necessary amenities including a restaurant. It's 2.5km north of the village by dirt roads.

El Naranjero (☎ 950 37 01 11; Calle Iglesia 1; mains €9.50-25; ✓ closed Sun) The nearest thing to a proper restaurant, situated at the entrance to the village. It specialises in fish and seafood.

Faro de Cabo de Gata & Around

Beyond the Salinas de Cabo de Gata, the road winds 4km round the cliffs to **Faro de Cabo de Gata**, the lighthouse at the promontory's tip. A turning by Café Bar El Faro, just before the lighthouse, leads to the **Torre Vigía Vela Blanca**, an 18th-century watchtower atop 200m cliffs, with awesome views. Here the road ends but a walking and cycling track continues down to Playa de Mónsul (one hour on foot).

San José
pop 175

San José, spreading round a bay on the eastern side of Cabo de Gata, becomes a mildly chic little resort in summer, but remains a small, pleasant, low-rise place.

ORIENTATION & INFORMATION

The road from the north becomes San José's main street, Avenida de San José, with the beach a couple of blocks down to the left. On Avenida de San José you'll find a **nature-park information office** (☎ 950 38 02 99; Calle Correo; ✓ 10am-2pm & 5-9.30pm Mon-Sat, 10am-2pm Sun), a bank and an ATM. The information office can tell you about bicycle rental, horse riding, boat trips and diving.

BEACHES

San José has a sandy beach but some of the best beaches on Cabo de Gata lie along a dirt road to the southwest. **Playa de los Genoveses**, a broad strip of sand about 1km long, with shallow waters, is 4.5km away. **Playa de Mónsul**, 2.5km further along, is a shorter length of grey sand, backed by huge lumps of volcanic rock. Away from the road, the coast between these two beaches is strung with a series of isolated, sandy cove beaches, the **Calas del Barronal**, which are reachable only on foot.

SLEEPING & EATING

Hostal Sol Bahía (☎ 950 38 03 07, fax 950 38 03 06; Avenida de San José; d €35-60; 🐱) The Sol Bahía and its sister establishment, **Hostal Bahía Plaza**, across the street, are in the centre of San José and have attractive, clean rooms in bright, modern buildings. Half a dozen other hostales and hotels have similar or higher prices.

Hotel Cortijo el Sotillo (☎ 950 61 11 00; www.hotel sotillo.com; Carretera Entrada a San José s/n; s €66-100, d €90-124; mains €8-14; P 🐱 🕭) This fun ranch-style complex, popular with families, has a host of great facilities, on-site riding and a huge, excellent restaurant serving regional cuisine.

Camping Tau (☎ 950 38 01 66; e@parquenatural .com; camping per adult/tent/car €4/4.75/5.50; 🕭 Apr-Sep) Set 250m from the beach, the shady Tau is very popular with families.

Mesón El Tempranillo (☎ 950 38 00 59; Puerto de San José 6-7; mains €9-15) One of a number of good fish restaurants, beneath colourful awnings near the harbour. Eat out on the shaded verandah.

Restaurante El Emigrante (☎ 950 38 03 07; Avenida de San José; fish & meat mains €6-12) Under the same ownership as the Bahía hostales, the Emigrante is a dependable option in the centre of town.

San José to Las Negras

The rugged coast northeast of San José allows only two small settlements, the odd fort and a few beaches before the village of Las Negras, 17km away as the crow flies. The road spends most of its time ducking inland.

The hamlet of **Los Escullos** has a short beach. You can walk here from San José, along a track starting at Cala Higuera bay. **Hotel Los Escullos** (☎ 950 38 97 33; d incl breakfast €51-85; 🐱), a small hotel near the beach, has reasonable air-con rooms and a restaurant serving limited fare between €8 and €15. The large **Camping Los Escullos** (☎ 950 38 98 11; camping per 2 adults, tent, car & powered sites €18.70; 🕭 year-round; P 🕭), 900m back from the beach, has a pool, a restaurant, a grocery store, an ATM and bikes for hire.

One kilometre further northeast, **La Isleta del Moro** is a tiny village with a beach and a couple of fishing boats. **Casa Café de la Loma** (La Isleta del Moro; s/d €30/42, Aug €36/48), on a small hill above the village, is a friendly, relaxed little place with terrific views.

From here the road heads inland past the former gold-mining village of **Rodalquilar**. About 1km past Rodalquilar is the turning to **Playa del Playazo**, a good beach between two headlands, 2km along a level track. From here you can walk near the coast to **Las Negras**, set on a pebbly beach and largely given over to seasonal tourism.

On Las Negras' main street, **Hostal Arrecife** (☎ 950 38 81 40; Calle Bahía 6, Las Negras; s/d €26/38) has cool, quiet, well-maintained rooms, some with sea views from their balconies. **Camping La Caleta** (☎ 950 52 52 37; camping per adult/tent/car €4.60/4.50/4.75; 🕭 year-round; P 🕭) lies in a separate cove 1km south of Las Negras. It can be fiercely hot in summer, but there is a good pool. Other accommodation in Las Negras is mostly holiday apartments and houses to let. **Restaurante La Palma** (☎ 950 38 80 42; mains €5-10), overlooking the beach, plays good music and serves excellent fish at medium prices.

Las Negras to Agua Amarga

There's no road along this secluded, cliff-lined stretch of coast, but walkers can take an up-and-down path of about 11km, giving access to several beaches. **Playa San Pedro**, one hour from Las Negras, is the site of a ruined hamlet with a castle. It's 1½ hours on from there to **Cala del Plomo** beach, with another tiny village, then 1½ hours further to **Agua Amarga**.

Drivers must head inland from Las Negras through Hortichuelas. A mostly un-sealed road heads northeast, cross-country from the bus shelter in Fernán Pérez. Keep to the main track at all turnings and after 10km you'll reach a sealed road running down from the N341 to Agua Amarga, a slow-paced tourist-cum-fishing village on a straight sandy beach that attracts cool young professional types. **Hotel Family** (☎ 950 13 80 14; fax 950 13 80 70; Calle La Lomilla; d with/without sea views €100/70) is relaxed, unpretentious and renowned for its excellent four-course *menú* (€16). Chic, slick **miKasa** (☎ 950 13 80 73; www.hotelmikasa.com; Carretera Carboneras s/n; d low season €80-174; P 🐱 🕭) is a romantic, intimate hideaway for the weekend crowd.

Getting There & Away

From Almería bus station buses run to San José (€2.40, 1¼ hours, four daily Monday to Saturday), Las Negras (€3.40, 1¼ hours, one daily Monday to Saturday) and Agua Amarga (€3.70, 1¼ hours, one daily Monday to Friday).

MOJÁCAR

pop 6000

Mojácar, northeast of Cabo de Gata, is actually made up of two towns: the old Mojácar Pueblo, a jumble of white, cube-shaped houses situated on a hilltop 2km inland; and Mojácar Playa, a modern beach resort strip 7km long but only a few blocks wide. Though dominated by tourism, the Pueblo is picturesque. Mojácar Playa has few high-rise buildings, a long, clean beach, and a lively summer scene.

From the 13th to 15th centuries, Mojácar found itself on the Granada emirate's eastern frontier, finally falling to the Catholic Monarchs in 1488. Tucked away in an isolated corner of one of Spain's most backward regions, it was decaying and half-abandoned by the mid-20th century, before its mayor started luring artists and others with giveaway property offers.

Orientation & Information

Pueblo and Playa are joined by a road that heads uphill from a junction by the Parque Comercial shopping centre, towards the northern end of Mojácar Playa.

The **tourist office** (☎ 950 47 51 62; Calle Glorieta; ◷ 10am-2pm & 5-7.30pm Mon-Fri, 10.30am-1.30pm Sat) is just off Mojácar Pueblo's main square, Plaza Nueva. In the same building are the post office and **Policía Local** (☎ 950 47 20 00).

Sights

Exploring the Pueblo is mainly a matter of wandering the winding streets, with their flower-decked balconies, and nosing into craft shops, galleries and boutiques. The **Mirador El Castillo**, at the topmost point, provides magnificent views. The fortress-style **Iglesia de Santa María** (Calle Iglesia) dates from 1560, and may have once been a mosque.

The most touching spot is the **Fuente Mora** (Moorish Fountain; Calle La Fuente) in the lower part of the Pueblo. Though remodelled in modern times, it maintains the medieval Islamic tradition of making art out of flowing water. An inscription records the moving speech made here, according to legend, by Alavez, the last Islamic governor of Mojácar, to the envoy of the Catholic Monarchs in 1488,

pleading for his people to be permitted to stay and 'continue working the land of our ancestors'.

Sleeping & Eating

MOJÁCAR PUEBLO

Hostal Mamabel's (☎ 950 47 24 48; www.mamabels.com; Calle Embajadores 5; d/ste €65/87) This exquisite small hotel hugs the very edge of the Pueblo, with rooms seemingly piled on top of each other. All are large and individually styled and some have fantastically precipitous views. The stylish restaurant here, **El Horno** (mains €10.50-16), offers the best home-cooked food in Mojácar, including a tasty couscous.

La Fonda del Castillo (☎ 950 47 30 22; www.elcastillomojacar.com in Spanish; Mirador El Castillo; d €48-54; ☒) A laid-back hostal with a no-fuss bohemian atmosphere and fantastic views.

Hostal Arco Plaza (☎ 950 47 27 77; fax 950 47 27 17; Calle Aire Bajo 1; s/d €42/54; ☒) Just off Plaza Nueva, the Arco Plaza has rooms in pretty pastel shades. The management are incredibly friendly and efficient.

Pensión El Torreón (☎ 950 47 52 59; Calle Jazmín 4; d without bathroom €50) This attractive hostal, with yet more great views, was allegedly the birthplace of Walt Disney, who locals maintain was the love child of a village girl and a wealthy landowner.

La Taberna (☎ 647-724367; Plaza del Cano 1; tapas & platos combinados from €4) This thriving little eatery, inside a warren of cave-like rooms, serves extremely well-prepared meals with plenty of tasty vegetarian options.

Restaurante El Viento del Desierto (Plaza Frontón; mains €5-6) This good-value Moroccan-cum-Spanish eatery is just by the church.

MOJÁCAR PLAYA

Hotel Río Abajo (☎ 950 47 89 28; www.mojacar.com/rio-abajo; Calle Río Abajo; d €45.10-57.10; ℗ ☒) Blue-and-white pueblo-style chalets are dotted among lush gardens with direct access to the broad sandy beach at the far north end of Mojácar Playa. A good place for kids.

Hotel Felipe San Bernabé (☎ 950 47 82 02; fax 950 47 27 35; Playa Las Ventanicas; d €45-66; mains €11-16; ℗ ☒) The San Bernabé is a swish and good-value hotel set back from one of the better beaches. It has a plush, conservatory-style restaurant providing excellent Spanish cooking, with a good selection of fish dishes.

Drinking & Entertainment

Classical music, live comedy acts and jazz concerts are staged at the lively **Café Bar Mirador del Castillo** (☎ 950 47 30 22; ☽ 11am-11pm or later) in Mojácar Pueblo. The Pueblo's better bars (which open in the evenings only, from around 8pm) include the Mexican-style **Caipirinha Caipirosa** (Calle Horno), the reggae **Azul Marino** (Calle Enmedio; ☽ 8pm-late Jun-Sep) and **La Muralla** (Calle Estación Nueva), which boasts the most romantic views from its terrace. Stylish **Time & Place** (Plaza de las Flores) keeps the drinks and conversation going till the early hours.

Alternatively, just hang out in the beachfront bar of the moment, **La Mar Salada** (Paseo del Mediterraneo 62; ☽ 10am-late Mon-Fri, 11am-late Sat) or lively **Tito's** (☎ 950 61 50 30; Playa de las Ventanicas; ☽ Apr-Oct), which features live music, including jazz.

Getting There & Around

Long-distance buses stop at the Parque Comercial and the Fuente stop at the foot of Mojácar Pueblo. The tourist office has timetables. Buses go to Murcia (€8.70, 2½ hours, four daily), Almería (€5.50, 1¾ hours, two daily), Granada (€13.75, 4¼ hours, two daily) and Madrid (€29.15, eight hours, two daily). Buses to Alicante, Valencia and Barcelona go from Vera, 16km north and served by several daily buses from Mojácar (€1, 45 minutes).

A local bus service (€0.75) runs a circuit from the southern to northern ends of Mojácar Playa, then back to the Parque Comercial, up to the Pueblo (Calle Glorieta), then back down to the Parque Comercial and the southern end of the Playa. It runs every half-hour, 9am to 11.30pm, from April to September, and every hour from 9.30am to 7.30pm between October and March.

Extremadura

A broad, sun-drenched and sparsely populated tableland bordering Portugal, Extremadura lies far off the tourist trail and remains one of the country's best-kept secrets. Extremadura is aptly named. A land of extremes (boiling in summer and bitingly cold in winter), it has known the depths of poverty and the riches of the Americas.

Reconquered from the Muslims in the 13th century, the land was handed to knights who turned it into one great sheep pen. Those who did not work the land often had only one choice – migration. Small wonder that many 16th-century conquistadors, including Pizarro and Cortés, sprang from this land. The riches they brought back from the Americas are to this day reflected in the lavish townhouses that litter many of the region's towns.

Long before Pizarro and Cortés, the Romans flourished in the city of Mérida, and plenty of evidence of this remains. The urban splendour continues in the old centre of Cáceres, while on a smaller scale towns such as Trujillo and Guadalupe are enchanting.

Wooded sierras rise up along the region's northern, eastern and southern fringes. The north in particular has a sequence of beautiful ranges and green valleys dotted with timeless old villages. Two of Spain's major rivers, the Tajo and the Guadiana, cross Extremadura from east to west. The craggy Parque Natural Monfragüe, straddling the Tajo between Plasencia and Trujillo, has some of Spain's most spectacular bird life.

Aside from the region's famed ham, *jamón de bellota* (acorn), another culinary highlight is the creamy sheep-milk cheese Torta del Casar. The north is *cereza* (cherry) country; try the sweet *licor de cereza* or opt for the acorn variety, *licor de bellota*.

HIGHLIGHTS

- Travel to Trujillo, home town of some of Latin America's most (in)famous **conquistadors** (p814)
- Discover the medieval nooks and crannies of **Cáceres** (p809)
- Spot majestic birds of prey as they swoop over the **Parque Natural Monfragüe** (p808)
- Explore fine Roman ruins in **Mérida** (p819)
- Commune with Carlos I at tranquil **Monasterio de Yuste** (p801)
- Enjoy the quiet, ancient stone village of **San Martín de Trevejo** (p806) in the hilly northwest
- Wander among white buildings in the southern town of **Zafra** (p825)
- Watch the ritual of **Los Empalaos** in Villanueva de la Vera (p802)
- Keep your bearings in the labyrinthine frontier castle of **Albuquerque** (p825)

San Martín de Trevejo ★
Monasterio de Yuste ★
★ Villanueva de la Vera
Plasencia ★
Parque Natural Monfragüe ★
Cáceres ★
★ Albuquerque
★ Trujillo
★ Mérida
★ Zafra

| ■ AREA: 41,634 SQ KM | ■ POP: 1,073,904 | ■ AVE SUMMER TEMP: HIGH 38°C, LOW 26°C |

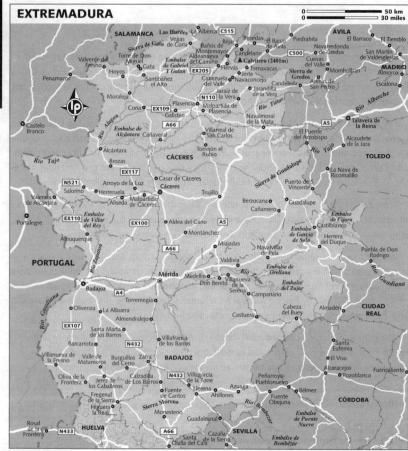

EXTREMADURA

NORTHERN EXTREMADURA

In the far north of Extremadura you're in the western reaches of the Cordillera Central, a jigsaw of uplands and valleys arching around Plasencia from the Sierra de Gredos in the east to the Sierra de Gata in the west. Northeast, three lush valleys – La Vera, the Valle del Jerte and the Valle del Ambroz – stretch down towards the old city of Plasencia. Watered by rushing mountain streams (*gargantas*) and dotted with ancient villages, these valleys offer a good network of places to stay and some fine walking routes.

The once remote Las Hurdes region in the northernmost tip of Extremadura has a harsh sort of beauty, while the Sierra de Gata in the northwest is pretty and more fertile.

LA VERA

The many crops of La Vera, occupying the northern side of the valley of the Río Tiétar, include raspberries, asparagus, figs and paprika (*pimentón*), sold in old-fashioned tins and locally called *oro rojo* (red gold). La Vera is also Spain's largest producer of tobacco (look out for the brick drying sheds with their honeycombs of air vents). Much of the production benefits from EU subsidies that could be threatened now that the EU has 10 new member states.

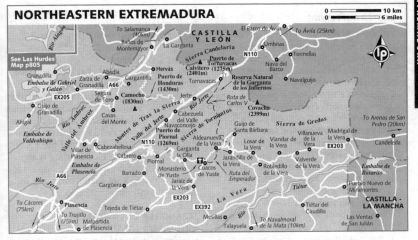

NORTHEASTERN EXTREMADURA

Typical too of La Vera are half-timbered houses leaning at odd angles, their overhanging upper storeys supported by timber or stone pillars.

Information

A good regional website is www.turismo extremadura.com. Useful websites for the valley, with tips on walks, villages and accommodation are www.aturive.com and www .comarcadelavera.com.

Tourist office (☎ 927 17 05 87; Avenida de la Constitución 167, Jaraíz de la Vera; ☼ 9.30am-2pm & 4.30-7.30pm Mon-Fri, 10am-2pm Sat & Sun) If you're here to hike, ask for its useful walking brochure, *Senderos con Encanto de La Vera de Extremadura*.

Tourist office (☎ 927 56 04 60; Plaza de la Constitución 1, Jarandilla de la Vera; ☼ 10am-2pm & 4-6pm Tue-Sat, 10am-2pm Sun)

Sights & Activities

Cuacos de Yuste, 45km northeast of Plasencia, is surrounded by typical La Vera half-timbered houses, including **Casa Juan de Austria** (Plaza Juan de Austria); look for the bust of Carlos I before it. Here, the emperor's illegitimate son (Don Juan of Austria, later a charismatic admiral who beat the Turks at the Battle of Lepanto in 1571) reputedly stayed while visiting his father at the Monasterio de Yuste.

Two kilometres northwest of Cuacos is the **Monasterio de Yuste** (☎ 927 17 21 30; www .yuste.org/monasterio; admission with guided tour in Spanish €2.50; ☼ 9.30am-12.30pm & 3-6pm Mon-Sat, 9.30-11.15am & 3-6pm Sun), to which the gouty

Carlos I of Spain retired in 1557 to spend his dying years. (Confusingly, he was known with equal frequency as Carlos V of Austria, Emperor of the Holy Roman Empire, having divided the world's biggest empire between his brother and his legitimate son, Felipe II.) The monastery is occupied by a closed order of Hieronymite monks, but you can visit the outlying church, with its Gothic and Plateresque cloisters, and the modest royal chambers, with the ailing monarch's bed placed to give him a direct view of the altar.

The road to the monastery continues 4km to **Garganta la Olla**, a picturesque village from where you can make the spectacular drive over the 1269m **Puerto de Piornal** pass to the Valle del Jerte.

Jarandilla de la Vera, 10km northeast of Cuacos de Yuste, has a 15th-century fortress-church on Plaza de la Constitución.

The **Ruta del Emperador**, a 10km walking trail, follows the Emperor's route from Jarandilla to the Monasterio de Yuste. Follow the sign south from the church below the town's *parador* (luxurious state-owned hotel) and turn right at a T-junction to leave town via Calle Marina.

Other La Vera villages with fine traditional architecture are **Valverde de la Vera** and **Villanueva de la Vera**. The former is particularly engaging, with its pretty Plaza de España lined with timber balconies and town water gushing down ruts etched into the middle of the cobbled lanes.

EASTER SUFFERING

Villanueva de la Vera is the scene, on Good Thursday, of one of the more curious of Spain's religious festivities, **Los Empalaos** (literally 'The Impaled'). Several penitent locals submit to this Via Crucis, their arms strapped to a beam (from a plough) and their naked bodies wrapped tight with cords from waist to armpits, and the length of the arms to the fingertips. Barefoot and with two swords strapped to their backs, veiled and wearing a crown of thorns, these 'walking crucifixes' follow a painful Way of the Cross, watched on in respectful silence by townsfolk and visitors from far and wide. Hanging from the timber are chains of iron that tinkle in a sinister fashion as the penitents make their painful progress. As they make their way, guided by *cirineos* (guides who light the way and help them if they fall), the *empalaos* occasionally cross paths. When this happens they kneel and rise again to continue their path. Doctors stay on hand as being so tightly strapped does nothing for blood circulation.

Sleeping & Eating

Many villages have camping grounds, often with good riverside positions. Some fine *casas rurales* (country houses) are also dotted about the area, along with the occasional good hotel. A handful of fine local restaurants are worth searching out.

CUACOS DE YUSTE

Hotel Moregón (☎ 927 17 21 81; www.moregon.com; Avenida de la Constitución 77; s/d €32/51.35; ✗) Handy for the Monasterio de Yuste, this modern place offers a varied range of rooms, most with elements of exposed brick wall, cool floor tiles and a colour scheme ranging from sunny yellow to wine red. On the premises you'll also find a good restaurant.

Camping Carlos I (☎ 927 17 20 92; camping per person/tent/car €3.10/3.10/3.10; ✆ Easter–mid-Sep; ☍ P) Just 1km east of Cuacos de Yuste, this is another shady spot with a tennis court and a restaurant.

GARGANTA LA OLLA

Restaurante La Fragua (☎ 927 17 95 71; Calle de Toril 4; meals €20-25) One of several welcoming eateries scattered about the cramped little lanes of this hamlet, La Fragua offers good local cooking in a busy dining room, all timber beams and exposed stone walls.

JARAIZ DE LA VERA

Finca Valvellidos (☎ 927 19 41 43; www.valvellidos .com; d €45-56) The area is laced with *casas rurales* but this is one of the best. In this impeccably restored farmhouse you find spacious double rooms; it also has bungalows and self-contained apartments, all in a soft country setting 2km in off the EX392, 2km south of Jaraiz. Horse riding is an option and downstairs is a small restaurant for guests – the €15 set menu combines local tastes with international caprice.

JARANDILLA DE LA VERA

Hotel Jaranda (☎ 927 56 02 06; www.hoteljaranda .com; Avenida de Soledad Vega Ortiz 101; s/d €30/60; ✗ ☐) From the lounge area of this hotel you espy the town's Castillo de los Condes de Oropesa (and *parador*, see following), while from some of the rooms guests enjoy vistas of the Sierra de Gredos and Valle Jaranda. Rooms are furnished in antique style, some with brass beds and others with dark-oak bedheads.

Parador (☎ 927 56 01 17; jarandilla@parador.es; Avenida de García Prieto 1; d €113.30; ✗ ☍ P) Push out the boat and emulate the emperor by staying overnight in this stylish castle-turned-hotel. Protected by the stout walls and turrets of this 15th-century castle are tastefully decorated rooms with period furniture.

Camping Jaranda (☎ 927 56 04 54; camping per person/tent/car €3.60/3.60/3.60; ✆ mid-Mar–mid-Sep; ☍ P) Located 1.25km west of Jarandilla, this site is particularly good for walkers and provides plans for gentle hikes in the area. The grounds sit next to a babbling brook and have a restaurant, plenty of shade and bungalows for those without tents.

VALVERDE DE LA VERA

Restaurante Tejabana (☎ 927 56 70 48, 687-832802; Calle de Mirlos 6; meals €30-35; ✆ lunch Fri-Sun) Hidden away in a charming yellow house on the elbow of a tight lane, this is a surprise packet, offering a cut above the standard local faves with an inventive whim. How does *solomillo de avestruz con frutas del bosque* (ostrich sirloin with wild fruits from the forest) sound?

Getting There & Away

Mirat (☎ 927 53 54 39; www.mirat.net) runs up to two buses daily between La Vera villages and Plasencia. The trip from Plasencia to the most distant villages (Madrigal de la Vera) takes 1¾ hours.

VALLE DEL JERTE
Orientation & Information

This valley, separated by the Sierra de Tormantos from La Vera, grows half of Spain's cherries and is a sea of white blossom in late March or early April. The Plasencia–Ávila N110 runs up the valley, crossing into Castilla y León by the Puerto de Tornavacas (1275m).

Tourist office (☎ 927 47 25 58; www.turismovalle deljerte.com; ☉ 10am-3pm Mon, 10am-3pm & 4-5.30pm Tue-Fri, 10am-2pm Sat) This office, 600m north of Cabezuela del Valle, covers the whole valley.

www.elvalledeljerte.com Another useful website.

Sights & Activities

Piornal (1200m), on the southeast flank of the valley and famous for its Serrano ham, makes a good base for walks along the Sierra de Tormantos.

In **Cabezuela del Valle**, Plaza de Extremadura, leading into Calle Hondón, has some fine houses with overhanging wooden balconies. A winding 35km road, easily the most spectacular drive in the region, leads from just north of Cabezuela over the 1430m Puerto de Honduras to Hervás in the Valle del Ambroz.

Jerte is another good base for walks in the beautiful **Reserva Natural de la Garganta de los Infiernos** (☎ 927 01 49 36; www.gargantade losinfiernos.com). This nature reserve of 'Hell's Gorge' has a small information office beside Camping Valle del Jerte. An easy 50-minute walk from the office takes you to Los Pilones, strangely smooth rock formations sliced in half by the emerald and sapphire crystal-clear water of the Río Jerte.

Tornavacas, yet another village with a huddled old quarter, is the starting point of the **Ruta de Carlos V**. This 28km trail (PR1) follows the route by which Carlos I was carried over the mountains to Cuacos de Yuste (see La Vera p801) via Jarandilla de la Vera. You can walk it in one day – just as Carlos' bearers did in the 1550s. The route crosses the Sierra de Tormantos by the 1479m Collado (or Puerto) de las Yeguas.

Sleeping & Eating

Camping Valle del Jerte (☎ 927 47 01 27; camping@ elvalledeljerte.com; camping per 2 people, tent & car €14.40; ☉ mid-Mar–mid-Sep; ☒ P) Just outside Jerte, the grounds boasts a tennis court, bar-restaurant and minimarket.

Camping Río Jerte (☎ 927 17 30 06; www.camping riojerte.com; camping per person/tent/car €3.50/3.50/3.50, bungalows €66.20; ☒ P) This camping ground is on the river's right bank, 1.5km southwest of Navaconcejo. It hires out bikes and has some attractive stone bungalows sleeping up to four. To cool off you can choose from the natural riverside pool or a standard artificial one.

Hospedería La Serrana (☎ 927 47 60 34; www .hospederialaserrana.com; Carretera Garganta la Olla s/n; s/d €40.25/58.05; ☒ P) Only 1km east of Piornal, you can look forward to large, well-furnished, excellent-value rooms in this low-slung house in the country. The location is ideal for exploring the sierra's signed walking trails.

Hotel Aljama (☎ 927 47 22 91; Calle de Federico Bajo s/n, Cabezuela del Valle; s/d with bathroom €25.70/45; ☒) Almost touching the church across the street, this place preserves some of the

---

DEHESAS

The Spanish word *dehesa* means, simply, 'pastureland', but in parts of Extremadura, where pastures are often dotted with evergreen oaks, it takes on a dimension that sends environmentalists into rapture. *Dehesas* of *encina* (holm oak) or *alcornoque* (cork oak) are textbook cases of sustainable exploitation. The bark of the cork oak can be stripped every nine years for cork *(corcho)* – you'll see the scars on some trees, a bright terracotta colour if they're new. The holm oak can be pruned about every four years and the wood used for charcoal. Meanwhile, livestock can graze the pastures, and in autumn pigs are turned out to gobble up the fallen acorns *(bellotas)* – a diet that produces the best ham of all.

Such, at least, is the theory. In practice a growing number of Extremadura's *dehesas* are used to less than their full potential. Some belong to absentee landlords, who use them only for shooting; others are left untended because people are finding easier ways of earning a crust.

traditional architecture (plenty of wood beams and it juts out into the narrow lane) typical of towns in this part of the region. Rooms are spacious and have a rustic touch. The restaurant is one of the best in town, offering generous main courses, mostly meat, and a *menú del día* (€15).

Hotel Los Arenales (☎ 927 47 02 50; www.hotel arenales.com; s/d €24.05/36.05; ✗ P) Just 1.5km southwest of Jerte on the N110, this is a decent roadside stopover with a restaurant. It is located about 500m from the Río Jerte and the Garganta de los Infiernos park.

The valley is known for its *casas rurales*, country homestays that are sometimes in the villages. They usually offer only a handful of rooms and are often booked well in advance on weekends. **El Cerezal de los Sotos** (☎ 927 47 04 29, 607-752197; elcerezaldelossotos@ hotmail.com; Jerte; d €50; ✗ P) is a fine example of the species. A sprawling stone house set amid gardens on the east bank of the Río Jerte (follow the signs from the N110), it is a splendid country home.

Getting There & Away

From Plasencia there's one weekday bus to Piornal and up to four along the valley to Tornavacas.

VALLE DEL AMBROZ

This broader valley west of the Valle del Jerte, once split by the Roman Vía de la Plata (Silver Route), nowadays carries the A66, running from Plasencia to Salamanca in Castilla y León. The area's **tourist office** (☎ 927 47 36 18; www.valleambroz.com; Calle de Braulio Navas 6; ☻ 10am-2.30pm & 4-6pm Tue-Fri, 10am-2pm Sat & Sun Oct-Apr; 10am-2.30pm & 5-7pm Tue-Fri, 10am-2pm Sat & Sun May-Sep) is in Hervás.

Hervás
pop 3846

This characterful town has Extremadura's best surviving **barrio judío** (Jewish quarter), which thrived until the 1492 expulsion of the Jews, when most families sought refuge in Portugal. For a fine view, climb up to the **Iglesia de Santa María**, on the site of a ruined Knights Templar castle.

The **Museo Pérez Comendador-Leroux** (☎ 927 48 16 55; Calle de Asensio Neila; admission €1.20, Sun free; ☻ 4-8pm Tue, 11am-2pm & 4-8pm Wed-Fri, 10.30am-2pm Sat & Sun), in an impressive 18th-century mansion on the main street, houses works

of Hervás-born, 20th-century sculptor Enrique Pérez Comendador and his wife, the French painter Magdalena Leroux.

The **Museo de la Moto Clásica** (☎ 927 48 12 06; www.museomotoclasica.com; Carretera de la Garganta; adult/child €10/5; ☻ 10.30am-1.30pm & 4-7pm Tue-Fri, 10.30am-1.30pm & 4-8pm Sat & Sun Sep-Jun; 10.30am-1.30pm & 5-9pm Tue-Fri, 10.30am-1.30pm & 4-9pm Sat & Sun Jul-Aug), on a hillock 200m north of the river, is home to a large collection of classic motorcycles, including models ranging from Harleys to Zundapps. In separate pavilions are collections of classic cars and horse-drawn carriages too. Round off a visit with a coffee on the terrace.

SLEEPING & EATING

Camping El Pinajarro (☎ 927 48 16 73; www.camping elpinajarro.com; camping per person/tent/car €3.90/3.90/ 3.90; ☻ mid-Mar–late Sep) On the EX205, 2¾km southwest of Hervás, this shady, top-class camping ground is run by a welcoming young couple. Environmentally friendly and warmly recommended, it rents out mountain bikes.

Hospedería Valle del Ambroz (☎ 927 47 48 28; www.hospederiavalledelambroz.com; Plaza del Hospital s/n; s/d €69.55/112.35; ✗ 🖭 P) Occupying a beautifully restored 17th-century monastery, this place is not all that it seems. The rustic monumental exterior belies a rather more modern interior, where instead of creaking period furniture you are confronted by soft pastel colours and contemporary art.

Granadilla

About 22km west of Hervás, **Granadilla** (admission free; ☻ 10am-1pm & 5-7pm Mon-Fri, 5-7pm Sat, 10am-1pm Sun) is a picturesque fortified village. Abandoned after the creation (in the 1960s) of the reservoir that laps around it, Grandilla is gradually being restored and is used as a centre for student rural retreats. The lush green setting adds a special touch to this ghostly place. To get here, drive to Zarza de Granadilla and follow the signs for the run-down 11km road.

Baños de Montemayor

Water and wicker bring visitors to this small spa town, 7km north of Hervás. Its two springs, both dispensing sulphurous waters at 43°C, were first tapped by the Romans, whose baths soothed the muscles of weary travellers along the Vía de la Plata. At the

Balneario de Baños de Montemayor (☎ 923 42 83 02; www.villatermal.com; Avenida de las Termas 52) you can follow a 45-minute water-based relaxation programme – and take a peek at the remains of the Roman bathhouse – for €36 (or €64 for two people together). A host of other treatment options from mudpacks to massage are also available.

Baskets of all shapes and sizes, mats, even hats, cascade from the wicker shops along the main street. Check the label if something takes your fancy; much of what's on sale nowadays comes from the Far East.

Getting There & Away

Alsa (☎ 902 422242; www.alsa.es) runs four to five buses daily between Cáceres, Plasencia and Salamanca via the Valle del Ambroz and stopping 2km outside Hervás.

LAS HURDES

Las Hurdes was long synonymous with poverty, disease and chilling tales of witchcraft, evil spirits and cannibalism. In 1922 the miserable existence of the *hurdanos* prompted Alfonso XIII to declare during a horseback tour, 'I can bear to see no more'. A decade later Luis Buñuel made *Las Hurdes – Terre Sans Pain* (Land without Bread), his short, harrowing documentary about rural poverty. Today Las Hurdes has shaken off the worst of its poverty, as evidenced by the slick roads and growth of could-be-anywhere housing, which has robbed much of the picturesque feel from its villages but notably improved locals' living standards. Outsiders are still a rare enough phenomenon to attract stares.

The austere, rocky terrain yields only small terraces of cultivable land along the riverbanks. The huddles of small stone houses, where they still exist, look almost as much like slate-roofed sheep pens as human dwellings and, in the hilly terrain, donkeys and mules remain more common than tractors. Here and there clusters of beehives produce high-quality honey.

Information

The **tourist office** (☎ 927 43 53 29; Avenida de Las Hurdes s/n; ☼ 10am-2pm & 4-7pm Tue-Sat, 10am-2pm Sun) is beside the EX204 in Caminomorisco, and is the area's lone information office.

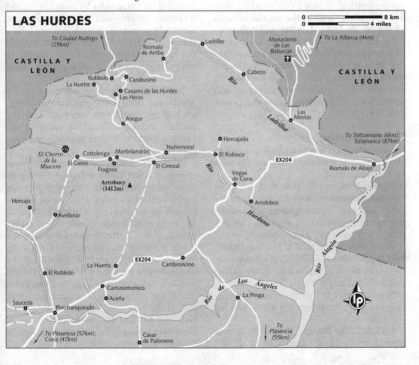

LAS HURDES

Sights & Activities

The heart of Las Hurdes is the valley of the Río Hurdano, which slices northwest from Vegas de Coria along the EX204. From **Nuñomoral**, 7.5km up the valley, a road heads west up a side valley to **El Gasco**, from where there's a particularly good half-hour walk (about 2km) to **El Chorro de la Miacera**, a 70m waterfall. This side valley is the most picturesque of the area, with hard-won farming terraces carved out of the steep banks on either side of the mountain stream, more donkeys and mules than tractors, a good whack of the old stone and slate-roofed houses huddled together in hamlets such as **Cottolengo**, and many of the older locals still wearing the simple dress of bygone years.

Back in the main valley, 9km northwest of Nuñomoral, **Casares de las Hurdes** has a pleasant main square with good views down the valley. Beyond Casares de las Hurdes, the road winds up through Carabusino and Robledo to the border of Salamanca province, from where you can continue 25km to Ciudad Rodrigo (p179).

Alternatively, a right turn 20m before the border marker will take you winding 9km down through forest to the isolated villages of **Riomalo de Arriba**, **Ladrillar** and **Cabezo** as far as **Las Mestas**, which lies on the junction of the wood-lined road that leads up into the Peña de Francia towards La Alberca (p188). Las Mestas is a pretty little stop, with a *piscina natural* (river swimming spot) and several local stores selling honey and pollen products.

Sleeping & Eating

Most of the main towns and villages of Las Hurdes have at least one hotel, usually with its own restaurant.

Pensión Hurdano (☎ 927 43 30 12; Avenida del Padre Rizabala; Nuñomoral; s/d €18/30) Deep into the valley and run by an engaging old couple, this is a little gem. There are some cheaper rooms without private bathroom.

Hostal Montesol (☎ 927 67 61 93; Calle de Lindón 7; d with/without bathroom €30/27; ✖ P) In Casares de las Hurdes, high up in the austere valley, this *hostal* (budget hotel) has rear rooms with great views. It also has a hearty restaurant and single travellers pay a little less for the same rooms.

Las Cabañas de Mestas (☎ 927 43 40 25; www .lasmestas.com; Finca La Viña Grande; d €45-55; ✖ P)

This charming timber lodging has a scattering of quaint cabins amid olive groves, each with a porch, kitchen and bit of garden. The bigger ones can accommodate up to four people.

Getting There & Away

One bus runs daily on weekdays from Plasencia to Vegas de Coria (€4.80, 1½ hours), Casares de las Hurdes (€5.90, 2¼ hours) and back. A local bus runs on weekdays between Riomalo de Arriba and Vegas de Coria (€2.20, 30 minutes).

SIERRA DE GATA

The Muslims built several castles all along the sierra. After the Reconquista in 1212 the area was controlled by the Knights Templar and Knights of Alcántara. Typical traditional architecture features granite stonework and external staircases.

Hoyos, formerly the summer residence of the bishops of Coria, has some impressive *casas señoriales* (mansions). The solid sandstone mass of its 16th-century Iglesia de Nuestra Señora del Buen Varón is surrounded on three sides by wide plazas and balconies bright with cascading flowers. About 5km out of central Hoyos (follow the signs for *piscina natural* just outside the east exit) is a popular local freshwater stream that widens out and is used as a local summer pool.

Santibáñez el Alto, high up on a lonely windswept ridge to the east, has the dinkiest bullring you'll ever see, built into the partially ruined walls of the mostly 13th-century castle that once guarded this vantage point.

Of all the hamlets in the sierra, the most engaging is **San Martín de Trevejo**. Lining up along cobblestone lanes with water coursing down central grooves, traditional houses jut out upon timber and stone barbicans. Set amid a landscape of oak and chestnut woods, it is a perfect place for a relaxing break. A couple of *casas rurales* offer rooms in the old village centre and food can be had in several bars and a restaurant. On the northern edge of the village you can stroll out along an original Roman road. Here and in the two next villages looking west, **Elvas** and **Valverde del Fresno**, the folk speak their own isolated dialect, a strange mix of Spanish and Portuguese.

Getting There & Away
From Coria, four buses run daily to Hoyos (€2.10), and up to two to Valverde del Fresno (€4.25, 1¾ hours). There's one bus daily on weekdays from Plasencia to Valverde del Fresno (2¾ hours) via San Martín de Trevejo. Two run from Plasencia to Hoyos and another to Santibáñez (one hour).

CORIA & AROUND
pop 12,600
South of the Sierra de Gata, what are claimed to be Europe's most perfectly preserved **Roman walls** surround the old, mostly pedestrianised, part of Coria, watched over by a mighty **keep**. The **tourist office** (☎ 927 50 13 51; www.coria.org; Avenida de Extremadura 39; ☺ 9.30am-2pm & 4.30-7pm Oct-Mar; 9.30am-2pm & 5-8pm Apr-Sep) has information on the town and surrounding area.

Sights & Activities
The **catedral** (Plaza de la Catedral; ☺ 10.30am-1.30pm & 5-7pm), primarily Gothic, has intricate Plateresque decoration around the main portals. Attached is a small **ecclesiastical museum** (admission €2). On the plain below stretches a fine stone bridge, abandoned in the 17th century by the Río Alagón, which now takes a slightly more southerly course.

The **Convento de la Madre de Dios** (Calle de las Monjas s/n; admission €1.50; ☺ 10am-noon & 4.30-6.15pm Sun-Fri, 4.30-6.15pm Sat) is a 16th-century, thriving convent with an elegant cloister. The sisters sell a variety of mouth-watering home-made sweets and pastries.

The **Museo de la Carcel Real** (Calle de las Monjas 2; adult/child €1.20/0.60; ☺ 10.30am-2pm & 5.30-8.30pm Wed-Sun) houses Coria's small but enjoyable archaeological museum.

Galisteo, 26km east of Coria on the EX108, has near-intact Muslim-era walls, the remains of a 14th-century fort with a curious octagonal cone-shaped tower and a Mudéjar brick apse to its old church.

Sleeping & Eating
Hotel los Kekes (☎ 927 50 40 80; Avenida de la Sierra de Gata 49; s/d €21.30/37.60) In the heart of town, these neat and well-furnished rooms make for an inviting stop. The prices rise a little in August.

Casa Campana (☎ 927 50 00 38; Plaza de San Pedro 5; meals €20-25; ☺ Wed-Mon) The slightly kitsch décor in the Casa Campana's dining room,

with its Roman walls and orange paint job, should not detract from the fine country cooking you'll get here. There is a great *menú del día* for €9.

Getting There & Away
The **bus station** (☎ 927 50 01 10; Calle de Chile) is in the new part of town, about 1km from the old quarter. Buses run to/from Plasencia and Cáceres (one daily).

PLASENCIA
pop 38,600
This pleasant, bustling town rising above a bend of the Río Jerte is the natural hub of northern Extremadura. Founded in 1186 by Alfonso VIII of Castilla, Plasencia only lost out to Cáceres as Extremadura's most important town in the 19th century. It retains an attractive old quarter of narrow streets and stately stone buildings, many emblazoned with noble heralds.

Orientation & Information
The heart of town is the lively Plaza Mayor, meeting place of 10 streets and scene of a Tuesday market since the 12th century. The **bus station** (Calle de Tornavacas 2) is about 1km east. The train station is off the Cáceres road, about 1km southwest of town. The **tourist office** (☎ 927 42 38 43; Calle de Santa Clara; ☺ 9am-2pm & 4-9pm Mon-Fri, 10am-2pm & 4-8pm Sat & Sun) is helpful.

Sights
The **catedral** (Plaza de la Catedral; ☺ 9am-1pm & 4-6pm Mon-Sat, 9am-1pm Sun Oct-Apr; 9am-1pm & 5-7pm Mon-Sat, 9am-1pm Sun Jun-Sep) is actually two *catedrals:* the Romanesque **Catedral Vieja** (admission €2) and the 16th-century **Catedral Nueva** (admission free), a mainly Gothic building with a handsome Plateresque façade. Within the Catedral Vieja are the fine Capilla de San Pablo, a lovely cloister, and the *catedral* museum with 15th- to 17th-century Spanish and Flemish art.

Nearby is the **Museo Etnográfico-Textil** (☎ 927 42 18 43; Plazuela del Marqués de la Puebla; admission free; ☺ 11am-2pm & 5-8pm Wed-Sat, 11am-2pm Sun), which displays local handicrafts and costumes.

The **Museo Municipal** (☎ 927 42 38 43; Calle de Santa Clara; admission free; ☺ 10am-2pm & 5-8pm Wed-Sun), housed in a former convent next door to the tourist office, is as interesting for the centuries-old building as the displays recounting the history of the town.

Among several old churches and mansions meriting a glance are the **Casa de las Dos Torres** (Calle de Santa Isabel), the **Iglesia de San Nicolás** (Plaza de San Vicente Ferrer) and the **Iglesia de San Martín** (Plazuela de San Martín), all dating from the 13th or 14th century. San Martín, now an exhibition hall, has an altarpiece with paintings by the noted 16th-century *extremeño* artist Luis Morales, known as El Divino Morales.

Sleeping

Hotel Rincón Extremeño (☎ 927 41 11 50; rincon@ infonegocio.com; Calle de las Vidrieras 6; s/d €30/39; ✖) This unpretentious hotel has good, clean rooms and also runs a popular restaurant in a busy little lane cluttered with eateries and bars just off Plaza Mayor.

Hotel Alfonso VIII (☎ 927 41 02 50; www.hotelal fonsoviii.com; Avenida de Alfonso VIII 32-34; s/d €67.40/ 116.70; ✖) Cool and gracious, on a busy street just outside the old city walls, this hotel offers sound-proofed, spacious rooms. The décor is a little dated but comfort is assured.

Parador (☎ 927 42 58 70; plasencia@parador.es; Plaza de San Vicente Ferrer s/n; s/d €113.50/128.10) Occupying an old convent, the fairly straightforward rooms here are arranged across an unforgettable setting, full of medieval splendour.

Eating

Tapas are the thing in Plasencia. At lunch time the bars on and around Plaza de Mayor fill up with eager punters, who sock away *cañas* (beer in a small glass) or the local *pitarra* red at €1 a shot. With each tipple comes a tapa for free. Depending on your tolerance for the grog, you can easily lunch this way!

La Pitarra del Gordo (☎ 927 41 45 05; Plaza Mayor 8) This is one of myriad busy tapas bars handing out little goodies with lunchtime tipples. It has four other branches around the town.

Casa Juan (☎ 927 42 40 42; Calle de Arenillas 5; meals €25-30; ✖ Fri-Wed) Tucked away in a quiet lane, this is a local favourite for well-prepared *extremeño* meat dishes.

Getting There & Away

Up to 10 buses daily run to/from Cáceres (50 minutes) and five to seven to Madrid (2½ hours). Local services, weekdays only, include La Vera (three daily), Hervás (two daily), Coria (three daily) and one each to Caminomorisco, Hoyos and Valverde del Fresno. Up to five services run to Salamanca (€7.15, 2½ hours).

Train destinations from Plasencia include Madrid (from €12.80, three to 3½ hours), Cáceres (from €2.70, 1¼ hours, two to three daily) and Mérida (€6.65, 2½ hours, two to three daily).

PARQUE NATURAL MONFRAGÜE

This natural park, straddling the Tajo valley, is home to some of Spain's most spectacular colonies of raptors, and more 75% of Spain's protected species. Among some 175 feathered varieties are around 200 pairs of black vultures (the largest concentration of Europe's biggest bird of prey) and populations of two other rare large birds: the Spanish imperial eagle and the black stork. The best time to visit is between March and October, since vultures, storks and others winter in Africa.

Orientation & Information

At the hamlet of Villarreal de San Carlos on the EX208 Plasencia–Trujillo road is an **information centre** (☎ 927 19 91 34; ✖ 9am-2.30pm & 4.30-7.30pm Apr-Sep; 9am-2.30pm & 4-6pm Oct-Mar). From Villarreal, several marked walking trails lead to good lookout points, some of which you can also drive to.

Sights & Activities

The hilltop **Castillo de Monfragüe**, a ruined 9th-century Muslim fort about 1½ hours' walk south from Villarreal (or a few minutes' drive), is a great spot for watching birds in flight from the Peña Falcón crag on the opposite (west) bank of the Río Tajo. Residents include 80 pairs of griffon vultures, three of black storks and one each of Egyptian vultures, peregrine falcons, golden eagles and eagle owls. The Salto del Gitano, by the road below the castle, gives a closer look at Peña Falcón.

Another walk (2½ hours return) goes west from Villarreal de San Carlos to **Cerro Gimio**, where you may see black vultures nesting. The **Mirador de la Tajadilla**, about a three-hour return walk from Villarreal (you can also drive there), is noted for griffon vultures and Egyptian vultures in flight.

WOOLLY WANDERERS

If you travel the byways of Extremadura, Castilla y León, Castilla-La Mancha or western Andalucía you may find your road crossing or running beside a broad grassy track, which might have signs saying *cañada real* (royal drove road) or *vía pecuaria* (secondary drove road). What you've stumbled upon is one of Spain's age-old livestock migration routes. The Visigoths were the first to take their flocks south from Castilla y León to winter on the plains of Extremadura – a practice that avoided the cold northern winter and allowed pastures to regenerate.

This twice-yearly *trashumancia* (migration of herds) grew to epic proportions in the late Middle Ages, when sheep became Spain's economic mainstay. The vast network of drove roads is estimated to have totalled 124,000km.

The biggest drove roads – veritable sheep freeways measuring up to 75m wide – were the *cañadas reales*. The Cañada Real de la Plata, which roughly followed the Roman Vía de la Plata from northwest to southwest Spain, passes just west of Salamanca, enters Extremadura by the Valle del Ambroz, crosses the Parque Natural Monfragüe, and then follows stretches of the EX208 to Trujillo.

In modern times the drove roads fell into disuse, although since the late 1990s some effort has been made to maintain some of them and even resuscitate the *trashumancia*. The most publicised example takes place in Madrid, where in autumn a flock of 2000 or so sheep is driven through the city centre as a symbolic act.

Sleeping

Camping Monfragüe (☎ 927 45 92 33; camping per person/tent/car €3.30/3.30/3; bungalows €40-55; ☺ year-round; ☒ ℗) This camping ground is the nearest sleeping place to the park, 14km north on the EX208. It rents out bikes. The nearest towns with accommodation are Torrejón el Rubio, 16km south of Villarreal de San Carlos, and Malpartida de Plasencia, 18.5km north.

CENTRAL EXTREMADURA

CÁCERES

pop 87,000

Extremadura's second-biggest city is a pleasant and lively place that successfully blends old with new, helped along by a sizable student population. At the heart of Cáceres stands a town so little changed since the 15th and 16th centuries that it's often used as a film set.

A key goal for anyone hoping to control Extremadura: the city was thrice captured from the Muslims by the Christian kingdom of León between 1142 and 1184 but retaken each time. The fourth conquest, by Alfonso IX of León in 1227, proved permanent. Noble Leónese families migrated here, and during the 15th and 16th cen-

turies turned its walled nucleus into one of the most impressive concentrations of ancient stonemasonry in Europe.

Orientation & Information

The heart of Cáceres is its 150m-long Plaza Mayor, with the walled old town, the Ciudad Monumental, rising on its eastern side. Around Plaza Mayor and the Ciudad Monumental, a tangle of humble old streets extend southwest to Avenida de España. From Plaza de América, at its southern end, Avenida de Alemania runs 1km southwest to the train and bus stations.

Ciberjust (Calle de Diego Maria Crehuet 7; per hr €2; ☺ 10am-2.30pm & 4.30pm-midnight Mon-Fri, noon-2.30pm & 5pm-midnight Sat, 5pm-midnight Sun) The closest Internet café to the Ciudad Monumental.

Main post office (Paseo de Primo de Rivera 2; ☺ 8.30am-8.30pm Mon-Fri, 9am-2pm Sat)

Provincial tourist centre (☎ 927 25 55 97; Calle de l'Amargura 1; ☺ 9am-9.30pm Mon-Fri, 10am-2pm & 5-8pm Sat, 10am-2pm Sun)

Tourist office Calle Ancha (☎ 927 24 71 72; Calle Ancha 7; ☺ 9.15am-2pm & 4.30-6.45pm Mon-Sat, 10am-2pm Sun); Plaza Mayor (☎ 927 01 08 34; Plaza Mayor 3; ☺ 9am-2pm & 5-7pm Mon-Fri Jun-Sep; 9am-2pm & 4-6pm Mon-Fri Oct-May; 9.45am-2pm Sat & Sun year-round)

Ciudad Monumental

The **Ciudad Monumental**, mostly surrounded by walls and towers rebuilt by the Almohads in the 12th century, merits at least two

CÀCERES

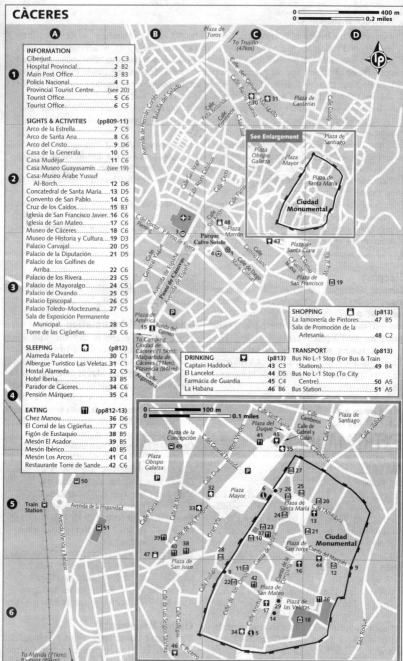

visits: one by day and one by night, the latter to enjoy the buildings illuminated. Many of its mansions – all carved with the heraldic shields of their founding families – are still in private, often absentee, hands; others are used by the provincial government, the local bishop and the Universidad Extremeña.

PLAZA DE SANTA MARÍA

Entering the Ciudad Monumental from Plaza Mayor through the 18th-century **Arco de la Estrella**, you'll see ahead the **Concatedral de Santa María** (☎ 927 24 52 50; Plaza de Santa María; ☽ 10am-2pm & 5-8pm Mon-Sat, 10am-2pm & 5-7.30pm Sun), Cáceres' 15th-century Gothic cathedral. On its southwest corner is a modern statue of San Pedro de Alcántara by the 20th-century *extremeño* sculptor Enrique Pérez Comendador. This particular San Pedro was a 16th-century *extremeño* ascetic who dedicated himself to reforming the Franciscan order. Inside, stick €0.50 in the slot to the right of the Santa Rita chapel to light up the magnificent carved 16th-century cedar altarpiece. Inside the cathedral is a small **museum** (admission €1) laden with mostly religious art. You can climb the **belltower** (admission €1; ☽ 11am-12.30pm & 5-6pm) for great views across the city.

Also on Plaza de Santa María, perhaps the Ciudad Monumental's most handsome plaza, are the **Palacio Episcopal** (Bishop's Palace), the **Palacio de Mayoralgo** and the **Palacio de Ovando**, all in 16th-century Renaissance style. Just off the plaza's northeast corner is the **Palacio Carvajal**, a late-15th-century mansion.

Not far away, in the northwest corner of the walled city, the **Palacio Toledo-Moctezuma** was once the home of a daughter of the Aztec emperor Moctezuma, who was brought to Cáceres as the bride of conquistador Juan Cano de Saavedra.

PLAZA DE SAN JORGE

Southeast of Plaza de Santa María, past the Renaissance-style **Palacio de la Diputación**, is Plaza de San Jorge, above which rises the **Iglesia de San Francisco Javier**, an 18th-century Jesuit church.

Nearby, the **Casa-Museo Árabe Yussuf Al-Borch** (Cuesta del Marqués 4; admission €1.50; ☽ irregular) is a private house decked out by its owner with an eccentric mix of Eastern and Islamic trappings. The **Arco del Cristo**, at the bottom of this street, is a Roman gate.

PLAZA DE SAN MATEO & PLAZA DE LAS VELETAS

From Plaza de San Jorge, Cuesta de la Compañía climbs to Plaza de San Mateo and the **Iglesia de San Mateo**, traditionally the church of the landowning nobility.

Just to the east is the **Torre de las Cigüeñas** (Tower of the Storks). This was the only Cáceres tower to retain its battlements when the rest were lopped off in the late 15th century, on Isabel la Católica's orders, to stop rivalry between the city's fractious nobility. You can sometimes wander in for temporary exhibitions.

Below the square is the excellent **Museo de Cáceres** (☎ 927 01 08 77; Plaza de las Veletas 1; admission €1.20, free with EU passport; ☽ 9am-2.30pm & 5-8.15pm Tue-Sat, 10.15am-2.15pm Sun mid-Apr–Sep; 9am-2.30pm & 4-7.15pm Tue-Sat, 10.15am-2.15pm Sun Oct–mid-Apr). This museum is housed in a 16th-century mansion built over an elegant 12th-century *aljibe* (cistern), the only surviving bit of Cáceres' Muslim castle. It has an impressive archaeological section, rooms devoted to traditional crafts and costumes, and a good little fine arts display, which includes works by El Greco, Picasso and Miró.

OTHER BUILDINGS

Also worth a look within the Ciudad Monumental are the **Palacio de los Golfines de Arriba** (Calle de los Olmos), which was briefly Franco's headquarters early in the civil war, and the **Casa Mudéjar** (Cuesta de Aldana 14), one of the few buildings in Cáceres still showing Muslim influence. On opposite sides of Plaza de los Caldereros are the **Casa de la Generala**, now the university law faculty, and the **Palacio de los Rivera**, the university's rectorate.

Just outside the old walls, the **Sala de Exposición Permanente Municipal** (Plaza de Publio Hurtado 3; admission free; ☽ 10.30am-2pm & 5-8.30pm Tue-Fri, 10am-2pm Sat & Sun) has bright, attractive, acrylic paintings of Cáceres and Extremadura by local artist Massa Solís.

South of the Ciudad Monumental by Plaza de San Francisco are the **Museo de Historia y Cultura** and **Casa Museo Guayasamín** (both ☎ 927 24 16 33; Casa Pedrilla; admission free; ☽ 11am-2pm & 5-8pm Tue-Fri, 11am-2pm Sat & Sun). The former houses a number of displays on history and culture, as well as a collection of works by *extremeño* painters, while the latter presents the very dark work of painter Oswaldo Guayasamín.

Festivals & Events

Every year since 1992 Cáceres has staged the Spanish edition of **Womad** (World of Music, Arts and Dance; www.bme.es/womad), with international bands ranging from reggae and Celtic to African, Indian and Australian Aboriginal, playing in the old city's squares.

The townsfolk turn out on the evening of 21 April for the **Fiesta de San Jorge**, their patron saint, with a night-time parade of the Virgen de la Montaña. More festivities, including bullfights, follow over the next two days.

The **Ferias de Cáceres** feature bullfights, concerts, fireworks and fun aplenty for a week around the end of May or June.

Sleeping

With more than 30 accommodation options, finding a place to sleep generally presents little problem. Quite a few places are clustered on or near Plaza Mayor, but the area can get noisy on summer and weekend nights.

Albergue Turístico Las Veletas (☎ 927 21 12 10; www.albergueturisticos.com; Calle del General Maragallo 36; dm €18; reception 🕒 5-9pm Mon, 10am-2pm & 5-9pm Tue-Sat, 10am-2pm Sun; 🖳) In rooms of two, four or more in this modern hostel, you'll find agreeable dorm-style accommodation.

Pensión Márquez (☎ 927 24 49 60; Calle de Gabriel y Galán 2; s/d €10/21) For clean, simple rooms (shared bathroom) in a family-run home, this is not a bad bet. Some rooms look onto Plaza Mayor.

AUTHOR'S CHOICE

Alameda Palacete (☎ 927 21 16 74; www.alamedapalacete.com; Calle del General Maragallo 45; d €60; 🞮) In a carefully renovated, elegant two-storey early 20th-century townhouse are eight beautifully arranged rooms (three of them as big as small studios that can sleep up to four). Exquisite ceramic floors, high ceilings and the small patio make for a pleasant stay. The main stairway features fine Venetian stucco work, done by a specialist brought in especially for the job by the house's one-time owner, the Conde de Aguasclaras. Some of the little details, such as flowers in the bathrooms, make all the difference. The hotel is just a short walk from the centre of the old town.

Hotel Iberia (☎ 927 24 76 34; iberiaplaza@hotmail.com; Calle de los Pintores 2; s/d €35/45; 🞮) Set in an 18th-century building just off Plaza Mayor, this little hotel is decorated with taste, and is full of character.

Hostal Alameda (☎ 927 21 12 62; Plaza Mayor 33; d €42; 🞮) A great deal on the 3rd floor; rooms here are spacious, with comfortable beds, tile floors, lounge with occasional furniture and shared toilets.

Parador de Cáceres (☎ 927 21 17 59; caceres@parador.es; Calle Ancha 6; s/d €96.70/120.80; 🞮) A grand 14th-century noble townhouse is the scene for this fine accommodation in the walled town. Sit around in the courtyard or dine in the fine restaurant attached.

Eating

El Corral de las Cigüeñas (Cuesta de Aldana 6; 🕒 8am-3pm Mon-Wed, 8am-3pm & 7pm-3am Thu-Sat, 5-11pm Sun) The sunny, quiet courtyard here, with its two towering palm trees, is the perfect spot for one of the best-value breakfasts around – generous orange juice, coffee and pastry or toast for €2!

Mesón Los Arcos (☎ 927 24 51 45; Plaza Mayor 22; meals €15) Of the several cheap and cheerful restaurants and cafés around the square, this is one of the better ones for a simple meal with *platos combinados* (combination plates; €5.50) and *raciónes* (meal-sized serving of tapas; €5) the order of the day.

Mesón El Asador (☎ 927 22 38 37; Calle de Moret 34; meals €30-35) Here you'll find pork with crackling that really crackles – you won't taste a better roast in town. Its bar also serves *bocadillos* (bread roll with filling) and a wide range of *raciónes*.

Mesón Ibérico (☎ 927 21 67 19; Plaza de San Juan 10; meals €25; Wed-Mon) Head upstairs from the bar to the tiny dining room for fresh local food. Start with a *tabla* (platter) of mixed cheeses and ham, then proceed to a hearty meat main. Round off with *técula mécula*, a divine and heavy dessert made of egg yoke, almonds and acorns.

Figón de Eustaquio (☎ 927 24 43 62, Plaza de San Juan 14; meals €40) In this low-beamed, multi-roomed top-end option you'll be treated to such dishes as *vacuno con salsa de anchoa*, strange bedfellows of steak topped with olives and anchovies.

Restaurante Torre de Sande (☎ 927 21 11 47; Calle de los Condes 3; meals €30-35; 🕒 Tue-Sat, lunch Sun) Dining in the gorgeous, high-walled courtyard is

Chez Manou (☎ 927 22 76 82; Plaza de las Veletas 4; meals €35-40; ☯ Tue-Sat, lunch Sun) Dark-wood tables and chairs are spread out beneath the lofty, sloping, timber ceiling of this fine old house within the walled town. On offer is an enticing mix of local and French dishes in a deliciously romantic setting. On cold winter's days it makes the perfect refuge but on a cracking hot summer's night you might prefer to eat under the stars on the terrace. They offer a set meal at €24.60.

as agreeable as inside at this old-town mansion. Cuisine is local and well prepared.

Drinking

The northern end of Plaza Mayor and offshoots such as Calle del General Ezponda (known to locals as Calle de los Bares), Calle de Gabriel y Galán and Plaza del Duque, are lined with lively late-night bars, most playing recorded music. Just beyond the walls on the south side of the Ciudad Monumental more bars, such as **Capitán Haddock** (7 Calle de Luis Sergio Sánchez) and **La Habana** (1 Calle de Luis Sergio Sánchez), line Calle de Pizarro and its continuation, Calle de Luis Sergio Sánchez. The new part of the city also offers plenty of *marcha* (action), including several clubs, in an area known as La Madrila on and around Calle del Doctor Fleming.

Farmácia de Guardia (Plaza Mayor 20; ☯ 6pm-2.30am) Far from being a pharmacy, this is a lively bar with a terrace.

El Lancelot (Rincón de la Monja 2; ☯ 6pm-2am Wed-Mon) All stained wood and rustic panelling, this is a great spot for a tipple and occasionally live (generally Irish) music.

El Corral de las Cigüeñas (Cuesta de Aldana 6; ☯ 8am-3pm Mon-Wed, 8am-3pm & 7pm-3am Thu-Sat, 5-11pm Sun) A cool place for a drink, this place also stages live music occasionally.

Shopping

A good shop for local hams, sausages, cheeses and fruit liquor is **La Jamonería de Pintores** (☎ 927 24 54 93; Calle de los Pintores 30).

At **Sala de Promoción de la Artesanía** (☎ 927 22 09 27; Calle de San Antón 17), run by the provincial government, you can see and buy typical *extremeño* handicrafts.

Getting There & Away

Bus services include Trujillo (€2.70, 45 minutes, eight daily), Badajoz (€5.70, 1½ hours, four daily) and Madrid (€16.60, 3½ hours, seven to nine daily).

At least two trains per day run to/from Madrid (from €15.60, 3½ to five hours) and Mérida (from €3.50, one hour).

Getting Around

Bus No L-1 from the stop outside the train station – close to the bus station – will take you into town.

AROUND CÁCERES

About 3km south of Malpartida de Cáceres (11km west of Cáceres on the N521) is the **Museo Vostell Malpartida** (☎ 927 01 08 12; www.museovostell.org; adult/student €1.20/0.60; ☯ 10am-1.30pm year-round; 5-7.30pm mid-Apr–mid-Jun; 6-9pm mid-Jun–Sep; 4-6.30pm Oct–mid-Apr; closed Mon & hols) in what was an old lakeside wool wash house. The museum, set up by Wolf Vostell (1932–98), a German-Spanish artist, contains over 200 weird and wonderful works by Vostell and a number of his contemporaries. The site is within **Los Barruecos**, a natural granite rock park, which alone is worth the visit. You need your own wheels to get here.

VALENCIA DE ALCÁNTARA
pop 4900

Just 7km short of the Portuguese frontier and 92km west of Cáceres, this pretty town boasts a well-preserved old centre – a curious labyrinth of whitewashed houses and mansions punctuated by gravestone entrances. One side of the old town is watched over by the ruins of a medieval castle and the **Iglesia de Rocamador** (which sounds like something from a Tolkien novel).

The surrounding area is known for its busy cork industry and some 50 ancient dolmens (Stone Age structures made of immense slabs of stone) littered about the countryside.

Up to three buses run daily from Cáceres (€4.40, 1½ hours).

ALCÁNTARA
pop 1740

Alcántara is Arabic for 'The Bridge'. A six-arched **Roman bridge** – 204m long, 61m high and much reinforced over the centuries – spans the Río Tajo west of town

EXTREMADURA & AMERICA

Extremeños jumped at the opportunities opened up by Columbus' discovery of the Americas in 1492.

In 1501 Fray Nicolás de Ovando from Cáceres was named governor of all the Indies. He set up his capital, Santo Domingo, on the Caribbean island of Hispaniola. With him went 2500 followers, many of them from Extremadura, including Francisco Pizarro, an illegitimate son of a minor noble family from Trujillo. In 1504 Hernán Cortés, from a similar family in Medellín, east of Mérida, arrived in Santo Domingo too.

Both young men prospered. Cortés took part in the conquest of Cuba in 1511 and settled there. Pizarro, in 1513, accompanied Vasco Núñez de Balboa (from Jerez de los Caballeros) to Darién (Panama), where they discovered the Pacific Ocean.

In 1519 Cortés led a small expedition to what's now Mexico, rumoured to be full of gold and silver. By 1524, with a combination of incredible fortitude, cunning, luck and ruthlessness, Cortés and his band had subdued the Aztec empire. Though initially named governor of all he had conquered, Cortés soon found royal officials arriving to usurp his authority. He returned to Spain in 1540, where he died seven years later.

Pizarro, after forays south of Panama had led to contact with the Inca empire, won royal backing for his plan to subject the territory and was named, in advance, governor of newly styled Nueva Castilla.

Before returning to Panama, Pizarro visited Trujillo, where he received a hero's welcome and picked up his four half-brothers – Hernando, Juan and Gonzalo Pizarro, and Martín de Alcántara – and other relatives and friends. Their expedition set off from Panama in 1531, with just 180 men and 37 horses. Pizarro and his force crossed the Andes and managed to capture the Inca emperor Atahualpa, despite the emperor having an army of 30,000 on hand. The Inca empire, with its capital in Cuzco and extending from Colombia to Chile, resisted until 1545, by which time Francisco had died (he is buried in the cathedral of Lima, Peru).

Altogether, 600 or 700 people of Trujillo made their way to the Americas in the 16th century, so it's hardly surprising that there are at least seven Trujillos in North, Central and South America today. There are even more Guadalupes, for conquistadors and colonists from all over Spain took with them the cult of the Virgen de Guadalupe in eastern Extremadura, one which remains widespread throughout Latin America today.

(62km northwest of Cáceres), below a huge dam retaining the Embalse de Alcántara. An inscription above a small Roman temple on the river's left bank honours the bridge's original architect, Caius Julius Lacer – though no-one knows how many, if any, of his original building blocks remain.

The town itself retains some of its old walls, the remains of a castle and several imposing mansions. From 1218 it was the headquarters of the Orden de Alcántara, an order of Reconquista knights that ruled much of western Extremadura as a kind of private kingdom.

Hostal Kantara Al Saif (☎ 927 39 08 33; Avenida de Mérida s/n; s/d Mon-Fri Sep-Jul €18/32, Sat & Sun Aug €27/36) is a modern, unexciting but comfortable place on the eastern edge of town as you enter.

Up to four buses run daily from Cáceres (€4.70, 1½ hours).

TRUJILLO
pop 9500

Romans, Visigoths and Muslims all settled here long before the Christians took it on 25 January 1232. They gradually expanded the defensive walls (which the Muslims had equipped with seven towers) and the castle, but the town only truly came into its own with the conquest of the Americas.

With its labyrinth of terracotta-tiled houses and mansions, leafy courtyards, fruit gardens and groves, churches and convents, and remnants thereof, all gathered on a rise overlooking the surrounding plains, Trujillo is a remarkable piece of living history and one of the most engaging small towns in Spain. Although Francisco Pizarro (its most famous son) and co enriched the city with a grand new square and a series of Renaissance mansions, in the following centuries decay set in.

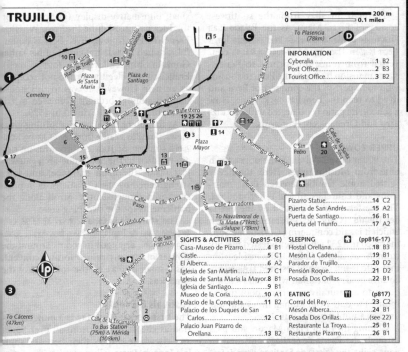

TRUJILLO

Information

Ciberalia (☎ 927 65 90 87; www.ciberalia.org; Calle de Tiendas 18; per hr €2; ⏰ 10.30am-midnight)

Post office (☎ 927 32 05 33; Calle de la Encarnación 28; ⏰ 8.30am-2pm Mon-Sat)

Tourist office (☎ 927 32 26 77; www.ayto-trujillo .com; Plaza Mayor s/n; ⏰ 9.30am-2pm & 4-7pm Oct-May; 9.30am-2pm & 5-8.30pm Jun-Sep)

Sights

A combined ticket (€4.70) will give you entry to the Iglesia de Santiago, Casa-Museo de Pizarro and castle, and includes a comprehensive guidebook available in English. To include the Iglesia de San Martín it costs €5.30, and it's €6.75 if you want to join a guided tour.

PLAZA MAYOR

A large equestrian **Pizarro statue** by American Charles Rumsey dominates Plaza Mayor. There's a tale that Rumsey originally sculpted it as a statue of Hernán Cortés to present to Mexico, but Mexico, which takes a poor view of Cortés, declined it, so it was given to Trujillo as Pizarro instead!

On the plaza's southern side, the corner of the **Palacio de la Conquista** sports carved images of Pizarro and his lover Inés Yupanqui (sister of the Inca emperor Atahualpa). To the right is their daughter Francisca Pizarro Yupanqui, with her husband (and uncle), Hernando Pizarro. The mansion was built in the 1560s for Hernando and Francisca after Hernando – the only Pizarro brother not to die a bloody death in Peru – emerged from 20 years in jail for the killing of Diego de Almagro. Above the corner balcony another carving shows the Pizarro family shield.

Overlooking the Plaza Mayor from the northeast corner is the mainly 16th-century **Iglesia de San Martín** (admission €1.30; ⏰ 10am-12.30pm & 4-7.30pm), which contains a number of noble tombs. It is one of the only churches still functioning in Trujillo.

Across the street from the church is the 16th-century **Palacio de los Duques de San Carlos** (admission €1.30; ⏰ 9.30am-1pm & 4.30-6.30pm Mon-Sat, 10am-12.30pm Sun), now a convent but open for visits. It has a classical patio and a grand staircase.

Through an alley from the southwest corner of Plaza Mayor is the **Palacio Juan Pizarro de Orellana** (admission free; ☼ 10am-1pm & 4-6pm Mon-Fri, 11am-2pm & 4.30-7pm Sat & Sun), converted from miniature fortress to Renaissance mansion by one of the Pizarro cousins who took part in the conquest of Peru and lived to reap the benefits back home. Now a school, its patio is decorated with the Pizarro and Orellana coats of arms.

UPPER TOWN
The 900m of walls circling the upper town date from Muslim times. Here, the newly settled noble families erected their mansions and churches after the Reconquista. The western end is marked by the **Puerta del Triunfo** (Gate of Triumph), through which it is said conquering Christian troops marched in 1232 when they wrested the city from the Muslims. About 100m inside from that gate is the recently restored **El Alberca**, a strange quarry-like affair with stairs leading down to a naturally occurring pool that is thought to date from Roman times and was used as a public baths until 1935.

Coming up from Plaza Mayor, you pass through the **Puerta de Santiago** and find to your right the **Iglesia de Santiago** (Plaza de Santiago; admission €1.30; ☼ 10am-2pm & 4-7.30pm). It was founded in the 13th century by the Knights of Santiago, whose conch-shell emblem is visible, and deconsecrated for lack of interest and funds in 1896. You can climb into the bell tower and visit the sacristan's sleeping quarters. If you're choosing your churches carefully, it's the least interesting.

The **Iglesia de Santa María la Mayor** (Plaza de Santa María; admission €1.25; ☼ 10am-2pm & 4.30-7.30pm) has a mainly Gothic nave and a Romanesque tower that you can ascend for fabulous views. It also has tombs of leading Trujillo families of the Middle Ages, including that of Diego García de Paredes (1466–1530), a Trujillo warrior of legendary strength who, according to Cervantes, could stop a mill wheel with one finger. The church has a fine altarpiece with Flemish-style 15th-century paintings.

The 15th-century **Casa-Museo de Pizarro** (☎ 927 32 26 77; Calle del Convento de las Jerónimas 12; admission €1.30; ☼ 10am-2pm & 4-7.30pm) was the ancestral home of the great conquistador family. Restored in the style of the 15th and 16th centuries, the house contains a small informative display (in Spanish) on the Inca empire and the Pizarros. Whether Francisco Pizarro ever lived here is doubtful. Though he was the eldest of his father Gonzalo's nine children (by four women) Francisco was illegitimate and not accepted as an heir. However, it was to this house that his siblings brought Francisco in triumph on his visit to Trujillo in 1529.

At the top of the hill and affording great views, Trujillo's **castle** (admission €1.30; ☼ 10am-2pm & 4-7.30pm), of 10th-century Muslim origin (evident by the horseshoe-arch gateway just inside the main entrance) and later strengthened by the Christians, is impressive, even though empty. Stroll along the battlements for the sweeping views.

The **Museo de la Coria** (☎ 927 32 18 98; Calle de Santa María de Trujillo; admission free; ☼ 11.30am-2pm Sat & Sun), arranged in rooms around the cloister of a partly ruined former convent, has a small display on the conquest of the Americas.

Festivals & Events
The first weekend in May is a pungent period as cheese makers from all over Spain and elsewhere display their best at Trujillo's **Feria del Queso** (Cheese Fair). The **Ferias y Fiestas de Trujillo**, with bullfights, music and partying, are spread over a few days in early June.

Sleeping
Mesón La Cadena (☎ 927 32 14 63; Plaza Mayor 8; s/d €30/37.30; ⌘) Occupying part of a 16th-century mansion on the grand central square, this place's location is unbeatable. Austere, cell-like rooms with timber bedheads, night

---

AUTHOR'S CHOICE

Posada Dos Orillas (☎ 927 65 90 79; www .dosorillas.com; Calle de Cambrones 6; d €90; ⌘ ▣) Just seven beautifully appointed double rooms are spread out over this tastefully renovated 16th-century mansion in the walled town that once served as a silk-weaving centre. Rooms deliberately ooze an air of Spanish colonial taste and reflect the 'seven Trujillos' in Extremadura and various conquered South American countries. Relax in the sunny patio in between forays to the old town.

tables and yellow bed covers are scrubbed clean and offer spartan comfort.

Pensión Roque (☎ 927 32 23 13; Calle del Domingo de Ramos 30; s/d €18/24) Best of several cheapies is this quiet little red house down a narrow cobbled street, with tilework on its entrance walls and ground floor. There are some cheaper rooms with shared bathroom.

Hostal Orellana (☎ 927 32 07 53; Calle de Ruiz de Mendoza 2; d €42; ✿) The lovingly restored rooms in this 16th-century house just a short walk away from the centre of the town are all the more attractive for the exposed stone walls, dark timber and warm décor.

Parador de Trujillo (☎ 927 32 13 50; trujillo@parador.es; Calle de la Santa Beatriz de Silva s/n; s/d €83.50/103.80; ✿ P) Set in a beautiful 16th-century former convent with a peaceful cloistered courtyard and gently bubbling fountains, this makes a fine, almost haughty retreat in the winding back streets of the old town.

Eating

Restaurante Pizarro (☎ 927 32 02 55; Plaza Mayor 13; meals €25-30; ✿ Wed-Mon) Much esteemed locally, this spot has been offering subtle versions of traditional fare and been winning prizes for it since 1985. The setting exudes a grand, noble air to accompany the house

---

AUTHOR'S CHOICE

Restaurante La Troya (☎ 927 32 13 64; Plaza Mayor 10; set meals €15) The restaurant and its owner, Concha Álvarez, whose dour countenance glowers from a wall full of photos of her with celebrities great and small, are *extremeño* institutions. Since shortly after WWII, Álvarez has stuck to a simple formula in this rambling, centuries-old mansion. You will be directed to one of several dining areas and there, without warning, be presented with a plate full of tortilla, chorizo and salad, served with wine and water. You are then asked in machine-gun fashion what you want for a first course (ranging from gazpacho to hearty bean stews and paella). Shortly thereafter staff will want to know your choice of main (*pruebas de cerdo*, lightly spiced cubes of roast pork, is good). The servings are more than any mortal can finish. When done, you'll be charged the standard €15 on the way out.

---

special of *gallina trufada* (chicken prepared with truffles) and various roasts.

Mesón Alberca (☎ 927 32 22 09; Calle de Cambrones 8; meals €25-30; ✿ Thu-Sun) Dark-timber tables laid with gingham cloths, set in an ageless and restored house within the old walled city, create a warm atmosphere for classic *extremeño* cooking. The speciality is coalfired oven roasts.

Posada Dos Orillas (☎ 927 65 90 79; www.dosorillas.com; Calle de Cambrones 6; meals €40-45) Just as the hotel (see boxed text p816) is a charming gem, so the restaurant is a place of quiet, refined eating. Try the *chuletón de buey aromatizado a hierba buena*, a generous chop of ox done in mint.

Corral del Rey (☎ 927 32 17 80; Corral del Rey 2; meals €30-40; ✿ Mon-Sat, lunch Sun) As if hiding away in a little corner chipped off the main square, this grand restaurant offers some worthy gastronomy. You can settle for a simple *menú del día* at €15 or be more adventurous and choose from a range of meat and fish options. A classic is the *rabo de toro estofado con setas* (oxtail stew with mushrooms).

Getting There & Away

The **bus station** (☎ 927 32 12 02; Avenida de Miajadas) is 500m south of Plaza Mayor. There are services to/from Madrid (€14 to €17.30, 2½ to 4¼ hours, up to 10 daily), Guadalupe (€5.20, two daily), Cáceres (€2.80, 45 minutes, up to eight daily), Mérida (€6.25, 1¼ hours, four daily) and Salamanca (one daily) via Plasencia.

GUADALUPE
pop 2200

Approached from the north along the EX118 road, the bright, white town of Guadalupe (from the Arabic meaning 'hidden river') appears as though from nowhere, huddled around the massive stone hulk of the largely 15th-century Real Monasterio de Santa María de Guadalupe. This engaging town, with its uneven cobbled squares, squat porticoed houses, bubbling fountains and terracotta ceilings is a bright jewel set in the green crown of the surrounding hill ranges and ridges of the Sierra de Villuercas. Thick woods of chestnut, oak and cork trickle down to a knitted mantle of olive groves and vineyards, great for peaceful walks and drives. In winter a glacial cold takes a hold of the place, especially at night.

Orientation & Information

Buses stop on Avenida del Conde de Barcelona near the town hall, a two-minute walk from central Plaza de Santa María de Guadalupe (or Plaza Mayor) and the monastery.

The **tourist office** (☎ 927 15 41 28; Plaza de Santa María de Guadalupe; ☷ 10am-2pm & 5-7pm Tue-Fri, 10am-2pm Sat & Sun Apr-Oct; 10am-2pm & 4-6pm Tue-Fri, 10am-2pm Sat & Sun Nov-Mar) is particularly helpful.

Real Monasterio de Santa María de Guadalupe

The **monastery** (☎ 927 36 70 00; Plaza de Santa María de Guadalupe s/n; ☷ 9.30am-1pm & 3.30-6.30pm), a Unesco World Heritage site, was founded in 1340 by Alfonso XI on the spot where, according to legend, a shepherd had found an effigy of the Virgin, hidden years earlier by Christians fleeing the Muslims. It remains one of Spain's most important pilgrimage sites.

In the 15th and 16th centuries, the Virgin of Guadalupe was so revered that she was made patron of all the territories conquered by Spain in America. On 29 July 1496, Columbus' Indian servants were baptised in the fountain in front of the monastery, an event registered in the monastery's first book of baptisms. The Virgin remains a key figure for many South American Catholics.

Inside the **church** (admission free) you will find the Virgin's image occupying the place of honour within the grand *retablo* (altarpiece) soaring behind the altar. The one-hour **guided tour** (adult/child €3/1.50) of other rooms, although only in Spanish, should not be missed.

At the centre of the monastery is a 15th-century Mudéjar cloister, off which are three museums. The **Museo de Bordados** contains wonderfully embroidered altar cloths and vestments; the **Museo de Libros Miniados** has a fine collection of illuminated choral song books from the 15th century onwards; and the **Museo de Pintura y Escultura** includes paintings by El Greco and Goya, and a beautiful little ivory crucifixion attributed to Michelangelo. The superbly decorated baroque **sacristía** (sacristy) is hung with 11 paintings by Zurbarán and a lantern

captured from the Turkish flagship at the Battle of Lepanto (1571). The **Relicario-Tesoro** houses a variety of other treasures, including an exquisite baroque chandelier and a 200,000-pearl cape for the Virgin. Finally the tour reaches the **camarín**, a chamber behind the church's *retablo*, where the image of the Virgin is revolved for the faithful to contemplate her at close quarters and kiss a fragment of her mantle.

Walking

The tourist office has plans and printed material in Spanish for walks in the area. One splendid option is to take the Madrid–Miajadas bus to the village of **Cañamero**, southwest of Guadalupe, and hike back along the **Ruta de Isabel la Católica**, a well-signed 17km trail. The tourist office has pamphlets suggesting a couple of shorter and easier circuits to country chapels, walks of about three to four hours' duration.

Festivals & Events

Colourful processions wind through the heart of the town during **Semana Santa**, between the 6 and 8 September, in honour of the Virgin of Guadalupe, and on 12 October. Wednesday is the local market day.

Sleeping

Camping Las Villuercas (☎ 927 36 71 39; camping per person/tent/car €3/3/2.50; ☷ ☷) The ground has a pretty site in a river valley a short distance off the EX102, 3km south of Guadalupe. It also has self-catering apartments (two/four people €34/52).

Hostal Isabel (☎ 927 36 71 26; Plaza de Santa María de Guadalupe 13; s/d €18/30; ☷) This lodging is virtually at the foot of the monastery steps. Straightforward rooms are scattered off a labyrinth of corridors and stairs, some with skylights and all with slightly saggy beds.

Posada del Rincón (☎ 927 36 71 14; www.posadadelrincon.com; Plaza de Santa María de Guadalupe 11; s/d €36.80/52) Located in the heart of the town, Posada del Rincón's warm-coloured rooms with exposed brick and stonework, dark-timber furniture and oak ceilings, makes it a fine option. The *posada* was first mentioned in the late 15th century.

Hospedería del Real Monasterio (☎ 927 36 70 00; Plaza de Juan Carlos I s/n; s/d €38.50/56.70; ☷ ☷) Centred on the monastery's beautiful 16th-century Gothic cloister, this is by far the most characterful sleeping option in Guadalupe. Some of the rooms look directly onto the heart of the cloister. Book well ahead as it is frequently full with wedding parties.

Parador Zubarán (☎ 927 36 70 75; guadalupe@parador.es; Calle del Marqués de la Romana 12; d €111.50; 🛇 🛱 🅿) Guadalupe's premier digs occupies a converted 15th-century hospital opposite the monastery. The spacious rooms are tastefully decorated and the internal courtyard is a pleasure to relax in.

Eating

A host of restaurants around the centre offer a *menú del día* for €8 to €10 as well as extensive if fairly repetitive *a la carta* options of *extremeño* dishes. You'll get solid if uninspiring grub at any of these. In addition to the following, the restaurants in the Parador Zubarán and Posada del Rincón are also worth inspecting.

Mesón El Cordero (☎ 927 36 71 31; Calle del Convento 11; meals €20-25; 🕑 Tue-Sun Mar-Jan) Although it is now clearly trading on past glory, this is still the best place in town for the house speciality, *cordero asado* (roast lamb). Wash it down with a porcelain jug of house *vino pitarra* (simple, robust red). The setting is rustic, with polished wooden floors, old leather and wood seats. Shame about the TV blaring in the background.

Hospedería del Real Monasterio (☎ 927 36 70 00; Plaza de Juan Carlos I s/n; meals €25) In summer it is a delight to take up a seat in the magnificent Gothic cloister. Otherwise, two grand dining halls rich with 17th-century timber furnishings and impressive ceramics are redolent of another era. Treat yourself to a competent range of meat dishes and a surprising set of fish options.

Shopping

You will quickly be overwhelmed by the handicrafts and souvenir shops around Plaza de Santa María de Guadalupe. Perhaps more interesting than the embroidery and ceramics are the food products, among them *vino pitarra*, *queso di Ibores* (local goat's cheese), various honeys and liqueurs produced in the monastery, and the rich, sweet *rosco di muégado* (made of a dough composed of wheat, flour, egg, aniseed, oil and cilantro, deep fried in strips and drenched in toasted honey). Take a look at the goodies at **Atrium** (☎ 927 36 70 40; Calle de Alfonso El Onceno 6).

Getting There & Away

Mirat generally runs one or two buses daily to/from Cáceres (€8.52, two to 2½ hours) via Trujillo. **La Sepulvedana** (☎ 91 530 48 00; www.lasepulvedana.es) has two daily buses (one on Sunday) to/from Madrid (€12.60) via Talavera de la Reina. The tourist office has timetables.

SOUTHERN EXTREMADURA

MÉRIDA

pop 51,500

Mérida stands on the site of the Roman Augusta Emerita, founded in 25 BC for veterans of Rome's campaigns in Cantabria. With more than 40,000 inhabitants it became the capital of the Roman province of Lusitania, the largest Roman city on the Iberian Peninsula, and its political and cultural hub. Mérida remained an important city under the Visigoths and held out against the Muslims until 713, after which it fell into decline.

A lively city has grown up around Spain's most complete Roman ruins. Since 1983 Mérida has been the seat of the Junta de Extremadura, the regional government. The orange-blossom perfume in the air and the bright, low houses along cobbled lanes lend a touch of Andalucía to the town centre.

Orientation

The **train station** (Calle de Cardero) is a 10-minute walk from central Plaza de España. From the **bus station** (Avenida de la Libertad), 400m west of the Río Guadiana, a 20-minute walk takes in a spectacular view of the Puente Romano from the modern suspension bridge and the Puente Lusitania, designed by Santiago Calatrava.

The most important Roman ruins are in easy walking distance on the east side of town. Pedestrianised Calle de Santa Eulalia, heading northeast from Plaza de España, is the main shopping street.

Information

@rroba.Com (Calle de Camilo José Cela 28; per hr €1-1.70; 🕑 11am-2pm & 5pm-midnight daily)
Post office (☎ 924 31 24 58; Plaza de la Constitución; 🕑 8.30am-8.30pm Mon-Fri, 9.30am-1pm Sat)

EXTREMADURA

MÉRIDA

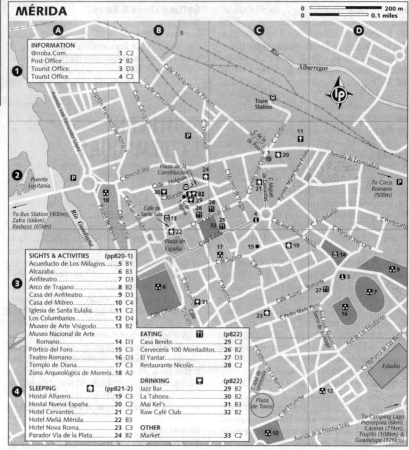

0 — 200 m
0 — 0.1 miles

INFORMATION	
@rroba.Com.	1 C2
Post Office	2 B2
Tourist Office	3 D3
Tourist Office	4 C2

SIGHTS & ACTIVITIES	(pp820-1)
Acueducto de Los Milagros	5 B1
Alcazaba	6 B3
Anfiteatro	7 D3
Arco de Trajano	8 C3
Casa del Anfiteatro	9 D3
Casa del Mitreo	10 C4
Iglesia de Santa Eulalia	11 C2
Los Columbarios	12 D4
Museo de Arte Visigodo	13 C2
Museo Nacional de Arte Romano	14 D3
Pórtico del Foro	15 C3
Teatro Romano	16 D3
Templo de Diana	17 C3
Zona Arqueológica de Morería	18 A2

SLEEPING	(pp821-2)
Hostal Alfarero	19 C3
Hostal Nueva España	20 C2
Hotel Cervantes	21 C2
Hotel Meliá Mérida	22 B3
Hotel Nova Roma	23 C3
Parador Vía de la Plata	24 B2

EATING	(p822)
Casa Benito	25 C2
Cervecería 100 Montaditos	26 B2
El Yantar	27 D3
Restaurante Nicolás	28 C2

DRINKING	(p822)
Jazz Bar	29 B2
La Tahona	30 B2
Mai Kel's	31 B3
Raw Café Club	32 B2

OTHER	
Market	33 C2

Tourist office (☎ 924 00 97 30; otmerida@bme.es; Avda de José Álvarez Saenz de Buruaga s/n; ☯ 9am-1.45pm & 5-7pm Mon-Fri, 9.30am-2pm Sat & Sun Jun-Sep; 9am-1.45pm & 4-6.30pm Mon-Fri, 9.30am-2pm Sat & Sun Oct-May) Right beside the gates to the Roman theatre and amphitheatre.

Tourist office (☎ 924 33 07 22; Calle de Santa Eulalia 64; ☯ 9.30am-2pm & 4.30-7.30pm) An alternative office run by the city council.

Roman Remains

You can buy a ticket for the Teatro Romano, Anfiteatro, Casa del Anfiteatro, Casa del Mitreo, Los Columbarios, Alcazaba, Iglesia de Santa Eulalia, Circo Romano and the **Zona Arqueológica de Morería** (adult/child €8/4; ☯ 9.30am-1.45pm & 5-7.15pm Jun-Sep; 9am-1.45pm & 4-6.15pm Oct-May). Santa Eulalia is closed on Sunday. Entry to just the Teatro Romano and the Anfiteatro is €5.50/3. With either ticket you get a detailed booklet in Spanish or English about Mérida's monuments. Individual tickets for each monument cost €2.80/1.40.

The **Teatro Romano**, built around 15 BC to seat 6000 spectators, has a dramatic and particularly well-preserved two-tier backdrop of stone columns. The adjoining **Anfiteatro**, opened in 8 BC for gladiatorial contests, had a capacity of 14,000. Nearby, the **Casa del Anfiteatro**, the remains of a 3rd-century mansion, boasts some reasonable floor mosaics. The **Casa del Mitreo** (Calle de Oviedo), a 2nd-century Roman house, has mosaics in almost every room and remarkable frescoes. **Los Columbarios** (Calle del Ensanche) is a Roman funeral site.

The **Puente Romano** over the Río Guadiana, 792m long with 60 granite arches, is one of the longest bridges built by the Romans. The 15m-high **Arco de Trajano** over Calle de Trajano may have served as the entrance to the provincial forum, from where Lusitania province was governed. The **Templo de Diana** (Calle de Sagasta) stood in the municipal forum, where the city government was based. Parts were incorporated into a 16th-century mansion, built within it. The restored **Pórtico del Foro** (Calle de Sagasta), the municipal forum's portico, is nearby.

Northeast of the amphitheatre are the remains of the 1st-century **Circo Romano**, the only surviving hippodrome of its kind in Spain, which could accommodate 30,000 spectators. Inside you can see a brief video (Spanish only) on Diocles, a champion *auriga* (chariot racer) who started his career driving *bigas* and *cuadrigas* (two- and four-horse-drawn chariots) in Mérida before going on to the big league in Rome. Further west is the **Acueducto Los Milagros** (Calle de la Marquesa de Pinares), highly favoured by nesting storks and which once supplied the Roman city with water from the dam at Lago Proserpina, about 5km out of town.

Museo Nacional de Arte Romano

This excellent **museum** (☎ 924 31 16 90; Calle de José Ramón Mélida; adult/child €2.40/1.20, Sat afternoon & Sun free; ❧ 10am-2pm & 6-9pm Tue-Sat, 10am-2pm Sun Mar-Nov; 10am-2pm & 4-6pm Tue-Sat, 10am-2pm Sun Dec-Feb) houses a superb collection of statues, mosaics, frescoes, coins and other Roman artefacts. Designed by the architect Rafael Moneo, the grand brick structure reminiscent of the best in Roman engineering is a remarkable home for the collection.

Alcazaba

This large **Muslim fort** (Calle de Graciano) was built in AD 835 on a site that already had many Roman and Visigothic remains. The 15th-century monastery in its northeast corner now serves as the Junta de Extremadura's presidential offices. The Aljibe (a grand well) at the centre includes marble and stone slabs with Visigothic decoration recycled by the Muslims. Climb up on to the walls to gaze out over the Guadiana.

Iglesia de Santa Eulalia

Originally built in the 5th century in honour of Mérida's patron saint (martyred in Roman times and, according to tradition, buried here – although Barcelona contests that claim with its own legend, see p282), this church on Avenida de Extremadura was completely reconstructed in the 13th century. A museum and open excavated areas enable you to identify Roman houses, a 4th-century Christian cemetery and the original 5th-century basilica.

Museo de Arte Visigodo

Many of the Visigothic objects unearthed in Mérida are exhibited in this **museum** (☎ 924 30 01 06; Calle de Santa Julia; admission free; ❧ 10am-2pm & 6-9pm Tue-Sat, 10am-2pm Sun Mar-Nov; 10am-2pm & 4-6pm Tue-Sat, 10am-2pm Sun Dec-Feb), just off Plaza de España.

Zona Arqueológica de Morería

This excavated Moorish quarter along Paseo de Roma contains the remains of a cemetery, walls and houses dating from Roman to post-Islamic times.

Festivals & Events

The prestigious summer **Festival de Teatro Clásico** (www.festivaldemerida.es; admission €10-30; ❧ around 11pm nightly Jul-Aug), at the Roman theatre and amphitheatre, features Greek and more recent dramatic classics, plus music and dance. Mérida lets its hair down a little later than most of Extremadura in its **Feria de Septiembre** (September Fair).

Sleeping

Hostal Alfarero (☎ 924 30 31 83; elalfarero@telefonica .net; Calle de Sagasta 40; s/d €30/40; ❀) A pretty little yellow house two blocks from the Pórtico del Foro, this is the choice budget option in the heart of town. A real effort has been made to create a warm atmosphere, with terracotta floors, rustic décor and a pleasant little internal patio.

Hostal Nueva España (☎ 924 31 33 56; Avenida de Extremadura 6; s/d €23/35; ❀) Bright, modern rooms with reasonable linen and a decent hot shower and bath make this central cheapie a reasonable choice.

Hotel Cervantes (☎ 924 31 49 61; www.hotelcervan tes.com; Calle de Camilo José Cela 8; s/d €40/60; ❀ P) A modern and somewhat listless sort of place, the Cervantes is nevertheless a comfortable mid-range option aimed mostly at a small, local business market.

Hotel Nova Roma (☎ 924 31 12 61; www.novaroma .com; Calle Suárez Somonte 42; s/d €71.90/90; ❄) What a bizarre place. The tall brick frontage hides a pseudo–Roman Empire interior, complete with heavy layers of marble and copies of headless statues. The rooms themselves are rather more staid, bright and spacious with light pastel-coloured décor but otherwise unremarkable. It often drops prices quite a bit, which is when it becomes an interesting option.

Parador Vía de la Plata (☎ 924 31 38 00; merida@ parador.es; Plaza de la Constitución 3; s/d €91.50/114; ❄ ⓡ Ⓟ) Easily the most charming of Mérida's hotels, this *parador's* site was originally part of a Roman temple and was later a convent, hospital and prison. The columns in the tranquil patio were pillaged from 5th-century buildings. Out the back, room balconies look onto a quiet garden with fountains.

Hotel Meliá Mérida (☎ 924 38 38 00; www.sol melia.com; Plaza de España 19; s/d to €133.80/155; ❄ ⓡ Ⓟ) The fine stone façade of this 19th-century mansion faces the orange-tree-lined square. Inside, this luxury hotel has overdone the décor in public areas but presents beautiful, spacious rooms with Roman-style mosaic décor and muted timber furniture.

Camping Lago Proserpina (☎ 924 12 30 55; camping per person/tent/car €3.30/3.30/3.30; ❄ Apr-Aug) About 5km north of Mérida, this ground lies by a reservoir held back by a Roman dam, which once supplied the city's water and is still a favourite cooling-off spot for summer-stunned locals.

Eating

Cervecería 100 Montaditos (Calle de Felix Valverde Lillo 3; mini-bocadillos €0.90-1.20; ❄ 8am-midnight) It's true, they really do make 100 different baby *bocadillos* here (with anything from Jabugo ham to salmon and cream-cheese filling), served on wood platters. This chatty corner joint is a popular local choice.

Casa Benito (☎ 924 33 07 69; Calle de San Francisco 3; meals €15-20) No bull, this place is the genuine article. Squeeze onto a tiny stool in the wood-panelled dining room out back, prop up the bar or take a seat on the sunny terrace for tapas and *raciónes* at this bullfight enthusiasts' hang-out. The walls are plastered with photos, posters and other memorabilia from down the years in the ring.

El Yantar (☎ 924 31 63 54; Avenida de José Álvare Saez de Buruaga; meals €25) This cheerful *mesór* (tavern) is popular for the freshness of the local produce it uses. Taste small servings o *extremeño* dishes. Gourmands should check out the shop – this is the place to stock up on top-quality ham, Torta del Casar cheese and other goodies.

Restaurante Nicolás (☎ 924 31 96 10; Calle de Felix Valverde Lillio 13; meals €30; ❄ Mon-Sat, lunch Sun Long a favourite with locals, this is one of the classier city dining options. Its relaxing ground-floor bar serves *raciónes*. Upstairs the food is decidedly more exciting than the restaurant's rather drab décor.

Entertainment

Calle de John Lennon is lined with noisy little bars, a couple of clubs, snack bars and eateries. You'll find a more diverse selection of bars scattered about Plaza de la Constitución.

La Tahona (☎ 924 31 35 01; Calle de Alvarado 5, ❄ 1pm-2.30am) This sprawling, spit-and-sawdust place, much beloved of local youth, belts out 'Span pop' hits of the 1990s, puts on Argentine grilled meat in its adjacent restaurant and occasionally gets in local bands to jam.

Raw Café-Club (☎ 605-063933; Plaza de la Constitución 2; ❄ 5pm-3am Wed-Mon) A cool café-bar lurks upstairs here, where you can chill and look out over the square.

Jazz Bar (☎ 666-709263; Calle de Alvarado 10; ❄ 4pm-2am Tue-Sat) For a soothing atmosphere while tippling, this is the best spot in the area.

Mai Kel's (☎ 924 30 25 51; Calle de John Lennon 19; ❄ 12.30-5am Thu-Sat) This is the spot to come and move your booty in downtown Mérida.

Getting There & Away

At least seven daily buses run to/from Badajoz (€3.80, 45 minutes) and Seville (€10.85, 2½ hours). At least four go to Cáceres (€4.20, one hour) and Trujillo (€6.50, 1¼ hours).

There are four trains to Madrid (from €19.20, 4½ to 7½ hours) and one to Seville (€11, 4½ hours) via Zafra. Up to three regional trains run to/from Cáceres (€3.30, one hour 10 minutes).

BADAJOZ

pop 138,400

Badajoz, provincial capital of the southern half of Extremadura, straddles the Río

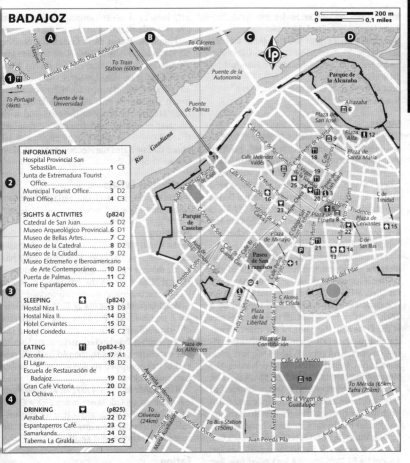

BADAJOZ

Guadiana just 4km from Portugal. It's a sprawling, primarily industrial city with a dilapidated historic heart that's (very) gradually being turned around.

Formerly the capital of a Muslim *taifa* (kingdom) and reconquered by Alfonso IX of León in 1230, Badajoz has had more than its share of strife over the centuries. It was first occupied by Portugal in 1385, and again in 1396, 1542 and 1660. It was besieged during the War of the Spanish Succession, then three times by the French in the Peninsular War. In 1812 the British expelled the French in a bloody battle that cost some 6000 lives. In the Spanish Civil War, the Nationalists carried out atrocious massacres when they took Badajoz in 1936.

Orientation

Plaza de España is the centre of the old town. The pedestrianised streets to its west are full of eateries and bars. The main commercial centre is to the south, around Avenida de Juan Carlos I and Paseo de San Francisco.

The **bus station** (Calle de José Rebollo López) is 1km south of the city centre. The **train station** (Avenida de Carolina Coronado) is 1.5km northwest of the city centre, across the river.

Information

Ciber Café Lucía (Calle de Meléndez Valdés; per hr €2; ⏰ 11.30am-2pm & 4.30pm-midnight Mon-Sat, 4.30pm-midnight Sun)

Junta de Extremadura Tourist Office (☎ 924 01 36 59; Plaza de la Libertad 3; ⏰ 9am-2pm & 5-7pm

Mon-Fri, 10am-2pm Sat & Sun Jun-Sep; 9am-2pm & 4-6pm Mon-Fri, 10am-2pm Sat & Sun Oct-May)

Municipal tourist office (☎ 924 22 49 81; Pasaje de San Juan s/n; ☿ 10am-2pm & 6-8pm Mon-Fri, 10am-2pm Sat Jun-Sep; 10am-2pm & 5-7pm Mon-Fri, 10am-2pm Sat Oct-May)

Post office (Plaza de la Libertad; 8.30am-8.30pm Mon-Fri, 9.30am-2pm Sat)

Sights

The **Catedral de San Juan** (☎ 924 22 39 99; Plaza de España; ☿ 11am-1pm & 6-8pm Tue-Sat), built in the 13th century on the site of a mosque and subsequently much altered, has some finely carved choir stalls and a dusty, gilded altarpiece, elaborate even by Spain's lavish standards. The **Museo de la Catedral** (☎ 924 23 90 27; Calle de San Blas s/n; admission €1; ☿ 11am-1pm & 5-7pm Tue-Sat) contains a treasure chest of religious objects and artworks.

The unkempt remains of the walled Arab **Alcazaba** stand on the hilltop north of the centre. Guarding all is the **Torre Espantaperros** (Scare-Dogs Tower), symbol of the city constructed by the Arabs and topped by a 16th-century Mudéjar bell tower. At its feet is the **Plaza Alta**, long one of the most dilapidated squares in all Spain and still undergoing cosmetic surgery. Within the fort area, a restored Renaissance palace houses the **Museo Arqueológico Provincial** (☎ 924 00 19 08; admission free; ☿ 10am-3pm Tue-Sun), with ancient artefacts from across the province and from prehistoric times through the Roman, Islamic and medieval Christian periods.

The **Museo de Bellas Artes** (☎ 924 21 24 69; Calle del Duque de San Germán 3; admission free; ☿ 10am-2pm & 6-8pm Tue-Fri, 10am-2pm Sat & Sun Jun-Aug; 10am-2pm & 4-6pm Tue-Fri, 10am-2pm Sat & Sun Sep-May) is an excellent gallery with works by Zurbarán, Morales, Picasso, Dalí and the 19th-century Badajoz-born artist Felipe Checa.

The **Puente de Palmas**, an impressive 582m-long granite bridge built in 1596, leads over the Río Guadiana from the 16th-century **Puerta de Palmas** city gate. It's so insensitively over-restored that it looks like something out of Disneyland.

Badajoz's pride and joy is the **Museo Extremeño e Iberoamericano de Arte Contemporáneo** (MEIAC; ☎ 924 01 30 60; Calle de la Virgen de Guadalupe 7; admission free; ☿ 10am-1.30pm & 5-8pm Tue-Sat, 10.30am-1.30pm Sun). This striking modern building, dedicated to Spanish, Portuguese and Latin American contemporary

art, houses a wide-ranging collection of avant-garde painting and sculpture.

The new **Museo de la Ciudad** (City Museum; ☎ 924 20 06 87; Plaza de Santa María; admission free; ☿ 10am-2pm & 6-9pm, 10am-2pm Sun Jun-Aug, 10am-2pm & 4.30-7.30pm, 10am-2pm Sun Sep-May) is above all part of an attempt to regenerate this much run-down part of old Badajoz. It is dedicated to the story of the city, told with illustrative panels and interactive displays that take you through the glory days of Islamic Badajoz and the Reconquista to today. It's all in Spanish.

Festivals & Events

Badajoz's big bash is the **Feria de San Juan**, celebrated for a full week around 24 June.

Sleeping

Hostal Niza II (☎ 924 22 31 73; fax 924 22 38 81; Calle del Arco Agüero 45; s/d €24/40; 🅿) This place has light, decent rooms. The newly renovated Hostal Niza I across the road at No 34 has less character but is more comfortable.

Hotel Cervantes (☎ 924 22 37 10; Calle de Trinidad 2; s/d €26/40; 🅿 🅿) This is a wonderful old time place, with ceramic walls in the green timber-banistered atrium and worn but evocative rooms in the old half; quieter and better equipped rooms are in the newer part out back.

Hotel Condedu (☎ 924 20 72 47; www.infonegocio .com/hotelcondedu; Calle Muñoz Torrero 27; s/d €34/50; 🅿 🅿) Housed in an attractive former private mansion, the rooms in this hotel are spacious, tranquil and spotless.

Eating

Gran Café Victoria (☎ 924 26 32 23; Calle del Obispo San Juan de Ribera 3; breakfasts €2-3) With its huge central lamp arrangement, tall dark pillars and wine-red couches, this café makes some effort at creating a dignified ambience for your morning coffee, with anything from a croissant to *migas* (fried bread crumbs)!

La Ochava (☎ 924 24 70 15; Calle de Zurbarán 15; meals €20-25; ☿ Mon-Sat) Out back from the friendly bar is a family restaurant where you can encounter such unexpected items as tofu kebab and vegetarian couscous among a range of meatier choices.

El Lagar (☎ 924 22 02 98; Calle de San Pedro Alcántara 10; meals €10-15; ☿ Tue-Sat, lunch Sun) On Tuesday to Thursday nights El Lagar does a huge, mixed grilled-meat platter with soup or salad to satisfy three people for €21 in total.

Azcona (☎ 924 27 24 07; Avenida de Adolfo Díaz Ambrona 20; meals €20-25; ⊕ Mon, Thu-Sat, lunch Tue, Wed & Sun) This cheerful yellow and wine-red house rewards the long haul across Puente de la Universidad with its hearty local fare, impeccably prepared.

Escuela de Restauración de Badajoz (☎ 924 22 99 97; Calle de la Virgen de la Soledad 6; ⊕ Mon-Sat, lunch Sun) Badajoz's restaurant training school is warmly recommended, whatever you're hankering after. The bar does good coffee and pastries, milk shakes and quality wine by the glass. Its restaurant, **Atalaya**, (meals €30-35) goes for creative, innovative cuisine while its sister restaurant, the **Alpéndiz** (lunch €15), serves more traditional Mediterranean fare.

Drinking

Taberna La Giralda (☎ 924 23 59 11; Calle de la Virgen de la Soledad 25b) For a more traditional locale, head for this typical *extremeño* wine tavern, where locals hotly discuss the days issues over a long glass of red, with perhaps a few tapas.

Late-night bars are scattered in and around the streets near the cathedral. Among the liveliest are **Espantaperros Café** (Calle de Hernán Cortés 14A; ⊕ 8pm-3am Mon-Thu & 4pm-4am Fri-Sun), **El Arrabal** (☎ 924 26 17 32; Calle de San Blas 14; ⊕ 5pm-2.30am), with its garden bar, and **Samarkanda** (☎ 924 22 53 68; Calle de la Virgen de la Soledad 5A; ⊕ 4.30pm-2.30am), the pick of the crop.

Getting There & Away

You can get buses to most main points in the region from Badajoz. Up to seven buses a day run to Madrid (€22.35, 4½ to 5½ hours), four to Lisbon (€14.10, 3½ hours) and five to Seville (€12.30, three hours 10 minutes) via Zafra.

Trains are much less frequent and the station awkwardly placed.

AROUND BADAJOZ
Albuquerque
Pop 5640

Looming large above the small town, 38km north of Badajoz, is the extraordinarily intact **Castillo de la Luna** (☎ 924 01 54 62; admission free; ⊕ guided visits in Spanish 11am-1pm & 4-6pm Tue-Sun). The centrepiece of a complex frontier defence system of forts, the castle was built on the site of its Muslim predecessor in the 13th century and expanded in the following

centuries. From the top, views dominate the Portuguese frontier (whence repeated attacks came until the Portuguese actually took the town for a few years in the early 18th century). Of the many curiosities is a hole set in the wall of one of the towers. It was used by the castle's masters as a loo, including when under siege, sending an unpleasant message to hostile forces below! A **youth hostel** (dm from €5.10) has been set up inside the castle. It generally caters for groups, so call ahead.

Up to four buses a day between Badajoz and San Vicente de Alcántara stop by here (€3.40, 45 minutes).

Olivenza
pop 11,000

Olivenza, 24km south of Badajoz, is a town that clings to its strong Portuguese heritage. The whitewashed houses, typical turreted defensive walls and predilection for blue-and-white ceramics pay testament to the fact that it has only been Spanish since 1801.

The town was fortified because of its strategic position as a Portuguese outpost on the fertile Guadiana plain. Smack bang in its centre is the 14th-century **castle**, dominated by the **Torre del Homenaje**, 37m high, from which there are fine views. The castle houses an **ethnographic museum** (☎ 924 49 02 22; admission €1; ⊕ 11am-2pm & 5-8pm Tue-Fri, 10am-2pm & 5-8pm Sat, 10am-2pm Sun May-Sep; 11am-2pm & 4-7pm Tue-Fri, 10am-2pm & 4-7pm Sat, 10am-2pm Sun Oct-Apr). Eternal Peter Pans will savour the collection of toy cars on the 1st floor. The most impressive section of the original **defensive walls** is around the 18th-century **Puerta del Calvario**, on the west side of town.

Buses to Badajoz (€1.40, 30 minutes) run almost hourly during the week from the bus station on Calle Avelino, five minutes' walk east of Plaza de España.

ZAFRA
pop 15,500

The gorgeous old town of Zafra, as white as any of Andalucía's *pueblos blancos* to the south, was originally a Muslim settlement and makes a serene, attractive stop en route between Seville and Mérida.

The **tourist office** (☎ 924 55 10 36; www.ayto -zafra.com; Plaza de España s/n; ⊕ 9.30am-2pm & 5-8pm Mon-Fri, 10am-1.30pm Sat & Sun Easter-Sep; 9.30am-2pm & 4-7pm Mon-Fri, 10am-1.30pm Sat & Sun Oct-Easter) is in the northeast corner of the square.

Zafra's 15th-century **castle**, now a *parador*, was built over the former Muslim *alcázar*. **Plaza Grande** and the adjoining **Plaza Chica**, arcaded and bordered by cafés, are a pair of charming squares. All over the town, churches and convents are scattered. Peek into the courtyard of the **ayuntamiento** (town hall) on Plaza del Pilar Redondo and the fine *retablos* inside the 16th-century **Iglesia de la Candelaria** (Calle de Tetuán). The colourful Easter week processions attract crowds and crank up hotel prices considerably.

Sleeping & Eating

Zafra offers around a dozen accommodation options.

Albergue Convento San Francisco (☎ 923 02 98 17; Calle Ancha 1; dm €15) This is the choice of walkers along the Ruta Vía de la Plata (the ancient Silver Route, which runs north–south from Andalucía to the Bay of Biscay). Just 18 beds are spread over simple but comfortable rooms of four and two beds in this former monastery.

Hotel Huerta Honda (☎ 924 55 41 00; www.hotel huertahonda.com; Calle de López Asme 30; r from €79.20; 🖭 🖳) Although the 'olde worlde' atmosphere is perhaps a trifle overdone, this charming boutique number with a sunny patio and beautifully appointed rooms (dark ceramic floors, timber ceilings and four-posters in some) is tempting.

Parador Hernán Cortés (☎ 924 55 45 40; zafra@ parador.es; Plaza del Corazón de María 7; s/d €83.10/103.90; 🖭 🖳 🅿) They say a man's home is his castle, well here it's the other way around. Spacious rooms with plenty of warm, dark wood are for sleeping in, and you can take your meal in the mighty courtyard.

Most of the hotels here have their own restaurants, which are very good in the parador and Hotel Huerta Honda. For a *coffee*, wine or a snack, try one of the many cafés and bars on Plaza Grande.

La Rebotica (☎ 924 55 42 89; Calle de las Boticas 12; meals €30-35; 🕑 Tue-Sat, lunch Sun) Set in a modest house just off Plaza Chica, here you will be treated to such exquisite dishes as *pechuga de pollo con salsa de moras* (chicken breast in mulberry sauce).

Getting There & Away

Zafra is on the main bus and train routes linking Seville in the south with Mérida and Badajoz.

AROUND ZAFRA

Roads through the rolling Sierra Morena into Andalucía head southwest through Fregenal de la Sierra into northern Huelva province, and southeast into the Parque Natural Sierra Norte in Sevilla province.

In **Fregenal de la Sierra**, you'll find a castle and adjoining church, both dating from the 13th century, together with a bullring and market square in an unusual grouping. Walled and hilly **Jerez de los Caballeros**, 42km west of Zafra, was a cradle of conquistadors and has a Knights Templar castle and several handsome churches, three of them with towers emulating the Giralda in Seville (the Iglesia de San Bartolomé is the most exuberant). Quiet **Burguillos del Cerro**, southwest of Zafra, is dominated by a 15th-century castle atop a grassy hill. Just outside **Casas de Reina** on the Guadalcanal road are impressive remains of a Roman theatre and a hilltop Muslim castle.

One bus per day (often none at weekends) runs between Zafra and Fregenal de la Sierra (one hour), Jerez de los Caballeros (one hour) and Burguillos del Cerro (30 minutes).

Directory

CONTENTS

ACCOMMODATION

There's generally no need to book ahead for a room in the low or shoulder seasons, but when things get busier it's advisable (and in high periods it can be essential) to make a reservation if you want to avoid a wearisome search for a room. At most places a phone call earlier the same day is all that's needed: they'll probably ask your approximate time of arrival and will tell you that they'll hold the room for you until a specific hour. Many hotels will help you book a hotel in the next city you're going to. It's also possible to make a reservation by mail, fax or email, but getting written confirmation is not always so easy.

Prices throughout this guidebook are generally high-season maximums. In many cases

---

PRACTICALITIES

- Use the metric system for weights and measures.

- Buy or watch videos on the PAL system.

- Plugs have two round pins, so bring an international adapter; the electric current is 220V, 50Hz.

- If your Spanish is up to it, try the following newspapers: *El País*, the country's leading daily; *El Mundo*, a left-of-centre paper once known for its investigative reports, although it has lost steam in recent years; the Barcelona-based *La Vanguardia*, which on Friday has a great listings magazine for that city; and *Marca*, an all-sports (especially football) paper.

- Tune into: Radio Nacional de España (RNE)'s Radio 1, with general interest and current affairs programmes; Radio 5, with sport and entertainment; and Radio 3 ('Radio d'Espop'), with admirably varied pop and rock music. The most popular commercial pop and rock stations are 40 Principales, Cadena 100 and Onda Cero.

- Switch on the box to watch Spain's state-run Televisión Española (TVE1 and La 2) or the independent commercial stations (Antena 3, Tele 5 and Canal Plus). Regional governments run local stations, such as Madrid's Telemadrid, Catalonia's TV-3 and Canal 33 (both in Catalan), Galicia's TVG, the Basque Country's ETB-1 and ETB-2, Valencia's Canal 9 and Andalucía's Canal Sur.

---

this means you may be pleasantly surprised if you travel off season. What constitutes low or high season depends on where and when. Most of the year is high season in Barcelona, especially when trade fairs are on. August can be pretty dead in the cities and room prices can actually fall then. Winter is high season in the Pyrenees and low season in the Balearic Islands (indeed, the islands seem to shut down between November and Easter). July and August in the Balearics offer plenty of sun and fun, but finding a place to stay without booking ahead can be a real pain. Weekends are high season for boutique hotels and *casas rurales* (country homes; see below) but bad for multi-star business hotels in Madrid and Barcelona (which often make generous offers then).

We divide accommodation categories into budget, mid-range and top end. As prices vary greatly from one part of the country to another, it is difficult to set an arbitrary dividing line. In places such as Barcelona and Madrid, and other popular tourist locations, a budget place can mean anything up to €40/60 for an *individual/doble* (single/double). At the higher end of this range you can generally expect to find good, comfortable rooms with private bathroom. Shave a few euros off and you may find the place only has shared bathrooms in the corridor. In less-travelled regions such as Extremadura, Murcia and Castilla it can be relatively easy to find perfectly acceptable single/double rooms (usually with shared bathroom) for around €20/35. If you want to go for rock bottom, youth hostels, where a bed can cost anything up to €22 but more often around €15 to €18, are probably the best bet.

Mid-range places in the big cities can range up to about €180 for a very nice double, and there are plenty of good and on occasion outright charming options for less. Anything above that price takes you into luxury level. Again, though, much depends on the location. In many parts of Spain you'd be hard-pressed to pay more than €120 for the best double rooms in town. Within each area we have divided up the offerings on the basis of local conditions. A double in a *parador* (see p830) in Castilla-La Mancha at around €100 might be rated top end; the same price will get you a nice mid-range room in Madrid.

A *habitación doble* (double room) is frequently just that: a room with two beds (which you can often shove together) if you want to be sure of a double bed *(cama matrimonial)*, ask for it!

Two websites with online hotel booking facilities are **Hotelkey** (in Spain ☎ 902 180743; www.hotelkey.com) and **Madeinspain** (www.madein spain.net).

Apartments, Villas & Casas Rurales

Throughout Spain there are many self-catering apartments and houses that you can rent for any length of time from one night upwards.

Villas and houses are widely available on the main holiday coasts and in popular country areas. Rural tourism continues to boom, with accommodation available in many new *casas rurales*. These are usually comfortably renovated village houses or farmhouses with a handful of rooms. Some just provide rooms, while others offer meals or self-catering accommodation. Prices typically hover around €25/45 (single/double) per night. Also known as *'agroturismo'*, this kind of place is being turned into a fine art in parts of the country, particularly the Balearic Islands and parts of Catalonia.

A simple one-bedroom apartment in a coastal resort for two or three people might cost as little as €25 per night, although more often you'll be looking at nearly twice that much, and prices can jump further in high season. These options are most worth considering if you plan to stay several days or more, in which case there will usually be discounts from the daily rate.

Tourist offices can supply lists of places for rent, and in Britain the travel sections of the broadsheet press carry private ads for such places. Agencies include:

Individual Travellers Spain (☎ 08700 780194; www.indiv-travellers.com)

Magic of Spain (☎ 0800 980 3378; www .magictravelgroup.co.uk)

Simply Spain (☎ 020-8541 2208, brochure line ☎ 020-8541 2222; www.simply-travel.com)

Spain at Heart (☎ 01373-814222; www .spainatheart.co.uk)

Top Rural (www.toprural.com)

Travellers' Way (☎ 01527-559000; www .travellersway.co.uk)

Camping & Caravan Parks

Spain has around 1000 officially graded *campings* (camping grounds). Some are well located in woodland or near beaches or rivers, but others are stuck away on the unattractive edges of towns or along highways. Few are near city centres, and camping isn't particularly convenient if you're relying on public transport.

Camping grounds are officially rated as 1st class (1ªC), 2nd class (2ªC) or 3rd class (3ªC). There are also a few that are not officially graded, usually equivalent to 3rd class. Facilities generally range from reasonable to very good, although any camping ground can be crowded and noisy at busy times (especially July and August). Even a 3rd-class camping ground is likely to have hot showers, electrical hook-ups and a café. The best ones have heated swimming pools, supermarkets, restaurants, laundry service, children's playgrounds and tennis courts. Sizes range from a capacity of under 100 people to over 5000.

Camping grounds usually charge per person, per tent and per vehicle – typically €3 to €4 for each. Children usually pay a bit less than adults. Many camping grounds close from around October to Easter.

The annual *Guía Oficial de Campings*, available in bookshops around the country, lists most of Spain's camping grounds and their facilities and prices. Tourist offices can always direct you to the nearest camping ground.

You sometimes come across a *zona de acampada* or *área de acampada*, a country camping ground with minimal facilities (maybe just tap water or a couple of barbecues), little or no supervision and little or no charge. If it's in an environmentally protected area, you may need to obtain permission from the local environmental authority to camp there.

With certain exceptions – such as many beaches and environmentally protected areas and a few municipalities that ban it – it is legal to camp outside camping grounds (but not within 1km of official ones!). Signs usually indicate where wild camping is not allowed. If in doubt you can always check with tourist offices. You'll need permission to camp on private land.

Hostels

Spain's 200 or so youth hostels – *albergues juveniles*, not be confused with *hostales* (budget hotels) – are often the cheapest places for lone travellers, but two people can usually get a double room elsewhere for a similar price. Some hostels are only moderate value, lacking in privacy, often heavily booked by school groups, and with night-time curfews and no cooking facilities (although if there is nowhere to cook there is usually a cafeteria). Others, however, are conveniently located, open 24 hours and composed mainly of double rooms or small dorms, often with private bathroom. An increasing number have

rooms adapted for people with disabilities. Some even occupy fine historic buildings.

Most Spanish youth hostels are members of the **Red Española de Albergues Juveniles** (REAJ, Spanish Youth Hostel Network; ☎ 91 347 77 00; www.reaj .com), the Spanish representative of **Hostelling International** (HI; www.hihostels.com).

Most Spanish hostels are also members of the youth hostel association of their region (Andalucía, Catalonia, Valencia etc). Each region usually sets its own price structure and has a central booking service where you can make reservations for most of its hostels. You can also book directly with hostels themselves. Central booking services include:
Andalucía (☎ 902 51 00 00; www.inturjoven.com)
Catalonia (☎ 93 483 83 41; www.tujuca.com)
Valencia (☎ 902 22 55 52; www.ivaj.es, in Spanish)

Just a few youth hostels are independent of regional associations – although they may still be REAJ and HI members!

Prices at youth hostels often depend on the season, and vary between €9 and €18 for under-26s (the lower rate is usually applied to people with ISIC cards too) and between €12 and €22 for those 26 and over. In some hostels the price includes breakfast. A few hostels require you to rent sheets (around €2 for your stay) if you don't have your own or a sleeping bag.

Most hostels require you to have an HI card or a membership card from your home country's youth hostel association; others don't require a card (even though they may be HI hostels), but may charge more if you don't have one. You can obtain an HI card in Spain at most hostels.

You will sometimes find independent *albergues* offering dormitory accommodation for around €10, usually in villages in areas that attract plenty of Spanish walkers and climbers. These are not specifically youth hostels – although the clientele tends to be aged under 35. They're a kind of halfway house between a youth hostel and a *refugio* (mountain shelter; see p830). Some will rent you sheets for a couple of euros if you need them.

Hotels, Hostales, Pensiones & Hospedajes

Officially, places to stay are classified into *hoteles* (hotels, one to five stars), *hostales* (one to three stars) and *pensiones* (one or two stars). These are the categories used by the annual *Guía Oficial de Hoteles*, sold in bookshops, which lists almost every such establishment in Spain, except for one-star *pensiones*, with approximate prices.

In practice, accommodation places use all sorts of overlapping names to describe themselves, especially at the budget end of the market. In broad terms, the cheapest are usually places just advertising *camas* (beds), *fondas* (traditionally a basic eatery and inn combined, though one of these functions is now often missing) and *casas de huéspedes* or *hospedajes* (guesthouses), not to be confused with *hostales* (budget hotels). Most such places will be bare and basic. Bathrooms are likely to be shared. Your room may be small, possibly lacking a window, and it may have alarming electrical fittings and erratic hot water – but in most cases it will be kept pretty clean. The beds may make you feel as though you're lying diagonally across a bumpy hillside – or they may be firm, flat and comfortable. In winter don't hesitate to ask for extra blankets. Singles/doubles in these places cost from around €12/20 to €15/25.

A *pensión* (basically a small private hotel) is usually a small step up from the above types in standards and price. Some cheap establishments forget to provide soap, toilet paper or towels. Don't hesitate to ask for these necessities. *Hostales* are in much the same category. In both cases the better ones can be bright and spotless, with rooms boasting full en suite bathroom. Prices can range up to €40/60 for singles/doubles in more popular/expensive locations.

The remainder of establishments call themselves *hoteles* and cover the full range of quality from straightforward roadside places, bland but clean, through charming boutique jobbies and on to super luxury hotels. Even in the cheapest hotels, rooms are likely to have an attached bathroom and there'll probably be a restaurant. Among the most tempting hotels for those with a little fiscal room to manoeuvre are the **Paradores** (www.parador.es), a state-run chain of hotels in stunning locations, among them towering castles and former medieval convents. Similarly, you can find stunning hotels in restored country homes and old city mansions, and these are not always particularly expensive. Seriously modern design hotels with androgynous staff and a fashion feel à la New York are also beginning to pop up in some of the big cities.

Many places to stay of all types have a range of rooms at different prices. At the budget end, prices will vary according to whether the room has only a *lavabo* (washbasin), *ducha* (shower) or *baño completo* (full bathroom), that is bath/shower, basin and loo. At the top end you may pay more for a room on the *exterior* (outside) of the building or with a *balcón* (balcony) and will often have the option of a suite. Seaside views frequently attract higher rates. Many places have rooms for three, four or more people where the per-person cost is lower than in a single or double, which is good news for families.

Checkout time is generally between 11am and noon.

Monasteries

An offbeat possibility is staying in a monastery. In spite of the expropriations of the 19th century and a sometimes rough run in the 20th, plenty of monastic orders have survived (albeit in diminishing numbers) across the country. Some offer rooms to outsiders – often fairly austere monks' or nuns' cells.

Monastery accommodation is generally a single-sex arrangement, and the idea in quite a few is to seek a refuge from the outside world and indulge in quiet contemplation and meditation.

Refugios

Mountain shelters *(refugios)* for walkers and climbers are quite liberally scattered around most of the popular mountain areas (mainly the Pyrenees), except in Andalucía, which has only a handful. They're mostly run by mountaineering and walking organisations. Accommodation – usually bunks squeezed into a dorm – is often on a first-come, first-served basis, although for some *refugios* you can book ahead. In busy seasons (July and August in most areas) they can fill up quickly and you should try to book in advance or arrive by mid-afternoon to be sure of a place. Prices per person range from nothing to €12 a night. Many *refugios* have a bar and offer meals (dinner typically costs around €10), as well as a cooking area (but not cooking equipment). Blankets are usually provided but you'll have to bring any other bedding yourself.

ACTIVITIES

The variety of landscape in Spain lends itself to an equally broad palette of outdoor activities. In the mountains, especially the Pyrenees, there is plenty of great skiing in winter and hiking in summer. Other mountain chains, such as the Picos de Europa and the Sierra de Gredos, exert equal fascination on hikers, while the Sierra Nevada in Andalucía is a frisky ski haven in the warm deep south of the country.

Many people's thoughts turn first to the seaside when thinking of Spain. As well as an endless variety of beaches and coves to swim at, you can dive or snorkel off the Costa Brava, surf off the Basque Country coast and windsurf off Tarifa. And sailors love to promenade up and down the coast or between the mainland and the Balearic Islands. White-water rafting, canoeing and hydrospeed are options along a handful of gushing northern rivers.

Cycling and mountain biking are increasingly popular around the country.

More offbeat sports can also be practised. Canyoning, bungee-jumping from high bridges (what the Catalans call *puonting*), and hang-gliding are among the most popular activities.

For details on a wide array of sports activities on offer in Spain, see the Spain Outdoors chapter (p78).

BUSINESS HOURS

Generally, Spaniards work Monday to Friday from about 9am to 2pm and then again from 4.30pm or 5pm for another three hours. Shops and travel agencies are usually open these hours on Saturday too, although many skip the evening session. The further south you go, the longer the afternoon break tends to be, with shops and the like staying closed until 6pm or so.

Big supermarkets and department stores, such as the nationwide El Corte Inglés chain, open from about 9am to 9pm Monday to Saturday. Shops in tourist resorts sometimes open on Sunday too.

Many government offices don't bother opening in the afternoon, any day of the year. In summer, offices tend to go on to *horario intensivo*, which means they can start as early as 7am and finish up for the day by 2pm.

Museums all have their own opening hours: major ones tend to open for something like normal Spanish business hours (with or without the afternoon break), but often have their weekly closing day on Monday.

Pharmacies have a wide variety of opening hours. The standard hours follow those of other shops. In the bigger centres you will find several that open 24 hours a day. Other shops have extended hours, say 8am to 10pm, usually on a rota basis. To find out where late-opening pharmacies are in the cities and bigger towns, pick up the local paper.

For bank and post office opening hours, respectively, see Money on p841 and Post on p842.

As a general rule restaurants open their kitchens for lunch from 1pm to 4pm and for dinner from 8pm to midnight. The further south you go, the later locals tend to go out to eat. While Barcelona restaurants may already be busy by 9.30pm, their Madrid counterparts are still half empty at this time. At lunch and dinner time you can generally linger quite a while after the kitchen closes. Some, but by no means all, places close one or two days a week. Some also shut for a few weeks' annual holiday – the most common period for this is during August.

Bars have a wider range of hours. Those that serve as cafés and snack bars can open from about 8am to the early evening. Those that are more nightlife bars may open in the early evening and generally close around 2am to 3am. Some places combine the two roles. As the bars close the clubs open (generally from around midnight or 1am to around 5am or 6am).

CHILDREN
Practicalities

As a rule Spaniards are very friendly to children. Any child whose hair is less than jet black will be dubbed *rubia* (blonde) if she's a girl or *rubio* if he's a boy. Accompanied children are welcome at all kinds of accommodation, as well as in many cafés, bars and restaurants, where outside tables often allow kids a bit of space and freedom while the grown-ups sit and eat or drink. Spanish children stay up late and at fiestas it's common to see even tiny ones toddling the streets at 2am or 3am. Visiting kids like this idea too – but can't always cope with it quite so readily.

Always make a point of asking staff at tourist offices if they know of family activities and for suggestions on hotels that cater for kids. Discounts are available for children (usually aged under 12) on public transport and for admission to sites. Those under four generally go free.

You can hire car seats for infants and children from most car-rental firms, but you should always book them in advance. You cannot rely on restaurants having high chairs and few have nappy-changing facilities. In better hotels you can generally arrange for childcare and in some places child-minding agencies cater to temporary visitors.

You can buy baby formula in powder or liquid form, as well as sterilising solutions such as Milton, at *farmacias* (pharmacies). Disposable nappies (diapers) are widely available at supermarkets and *farmacias*. Fresh cow's milk is sold in cartons and plastic bottles in supermarkets in big cities, but can be hard to find in small towns, where UHT is often the only option.

Sights & Activities

As well as the obvious attractions of beaches (and all the seaside activities), swimming pools and playgrounds, there are plenty of other good options. Aquaparks, zoos and aquariums are generally winners. Barcelona's **Aquàrium** (p287), with its extraordinary walk-through shark-infested tunnel, is one of the best in all Europe.

Most kids and not a few adults succumb to the siren call of extravagant theme parks like **Warner Brothers Movie World** near Madrid (p164) and Catalonia's **Universal Mediterrània** (p381). On a slightly different note are Mini Hollywood and other Western movie sets in the Almería desert (p793).

Keep an eye out for sights that might be of special interest to children. Castles, of which Spain is full (they are especially numerous across the two Castillas), are often the easiest sights to sell to young ones.

Certain museums will also interest children. The **Museu Marítim** (p281) in Barcelona, for instance, has imaginative seafaring displays that will appeal to the imagination of older children. Equally, Valencia's **Ciudad de las Artes y las Ciencias** (p577) is another magnificent attraction.

Most younger children are fascinated by the ubiquitous street-corner *kioscos* selling sweets or *gusanitos* (corn puffs) for a few *céntimos*. The magnetism of these places often overcomes a child's inhibitions enough for them to carry out their own first Spanish transactions.

For further information, see Lonely Planet's *Travel with Children* or the websites www.travelwithyourkids.com and www.familytravelnetwork.com.

CLIMATE CHARTS

The *meseta* (the high tableland of central Spain) and Ebro basin have a continental climate: scorching in summer, cold in winter, and dry. Madrid regularly freezes in December, January and February and temperatures climb above 30°C in July and August. Valladolid on the northern *meseta* and Zaragoza in the Ebro basin are even drier, with only around 300mm of rain a year (little more than Alice Springs in Australia). The Guadalquivir basin in Andalucía is only a little wetter and positively broils in high summer, with temperatures of 35°C-plus in Seville that kill people every year.

The Pyrenees and the Cordillera Cantábrica backing the Bay of Biscay coast bear the brunt of cold northern and northwestern airstreams, which bring moderate temperatures and heavy rainfall (three or four times as much as Madrid's) to the north coast. Even in high summer you never know when you might get a shower.

The Mediterranean coast and Balearic Islands get a little more rain than Madrid and the south can be even hotter in summer. The Mediterranean, particularly around Alicante, also provides Spain's warmest waters (reaching 27°C or so in August). Barcelona's weather is typical of the coast – milder than in inland cities but more humid.

In general you can usually rely on pleasant or hot temperatures just about everywhere from April to early November. In Andalucía there are plenty of warm, sunny days right through winter. In July and August, temperatures can get unpleasantly hot inland.

Snowfalls in the mountains can start as early as October and some snow cover lasts all year on the highest peaks.

COURSES

A spot of study in Spain is a great way not only to learn something but also to meet people – Spaniards as well as other travellers – and get more of an inside angle on local life than the average visitor. More than

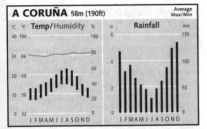

A CORUÑA 58m (190ft)

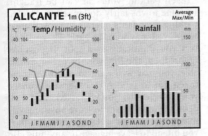

ALICANTE 1m (3ft)

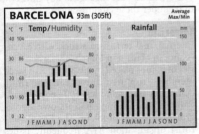

BARCELONA 93m (305ft)

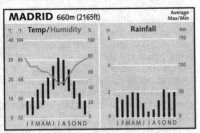

MADRID 660m (2165ft)

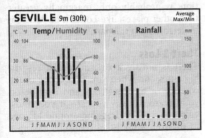

SEVILLE 9m (30ft)

anything else, people are drawn to Spain from all over Europe and North America for language courses – after all, Spanish is the world's third most spoken tongue after Chinese and English!

The **Instituto Cervantes** (www.cervantes.es), with branches in over 30 cities around the world, promotes the Spanish language and culture. It's mainly involved in Spanish teaching and in library and information services. The institute's London branch has a **library** (☎ 020-7235 0353; 102 Eaton Square, London SW1 W9AN) with a wide range of reference books, periodicals, videos (including feature films), language-teaching material, electronic databases and music CDs. You can find more addresses on the institute's website. It can send you long lists of places offering Spanish-language courses in Spain. Some Spanish embassies and consulates can also provide information on courses.

A number of Spanish universities offer good-value language courses. Seville (p689), Granada (p767), Madrid (p136), Barcelona (p298) and Salamanca (p182) are popular places to study Spanish. The **Escuela Oficial de Idiomas** (EOI; www.eoidiomas.com in Madrid) is a nationwide language institution where visitors can learn Spanish and locals other languages. Classes can be large and busy but are generally fairly cheap. There are branches in many major cities. The Madrid website has contact details for other EOIs around the country.

Private language schools as well as universities cater for a wide range of levels, course lengths, times of year, intensity and special requirements. Many courses have a cultural component as well as pure language. University courses often last a term, although some are as short as two weeks or as long as a year. Private colleges can be more flexible. One with a good reputation is **¿?don Quijote** (www.donquijote.com), with branches in Barcelona, Granada, Madrid, Salamanca, Seville and Valencia.

Costs vary widely. A typical 40-hour course over two to four weeks will cost around €300 at a university. At private schools you could be looking at around €650 to €700 for a month at 20 to 25 hours a week. Accommodation can be arranged with families, or in student flats or residences. You might pay €450 per month in a flat or €800 to €900 for full board in a family.

It's also worth finding out whether your course will lead to any formal certificate of competence. The Diploma de Español como Lengua Extranjera (DELE) is recognised by Spain's Ministry of Education and Science.

CUSTOMS

Duty-free allowances for travellers entering Spain from outside the EU include 2L of wine (or 1L of wine and 1L of spirits), and 200 cigarettes or 50 cigars or 250g of tobacco.

Duty-free allowances for travel between EU countries were abolished in 1999. There are no restrictions on the import of duty-paid items into Spain from other EU countries for personal use. You *can* buy VAT-free articles at airport shops when travelling between EU countries.

DANGERS & ANNOYANCES

Spain is generally a pretty safe country. The main thing to be wary of is petty theft (which may of course not seem so petty if your passport, cash, travellers cheques, credit card and camera go missing). Most visitors to Spain never feel remotely threatened, but a sufficient number have unpleasant experiences to warrant an alert. What follows is intended as a strong warning rather than alarmism.

Scams

There must be 50 ways to lose your wallet. As a general rule, talented petty thieves work in groups and capitalise on distraction. More imaginative strikes include having someone dropping a milk mixture on to the victim from a balcony. Immediately a concerned citizen comes up to help you brush off what you assume to be pigeon poo, and thus suitably occupied you don't notice the contents of your pockets slipping away.

Beware: not all thieves look like thieves. Watch out for an old classic: the ladies offering flowers for good luck. We don't know how they do it, but if you get too involved in a friendly chat with these people, your pockets always wind up empty.

On some highways, especially the AP7 from the French border to Barcelona, bands of delinquents occasionally operate. Beware of men trying to distract you in rest areas and don't stop along the highway if people driving alongside indicate you have a problem with the car. While one inspects the rear of the car with you, his pals will empty your vehicle. They have even been reported puncturing tyres of cars stopped in rest areas. They then follow and 'help' the victim when they stop to change the wheel. Hire cars and those with foreign plates are especially targeted. When you do call in at highway rest stops, try to park close to the buildings and leave nothing of value in view.

Even parking your car can be fraught. In some towns fairly dodgy self-appointed parking attendants operate in central areas where you may want to park. They will direct you frantically to a spot. If possible, ignore them and find your own. If unavoidable, you may well want to pay them some token not to scratch or otherwise damage your vehicle after you've walked away. You definitely don't want to leave anything visible in the car (or open the boot/trunk if you intend to leave luggage or anything else in it) under these circumstances.

Terrorism

International terrorism struck with a vengeance in Madrid in March 2004 when a series of bombs placed by suspected Al-Qaeda members ruptured three early-morning commuter trains and left 190 people dead.

But Spain has long had its own homegrown terrorism problem. The Basque terrorist organisation ETA frequently issues chilling warnings to tourists to stay away from Spain, although on the ground the bulk of their attacks have in recent years been aimed at specific local figures – politicians, police and the like.

Repeated arrests of ETA members and a tough stance by the central government and French authorities seem to have dented the group's capacity to strike, but this doesn't stop them from trying. Overall, the chances of being in the wrong place at the wrong time is probably only marginally greater than other places, like London or Paris, hit by terrorism in the past.

Theft & Loss

Theft is mostly a risk in tourist resorts, big cities and when you first arrive in the country or at a new city and may be off your guard. Clearly you are at your most vulnerable when dragging around luggage to or from your hotel (consider taking a taxi). Barcelona, Madrid and Seville have the worst reputations for theft and, on occasion, muggings.

The main things to guard against are pickpockets, bag snatchers and theft from cars. It appears muggings are on the increase and in the big cities can occur around the sights and areas frequented by tourists, on the metro (trains and stations) and at main points of arrival. Some thieves operate in groups and on occasion have no scruples about attacking in broad daylight in crowded areas. The significant change in the past few years has been the appearance of more gangs, their preparedness to use violence and their daylight daring. Unfortunately, police are thin on the ground and generally seem fairly blasé about such incidents (they've seen it all before and know they can do little or nothing).

It is difficult to gauge the chances of falling victim to such an assault. In any event, you should take certain precautions. Carry any valuables under your clothes if possible – not in a back pocket, a day pack or anything that could be snatched away easily – and keep your eyes open for people who get unnecessarily close to you in public transport or on the streets. Don't leave baggage unattended and avoid crushes. Also be cautious with people who come up to offer or ask you something (such as the time or directions) or start talking to you for no obviously good reason. These could be attempts to distract you and make you an easier victim. Ignore demands to see your passport unless they come from a uniformed police officer; some gangs recycle stolen passports. Keep a firm grip on day packs and bags at all times.

Always remove the radio and cassette player from your car and never leave any belongings visible when you leave the car.

Anything left lying on the beach can disappear in a flash when your back is turned. Avoid dingy, empty city alleys and backstreets, or anywhere that just doesn't feel 100% safe, at night.

You can also help yourself by not leaving anything valuable lying around your room, above all in any hostel-type place. Use a safe if one is available.

If anything valuable does go missing, you need to report it to the police and get a copy of the report if you want to make an insurance claim. In most cases the chances of recovering any property are next to zero. If your passport has gone, contact your embassy or consulate for help in issuing a replacement. Embassies and consulates can also give help of various kinds in other emergencies, but as a rule cannot advance you money to get home. Many countries have consulates in a few cities around Spain (such as Alicante, Barcelona, Málaga, Palma de Mallorca, Seville and Valencia) and your embassy can tell you where the nearest one is (see p836).

DISABLED TRAVELLERS

Spain is not overly disabled-friendly but some things are slowly changing. Disabled access to some museums, official buildings and hotels represents something of a sea change in local thinking, although it remains a minority phenomenon. In major cities more is slowly being done to facilitate disabled access to public transport and taxis.

Organisations

Accessible Travel & Leisure (☎ 01452-729739; www.accessibletravel.co.uk; Avionics House, Naas Lane, Gloucester GL2 2SN) Claims to be the biggest UK travel agent dealing with travel for the disabled and encourages the disabled to travel independently.

Holiday Care (☎ 0845 124 9971; www.holidaycare.org .uk; 2nd fl, Imperial Buildings, Victoria Rd, Horley, Surrey RH6 7PZ) Information on hotels with disabled access, where to hire equipment and tour operators dealing with the disabled.

ONCE (☎ 91 436 53 00; www.once.es; Calle de José Ortega y Gasset 22-24, Madrid) The Spanish association for the blind. You may be able to get hold of guides in Braille to a handful of cities, including Madrid and Barcelona, although they are not published every year.

Royal Association for Disability & Rehabilitation (RADAR; ☎ 020-7250 3222; www.radar.org.uk; Unit 12, City Forum, 250 City Rd, London EC1V 8AF) RADAR publishes *European Holidays & Travel Abroad: A Guide for Disabled People*, which provides a good overview of facilities available to disabled travellers throughout Europe.

DISCOUNT CARDS

At museums, never hesitate to ask if there are discounts for students, young people, children, families or the elderly.

Senior Cards

There are reduced prices for people over 60, 63 or 65 (depending on the place) at various museums and attractions (sometimes restricted to EU citizens only) and occasionally on transport. Some of the luxurious Paradores (see Hotels, Hostales, Pensiones & Hospedajes, p829) offer discounts of 35% for people over 60. You should also seek information in your own country on travel packages and discounts for senior travellers, through senior citizens organisations and travel agents.

Student & Youth Cards

At some sights discounts (usually half the normal fee) are available to students and people aged under 18. You will need some kind of identification to prove age or student status. An ISIC (International Student Identity Card; www.isic.org) may come in handy (there is also a teachers' version, ITIC) for travel discounts but is not accepted at many sights.

You'll have more luck with a Euro<26 (www.euro26.org) card (known as Carnet Joven in Spain), which is useful for those under 26. For instance, Euro<26 card holders enjoy 20% or 25% off most 2nd-class train fares; 10% or 20% off many Trasmediterránea ferries and some bus fares; good discounts at some museums; and discounts of up to 20% at some youth hostels.

For non-travellers under 25 there is also the International Youth Travel Card (IYTC; www.istc.org), which offers similar benefits.

Student cards are issued by hostelling organisations, student unions and some youth travel agencies worldwide.

EMBASSIES & CONSULATES
Spanish Embassies & Consulates

Spanish embassies and consulates can be found in:

Andorra (☎ 800 030; embespad@correo.mae.es; Carrer Prat de la Creu 34, Andorra la Vella)

Australia Canberra (☎ 02-6273 3555; www.embaspain.com; 15 Arkana St, Yarralumla ACT 2600); Melbourne (☎ 03-9347 1966; 146 Elgin St, Vic 3053); Sydney (☎ 02-9261 2433; Level 24, St Martin's Tower, 31 Market St, NSW 2000)

Canada Ottawa (☎ 613-747 2252; www.embaspain.ca; 74 Stanley Ave, Ontario K1M 1P4); Montreal (☎ 514-935 5235; Ste 1456, 1 Westmount Sq, Québec H3Z 2P9); Toronto (☎ 416-977 1661; Simcoe Place, Ste 2401, 200 Front St, Ontario M5V 3K2)

France (☎ 01 44 43 18 00; www.amb-espagne.fr; 22 ave Marceau, 75008 Paris)

Germany Berlin (☎ 030-254 00 70; www.spanische botschaft.de; Lichtensteinallee 1, 10787); Düsseldorf (☎ 0211-43 90 80; Hombergerstr 16, 40474); Frankfurt am Main (☎ 069-959 16 60; Nibelungenplatz 3, 60318); Munich (☎ 089-998 47 90; Oberföhringerstr 45, 81925)

Ireland Dublin (☎ 01-269 1640; 17A Merlyn Park, Ballsbridge, Dublin 4)

Japan Tokyo (☎ 03-3583 8533; embesjp@mail.mae.es; 1-3-29 Roppongi Minato-Ku, Tokyo 106)

Morocco Rabat (☎ 07-26 80 00; ambespma@mail.mae.es; 3 Zankat Madnine); Casablanca (☎ 02-22 07 52; 31 rue d'Alger); Tangier (☎ 09-93 70 00; 85 Ave Président Habib Bourghiba)

Netherlands The Hague (☎ 070-302 49 99; www.claboral.nl; Lange Voorhout 50, 2514 EG)

New Zealand See Australia

Portugal Lisbon (☎ 01-347 2381; embesppt@correo.mae.es; Rua do Salitre 1, 1269-052)

UK London (☎ 020-7235 5555; spain.embassyhomepage.com; 39 Chesham Place, SW1X 8SB); Edinburgh (☎ 0131-220 1843; 63 North Castle St, EH2 3LJ); London consulate (☎ 020-7589 8989; 20 Draycott Place, SW3 2RZ); Manchester (☎ 0161-236 1262; 1a Brook House, 70 Spring Gardens)

USA Washington DC (☎ 202-728 2332; 2375 Pennsylvania Ave NW, 20037); Boston (☎ 617-536 2506); Chicago (☎ 312-782 4588); Houston (☎ 713-783 6200); Los Angeles (☎ 213-938 0158); Miami (☎ 305-446 5511); New York (☎ 212-355 4080); San Francisco (☎ 415-922 2995)

Embassies & Consulates in Spain

The embassies are in Madrid. Some countries also maintain consulates in major cities, particularly in Barcelona. Embassies and consulates include:

Australia Madrid (Map p113; ☎ 91 441 60 25; www.spain.embassy.gov.au; Plaza del Descubridor Diego de Ordás 3); Barcelona (Map pp266-7; ☎ 93 490 90 13; 9th fl, Gran Via de Carles III 98)

Canada Madrid (Map pp108-9; ☎ 91 423 32 50; www.canada-es.org; Calle de Núñez de Balboa 35); Barcelona (Map pp266-7; ☎ 93 204 27 00; Carrer d'Elisenda de Pinós 10; FGC Reina Elisenda)

France Madrid (Map pp106-8; ☎ 91 423 89 00; www.amba france-es.org; Calle de Salustiano Olózaga 9); Barcelona (Map pp270-2; ☎ 93 270 30 00; Ronda de l'Universitat 22B)

Germany Madrid (Map pp108-9; ☎ 91 557 90 00; www.embajada-alemania.es; Calle de Fortuny 8); Barcelona (Map pp268-9; ☎ 93 292 10 00; Passeig de Gràcia 111)

Ireland Madrid (Map pp108-9; ☎ 91 436 40 93; embajadairlanda@terra.es; Paseo de la Castellana 46); Barcelona (Map pp266-7; ☎ 93 491 50 21; Gran Via de Carles III 94)

Netherlands Madrid (Map p113; ☎ 91 353 75 00; www.embajadapaisesbajos.es; Avenida del Comandante Franco

32); Barcelona (Map pp266-7; ☎ 93 363 54 20; Avinguda Diagonal 601); Palma de Mallorca (Map p621; ☎ 971 71 64 93; Calle de San Miquel 36)

New Zealand Madrid (Map pp114-6; ☎ 91 523 02 26; nzembmadrid@santandersupernet.com; Plaza de la Lealtad 2); Barcelona (Map pp268-9; ☎ 93 209 03 99; Travessera de Gràcia 64; FGC Gràcia)

UK Madrid (Map pp108-9; ☎ 91 700 82 00; www.ukinspain .com; Calle de Fernando el Santo 16); Consulate (Map pp108-9; ☎ 91 524 97 00; Paseo de Recoletos 7/9); Barcelona (Map pp268-9; ☎ 93 366 62 00; Avinguda Diagonal 477); Palma de Mallorca (Map p621; ☎ 971 71 20 85; Plaza Mayor 3D)

USA Madrid (Map pp108-9; ☎ 91 587 22 00; www.embusa .es; Calle de Serrano 75); Barcelona (Map pp266-7; ☎ 93 280 02 95; Passeig de la Reina Elisenda de Montcada 23-25; FGC Reina Elisenda); Palma de Mallorca (Map p621; ☎ 971 72 50 51; Edificio Reina Costanza, Carrer de Porto Pi 8)

FESTIVALS & EVENTS

Spaniards like nothing more than indulging in their love of colour, noise, crowds, dressing up and partying at innumerable local fiestas (festivals) and *ferias* (fairs); even small villages will have at least one, probably several, in the year, all with unique twists and local peculiarities. Many fiestas are religion-based but are celebrated with an earthy party spirit. A few of the most outstanding include the following:

January
Festividad de San Sebastián (p450; 20 January) During this festival everyone in San Sebastián dresses up and goes berserk.

February/March
Carnaval This event involves several days of fancy-dress parades and merrymaking. It is at its wildest in Cádiz (p707) and Sitges (p321), but is also good in Ciudad Rodrigo (p186). It usually ends just before Lent, on the Tuesday 47 days before Easter Sunday.

March
Las Fallas (15–19 March) This festival consists of several days of all-night dancing and drinking, first-class fireworks and processions. Its principal stage is Valencia city (p582), but it is also celebrated in Gandia (p596) and Benidorm (p600).

Semana Santa (Holy Week) The week leading up to Easter Sunday entails parades of *pasos* (holy images) and huge crowds. It is most extravagantly celebrated in Seville (see the boxed text, p690), but is also big in Málaga (p737), Córdoba (p755), Toledo (p244), Ávila (p176), Valladolid (p196 and Zamora (p204). Holy Week can also fall in April or across the two months.

April
Moros y Cristianos (p610; 22–24 April). Colourful parades and 'battles' between Christian and Muslim 'armies' in Alcoy, near Alicante, make this one of the most spectacular of several similar events in Valencia and Alicante provinces through the year.

Feria de Abril (p689; late April) This is a week-long party in Seville held after the religious fervour of Semana Santa.

Romería de la Virgen de la Cabeza (last Sunday in April) Hundreds of thousands of people make a mass pilgrimage to the Santuario de la Virgen de la Cabeza near Andújar, in Jaén province (p782).

May
Feria del Caballo (p715; early May) A colourful equestrian fair in Andalucía's horse capital, Jerez de la Frontera. **Concurso de Patios Cordobeses** (see the boxed text, p755; early to mid-May) Scores of beautiful private courtyards are opened to the public for two weeks in Córdoba. **Fiesta de San Isidro** (p137; 15 May) Madrid's major fiesta features bullfights, parades, concerts and more. Some of the events, such as the bullfighting season, last a month.

May/June
Romería del Rocío (see the boxed text, p701) Focused on Pentecost weekend, the seventh after Easter, this is a festive pilgrimage by up to one million people to the shrine of the Virgin at the Andalucian village of El Rocío. **Corpus Christi** Falls on the Thursday of the ninth week after Easter. Religious processions and celebrations in Toledo (p244) and other cities.

June
Hogueras de San Juan (23 June) Midsummer bonfires and fireworks, notably along the southeast and south coasts, on the eve of the Fiesta de San Juan (24 June).

July
Fiesta de San Fermín or Sanfermines (p471; 6 to 14 July) For many the highlight of this week-long nonstop festival and party is the *encierro* (running of the bulls) in Pamplona, an activity also pursued in dozens of other cities and towns through the summer.

Día de la Virgen del Carmen (16 July) Around this date at most coastal towns, the image of the patron of fisherfolk is carried into the sea or paraded on it amid a flotilla of small boats.

Día de Santiago (Feast of St James, 25 July) This is the national saint's day and is spectacularly celebrated in Santiago de Compostela (p538), site of his tomb.

August
Semana Grande or Aste Nagusia Dates vary from place to place for this week of general celebration, heavy drinking and bad hangovers on the north coast.

La Tomatina (see the boxed text p588; second-last or last Wednesday in August) This massive tomato-throwing festival in Buñol, Valencia, must be one of the messiest festivals in the country.

September

Festes de la Mercè (p300; around 24 September) Barcelona's gigantic party marks the end of summer and is held over several days with parades, concerts, theatre and more.

FOOD

Glorious food. There's plenty of it in Spain and the regional variety is remarkable. From myriad seafood curiosities in Galicia to the venison of Castilla and the avantgarde *nueva cocina* that's cooking in Barcelona, Madrid and the Basque Country, Spain offers no shortage of surprises. For an overview of what's in store in Spain's kitchens, see p94.

In the course of this guidebook we provide a broad selection of eateries. In order to provide a guide to what you might pay for your grub, we divide listings into Budget (up to €15 for a full meal), Mid-Range (€16 to €45) and Top End (€45 and up). On some occasions, dining listings have been ordered by type (café, restaurant etc). This division is rather arbitrary and based on the situation in the big cities. You may well find yourself eating like royalty in out-of-the-way towns and spending less than this split would indicate. A budget place in Madrid might well be a lower mid-range joint in Murcia. We take this into account with listings; a place listed as mid-range in Andalucía would fall in Madrid's budget range.

GAY & LESBIAN TRAVELLERS

Homosexuality is legal in Spain and the age of consent is 16 years old, as for heterosexuals. In 1996 the conservative Partido Popular (PP) government put the brakes on a law intended to establish the legal rights of de facto gay couples (the arrival of a new Socialist government in March 2004 has fuelled hopes that this situation might now be reversed). The regional governments of Catalonia and Aragón have both approved such laws. In Navarra a landmark case in 2004 granted a lesbian couple custody of a child born to one of the couple.

Lesbians and gay men generally keep a fairly low profile, but are more open in the cities. Madrid, Barcelona, Sitges, Torremolinos and Ibiza have particularly lively scenes. Sitges is a major destination on the international gay party circuit; gays take a leading role in the wild Carnaval there in February/March (p321). As well, there are gay parades, marches and events in several cities on and around the last Saturday in June, when Madrid's gay and lesbian pride march takes place.

A couple of informative free magazines are in circulation in gay bookshops and gay and gay-friendly bars. One is the biweekly *Shanguide*. It is jammed with listings and contact ads and aimed principally at readers in Barcelona and Madrid. A companion publication is *Shangay Express,* better for articles and a handful of listings and ads. Also worth looking for in gay bookshops is *Punto Guía de España para Gays y Lesbianas,* a countrywide guide for gay and gay-friendly bars, restaurants, hotels and shops around the country. The monthly *MENsual* (€3.60) is available at newsstands. There is a Web version at www.mensual.com.

Check out the following queer sites on the Internet:

Chueca.com (www.chueca.com) You have to become a member of Chueca XL (€18 a year) if you want to access the site's Guía Nocturna for bars and clubs.

Coordinadora Gai-Lesbiana (www.cogailes.org) A good site presented by Barcelona's main gay and lesbian organisation, with nationwide links. Here you can zero in on information ranging from bar, sauna and hotel listings through to contacts pages.

Corazon Gay (www.corazongay.com) Gay personals and website search engine.

Esdificil.com (www.esdificil.com) A gay website with listings ranging from bars and restaurants to shops and hairdressers.

GayBarcelona.Net (www.gaybarcelona.net) News and views and an extensive listings section covering bars, saunas, shops and more in Barcelona and Sitges.

Nación Gay (www.naciongay.com) News on the gay community across Spain.

Voz Gay (www.vozgay.com) A Spanish community website with listings for the whole country.

Organisations

Casal Lambda Barcelona (Map pp270-2; ☎ 93 319 55 50; www.lambdaweb.org; Carrer de Verdaguer i Callis 10). A gay and lesbian social, cultural and information centre.

Colectivo de Gais y Lesbianas de Madrid (Map pp110-2; ☎ 91 522 45 17; www.cogam.org; Calle de Fuencarral 37) Offers an information office and social centre and runs an information line (☎ 91 523 00 70) from 5pm to 9pm on Fridays. The Comunidad de Madrid also has an information line (toll free ☎ 900 72 05 69; ☺ 10am-2pm & 5-9pm Mon-Fri).

Coordinadora Gai-Lesbiana Barcelona (Map pp266-7; ☎ 902 12 01 40, from abroad ☎ 93 298 10 88; www .cogailes.org; Carrer de Finlàndia 45). The city's main coordinating body for gay and lesbian groups. It also runs an information line, the Línia Rosa (☎ 900 60 16 01).

Fundación Triángulo Madrid (Map pp110-2; ☎ 91 593 05 40; www.fundaciontriangulo.es; Calle de Eloy Gonzalo 25) Another source of information on gay issues.

HOLIDAYS

The two main periods when Spaniards go on holiday are Semana Santa (the week leading up to Easter Sunday) and August. At these times accommodation in resorts can be scarce and transport heavily booked, but other places are often half-empty.

There are at least 14 official holidays a year – some observed nationwide, some locally. When a holiday falls close to a weekend, Spaniards like to make a *puente* (bridge), meaning they take the intervening day off too. On the odd occasion when some holidays fall close, they make an *acueducto* (aqueduct)! National holidays are:

Año Nuevo (New Year's Day) 1 January
Viernes Santo (Good Friday) March/April
Fiesta del Trabajo (Labour Day) 1 May
La Asunción (Feast of the Assumption) 15 August
Fiesta Nacional de España (National Day) 12 October
La Inmaculada Concepción (Feast of the Immaculate Conception) 8 December
Navidad (Christmas) 25 December

Regional governments set five holidays and local councils two more. Common dates for widely observed holidays include:

Epifanía (Epiphany) or **Día de los Reyes Magos** (Three Kings' Day) 6 January
Día de San José (St Joseph's Day) 19 March
Jueves Santo (Good Thursday) March/April. Not observed in Catalonia and Valencia.
Corpus Christi June. This is the Thursday after the eighth Sunday after Easter Sunday.
Día de San Juan Bautista (Feast of St John the Baptist) 24 June
Día de Santiago Apóstol (Feast of St James the Apostle) 25 July
Día de la Constitución (Constitution Day) 6 December

INSURANCE

A travel-insurance policy to cover theft, loss and medical problems is a good idea. It may

also cover you for cancellation or delays to your travel arrangements. Paying for your ticket with a credit card can often provide limited travel-accident insurance and you may be able to reclaim the payment if the operator doesn't deliver. Ask your credit-card company what it will cover.

Basic medical care is available free of charge to EU nationals carrying an E111 form, which you must obtain from your local health authority (or post office in the case of the UK) before travelling. For most short holidays private insurance is by far the best option.

You may prefer a policy that pays doctors or hospitals directly, rather than you having to pay on the spot and claim later; if you have to claim later make sure you keep all documentation. Some policies ask you to call back (reverse charges) to a centre in your home country, where an immediate assessment of your problem is made.

Check that the policy covers ambulances or an emergency flight home. For details of car insurance, see p859.

INTERNET ACCESS

Travelling with a portable computer is a great way to stay in touch with life back home, but unless you know what you're doing it's fraught with potential problems. Make sure you have a universal AC adapter, a two-pin plug adapter for Europe and a reputable 'global' modem. Spanish telephone sockets are the US RJ-11 type. A growing number of the better hotels are set up with Internet connections, and sometimes just plugging into the hotel room's phone socket will be sufficient (although frequently this will not work, as you have to go through a switchboard). For more details on travelling with a portable computer, see www.teleadapt.com.

Major Internet service providers (ISPs) like CompuServe (http://webcenters.com puserve.com) have dial-in nodes in Spain; download a list of the dial-in numbers before you leave home.

Some Spanish servers can provide short-term accounts. Tiscali (www.tiscali.es) is a reliable one. Another is Terra (www.terra.es).

If you intend to rely on cybercafés, you'll need to carry three pieces of information: your incoming (POP or IMAP) mail-server name, your account name and your password. You typically have to pay about €1.50 to €2 per hour to go online in most cybercafés.

LEGAL MATTERS

If you're arrested you will be allotted the free services of a duty solicitor (abogado de oficio), who may speak only Spanish. You're also entitled to make a phone call. If you use this to contact your embassy or consulate, the staff will probably be able to do no more than refer you to a lawyer who speaks your language. If you end up in court, the authorities are obliged to provide a translator.

In theory, you are supposed to have your national ID card or passport with you at all times. If asked for it by the police, you are supposed to be able to produce it on the spot. In practice it is rarely an issue and many people choose (understandably) to leave passports in hotel safes.

Drugs

The only legal drug is cannabis and it's only legal in amounts for personal use, which means very small amounts. Public consumption of any drug is illegal, although in a few bars you may find people smoking joints openly. Travellers entering Spain from Morocco should be prepared for drug searches, especially if they have a vehicle.

Police

Spain is well endowed with police forces. The Policía Local or Policía Municipal operates at a local level and deals with such issues as traffic infringements and minor crime. If your car is towed, it's because these guys called up the removal truck.

The Policía Nacional is the state police force, dealing with major crime and operating especially in the cities. The military-linked Guardia Civil (created in the 19th century to deal with banditry) is largely responsible for highway patrols, borders

---

LEGAL AGE

- The right to vote: 18 years old
- Age of consent: 16 years old (heterosexual and homosexual)
- Driving age: 18 years old

---

and security, and often has a presence in more remote areas where there is no Policía Nacional station (comisaría). They also deal with major crime and terrorism and there is frequently an overlap (and occasional bickering) with the Policía Nacional. Indeed, in the wake of the March 2004 terror bombings in Madrid a joint terrorism task force between the two forces was set up to streamline coordination.

Just to complicate matters, several regions have their own police forces, such as the Mossos d'Esquadra in Catalonia and the Ertaintxa in the Basque Country.

MAPS

In early 2004 some major highway codes were changed across Spain. Several regions have also changed highway codes within their regional boundaries. You should therefore look for the very latest maps of Spain and its regions (those arriving on the bookshelves in 2004 were caught short). The most significant changes involve toll-paying motorways (autopistas) and dual carriageway highways (autovías). What was the A7, running from the French border through the Mediterranean coastal regions of the country, is now the AP7. Like a row of toothpicks moved to one side, the A denomination now applies to some (but not all!) national highways. Thus the former NII from Barcelona to Madrid is now the A2, not to be confused with the toll highway AP2 running between the same cities (which used to be the A2!).

City Maps

For finding your way around cities, the free maps handed out by tourist offices are often adequate, although more detailed maps are sold widely in bookshops. The best Spanish series of maps are produced by Telstar, Alpina and Everest, while Lonely Planet produces a sturdy and helpful Barcelona City Map.

Small-Scale Maps

Some of the best maps for travellers are published by Michelin, which produces the 1:1,000,000 Spain Portugal map and six 1:400,000 regional maps covering the whole country. These are all pretty accurate, even down to the state of minor country roads, are frequently updated and detailed yet easy to read. They're widely available in Spain if you don't manage to pick them up before you go. Also good are the GeoCenter maps published by Germany's RV Verlag.

Probably the best physical map of Spain is *Península Ibérica, Baleares y Canarias* published by the Centro Nacional de Información Geográfica (CNIG; www.cnig .es), the publication arm of the Instituto Geográfico Nacional (IGN). Ask for it in good bookshops.

Walking Maps

Useful for hiking and exploring some areas (particularly in the Pyrenees) are Editorial Alpina's *Guía Cartográfica* and *Guía Excursionista y Turística* series. The series combines information booklets in Spanish (and sometimes Catalan) with detailed maps at scales ranging from 1:25,000 (1cm to 250m) to 1:50,000 (1cm to 500m). They are an indispensable hiker's tool but they do have their inaccuracies. The Institut Cartogràfic de Catalunya puts out some decent maps for hiking in the Catalan Pyrenees that are often better than their Editorial Alpina counterparts. Remember that for hiking only maps scaled at 1:25,000 are seriously useful. The CNIG also covers most of the country in 1:25,000 sheets.

You can often pick up Editorial Alpina publications and CNIG maps at bookshops near trekking areas, and at specialist bookshops such as Librería Desnivel (p117) or Altaïr (p277) or Quera (p277) in Barcelona. Some map specialists in other countries, such as **Stanfords** (☎ 020-7836 1321; www.stanfords .co.uk; 12-14 Long Acre, London WC2E 9LP) in the UK, also have a good range of Spain maps.

MONEY

As in 11 other EU nations (Austria, Belgium, Finland, France, Germany, Greece, Ireland, Italy, Luxembourg, the Netherlands and Portugal), the euro has been Spain's currency since 2002. The euro is divided into 100 cents. Coin denominations are one, two, five, 10, 20 and 50 cents, €1 and €2. The notes are €5, €10, €20, €50, €100, €200 and €500.

Exchange rates are given on the inside front cover of this book and a guide to costs can be found on p13.

Spain's international airports have bank branches, ATMs and exchange offices. They are less frequent at road crossings now as Spain's neighbours – Andorra, Portugal and France – all use the euro. If you're coming from Morocco, get rid of any dirham before you leave.

Banks and building societies tend to offer the best exchange rates, and are plentiful: even small villages often have at least one. They mostly open from about 8.30am to 2pm Monday to Friday. Some also open Thursday evening (about 4pm to 8pm) or Saturday morning.

Ask about commissions before changing (especially in exchange bureaux).

ATMs

Many credit and debit cards (Visa and MasterCard are the most widely accepted) can be used for withdrawing money from *cajeros automáticos* (automatic telling machines). This is handy because many banks do not offer an over-the-counter-cash advance service on foreign cards (and where they do the process can be wearisome). The exchange rate used for credit and debit card transactions is usually more in your favour than that for cash exchanges. Bear in mind, however, the costs involved. There is usually a charge (hovering around 1.5% to 2%) on ATM cash withdrawals abroad. This charge will appear on your statements.

Cash

There is little advantage in bringing foreign cash into Spain. True, exchange commissions are often lower than for travellers cheques, but the danger of losing the lot far outweighs such gains.

Credit & Debit Cards

You can use plastic to pay for many purchases (including meals and rooms, especially from the middle price range up). You'll often be asked to show your passport or some other identification when using cards. Among the most widely usable cards are: Visa, MasterCard, American Express (AmEx), Cirrus, Maestro, Plus, Diners Club and JCB. Many institutions add 2.5% to all transactions (cash advance or purchases) on cards used abroad – this charge does not generally appear on your bank statements.

If your card is lost, stolen or swallowed by an ATM, you can telephone toll free to have an immediate stop put on its use. For

MasterCard the number in Spain is ☎ 900 971231; for Visa it's ☎ 900 991124; and for Diners Club ☎ 91 701 59 00 or ☎ 901 101011.

AmEx is also widely accepted (although not as commonly as Visa or MasterCard). If you lose your AmEx card, call ☎ 900 994426.

Moneychangers

As well as at banks, you can exchange both cash and travellers cheques at exchange offices – usually indicated by the word *cambio* (exchange). They abound in tourist resorts and other places that attract high numbers of foreigners. Generally they offer longer opening hours and quicker service than banks, but worse exchange rates. Their commissions are, on occasion, outrageous.

Taxes & Refunds

In Spain, value-added tax (VAT) is known as IVA (*ee-ba*; *impuesto sobre el valor añadido*). On accommodation and restaurant prices, it's 7% and is often included in quoted prices. On retail goods and car hire, IVA is 16%. To ask 'Is IVA included?', say '¿*Está incluido el IVA?*'.

Visitors are entitled to a refund of the 16% IVA on purchases costing more than €90.15 from any shop if they are taking them out of the EU within three months. Ask the shop for a Cashback refund form showing the price and IVA paid for each item, and identifying the vendor and purchaser. Then present the refund form to the customs booth for IVA refunds at the airport, port or border from which you leave the EU. This works best at airports, where you will need your passport and a boarding card that shows you are leaving the EU. The officer will stamp the invoice and you hand it in at a bank at the departure point for immediate reimbursement. Otherwise you will have to send the forms off from your home country and have the amount credited to your credit card.

Tipping

The law requires menu prices to include a service charge; tipping is a matter of choice. Most people leave some small change if they're satisfied: 5% is normally fine and 10% generous. Porters will generally be happy with €1. Taxi drivers don't have to be tipped, but a little rounding up won't go amiss.

Travellers Cheques

Travellers cheques usually bring only a slightly better exchange rate than cash, usually offset by the charges for buying them in the first place.

The advantage, of course, is that they protect your money because they can be replaced if lost or stolen. Visa, AmEx and Travelex are widely accepted brands with (usually) efficient replacement policies. AmEx offices will cash AmEx travellers cheques commission-free – but you should always compare exchange rates with those offered in banks. Take along your passport when you cash travellers cheques.

Get most of your cheques in fairly large denominations (the equivalent of €100 or more) to save on any per-cheque commission charges.

If you lose your AmEx cheques, call a 24-hour freephone number (☎ 900 994426). For Visa cheques call ☎ 900 948973; for MasterCard cheques call ☎ 900 948971. It's vital to keep your initial receipt, and a record of your cheque numbers and the ones you have used, separate from the cheques themselves.

POST

The Spanish postal system, **Correos** (☎ 902 197197; www.correos.es), is generally reliable, if a little slow at times. Central post offices in most cities open around 8.30am to 9.30pm, Monday to Saturday. Most branch post offices open 8am to 2pm, Monday to Friday.

Postal Rates & Services

A postcard or letter weighing up to 20g costs €0.52 from Spain to other European countries, and €0.77 to the rest of the world. The same would cost €2.71 and €2.96 respectively for *certificado* (registered) mail. Sending such letters *urgente*, which means your mail may arrive two or three days quicker than normal, costs €2.35 and €2.65 respectively. You can send mail both *certificado* and *urgente*. Stamps for regular letters, including those being sent abroad, can also be bought at most tobacconists (look for the 'Tabacos' sign).

Receiving Mail

Delivery times are similar to those for outbound mail. All Spanish addresses have five-digit postcodes; using postcodes will help your mail arrive more quickly.

Lista de correos (poste restante) mail can be addressed to you anywhere in Spain that has a post office. It will be delivered to the place's main post office unless another is specified in the address. Take your passport when you pick up mail. A typical *lista de correos* address looks like this:

Jenny JONES
Lista de Correos
28080 Madrid
Spain

AmEx card or travellers cheque holders can use the free client mail-holding service at the AmEx office. Take your passport when you pick up mail. AmEx offices only accept standard letters, no packets.

Sending Mail

Delivery times are erratic but ordinary mail to other Western European countries can take up to a week; to North America up to 10 days; and to Australia or New Zealand up to two weeks.

SHOPPING

There are some excellent *mercadillos* (flea markets) and *rastros* (car-boot sales) around the country, and craft shops can be found in many villages and towns. You may also pick up crafts at weekly or daily markets. The single most likely place you'll find any particular item in most cities is the nationwide department store El Corte Inglés.

Bargaining

Bargaining is not really an option in department stores and high street shops. At markets and more souvenir-oriented stores you can try your luck (you've got nothing to lose, after all).

Clothes & Textiles

Label lovers and fashion victims can keep themselves well occupied in the big cities, such as Madrid and Barcelona, where local and international names present a broad range of options. Ibiza in summer is also a bit of a magnet for clubbing and summer-wear seekers.

Inexpensive rugs, blankets and hangings are made all over the country, notably in Andalucía and Galicia. In Andalucía head for Las Alpujarras and Níjar for colourful rugs and blankets. Items known as *jarapas* feature weft threads made of different types of cloth. Other textiles include lace tablecloths and pillowcases (especially from Galicia), and embroidery. Places particularly known for their embroidery include Segovia, La Alberca (Salamanca province), Carbajales (Zamora province), and Lagartera, Oropesa and Talavera (Toledo province).

In Andalucía, every major city centre has a cluster of flamenco shops selling embroidered shawls, hand-painted fans, flat-top Cordoban hats and of course lots of very colourful flouncy dresses.

Leather

Prices of leather goods aren't as low as they used to be, but you can get good deals on jackets, bags, wallets, belts, shoes and boots in many places. Mallorcan shoe brands like Camper and Farrutx have become international beacons – their products are stylish, moderately priced and, especially in the case of Camper, easily found all over Spain.

Pottery

Crockery, jugs, plant pots, window boxes and tiles are cheap. Islamic influence on design and colour is evident in much of the country. Original techniques include the use of metallic glazes and *cuerda seca* (dry cord), in which lines of manganese or fat are used to separate areas of different colour. Toledo, Talavera de la Reina, Seville, Granada and Úbeda are centres of production.

Other Crafts

Damascene weapons (made of steel encrusted with gold, silver or copper) are still produced in Toledo. There's some very pleasing woodwork available, such as Granada's marquetry boxes, tables and chess sets, some of which are inlaid with bone or mother-of-pearl. Baskets and furniture made from plant fibres are produced throughout Spain but are most evident near the coasts.

SOLO TRAVELLERS

About the only real practical disadvantage of travelling solo in Spain is the cost of accommodation. As a rule, single rooms (or doubles let as single rooms) cost around two-thirds of the price of a double. Some hotels make little or no discount on double-room rates.

Sole female travellers should generally encounter no problems either, at least in more travelled parts of the country. In more out-of-the-way places the sight of a lone female traveller may raise local eyebrows. You should be choosy about your accommodation too. Bottom-end fleapits with all-male staff can be insalubrious locations to bed down for the night. Lone women should also take care in city streets at night – stick with the crowds. Hitching for solo women travellers, while feasible, is risky.

TELEPHONE

The ubiquitous blue payphones are easy to use for international and domestic calls. They accept coins, phonecards issued by the national phone company Telefónica (*tarjetas telefónicas*) and, in some cases, various credit cards. *Tarjetas telefónicas* come in €6 and €12 denominations and, like postage stamps, are sold at post offices and tobacconists.

Public phones inside bars and cafés, and telephones in hotel rooms, are almost always a good deal more expensive than street payphones.

Mobile Phones

Spaniards adore *teléfonos móviles* (mobile/cell phones). Sales in 2004 are expected to be around 14 million (13 million in 2003). Shops on every high street sell phones with prepaid cards from around €70.

Spain uses GSM 900/1800, which is compatible with the rest of Europe and Australia but not with the North American GSM 1900 or the totally different system used in Japan. (Some North Americans, however, have GSM 1900/900 phones that do work in Spain.)

You can rent a mobile phone by calling the Madrid-based **Cellphone Rental** (☎ 91 523 21 59, 656-266844; www.onspanishtime.com/web). In Madrid, delivery and pick-up are done in person at a cost of US$20 (US$25 on weekends and holidays). The basic service costs US$30 a week for the phone plus postal costs (except in Madrid). You also pay US$150 to discourage scarpering with the phone. The whole operation is done on the web.

Phonecards

Cut-rate phonecards can be good value for international calls. They can be bought from *estancos* (tobacconists) and newsstands in

the main cities and tourist resorts – compare rates if possible because some are better than others. *Locutorios* (private call centres) that specialise in cut-rate overseas calls have popped up all over the place in the centre of bigger cities. Again, compare rates – as a rule the phonecards are better value and more convenient.

Phone Codes

Dial the international access code (☎ 00 in most countries), followed by the code for

Spain (☎ 34) and the full number (including the code, 91, which is an integral part of the number. For example to call the number ☎ 91 455 67 83 in Madrid you need to dial the international access code followed by ☎ 34 91 455 67 83.

The access code for international calls from Spain is 00. To make an international call dial the access code, wait for a new dialling tone, then dial the country code, area code and number you want.

International collect calls are simple: dial 900 followed by a code for the country you're calling:

Australia ☎ 99 00 61
Canada ☎ 99 00 15
France ☎ 99 00 33
Germany ☎ 99 00 49
Ireland ☎ 99 03 53
Israel ☎ 99 09 72
New Zealand ☎ 99 00 64
UK for BT ☎ 99 00 44, for Cable & Wireless ☎ 99 09 44
USA for AT&T ☎ 99 00 11, for Sprint and various others ☎ 99 00 13

You'll get straight through to an operator in the country you're calling. The same numbers can be used with direct-dial calling cards.

If for some reason the above information doesn't work for you, in most places you can get an English-speaking Spanish international operator on ☎ 1008 (for calls within Europe) or ☎ 1005 (rest of the world).

For international directory inquiries dial ☎ 11825. Be warned: a call to this number costs €2!

Within Spain, you must always dial the full area code with the number. All numbers have nine digits and begin with 9. Dial ☎ 1009 to speak to a domestic operator, including for a domestic reverse-charge (collect) call (llamada por cobro revertido). For national directory inquiries dial ☎ 11818.

Mobile phone numbers start with 6. Numbers starting with 900 are national toll-free numbers, while those starting 901 to 905 come with varying conditions. A common one is 902, which is a national standard rate number. In a similar category are numbers starting with 803, 806 and 807.

TIME

Mainland Spain and the Balearic Islands have the same time as most of the rest of Western Europe: GMT/UTC plus one hour during winter and GMT/UTC plus two hours during the daylight-saving period, which runs from the last Sunday in March to the last Sunday in October.

The UK, Ireland, Portugal and the Canary Islands, a part of Spain out in the Atlantic Ocean, are one hour behind mainland Spain.

Spanish time is normally USA Eastern Time plus six hours, and USA Pacific Time plus nine hours. But the USA tends to start daylight saving a week or two later than Spain, so you must add one hour to the time differences in the intervening period.

Morocco is on GMT/UTC year-round. From the last Sunday in March to the last Sunday in October, subtract two hours from Spanish time to get Moroccan time; the rest of the year, subtract one hour.

In the Australian winter (Spanish summer), subtract eight hours from Australian Eastern Standard Time to get Spanish time; in the Australian summer subtract 10 hours. The difference is nine hours for a few weeks in March.

Although the 24-hour clock is used in most official situations, you'll find people generally use the 12-hour clock in everyday conversation.

TOURIST INFORMATION
Local Tourist Offices

All cities and many smaller towns have an oficina de turismo or oficina de información turística. In provincial capitals you'll sometimes find more than one tourist office – one specialising in information on the city alone, the other carrying mostly provincial or regional information. There seems, however, to be no set rule on this division of labour. National and natural parks also often have visitor centres offering useful information. Their opening hours and quality of information vary widely.

Turespaña (www.tourspain.es), the country's national tourism body, presents a variety of general information and links on the entire country in its Web pages. There is also a nationwide tourist information line in several languages, which might come in handy if you are calling from elsewhere in Spain. For basic information in Spanish, English, French and German call ☎ 901 300600 from 9am to 10pm daily.

DIRECTORY

Tourist Offices Abroad

Information on Spain is available from the following branches of Turespaña abroad:

Canada (☎ 416-961 3131; www.sispain.org; 2 Bloor St W, 34th fl, Toronto M4W 3E2)

France (☎ 01 45 03 82 50; www.espagne.infotourisme .com; 43 rue Decamps, 75784 Paris)

Germany (☎ 030-882 6543; berlin@tourspain.es; Kurfürstendamm 63, 10707 Berlin) Branches in Düsseldorf, Frankfurt am Main and Munich.

Netherlands (☎ 070-346 59 00; www.spaansverkeers bureau.nl; Laan van Meerdervoor 8a, 2517 The Hague)

Portugal (☎ 21-354 1992; lisboa@tour spain.es; Avenida Sidónio Pais 28 3° Dto, 1050-215 Lisbon)

UK (☎ 020-7486 8077; www.tourspain.co.uk; 22-23 Manchester Square, London W1M 5AP)

USA (☎ 212-265 8822; www.okspain.org; 666 Fifth Ave, 35th fl, New York, NY 10103) Branches in Chicago, Los Angeles and Miami.

VISAS

Spain is one of 15 member countries of the Schengen Convention, an agreement whereby all the then EU member countries (except the UK and Ireland) plus Iceland and Norway abolished checks at internal borders in 2000. As of 1 May 2004, the EU is made up of 25 countries. For detailed information on the EU, including which countries are member states, see http://europa.eu.int.

EU, Norwegian and Icelandic nationals need no visa, regardless of the length or purpose of their visit to Spain (there may be exceptions to this rule for the 10 new member states that joined the EU in May 2004). If they stay beyond 90 days they are required to register with the police (although many do not). Legal residents of one Schengen country (regardless of their nationality) do not require a visa for another Schengen country.

Nationals of many other countries, including Australia, Canada, Israel, Japan, New Zealand, Switzerland and the USA, do not need a visa for tourist visits of up to 90 days in Spain, although some of these nationalities may be subject to restrictions in other Schengen countries and should check with consulates of all Schengen countries they plan to visit. If you wish to work or study in Spain, you may need a specific visa, so contact a Spanish consulate before travel. If you are a citizen of a country not mentioned in this section, check with a Spanish consulate whether you need a visa.

The standard tourist visa issued by Spanish consulates is the Schengen visa, valid for up to 90 days. A Schengen visa issued by one Schengen country is generally valid for travel in all other Schengen countries.

Those needing a visa must apply *in person* at the consulate in the country where they are resident. You may be required to provide proof of sufficient funds, an itinerary or hotel bookings, return tickets and a letter of recommendation from a host in Spain. Issue of the visa does *not*, however, guarantee entry.

You can apply for no more than two visas in any 12-month period and they are not renewable once in Spain. Various transit visas also exist.

Coming from Morocco, you are unlikely to get into Spain's North African enclaves of Ceuta or Melilla without a Spanish visa (if you are supposed to have one), and passports are generally checked again when you head on to the peninsula. You may well be able to board a boat from Tangier (Morocco) to Algeciras and certainly to Gibraltar but, again, passports are generally closely checked by the Spaniards at Algeciras and you could be sent back to Morocco. If you go via Gibraltar, you may just sneak across at La Línea without having your passport checked – but you can't bank on it.

Extensions & Residence

Schengen visas cannot be extended. Nationals of EU countries, Norway and Iceland can enter and leave Spain at will. Those wanting to stay in Spain longer than 90 days are supposed to apply during their first month for a *tarjeta de residencia* (residence card).

People of other nationalities who want to stay in Spain longer than 90 days are also supposed to get a residence card, and for them it's a drawn-out process, starting with a residence visa issued by a Spanish consulate in your country of residence. Start the process well in advance.

Non-EU spouses of EU citizens resident in Spain can apply for residency too. The process is lengthy and those needing to travel in and out of the country in the meantime who would normally require a visa could ask for an *exención de visado* – a visa exemption. In most cases, the spouse is obliged to make the formal application in their country of residence.

Photocopies

All important documents (passport data page and visa page, credit cards, travel insurance policy, air/bus/train tickets, driving licence etc) should be photocopied before you leave home. Leave one copy with someone at home and keep another with you, separate from the originals.

WOMEN TRAVELLERS

Travelling in Spain is as easy as travelling anywhere in the Western world. Spanish women now travel widely around their own country without men, and Spaniards are quite accustomed to foreign women travelling in Spain without men. Spanish men under about 35, who have grown up in the liberated post-Franco era, conform less to old-fashioned sexual stereotypes, although you might notice that sexual stereotyping becomes more pronounced as you move from north to south in Spain, and from city to country.

Women travellers should be ready to ignore stares, catcalls and unnecessary comments, although harassment is less frequent than you might expect. Learn the word for help (*socorro*) in case you need to draw other people's attention.

By and large, Spanish women have a highly developed sense of style and put considerable effort into looking their best. While topless bathing and skimpy clothes are in fashion in many coastal resorts, people tend to dress more modestly elsewhere.

There are women's bookshops in Madrid, Barcelona and a few other cities that are also useful sources of information on women's organisations and activities. The websites of many women's organisations can be reached through the feminist website www.nodo50.org/mujeresred.

WORK

With one of the EU's highest unemployment rates, Spain doesn't exactly have a labour shortage. You could possibly look for casual work in fruit picking or harvests, but this is generally done with imported labour from Morocco and Eastern Europe with pay and conditions that can best be described as dire. There are a few other ways of earning your keep (or almost) while you're here.

Nationals of EU countries, Switzerland, Norway and Iceland may work in Spain without a visa, but for stays of more than three months they are supposed to apply within the first month for a *tarjeta de residencia* (residence card). If you are offered a contract, your employer will usually steer you through the labyrinth.

Virtually everyone else is supposed to obtain, from a Spanish consulate in their country of residence, a work permit and, if they plan to stay more than 90 days, a residence visa. These procedures are well nigh impossible unless you have a job contract lined up before you begin them. Quite a few people do work, discreetly, without bothering to tangle with the bureaucracy.

Translating and interpreting could be an option if you are fluent in Spanish and a language in demand.

Another option might be au pair work, organised before you come to Spain. A useful guide is *The Au Pair and Nanny's Guide to Working Abroad*, by Susan Griffith and Sharon Legg. Susan Griffith's *Work Your Way Around the World* is also worth looking at.

University students or recent graduates might be able to set up an internship with companies in Barcelona. The **Association of International Students for Economics and Commerce** (www.aiesec.org), with branches throughout the world, helps member students find internships in related fields. For information on membership, check out the website.

Language Teaching

This type of work is an obvious option for which language-teaching qualifications are a big help. There are lots of language schools in all the big cities and often one or two in smaller towns. They're listed under 'Academias de Idiomas' in the Yellow Pages. Getting a job is harder if you're not an EU citizen. Some schools do employ people without work papers, usually at lower than normal rates. Giving private lessons is another avenue, but is unlikely to bring you a living wage straight away.

Sources of information on possible teaching work – in a school or as a private tutor – include foreign cultural centres (the British Council, Alliance Française etc), foreign-language bookshops, universities and language schools. Many have notice boards where you may find work opportunities or can advertise your own services.

Tourist Resorts

Summer work on the Mediterranean coasts is a possibility, especially if you arrive early in the season and are prepared to stay a while. Many bars (especially of the UK and Irish persuasion), restaurants and other businesses are run by foreigners. Check any local press in foreign languages, such as the Costa del Sol's *Sur In English*, which has some ads for waiters, nannies, chefs, baby-sitters, cleaners and the like.

Yacht Crewing

It is possible to stumble upon work as crew on yachts and cruisers. The best ports to look include (in descending order) Palma de Mallorca, Gibraltar and Puerto Banús.

In summer the voyages tend to be restricted to the Mediterranean, but from about November to January a few boats head for the Caribbean. Such work is usually unpaid and about the only way to find it is to ask around on the docks.

Transport

CONTENTS

GETTING THERE & AWAY

Spain is one of Europe's top holiday destinations and is well linked to other European countries by air, rail and road. Regular car ferries and hydrofoils run to and from Morocco and there are ferry links to the UK, Italy and the Canary Islands.

As competition in the air grows, flying is increasingly the cheapest and fastest option from other European countries.

Some good direct flights are available from North America. Those coming from Australasia have fewer choices and will usually have to make at least one change of flight.

ENTERING THE COUNTRY
Passport

Citizens of the 25 European Union (EU) member states and Switzerland can travel to Spain with their national identity card alone. If such countries do not issue ID cards – as in the UK – travellers must carry a full valid passport (UK visitor passports are not acceptable). All other nationalities must have a full valid passport.

If applying for a visa (see p845), check that your passport's expiry date is at least

> **THINGS CHANGE...**
>
> The information in this chapter is particularly vulnerable to change: prices for international travel are volatile, routes are introduced and cancelled, schedules change, special deals come and go, and rules and visa requirements are amended. You should check directly with the airline or a travel agent to make sure you understand how a fare (and ticket you may buy) works and be aware of the security requirements for international travel.
>
> The upshot of this is that you should get opinions, quotes and advice from as many airlines and travel agents as possible before you part with your hard-earned cash. The details given in this chapter should be seen as pointers and are not a substitute for your own careful, up-to-date research.

six months away. If you are not an EU citizen you may be required to fill out a landing card (at airports only), scattered about in the area just prior to passport control.

By law you are supposed to have your passport or ID card with you at all times in Spain. It doesn't happen often, but it could be embarrassing if you are asked by the police to produce a document and you don't have it with you. You will need one of these documents for police registration when you book a hotel room.

AIR

High season in Spain generally means Christmas/New Year, Easter and roughly June to September. This varies somewhat, however, depending on the specific destination. You may find reasonably priced flights available to places such as Madrid in August because it is stinking hot and everyone else has fled to the mountains and the sea. As a general rule, November to March is when air fares to Spain are likely to be at their lowest, and the intervening months can be considered shoulder periods. With the proliferation of low-cost, first-come-best-served airlines, it is becoming increasingly difficult to nail airfare price

TRANSPORT

ranges within Europe. Very roughly speaking, a return fare might cost UK£60/250 to main destinations in the low/high season from the UK; US$500/900 from the USA; C$700/1400 from the Canadian east and C$900/1800 from the Canadian west coast; and A$1800/2200 from Australia.

Airports & Airlines

The main gateway to Spain is Madrid's **Barajas airport** (Aeropuerto de Barajas; ☎ 91 393 60 00, flight information ☎ 902 353570; www.aena.es), although many European direct flights serve other centres, particularly Barcelona's **Aeroport del Prat** (☎ 93 298 38 38; www.aena.es), Málaga and Palma de Mallorca. Charter flights and low-cost airlines (mostly from the UK) also fly into other airports, such as Alicante, Bilbao, Girona (for the Costa Brava and Barcelona), Ibiza and Murcia.

Iberia, Spain's main national carrier, flies to most Spanish cities (many via Madrid) from around the world but is generally the expensive way to go.

Among the airlines that fly to and from Spain are the following:

Aer Lingus (code EI; ☎ 0818 365000 in Ireland; www.aerlingus.ie) Flies to Alicante, Barcelona, Bilbao, Madrid, Málaga and Palma de Mallorca, as well as to Alicante, Barcelona and Málaga from Cork.

Air Berlin (code AB; ☎ 01805 737800 in Germany, ☎ 901 11 64 02 in Spain; www.airberlin.com) German budget airline with flights to Mallorca and on to Barcelona and Madrid from cities all over Germany. Also London (Stansted) to Madrid, Barcelona and other destinations via Palma de Mallorca.

Air Europa (code UX; ☎ 08702 401501 in the UK, ☎ 902 40 15 01 in Spain; www.aireuropa.com) Flies to Madrid from London, Paris, Rome, Milan and New York, and from destinations all over Spain.

Air Madrid (code DRI; ☎ 902 51 52 51 in Spain; www.airmadrid.com) A new intercontinental budget airline linking Madrid with various South American destinations, including Brasil, Colombia, Costa Rica, Mexico and Peru.

Air Scotland (code GRE; ☎ 0141 222 2363 in UK; www.air-scotland.com) Flies from Edinburgh and Glasgow to Barcelona, Alicante and Málaga.

Basiq Air (code HV; ☎ 0900 0737 in the Netherlands, ☎ 902 11 44 78 in Spain; www.basiqair.com) Low-cost flights from Amsterdam to Alicante, Barcelona, Girona, Madrid and Málaga.

BMI (code BD; ☎ 08706 070555 in UK; www.flybmi.com) Flights from Heathrow airport (London) to Madrid and Palma de Mallorca.

BMI Baby (code WW; ☎ 08702 642229 in the UK, ☎ 902 10 07 37 in Spain; www.bmibaby.com) A British

Midlands budget subsidiary, it flies to Alicante, Barcelona, Ibiza, Málaga, Murcia and Palma de Mallorca from East Midlands and Manchester airports, and in some cases from Teeside and Cardiff.

British Airways (code BA; ☎ 08708 509850 in the UK, ☎ 902 11 13 33 in Spain; www.britishairways.com)

Brussels Airlines (code SN; ☎ 902 90 14 92 in Spain, ☎ 070 351111 in Belgium; www.flysn.com) Flies from Brussels to Barcelona, Bilbao, Madrid and Seville.

CityJet (code WX; ☎ 01-870 0100 in Ireland, ☎ 952 04 88 38 in Spain; www.cityjet.com) Direct flights from Dublin to Málaga.

Delta Air Lines (code DL; ☎ 800 241 4141 in USA, ☎ 901 11 69 46 in Spain; www.delta.com) Flies from New York direct to Madrid (and on to Barcelona) daily.

EasyJet (code U2; ☎ 08706 000000 in the UK, ☎ 902 29 99 92 in Spain; www.easyjet.com) Flies to Alicante, Barcelona, Bilbao, Ibiza, Madrid, Málaga and Palma de Mallorca from various London and other UK airports. Some of these destinations are also served from Berlin (Schönefeld), Dortmund, Geneva and Paris (Orly).

Germanwings (code 4U; ☎ 91 514 08 25 in Spain, ☎ 01805 955855 in Germany; www.germanwings.com) Flies from Cologne, Stuttgart and other cities to Barcelona, Ibiza, Málaga, Madrid and Palma de Mallorca.

Iberia (code IB; ☎ 902 40 05 00 in Spain; www.iberia.es)

Jet2 (code LS; ☎ 08707 378282 in the UK, ☎ 902 02 02 64 in Spain; www.jet2.com) A budget airline that flies from Leeds to Alicante, Barcelona, Málaga, Murcia and Palma de Mallorca.

LTU (code LT; ☎ 901 33 03 20; www.ltu.com) Flights from all over Germany to Alicante, Almería, Ibiza, Maó, Málaga, Palma de Mallorca and Seville. It also offers all-in packages.

Meridiana (code IG; ☎ 199 111333 in Italy; www.meridiana.it) Flights from Florence to Barcelona and connections throughout Italy.

Monarch (code ZB; ☎ 08700 405040 in the UK, ☎ 902 502737 in Spain; www.flymonarch.com) Has scheduled flights from London Gatwick to Alicante and Málaga; London Luton to Alicante, Málaga and Menorca; and Manchester to Alicante, Barcelona, Málaga and Palma de Mallorca. The airline also has charter flights to several Spanish destinations.

Royal Air Maroc (code AT; ☎ 09000 0800 in Morocco; www.royalairmaroc.com) Also known as RAM, it covers much of the air traffic between Spain and Morocco.

Ryanair (code FR; ☎ 08712 460000 in the UK, ☎ 0181 303030 in Ireland, ☎ 807 22 00 22 in Spain; www.ryanair.com) Flies to Girona from London Stansted, Birmingham, Bournemouth, Glasgow, Liverpool, Dublin (weekends only), Alghero (Sardinia), Bergamo (for Milan), Brussels (Charleroi), Eindhoven, Frankfurt (Hahn), Karlsruhe, Paris (Beauvais), Rome (Ciampino), Treviso (for Venice) and Turin. Also flies to Jérez, Málaga, Murcia and Reus (108km south of Barcelona for Salou).

panair (code JK; ☎ 902 13 14 15 in Spain; www
spanair.com) Flights to Barcelona, Ibiza, Málaga, Madrid
nd Valencia from Copenhagen, Oslo, Stockholm, Frank-
urt, Munich and Vienna. Flights to Madrid from various US
destinations and Rio de Janeiro.

wiss (code LX; ☎ 901 11 67 12 in Spain; ☎ 0848
52000 in Switzerland; www.swiss.com) It flies from
Geneva and Zurich to Barcelona, Málaga, Madrid, Palma de
Mallorca, Seville and Valencia.

Virgin Express (code TV; ☎ 070 353637 in Belgium,
☎ 902 88 84 59 in Spain; www.virgin-express.com)
Regular flights from Brussels to Barcelona, Málaga, Madrid
and Palma de Mallorca.

Volare (code VA; ☎ 899 700007 in Italy, ☎ 900 81 00
42 in Spain; www.volareweb.com) Flights to Barcelona
from Bari, Catania, Milan, Rome and Venice), Bilbao (from
Milan and Rome), Ibiza (from Rome and Venice), Madrid
(from Venice), Palma de Mallorca (from Milan and Venice)
and Valencia (from Milan and Venice).

Vueling (code VLG; ☎ 902 33 39 33 in Spain; www
vueling.com) A Barcelona-based budget airline that
started in mid-2004 with flights to Brussels and Paris (as
well as some internal flights).

Tickets

World aviation has never been so competitive and the Internet is fast becoming the
easiest way of locating and booking reasonably priced seats.

Full-time students and those under 26
have access to discounted fares. You have
to show a document proving your date of
birth or a valid International Student Identity Card (ISIC) when buying your ticket.
Other cheap deals include the discounted
tickets released to travel agents and specialist discount agencies. One exception to this
rule is the expanding number of 'no-frills'
carriers, which sell direct to travellers. Many
airlines also offer excellent fares to Internet
surfers, and there is an increasing number
of online agents:

www.cheaptickets.com
www.expedia.com
www.openjet.com
www.opodo.com
www.planesimple.co.uk
www.travelocity.co.uk

Africa

From South Africa a host of major airlines service Spain but usually via major
European hubs such as Frankfurt, London
and Paris. British Airways, Air France and
Lufthansa are among the airlines offering

the best deals flying out of Cape Town,
Durban and Johannesburg. **Flight Centre**
(☎ 0860 400727; www.flightcentre.co.za) has offices
in Johannesburg, Cape Town and Durban,
and **STA Travel** (☎ 0800 004103; www.statravel.co.za)
has offices in Johannesburg, Pretoria and
Bloemfontein.

Morocco's national airline, Royal Air
Maroc, dominates the flying trade from Morocco to major Spanish cities, with flights
to Madrid, Barcelona and Málaga. Most of
the direct flights are from Casablanca. Morocco's Regional Air Lines operates some
flights in codeshare with RAM to Málaga
from Casablanca and Tangier. Iberia also
flies to Casablanca and a few other Moroccan destinations.

The Iberia subsidiary Iberia Regional-Air
Nostrum flies to/from Málaga (up to six times
daily), Almería, Granada and Madrid from
Melilla, the Spanish enclave on the Moroc-
can coast. The Moroccan crossing point into
Melilla is the neighbouring town of Nador.

Asia

Bangkok, Singapore and Hong Kong are
the best places to shop around for discount
tickets. **STA Travel** (www.statravel.com) has offices in Hong Kong, Singapore, Taiwan
and Thailand. In Hong Kong many travellers use the **Hong Kong Student Travel Bureau**
(☎ 2730 3269; www.hkst.com.hk in Chinese).

Singapore Air and Thai Airways serve
most of Western Europe and also connect
with Australia and New Zealand. Similarly,
discounted fares can be picked up from
Qantas, which usually transits in Kuala
Lumpur, Bangkok or Singapore.

Australia

Cheap flights from Australia to Europe generally go via Southeast Asian capitals. As a
rule there are no direct flights from Australia to Spain. You will have to fly via Asia
and probably another European destination, changing flights along the way. Flights
from Perth are generally a few hundred dollars cheaper than from the east coast.

STA Travel (☎ 1300 733 035; www.statravel.com
.au) and **Flight Centre** (☎ 133 133; www.flightcentre
.com.au) are major dealers in cheap air fares,
although discounted fares can also be found
at your local travel agent. Look at the travel
ads in the Saturday editions of Melbourne's
Age and the *Sydney Morning Herald*.

TRANSPORT

Canada

Scan the travel agencies' advertisements in the *Toronto Globe & Mail, Toronto Star* and *Vancouver Sun*. **Travel CUTS** (☎ 1-888 359 2887; www.travelcuts.com), called Voyages Campus in Quebec, has offices in all major cities in Canada.

Iberia has daily flights from Toronto via London to Madrid. Other major European airlines offer competitive fares to most Spanish destinations via other European capitals.

Canary Islands

Few visitors to the Canary Islands combine their trip with another to mainland Spain (or vice versa). There is no financial incentive to do so, as flights from other parts of Europe to the Canaries are often cheaper than those between the islands and the mainland.

Iberia, Spanair, Air Europa and charters fly from Santa Cruz de Tenerife, Las Palmas de Gran Canaria and, less frequently, Lanzarote and Fuerteventura to Madrid, Barcelona and other mainland destinations.

Continental Europe

Air travel between Spain and other places in continental Europe is worth considering if you are short on time. Short hops can be expensive, but for longer journeys you can often find air fares that beat overland alternatives.

In France the student travel agencies **OTU Voyages** (☎ 0820 817817; www.otu.fr, in French) and **Travel Connections** (☎ 0825 082525; www.travelclub-voyages.com, French only) are a safe bet for cut-price travel.

In Germany, Munich is a haven of budget travel outlets such as **STA Travel** (☎ 01805 456422; www.statravel.de, in German), which is one of the best and has offices throughout the country. **Kilroy Travel Group** (www.kilroytravels.com) offers discounted travel to people aged 16 to 33, and has representative offices in Denmark, Sweden, Norway, Finland and the Netherlands.

Amsterdam is a popular departure point and a good budget flight centre. Try the bucket shops along Rokin. Or try **Air Fair** (☎ 020 620 51 21; www.airfair.nl, in Dutch).

The best place to look for cheap fares in Italy is at **CTS** (Centro Turistico Studentesco e Giovanile; www.cts.it), which has branches in cities throughout the country.

In Lisbon, Portugal, **Tagus** (☎ 311 30 37; Rua Camilo Castelo Branco 20) is a reputable travel agency.

New Zealand

Unfortunately, there are no direct flights between New Zealand and Spain. The *New Zealand Herald* has a travel section in which travel agencies advertise fares. **STA Travel** (☎ 0508 782872; www.statravel.co.nz) has offices in Auckland, as well as in Hamilton, Palmerston North, Wellington, Christchurch and Dunedin. **Flight Centre** (☎ 0800 243544; www.flightcentre.co.nz) has branches in Auckland and throughout the country.

South America

Iberia and a series of South American national airlines connect Spain with Latin America. Most flights converge on Madrid, although some continue to Barcelona.

Asatej (www.almundo.com) is a Hispanic youth travel organisation, with offices in Argentina, Chile, Mexico and Spain.

The UK & Ireland

Discount air travel is big business in London. Advertisements for many travel agencies appear in the travel pages of the weekend newspapers, such as the *Independent*, the *Guardian* on Saturday and the *Sunday Times*.

STA Travel (☎ 0870 160 0599; www.statravel.co.uk) and **Trailfinders** (☎ 020 7937 1234; www.trailfinders.com), both of which have offices throughout the UK, sell discounted and student tickets. Other good sources of discounted fares are www.etn.nl, www.ebookers.com and www.flynow.com.

No-frills airlines are increasingly big business for travel between the UK and Spain. EasyJet is the main operator, getting a little competition from Ryanair, Jet2 and BMI Baby. Prices vary wildly according to season and also depend on how far in advance you can book them.

The two national airlines linking the UK and Italy are British Airways and Iberia. They both operate regular direct flights to Madrid and Barcelona.

Most British travel agents are registered with the ABTA (Association of British Travel Agents). If you've paid for your flight with an ABTA-registered agent who goes bust, ABTA will guarantee a refund or an alternative.

Good agencies for charter flights from the UK to Spain include **Avro** (☎ 08704 582841; www.avro.com), **JMC** (☎ 08707 505711; www.jmc.com) and **Lunn Poly** (☎ 08701 655000; www.lunnpoly.com).

From Ireland, check out offers from Aer Lingus and CityJet.

USA

Several airlines fly 'direct' (many flights involve a stop elsewhere in Europe en route) to Spain, landing in Madrid and Barcelona. These include Iberia, British Airways and KLM.

Discount travel agencies in the USA are known as consolidators. San Francisco is the ticket consolidator capital of America, although some good deals can be found in other big cities. The *New York Times,* the *Los Angeles Times,* the *Chicago Tribune* and the *San Francisco Examiner* all produce weekly travel sections. **STA Travel** (☎ 800 781 4040; www.statravel.com) has offices around the country.

Discount and rock-bottom options from the USA include charter, stand-by and courier flights. Stand-by fares are often sold at 60% of the normal price for one-way tickets. **Courier Travel** (☎ 303 570 7586; www.couriertravel.org) is a search engine for courier and stand-by flights. You can also check out **Now Voyager** (☎ 212 459 1616; www.nowvoyagertravel.com) or the **International Association of Air Travel Couriers** (IAATC; ☎ 308 632 3273; www.courier.org).

LAND

You can enter Spain by train, bus and private vehicle along various points of its northern border with France (and Andorra) and the western frontier with Portugal. Bus is generally the cheapest option but the train is more comfortable, especially for long-haul trips.

Border Crossings

The main road crossing into Spain from France is the highway that links up with Spain's AP7 tollway, which runs down to Barcelona and follows the Spanish coast south (with a branch, the AP2, going to Madrid). A series of links cut across the Pyrenees from France and Andorra into Spain, as does a coastal route that runs from Biarritz in France into the Spanish Basque Country.

The A5 freeway linking Madrid with Badajóz crosses the Portuguese frontier and continues on to Lisbon, but there are many road connections up and down the length of the Hispano-Portuguese frontier.

As Spain, France and Portugal are members of the EU and the Schengen area (see p845) there are usually no border controls between them. The tiny principality of Andorra is not in the EU and border controls between it and its big neighbours, Spain and France, remain in place.

Bus

Eurolines (www.eurolines.com) and its partner bus companies run an extensive network of international buses across 24 European countries and Morocco. In Spain they serve many destinations from the rest of Europe, although services often run only a few times a week.

Car & Motorcycle

When driving in Europe always carry proof of ownership of a private vehicle. Third-party motor insurance is required throughout Europe (see p859).

BUS PASSES

Travellers planning broader European tours that include Spain could find one of the following passes useful.

Busabout (☎ 020-7950 1661; www.busabout.com; 258 Vauxhall Bridge Rd, London SW1V 1BS) is a UK-based hop-on, hop-off bus service aimed at younger travellers. It has passes of varying durations allowing you to use a network of 41 cities in 11 countries. The passes are of interest only to those who intend to travel a lot beyond Spain (where there are 11 stops). Passes lasting from two weeks to six months cost from UK£239 to UK£819 (UK£219 to UK£729 for under-26s).

Eurolines (www.eurolines.com) offers a low-season pass valid for 15/30/60 days that costs UK£149/209/265 (UK£129/169/211 for under-26s and senior citizens over 60). This pass allows unlimited travel between 37 European cities. The only Spanish cities included are Barcelona and Madrid. Fares increase to UK£195/290/333 (UK£165/235/259) between June and mid-September. The pass is available at Eurolines offices across Europe.

Every vehicle travelling across an international border should display a nationality plate of its country of registration. A warning triangle (to be used in the event of a breakdown) is compulsory. In Spain a reflective jacket is also compulsory. Recommended accessories are a first-aid kit, spare-bulb kit and fire extinguisher.

Pre-booking a rental car before leaving home will enable you to find the cheapest deals (multinational agencies are listed on p858). No matter where you hire your car, make sure you understand what is included in the price and what your liabilities are.

Spain is great for motorcycle touring and motorcyclists swarm into the country in summer to tour the scenic roads. With a bike you rarely have to book ahead for ferries and can enter restricted traffic areas in cities.

An interesting website loaded with advice for people planning to drive in Europe is www.ideamerge.com.

Be aware that your vehicle could be subject to search on arrival from Andorra. Spanish customs are on the look out for contraband duty-free products destined for illegal resale in Spain. In the same way, your vehicle will also generally be subject to a search on arrival from Morocco or the Spanish North African enclaves of Ceuta and Melilla (see p856). In this case the search is for hash (or any other controlled substances).

See pp858–9 for information on road rules, petrol and other driving tips for Spain.

Train

The principal rail crossings into Spain pierce the Franco-Spanish frontier along the Mediterranean coast and via the Basque Country. Another minor rail route runs inland across the Pyrenees from Latour-de-Carol to Barcelona. From Portugal, the main line runs from Lisbon across Extremadura to Madrid.

Direct trains link Barcelona with Geneva, Zürich, Turin and Milan at least three times a week. You can check details of these on the **Spanish national railways** (Renfe; www.renfe .es) website. Reaching other major destinations in Europe beyond these will require a change in these cities or in Paris.

Andorra

Regular buses connect Andorra with Barcelona (including winter ski buses and direct services to the airport) and other destinations

in Spain (including Madrid) and France. For details see p388.

France
BUS

Eurolines (www.eurolines.fr) heads to Spain from Paris and more than 20 other French cities and towns. It connects with Madrid (17½ hours), Barcelona (15¼ hours) and many other destinations. There is at least one departure per day for main destinations.

TRAIN

About the only truly direct trains to Madrid and Barcelona are the *trenhoteles*, which are expensive sleeper trains. The Barcelona service leaves from Paris at 8.32pm daily and arrives at 8.24am (stopping at Les Aubrais, Limoges, Figueres, Girona and Barcelona Sants). The Madrid equivalent leaves from Paris at 7.43pm daily and arrives in Madrid Chamartín at 9.13am (stopping at Blois, Poitiers, Vitoria, Burgos and Valladolid).

There are several other less luxurious possibilities. Two or three TGV trains leave from Paris Montparnasse for Irún, where you change to a normal train for the Basque Country and on towards Madrid. Up to three TGVs also put you on the road to Barcelona (leaving from Paris Gare de Lyon), with a change of train at Montpellier or Narbonne. Two daily direct Talgo services connect Montpellier with Barcelona (and on to Murcia). Some other slower services (with a change at Portbou) also make this run. All stop in Perpignan. A slow overnight train also runs from Paris to Latour-de-Carol, where you change for a local regional train to Barcelona. There is an alternative train, with a change at Portbou (on the coast).

For more information on French rail services contact the **SNCF** (www.voyages-sncf.com).

Morocco

Buses from several Moroccan cities converge on Tangier to make the ferry crossing to Algeciras and then fan out across to main Spanish centres.

Portugal
BUS

AutoRes (☎ 902 020052 in Spain, ☎ 218 94 02 50 in Portugal; www.auto-res.net) runs one or two buses a day from Lisbon to Madrid via Badajoz. The trip takes about seven hours.

RAIL PASSES

The InterRail Pass and Rail Europe Senior Card are available to people who have lived in Europe for six months or more. They can be bought at most major stations and student travel outlets.

Eurail passes and Eurail Selectpass are for those who have lived in Europe for less than six months and are supposed to be bought outside Europe. They are available from leading travel agencies and online at www.eurail.com.

InterRail Pass

The InterRail (www.interrail.net) map of Europe is divided into zones, one of which comprises Spain, Portugal and Morocco. The pass is designed for people aged under 26, but there is a more expensive version for older folk: the InterRail 26+. There are three types of ticket: 16 days in one zone under 26/over 26 (€210/299), 22 days in two zones (€289/409) and one month in all zones (€399/559). Cardholders get discounts on travel in the country where they purchase the ticket.

Senior Railcard

Senior citizens can get a Rail Europe Senior Card (available at all major stations), which is valid for a year for trips that cross at least one border and which entitles you to 30% off standard fares. In the UK the card costs UK£5 but you must already have a **Senior Railcard** (www.senior-railcard.co.uk; UK£18).

Eurail Passes

Eurail passes are good for travel in 18 European countries (not including the UK) but forget it if you intend to travel mainly in Spain. People aged over 26 pay for a 1st-class pass (Eurailpass) and those aged under 26 for a 2nd-class pass (Eurailpass Youth). Passes are valid for 15 or 21 days or for one, two or three months. These cost US$588/762/946/1338/1654 respectively for the Eurailpass. Children aged between four and 11 pay half-price for 1st-class passes. The Eurailpass Youth comes in at US$414/534/664/938/1160.

Eurail Selectpass

Previously called the Europass, this provides between five and 15 days of unlimited travel within a two-month period in 17 European countries. As with Eurail passes, those aged over 26 pay for a 1st-class pass, while those aged under 26 can get a cheaper Europass Youth for travel in 2nd class. The basic five-day pass costs US$438/307 for the adult/youth version. There is also a Europass Saver that works like the Eurailpass Saver and costs US$374 per person.

Other services from the Portuguese capital run to Seville via Aracena; to Málaga via Badajoz, Seville, Cádiz, Algeciras and the Costa del Sol; to Granada via Albufeira, Huelva, Seville, Málaga and Almuñécar.

Another service runs north via Porto to Tui, Santiago de Compostela and A Coruña in Galicia. Local buses cross the border from towns such as Huelva in Andalucía, Badajoz in Extremadura and Ourense in Galicia.

TRAIN

A daily train runs between Lisbon and Madrid. Another train operates between Vigo in Galicia and Porto, running via Tui. Yet another connects Irún with Lisbon.

UK
BUS

Eurolines (☎ 08705 143219; www.nationalexpress.com/eurolines; 52 Grosvenor Gardens SW1, London) runs buses to Barcelona, Madrid and other Spanish destinations several times a week. The London terminal is at Victoria Coach Station on Buckingham Palace Rd. Journey times can range from 24 to 26 hours to Barcelona and 28 to 35 hours to Madrid.

CAR & MOTORCYCLE

You can take your car across to France by ferry or via the Channel Tunnel on **Eurotunnel** (☎ 08705 353535; www.eurotunnel.com). The latter runs four crossings (35 minutes)

TRANSPORT

an hour between Folkestone and Calais in the high season.

For breakdown assistance both the **AA** (☎ 08706 000371; www.theaa.com) and the **RAC** (☎ 08700 106382; www.rac.co.uk) offer comprehensive cover in Europe.

TRAIN

The passenger-train service **Eurostar** (www.eurostar.com) travels between London and Paris, from where you can connect with trains to Spain. Alternatively, you can purchase a train ticket that includes crossing the English Channel by ferry, SeaCat or hovercraft.

For the latest fare information on journeys to Spain, including the Eurostar, contact the **Rail Europe Travel Centre** (☎ 08705 848848; www.raileurope.co.uk). Another source of rail information for all of Europe is **Rail Choice** (www.railchoice.com). Travel times depend in large measure on what connections you make in Paris.

SEA

Ferries run to mainland Spain regularly from the Canary Islands, Italy, North Africa (Algeria, Morocco and the Spanish enclaves of Ceuta and Melilla) and the UK.

Algeria

Romeu y Compañia (☎ 96 514 70 10) runs a regular ferry from Alicante to Oran in Algeria. Contact the agents in the Puerto Maritimo in Alicante and check the security situation before travelling.

Canary Islands

A **Trasmediterránea** (☎ 902 454645; www.trasmediterranea.es) car ferry leaves from Santa Cruz de Tenerife (10am) and Las Palmas de Gran Canaria (2.30pm) every Saturday for Cádiz. It's a long and bumpy ride, taking about 48 hours from Santa Cruz.

Italy

The Grimaldi group's **Grandi Navi Veloci** (☎ 010 209 45 91; www1.gnv.it) operates a high-speed, roll-on, roll-off ferry service (which takes 18 hours) from Genoa to Barcelona three times a week. For more information see p317.

Morocco

You can sail from the Moroccan ports of Tangier and Nador, as well as from Ceuta or Melilla (Spanish enclaves on the Moroccan coast) to Almería, Málaga, Algeciras, Gibraltar and Tarifa. The routes are: Melilla–Almería, Nador–Almería, Melilla–Málaga, Tangier–Gibraltar, Tangier–Algeciras, Ceuta–Algeciras and Tangier–Tarifa. All routes usually take vehicles as well as passengers.

The most frequent sailings are to/from Algeciras. Usually at least 16 sailings a day ply the route between Algeciras and Tangier (taking 1¼ to 2½ hours) and 16 between Algeciras and Ceuta (35 minutes). Extra services are put on during the peak summer period (mid-June to mid-September) and the Tangier–Tarifa route may be restricted to people with EU passports or EU residence papers during this period. For more details, see the appropriate sections in the Andalucía chapter.

UK

PLYMOUTH–SANTANDER

From Milbay Docks in Plymouth, **Brittany Ferries** (☎ 08703 665333; www.brittanyferries.co.uk) runs a car ferry twice a week to Santander from mid-March to mid-November. See also p496.

PORTSMOUTH–BILBAO

Throughout the year **P&O European Ferries** (☎ 08705 202020; www.poportsmouth.com) operates a service from Portsmouth to Bilbao. As a rule there are two sailings a week. See also p464.

VIA FRANCE

You can transport your car by Hoverspeed or ferry to France from the UK. **Hoverspeed** (☎ 08702 408070; www.hoverspeed.com) fast boats take about two hours to cross from Dover to Calais or Newhaven to Dieppe. **P&O Stena Line** (☎ 08705 202020; www.poferries.com) also has frequent car ferries from Dover to Calais (1¼ hours).

GETTING AROUND

You can reach almost any destination in Spain by train or bus, and services are generally efficient and cheap. For longer distances there are plenty of domestic air services, although generally it's not the cheapest way to get around. Your own wheels give you the most freedom.

AIR
Airlines in Spain
Iberia and its subsidiary, Iberia Regional-Air Nostrum, have an extensive network covering all Spain. Competing with Iberia are Spanair and Air Europa. They both compete with Iberia on the busy Madrid–Barcelona run and fly to a host of other Spanish destinations. For airline contact details see p850.

The cheapest return fare between Madrid and Barcelona with any of these airlines hovers around €90, but it can range up to €250. Cheaper tickets are generally nonrefundable, must be booked up to two weeks in advance and allow no changes. All applicable airport taxes are factored into the price of your ticket.

A new Barcelona-based budget airline, Vueling (see p850), started flying daily between Barcelona, Valencia, Palma de Mallorca and Ibiza in mid-2004.

BICYCLE
Years of highway improvement programmes across the country have made cycling a much easier prospect than it once was. There are plenty of options, from mountain biking in the Pyrenees to distance riding along the coast.

If you get tired of pedalling it is often possible to take your bike on the train. All regional trains have space for bikes (usually marked by a bicycle logo on the carriage), where you can simply load the bike. Bikes are also permitted on most cercanías (local area trains around big cities such as Madrid and Barcelona). On long-distance trains there are more restrictions. As a rule you have to be travelling overnight in a sleeper or couchette to have the (dismantled) bike accepted as normal luggage. Otherwise, it can only be sent separately as a parcel. It's often possible to take your bike on a bus – usually you'll just be asked to remove the front wheel.

In the UK the **Cyclists' Touring Club** (CTC; ☎ 08708 730060; www.ctc.org.uk; Cotterell House, 69 Meadrow, Godalming, Surrey GU7 3HS) can help you plan your own bike tour or organise guided tours. Membership costs UK£30.50 per annum (UK£11 for those under 26).

Hire & Purchase
Bicycle rental is not too common in Spain, although it is more so in the case of mountain bikes (bici todo terreno) and in some of the more popular regions such as Andalucía and in some coastal spots like Barcelona. Costs vary considerably but you can be looking at around €5/15/50 per hour/day/week. You can purchase any kind of bicycle you want in the bigger centres and prices are average by European standards. A basic city bike with no gears won't come for much less than €100. For a decent mountain bike with 16 gears you're looking at €250 or more and racing bikes can be more expensive still.

BOAT
Ferries and hydrofoils link the mainland (La Península) with the Balearic Islands and Spain's North African enclaves of Ceuta and Melilla. For details of the latter, see opposite and the relevant sections in the Andalucía chapter. For more on ferries between the mainland and the Balearic Islands, see p617.

The main national ferry company is **Trasmediterránea** (☎ 902 454645; www.trasmediterranea.es). It runs a combination of slower car ferries and modern high-speed, passenger-only Fast Ferries and hydrofoils. On overnight services between the mainland and the Balearic Islands you can opt for seating or sleeping accommodation in a cabin.

BUS
A plethora of companies provide bus links, from local routes between villages to fast intercity connections. It is often cheaper to travel by bus than by train, particularly on long-haul runs, but also less comfortable.

Local services can get you just about anywhere, but most buses connecting villages and provincial towns are not geared to tourist needs. Frequent weekday services drop off to a trickle on weekends. Often just one bus runs daily between smaller places during the week and none operate on Sunday. It's usually unnecessary to make reservations; just arrive early enough to get a seat.

On many regular runs (say, from Madrid to Toledo) the ticket you buy is for the next bus due to leave and cannot be used on a later bus. Advance purchase in such cases is generally not possible.

For longer trips (such as Madrid–Seville, or to the costas, coasts), and certainly in peak season, you can (and should) buy your ticket in advance. On some routes you have the choice between express and all-stops services. The faster services sometimes cost more.

In most larger towns and cities, buses leave from a single bus station (*estación de autobuses*). In smaller places, buses tend to operate from a set street or plaza, often unmarked. Locals will know where to go. Usually a specific bar sells tickets and has timetable information, although in some cases you may have to purchase tickets on the bus.

Bus travel within Spain is not overly costly. The trip from Madrid to Barcelona costs around €24 one way. From Barcelona to Seville, about one of the longest trips you could do (15 to 17 hours) you would pay up to €77 one way for the faster services.

People under 26 should ask about discounts on long-distance trips. Occasionally a return ticket is cheaper than two singles.

Alsa (☎ 902 422242; www.alsa.es) has routes all over the country that it operates in association with various companies, such as Enatcar and Eurobus. From Madrid it runs buses to Barcelona, Zaragoza, Tarragona, Ávila, Segovia, Valladolid, León, major towns in Galicia, Alicante, Murcia and Almería. From Seville buses run up through Extremadura and Salamanca into Galicia, as well as through Córdoba through the east of the country to Barcelona.

Alsina Graells (☎ 93 265 65 92; www.alsinagraells .es) operates main routes across Catalonia from Barcelona. It also runs buses across Andalucía in tandem with Continental-Auto (see below).

AutoRes (☎ 902 020999; www.auto-res.net) operates buses from Madrid to Extremadura, western Castilla y León (eg Tordesillas, Salamanca and Zamora) and Valencia via eastern Castilla-La Mancha (eg Cuenca).

Continental-Auto (☎ 902 330400; www.continental -auto.es) runs from Madrid to Burgos, Logroño, Navarra, the País Vasco, Santander, Soria, Alcalá de Henares, Guadalajara, Granada and Toledo.

La Sepulvedana (☎ 915304800; www.lasepulvedana .es) has buses to Segovia, parts of Castilla-La Mancha and Extremadura from Madrid.

Socibus (☎ 902 229292; www.socibus.es) operates services between Madrid and western Andalucía, including Cádiz, Córdoba, Huelva and Seville.

CAR & MOTORCYCLE
Automobile Associations
The **Real Automóvil Club de España** (Map pp106-8; RACE; ☎ 902 40 45 45; www.race.es) Calle de Eloy Gonzalo) is the national automobile club. In an emergency you can call its road assistance service on ☎ 902 30 05 05. You will be charged for this service and should thus obtain a contact number from your own national insurer before heading to Spain.

Bring Your Own Vehicle
If bringing your own car, remember to have your insurance and other papers in order (see p853).

Driving Licence
All EU member states' driving licences are fully recognised throughout Europe. Those with a non-EU licence are supposed to obtain a 12-month International Driver's Permit (IDP) to accompany their national licence, which your national automobile association can issue. People who have held residency in Spain for one year or more must apply for a Spanish driving licence. If you want to hire a car or motorcycle you will need to produce your driving licence.

Fuel & Spare Parts
Gasolina (petrol) in Spain is pricey, but generally cheaper than in its major EU neighbours (including France, Germany, Italy and the UK). About 30 companies, including several foreign operators, run petrol stations in Spain, but the two biggest are the home-grown Repsol and Cepsa.

Prices vary between service stations (*gasolineras*). Lead free (*sin plomo*; 95 octane) costs an average €0.88/L. A 98-octane variant costs €0.96/L, while the 97-octane type, introduced to replace leaded super (many cars in Spain still ran on super when leaded petrol was banned in January 2002), costs €0.95/L. Diesel (*gasóleo*) comes in at €0.74/L.

Petrol is about 10% cheaper in Gibraltar than in Spain and 15% cheaper in Andorra. It's about 40% cheaper in Spain's tax-free enclaves of Ceuta and Melilla in North Africa.

You can pay with major credit cards at most service stations.

Most vehicle makes can be dealt with by local mechanics, but some of the more popular brands include Seat, Volkswagen, Renault and Fiat.

Hire
The most competitive multinational car rental agencies are listed below.

ROAD DISTANCES (km)

	Alicante	Badajoz	Barcelona	Bilbao	Córdoba	Granada	A Coruña	León	Madrid	Málaga	Oviedo	Pamplona	San Sebastián	Seville	Toledo	Valencia	Valladolid	Zaragoza
Alicante	---																	
Badajoz	696	---																
Barcelona	515	1022	---															
Bilbao	817	649	620	---														
Córdoba	525	272	908	795	---													
Granada	353	438	868	829	166	---												
A Coruña	1031	772	1118	644	995	1043	---											
León	755	496	784	359	733	761	334	---										
Madrid	422	401	621	395	400	434	609	333	---									
Málaga	482	436	997	939	187	129	1153	877	544	---								
Oviedo	873	614	902	304	851	885	340	118	451	995	---							
Pamplona	673	755	437	159	807	841	738	404	407	951	463	---						
San Sebastián	766	768	529	119	869	903	763	433	469	13	423	92	---					
Seville	609	217	1046	933	138	256	947	671	538	219	789	945	1007	---				
Toledo	411	368	692	466	320	397	675	392	71	507	510	478	540	458	---			
Valencia	166	716	349	633	545	519	961	685	352	648	803	501	594	697	372	---		
Valladolid	615	414	663	280	578	627	455	134	193	737	252	325	354	589	258	545	---	
Zaragoza	498	726	296	324	725	759	833	488	325	869	604	175	268	863	396	326	367	---

TRANSPORT

Autos Abroad (☎ 08700 667788 in the UK; www
.autosabroad.com)

Avis (☎ 902 135531 in Spain; www.avis.com)

Budget (☎ 1-800 472 33 25 in the USA; www.budget
.com)

Europcar (☎ 902 105030 in Spain; www.europcar.com)

Hertz (☎ 902 402405 in Spain; www.hertz.com)

National/Atesa (☎ 902 100101 in Spain; www.atesa.es)

Pepecar (☎ 807 212121 in Spain; www.pepecar.com)
This low-cost company specialises in cheap rentals of
Mercedes Class A cars and Smarts. They have outlets in
Barcelona, Ibiza, Madrid, Palma de Mallorca, Seville and
Valencia. If you book far enough ahead, it can cost you
around €12 per day (with 100km free), plus a credit card
handling fee and a €12 cleaning charge.

Most tourist offices and hotels can provide
information about car or motorcycle rental.
To rent a car in Spain you have to have
a licence, be aged 21 or over and, for the
major companies at least, you have to have
a credit card. Smaller firms in areas where
car hire is particularly common (such as
the Balearic Islands) can sometimes live
without this requirement. Although those
with a non-EU licence should also have an
IDP, you will find in practice that national
licences from countries such as Australia,
Canada, New Zealand and the USA are
often accepted.

Insurance
Third-party motor insurance is a minimum
requirement in Spain and throughout Europe. Ask your insurer for a European Accident Statement form, which can simplify
matters in the event of an accident. A European breakdown assistance policy such as
the AA Five Star Service or RAC Eurocover
Motoring Assistance is a good investment.

Car-hire companies also provide this
minimum insurance but be careful to understand what your liabilities and excess are
and what waivers you are entitled to in case
of accident or damage to the hire vehicle.

Road Rules
Drive on the right. In built-up areas the
speed limit is 50km/h, which rises to
100km/h on major roads and up to 120km/h
on *autovías* and *autopistas* (toll-free and
tolled dual-lane highways, respectively).

Cars towing caravans are restricted to a maximum speed of 80km/h. The minimum driving age is 18.

Motorcyclists must use headlights at all times and wear a crash helmet if riding a bike of 125cc or more. The minimum age for riding motorbikes and scooters of 80cc and over is 16 and for those 50cc and under is 14. A licence is required.

Spanish truck drivers often have the courtesy to turn on their right indicator to show that the way ahead of them is clear for overtaking (and the left one if it is not and you are attempting this manoeuvre).

Vehicles in traffic circles (roundabouts) have the right of way.

The blood-alcohol limit is 0.05%. Breath tests are becoming more common and if found to be over the limit you can be judged, condemned, fined and deprived of your licence within 24 hours. Fines range up to around €600 for serious offences. Nonresident foreigners will be required to pay up on the spot. Pleading linguistic ignorance will not help – your traffic cop will produce a list of infringements and fines in as many languages as you like. If you don't pay, or have a Spanish resident go guarantor for you, your vehicle will be impounded.

HITCHING

Hitching is never entirely safe and we don't recommend it. Travellers who decide to hitch should understand that they are taking a small but potentially dangerous risk. You'll also need plenty of patience and common sense. Women should avoid hitching alone, and even men should consider the safer alternative of hitching in pairs.

Hitching is illegal on *autopistas* and *autovías*, and difficult on other major highways. Choose a spot where cars can safely stop before highway slipways, or use minor roads. The going can be slow on the latter, as the traffic is often light. Overall, Spain is not a hitchhiker's paradise. It is more difficult still in the south, where drivers tend to be more wary of strangers.

LOCAL TRANSPORT

All the major cities have good transport. Madrid and Barcelona have extensive bus and metro systems and other major cities also benefit from generally efficient public transport.

Bicycle

Few of the big cities offer much in the way of encouragement to cycle. Barcelona is an exception, where cycling lanes have been laid out along main roads and several hire outlets make it possible for visitors to enjoy them. Driver attitudes are not always so enlightened, so beware.

Bus

Cities and provincial capitals all have reasonable bus networks. You can buy single tickets (up to €1.15, depending on the city) on the buses or at tobacconists, but, in the case of cities such as Madrid and Barcelona, you are better off buying combined 10-trip tickets (see Metro below) that allow the use of a combination of bus and metro, and which work out cheaper per ride. These can be purchased in any metro station.

Regular buses run from about 6am to shortly before midnight. In the big cities a night bus service generally kicks in on a limited number of lines in the wee hours. In Madrid they are known as *búhos* (owls) and in Barcelona more prosaically as *nitbusos* (night buses).

Metro

Madrid has the country's most extensive metro network, which has been rapidly expanded and modernised in recent years. Barcelona follows in second place with a reasonable system. Valencia and Bilbao also have limited metros. Tickets must be bought in metro stations (from counters or vending machines). Single tickets cost the same as for buses (ie up to €1.15). The best value for most visitors wanting to move around the major cities over a few days are the 10-trip tickets, known in Madrid as Metrobús (€5.35) and in Barcelona as T-10 (€6). Monthly and season passes are available but are only of interest to regular commuters over a longer period.

If you are caught without a ticket you will be fined (€18 in Madrid, €40 in Barcelona).

Taxi

You can usually find taxi ranks at train and bus stations or you can telephone for radio taxis. In larger cities taxi ranks are also scattered about the centre and taxis will stop if you hail them in the street. Look for the green light and/or the *Libre* sign on the passenger side of the windscreen. The bigger cities are well populated with taxis, although finding one when you need to get home late on a Friday or Saturday night in places such as Madrid and Barcelona can be next to impossible. No more than four people are allowed in a taxi.

Flagfall is around €1.20 to €1.55. You then pay around €0.70 to €0.90 per kilometre depending on the time of day. There are airport and luggage surcharges. A cross-town ride in a major city will cost about €5 to €8, while a taxi between the city centre and airport in either Madrid or Barcelona should not cost more than €20 with luggage.

Tram

Trams were stripped out of Spanish cities decades ago but they are making a timid comeback in some. Barcelona has a couple of new suburban tram services in addition to its tourist Tramvia Blau run to Tibidabo. Valencia has some useful trams to the beach.

TRAIN

Renfe (☎ 902 240202; www.renfe.es) is the national state train system that runs most of the services in Spain. A handful of small private railway lines are noted in the course of this book.

Spain has several types of trains. For short hops, bigger cities such as Madrid, Barcelona, Bilbao, Málaga and Valencia have a local network known as *cercanías*. Long-distance (aka *largo recorrido*) trains come in all sorts of different flavours. They range from the all-stops *regionales* to the high-speed AVE trains that link Madrid with Seville and Lleida (and, one day, Barcelona). Similar trains used on conventional Spanish track (which differs from the standard European gauge) connect Barcelona with Valencia in the Euromed service. A whole host of modern intermediate speed services (Intercity, Talgo, Talgo 200, Alaris, Altaria and Arco) offer an increasingly speedy and comfortable service around the country.

You'll find *consignas* (left-luggage facilities) at all main train stations. They are usually open from about 6am to midnight and charge from €3 to €4.50 per day per each piece of luggage.

Classes & Costs

All long-distance trains have 2nd and 1st classes, known as *turista* and *preferente*, respectively. The latter is about 40% more expensive. Fares vary enormously depending on the service (faster trains cost more) and, in the case of some high-speed services such as the AVE, on the time and day of travel. If you get a return ticket, it is worth checking whether your return journey is by the same kind of train. If you return on a slower train than the outward-bound trip you may be entitled to a modest refund on the return leg. Alternatively, if you return by a faster train you will need to pay more to make your return ticket valid for that train.

Children aged between four and 12 years are entitled to a 40% discount; those aged under four travel free. Buying a return ticket gives you a 20% discount on the return trip. Students and people up to 25 years of age with a Euro<26 card (Carnet Joven in Spain) are entitled to up to 25% off some prices. Senior citizens need a pass (see right).

On overnight trips within Spain it's worth paying extra for a *litera* (couchette; a sleeping berth in a six- or four-bed compartment). The cost depends on the type of train and length of journey. Only a few trains offer this service now. A more comfortable and expensive way to go is by *trenhotel*, which offers *turista* (sitting up or sleeping), *preferente* (sleeping single or double) and *gran clase* (luxury sleeping, single or double) classes. The lines covered are Madrid–La Coruña, Barcelona–Córdoba–Seville, Barcelona–Madrid (and on to Lisbon) and Barcelona–Málaga.

Reservations

Reservations are recommended for long-distance trips, such as Madrid–Barcelona. You can make reservations in train stations, Renfe offices, travel agencies and online. There is generally no fee for booking unless you ask to have tickets mailed to you. Holders of InterRail and Eurail cards will be charged a booking fee of €3 (or €15 for a sleeping berth).

Train Passes

Renfe offers its own discount passes for travel within the country. These include the **Carta Dorada** (€3; valid one year) for people aged 60 years and over and resident in Spain, which entitles holders to discounts of 25% to 40%.

Eurodominó is designed for people resident outside Spain but in Europe for at least six months. The ticket entitles you to three to eight days' rail travel in Spain within a one-month period. The ticket costs from €113 to €263 for adults and €95 to €220 for people under 26. Senior citizens pay marginally more.

For people resident outside Europe there is the **Spain Flexipass**, which entitles holders to three to 10 days' unlimited rail travel in a two-month period. It costs US$175 to US$385 in *turista* class and US$225 to US$470 in *preferente*. Within Spain it can only be bought at main Renfe stations in Barcelona, Madrid (and at the airport), Seville and Valencia. Similar passes include **Iberic Railpass** (which covers Spain and Portugal) and **France 'n Spain** (which is for Spain and France).

Health

BEFORE YOU GO

Prevention is the key to staying healthy while abroad. Some predeparture planning will save trouble later. See your dentist before a long trip, carry a spare pair of contact lenses and glasses, and take your optical prescription with you. Bring medications in their original, clearly labelled, containers. A signed and dated letter from your physician describing your medical conditions and medications, including generic names, is also a good idea. If carrying syringes or needles, be sure to have a physician's letter documenting their medical necessity.

INSURANCE

If you're an EU citizen, an E111 form, available from health centres or, in the UK, post offices, covers you for most medical care. The E111 will not cover you for nonemergencies or emergency repatriation home. So even with an E111, you will still have to pay for medicine bought from pharmacies, even if prescribed, and perhaps for a few tests and procedures. An E111 is no good for private medical consultations and treatment in Spain; this includes virtually all dentists, and some of the better clinics and surgeries. Citizens from other countries should find out if there is a reciprocal arrangement

for free medical care between their country and Spain. If you do need health insurance, strongly consider a policy that covers you for the worst possible scenario, such as an accident requiring an emergency flight home.

Find out in advance if your insurance plan will make payments directly to providers or reimburse you later for overseas health expenditures. The former option is generally preferable, as it doesn't require you to pay out of your own pocket in a foreign country.

RECOMMENDED VACCINATIONS

No jabs are necessary for Spain. However, the World Health Organization (WHO) recommends that all travellers should be covered for diphtheria, tetanus, measles, mumps, rubella and polio, regardless of their destination. Since most vaccines don't produce immunity until at least two weeks after they're given, visit a physician at least six weeks before departure.

INTERNET RESOURCES

International Travel and Health, a WHO publication, is revised annually and is available online at www.who.int/ith/. Other useful websites include www.mdtravelhealth.com (travel health recommendations for every country; updated daily), www.fitfortravel .scot.nhs.uk (general travel advice for the lay person); www.ageconcern.org.uk (advice on travel for the elderly); and www.mariestopes .org.uk (information on women's health and contraception).

IN TRANSIT

DEEP VEIN THROMBOSIS (DVT)

Blood clots may form in the legs during plane flights, chiefly because of prolonged immobility. The chief symptom of DVT is swelling or pain of the foot, ankle or calf, usually but not always on just one side. When a blood clot travels to the lungs, it may cause chest pain and breathing difficulties. Travellers with any of these symptoms should immediately seek medical attention.

To prevent the development of DVT on long flights you should walk about the cabin, contract your leg muscles while sitting, drink plenty of fluids, and avoid alcohol and tobacco.

IN SPAIN

AVAILABILITY OF HEALTH CARE

If you need an ambulance, call ☎ 061. For emergency treatment go straight to the *urgencias* (casualty) section of the nearest hospital.

Good health care is readily available, and *farmacias* (pharmacies) offer valuable advice and sell over-the-counter medication. In Spain, a system of *farmacias de guardia* (duty pharmacies) operates so that each district has one open all the time. When a pharmacy is closed, it posts the name of the nearest open one on the door.

TRAVELLER'S DIARRHOEA

If you develop diarrhoea, be sure to drink plenty of fluids, preferably an oral rehydration solution, such as Dioralyte. If diarrhoea is bloody, persists for more than 72 hours or is accompanied by a fever, shaking, chills or severe abdominal pain, you should seek medical attention.

ENVIRONMENTAL HAZARDS
Altitude Sickness

Lack of oxygen at high altitudes (over 2500m) affects most people to some extent. Symptoms of Acute Mountain Sickness (AMS) usually develop during the first 24 hours at altitude but may be delayed up to three weeks. Mild symptoms include headache, lethargy, dizziness, difficulty sleeping and loss of appetite. AMS may become more severe without warning and can be fatal. Severe symptoms include breathlessness, a dry, irritative cough (which may progress to the production of pink, frothy sputum), severe headache, lack of coordination and balance, confusion, irrational behaviour, vomiting, drowsiness and unconsciousness. There is no hard-and-fast rule as to what is too high: AMS has been fatal at 3000m, although 3500m to 4500m is the usual range.

Treat mild symptoms by resting at the same altitude until recovery, usually for a day or two. Paracetamol or aspirin can be taken for headaches. If symptoms persist or become worse *immediate descent is necessary*; even 500m can help. Drug treatments should never be used to avoid descent or to enable further ascent.

Diamox (acetazolamide) reduces the headache caused by AMS and helps the body acclimatise to the lack of oxygen. It is only available on prescription and those who are allergic to the sulfonamide antibiotics may also be allergic to Diamox.

In the UK, fact sheets are available from the British Mountaineering Council, 177–179 Burton Rd, Manchester, M20 2BB.

Heat Exhaustion & Heatstroke

Heat exhaustion occurs following excessive fluid loss with inadequate replacement of fluids and salt. Symptoms include headache, dizziness and tiredness. Dehydration is happening by the time you feel thirsty – aim to drink sufficient water to produce pale, diluted urine. Replace lost fluids by drinking water and/or fruit juice, and cool the body with cold water and fans. Treat salt loss with salty fluids, such as soup, or add a little more table salt to foods than usual.

Heatstroke is much more serious, resulting in irrational and hyperactive behaviour, and eventually loss of consciousness and death. Rapid cooling by spraying the body with water and fanning is ideal. Emergency fluid and electrolyte replacement by intravenous drip is recommended.

Bites & Stings

Bees and wasps only cause real problems to those with a severe allergy (anaphylaxis). If you have a severe allergy to bee or wasp stings, carry an 'epipen' or similar adrenaline injection.

In forested areas watch out for the hairy reddish-brown caterpillars of the pine processionary moth. They live in silvery nests up in the pine trees and, come spring, they leave the nest to march in long lines (hence the name). Touching the caterpillars' hairs sets off a severely irritating allergic skin reaction.

Some Spanish centipedes have a very nasty but nonfatal sting. The ones to watch out for are those with clearly defined segments, which may be patterned with, for instance, black and yellow stripes.

Jellyfish, with their stinging tentacles, generally occur in large numbers or hardly at all, so it's fairly easy to know when not to go in the sea.

Mosquitoes are found in most parts of Europe. They may not carry malaria, but can cause irritation and infected bites. Use a DEET-based insect repellent.

Sandflies are found around the Mediterranean beaches. They usually cause only a nasty itchy bite but can carry a rare skin disorder called cutaneous leishmaniasis.

Scorpions are found in Spain and their sting can be distressingly painful, but not considered fatal.

The only venomous snake that is even relatively common in Spain is Lataste's viper. It has a triangular-shaped head, is up to 75cm long, and grey with a zigzag pattern. It lives in dry, rocky areas, away from humans. Its bite can be fatal and needs to be treated with a serum, which state clinics in major towns keep in stock. Also to be avoided is the Montpellier snake, which is blue with a white underside and prominent ridges over the eyes. It lives mainly in scrub and sandy areas, but keeps a low profile and is unlikely to be a threat unless trodden on.

Check for ticks if you have been walking where sheep and goats graze: they can cause skin infections and other more serious diseases.

Hypothermia

The weather in Spain's mountains can be extremely changeable at any time of year. Proper preparation will reduce the risks of getting hypothermia. Even on a hot day the weather can change rapidly; carry waterproof garments and warm layers, and inform others of your route.

Hypothermia starts with shivering, loss of judgment and clumsiness. Unless rewarming occurs, the sufferer deteriorates into apathy, confusion and coma. Prevent further heat loss by seeking shelter, warm dry clothing, hot sweet drinks and shared bodily warmth.

Water

Tap water is generally safe to drink in Spain. If you are in any doubt, ask *¿Es potable el agua (de grifo)?* (Is the (tap) water drinkable?). Do not drink water from rivers or lakes as it may contain bacteria or viruses that can cause diarrhoea or vomiting.

TRAVELLING WITH CHILDREN

Make sure your children are up to date with routine vaccinations, and discuss possible travel vaccines well before departure as some vaccines are not suitable for children under one year of age.

WOMEN'S HEALTH

Travelling during pregnancy is usually possible but always seek a medical check-up before planning your trip. The most risky times for travel are during the first 12 weeks of pregnancy and after 30 weeks.

SEXUAL HEALTH

Condoms are widely available, but emergency contraception may not be so take the necessary precautions. When buying condoms, look for a European CE mark, which means they have been rigorously tested. Remember to also keep them in a cool, dry place so that they don't crack and perish.

HEALTH

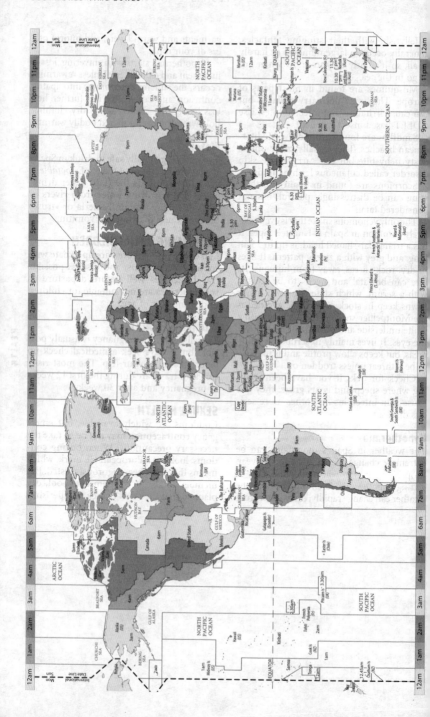

Language

CONTENTS

Spanish (*español*), or Castilian (*castellano*) as it is more precisely called, is spoken throughout Spain, but there are also three important regional languages: Catalan (*català*), another Romance language with close ties to French, spoken in Catalonia, the Balearic Islands and Valencia; Galician (*galego*), similar enough to Portuguese to be regarded by some as a dialect, spoken in Galicia; and Basque (*euskara*), of obscure, non-Latin origin, spoken in the Basque Country and Navarra.

English isn't as widely spoken as many travellers expect, though you're more likely to find people who speak some English in the main cities and tourist areas. Generally, however, you'll be better received if you try to communicate in Spanish.

For a more comprehensive guide to the Spanish language than we're able to offer here, get a copy of Lonely Planet's *Spanish Phrasebook*. For information on language courses available in Spain, see p832.

PRONUNCIATION

Spanish pronunciation isn't difficult – many Spanish sounds are similar to their English counterparts, and there's a clear and consistent relationship between pronunciation and spelling. If you stick to the following rules you should have very few problems making yourself understood.

Vowels

Unlike English, each of the vowels in Spanish has a uniform pronunciation that doesn't vary. For example, the Spanish **a** has only one pronunciation, similar to the 'u' in 'nut'. Many Spanish words are written with an acute accent (eg *días*) – this normally indicates a stressed syllable and doesn't change the sound of the vowel. Vowels are pronounced clearly even if they are unstressed.

Spanish Pronunciation Guide

Spanish		
a	a	as the 'u' in 'nut'
ai	ai	as in 'aisle'
au	ow	as in 'cow'
e	e	as in 'met'
ei	ey	as in 'they'
i	ee	as in 'keep'
ia	ya	as in 'yard'
ie	ye	as in 'yes'
o	o	as in 'hot'
oy	oy	as in 'boy'
u	oo	as in 'hoof'
	–	silent after **q** and in *gue/gui*
ue	we	as in 'wet'
uy	ooy	as the 'oy' in 'boy'
ü	w	as in 'wet'

Semiconsonant

Spanish also has the semiconsonant **y**. When occuring at the end of a word or standing alone (meaning 'and') it's pronounced like the Spanish **i**. As a consonant, it's somewhere between the 'y' in 'yonder' and the 'g' in 'beige', depending on the region you're in.

Consonants

Some Spanish consonants are the same as their English counterparts. The pronunciation of others varies according to which vowel follows and which part of Spain you happen to be in. The Spanish alphabet also contains three consonants that are not found within the English alphabet: **ch**, **ll** and **ñ**. In newer dictionaries the letters **ch** and **ll** are listed under **c** and **l** respectively, but **ñ** is still treated as a separate letter and comes after **n**.

Spanish Pronunciation Guide

b	b	as in 'book' when at the start of a word or preceded by **m** or **n**; elsewhere as the 'v' in 'van'
c	k	as in 'cat' when followed by **a**, **o**, **u** or a consonant
	th	as in 'thin' before **e** and **i**
ch	ch	as in 'church'
cu	kw	as the 'qu' in 'quite'
d	d	as in 'dog' when word-initial or when preceded by **l** or **n**
	th	as in 'then'
	–	sometimes not pronounced at all – *partido* (divided) is pronounced par·*tee*·o
f	f	as in 'frame'
g	g	as in 'get' when initial and before **a**, **o** and **u**
	kh	as the 'ch' in the Scottish *loch* before **e** or **i**
h	–	always silent
j	kh	as the 'ch' in the Scottish *loch*
l	l	as in 'let'
ll	ly	as the 'lli' in 'million'; some people pronounce it like the 'y' in 'yellow'
m	m	as in 'many'
n	n	as in 'nana'
ñ	ny	as the 'ni' in 'onion'
p	p	as in 'pop'
q	k	as in 'kick'
r	r	a rolled 'r' sound; longer when initial or doubled
s	s	as in 'see'
t	t	as in 'top'
v	b	as in 'bus'
vu	vw	as the 'voi' in the French *voir*
x	ks	as in 'taxi' when between two vowels
	s	as in 'see' when preceding a consonant
z	th	as in 'thin'

WORD STRESS

Stress is indicated by italics in the pronunciation guides included with all the words and phrases in this language guide. In general, words ending in vowels or the letters **n** or **s** have stress on the next-to-last syllable, while those with other endings have stress on the last syllable. Thus *vaca* (cow) and *caballos* (horses) both carry stress on the next-to-last syllable, while *ciudad* (city) and *infeliz* (unhappy) are both stressed on the last syllable.

Written accents indicate a stressed syllable, and will almost always appear in words that don't follow these rules, eg *sótano* (basement) and *porción* (portion).

GENDER & PLURALS

Spanish nouns are marked for gender (masculine or feminine) and adjectives will vary according to the gender of the noun they modify. There are rules to help determine gender – with exceptions, of course! Feminine nouns generally end with -a or with the groups -ción, -sión or -dad. Other endings typically signify a masculine noun. Endings for adjectives also change to agree with the gender of the noun they modify (masculine/feminine -o/-a).

Where necessary, both forms are given for the words and phrases below, separated by a slash and with the masculine form first, eg *perdido/a* (lost).

If a noun or adjective ends in a vowel, the plural is formed by adding **s** to the end. If it ends in a consonant, the plural is formed by adding **es** to the end.

ACCOMMODATION

I'm looking for ...	Estoy buscando ...	e·*stoy* boos·*kan*·do ...
Where is ...?	¿Dónde hay ...?	*don*·de ai ...
a hotel	un hotel	oon o·*tel*
a boarding house	una pensión/ un hospedaje	oo·na pen·*syon*/ oon os·pe·*da*·khe
a youth hostel	un albergue juvenil	oon al·*ber*·ge khoo·ve·*neel*

I'd like a room.	Quisiera una habitación ...	kee·*sye*·ra oo·na a·bee·ta·*thyon* ...
double	doble	*do*·ble
single	individual	een·dee·vee·*dwal*
twin	con dos camas	kon dos *ka*·mas

How much is it per ...?	¿Cuánto cuesta por ...?	*kwan*·to *kwes*·ta por ...
night	noche	*no*·che
person	persona	per·*so*·na
week	semana	se·*ma*·na

May I see the room?

¿Puedo ver la habitación?	*pwe*·do ver la a·bee·ta·*thyon*

Does it include breakfast?

¿Incluye el desayuno?	een·*kloo*·ye el de·sa·*yoo*·no

don't like it.
No me gusta.   no me *goos*·ta

t's fine. I'll take it.
OK. La alquilo.   o·*kay* la al·*kee*·lo

'm leaving now.
Me voy ahora.   me *voy* a·*o*·ra

full board	pensión completa	pen·*syon* kom·*ple*·ta
private/shared	baño privado/	*ba*·nyo pree·*va*·do/
bathroom	compartido	kom·par·*tee*·do
too expensive	demasiado caro	de·ma·*sya*·do *ka*·ro
cheaper	más económico	mas e·ko·*no*·mee·ko
discount	descuento	des·*kwen*·to

MAKING A RESERVATION
(for phone or written requests)

To ...	A ...
From ...	De ...
Date	Fecha
I'd like to book ...	Quisiera reservar ... (see Accommodation on p868 for bed/room options)
in the name of ...	en nombre de ...
for the nights of ...	para las noches del ...
credit card ...	tarjeta de crédito ...
number	número
expiry date	fecha de vencimiento
Please confirm ...	Puede confirmar ...
availability	la disponibilidad
price	el precio

CONVERSATION & ESSENTIALS

When talking to people familiar to you or younger than you, use the informal form of 'you', *tú*, rather than the polite form *Usted*. Wait for your Spanish friends to suggest you use the *tú* form. The polite form is used in all cases in this guide; where options are given, the form is indicated by the abbreviations 'pol' and 'inf'.

Hello.	Hola.	o·la
Good morning.	Buenos días.	*bwe*·nos *dee*·as
Good afternoon.	Buenas tardes.	*bwe*·nas *tar*·des
Good evening/ night.	Buenas noches.	*bwe*·nas *no*·ches
Goodbye.	Adiós.	a·*dyos*
Bye/See you soon.	Hasta luego.	*as*·ta *lwe*·go
Yes.	Sí.	see
No.	No.	no

Please.	Por favor.	por fa·*vor*
Thank you.	Gracias.	*gra*·thyas
Many thanks.	Muchas gracias.	*moo*·chas *gra*·thyas
You're welcome.	De nada.	de *na*·da
Pardon me.	Perdón/	per·*don*/
(getting attention)	Discúlpeme.	dees·*kool*·pe·me
Sorry.	Lo siento.	lo see·*en*·to
(when apologising)		
Excuse me.	Permiso.	per·*mee*·so
(when asking to get past someone)		

How are things?
¿Qué tal?   ke tal

What's your name?
¿Cómo se llama Usted?   *ko*·mo se *lya*·ma oo·ste (pol)
¿Cómo te llamas?   *ko*·mo te *lya*·mas (inf)

My name is ...
Me llamo ...   me *lya*·mo ...

It's a pleasure to meet you.
Mucho gusto.   *moo*·cho *goos*·to

Where are you from?
¿De dónde es/eres?   de *don*·de es/e·res (pol/inf)

I'm from ...
Soy de ...   soy de ...

Where are you staying?
¿Dónde está alojado/a?   *don*·de es·*ta* a·lo·*kha*·do/da (pol)
¿Dónde estás alojado/a?   *don*·de es·*tas* a·lo·*kha*·do/da (inf)

May I take a photo?
¿Puedo hacer una foto?   *pwe*·do a·*ther* *oo*·na *fo*·to

DIRECTIONS
How do I get to ...?
¿Cómo puedo llegar a ...?   *ko*·mo *pwe*·do lye·*gar* a ...

Is it far?
¿Está lejos?   es·*ta* *le*·khos

Go straight ahead.
Siga/Vaya derecho.   *see*·ga/*va*·ya de·*re*·cho

Turn left.
Doble a la izquierda.   *do*·ble a la eeth·*kyer*·da

Turn right.
Doble a la derecha.   *do*·ble a la de·*re*·cha

SIGNS

Abierto	Open
Cerrado	Closed
Comisaría	Police Station
Entrada	Entrance
Prohibido	Prohibited
Prohibido Fumar	No Smoking
Salida	Exit
Servicios/Aseos	Toilets
Hombres	Men
Mujeres	Women

LANGUAGE

Can you show me (on the map)?
¿Me lo podría indicar (en el mapa)?		me lo po·dree·a een·dee·kar (en el ma·pa)

here	aquí	a·kee
there	allí	a·lyee
avenue	avenida	a·ve·nee·da
street	calle/paseo	ka·lye/pa·se·o
traffic lights	semáforos	se·ma·fo·ros
north	norte	nor·te
south	sur	soor
east	este	es·te
west	oeste	o·es·te

EMERGENCIES

Help!	¡Socorro!	so·ko·ro
Fire!	¡Incendio!	een·then·dyo
Go away!	¡Vete!/¡Fuera!	ve·te/fwe·ra

Call ...!
¡Llame a ...!		lya·me a
an ambulance		
una ambulancia		oo·na am·boo·lan·thya
a doctor		
un médico		oon me·dee·ko
the police		
la policía		la po·lee·thee·a

It's an emergency.
Es una emergencia.
es oo·na e·mer·khen·thya

Could you help me, please?
¿Me puede ayudar, por favor?
me pwe·de a·yoo·dar por fa·vor

I'm lost.
Estoy perdido/a.
es·toy per·dee·do/da

Where are the toilets?
¿Dónde están los baños?
don·de es·tan los ba·nyos

HEALTH
I'm sick.
Estoy enfermo/a.
es·toy en·fer·mo/ma
I need a doctor.
Necesito un médico
(que habla inglés).
ne·the·see·to oon me·dee·ko
(ke a·bla een·gles)
Where's the hospital?
¿Dónde está
el hospital?
don·de es·ta
el os·pee·tal
I'm pregnant.
Estoy embarazada.
es·toy em·ba·ra·tha·da

I've been vaccinated.
Estoy vacunado/a.
es·toy va·koo·na·do/da

I'm allergic to ...
Soy alérgico/a a ...	soy a·ler·khee·ko/ka a ...
antibiotics	
los antibióticos	los an·tee·byo·tee·kos
penicillin	
la penicilina	la pe·nee·thee·lee·na
nuts	
las nueces	las nwe·thes
peanuts	
los cacahuetes	los ka·ka·we·tes

I'm ...
Soy ...	soy ...
asthmatic	
asmático/a	as·ma·tee·ko/ka
diabetic	
diabético/a	dya·be·tee·ko/ka
epileptic	
epiléptico/a	e·pee·lep·tee·ko/ka

I have ...
Tengo ...	ten·go ...
a cough	
tos	tos
diarrhea	
diarrea	dee·a·re·a
a headache	
un dolor de cabeza	oon do·lor de ka·be·tha
nausea	
náusea	now·se·a

LANGUAGE DIFFICULTIES
Do you speak (English)?
¿Habla/Hablas (inglés)?	a·bla/a·blas (een·gles) (pol/inf)
Does anyone here speak English?
| ¿Hay alguien que | ai al·gyen ke |
| hable inglés? | a·ble een·gles |
I (don't) understand.
| Yo (no) entiendo. | yo (no) en·tyen·do |
How do you say ...?
| ¿Cómo se dice ...? | ko·mo se dee·the ... |
What does ...mean?
| ¿Qué quiere decir ...? | ke kye·re de·theer ... |

Could you please ...?
¿Puede ..., por favor?	pwe·de ... por fa·vor
repeat that	
repetirlo	re·pe·teer·lo
speak more slowly	
hablar más despacio	a·blar mas des·pa·thyo
write it down	
escribirlo	es·kree·beer·lo

LANGUAGE

NUMBERS

0	zero	the·ro
1	uno	oo·no
2	dos	dos
3	tres	tres
4	cuatro	kwa·tro
5	cinco	theen·ko
6	seis	seys
7	siete	sye·te
8	ocho	o·cho
9	nueve	nwe·be
10	diez	dyeth
11	once	on·the
12	doce	do·the
13	trece	tre·the
14	catorce	ka·tor·the
15	quince	keen·the
16	dieciséis	dye·thee·seys
17	diecisiete	dye·thee·sye·te
18	dieciocho	dye·thee·o·cho
19	diecinueve	dye·thee·nwe·be
20	veinte	veyn·te
21	veintiuno	veyn·tyoo·no
30	treinta	treyn·ta
31	treinta y uno	treyn·tai oo·no
40	cuarenta	kwa·ren·ta
50	cincuenta	theen·kwen·ta
60	sesenta	se·sen·ta
70	setenta	se·ten·ta
80	ochenta	o·chen·ta
90	noventa	no·ven·ta
100	cien	thyen
101	ciento uno	thyen·to oo·no
200	doscientos	dos·thyen·tos
500	quinientos	keen·yen·tos
1000	mil	meel
5000	cinco mil	theen·ko meel

SHOPPING & SERVICES

I'd like to buy ...
Quisiera comprar ...   kee·sye·ra kom·prar ...
I'm just looking.
Sólo estoy mirando.   so·lo es·toy mee·ran·do
May I look at it?
¿Puedo mirar(lo/la)?   pwe·do mee·rar·(lo/la)
How much is it?
¿Cuánto cuesta?   kwan·to kwes·ta
That's too expensive for me.
Es demasiado caro   es de·ma·sya·do ka·ro
para mí.   pa·ra mee
Could you lower the price?
¿Podría bajar un poco   po·dree·a ba·khar oon po·ko
el precio?   el pre·thyo

I don't like it.
No me gusta.   no me goos·ta
I'll take it.
Lo llevo.   lo lye·vo

Do you accept ...?
¿Aceptan ...?   a·thep·tan ...
　　credit cards
　　tarjetas de crédito   tar·khe·tas de kre·dee·to
　　travellers cheques
　　cheques de viajero   che·kes de vya·khe·ro

less	menos	me·nos
more	más	mas
large	grande	gran·de
small	pequeño/a	pe·ke·nyo/nya

I'm looking for the ...
Estoy buscando ...   es·toy boos·kan·do ...
　　ATM
　　el cajero automático   el ka·khe·ro ow·to·ma·tee·ko
　　bank
　　el banco   el ban·ko
　　bookstore
　　la librería   la lee·bre·ree·a
　　chemist/pharmacy
　　la farmacia   la far·ma·thya
　　embassy
　　la embajada   la em·ba·kha·da
　　laundry
　　la lavandería   la la·van·de·ree·a
　　market
　　el mercado   el mer·ka·do
　　post office
　　correos   ko·re·os
　　supermarket
　　el supermercado   el soo·per·mer·ka·do
　　tourist office
　　la oficina de turismo   la o·fee·thee·na de too·rees·mo

What time does it open/close?
¿A qué hora abre/cierra?
a ke o·ra a·bre/thye·ra
I want to change some money/travellers cheques.
Quiero cambiar dinero/cheques de viajero.
kye·ro kam·byar dee·ne·ro/che·kes de vya·khe·ro
What is the exchange rate?
¿Cuál es el tipo de cambio?
kwal es el tee·po de kam·byo
I want to call ...
Quiero llamar a ...
kye·ro lya·mar a ...

airmail	correo aéreo	ko·re·o a·e·re·o
letter	carta	kar·ta

registered		
mail	*correo*	ko·*re*·o
	certificado	ther·tee·fee·*ka*·do
stamps	*sellos*	se·lyos

TIME & DATES

What time is it?
¿Qué hora es?   ke *o*·ra es
It's one o'clock.
Es la una.   es la *oo*·na
It's seven o'clock.
Son las siete.   son las *sye*·te
midnight
medianoche   me·dya·*no*·che
noon
mediodía   me·dyo·*dee*·a
half past two
dos y media   dos ee *me*·dya

today	*hoy*	oy
tonight	*esta noche*	es·ta *no*·che
tomorrow	*mañana*	ma·*nya*·na
yesterday	*ayer*	a·*yer*

Monday	*lunes*	*loo*·nes
Tuesday	*martes*	*mar*·tes
Wednesday	*miércoles*	*myer*·ko·les
Thursday	*jueves*	*khwe*·bes
Friday	*viernes*	*vyer*·nes
Saturday	*sábado*	*sa*·ba·do
Sunday	*domingo*	do·*meen*·go

January	*enero*	e·*ne*·ro
February	*febrero*	fe·*bre*·ro
March	*marzo*	*mar*·tho
April	*abril*	a·*breel*
May	*mayo*	*ma*·yo
June	*junio*	*khoo*·nyo
July	*julio*	*khoo*·lyo
August	*agosto*	a·*gos*·to
September	*septiembre*	sep·*tyem*·bre
October	*octubre*	ok·*too*·bre
November	*noviembre*	no·*vyem*·bre
December	*diciembre*	dee·*thyem*·bre

TRANSPORT
Public Transport
What time does ... leave/arrive?
¿A qué hora sale/llega ...?   a ke *o*·ra *sa*·le/*lye*·ga ...?
   the bus
     el autobús   el ow·to·*boos*
   the plane
     el avión   el a·*vyon*
   the ship
     el barco   el *bar*·ko
   the train
     el tren   el tren

airport
el aeropuerto   el a·e·ro·*pwer*·to
bus station
la estación de autobuses   la es·ta·*thyon* de ow·to·*boo*·ses
bus stop
la parada de autobuses   la pa·*ra*·da de ow·to·*boo*·ses
luggage check room
consigna   kon·*seeg*·na
taxi rank
la parada de taxi   la pa·*ra*·da de *tak*·see
ticket office
la taquilla   la ta·*kee*·lya
train station
la estación de tren   la es·ta·*thyon* de tren

The ... is delayed.
El/La ... está   el/la ... es·*ta*
retrasado/a.   re·tra·*sa*·do/da
I'd like a ticket to ...
Quiero un billete a ...   *kye*·ro oon bee·*lye*·te a ...
Is this taxi free?
¿Está libre este taxi?   e·*sta lee*·bre es·te *tak*·see
What's the fare to ...?
¿Cuánto cuesta hasta ...?   *kwan*·to *kwes*·ta *a*·sta ...
Please put the meter on.
Por favor, ponga el   por fa·*vor pon*·ga el
taxímetro.   tak·*see*·me·tro

a ... ticket	*un billete de ...*	oon bee·*lye*·te de ...
one-way	*ida*	*ee*·da
return	*ida y vuelta*	*ee*·da ee *vwel*·ta
1st-class	*primera clase*	pree·*me*·ra *kla*·se
2nd-class	*segunda clase*	se·*goon*·da *kla*·se
student	*estudiante*	es·too·*dyan*·te

Private Transport
I'd like to hire a/an ...
Quisiera alquilar ...   kee·*sye*·ra al·kee·*lar* ...
   4WD
     un todoterreno   oon to·do·te·*re*·no
   car
     un coche   oon *ko*·che
   motorbike
     una moto   *oo*·na *mo*·to
   bicycle
     una bicicleta   *oo*·na bee·thee·*kle*·ta

Is this the road to ...?
¿Se va a ... por esta carretera?   se va a ... por es·ta ka·re·te·ra
Where's a petrol station?
¿Dónde hay una gasolinera?   *don*·de ai *oo*·na ga·so·lee·*ne*·ra
Please fill it up.
Lleno, por favor.   *lye*·no por fa·*vor*

ROAD SIGNS

Acceso	Entrance
Aparcamiento	Parking
Ceda el Paso	Give Way
Despacio	Slow
Desvío	Detour
Dirección Única	One Way
Frene	Slow Down
No Adelantar	No Overtaking
Peaje	Toll
Peligro	Danger
Prohibido Aparcar	No Parking
Prohibido el Paso	No Entry
Vía de Accesso	Freeway Exit

I'd like (20) litres.
Quiero (veinte) litros.
kye·ro (veyn·te) lee·tros

diesel	*diesel*	dee·sel
leaded (regular)	*gasolina normal*	ga·so·lee·na nor·mal
petrol	*gasolina*	ga·so·lee·na
unleaded	*gasolina sin plomo*	ga·so·lee·na seen plo·mo

(How long) Can I park here?
¿(Por cuánto tiempo) Puedo aparcar aquí?
(por kwan·to tyem·po) pwe·do a·par·kar a·kee

Where do I pay?
¿Dónde se paga?
don·de se pa·ga

I need a mechanic.
Necesito un mecánico.
ne·the·see·to oon me·ka·nee·ko

The car has broken down at ...
El coche se ha averiado en ...
el ko·che se a a·ve·rya·do en ...

The motorbike won't start.
No arranca la moto.
no a·ran·ka la mo·to

I have a flat tyre.
Tengo un pinchazo.
ten·go oon peen·cha·tho

I've run out of petrol.
Me he quedado sin gasolina.
me e ke·da·do seen ga·so·lee·na

I've had an accident.
He tenido un accidente.
e te·nee·do oon ak·thee·den·te

TRAVEL WITH CHILDREN

I need ...
Necesito ... ne·the·see·to ...

Do you have ...?
¿Hay ...? ai ...

a car baby seat
un asiento de seguridad para bebés
oon a·thyen·to de se·goo·ree·da pa·ra be·bes

a child-minding service
un servicio de cuidado de niños
oon ser·vee·thyo de kwee·da·do de nee·nyos

a children's menu
un menú infantil
oon me·noo een·fan·teel

a crèche
una guardería
oo·na gwar·de·ree·a

(disposable) nappies/diapers
pañales (de usar y tirar)
pa·nya·les (de oo·sar ee tee·rar)

an (English-speaking) babysitter
un canguro (de habla inglesa)
oon kan·goo·ro (de a·bla een·gle·sa)

formula (milk)
leche en polvo
le·che en pol·vo

a highchair
una trona
oo·na tro·na

a potty
un orinal de niños
oon o·ree·nal de nee·nyos

a stroller
un cochecito
oon ko·che·thee·to

Do you mind if I breast-feed here?
¿Le molesta que dé de pecho aquí?
le mo·les·ta ke de de pe·cho a·kee

Are children allowed?
¿Se admiten niños?
se ad·mee·ten nee·nyos

Also available from Lonely Planet:
Spanish Phrasebook

Glossary

Unless otherwise indicated, these terms are in Castilian Spanish. For help in decoding menus, see p99.

abierto – open
abogado de oficio – duty solicitor
absenta – absinthe
acequia – Islamic-era canals
aficionado – enthusiast
agroturismo – rural tourism, see also *turismo rural*
ajuntament – Catalan for *ayuntamiento*
alameda – tree-lined avenue
albergue – refuge
albergue juvenil – youth hostel
alcalde – mayor
alcázar – Muslim-era fortress
alfiz – rectangular frame about the top of an arch in Islamic architecture
aljibe – cistern
altar mayor – high altar
alud – avalanche
años de hambre – literally 'years of hunger'; a period in the late 1940s when Spain was hit by a UN-sponsored trade boycott
apartado de correos – post-office box
área de acampada – see *zona de acampada*
armadura – wooden *Mudéjar* ceiling
arroyo – stream
artesonado – wooden *Mudéjar* ceiling with interlaced beams leaving a pattern of spaces for decoration
auriga – chariot racer
auto-da-fé – elaborate execution ceremony staged by the Inquisition
autonomía – autonomous community or region: Spain's 50 *provincias* are grouped into 17 of these
autopista – tollway
autovía – toll-free highway
AVE – Tren de Alta Velocidad Española; high-speed train
ayuntamiento – city or town hall
azulejo – glazed tile

bailaor – male flamenco dancer
bailaora – female flamenco dancer
baile – dance in a flamenco context
bakalao – ear-splitting Spanish techno music
balcón – balcony
balneario – spa
baño completo – full bathroom with toilet, shower and/or bath and washbasin
barranco – dry riverbed
barrio – district/quarter (of town or city)

bata de cola – frilly flamenco dress
bateas – platforms where mussels, oysters and scallops are cultivated
batipuertas – wooden half-doors
biblioteca – library
bici todo terreno (BTT) – mountain bike
bodega – cellar (especially wine cellar); also a winery or a traditional wine bar likely to serve wine from the barrel
bomberos – fire brigade
bota – sherry cask or animal-skin wine vessel
botijo – jug, usually earthenware
buceo – snorkelling; also used to mean diving; see *submarinismo*
búhos – night-bus routes
butaca – seat
buzón – letter box

cabrito – kid
cajero automático – automated teller machine (ATM)
cala – cove
calle – street
callejón – lane
cama – bed
cambio – change; also currency exchange
campings – officially graded camping grounds
caña – small glass of beer
canguro – babysitter
cante jondo – literally 'deep song'; song of the *gitanos*
capea – amateur bullfight
capilla – chapel
capilla mayor – chapel containing the high altar of a church
carmen – walled villa with gardens, in Granada
carnaval – traditional festive period that precedes the start of Lent; carnival
carretera – highway
carta – menu
casa de huéspedes – guesthouse; see also *hospedaje*
casa de labranza – *casa rural* in Cantabria
casa de pagès – *casa rural* in Catalonia
casa rural – village or country house or farmstead with rooms to let
casco – literally 'helmet'; often used to refer to the old part of a city; more correctly, *casco antiguo/histórico/viejo*
castellano – Castilian; used in preference to *'español'* to describe the national language
castellers – Catalan human-castle builders
Castile – Castilla
castillo – castle
castizo – literally 'pure'; refers to people and things distinctly from Madrid

castro – Celtic fortified village

catalá – Catalan language; a native of Catalonia

catedral – cathedral

caudillo – Franco's title; roughly equivalent to the German Führer

caza – hunting

centro de salud – health centre

cercanía – local train network

cerrado – closed

certificado – certified mail

cervecería – beer bar

chato – glass

churrigueresque – ornate style of baroque architecture named after the brothers Alberto and José Churriguera

cigarrales – country estates

ciudad – city

claustro – cloister

CNIG – Centro Nacional de Información Geográfica; producers of good-quality maps

cofradía – see *hermandad*

colegiata – collegiate church

coll – Catalan for *collado*

collado – mountain pass

comarca – district; grouping of *municipios*

comedor – dining room

comisaría – national police station

completo – full

comunidad – fixed charge for maintenance of rental accommodation (sometimes included in rent); community

comunidad autónoma – see *autonomía*

condones – condoms

conquistador – conqueror

consigna – left-luggage office or lockers

converso – Jew who converted to Christianity in medieval Spain

copas – drinks; literally 'glasses'

cordillera – mountain range

coro – choir; part of a church, usually in the middle

correos – post office

corrida de toros – bullfight

cortado – short black coffee with a little milk

Cortes – national parliament

costa – coast

coto – woodland and scrub

cruceiro – standing crucifix found at many crossroads in Galicia

cuenta – bill, cheque

cuesta – lane, usually on a hill

custodia – monstrance

dehesa – pastureland

DELE – Diploma de Español como Lengua Extranjera; language qualification recognised by the Spanish government

día del espectador – cut-price ticket day at cinemas; literally 'viewer's day'

diapositiva – slide film

dolmen – prehistoric megalithic tomb

ducha – shower

duende – spirit

embalse – reservoir

embarcadero – pier or landing stage

encierro – running of bulls Pamplona-style; also happens in many other places around Spain

entrada – entrance

ermita – hermitage or chapel

església – Catalan for *iglesia*

estació – Catalan for *estación*

estación – station

estación de autobuses – bus station

estación de esquí – ski station or resort

estación de ferrocarril – train station

estación marítima – ferry terminal

estanco – tobacconist shop

estanque – pond

estany – lake

Euskadi Ta Askatasuna (ETA) – the name stands for Basque Homeland and Freedom

extremeño – Extremaduran; a native of Extremadura

fallas – huge sculptures of papier-mâché on wood used in Las Fallas festival of Valencia

farmacia – pharmacy

faro – lighthouse

feria – fair; can refer to trade fairs as well as to city, town or village fairs that are basically several days of merry-making; can also mean a bullfight or festival stretching over days or weeks

ferrocarril – railway

FEVE – Ferrocarriles de Vía Estrecha; a national train company

fiesta – festival, public holiday or party

fin de semana – weekend

flamenco – flamingo or Flemish; also means flamenco music and dance

frontón – walled court where *pelota vasca* is played

funicular aereo – cable car; also called *telefèric*

fútbol – football (soccer)

gaditano – person from Cádiz

gaita – Galician version of the bagpipes

gallego – Galician; a native of Galicia

galería – Galician glassed-in balcony

garum – a spicy, vitamin-rich sauce made from fish entrails throughout the Roman Empire, used as a seasoning or tonic

gasolina – petrol

gatos – literally 'cats'; also a colloquial name for *madrileños*

gitanos – the Roma people (formerly known as Gypsies)

glorieta – big roundabout/traffic circle

Gran Vías – main thoroughfares

GRs – senderos de Gran Recorrido; extensive network of long-distance paths

guardía civil – police

gusanitos – corn puffs sold at *kioscos*

habitaciones libres – literally 'rooms available'

hermandad – brotherhood (including men and women), in particular one that takes part in religious processions

hórreo – Galician or Asturian grain store

hospedaje – guesthouse

hostal – cheap hotel

hostal-residencia – *hostal* without any kind of restaurant

huerta – market garden; orchard

humedal – wetland

iglesia – church

infanta/infante – princess/prince

interiores – room without a street view

IVA – *impuesto sobre el valor añadido,* or value-added tax

jai-alai – Basque name for *pelota vasca*

jardines – gardens

jondura – depth

jondo – short for *cante jondo;* early form of flamenco

judería – Jewish *barrio* in medieval Spain

kiosco – kiosk; newspaper stand

la gente guapa – literally 'the beautiful people'

lavabo – washbasin

lavandería – laundrette

levante – easterly

librería – bookshop

lidia – the art of bullfighting

lista de correos – poste restante

litera – couchette or sleeping carriage

llegada – arrival

locutorio – private telephone centre

lugares colombinos – Columbus sites

luz – light; also a common name for household electricity

macarras – Madrid's rough but (usually) likable lads

madrileño/a – a person from Madrid

madrugada – the 'early hours', from around 3am to dawn

manchego – La Manchan; a person from La Mancha

marcha – action, life, 'the scene'

marismas – wetlands

marisquería – seafood eatery

martinete – early form of flamenco song

mas tasas – plus tax

medina – Arabic word for town or city

mercadillo – flea market

mercado – market

mercat – Catalan for *mercado*

meseta – the high tableland of central Spain

mihrab – prayer niche in a mosque indicating the direction of Mecca

mirador – lookout point

Modernisme – literally 'modernism'; the architectural and artistic style, influenced by Art Nouveau and sometimes known as Catalan modernism, whose leading practitioner was Antoni Gaudí

Modernista – an exponent of *modernisme*

mojito – popular Cuban-based rum concoction

monasterio – monastery

morería – former Islamic quarter in a town

morisco – a Muslim who converted (often only superficially) to Christianity in medieval Spain

moro – 'Moor' or Muslim (usually in a medieval context)

movida – similar to *marcha;* a *zona de movida* is an area of a town where lively bars and discos are clustered

Mozarab – Christian living under Muslim rule in early medieval Spain

mozarabic – style of architecture developed by Mozarabs, adopting elements of classic Islamic construction to Christian architecture

Mudéjar – Muslims who remained behind in territory reconquered by Christians; also refers to a decorative style of architecture using elements of Islamic building style applied to buildings constructed in Christian Spain

muelle – wharf or pier

municipio – municipality, Spain's basic local administrative unit

muralla – city wall

murgas – costumed groups

museo – museum

museu – Catalan for *museo*

muwallad – descendant of Christians who converted to Islam in medieval Spain

nitbusos – night buses

novilleras – novice bullfights

número uno – best, literally number one

objetos perdidos – lost-and-found office

oficina de turismo – tourist office; also *oficina de información turística*

Páginas Amarillas – phone directory; the Yellow Pages

palloza – traditional circular, thatch-roofed house

Pantocrator – Christ the All-Ruler or Christ in Majesty, a central emblem of Romanesque art

parador – luxurious state-owned hotels, many of them in historic buildings

parque nacional – national park; strictly controlled protected area

parque natural – natural park; protected environmental area

paseo – promenade or boulevard; to stroll

pasos – figures carried in *Semana Santa* parades

pelota vasca – Basque form of handball, also known simply as pelota, or *jai-alai* in Basque

peña – a club, usually of flamenco *aficionados* or Real Madrid or Barcelona football fans; sometimes a dining club

pensión – small private hotel

pinchadiscos – DJs

pinchos – snacks

pinsapar – woodland of the rare and beautiful Spanish fir

pintxos – Basque for *tapas*

piscina – swimming pool

plaça – plaza; square

Plateresque – early phase of Renaissance architecture noted for its intricately decorated façades

platja – Catalan for *playa*

playa – beach

plaza de toros – bullring

poniente – westerly

porrón – jug with a long, thin spout through which you (try to) pour wine into your mouth

port – Catalan for *puerto*

PP – Partido Popular (People's Party)

PRs – *senderos de Pequeño Recorrido;* footpaths for day or weekend walks

presa – dam

preservativos – condoms

prohibido – prohibited

pronunciamiento – pronouncement of military rebellion

provincia – province; Spain is divided into 50 of them

PSOE – Partido Socialista Obrero Español (Spanish Socialist Worker Party)

pueblo – village

puente – bridge; also means the extra day or two off that many people take when a holiday falls close to a weekend

puerta – gate or door

puerto – port or mountain pass; see also *port*

punta – point or promontory

RACE – Real Automóvil Club de España

rambla – avenue or riverbed

rastro – flea market; car-boot sale

REAJ – Red Española de Albergues Juveniles, which is the Spanish HI youth hostel network

real – royal

Reconquista – the Christian reconquest of the Iberian Peninsula from the Muslims (8th to 15th centuries)

refugi – Catalan for *refugio*

refugio – mountain shelter, hut or refuge

refugios vivac – stone shelters with boards to sleep on

reja – grille, especially a wrought-iron one dividing a chapel from the rest of a church

Renfe – Red Nacional de los Ferrocarriles Españoles; the national rail network

reredos – decoration behind an altar

reservas nacional de caza – national hunting reserves, where hunting is permitted but controlled

retablo – altarpiece

Reyes Católicos – Catholic Monarchs; Isabel and Fernando

ría – estuary

río – river

riu – Catalan for *río*

rodalies – Catalan for *cercanías*

romería – festive pilgrimage or procession

ronda – ring road

sacristía – sacristy; the part of a church in which vestments, sacred objects and other valuables are kept

sagrario – sanctuary

sala capitular – chapter house

salida – exit or departure

salinas – salt-extraction lagoons

santuario – shrine or sanctuary

según mercado – meaning 'according to market price'

Semana Santa – Holy Week, the week leading up to Easter Sunday

Sephardic Jews – Jews of Spanish origin

servicios – toilets

seu – cathedral (Catalan)

sevillana – Andalucian folk dance

SGE – Servicio Geográfico del Ejécito (Army Geographic Service); producers of good-quality maps

sida – AIDS

sidra – cider

sidrería – cider bar

sierra – mountain range

s/m – on menus, an abbreviation for *según mercado*

s/n – sin número (without number), sometimes seen in addresses

submarinismo – scuba diving

supermercado – supermarket

tablao – tourist-oriented flamenco performances

tacaor – male flamenco guitarist

tacaora – female flamenco guitarist

taifa – small Muslim kingdom in medieval Spain

tajines – earthenware dishes with pointed lids

tapeo – tapas-bar crawl

taquilla – ticket window

taracea – marquetry

tarjeta de crédito – credit card

tarjeta de residencia – residence card

tarjeta telefónica – phonecard

tasca – tapas bar

techumbre – roof; specifically a common type of *armadura*

telefèric – cable car; also called *funicular aereo*

temporada alta/media/baja – high/mid/low season
terraza – terrace; pavement café
terrazas de verano – open-air late-night bars
tertulia – informal discussion group or other regular social gathering
tetería – teahouse, usually in Middle Eastern style, with low seats around low tables
tienda – shop or tent
topoguías – detailed Spanish walking guides
toque – guitar-playing
toreros – bullfighters
torno – revolving counter in a convent by which nuns can sell cakes, sweets and other products to the public without being seen
torre – tower
transept – the two wings of a cruciform church at right angles to the nave
trascoro – screen behind the *coro*
trenet – little train
trono – literally 'throne'; also the platform on which an image is carried during a religious procession
tunas – university students dressed up in medieval garb and busking towards the end of the academic year

turismo – means both tourism and saloon car; el turismo can also mean 'tourist office'
turismo rural – rural tourism; usually refers to accommodation in a *casa rural* and associated activities, such as walking and horse riding
tympanum – semicircular or triangular space above the lintel of the main entrance to a church or other public building

urbanització – Catalan for *urbanización*
urbanización – suburban housing development
urgencia – emergency

vall – Catalan for *valle*
valle – valley
venta de localidades – ticket office
villa – small town
VO – abbreviation of versión original; a foreign-language film subtitled in Spanish

zarzuela – Spanish mix of theatre, music and dance
zona de acampada – country camp site with no facilities, no supervision and no charge; also called *área de acampada*

Behind the Scenes

THIS BOOK

For this 5th edition of *Spain,* Damien Simonis coordinated a skilled team of authors comprising Sarah Andrews, Susan Forsyth, Anthony Ham, John Noble, Miles Roddis and Daniel C Schecter. Damien, Susan, John and Miles also made major contributions to previous editions, as did Fiona Adams, Mark Armstrong, Fionn Davenport, Tim Nollen, Andrea Schulte-Peevers, Corinne Simcock and Elizabeth Swan. Contributing authors for this edition include Nancy Frey, Richard Sterling and Dr Caroline Evans.

THANKS from the Authors

Damien Simonis In Barcelona I'd like to thank: Edith López García, María Barbosa Pérez (and Enric), Silvia Folch, Susan Kempster, Michael van Laake and Rocio Vázquez, Susana Pellicer (and the Ceba gang), Ottobrina Voccoli, Nicole Neuefeind, Armin Teichmann, José María Toro & Eduard Antonijuan (the world's friendliest bankers!), Stephan Rundel, Simona Volonterio, Oscar Elias, Steven Muller & Veronika Brinkmann, Núria Vilches, Xavi Orfells, Geoff Leaver-Heaton (and Lola and little Natalia) and a host of others.

Thanks to Silvana Solivella in Lausanne for some handy art tips. It was great catching up with my old pals Roberto Fortea (and friends), Pablo García Tobin (and Sara) in lazy Formentera. Miles Roddis provided me with some helpful tips before I set off for Extremadura – cheers! Staff at tourist offices around Catalonia, the Balearics and Extremadura were always forthcoming. *Sobretodo, esto es para Janique.*

Sarah Andrews The book just wouldn't be the same without the help of countless people who took me along to their favourite restaurants, drew me maps so that I could find some hidden little bar that I just had to include, and told me all the secrets of life in Madrid. I want to give an especially big thanks to Nuria Pardina and Fede Alvarez, who opened so many doors for me, and to my friend and travelling companion Theresa Coryn. Thanks are also in order for Pilar Ballesteros, Carlos Barrio, Simon Hunter, Cristina Lobillo, Andrés Madrigal, Ana Maeso, Genevieve McCarthy, Ed McCullough and the crew at AP, Miguel Montañez, Clayton Maxwell, Belén Ramírez, Rafa Ruíz, Ramón Urgarte and Gisela Williams. As always, my biggest helper and supporter was my wonderful husband, Miquel, who was with me every step of the way both on the road and back at home.

Anthony Ham I've been very lucky throughout the researching and writing of this book to have had so many Spanish friends who shared their local knowledge. Particular thanks go to my father-in-law, Alberto, for his expert food insights; Leo for the pleasure of his company in Toledo and rigorous attention to detail; Alejandro, Dulce, Javier and Patricia for sharing their love and knowledge of northern Spain. Thanks also to Veronica, Eva, Nacho, Javier, Noelia, Marina, Beatriz, and *el colchonero,* José. Tourist office staff across Spain were particularly helpful, especially in Bilbao, San Sebastián, León, Olite, Haro and Sigüenza. In San Sebastián, Amaia's local knowledge was as valuable as her company was enjoyable. To my

THE LONELY PLANET STORY

The story begins with a classic travel adventure: Tony and Maureen Wheeler's 1972 journey across Europe and Asia to Australia. There was no useful information about the overland trail then, so Tony and Maureen published the first Lonely Planet guidebook to meet a growing need.

From a kitchen table, Lonely Planet has grown to become the largest independent travel publisher in the world, with offices in Melbourne (Australia), Oakland (USA) and London (UK). Today Lonely Planet guidebooks cover the globe. There is an ever-growing list of books and information in a variety of media. Some things haven't changed. The main aim is still to make it possible for adventurous travellers to get out there – to explore and better understand the world.

At Lonely Planet we believe travellers can make a positive contribution to the countries they visit – if they respect their host communities and spend their money wisely. Every year 5% of company profit is donated to charities around the world.

mother, Jan, special thanks for having been born with a Spanish soul, and to Ron, Lisa, Greg, Alex, Greta, Damien, Quetta, Scout, Harrison (born during the life of this book) and Rachael. Thanks also to Heather Dickson and Damien Simonis for the clarity of their instructions and for their helpfulness throughout – it's been a pleasure to work with you. To my co-author Miles Roddis, who gave me my first Spanish dictionary and has ever since has been a wonderful friend, a very big thank you. Finally to my wife, Marina – you represent everything that I love most about Spain.

John Noble & Susan Forsyth John thanks Paula Hardy and Heather Dickson, whose work for LP's *Andalucía 4* formed the basis of large parts of this book's Andalucía chapter, Damien Simonis for his as ever beautifully uncomplicated approach to co-ordination, the hoteliers of Sierra Norte de Sevilla for their hospitality, the people of Cádiz for their warmth, John King, Nick Selby, Daniel Schechter and James Lyon, the best of a long list of very fine co-authors, Michelle de Kretser, the best editor, and Susan, Izzy and Jack for putting up with life with a Lonely Planet author.

Miles Roddis A packful of thanks to Ingrid, who drove me all around Murcia and the Comunidad Valenciana. Also to students of the Rutgers University Study Abroad programme, who shared the rich fruits of their nocturnal researches with me, and to Marina López and Anthony Ham for their hospitality.

Thank you also to: in Andorra, the ever-helpful team in Canillo's tourist office, Lourdes and Meritxell (Andorra la Vella), Laura (La Massana), Xesca (Ordino), Sylvia and Jordi (Pas de la Casa) and Anna Gascón in the Centre d'Interpretació de la Natura, Ordino; in Valencia, Soco (Benicàssim), Nuria (Peñiscola), Carmina Fenollosa (Castellón), María Jover (Valencia), Salvador Bellver (Gandia), Carol (Jávea), Maria-José (Calpe), Pedro (Benidorm), Rosa (Alicante), Paqui (Santa Pola), Mirella (Torrevieja), Puri (Villena), Begonia and Felipe (Novelda), Joan Carles Martí i Casanova and Vanessa (Elx); in Murcia, Mari-José (Cartagena) and Mari-Paz (Lorca).

Daniel Schechter Throughout this Iberian journey, I've benefited from the warmth and generosity of both the Spaniards and those who've adopted Spain as their home. At the outset, Paul Day and Astrit Fernández helped smooth my transition, and John Noble provided invaluable background. Along the way, numerous tourism personnel impressed me with their enthusiasm, in particular: Marta Crego at the Oviedo regional office, Alicia

Palacios in Cangas de Onis, Barbra Fogarty in Arenas de Cabrales, and Celalba Rivera at Santiago de Compostela's municipal office. And during the final write-up phase, the whole town of Cedeira, Galicia, showed a generally helpful attitude, especially María del Mar at the tourist office and Ángeles Fernández at the public library, while Nicola Harris, Jane Danko, Antonio Loureiro and Alicia Beatriz Freire Vera helped me appreciate the texture of their land. As usual, my wife, Myra Ingmanson, contributed navigational skills, editorial commentary and emotional ballast.

CREDITS

This title was commissioned and developed in Lonely Planet's London office by Heather Dickson. Cartography for this guide was developed by Mark Griffiths. Coordinating the production of this magnificent 5th edition of *Spain* were Lou McGregor (editorial) and Jimi Ellis (cartography). Kaitlin Beckett and Michael Ruff laid the book out. Adrienne Costanzo and Owen Eszeki also held the reins coordinating editorial and cartography, respectively, while Lou and Jimi were up to no good. Overseeing production were Eoin Dunlevy and Celia Wood (project managers). Darren O'Connell and Jennifer Garrett (managing editors).

Helping behind the scenes were a talented list of editors, proofers and indexers: David Andrew, Adam Bextream, Hilary Erickson, Kyla Gillzan, Charlotte Harrison, Victoria Harrison, Kim Hutchins, Laura Jane, Evan Jones, Thalia Kalkipsakis, Brooke Lyons, Kate McLeod, Lucy Monie, Kristin Odijk and Simon Williamson. The language content coordinator was Quentin Frayne. Thanks also go to the very lovely Sally Darmody, Kate McDonald and Adrianna Mammarella for layout checks.

Assisting with mapping were Tony Dupcinov, Tadhgh Knaggs, Joelene Kowalski, Valentina Kremenchutskaya, Laurie Mikkelsen, Emma McNicol, Anthony Phelan, Charles Rawlings-Way, Jacqui Saunders, Kelly Stanhope, Chris Thomas, Chris Tsismetzis, Natasha Velleley, Celia Wood. The fabulous colour-map section was done by (och) Jimi. The cover and artwork were designed by Brendan Dempsey. Wayne Murphy did the back-cover map. Technical support was provided by Mark Germanchis, Chris LeeAck, Paul Piaia, Lachlan Ross.

THANKS from Lonely Planet
Many thanks to the following travellers who used the last edition and wrote to us with helpful hints, useful advice and interesting anecdotes.
A Chloe Adams, Richard Adams, Eve Addis, Sabine Agena, Therese Agståhl, Rosey Aindow, Abe Akresh, Jan Alexander, Neil Allies, Jose

Alonso, Esteban Altamirano, Sine Andersen, Phil & Hilary & Pippa Andre, Sandra Andtfolk, Ted Angell, Robert Angert, Rachel Antell, Edward Archibald, Joy Armstrong, Sarah Armstrong, Robert Aronson, Rikard Åström, Amy Atzell **B** Margaret Baker, Chris & Peter Baldwin, Heike Balzer, Martin Bamford, Alison Barber, Dr Elaine Barry, Michael Barry, Simon Beavington Penney, Isabelle Béjin, Monica Belford, Mike & Daphne Bell, Tony Bellette, Alex Benarroch, Alessandro Benvenuti, Edward Benz, Alicia Berger, Andrew Berns, Magda Biesemans, Owen Billing, Burke Bindbeutel, Tamas Biro, John Birthistle, Jeroen Blansjaar, Brian W Boag, Julien Bodart, Danny Boer, Jennifer Boger, Andre Bookelmann, A Th Bookleman, Figa Borova, Joseph Bosco, Pauline Bourhill, Pamela & Geroge Bours, Paul Bouwman, Julie Bowden, Jess Boydell, Glenn Boyes, Mihael Bracko, Robert Braiden, Fiona Brawley, Nathaniel S. Brigham, Evan Brinton, Dr Olivier Brunel, Lisbeth Brunthaler, Nina Brydolf, Peter Bubbear, Ian Buchanan, Jane Buenaventura, Philippa Burbeck, Larry Burrows, Timothy Burrows, Belinda Byrne **C** James & Janet Calladine, Camino Galan Camon, Juan Manuel Perez Campo-Cossio, Judy Capps, Mauro Carlieri, Laetitia Carquet, Slivio Filipe Carvalheira Fonte, George Casley, Jarret Cassaniti, Patrick Cavanagh, J C Cazorla, Bryan Chambers, Cherie Chaperon, Michael Chapman, Pep Charusanti, Rita Chawdhuri, Nikitas Chondroyannos, Alfred Choy, Shelia Christos, Mollie Churchill, Anna Cifani, Melinda Clark, Mona Clark, Mary Clarke, Katherine & Cassie Clift, Barbara Coddington, Tamar Cohen, Clark Colahan, Ian Coldicott, Mary Collow, Anna & Robin Cooper, Maria Benedita Costa, Robert Cotter, Nicholas Covelli, David Cox, Elisabeth Cox, John Cox, Stuart Cruickshank, Drew Cummings, Elizabeth Cunliffe, Stuart Cunningham, Trevor Curnow, P Cuypers **D** Roanna Dalziel, Kathy Davidow, Abduraghmaan Dawood, Maria De Matos, Boris De Wolf, Marco De Zwart, Annemieke Dekker, Christophe Delaunay, Liz DeLoughrey, Dr Mike Dodd, Thomas Donegan, Mirka Doubravova, Kate Downer, Catherine Downie, Elizabeth Downing, Jenni Duncan **E** Robert Eastham, Stephen Edwards, Alex Egerton, Jack Egerton, Martin Egerup, Pippa Ellwood, Henrik Elonheimo, Erik En Inez Van Ginneken, Marleen Enschede, Aaron Epstein, Jacobien Erbrink, Silvina Errecalde, Nicola Escario **F** Grahame Fearon-Wilson, Iain Fielden, Jennifer File, Cathrin Flentje, Karel Fluijt, Marek Fodor, Jay Fonkert, Arsenio Formoso, Max Francis **G** Richard G. Gabriel, Ainsley Gallagher, Saul Gallagher, Graeme Galloway, Elizabeth Garber, Nick Garcia, Jose Garcia de Dios, Julio Garcia Lopez, Alejandro Garduno, Mr & Mrs Gaudet, Ariel Gejman, Megan Gibbs, Kathleen Gillett, Nicole Goodfellow, Teresa Goss, Alexander Goutbeek, Meahan Grande, Gordon Grant, Lindsay Grant, Tom Gray, Kate Greenwood, Romualdo Grillo, Lilian Grundström, Catherina Grunwald, Andrea Gulli, Paul Gurn **H** Bud Haas, Samantha Hack, Benjamin Hagard, Janet Hall, Eric Halvorson, Alex Hammond, Nora Handsher, Jill Hardy, Chris Harkensee, Alison Harris, I W Harris, W Harrison, Georg Hasse, Olaf Hauk, Patricia Havekost, Paul Heidelberg, Sylvia Henriksen, Adrian Hervey, Kaj Heydorn, Michael Hicks, Laura Higgins, N Hill, Sarah Hird, Martin Hlawon, Sim Sim Hockney, Stefan Hofer, Jan Hooper, George Houston, Suzanne Hudson, Kimberly Huie, Barbara Huppauf, Sara Huston **I** John Iaquinto, Edouard Imbeau, Shamin Islam **J** Emma Jacobs, Ted & Pixie James, Peter Jaskiewicz, Craig Jenkins, Robin Jett, Judith Johnson, Kirk Johnson, Linds Johnson, Barry Johnston, Anita Jones, Sara Jones, Sarah Jones, Hans Jonsson, Roger Jubin **K** Alex Anna Kamenski, Cynthia Karena, Jakob Kejerud, Erin Kelli, Simon Kerby, Manon Kerssemeeckers, Yu Fay Khan, Zia Asad Khan, Philip Kim, Hannah King, Phil Kirkley, Alison Kirsch, Dave Klassen, Amanda Kliefoth, Brent Knevett, Suzanne Kocher, George & Heike Koenig, Daan Korten, Sharon Kristoff, Petra Kubalcik, Mari Kuraishi, Martin Kuster **L** Lucien Lahaye, Fernando Landro, Sascha Lange, Isabella Lattanzi, Vince Lauzon, Annette Lawrence, Margaret Lee, Gail & Ken Lefever, Frances & Andrea Lench, Rebecca LeSeelleur, Rebecca Letven, Dan Liberman, Hui Ling, Zhiyu Liu, Nick Lloyd, Friedel Loenen, Jonathan Lord, Matt Loughney, Benny Lövström **M** Christine Mackay, Sara Macmillan, Linda Magno, Edith Maker, Fay Mander-Jones, Jill Manning Press, Brian Mannix, Marisa Manzin, Calos Marcos, Giles Marshall, Jordi Sanchez Marti, Lukas Martin, Eliane Martinez, Dubravka Martinovic, Jill Matthews, Jeremy May, Kirsty McFarlane, Mary McGinn, Annette McGuinness, Andrew McMenamin, Mrs Mcpryer, Janet Mead, Karen & Loyal Mealer, Alison Metcalfe, John & Lynn Midgley, Codrin Mihai, Susan & David Millar, Brett Mitchell, Glen Mitchell, Naomi Mitchell, Charlene Mogdan, Andre Monteyne, Jordi Vidal Morgades, Johnny Morgan, Nicole Morris, Bea Morrow, Raymond Mosher, Geronimo Mosso, Greg Mossop, Stuart Mould, Schloy Mualem, K Mulzer, Carol Murphy, Casey Murphy, Roberta Murray **N** Seth Nagel, Phil Nery, Phil Newnham, Brad & Rhea Ng, Julie Nichols, Maria Mejer Nielsen, Bente Nystad **O** Michael O'Donoghue, Christopher O'Brien, Jacob Odland, Fleur & Hugh Ogilvie, Don O'Hara, Karen Olch, Sam Oldershaw, Robert Olsson, Ros Osborne, Alyson O'Shannessy, Ian

SEND US YOUR FEEDBACK

We love to hear from travellers – your comments keep us on our toes and help make our books better. Our well-travelled team reads every word on what you loved or loathed about this book. Although we cannot reply individually to postal submissions, we always guarantee that your feedback goes straight to the appropriate authors, in time for the next edition. Each person who sends us information is thanked in the next edition – and the most useful submissions are rewarded with a free book.

To send us your updates, and find out about Lonely Planet events, newsletters and travel news, visit our award-winning website: **www .lonelyplanet.com/feedback**.

Note: We may edit, reproduce and incorporate your comments in Lonely Planet products such as guidebooks, websites and digital products, so let us know if you don't want your comments reproduced or your name acknowledged. For a copy of our privacy policy visit www.lonelyplanet.com/privacy.

Ostbye, Patric Öström **P** Carolyn Parker, Mark Parkes, Nikolaos Patelis, Jorge Peixoto, Jan Pennington, Ilan Peri, Janet & Neil Perkins, Marianne Persson, Nicolas Pesenti, Genevieve Peterson, Jenny Peterson, David Pickering, Lizzy Pike, Martin Pilon, Tiago Pinto, Mark Pitt, L Podlesak, Korbinian Poeschl, Scott Pope, Wendy & Joe Postier, LaMont Powell, Millie Powell, Elise Power, Alexandra Prichard, Paul Proulx, Rich Proulx, Duncan Purvis, Madeline Pyle **R** Mobeena Rahmatullah, John S Ramsay, Luca Randolfi, Paul Ratcliffe, Priyadarshini Rath, Cadence Reed, Jon Reimer, Spela Repic, Riccardo Ricci, Dave Richards, Tony Richmond, Felice Riedel, Peter & Yumiko Riley, Petro Rinaldi, Janis Ringuette, Graham Rinzai, Nikki Rizza, Barbara Roberts, Daniella Robinson, Cynthia Rocha, Christiane Rochon, Anne & Peter Rolston, Andres N Roman, Kelly Rose, Bill Roth, Orea Roussis, Gustavo Rubio, Antje Runschke **S** Julie Sadigursky, Helen Sage, Juan Carlos Sanchez, Vivienne Sandy, Eric Sarlet, Joy Sarte, T E Savage, Alison Saville, Carlos Schaap, Paul Schilder, Benny Schiller, Ulrike Schipf, Steffi Schott, Jaap & Maria Schouten, Guy Seinet, Heather Selin, Sonia Sereno, Selina Serio, Tasha Seuren, Chris Seymore, Eyal Shaham, Gwen & Norm Shannon, Sue Shelley, John Sheppard, Seb Sheppard, Mike Shillitoe, Adele Sidhom, Ann Silverstein, Kevin Skinner, Emma Smith, Margot Smith, Paul Smith, Richard Smith, Danielle Snyder, Rael Solomon, Christiana Souza, Luca Spadotto, Eve Spence, Simon Spence, Bronwyn Spiteri, Suzanne Stahlie, Sue Stanton, Andy Starke, Alberto Di Stefano, Eric Steiner, Giorgio Stenner, Rebecca Stephenson, Peter Stibal, David Stone-Resneck, Bill & Ann Stoughton, Rafael Iglesias Stoutz, Michael Stringer, Barbara Stuart, Philip Stynen, Mark Sukhija, Lisa Sullivan, Eil Synnott

T Terence Tam, Alan Tan, Christine Tanhueco, Ian Taylor, Marcel ter Veld, Margaret Thresh, Michel Thuis, Chris Thurman, Nenad Tkalec, Alex Tobaschus, Michael Tobin, Markus Tomschitz, Clayton Trapp, Kristian Tryggvason, Heidi Tsao, Hau Yen Tsen, Liz Turner **U** Andreas Uthmann **V** Javier Valbuena, Pieter-Jan Van De Velde, J W Van Der Graaf, Freek Van Gijn, Joost Van Iersel, Sandra Van Maasakkers, Wim Vandenbussche, Xiris Vazquez, Holly Venable, Francesca Vendramin, J D R Vernon, Jacques Vialla, Mari Christina Di Vito, Mirjam Volgmann **W** Kjell-Tore Waale, Jason Muir Walker, N C Walker, Rob Walker, Leanne Wallinger, Barbara Walter, Nathan Walter, Jane Wastell, Georgie Wates, Paul Watkinson, Adrian Waugh, Sabine Wehinger, Gwyn Welles, Andrew Wenrick, James Whaley, Kristin White, B M Whitehead, Roy Wiesner, Hannah Wilberforce, Ed Wilde, Mark Wildon, Claire Wilhelm, Catherine Williamson, Matthew Willner-Reid, Maggie Willsher, Tom Wingfield, Kori Wolfard, Murray Woodburn, Glen Woods, Lucy Woodward, Nicholas Woyevodsky, Cecilia Wrebström, Roger Wu **Y** Andrew Yale, Elisabeth Yunarko **Z** Jabi Zabala, Mark Zappala, Matthew Zealand, Mara Zepeda, Sue Zyrich.

ACKNOWLEDGMENTS

Many thanks to the following for the use of their content:

Globe on back cover © Mountain High Maps 1993 Digital Wisdom, Inc.

Thanks also to Madrid Metro Map © 2004 Metro de Madrid S.A. and Barcelona Metro Map © 2004 TMB.

Index

INDEX

INDEX

INDEX

INDEX

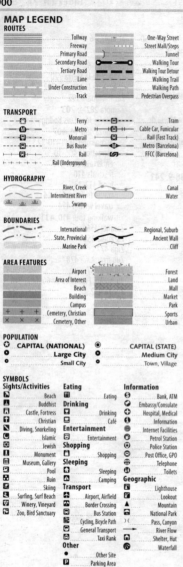

MAP LEGEND
ROUTES

Tollway		One-Way Street
Freeway		Street Mall/Steps
Primary Road		Tunnel
Secondary Road		Walking Tour
Tertiary Road		Walking Tour Detour
Lane		Walking Trail
Under Construction		Walking Path
Track		Pedestrian Overpass

TRANSPORT

Ferry		Tram
Metro		Cable Car, Funicular
Monorail		Rail (Fast Track)
Bus Route		Metro (Barcelona)
Rail		FFCC (Barcelona)
Rail (Underground)		

HYDROGRAPHY

River, Creek		Canal
Intermittent River		Water
Swamp		

BOUNDARIES

International		Regional, Suburb
State, Provincial		Ancient Wall
Marine Park		Cliff

AREA FEATURES

Airport		Forest
Area of Interest		Land
Beach		Mall
Building		Market
Campus		Park
Cemetery, Christian		Sports
Cemetery, Other		Urban

POPULATION

◎ CAPITAL (NATIONAL)	◉ CAPITAL (STATE)
● Large City	◉ Medium City
● Small City	◉ Town, Village

SYMBOLS

Sights/Activities
- Beach
- Buddhist
- Castle, Fortress
- Christian
- Diving, Snorkeling
- Islamic
- Jewish
- Monument
- Museum, Gallery
- Pool
- Ruin
- Skiing
- Surfing, Surf Beach
- Winery, Vineyard
- Zoo, Bird Sanctuary

Eating
- Eating

Drinking
- Drinking
- Café

Entertainment
- Entertainment

Shopping
- Shopping

Sleeping
- Sleeping
- Camping

Transport
- Airport, Airfield
- Border Crossing
- Bus Station
- Cycling, Bicycle Path
- General Transport
- Taxi Rank

Other
- Other Site
- Parking Area

Information
- Bank, ATM
- Embassy/Consulate
- Hospital, Medical
- Information
- Internet Facilities
- Petrol Station
- Police Station
- Post Office, GPO
- Telephone
- Toilets

Geographic
- Lighthouse
- Lookout
- Mountain
- National Park
- Pass, Canyon
- River Flow
- Shelter, Hut
- Waterfall

LONELY PLANET OFFICES

Australia
Head Office
Locked Bag 1, Footscray, Victoria 3011
☎ 03 8379 8000, fax 03 8379 8111
talk2us@lonelyplanet.com.au

USA
150 Linden St, Oakland, CA 94607
☎ 510 893 8555, toll free 800 275 8555
fax 510 893 8572, info@lonelyplanet.com

UK
72–82 Rosebery Ave,
Clerkenwell, London EC1R 4RW
☎ 020 7841 9000, fax 020 7841 9001
go@lonelyplanet.co.uk

Published by Lonely Planet Publications Pty Ltd
ABN 36 005 607 983

© Lonely Planet 2005

© photographers as indicated 2005

Cover photographs by Lonely Planet Images: *Toro* (bull) on the road north to Benavente – Castilla y León, Damien Simonis (front); fiery red sunset over Puerta de Alcalá in Madrid, Bill Wassman (back). Many of the images in this guide are available for licensing from Lonely Planet Images: www.lonelyplanetimages.com

Printed through The Bookmaker International Ltd
Printed in China